Dictionary

Afrikaans - English
Engels - Afrikaans

COETZEE COETZEE
Woordeboek Dictionary

Afrikaans – Engels Afrikaans – English
Engels – Afrikaans English – Afrikaans

Uitspraak woordeboek Pronouncing dictionary
met oor die containing more than
39,000 inskrywings 39,000 entries

COLLINS
Johannesburg
Glasgow

First published in this edition 1969
Latest reprint 1986

ISBN 0 00 433415 9

Printed in Great Britain by
Collins Clear-Type Press

INHOUD · CONTENTS

AFRIKAANS - ENGLISH
AFRIKAANS - ENGELS

Edited and compiled by
ABEL COETZEE
M.A., D.Litt. (Witwatersrand), D. Lit. et. Phil. (Nijmegen)
Professor Emeritus
University of the Witwatersrand

NOTES ON THE AFRIKAANS-ENGLISH SECTION

A. Grammar

1. *Nouns*

(i) Most Afrikaans nouns form their plural by adding *-s, -e, -ens,* or *-ers* to the form for the singular; in the Dictionary this is indicated as follows:

>man, (*-s*), which signifies: *sing.* man, *pl.* mans;
>vurk, (*-e*), *sing.* vurk, *pl.* vurke;
>vrou, (*-ens*), *sing.* vrou, *pl.* vrouens;
>kind, (*-ers*), *sing.* kind, *pl.* kinders.

(ii) In some cases nouns may have more than one plural form, without any difference in meaning; this is indicated as follows:

>vrou, (*-e, -ens*); vereniging, (*-s, -e*).

(iii) Where the suffix of a noun has a mutation of the vowel in the plural, or where a difference of spelling occurs in the plural suffix only, it is given in full:

>seer, (*sere*).
>vokaal, (*vokale*).

(iv) In cases such as man, (*-ne*), *pl.* manne, bom, (*-me*), *pl.* bomme, the doubling of the consonant merely serves as indication that the root vowel remains short in the plural.

(v) Where other mutations occur in the plural, the plural form is given in full:

>brug, (*brûe*); oog, (*oë*); maag, (*mae, mage*); boom, (*bome*).

(vi) Compounds with *-ge-* between the two parts often are derived from past participles of verbs; where such compounds are not given as main entries or as secondary entries, the reader must refer to the form without *-ge-*.

2. *Adjectives/Adverbs*

(i) The positive of an adjective usually has two forms in Afrikaans: inflected and uninflected, ordinarily depending on whether it is used as an adjective or as part of the verb, *e.g.*: *die man is* oulik; *die* oulike *man.* The comparative is formed by adding *-er,* and the superlative by adding *-ste* to the positive. Often some modification takes place in the spelling. All these facts are indicated as follows in the Dictionary:

>oulik, (*-e*; *-er, -ste*)—oulik, oulike—ouliker—oulikste;
>seldsaam, (*seldsame*; *seldsamer, -ste*)—seldsaam, seldsame—seldsamer—seldsaamste;
>dierbaar, (*dierbare*; *-der, -ste*)—dierbaar, dierbare—dierbaarder, dierbaarste.

(ii) Some adjectives form the degrees of comparison by means of *meer* and *mees,* which is indicated thus:

>ontevrede, (*meer-, mees-*), *i.e.* ontevrede, meer ontevrede, mees ontevrede.

(iii) Where an adjective normally has no degree of comparison, but only an inflected positive, it is indicated as follows:

>absoluut, (*absolute*).

(iv) Irregular forms are given in full:

>goed (*goeie, beter, beste*).

3. Verbs

(i) The past participle of the Afrikaans verb can be formed without a prefix, or with the prefix *ge-*; where *ge-* is used, it can either be in the form of a prefix or of an infix. In the Dictionary this is represented as follows:

begin, (-), *i.e. inf.* (*om te*) **begin;** *pp.* (*het*) **begin**—without prefix; normally this is the case where the verb already has an unaccented prefix *be-, ge, her-, er-, ont-, ver-* in the infinitive:

staan, (*ge-*), *i.e. inf.* **staan;** *pp.* **gestaan;**
this is the predominant form in Afrikaans;

voorloop, (-*ge-*), *i.e. inf.* **voorloop;** *pp.* **voorgeloop;**
this usually is the case where a separably compounded verb is concerned.

(ii) Forms in which deviations in the spelling occur, are given in full, *e.g.*:

eer, (*gēer*); *erf,* (*geërf*).

(iii) The different forms of the few remaining irregular auxiliary verbs in Afrikaans are given in full:

is, (*was, gewees*); **sal,** (*sou*); **kan,** (*kon*).

4. General

(i) Two slightly different forms of a word, both of which are recognised as correct usage, are represented thus:

feit(e)lik, vind(e), *i.e.* **feitlik/feitelik, vind/vinde.**

(ii) Where a main entry recurs in an illustrative example, it is not repeated, but replaced by a dash, *e.g.*:

mostert, - *na die maal.*

(iii) Compounds not given in the Dictionary, are to be looked up under the component parts, thus **oggendduur** may be looked up under **oggend** (*morning*) and **uur** (*hour*), **deurkosyn** under **deur** (*door*) and **kosyn** (*frame*).

(iv) Derivatives and compounds are, as a rule, not given as main entries, but as secondary entries.

(v) The equal-sign (=) is used to indicate that the meaning of both words concerned, are equivalent; where *cp.* or the equal-sign is used in an entry, it serves as indication that the word referred to, should be compared for more information on the meaning.

B. Pronunciation

In a country where two languages are in daily use in all walks of life, practical exigence demands of a bilingual dictionary the necessary indications for the pronunciation of those words which do not form part of the speaker's mother tongue. A system has been devised by the editor, which can be understood by any person of ordinary intelligence who knows English. To apply this system, no knowledge of Phonetics is required, because use is made of key words to illustrate particular sounds. It must, however, be pointed out that no ordinary system can represent the exact sounds of Afrikaans in terms of English; the nearest we can approach will be a very close proximation, near enough to be easily understood by Afrikaans speakers. The student of Afrikaans should, therefore, avail himself of every opportunity to listen carefully to spoken Afrikaans and try to master the exact sounds by imitation. In this way the practical value of the information supplied in the Dictionary will be increased.

1. Afrikaans Consonants

Afrikaans *English*

b, pronounced as in English, except at the end of a syllable or word, when it is pronounced - - - - - - - p

d, pronounced as in English, except at the end of a word or syllable, when it is pronounced - - - - - - t

g, initially or finally, pronounced as **ch** in Scottish **loch**; represented by - - - - - - - - - - - ch

h, differs from English in that it is not a forceful aspiration, but is pronounced voiced throughout; represented by - - - h

j, pronounced as in English **yes**; represented by - - - y

r, is rolled as in Scottish pronunciation; represented by - - R

s, is always a voiceless sound as in **say, cease**; represented by - s

v, is pronounced as in **free, off**; represented by - - - f

w, pronounced as in **very, vain**; represented by - - - v

pronounced as in **water**; represented by - - - - w

f, l, m, n, pronounced as in English; represented by - f, l, m, n

k, p, t, pronounced as in English, but no aspiration at close of sound; represented by - - - - - - - - - k, p, t

-ng, pronounced as in **king, hang**; represented by - - - -ng

-nk, pronounced as in **think, kink**; represented by - - - -nk

vowel + n + s, in a syllable built up in this way, the **n** is not pronounced, but the vowel is nasalised as in French **bon**; represented by - - - - - - - - - - - - n

-tj(ie), no English equivalent, but it can be approximated by pronouncing the **k** against the hard palate in the front part of the mouth; represented by - - - - - - - K

2. Afrikaans Vowels and Diphthongs

a, pronounced as in Scottish **man**; represented by - - - a

aa, pronounced as in **father**; represented by - - - ā

e, pronounced as **e** in **father**; represented by - - - ə

e, pronounced as in **bed, men**; represented by - - - - e

ê, as in **air, fare, fair, there**; represented by - - - ε

eë, pronounced as in **fear, bear**; represented by - - - ε̄

eu, pronounced as in **fear**, but with pouted lips;

short, represented by - - - - - - - œ

long, represented by - - - - - - - œ̄

the nearest approximation is the French **oeu** in **coeur de lion** (*Lionheart*)

i, pronounced as **e** in **father**;

short, represented by - - - - - - - - ə

long, represented by - - - - - - - - ɜ

ie, pronounced as in **quick, seen**;

short, represented by - - - - - - - i

long, represented by - - - - - - - ī

o, pronounced as in **moth**; represented by - - - - - o

ô, pronounced as in **ore, awl, caul**; represented by - - au

oo, pronounced as in **moor, boor**; represented by - - ō

oe, pronounced as in **foot**;

short, represented by - - - - - - - u

long, represented by - - - - - - - ū

u, pronounced as in **putty, nut**, but with pouted lips;

short, represented by - - - - - - - ʌ

long, represented by - - - - - - - ʌ̄

uu, pronounced as **y** in French; represented by - - - ew

ai, pronounced as in **tight;** represented by - - - - ai
aai, pronounced as in **mine, buy;** represented by - - āï
ei, y, pronounced as in **prey, say;** represented by - - - ay
eeu, pronounced as **eo** in **leopold, Cleopatra;** represented by - eo
oi, pronounced as in **coin;** represented by - - - - oi
ooi, pronounced as long **o (moor)** plus **i;** represented by - - ōï
ou, pronounced as in **boat;** represented by - - - - oa
ui, pronounced as **ay** in **say,** but with pouted lips; represented by œi
oei, pronounced as **oo (foot)** plus **i;** represented by - - - ui

C. Stress

The main stress of the words in our Dictionary is indicated by means of an acute stress mark in front of the stressed syllable, as follows:
versper, (feR′spεR), obstruct, *i.e.* **-sper** has the main stress.

D. Abbreviations and Contractions used in this Dictionary

a.	-	-	adjective	*pron.*	-	-	pronoun
av.	-	-	adverb	*p.p.*	-	-	past participle
n.	-	-	noun	*pres. p.*	-	-	present participle
masc.	-	-	masculine	*conj.*	-	-	conjunction
fem.	-	-	feminine	*inf.*	-	-	infinitive
sing.	-	-	singular	*interj.*	-	-	interjection
pl.	-	-	plural	*dim.*	-	-	diminutive
v.t.	-	-	verb transitive	*var.*	-	-	variant
v.i.	-	-	verb intransitive	*i.e.*	-	-	that is
v. refl.	-	-	reflexive verb	*e.g.*	-	-	for example
v. aux.	-	-	auxiliary verb	*cp.*	-	-	compare
prep.	-	-	preposition				

aanm. aanmerking, *remark.*

A.Asb. antwoord asseblief, *R.S.V.P.*

advt(s). advertensie(s), *advt(s), ad(s).*

afb. afbeelding, *illus.*

alg. algemeen, *general.*

antw. antwoord, *ans.*

a.s. aanstaande, *next.*

bep. bepaling, *def(n).*

bepk., bpk. beperk, *Ltd.*

bet. betekenis, *meaning.*

betd., btd. betaal(d), *pd.*

bl(s). bladsy, *p.*

b.o. blaai om, *P.T.O.*

B.O.A. Brits-Oos-Afrika, *B.E.A.*

bv., byv. byvoorbeeld, *e.g.*

byl. bylae, *enc(l).*

C. sent, *cent, c.*

C.J.V. Christelike Jongeliedevereniging, *Y.M.C.A., Y.W.C.A.*

C.N.O. Christelik Nasionale Onderwys, *C.N.E.*

C.S.V. Christelike Strewersvereniging, *C.S.A.*

ct. sentenaar, *cwt.*

dat. datum, *date, dat.*

dd. gedagteken, *dated, dd.*

des. deser, *inst.*

dgl. dergelike, *such.*

d.i. dit is, *i.e.*

diensw. dienswillige, *obed.*

dies. dieselfde, *do.*

dist. distrik, *dist.*

dm. duim, desimeter, *in.; dm.*

dnr. dienaar, *servant.*

dos. dosyn, *doz.*

D.P.W. Department van Publieke Werke, *P.W.D.*

dr. dokter; dokter, *Dr.*

ds. dominee, *Rev.*

dt. debet, debiteur, *Dr.*

dw. dienswillige, *obed.*

d.w.s. dit wil sê, *that is to say.*

e.a. en ander, *etc.*

Ed. Edele, *Hon.*

e.d.m. en dergelike meer, *etc.*

eerw. eerwaarde, *Rev.*

e.k. eerskomende, *next.*

eks. eksemplaar, *copy.*

ens. en so voort, *etc.*

e.s.m. en so meer, *etc.*

EVKOM. Elektrisiteitsvoorsieningkommissie, *Electricity Supply Commission, ESCOM.*

F.A.K. Federasie van Afrikaanse Kultuurvereniginge.

F.A.T.S.A. Federasie van Amateur - Toneelgeselskappe, Suid-Afrika.

F. & W.U. Foute en Weglatings Uitgesonder, *E. & O.E.*

geb. gebore, *b.; ne(e).*

Gebr. Gebroeders, *Bros.*

geïll. geïllustreer(de), *illustr.*

get. geteken; getuie, *sgd.; witness.*

gew. gewig, *wt.*

G.G.D. Grootste Gemene Deler, *G.C.M.; H.C.F.*

H.d.L. Heil die Leser, *L.S.*

H.Ed. Hoog-Edele, *(Rt.) Hon.*

H.Ed.Gestr. Hoogedel-Gestrenge, *Rt. Hon.*

hfst. hoofstuk, *ch.; cap.*

hh. here, menere, *messrs.*

Holl. Hollands, *Dutch.*

H.P.K. Hoofposkantoor, *G.P.O.*

hs(s). handskrif(te), *MS(S).*

h/v. hoek van, *cor.*

i.p.v. in pleks (plaas) van, *instead of, vice.*

i.s. insake, *re.*

I.H.M.D. In Haar Majesteit se Diens, *O.H.M.S.*

I.S.M.D. In Sy Majesteit se Diens, *O.H.M.S.*

jl. jongslede, *ult.*

jt. jaart, *yd.*

kapt. kaptein, *Capt.*

k.b.a. kontant by aflewering, *C.O.D.*

K.G.V. Kleinste Gemene Veelvoud, *L.C.M.*

Kie. kompanjie, *Co(y).*

kol. kolonel, *Col.*

K.P. Kaap-Provinsie, *C.P.*

kt. krediteer, krediteur, *Cr.*

kurs. kursief(druk), *ital.*

L.C. loco citati (op die aangehaalde plek), *l.c.*

ll. laaslede, *ult.*

l.n.r. links na regs, *left to right.*

L.P.R. Lid van die Provinsiale Raad, *M.P.C.*

L.S. Lectori Salutem (H.d.L.), *L.S.*

L.U.K. Lid van die Uitvoerende Komitee, *M.E.C.*

L.V. Lid van die Volksraad, *M.P.*

L.W. Let Wel, *N.B.*

maj. majoor, *Maj.*

m.a.w. met ander woorde, *in other words.*

mej(j). mejuffrou(e), *Miss(es).*

mem(o). memorandum, *mem(o).*

mev(r). mevrou, *Mrs.*

m.i. myns insiens, *in my opinion.*

min. minister; minuut, *Min.*

mnr(e). meneer (menere), *Mr., Esq.*; *Messrs.*

m.p.u. myl per uur, *m.p.h.*

ms(s). manuskrip(te), *MS(S).*

My. maatskappy, *Co(y).*

nC. na Christus, *A.D.*

Ndl. Nederlands, *Dutch (High).*

nl. naamlik, *viz.*

nm. namiddag, *p.m.*

no. nommer, *No.*

N.O.I.K. Nederlands Oos-Indiese Kompanjie, *D.E.I.C.*

NOK. Nywerheidsontwikkelingskorporasie, *IDC.*

N.P. Nasionale Party, *N.P.*

Ns. naskrif, *P.S.*

O. oos, *E.*

o.a. onder andere, *inter alia.*

o.m. onder meer, *inter alia.*

oorl. oorlede, *ob.*

opm. opmerking, *note*; rem.

Ord. Ordonnansie, *ord.*

O.V.S. Oranje-Vrystaat, *O.F.S.*

p/a. per adres, *c/o.*

p.j. per jaar, *p.a.*

Pk. Poskantoor, *P.O.*

R. Rand, *R.*

red. redakteur; redaksie, *ed.*

reg. regering, *govt.*

R.S.A. Republiek van Suid-Afrika, *R.S.A.*

S.A. Suid-Afrika, *S.A.*

S.A.P. Suid-Afrikaanse Polisie; Suid-Afrikaanse Party, *S.A.P.*

S.A.S. (& H.) Suid-Afrikaanse Spoorweë (en Hawens), *S.A.R. & H.*

S.A.U.K. Suid-Afrikaanse Uitsaaikorporasie, *S.A.B.C.*

S.Ed. Sy Edele, *His Hon.*

sekr. sekretaris, *sec(y).*

S.Eks. Sy Eksellensie, *His Exc.*

sen., snr. senior, *sen(r).*

sg. sogenoemde, *so-called*

S.M. Sy Majesteit, *H.M.*

sr. senior, *sen(r).*

str. straat, *st.*

S.W.A. Suidwes-Afrika, *S.W.A.*

t.a.p. ter aangehaalde plaas, *loc. cit.*

tel. telefoon; telegram, *tel.*; *teleg.*

t.o.v. ten opsigte van, *with regard to.*

Tvl. Transvaal, *Tvl.*

t.w. te wete, *viz.*

U dw. dnr. U dienswillige dienaar, *your obed. servant.*

U Ed. U Edele, *Your Hon.*

UNISA. Universiteit van Suid-Afrika, *UNISA.*

v.C. voor Christus, *B.C.*

v.d. van die, *of the.*

V.D.M. Verbi Domini Minister (predikant), *Rev.*

vgl. vergelyk, *cf.*; *cp.*

vk. vierkant, *sq.*

vm. voormiddag, *a.m.*

V.R. Vrederegter, *J.P.*

V.S.A. Verenigde State van Amerika, *U.S.A.*

vt. voet, *ft.*

waarn. waarnemende, *acting.*

w.g. was geteken, *sgd.*

W.N.N.R. Wetenskaplike en Nywerheidsnavorsingsraad, *C.S.I.R.*

w.o. waaronder, *among which.*

W.P. Westelike Provinsie, *W.P.*

AFRIKAANS—ENGLISH

A

a [ă] n. (-'s) a, *van-tot* Z from beginning to end; *-ja-* certainly, decidedly; *-nee-* (!) oh no, not at all.

'aai ['āi] v. (-ge-) caress, stroke.

'aaklig ['āklǝch] a. & av. (-e, -er, -ste) horrible, awful, wretched; **-heid** n.

'aalmoes ['ālmus] n. (-e) alms, charity; **-e'nier** n almoner; **-e'nierskap** n almonership.

'aalwee ['ālvē] n. (-s) = **aalwyn**.

'aalwyn ['ālvɐyn] n. (-e) aloe; **-bitter** n. aloin; **-blaar** n. aloe-leaf; **-boom** n. aloe-plant; **-hars** n. aloetic resin.

'aam [ām] n. (*ame*) aum, *cp.* **half-aam**.

'aambeeld ['āmbĕlt] n. (-e) anvil; *altyd op dieselfde-slaan* to harp on the same string.

'aambei ['āmbay] n. (-e) haemorrhoids.

aam'borstig [ām'boRstǝch] a. (-e; -er, -ste), asthmatic, hoarse, husky; **-heid** n. asthma, hoarseness.

'aan ['an] prep. & av. at, on, near, next to, upon, by, in, of against; *-die slaap* asleep; *-boord* aboard; *dit kom nie daarop-nie* it does not matter.

'aan-'afskakelaar ['ăn-'afskākǝlăR] n. (-s) on-and-off switch.

'aanbel ['āmbel] v. (-ge-) ring, give a ring.

'aanbestee ['āmbǝstĕ] v. (-) put out to contract; call for tenders; **'aanbestede werk** a. contract-work; **'aanbesteding** n. letting out on contract, calling for tenders; contract; tender; *by aanbesteding* by contract.

'aanbetref ['āmbǝtRef] v. (-) concern; *wat dit —* as regards this.

'aanbeur ['āmbĕR] v. (-ge-) struggle along.

'aanbeveel ['āmbǝfĕl] v. (-) commend, recommend; **'aanbeveling** n.; **'aanbevelingsbrief** n. letter of introduction; **'aanbevelenswaardig** a. laudable; **-baar** a. (-bare) laudable.

'aanbevole ['āmbǝfŏlǝ] a. = **aanbeveel**.

aan'bid [ām'bǝt] v. (-) adore, idolize, worship; **-delik** a. (-e; -er, -ste) adorable; **-delikheid** n. adorableness; **-der** n. (-s) adorer; **-ding** n. adoration, worship; **'aangebede** a. adored, worshipped; **'aangebedene** n. (-s) adored one, idol.

'aanbied ['āmbit] v. (-ge-) bid, offer, tender, proffer, present; propose;

as die geleentheid hom — if the opportunity occurs; **-ing** n. (-e, -s).

'aanbind ['āmbǝnt] v. (-ge-) tie, bind, fasten; *die stryd-met* join issue with.

'aanblaas ['āmblās] v. (-ge-) blow, fan; rouse, stir up, foment; **'aanblaser** n fomenter, instigator; **'aanblasing** n.

'aanblaf ['āmblaf] v. (-ge-) bark at.

'aanblik ['āmblǝk] n. sight, look, glance, view; aspect; v. (-ge-) glance at, look at.

'aanbly ['āmblay] v. (-ge-) continue, remain, stay.

'aanbod, 'aanbot ['āmbot] n. (*aanbotte, aanbiedinge*) = **aanbieding**; *vraag en —* demand and supply.

'aanboor ['āmbŏR] v. (-ge-) strike (ore, minerals); broach, tap; continue boring.

'aanbou ['āmboa] v. (-ge-) add by building, build against; n. annexe construction, erection; **-sel** n. annexe.

'aanbrand ['āmbRant] v. (-ge-) burn, scorch, stick to as a consequence of burning; **-sel** n. (-s) scorched crust resulting from burning.

'aanbreek ['āmbRĕk] v. (-ge-) commence, broach, cut into; n. beginning, commencement.

'aanbring ['āmbRǝng] v. (-ge-) bring, bring in, bring on, bring about, install, make.

'aand ['ănt] n. (-e) evening; **-besoek** n. evening-call; **-blom** n. Freesia; **-diens** n. evensong; **-jie** ['aingKi] *dim.* social evening; **-klok** n. curfew; **-lig** n. twilight; **-pak** n. dress-suit; **-rok** n. evening-dress; **-praatjies** n. *sy-praatjies en morepraatjies kom nie ooreen nie* what he says today, contradicts what he said yesterday.

aan'dadig [an'dădǝch] a. (-e) *-aan* instrumental in, implicated in; **-e** n. (-s) accomplice, *cp.* **medepligtige**.

'aandag [ăndach] n. attention, notice, observation; *gee-aan* pay attention to; *met —* attentively; *die-boei* hold the attention; **-streep** n. dash; **'aan'dagtig** a. (-e; -er, -ste) attentive; **aan'dagtiglik** av. attentively; **aan'dagtigheid** n. attention, attentiveness.

'aandeel ['āndĕl] n. (*aandele*) portion, part; share; **aandele** *pl.* stock; **-bewys** n. share-certificate; **-houer** n. (-s) shareholder; **'aandelemark** n. share market.

I

'**aandenking** ['ǎndenkəng] *n.* (-e, -s) memory, remembrance; memento, souvenir.

'**aandete** ['ǎntētə] *n.* supper.

'**aandien** ['ǎndin] *v.* (-ge-) announce, usher in.

'**aandig** ['ǎndəch] *v.* (-ge-) impute; -ting *n.*

'**aandik** ['ǎndək] *v.* (-ge-) thicken; emphasize; exaggerate; -ing *n.*

'**aandoen** ['ǎndun] *v.* (-ge-, *aange-daan*) call at (*port*); cause, inflict, give, move, touch; -ing *n.* (-e, -s), infection, affection, emotion; **aan'doenlik** *a.* (-e; -er, -ste); moving, touching; sensitive; **aan'doenlikheid** *n.* pathos; sensitiveness; '**aangedaan** *a.* affected, moved, agitated.

'**aandra** ['ǎndRǎ] *v.* (-ge-) carry, fetch; blab, tell (*tales*); -er *n.* carrier, tell-tale.

'**aandraai** ['ǎndRǎi] *v.* (-ge-) fasten, fix on, screw tighter, tighten; turn on, switch on.

'**aandraf** ['ǎndRaf] *v.* (-ge-) come running along; trot faster.

'**aandrang** ['ǎndRang] *n.* impetus, urge, impulse; instigation.

'**aandrentel** ['ǎndRentəl] *v.* (-ge-) saunter along.

'**aandrif** ['ǎndRəf] *n.* = aandrang.

'**aandring** ['ǎndRəng] *v.* (-ge-) urge, press on, insist on.

'**aandruk** ['ǎndRak] *v.* (-ge-) clasp, hug, press against; press on; press forward.

'**aandryf** ['ǎndRayf] *v.* (-ge-, *aange-drywe*) wash ashore; float along; actuate, incite, impel; '**aandrywer** *n.* mover; prompter; '**aandrywing** *n.* (-e, -s) driving, incitement.

'**aandui** ['ǎndœi] *v.* (-ge-) indicate, show; mark; denote; argue; specify; -ding *n.* (-e, -s).

'**aandurf** ['ǎndʌRf] *v.* (-ge-) dare, risk, venture upon.

aan'een [an'ēn] *prep.* together, connected, consecutively, without break.

aan'eenskakel [an'ēnskākəl] *v.* (-ge-) link together, couple; **aan'eenge-skakelde** *a.* connected; -end *a.* copulative; -ing *n.* sequence, series, string.

aan'eensluit [an'ēnslœit] *v.* (-ge-) close, join, link, unite; rally; **aan'eengeslote, aan'eengesluit** *a.* coherent, connected, united; -ing *n.*

'**nangaan** ['ǎnchǎn] *v.* (-ge-) proceed, continue; burn; conclude; *aan'gaande prep.* with regard to.

'**aangaap** ['ǎnchǎp] *v.* (-ge-) gape, stare at.

'**aangebore** ['ǎnchəbōRə] *a.* inborn, innate, connate.

'**aangedaan** ['ǎnchədǎn] *av.* cp. aandoen.

'**aangee** ['ǎnchē] *v.* (-ge-) pass on; indicate; record; notify; *n.* ('*aangeē*) passes (*football*); '**aangeēr, aangewer** *n.* recorder; informer; '**aange-**

'**gewe** *a.* given, recorded; indicated; alleged; reported.

'**aangehuud** ['ǎnchəhēwt] *a.* ('*aange-hude*) related by marriage.

'**aangeklaagde** *cp.* aankla.

'**aangeklam** ['ǎnchəklam] *a.* (-de) tipsy.

'**aangekool** ['ǎnchəkōl] (-de) *a.* carbonized.

'**aangeleë** ['ǎnchəlēə] *a.* adjacent, adjoining.

'**aangeleentheid** ['ǎnchəlēntayt] *n.* ('*aangeleenthede*) affair, matter; importance, moment.

'**aangeleer** (-de) *cp.* aanleer.

'**aangenaam** ['ǎnchənǎm] *a.* ('*aan-gename*) agreeable, pleasant.

'**aangenome** ['ǎnchənōmə] *a.* accepted; assumed; adopted; *conj.* assuming; granted.

'**aangepak** ['ǎnchəpak] *a.* coated.

'**aangesetene** ['ǎnchəsētənə] *n.* (-s) guest.

'**aangesien** ['ǎnchəsin] *conj.* considering, whereas, since.

'**aangesig** ['ǎnchəsəch] *n.* (-te) countenance, visage, face; met twee -te, double-faced; *van-tot-*, face to face.

'**aangeskrewe, 'aangeskrywe** ['ǎnchəskRēvə] *a.* estimated, reputed.

'**aangeslaan** *cp.* aanslaan.

'**aangespe** ['ǎnchespə] *v.* buckle on, gird on.

'**aangetroud** ['ǎnchətroat] *a.* (-de) *cp.* aangehuud.

'**aangewese** ['ǎnchəwēse] *a.* cp. aan-wys.

'**aangifte** ['ǎnchəftə] *n.* declaration; information.

'**aangluur** ['ǎnchlēwR] *v.* (-ge-) leer at, glower at.

'**aangooi** ['ǎnchōi] *v.* (-ge-) cast along, pass on, pass to; *die geweer-level a gun.

'**aangord** ['ǎnchoRt] *v.* (-ge-) gird on, gird up.

'**aangrens** ['ǎnchRɛŋs] *v.* (-ge-) adjoin, border on; -end *a.* (-e) adjacent, contiguous.

'**aangroei** ['ǎnchRœi] *v.* (-ge-) accrue, wax, swell; grow faster; set (bone); -ing *n.* augmentation, waxing.

'**aangryns** ['ǎnchRayns] *v.* (-ge-) grin at, stare in face.

'**aangryp** ['ǎnchRayp] *v.* (-ge-) catch, fasten upon, grip; seize; affect; **aan'grypend** *a.* (-e) affecting, gripping; -(ings)punt *n.* point of attack; centre.

'**aanhaak** ['ǎnhǎk] *v.* (-ge-) couple, fasten, hitch to; inspan.

'**aanhaal** ['ǎnhǎl] *v.* (-ge-) fetch; tighten; cite, quote; coax, caress; **aan'halerig** *a.* (-e) affectionate, coaxing, sweet; **aan'halerigheid** *n.* winning ways; '**aanhaling** *n.* (-e, -s) citation, quotation; '**aanhalings-teken** *n.* quotation mark.

'**aanhang** ['ǎnhang] *n.* adherents, following, partisans; favour, support; *v.* (-ge-) adhere to, favour,

support; attach, append; -er n. (-s)
adherent, supporter; aan'hangig av.
(-e) under consideration; -motor n.
outboard-motor; -sel n. (-s) addendum; extremity.
'aan'hanklik ['an'hanklǝk] a. & av.
(-e) attached, dependent, devoted;
-heid n.
'aanhark ['ǝnhaRk] v. (-ge-) rake up.
'aanhê ['ǝnhɛ] v. ('aangehad) have
on, wear, be dressed in.
'aanhef ['ǝnhef] v. (-ge-) begin,
commence; raise; n. beginning,
preamble.
'aanheg ['ǝnhech] v. (-ge-) affix,
attach; -sel n. (-s) addendum,
enclosure; -ting n. (-e, -s) attach-
ment; insertion (botany).
'aanhelp ['ǝnhelp] v. (-ge-) assist,
help along.
'aanhink ['ǝnhɪnk] v. (-ge-) hobble
along.
'aanhits ['ǝnhǝts] v. (-ge-) incite,
instigate, set on; -er n. (-s) inciter,
instigator; -ing n. (-e, -s) incitement.
'aanhoor ['ǝnhoR] v. (-ge-) give a
hearing to, listen to; -der n. (-s)
hearer, listener; pl. (-s) audience;
'aanhore n. ten-van in the hearing
of.
aan'horig ['an'hoRǝch] a. (-e) apper-
taining to, belonging to; -e n. (-s)
relative; retainer; -heid n. depen-
dence, appurtenance.
'aanhou ['ǝnhoa] v. (-ge-) continue,
insist, persist, keep on; apprehend,
arrest; hold up; keep; keep up;
aan'houdelik a. & av. (-e) continual,
persistent; aan'houdend a. (-e) constant, incessant, continuous; aan'-
houdendheid n. persistence; 'aanhouding n. detainment; 'aanhouer
n. perseverer. -wen dogged does it.
'aanhu ['ǝnhew] v. (-ge-) obtain by
marriage; -wing n. alliance by
marriage.
'aanja(ag) ['ǝnyā(ch)] v. (-ge-) hurry
along, hurry on; drive, urge on,
boost; skrik- to frighten; vrees-
incite; 'aanjaer n. (-s) driver,
booster; 'aanjaging n. boost.
aan'kant [ang'kant] av. -maak put in
order, straighten, tidy.
'aankla(ag) 'aanklae ['ǝnklā(ch)] v.
(-ge-) accuse, indict (for), charge
(with); 'aanklaer n. accuser, prosecutor, openbare- public prosecutor;
'aanklaagster fem.; 'aanklag n. (-te,
-tes) accusation, charge, complaint;
'aangeklaagde n. (-s) accused.
'aanklam ['ǝngklam] v. (-ge-) become
moist; moisten, wet; to condition.
'aanklee(d) ['ǝngklē(t)] v. (-ge-)
attire, clothe, dress, rig out;
present; 'aankleding n.
'aankleef, 'aanklewe ['ǝngklēf] v.
(-ge-) adhere to; -sel n. appurtenance, appendage; 'aanklewer n.
adherent, supporter; 'aanklewing n.
adhesion.
'aanklop ['ǝngklop] v. (-ge-) knock at

the door; om hulp-by iemand apply
to someone for help.
'aanknoop ['ǝnknop] v. (-ge-) button
on; enter into, establish; 'aan-
knoping n.; -pingspunt n. point of
contact.
'aankom ['ǝngkom] v. (-ge-) come,
come along; begin; arrive; improve;
happen; 'aankomeling n. (-e) new-
comer, beginner; 'aankomend a. (-e)
arriving; future; prospective; 'aan-
kom(en)de a. next, following; 'aankoms n. arrival.
'aankondig ['ǝngkondǝch] v. (-ge-)
announce, inform; foreshadow; pre-
dict; review (a book); 'aankondiger
n. (-s) announcer, reviewer; 'aankondiging n. (-e, -s) announcement;
notification; review.
'aankool ['ǝngkōl] v. (-ge-) to
carbonize; 'aankoling n.
'aankoop ['ǝngkōp] n purchase; v.
(-ge-) buy, purchase; -som n.
purchase-price; 'aankoper n. buyer,
purchaser.
'aankoppel ['ǝngkopǝl] v. (-ge-)
couple, join, link.
'aankruie ['ǝngkRœiǝ] v. (-ge-) convey in a wheelbarrow; struggle
along.
'aankry ['ǝngkRay] v. (-ge-) get into
(clothes), put on; set alight (fire).
'aankweek ['ǝngkwēk] v. (-ge-) cultivate, raise, foster; train; n.
cultivation; 'aankweking n. cultivation, raising.
'aankyk ['ǝngkayk] v. (-ge-) look at.
'aanlag ['ǝnlach] v. (-ge-) favour,
smile at, smile upon.
'aanland ['ǝnlant] v. (-ge-) arrive
(at); -ing n.
'aanlap ['ǝnlap] v. (-ge-) sew on.
'aanlas ['ǝnlas] v. (-ge-) attach to,
join on; exaggerate (story).
'aanlê ['ǝnlɛ] v. (-ge-) recline (at
table); moor; stand to, call at (port);
point a gun; build (a fire); install;
found; manage (things); 'aanleg n.
arrangement; plant, design; ability,
aptitude, disposition; 'aanlêhawe n.
port of call.
'aanleer ['ǝnlēR] v. (-ge-) acquire
(a habit); learn.
'aanleg ['ǝnlech] n. talent, knack,
bent; plant (pl. -te).
'aanlei ['ǝnlay] v. (-ge-) lead on; contribute to, induce; -dende a
contributive, contributory; -ding n.
(-e, -s) cause, motive, reason; na-
van as a result of; sonder- without
provocation; -gee give cause for.
'aanlok ['ǝnlok] v. (-ge-) allure,
entice, tempt; seduce; -king n. (-e,
-s); -kingsmiddel n. bait; aan'loklik
a. (-e; -er, -ste) alluring, charming;
aan'loklikheid n. charm, allure-
ment; -sel n. bait, decoy.
'aanloop ['ǝnlop] v. (-ge-) walk along;
quicken pace; by iemand- give
someone a look-in; collide; n.
patronage; preamble; take-off;

-hawe n. port of call; -plank n. spring-board.

'aanmaak ['āmāk] v. (-ge-) mix, prepare, make, light; n. fabrication, mixing.

'aanmaan ['āmān] v. (-ge-) urge; warn; press for; 'aanmaning n. (-s) n. reminder; warning; relapse, touch (disease).

'aanmatig ['āmātəch] v. (-ge-) arrogate to oneself, presume, usurp; -end (-e) a. arrogant, presumptive; -ing n. arrogance, presumption.

'aanmeet ['āmēt] v. (-ge-) take a person's measure (for suit).

'aanmeld ['āmelt] v. (-ge-) announce, report; come forward; apply; -ing n. (-e, -s).

aanme'kaar [amə'kāR] conj., av. together; on end, consecutively; -raak v. (-ge-) fight, quarrel; -spring v. fight.

'aanmerk ['āmeRk] v. (-ge-) consider; observe; remark; note, mark; criticize; -ing n. (-e, -s) consideration; remark; criticism; objection; in-neem take into consideration; op- en -s remarks and comments; aan'merklik a. (-e) considerable.

aan'minlik [ā'mənlək] a. (-e) amiable, charming, sweet; -heid n.

aan'minnig [ā'mənəch] a. (-e; -er, -ste) = aanminlik.

'aanmoedig ['āmudəch] v. (-ge-) encourage; -er n. (-s) supporter; -ing n. encouragement.

'aannaai ['ānāi] v. (-ge-) sew, stitch on.

'aanneem ['ānēm] v. (-ge-) accept, take, receive; assume (name), contract (habit), embrace (faith); suppose; pass (bill); undertake; engage (labourers); agree; confirm; adopt; 'aanneme n. confirmation (church); aan'neemlik a. (-e; -er, -ste) acceptable; aan'neemlikheid n. credibility; reasonableness; 'aanneming n. acceptance; adoption; confirmation; by- by contract; 'aannemeling n. (-e) candidate for confirmation; 'aannemer n. (-s) contractor, builder, undertaker; 'aangenome (pp.) a. adopted; granted.

'aanolie ['ānōli] v. (-ge-) aangeolie raak to oil up.

aanpak ['āmpak] v. (-ge-) seize, catch; form a crust, adhere to; undertake, tackle; attack; die vuur- lay the fire; -sel n. (-s) accretion.

'aanpas ['āmpas] v. (-ge-) fit, try on (shoes, clothes); adapt (to environment); -sing n. (-e, -s) adaptation; adjustment; -singsvermoë n. adaptability; accommodation.

'aanpiekel ['āmpikəl] v. (-ge-) drag along; move with difficulty.

'aanplak ['āmplak] v. (-ge-) paste up (notice), stick (bills); -biljet n. (-le) placard, poster; -bord n. hoarding; bill-board; -ker n. bill-poster.

'aanplant ['āmplant] v. (-ge-) plant, grow, cultivate; extend by planting; n. cultivation; plantation; -ing n. = aanplant n.

'aanpor ['āmpoR] v. (-ge-) rouse, prod, spur on; urge, instigate; -ring n. (-e, -s).

'aanprys ['āmpRays] v. (-ge-) commend, eulogize; -ing n.

'aanraai ['ānRāi] v. (-ge-) advise, suggest, recommend.

'aanraak ['ānRāk] v. (-ge-) touch, come in contact with; 'aanraking n. (-e, -s) contact, touch; g'n punte van-hê nie have nothing in common.

'aanrand ['ānRant] v. (-ge-) assail, assault; -er n. (-s) assailant, assaulter; -ing n.

'aanreik ['ānRayk] v. (-ge-) hand, pass, reach; -er n. server (table).

'aanrig ['ānRəch] v. (-ge-) cause, commit, bring about; skade- cause damage.

'aanrit [ānRət] n. (-le) ramp; cp. oprit afrit.

'aanroep ['ānRup] v. (-ge-) hail; challenge; invoke; -ing n.

'aanroer ['ānRuR] v. (-ge-) touch, mention; hurry, quicken; 'n tere snaar- touch a sensitive spot; -ing n. mention.

'aanruk ['ānRʌk] v. (-ge-) advance, march upon; -king n.

'aanry ['ānRay] v. (-ge-) keep on riding; drive faster; bring or convey (by vehicle); pull up somewhere (for call); -teen crash into.

'aanrye, 'aanryg ['ānRayə] v. (-ge-) string (beads); tack (dress); lace up (boots).

'aans ['āñs] conj. presently; possibly.

'aansê ['āñse] v. (-ge-) announce; notify; inform; 'aansegging n.

'aansien ['āñsin] v. (-ge-) look at; consider, regard; uit die hoogte- look down upon; met die nek- give the cold shoulder; n. appearance; consideration, esteem, respect; 'aangesien conj. considering, whereas, since; aan'sienlik a. (-e) considerable; notable; aan'sienlikheid n. distinction, importance.

'aansig ['āñsəch] n. (-te) view, elevation.

'aansit ['āñsət] v. (-ge-) start (motor); to fit; sit down (at table); put on (ring); incite; n. starting; -ter n. (-s) self-starter; guest; motor n. starting-motor; -slinger n. starting-handle; -tende n. (-s) guest.

'aanskaf ['āŋskaf] v. (-ge-) buy, procure, obtain; -fing n.

'aanskiet ['āñskit] v. (-ge-) whip on (clothes); -op rush at.

aan'skou [an'skoa] v. (-) look at, behold; contemplate; n. in-neem to examine, inspect; -(e)lik a. (-e) clear; graphic; realistic; -(e)likheid n. clearness, realism; -er n. (-s) spectator, beholder; -ing n. contemplation; observation; intuition;

-ings-vermoë n. power of intuition.

'aanskroef, 'aanskroewe ['ǎnskRuf] v. (-ge-) screw on, screw home; iemand- press someone for payment of debt.

'aanskryf, 'aanskrywe ['ǎnskRayf] v. (-ge-) notify; demand payment; summon; 'aangeskrewe a. estimated, reputed; 'aanskrvwing n. (-s) letter of demand, summons, writ.

'aanslaan ['ǎnslǎn] v. (-ge-) strike (note); start, switch on (light); apply (brakes); get smoky, blurred, become black; tarnish; assess, rate, estimate; knock on (football); hoog- value highly; 'n hoë toon- to ride the high horse.

'aanslag ['ǎnslach] n. ('aanslae) touch (piano); attack, attempt, outrage; assessment, rating; sediment, fur (kettle); bloom (lens); knock-on (football); -biljet n. notice of assessment.

'aansleep ['ǎnslêp] v. (-ge-) drag along.

aanslib ['ǎnsləp] v. (-ge-) increase (by sedimentation); silt up; -bing n. (-e, -s) alluvial deposit of land; -sel n. (-s) alluvium, silt.

'aansluip ['ǎnslœip] v. (-ge-) approach stealthily; steal upon.

'aansluit ['ǎnslœit] v. (-ge-) join; link; enrol; follow; -ing n. connection, junction.

aansmee ['ǎnsmê] v. (-ge-) forge or weld on.

'aansmeer ['ǎnsmêR] v. (-ge-) apply put on (ointment); daub (wall); grease; iemand iets- smear a person with something.

'aansnou ['ǎnsnoa] v. (-ge-) snarl at.

'aansny ['ǎnsnay] v. (-ge-) give the first cut; add to by cutting.

'aansoek ['ǎnsuk] n. (-e) application, proposal.

'aanspeld(e) ['ǎnspelt, 'ǎnspələ] v. (-ge-) pin on.

'aanspoor ['ǎnspôR] v. (-ge-) spur on (horse), urge on (person); incite, rouse, stimulate; 'aansporing n. (-e, -s) inducement.

aanspraak ['ǎnspRǎk] n. claim, right, title; sonder-wees be without company.

'aanspreek ['ǎnspRêk] v. (-ge-) address, speak to; draw upon, break into (one's capital); talk seriously to a person about something; aan'spreeklik a., av. (-e) accountable, liable, responsible; aan'spreeklikheid n. liability; 'aanspreking n. address, apostrophe; salutation (in letter).

'aanstaan ['ǎnstǎn] v. -ge-) please, like, suit; stand nearer.

aan'staande [ǎn'stǎndə] a. next (week); forthcoming, approaching; imminent; prospective (bride); expectant (mother); av. Paasfees is-Easter is drawing near; n. fiancée, spouse to be, intended (spouse).

'aanstaar ['ǎnstǎR] v. (-ge-) gaze or stare at.

'aanstalte(s) ['ǎnstaltə(s)] n. preparation(s); -maak get ready.

'aansteek ['ǎnstêk] v. (-ge-) pin on (flower), put on (ring); kindle (fire), light (lamp); contaminate, infect; aan'steeklik a. (-e; -er, -ste) contagious, infectious; aan'steeklikheid n. contagiousness; 'aansteker n. igniter, lighter; 'aansteking n. kindling; infection, contagion.

'aanstel ['ǎnstel] v. (-ge-) appoint (to post); pretend, show off; -ler n. (-s) humbug, pretender; appointer; -lerig a. (-e) affected, conceited; -lerigheid n. affectation, conceit; -lery n. = aanstellerigheid: -ling n. (-e, -s) appointment, commission; -lings pl. airs.

'aansterk ['ǎnsteRk] v. (-ge-) rally, recuperate, recover; -ing n.

'aanstip ['ǎnstəp] v. (-ge-) jot down, touch on (subject).

'aanstons ['ǎnstauñs] conj. forthwith; presently.

'aanstook ['ǎnstôk] v. (-ge-) stir (fire); foment (quarrel); incite; 'aanstoker n. (-s) agitator, instigator.

'aanstoot ['ǎnstôt] v. (-ge-) push; nudge; knock against; clink (glasses); make a move (chess); offend; n. offence, scandal; steen des -s stumbling block; aan'stootlik a. (-e) indecent, offensive, shocking; aan'stootlikheid n. indecency.

'aanstreep ['ǎnstRêp] v. (-ge-) underline; straggle along (in single file).

'aanstrompel ['ǎnstRompəl] v. (-ge-) stumble along.

'aanstruikel ['ǎnstRœikəl] v. (-ge-) = aanstrompel.

'aanstryk ['ǎnstRayk] v. (-ge-) apply (with brush); toddle along; quicken one's pace; keep on walking.

'aanstuur ['ǎnstewR] v. (-ge-) pass on, forward; -op head for.

'aansuiwer ['ǎnsœivəR] v. (-ge-) settle (account); 'n tekort- make good a deficit; adjust; -ing n.

'aansukkel ['ǎnsʌkəl] v. (-ge-) trudge, struggle along.

aansweef, 'aanswewe ['ǎnswêf] v. (-ge-) float, glide along.

'aansweep ['ǎnswêp] v. (-ge-) egg on, lash up, incite.

'aanswel ['ǎnswel] v. (-ge-) swell out, rise; increase.

'aanswoeg ['ǎnswuch] v. (-ge-) struggle along.

'aansyn ['ǎnsayn] n. being, existence, life; presence.

'aantal ['ǎntal] n. (-le) number.

'aantas ['ǎntas] v. (-ge-) affect; touch; attack; iemands se eer-injure a person's honour; -baar a. ('aantasbare) assailable; -ting n.

'aanteel ['ǎntêl] v. (-ge-) breed, rear; increase; n. breeding; increase; -merrie n. brood-mare; -vee n. breeding cattle.

'**aanteken** ['äntēken] v. (-ge-) note, take note, mark; register (letter), enter, record; **aangeteken afstuur** send by registered post; **-ing** n. (-e, -s) n. **-ingboek** n. notebook; **-koste** n. registration-fee.

'**aantog** ['äntoch] n. in-, approach, advance.

'**aantoon** ['äntōn] v. (-ge-) show, indicate, prove; **aantonende wys** indicative mood.

'**aantree** ['äntRē] v. (-ge-) fall into line, line up.

'**aantref** ['äntRef] v. (-ge-) meet (with), come across, stumble upon (by accident).

'**aantrek** ['äntRek] v. (-ge-) draw; attract, appeal to; tighten; put on, dress; take to heart; **-king** n. attraction, gravitation; **aan'treklik** a. (-e) attractive; sensitive; **aan'treklikheid** n. charm; sensitiveness; **aan'treklikhede** pl. attactions.

'**aantrou** ['äntroa] v. (-ge-) obtain by marriage.

'**aantyg** ['äntaych] v. (-ge-) impute, accuse of, charge with; **-ing** n. (-e, -s).

'**aanvaar** ['änfaR] v. (-ge-) 'aangevaar teen crash into, collide with.

aan'vaar [än'faR] v. (-) begin, commence; assume (office); undertake; doubt; accept, take; **-baar** a. (aan'vaarbare) acceptable; **-baarheid** n. acceptableness; **-ding** n.

'**aanval** ['änfal] v. (-ge-) attack, charge; fall to (at table); n. attack, charge; fit, touch; **-lend** a. (-e) aggressive; **-lenderwys(e)** av. aggressively; **-ler** n. (-s) assailant, aggressor; **aan'vallig** a. (-e; -er, -ste) charming, lovely; **aan'valligheid** n. charm.

'**aanvang** ['änfang] v. (-ge-) begin, commence; **wat het jy nou weer aangevang** what have you been up to; n. commencement; initial; origin, start; **aan'vanklik** a. (-e) initial, original; av. at first.

'**aanvat** ['änfat] v. (-ge-) take hold of, begin.

aan'vegbaar [än'fechbaR] a. (aan'-vegbare) assailable, contentious.

'**aanvegting** ['änfechtəng] n. (-e, -s) impulse; temptation.

'**aanverwant** ['änfəRvant] a. (-e) allied, cognate, related; **-skap** n. affinity.

'**aanbly** ['änblay] v. (-ge-) nestle against.

'**aanvoeg** ['änfuch] v. (-ge-) add, join; **-ende wyse** subjunctive mood; **-ing** n.; **-sel** n. addendum.

'**aanvoel** ['änful] v. (-ge-) feel, touch; experience; sense; **-ing** n.

'**aanvoer** ['änfuR] v. (-ge-) bring, convey; supply; import; advance (reason), raise (objection); adduce (proof), cite; command (army); n. supply; **-der** n. (-s) commander, leader; **-ing** n. command, leadership.

'**aanvoor** ['änfôR] v. (-ge-) begin, commence, start; **'n saak-** take initial steps in a matter.

aanvra ['änfRa] v. (-ge-) apply for, request; **-er** n. applicant.

'**aanvraag** ['änfRach] n. enquiry; request, requisition; demand; **-en** aanbod demand and supply.

'**aanvreet** ['änfRēt] v. (-ge-) corrode.

'**aanvryf**, '**aanvrywe** ['änfRayf] v. (ge-) rub against; **iemand iets-** lay something at a person's door = **aansmeer.**

'**aanvul** ['änfʌl] v. (-ge-) replenish (stock); eke out (meal); complete; augment; supplement; **-ling** n. addition; completion; supplement; **-lingsbegroting** n. supplementary estimates; **-sel** n. complement; padding; **-lend** a. (-e) complement-ary, supplementary.

'**aanvuur** ['änfewR] v. (-ge-) fire (imagination), incite, inspire, en-courage; '**aanvuring** n.; **-der** n. (-s) inciter.

'**aanwaggel** ['änvachəl] v. (-ge-) stagger, waddle along.

'**aanwakker** ['änvakaR] v. (-ge-) animate, rouse, stir up; liven up; **-ing** n.

'**aanwas** ['änvas] v. (-ge-) wax, increase, grow; rise; n. increase.

'**aanwen** ['änven] v. (-ge-) acquire (habit); get accustomed to; reclaim (land), increase; **-sel** n. (-s) habit.

'**aanwend** ['änvent] v. (-ge-) apply, use; appropriate; **-ing** n. application, use.

'**aanwerf**, **aanwerwe** ['änveRf, 'an-veRvə] v. (-ge-) enlist, recruit; '**aanwerwing** n.

'**aanwerk** ['änveRk] v. (-ge-) sew on; work faster; keep on working.

aan'wesig [än'vēsəch] a. (-e) present, on hand; **-e** n. (-s) audience; **-heid** n. presence, existence.

'**aanwinning** ['änvənəng] n. reclama-tion (of land).

'**aanwins** ['änvəns] n. (-te) gain, profit; acquisition.

'**aanwys** ['änvays] v. (-ge-, -gewese) indicate, show; allot, assign; **op jouself aangewys** thrown on one's own resources; **-end** a. (-e) indicat-ing; demonstrative (pron.); **-er** n. (-s) n. indicator; **-ing** n. allocation; indication; instruction: clue.

'**aap** ['äp] n. (ape) ape; monkey; **die-is uit die mou** the cat is out of the bag; '**n-** a foolish person; **jy lyk 'n mooi-** you fancy yourself; **-agtig** a. (-e) apish; **-skilloeder** n. black-guard, blighter; **-stert** n. sjambok; **stuipe** n. **die-kry** fly into a rage.

'**aar** ['aR] n. (are) ear (wheat), spike (bot.), vein (body), nerve (leaf); underground watercourse, lode, seam; core; **-ontsteking** n. plebitis; **-pers** n. tourniquet.

'**aarbei** ['aRbay] n. (-e) strawberry.

'**aard** ['aRt] n. character, disposition,

nature; kind, sort; v. (ge-) thrive, get on well; -na take after; -ig a., av. agreeable, nice; smart, witty; queer, unpleasant; -igheid n. fun, joke, pleasantry.

'aard ['aRt] v. (ge-) to earth, to ground (elect.); -kabel n. (-s) earth cable, earth strap.

'aarde ['aRdə] n. earth; soil; terbestel inter; op die-! interj. my word!; -werk n. earthenware, pottery.

'aard- n. = aarde.

'aardig ['aRdəch] a. (-; -er, -sie), agreeable; queer, strange.

'aards ['aRts] a. (-e) earthly, terrestrial, wordly, mundane; -gesind a. (-e) wordly-minded; -gesindheid n. worldliness.

'aars ['aRs] n. anus.

'aarsel ['aRsəl] v. (ge-) hesitate, waver; -end av. (-e) hesitant, wavering; -ing n.

'aartappel ['aRtapəl] n. potato; numskull.

'aarts- ['aRts] pref. consummate; -dom a. utterly stupid; -skelm n. arrant knave; -vader patriarch.

aas ['as] n. (ase) ace (cards); god (heathen); bait, carrion, prey; v. (ge-) feed, prey on; -voël n. (-s) vulture; -vretend a. (-e) necrophagous.

aaskewer ['askɛvər] n. (-s) carrion (sexton) beetle.

abakus ['abakʌs] n. (-se) abacus.

'abba ['aba] v. (ge-) pick-a-back; -kaggel n. outside chimney.

'abelspel ['abəlspɛl] n. ('abelspele), medieval secular drama.

ab'jater [ap'yatəR] n. (-s) scamp, urchin.

abnor'maal [apnoR'mal] a. (abnormale; abnormaler, abnormaalste) abnormal.

abon'nee [abo'ne] n. subscriber; -r v. (ge-) subscribe; abonne'ment n. subscription.

ab'sent [ap'sent] a. absent.

ab'ses [ap'ses] n. abscess.

ab'sint [ap'sənt] n. absinthe, wormwood.

abso'luut [apso'lewt] a. (abso'lute) absolute; av. opsluit absolutely.

absor'beer [apsoR'bɛR] v. (ge-) absorb; -gaas n. absorbent gauze; ab'sorberend a. (-e) absorbent; ab'sorbsie n. absorption; ab'sorpsievermoë n. absorptive power.

abstra'heer [apstRa'hɛR] v. (ge-) abstract; -hering n.

ab'strak [ap'stRak] a. (-te) abstract; -sie n. abstraction; -theid n. abstractness.

ab'surd [ap'sʌRt] a. preposterous, absurd; -i'teit n.

a'buis [a'bœis] n. error, mistake, oversight; per- by mistake.

'adamsappel ['adamsapəl] n. (-s) Adam's apple.

adap'tasie [adap'tasi] n. adaptation; adap'teer v. (ge-) adapt.

ad'dendum [a'dendʌm] n. addendum.

'adder ['adəR] n. (-s) snake, viper, serpent; -gebroedsel n. viperous brood.

addisio'neel [adisyo'nel] a. (addisio'nele) additional.

addi'tief [adi'tif] n. (additi'ewe) additive.

'adel 'adəl] n. nobility; v. (ge-) raise to peerage; ennoble; arbeid- labour ennobles; -dom n. nobility; -lik a. (-e) noble; titled; -likheid n. nobleness; -stand n. peerage.

'adelaar ['adəlaR] n. (-s) eagle, cp. arend.

'adem ['adəm] n. = asem; v. (ge-) breathe; -haling n. = asemhaling; -loos a. ('ademlose) breathless; -tog n. breath, gasp.

'ader- ['adəR] n. cp. aar-; -laat v. = bloedlaat; -lik a. (-e) venous.

ad'hesie [at'hɛsi] n. adhesion.

a'dieu [a'dyœ] n. (-s) goodbye.

adjek'tief [atyek'tif] n. (adjek'tiewe) adjective; adjek'tiwies a. adjectival.

adju'dant [atyew'dant] n. (-e) adjutant, aide-de-camp.

ad'junk [at'yʌnk] n. (-te) adjunct, assistant, deputy.

adminis'trasie [atmənə'stRasi] n. administration; management; administra'tief a. (administra'tiewe) administrative; adminis'treer v. (ge-) administer, manage.

'administra'teur [atmənəstRa'tœR] n. (-s) administrator, manager.

admi'raal [atmə'Ral] n. (-s) admiral; admirali'teit n. admirality; admirali'teitshof n. admirality-court.

adoles'sensie [adolə'sensi] n. adolescence; adoles'sent a. & av. (-e) adolescent.

a'doons [a'dons] n. monkey, jacko; ugly person.

adop'teer [adop'tɛR] v. (-) to adopt; adop'tasie n. adoption; adop'tief a. (adop'tiewe) adoptive.

adrena'lien, adrena'line [atRena'lin, atRena'linə] n. adrenalin.

a'dres [a'dRes] n. (-se) address; direction; petition; memorial; percare of; -'sant n. (-e) petitioner, sender; adres'seer v. (ge-) to address, label.

ad'verbium [at'fɛRbiʌm] n. (ad'verbia) adverb; adverbi'aal a. (ad'verbiale) adverbial.

adver'teer [atfəR'tɛR] v. (-) advertise; adver'tensie n. (-s) advertisement.

ad'vies [at'fis] n. advice; opinion; advi'seer v. (ge-) to advise; advi'serend a. (-e) advisory; advi'seur n. (-s) adviser.

advo'kaat [atfo'kat] n. (advo'kate) advocate, barrister; egg-flip; praat soos 'n- to have the gift of the gab; advo'katestreek n. clever trick.

'af ['af] pref. off; down; from; -en

toe off and on; *die werk is-* the work
is finished.

afa'sie [afa'si] n. aphasia.

'**afbaken** ['afbākən] v. (-ge-) delimit;
define; **-ing** n. delimitation; demarcation.

'**afbeeld** ['afbēlt] v. (-ge-) depict,
paint, represent; **-ing** n.; **-sel** n. (-s)
image, portrait.

'**afbeen** ['afbēn] a. crippled; n. a
cripple.

'**afbel** ['afbel] v. (-ge-) ring off.

'**afbestel** ['afbəstel] v. (-) counter-
mand, cancel (*an order*); **-ling** n.

'**afbetaal** ['afbətāl] v. (-) pay off;
clear (*debt*); pay on account;
'**afbetaling** n.; '**afbetalingstelsel** n.
instalment-system.

'**afbeul** ['afbœl] v. (-ge-) fag out.

'**afbind** ['afbənt] v. (-ge-) underbind,
tie off (*wart*); ligate (*vein*); butt;
-ing n. ligature.

'**afblaas** ['afblās] v. (-ge-) blow off
(*steam*); deflate; sound the retreat.

'**afborsel** ['afbauRsəl] v. (-ge-) brush
up (*off*).

'**afbraak** ['afbRāk] n. demolition.

'**afbrand** ['afbRant] v. (-ge-) set on
fire; burn down; **-ing** n.

'**afbreek** ['afbRēk] v. (-ge-) break off;
snap; divide; disconnect; break
down; '**afbreker** n. demolisher;
'**afbreking** n.

'**afbreuk** ['afbrœk] n. damage, injury; cp. **afbreek**.

'**afbring** ['afbRəng] v. (-ge-) bring
down, reduce; come off, get off,
escape.

'**afbuig** ['afbœich] v. (-ge-) bend
down, bend aside; **-ing** n. curving.

'**afbyt** ['afbayt] v. (-ge-) bite off; *die
spit-* bear the brunt.

'**afdaal** ['afdāl] v. (-ge-) to descend;
to stoop; '**afdaling** n.

'**afdak** ['afdak] n. lean-to, shed.

'**afdam** ['afdam] v. (-ge-) to dam up;
-ming n. (-e, -s) barrage.

'**afdank** ['afdank] v. (-ge-) dismiss;
discharge; scrap; cast off; **-ing** n;
'**afgedank(s)te** a. '*n - pakslae* a
severe hiding.

'**afdek** ['afdek] v. (-ge-) clear the
table.

'**afdeling** 'afdēlang] n. classification; detachment; section; department.

'**afdig** ['afdəch] v. (-ge-) to seal, blank
off; **-ting** n. seal, sealing.

'**afding** ['afdəng] v. (-ge-) to bargain,
haggle; disparage someone's merits.

'**afdoen** ['afdun] v. (-ge-, 'afgedaan)
detract from; settle (*business*); do
(*work*); **-de** a. conclusive, decisive;
effective.

'**afdop** ['afdop] v. (-ge-) peel, shell.

'**afdra** ['afdRā] v. (-ge-) carry down
(*steps*); wear out (*clothes*); hand over
(*money*); '**afdraand**, '**afdraans** av.
downhill; '**afdraande(s)** n. declivity,
slope.

'**afdraai** ['afdRāi] v. (-ge-) turn off

(*tap*), twist off (*neck*), run off (*film*),
play (*record*), branch off (*road*);
uncoil (*thread*), strip (*bolt*).

'**afdrink** ['afdRənk] v. (-ge-), *dit-* to
settle it over a glass.

'**afdroë**, '**afdroog** ['afdRōə, 'af-
dRōch] v. dry (*tears*); dry off; wipe
off; '**afdroogdoek** n. kitchen-cloth.

'**afdruk** ['afdRʌk] v. (-ge-) press
down; impress; print, reproduce; n.
(-ke) copy, impression; **-sel** n. (-s)
impression, print.

'**afdryf**, '**afdrywe** ['afdRayf, 'af-
dRayvə] v. (-ge-) drift down; force
down, abort; **-sel** n. flotsam;
'**afdrywend** a. (-e) purgative, aborti-
facient; '**afdrywing** n. expulsion;
refining: abortion.

'**afdwaal** ['afdwāl] v. (-ge-) stray;
digress; err.

'**afdwing** ['afdwəng] v. (-ge-) extort,
wring from, force out of; coerce;
-baar a. (-bare) actionable.

affek'teer [afek'tēR] v. (ge-) to
affect.

af'fêre [a'fɛrə] n. (-s) affair, business,
thing; '*n mooi-* a pretty kettle of
fish.

affili'eer [afili'ēR] v. (ge-) to affiliate;
affili'asie n.

affini'teit [afini'tayt] n. affinity.

affodil [afo'dəl] n. (-le) daffodil,
asphodel.

af'front [a'fRont] n. affront; **-'eer**
v. (ge-) to insult; **-'asie** n.

'**afgaan** ['afchān] v. (-ge-) go down;
part, leave; *-de koors* remittent
fever; *-de maan* waning moon.

'**afgebroke** ['afchəbRōkə] a. broken;
intermittent.

'**afgedankste** ['afchədankstə] a. confounded, deuced, severe; cp. **afdank**.

'**afgee** ['afchē] deliver, hand over,
tender, surrender, leave (*one's card*),
give out (*off*), emit; *- met iemand* to
keep company below one's station;
die kleur gee af the colour comes off,
stains.

'**afgeknot** ['afchəknot] a. (-te) stunted; truncated.

'**afgeleë** ['afchəlēə] a. distant, off the
beaten track.

'**afgeleef** ['afchəlēf] a. (-de) decrepit,
worn out (*with age*); **-dheid** n.

'**afgelei** ['afchəlay] cp. **aflei**.

'**afgelope** cp. **afloop**.

'**afgemat** ['afchəmat] a. (-te) tired,
weary; **-heid** n.

'**afgemete** ['afchəmētə] cp. **afmeet**.

'**afgerem** ['afchəRem] a. worn out,
fagged, jaded.

'**afgerig** ['afchəRəch] a. (-te) trained.

afgerond cp. **afrond**.

afgesaag ['afchəsāch] a. (-de) hack-
neyed; stale; sawn off, cp. **afsaag**.

'**afgesant** ['afchəsant] n. (-e) ambassador.

'**afgesien** ['afchəsin] conj. *-van* notwithstanding, irrespective of; av.
-van apart from.

'**afgeskeidene** ['afchəskaydənə] n.

(-s) dissenter, nonconformist; '**afge-skeidenheid** n. privacy, seclusion; '**afgeskeie** a. separate, dissenting.

'**afgesloof** cp. **afsloof**.

'**afgeslote** cp. **afsluit**.

'**afgesonder** cp. **afsonder**.

'**af'gespe(r)** ['af'chespə(R)] v. (-ge-) unbuckle, unclasp.

'**afgestorwe** ['afchəstoRvə] a. deceased, dead; -**ne** n. (-s).

'**afgetob** ['afchətop] a. (-de) worn out, weary.

'**afgetrokke** ['afchətRokə] a. abstract, absentminded; -**selfstandige naamwoord** abstract noun; -**nheid** n.

afgevaardigde ['afchəfaRdəchdə] n. (-s) delegate, representative.

afgevallene ['afchəfalənə] n. (-s) apostate, renegade.

'**afgewerk** ['afchəveRk] a. (-te) tired, worn out; finished.

'**afgiet** ['afchit] v. (-ge-) pour off; drain; cast, mould; -**sel** n. (-s) cast, copy, mould; -**seldiertjies** pl. infusoria.

'**afgod** ['afchot] n. ('afgode) idol, fetish; '**afgodies** a. (-e) idolatrous; **afgo'dis** a. (-te) idolator; '**afgodsbeeld** n. idol.

'**afgooi** ['afchŏi] v. (-ge-) throw down, throw off.

'**afgrond** ['afchRont] n. (-e) abyss, precipice.

af'gryslik [af'chrayslək] a. (-e) ghastly, horrible, dreadful; -**heid** n.

'**afguns** ['afchʌns] n. jealousy, spite; **af'gunstig** a. (-e) envious, jealous; **af'gunstigheid** n.

afhaak ['afhàk] v. (-ge-) unhook, detach; let go, let rip; get married.

afhaal ['afhàl] v. (-ge-) bring down; fetch, collect; meet; iemand- insult a person; -**wa** n. collecting-van.

'**afhaar** ['afhàR] v. (-ge-) depilate; string beans.

'**afhandel** ['afhandəl] v. (-ge-) conclude, settle; -**ing** n.

af'handig [af'handəch] av. iemand iets-maak filch something from a person.

'**afhang** ['afhang] v. (-ge-) hang down; droop; depend on; -**end** a. (-e) hanging, drooping, pendulous; **af'hanklik** a. (-e) dependent; **af'hanklikheid** n.

'**afheg** ['afhech] v. (-ge-) cast off (knitting).

'**afhel** ['afhel] v. (-ge-) slant down, decline.

'**afhelp** ['afhelp] v. (-ge-) hand down, help off; rid a person of something.

'**afhou** ['afhoa] v. (-ge-) keep off, keep at bay; withhold.

'**afjak** ['afyak] v. (-ge-) to affront, scold, snub; n. affront, rating, rebuff.

afjakker ['afyakəR] v. (-ge-) to overwork, overdrive, wear out.

'**afkam** ['afkam] v. (-ge-) to comb off; disparage.

'**afkant** ['afkant] v. (-ge-) to chamfer; -**ing** n. chamfer.

af'kap ['afkap] v. (-ge-) chop off; cut down; abbreviate (word); -**ping** n.; -**pingsteken** n. apostrophe.

af'keer ['afkèR] v. (-ge-) avert; parry; turn aside (water in canal); n. dislike, repugnance; '**afkerig** av. -**van** averse to; '**afkerigheid** n.

af'keur ['afköR] v. (-ge-) disavow, disapprove, condemn; denounce, reject; ban; -**ens'waardig** a. (-e) blameworthy, objectionable; -**ens-'waardigheid** n. blameworthiness; -**ing** n.

af'klim ['afkləm] v. (-ge-) climb down, descend.

'**afknibbel** ['afknəbəl] v. (-ge-) nibble off; haggle.

'**afknip** ['afknəp] v. (-ge-) cut off, trim; clip; crop (hair).

'**afknou** ['afknoa] v. (-ge-) to hurt, bully.

'**afknyp** ['afknayp] v. (-ge-) to pinch off; use sparingly.

af'koel ['afkul] v. (-ge-) to cool down; to calm down; refrigerate.

af'kom ['afkom] v. (-ge-) come down; -**van** get off; get rid of; be descended from (a family), derived from (a language); -**s** n. birth, descent; derivation; **af'komstig** av. descended from, derived from.

'**afkondig** ['afkondəch] v. (-ge-) declare, promulgate; -**ing** n.

'**afkonkel** ['afkonkəl] v. (-ge-) to entice away from.

af'kook ['afkŏk] v. (-ge-) decoct; -**sel** n. (-s) decoction, extract.

af'koop ['afkŏp] v. (-ge-) buy off, redeem; ransom; 'n polis- surrender a policy; n. redemption; ransom; -**baar** a. (-bare) redeemable; -**boete** n. (-s) spot fine; -**waarde** n. (-s) surrender value.

af'kort ['afkoRt] v. (-ge-) abbreviate (word); abridge (story); -**ing** n.

afkry [afkRay] v. (-ge-), to finish (task); to remove (stain); to get free (day).

'**afkyk** ['afkayk] v. (-ge-) look down; to crib.

'**aflaai** ['aflài] v. (-ge-) unload, offload, discharge.

'**aflaat** ['aflàt] n. indulgence.

'**aflê** ['aflè] v. (-ge-) lay down (arms); cover (distance); die eed- take the oath; n. besoek- to pay a visit; discard (clothes); '**aflegging** n.

'**afleer** ['aflèR] v. (-ge-) unlearn (habit); forget (language).

'**aflees** ['aflès] v. (-ge-) read out, call out (names).

'**aflei** ['aflay] v. (-ge-) lead down, away; divert; conclude; deduce; derive; trace back to; -**ding** n. (-e, -s); -**er** n. lightning-conductor.

'**aflewer** ['aflèvəR] v. (-ge-) deliver (goods); turn out (graduates); -**ing** n. delivery; instalment (journal)-**diens**

n. (-te) delivery service; -wa n. (-ens) delivery van.

'afloer ['aflůR] v. (-g-) to peep, spy out; -der n. (-s) peeping Tom.

'afloop ['aflôp] v. (-ge-) flow down; expire; drain; slope; n. termination, end: issue; denouement.

'aflos ['aflos] v. (-ge-) to relieve, take turns; redeem, pay off; -baar a. (-bare) redeemable; -sing n.

'aflui ['aflœi] v. (-ge-) ring off.

'afluister ['aflœistəR] v. (-ge-) eaves-drop; -aar n. eavesdropper.

'afmaak ['afmǎk] v. (-ge-) finish (task); settle (quarrel); kill, slaughter; shell (cobs); 'afmaker n. sheller.

'afmat ['afmat] v. (-ge-) to tire out, exhaust; 'afgematte a. exhausted; 'afgematheid n. exhaustion; 'afmat-tend a. (-e) tiring, gruelling, trying; -ting n.

'afmeet ['afmět] v. (-ge-) measure off; 'afmeting n. dimension, size.

'afname ['afnǎmə] n. decline, decay, cp. afneem.

'afneem ['afněm] v. (-ge-) remove, take down; deprive of; decrease; abate; subside; decline; wane, slacken; to photograph; -baar a. (-bare) removable, detachable; 'af-nemer n. (-s) photographer.

'afoes ['afus] v. (-ge-) to reap.

afo'nie [afo'ni] n. aphony.

afor'isme [afo'Rəsmə] n. (-s) aphor-ism, adage; afor'isties a. (-e) aphoristic.

'afpaar ['afpǎR] v. (-ge-) pair off (anglicism).

'afpak ['afpak] v. (-ge-) unpack, unload.

'afpen ['afpen] v. (-ge-) peg off.

'afperk ['afpeRk] v. (-ge-) fence in; circumscribe; -ing n. demarcation.

'afpers ['afpeRs] v. (-ge-) extort; draw (tears); -ing n.

'afpluk ['afplʌk] v. (-ge-) pick, pluck, gather.

'afpoets ['afputs] v. (-ge-) clean, polish.

'afpraat ['afpRǎt] v. (-ge-) arrange, agree upon.

'afraai ['afRǎi] v. (-ge-) advise against, discourage.

'afraak ['afRǎk] v. (-ge-) to stray from; get away from; get rid of.

'aframmel ['afRaməl] v. (-ge-) rattle off.

'afransel ['afRǎnsəl] v. (-ge-) thrash, flog; -ing n.

'afraspe(r) ['afRaspə(R)] v. (-ge-) rasp off.

'afreis ['afrays] v. (-ge-) depart, set out on journey; die land- travel all over country; n. departure.

'afreken ['afRěkən] v. (-ge-) settle accounts; -ing n.

'afrig ['afRəch] v. (-ge-) coach, train, break in (horse); -ter n. coach, trainer; -ting n.

'Afrika ['ǎfRikǎ] n. Africa; Afri-

'kaans n., a. (-e) Afrikaans; of Africa; Afri'kaner n. (-s) Africander; European in S. Africa; Mexican marigold; Afri'kanertjie dim. (-s) gladiolus.

'afrit ['afRət] n. (-te) ramp (down); cp. aanrit.

'afrokkel ['afRokəl] v. (-ge-) entice away.

'afrol ['afRol] v. (ge-) roll down; unroll; uncoil.

'afrond ['afRont] v. (-ge-) finish off, round off; -ing n.; 'afgeronde a. finished off.

'afroom ['afRôm] v. (-ge-) take cream off, skim.

'afruk ['afRʌk] v. (-ge-) pull, tear down, tear away.

'afry ['afRay] v. (-ge-) drive off; cover by driving; wear out.

'afsaag ['afsǎch] v. (-ge-) saw off; 'afgesaag a. (-de) sawn off; hack-neyed, stale.

'afsaal ['afsǎl] v. (-ge-) off-saddle.

'afsak ['afsak] v. (-ge-) slip, sag down, subside; -sel n. deposit, silt.

afsê ['afse] v. (-ge-) cancel, call off; sack; 'afsegging n.

'afsend ['afsent] v. (-ge-) consign, dispatch, forward, send off; -er n. (-s) sender; -ing n.

'afset ['afset] n. sale, turnover; v. (-ge-) victimize; amputate; -baar a. (-bare), marketable, disposable; -sel n. trimming, sediment; -ter n. cheat, swindler; -tery n. swindling; -ting n. amputation; dismissal; sediment.

'afsien ['afsin] v. (-ge-) abandon; forego; af'sienbaar a. (af'sienbare) -toekoms near or immediate future, foreseeable.

af'sigtelik [af'səchtələk] a. (-e) hideous, ugly; af'sigtelikheid n.

'afsit ['afsət] v. (-ge-) start, run off; remove; dismiss; amputate.

'afskaf ['afskaf] v. (-ge-) abolish; abrogate; give up; -fer n. abolisher; teetotaller; -fing n. abolition; tee-totalism; -fingsbeweging n. temper-ance-movement.

'afskeep ['afskěp] v. (-ge-) treat shabbily; neglect someone; botch one's work; 'afskepery n. neglect; bungling.

'afskeer ['afskěR] v. (-ge-) shave off, shear off.

'afskei ['afskay] v. (-ge-) separate, sever; secrete; dissociate; -d n. departure; -ding n. separation; secession; secretion; -er n. separator.

'afskep ['afskep] v. (-ge-) skim; scoop off.

'afskets ['afskets] v. (-ge-) sketch.

'afskeur ['afskěR] v. (-ge-) peel, tear off; secede; -ing n.

'afskiet ['afskit] v. (-ge-) discharge, fire; shoot down; shoot off.

'afskil ['afskəl] v. (-ge-) peel, pare, bark (tree).

'afskilfer ['afskəlfəR] v. (-ge-) peel off, flake away.

'**afskop** ['afskop] v. (-ge-) kick off; kick down (stairs); n. kick-off (football).

'**afskort** ['afskoRt] v. (-ge-) partition off; **-ing** n.

'**afskot** ['afskot] n. = **afskorting**.

'**afskraap** ['afskRāp] v. (-ge-) scrape off, scale (fish); **-sel** n. scrapings.

'**afskram** ['afskRam] v. (-ge-) glance off.

'**afskrif** ['afskRəf] n. (-te) copy, duplicate.

'**afskrik** ['afskRək] v. (-ge-) deter; frighten; dishearten; n. horror; deterrent; aversion; **-'wekkend** a. (-e; -er, -ste) terrifying, deterring.

'**afskroef** ['afskRuf] v. (-ge-) unscrew.

'**afskroei** ['afskRui] v. (-ge-) singe (off).

'**afskrop** ['afskRop] v. (-ge-) scrub, scour (floor); scrape off (soil).

'**afskryf**, '**afskrywe** ['afskRayf, 'afskRayvə] v. (-ge-) copy, transcribe; crib; cancel; sack; write off (depreciation); '**afskrywing** n. (-e, -s).

'**afsku** ['afskew] n. abhorrence, horror; **-wekkend** a. (-e; -er, -ste), horrifying, hideous; '**afskuwelik** a. (-e; -er, -ste) horrible, hideous, abominable, vile; '**afskuwelikheid** n. atrociousness, horribleness.

'**afskud** ['afskʌt] v. (-ge-) shake off.

'**afskuif**, '**afskuiwe** ['afskœif, 'afskœivə] v. (-ge-) slide down; push back (bolt); slip off (ring).

'**afskuim** ['afskœim] v. (-ge-) skim, remove froth.

'**afskuins** ['afskœiñs] v. (-ge-) to bevel; **-ing** n. bevelling.

'**afskut** ['afskʌt] v. (-ge-) partition off; **-ting** n.

'**afskuur** ['afskēwR] v. (-ge-) scour off, grind.

'**afslaan** ['afslān] v. (-ge-) beat off; repel; decline; tee off (golf); '**afslag** n. reduction; '**afslaer** n. (-s) auctioneer.

'**afslag** ['afslach] v. (-ge-) flay, skin.

'**afslof** ['afslof] v. (-ge-) wear out; shuffle down.

'**afsloof**, '**afslowe** ['afslôf, 'afslōvə] v. (-ge-) wear out.

'**afsluit** ['afslœit] v. (-ge-) lock; cut off; shut off; block; disconnect; close, wind up (account); conclude (treaty); **-er** n. stop-valve; cut-out; **-ing** n.

'**afslyt** ['afslayt] v. (-ge-) wear away; **-ing** n.

'**afsmeer** ['afsmēR] v. (-ge-) palm off.

'**afsnoer** ['afsnūR] v. (-ge-) separate; **-ing** n.

'**afsnou** ['afsnoa] v. (-ge-) snub, snarl at.

'**afsny** ['afsnay] v. (-ge-) cut off; intercept; amputate; **-ding** n.

'**afsonder** ['afson(d)əR] v. (-ge-) separate; isolate; jou-van, retire from; seclude; **-ing** n.; '**afsonderlik** a. (-e) separate; individual; av.

separately; '**afgesonder** a. (-de) separated.

'**afspit** ['afspət] v. (-ge-) dig off.

'**afsplinter** ['afspləntəR] v. (-ge-) splinter off.

'**afsplits** ['afspləts] v. (-ge-) split off; **-ing** n.

'**afspoel** ['afspul] v. (-ge-) rinse, wash.

'**afspons** ['afspauñs] v. (-ge-) sponge down.

'**afspraak** ['afspRāk] n. appointment; agreement.

'**afspreek** ['afspRēk] v. (-ge-, '**afgesproke**) agree upon, arrange; '**afgesproke!** interj. agreed! done!

'**afspring** ['afspRəng] v. (-ge-) jump off, alight; crack off (paint), burst off (button), break off (negotiation).

'**afstaan** ['afstān] v. (-ge-) cede, give up, renounce; **afstand** n.

'**afstam** ['afstam] v. (-ge-) -van be descended from; **-meling** n. descendant; **-ming** n. descent, derivation.

'**afstamp** ['afstamp] v. (-ge-) bump, knock off.

'**afstand** ['afstant] n. distance, range; interval; cession; renunciation; waiver.

'**afstap** ['afstap] v. (-ge-) step off, alight; cover by walking; -van change, dismiss, drop (subject).

'**afsteek** ['afstēk] v. (-ge-) cut (sods), mark out (with spade); chisel off; make a speech; push off from shore; to cut a bad figure.

'**afstel** ['afstel] v. (-ge-) disengage, disconnect; cancel (appointment); n. cancellation.

'**afstem** ['afstem] v. (-ge-) reject, turn down; **-ming** n.

'**afstempel** ['afstempəl] v. (-ge-) cancel by means of a stamp; **-ing** n. cancellation.

'**afsterf**, '**afsterwe** ['afstēRf, 'afstēRvə] v. (-ge-) die, die off; mortify (organs); die out (friendship); forget (friendship); '**afsterwing** n.

'**afstig** ['afstəch] v. (-ge-) secede and form new organisation.

'**afstof** ['afstof] v. (-ge-) dust.

'**afstomp** ['afstomp] v. (-ge-) blunt; deaden (feelings); **-ing** n.

'**afstoot** ['afstōt] v. (-ge-) thrust off, repel, repulse; alienate (people); af'**stootlik** a. (-e; -er, -ste) forbidding, repulsive; af'**stootlikheid** n. repulsiveness; af'**stotend** a. (-e; -er, -ste) = **afstootlik**.

'**afstraal** ['afstRāl] v. (-ge-) radiate, reflect.

'**afstraf** ['afstRaf] v. (-ge-) punish; reprove; **-fing** n.

'**afstroop** ['afstRōp] v. (-ge-) flay, strip (animal); plunder (country); roll down (sleeves).

'**afstuit** ['afstœit] v. (-ge-) rebound, recoil; be frustrated by.

'**afstyg** ['afstaych] v. (-ge-) get down, dismount.

'**afsweer** ['afswēR] v. (-ge-) abjure, forswear, renounce; '**afswering** a.

'aftakel ['aftǎkəl] v. (-ge-) dismantle; thrash.

'aftap ['aftap] v. (-ge-) tap, draw off, bottle; drain; -prop n. (-pe) drain plug.

'aftas ['aftas] v. (-ge-) scan, sweep (radar); -ter n. (-s) scanner, viewer; -ting n. (-s) scanning, sweep.

'aftel ['aftel] v. (-ge-) count out; lift off (down).

'aftog ['aftoch] n. retreat.

'aftorring ['aftoRəng] v. (-ge-) unrip.

'aftrap ['aftRap] v. (-ge-) step down; 'n stel- put one's foot into it.

aftree ['aftRē] v. (-ge-) descend; retire; resign; place; 'aftreding n.

'aftrek ['aftRek] v. (-ge-) deduct; extract; pull down; divert (attention); pull trigger; n. reduction; demand, sale; -king n.; -teken n. minus sign; -sel n. extract, infusion.

'aftuimel ['aftœiməl] v. (-ge-) tumble down.

'afvaardig ['afǎRdəch] v. (-ge-) delegate, depute; elect; -ing n.

'afval]'afal] v. (-ge-) drop off; lose weight; secede from; n. garbage, refuse; scrap; tripe and trotters; -lend a. (-e) deciduous; af'vallig a. (-e; -er, -ste) disloyal, faithless; af'valligheid n. defection; desertion.

'afvee(g) ['afē(ch)] v. (-ge-) wipe, mop, dust, sweep, polish.

'afvloei ['aflui] v. (-ge-) flow down, run off, drain; n. drainage; -ing n.

'afvoer ['afūR] v. (-ge-) remove, lead away; n. removal; carrying off.

'afvryf, 'afvrywe ['afRayf, 'afRay-və] v. (-ge-) rub off, polish.

'afvuur ['afēwR] v. (-ge-) discharge, fire (gun).

'afvyl ['afayl] v. (-ge-) file down.

'afwaai ['avǎi] v. (-ge-) blow off; 'afgewaaide vrugte windfall.

'afwaarts ['avǎRts] av. downward.

'afwag ['avach] v. (-ge-) await, bide; tend a. (-e) waiting; -ting n.

'afwas ['avas] v. (-ge-) wash, wash off.

'afwater ['avǎtəR] v. (-ge-) drain, pour off; weaken, water down; -ing n.

'afweer ['avēR] v. (-ge-) avert (danger), prevent; parry, keep at bay; n. defence; 'afwering n. defence.

'afwen ['aven] v. (-ge-) unlearn, break off a habit; unreel.

'afwend ['avent] v. (-ge-) avert; divert; stave off; -ing n.

'afwentel ['aventl] v. (-ge-) roll away.

'afwerk ['aveRk] v. (-ge-) complete, finish off; work off (debt); conclude (program); -ing n. workmanship, finish.

'afwerp ['aveRp] v. (-ge-) cast, shed; yield; shake off (feeling).

af'wesig [av'ēsəch] a. (-e) absent; -e n. (-s) absent person; -heid n. absence.

'afwikkel ['avəkəl] v. (-ge-) unwind, uncoil; wind up, liquidate; -ing n.

'afwissel ['avəsəl] v. (-ge-) alternate, vary; -end a. (-e) varied, alternate; varying; -ing n.

'afwit ['avət] v. (-ge-) whitewash.

'afwyk ['avayk] v. (-ge-) diverge, deviate, deflect; -end a. (-e; -er, -ste) devious, divergent; abnormal; -ing n.

'afwys ['avays] v. (-ge-) turn away; reject, decline; -end a. (-e) negative; -ing n.

'ag ['ach] v. (-ge-) esteem, value; regard; n. attention, care; -ting n.; interj. -! ah! alas!; -baar a. (-bare) honourable, venerable; -baarheid n. respectability, venerableness; -tens-'waardig a. (-e) venerable; -tens-'waardigheid n. respectability.

'ag(t) ['ach(t)] n. eight.

a'gaat [a'chǎt] n. agate.

aga'pant [acha'pant] n. agapanthus.

a'geer [a'chēR] v. (ge-) act; a'gerend a. (-e) acting.

a'genda [a'chenda] n. (-s) agenda.

a'gent [a'chent] n. (-e) agent; policeman; -skap n. agency.

aggre'gaat [achRə'chǎt] n. aggregate.

'agie ['ǎchi] n. nuuskierige- Miss Curiosity.

agi'tasie [achi'tǎsi] n. agitation; agi'tator n. (-s) agitator; agi'teer v. (ge-) agitate.

a'grariër [a'chRǎRiəR] n. (-s) agrarian; a'graries a. (-e) agrarian.

a'gressie [a'chResi] n. aggression; agres'sief a. (-we; -wer, -ste) aggressive; agressiwi'teit n. aggressiveness.

'ag(t)ste ['ach(t)stə] ord. eighth.

'agteloos ['achtəlōs] a. careless, inattentive; negligent; agte'losig a. av. (-e; -er, -ste) = agteloos; -heid, 'agtelosigheid n.

agtens'waardig [achtəfis'vǎRdəch] a. (-e; -er, -ste) respectable, estimable.

'agter ['achtəR] prep. behind (door), at back (of house), in arrears; av. in the rear; my oorllosie is- my watch is slow; hy kom van - af he came up from the rear; ek gaan gou - toe I'm going to the lavatory.

'agteraan ['achtəRǎn] av. behind, at the back, in the rear; -aankom v. (-ge-) bring up the rear; 'agteraf av. backward, secretly; poor; out of the way; a. backward, 'n-straat back street; 'agterbaks a. (-e) sly, underhand; av. secretly, on the sly.

'agteras ['achtəRas] n. (-te) rear or back axle.

'agterbly ['achtəRblay] v. (-ge-) remain, stay behind; lag behind; survive; -er n. (-s) laggard, straggler; -wende n. (-s) survivor.

'agterbuurt ['achtəRbēwRt] n. slum.

'agterdeur ['achtəRdēR] n. backdoor; loop-hole; by die - inkom to attain a position by underhand methods.

'agter'dog ['achtəRdoch] n. suspicion; -tig a. (-e; -er, -ste) suspicious; -tigheid n.

agter'een [achtəR'ēn] av. = aaneen; -'volgende a. consecutive; -'volgens av. consecutively.

'agterend ['achtəR'ent] n. hind-part; backside.

'agtergrond ['achtəRchRont] n. background.

agter'haal [achtərhāl] v. (-) overtake, catch up with.

'agterhoede ['achtəRhudə] n. rearguard, rear.

'agterhou ['achtəRhoa] v. (-ge-) keep back; withhold; conceal; agter'houdend a. (-e; -er, -ste) close, reserved; agter'houdendheid n.

'agterhuis ['achtəRhœis] n. back part of house; - in av. at the back.

'Agter-'Indië Further India.

'agteringang ['achtəRəngang] n. (-e) rear entrance, entry.

'agterklap ['achtəRklap] n. slander.

'agterkleinkind ['achtəRklayngkənt] n. (-ers) great-grandchild.

'agterkom ['achtəRkom] v. (-ge-) discover, find out, uncover the truth; hy kom agter die waarheid he discovers the facts.

'agterkop ['achtəRkop] n. (-pe) occiput; 'n plan in sy - hê to have a plan in mind.

'agterlaat ['achtəRlāt] v. (-ge-) leave behind.

'agterlamp ['achtəRlamp] n. (-e) rear lamp.

'agterlig ['achtəRləch] n. (-te) rear light.

'agterlik ['achtəRlək] a. (-e; -er, -ste) backward, outmoded, lagging; -heid n.

agterlosig ['achtəlōsəch] a. careless.

'agterlyf ['achtəRlayf] n. ('agterlywe) rear part of body, buttocks, haunches.

agterme'kaar [achtəRmə'kāR] a. neat, orderly, 'n-huis an orderly house; av. on end, without end or pause, dinge gebeur - things happen incessantly.

agter'middag ['achtəRmədach] n. cp. middag afternoon.

agter'na [achtəR'nā] av. subsequently, afterwards.

'agternaam ['achtəRnām] n. ('agtername) surname.

agter'nasit [achtəR'nasət] v. (-gesit) pursue.

'agterom ['achtəRom] av. round the back (way).

'agterop ['achtəRop] av. behind, at the back.

agter'opskop [achtəR'opskop] v. (-opge-) frisk.

'agteros ['achtəRos] n. (-se) rear ox, the slow one.

'agterplaas ['achtəRplās] n. ('agterplase) backyard.

agter'stallig [achtəR'staləch] a. due, overdue.

'agterste ['achtəRstə] a. last, hindmost; n. hinder parts = agterlyf.

'agterstand ['achtəRstant] n. arrears.

'agterstel ['achtəRstel] v. (-ge-) place behind, put at disadvantage; n. back, behind; rear-chassis; -ling n.

agtereste'voor [achtəRstə'fōR] av. back-to-front, topsy-turvy.

agter'uit [achtəR'œit] av. back, backward; -ry v. (-gery) reverse, ride backwards.

'agterveld ['achtəRfelt] n. backveld; -er n. (-s) backvelder.

'agtervoeg ['achtəRfuch] v. (-ge-) add, affix, subjoin; -ing n. addition, paragoge; -sel n. (-s) suffix.

agter'volg [achtəR'folch] v. (-) chase, follow, pursue; -er n. (-s) pursuer; persecutor; -ing n.

'agtien ['achtin] num eighteen; -de n., a. eighteenth.

'agting ['achtəng] n. esteem.

'agtuur ['achtāWR] n. eight o'clock; breakfast.

a'gurkie [a'chəRkī] dim. (-s) gherkin.

'ai ['ai] interj. ah! ow! ouch!

'aia ['aya] n. (-s) ayah, native nursemaid, old native woman.

'aikôna ['(h)aikauna] interj. not at all! emphatically no!

'aitsa ['aitsa] interj. my! look out! sorry!

aka'demie [aka'dēmī] n. (-s) academy; -s a. (-e) academic.

a'kant [ā'kant] n. acanthus.

a'kasia [a'kāsia] n. acacia.

ake'lei [akə'lay] n. columbine, aquilegia.

'Aken ['akə] Aix-la-Chapelle.

'akkedis [akə'dəs] n. lizard, newt.

'akker ['akəR] n. (-s) field, plot; acre; acorn; -boom n. oaktree; -bou n. agriculture; -hout n. oak; -tjie dim. bed (flower).

akkomo'deer [akomə'dēR] v. (ge-) accommodate.

akkompan'jeer [akompan'yēR] v. (ge-) accompany.

ak'koord [a'kōRt] n. (-e) agreement, arrangement; chord (music); -! OK!

akkor'deer [aka'dēR] v. (ge-) agree, come to terms; get on with.

akku'raat [akew'Rāt] a. (akku'rate; akku'rater, -ste) accurate, precise; -heid n.

akkusa'tief [a'kewsatif] n. (akkusa-'tiewe) accusative.

akoes'tiek [akus'tik] n. acoustics; a'koesties a. (-e) acoustic.

akro'baat [akRo'bāt] n. (akro'bate) acrobat; akro'baties a. (-e) acrobatic.

'aks ['aks] n. eighth (of an inch); wee bit.

ak'sent [ak'sent] n. (-e) accent; aksentu'asie n. accentuation; aksentu'eer v. (ge-) accentuate, stress.

aksep'teer [aksep'tēR] v. (ge-) accept; aksep'tasie n.

'aksie ['aksi] *n.* agitation; law-suit; -s *pl.* airs.

aksi'oma [aksi'ōma] *n.* (-s) axiom; aksio'maties *a.* (-e) axiomatic.

aksio'naris [aksio'nāRəs] *n.* shareholder.

ak'syns [ak'sayns] *n.* excise; -pligtig *a.* (-e) excisable.

'akte ['aktə] *n.* (-s) deed; certificate; -tas *n.* brief-case; -trommel *n.* (-s) deed-box.

ak'teur [aktœR] *n.* (-s) actor, player; *cp.* toneelspeler.

ak'tief [ak'tif] *a.* (ak'tiewe; ak'tiewer, -ste) active, energetic; ak'tiewe diens active service; aktiwi'teit *n.*

aktuali'teit [aktew'alitayt] *n.* actuality.

aktu'ari(u)s [aktew'āRi(ʌ)s] *n.* actuary; aktuari'eel *a.* (aktu'ariéle) actuarial.

aktu'eel [aktew'ēl] *a.* (aktu'ele; aktu'ele, -ste), actual.

a'kuut [akewt] *a.* (akute), acute.

akwa'duk [akwa'dʌk] *n.* (-te) aqueduct.

akwa'rel [akwa'Rel] *n.* (-le) aquarelle.

a'kwarium [a'kwāRiʌm] *n.* (-s) aquarium.

'al *a.* (-le) all, each, every, -twee both; -dae every day; *av.* already, yet; -te veel overmuch; -lank- long ago; geheel en- altogether; *conj.* though, even if, even though; -honderd en tien keer even so.

a'larm [a'laRəm] *n.* alarm, uproar; alar'merend *a.* (-e) alarming; alar'mis *n.* (-te) scaremonger; alar'misties *a.* (-e) alarming.

Al'banië [al'bāniə] Albania: alba'nees *a., n.* (Al'banese) Albanian; Al'banies *a.* (-e) Albanian.

al'baster [al'bastəR] *n.* (-s) marble; alabaster.

al'bei ['albay] *n.* both.

al'bino [al'binō] *n.* (-s) albino.

albu'mine [albew'minə] *n.* albumen; eiwit(stof).

al'chemie [alshə'mi] *n.* alchemy.

al'daar [al'dāR] *av.* there, at that spot.

'aldag [al'dach] *av.* every day.

'aldeur [al'dœR] *av.* all along, throughout.

al'dus [al'dʌs] *av.* thus, therefore.

al'eer [al'ēR] *conj.* before, ere.

Alemanne ['āləmanə] Alemanni.

'alfa ['alfa] *n.* alpha; die-en omega the beginning and end.

alfa'bet [alfa'bet] *n.* (-te) alphabet; alfa'beties *a.* (-e) alphabetic.

'algar ['alchəR] *pron.* all, everybody.

'alge ['algə] *pl.* n. algae.

'algeheel ['alchəhēl] *a.* ('algehele) complete, utter; *av.* completely, utterly.

'algemeen ['alchəmēn] *n.* in die in general; *a.* ('algemene; 'algemener, -ste) general; common; 'algemene

verkiesing general election; -heid *n.* commonness.

al'hier [al'hiR] *av.* here, at this place.

alhoe'wel [alhu'vel] *conj.* (al)though.

'alkant(e) ['alkant(ə)] *n.* (on) all sides.

al'koof [al'kōf] *n.* (al'kowe) alcove.

'alla ['ala] *interj.* -'mapstieks, -'maskas, -'mastig, -'mensig, -'mintig, -'wêreld goodness! gracious!

'alledaags ['alədāchs] *a.* (ee; -er, -ste) common; daily, ordinary; -heid *n.* commonness; triviality.

al'leen [a'lēn] *av.* alone, lonely; -heerser *n.* (-s) autocrat; -lik *av.* only, merely; -staande *a.* isolated, solitary.

al'leenhandel [a'lēnhanl] *n.* monopoly.

allego'rie [alachō'Ri] *n.* allegory; alle'gories *a.* (-e) allegoric(al).

'alleman, Jan - ['yan 'aləman] *n.* John Citizen, Everyman, everybody.

'allengs ['alengs] *av.* gradually.

al'lenig = alleen.

'aller- [aləR] *pref.* denoting the highest degree of.

aller'gie [aleR'chi] *n.* allergy.

'allerhande ['aləRhande] *a.* all kinds of.

'allerlei ['aləRlay] *a.* miscellaneous, *cp.* allerhande.

aller'syds [aləR'sayts] *av.* on all sides.

'allerweë ['aləRvēə] *av.* everywhere.

'alles ['aləs] *n.* all, everything.

allesbe'halwe [aləsbə'halvə] *av.* anything but.

'allesins ['aləsəns] *av.* in every respect.

'allig ['aləch] *av.* probably.

al'looi [a'lōi] *n.* alloy.

alluvi'aal [aluvi'āl] *a.* (alluvi'ale) alluvial.

'almag ['almach] *n.* omnipotence; Almagtige, die- the Almighty.

'almal ['almal] *n.* all, everybody.

alma'nak [alma'nak] *n.* (-ke) almanac, calendar.

'almelewe ['amələvə] *av.* always.

'almiddel ['almədəl] *n.* (-s) panacea; = geneesal.

almis'kie [alma'ski] *av.* nevertheless.

al'om [al'om] *av.* everywhere.

'alomvattend ['alomfatənt] *a.* (-e) all-embracing.

al'oue [al'oaə] *a.* ancient.

'Alpe, die- the Alps; -roos *n.* rhododendron; -viooltjie *n.* cyclamen.

al'reeds [al'Rēts] *av.* already.

'alrisikopolis ['alRisikōpōləs] *n.* (-se) all-risks policy.

'als(em) ['als(əm)] *n.* wormwood.

al'so [al'sō] thus.

'alsolie ['alsōli] *n.* absinthe oil.

al'sydig [al'saydəch] *a.* (-e; -er, -ste) all-round; versatile; -heid *n.*

al'tans [al'tāns] *conj.* at least, anyway, anyhow.

'alte ['altə] *av.* very, too.

alte′mit(s) [altə′mət(s)] *av.* perhaps, maybe.

alterna′tief [alteRna′tif] *n.*, *a.* (*alterna′tiewe*) alternative.

′altesaam, ′altesame [′altesām] *av.* altogether.

′altoos [′altōs] *av.* always.

altyd [′altayt] *av.* always.

′altyddeur [′altayd(ŒR] *av.* always, ever and anon.

al′vas [al′fas] *av.* meanwhile.

′alvleesklier [′alflĕskliR] *n.* pancreas.

al′vorens [al′fōRəns] *prep.* before.

al′waar [al′vāR] *av.* where.

al′weer [al′vĕR] *av.* again.

al′wetend [al′vĕtənt] *a.* (-*e*) omniscient.

alwys [′alvays] *a.* (-*e*) all-wise.

a′mandel [a′mandəl] *n.* (-*s*) almond; tonsil.

ama′rant [ama′Rant] *n.* amaranthus.

ama′ril [ama′Rəl] *n.* emery; **-doek** *n.* emery cloth; **-papier** *n.* emery paper; **-skyf** *n.* (*skywe*) emery wheel; **-steen** *n.* (*stene*) emery stone.

ama′teur [ama′tŒR] *n.* amateur, novice.

′ambag [′ambach] *n.* (-*te*) trade, craft, profession; *′n man van twaalf ambagte en dertien ongelukke* Jack-of-all-trades; **-sman** *n.* (-*ne*) artisan.

ambas′sade [′ambə′sādə] *n.* (-*s*) embassy; **ambassa′deur** *n.* (-*s*) ambassador.

′amberboom [′ambəRbōm] *n.* sweetgum, liquid amber.

ame′tis [ama′təs] *n.* amethyst.

ameubel′ment [amŒbəlment] *n.* furniture.

ammoniak [amoni′ak] *n.* ammonia.

ammu′nisie [amə′newsi] *n.* ammunition.

a′mok [a′mok] *n.* amuck; *-maak* run amuck.

amo′raal [′amō′Rāl] *a.* & *av.* amoral.

′amp [′amp] *n.* (-*te*) function, office, duty; **-telik** *a.*, *av.* (-*e*) official(ly); **-tenaar** *n.* (′*amptenare*) official, clerk.

′amp [′amp] *n.* (-) (*electr.*) amp.

ampsgenoot [′ampschənōt] *n.* (′*ampsgenote*) colleague.

′amper [′ampəR] *av.* almost, nearly.

amu′sant [amew′sant] *a.* (-*e*; -*er*, -*ste*) amusing.

analfabeet [′analfabēt] *n.* (′*analfabete*) illiterate person.

ana′lise [ana′lisə] *n.* (-*s*) analysis; **anali′seer** *v.* (ge-) analyse.

anar′gie [anaR′chi] *n.* anarchy; **anar′gisties** *a.* (-*e*) anarchic.

′ander [′an(d)əR] *n.*, *a.* other, another.

′anderhalf [′an(d)əRhalf] *n.* one and a half.

′anderkant [′an(d)əRkant] *prep.* across, beyond.

′anderland [′anəRlant] *n.* foreign country.

′andermaal [′an(d)Rəmal] *av.* again, once more.

′anders [′an(d)əRs] *a.*, *av.* different; otherwise.

′andersdenkend [′anəRsdenkənt] *a.* (-*e*) of a different opinion.

′andersins [′an(d)əRsôfis] *av.* otherwise.

′andersyds [′an(d)əRsayts] *av.* on the other hand.

′angel [′angəl] *n.* (-*s*) sting, barb.

ange′lier [angə′liR] *n.* (-*e*) carnation.

′angs [′angs] *n.* fear; **-tig** *a.* (-*e*; -*er*, -*ste*) fearful; anxious; **-tigheid** *n.* **-vallig** *a.* (-*e*) conscientious; **-valligheid** *n.* scrupulousness, **-wekkend** *a.* (-*e*) alarming.

anhi′dreer [anhi′dRĕR] *v.* (ge-) dehydrate.

′anker [′angkəR] *n.* (-*s*) anchor; armature; brace; stay; *v.* (ge-) drop anchor; brace; **-wikkeling** *n.* armature-winding.

′ankertou [′angkəRtoa] *n.* (-*e*) guy rope.

ano′niem [ano′nim] *a.* (-*e*) anonymous.

′anorganies [′anoRchānis] *a.* (-*e*) inorganic.

an′tenne [an′tenə] *n.* *pl.* antenna, aerial.

′anti′stolmiddel [′anti′stolmədəl] *n.* (-*s*) anti-coagulant.

′Antjie [′anKi] -Taterrat Annie the Tattler, chatterbox.

′antwoord [′antvōRt] *n.* (-*de*) answer, reply; *v.* (ge-) to answer, reply.

a′part [a′paRt] *a.* (-*e*) separate, apart.

apos′troof [apos′tRōf] *n.* (*apos′trowe*) apostrophe.

′appel [′apəl] *n.* (-*s*) apple; pupil (*eye*); pommel.

ap′pél [ap′pel] *n.* appeal; **-hof** *n.* court of appeal.

appelde′liefde [apəldə′lifdə] *n.* gooseberry.

appel′koos [apel′kōs] *n.* (*appel′kose*) apricot; **-siekte** *n.* diarrhoea.

a′prilgek [a′pRəlgek] *n.* (-*ke*) April-fool.

ap′teek [ap′tĕk] *n.* (*ap′teke*) pharmacy; **ap′teker** *n.* (-*s*) chemist, druggist; **-sparaffien** *n.* liquid paraffin = **mediese paraffien**.

arbei [′aRbay] *v.* (ge-) to labour, toil, work.

′arbeid [′aRbayt] *n.* labour, work; **-ende** *a.* **-klas** *n.* working class; **-er** *n.* (-*s*) labourer; **ar′beidsaam** *a.* (*ar′beidsame*; *ar′beidsamer*, -*ste*) industrious; **ar′beidsaamheid** *n.* diligence; **-ster** *n.* working-woman.

′arend [′āRənt] *n.* (-*e*) eagle; **-sneus** *n.* aquiline nose.

′argeloos [′aRchəlōs] *a.* (′*argelose*) guileless.

ar′gief [aR′chif] *n.* (*ar′giewe*) archive; **ar′givaris** *n.* (-*se*) archivist.

argi′tek [aRchi′tek] *n.* (-*te*) architect.

arg'listig [aRch'ləstəch] a. (-e; -er, -ste), crafty; -heid n.

'argwaan ['aRchvān] n. -hê have suspicion; **'argwanend** a. (-e) suspicious.

'arm ['aRəm] n. (-s) arm; crank, lever; branch; a. poor, needy; (-e; -er, -ste) unfortunate; **-band** n. bracelet; **-blanke** n. poor-white; **-lastig** a. -wees be a charge upon the parish; **-e** n. (-s) pauper; **-lik** a. (-e) poor, shabby.

'arm(e)sorg ['aRəm(ə)soRch] n. care for the needy.

'arm'hangverband ['arəm'hangfəR-bant] n. (-e) arm sling.

'armoede ['aRmudə] n. indigence, poverty, want; **ar'moedig** a. (-e; -er, -ste) needy, poverty-stricken, shabby; **ar'moedigheid** n. poverty, poorness.

arm'salig [aRəm'sāləch] a. (-e; -er, -ste) pitiful, miserable.

'aronskelk ['aRonskelk] n. arum-lily.

ar'res [a'res] n. arrest; detention.

ar'seer [aR'sēR] v. (ge-) shade.

ar'tikel [aR'tikəl] n. article.

'arts ['arts] n. (-e) doctor, physician, practitioner; **-e'ny** n. (-e) medicine; **-e'nykunde** n. pharmacology; **-e'nymiddel** n. (-s) drug.

'as ['as] n. (-se) ash, ashes, cinders; (-se, -te) axle, axle-tree, axis, spindle, shaft; av., conj. prep. as, like; in the capacity of; when; if; as if.

'asbakkie ['asbaki] n. (-s) ash-tray.

as'bes [as'bes] n. asbestos.

'asem ['āsəm] n. breath; **-skep** breathe; **uit-** breathless; **na-hyg** gasp; v. (ge-) breathe; **-haal** v. (-ge-) breathe; **-haling** n. breathing, respiration; **-halingsorgaan** n. respiratory organ; **-loos** a. (-lose) breathless; **-tog** n. (-te) gasp, breath.

asi'aat [asi'āt] n. (asi'ate) Asiatic.

'asjas ['asyas] n. (-se) good-for-nothing, scoundrel.

'askas ['askas] n. (-te) axle box.

'aslaer ['aslāR] n. (-s) axle bearing.

'aslas ['aslas] n. (-te) axle load.

as'of [as'of] conj. as if, as though.

'aspakking ['aspakəng] n. (-s) shaft packing.

aspi'rant [aspi'Rant] n. (-e) aspirant, applicant; **aspi'rasie** n. aspiration; **aspi'reer** v. (ge-) aspires.

'aspoestertjie ['aspustəRKi] n. Cinderella.

asse'blief [asə'blif] conj. please.

asse'gaai [asə'chāi] n. (-e) assegai.

assimi'lasie [asəmə'lāsi] n. assimilation; **assimi'leer** v. (ge-) assimilate.

assis'tent [asəs'tent] n. (-e) assistant; **-'e** sing. fem.

assosi'asie [asōsi'āsi] n. (-s) association; **assosi'eer** v. (ge-) associate.

assu'ransie [asew'Rānsi] n. assurance, insurance.

a'strant [as'tRant] av. (-e; -er, -ste) impudent, cool, bold; **-heid** n.

'asvaal ['asfāl] av. ashen, pale.

a'syn [a'sayn] n. vinegar; **-stelletjie** n. cruet stand; **-vliegies** n. pl. vinegar flies.

atel'jee [atl'yē] n. (-s) studio.

'atjar ['atyaR] n. pickles.

at'leet [at'lēt] n. (at'lete) athlete; **atle'tiek** n. athletics; **at'leties** a. (-e) athletic.

'atmosfeer ['atmosfēR] n. atmosphere; **'atmos'feries** a. (-e) atmospheric.

a'toom [a'tōm] n. (a'tome) atom; **-gewig** n. atomic weight.

at'tensie [a'tensi] n. attention, consideration; **at'tent** a. (-e) attentive, considerate.

attes'taat [atəs'tāt] n. (attes'tate) certificate.

attribu'tief [atRəbew'tif] n. (attribu-'tiewe) attributive.

'au ['a-u] interj. ouch!

'avondmaal ['āfontmāl] n. Holy Communion.

avon'tuur [afon'tēwR] n. adventure; **avon:u'rier** n. (-s) adventurer; **-lik** a. (-e) adventurous.

'aweregs ['āvəRechs] a. (-e) wrong, perverse.

awe'ry [avə'Ray] n. average, damage to ship or cargo.

B

B.H.F. ['bē'hā'ef] n. (baie hoë frekwensie) VHF (very high frequency).

b-'dur [bē'dewR] n. B sharp.

b-'mol [bē'mol] n. B flat.

'ba! [bā] interj. bah!

'baadjie ['bāiKi] n. (-s) jacket, coat; op jou-kry get a hiding; **-pak** n. costume.

'baai ['bāi] n. baize; (-e) bay; v. (ge-) bathe.

'baaierd ['bāiəRt] n. chaos.

'baal ['bā] n. (bale) bale; ten reams (paper); v. (ge-) to bale; **-tjie** dim.

'baan ['bān] n. (bane) path, course, track, orbit, strip (flag), rink, floor (dance), trajectory, trunk; 'n-opskop kick up a row; v. (ge-) pave (the way) force (one's way through), ge-de weg beaten track; **-brekend** a. (e-) pioneer-; **-breker** n. (-s) pioneer; **-tjie** dim. job; **-s** vir boeties jobs for pals.

'baan- ['bān-] in compounds orbital.

'baar ['bāR] n. (bare) wave, billow; bier, litter; ingot (gold); a. raw, unskilled, inexperienced; v. (ge-) bear, give birth; cause; opsien-cause a stir; **-kleed** n. pall; **-moeder** n. womb.

'baard ['bāRt] n. (-e) beard, whiskers; bit (key); **-angelier** n. sweet william.

'baars ['bāRs] n. perch, bass.

'baas ['bās] n. (base) boss, master; head, overseer; crack, champion;

-raak v. (ge-) overcome, defeat; -speel v. (-ge-) domineer, bully.

'baat ['bāt] n. benefit, profit, cp. bate; v. (ge-) avail; dit sal jou niksnie it will be of no avail; -sug n. selfishness; -sugtig a. (-e, -er, -ste) selfish; -sugtigheid n. selfishness.

'babbel ['babəl] v. (ge-) chatter, babble; chat; -aar n. (-s) chatterbox; -(a)ry n. chattering; -bek n. = babbelaar; -kous n. = babbelaar; -sug n. talkativeness.

'bad ['bat] n. (baaie) bath, hot springs, spa; (-de, -dens) bath; v. (ge-) to bath, have a bath; -borsel n. bath brush; -broek n. bathing trunks; -gas n. seaside visitor, visitor to a watering place; -handdoek n. bath-towel; -huis n. bathhouse; -jie dim.; -kamer n. bathroom; -kristalle n. bath crystals; -olie n. bath oil; -seep n. bath soap; -sout n. bathsalts; -spons ['spauns] n. bath sponge; -termometer n. bath thermometer; -water n. bathwater.

ba'gasie [bə'chāsi] n. baggage; -wa n. luggage-van.

'bagger ['bachəR] v. (ge-) dredge.

'baie ['baiə] indef. num. (meer, meeste) much, many; av. very; much; many; far; -meer far more; -keer av. frequently; -mal av. = baiekeer.

bajo'net [ba-yō'net] n. (-te) bayonet, met gevelde- with fixed bayonets.

'bak ['bak] n. (-ke) bowl, dish, bucket, can; -bees n. giant, colossus; -kie dim.; -kies dim. sing. face; -kiespomp n. Persian wheel; -ore n. plur. prominent ears; v. (ge-) bake, fry, bask; iemand 'n poets- play a trick on; -ker n. (-s) baker; -kersbrood n. baker's-bread; -kery n. bakery, baking; -oond n. oven; -sel n. (-s) batch; -steen n. brick.

'bak ['bak] n. (-ke) body (of vehicle); -bou n. body-building; -bouer n. body-builder; -werk n. bodywork.

baka'tel [baka'təl] n. bagatelle; trifle.

bakboord ['bak'bōRt] n. port, portside.

'baken ['bākən] n. (-s) beacon, land-(sea)mark.

'baker ['bākəR] n. (-s) (dry-)nurse; v. (ge-) to (dry-)nurse; -mat n. birthplace, cradle; -rympie n. nursery-rhyme.

'bakkie ['baki] n. (-s) light (delivery) van.

ba'klei [bə'klay] v. (ge-) fight, scuffle, scrap; -erig a. (-e, -er, -ste) quarrelsome; -ery n. fighting.

'baksteen ['bakstēn] n. (-stene) brick.

bak'terie [bak'tēRi] n. (-ë) bacterium.

bakvis(sie) ['bakfəs(i)] n. (-s) flapper.

'bal ['bal] n. (-le) ball; testicle; (-s) ball, dance; gemaskerde- masked ball; v. (ge-) clench.

ba'lans [ba'lāns] n. balance, balance-

sheet; -'eer v. (ge-) balance, poise; -staat n. balance-sheet.

bal'dadig [bal'dādəch] a. (-e; -er, -ste) rowdy, boisterous, frisky.

bal'horig [bal'hōRəch] a. (-e; -er, -ste) refractory, stubborn.

'balie ['bāli] n. tub; bar (law).

bal'jaar [bal'yāR] v. (ge-) frolic, frisk; kick up row.

bal'ju [bal'yew] n. (-'s) bailiff.

'balk ['balk] n. (-e) beam, rafter; -ie dim. bar (on boot).

bal'kon [bal'kon] n. (-ne) balcony.

bal'lade [ba'lādə] n. (-s) ballad.

bal'let [ba'let] n. ballet.

'balling ['baləng] n. exile; -skap n. exile, banishment.

'balsem ['balsəm] n. balm; v. (ge-) balm.

'ban ['ban] n. excommunication, ban; v. (ge-) banish, exile.

ba'naal [ba'nāl] a. ('banale; 'banaler, -ste) banal, trivial.

'band [bant] n. (-e) band, string, ribbon, bandage, tape, belt, strap; hy is almal se- he is second to none; aan -e lê to restrict; -eloos a. ('bandelose; bandeloser, -ste) lawless; unrestrained.

'band [bant] n. (-e) tyre; -breuk n. tyre failure; -druk n. tyre pressure; -grootte n. tyre size; -ligter n. tyre lever; -loopvlak n. tyre tread; -lugdruk n. inflation pressure; -versoling n. tyre retreading; -wand n. tyre wall.

bande'lier [bandə'liR] n. (-e) bandoleer, bandolier.

ban'diet [ban'dit] n. (-e) convict.

'bandmaat ['bantmāt] n. tape-measure.

'bandopnemer ['bantopnēməR] n. (-s) tape recorder.

'bantom ['bantom] n. (-s) bantam, pebble.

'bang ['bang] a., av. (-er, -ste) afraid, frightened; cowardly, timid; -broek n. coward; -erig a., av. nervous; -heid n.; -makery n. intimidation; -pratery n. intimidation.

ba'nier [ba'niR] n. (-s) banner.

'bank ['bangk] n. (-e) bench, seat, sofa, settee, pew; -oortreksel n. (-s) seat cover; -steller n. seat adjuster; deur die- on the average; bank; v. (ge-) to bank (money); -ier n. (-s) banker; -boekie n. (-s) pass book; -oordrag n. (-te) bank transfer; - n. (ouklip) pan.

ban'ket [bang'ket] n. banquet; confectionery; (gold-bearing) geological formation.

bank'rot [bang'kRot] a. bankrupt, insolvent.

'banneling ['banələng] n. = balling.

bantoeïs'tiek [bantuəs'tik] n. Bantu studies.

'bar [baR] a. (-re) barren; gruff; inclement; av. terribly, horribly.

bar'baar [baR'bāR] n. (bar'bare)

barbarian, savage; **-s** a. (**-e**) barbarous, barbarian.

bar'bier [baR'biR] n. barber.

barm'hartig [baRəm'haRtəch] a. (**-e**; **-er**, **-ste**) merciful, charitable; **-heid** n. mercy, charity.

ba'ron [ba'Ron] n. (**-ne**) baron; **-'es** n. (**-se**) baroness.

'bars ['baRs] n. (**-te**) crack; burst; chap; a. (**-**, **-e**) harsh, rough; blunt; av. sternly, harshly, **-aanspreek** v. browbeat; v. (ge-) burst, crack; **-tens** tot-toe to the utmost.

'bas ['bas] n. (**-se**) bass; (**-te**) bark, bast.

ba'saar [bə'saR] n. (**-s**) bazaar, church fair.

'basboom ['basbōm] n. wattle.

ba'seer [ba'sēR] v. (ge-) base on; **ba'sies** a. (**-e**) basic; **ba'sis** n. (**-se**) base; basis.

'basta ['basta] interj. stop it! shut up!

'baster ['bastəR] n. (**-s**) bastard, half-caste; av. kind of, rather, quite; v. (ge-) hybridize, interbreed; **-geslag** n. (**-te**) mongrel race.

ba'suin [ba'sœin] n. (**-e**) trumpet, trombone; v. (**-ge-**) make known loudly.

batal'jon [batal'yon] n. (**-ne**, **-s**) battalion.

'bate en 'laste ['bātən'lastə] n. assets and liabilities.

'batige ['bātəchə] a. **-saldo** credit balance.

batte'ry [batə'ray] n. (**-e**) battery. **-aansluiter** n. (**-s**) battery terminal; **-aardkabel** n. (**-s**) battery earth cable; **-bak** n. (**-ke**) b. case; **-houer** n. (**-s**) b. container; **-kabel** n. (**-s**) b. cable; **-kas** n. (**-te**) b. box; **-laaier** n. (**-s**) b. charger; **-'sel** n. (**-le**) b. cell; **-spuit** n. (**-e**) b. syringe; **-sterkte** n. state of charge of b.; **-suur** n. b. acid; **-toetser** n. b. tester; **-vuller** n. b. filler.

bayrum = **lourier en rum**.

be'aam [bə'ām] v. (**-**) assent to; approve; **be'aming** n. assent.

be'ampte [bə'amptə] n. (**-s**) official.

be'angs [bə'angs] a., av. (**-te**) anxious, alarmed.

be'antwoord [bə'antvōRt] v. (**-**) answer, reply; return; be suitable; **-ing** n.

be'arbei [bə'aRbay] v. (**-**) work; cultivate; treat; ply with arguments; try to persuade.

be'bloed [be'blut] a. (**-e**) bloody.

be'boet [be'but] v. (**-**) to fine.

be'bou [bə'boa] v. (**-**) build up; till.

be'brou [bə'bRoa] v. (**-**) mess up, spoil.

bed [bet] n. (**-de**, **-dens**) bed; **-ding** n. (**-s**) seedbed, bed of river; **-dinkie** dim. seedbed.

be'daag(d) [bə'dāch(t)] a. (**-e**) elderly.

be'daar [bə'dāR] v. (**-**) calm down; subside; **-d** a. (**-e**; **-er**, **-ste**) calm.

be'dag [bə'dach] av. **-wees op** be

mindful of; **-saam** a. (**-same**; **-samer**, **-ste**) thoughtful, considerate; **-saamheid** n. thoughtfulness.

be'dags [bə'dachs] av. during day.

be'dank [bə'dank] v. (**-**) thank; resign; decline; **-ing** n. (**-e**, **-s**).

'beddegoed ['bedəchut] n. bedding, bed-clothes.

'bedding ['bedəng] n. (**-s**) river bed; flower bed.

'bede ['bēdə] n. (**-**) prayer, entreaty; **-huis** n. church.

be'deel [bə'dēl] n. (**-**) endow; bestow upon; **-d** av. **-met** endowed with; **be'deling** n. endowment; order of things.

be'dees(d) [bə'dēs(t)] a. (**-de**; **-der**, **-dste**) bashful; self-conscious.

be'dek [bə'dek] v. (**-**) cover, conceal, hide; mulch; **-te** a. covered, concealed; **-king** n.; **-telik** av. covertly.

'bedel ['bēdəl] v. (ge-) beg; cadge; **-aar** n. (**-s**) beggar; **-a'res** n. beggarwoman; **-a'ry** n.; **-staf** n. beggar's staff, tot die **-bring**, reduce to begging.

be'denking [bə'dengkəng] n. (**-e**, **-s**) consideration; objection; **bedenklik** a. (**-e**; **-er**, **-ste**) critical; dangerous; suspicious.

be'derf, **be'derwe** [bə'deRf, bə'deRvə] v. (**-**) rot, decay, spoil, ruin, mar; n. decay, rotting, decomposition; **-baar** a. (**-bare**; **-der**, **-ste**) perishable **-lik** a. (**-e**; **-er**, **-ste**) perishable, corruptible; **be'derwer** n. (**-**) spoiler.

be'derfwerend [bə'deRvēRənt] a. (**-e**) antiseptic, preservative.

'bedevaart ['bēdəfāRt] n. pilgrimage.

be'dien [bə'din] v. (**-**) serve, attend to, to operate; make use of, avail; **-aar** n. (**-s**) **-van die Woord** preacher; **-de** n. (**-s**) servant, waiter; **-er** n. (**-s**) operator; **-ing** n. service; serving; preaching; **-ing** n. operation, working.

be'ding [bə'dəng] v. (**-**) stipulate; n. stipulation, condition.

be'dink [bə'dənk] v. (**-**) bear in mind; devise.

be'dissel [bə'dəsəl] v. (**-**) arrange, manage.

'bedlêend ['betlēənt] a. (**-e**) bed-ridden.

be'doel [bə'dul] v. (**-**) mean; intend; **-ing** n. (**-e**, **-s**).

be'dolwe [bə'dolvə] av. buried.

be'dompig [bə'dompəch] a. (**-e**; **-er**, **-ste**) stuffy, sultry; **-heid** n.

be'dons [bə'dauñs] av. crazy, mad.

be'dorwe [bə'dauRvə] a. (**meer-**, **mees-**) tainted; rotten, putrid; spoilt; **- brokkie** a spoilt child, brat.

be'dot [bə'dot] v. (**-**) trick, fool.

be'dra [bə'dRā] v. (**-**) amount to; **be'drag** n. (**be'drae**).

be'dreig [bə'dRaych] v. (**-**) threaten, menace; **-ing** n. (**-e**, **-s**).

be'drewe [bə'dRēvə] a., av. (**-ner**, **-nste**) skilled, skilful.

be'drieg, be'drieë [be'dRich, be-dRiə] v. (-) deceive, cheat; be'drieër n. (-s) swindler, fraud; -lik a., av. (-e; -er, -ste) deceptive, deceitful; -ster fem. of bedrieër; be'droë av. deceived.

be'droef [bə'dRuf] v. (-) grieve; a. (-de) grieved; av. -min precious little; -dheid n. grief, sorrow; be'droewend a., av. (-e) sad, pitiful.

be'drog [bə'dRoch] n. deceit, circumvention; cp. bedrieg.

be'druk [bə'dRʌk] v. (-) print on; a., av. (-te; -ter, -ste) dejected, downcast; printed; -theid n. dejection, depression.

be'dryf [bə'dRayf] n. (be'drywe) deed; trade, profession; industry; act (play); v. be'drywe (-) commit, do; -skapitaal n. working-capital; be'drywende vorm a. active voice; be'drywigheid n. activity.

be'dug [bə'dʌch] av. afraid, apprehensive; -theid n.

be'dui(e) [bə'dœiə] v. (-) mean, signify; portend, indicate; gesticulate; direct; -dend a., av. (-e; -er, -ste) considerable; -denis n. meaning, significance; -ery n. gesticulation.

be'duiweld [bə'dœivəlt] a., av. (-e) mad, crazy, daft; devilish; n. soos 'n-e like mad.

be'dwang [bə'dwang] n. control, restraint; in-hou keep under control.

be'dwelm [bə'dweləm] v. (-) daze, stun, intoxicate; -d a. (-e) stunned, dazed; comatose; -end a. (-e; -er, -ste) stunning, intoxicating; -ing n.

be'dwing [bə'dwəng] v. (-) control, hold in check, curb; cp. bedwang; -baar a. (-bare; -der, -ste) restrainable.

be'ëdig [bə'ədəch] v. (-) swear in; swear to; -de a. sworn; -ing n.

'beef, 'bewe [bêf, bêvə] v. (ge-) tremble, shake.

be'ëindig [bə'ayndəch] v. (-) finish, end, terminate; -iging n.

'beeld [bêlt] n. (-e) image; reflection; statue; symbol; notion; -jie dim. figurine; v. (ge-) form, shape; depict, portray; -end a. (-e) plastic; hou v. (-ge-) carve, sculpture; -houer n. (-s) sculptor; -houkuns n. sculpture; -houwerk n. sculpture; carving; -jie dim. (-s) statuette; -opnemer n. pick-up (radar); -ryk a. (-e; -er, -ste) ornate; -sel n. (-s) effigy; -skoon a. (-skone; -skoner, -ste) of rare beauty; -spraak n. metaphor; -tenis n. image, likeness, portrait.

'been [bên] n. (bene) bone; leg; harde bene kou suffer hardship; jou bene dra leg it; -af av. with a broken leg; in love; -agtig a. (-e; -er, -ste) bony; -bekleding n. leggings; -eter n. caries; -tjie [-Kî] dim. jou beste-voor sit put one's best foot foremost; -windsels pl. puttees.

'beer ['bêr] n. (bere) bear; boar; buttress; -tjie dim. Teddy bear; -klou n. acanthus.

be'ërf [bə'eRf] v. (-) inherit.

'bees ['bês] n. (-te) beast; brute; interj. ou-! by gum!; -te pl. cattle; -'agtig a. (-e; -er, -ste) beastly, brutal, bestial; av. in a beastly way; -vleis n. beef; -wagter n. cattle-herd; -brommer n. screwworm (cattle).

'beet ['bêt] n. beetroot.

'beethê ['bêths] v. ('beetgehad) have got hold of.

'beetkry, 'beetneem, 'beetpak ['bêt-kRay, 'bêtnêm, 'bêtpak] v. (-ge-) take hold of; iemand beetneem make a fool of somebody.

be'faamd [bə'fâmt] a. (-e; -er, -ste) famous, renowned.

be'floers [bə'flûRs] v. (-) muffle.

be'foeter [bə'futəR] v. (-) mess up; -d a. (-e) crazy, daft; devilish; -dheid n. craziness.

be'gaaf(d) [bə'châf(t)] a. (-de) gifted, talented; -dheid n. ability.

be'gaan [bə'chân] v. (-) tread; go; 'n fout- commit an error; laat hom-let him have his way; a. (be'gane) beaten; upset, anxious; -baar a. (-bare) passable; -baarheid n. passability.

be'geef, be'gewe [bə'chêf, bə'chêvə] v. (-) forsake; in gevaar- expose to danger; -na 'n plek proceed to a place.

be'geer [bə'chêR] v. (-) desire, want, covet; -lik a. (-e; -er, -ste) desirable, enticing; -likheid n. desirability; be'gerig av. desirous, covetous; -te n. wish, desire; lust.

bege'lei [bəchə'lay] v. (-) accompany, escort; -dend a. (-e) accompanying; -er n. attendant; accompanist; -ding n.; -dster fem. of begeleier.

bege'nadig [bəchə'nâdəch] v. (-) pardon, reprieve; favour; -de a. pardoned, reprieved; favoured; -ing n.

be'giftig [bə'chəftəch] v. (-) endow; -ing n.; -er n. donor; -de n. (-s) donee.

be'gin [bə'chən] v. (-) begin, start, commence; n. beginning, outset; -ner n. (-s) beginner, novice; -punt n. starting-point; -sel n. (-s) principle.

be'goël [bə'chœəl] v. (-) bewitch; delude.

be'graaf, be'grawe [bə'chRâf, bə'chRâvə] v. (-) bury; -plaas n. cemetery; be'grafnis n. funeral.

be'grens [bə'chRɛñs] v. (-) limit; -d a. (-e) limited, confined; -dheid n. limitedness; -sing n. limitation, bounds.

be'grepe cp. bergyp.

be'grip [bə'chRəp] n. idea, conception, notion; vlug van- quick-witted; cp. begryp.

be'groei [bə'chRul] v. (-) overgrow; -d a. (-e) overgrown.

be'groet [bə'chRut] v. (-) greet, salute; -ing n.

be'groot [bə'chRôt] v. (-) estimate, rate; -ing n. (-s) budget, estimates.

be'gryp [bə'chrayp] v. (-) understand, comprehend, grasp, conceive; -er n. 'n goeie-het 'n halwe woord nodig a word to the wise is enough; -lik a. (-e) comprehensible, understandable, conceivable; -likerwyse av. obviously; -likheid n. comprehensibility.

be'gunstig [bə'chʌnstəch] v. (-) favour; benefit; -de n. (-s) beneficiary; patronize; -ing n.

be'haag [bə'hâch] v. (-) please; -lik a. (-e; -er, -ste) pleasant, comfortable; -likheid n. pleasantness; comfort; -siek a. (-e) coquettish; over-anxious to please; -sug n. (-s) coquettishness; be'hae n. pleasure, delight.

be'haal [bə'hâl] v. (-) gain, score; get; obtain, win.

be'halwe [bə'halvə] conj. except, but, save.

be'handel [bə'handəl] v. (-) treat; deal with; manage; attend; discuss; do; -ing n.

be'hang [bə'hang] v. (-) decorate with, to drape; n. wall-paper; -er n. (-s) paper-hanger; -sel n. paper-hangings, wall-paper.

be'hartig [bə'haRtəch] v. (-) look after, serve, further, promote; be'hartenswaardig a. (-e) worthy of consideration; -ing n.

be'heer [bə'hêR] v. (-) manage, control, administer; n. management, control; -der n. (-s) manager, director.

be'heers [bə'hêRs] v. (-) control (passions), master; govern (people); be master of (situation), dominate; -er n. (-s) master, ruler; -ing n.

be'help [bə'help] v. (-) make shift.

be'hels [bə'hels] v. (-) comprise; contain.

be'hendig [bə'hendəch] a. (-e; -er, -ste) dexterous, clever, adroit; -igheid n.

be'hep [bə'hep] av. possessed by, afflicted with.

be'hoed [bə'hut] v. (-) guard, protect, preserve; -er n. protector, -ster fem. behoeder; -saam a. (-same; -samer, -ste) cautious, wary.

be'hoefte [bə'huftə] n. (-s) need, want; be'hoeftig a. (-e; -er, -ste) needy, indigent; be'hoeftigheid n. neediness, indigence, penury; be-'hoewe ten-van on behalf of, in aid of.

be'hoort [bə'hôRt] v. (-) belong; be proper; be'hoorlik [bə'hôRlək] a. (-e) proper; becoming; decent; av. properly, decently; -heid n. propriety; -heidshalwe av. for the sake of propriety; be'hore na- properly, fittingly.

be'hou [bə'hoa] v. (-) keep; retain;

maintain; -d n. keeping; retention; maintenance; salvation; -end a. (-e) conservative (party); -denis n. salvation; -dens prep. except for, subject to; -e av. safe, unhurt.

be'huis [bə'hœis] v. (-) provide dwelling; -ing n.

be'hulp [be'hʌlp] n. met-van by means of; -saam a. (-same) helpful; -saamheid n. helpfulness.

'beide ['baydə] n. both.

be'invloed [bə'ənflut] v. (-) influence, affect; -ing n.

'beitel ['baytəl] v. chisel.

be'jaard [bə'yâRt] a. (-e; -er, -ste) elderly; -heid n. elderliness.

be'jammer [bə'yaməR] v. (-) bewail; deplore; -enswaardig a. (-e) pitiable, deplorable.

be'jeën [bə'yëən] v. (-) act towards.

'bek ['bek] n. (-ke) mouth; beak; snout; muzzle; jaws; opening; hou jou-! shut up!; -af a., av. down in the mouth, downhearted; fatigued; -drywer n (-s) back-seat driver.

be'keer [bə'kêR] v. (-) convert; reform; -d a., av. (-e) converted; -de n. (-s) convert; -ling n. convert.

be'ken [bə'ken] v. (-) acknowledge, admit; see, recognize; skuld- plead guilty; -tenis n. confession.

be'kend [bə'kent] a. (-e; -er, -ste) known, well-known; familiar; noted for; -maak announce; -e n. (-s) acquaintance; -heid n. name, reputation; acquaintance; -making n. (-e, -s) announcement; notice.

'beker ['bëkəR] n. (-s) mug; jug; beaker; cup, trophy.

'bekken ['bekən] n. (-s) basin; catchment area; font; cymbal; -holte n. pelvic cavity.

be'kla(ag) [bə'klâ(ch)] v. (-) pity; lament; bemoan.

be'klad [bə'klat] v. (-) blot, stain, sully.

be'klag [bə'klach] n. complaint.

be'klee [bə'klë] v. (-) clothe; upholster, cover, drape; occupy; hold (office); invest (with power); a. lagged; -dsel n. (-s) covering, upholstery; be'kleër n. (-s) upholsterer; holder (office); be'kleding n. covering; upholstery; investiture.

be'klem [bə'klem] v. (-) oppress; stress; -d a. (-e) oppressed, heavy; accentuated; -dheid n. oppression, heaviness; -ming n. oppression; strangulation (hernia); angina (chest) -toon v. (-) accent, stress.

be'klim [bə'kləm] v. (-) climb; ascend; mount; scale.

be'klink [bə'klənk] v. (-) clinch, settle; rivet.

be'knel [bə'knel] v. (-) pinch, oppress.

be'knop [bə'knop] a. (-te; -ter, -ste) concise, condensed, compact, confined; av. concisely; -theid n. conciseness, brevity.

be'kom [bə'kom] v. (-) get, obtain;

agree with; *dit sal jou suur-* you'll
regret it; *-s* n. *jou-eet* eat one's fill.

be'kommer [bə'koməR] *v.* (-) worry
about, feel uneasy; *-d* a. (*-e*; *-er*, *-ste*)
worried, concerned; *-dheid* n. an-
xiety; *-ing* n. (*-e*); *-nis* n. anxiety.

be'koor [bə'kôR] *v.* (-) charm,
fascinate; tempt; *-der* n. (*-s*)
charmer, tempter; *-lik* a. (*-e*; *-er*,
-ste) fascinating; *-likheid* n. charm,
fascination; **be'koring** n. charm.

be'kostig [bə'kostəch] *v.* (-) afford.

be'kragtig [bə'kRachtəch] *v.* (-)
ratify; confirm; *-ing* n.

be'krompe [bə'kRompə] a. confined,
narrow; narrowminded; *- nheid* n.

be'kroon [bə'kRôn] *v.* (-) crown;
award (*prize*); **be'kroning** n.

be'kruip [bə'kRœip] *v.* (-) stalk,
steal upon.

be'kwaam [bə'kwäm] *v.* (-) train,
study for; qualify; **be'kwame** a. (*-r*, *be-
kwaamste*) able, competent; mature;
-heid n. ability, capacity.

be'kwaald [bə'kwält] a., av. (*-e*)
sickly.

be'kyk [bə'kayk] *v.* (-) look at, view.

'**bel** ['bel] n. bell; ear-drop; wattle
(*turkey*); *v.* (ge-) ring; telephone.

be'laai [bə'läi] *v.* (-) to load, burden.

be'laglik [bə'lachlək] a. (*-e*, *-er*, *-ste*)
ridiculous; *-heid* n.

be'land [bə'lant] *v.* (-) *in 'n sloot*
land in a ditch; *waar moet ek-?* what
is to become of me?

be'lang [bə'lang] n. (*-e*) interest;
importance; concern; *-eloos* a.
(*be'langlose*) disinterested; *-hebbend*
a. (*-e*) interested; *-rik* a. (*-e*, *-er*, *-ste*)
important; *-rikheid* n.; *-stel* v. (ge-)
be interested in; *-stellend* a. (*-e*)
interested; *-stellendes* pl. those
interested; *-stelling* n. interest;
-wekkend a. (*-e*) interesting.

be'las [bə'las] *v.* (-) load, burden,
taxed; rate, tax, assess; a. (*-te*)
loaded, burdened; taxed; *-baar* a.
(*-bare*) taxable, dutiable; *-baarheid*
n. taxability; *-ting* n.

be'lê [bə'lê] *v.* (-) cover, invest; call
(*meeting*); **be'legging** n.

be'ledig [bə'lêdəch] *v.* (-) offend,
insult; *-de* a. insulted, n. (*-s*) insulted
person; *-end* a., av. (*-e*, *-er*, *-ste*)
offensive, insulting; *-ing* n. (*-e*, *-s*).

be'leë [bə'lêə] a. mature, ripe.

be'leef, be'lewe [bə'lêf, bə'lêvə] *v.* (-)
experience; witness.

be'leef(d) [bə'lêf(t)] a. (*-e*; *-er*, *-ste*)
polite, courteous, civil; av. politely;
-heid n.; *-heidshalwe* av. out of
politeness; *-heidsvorm* n. formality.

be'leër [bə'lêəR] *v.* (-) besiege.

be'leg [bə'lech] n. siege.

be'legging [bə'lechəng] n. (*-e*, *-s*)
investment; convening.

be'leid [bə'layt] n. management;
tact; policy.

be'lemmer [bə'leməR] *v.* (-) impede,
hamper; stunt; *-ing* n. (*-e*, *-s*).

be'lese [bə'lêsə] a. (*meer*, *mees*) well-
read, erudite.

be'let [bə'let] *v.* (-) prevent, forbid;
-vra make an appointment for a
social call.

be'lewe [bə'lêvə] *v.* (-) experience,
witness, live to see.

'**belg** [belch] *v.* (ge-) *ge-wees* angry,
offended.

'**Belg** ['belch] Belgian.

'**België** ['belchiə] Belgium.

'**belhamel** ['belhäməl] n. (*-s*) ring-
leader.

be'lig [bə'lech] *v.* (-) light; elucidate;
-ting n.

be'liggaam [bə'lechäm] *v.* (-) em-
body; **be'liggaming** n.

belle'trie [belə'tri] n. belles-lettres.

be'loer [bə'lûR] *v.* (-) watch, spy
upon.

be'loof, be'lowe [bə'lôf, bə'lôvə] *v.*
(-) promise; **be'lofte** n. (*-s*).

be'loon [bə'lôn] *v.* (-) reward,
recompense.

be'luister [bə'lœistəR] *v.* (-) eaves-
drop, listen to.

be'ly [bə'lay] *v.* (-) profess; avow;
-denis n. confession, creed.

be'magtig [bə'machtəch] *v.* (-) seize;
usurp.

be'man [bə'man] *v.* (-) to man; *-ning*
n.

be'merk [bə'meRk] *v.* (-) notice,
perceive; *-baar* a. (*-bare*) noticeable;
-ing n.

be'mes [bə'mes] *v.* (-) manure,
fertilise.

be'middeld [bə'mədəlt] a. (*-e*) well-
to-do, wealthy.

be'min [bə'mən] *v.* (-) love; *-d* a. (*-e*)
loved, beloved; *-de* n. (*-s*) lover;
-lik (*-e*; *-er*, *-ste*) lovable; *-nens-
waardig* a. (*-e*) lovable.

be'moedig [bə'mudəch] *v.* (-) en-
courage.

be'moei [bə'mui] *v.* (-) meddle with;
-al n. busy-body; *-ing* n.; *-siek* a.
(*-e*) meddlesome; *-sug* n. meddle-
someness.

be'mors [bə'moRs] *v.* (-) to soil,
dirty.

be'nadeel [bə'nädêl] *v.* (-) to harm,
injure; **be'nadeling** n.

be'nader [bə'nädəR] *v.* (-) approach;
estimate.

be'nard [bə'naRt] a. (*-e*) critical.

'**hende** ['bendə] n. (*-s*) gang.

be'nede [bə'nêdə] av. down, below,
downstairs; *prep.* under, below,
beneath.

be'neem [bə'nêm] *v.* (-) deprive of.

be'nepe [bə'nêpə] a. cramped, petty.

be'newel [bə'nêvəl] *v.* (-) befog.

be'newens [bə'nêvôns] *prep.* besides.

be'nodig [bə'nôdəch] a. (*-de*) required; *-hede* n. pl. requirements,
accessories.

be'noem [bə'num] *v.* (-) to nominate,
appoint; *-baar* a. (*-bare*) eligible;
-de a. nominated; *-ing* (*-e*, *-s*)
nomination; appointment.

be'noud [bə'noat] *a.* (-e; -er, -ste) close, oppressed; -e bors *n.* asthma; -heid *n.* stuffiness; oppression; **be'nouing** *n.* oppression.

be'nul [bə'nʌl] *n. nie die minste-hê nie* without the slightest notion of ...

be'nut [bə'nʌt] *v.* (-) utilize.

be'ny [bə'nay] *v.* (-) to envy; -denswaardig *a.* (-e) enviable.

be'oefen [bə'ufən] *v.* (-) follow, exercise, study.

be'oog [bə'ôch] *v.* (-) aim at.

be'oordeel [bə'ôRdêl] *v.* (-) judge; adjudicate; review; **be'oordelaar** *n.* (-s) judge; reviewer; **be'oordeling** *n.*

be'paal [bə'pâl] *v.* (-) fix; appoint; decide; ascertain; define; -baar *a.* (-bare) definable; -d *av* (-e) positively, decidedly; **be'palend** *a.* (-e) qualifying, modifying; **be'paling** *n.* (-e, -s) determination, stipulation.

be'peins [bə'pãῦns] *v.* (-) ponder on; -ing *n.*

be'perk [bə'peRk] *v.* (-) limit, restrict; reduce; -end *a.* (-e) limiting, restrictive; -ing *n.* (-e, -s); -theid *n.* limitedness; restriction.

be'pleit [bə'playt] *v.* (-) plead, champion; advocate.

be'proef [bə'pRuf] *v.* (-) attempt; test; afflict; -d *a.* (-) tried, trusty; bereaved; **be'proewing** *n.* (-e, -s).

be'raadslaag [bə'Râtslâch] *v.* (-) consult with, consult, deliberate on; **be'raadslaging** *n.* (-e, -s).

be'raam [bə'Râm] *v.* (-) devise, contrive; frame; estimate; **be'raming** *n.* devising, estimation.

'berde ['beRdə] *n. iets te-bring* broach a subject.

'bêre, berg ['bERə, 'beRch] *v.* (ge-) put away; store; hide; save oneself; salve; -plek *n.* storehouse, shed; **'berging** *n.* salvage.

be'redder [bə'redəR] *v.* (-) put in order; administer (*estate*); -aar *n.* (-s) administrator (*estate*); -ing *n.* liquidation.

be'rede [bə'Rêdə] *a.* mounted (*police*).

be'rei [bə'Ray] *v.* (-) prepare, get ready, compound; curry; dress; cure; -d *a.*, *av.* (-e) prepared, willing; -der *n.* dresser; -ding *n.* preparation; dressing; -dvaardig *a.* (-e; -er, -ste) willing; -dwillig *a.* (-e) willing; -dwilligheid *n.* willingness.

be'reik [bə'Rayk] *v.* (-) reach; attain; achieve; *n.* reach, grasp, range; -baar *a.* (-bare) attainable; -ing *n.* achievement, attainment.

be'reken [bə'Rêkən] *v.* (-) calculate, evaluate, compute; -aar *n.* (-s) computer; -de *a.* calculated, computed; deliberate; -baar *a.* (-bare) calculable; -end *a.* (-e) calculating; scheming; -ing *n.*

'berg [beRch] *v.* (-) = **bêre** *n.* (-e) mountain; -agtig *a.* (-e; -er, -ste) mountainous; -er *n.* (-s) salvor; -ing *n.* cp. **bêre** salvage; -af *av.* down-

hill, slope; -op *av.* up-hill; **bergrede** *n.* Sermon on the Mount.

be'rig [bə'Rəch] *v.* (-) report; inform, notify; *n.* (-te) tidings, news; report; -gewer *n.* (-s) reporter.

be'rispe [bə'Rəspə] *v.* (-) reprimand, rebuke, censure; **be'risping** *n.*

be'roem [bə'Rum] *v.* (-) *jou-op* take a pride in; boast of; -d *a.* (-e; -er, -ste) famous, celebrated; -dheid *n.* fame, celebrity.

be'roep [bə'Rup] *v.* (-) call (*minister of religion*); -op appeal to; *n.* calling, occupation; vocation; invitation; appeal; -baar *a.* (-bare) eligible (*minister*); -shalwe *av.* by virtue of one's calling; -sgevaar *n.* (*be'roepsgevare*) occupational hazard.

be'roer [bə'RûR] *v.* (-) stir, disturb; perturb; -d *a.* (-e; -er, -ste) miserable, rotten; confounded; -dheid *n.* wretchedness; rottenness; -ing *n.*; -te *n.* apoplexy.

be'rokken [bə'Rokən] *v.* (-) cause, give, bring upon.

be'roof, be'rowe [bə'Rôf, bə'Rôwə] *v.* (-) rob; deprive; bereave; **be'rowing** *n.*

be'rou [bə'Roa] *v.* (-) repent, regret; *n.* repentance, remorse; -vol *a.* (-le; -ler, -ste) penitent, repentant, contrite.

be'rug [bə'Rʌch] *a.* (-te; -er, -ste) notorious; -theid *n.*

be'rus [bə'Rʌs] *v.* (-) -by rest with; submit to, reconcile oneself to; -tend *a.* (-e) submissive; -ting *n.* resignation.

be'rym [bə'Raym] *v.* (-) put to verse.

'bes ['bes] *n.* best; *av.* very well; -moonltik very likely.

be'sadig(d) [bə'sâdəch(t)] *a.* (-de) coolheaded, calm; moderate; -dheid *n.* moderation.

be'sef [bə'sef] *v.* (-) realize; *n.* idea; realization.

'besem ['bêsəm] *n.* (-s) broom, besom; -stok *n.* broom-stick.

be'sending [bə'sendəng] *n.* consignment.

be'set [bə'set] *v.* (-) occupy; cast (*a play*); set; trim; garrison; *a.* (-te) engaged, occupied; **be'sete** *a.* possessed (*by devil*); **be'setene** *n.* (-s) one possessed; -sel *n.* trimming; -ting *n.*

'besie ['bêsi] *n.* (-s) cicada.

be'siel [bə'sil] *v.* (-) inspire; animate; -d *a.* (-e) inspired; animated; -end *a.* (-e; -er, -ste) inspiring; -ing *n.*

be'sien [bə'sin] *v.* (-) look at, view; -swaardig *a.* (-e) worth seeing.

'besig ['bêsəch] *v.* (ge-) use, make use of; -e *a.* (-r, besigste) busy, engaged; -heid *n.* business; -hou *v.* (-ge-) to keep occupied; -ing *n.* use.

be'sin [bə'sən] *v.* (-) reflect; change one's mind; -ning *n.* consciousness; *tot-kom* come to one's senses.

be'sink [bə'sənk] *v.* (-) subside, settle; -sel *n.* sediment, dregs.

be'sit [bə'sət] v. (-) possess, have, own; n. possession, assets; -lik a. (-e) possessive (pron.); -tend (-e) propertied (class); -ter n. (-s) possessor; -ting n. (-e, -s) possession, property.

be'skaaf, be'skawe [bə'skāf, bə-'skāvə] v. (-) refine, civilize; -d a. (-e; -er, -ste) civilized; refined; polished; -dheid n. refinement, breeding; be'skawing n. civilization; refinement.

be'skaam [bə'skām] v. (-) put to shame; disappoint.

be'skadig [bə'skādəch] v. (-) damage, injure.

be'skeid [bə'skayt] n. answer.

be'skeidenheid [bə'skaydnyt] n. discretion, modesty.

be'skeie [bə'skayə] a. modest; unobtrusive.

be'skerm [bə'skeRəm] v. (-) protect, screen; patronize; -end a. (-e) protective; -engel n. guardian-angel; -er n. (-s) protector; patron; -heer n. patron; -ing n.

be'skik [bə'skək] v. (-) arrange; dispose; -baar a. (-bare) available; -king n.

be'skimmeld [bə'skəmɛlt] a. (-d) mouldy.

be'skinder [bə'skənəR] v. (-) slander.

be'skonke [bə'skonkə] a. intoxicated.

be'skore [bə'skōRə] a. allotted, granted to.

be'skot [bə'skot] n. wainscoting.

be'skou [bə'skoə] v. (-) look at, view; contemplate; -end a. (-e) speculative; -ing n.

be'skroomd [bə'skRōmt] a. (-e; -er, -ste) shy, timid.

be'skryf, be'skrywe [bə'skRayf, bə'skRayvə] v. (-) describe; put in writing; write on; be'skrywend a. (-e) descriptive; be'skrywing n.

be'skuit [bə'skœit] n. rusk; biscuit; -jie dim. biscuit.

be'skuldig [bə'skʌldəch] v. (-) accuse; charge; incriminate; blame; -de n. (-s) accused; -er n. (-s) accuser; -ing n.

be'skut [bə'skʌt] v. (-) protect, shelter; guard; -ting n. protection; impalement.

be'slaan [bə'slān] v. (-) shoe (horse); mount (with metal); stud (nails); occupy (time, space); become dimmed (pane); tarnish (metal); extend over; -de a. shod; coated; steamy.

be'slag [bə'slach] n. mounting; fittings; -lê op seize.

be'sleg [bə'slech] v. (-) settle.

be'slis [bə'sləs] v. (-) decide; arbitrate; -te a. decided, resolute; definite; av. decidedly, positively; -send a. (-e) decisive, casting; -theid n. resoluteness.

be'slommering [bə'sloməRəng] n. trouble, worry; be'slommernis = beslommering.

be'sluit [bə'slœit] v. (-) decide; end, wind up; infer; n. (-e) conclusion, close; decision; -eloos a. (-lose) undecided, wavering; -eloosheid n. indecision.

be'smeer [bə'smēR] v. (-) smear, soil.

be'smet [bə'smet] v. (-) infect; pollute; defile; -te a. infected; contaminated; defiled; -lik a. (-e; -er, -ste) contagious, infectious; -ting n. contagion.

be'snoei [bə'snui] v. (-) prune; curtail; retrench; -ing n.

be'sny [bə'snay] v. (-) circumcise; -denis n. circumcision; be'snede a. circumcised.

be'soedel [bə'sudəl] v. (-) = besmet.

be'soek [bə'suk] v. (-) visit, call on; attend; n. (-e) visit, call; ons het we have visitors; -ing n. affliction; -uur n. visiting-hour.

be'soldig [bə'soldəch] v. (-) pay; -ing n. wages.

be'sonder [bə'sondəR] n. in die in particular; a. (-e) special; strange; individual; av. particularly, exceedingly; uncommonly; -heid n. detail, particular; -lik (-e) = besonder, av.; -s a. (-e) = besonder a.

be'sondig [bə'sondəch] v. (-) commit sin, transgress.

be'sonne [bə'sonə] a. considerate, well-considered.

be'sope [bə'sōpə] a. intoxicated, fuddled.

be'sorg [bə'soRch] v. (-) give cause; provide, furnish; attend to; -d a. anxious, uneasy; -dheid n. anxiety; -ing n. delivery.

be'spaar [bə'spāR] v. (-) save; be'sparing n. saving.

be'speel [bə'spēl] v. (-) play, play on.

be'speur [bə'spēR] v. (-) observe, notice; -baar a. (-bare) observable, noticeable.

be'spied [bə'spit] v. (-) spy on; -ing n.

be'spoedig [bə'spudəch] v. (-) expedite.

be'spot [bə'spot] v. (-) mock; -lik a. (-e) ridiculous; -ting n. ridicule.

be'spreek [bə'spRēk] v. (-) discuss; reserve; review; be'spreking n. (-e, -s); be'sproke a. reserved.

be'sproei [bə'spRui] v. (-) spray, irrigate; -ing n.

'bessie ['besi] n. (-s) berry.

be'staan [bə'stān] v. (-) exist; live; subsist; n. existence: livelihood; -baar a. (-bare) possible; reasonable; compatible with; -de a. existing; be'stand n. -teen proof against; -sbeveiliging n. social security.

'beste ['bestə] n. best; a. best, first class; excellent; my ou- my better half, spouse.

be'stee [bə'stē] v. (-) spend.

be'stek [bə'stek] n. (-ke) compass; specifications.

be'stel [bə'stel] v. (-) order; arrange; appoint; -ling n.

be'stem [bə'stem] v. (-) destine; set apart; fix; -de a. destined, intended (for); -ming n. destination, destiny.

be'storwe [bə'stoRvə] a. livid, deadly pale; -boedel n. (-s) legacy.

be'straf [bə'stRaf] v. (-) reprimand, rebuke; punish.

be'stry [bə'stRay] v. (-) fight; combat; oppose; -ding n.

bestu'deer [bəstew'deÊR] v. (-) study.

be'stuif, be'stuiwe [bə'stœif] v. (-) dust; pollinate.

be'stuur [bə'stÊwR] v. (-) drive, pilot; guide, run; control, manage; n. (be'sture) management, control; rule, government; -baar a. (-bare) manageable; -der n. driver; manager.

be'suinig [bə'sœinəch] v. (-) economize; -ing n.

be'swaar [bə'swÊR] v. (-) load, burden; n. (be'sware) objection; scruple; -de a. oppressed; mortgaged; -lik a. hardly; be'swarend a. (-e) aggravating.

be'swadder [bə'swadəR] v. (-) slander.

be'sweer [bə'svÊR, bə'swÊR] v. (-) adjure; exorcise, lay (ghost); entreat, beseech; allay; -der n. -s) one who exorcises; -ing n. (-s, -e) exorcism; incantation; charming.

'beswil ['bəsvəl] n. vir jou eie- for your own good.

be'swyming [bə'swaymong] n. (-s) trance; in - val to swoon.

be'taal [bə'tÊl] v. (-) pay; pay for; settle; -baar a. (-bare) payable; be'taling n.

be'taam [bə'tÊm] v. (-) behove, become; -lik a. (-e) proper, fit, decent.

be'teken [bə'tÊkən] v. (-) mean; imply; represent; spell (ghost); -is n. (-se) -isvol a. (-le; -ler, -ste) significant.

be'ter ['bÊtəR] n. niks -s nie nothing better a., av. better; -skap n. improvement; -wete n. teen sy- against his own conviction; -weter n. (-s) wiseacre.

be'teuel [bə'tÊəl] v. (-) restrain; curb; repress; -ing n.

be'teuterd [bə'tÊtəRt] a. (-e) confused, puzzled.

be'ton [bə'ton] n. concrete; be-wapende - reinforced concrete.

be'toog [bə'tÔch] v. (-) argue; n. (be'toë); be'toging n. demonstration.

be'toon [bə'tÔn] v. (-) show; accentuate; n. display; manifestation.

be'tower [bə'tÔvəR] v. (-) enchant; fascinate; -de a. bewitched, enchanted; -end a. (-e) bewitching; charming; -ing n. charm, spell.

be'trag [bə'trach] v. (-) do (duty); contemplate; -ting n. discharge (of duty); contemplation.

be'trap [bə'tRap] v. (-) tread upon; detect.

be'tref [bə'tRef] v. (-) concern; -fende av. concerning.

be'trek [bə'tRek] v. (-) move into, take; become overcast: entangle in; surprise; -king n. situation; relation; reference; -lik a. (-e; -er, -ste) comparative; av. relatively.

be'treur [bə'tRÊR] v. (-) deplore, regret; -enswaardig a. (-e) deplorable.

be'trou [bə'tRoa] v. (-) trust; -baar a. (-bare; -der, -ste) reliable.

be'twis [bə'twəs] v. (-) dispute, challenge, deny.

be'twyfel [bə'twayfəl] v. (-) doubt, question.

be'tyds [bə'tayts] av. in time.

'beuel ['bÊl] n. (-s) bugle, trumpet.

'beuk ['bÊk] n. (-e) beech; v. (ge-) beat, thrash; -elaar n. (-s) tenderizer (butcher).

'beul ['bÊl] n. (-s) executioner.

'beur [bÊR] v. (ge-) drag, strain; struggle.

'beurs [bÊRs] n. purse; scholarship; exchange; -ie dim. purse.

'beurt [bÊRt] n. (-e) turn, innings, opportunity; -elings av. alternately, in turn.

'beusel ['bÊsəl] v. (ge-) trifle, dawdle; -'agtig a. (-e) trivial.

be'vaar [bə'fÊR] v. (-) navigate, sail; -baar a. (-bare; -der, -ste) navigable.

be'val [bə'fal] v. (-) please; give birth to; -lig a. (-e; -er, -ste) charming; -ligheid n. charm; -ling n. (-e, -s) confinement.

be'vange [bə'fange] a. seized; foundered.

be'vat [bə'fat] v. (-) contain; comprehend; -lik a. (-e) clear; intelligent; -ting n.; -tingsvermoë n. comprehension.

be'veel [bə'fÊl] v. (-) command, charge; commend; be'vel n. (be'vele) command; be'velhebber n. (-s) commander; be'velvoerder n. (-s) = bevelhebber; be'velvoerend a. (-e) commanding.

be'veg [bə'fech] v. (-) oppose.

be'vel [bə'fel] n. (-) order, command.

be'vestig [bə'festəch] v. (-) attach, fasten; fix; confirm; affirm; consolidate; induct, ordain; -end a. (-e) affirmative; -ing n.

be'vind [bə'fant] v. (-) find; jou in gevaar- be in danger; jou in die stad- be in the city; -ing n. (-e, -s) finding (of commission).

be'voeg [bə'fuch] a. (-de) competent.

be'volk [bə'folk] v. (-) to people; -te a. populated; -ing n. (-e, -s) n.

be'voordeel [bə'fÔRdêl] v. (-) benefit.

be'vooroordeel [bə'fÔRÔRdêl] a. (-de) prejudiced.

be'vorder [bə'foRdəR] v. (-) promote; -ing n.; -lik a. (-e; -er, -ste) beneficial, conducive.

be'vrag [bə'fRach] v. (-) to charter; -ing n.

be'vredig [bə'fRêdəch] (v. -) satisfy, gratify; -end a. (-e) satisfactory; -ing n.

be'vrees [bə'fRẽs] a., av. (-de) afraid, apprehensive.

be'vriend [bə'fRint] a. (-e) friendly.

be'vries [bə'fRis] v. (-) freeze.

be'vrore [bə'fRõRə] a. frozen, cp. bevries p.p.

be'vrug [bə'fRʌch] v. (-) impregnate; fertilize; -ting n.

be'vry [bə'fRay] v. (-) set free; -ding n.

be'waak [bə'vãk] v. (-) guard, keep watch; be'waking n.

be'waar [bə'vãR] v. (-) save; keep (secret); maintain; preserve; protect; -der n. (-s) keeper; warder; be'waring n.; -skool n. infant-school.

be'wapen [bə'vãpən] v. (-) arm; -ing n.

be'weeg [bə'vẽch] v. (-) move; stir; shift; prevail upon, persuade; -baar a. (-bare, -der, -ste) movable; -grond n. (-e) motive; -lik a. (-e; -er, -ste) movable; mobile; be'wegend a. (-e) moving; be'weging (-e, -s) n.

be'weegrede [bə'vẽchRẽdə] n. (-s) motive.

be'weer [bə'vẽR] v. (-) maintain, assert; contend; be'wering n. (-e, -s).

'bewe ['bẽvə] v. (ge-) tremble; shiver; waver; = beef; be'werasie n. shivering; the shakes; -rig a. (-e; -er, -ste) trembling; shaky; be'wing n. trembling; fear.

'bewer ['bẽvər] n. (-s) beaver.

be'werk [bə'veRk] v. (-) cultivate; treat; bring to pass; revise; adapt.

be'wind [bə'vənt] n. government.

be'wonder [bə'von(d)əR] v. (-) admire; -aar n. (-s) admirer; -ens'waardig a. (-e) admirable; -ing n.

be'woë [bə'võə] a. moved; agitated.

be'woon [bə'võn] v. (-) inhabit, occupy, dwell in; -baar a. (-bare) habitable; be'woner n. (-s) inhabitant; be'woning n.

be'wus [bə'vʌs] a. (-te) conscious, aware; die-te persoon the person in question; -syn n. consciousness; cognition; -teloos a. (-lose) unconscious; comatose; -theid n. consciousness.

be'wys [bə'vays] v. (-) prove; demonstrate; do (favour); render (service); eer- pay homage; n. (-e) proof; evidence; sign; token; promissory note; receipt; voucher; certificate; -baar a. (-bare) provable, demonstrable; -grond n. (-e) argument; -ie dim. cp. bewys n.; -plaas n. reference; -voering n. argumentation.

be'ywer [bə'ayvəR] v. (-) exert oneself, endeavour.

'bibber ['bəbəR] v. (ge-) shiver, tremble, jitter (radar); cp. bewe.

biblio'teek [bəbliʊ'tẽk] n. (biblio'teke) library; bibliote'karis n. (-se) librarian; biblioteka'resse n. fem.

'bid ['bit] v. (ge-) pray; say grace; beseech; -der n. (-s) one who prays.

'bied ['bit] v. (ge-) offer; bie v. (ge-) bid; bie(d)er n. bidder.

'bieg ['bich] v. (ge-) confess; n. confession.

'bier ['biR] n. beer.

'bies ['bis] n. beestings, colostrum.

'biesie ['bisi] n. (-s) rush, reed.

'bietjie ['biKi] n. (-s) a little; moment; wag 'n-! wait a moment; av. rather, somewhat; 'n-baie rather much; -bietjie av. bit by bit.

biga'mie [bicha'mi] n. bigamy.

'biggel ['bəchəl] n. (ge-) trickle (tears).

bilate'raal [bilatə'Rãl] a. (bilate'rale) bilateral.

bil'jart [bəl'yaRt] n. billiards; v. (ge-) play billiards.

'biljet [bəl'yet] n. poster, handbill; note (bank).

bil'joen [bəl'yun] num. (-e) billion.

'billik ['bələk] a. (-e; -er, -ste) reasonable; fair; just; v. (ge-) approve of; -erwyse av. in fairness; -heid n. fairness, justice; -heidshalwe av. in fairness.

'biltong ['bəltong] n. strips of dried meat.

'bind ['bint] v. (ge-) tie; fasten; bind; -end a. (-e) binding; -er n. (-s) binder; bond (mech.); -doek n. (-e) binder.

'binne ['bənə] prep. within, inside; av. in, inside, within; -goed n. entrails; -in av. right inside; -kant av. inside; -kort av. ere long, shortly; -land n. inland, interior; -nsmonds a., av. -praat mumble; -ste n. inside, interior; a. innermost, inner; -stebuite av. inside out.

'binneband ['bənəbant] n. (-e) tube.

'binnebuis ['bənəbœis] n. (-e) inner tube.

'binnesool ['bənəsõl] n. ('binnesole) tyre gaiter; inner sole (shoe); -tjie dim.

bio'graaf [biʊ'chRãf] n. (bio'grawe) biographer; biogra'fie n. biography; bio'grafies a. (-e) biographic.

biolo'gie [biʊlʊ'chi] n. biology; bio'loog n. (bio'loë) biologist.

bio'skoop [biʊ'skõp] n. (bio'skope) bioscope, cinema.

'bis ['bəs] n. encore.

'bits ['bəts] a., av. sharp, tart, harsh; -ig a., av. = bits; -igheid n. acrimony.

'bitter ['bətəR] a. (-) (-e; -der, -ste) bitter; sore; av. bitterly; -min precious little; -agtig a. (-e) bitterish; -einder n. (-s) die-hard; -heid n. bitterness; -lik a. (-e) bitterly.

'bitterhoutjies ['bətəRhoakis] n. quassia chips.

'blaadjie ['blãiKi] dim. leaflet; petal; tract; cp. blaar, blad.

'blaai ['blãi] v. (ge-) turn over the pages.

'blaak ['blãk] v. (ge-) glow, burn.

'blaam ['blãm] n. blame; reproach.

'blaar ['blɑ̄r] n. (blare) leaf; blister; -loos a. (-lose) leafless; -tjie dim.

'blaas ['blɑ̄s] n. (blase) bag, bladder; cyst; bubble; v. (ge-) blow; breathe; -balk n. bellows; -op n. toby, frog; grasshopper; -orkes n. brass band; -pyp n. blowpipe; -pootjie n. thrips.

'blad ['blat] n. (blaaie) leaf, sheet; paper; shoulder; -breker n. subsoiler; -sak n. knapsack; -steek v. (-ge-) shake hands; -sy n. (-e) page; -vulling n. padding; -wisselend a. (-e) deciduous; -wyser n. bookmark.

'blaf ['blaf] v. (ge-) bark; cough; n. bark.

'blakend ['blɑ̄kənt] a. (-e; -er, -ste) burning, glowing.

'blaker ['blɑ̄kəR] n. (-s) candle-stick.

blameer [bla'mēR] v. (ge-) to blame, cp. blaam.

'blank ['blank] a. (-e) white, fair; unstained, untarnished; blank (verse); -e n. (-s) white person, European; -heid n. whiteness; purity; -o a. -tjek blank cheque.

'blas ['blas] a. dark, sallow.

'blatjang ['blatyang] n. chutney.

'bleek ['blēk] a. pallid, pale; n. bleaching; v. (ge-) bleach, whiten; -blou n. pale blue; -siekte n. anaemia; -sug n. = -siekte chlorosis.

'bleik [blayk] = bleek; -poeier n. bleaching powder.

'blêr [blɛ̄R] v. (ge-) bleat; bellow, howl.

'blies ['blies] n. (-se) blaze (of horse); horse with blaze; bald head; -kop n. bald head.

'blik [blək] n. (-ke) tin (receptacle); tin-plate; look, glance; jou-! you blighter!; -beker n. tin mug; -kantien n. tin can; dis laaste sien van die he's gone with the wind; -kiesdorp n. tin town, shanty town, slums; -kieskos n. tinned food; -kiesmelk n. condensed milk.

'bliksem ['bləksəm] n. lightning; jou-! you damned scoundrel!; v. (ge-) lighten, flash; -sl interj. the deuce!

'bliksnyer ['bləksnayəR] n. (-s) tin-opener.

'blind [blənt] a. (-e; -er, -ste) blind; false; blank; av. blindly; -doek n. bandage for blindfolding; v. (ge-) to blindfold, deceive, hoodwink; -e n. (-s) blind person; -ederm n. appendicitis; appendix, caecum; -ebult n. blind rise; -ehoek n. blind corner; -ekol n. blind spot; -enadering n. blind approach; -elings av. blindly; -eskrif n. braille; -heid n. blindness; -ing n. (-s) shutter, blind.

'blink [blənk] a. (-e; -er, -ste) shining, bright; sleek; radiant; 'n-gedagte a brain-wave.

'blits ['bləts] n. lightning; v. (ge-) flash, lighten; -snel av. quck as lightning; -vinnig av. = -snel;

-motor n. (-s) flying squad car; -patrollie n. (-s) flying squad.

'bloed ['blut] n. blood; -agtig a. (-e) bloodlike; -arm a. anaemic; -armoede n. anaemia; -bad n. carnage; -'dorstig a. (-e; -er, -ste) bloodthirsty; -erig a. (-e) bloody; -ig a. (-e; -er, -ste) bloody; blazing (hot) av. -kwaad furiously angry; -ing n. haemorrhage; -jie dim. (-s) poor mite; -klont n. clot of blood; -liggaampie n. blood corpuscle; -menging n. mixture of blood; -min a. very little; -vat n. bloodvessel.

'bloedbad ['blutbat] n. massacre.

'bloedskande ['blutskanə] n. incest.

'bloedskenker ['blutskengkəR] n. (-s) blood donor.

bloedstelp'stiffie [blutstelp'stəfi] n. (-s) styptic pencil.

'bloedsuiweraar ['blutsœivəRɑ̄R] n. blood purifier.

'bloedverwant ['blutfəRvant] n. (-e) kinsman.

'bloei ['blui] v. (ge-) bloom, flourish, prosper; bleed; n. prosperity, bloom; -sel n. (-s) blossom.

bloe'mis [blu'məs] n. (-te) florist.

'bloemlesing ['blumlēsəng] n. (-s) anthology.

'bloesend ['blusənt] a. (-e; -er, -ste) florid, rosy.

'blok ['blok] n. (-ke) block; log; stocks (for offenders); handicap; v. (ge-) cram, swot.

'blom ['blom] n. (-me) flower; blossom; flour; the pick, choice; v. (ge-) to flower, bloom; -kool n. cauliflower; -kweker n. (-s) floriculturist; -swa(w)el n. flowers of sulphur; -tuil n. posy.

'blond ['blont] a. (-e; -er, -ste) blond.

'bloos ['blōs] v. (ge-) blush, flush.

'bloot ['blōt] a. (blote) bare; mere; bald (fact); av. merely; -s a. unsaddled, bare-backed; -stel v. (ge-) expose; subject; -lê v. (-ge-) denude; uncover.

'blootshoofds ['blōtshōfs] a. bareheaded.

'blos ['blos] n. blush.

'blou [bloa] n. blue; a. (-e; -er, -ste) blue; blou-blou iets-laat let the matter rest; -druk n. blue-print; -druifie n. grape hyacinth; -sel n. blue; -tjie dim. carbon-copy, 'n-loop be refused as suitor; -reën n. wistaria.

'blousuur ['bloasȳwR] n. prussic acid.

'blus ['blʌs] n. sy-is uit his bolt is shot; v. (ge-) extinguish (fire); slake (lime).

'bly [blay] a. (-) (-e; -er, -ste) glad, joyful, happy; v. (ge-) stay; live; keep on; -dskap n. joy; -held n. joy; -moedig a. (-e; -er, -ste) cheerful, jovial; -spel n. comedy; -wend a. (-e; -er, -ste) lasting, enduring.

'blyk ['blayk] n. (-e) token; sign; v. (ge-) appear, be obvious; show; -baar *a.* (*-bare*) apparent, obvious; *av.* apparently, evidently; *-ens prep.* as appears from.

'**blyspel** ['blayspel] *n.* (*-e*) comedy.

'**bo**, '**bowe** ['bŏ, 'bŏvə] *prep.* above, over, past, beyond; *av.* above, upstairs, on high; *te-gaan* exceed; *te-kom* overcome; — **-aan** *av.* at the top; '**boaards** *a.* (*-e*) superterrestrial; — **-af** *av. van-* from the top; — **-al** *av.* above all; — **-arm** *n.* upper-arm; **-baadjie** *n.* (*-s*) jacket, coat; **-baas** *n.* champion, top-dog; **-bemesting** *n.* top-dressing; — **-end** *n.* head, upper-end; — **-mentioned** *a.* above-mentioned; — **-in** *av.* (*in*) at the top; **-gronds** *a.* overhead; — **-kant** *n.* upper side; *av.* over, above; **-loop** *n.* headwaters; **-lyf** *n.* upper part of body; — **-oor** *av.* over the top; — **-op** *av.* at the top, on top; **-staande** *a.* above-mentioned; **-stel** *n.* body (*of vehicle*).

bobbe'jaan [bobə'yăn] *n.* (*bobbe'jane*) baboon, monkey.

bo'botie [bo'bŏti] *n.* curried minced meat.

'**bod**, '**bot** ['bot] *n.* (*-te*) bid, offer.

'**bode** ['bŏdə] *n.* (*-s*) messenger.

'**bodem** ['bŏdəm] *n.* (*-s*) bottom (*of sea*); soil, territory; ship; **-loos** *a.* (*-lose*) bottomless.

'**boedel** ['budəl] *n.* (*-s*) estate, property; *-oorgee* become bankrupt, feed the fishes.

'**boef** [buf] *n.* (*boewe*) villain, knave.

'**boeg** ['buch] *n.* bow (*of ship*); shoulder, chest; **-lam** *a.* fatigued.

'**boegoe** ['buchu] *n.* buchu (*Barosma betulina*).

boei ['bui] *n.* (*-e*) handcuff, shackle; buoy; *v.* (*ge-*) to handcuff, fetter; absorb (*attention*); **-end** *a.* (*-e*; *-er*, *-ste*) absorbing, compelling.

'**boek** ['buk] *n.* (*-e*) book; quire (*paper*); *v.* (*ge-*) enter, book; **-agtig** *a.* (*-e*; *-er*, *-ste*) bookish; **-deel** *n.* volume; **-enhout** *n.* S. African beech; **-ery** *n.* (*-e*) collection of books, library; **-evat** *v.* (*-ge-*) hold family-prayers; **-hou** *n.* book-keeping; *v.* (*ge-*) keep accounts, keep the books; **-houer** *n.* (*-s*) book-keeper; **-jaar** *n.* financial year; **-staaf** *v.* (*ge-*) put on record; **-wurm** *n.* bookworm.

boe'ket [bu'ket] *n.* bouquet (*of wine*).

'**boekstaaf** ['bukstăf] *v.* (*ge-*) put on record.

'**boel** ['bɁl] *n.* lot, crowd.

'**boemel** ['buməl] *v.* (*ge-*) loaf, be a hobo; **-trein** *n.* slow train; **-aar** *n.* hobo.

'**boen** ['bun] *v.* (*ge-*) polish, shine.

'**boender** ['bun(d)əR] *v.* (*ge-*) chase, drive away.

'**Boer** ['bŭR] *n.* (*-e*) Afrikaans speaking S. African of European descent.

'**boer** ['bŭR] *n.* (*-e*) farmer; peasant; Jack (*cards*); *v.* (*ge-*) farm; *by 'n*

plek- to frequent a place; **-dery** *n.* (*-e*) farming, farm; **-ebedrog** *n.* swindling; **-everneuker** *n.* swindler; **-kool** *n.* borecole; **-plek** *n.* haunt; **-s** *a.* (*-e*) boorish, rustic; **-seep** *n.* home-made soap; **-ewors** *n.* boer-sausage.

'**boesel** ['busl] *n.* (*-s*) bushel.

'**boesem** ['busəm] *n.* (*-s*) bosom, breast.

'**boet** ['but] *v.* (*ge-*) pay; suffer; **-e** *n.* (*-s*) fine, penalty, penance.

'**boeteling** ['butələng] *n.* penitent person.

boet'vaardig [but'făRdəch] *a.* penitent, contrite.

'**bof** ['bof] *n.* (*bowwe*) den, home (*games*); tee (*golf*); **-bal** *n.* baseball.

'**bog** ['boch] *n.* (*-te*) bend, bight; nonsense, trash; **-gel** *n.* (*-s*) hump, hunch; **-kind** *n.* mere child; **-praatjies** *pl.* piffle; **-terig** *a.* (*-e*) trifling; **-tery** *n.* nonsense, nuisance.

'**bogronds** ['bŏchRonds] *a.* (*-e*) overhead.

'**bok** ['bok] *n.* (*-ke*) goat, buck (*wild*); buck (*of wagon*); trestle; blunder; *v.* (*ge-*) flirt; **-baard** *n.* goatee (*beard*); **-haar** *n.* mohair; **-kie** *dim.* (*-s*) kid; **-leer**: *n.* kid; spring *v.* (*ge-*) caper; **-wa** *n.* (*eens*) buck-wagon.

'**bokkem** ['bokəm] *n.* (*-s*) Cape herring.

'**boks** ['boks] *v.* (*ge-*) box.

'**bol** ['bol] *n.* (*-le*) ball; globe; sphere; crown (*hat*); bulb (*plant*); *a.* (*-*, *-le*) convex, round; *v.* (*ge-*) bulge; **-agtig** *a.* (*-e*) bulbous; **-heid** *n.* convexity; **-hol** *a.* convexo-concave; **-la** *n.* (*-'s*) bun (*of hair*); **-(le) makiesie** *a.* head over heels; **-rond** *a.* (*-e*) convex; **-vorm** *n.* spherical shape; **-werk** *n.* bulwark.

'**bolspuit** ['bolspœit] *n.* ball syringe.

'**Boland** ['bŏlant] Western Cape Province.

'**bom** ['bom] *n.* (*-me*) bomb; **-ar'deer** *v.* (*ge-*) to bombard; **-vry** *a.* shell-proof; **werper** *n.* (*-s*) bomber (*aeroplane*).

'**bomaats** ['bŏmăts] *av.* oversize.

'**bond** ['bont] *n.* (*-e*) league, union; **-genoot** *n.* (*'bondgenote*) *n.* ally; **-staat** *n.* federal state.

'**bondel** ['bon(d)əl] *n.* (*-s*) bundle, cluster, sheaf; *v.* (*ge-*) bundle; **-draer** *n.* (*-s*) pedlar, tramp, loafer.

'**bondig** ['bondəch] *a.* (*-e*; *-er*, *-ste*) concise, terse.

'**bonk** ['bonk] *v.* (*ge-*) lump; thump; **-ig** *a.* (*-e*) bony.

'**bons** ['bauñs] *n.* thump; *v.* (*ge-*) bump.

'**bont** ['bont] *n.* fur; **-jas** *n.* fur-coat; **-kraag** *n.* fur collar; **-werk** *n.* fur goods; **-werker** *n.* furrier.

'**bont** ['baunt] *a.* (*-e*; *-er*, *-ste*) pied, piebald; **-heid** *n.* variegation; **-praat** *v.* (*-ge-*) ramble; contradict oneself; seep *n.* mottled soap; **-span** *n.* motley crowd; **-staan** *v.* (*-ge-*) try hard.

'**boodskap** ['bŏtskap] n. (-pe) message, errand; v. (ge-) bring word; -per n. (-s) messenger.

'**boog** ['bŏg] n. (boē) bow; arch; arc; v. (ge-) -op boast of, glory in; -**brug** n. arched bridge; -**lamp** n. arc-lamp; -**skiet** n. archery; -**skutter** n. archer; -**venster** n. bow-window; -**vormig** a. (-e) arched.

'**boom** ['bŏm] n. (bome) tree; beam, barrier, pole; bottom, floor; v. (ge-) punt; -**agtig** a. (-e) arboreous; -**loos** a. (-lose) treeless; -**pie** dim.; -**skraap** a. empty; -**vormig** a. (-e) tree-shaped; -**wol** n. kapok.

'**boon** ['bŏn] n. (bone) bean; -**tjie** dim.; -**tjiesop** n. bean-soup.

'**boonop** ['bŏnop] av. moreover, besides; cp. **bo**.

'**boonste** ['bŏnsta] n. top, upper part; a. topmost, upper.

'**boor** ['bŏR] n. (bore) bit; drill; jumper; gimlet; v. (ge-) drill, bore; -**der** n. (-s) borer; -**gat** n. borehole; -**poeier** n. boracic powder; -**salf** n. boracic ointment; -**suur** n. boracic acid; -**tjie** dim. gimlet.

'**boortoring** ['bŏRtŏraŋ] n. (-s) derrick.

'**boord** [bŏRt] n. (-e) orchard; border, edge; board (ship); -**jie** n. collar; -**jieknoop** n. collar-stud.

'**boorsel** ['bŏRsəl] n. (-s) edging.

'**boos** ['bŏs] a. (bose) angry, cross; wicked; malignant; -'**aardig** a. (-er, -ste) malicious, malign; -'**aardigheid** n. malice; -**doener** n. (-s) evildoer; -**heid** n. evil; anger; -**wig** n. (-te) criminal.

'**boot** ['bŏt] n. (bote) boat, ship.

'**bord** ['bauRt] n. (-e) plate; board; blackboard; -**jie** dim.

bor'duur [boR'dēWR] v. (ge-) embroider; -**sel** n. embroidery; -**ster** n. fem. embroiderer.

'**borg** ['boRch] n. (-e) guarantee; security; bail; -**staan** v. (-ge-) go bail, stand surety; -**akte** n. (-s) security bond; -**steller** n. surety; -**stelling** n. surety, bail; -**teken** n. (-ge-) = -**staan**; borg- secure, lock.

'**borrel** ['boRəl] n. (-s) bubble; apéritif, tot; v. (ge-) bubble.

'**borrie** ['boRi] n. turmeric.

'**bors** ['bauRs] n. (-te) breast; bosom, chest; thorax; brisket; front (shirt); bust; -**beeld** n. (-e) bust, effigy; -**hemp** n. 'borshemde) dress-shirt; -**lap** n. (-pe) bib; -**lyfie** n. bust-bodice; -**trok** n. corset; -**slag** n. breast-stroke; -**speld** n. (-e) brooch; -**suiker** n. sugar-stick, barley sugar; -**wering** n. parapet.

'**borsel** ['bauRsəl] n. (-s) brush; bristle.

'**bos** ['bos] n. (-se) forest; bush; bunch; shock (hair); -**agtig** a. (-e; -er, -ste) woody; -**baadjie** n. (-s) lumber-jacket; -**bou** n. forestry; -**luis** n. tick; -**ryk** a. (-e) woody; well-wooded; -**sie** dim.; -**siedokter**

n. (-s) herbalist; quack; -**siestee** n. bush-tea; -**veld** n. bush-veld; -**wêreld** n. bush country; -**wese** n. (dept. of) forestry.

'**bose** ['bŏsə] n. die B- the Evil One.

'**bossuiker** = **borssuiker**.

'**bot** ['bot] n. (-te) flounder (fish); bone; a. (-te; -ter, -ste) blunt, dull; indolent; v. (ge-) bud, sprout; -**heid** n. dullness; -**sel** n. bud; -**weg** av. bluntly.

'**bots** ['bots] v. (ge-) collide; clash, disagree; -**ing** n. (-s) collision; clash.

'**bottel** ['botəl] n. (-s) bottle; v. (ge-) to bottle; -**ier** n. (-s) steward (cp. butler); -**stoor** n. (-store) wine and spirit merchant; -**eer** v. (ge-) to bottle; -**bottellering** n. bottling.

'**botter** ['botəR] n. butter; -**blom** n. buttercup, gazania; -**broodjie** n. scone; -**kop** n. (-pe) dunce; -**tande** -uitrek do without butter.

'**botvier** ['botfiR] v. (-ge) give rein to.

'**bou** ['boa] v. (ge-) build, erect, construct; rely on; 'n. build (body); construction; structure; framework (novel); — -**aannemer** n. (-s) contractor; -**er** n. (-s) builder; -**ery** n. building; -**kunde** n. architecture; -'**kundige** n. (-s) architect; -**kuns** n. architecture; -**val** n. (-le) ruin(s); -**vallig** a. (-e; -er, -ste) dilapidate.

'**boud** [boat] n. (-e) buttock; leg, hindquarter.

'**boul** ['boal] v. (ge-) bowl.

'**bout** ['boat] n. (-e) bolt; rivet; pin; -**jie** dim.

bowen'dien [bŏvən'din] prep., av. besides, moreover, also.

'**bra** [bRă] av. very; rather.

'**braaf** ['bRăf] a. (brawe) brave; virtuous; respectable.

'**braai** ['bRăi] v. (ge-) roast, grill, fry, broil; -**boud** n. roast leg of mutton; -**ribbetjie** n. roasted rib; -**vet** n. dripping; -**vleis** n. roast (meat).

'**braak** ['bRăk] a. fallow; v. (ge-) break up, fallow; vomit, retch; -**land** n. (-e) fallow land; -**middel** n. (-s) emetic; -**sel** n. vomit; -**neut** n. nux vomica.

'**braam** ['bRăm] n. bramble; blackberry; wire edge (of knife).

'**brabbel** ['bRabəl] v. (ge-) chatter, jabber; -**taal** n. jargon.

'**brak** ['bRăk] n. (-ke) little dog; mongrel; salt-lick; brackish spot; a. brackish, saltish, alkaline; -**bos** (sie) n. lye-bush; -**hond** n. mongrel; -**kie** dim.; -**plek** n. brackish spot.

'**brand** ['bRant] n. (-e) fire, conflagration; burnt veld; smut; v. (ge-) burn, be on fire; roast; scorch; cauterise; yearn; -**arm** a penniless; -**baar** a. (-bare) combustible; -**assies** n. pl. midges, punkies; -**blaar** n. (-blare) blister; -**end** a. (-e) burning; ardent; -**er** n. (-s) wave, breaker; burner; rebuke; -**erig** a. (-e) smarting; -**ewyn** n. brandy; -**glas** n. lens; -**hout** n. fire-wood; -**kas** n. safe; -**kraan** n.

fire-cock; **-maer** a. skinny, scraggy; **-merk** n. stigma; **-mier** n. fire ant; **-punt** n. focus; **-seer** n. (-sere) veldsore; **-siekte** n. scab; **-skatting** n. ransom; **-spiritus** n. methylated spirits; **-stapel** n. stake; **-stigting** n. arson; **-trap** n. (-pe) fire escape; **-vry** a. fire-proof; **-wag** n. (-te) outpost, sentry, picket; **-weer** n. fire-brigade; **-blusser** n. fire extinguisher; **-byl** n. fire axe; **-olie** n. fuel oil; **-slang** n. fire hose.

'**brandstof** ['bRantstof] n. fuel; **-pomp** n. (-e) fuel pump; **-tenk** n. (-s) fuel tank; **-verbruik** n. fuel consumption.

'**brandemalje** ['bRantĕmalyə] n. baked enamel.

'**bredie** ['bRĕdi] n. ragout.

'**breed** [bRĕt] a. (breĕ; breĕr, -ste) broad, wide; **-heid** n. breadth, width; **-te** n. (-s) width; **-voerig** a. (-e; -er, -ste) full, detailed.

'**breek** ['bRĕk] v. (ge-) break; smash, crush; refract; **-baar** a. (-bare) breakable, fragile; **-goed** n. pl. crockery; **-mielies** n. crushed maize; **-spul** n. smash-up, mess; **-yster** n. crowbar; **breking** n. refraction; **-skade** n. breakage.

'**brei** ['bRay] v. (ge-) knit; curry (hide); knead, train, make robust; **-er** n. (-s) knitter; trainer, coach; **-goed** n. (collective) knitting.

'**breidel** ['bRaydl] n. bridle, curb.

'**brein** ['bRayn] n. (-s) brain; **— harsings.**

'**brekfis** ['bRekfəs] n. breakfast (angl.); dis sommer 'n- it is child's play.

'**brem** ['bRem] n. broom.

'**bres** ['bRes] n. (-se) breach.

'**breuk** ['bRĕk] n. breach; rupture; fracture; fraction; **-band** n. truss.

'**briek** ['bRiek] n. (-e) brake; v. (ge-) apply brakes.

'**bries** ['bRis] n. (-e) breeze; **-end** a. (-e; -er, -ste) furious.

'**bril** ['bRil] n. (-le) spectacles, glasses; v. (ge-) wear spectacles; **-doos** n. spectacle-case; **-slyper** n. (-s) optician.

'**bring** ['bRing] v. (ge-) bring, convey; entail.

'**Brit** ['bRət] n. (-te) Britisher, Briton; **-s** a. British.

'**broeder** ['bRudəR] n. (-s) brother; geliefde (-s) brethren; **-lik** a. (-e; -er, -ste) brotherly; **-skap** n. brotherhood.

'**broei** ['bRui] v. (ge-) hatch; brood; ferment; incubate; get hot; brew; **-erig** a. (-e) stifling, sultry, muggy; **-nes** n. hot-bed; **-s** a. broody; **-sel** n. clutch.

'**broek** ['bRuk] n. (-e) pair of trousers, breeches, pants, shorts; bloomers, knickers; **-sband** n. waist-band; **-skeur** av. dit gaan- it is uphill work.

'**broer** ['bRūR] n. brother; cp. roed er; **-skind** n. nephew, niece; **-tjie** dim.

'**brok** ['bRok] n. (-ke) piece, lump; cp. **breek**; **-kel** v. (ge-) crumble; **-kelrig** a. (-e) crumbly, friable; **-kie** dim.; **-sgewyse** av. piece-meal; **-stuk** n. (-ke) **— brok.**

'**brom** ['bRom] v. (ge-) drone; grumble, grouse; **-mer** n. (-s) blowfly; **-merig** a. (-e) grumpy; **-pot** n. grouser.

bro'mied, bro'mide [bRŏ'mit] n. bromide.

'**bron** ['bRon] n. (-ne) spring, well; source; **-kors** n. water-cress.

'**brons** ['bRauñs] n. bronze; heat, rut; **-tig** a. (-e) rutting.

'**bronstyd** ['bRauñstayt] n. rutting season.

'**brood** ['bRŏt] n. (brode) n. bread; loaf; **-sgebrek** n. starvation; **-jie** dim.; mooi-s bak eat humble pie; **-nodig** av. highly necessary; **-nyd** n. professional jealousy; **-skrywer** n. (-s) hack-writer; **-winner** n. bread-winner.

'**broom** ['bRŏm] n. bromine.

'**broos** ['bRŏs] a. (brose; broser, -ste) fragile, frail, delicate; **-heid** n. fragility.

'**bros** ['bRos] a. brittle, crisp, crumbly; **-brood** n. shortbread.

'**brou** ['bRoa] v. (ge-) brew; bungle; **-ery** n. brewery; **-sel** n. brew, concoction.

'**brug** [bRʌch] n. (brûe, brûens, brugge) bridge; parallel bars (gymn.); gangway (ship); card-game; **-hoof** n. bridge-head.

'**bruid** [bRœit] n. (-e) bride; **-egom** n. (-s) bridegroom; **-sdae** n. bridal days; **-skat** n. dowry; **-skrans** n. bridal wreath; **-srok** n. wedding dress; **-sruiker** n. bridal bouquet.

'**bruikbaar** ['bRœikbaR] a. (-bare) serviceable.

'**bruikleen** ['bRœiklĕn] n. loan.

'**bruilof** ['bRœilof] n. wedding; **-sfees** n. wedding party; **-sgas** n. wedding guest.

'**bruin** ['bRœin] n. brown; Brown (bear); a. (-e) brown; **-agtig** a. (-e) brownish; **-e** n. (-s) brown one; **-erig** a. (-e) brownish; **-kool** n. brown coal; **-mense** n. (collective) coloured people; **-vis** n. (-se) porpoise.

brui'neer [brœi'nĕR] v. (-) burnish; **-der** n. (-s) burnisher.

'**bruis** ['bRœis] v. (ge-) effervesce, bubble; seethe; **-end** a. (-e) foaming, seething.

'**brul** ['bRʌl] v. (ge-) roar, bellow; n. (-le) roar, bellow; **-padda** n. (-s) bullfrog; **-voël** n. bittern.

bru'taal [bRew'tãl] a. (bru'tale; bru'taler, -ste) impudent, audacious, saucy; av. impudently; **bru'taliteit** n. impudence.

'**bruto** ['bRewtŏ] a. gross; **-gewig** n. gross weight; **-ontvangste** n. gross receipts.

'**bruusk** ['bRewsk] a. brusque.

'**bruut** ['bRewt] n. brute; a. (brute) brute (force).

'**bry** ['bRay] v. (ge-) speak with a burr; n. pulp.

'**buffel** ['bʌfəl] n. (-s) buffalo; churl; -**agtig** a. (-e; -er, -ste) churlish; -**agtigheid** n. churlishness.

'**buffer** ['bʌfəR] n. buffer, bumper.

buf'fet- [bʌ'fet] n. (-te) sideboard; bar (refreshment).

'**bui** ['bœi] n. (-e) shower; mood; fit; -**erig** a. (-e; -er, -ste) showery; moody, capricious.

'**buidel** ['bœidl] n. (-s) pouch; purse; -**wa** n. (-ens) straddle truck.

'**buig, 'buie** [bœich, bœiə] v. (ge-) bend, bow; curve; stoop; -**baar** a. (-bare) flexible; declinable; -**ing** n. (-s, -e) curtsey; curve; declension; -**ingsleer** n. accidence; -**ingsuitgang** n. (-e) inflexion; -**saam** a. (-same; -samer, -saamst) pliant; yielding.

'**buik** ['bœik] n. (-e) abdomen, stomach; bottom (wagon); -**loop** n. diarrhoea; -**vol** n. fed-up.

'**buikspreker** ['bœikspRēkəR] n. ventriloquist.

'**buis** [bœis] n. (-e) tube, pipe, duct; -**ie** dim.; -**loos** a. (-lose) ductless (gland); -**vormig** a. (-e) tubular.

'**buit** [bœit] n. booty; v. (ge-) seize.

'**buite** ['bœitə] av. outside; out of doors; out of town; prep. outside (a place); beyond: -**bly** v. (-ge-) remain outside; -**deur** n. outer door; —**egtelik** a. (-e) out of wedlock; -**kans** n. windfall; -**kant** n. outside; prep. outside, beyond; -**land** n. foreign country; -**s** a. (-e) foreign; -**n** prep. except, besides; -**ndien** prep. besides, moreover; -**nsporig** a. (-e) excessive; -**nste** n. exterior; a. outer; -**pos** n. outpost; -**staander** n. outsider.

'**buiteband** ['bœitəbant] n. (-e) tyre; -**verf** n. tyre paint.

'**buitenshuis** ['bœitənshœis] a. & av. (-e) outdoor(s).

'**buk** ['bʌk] v. (ge-) bend, stoop, bow.

'**buks** ['bʌks] n. air-gun; little fellow; -**ie** dim.

'**bul** ['bʌl] n. (-le) bull (papal), diploma; bull (animal); thumper, colossus, giant; -**hond** n. bulldog; -**letjie** dim.

'**bulder** ['bʌldəR] v. (ge-) roar, bellow; boom; -**end** a. (-e) roaring, raging.

'**bulk** [bʌlk] v. (ge-) bellow, low, moo.

'**bullebak** ['bʌləbak] n. bully.

'**bulsak** ['bʌlsak] n. feather-bed.

'**bult** [bʌlt] n. (-e) bump, lump, protuberance, hunch; hill, ridge; -**enaar** n. hunchback; -**erig** a. (-e; -er, -ste) bumpy, hilly; — v. (ge-) to bulge.

'**bundel** ['bʌndəl] n. (-s) collection; volume; beam; v. (ge-) collect, publish in bookform.

'**burg** ['bʌRch] n. (-e) hog; stronghold; -**emeester** n. (-s) mayor;

—**emeeste'res** n. fem. mayoress; —**emeestersvrou** n. mayor's wife.

'**burger** ['bʌRgəR] n. (-s) citizen, civilian; -**'es** fem.; -**lik** a. (-e) civil, civilian; -**mag** n. (-te) civilian force; -**skap** n. citizenship.

bu'ro [bew'Rõ] n. (-s) bureau.

'**bus** ['bʌs] n. (-se) omnibus; box; bush; -**kruit** n. gunpowder.

'**buur** ['bēwR] n. (bure) neighbour; -**man** n. neighbour; -**praatjies** n. gossip; -**skap** n. neighbourly relations; -**t** n. (-e, -es) neighbourhood; -**vrou** n. = buur fem.

'**buuste** ['bēwstə] n. bust.

'**by** ['bay] n. (-e) bee; prep. by, with, near, at; av. present, there; -**baantjie** n. side-line; -**bedoeling** n. ulterior motive; -**behorend** a. (-e) belonging to it; -**behores, -behoorsels** n. accessories; -**betaling** n. excess payment; -**betekenis** n. secondary meaning; -**blad** n. supplement (of journal); -**bly** v. (-ge-) keep up to; -**dam** v. (-ge-) accost; -**derhand** av. close by; -**dra** v. (-ge-) contribute; -**drae** n. (-s) contribution; -'**eenkoms** n. (-te) assembly; -**figuur** n. secondary figure; -**gaande** a. accompanying; -**gedagte** n. (-s) afterthought; -**geloof** n. superstition; -**geval** av. in case; -**gevolg** av. consequently; -**hou** v. (-ge-) keep pace; -**kans** av. almost -**kom** v. (-ge-) get at, get hold of; be included; -**komend** a. (-e) inclusive; -'**komstig** a. (-e) subsidiary; -**me'kaar** av. together; -**na** av. almost; -**naam** n. nickname; -**produk** n. (-te) by-product; -**saak** n. matter of minor importance; -**siende** a. short-sighted; -**siendheid** n. myopia; -**sin** n. (-ne) subordinate sentence or clause; -**staan** v. (-ge-) assist; -**tel** v. (-ge-) add; -**val** n. approval; -**voeg** v. (-ge-) add; -'**voeglik** a. (-e) adjectival; -**voegsel** n. (-s) supplement; -'**voorbeeld** n. for example; -**woner** n. (-s) subfarmer, squatter; -**woord** n. adverb.

'**bykom** ['baykom] v. (-ge-) resuscitate, revive.

'**bysit** ['baysət] n. concubine.

'**bysmaak** ['baysmāk] n. ('bysmake) taint.

'**bystand** ['baystant] n. assistance, support.

'**bysyn** ['baysayn] n. presence.

'**byl** ['bayl] n. (-e) hatchet, axe; -**tjie** dim.

'**byster** ['baystəR] a. die spoor-wees be at a loss; av. extremely.

'**byt** ['bayt] v. (ge-) bite, snap at; n. bite; -**end** a. (-e) biting; -**erig** a. (-e) snappish; -**soda** n. caustic soda; -**middel** n. (-s) corrosive.

'**bytel** ['baytəl] v. (-ge-) count in, add.

'**byvul** ['bayfʌl] v. (-ge-) top up; -**ling** n. topping up.

C

(For words not found under C,
see K or S.)

c. (cent) ['sent] *n.* (-e) c.(ent).

ca'chet [ka'shet] *n.* (-te) cachet,
mark, stamp.

ca'lendae [ka'lendāi] *n. pl.* calends.

Cal'vyn [kal'fayn] *n.* Calvin; **calvi-
nis** *n.* (-te) Calvinist.

camou'flage [kamu'flāsh] *n.* camouflage; **camou'fleer** *v.* (ge-) to camouflage.

cause'rie [koasə'ri] *n.* (-ĕ, -s) causerie,
talk; **cau'seur** *n.* (-s) conversational-
ist.

ce'dille [se'dələ] *n.* (-s) cedilla.

cein'tuur [sayn'tēWR] *n.* (*cein'ture*,
-s) belt.

cen'taur [sen'tauR] *n.* (-e, -i) centaur.

'cerebrum ['sēRəbrʌm] *n.* cerebrum;
cere'braal = serebraal; **cere'bel-
lum** *n.* cerebellum.

ce'suur [se'sēWR] *n.* caesura.

Chal'deë [chal'dēə] *n.* Chaldea; **-r** *n.*
(-s) Chaldean; **Chal'deeus** *a.* (-e)
Chaldean.

chan'son [shāñ'saung] *n.* (-s) chan-
son.

chape'ron [shapə'Rõn] *n.* (-ne, -s)
chaperon; *v.* (ge-) to chaperon.

charla'tan [shaRla'tan] *n.* (-s) char-
latan.

'charme [shaRmə] *n.* charm.

'charter ['tshāRtəR] *n.* (-s) charter.

chau'ffeur [shŏ'fēR] *n.* (-s) chauffeur.

chauve'nis [shofi'nəs] *n.* (-te)
chauvinist; **-me** *n.* chauvinism; **-ties**
a. (-e) chauvinistic.

chef ['shef] *n.* (-s) chef, chief.

che'mie [chě'mi] *n.* chemistry;
'chemies *a.* (-e) chemical; **'chemikus**
n. (-se) chemist; **chemi'kalië** *n. pl.*
chemicals.

chic ['shik] *a.* (-, -e) chic, stylish.

chi'rurg [shi'RʌRch] *n.* (-e) surgeon;
chirur'gie *n.* surgery.

'chloor ['chlŏR] *n.* chlorine.

chloroform [klŏRŏ'foRəm] *n.*
chloroform.

'cholera ['chŏləRa] *n.* cholera.

'Christus ['chRəstʌs] *n.* Christ;
'christen *n.* (-e) christian; **chris'tin**
n. fem.; **'christelik** *a.* (-e, -er, -ste)
christianlike; **'christelikheid** *n.*
Christianity; **'christendom** *n.*
Christiandom.

chro'maties [chRŏ'mātis] *a.* (-e)
chromatic.

'chronies ['kRŏnis] *a.* (-e) chronic.

chronolo'gie [kRŏnŏlŏ'chi] *n.* chro-
nology.

chroom ['kRŏm] *n.* chromium.

clairvo'yance [kleRva'yāñs] *n.* clair-
voyance.

'classis ['klasəs] *n.* (*classes*) classis,
presbytery (*of church*).

cli'chĕ [kli'shĕ] *n.* (-s) cliche;
hackneyed phrase.

cochi'nille [kosha'nilyə] *n.* cochineal.

Cons'tantia [kauñs'tāñsia] *n.* Con-
stantia.

'cosecans ['kŏsəkans] *n.* (-e, *'cose-
cante*) cosecant.

'cosinus ['kŏsinʌs] *n.* (-se) cosine.

'cotangens ['kŏtang-chens] *n.* ('*co-
tangente*) cotangent.

'crème ['kRɛm] *n.* crème, cream.

'crêpe ['kRɛp] *n.* crêpe.

'Cyprus ['sipRʌs] *n.* Cyprus.

D

dB (*desibel*), **d.B.** (*decibel*).

daad ['dāt] *n.* (*dade*) act, action,
deed, achievement, move; exploit;
op die- at once; *op heter-betrap* to
catch red-handed; **-'kragtig** *a.* (-e)
energetic; **-'werklik** *a.* (-e) actual,
de facto.

'daagliks ['dāchləks] *av.* (-e) daily,
everyday.

daal ['dāl] *v.* (ge-) descend; sink;
decline; **daling** *n.* (-e, -s) slump.

daalslag ['dālslach] *n.* ('*daalslae*)
downstroke.

'daalder ['dāləR] *n.* (-s) one shilling
and sixpence (fifteen cents).

'daar ['dāR] *av.* there; then; *conj.*
as, because, since; **-aan** *av.* by that,
to that, attached to it; **-agter** *av.*
behind it; **-be'newens** *av.* besides;
-'binne *av.* in there, within; **-bo** *av.*
up there, above, upwards; **-buite**
av. outside; **-'by** *av.* besides; **-die**
['dāRi] *pron.* that, *pl.* those; **-en-
'bowe** *av.* furthermore; **-en'teë/teen**
av. on the other hand; **-gelate** *av.*
not to mention, apart from; **-'ginds**
av. over there; **-heen** *av.* thither; **-in**
av. in that; **-mee** *av.* therewith; **-'na**
av. afterwards, next; accordingly;
-'naas *av.* next to that, besides that;
-natoe *av.* underneath; among; **-oor**
av. about that; because of that;
across that; **-'op** *av.* upon that,
thereupon; **-so** *av.* there, yonder;
-'sonder *av.* without that; whereas;
-teenoor *av.* opposite; on the other hand;
-toe *av.* to that end; **-tussen** *av.* in
between, among them; **-uit** *av.* from
that, thence; **-van** *av.* of that, from
that, thereof; **-vandaan** *av.* hence;
thence; **-voor** *av.* for that, therefore;
-'voor *av.* before that; in front of
that.

daarstel ['dāRstel] *v.* (-ge-) cause,
introduce, accomplish, erect; **-ling**
n. accomplishment, erection, introduction.

'dadel ['dādl] *n.* (-s) date; *daar kom-s
van nothing of the kind!*

'dadelik ['dātlək] *av.* at once,
promptly.

'daeraad ['dāRāt] *n.* dawn =
dagbreek.

dag ['dach] *n.* (*dae*) day; *die jongste-*

Doomsday; *die laaste der dae* the last days; -aan-, -vir- day by day; *aan die-kom* come to light; -blad n. (-blaaie) daily paper; -bladpers n. daily press; -boek n. diary; -breek n. daybreak; -dief n. (-diewe) idler; -diens n. day-duty; 'dag-en-'nagewening n. equinox; 'dageraad = dagbreek; -geld n. day's pay; -lig n. daylight; -loner n. (-s) daylabourer; -loon n. = daggeld; -lumier n. = dagbreek; -ploeg n. day-shift; -taak n. daily work (task); -teken v. (ge-) date.

'dagbloeiend ['dachbluïant] a. (-e) hemeranthic.

'dagga ['dacha] n. wild hemp.

'dagvaar ['dachfaR] v. (ge-) summon(s), cite, subpoena; -ding n.

'dagverhaal ['dachfaRhāl] n. diary.

'dahlia ['dālia] n. (-s) dahlia.

dak ['dak] n. (-ke) roof; hanging layer; *onder-bring* accommodate; -bedekking n. roofing; -drup n. eaves; -geut n. (-e) gutter; -kamer n. attic; -lig n. sky-light; -loos a. (-lose) homeless; -pan n. (-ne) tile; -rak n. roof carrier; -rand n. eaves; -venster n. attic window; -vors n. ridge.

dak'tiel [dak'til] n. dactylus; dactilies a. (-e) dactylic.

dal ['dal] n. (dale), valley, vale, dale, dell.

'daling cp. daal.

dalk ['dalk] av. perhaps, possibly; -ies dim. by-and-by, presently.

dam ['dam] n. (-me) dam; barrage, weir, reservoir; v. (ge-) dam (up); crowd together; play draughts; -bord n. draught-board; -hert n. fallow-deer; -skrop n. dam-scraper; -wal n. embankment of dam; -water n. water from storage dam.

da'mas [da'mas] n. damask; -'seer v. (ge-) damascene; -sy n. damasksilk.

'dame ['dāmə] n. (-s) lady, (gentle) woman; -saal n. side-saddle; damesgeruit n. zephyr; -tjie [-Ki] dim. (-s) little lady.

'damp ['damp] n. (-e) vapour, fumes; -kap n. hood.

dan ['dan] av. then; than.

'danig ['dānəch] a. (-e) thorough; tremendous; av. much; intimate; awfully; -heid n. intimacy; posh affair.

dank ['dank] n. acknowledgement, thanks; *stank vir-kry* get small thanks; *teen wil en-* willy nilly; -sy God thank God; v. (ge-) thank, give thanks; say grace; be indebted to; -jou *die duiwel* like hell! -baar a. (-bare, -der, -ste) grateful, thankful; -baarheid s. gratitude; -betuiging n. (-e, -s) expression of thanks; 'danke *te-aan* due to; -ie int. thanks! -ie sé v. (-ge-) to thank; say grace; -segging n. thanksgiving; grace.

dans ['dãns] n. (-e) dance, ball; v. (ge-) dance; -er n. (-s) dancer; -e'res n. fem. (-se) dancer; -ie dim. dance, hop; -woede n. dancing mania.

'dapper ['dapəR] a. brace, plucky, valiant; n. *met-en stapper* on foot; -heid n. bravery, valour.

'darem ['daRəm] av. after all, all the same, surely, though, really.

'dartel ['daRtəl] v. (ge-) frisk, frolic, gambol; a. frisky, playful; skittish; -heid n.

das ['das] n. (-se) necktie; coney; -sie dim.; -siespis n. hyraceum; -speld n. tie (scarf) pin.

dat ['dat] conj. that, so that; -jie [daiKi] n. *ditjies en -s* this and that, unimportant things.

da'teer [da'tēR] v. (ge-) date.

'datief ['dātif] n. ('datiewe) dative.

'datum ['dātəm] n. (-s) date.

'davib = dawee.

'dawee ['dāvē] n. tamarisk.

'dawer ['dāvəR] v. (ge-) boom, roar, thunder; -end a. (-e) roaring, thundering.

de ['də] = die article used emphatically, -duiwel in wees have one's monkey up.

dè ['de] v. imperative take!

de'bat [də'bat] n. (-te) debate, discussion; -'teer v. (ge-) debate, discuss.

de'biet [də'bit] n. (-e) debit; sale, market; debi'teer v. (ge-) debit, charge.

de'buut [də'bewt] n. debut, first appearance.

dé'cor [dē'kauR] n. scenery.

deeg ['dēch] n. dough; -agtig a. (-e) doughy; 'deegerig a. (-e) doughy.

'deeglik ['dēchlək] a. (-e) sound, substantial, thorough; -heid n.

'deel ['dēl] n. (dele) deal, board, plank; part, portion, share; volume; *ten dele* partly; v. (ge-) divide, participate, share; -'agtig a. *ietsword, participating;* -baar a. (-bare, -der, -ste) divisible; -baarheid n. divisibility; -genoot n. ('deelgenote) partner; -hebber n. (-s) participant; -lyn n. bisector (*of an angle*); -neem v. (-ge-) participate; -nemend a. (-e) compassionate; -nemer s. (-s) participant, competitor; -neming n. participation, compassion; -s av. partly; -sgewyse av. bit by bit; -teken n. division sign (*arith.*); -tjie ['dēlKi] dim.; -woord n. participle.

'deemoed ['dēmut] n. humility, submission; dee'moedig a. (-e) humble, submissive; dee'moedigheid n.

deer ['dēR] v. (ge-) harm, hurt, injure; -lik a. (-e) sad, pitiful; -nis n. pity, compassion; -nis'wekkend a. (-e; -er, -ste) pitiful.

de'fek [dē'fek] n. (-te) defect, flaw; a. defective; av. out of order; n. breakdown.

defi′nisie [defə′nisi] n. (-s) definition; defini′eer v. (ge-) define.

defini′tief [defənə′tif] a. & av. (defini′tiewe) definite(ly).

de′fleksie [də′fleksi] n. deflection; deflek′teer v. (ge-) deflect.

′deftig [′deftəχ] a. (-e; -er, -ste) stately, dignified, smart, grand; -heid n.

′degen [′dēχən] n. (-s) sword, foil.

degene′rasie [dēχənə′Rāsi] n. degeneration, degeneracy; **degene′reer** v. (ge-) degenerate.

′degerig a. cp. **deeg.**

′dein [′dayn] v. (ge-) heave, swell, roll; fade (radio); -ing n. (-e, -s).

deins [′dayns] v. (ge-) recoil, shrink.

dek [′dek] n. (-ke) cover(ing); deck; v. (ge-) cover, slate, thatch; -cover, serve; defray; make good; -blaar n. (-blare), perlanth-leaf; -geld n. stud-fee; tiling (thatching) costs; -gras n. thatch; -hings n. stud-stallion; -king n. cover, protection; service (animals); -laag n. upper layer; -lading n. deck cargo; -lood n. sheet-lead; -mantel n. colour; disguise, pretext; -punt n. cover-point; -riet n. thatch (-reed); -seil n. tarpaulin; -strooi n. thatch (-grass); weefsel n. epithelium.

de′kaan [dē′kān] n. (de′kane) dean.

de′kade [dē′kādə] n. (-s) decade.

deka′densie [dēka′densi] n. decadence; **deka′dent** a. decadent.

′deken [′dēkən] n. (-s) counterpane; doyen.

′dekgras [′dekhRas] n. thatch grass.

′deklaag [′deklāχ] n. mulch.

dekla′rasie [dēkla′rāsi] n. (-s) declaration.

dekli′nasie [dēkli′nāsi] n. declination; variation; **dekli′neer** v. (ge-) decline.

dekora′tief [dēkōRa′tif] a. (dekora′tiewe) decorative, ornamental.

deko′reer [dēkō′RēR] v. (ge-) decorate.

′deksel [′deksəl] n. (-s) cover, lid; operculum; wat de-! what the deuce! -s a. (-e) blessed, confounded; av. confoundedly; interj. the deuce!

′deler [′dēlər] n. (-s) divider, devisor; cp. **deel.**

delf, ′delwe [′delf, ′delvə] v. (ge-) delve, dig, mine; -stof n. (-stouwe) mineral.

delg [′delχ] v. (ge-) clear, redeem; extinguish; -ing n.

′deling]′dēləng] n. division, partition, fission; cp. **deel.**

′delwe = **delf**; -r n. (-s) digger; -ry n. (-e) diggings.

dema′goog [dēma′χōχ] n. demagogue; **demago′gie** n. demagogy.

de′missie [dē′misi] n. dismissal.

demobili′sasie [dēmobili′sāsi] n. demobilization; **demobili′seer** v. (ge-) demobilize.

demo′kraat [dēmō′kRāt] n. (demo-

′krate) democrat; **demo′kraties** a. (-e) democratic; **demokra′sie** n. (-ë) democracy.

′demon [′dēmon] n. (de′mone) demon, devil; **de′monies** a. (-e) demoniacal.

demon′strasie [dēmon′stRāsi] n. (-s) demonstration; **demon′streer** v. (ge-) demonstrate.

demorali′seer [dēmōRali′sēR] v. (ge-) demoralize.

′demp [′demp] v. (ge-) fill up; quell; dim; quench; -er n. (-s) damper, silencer.

′den [′den] n. (-ne) fir, pine; -neteer n. pine tar.

′denkbaar [′denkbāR] a. (′denkbare) conceivable; **′denkbeeld** n. (-e) idea; **denk′beeldig** a. (-e) imaginary, illusory; **denker** n. (-s) thinker; philosopher; **denkkrag** n. power of thought; **denklik** a. (-e) possible; **denkvermoë** n. intellectual capacity; **denkwyse** n. opinion; mental attitude.

densi′teit [densi′tayt] n. density.

den′taal [den′tāl] a. (den′tale) dental.

departe′ment [dəpaRtə′ment] n. (-e) department; **departemen′teel** a. (departmen′tele) departmental.

depo′neer [dēpō′nēR] v. (ge-) put down; deposit; lodge.

depor′tasie [dēpor′tāsi] n. deportation; **depor′teer** v. (ge-) deport.

de′posito [dē′pōsitō] n. (-′s) deposit.

′depper [′depəR] n. (-s) swab; -tang n. (-e) swab forceps.

de′pressie [dē′pResi] n. depression.

depu′tasie [dēpew′tāsi] n. (-s) deputation; **depu′teer** v. (ge-) depute.

der [′deR] article for emphasis, cp. **de, die.**

′derde [′dɛRdə] ordinal third; -mag n. cube; -mannetjie [-manəKi] n. game; unwelcome third member of a party; -rangs a. (-e) third-rate.

′dergelik [′deRchələk] a. (-e) such-like, similar; -s a. iets -s something like it.

′derhalwe [′deRhalvə] av. consequently.

′derm [′deRəm] n. (-s) intestine; gut, entrails; -ontsteking n. enteritis; -snaar n. (-snare) catgut.

′dermate [′deRmātə] av. to such an extent.

′dertien [′deRtin] num. thirteen; -de ordinal thirteenth.

′dertig [′deRtəχ] num. thirty.

′derwaarts [′deRvāRts] av. thither.

′derwe [′deRvə] v. (ge-) lack, want, miss.

′deser [′dēsəR] n. die 10de- the 10th instant.

′desgelyks [′desχələyks] av. likewise.

desi′maal [desi′māl] n. (desi′male) decimal place; a. (desi′male) decimal.

′desinfeksie [′desənfeksi] n. disinfection.

des'kundig [des'kʌndəch] a. (-e) expert; -e n. (-s) expert.

'desnoods ['desnōts] av. if need be.

'desorganisasie ['desoRchanisāsi] n. disorganization.

'destyds ['destayts] av. at that time.

de'tail [dē'tāi] n. (-s) detail.

determi'neer [dēteRmə'nēR] v. (ge-) determine, define.

deug ['dēch] n. (-de) virtue, excellence; v. (ge-) be good for, serve a purpose; -delik a. (-e; -er, -ste) reliable; valid; durable; -niet n. good-for-nothing; -saam a. (-same; -samer, -ste) excellent, virtuous.

deuk ['dēk] n. (-e) dent, cavity; v. (ge-) dent, indent.

'deuntjie ['dēng-Ki] n. (-s) air, ditty, tune.

deur ['dēR] n. (-e) door; prep. through, throughout; by; on account of; -bel n. door-bell; v. (-ge-) phone through; -'boor v. (-ge-) pierce, stab; -braak n. breach, break-through; -bring v. (-ge-) spend; waste; -'dag a. & av. well-planned; -dat conj. as, because; -dring v. (-ge-) penetrate, pierce; -'dring v. (-) permeate, pervade, impress; -'dringend a. (-e) pungent; -'dronge av. -van impressed with, fully convinced of; -en- av. thoroughly; -entyd av. always; -gaans av. commonly, generally; -gang n. passage, gangway; -gelê av. hy is- he has bedsores; -grendel n. door-bolt; -'grond v. (-) fathom, penetrate; -haal v. (-ge-) cancel; -hang v. (-ge-) sag; -'knee(d) a. thoroughly versed in; -kom v. (-ge-) get through; pass; escape; survive; -'kruis v. (-) traverse, scour; -kyk v. (-ge-) glance through; check; size up; -'leef v. (-) experience; -loop n. passage, arcade; v. (-ge-) walk through; wear out by walking; punish; -lopend a. (-e) continuous; -maak v. (-ge-) = deurleef; -me'kaar a. in confusion, pell-mell; delirious, insane; -me'kaarspul n. chaos, babel; -send v. (-ge-) relay; -settingsvermoë n. perseverance; -sig n. discernment, insight; -'sigtig a. (-e; -er, -ste) clear; obvious; transparent; -'skynend a. (-e) transparent; -slag n. punch; -slagpapier n. carbon-paper; -snee n. section; -'spek a. (-te) interlarded; -'staan v. (-) endure; -'tastend a. (-e; -er, -ste) decisive, energetic, sweeping; -trapte a. consummate; -'trokke a. imbued, steeped; -waarder n. (-s) porter; -'wrog a. (-te) elaborate; well-planned.

'deurklink ['dēRklɔngk] n. (-e) door latch; -knip n. door catch.

'deurry ['dēRay] v. (-ge-) pass through; chafe by riding.

deur'skote [dēꞓRskōtə] a. interleaved.

'deurslagveer ['dēRslachfēR] n.

(vere), ('deurslagvere) bump spring.

devalu'asie [dēvalew'āsi] n' devaluation; devalu'eer v. (ge-) devaluate.

diag'nose [diach'nōsə] n. (-s) diagnosis; diagno'seer v. (ge-) diagnose.

diago'naal [diachō'nāl] n. (diago-'nale) diagonal.

dia'gram [dia'chRam] n. (-me) diagram.

di'aken [də'yākən] n. (-s) deacon; diako'nie n. church board of charity.

dia'lek [dia'lek] n. (-te) dialect; -geogra'fie n. dialectal geography; -ties a. (-e) dialectal.

dia'loog [dia'lōch] n. (dia'loë) dialogue.

dia'mant [dia'mant] n. (-e) diamond.

dia'meter [dia'mētəR] n. (-s) diameter.

dia'rree [dia'Rē] n. diarrhoea.

di'aspora [di'āspōRa] n. diaspore.

didak'tiek [didak'tik] n. didactics; di'dakties a. (-e) didactic; di'daktikus n. (-se) didactician.

die ['di] art. the; dié demonstr. pron. this.

di'eet [di'ēt] n. (diëte) diet, regimen.

dief ['dif] n. (diewe) thief; -agtig a. (-e) thievish; -stal n. theft.

'diegene ['dichēnə] n. (-s) he, she, those.

dien ['din] v. (ge-) serve; wait on, minister; jy-te weet you ought to know; -aar n. ('dienare, -s) servant; -a'res n. (-se) fem. servant; -der n. (-s) policeman; -lik a. (-e; -er, -ste) serviceable; -likheid n. utility.

diens ['dins] n. (-te) duty; function; service; 'n-bewys render a service; -baar a. (-bare) serviceable; sub-servient; -bode n. (-s) domestic servant; -doende a. acting; -jaar n. year of service; financial year; -kneg n. (-te) (man-)servant; -maag n. (-de) (maid-)servant; -meisie n. (-s) maid; -plig n. compulsory service (mil.); -'pligtig a. (-e) liable to military service; -ure n. hours of business (duty); -'vaardig a. (-e) obliging; -verlating n. desertion; -voorwaardes n. conditions of service; -willig a. (-e) obedient.

diep ['dip] a. (-e; -er, -ste) deep, profound; av. deeply, profoundly; -gaande a. (-e) searching, thorough; -gang n. draught (ship); -lood n. sounding-lead; -'sinnig a. (-e; -er, -ste) abstruse, profound; -te n. (-s) depth; profundity.

'dienstig ['dīnstəch] a. (-e; -er, -ste) serviceable, useful.

'dier ['diR] n. (-e) animal, beast; brute; -lik a. (-e; -er, -ste) animal; bestial; -tjie [-Ki] dim.

die'rasie [di'Rāsi] n. (-s) devil, beast, monster.

'dierbaar ['diRbāR] a. ('dierbare; -der, -ste) beloved, dear; -heid n.

'diereriem ['diRəRim] n. zodiac;

'diereryk n. animal-kingdom; diere-temmer n. (-s) animal-tamer; dieretuin n. zoo.

'dierkunde ['diRkʌndə] n. zoology.

die'selfde [di'selfdə] n. the same.

'Diets ['dits] n. Middle Dutch; Pan-Dutch (Netherlands, Flemish & Afrikaans); iemand iets-maak gull, deceive a person.

'diewery ['divəRay] n. thieving, cp. dief.

differensi'aal [dəfəRensi'āl] a. (differensi'ale) differential; -rekening n. (differential) calculus.

differensi'eer [dəfəRensi'ēR] v. (ge-) differentiate; differensi'ëring n. differentiation.

difte'rie [dəftə'Ri] n. diphtheria.

'diftong ['dəftaung] n. (-e) diphthong.

dig ['dəch] a. (-te; -ter, -ste) closed, shut; tight, dense; v. (ge-) write poetry; -by av. close by, near; -hou v. (-ge-) keep secret; -kuns n. poetic art; -maat n. metre; -soort n. kind of poetry; -ste: n. (-s) poet; -te'res n. (-se) poetess; -terlik a. (-e; -er, -ste) poetic; -theid n. density.

dig ['dəch] v. (ge-) to seal, seal off; -ting n. sealing; -tingaring n. (-e) sealing ring, seal.

di'gestie [di'chesti] n. digestion.

dik ['dək] a. (-ke; -ker, -ste) thick, bulky, dense; stout; close (friends); fed-up; n. deur-en dun under all circumstances; -buik n. pot-belly; -derm n. colon; -huid n. pachyderm; -kerig a. (-e; -er, -ste) corpulent; -melk n. curdled milk; -te n. (-s) thickness.

'diksie ['diksi] n. diction.

dik'taat [dək'tāt] n. dictation, notes; dik'tator n. (-s) dictator; diktatori-'aal a. (diktatori'ale) dictatorial.

dik'tee [dək'tē] n. dictation; -r v. (ge-) dictate.

'dikwels ['dəkvəls] av. frequently, often.

dille'tant [dələ'tant] n. (-e) dilettante, amateur; -ies a. (-e) amateurish.

diminu'tief [diminew'tif] n. (diminu-'tiewe) diminutive.

di'namies [di'nāmis] a. (-e) dynamic.

dina'miet [dina'mit] n. dynamite.

di'namika [di'nāmika] n. dynamics.

di'namo [di'nāmō] n. (-'s) dynamo.

dinas'tie [dinas'ti] n. (-ē) dynasty.

di'nee [di'nē] n. (-s) dinner; -r v. (ge-) dine.

ding ['dəng] n. (-e) thing, affair; gadget; v. (ge-) compete; sue; stand for; -es n. what-do-you-call-it; -etjie [-eKi] dim. trifle; little dear.

dink ['dənk] v. (ge-; past tense also: dag, dog; pp. gedink, gedog gedag) think; expect; be of opinion.

Dinsdag ['dənsdach] n. Tuesday.

diok'sied [di-ok'sit] n. dioxide.

dip ['dəp] n. (-pe) dipping; v. (ge-) dip; -stof n. dip.

di'ploma [də'plōma] n. (-s) diploma; -'sie n. diplomacy; diplo'maat n. (diplo'mate) diplomat; diplo'maties a. (-e) diplomatic.

di'rek [di'Rek] a. (-te) direct, prompt; -sie n. (-s) management, board (of directors); direk'teur n. (-s, -e) director.

diri'geer [dəRə'chēR] v. (ge-) conduct (orchestra); diri'gent n. (-e) conductor (orchestra).

dis ['dəs] n. table, board; -genoot n. (disgenote) fellow-guest.

dis = dit is it is, that is.

dis- ['dəs-] prefix denotes negation, opposition, deprivation; indicates undoing of action of the simple verb; -inte'grasie n. disintegration; -inte'greer v. (ge-) disintegrate; -kon'teer v. (ge-) discount; -'konto n. discount; -krediet n. discredit; -'kreet a. (dis'krete) discreet, modest; -'kresie n. discretion; -'kussie n. discussion, argument; -kwalifikasie n. disqualification; -kwalifi'seer v. (ge-) disqualify; -pepsie n. dyspepsia; -pu'teer v. (ge-) argue, dispute; -sosiasie n. dissociation; -sosi'eer v. (ge-) dissociate; -til'lasie n. distillation; -til'leer v. (ge-) distil; -til'leerder n. (-s) distiller; -til'leerdery n. distillery; -tin'geer v. (ge-) to distinguish oneself; -'tinksie n. distinction; -tribu'eer v. (ge-) distribute; -tri'busie n. distribution.

disente'rie [dəsəntē'Ri] n. dysentery.

diskus ['dəskʌs] n. (-se) discus, disc.

dis'nis [dəs'nəs] av. -loop beat, outdo thoroughly.

'dissel ['dəsəl] n. (-s) adze.

'dispens = spens.

dis'sipel [di'sipəl] n. (-s) disciple.

dissi'pline [dəsə'plinə] n. discipline; dissipli'neer v. (ge-) discipline; dissipli'nêr a. (-e) disciplinary.

dis'tansie [dəs'tānsi] n. (-s) distance.

distel ['dəstl] n. (-s) thistle.

dis'trik [dəs'trək] n. (-te) district.

'dit ['dət] pron. this, it.

di'van [di'fan] n. (-s) divan.

di'verse [di'feRsə] n. sundries; incidental expenses.

divi'dend [divi'dent] n. (-e) dividend.

di'visie [di'visi] n. (-s) division.

'dobbel ['dobəl, 'dovəl] v. (ge-) gamble; -ary n. gambling; -aar n. (-s) gambler; -spel n. gambling; -steen n. die.

'dobber ['dobəR, 'dovəR] n. (-s) float; buoy; v. (ge-) bob, drift about; fluctuate; -tjie [-Ki] dim. float.

'dodelik ['dōdəlik] a. (-e; -er, -ste) mortal, fatal, deadly, lethal.

doe'ane [du'āne] n. customs.

doe'blet [du'blet] n. double.

'doedelsak ['dudisak] n. bagpipe.

doek ['duk] n. cloth, linen; canvas; painting; -ies dim. pl. geen-omdraai nie not mince matters; -steen n. asbestos; silwer- n. screen (cinema).

doel ['dul] n. (-e, -eindes) aim; design; goal; purpose; v. (ge-) aim at; refer to; -bewus a. (-te) purposeful, unswerving; -einde = doel; -loos a. (-lose) aimless, purposeless; -'matig a. (-e) adequate, efficient; -'treffend a. (-e; -er, -ste) effective; -wit n. = doel.

doem ['dum] n. doom; v. (ge-) doom, condemn.

doen ['dun] v. (ge-) do, make, perform, effect; -de av. al-de leer mens practice makes perfect; -ig av. doing, active; -lik a. (-e) feasible.

doenigheid ['dunəchayt] n. activity.

'doenlik ['dunlək] av. practicable.

'doepa ['dupa] n. dope, potion, charm.

'doeselig ['dusələch] a. (-e) drowsy, dreamy.

dof ['dof] a. (dowwe) dull, faint, dim; -heid n.; -geel a. buff.

dog ['doch] conj. but, still.

dogma ['dochma] n. (-s) dogma; **dog'maties** a. (-e) dogmatic.

'dogter ['dochtəR] n. (-s) daughter, girl.

dok ['dok] n. (-ke) dock.

'dokter ['doktəR] n. (-s) medical practitioner, doctor; v. (ge-) doctor, nurse; revise, cook.

'doktor ['doktəR] n. (-e, -s) doctor (divinity, laws, etc.).

doku'ment [dokew'ment] n. (-e) document; **dokumen'teer** v. (ge-) document; **dokumen'têr** a. (-e) documentary.

dol ['dol] a. (-le) mad; frantic, wild, crazy; -graag av. ever so much; -heid n. folly; -leeg a. absolutely empty; -os n. (-se) knuckle-bone, dib.

'doldraai ['doldRāī] v. (-ge-) strip (nut).

dol'sinnig [dol'sənəch] a. (-e) rash.

dolk ['dolk] n. (-e) dagger.

'dolwe ['dolvə] v. (ge-) dig deep, delve, trench.

dom ['dom] n. (-me) dome; church; a. (-me, -mer, -ste) dense, fatuous, silly; doltish; -astrant a. (-e) cheeky, impudent; -kerk n. cathedral; -kop n. blockhead, dunce, dunderhead, ignoramus; -migheid n. stupidity; -oor n. = domkop.

do'mein [dō'mayn] n. (-e) domain.

'dominee ['dōmənī] n. (-'s) clergyman, parson.

domi'neer [dōmə'nēR] v. (ge-) dominate; **domi'nerend** a. (-e) dominating, domineering.

domi'silie [dōmi'silī] n. domicile.

'domkrag ['domkRōch] n. (-te) n. jack.

'dommel ['doməl] v. (ge-) doze, drowse.

'dom-oor ['domōR] n. dunce.

'domp ['domp] v. (ge-) to dip (light).

'dompel ['dompəl] v. (ge-) plunge, duck, dive.

'domper ['dompəR] n. (-s) extin-

guisher; -skakelaar n. (-s) dipper (switch).

do'nasie [dō'nāsi] n. (-s) donation; **dona'teur** n. (-s) donor, patron.

'Donau ['dōna-u] n. Danube.

'donder ['donəR] n. thunder; v. (ge-) thunder, boom; rave; -s a. & av. (-e) confounded(ly).

'Donderdag ['donəRdach] n. Thursday.

'donker ['donkəR] n. dark, darkness; a. (-; -der, -ste) dark, dull, dusky, gloomy; -agtig a. (-e) darkish; -heid n. darkness, obscurity; -te n. dark, darkness; -werk n. -is konkelwerk bungling in the dark.

'donkie ['donki] n. (-s) donkey; dunce.

dons ['dauns] n. (-e) down, fluff; -agtig a. (-e) downy, fluffy; -erig a. (-e) downy; -harig a. (-e) pubescent.

dood ['dōt] n. death, decease, demise; a. dead, demised, deceased; v. (ge-) kill, slay; mortify; av. quite, extremely; -alleen all (quite) alone; -goed wees good to a fault; -hou n. death blow; doodskis n. (-te) coffin; -kry v. (-ge-) kill; -s a. (-e) deathlike, deathly; -sonde n. mortal sin; -straf n. capital punishment; doodsvonnis n. sentence of death; a. (dooie) dead, deceased.

'doodluiters ['dōtlœitəRs] a. unembarrassed, unabashed.

'doodsbleek ['dōtsblēk] av. ghastly.

'doodveilig ['dōtfayləch] a. (-e) -e aandele gilt-edged shares.

doof ['dōf] a. (dowe; dower, doofste) deaf; v. (ge-, gedowe) extinguish; quench; fade; -stom a. deaf and dumb.

dooi ['dōi] v. (ge-) thaw.

'dooier ['dōiəR] n. (-s) yolk.

'dooierig ['dōiəRəch] a. (-e) listless, lifeless, apathetic.

dool ['dōl] v. (ge-) ramble, rove; err; -hof n. labyrinth, maze.

doop ['dōp] n. baptism; v. (ge-) baptise; initiate; -seël n. (-s) baptismal certificate.

'door ['dōR] n. = dooier.

doos ['dōs] n. (dose) box, case; uit die ou- old-fashioned; dosie dim.

'dop ['dop] n. (-pe) shell, husk, pod; cap; brandy, tot; v. (ge-) shell (peas), fail (test); -emmer n. (-s) milking-pail; -ertjies n. green peas; -pie dim.

'dophou ['dophoa] v. (-ge-) keep an eye on, watch.

'dopluise ['doplœisə] n. pl. scale insects.

'dopsleutel ['dopslœtl] n. (-s) box spanner.

dor ['doR] a. (-re) dry, barren, arid; -heid n.

'doring ['dōrəng] n. thorn, spike; -agtig a. (-e) thorny, spinous; -draad n. barbed wire; -loos a. (-lose) spineless; **Doringrosie** n. Sleeping Beauty (fairy princess).

dorp ['doRp] n. (-e) village; -ensar

n. (-s) villager; -e a. (-e) rustic; -spraatjies n. village-gossip; -sveld n. commonage.

dors ['dauRs] n. thirst; a. thirsty; v. (ge-) thresh; Dorsland n. waterless region in Botswana; -masjien n. threshing machine; -tig a. (-e) thirsty; -tyd n. threshing-time; -vloer n. threshing-floor.

dos ['dos] v. (ge-) array, dress.

do'seer [dŏ'sēR] v. (ge-) lecture; teach; dose, give a dose of.

do'sent [dŏ'sent] n. (-e) lecturer.

'dosis ['dōsəs] n. (-se) dose.

do'syn [du'sayn] n. (-e) dozen.

dou ['doə] n. dew; v. (ge-) dew; -spoor n. track in dew; -voordag av. before daybreak.

'dowe ['dōvə] n. (-s) deaf person; -rig a. (-e) slightly deaf, cp. doof.

dra ['dRā] v. carry (of news); bear; wear; run, suppurate; be with young; -baar a. (-bare) bearable; portable; wearable; n. stretcher; -krag n. carrying capacity; range.

draad ['dRāt] n. (drade) thread; grain (of wood); string (of pod); wire, fence; ply; -jie dim.; -loos n. radio, wireless; -werk n. wiring, vol-wees full of fads and fancies; 'draderig a. (-e) stringy, ropy, fibrous; -maas n. wire mesh; -maat n. (-mate) gauge; -opnemer n. wire recorder; -skut n. wire guard; -werker n. wireman.

draag = dra; -baar n. bier, stretcher; -hout n. neck-bar; -lik a. (-e) tolerable; -tyd n. gestation; -wydte n. range.

draai ['dRāi] n. (-e) turn; twist; curve; kink; v. (ge-) turn; spin, rotate, revolve, whirl; dawdle; stokkies- play truant; -baar a. (-bare) revolvable; -bank n. lathe; -boek n. scenario (for film); -erig a. (-e) dizzy; loitering; -ery n. delay, tarrying; -hek n. turnstile; -kous n. dawdler; -tafel n. revolving table; -trap n. winding staircase; -werk n. turnery.

draak [dRāk] n. (drake) dragon; die-steek poke fun at.

draal ['dRāl] v. (ge-) dawdle.

dra'bok [dRa'bok] n. darnel.

draderig cp. draad.

'drae = dra; -r n. (-s) bearer, carrier.

draf ['dRaf] n. trot; swill; drawwe v. (ge-) trot.

drag ['dRach] n. (-te) costume, dress; burden, load; litter, crop; -tig a. (-e) pregnant; -gie dim.

'drama ['dRāma] n. (-s) drama, play; drama'tiek n. the drama, dramatic art; dra'maties a. (-e) dramatic; -ti'seer v. (ge-) dramatize; -'turg n. (-e) dramatist.

drang ['dRang] n. (-e) pressure; urgency; impulse, urge.

drank ['drank] n. (-e) drink; draught; liquor; -sug n. dipsomania; -sugtig a. bibulous; -ver-

gunning n. liquor licence; -wet n. liquor law.

drape'rie [dRapə'ri] n. (-ē) drapery, hangings; dra'peer v. (ge-) drape; dra'pering n. draping.

'drassig ['dRasəch] a. (-e) marshy.

'drasties ['dRastis] a. (-e) drastic.

'dreef ['dRēf] n. op - kom get into your stride.

dreig ['dRaych] v. (ge-) threaten; intend; -e'ment n. (-e) threat; -end a. (-e) threatening; imminent; -ing n. = dreigement.

drei'neer [dRay'nēR] v. (ge-) drain; -'nering n. drainage.

'drek ['dRek] n. muck, dung.

'drel ['dRel] n. (-le) indecent woman.

drenk ['dRenk] v. (ge-) drench; soak, steep; -eling n. (-e) drowning person (drowned).

'drentel ['dRentəl] v. (ge-) loiter; -gang n. saunter; -kous n. loiterer.

dreun ['dRēn] v. (ge-) boom, roar; drone; n. booming, rumbling; chant; -ing n. (-s) rumbling, rolling.

drie ['dri] num. three; try (rugby) -been n. three-legged, triad; -delig a. (-e) tripartite; -draads a. (-e) three-plied; -hoek n. (-e) triangle; -hoeksmeting n. trigonometry; -ling n. (-e) triplets; -manskap n. triumvirate; -sprong n. junction of three roads, parting of the ways; -tand n. trident; -voet n. tripod.

'dries ['dris] v. (ge-) break up virgin soil; n. fallow land.

drif ['dRəf] n. anger, heat; n. (-te, driwwe) ford, drift; -kop n. hothead; -tig a. (-e) angry, touchy, choleric, irascible.

dril ['dRəl] n. drill (material; implement; exercise); v. (ge-) bore, drill, coach; quiver.

dring ['dRəng] v. (ge-) push, throng; urge; -end a. (-e, -er, -ste) urgent, cogent.

drink ['dRənk] v. (ge-) drink; to take alcohol; -baar a. (-bare; -der, -ste) drinkable; -beker n. mug; -ebroer n. boozer; -gelag n. carouse; -water n. drinking water.

'droë, droog ['dRōə, 'dRŏch] v. (ge-) dry; wipe; evaporate; a. (-) dry; -land n. dry land; -r n. drier.

droef ['dRuf] a. (droewe) afflicted, dejected, sad; -(e)nis n. grief, sorrow; -'geestig a. (-e; -er, -ste) dejected, gloomy, sad; -heid n. sorrow; droewig a. (-e) pitiful, sad.

'drogbeeld ['drochbēlt] n. (-e) chimera, illusion; 'drogrede n. fallacy; -redenaar n. casuist.

drom ['dRom] n. (-me) crowd; drum; ear-drum.

'dromer ['dRōməR] n. (-s) dreamer, visionary; cp. droom; -ig a. (-e; -er, -ste) dreamy; -y n. reverie.

'drommel ['dRoməl] n. (-s) beggar, wretch; the deuce! -s a. (-e) confounded, deuced; -s! interj. the deuce!

dronk ['dRonk] a. (-e) intoxicated; -aard n. (-s) drunkard; -enskap n. intoxication; -lap n. boozer; -slaan v. (-ge-) dumbfound.

droog ['dRôch] v. (ge-) desiccate; a. (droë) cp. **droë**; dry, arid, parched; dull; -lê v. (-ge-) drain, reclaim; -maak v. (-ge-) dry, cure; -sit v. (-ge-) oust, get the better of; -skoonmaker n. (-s) dry cleaner; -te n. (-s) dryness, drought; -voets a. dry-shod; drogies av. drily; dro'gis n. (-te) druggist.

droom ['dRôm] n. (drome) dream; v. (ge-) dream; moon about; -beeld n. illusion; -wêreld n. dream-world.

drop ['dRop] n. liquorice.

dros ['dRos] v. (ge-) abscond, desert; -ter n. (-s) absconder, deserter; -tery n. absconding.

dros'dy ['dRos'day] n. (-e) magistracy; residency.

druif ['dRœif] n. (druiwe) grape.

druip ['dRœip] v. (ge-) drip; fail; -eling n. (-e) person who failed; -nat a. drenched; -stert av. -wegdros sneak off.

druis ['dRœis] v. (-ge-) roar, swish.

'druiwe ['dRœivə] n. grapes; -suiker n. glucose.

druk ['dRɅk] n. (-ke) pressure; burden; squeeze; print, type; edition; a. (-) busy, lively; crowded; v. (ge-) press, squeeze; weigh down; oppress; print; -kend a. (-e) burdensome, onerous; close; -ker n. (-s) printer; -ke'ry n. printing-office; -king n. pressure; -koste n. printing expenses; -letter n. printing type, type letter; -te n. stir, fuss.

'druklug ['dRɅklɅch] n. compressed air; -boor n. pneumatic drill.

'druksmering ['drɅksmērəng] n. force-feed lubrication.

'drukwyser ['drɅkvaysər] n. (-s) pressure indicator.

'drumpel ['drɅmpəl] n. (-s) threshold, doorstep.

drup ['dRɅp] n. eaves; v. (ge-) drip, drop; -pel n. (-s) drop, bead, globule; v. (ge-) drip; -bottel n. drop bottle; -per n. dropper.

dryf. ['dRayf] v. (ge-) float, drift; drive, propel; urge, hurry; conduct; prompt; -hou n. drive; -krag n. driving force; -sand n. drift sand; -veer n. motive; mainspring; -as n. driving shaft; -band n. belt; -krag n. driving power; -rat n. driving gear.

'drywe ['drayvə] v. (ge-) = dryf; -nd a. (-e) drifting, floating; -r n. (-s) driver; fanatic; -ry n. driving; fanaticism.

'dubbel(d), 'duwwel(d) ['dɅbəlt, 'dɅvəlt] a. (-e) double, twice; -ganger n. double, second self; -punt n. colon; -'sinnig a. (-e; -er, -ste) ambiguous; obscene; -tjie [-Ki] dim. penny; devil's thorn; dubbel-double, dual, twin.

du'et [dəw'et] n. (-te) duet.

'duidelik ['dœidələk] a. & av. (-e; -er, -ste) clear, plain; explicit; legible.

duif ['dœif] n. (duiwe) dove, pigeon; -ie dim.

duik ['dœik] v. (ge-) dive, plunge; -boot n. submarine; -el v. (ge-) turn somersault; -er n. (-s) diver; cormorant; antelope; -weg n. subway; -n. dent; -klopper n. panel beater; -kloppery n. panel beating.

duim ['dœim] n. (-e) thumb; inch; -pie dim. Klein Duimpie Tom Thumb; -spykertjie n. drawing pin; -stok n. footrule; -suiery n. fabrication.

'duimgooi ['dœimchôi] v. (-ge-) to thumb a lift; 'duimgooiery n. (-ge-) to hitchhike; 'duimgooiryer n. hitchhiker.

duin ['dœin] n. (-e) dune; -tjie dim.

'duisel ['dœisəl] v. (ge-) get dizzy; -ig a. (-e) dizzy, giddy; -ing n. dizziness; -ing'wekkend a. (-e) giddy.

'duisend ['dœisənt] num. (-e) thousand; -erlei a. of a thousand kinds; -poot n. millipede; -skoon n. sweet William; -ste ordinal thousandth; -tal n. a thousand.

'duister ['dœistəR] n. dark, darkness, cp. donker; a. dark; obscure; gloomy; -heid n. mystery, obscurity; -nis n. dark(ness).

duit ['dœit] n. (-e) farthing.

Duits ['dœits] n. German; a. (-e) German; -er n. German; -land n. Germany.

'duiwel ['dœivəl] n. (-s) devil, satan; bogy; -agtig a. (-e; -er, -ste) devilish, fiendish; -s a. (-e) devilish; -drek n. asafoetida; -sterk n. very strong cloth, drill, corduroy; -tjie dim.

duld ['dɅlt] v. (ge-) bear; tolerate; allow; -baar a. (-bare) tolerable.

dun ['dɅn] a. (-ner, -ste) thin; slender; rare; scanty; sparse; v. (ge-) thin, thin out; -heid n. thickness.

dunk ['dɅnk] n. idea, opinion.

'duplikaat [dewpli'kât] n. ('duplikate) duplicate.

dupli'seer [dewpli'sēR] v. (ge-) duplicate.

durf ['dɅRf] n. pluck, daring; v. (ge-) dare, risk.

,dus ['dɅs] conj. consequently, so, thus.

'duskant = **deuskant**.

'dusver ['dɅsfeR] av. thus far.

dut ['dɅt] v. (ge-) doze; -jie ['dɅKi] dim. nap.

duur ['dēwR] n. duration; a. (dure) dear, expensive; v. (ge-) continue; endure; keep; -saam a. (-same; samer, -ste) durable; -te n. dearness; -tetoeslag n. cost of living allowance.

'duusman [dewsman] n. European.

'duwweld = **dubbeld**.

dwaal ['dwâl] v. (ge-) roam, wander; err; -gees n. ghost; -leer n. heresy;

-lig n. will-o'-the-wisp; **dwaling** n. mistake; error.

dwaas ['dwās] n. (*dwase*) fool, ass; a. (*dwase*) foolish, absurd, silly, doltish; -lik av. foolishly.

dwang ['dwang] n. compulsion; -buis n. straight jacket = **dwangbaadjie**.

dwarrel ['dwaRəl] v. (ge-) whirl, flutter; -ing n. whirling; -wind n. whirlwind.

dwars ['dwaRs] a. transverse; across, contrary, perverse; -deur av. right through; -drywer n. perverse fellow; -hou n. cross-stroke; -lêer n. (-s) sleeper (*rail*); -oor av. right across; -te n. across, athwart; -trek av. (-ge-) quarrel; -weg av. iemand-antwoord to give a surly answer.

dwarsboom ['dwaRsbōm] v. (ge-) to thwart.

dwarsstraat ['dwaRstRāt] n. crossstreet.

dweep ['dwēp] v. (ge-) be fanatical, idolize; -siek a. (-e) enthusiastic, fanatic; -sug n. fanaticism; **dwepend** a. (-e) fanatical; **dweper** n. (-s) bigot, fanatic; **dwepery** n. bigotry, fanaticism.

dweil ['dwayl] n. (-e) mop; swab; v. (ge-) mop, scrub, wash, swab.

dwerg ['dweRch] n. dwarf, pigmy; -agtig a. (-e) dwarfish.

dwing ['dwəng] v. (ge-) force, compel; be on the point of; -eland n. tyrant.

dy ['day] n. (-e) thigh; v. (ge-) thrive; -been n. thighbone, femur.

dyk ['dayk] n. (-e) dyke, bank.

dykouse ['daykoasə] n. thigh stockings.

dynserig ['daynsəRəch] a. (-e; -er, -ste) cloudy, hazy.

E

EVKOM (*Elektrisiteitsvoorsieningskommissie*) ESCOM (*Electricity Supply Commission*).

eau-de-co'logne [ōdəkə'launye] n. eau-de-Cologne.

eb ['ep] n. ebb-tide.

'ebbehout ['ebəhoat] n. ebony.

'edel ['ēdəl] a. (-e; -er, -ste) noble; generous; precious; -'agbaar a. (-bare) honourable, worshipful; -es n. pl. the nobility; -gesteente n. (-s) jewel, precious stone; -man n. (-liede, -es) nobleman, noble; -'moedig a. (-e) generous, magnanimous; -steen n. = edelgesteente.

'edik ['ēdək] n. (-te) edict, decree.

e'disie [ē'disi] n. edition, issue.

'eed ['ēt] n. (ede) oath; kommissaris van ede, commissioner of oaths; -breuk n. breach of oath; -genoot n. (eedgenote) confederate.

'eekhorinkie ['ēkhōRənki] n. squirrel.

'eelt ['ēlt] n. (-e) callus, horny skin; -agtig a. (-e) callous; -sweer n. bunion.

'een ['ēn] n. & pron. one; someone; something; a. & av. a, a certain, one; mono-, uni-; -akter n. (-s) one-act play; -dekker n. (-s) monoplane; -drag n. concord; -heid n. unity; -ling n. individual; -lopend a. (-e) single, unmarried; -saam a. (-same, -samer, -ste) solitary, lonely; -'selwig a. (-e) reserved, solitary; -parig a. (-e) unanimous; -'stemmig a. (-e) unanimous; -'sydig a. (-e) one-sided; partial; -tjie dim. one, a small one; -'tonig a. (-e) monotonous; -'vormig a. (-e) uniform; -voud n. simplicity; -'voudig a. (-e) plain, simple.

'eend ['ēnt] n. (-e) duck; -agtig a. (-e) duck-like.

'eendag ['ēndach] av. once (upon a time), some day; -svlieg n. mayfly.

'eendrag ['ēndRach] n. concord, -maak mag unity is strength.

'eenkeer = eendag.

'eenling ['ēnləng] n. eccentric; lonely person.

'eenmaal ['ēnmāl] av. once, one day

een'parig ['ēm'pāRəch] a., av. (-e) unanimous.

'eens ['ēns] a. & av. once, one day; just, even; unanimous; -gesind a. (-e) in harmony; -klaps av. suddenly.

een'stemmig [ēñ'steməch] a. (-e) unanimous.

een'sydig [ēñ'saydəch] a. (-e) partial.

een'talig [ēn'tāləch] a. (-e) unilingual.

een'tonig [ēn'tōnəch] a. (-e) monotonous, tedious.

'eenvoud ['ēñfoat] n. simplicity; -ig a. simple.

'eer ['ēR] n. credit, honour, repute; die laaste-bewys render the funeral honours; av. & conj. before, rather, sooner, cp. liewer; v. (ge-) honour, respect, revere; -baar a. (-bare) chaste, honest, virtuous; -betoon n. homage, tribute; -bied n. regard, veneration; -'biedig a. (-e) respectful, reverent; v. (ge-) respect; -biedwaardig a. (-e; -er, -ste) respectable; -der av. rather; sooner; -gevoel n. sense of honour; -gevoelig a. (-e; -er, -ste) proud, touchy; -'gierig a. (-e) ambitious; -lik a. (-e; -er, -ste) honest; -likheid n. honesty; -loos a. (-lose) dishonourable; -skennis n. defamation; -sug n. ambition; -'sugtig a. (-e) ambitious; -vergete a. infamous, vile; -vol a. (-le) honourable; -waarde a. reverend; -'waardig a. (-e) venerable.

'eergister ['ēRchəstəR] n. the day before yesterday.

'eerlang ['ēRlang] av. before long.

'eertyds ['ēRtayts] a. & av. (-e) former(ly).

eers ['ēRs] av. first, formerly; once; only, not even; before; -daags av. shortly, soon; -geborene n. (-s) first-born; **-genoemde** n. & a. former; **-komende** a. following, next; **-volgende** a. following, next; **-sterwende** n. the first-dying (of an estate).

'eerste ['ĕRstə] a. & av. first, chief, leading; **-hands** a. (-e) first-hand (information); **-klas** a. & av. first-rate, topping, first-class **-ling** n. (-e) first-born; firstling; **-ns** av. firstly; **-rangs** a. & av. first-rate.

'eerstehulp ['ĕRstəhʌlp] n. first-aid; **-kas** n. first-aid box.

'eet ['ĕt] v. (ge-) eat; dine; feed; **-baar** a. (-bare; -der, -ste) eatable, edible; **-goed** n. eatables; **-kamer** n. (-s) dining-room; **-lepel** n. (-s) tablespoon; **-lus** n. appetite; **-luswekkend** a. (-e; -er, -ste) appetizing; **-maal** n. meal; banquet; **-servies** n. dinner-service; **-ware** n. eatables, provisions.

'eeu ['ĕö] n. age; century; **-elang** (-lank) a. (-e) age-long; **-e-oud** a. time-honoured; **-fees** n. (-te) centenary.

'effe ['efə] a. & av. even, level; plain.

'effek [ĕ'fek] n. (-te) effect, result; **-bejag** n. straining after effect; **-te** pl. bonds, stocks, shares; **-tebeurs** n. exchange; **-tekoers** n. price of stocks; **-'tief** a. (-tiewe) effective, real.

'effen ['efən] v. (ge-) make even, level; **-aar** n. equalizer; **-heid** n. evenness.

'effens ['efŏns] av. slightly.

'effentjies = **effens.**

'efod ['ĕfot] n. ephod.

eg ['ech] n. (-ge, êe) harrow; marriage; **-skeiding** n. divorce; **-telik** a. (-e) conjugal; true; **-theid** n. genuineness; **-genoot** n. (eggenote) spouse; **-genote** n. (-s) wife; **-paar** n. couple; **-telik** a. (-e) connubial.

'ega ['ĕcha] n. spouse.

e'gaal [ĕ'chāl] av. even, level, smooth; e'**galig** a. (-e; -er, -ste) level; uniform.

'egbreuk ['ech'brĕk] n. adultery.

'eggo ['echō] n. echo.

E'gipte [ĕ'chəptə] n. Egypt; **-naar** n. (-s) Egyptian; **-ties** a. (-e) Egyptian.

'ego ['ĕchō] n. self; **-'is** n. egoist; **-'isties** a. (-e) selfish; **-'sentries** a. (-e) self-centred.

'egter ['echtəR] conj. however, nevertheless, yet.

'eie ['ayə] a. own, private; natural; peculiar; intimate; **-baat** n. egoism; **-belang** n. self-interest; **-beweging** n. free motion; **-dunk** n. self-conceit; **-ge'regtig** a. (-e) self-righteous; **-liefde** n. egotism; **-'magtig** n. arbitrary; **-naam** n. proper name; **-'sinnig** a. (-e) obstinate; **-waan** n. self-conceit; **-wys** a. obstinate.

'eien ['ayən] v. (ge-) appropriate; possess; recognize; **-aar** n. (-s) owner; **-a'res** n. (-se) fem. owner; **-'aardig** a. (-e; -er, -ste) peculiar,

curious; **-'aardigheid** n. peculiarity; **-dom** n. (-me) property, possession; **-domsbewys** n. title-deed; **-domsreg** n. right of possession; **-doms** (patent) n. proprietary (patent); **-skap** n. (-pe) quality, attribute.

'eiegewig ['ayəchəvəch] n. tare.

'eier ['ayəR] n. (-s) egg; op-s loop go very slowly; **-kelkie** n. (-s) eggcup; **-klitser** n. egg-beater; **-rond** a. (-e) ovate; **-vormig** a. (-e) ovoid; **-sakkie** n. ovisac; **-struif** n. omelette; **-tjie** [-Kl] dim.

'eierstok ['ayəRstok] n. ovary.

eie'sinnig ['ayəsənəch] a. (-e) obstinate.

'eiewys [ayə'vays] a. headstrong.

eik ['ayk] n. (-e) oak; **-ehout** n. oak.

'eiland ['aylant] n. (-e) island; **-bewoner** n. (-s) islander; **-jie** ['aylaingKi] dim.

'eina! ['ayna] interj. ow!

eind, 'einde ['aynt, 'ayndə] n. & a. end; -goed, al goed all is well that ends well; **-beslisser** n. umpire; **-bestemming** n. destination; **-doel** n. final aim; **-e** n. close, conclusion, end; ten -e in order to; **-delik** a. & av. last, final(ly); **-eloos** a. (eindelose) endless; **-ig** v. (ge-) conclude, end, finish; finalize; **-paal** n. limit; goal; **-punt** n. end, terminal; **-sitting** n. final session; **-snelheid** n. final velocity; **-wedstryd** n. final match.

'einste ['aynstə] a. same; cp. **eien.**

'eintlik ['ayntlək] a. (-e) actual, real.

eis ['ays] n. (-e) claim, demand; petition; v. (ge-) claim; require; **-er** n. (-s) claimant, plaintiff; **-e'res** n. (-se) = fem. **eiser.**

'eiwit ['ayvət] n. albumen; cp. **eier.**

ek ['ek] pron. I; **-heid** n. the ego; **-kerig** a. (-e) egotistic; subjective; **-'self** emphatic I myself; **'ander -'** n. alter ego.

e'klips [ĕ'kləps] n. eclipse.

ekono'mie [ĕkŏnŏ'mi] n. economy; economics; **eko'nomies** a. (-e) economic(al); **eko'noom** n. (eko'nome) n. economist.

ek'sak [ek'sak] a. (-te) exact, precise; **-theid** n. exactness.

eksal'tasie [eksal'tāsi] n. exaltation; **eksal'teer** v. (ge-) exalt.

ek'samen [ek'sāmən] n. (-s) examination; 'n-aflê sit for an examination; in 'n-slaag (druip) pass (fail) an examination; **-rooster** n. examination time-table; **eksami'nator** n. (eksamina'tore) examiner; **eksami'neer** v. (ge-) examine.

ekse'kusie [eksə'kewsi] n. execution; **ekseku'teur** n. (-s) executor; **ekseku'trise** n. (-s) executrix.

eksel'lensie [eksə'lɛ̃si] n. (-s) excellency; **-sel'lent** a. & av. (-e) excellent.

eksem'plaar [eksem'plāR] n. (eksem'plare) specimen, sample, copy.

eksen'triek [eksen'tRik] a. (-e)

eccentric, cranky, odd; -'sentries *a.* (*-e*) eccentric; **eksentrisi'teit** *n.* eccentricity.

ek'sepsie [ek'sepsi] *n.* (*-s*) exception.

ek'serp [ek'seRp] *n.* (*-te-*) excerpt; **ekser'peer** *v.* (ge-) make an excerpt.

ek'ses [ek'ses] *n.* (*-se*) excess; -'sief *a.* (*-siewe*) excessive.

'eksie-per'feksie ['eksi-pəR'feksi] *a.* perfect, smart.

eksis'tensie [eksəs'tensi] *n.* existence.

eksklu'sief [eksklew'sif] *a. & av.* (*eksklu'siewe*) exclusive(ly).

eks'kursie [eks'kʌRsi] *n.* excursion.

eks'kuus [eks'kEWs] *n.* apology; excuse; **eksku'seer** *v.* (ge-) excuse, pardon.

'eksodus ['eksōdʌs] *n.* exodus.

eksoga'mie [eksōcha'mi] *n.* exogamy.

ek'soties [ek'sōtis] *a.* (*-e*) exotic.

ekspe'disie [ekspə'disi] *n.* expedition; forwarding.

eksperi'ment [ekspeRi'ment] *n.* (*-e*) experiment; **eksperomen'teel** *a.* (*eksperimen'tele*) experimental.

eks'pert [eks'peRt] *n.* expert.

eksploi'tasie [eksploi'tāsi] *n.* exploitation; **eksploi'teer** *v.* (ge-) exploit.

eksplorasie [eksplō'Rāsi] *n.* exploration; **eksplo'reer** *v.* (ge-) *v.* (ge-) explore.

eksplo'sief [eksplō'sif] *n. & a.* (*eksplo'siewe*) explosive.

'eksport ['ekspoRt] *n.* export; **ekspor'teer** *v.* (ge-) export; **ekspor'teur** *n.* (*-s*) exporter.

eks'pres [eks'pRes] *n.* express (train); *a.* on purpose.

eks'pressie [eks'pResi] *n.* (*-s*) expression; **ekspres'sief** *a. & av.* (*ekspres'siewe*) expressive(ly); **ekspressio'nis** *n.* (*-te*) expressionist.

eks'tase [eks'tāsə] *n.* ecstasy.

eksten'sief [eksten'sif] *a.* (*eksten-'siewe*) extensive.

'ekstern ['eksteRn] *a.* (*-e*) external.

'ekstra ['ekstRa] *n.* (*-s*) extra, spare; *a.* extra, additional, special; *av.* specially; -tjie *dim.*

eks'trak [eks'tRak] *n.* (*-te*) extract.

ekstre'mis [ekstRē'məs] *n.* (*-te*) extremist; **ekstre'misties** *a.* (*-e*) extremistic.

ekstrin'siek [ekstRin'sik] *a.* (*-e*) extrinsic.

e'kwator [ē'kwātoR] *n.* equator; **ekwator'iaal** *a.* (*ekwatori'ale*) equatorial.

ekwi'noks [ēkwi'noks] *n.* equinox, -i'aal *a.* (*-iale*) equinoctial.

ekwiva'lent [ēkwiva'lent] *n.* (*-e*) equivalent.

el ['el] *n.* (*-le*) ell, yard.

'eland ['ēlant] *n.* (*-e*) eland (S.A.); elk (Europe).

elas'tiek [ēlas'tik] *n.* elastic; **e'lasties** *a.* (*-e*) elastic; **elastisi'teit** *n.* elasticity.

'elders ['eldəRs] *av.* elsewhere.

ele'gant [ēlə'chant] *a.* (*-e*) elegant.

ele'gie [ēlə'chi] *n.* elegy; **e'legies** *a.* (*-e*) elegiac.

e'leksie [ē'leksi] *n.* election.

e'lektries [ē'lektris] *a.* (*-e*) electric; *av.* electrically; **elektrifi'kasie** *n.* electrification; **elektrifi'seer** *v.* (ge-) electrify; **elektrisi'ën** *n.* electrician; **elektrisi'teit** *n.* electricity; **e'lektron** *n.* electron.

e'lektroteg'niek [ē'lektRōtech'nik] *n.* electrical engineering.

ele'ment [ēlə'ment] *n.* element; cell (*electr.*); **elemen'têr** *a.* (*-e*) elementary.

'elf ['elf] *n.* (*elwe*) elf, fairy; *n.* (*-s*, *elwe*) eleven; -de *ordinal* eleventh; **elf-en-dertigste** *op sy-wees* in a very critical condition; -tal *n.* number eleven; team of eleven.

elimi'nasie [ēləmə'nāsi] *n.* elimination; **elimi'neer** *v.* (ge-) eliminate.

e'lisie [ē'lisi] *n.* elision; **eli'deer** *v.* (ge-) elide.

elk ['elk] *pron.* (*-e*) each, every, any; -een *n.* everyone, anybody.

el'lende [ē'lendə] *n.* distress, misery; -ling *n.* villain, wretch; **el'lendig** *a.* (*-e*) miserable, wretched.

'ellepyp ['eləpayp] *n.* ulna.

'elmboog ['eləmbōch] *n.* (*'elmboë*) elbow.

elo'kusie [ēlō'kewsi] *n.* elocution.

els ['els] *n.* (*-e*) awl; alder.

e'malje [ē'malyə] *n.* enamel; emal-'jeer *v.* (ge-) enamel.

emansi'pasie [ēmansi'pāsi] *n.* emancipation; **emansi'peer** *v.* (ge-) emancipate.

embleem [em'blēm] *n.* (*em'bleme*) emblem; **emble'maties** *a.* (*-e*) emblematic.

'embrio ['embRiō] *n.* (*-s*) embryo; -lo'gie *n.* embryology.

em'fase [em'fāsə] *n.* emphasis; **em'faties** *a.* (*-e*) emphatic.

emi'grasie [ēmi'chRāsi] *n.* emigration; **emi'grant** *n.* (*-e*) emigrant; **emi'greer** *v.* (ge-) emigrate.

emi'nent [ēmi'nent] *a.* (*-e*) eminent.

'emmer ['eməR] *n.* (*-s*) bucket, pail, measure.

e'mosie [ē'mōsi] *n.* (*-s*) emotion; **emosio'neel** *a.* (*emosio'nele*) emotional.

empi'rie [empi'Ri] *n.* empiricism; **em'piries** *a.* (*-e*) empirical.

emplo'jeer [amplō'yēR] *v.* (ge-) employ.

e'mulsie [ē'mʌlsi] *n.* emulsion.

end ['ent] *n.* end, close, conclusion.

'endelderm ['endəldeRəm] *n.* rectum.

endos'seer [endo'sēR] *v.* (ge-) endorse; **endos'sant** *n.* endorser; **endosse'ment** *n.* endorsement; **endos'sering** *n.* endorsement.

'end-uit ['ent-œit] *av.* to the end.

e'nemmel = emalje.

ener'gie [ēneR'shi] *n.* energy; **ener'giek** *av.* (*-e*) energetic.

'**eng** ['eng] *a. & av.* narrow, tight; narrow-minded; **-heid** n.; **-te** n. narrowness; defile; strait; isthmus.

'**engel** ['engəl] n. (-e) angel; **-agtig** *a.* (-e) angelic; **-ebak** n. the gods (theatre); **-tjie** *dim.*

'**Engels** ['engəls] n. English; *a.* (-e) English; **-man** n. Britisher.

'**enigeen** ['ēnəchēn] n. anyone.

'**enigermate** ['ēnəchəRmātə] *av.* to some extent.

'**enigheid** ['ēnəchayt] n. loneliness, solitude.

'**enigsins** ['ēnəchsəns] *av.* somewhat.

'**enigste** ['ēnəchstə] *a.* only.

en**jambe'ment** [enyambə'ment] n. enjambment.

'**enjin** ['enyən] n. (-s) engine, machine; **-kap** n. (-pe) bonnet, hood.

'**enkel** ['enkəl] n. (-s) ankle; *a.* (-e) single; *av.* only, merely; **-ing** n. (-e) individual; **-skut** n. ankle-guard; **-spel** n. singles; **-voud** n. singular; '**-voudig** *a.* (-e) singular.

e'**norm** [ē'noRəm] *a.* (-e) enormous.

ensiklope'**die** [ensiklōpə'di] n. encyclopedia; **ensiklo'pedies** *a.* (-e) encyclopedic.

'**ensovoorts** ['ɛñsəfōRts] n. etcetera.

ent ['ent] n. (-e) end; piece; graft, vaccination; *v.* (ge-) graft, innoculate, vaccinate; **-jie** ['engKi] *dim.*; **-stof** n. vaccine.

entoesi'**as** [entusi'as] n. (-te) enthusiast; **-me** n. enthusiasm; **-ties** *a.* (-e) enthusiastic.

'**envelop** ['âñvəlop] n. (-pe) envelope, *cp.* **koevert**.

epide'**mie** [epidə'mi] n. (-ē, -s) epidemic; **epi'demies** *a.* (-e) epidemic.

e'**piek** [ē'pik] n. epic poetry; '**epies** *a.* (-e) epic.

epi'**lepsie** [ēpi'lepsi] n. epilepsy; **epi'lepties** *a.* (-e) epileptic.

epi'**loog** [ēpi'lōch] n. epilogue.

epi'**sode** [ēpi'sōdə] n. (-s) episode; **epi'sodies** *a.* (-e) episodic.

e'**pistel** [ē'pəstəl] n. (-s) epistle.

epi'**teel** [ēpi'tēl] n. epithelium.

e'**pitheton** [ē'pitətǝn] n. (-s) epithet, epithet.

'**epos** ['ɛpos] n. epic poem.

er'**barm** [eR'baRəm] *v.* (ge-) have pity on; **-ing** n. mercy; **-lik** *a.* (-e; -er, -ste) lamentable, pitiful.

erd ['eRt] n. earth, clay; compost; *v.* (ge-) earth (mould) up.

'**erd(e)-** ['eRə-] *pref.* earthen, clay; **-pot** n. (-te) clay pot; **-skottel** n. (-s) earthenware-dish; **-werk** n. crockery; **-vark** n. ant-eater; **-wurm** n. glow-worm.

'**ere** ['ēRə] n. honour, *ter-van* in honour of, *cp.* **eer**; **-baantjie** n. post of honour; **-burger** n. freeman; **-diens** n. public worship; **-doktor** n. doctor honoris causa; **-gas** n. (-te) guest of honour; **-graad** n. honorary degree; **-lid** n. honorary member; **-woord** n. word of honour.

'**erens** ['ɛRǝñs] *av.* somewhere.

erf ['eRf] n. (erwe) erf (S.A.) (pl. erven) plot, site; huis en- premises; *v.* (ge-) inherit; **-deel** n. heritage; **-geld** n. inherited money; **-genaam** n. heir; **-goed** n. heritage; **-later** n. testator; **-lik** *a.* (-e; -er, -ste) hereditary; **-likheid** n. heredity; **-nis** n. heritage, inheritance; **-opvolging** n. succession; **-porsie** n. = **erfgoed**; **-reg** n. law of succession; **-sonde** n. original sin; **-stuk** n. heirloom.

erg ['eRch] n. suspicion; malice; *a.* bad; ill; severe; *v.* (ge-) annoy, vex, offend; **-erlik** ['eRgǝRlǝk] *a.* (-e; -er, -ste) aggravating, offensive; **-ernis** n. annoyance, nuisance; chagrin; **-ste** n. worst.

er'**ken** [eR'ken] *v.* (-) acknowledge; recognize; avow; admit; **-de** *a.* acknowledged, recognized, admitted, approved; **-ning** n.; **-tlik** *a.* (-e; -er, -ste) grateful, thankful; **-tlikheid** n. gratitude.

er'**lang** [eR'lang] *v.* (-) acquire, obtain.

erns ['eRns] n. earnestness, gravity; **-tig** *a. & av.* (-e; -er, -ste) earnest, serious, grave.

e'**rosie** [ē_Rōsi] n. erosion.

e'**roties** [ē'Rōtis] *a.* (-e) erotic.

'**ertappel** ['ertapəl] n. (-s) potato.

'**ertjie** [eRKi] n. (-s) pea.

erts ['eRts] n. ore.

e'**rupsie** [ē'Rʌpsi] n. (-s) eruption.

er'**vaar** [eR'fāR] *v.* (-) experience.

er'**vare** [eR'fāRə] *a.* (meer, mees) experienced; **-nheid** n. experience; er'**varing** n. experience.

es ['es] n. ash tree; sharp turn; kitchen hearth.

'**esel** ['ēsəl] n. (-s) ass; dunce; easel; **-agtig** *a.* (-e) asinine; stupid; **-hings** n. (-te) jackass; **-'in** (-ne) jenny-ass; **-werk** n. drudgery.

es'**kader** [es'kādəR] n. (-s) squadron.

'**Eskimo** ['eskimō] n. (-'s) Eskimo.

E'**sopus** [ē'sōpʌs] n. Aesop.

'**essens** ['esəns] n. essence.

es'**sensie** [e'sensi] n. essence; **essensi'eel** *a.* (essensiële) essential.

este'**tiek** [estē'tik] n. aesthetics; **es'teties** *a.* (-e) aesthetic(al).

'**ete** ['ētə] n. food, meal; *cp.* **eet**; **-nstyd** n. meal-time; **-nsuur** n. dinner-hour.

'**eter** ['ētəR] n. (-s) eater; ether; **-y** n. eating.

e'**teries** [ē'tēRis] *a.* (-e) ethereal.

e'**tiek** [ē'tik] n. ethics.

'**etika** ['ētika] n. = **etiek**.

eti'**ket** [ēti'ket] n. label; etiquette.

etimolo'**gie** [ētimōlō'chi] n. etymology; **etimo'logies** *a.* (-e) etymological.

'**etlike** ['etləkə] *a.* several, some.

et'**maal** ['etmāl] n. twenty-four hours.

ets ['ets] n. (-e) etching; *v.* (ge-) etch.

'**etter** ['etəR] n. discharge, pus; *v.* (ge-) fester; **-agtig** *a.* (-e) purulent; **-end** *a.* (-e) festering.

Eu'fraat [œ'fRãt] n. Euphrates.
euka'liptus [œka'ləptʌs] n. eucalyptus.
Eu'klides [œ'klidẽs] n. Euclid.
Eu'ropa [œ'Rõpa] n. Europe; Europe'aan n. (Europe'ane) European; Euro'pees a. (Euro'pese) European.
'euwel ['œvəl] n. (-s) evil; defect.
evan'gelie [ēfang-'chĕli] n. (-s) gospel; -s (-e) evangelic.
eventu'eel [ēfentew'ēl] a. & av. (eventu'ele) possible, potential.
evo'lusie [ēvõ'lewsi] n. evolution.
'ewe ['ēvə] n. dis my om die- it is all the same to me; a. even = gelyk; av. as, even, just, equally; -beeld n. counterpart, likeness, image; -'kansig a. (-e) random; -neens av. also, likewise, too; -knie n. equal, match; -mens n. fellow-man; -min av. just as little; -naar n. equator; differential; -wel, ewenwel av. however; -'redig a. (-e) proportional, proportionate; -seer av. as much as; -so av. likewise; -veel av. as much, the same; -'ver (-'feR) av. equally so; -wig n. balance, poise, equilibrium; -wigtig a. (-e; -er, -ste) well-balanced; level-headed; -'wigtigheid n. balance; level-headedness; -'wydig a. (-e) parallel.
'eweneens ['ēvənēns] av. similarly.
'ewig ['ēvach] a. & av. (-e) eternal, perpetual; -'durend a. (-e) everlasting, incessant; -heid n. eternity.

F

faal ['fãl] v. (ge-) fail.
'faam ['fãm] n. fame, reputation, repute.
'fabel ['fãbəl] n. (-s) fable; fiction; -agtig a. (-e; -er, -ste) fabulous, incredible; -leer n. mythology.
fa'briek [fa'bRik] n. (-e) factory; -swese n. industry; fabri'kaat n. (fabrie'kate) manufacture; fabric; fabri'kant n. (-e) manufacturer; fabri'kasie n. manufacture; fabri'seer v. (ge-) manufacture, produce; fabricate.
fagot ['fachot] n. (-te) bassoon.
'fakkel ['fakəl] n. (-s) torch, flare.
'fakties ['faktis] a. (-e) actually.
fak'toor [fak'tõR] n. (fak'tore) agent, factor.
'faktor ['faktoR] n. (fak'tore) factor.
fak'tuur [fak'tēwR] n. bill, invoice; faktu'reer v. (ge-) invoice.
fakul'teit [fakʌl'tayt] n. faculty.
fa'lanks [fa'lanks] n. (-e) phalanx.
fal'set [fal'set] n. falsetto.
familiari'teit [familiaRi'tayt] n. familiarity.
fa'milie [fa'mĭli] n. (-s) family; relatives; -betrekking n. (-e) relative; -gek a. over-fond of one's relatives; -goed n. family-estate; -kring n. family-circle; -lid n. (-lede) member

of a family; -stuk n. heirloom; -wapen n. coat-of-arms.
fa'natikus [fa'nãtikʌs] n. fanatic; fana'tiek a. (-e) fanatic.
fanta'sie [fanta'si] n. fantasy; imagination; fantasia; fanta'seer v. (ge-) fancy, imagine; improvize; fan'tasties a. (-e) fantastic.
'Farao ['fãRaõ] n. Pharaoh.
fa'rinks ['fãRənks] n. pharynx; farin'gitis n. pharyngitis.
fari'seër [faRi'sēəR] n. (-s) hypocrite; Pharisee; fari'sees a. (fari'sese) hypocritical.
farmakolo'gie [faRmakõlõ'chi] n. pharmacology; farmako'loog n. (farmakoloë) pharmacologist; farma'seut n. chemist.
fas'cis [fa'shəs] n. fascist; -ties a. (-e) fascist.
'fase ['fãsə] n. (-s) phase, stage.
fa'set [fa'set] n. (-te) facet.
fasilil'teit [fasili'tayt] n. (-e) facility.
fa'taal [fa'tãl] a. (fa'tale) fatal; fatali'teit n. fatality.
fat'soen [fat'sun] n. (-e) shape; cut; fashion; decency; -'eer v. (ge-) fashion, mould; -lik a. (-e; -er, -ste) decent, respectable; av. decently, properly.
'Februarie ['fēbəRvãRi] n. February.
fede'raal [fēdə'Rãl] a. (fede'rale) federal; feder'asie n. federation; fede'reer v. (ge-) federate.
fee ['fē] n. (feë) fairy; -agtig a. (-e) fairy-like.
feeks ['fēks] n. vixen.
fees ['fēs] n. (-te) feast, festival; -maal n. banquet; -telik a. & av. (-e; -er, -ste) festal, festive, convivial; -telikheid n. festivity.
'feil ['fayl] n. a. (-e) fault, error.
'feilbaar ['faylbãR] a. ('feilbare; -der, -ste) fallible; -baarheid n. fallibility; -loos a. (-lose) faultless.
feit ['fayt] n. (-e) fact; -lik a. & av. (-e) actual(ly), real(ly).
fel ['fel] a. (-le) fierce, keen, sharp; -heid n. severity, violence.
felisi'teer [fələsə'tēR] v. (ge-) congratulate.
'feniks ['fēnəks] n. phoenix.
feno'meen [fēnõ'mēn] n. (feno'mene) phenomenon; fenome'naal a. (fenomenale) phenomenal.
feo'daal [fēõ'dãl] a. (feo'dale) feudal.
ferm ['feRəm] a. (-e) firm, steady, strong; -heid n. firmness.
fer'weel [fəR'vēl] n. corduroy, velvet; -tjie dim. sparaxis.
'fetisj ['fetish] n. (-e) fetish.
'fetus ['fētʌs] n. foetus, fetus.
'fiemies ['fimis] n. capriciousness; whims.
fier ['fiR] a. (-e) high-minded, proud; -heid n. pride.
fieter'jasies [fitəR'yasis] n. frills, flourishes.
fiets ['fits] n. (-e) bicycle; v. (

cycle; a. (-e) smart; -baan n. cycle lane, track; -ryer n. cyclist; -pad n. (-paaie) cycle path.

figu'rant [fichew'rant] n. puppet, figure, dummy.

fi'guur [fə'chēwR] n. (fi'gure) figure; figura'tief a. (figura'tiewe) figurative; figu'reer v. (ge-) figure, pose; -lik a. & av. figurative(ly); -tjie dim.

fiks ['faks] a. (-e) healthy, robust, energetic.

fik'seer [fak'sēR] v. (ge-) fix, stare at (a person).

'fiksie ['fiksi] n. fiction; fik'tief a. (fik'tiewe) fictitious.

filan'troop [filan'trŏp] n. a. (filan'trope) philanthropist; filan'tropies a. (-e) philanthropic.

fili'aal [fili'āl] n. (fili'ale) branch (office).

film ['fələm] n. film; v. (ge-) film.

filolo'gie [filŏlŏ'chi] n. philology; filo'logies a. (-e) philologic; filo'loog n. (filo'loë) philologist.

filo'soof [filŏ'sŏf] n. (filo'sowe) philosopher; filoso'fie n. philosophy; filo'sofies a. (-e) philosophic; filoso'feer v. (ge-) philosophize.

'filter ['fəltəR] n. (-s) filter, percolator, strainer; screen; fil'traat n. (fil'trate) filtrate; fil'trasie n. filtration; fil'treer v. (ge-) filter, strain.

fi'naal [fi'nāl] a. (fi'nale) final, complete, total; fi'nale n. (-s) final, finale; finali'teit n. finality.

fi'nansië [fi'nansië] n. finance; finances; finansi'eel a. (finansi'ële) financial; finansi'eer v. (ge-) finance; finan'sier n. financier; fi'nansies n. = finansië.

fi'nesse [fi'nes] n. (-s) finesse, nicety.

fin'geer [fang'chēR] v. feign, invent, pretend.

'firma ['fəRma] n. (-s) concern, firm.

firma'ment [fəRma'ment] n. sky.

fi'sant [fi'sant] n. (-e) pheasant.

fi'siek [fə'sik] n. (-e) physique; a. (-e) physical; 'fisies a. (-e) physical.

'fisika ['fisika] n. physics.

fisiolo'gie [fisiŏlŏ'chi] n. physiology; fisio'logies a. (-e) physiological.

fisiono'mie [fisiŏnŏ'mi] n. physiognomy.

fis'kaal [fəs'kāl] n. (fis'kale, -s) fiscal; butcher-bird.

'fistel ['fəstəl] n. (-s) fistula.

fjord ['fyort] n. (-s) fjord.

'fladder ['fladəR] v. (ge-) flutter, flap, flit.

fla'grant [fla'chRant] a. (-e) flagrant, glaring.

fla'mink [fla'mənk] n. (-e) flamingo.

flank ['flank] n. (-e) flank, side; -'eer v. (ge-) flank, gad about.

flans ['flāns] v. (ge-) flange, knock together.

flap ['flap] n. (-pe) iris; long-tailed widow-bird.

'flarde ['flaRdə] n. pl. aan- in rags, tatters.

'flater ['flātəR] n. (-s) blunder, mistake.

fleg'maties [flech'mātis] a. (-e) phlegmatic.

'fleksie ['fleksi] n. flection; -loos a. (-lose) without inflection.

'flennie ['fleni] n. flannel; -agtig a. (-e) flannelly.

'flens ['fleñs] n. flange, bead; -dop n. flanged cap; -loos a. flangeless.

'flenter ['flentəR] n. (-s) rag, tatter, splinter; g'n-omgee nie not care two hoots; v. (ge-) gad about; -s av. in rags.

'flerrie ['flɛRi] n. (-s) flirt; v. (ge-) flirt; gad about.

fles ['fles] n. (-se) bottle, flask; -sie dim. phial.

flets ['flets] a. (-e) faded, pale; wilted, flat.

fleur ['flœR] n. flower, bloom, prime; -ig a. (-e) blooming, lively.

'flikflooi ['fləkflŏi] v. (ge-) cajole, wheedle.

'flikker ['fləkəR] v. (ge-) glitter, sparkle, twinkle; -ing n. flickering, twinkling; -s n. pl. capers; -s gooi cut capers.

flink ['flənk] a. (-, -e) fine, robust; energetic; substantial; av. energetically; firmly.

flirt ['flaRt] = flerrie.

flits ['flats] n. (-e) flash; torch; v. (ge-) flash.

'flitslig ['flətsləch] n. flash light, torch.

'floers ['flūRs] n. crape.

'flonker ['flonkəR] v. (ge-) sparkle; -ing n. sparkle, sparkling.

flo'reer [flŏ'RēR] v. (ge-) flourish; flo'rerend a. (-e) flourishing.

flo'teer [flŏ'tēR] v. (ge-) float.

flou ['flŏa] a. (-, -e; -er, -ste) flat, insipid; feeble; dim; dull; -val v. (ge-) faint; -heid n.; -i'teit n. silly joke; -te n. fainting spell; -tjies av. dim. feebly.

flous ['flŏas] v. (ge-) cheat.

fluim ['flœim] n. phlegm.

'fluister ['flœistəR] v. (ge-) whisper; -erend a. (-e) in a whisper; -ing n. whispering.

fluit ['flœit] n. (-e) flute; whistle; v. (ge-) whistle; play on the flute; na iets- whistle for something; fluit-fluit av. easily; -tjie dim. whistle, mouth-organ.

fluks ['flaks] a. & av. (-e; -er, -stə) energetic, willing; quick.

fluktu'asie [flʌktəw'āsi] n. fluctuation; fluktu'eer v. (ge-) fluctuate.

'flus ['flʌs] av. directly, a moment ago.

flu'weel [flew'vēl] n. velvet; -agtig a. (-e) velvety.

'fnuik ['fnœik] v. (ge-) clip, nip in the bud.

foei ['fui] interj. shame! fie!

'foelie ['fuli] n. mace.

'foeter ['futəR] v. (ge-) bother, trouble; thrash.

foli'ant [fŏli'ant] n. (-e) folio, volume.
'folio [fŏliŏ] n. *folio*; **-papier** n. foolscap.
'folter ['foltəR] v. (ge-) torture; **-aar** n. (-s) torturer; **-end** a. (-e) agonizing, racking; **-ing** n. torture.
fonda'ment [fonda'ment] n. (-e) foundation; anus.
fon'deer [fon'dēR] v. (ge-) lay foundation stone; **fon'dering** n. foundation.
fonds [fonts] n. (-e) fund.
fono'graaf ['fŏnŏchRâf] n. (fono'grawe) phonograph.
fono'gram [fŏnŏ'chRam] n. (-me) phonogram.
fon'tein [fon'tayn] n. (-e) fountain; **-tjie** dim.
fooi ['fŏi] n. (-e) tip; **-tjie** dim.; v. (ge-) tip.
fop ['fop] v. (ge-) cheat; hoax; **-pertjie** dim. dummy, soother; **-pery** n. cheating, chicanery; **-speen** n. = **foppertjie**.
fo'rel [fŏ'Rel] n. (-le) trout.
for'maat [foR'māt] n. (for'mate) size; shape.
formali'teit [foRmali'tayt] n. (-e) formality.
for'masie [foR'māsi] n. (-s) formation.
for'meel [foR'mēl] a. (for'mele) formal.
for'mule [foR'mēWlə] n. (-s) formula; **formu'leer** v. (ge-) formulate; **formu'lering** n. formulation; wording, statement; **formu'lier** n. form; formulary.
fors ['foRs] a. (-, -e; -er, -ste) bold, robust.
for'seer [foR'sēR] v. (ge-) force, coerce, compel; strain.
fort ['foRt] n. (-e) fortress; **-ifi'kasie** n. fortification; **-ifi'seer** v. (ge-) fortify.
for'tuin [foR'tœin] n. fortune, wealth; **-soeker** n. adventurer.
fos'faat [fos'fât] n. phosphate.
'fosfor ['fosfoR] n. phosphorus.
fos'siel [fo'sil] n. (-e) fossil; a. (-e) fossil.
'foto ['fŏtŏ] n. (-'s) photo; **-'graaf** n. (-grawe) photographer; **-gra'feer** v. a. (ge-) photograph; take a photo; **-gra'fie** n. photography; **-flitslamp** n. photo flash bulb.
fout ['foat] n. (-e) fault, error, mistake, defect; blunder; **fou'teer** v. (ge-) err, make a mistake; **fou'tief** a. (fou'tiewe) faulty, wrong.
fraai ['fRâi] a. (-e; -er, -ste) beautiful, pretty.
frag'ment [fRach'ment] n. (-e) fragment; **fragmen'taries** a. (-e) fragmentary.
'fraiing ['fRâyəng] n. (-s) fringe, edging; tassel.
frak'tuur [fRak'tēwR] n. (frak'ture) fracture.
fram'boos [fRam'bŏs] n. raspberry.
frank ['fRank] a. frank, free;

fran'keer v. (ge-) frank, stamp; **fran'kering** n. postage.
'Frankryk ['frankrayk] n. France.
Frans ['fRâns] a. (-e) French; **-man** n. Frenchman.
'frase ['fRâsə] n. (-s) phrase.
frats ['fRats] n. (-e) caprice, whim; clownery.
fre'kwensie [fRě'kwensi] n. frequency.
'fresia ['frēsia] n. freesia.
frikka'del [fRəkə'del] n. (-le) rissole.
fris ['fRəs] a. (-se; -ser, -ste) fresh, cool; fit; **-heid** n. coolness, freshness; strength.
'frokkie ['fRoki] n. (-s) vest.
'frommel ['fRoməl] n. (-s) home-made vermicelli; v. (ge-) crumple; crease; fumble.
frons ['fRauns] n. (-e) frown, scowl; v. (ge-) knit one's brow, frown, scowl.
front ['fRont] n. (-e) front, facade.
fuga ['fewcha] n. (-s) fugue.
fuif ['fœif] n. (fuiwe) spree, celebration, binge; v. (ge-) feast, revel.
'fuik ['fœik] n. (-e) fish-trap, coop.
funda'ment = **fondament**; **fundamen'teel** a. (fundamen'tele) fundamental.
fungeer cp. **funksie**.
'funksie ['fʌnksi] n. (-s) function; capacity; **fun'geer** v. (ge-) function; **funksio'neer** v. (ge-) function as.
fusil'leer [fewsə'lēR] v. (ge-) fusillade.
fut ['fʌt] n. go, push, vim; **-loos** a. (-lose) spiritless.
fu'tiel [few'til] a. (-e) futile.
fyn ['fayn] a. (-e; -er, -ste) fine; delicate; lovely; choice; subtle; **-gevoelig** a. (-e) sensitive; **-heid** n. delicacy, nicety; **-ighede** n. finesse; **-proewer** n. (-s) connoisseur; **-tjies** av. dim. cleverly, smartly.
'fynekam ['faynəkam] n. fine-comb.
'fyntalk ['fayntalk] n. French chalk.
fyt ['fayt] n. whitlow.

G

ga! ['cha] *interj.* phew!
gaaf ['châf] a. & av. (gawe; gawer, -ste) fine, good; excellent, sound; undamaged; **'n gawe kêrel** a jolly fellow.
gaan ['chân] v. (ge-) go; move, walk; **hoe-dit?** how are you? **dit-jou goed!** good luck to you! **dit-jou nie aan nie** it doesn't concern you; **-de** av. wat is **-de?** what is afoot? **'n beweging is -de?** a movement is on foot; **-deweg** av. gradually.
gaap ['châp] v. (ge-) yawn; gape; **'gapend** a. (-e) yawning.
gaar ['châR] a. & av. cooked, done; **die gort is-** the fat is in the fire.
'gaarne ['châRnə] av. gladly, readily; cp. **graag**; yearn.

gaas]'chās] *n.* gauze; **-doek** *n.* cambric; **-draad** *n.* gauze-wire.

gaatjie [chāiKi] *n. dim.* (-s) little hole; ventage; **-svisier** *n.* peephole.

gade ['chādə] *n.* (-s) spouse.

'**gadeslaan** ['chādəslān] *v.* (-ge-) observe.

'**gading** ['chādəng] *n.* inclination; *dis nie van my-nie* it is not in my line.

'**gaffel** ['chafəl] *n.* (-s) pitchfork; prong.

gaip ['chaip] *n.* (-e) lout.

gal ['chal] *n.* bile, gall; **-agtig** *a.* (-e) bilious; **-bitter** *a. & av.* as bitter as gall; **-blaas** *n.* gall-bladder; **-buis** *n.* bile-duct; **-bult** *n.* urticaria.

'**gala** ['chāla] *n.* (-s) festival, gala.

ga'lant [cha'lant] *a.* (-e) gallant, courteous.

gale'ry [chalə'Ray] *n.* gallery; drive.

galg ['chalch] *n.* (-e) gallows.

'**Galliëe** ['chaliə] *n.* Gaul; '**Gallies** *a.* (-e) Gallic, Gaulic.

gal'lon = gelling.

galm ['chaləm] *n.* (-e) booming, peal; *v.* (ge-) bawl, resound.

'**galmuggies** ['chalmʌchis] *n. pl.* gall midges.

ga'lop [cha'lop] *n.* galop (*dance*); gallop (*horse*); *v.* (ge-) gallop; **-'peer** *v.* (ge-) = **galop** *n.*

'**galsterig** ['chalstəRəch] *a.* (-e) rancid.

gal'vanies [chal'fānis] *a.* (-e) galvanic; **galvani'seer** *v.* (ge-) galvanize.

Gam ['cham] *n.* Ham.

'**gamat** [chamat] *n.* (-s. -te) Cape Malay.

gang ['chang] *n.* (-e) passage; gait; pace; trend; *sy eie-gaan* go his own way; gear, speed, **eerste - ** *a.* first (gear), **tweede - ** *a.* second (gear), **derde - ** *a.* third (gear), **hoogste - ** *a.* top (gear), **laagste - ** *a.* low (gear); **-baar** *a.* (-bare/ -der, -ste) current, passable; **-etjie** *n.* (-s) *dim.* narrow passage; **-maker** *n.* (-s) pace-maker.

'**Ganges** ['changes] *n.* Ganges.

'**ganglion** ['changlion] *n.* ganglion.

'**ganna** ['chana] *n.* (-s) ganna, lye-bush.

gans ['chāns] *n.* (-e) goose; *a.* (-e) all, entire, whole; *av.* absolutely; **-ie** *dim.* gosling.

ganse/gaar ['chānsə'chaR] *av.* entirely.

'**gapend** *cp.* **gaap.**

'**gaping** ['chāpəng] *n.* (-s; -e) gap, hiatus.

ga'rage [ga'Rāsh] *n.* (-s) garage.

ga'ransie [cha'ransi] *n.* guarantee, **garan'deer** *v.* (ge-) guarantee.

'**garde** ['chaRdə] *n.* guard, *die ou-* veterans.

gar'denia [chaR'dēnia] *n.* gardenia.

'**gare = garing.**

'**garing** ['charəng] *n.* yarn, thread; **-boom** *n.* agave; **-klip** *n.* asbestos.

gar'naal [chaR'nāl] *n.* (*gar'nale*) shrimp.

gar'neer [chaR'nēR] *v.* (ge-) trim; garnish; **gar'neersel** *n.* trimming; **gar'nering** *n.* trimming; **garni'tuur** *n.* trimming.

garni'soen [chaRni'sun] *n.* (-e) garrison.

gars ['chaRs] *n.* barley.

gas ['chas] *n.* (-te) guest; *n.* (-se) gas; **-agtig** *a.* (-e) gaseous; **-sheer** *n.* host; **-vry** *a.* hospitable; **-vryheid** *n.* hospitality; **-vormig** *a.* (-e) gaseous.

ga'sel [cha'sel] *n.* (-s) gazelle.

'**gasie** ['chāsi] *n.* pay, wages.

'**gasvrou** ['chasfRoa] *n.* (-e, -ens) hostess.

'**gasvry** ['chasfRay] *a.* hospitable.

gat ['chat] *n.* (-e) hole, gap; *n.* (-te) anus; **-erig** *a.* (-e) holey; **-kant** *n.* back, backside; **-kruiper** *n.* (-s) toady; **-s!** *interj.* gosh!

'**gawe** ['chāvə] *n.* (-s) gift, talent; donation; **-rig** *a.* (-e) fine, good, nice.

ge'aard [chə'āRt] *a. & av.* disposed, tempered; **-heid** *n.* disposition, nature, temper.

ge'ag [chə'ach] *a.* (-te) esteemed, respected.

gealli'eer(d) [chəali'ēRt] *a.* (-e) allied; **-es** *n.* allies.

ge'baande [chə'bāndə] *a.* beaten; *die-pad* the beaten track.

ge'baar [chə'bāR] *n.* (ge'bare) gesture, gesticulation.

ge'babbel [chə'babəl] *n.* chatter, prattle.

ge'bak [chə'bak] *n.* cake, pastry; *a.* (-te) baked, fried.

ge'barespel [chə'bāRəspel] *n.* gestures; pantomime; **ge'baretaal** *n.* language of signs.

ge'barste [chə'baRstə] *a.* burst, cracked.

ge'basel [chə'bāsəl] *n.* empty talk.

ge'bed [chə'bet] *n.* (ge'bede) prayer.

ge'bedel [chə'bēdəl] *n.* begging.

ge'beente [chə'bēntə] *n.* bones.

ge'belg [chə'belch] *a.* (-de) angry, incensed, piqued.

ge'bergte [chə'beRchtə] *n.* (-s) mountain-chain.

ge'beur [chə'bēR] *v.* (-) chance, come to pass; **-de** *n.* *die-de* the event; **-lik** *a.* (-e) contingent; **-likheid** *n.* contingency; **-tenis** *n.* (-se) event.

ge'bied [chə'bit] *n.* (-e) territory; area; jurisdiction; domain; *v.* (-) command, direct; **-end** *a.* commanding, compelling; **-enderwys(e)** *av.* authoritatively; **-er** *n.* master, ruler.

ge'bint [chə'bənt] *n.* (-e) cross-beam, truss.

ge'bit [chə'bət] *n.* (-te) denture dentition; bit.

ge'blaas [chə'blās] *n.* hissing.

ge'bladerte [chə'blādəRtə] *n.* foliage.

ge'blaf [chə'blaf] *n.* barking.

ge'blêr [chə'blɛR] *n.* bleating.

ge'blinddoek [chə'blənduk] *a.* (-te) blindfolded.

ge'blom [chə'blom] a. (-de) floral.

ge'blus [chə'blʌs] a. (-te) slaked.

ge'bod [chə'bot] n. (ge'booie) command, order; pl. banns.

ge'boë [chə'bōə] a. arched, bent.

ge'boggel [chə'bochəl] a. (-de) hunch-backed.

ge'bonde [chə'bondə] a. bound; latent; poetic; -nheid n. lack of freedom.

ge'boomte [chə'bōmtə] n. trees.

ge'boorte [chə'bōRtə] n. (-s) birth.

ge'bore [chə'bōRə] a. born; native.

ge'bou [chə'boa] n. (-e) building; -de a. built.

ge'braad [chə'bRāt] n. roast.

ge'braai [chə'bRāi] a. (-de) roasted, broiled; poached.

ge'brabbel]chə'bRabəl[n. jargon, gibberish.

ge'brand [chə'bRant] a. (-e) burnt, roasted.

ge'breek [chə'bRēk] a. (-re) broken.

ge'brei [chə'bRay] a. (-de) knitted.

ge'brek [chə'bRek] n. (ge'breke) lack, want, dearth; poverty; defect, flaw; -kig a. (-e; -er, -ste) defective; -lik a. (-e; -er, -ste) crippled, deformed; -likheid n. deformity.

ge'broeders [chə'bRudəRs] n. brothers, Bros.

ge'broke [chə'bRōkə] a. broken.

ge'brom [chə'bRom] n. murmur.

ge'bruik [chə'bRœik] n. (-e) use; custom; application; consumption; a. (-te) used; second-hand; v. (-) use; employ; partake; -er n. (-s) user, consumer; -lik a. (-e) customary.

ge'bruis [chə'bRœis] n. seething; effervescence.

ge'brul [chə'bRʌl] n. roaring.

ge'bukkend [chə'bʌkənt] a. (-e) stooping.

ge'bulder [chə'bʌldəR] n. rumbling, booming.

ge'bulk [chə'bʌlk] n. bellowing, mooing.

ge'bundel [chə'bʌndəl] a. (-de) collected.

ge'daagde [chə'dāchdə] n. (-s) respondent.

ge'daan [chə'dān] a. (ge'dane) done; exhausted.

ge'daante [chə'dāntə] n. (-s) figure, shape; spectre.

ge'dagte [chə'dachtə] n. (-s) idea, thought; memory; reflection; opinion; -gang n. line of thought; -loos a. (-lose) thoughtless, absentminded; -nis n. (-se) memory, remembrance; memento; -streep n. dash; ge'dagtig a. mindful.

ge'dawer [chə'dāvəR] n. booming.

ge'deelte [chə'dēltə] n. (-s) portion, share, instalment; -telik a. & av. partial, partly.

ge'dek [chə'dek] a. (-te) covered; secured.

ge'demp [chə'demp] a. (-te) filled up; muffled.

ge'denk [chə'denk] v. (-) bear in mind, remember; -boek n. album; -dag n. anniversary; -rol n. roll of honour, annals.

gedenk'waardig [chə'dənkvāRdəch] a. (-e) memorable.

ge'dienstig [chə'dīnstəch] a. (-e) attentive, obeying; -heid n. politeness.

ge'dierte [chə'diRtə] n. (-s) animals, beasts, creatures; vermin; monster.

ge'dig [chə'dəch] n. (-te) poem.

ge'ding [chə'dəng] n. (-e) action, lawsuit; quarrel.

gedissipli'neer [chədəsəpli'nēR] a. (-de) disciplined.

gedistil'leer [chədəstə'lēR] a. (-de) distilled.

ge'doe [chə'du] n. bustle, fuss.

ge'doente [chə'duntə] n. (-s) = gedoe.

ge'doog [chə'dōch] v. (-) allow, tolerate.

ge'doriewaar [chə'dōRivāR] interj. by gum!

ge'dra [chə'dRā] v. (-) act, behave, conduct oneself.

ge'draai [chə'dRāi] n. delay, tarrying; twisting; a. (-de) twisted.

ge'draal [chə'dRāl] n. delay, tarrying.

ge'drag [chə'drach] n. behaviour, deportment; cp. gedra.

ge'drang [dhə'dRang] n. crowd, throng.

ge'dreun [chə'dRœn] n. din.

ge'drog [chə'droch] n. (-te) monster, monstrosity; -telikheid n. monstrosity.

ge'dronge [chə'drongə] a. compact, terse; obliged.

ge'druis [chə'dRœis] n. noise, rush, roar.

ge'druk [chə'dRʌk] n. = gedrang; a. (-te) printed; dejected.

ge'dug [chə'dʌch] a. (-te) doughty; formidable.

ge'duld [chə'dʌld] n. patience; -ig a. (-e; -er, -ste) patient.

ge'durende [chə'dēwRəndə] av. during; ge'durig a. (-e) constant; ge'duriglik av. constantly.

ge'dwee [chə'dwē] a. docile; -heid n. meekness.

ge'dwonge [chə'dwongə] a. compulsory; constrained; enforced.

ge'dy [chə'day] v. (-) prosper, thrive.

gee ['chē] v. (ge-) give.

ge'ëer [chə'ēR] a. (-de) honoured.

'geen-eis-bonus ['chēn-ays-bōnʌs] n. (-se) no-claim bonus.

'geel ['chēl] n. yellow; a. yellow; -agtig a. (-e) yellowish; -baadjie -aanhê be jealous; -heid n. yellowness; -ka'pel n. yellow cobra; -koper n. brass; -rys n. curried rice; -sug n. jaundice.

geen, 'g'n ['chēn, 'chən] a. & pron. no, not a, not any, none.

geen'een [c hən'ēn] pron. no one.

'ge ensins['chēnsəns] av. not at all.

ge'ënt [chə'ent] *a.* (-e) grafted; vaccinated.

gees ['chēs] *n.* (-te) spirit; mind; wit; genius; spectre; **-dodend** *a.* (-e; -er, -ste) soul-deadening, monotonous; **-drif** *n.* enthusiasm; **-tig** *a.* (-e; -er, -ste) enthusiastic; **-telike** *n.* (-s) clergyman, parson; **-telikheid** *n.* clergy; **-teloos** *a.* (*geestelose*) dull; **-verwant** *a.* (-e) congenial.

'geesryk ['chēsRayk] *a.* spirituous, heady; witty.

ge'flikker [chə'fləkəR] *n.* flashing, glittering.

ge'fluister [chə'flœistəR] *n.* whispering.

ge'fluit [chə'flœit] *n.* whistling.

ge'foeter [chə'futəR] *n.* botheration.

ge'gaap [chə'chāp] *n.* yawning.

ge'gewe [chə'chēvə] *n.* (-ns) datum *pl.* data; *a.* given.

ge'giggel [chə'chəchəl] *n.* giggling.

ge'goed [chə'chut] *a.* (-e) well-off.

ge'gons [chə'chauñs] *n.* humming.

ge'gote [chə'chōtə] *a.* cast.

gegradu'eerde [chəchRadew'ēRdə] *n.* (-s) graduate.

ge'grond [chə'chRont] *a.* (-e) well-founded.

ge'haas [chə'hās] *n.* hurry.

ge'halte [chə'haltə] *n.* (-s) quality.

ge'hard [chə'haRt] *a.* (-e) tempered; hardened.

ge-hawend [chə'hāvənt] *a.* (-e) battered; in rags.

ge'heel [chə'hēl] *n.* (*ge'hele*) whole; *a.* complete, entire; *av.* all, completely.

ge'heg [chə'hech] *a.* (-te) devoted.

ge'heim [chə'haym] *n.* (-e) secret; mystery; *a.* (-e) secret; occult; **-enis** *n.* mystery; **-nisvol** *a.* (-le) mysterious; **-houding** *n.* secrecy; **'-sinnig** *a.* (-e; -er, -ste) dark, mysterious.

ge'hekel [chə'hēkəl] *n.* cavilling; **-de** *a.* crocheted.

ge'hemelte [chə'hēməltə] *n.* palate.

ge'heue [chə'hœə] *n.* memory; mind; **-nis** *n.* memory.

ge'hoor [chə'hōR] *n.* hearing; audience; **-pyp** *n.* ear-trumpet; stethoscope; **-saam** *a.* (-same; -samer, -ste) obedient.

ge'hoorsaal [chə'hōRsāl] *n.* (*ge'hoorsale*) auditorium.

ge'hoorstuk [chə'hōRstʌk] *n.* receiver.

ge'hude [chə'hewdə] *n.* (-s) married person.

ge'hug [chə'hʌch] *n.* (-te) hamlet.

ge'huigel [chə'hœichəl] *n.* hypocrisy; **-de** *a.* feigned.

ge'hunker [chə'hʌnkəR] *n.* craving, hankering.

ge'hyg [chə'haych] *n.* gasping.

geil ['chayl] *a.* fertile, rank; lewd, lustful.

ge'ïnkorporeerde [chə'ənkoRpōRēRdə] *a.* collegiate.

'geiser ['chaysəR] *n.* (-s) geyser.

'geitjie ['chayKi] *n.* (-s) lizard.

ge'juig [chə'jœich] *n.* cheering, exultation.

gek ['chek] *n.* (-ke) fool; lunatic; *a.* (-ke; -ker, -ste) foolish; mad; funny; *v.* (ge-) joke; **-heid** *n.* folly; **-kerny** *n.* tomfoolery; **-kigheid** *n.* folly; **-skeer** *v.* (-ge-) banter.

ge'kant [chə'kant] *av.* **-teen** set against.

ge'kerm [chə'keRəm] *n.* groaning.

'gekkerny ['chekəRnay] *n.* tomfoolery, pest.

ge'kleed [chə'klēt] *a.* (*ge'klede*) dressed; dressy.

ge'klets [chə'klets] *n.* tattle.

ge'kletter [chə'klietəR] *n.* clattering.

ge'kleur [chə'klœR] *a.* (-de) coloured; **-de** *n.* (-s) = **kleurling**.

'geklik ['cheklək] *a.* silly.

ge'klik [chə'klək] *n.* ticking.

ge'kneus [chə'knœs] *a.* (-de) bruised.

ge'knoei [chə'knui] *n.* bungling; scheming.

ge'konfyt [chə'kaumfayt] *a.* **-in** well-versed in, skilled.

ge'konkel [chə'konkəl] *n.* = **geknoei**.

ge'krenk [chə'kRenk] *a.* (-te) hurt, offended; deranged.

ge'kreun [chə'krœn] *n.* groaning.

ge'krui [chə'krœi] *a.* (-de) spiced, spicy.

ge'krul [chə'kRʌl] *a.* (-de) curly, wavy.

ge'kuip [chə'kœip] *a.* intriguing.

ge'kunsteld [chə'kʌñstelt] *a.* (-e) affected, artificial.

ge'kwalifiseerd [chəkwalifi'sēRt] *a.* (-e) qualified.

ge'laat [chə'lāt] *n.* (*ge'late*) face, countenance.

ge'lag [chə'lach] *n. die-betaal* pay the score; laughter; **-kamer** *n.* tap-room.

ge'lang [chə'lang] *n. na-van* in accordance with.

ge'las [chə'las] *v.* (-) charge, command, order; *a.* (-te) joined, welded; **-tigde** *n.* (-s) deputy, delegate.

ge'late [chə'lātə] *a.* resigned; **-nheid** *n.* resignation.

geld ['chelt] *n.* money; *v.* (ge-) apply, be in force, valid; **-elik** *a.* (-e) monetary; **-end** *a.* (-e) current; accepted; **-'gierig** *a.* (-e; -er, -ste) avaricious; **sig** *a.* (-e; -er, -ste) valid, binding, legal; **-igheid** *n.* validity; **-skieter** *n.* (-s) money-lender.

ge'lede [chə'lēdə] *a.* suffered, *cp.* ly; *av.* ago.

ge'leding [chə'lēdəng] *n.* articulation.

ge'leë [chə'lēə] *a. & av.* convenient; situated.

ge'leende [chə'lēndə] *a.* borrowed.

ge'leentheid [chə'lēntayt] *n.* (*ge-'leenthede*) occasion, opportunity.

ge'leerd [chə'lēRt] *a.* (-e) learned; trained; scholarly; **-e** *n.* (-s) scholar, savant; **-heid** *n.* erudition, learning.

ge'lei [chə'lay] *n.* jelly; *v.* (-) lead

conduct, accompany; **-de** n. (-s)
escort, guard; **-der** n. conductor;
-dend a. (-e) conductive; **-delik** a.
(-e; -er, -ste) gradual; **-ding** n.
conducting; conduction.
ge'letter [chə'letəR] a. (-de)
lettered, learned.
ge'lid [chə'lət] n. (ge'ledere) rank, file.
ge'liefde [chə'lifde] n. (-s) dearest.
ge'liefkoosde [chə'lifkōsdə] a.
favourite.
ge'liewe [chə'livə] v. -my te berig
please inform me.
'gelling ['chəlɪŋ] n. (-s) gallon.
ge'lofte [chə'loftə] n. (-s) vow.
Ge'loftedag [chə'loftədach] n. Day
of the Covenant (16 Dec.).
ge'loof [chə'lōf] n. (ge'lowe) belief,
faith; creed; v. = glo; **-baar** a.
(-bare) believable; **-lik** a. (-e) =
geloofbaar; **-shalwe** av. for the sake
of one's belief (religion).
ge'lowig ['chə'lōvəch] a. (-e; -er, -ste)
faithful, pious; **-e** n. (-s) believer;
-heid n. piety; cp. geloof.
ge'luid [chə'lœit] n. (-e) sound, noise.
ge'luk [chə'lʌk] n. (-ke) bliss; joy;
fortune, luck; success; v. (-) succeed;
-kig a. (-e; -er, -ste) happy, fortunate;
-kige n. (-s) fortunate person;
-'salig a. (-e) blessed; **-beentjie** n.
wish-bone; **-ekind** n. lucky dog;
-wens v. (-ge-) congratulate.
ge'lukbringer [chə'lʌkbrəngəR] n.
(-s) mascot.
ge'lyk [chə'layk] n. -hê be right; meer
-e as eie similarity is not identity; a.
(-e; -er, -ste) alike; even; flush, level;
av. equally; simultaneously; **-e** n.
(-s) equal, peer; **-end** a. (-e) like;
-enis n. likeness; parable; **-lik** av.
(-e) equally; **-maak** v. (-ge-) equalize;
level; **-making** n. equation; **-'matig**
a. (-e; -er, -ste) equable; gelyk-op av.
equally; deuce, draw, tie; **-stel** v.
(-ge-) put on a par, equate; **-'tydig**
a. & av. (-e) simultaneous.
ge'lykstroom [chə'laykström] n.
continuous, direct current (electr.).
gelyk'vloers [chəlayk'flūRs] a. on
the ground floor; dreary.
ge'maal [chə'māl] n. (ge'male)
consort, spouse; grinding; worry;
a. (de-) ground, minced.
ge'magtigde [chə'machtəchdə] n.
(-s) deputy, proxy.
ge'mak [chə'mak] n. comfort;
leisure; convenience; **-huis** n. convenience; **-lik** a. & av. (-e; -er, -ste)
easy, convenient.
ge'matigd [chə'mātəcht] a. (-e)
moderate.
ge'meen [chə'mēn] a. & av.
(ge'mene) common; joint; general;
-goed n. common property; **-heid** n.
meanness; **-lik** av. commonly;
-saam a. (-same) familiar, intimate;
-skap n. -pe) community, in -skap
van gœdere (married) in community
of property; **-te** n. (-s) congregation,
parish; **-telik** a. (-e) municipal.

ge'menebes [chə'mēnəbəs] n.
commonwealth.
ge'meng [chə'meng] a. (-de) mixed,
miscellaneous.
ge'middeld [chə'mədəlt] a. (-e)
average; **-e** n. (-s) average, mean.
ge'mis [chə'məs] n. lack, want.
'gemmer ['chəməR] n. ginger.
ge'moed [chə'mut] n. (-ere) mind,
heart.
ge'moedelik [chə'mudəlik] a. (-e)
genial, jovial.
ge'moei(d) [chə'mui(t)] mee- at stake.
ge'mors [chə'moRs] n. mess, filth.
ge'munt [chə'mʌnt] a. (-e) coined;
aimed at.
ge'mymer [chə'mayməR] n. meditation, reverie.
ge'naak [chə'nāk] v. (-) approach.
ge'naamd [chə'nāmt] a. (-e) called,
named.
ge'nade [chə'nādə] n. grace; mercy;
pardon; interj. gracious! ge'nadig a.
(-e, -er, -ste) gracious; merciful;
lenient; ge'nadigheid n. grace,
mercy, clemency.
ge'nant [chə'nant] n. (-e) namesake.
ge'neë [chə'nēə] av. disposed,
inclined.
ge'neentheid [chə'nēntayt] n. inclination; cp. geneë.
ge'neer [chə'nēR] v. (-) feel
embarrassed.
ge'nees [chə'nēs] v. (-) cure, heal,
restore; recover; **-al** n. panacea;
-baar a. (-bare; -der, -ste) curable;
-kunde n. medicine; **-lik** a. (-e)
curable.
ge'neig [chə'naych] a. disposed to;
prone to.
gene'raal [chənə'Rāl] n. (-s)
general.
gene'rasie [chənə'Rāsi] n. generation.
gene'rator [chənə'RātoR] n. (-s)
generator; gene'reer v. (ge-) bring
forth.
ge'neul [chə'nœl] n. nagging.
Ge'nêve [shə'nēf] n. Geneva.
geni'aal [shēni'āl] a. (geni'ale)
brilliant.
ge'nie [shə'ni] n. (-ë) genius.
ge'niepsig [chə'nipsəch] a. (-e)
bullying; underhand, sly; **-heid** n.
ge'niet [chə'nit] v. (-) enjoy; **-baar**
a. (-bare) enjoyable; **-ing** n. enjoyment.
geni'tief [chēnə'tif] n. genitive.
ge'noeë [chə'nuə] n. (-ns) delight,
pleasure.
ge'noeg [chə'nuch] n. a. & av.
enough, sufficient; satisfaction;
satisfaction; **-lik** a. (-e) agreeable,
pleasant; **-saam** a. (-same) sufficient.
ge'noemde [chə'numdə] a. called,
named.
genomi'neerde [chənōmə'nēRdə] n.
(-s) nominated (person), nominee.
ge'noot [chə'nōt] n. (ge'note)
associate, partner; **-skap** n. company.

ge'not [chə'not] n. (ge'nietinge) delight, joy, enjoyment; -sug n. hedonism = -sugleer n.

'genre ['shănRə] n. (-s) genre.

Gent ['chent] n. Ghent.

ge'nugtig [chə'nʌchtəch] interj. goeie-! good gracious!

geo'graaf [chĕŏ'chRăf] n. (geografwe) geographer; geogra'fie n. geography; geo'grafies a. (-e) geographic.

geolo'gie [chĕŏlŏ'chi] n. geology; geo'logies geological.

geome'trie [chĕŏmĕ'tri] n. geometry; geo'metries a. (-e) geometric.

ge'paard [chə'păRt] a. & av. (-e) coupled, paired.

ge'pantser [chə'pantsəR] a. (-de) armoured.

ge'pas [chə'pas] a. (-te) apt, suitable.

ge'pelde(rys) [chə'peldə] a. hulled.

ge'peupel [chə'pœpəl] n. populace, raffle.

ge'piep [chə'pip] n. squeak.

ge'pier [chə'piR] cheated.

ge'ploeter [chə'plutəR] n. plodding.

ge'pluisde(saad) [chə'plœisdə] a. ginned (seed).

ge'raak [chə'răk] a. (-te) huffed, nettled; vexed; -theid n. pique, irritability.

ge'raamte [chə'Rămtə] n. (-s) skeleton; framework.

ge'raas [chə'Răs] n. din, noise.

ge'rade [chə'Rădə] av. advisable.

ge'rammel [chə'Raməl] n. clanking, rattle.

ge'redelik [chə'Rĕdələk] a. & av. (-e) prompt(ly), ready(-ily).

ge'reed [chə'Rĕt] av. ready; finished; prepared; -heid n. readiness; -hou v. (-ge-) be prepared; -maak v. (-ge-) get ready; -skap n. tools.

ge'reëld [chə'Rĕlt] a. (-e) fixed, regular.

ge'reg [chə'Rech] n. justice; (-te) course, dish; -te a. just; -telik a. (-e) judicial, legal; -tig av. entitled; -tigheid n. justice.

ge'rek [chə'Rek] a. (-te) tedious, long-drawn.

gereser'veer [chəRəsəR'fĕR] a. (-de) reserved.

gerf ['cheRf] n. (gerwe) sheaf.

ge'rief [chə'Rif] n. (ge'riewe) convenience; v. (-) accommodate, oblige; -lik a. (-e) commodious.

ge'rig [chə'Rech] n. die jongste-Doomsday; - (rig-) a. (-te) beamed, directional, directive.

ge'ringskat [chə'Rəngskat] v. (-geskat) underestimate.

ge'ring [chə'Rəng] a. & av. (-e; -er, -ste) slight, small, scanty.

Ger'maan [cheR'măn] n. German; Teuton; -s a. (-e) Teutonic; Germa'nis n. (-te) Germanic scholar.

ge'rond [chə'Ront] a. (-e) rounded.

ge'rug [chə'Rʌch] n. (-te) report, rumour.

ge'ruime [chə'Rœimə] a. considerable.

ge'ruis [chə'Rœis] n. (-e) noise; -loos (-lose) a. noise free; -peil n. noise level; -vry a. noise free.

ge'ruit [chə'Rœit] a. (-e) chequered.

ge'rus [chə'Rʌs] a. (-te) calm, quiet; av. safely, undoubtedly; -stel v. (-ge-) soothe, relieve; -stellend a. (-e) reassuring; -theid n. calm, confidence.

ge'saaide [chə'săidə] n. (-s) crop.

ge'sag [chə'sach] n. authority, power, prestige; -hebbend a. (-e) authoritative, influential.

ge'salfde [chə'salfdə] n. (-s) anointed.

ge'samentlik [chə'săməntlək] a. (-e) complete, total; av. collectively.

ge'sang [chə'sang] n. (-e) singing; hymn; die-insit lead the singing (hymn); start crying (tronical).

ge'sanik [chə'sănək] n. tattle, incessant talking.

ge'sant [chə'sant] n. (-e) ambassador, envoy; -skap n. (-pe) embassy.

ge'seën [chə'sĕən] a. (-de) blessed.

ge'segde [chə'sechdə] n. (-s) expression; predicate.

ge'seglik [chə'sechlək] a. (-e) amenable, docile.

'gesel ['chĕsəl] n. (-s) cane, lash; v. (ge-) flog.

ge'sel [chə'sel] n. (le) companion, mate; -lig a. (-e; -er, -ste) convivial, cosy; -ligheid n. cosiness, snugness; social meeting.

ge'sels [chə'sels] v. (-) chat, confabulate, converse; -erig a. (-e) talkative; -ery n. chatting; -kap n. conversation, company.

ge'set [chə'set] a. (-te) corpulent, stout; -te a. fixed, appointed; ge'sete a. seated; substantial.

ge'sien [chə'sin] a. (-e) esteemed, respected.

ge'sig [chə'sech] n. (-te) sight; face; view; vision; -gie n. dim. little face; pansy; -seinder n. horizon.

ge'sin [chə'sən] n. (-ne) family, household.

ge'sind [chə'sənt] a. (-e) disposed, inclined; -heid n.; -te n. denomination.

ge'sis [chə'səs] n. hissing.

ge'skape [chə'skăpə] a. created.

ge'skater [chə'skătəR] n. peals of laughter.

ge'skenk [chə'skenk] n. (-e) gift.

ge'skep [chə'skep] a. (-te) -te papier mould-made paper.

ge'skied [chə'skit] v. (-) happen, come to pass; -enis n. (-se) history; story; -'kundig a. (-e) historical; -'kundige n. (-s) historian.

ge'skik [chə'skək] a. (-te) able, appropriate, suitable, eligible; -theid n. ability; suitability.

ge'skil [chə'skəl] n. (-le) difference, dispute.

ge'skrif [chə'skRəf] n. (-te) document.

ge'skut [chə'skʌt] n. artillery.

ge'slaag [chə'slãch] a. (-de) successful.

ge'slag [chə'slach] n. (-te) generation; lineage; sex; a. (-te) slaughtered; **-loos** a. (-lose) sexless; **-telik** a. (-e) sexual.

ge'slepe [chə'slepə] a. (-ner, -nste) cunning; **-nheid** n.

ge'slote [chə'slótə] a. closed; locked; reticent; sealed.

ge'smelt(e) [che'smelt(ə)] a. **-sekering** blown fuse.

ge'sog [chə'soch] a. (-te) in demand.

ge'sond [chə'sont] a. (-e; -er, -ste) healthy, sound, sane; **-e** n. (-s) healthy person; **-heid** n.

ge'sout [chə'soat] a. (-e) salted; cured; immunized.

'gespe(r) ['chespə(R)] n. (-s) clasp, buckle; v. (ge-) strap on, clasp.

ge'spier [chə'spiR] a. (-de) muscular.

ge'spikkeld [chə'spəkəlt] a. (-e) speckled.

ge'sprek [chə'spRek] n. (-ke) conversation.

ge'spuis [chə'spœis] n. rabble, scum.

ge'stadig [chə'stãdəch] av. (-e) continually, gradually.

ge'stalte [chə'staltə] n. (-s) build, figure, stature; **-nis** n. figure, shape.

ge'stand [chə'stant] av. sy belofte-doen keep one's word.

ge'steente [chə'stēntə] n. (-s) (precious) stones; formation.

ge'stel [chə'stel] n. constitution, system; conj. suppose, supposing; **-dheid** n. condition.

ge'steurd [chə'stȇRt] a. (-e) piqued, annoyed.

ge'stig [chə'stəch] n. (-te) institution; asylum; **-te** a. established.

ge'streep [chə'stRēp] a. (-te) striate.

ge'swel [chə'swel] n. (-le) growth, swelling, tumour.

ge'swets [chə'swets] n. blasphemy.

ge'swind [chə'swənt] a. (-e) quick, rapid.

ge'swoeg [chə'swuch] n. drudgery.

ge'swore [chə'swõRə] a. sworn; cp. sweer.

ge'tal [chə'tal] n. (-le) number; **-sterkte** n. numerical strength.

ge'tier [chə'tiR] n. clamour, noise.

ge'tik [chə'tək] a. dotty, balmy.

ge'tob [chə'top] n. drudgery, worry.

ge'torring [chə'toRəng] n. nagging, teasing.

ge'trappe n. [chə'tRapəl] n. stamping, trampling.

ge'trou [chə'troa] a. (-e; -er, -ste) faithful, devoted.

ge'troud [chə'troat] a. (-e) married.

ge'trouheidswaarborg [chə'tRoahaytsvãRboRch] n. fidelity guarantee.

ge'tuie [chə'tœiə] n. (-s) witness; v. (-getuig) testify; **-nis** n. testimony.

ge'twis [chə'twʌs] n. quarrelling.

ge'ty [chə'tay] n. (-e) tide.

geul ['chœl] n. (-e) gully.

geur ['chȇR] n. (-e) flavour, scent, fragrance, aroma; **-ig** a. (-e; -er, -ste) fragrant; **-igheid** n. fragrance, perfume; **-tjie** dim. daar is 'n-aan there is something fishy going on.

geut ['chȇt] n. (-e) gutter; drain, duct; **-werk** n. channelling, trenching.

ge'vaar [chə'fãR] n. (ge'vare) danger, peril, risk; **-lik** a. (-e; -er, -ste) dangerous, perilous, hazardous; **-te** n. (-s) colossus, monster; **-vol** a. (-le) = **gevaarlik**.

ge'val [chə'fal] n. (-le) case, event; matter; v. (-) please, suit; **-lig** a. (-e) agreeable.

ge'vange [chə'fangə] a. captive, imprisoned; **-ne** n. (-s) prisoner, captive; **-nis** n. (-se) prison; **ge'vanklik** a. captive.

ge'vat [chə'fat] a. (-te) clever, witty; **-heid** n. shrewdness.

ge'veg [chə'fech] n. (-te) action, battle.

ge'veins [chə'fayns] a. (-de) false, feigned; **-de** n. (-s) hypocrite, dissembler; **-dheid** n. hypocrisy.

ge'vestig [chə'festəch] a. (-de) fixed, established.

ge'vierd [chə'fiRt] a. (-e) popular, famous.

ge'vleueld [chə'flœlt] a. (-e) winged.

ge'voeglik [chə'fuchlək] a. (-e) fit, proper; suitable; av. appropriately.

ge'voel [chə'ful] n. (-ens) feeling, emotion; sentiment; **-ig** a. (-e; -er, -ste) sensitive; **-igheid** n. sensitiveness; **-loos** a. (-lose) apathetic; numb; callous; **-vol** a. (-le) tender.

ge'volg [chə'folch] n. (-e) consequence; retinue; **-lik** av. accordingly.

ge'volmagtigde [chə'folmachtəchdə] n. (-s) plenipotentiary; proxy.

ge'vreet [chə'fRēt] n. face, mug (slang).

ge'waad [chə'vãd] n. (ge'wade) dress, raiment.

ge'waarword [chə'vãRvort] v. (-ge-) experience; **-ing** n. (-e, -s) experience, perception, aura.

ge'walste [chə'vals(tə)] a. rolled.

ge'was [chə'vas] n. (-se) growth; crop; plant.

ge'weer [chə'vēR] n. (-s, gewere) fire-arm, rifle.

'gewel ['chēvəl] n. (-s) facade, gable.

ge'weld [chə'velt] n. force, violence; **gewel'dadig** a. (-e) violent; **-enaar** n. (-s) tyrant; **-ig** a. (-e; -er, -ste) enormous, powerful, violent, av. violently.

ge'welf [chə'velf] n. (ge'welwe) arch, dome, vault.

ge'wente = **gewoonte**.

ge'wes [chə'ves] n. (-te) province, region; **-telik** a. (-e) provincial, regional; dialectal.

ge'wete [chə'vētə] n. (-ns) conscience;

-nloos a. (ge'wetenlose) unscrupulous; **-nsregter** n. casuist.

ge'wettig [chə'vetəch] a. (-de) justified, legitimate.

ge'wig [chə'vəch] n. (-te) weight, importance; **-stoot** n. (-ge-) putting (the shot); **-tig** a. (-e; -er, -ste) important.

ge'wiks [chə'vəks] a. (-te) sharp, smart, quick.

ge'wild [chə'vəlt] a. (-e; -er, -ste) popular; **-heid** n.

ge'willig [chə'vələch] a. (-e; -er, -ste) willing, docile; **-heid** n. willingness.

ge'wis [chə'vəs] a. (-se) certain, sure; av. certainly; **-heid** n. certainty.

ge'woel [chə'vul] n. bustle, throng.

ge'woon [chə'vôn] a. & av. (ge'wone) accustomed, common, usual; **-d** a. accustomed; **-lik** av. usually; **-te** n. custom, habit; **-weg** av. downright, simply.

ge'wrig [chə'vRəch] n. (-te) joint; wrist; **-sontsteking** n. arthritis.

ge'wrog [chə'vRoch] n. (-te) creation, production.

ge'wyd [chə'vayt] a. (-e) consecrated, sacred.

ge'yk [chə'ayk] a. (-te) assessed; stereotyped.

ghries ['gRis] n. grease; **-dop** n. (-pe) grease cup; **-prop** n. grease plug; **-spuit** n. grease gun.

ghrop ['gRop] n. cultivator; v. (ge-) cultivate.

ghwar ['gwaR] n. lout.

gids ['chəts] n. (-e) guide; directory.

gier ['chiR] n. (-e) caprice, fancy, fad; v. (ge-) scream; **-ig** a. (-e; -er, -ste) avaricious; **-igaard** n. (-s) miser; **-igheid** n. avarice.

giet ['chit] v. (ge-) pour; cast; **-er** n. (-s) watering can; **-sel** n. (-s) casting; **-lepel** n. casting ladle; **-staal** n. cast steel; **-stuk** n. casting; **-werk** n. casting; **-yster** n. cast iron.

gif ['chəf] n. gift, donation; poison; **-tig** a. (-e; -er, -ste) poisonous.

'giggel ['chəchəl] v. (ge-) giggle.

gil ['chəl] n. (-le) yell, scream; v. (ge-) yell.

'gilde ['chəldə] n. (-s) guild.

gim'nas [chəm'nas] n. (-te) gymnast; **-i'aal** a. (gimnasi'ale) of a gymnasium; **gim'nasium** n. (-s) gymnasium; **gimnas'tiek** n. gymnastics.

ginds ['chəns] av. yonder.

ginekolo'gie [chinēkŏlŏ'chi] n. gynaecology.

'ginnegap ['chənəchap] v. (ge-) giggle, titter, play the fool.

gips ['chəps] n. gypsum; gebrandeplaster of Paris; **-skêr** n. plaster shears; **-spalk** n. plaster of Paris splint; **-verband** n. plaster of Paris bandage.

gis ['chəs] n. yeast; v. (ge-) guess; **-sing** n. (-e, -s) conjecture; **-ting** n. fermentation; excitement; gissing en vergissing trial and error.

'gister ['chəstəR] n. yesterday.

git ['chət] n. jet.

gits ['chəts] interj. gosh! cp. **gats.**

glad ['chlat] a. (-de) smooth; av. altogether, quite; **-digheid** n. smoothness; cuteness; **-weg** av. flatly.

glans ['chlâns] n. gloss, lustre, splendour; v. (ge-) gleam, glisten; **-end** a. (-e) gleaming, glossy; **-erig** a. (-e) glossy; **-loos** a. (-lose) lustreless, dull; **-ryk** a. (-e) brilliant, glorious.

glas ['chlas] n. (-e) glass; tumbler; **-agtig** a. (-e) glassy, glass-like; **-erig** a. (-e) glassy, glazed; **gla'suur** n. enamel; glaze; v. (ge-) glazed.

'gletser ['chletsəR] n. (-s) glacier.

gleuf ['chlœf] n. (gleuwe) groove, slit.

'glibberig ['chləbəRəch] a. (-e) slippery, slimy.

glieps ['chlips] n. (-e) mistake, slip.

glim ['chləm] v. (ge-) gleam.

'glimlag ['chləmlach] n. smile; v. (ge-) smile; **-gie** dim. grin.

glimp ['chləmp] n. glimpse.

'glimstrook ['chləmstRôk] n. ('glimstroke) luminous strip.

'glimwurm ['chləmvʌRəm] n. (-s) glowworm.

'glinster ['chlənstəR] v. (ge-) glitter; **-ing** n. glittering, sparkle.

glip ['chləp] v. (ge-) slip, slide; **-pe** pl. slips (cricket); **-perig** a. (-e; -er, -ste) slippery; **-s** n. = **glieps.**

glise'rien ['chləsə'Rin] n. glycerine.

glo ['chlô] av. evidently; seemingly; v. (ge-) believe.

gloed ['chlut] n. glow, blaze; ardour; **-vol** a. (-le) glowing.

gloei ['chlui] v. (ge-) glow, incandesce; cp. **gloed**; **-end** a. (-e) glowing; a. burning; **-draad** n. filament; **-lamp** n. (-e) bulb.

glooi ['chlôi] v. (ge-) slope; **-end** a. (-e) sloping; **-ing** n. slope.

'glorie ['chlôRi] n. glory; hy is in syutterly satisfied.

gluur ['chlêwR] v. (ge-) peep; pry; leer.

g'n = **geen.**

gô ['chau] n. sy-is uit; he is played out; cp. **blus.**

God ['chot] n. God; **-dank** interj. thank God!

god ['chot] n. (gode) idol, god; **-delik** a. (-e) divine; **-deloos** a. (godelose) wicked; **-deloos** av. shamelessly; **-geleerde** n. (-s) theologian; **-geleerdheid** n. theology; **-heid** n. deity; **-jie** [choiKi] dim.; **-sdiens** n. religion; **-s'dienstig** a. (-e) pious.

goed ['chut] n. good, **-en** kwaad good and evil; n. (-ere) goods, assets; things; a. (goeie) good, good-natured; kind; well; av. well, correctly, rightly; **-aardig** a. (-e; -er, -ste) good-natured; **-dunke** n. na- at will; **-geefs** a. generous; **-gesind** a. (-e) favourable; **-ig** a. (-e) good-natured; **-heid** n. goodness; **-hou** v.

(-ge-) keep; control (*yourself*); **-jies** *dim.* ['chuiKis] trifles; **-keur** *v.* (-ge-) approve; pass; **-keurend** *a.* (-e) approving; **-keuring** *n.* approval; **-koop** *a.* cheap; **-maak** *v.* (-ge-) make good, make up for; **-praat** *v.* (-ge-) explain away; **-smoeds** *av.* deliberately; **-vind** *v.* (-ge-) approve of; **-'willig** *a. & av.* (-e) willing(ly).

goed'gunstig [chut'chʌn̄stəch] *av.* kindly.

'goedskiks ['chutskəks] *av.* willingly, gracefully.

'goeie ['chuyə] *a.* good; **-naand** good evening! **-dag** good day!

'goël ['chɵəl] *v.* (ge-) conjure, juggle; **-aar** *n.* (-s) conjurer, juggler, magician; **-ry** *n.* conjuring; magic.

'goeters ['chutəRs] *n. pl.* things, *cp.* **goed** (-ere).

goewer'ment [chuvəR'ment] *n.* (-e) government.

goewer'neur [chuvəR'nɵəR] *n.* (-s) governor.

'gogga ['chocha] *n.* (-s) insect, vermin; bogey.

golf ['cholf] *n.* (golwe) billow, wave; bay, gulf; **-band** *n.* wave band; **-lengte** *n.* (-s) wave length; golfundulatory.

'golwend ['cholvənt] *a.* (-e) waving, rolling; **'golwing** *n.* undulation.

gom ['chom] *n.* (-s) gum; glue; *v.* (ge-) gum, glue.

gomlas'tiek [chomlas'tik] *n.* rubber.

gonna ['chona] *interj.* oh my!

gons ['chauns] *v.* (ge-) buzz, drone, hum.

gooi ['chɵi] *v.* (ge-) throw, cast, fling, pitch; **-gaffel** *n.* pitchfork.

goor ['chɵR] *a.* (gore) rancid; dingy; **-maag** *n.* bilious attack.

gord ['choRt] *n.* (-e) belt, girdle; *v.* (ge-) gird.

'gordel ['choRdəl] *n.* (-s) belt, circle, girdle.

gor'dyn [chəR'dayn] *n.* (-e) curtain, blind.

'gorrel ['choRəl] *n.* (-s) gullet, throat; *v.* (ge-) gargle.

gort ['choRt] *n.* groats; *die gort is gaar* the fat is in the fire; **-water** *n.* barleywater.

gou ['choa] *a. & av.* quick(ly), rapid(ly), swift(ly); **gou-gou** *av.* quickly; **-igheid** *n.* dexterity; haste.

goud ['cheat] *n.* gold.

'goudief ['choadif] *n.* pickpocket.

'goue ['choaə] *a.* golden, gold.

'gouekelk ['choa-əkelk] *n.* (plant) cup of gold.

'gousblom ['choasblom] *n.* (-me) calendula.

graad ['chRāt] *n.* (grade) degree; grade; stage; **-boog** *n.* protractor.

graaf ['chRāf] *n.* (grawe) earl; spade; *v.* (ge-) dig; **-lik** *a.* (-e) of (like) an earl (count); **-skap** *n.* county, countship, earldom; **-werk** *n.* digging.

graag ['chRāch] *av.* gladly, readily, **-te** *n.* eagerness.

graan ['chRān] *n.* (grane) grain, corn; cereals; **-etend** *a.* (-e) granivorous; **-suier** *n.* (-s) grain-elevator.

graat ['chRāt] *n.* (grate) fishbone; **-jie** *dim.* ('chraiKi) meercat; thin child.

'grabbel ['chrabəl] *v.* (ge-) *iets te -gooi* something to scramble for.

gra'deer [chRa'dēR] *v.* (ge-) grade; **gra'dering** *n.* grading, graduation; **gradu'eel** *a.* (gradu'ele) gradual; **gradu'eer** *v.* (ge-) graduate.

graf ['chRaf] *n.* (-te, -tes) grave.

gra'fiek [chRa'fik] *n.* (-e) graph; **grafies** *a.* (-e) graphic.

'grafskrif ['chRafskRəf] *n.* epitaph.

grama'doelas [chRama'dulas] *n. pl.* rough country, outposts, backveld.

gram'matika [chRa'mātika] *n.* grammar; **gram'maties** *a.* (-e) grammatical; **grammati'kaal** *a.* (grammati-kale) grammatical; **gram'matikus** *n.* (-se) grammarian.

grammo'foon [chRamə'fōn] *n.* (grammo'fone) gramophone.

'gramskap ['chRamskap] *n.* anger, wrath.

gra'niet [chRa'nit] *n.* granite.

grap ['chRap] *n.* (-pe) fun, jest, joke; **-maker** *n.* (-s) joker, jester, buffoon; **-perig** *a.* (-e) amusing, comic; **-perigheid** *n.* fun, drollery.

gras ['chRas] *n.* grass; **-agtig** *a.* (-e) grassy; grass-like; **-duin** *v.* (ge-) browse; **-etend** *a.* (-e) herbivorous.

'grasie ['chRāsi] *n.* favour, grace, pardon.

grasi'eus [chRasi'ɵ̄s] *a.* (-e) elegant, graceful.

gratifi'kasie [chRatifi'kāsi] *n.* gratuity.

'gratis ['chRātəs] *a. & av.* free, gratis.

gra'veer [chRa'fēR] *v.* (ge-) engrave; **-der** *n.* (-s) engraver; **gra'vure** *n.* (-s) engraving, print.

gra'weel [chRa'vēl] *n.* (medical) calculus, stone.

greep ['chRēp] *n.* (grepe) clutch, grip; hilt.

grein ['chRayn] *n.* grain; **-hout** *n.* deal, white pine; **-tjie** *dim.* scrap, shred, morsel.

grena'della [chRənə'dela] *n.* granadilla, passion-fruit.

grena'dier [chRəna'dIR] *n.* (-s) grenadier.

'grendel ['chRendəl] *n.* (-s) bolt; *v.* (ge-) bolt.

grens ['chRɛns] *n.* (-e) boundary, frontier; limit; *v.* (ge-) adjoin; cry; **-loos** *a.* (-lose) boundless; **-geval** *n.* borderline case; **-hou** *n.* boundary (cricket).

'grensbalie ['chRɛnsbāli] *n.* (-s) crybaby.

'greppel ['chRepəl] *n.* (-s) furrow, trench.

'gretig ['chRĕtəch] a. (-e; -er, -ste) eager, greedy; -heid n.

grief ['chRif] n. (griewe) grievance; wrong; v. (ge-) grieve, hurt; 'griewend a. (-e) mortifying.

Griek ['chRik] n. (-e) Greek; -s a. (-e) Greek; -eland n. Greece.

'Griekwa ['chRikwa] n. (-s) Griqua.

griep ['chRip] n. influenza.

griesel ['chRisəl] v. (ge-) shudder; -ig a. (-e; -er, -ste) creepy, gruesome; -tjie dim. morsel.

Griet ['chrit] interj. grote-! great Scott!

'griewend cp. grief.

grif ['chRəf] av. promptly, readily; v. (ge-) impress, engrave; -fel n. (-s) slate-pencil; gri'fier n. (-s) clerk of the court, registrar; -weg av. = grif.

gril ['chRəl] n. (-le) whim; shudder; v. (ge-) shiver, shudder; -lerig a. (-e; -er, -ste) creepy; -lig a. (-e; -er, -ste) capricious, fantastic.

gri'mas ['chRə'mas] n. (-se) grimace.

gri'meer [chRi'mēR] v. (ge-) make up.

'grimlag ['chRəmlach] n. grin.

'grimmig ['chRəməch] a. (-e; -er, -ste) angry; grim; -heid n. anger, fury.

'grinnik ['chRənək] v. (ge-) grin, chuckle.

grint ['chRənt] n. gravel, grit.

grip ['chRəp] n. (-pe) ditch, groove.

groef ['chRuf] n. (groewe) groove, furrow, wrinkle; cp. groewe; v. (ge-) chase; ditch; groove.

groei ['chRui] v. (ge-) grow, increase; -saam a. (-same) favourable to growth.

groen ['chRun] n. green; greenery; a. green; verdant; immature; -agtig a. (-e) greenish; -e n. (-s) freshman; -erig a. (-e) greenish; -igheid n. greenness; green grass; greens; -te n. (-s) vegetables; -tjies dim. -; groene; -tyd n. freshmanship; -voer n. fresh green fodder.

groep ['chRup] n. (-e) group, cluster; -'eer v. (ge-) group, classify; groe'pering n. grouping, classification; -sgewyse av. in batches.

'groet ['chRut] n. (-e) greeting, salute; salutation; sê-e aan give my regards to; met vriendelike-e with kind regards; v. (ge-) greet, salute, shake hands, take leave; -e, -nis n. regards, greetings.

'groewe ['chRuvə] n. pit, quarry.

grof ['chRof] a. (growwe) rough, coarse, gross, bad; -geskut n. heavy artillery; -heid n. coarseness, rudeness; roughness; -smid n. blacksmith.

grond ['chRont] n. (-e) ground, earth, soil, land; bottom, foundation; reason; fundamentals; v. (ge-) base, found; -beginsel n. (-s) rudiment; -betekenis n. original meaning; -boontjie n. pea-nut; -e n. te-

gaan go to rack and ruin; -eloos a. (grondelose) bottomless; -erig a. (-e) earthy, muddy; -ig a. (-e; -er, -ste) thorough, profound; -kleur n. basic colour; -laag n. primary coat (paint), primary layer; -lêer n. (-s) founder; -legging n. foundation; -plan n. fundamental plan; -reël n. (-s) fundamental rule; -slag n. (-slae) basis, foundation; -stof n. raw material; -toon n. keynote; -verf n. primer; -ves v. (ge-) found, lay foundation of; -wet n. constitution; -'wettig a. (-e) constitutional.

groot ['chRōt] a. (grote; groter; -ste) great, large, vast; grown-up; grand; -bek n. braggart; -boek n. ledger; -doenery n. swagger; -handel n. wholesale; -'hartig a. (-e) generous; -heid n. greatness, largeness; magnitude, quantity; -hou v. (-ge-) keep stiff upper lip; -jie dim. ['chroiKi] great grandfather (mother); -liks av. greatly, largely; -maak v. (-ge-) rear, raise; -mens n. (-e) adult; -moedig a. (-e; -er, -ste) generous; -ouers n. grandparents; -pad n. highway; -praat v. (-ge-) brag; -s a. & av. (-e) grand, ambitious; -skeeps a. & av. (-e) grand, princely, royal; -te n. (-s), size; -vuur n. hell; -woord n. blasphemy.

'grootharsings ['chRōthaRsəngs] n. pl. cerebrum.

'grootheidswaan ['chRōthaytsvān] n. megalomania.

'grootvader ['chRōtfādəR] n. grandfather.

'grootwild ['chRōtvəit] n. big game.

gros ['chRos] n. (-se) gross; mass; average.

grot ['chRot] n. (-te) grotto, cave.

grotendeels ['chRōtəndēls] av. largely, chiefly.

grou ['chRoa] a. gray, grey; v. (ge-) growl, snarl.

'growwekam ['chRovəkam] n. (-me) rake, comb.

'growwerig ['chRovərəch] a. (-e; -er, -ste) rather coarse.

gruis ['chRœis] n. grit, gravel.

'grusaam ['chRewsām] a. ('grusame) gruesome; -heid n.

'gruwel ['chRewvəl] n. (-s) atrocity, crime; -daad n. atrocity; -ik a. (-e; -er, -ste) atrocious, horrible; naughty; -ikheid n. atrocity; naughtiness.

gryns ['chRayns] v. (ge-) sneer; -lag n. sardonic smile, sneer.

gryp ['chRayp] v. (ge-) catch, clutch, grab, grip.

'grys ['chRays] a. (-e; -er, -ste) grey, hoary; -aard n. (-s) grey-haired man; -erig a. (-e) greyish; -heid n. greyness.

'gul ['chʌl] a. (-le; -ler, -ste) cordial, genial, generous.

gul'hartig [chʌl'haRtəch] a. (-e) cordial, liberal.

'gulp ['chʌlp] n. (-e) slit; fly; v. (ge-) gush, spout.

'**gulsig** ['chʌlsech] *a.* (*-e*; *-er*, *-ste*) greedy; **-aard** *n.* (*-s*) glutton; **-heid** *n.* gluttony.

'**gulweg** ['chʌlvəch] *av.* frankly, genially.

'**gummie** ['chʌmi] *n.* rubber.

gun ['chʌn] *v.* (*ge-*) allow, grant; not to envy; **-s** *n.* (*-te*) favour; patronage; **-sbewys** *n.* (*-e*) favour; **-steling** *n.* (*-e*) favourite; **-stig** *a.* (*-e*; *-er*, *-ste*) favourable, advantageous.

'**gunter** ['chʌntəR] *av.* yonder.

guts ['chʌts] *v.* (*ge-*) gush, spout, *cp.* gulp *v.*

'**guttural** ['chʌtə'Rāl] *n.* *&* *a.* ('*gutturale*) guttural.

guur ['chēwR] *a.* (*gure*) bleak, raw, inclement; **-heid** *n.*

'**gyselaar** ['chaysəlāR] *n.* (*-s*) hostage; '**gyseling** *n.* imprisonment for debt.

H

haag ['hāch] *n.* (*hae*, *hage*) hedge.

'**haai** ['hāi] *n.* (*-e*) shark; **-!** *interj.* heigh! I say! **-vlakte** *n.* desolate plain.

haak ['hāk] *n.* (*hake*) hook, clasp; square; bracket; peg; crook; clamp; *uit die-* out of square; *v.* (*ge-*) hook; crotchet; **-plek** *n.* difficulty, hitch, obstruction; **-s** *av.* (*-e*) square; *-met mekaar* be at loggerheads; **-speld** *n.* safety-pin; **hakie** *n. dim. hakies en ogies* hooks and eyes; *tussen hakies* in brackets.

haal ['hāl] *v.* (*ge-*) fetch, go for, catch; recover.

haan ['hān] *n.* (*hane*) cock, rooster; hammer (*gun*); *hy is 'n ou-* he is a topper; **-tjie** *dim.* cockerel; quarrelsome fellow.

haar ['hāR] *n.* (*hare*) hair; *a.* right, *hot en-* right and left; *pron.* her; (*poss.*) her; **haar-af** *a.* the hair is coming out; **-fyn** *av.* in detail, subtle; **-kant** *n.* right side; **-laat** *v.* (*-ge-*) get into a scrape; **-loos** *a.* (*-lose*) hairless; **-kruller** *n.* haircurler; **-middel** *n.* hair lotion; **-naald** *n.* hair-pin; **-spoelmiddel** *n.* hair rinse; **-snyer** *n.* hairdresser; **-sproeier** *n.* hair spray; **-was** (*middel*) *n.* shampoo; **-waspoeier** *n.* shampoo.

haard ['hāRt] *n.* (*-e*) fireplace; source (*infection*).

'**haarklowery** ['hāRklōvəRay] *n.* hair-splitting, chicanery.

'**haarknipper** ['hāRknəpəR] *n.* (*-s*) hair-clippers.

'**haarom** ['hāRom] *av.* clockwise.

haas ['hās] *n.* (*hase*) hare; hurry, haste, speed; *av.* almost, nearly; *v.* (*ge-*) make haste, hurry; **-bek** *n.* having a tooth missing; **-tig** *a.* (*-e*; *-er*, *-ste*) hasty, hurried.

'**haaslip** ['hāsləp] *n.* hare-lip.

haat ['hāt] *n.* hatred; *v.* (*ge-*) hate, detest; **-draend** *a.* (*-e*) revengeful,

vindictive; **-lik** *a.* (*-e*) detestable, hateful.

hael ['hāl] *n.* hail; shot; *v.* (*ge-*) hail.

'**haglik** ['hachlək] *a.* (*-e*; *-er*, *-ste*) critical, precarious.

'**haikona** ['haikauna] *av.* no, never.

hak ['hak] *n.* (*-ke*) heel; *v.* (*ge-*) chop, cut; **-kel** *v.* (*ge-*) stammer; **-kelaar** *n.* stammerer; **-kerig** *a.* (*-e*) inclined to hitch.

'**hakskeen** ['hakskēn] *n.* ('*hakskene*) heel.

half ['half] *n.*, *a.* *&* *av.* (*halwe*) half, semi; **-'aam** *n.* half-aum; **-'naatjie** *n.* (*-s*) half-caste; **-was** *a.* (*-se*) half grown; **-eer** [hal'fēR] *v.* (*ge-*) bisect; **-kleurdiepte** *n.* half tone.

'**halfrond** ['halfRont] *n.* (*-e*) hemisphere.

'**halfslyt** ['halfslayt] *a.* second-hand.

'**hallo** ['halō] *interj.* hullo!

halm ['haləm] *n.* (*-e.* *-s*) blade, stalk.

hals ['hals] *n.* (*-e*) neck; **-aar** *n.* jugular vein; **-band** *n.* collar, neckband; **-oorkop** *av.* head over heels; **-'starrig** *a.* (*-e*; *-er*, *-ste*) stubborn, headstrong.

hait ['halt] *interj.* stop! **-e** *n.* (*-s*) halt; **-er** *n.* (*-s*) halter.

ham ['ham] *n.* (*-me*) ham.

'**hamel** ['hāməl] *n.* (*-s*) wether.

'**hamer** ['hāməR] *n.* (*-s*) hammer; mallet; *v.* (*ge-*) hammer; **-baar** *a.* (*-bare*) malleable.

hand ['hant] *n.* (*-e*) hand; **-gee** *v.* (*-ge-*) shake hands; *-e tuis!* (*command*) hands off! **-byltjie** *n. dim.* hatchet; **-doek** *n.* (*-e*) towel; **-druk** *n.* (*-ke*) hand-shake; **-gemeen -gemeen raak** come to blows; **-haaf** *v.* (*ge-*) maintain; **-hawing** *n.* maintenance; **-ig** *a.* (*-e*; *-er*, *-ste*) handy, deft; **-langer** *n.* (*-s*) handyman, helper; **-leiding** *n.* (*-s*) handbook, guide; **-skoen** *n.* (*-e*) glove; **-skrif** *n.* handwriting; **-'tastelik** *v. -word* manhandle; **-'tastelikheid** *n.* assault, violence; **-tekening** *n.* signature; **-vatsel** *n.* (*-s*) handle; **-ves** *n.* (*-te*) charter; **-vol** *av.* handful.

'**hand-** ['hant-] *pref.* hand-, manual.

hande-'viervoet [hanə'fiRfut] *av.* on all fours.

'**handel** ['handəl] *n.* commerce; business; trade; *v.* (*ge-*) act; deal, trade; **-aar** *n.* (*-s*) dealer, trader; **-baar** *a.* (*-bare*) docile; **-drywende** *a.* (*-e*) commercial, trading; **-end** *av.* (*-e*) *-optree* take action; **-ing** *n.* (*-e*, *-s*) action, act; **-wyse** *n.* procedure, proceeding.

'**handroom** ['hantRōm] *n.* hand cream.

'**handrug** ['hantRʌch] *n.* backhand.

'**handskrifkunde** ['hantskRəfkʌndə] *n.* graphology.

'**hanebalk** ['hānəbalk] *n.* (*-e*) roofbeam, rafter.

'**hanepoot** ['hānəpōt] *n.* muscat grapes.

'**hanerig** ['hānəRəch] *a.* cocky.

'hanetreetjie ['hänətRёKi] n. short distance.

hang ['hang] n. (-e) slope; v. (ge-) hang, droop; be suspended; -brug n. suspension bridge; -end av. pending; -kas n. (-te) wardrobe; -mat n. (-te) hammock; -slot n. padlock.

'hangertjie ['hangəRKi] n. (-s) pendant.

hans ['häns] a. orphan; -grootmaak feed out of hand; -kalf n. hand-fed calf; -lam n. hand-fed lamb; -wors n. buffoon.

han'teer [han'tёR] v. (ge-) handle, manipulate; han'tering n.

hap ['hap] n. (-pe) bite; bit, morsel; v. (ge-) bite, snap; -pie dim. tit-bit.

'haper ['häpəR] v. (ge-) not function properly; -ing n. impediment, hitch.

hard ['haRt] a. & av. (-e; -er, -ste) hard, loud, glaring; stern; unkind; v. (ge-) harden, temper; -epad n. hard labour, convict-labour; -er n. (-s) Cape herring; -'handig a. (-e) harsh, rude, violent; -heid n. hardness, sternness; -'horend a. (-e) dull of hearing; -'koppig a. (-e; -er, -ste) obstinate; -loop v. (ge-) run; -'lywig a. (-e) constipated; -'nekkig a. & av. (-e) obstinate, dogged; -op av. aloud; -'vogtig a. (-e; -er, -ste) callous; -werkend a. (-e) industrious.

'harder ['haRdəR] n. (-s) herring.

'harig ['häRəch] a. hairy, hirsute.

'haring ['häRəng] n. (-s) herring.

hark ['haRk] n. (-e) rake; v. (ge-) rake.

harle'kyn [haRlə'kayn] n. (-e) buffoon.

harmo'nie [haRmō'ni] n. harmony; harmoni'eer v. (ge-) harmonize; har'monies a. (-e) harmonious.

'harnas ['haRnas] n. (-se) armour; iemand in die-jaag antagonize a person; v. (ge-) arm oneself against.

har'puis [haR'pœis] n. resin.

hars = harpuis.

'harsings ['harsəngs] n. pl. brain; intellect; 'harsing-skudding ['haRsəng'skʌdəng] n. concussion of the brain.

'harslag ['haRslach] n. (-te) pluck.

harspan ['haRspan] n. cranium.

hart ['haRt] n. (-e) heart; courage; core; mind; body; -eloos a. ('harte-lose) heartless; -elus n. na- to one's heart's content; -ens n. hearts (cards); -'grondig a. (-e) profound; -jie dim. darling; -lam n. = hartjie; -lik a. (-e; -er, -ste) cordial, hearty; -'roerend a. (-e) touching; -seer n. grief; -slag n. heart-beat; -stog n. passion.

'hartkamer ['haRtkamər] n. (-s) auricle.

'hartkloppings ['haRtklopəngs] n. pl. palpitation.

'hartkramp ['haRtkRamp] n. (-e) angina.

harts'togtelik [harts'tochtələk] a. (-e) passionate.

'hartwater ['haRtvātəR] n. heart-water (cattle disease).

'harwar ['haRvaR] n. confusion.

'hasepad ['häsəpat] n. die-kies take to one's heels.

'haspel ['haspəl] n. (-s) reel, windlass.

'hawe ['hävə] n. goods, property; n. (-ns, -s) harbour, port; haven; -hoof n. pier, jetty; -loos a. (-lose) poor, homeless.

'hawer ['hävər] n. oats.

hè? ('hè?] interj. what!

hê ['he] v. (gehad) have, possess, want.

'hebbelikheid ['hebələkayt] n. habit, idiosyncracy.

'hebsug ['hepsʌch] n. greed; heb-'sugtig a. (-e; -er, -ste) greedy.

'hede ['hēdə] av. today, at the moment; -! interj. lord! -ndaags a. (-e) modern, present.

'hedera ['hēdəRa] n. ivy.

heel ['hēl] a. (hele) entire; complete; av. quite, very; v. (ge-) heal, cure; v. (ge-) connive, cooperate (with thieves); -'al n. universe; -baar a. (-bare) curable; -dag av. the whole day long, always; -huids av. without an injury; -krag n. curative power; -kunde n. surgery; -meester n. surgeon; -temal av. entirely; -wat a. considerable.

heen ['hēn] av. away; -gaan v. (-ge-) go away, die; -kome n. refuge.

heer ['hēR] n.(here) army; gentleman; -lik a. (-e; -er, -ste) delightful; -likheid n. glory.

Heer, 'Here ['hēR, 'hēRə] n. the Lord.

'heers ['hēRs] v. (ge-) rule, govern; prevail; -end (-e) prevailing; ruling; -er n. (-s) ruler; -skap n. master, lord; -skap'py n. rule, sovereignty; -sug n. ambition.

hees ['hēs] a. (-, hese; heser, -ste) hoarse; -heid n.

heet ['hēt] a. (hete) heter, -ste) hot, burning; torrid; v. (ge-) call, name.

'heethoofdig ['hēthōfdəch] a. (-e) hot-headed.

hef ['hef] n. (-te, hewwe) haft, handle; hilt; v. (ge-) lift; impose, levy; -boom n. lever; -fing n. imposition, levy; -tig a. (-e) vehement.

heg ['hech] v. (ge-) affix, attach; n. (-ge) hedge; -tenis n. custody; -theid n. firmness, solidity; -naald n. (-s) suture needle.

'hei ['hay] v. (ge-) pile driving, to drive in piles; -paal. n. (-pale) piling stakes; -werk n. piling.

'heide ['haydə] n. pl. heath; -veld n. moorland.

'heiden ['haydən] n. (-e, -s) heathen; -dom n. heathendom; -s a. (-e) heathen(ish); hei'din n. fem. heathen.

'heil ['hayl] n. welfare, salvation; -ig a. (-e; -er, -ste) holy; -ig v. (ge-) hallow; -ige n. (-s) saint; -iging n. hallowing; -loos a. (-lose) wicked, disastrous; **-saam** a. (-same; -samer, -ste) beneficial.

'**Heiland** ['haylant] n. Saviour.

'**heimlik** ['haymlək] a. (-e) clandestine, secret.

'**heimwee** ['haymvē] n. homesickness.

'**heining** ['haynəng] n. (-s) fence, hedge.

hek ['hek] n. (-ke) gate, boom.

'**hekel** ['hēkəl] v. (ge-) heckle; crochet; criticize, satirize; **-dig** n. satire; **-ing** n. satirizing, heckling.

'**heks** ['heks] n. witch; vixen; **-ery** n. sorcery.

hel ['hel] n. hell; a. bright, gleaming, glaring; v. (ge-) incline, slope; **-lend** a. (-e) sloping; **-ling** n. slope, incline; **-s** a. & av. devilish, hellish.

he'laas [hē'las] interj. alas!

held ['helt] n. (-e) hero; **-'haftig** a. (-e) heroic, brave.

'**helder** ['heldəR] a. (-e; -der, -ste) clear, vivid; **-heid** n.; **-siende** a. clairvoyant.

'**helfte** ['helftə] n. (-s) half.

'**helling** ['heləng] n. (-s) slope.

helm ['heləm] n. (-e, -s) helmet; helm; caul.

help ['help] v. (ge-) help, aid, assist; **-end** a. (-e) helping; **-er** n. (-s) helper; **-ster** n. (-s) fem. helper.

hemel ['hēmǝl] n. (-e, -s) heaven; firmament; sky; canopy; **-!** interj. good heavens! **-ing** n. (-e) inhabitant of Heaven; **-s** a. (-e) heavenly.

'**hen** ['hen] n. (-ne) hen.

'**hennep** ['henǝp] n. hemp.

hensop ['heñsop] v. (ge-) to put one's hands up, surrender; **-per** n. (-s) surrenderer.

'**hengel** ['hengǝl] v. (ge-) angle, fish; **-aar** n. (-s) angler.

'**herberg** ['heRbeRch] n. (-e) inn, tavern; accommodation; v. (ge-) accommodate, lodge; **her'bergsaam** a. (her'bergsame) hospitable.

her- ['heR-] prefix, (-ge) again; **-'bore** a. reborn; **-bou** v. (-) rebuild; **-de band** n. rebuilt tyre; **-'denk** v. (-) commemorate; **-'denking** n. commemoration; **-doop** n. rebaptism; **-'doop** v. (-) re-baptize, rename; **-'druk** n. (-ke) reprint; **-'druk** v. (-) reprint; **-'enig** v. (-) reunite; **-'haal** v. (-) recapitulate, repeat; **-'haalde** a. repeated; **-'haaldelik** av. repeatedly; **-'haling** n. repetition; **her'rinner** v. (-) call to mind, recollect; **-'ken** v. (-) recognize; **-'kenbaar** a. (her'kenbare) recognizable; **-'lei** v. (-) reduce, convert; **-'open** v. (-) re-open; **-'roep** v. (-) revoke; **-'sien** v. (-) revise; **-'skape** a. reborn; **-'stel** n. restoration, v. (-) mend, repair, redress; **-'vat** v. (-) resume; **-'vorm** v. (-) reform, amend; **-'wonne** a. regained.

'**herder** ['heRdǝR] n. (-s) shepherd; clergyman; **-lik** a. pastoral.

'**herereg** ['hēRǝRech] n. (-te) transfer-dues (property).

herfs ['heRfs] n. autumn.

her'haal [heR'hāl] v. (-) repeat; **-de** a. repeated; **-delik(e)** av. repeatedly; **-ing** n. (-s) repeat, recurrence; **-voorskrif** n. (-te) repeat prescription.

'**herkoms** ['heRkoms] n. derivation, descent, source.

her'lei [heR'lay] v. (-) convert; reduce; translate; **-ding** n.

her'nuwe [heR'newǝ] v. (-) renew; revive.

he'roïes [he'Rǒis] a. (-e) heroic.

her'roep [hĕ'Rup] v. (-) revoke, rescind.

'**hersenskim** ['heRsǝnskǝm] n. (-me) phantasm.

'**hersenskudding** ['heRsǝngskʌdǝng] n. concussion = harsingskudding.

'**herrie** ['heRi] n. din, row, racket, confusion.

her'stel [heRstel] v. (-) reinstate, revive; repair.

hert ['heRt] n. (-e) stag, deer.

'**hertog** ['heRtoch] n. ('hertoë) duke; **herto'gin** n. duchess.

'**heruitsend** ['heRœitsent] v. (-) relay, rebroadcast; **-ing** n. relay(ing).

her'vul [heR'fʌl] v. (-) refill; **-ling** n. (-s) refill.

'**herwaarts** ['heRvāRts] av. hither.

her'win [heR'vǝn] v. (-) reclaim; regain.

'**heserig** ['hēsǝRǝch] a. (-e) husky, slightly hoarse.

het v. = has.

heug ['hĕch] n. teen-en meug against one's liking; v. (ge-) dit-my nog I still remember; **-enis** n. memory; **-lik** a. (-e; -er, -ste) memorable.

heul ['hǝl] v. (ge-) collude with.

'**heuning** ['hœnǝng] n. honey.

heup ['hœp] n. (-e) hip.

'**heuwel** ['hœvǝl] n. (-s) hill; **-agtig** a. (-e) hilly; **-tjie** dim.

'**hewel** ['hēvǝl] n. (-s) siphon; v. (ge-) siphon.

'**hewig** ['hēvǝch] a. (-e; -er, -ste) violent, heavy.

hiel ['hiil] n. (-e) heel.

hi'ëna [hi'ēna] n. (-s) hyena.

hier ['hiR] av. here; **-by** av. hereby; **-deur** av. by this; **-die** pron. this; **-heen** av. hither; **-mee** av. herewith; **-'na** av. hereafter; **-natoe** av. this way; **-oor** av. about this; **-op** av. upon this, hereupon; **-teenoor** av. opposite, against this; **-uit** av. from this, hence.

hier'namaals [hiR'nāmāls] n. the great beyond.

hiet ['hit] v. (ge-) order; cp. heet v.

higi'ëne [hichi'ēnǝ] n. hygiene; **higiënies** a. (-e) hygienic.

hik ['hǝk] n. (-ke) hiccup; v. (ge-) hiccup.

'**hinder** ['hǝnǝR] v. (ge-) hinder, hamper; **-laag** n. (-lae) ambush; **-lik** *a.* (-e; -er, -ste) annoying; **-nis** *n.* hindrance.

hings ['həngs] *n.* (-te) stallion.

'hingsel ['həngsəl] *n.* (-s) handle.

hink ['hənk] *v.* (ge-) limp.

'hinnik ['hənək] *v.* (ge-) neigh.

hip'nose [hip'nōsə] *n.* hypnosis.

hipo'konders [hipə'koneRs] *n.* hypochondria; **hipo'kondries** *a.* (-e) hypochondriac.

hipo'teek [hipō'tēk] *n.* (hipo'teke) mortgage.

hipo'tese [hipō'tēsə] *n.* hypothesis.

histe'rie [histē'Ri] *n.* hysteria; **his'teries** *a.* (-e) hysterical.

his'tories [his'tōRis] *a.* (-e) historic; **his'torikus** *n.* (-se) historian.

hits ['həts] *v.* (ge-) incite; **-ig** *a.* (-e) hot; in heat; lewd.

'hitte ['hətə] *n.* heat.

hoe ['hu] *av.* how, what.

hoed ['hut] *n.* (-e) hat; bonnet; *v.* (ge-) heed, watch, guard, take care of; **-e** *n.* care, protection; **-er** *n.* (-s) keeper, guardian.

hoe'danig [hu'dānəch] *av.* (-e) how, what, what kind of.

hoef ['huf] *n.* (hoewe) hoof; *v.* (-) need, *jy-dit nie te doen nie* you needn't do it; **-yster** *n.* (-s) horseshoe.

'hoëfre'kwensie ['hōəfRə'kwensi] *n.* high frequency.

'hoegenaamd ['huchənāmt] *av.* *-nie* not at all.

hoek ['huk] *n.* (-e) corner; angle; hook; glen; **-ie** *dim.* nook; **-ig** *a.* (-e; -er, -ste) angular; **-anker** *n.* (-s) angle stay; **-lyn** *n.* diagonal; **-staal** *n.* angle steel; **-steun** *n.* angle (corner) bracket.

'hoeka ['huka] *n.* *van-af* of old.

'hoekom ['hukom] *av.* why.

'hoelank ['hulank] *av.* how long.

'hoender ['hunəR] *n.* (-s) fowl, chicken; *die-s in wees* angry; **-kop** *av. hy is-* he is tipsy; **-vel** *n. & av.* goose-skin.

'hoepel ['hupəl] *n.* (-s) hoop; **-been** *n.* bandy-leg.

hoer ['huR] *n.* (-e) harlot; *v.* (ge-) whore.

hoërskool ['hōəRskōl] *n.* (hoërskole) high school.

hoes ['hus] *v.* (ge-) cough; **-te** (-te) cough.

'hoeveel ['hufēl] *av.* how much, how many; **hoe'veelheid** *n.* quantity.

'Hoëveld ['hōəfelt] *n.* High Veld.

'hoever ['hufeR] *av.* how far.

'hoewe ['huvə] *n.* (-s) smallholding.

hoe'wel [hu'vel] *conj.* although, though.

hof ['hof] *n.* (howe) court; *'n meisie die-maak* court a girl; **-lik** *a.* (-e) courteous.

'hofie ['hōfi] *n.* (-s) heading, caption.

'hofsaak ['hofsāk] *n.* lawsuit.

hok ['hok] *n.* (-ke) kennel, pen, sty, cage, booth, cubicle; *v.* (ge-) *byme-kaar-* huddle together; **-slaan** *v.*

(-ge-) deny pleasure to someone; *-vas a.* (-te) *hy is-* he is a home-bird.

hol ['hol] *n.* (-le) hole; cave; lair; resort; anus; *iemand op -bring* turn a person's head; *a.* (-le; -ler, -ste) hollow, empty; *v.* (ge-) scamper, bolt; **-heid** *n.* hollowness; **-rond** *a.* (-e) concave; **-rug** *a.* *iets-ry* ride something to death; **-te** *n.* (-s) cavity.

'holderste'bolder ['holəRstə'boləR] *av.* topsy-turvy.

hom ['hom] *pron.* him, it.

homp ['homp] *n.* (-e) lump, chunk.

hond ['hont] *n.* (-e) dog, hound, cur; **-ehok** *n.* kennel; **-eweer** *n.* dog's life; **-eweer** *n.* beastly weather; **-jie** *dim.* pup; **-lelik** *a.* (-e) ugly as sin; **-mak** *a.* very tame.

'honderd ['honəRt] *n.* (-e) hundred; **-delig** *a.* (-e) centesimal.

'hondsdolheid ['haunsdolayt] *n.* rabies.

'honger ['hongəR] *n.* hunger; *a.* hungry; *v.* (ge-) hunger, be hungry; **-erig** *a.* (-e) hungry; **-snood** *n.* famine.

hon'neurs [ho'nœRs] *n.* honours.

hono'rarium [hono'RāRIʌm] *n.* fee, honorarium.

hono'rêr [hono'RɛR] *a.* (-e) honorary.

ho'noris 'causa [ho'nauRəs 'ka-usa] *a.* honorary.

hoof ['hōf] *n.* (-de) head; chief; heading; principal; main; **hoof-** *a.* chief, main; **-delik** *a.* (-e) per head; *'as n.* main shaft (axle); **-knik** *n.* (-ke) nod; **-kussing** *n.* (-s) pillow; **-laer** *n.* (-s) main bearing; **-letter** *n.* (-s) capital; **-pad** *n.* highway; **-s** *a.* (-e) courtly; **-'saaklik** *av.* chiefly; **-stad** *n.* (-stede) capital; **-stuk** *n.* (-ke) chapter; **-telwoord** *n.* numeral; **-weg** *n.* highway.

'hoof- ['hōf] *n.* *pref.* master, main; **-leiding** *n.* main; **-lig** *n.* main light; **-lyn** *n.* trunk line; **-si'linder** *n.* master cylinder; **-skag** *n.* main shaft; **-skakelaar** *n.* main switch; **-veer** *n.* (vere) mainspring.

'hoofkaas ['hōfkās] *n.* brawn.

'hoofpyn ['hōfpayn] *n.* headache.

'hoofrekene ['hōfRēkənə] *n.* mental arithmetic.

'hoofslagaar ['hōfslachāR] *n.* ('hoofslagare) aorta.

hoog ['hōch] *a.* (hoë; hoër, -ste) high, lofty, tall; **-ag** *v.* (-ge-) esteem, respect; **-agtend** *av.* respectfully; **-agting** *n.* respect, regard; **-drawend** *a.* (-e; -er, -ste) bombastic; **-edele** *n.* right honourable; **-hartig** *a.* (-e; -er, -ste) haughty; **-heid** *n.* highness; **-hou** *v.* (-ge-) uphold, maintain; **-leraar** *n.* professor; **-moed** *n.* pride; **-'moedig** *a.* (-e; -er, -ste) proud; **-e** *av.* highly; **-staande** *a.* distinguished; **-ste** *a.* highest; **-stens** *av.* at best; **-te** *n.* (-s) height, elevation; **-ty** *n.* *-vier* be rampant; **-vlakte** *n.* plateau.

'hoogland ['hōchlant] *n.* plateau.

'hoogspanning ['hŏchspanəng] n. high tension (pressure, voltage).

hooi ['hŏi] n. hay; -maand n. July; -mied n. (-e, -ens) haystack.

hoon ['hŏn] n. scorn, derision, contumely; v. (ge-) scorn, deride.

hoop ['hŏp] n. (hope) heap, pile; hope; v. (ge-) hope; -vol a. (-le) hopeful, promising.

hoor ['hŏR] n. hearing; v. (ge-) hear, learn; -baar a. (-bare; -der, -ste) audible; -der n. (-s) hearer, listener.

hoort ['hŏRt] v. (ge-) dit-so that is as it should be; hy-nie hier nie he doesn't belong here.

'hopeloos ['hŏpəlŏs] a. ('hopelose) hopeless, desperate.

'horing ['hŏRəng] n. (-s) horn; bugle; hooter; -agtig a. (-e) horny; -droog a. dry as dust; -oud a. as old as the hills; -vee n. horned cattle; -vlies n. cornea.

'horison ['hŏRison] n. (-te, -ne) horizon; -'taal a. (-tale) horizontal.

hor'losie [hoR'lŏsi] n. (-s) watch, clock.

'horrelpoot ['hoRəlpŏt] n. club-foot.

'horrelpyp ['hoRəlpayp] n. hornpipe.

'horrelvoet = horrelpoot.

'horries ['hoRis] n. pl. horrors, delirium tremens.

'horte ['hoRtə] n. pl. jerks, bolts.

hor'tensia [hoR'tensia] n. hydrangea.

'hortjie ['hoRKi] n. (-s) louvre, shutter.

hospi'taal [hospi'tāl] n. (hospi'tale) hospital.

hot ['hot] n. left; -om av. counter-clockwise.

hotnots'got [hotnots'chot] n. (-te) mantis.

hou ['hoə] n. (-e) blow, stroke; v. (ge-) hold, contain, keep; hew, cut; deliver; -baar a. (-bare) tenable; -ding n. (-e, -s) bearing; attitude; deportment; -er n. (-s) holder; bearer; container; -vas n. hold, support.

'hout ['hoat] n. (-e) wood; -erig a. (-e) wooden; stiff; -gerus av. at ease, unworried, unconcerned; -jie dim. iets op eie-doen do something off one's own bat; -skool n. charcoal; -wol n. wood-wool.

'houtsnee ['hoatsnē] n. woodcut.

'houtteer ['hoatēR] n. wood tar.

'hou-vir-'hou-oor'eenkoms ['hoafəR-'hoa-ōrēŋkoms] n. knock-for-knock agreement (motor insurance).

ho'vaardig [hŏ'fāRdəch] a. (-e) haughty.

hovaar'dy [hŏfaR'day] n. arrogance.

'howeling ['hŏvələng] n. (-e) courtier.

howe'nier [hŏvə'niR] n. (-s) gardener.

hu ['hew] v. (ge-) marry; -baar a. (-bare) marriageable.

'hugenoot ['hewchənŏt] n. ('hugenote) Huguenot.

huid ['hœit] n. hide, skin, pelt.

'huid- ['hœit-] n. pref. dermal-.

'huidige ['hœidəche] a. modern, present.

huig ['hœich] n. uvula.

'huigel ['hœichəl] v. (ge-) dissemble, feign; -aar n. (-s) hypocrite; -agtig a. (-e; -er, -ste) canting, hypocritical; -ary n. canting, hypocrisy; -taal n. cant.

huil ['hœil] v. (ge-) cry, howl, weep; -erig a. (-e) tearful; -ery n. crying, sobbing.

huis ['hœis] n. (-e) house, dwelling, home; family; firm; -baas n. landlord; -besoek n. house-to-house call; -bewoner n. householder; -braak n. housebreaking; -dier n. (-e) domestic animal; -genoot n. (huisgenote) inmate, family; -gesin n. (-ne) family; -hou v. (-ge-) keep house, run the house; -'houdelik a. (-e) domestic; -houding n. household, family; -houdster n. fem. housekeeper; -huur n. rent; -huurder n. (-s) tenant; -lik a. (-e) domestic, homely; -raad n. furniture; -ves v. (ge-) accommodate, lodge; -vesting n. accommodation; -vlyt n. home-industry; -vrou n. (-e, -ens) housewife.

'huiwer ['hœivəR] v. (ge-) shiver, hesitate, shrink; -ig a. (-e) afraid, trembling, hesitating; -ing n. hesitation.

hul = hulle.

'hulde ['hʌldə] n. homage, tribute; 'huldig v. (ge-) to pay homage, honour; 'huldiging n. homage, apotheosis.

'hulle ['hʌlə] pron. they; them; their.

hulp ['hʌlp] n. help, aid; -behoewend a. (-e) needy; -eloos a. ('hulpelose) helpless, needy; -werkwoord n. auxiliary verb.

'hulp- ['hʌlp] n. pref. auxiliary, ancillary, subsidiary.

huis ['hʌls] n. (-e) bush, sleeve; case; shell; -sel n. (-s) covering, wrap.

huma'nis [hewma'nəs] n. (-te) humanist.

hu'meur [hew'mœR] n. humour, temper, mood; -ig a. (-e) capricious; sulky.

'humus ['hewmʌs] n. vegetable mould.

'hunker ['hʌnkəR] v. (ge-) ache for, hanker after; -end a. (-e) craving, hankering; -ing n.

'huppel ['hʌpəl] v. (ge-) hop, frisk; -end a. (-e) hopping, frisky.

hups ['hʌps] a. (-e) polite; lively.

hurk ['hʌRk] n. (-e) -e haunches; v. (ge-) squat.

'husse ['hʌsə] n. -met ore curiosity killed the cat.

hut ['hʌt] n. (-te) cottage, cot; hut, hovel; cabin; -jie dim.

'hutspot ['hʌtspot] n. hotchpotch.

huur ['hēwR] n. hire, rent(al); lease; v. (ge-) hire, rent, engage, charter; -der n. (-s) lessee, tenant, hirer;

-**kontrak** n. (-*te*) lease, agreement of tenancy; -**ling** n. (-*e*) hireling.
'**huurkoop** ['hēwRkŏp] n. hire-purchase.
'**huwelik** ['hewvəlik] n. (-*e*) marriage, wedding; -**sgebooie** n. *pl.* banns; -**sreg** n. conjugal rights; -**voorwaarde** n. (-*s*) antenuptial contract.
hy ['hay] *pron.* he, it.
hyg ['haych] *v.* (ge-) gasp; pant; yearn; -**end** *a.* (-*e*) gasping, panting; -**ing** n.
hys ['hays] *v.* (ge-) hoist; -**bak** n. cage, skip; lift; -**er** n. (-*s*) hoist, crane; lift; elevator; -**kraan** n. crane.

I

I'berië [i'bēRiə] n. Iberia.
ide'aal [idē'ăl] n. (*ide'ale*) ideal.
idea'lis [idēa'ləs] n. (-*te*) idealist; **ideali'seer** *v.* (ge-) idealize; **idea-'listies** *a.* (-*e*) idealistic.
i'dee [i'dē] n. (-*ë*) idea, notion, opinion.
'**idem** ['idem] n. ditto.
iden'tiek [iden'tik] *a. & av.* (-*e*) identical; **identifi'kasie** n. identification; **identifi'seer** *v.* (ge-) identify; **identi'teit** n. identity.
ideolo'gie [idĕŏlŏchi] n. ideology.
i'dille [i'dilə] n. (-*s*) idyll; **i'dillies** *a.* (-*e*) idyllic.
idi'oom [idi'ŏm] n. (*idi'ome*) idiom; **idio'maties** *a.* (-*e*) idiomatic.
idi'oot [idi'ŏt] n. (*idi'ote*) idiot, imbecile.
'**ieder** ['idəR] *pron.* (-*e*) each, every; -**een** *pron.* anyone, everybody.
'**iemand** ['imant] *pron.* anybody, someone.
Ier ['iR] n. (-*e*) Irishman; -**s** *a.* (-*e*) Irish.
'**iesegrim** ['isechrəm] n. (-*me*) bear, grumbler; -**mig** *a.* (-*e*) bearish, surly.
iets ['its] *pron.* anything, something; *av.* somewhat, rather; -**ie** n. *dim.* a bit, a shade.
'**iewers** ['ivəRs] *av.* somewhere.
igno'reer [ichnŏ'RēR] *v.* (ge-) ignore, cut.
illumi'nasie [ilewmi'năsi] n. illumination; **illumi'neer** *v.* (ge-) illuminate.
il'lusie [i'lewsi] n. (-*s*) illusion.
illus'trasie [ilʌs'tRăsi] n. (-*s*) illustration; **illus'treer** *v.* (ge-) illustrate.
imbe'siel ['imbə'sil] n. (-*e*) imbecile, idiot.
imi'tasie [imi'tăsi] n. imitation; **imi'teer** *v.* (ge-) imitate.
'**immer** ['əməR] *av.* always, ever; -**s** *av.* but, yet; indeed; *cp.* **mos** *av.*; -**meer** *av.* evermore.
im'mersie [i'meRsi] n. immersion.
immi'grant [iml'chRant] n. (-*e*) immigrant; **immi'grasie** n. immigration; **immi'greer** *v.* (-) immigrate.

immo'reel [imŏ'Rēl] *a.* (*immo'rele*) immoral.
immuni'teit [imewni'tayt] n. immunity.
im'muun [i'mewn] *a.* immune.
impera'tief [impĕRa'tif] n. imperative (*mood*); *a.* (*impera'tiewe*) imperative, urgent.
imperi'aal [impĕRi'ăl] *a.* (*imperi'ale*) imperial.
'**impi** ['impi] n. (-'*s*) Impi.
impli'kasie [impli'kăsi] n. (-*s*) implication; **impli'seer** *v.* (ge-) implicate, imply.
impo'neer [impŏ'nēR] *v.* (ge-) impress; **impo'nerend** *a.* (-*e*; -*er*, -*ste*) imposing.
impor'tasie [impoR'tăsi] n. importation; **impor'teer** *v.* (ge-) import; **impor'teerder** n. (-*s*) importer; **impor'teur** n. (-*s*) importer.
impo'sant [impŏ'sant] *a.* (-*e*; -*er*, -*ste*) imposing.
impo'tent [impŏ'tent] *a.* (-*e*) impotent; **impo'tensie** n. impotence.
im'pressie [im'pResi] n. impression.
improvi'sasie [impRŏvi'săsi] n. (-*s*) improvisation; **improvi'seer** *v.* (ge-) improvise.
'**impuls** [im'pʌls] n. (-*e*) impulse; **impul'sief** *a.* (*impul'siewe*) impulsive.
in [ən] *prep.* in, into, within; during; *v.* (ge-) collect.
in'agneem [ən'achnĕm] *v.* (*inagge-*) consider; observe; **in'agneming** n. observance.
'**inbed** ['əmbet] *v.* (-ge-) to seat (*mech.*).
'**inbeeld** ['əmbĕlt] *v.* (-ge-) imagine.
'**inbegrepe** ['əmbachRēpə] *a.* included.
'**inbegrip** ['əmbachRəp] n. inclusion.
'**inboedel** ['əmbudl] n. furniture and effects.
'**inboesem** ['əmbusəm] *v.* (-ge-) inspire, fill with.
'**inboet** ['əmbut] *v.* (-ge-) replace; lose.
'**inboorling** ['əmbŏRləng] n. (-*e*) native.
'**inbors** ['əmboRs] n. character.
'**inbou** ['əmboa] *v.* (-ge-) build in; **ingebou(de)** *a.* built in.
'**inbraak** ['əmbRăk] n. burglary.
'**inbreek** ['əmbRēk] *v.* (-ge-) break into, burgle; -**breker** n. (-*s*) burglar; '**inbreuk** n. infringement.
'**inburger** ['əmbʌrgəR] *v.* (-ge-) naturalize.
in'daba [in'dăba] n. (-*s*) indaba, consultation.
in'dagtig [ən'dachtəch] *a.* mindful of.
in'deel ['əndĕl] *v.* (-ge-) classify.
'**indeks** ['əndeks] n. (-*e*) index.
inder'daad [əndəR'dăt] *av.* indeed, really.
inder'haas [əndəR'hăs] *av.* hurriedly.
'**indertyd** ['əndəRtayt] *av.* at the time.
in'dien [ən'din] *conj.* if, in case.

'**indien** ['əndin] v. (-ge-) introduce.

indi'kasie [indi'kāsi] n. (-s) indication; in'**dikatief** n. indicative (mood).

'**indirek** ['indiRek] a. & av. (-te) indirect.

indivi'du [indivi'dew] n. (-e, -'s) individual; **individu'eel** a. & av. (individuele) individual(ly).

'**indommel** ['əndoməl] v. (-ge-) doze off.

'**indompel** ['əndompəl] v. (-ge-) immerse.

'**indoop** ['əndōp] v. (-ge-) dip.

'**indring** ['əndRəng] v. (-ge-) intrude; penetrate; -er n. (-s) intruder, interloper.

'**indruis** ['əndRœis] v. (-ge-) clash, conflict.

'**indruk** ['əndRʌk] n. impression; v. (-ge-) impress; press in; force one's way in; -'wekkend a. (-e) impressive.

in'eengedronge [ən'ēnchədRonge] a. thick-set.

in'eens [ən'ēns] av. suddenly; at the same time.

in'eenstort [ən'ēnstoRt] v. (-gestort) collapse.

'**inent** ['ənent] v. (-ge-) vaccinate.

infinitief [ənfəne'tif] n. (infini'tiewe) infinitive (mood).

inflam'masie [ənflə'māsi] n. inflammation.

in'flasie [ən'flāsi] n. inflation.

in'fleksie [ən'fleksi] n. inflection; **inflek'teer** v. (ge-) inflect.

influ'ensa [ənflew'ēnsa] n. influenza.

infor'masie [ənfoR'māsi] n. information; **infor'meer** v. (ge-) inquire; inform.

infor'mele [ənfoR'mēl] a. (infor'mele) informal.

'**ingang** ['ənchang] n. (-e) entrance.

'**ingangs-** ['ənchangs] pref. entrance.

'**ingebore** ['ənchəbōRə] a. inborn.

'**ingedagte** ['ənchədachtə] av. lost in thought, absentminded.

'**ingelyfde** ['ənchəlayfdə] a. collegiate.

ingen'leur [ənchən'yōR] n. (-s) engineer.

'**ingenome** ['əng-chənōmə] a. pleased.

'**ingerig** ['əng-chəRəch] a. (-te) arranged, furnished.

'**ingesetene** ['ənchəsētənə] n. (-s) inhabitant.

'**ingetoë** ['ənchətōə] a. modest, reserved.

'**ingevreet** ['ənchəfRēt] a. pitted.

'**ingewande** ['ənchəvanə] n. entrails.

'**ingewikkeld** ['ənchəvəkəlt] a. (-e) complex, complicated, intricate.

'**ingewing** ['ənchēvəng] n. inspiration.

'**ingryp** ['ənchRayp] v. (-ge-) interfere, intervene; -end a. (-e; -er, -ste) drastic.

'**inhaal** ['ənhāl] v. (-ge-) overtake.

in'halig [ən'hāləch] a. (-e; -er, -ste) covetous; -heid n. greed.

'**inham** ['ənham] n. (-me) bay, creek, inlet.

'**inheems** ['ənhēms] a. (-e) indigenous.

'**inhoud** ['ənhoat] n. contents.

inisa'tief [inisa'tif] n. initiative.

'**ink** ['ənk] n. ink.

'**inkeer** ['əng-kēR] n. repentance.

in'kennig [əng-'kennəch] a. shy, timid.

in'kluis [əng'klœis] a. included.

inklu'sief [ənklew'sif] a. (inklu'siewe) inclusive.

'**inkomste** ['əng-komstə] n. income, revenue, earnings.

inkonse'kwent [inkonsə'kwent] a. (-e) inconsistent.

'**inkopie** ['əng-kōpi] n. (-s) small purchase; -s doen to go shopping.

'**inlaat-** ['ənlāt-] pref. entry, inlet.

'**inlig** ['ənləch] v. (-ge-) enlighten, inform; -ting n. information.

'**inlos** ['ənlos] v. (-ge-) redeem.

inme'kaar [əmə'kāR] av. close, together, entangled.

'**inmeng** ['əmeng] v. (-ge-) interfere.

in'nemend [ə'nēmənt] a. (-e) attractive.

in'nerlik ['ənəRlək] a. (-e) inner, internal, intrinsic.

'**innig** ['ənəch] a. (-e; -er, -ste) close; earnest; fervent.

'**inprent** ['əmprent] v. (inge) impress, inculcate.

'**inrig** ['ənRəch] v. (-ge-) adapt, arrange; fit; furnish; -ting n. (-e, -s) institution; arrangement.

'**insae** ['ənsā] n. ter - lê lie for inspection.

'**insê** ['ənse] v. (-ge-) iemand- give a person a bit of one's mind.

'**insek** ['ənsek] n. (-te) insect; -weerder n. insect repellent.

insgelyks ['ənschəlayks] av. likewise.

'**insien** ['ənsin] v. (-ge-) glance over, look into; realize.

'**insig** ['ənsəch] n. (-te) insight.

in'skiklik [ən'skəklək] a. (-e) accommodating; obliging.

'**insluit** ['ənslœit] v. (-ge-) enclose.

'**inslurp** ['ənslʌRp] v. (-ge-) gulp down.

'**insny** ['ənsnay] v. (-ge-) undercut.

insol'vent [ənsol'fənt] a. (-e) insolvent.

in'sonderheid [ən'sonəRayt] av. especially.

inspek'teur [ənspek'tōR] n. (-s) inspector.

inspi'rasie [ənspə'Rāsi] n. inspiration; **inspi'reer** v. (ge-) inspire.

'**instel** ['ənstel] v. (-ge-) align, tune; establish; adjust.

'**instem** [enstem] v. (-ge-) agree; -ming n. approval, agreement.

'**instink** ['ənstənk] n. (-te) instinct; **instink'tief** a. instinctive.

'**instort** ['ənstoRt] v. (inge-) collapse.

instru'eer [ənstRew'ēR] v. (ge-) instruct; **in'struksie** n. (-s) instruction; **instruk'teur** n. (-s) instructor; **instruk'tief** a. (instruktiewe) instructive.

instru'ment [ənstRew'ment] n. (-e) instrument, tool.

insu'lêr [ənsew'lɛR] a. (-e) insular.

'insuur ['ənsɵWR] v. (-ge-) prepare yeast.

'insweer ['ɵ̃nsvɛR] v. (-ge-) administer oath of office.

in'teendeel [ən'tɛndɛl] av. on the contrary.

intellek ['əntələk] n. (-te) intellect; intellektu'eel a. (intellektu'ele) intellectual.

intelli'gensie [intelə'cheñsi] n. intelligence; intelli'gent a. (-e; -er, -ste) intelligent.

in'tens [ən'tens] a. (-e) intense; inten'sief a. (inten'siewe) intensive.

interes'seer [əntəRə'sɛR] v. (ge-) interest.

in'tern [ən'teRən] a. (-e) internal.

internasio'naal [əntəRnashō'nâl] a. (internasio'nale) international.

inter'neer [əntəR'nêR] v. (ge-) intern.

inter'nis [əntəR'nəs] n. physician.

inter'punksie [intəR'pʌnksi] n. punctuation.

in'tiem [ən'tim] a. (-e) intimate.

into'nasie [əntō'nâsi] n. intonation.

'intrede ['əntRêdə] n. entrance; 'intree v. (-ge-) enter.

'intrek ['əntRek] v. (-ge-) to move in; draw (breath); cancel, withdraw; -king n. cancellation.

in'trige [in'tRichə] n. (-s) intrigue.

intu'ïsie [əntew'isi] n. intuition; intuï'tief a. (intuïtiewe) intuitive.

in'tussen [ən'tʌsən] av. meanwhile.

inven'taris [əmfən'tâRəs] n. (-se) inventory.

in'versie [əm'feRsi] n. inversion.

in'vloed [əmflut] n. influence.

'invoeg ['əmfuch] v. (-ge-) insert; -sel n. insertion.

'invoer ['ənfûR] v. (-ge-) import; -der n. (-s) importer; -ing n. importation.

'invorder ['əmfoRdəR] v. (-ge-) collect; recover; -baar a. (-bare) leviable; recoverable.

'invreting ['ənfRêtəng] n. pitting.

'inwen ['əmven] v. (-ge-) collect.

in'wendig [ən'vendəch] a. (-e) inner; internal; av. inwardly.

'inwillig ['əmnvələch] v. (inge-) accede.

'inwin ['əmvən] v. (-ge-) obtain.

'inwoner ['əmvōnər] n. (-s) inhabitant; 'inwoning n. lodging; -woon v. (-ge-) lodge, stay with.

'inwortel ['əmvoRtəl] v. (inge-) take root.

'inwy ['əmvay] v. (-ge-) initiate, consecrate.

iro'nie [iRō'ni] n. irony; ir'onies a. (-e) ironical.

irri'gasie [iRə'châsi] n. irrigation.

iso'lasie [isō'lâsi] n. isolation; iso-'leer v. (ge-) isolate; isole'ment n. isolation.

i'voor [i'fōR] n. ivory; -agtig a. (-e) ivory-like.

J

ja ['yâ] av. yes, yea, aye.

ja(ag), jae ['yâ, 'yâch, 'yâə] v. (ge-) chase; hurry; race; -baan n. racecourse; -duiwel n. speed merchant; -strik n. speed trap; -spinnekop n. lynx spider.

jaar [yâR] n. (jare) year; -blad n. annual; -gang n. (-e) volume; -gety n. (-e) season; -liks a. & av. (-e) yearly, annual(ly); -plant n. annual.

jaart ['yâRt] n. (-s) yard.

'jabroer ['yâbRûR] n. yes-man, spineless fellow.

jag ['yach] n. hunting, chase; yacht; v. (ge-) hunt, chase; -s a. (-e) on heat; -ter n. (-s) hunter.

'jakkals ['yakals] n. (-e) jackal; wily one; -draai n. evasion, pretext; -streek n. (-streke) cunning, slyness.

'jakker ['yakəR] v. (ge-) gad about; fag.

'jakkie ['yaki] n. (-s) coatee.

'Jakob ['yâkop] n. James, Jacob; die ware- Mr. Right; jakob-regop n. zinnia.

ja'loers [ya'lûRs] a. (-e) jealous, envious; jaloe'sie n. jealousy.

'jambe ['yambə] n. iamb(us).

'jammer ['yaməR] a. sorry; v. (ge-) lament; -lik a. (-e) miserable; -te n. pity; sorrow.

Jan ['yan] n. John; met - Tuisbly se kar ry stay at home.

ja-'nee [ya-'nê] av. sure!

'Januarie [yanə'vâri] n. January.

'japie ['yâpi] n. dim. of Jakob; simpleton.

ja'pon [ya'pon] n. (-ne) dress.

jap'snoet [yap'snut] n. impertinent child, imp.

jas ['yas] n. (-se) overcoat, greatcoat.

'jaspis ['yaspəs] n. jasper.

ja'wel [ya'vel] av. indeed, yes.

'jawoord [ya'vâvōRt] n. consent.

jee ['yê] interj. oh! oh dear!

'jeens ['yêñs] prep. to, towards, by, with.

'jellie ['yeli] n. (-s) jelly.

je'newer [yə'nêvəR] n. gin.

Je'rusalemblom [yə'rewsəlemblom] n. Maltese Cross (lily).

Je'saja [ye'sâyə] n. Isaiah.

Jesus ['yêsʌs] n. Jesus.

jeug ['yêch] n. youth; -dig a. (-e) young, youthful.

jeuk ['yêk] v. (ge) itch; n. itching; -erig a. (-e) itchy.

jig ['yəch] n. arthritis, gout.

jil ['yəl] v. (ge-) jest, joke.

'jodekers ['yōdəkəRs] n. Chinese lantern.

'jodium ['yōdiʌm] n. iodine.

joel ['yul] v. (ge-) bawl, shout, frolic.

joerna'lis [yuRna'ləs] n. (-te) journalist.

'joggie ['yochi] n. (-s) boy, kid; caddy.

jok ['yok] v. (ge-) fib, lie.

'jokkie ['yoki] n. (-s) jockey.

jol ['yol] v. (ge-) make merry, frolic; -ig a. (-e) jolly, merry; -igheid n. merriment.

jo'lyt [jŏ'layt] n. feasting, jollity.

jong ['yong] n. (-ens) non-European servant; youth; a. (pred. jonk) young; v. (ge-) bring forth young; -eling n. lad, youth; -etjie n. (-s) dim. boy, youth; -ie n. dim. laddie, sonny; -kêrel n. young-man, lover; -mens n. youngster, youth; -s van-af from childhood; -span n. children.

'jonker ['yonkəR] n. young man, lover.

'jonkman ['yonkman] n. young man, lover.

Jood ['yŏt] n. (Jode) Jew.

'jood ['yŏt] n. iodine = iodium.

jool ['yŏl] n. fun; students' rag.

joos ['yŏs] n. dit weet- deuce knows.

'josefskleed ['yŏsəfsklĕt] n. coleus.

'josie ['yŏsi] n. devil, die-in wees be angry.

jota ['yŏta] n. g'n-nie not a jot.

jou [yoa] pron. you; -e, -ne poss. yours; v. (ge-) boo, hoot.

jovi'aal [yŏvi'ăl] a. (jovi'ale) genial, jovial, debonair.

jubel ['yewbəl] v. (ge-) jubilate; -fees n. jubilee.

'juffer ['yʌfəR] n. (-s) young lady, miss; -tjie n. dim. lassie.

'juffrou ['yʌfRoa] n. lady, madam; teacher.

juig ['yœich] v. (ge-) exult, rejoice.

juis ['yœis] a. (-te; -ter, -ste) correct; precise; just; av. precisely; -theid n. accuracy.

'juk ['yʌk] n. (-ke) yoke; -been n. cheek-bone.

julle ['yʌlə] pron. pl. you; poss. pl. yours.

'Junie ['yewni] n. June.

'jurie ['yewRi] n. jury.

juris'diksie [yewRəs'diksi] n. jurisdiction.

jurk ['yʌRk] n. (-e) dress, frock.

jus'tisie [yʌs'tisi] n. justice.

ju'weel [yew'vĕl] n. (ju'wele) jewel; jewe'lier n. (-s) jeweller.

jy ['yay] pron. you.

K

kaai ['kăi] n. (-e) quay.

kaak ['kăk] n. (kake) jaw.

kaal ['kăl] a. (kale; kaler- -ste) bald; callow; bare; naked; barren; -heid n. baldness; -kop n. baldhead; a. & av. baldheaded.

kaap ['kăp] n. (kape) cape, headland; v. (ge-) capture, practise piracy; die Kaap n. Cape of Good Hope; Kaaps av. Cape; Kaapse draai, sharp turn.

'kaapstander ['kăpstandəR] n. (-s) capstan.

kaart ['kaRt] n. (-e) card; map; ticket; -jie dim. visiting card; ticket;

-mannetjie n. jack-in-the-box; -stelsel n. card-index system.

kaas ['kăs] n. (kase) cheese; -agtig a. (-e) caseous; -kop n. blockhead; Hollander.

kaats ['kăts] v. (ge-) play at ball (tennis).

ka'baai [ka'băi] n. night-gown.

ka'baal [ka'băl] n. clamour, hubbub, noise.

'kabbel ['kabəl] v. (ge-) ripple, murmur, babble; -ing n. (-e, -s).

'kabel ['kăbəl] n. (-s) cable, hawser; v. (ge-) cable; -'jou n. cod; -rem n. cable brake.

kabi'net [kabə'net] n. (-te) cabinet, ministry.

ka'bouter [ka'boatəR] n. (-s) brownie, elf, gnome.

ka'dans [ka'dăns] n. cadence.

'kader ['kădəR] n. frame, scheme, skeleton.

ka'do [ka'dŏ] n. (-'s) present, gift.

ka'driel [ka'dRil] n. quadrille.

ka'duks [ka'dʌks] a. decayed, exhausted, broken.

kaf ['kaf] n. chaff; n. (-te) book-jacket, wrapper.

ka'fee [ka'fĕ] n. (-s) café.

'kafferkoring ['kafəRkŏRəng] n. sorghum.

'kafferpak ['kafəRpak] n. sound thrashing.

'kafpraatjies ['kafpRăiKis] n. nonsense, trash.

'kaggel ['kachəl] n. (-s) chimney, flue (pipe).

'kaiing ['kayəng] n. (-s) greaves, browsels.

ka'juit [ka'yœit] n. (-e) cabin.

'kakebeen ['kăkəbĕn] n. ('kakebene) jaw, jowl.

'kakie ['kăki] n. (-s) khaki; British Tommy.

'kakkerlak ['kakəRlak] n. (-ke) cockroach.

ka'lant [kə'lant] n. (-e) sly fox, rogue, scamp.

kal'bas [kəl'bas] n. (-se) calabash, gourd.

ka'lender [ka'lendəR] n. (-s) calendar, almanac.

kalf ['kalf] n. (kalwers) calf; v. (ge-; gekalwe) calve; cave in; -ie dim.; -s-oog n. poached egg.

kal'fater [kəl'fătəR] v. (ge-) caulk, patch up.

ka'liber [ka'libəR] n. calibre; bore.

'kaliko ['kălikŏ] n. calico.

kalk ['kalk] n. lime; v. (ge-) white-wash, lime wash; -agtig a. (-e) calcareous, limy; -houdend a. (-e) calciferous; -lig n. limelight.

kal'koen [kəl'kun] n. (-s) turkey.

kalm ['kaləm] a. (-e; -er, -ste) calm, cool, quiet; kal'meer v. (ge-) calm down, compose; -'meermiddel n. (-s) calmative, sedative; -'meerstroop n. soothing syrup; -'erend a. (-e) calming, soothing, sedative; -pies av. calmly, quietly; -te n.

calm(ness), composure; **-weg** *av.* calmly.
kalo'rie [kalŏ'Ri] *n.* (*-ë*) calorie.
ka'lossie, 'klossie [ka'losi, 'klosi] *n.* ixia.
ka'lotjie [ka'loiKi] *n.* (*-s*) skull-cap.
'kalwe ['kalvə] *v.* (*ge-*) calve; = **kalf** *v.*
'kalwerliefde ['kalvəRlifdə] *n.* calf-love.
'kam ['kam] *n.* (*-me*) comb, crest, cam, cog; *v.* (*ge-*) comb, card.
ka'mas [ka'mas] *n.* (*-te*) legging.
ka'meel [ka'mēl] *n.* (*ka'mele*) camel; giraffe.
'kamer ['kāməR] *n.* (*-s*) chamber, room; ventricle; **-doek** *n.* cambric; **-japon** *n.* dressing-gown.
'kamera ['kāmərə] *n.* camera.
kame'raad [kamə'Rāt] *n.* (*kame-'rade*) comrade, mate; **-skap** *n.* comradeship.
'kamma ['kama] *av.* quasi, as if, make believe.
'kammetjie ['kaməKi] *n.* (*-s*) freesia.
kamp ['kamp] *n.* (*-e*) camp, combat, fight; *v.* (*ge-*) camp, encamp; fight; **kam'peer** *v.* (*ge-*) camp, encamp; **-vegter** *n.* (*-s*) champion, advocate.
kam'panje [kam'pãñyə] *n.* (*-s*) campaign.
kampi'oen [kampi'un] *n.* (*-e*) champion; **-skap** *n.* championship.
kam'pong [kam'paung] *n.* (*-s*) compound.
'kamrat ['kamRat] *n.* cog wheel.
'kamstof ['kamstof] *n.* worsted.
'kamta(g) = **kamma**.
kan ['kan] *n.* (*-ne*) can, jar, jug; *v.* (*kon*) can, may, be able.
ka'naal [ka'nāl] *n.* (*ka'nale*) canal, channel, passage, duct.
ka'narie [ka'nāRi] *n.* (*-s*) canary.
'kandelaar ['kandə'lāR] *n.* (*-s*) candle-stick; agapanthus.
kandi'daat [kandi'dāt] *n.* (*kandi-'date*) candidate; **kandida'tuur** *n.* candidature.
kan'dy [kan'day] *n.* candy.
ka'neel [ka'nēl] *n.* cinnamon.
'kanfer ['kamfəR] *n.* camphor.
'kanker ['kankəR] *n.* cancer.
'kanna ['kana] *n.* (*-'s*) canna.
kanni'baal [kani'bāl] *n.* (*kanni-'bale*) cannibal.
ka'non [ka'non] *n.* (*-ne*) cannon, gun.
kans [kāns] *n.* (*-e*) chance, opportunity, prospect.
'kansel ['kānsəl] *n.* (*-s*) pulpit; **-a'ry** *n.* (*-e*) chancellory; **-e'lier** *n.* (*-s*) chancellor.
kansel'leer [kānsə'lēR] *v.* (*ge-*) cancel.
kant ['kant] *n.* (*-e*) lace; side; border, edge; direction; *a.* **-en klaar**, ready, finished; *v.* (*ge-*) oppose; **-ig** *a.* (*-e*) angular; **-jie** *dim.* side, edge, margin; **-werk** *n.* lace.
'kantel ['kantəl] *v.* (*ge-*) topple, overturn, capsize, tilt; **-wa** *n.* side-tip truck.
kan'toor [kan'tŏR] *n.* (*kan'tore*) office.

kap ['kap] *n.* (*-pe*) hood, cowl, shade, cope; *v.* (*ge-*) fell, cut down **-hou** *n.* chop-stroke; **-mes** *n.* billhook, hackknife.
ka'pater [ka'pātəR] *n.* (*-s*) wether; *v.* (*ge-*) castrate.
kapasi'teit [kapasi'tayt] *n.* (*-e*) capacity; ability.
kapi'taal [kap'itāl] *n.* capital, principal; *a.* (*kapi'tale*) excellent; **kapita'lis** *n.* (*-te*) capitalist; **kapitali-'seer** *v.* (*ge-*) capitalize; **kapata'listies** *a.* (*-e*) capitalistic.
ka'pittel [ka'pətəl] *n.* (*-s*) chapter; *v.* (*ge-*) rebuke.
kapitu'lasie [kapitew'lāsi] *n.* capitulation; **kapitu'leer** *v.* (*ge-*) capitulate.
ka'poen [ka'pun] *n.* (*-e*) capon.
ka'pok [ka'pok] *n.* kapok; snow; **-haan(tjie)** *dim.* bantam-cock; fire-brand.
ka'pot [ka'pot] *av.* broken, exhausted, out of order.
'kapploeg ['kapluch] *n.* (*kapploeë*) rotavator.
kapri'ol [kapər'yol] *n.* (*-le*) **-le maak** cut capers.
'kapsel ['kapsəl] *n.* (*-s*) coiffure.
'kapsie ['kapsi] *n.* **-maak** raise objections.
'kapstok ['kapstok] *n.* (*-ke*) hat-rack.
kap'sule [kap'sēwlə] *n.* (*-s*) capsule.
kap'tein [kap'tayn] *n.* (*-s*) captain, chief.
kar ['kaR] *n.* (*-re*) cart; car; **-retjie** *dim.*
ka'raat [ka'Rāt] *n.* (*ka'rate*) carat.
ka'rakter [ka'RaktəR] *n.* (*-s*) character; rôle; mark; nature; **-i'seer** *v.* (*ge-*) characterize; **-i'sering** *n.* description; **-is'tiek** *n.* (*-e*) characteristic; *a.* (*-e*) characteristic; **-loos** *a.* (*-lose*) characterless; **-trek** *n.* (*-ke*) characteristic.
kar'ba [kaR'bā] *n.* (*-'s*) carboy, wicker-bottle.
kar'bied [kaR'bit] *n.* carbide.
karbo'naat [kaRbo'nāt] *n.* carbonate.
kardi'naal [kaRdi'nāl] *n.* (*kardi'nale*) cardinal; *a.* (*kardi'nale*) cardinal.
kar'does [kaR'dus] *n.* (*-se*) paper-bag, cartouche.
'karig ['kāRəch] *a. & av.* (*-e*; *-er*, *-ste*) scanty, slender, frugal; chary.
karika'tuur [kaRika'tēwR] *n.* (*kari-ka'ture*) caricature; **-agtig** *a.* (*-e*) exaggerated, ridiculous.
karil'jon [kaRə'yauñ] *n.* (*-s*) carillon.
kar'katjie [kaR'kaiKi] *n.* (*-s*) sty.
'karkas ['kaRkas] *n.* (*-se*) carcase.
karme'naadjie [kRəm'nāiKi] *n.* (*-s*) cutlet, choice piece of meat.
karmo'syn [kaRmŏ'sayn] *n.* crimson.
kar'nallie [kəR'nali] *n.* (*-s*) rascal.
kar'nuffel [kəR'nʌfəl] *v.* (*ge-*) cuddle; bully.
ka'ros [ka'Ros] *n.* (*-se*) skin-rug.
'karring ['kaRəng] *n.* (*-s*) churn; *v.* (*ge-*) churn; **-melk** *n.* buttermilk.

kar'tel [kaR'tel] n. (-s) cartel, trust.

'kartel [kaR'təl] v. (ge-) wave, curl, to knurl; **-middel** n. setting lotion.

kar'ton [kaR'ton] n. cardboard.

kar'wats [kəR'vats] n. riding whip.

kar'wei [kaR'vay] v. (ge-) convey, transport.

kas ['kas] n. (-te) case; socket; box; chest; cash; v. (ge-) deposit; **-'sier** n. (-s) cashier.

ka'sarm [kə'saRəm] n. barracks.

ka'serne = kasarm.

kaske'nade [kaskə'nādə] n. (-s) prank; uproar; gasconade.

kas'tailing [kas'tayəng] n. (-s) chestnut.

'kaste ['kastə] n. (-s) caste.

kas'teel [kas'tēl] n. (kas'tele) castle.

kasterolie ['kastəRōli] n. castor-oil.

kastig = kamma.

kas'treer [kas'tRēR] v. (ge-) castrate.

kas'trol [kas'tRol] n. (-le) casserole, saucepan.

kas'ty [kas'tay] v. (ge-) castigate, chastise; **-ding** n. castigation, chastisement.

kat ['kat] n. (-te) cat; **-agtig** a. (-e) feline; **-terig** a. (-e; -er, -ste) cattish; **-s** n. lash; **-swink** a. dazed; **-tekwaad** n. pranks, mischief.

ka'talogus [ka'tālŏchʌs] n. (-se) catalogue; **katalogi'seer** v. (ge-) catalogue.

katas'trofe [katas'tRōfə] n. (-s) catastrophe.

katego'rie [katəchŏ'Rī] n. (-ë) category— **kata'gories** a. (-e) categorical.

'katel ['kātəl] n. (-s) bedstead.

'kater ['kātəR] n. tom-cat.

ka'toen [ka'tun] n. cotton.

kato'liek [katŏ'lik] n. & a. (-e) catholic.

ka'trol [ka'tRol] n. (-le) pulley.

'katswink ['katswənk] a. unconscious, dazed.

'kattebak ['katəbak] n. dickey seat.

'kattekwaad ['katəkwāt] n. mischief.

'kattemusiek ['katəmewsik] n. caterwauling.

'katwilg ['katvəlch] n. pussy willow.

keb ['kep] n. (-s) cab.

keel ['kēl] n. (kele) throat, gullet; **-holte** n. pharynx; **-seer** n. sore throat; **-kwassie** n. throat brush; **-sweer** n. (swere) quinsy; **-verf** n. throat paint; **-verstuiwer** n. throat atomizer.

keep ['kēp] n. notch, nick; v. (ge-) notch; **keep-** n. pref. notching-.

keer ['kēR] n. (kere) chance; turn; time; v. (ge-) turn; prevent; defend; check; oppose; **-punt** n. turning point; **-sy** n. reverse.

'keerkring [kēRkRəng] n. (-e) tropic.

kees ['kēs] n. (kese) monkey.

kef ['kef] v. (ge-) yap, bark; **-fertjie** n. yapper, small dog.

kegel, 'keël ['kechəl, 'kēəl] n. (-s) cone; icicle; skittle.

kei ['kay] n. (-e) cobble-stone.

keil ['kayl] n. (-e) wedge; top-hat; v. (ge-) drive in wedge.

'keiser ['kaysəR] n. (-s) emperor; **-'in** fem.; **-snee** n. Caesarean section.

'kekkel ['kekəl] v. (ge-) cackle; chatter; **-bek** n. chatterbox.

'kelder ['keləR] n. (-s) cellar; v. (ge-) sink, go down.

kelk ['kelk] n. (-e) chalice, cup; calyx; **-ie** dim. wineglass.

'kelner ['kelnəR] n. (-s) waiter, steward.

ken ['ken] n. (-ne) chin; v. (ge-) know, understand, recognise; **-merk** n. (-e) characteristic; **-merkend** a. (-e) distinctive; **-ner** n. (-s) connoisseur; **-teken** n. (-s) characteristic.

kenkaartjie ['kenkāRki] n. (-s) tab, tag.

'kennis ['kenəs] n. knowledge; acquaintance; **-gewing** n. (-s) notice; **-skets** v. (ge-) characterize.

'kenstrokie ['kenstRōki] n. = **kenkaartjie**.

'kenter ['kentəR] v. (ge-) turn; **-ing** n. change, turn.

'keperstof ['kēpəRstof] n. twill.

'kêrel ['kɛRəl] n. (-s) chap, fellow; lover, fiancé; **-tjie** dim. little fellow; stripling.

kerf ['keRf] n. (kerwe) nick, notch, incision; v. (ge-) carve, cut, slice.

ker'jakker [kəR'yakəR] v. (ge-) romp, career.

kerk ['keRk] n. (-e) church, chapel; **sy-is uit** he is finished; **-er** n. (-s) prison; dungeon; **-hof** n. (-howe) churchyard, cemetery; **-lik** a. (-e) ecclesiastical; **-s** a. (-e) devout, pious.

kerm ['keRəm] v. (ge-) groan, lament.

'kermis ['keRməs] n. (-se) fair, fête.

'kermis-bed ['keRməsbet] n. shakedown.

kern ['keRn] n. (-s) kernel, pith, core, heart, gist; **-agtig** a. (-e; -er, -ste) terse; **kern-** n. pref. core.

'kerrie ['keRi] n. curry.

kers ['kɛRs] n. (-e) candle; **-ie** dim. cherry.

Kersfees ['kersfēs] n. Christmas, Kersaand n. Christmas Eve; Kersdag n. Christmas Day.

'kersten ['keRstən] v. (ge-) christianize.

kerwel ['keRvəl] n. chervil.

kês ['kɛs] n. boiled sour milk; **-kuiken** n. (-s) chicken, youngster.

'ketel ['kētəl] n. (-s) kettle; **-pak** n. boiler suit.

'kets ['kets] v. (ge-) miss, misfire.

'ketter ['ketəR] n. (-s) heretic; **-s** a. (-e) heretical; **-y** n. heresy.

'ketting ['ketəng] n. (-s) chain.

keur ['kœR] n. selection, choice; v. (ge-) examine, judge, test, inspect; **-der** n. (-s) inspector, taster, assayer, selector; **-ig** a. (-e; -er, -ste) exquisite, dainty, choice; **-ing** n. inspection; selection; choice.

'**keuse** ['kœsə] n. (-s) choice, option.

'**keuwel** ['kœvəl] v. (ge-) chat, gossip.

'**kewer** ['kèvəR] n. (-es) beetle.

'**kibbel** ['kəbəl] v. (ge-) bicker, wrangle; **-aar** n. wrangler.

'**kiek** ['kik] v. (ge-) snap; **-ie** n. snapshot.

kiel ['kil] n. (-e) keel.

'**kielhouer** ['kilhoaəR] n. pick-axe.

'**kielie** ['kili] v. (ge-) tickle; **-bak** n. armpit; **-rig** a. (-e; -er, -ste) ticklish.

kiem ['kim] n. (-e) germ; seed, bud; v. (ge-) germinate, sprout; **-ing** n. germination; **-drywer** n. germicide; **-plasma** n. germ plasm.

'**kiemvry** ['kimfray] a. sterilized.

kiep ['kip] interj. to drive off fowls; **kiep-kiep!** interj. chuck! chuck!

'**kierang** ['kiRang] n. cheating, deception; jou-sal braai the deception will be proved.

'**kierie** ['kiRi] n. (-s) walking-stick.

kies ['kis] n. (-te) molar-tooth; pyrites; a. (-e) considerate, dainty; v. (ge-) choose, select, elect, vote; **-baar** a. (-bare) eligible; **-er** n. (-s) constituent, voter; -'**keurig** a. (-e; -er, -ste) fastidious, dainty.

kik ['kək] n. (-ke) sound.

'**kikvors** ['kəkfoRs] n. (-e) frog.

kil ['kəl] a. (-le) chilly, cold.

kim ['kəm] n. (-me) horizon; mould.

kin = ken n.

'**kina** ['kina] n. quinine.

'**kind** ['kənt] n. (-ers) child, baby, infant; **-eragtig** a. (-e) childish, puerile; **-erjare** n. childhood; **-erlik** a. (-e) childlike, filial; **-erloos** a. (kinderlose) childless; **-erpokkies** n. chicken-pox; **-ertuin** n. kindergarten; -jie n. ['kəŋKi] baby, babe; **-s** a. (-e) doting, senile; **-sbeen** n. van-af from childhood; **-sheid** n. dotage.

kink ['kəŋk] n. kink, knot; v. (ge-) turn, twist; **-el** n. (-s) = kink n.

'**kinnebak** ['kənəbak] n. jawbone.

kir ['kəR] v. (ge-) coo.

kis ['kəs] n. (-te) box, case; chest; coffin; v. (ge-) place in coffin; **-klere** n. best clothes; **-sie** dim.

ki'taar [kə'tàR] n. (ki'tare, -s) guitar.

kits ['kəts] n. in 'n- in a jiffy.

klaag ['klàch] v. (ge-) complain, lament; **-lik** a. (-e) plaintive.

klaar ['klàR] a. (klare) clear; evident; finished; -'**blyklik** a. & av. (-e) evident, obvious, manifest; **-heid** n. clarity; **-kom** v. (ge-) manage, get ready; **-kry** v. (-ge-) get ready, get done, finish; **-praat** av. -met hom he is finished, he is done for; **-speel** v. (-ge-) pull it off.

'**klaargaar**- ['klàRchàR] pref. precooked.

klad ['klat] n. (-de) blot, stain, blotch, smudge; rough copy; v. (ge-) blot, stain; scribble; **-papier** n.

blotting-paper; **-werk** n. rough copy, scribbled notes.

klae = **klaag**; **-nd** a. (-e) complaining; **-r** n. (-s) complainant; **-rig** a. (-e) seedy, peevish.

klag ['klach] n. (-te, -tes) complaint, accusation, lamentation.

'**klakkeloos** ['klakəlòs] a. & av. groundless; off-hand.

klam ['klam] a. (-me) clammy, damp; **-heid** n. dampness; **-merig** a. (-e) slightly damp; **-te** n. = **klam-heid**.

klamp ['klamp] n. (-e) batten; cramp; clamp, cleat; v. (ge-) clamp, cleat.

klan'disie [klan'disi] n. custom, clientele, patronage.

klank ['klank] n. (-e) sound; **-leer** n. phonetics; **-demper** n. silencer, muffler; **-loos** a. (-lose) soundless, toneless; **-ryk** a. (-e) sonorous; **-baan** n. sound track; **-dig** a. (-te) sound-proof; **-effek** n. sound effect; **-film** n. sound film; **-golf** n. sound wave; **-prent** n. sound film.

klant ['klant] n. (-e) customer, client; 'n ou- an old fox, cp. kalant.

klap ['klap] n. (-pe) slap, blow; stroke, crack; **-per** n. (-s) cracker; coconut; index; rattler; v. (ge-) rattle, chatter; **-perdop** n. head; **-perhaar** n. coir; **-perolie** n. coconut-oil.

'**klappertand** ['klapəRtant] v. (ge-) shiver.

klas ['klas] n. (-se) class; form; grade; category.

klas'siek [kla'sik] a. & av. (-e) classic(al); **-e** n. die- the classics.

klassifi'kasie [klasifi'kàsi] n. classification; **klassifi'seer** v. (ge-) classify; **klassifi-sering** n. classifying, classification.

'**klatergoud** ['klàtəRchoat] n. tinsel, leaf-brass; **klatergoudstof** n. tinsel.

kla'vier [kla'fiR] n. (-e) piano.

'**klawer** ['klàvəR] n. clover, shamrock; **-s** n. clubs (cards).

'**kleding** ['klèdəng] n. clothes, dress, attire; **-stuk** n. (-ke) garment.

klee ['klè] v. (ge-) clothe, dress; **-rtjies** dim. baby-clothes.

kleed ['klèt] n. dress, garment; **-jie** dim. (-s) cloth, table-cloth.

kleef, 'klewe ['klèf, 'klèvə] v. (ge-) cleave, adhere; **-pleister** n. adhesive plaster.

klei ['klay] n. clay; **-agtig** a. (-e; -er, -ste) clayish; **-erig** a. (-e; -er, -ste) = **kleiagtig**; **-werk** n. clay-modelling.

klein ['klayn] a. & av. little, small; petty; **klei'neer** v. (ge-) disparage, belittle; -'**ering** n. belittlement, disparagement; -'**geestig** a. (-e; -er, -ste) narrow-minded, petty; **-geld** n. change; **-goed** n. kids; **-heid** n. smallness, pettiness; **-igheid** n. trifle; **-kind** n. grandchild; **-kry** v. (-ge-) master; **-maak** v. (-ge-) change; **-neef** n. second cousin; -'**serig** a. (-e) oversensitive; **-seun** n. grandson; -'sielig a. (-e) petty; **-span** n. kids; **-ste** a. smallest; **-tjie** dim. little one.

'kleinlik ['klaynlək] a. (-e) petty.

'kleinood ['klaynŏt] n. ('kleinode) jewel, gem.

'kleintongetjie ['klayntongəKi] n. uvula.

'kleinvee ['klaymfē] n. small live-stock.

klem ['klem] n. accent, lockjaw; trap; clamp; v. (ge-) clamp, tighten, clench; **-mend** a. (-e) forcible, cogent; **-teken** n. accent, stress; **-toon** n. accent; **klem–** n. pref. cleat, clip.

klep ['klep] n. (-pe) valve, key, flap; **-loos** a. (-lose) valveless; **-ligter** n. (-s) tappet; **-kop** n. valve head; **-reëling** n. valve timing; **-slyper** n. valve grinder; **-stoter** n. tappet; **-veer** n. valve spring.

'klepel ['klēpəl] n. (-s) clapper, tongue.

kle'rasie [klē'Rāsi] n. clothing.

'klere ['klēRə] n. pl. clothes; **-drag** n. dress, fashion.

kleri'kaal [klēRi'kāl] a. (kleri'kale) clerical.

klerk ['kleRk] n. (-e) clerk.

klets ['klets] v. (ge-) yap, chatter; splash, swish; **-ery** n. twaddle; **-nat** a. soaking wet; **-praatjie** n. small talk, gossip.

'kletskous ['kletskoas] n. gossip, chatterbox.

kleur ['klē̄R] n. (-e) colour, hue; timbre; dye; v. (ge-) colour; flush, blush; dye; kleur-eg a. (-te) fadeless; **-ig** a. gay, colourful; **-ling** n. (-e) coloured person; **-loos** a. (-lose) colourless; **-sel** n. colouring; **-wiel** n. colour wheel.

'kleuter ['klē̄tǝR] n. (-s) toddler, kiddy.

klewe = kleef; **-rig** a. (-e) adhesive, tacky.

klief ['klif] v. (ge-) cleave.

kliek ['klik] n. clique, coterie.

kli'ënt [kli'ent] n. (-e) client, customer; cp. klant.

klier ['kliR] n. (-e) gland.

'klik– ['klik–] n. pref. click-, pilot-, tell-tale-.

klim ['kləm] v. (ge-) climb, ascend, rise; **-mend** a. (-e) ascending; **-op** n. creeper.

kli'maat [klə'māt] n. climate; kli-mato'logies a. (-e) climatic.

'klimaks ['klimaks] n. climax.

'klimop ['kləmop] n. creeper.

'klimplant ['kləmplant] n. (-e) rambler, creeper.

kli'niek [klə'nik] n. (-e) clinic; 'klinies a. (-e) clinical.

klink ['klənk] v. (ge-) sound; n. latch, catch; **-end** a. (-e) resonant; **-er** n. (-s) vowel; clinker, biscuit; **-dig** n. sonnet.

'klinknael ['klənknāl] n. (-s) rivet.

klip ['kləp] n. (-pe, -pers) stone,

pebble; **-hard** a. & av. hard as stone; **-perig** a. (-e) stoney, rocky; **-rug** n. ridge; **-steenhard** a. & av. very hard; **-sweet** a. hyraceum.

'klisma ['kləsma] n. enema.

klits ['klots] v. (ge-) beat (eggs); thrash, smack; n. burr.

kloek ['kluk] a. bold, brave, strong.

klok ['klok] n. (-ke) bell, clock; **-huis** n. core (fruit); **-kie** n. dim.; **-slag**, n. stroke of the clock; **-sgewys(e)** a. & av. clockwise.

klomp ['klomp] n. (-e) crowd; lump; wooden shoe; **-ie** dim. a few, a small heap.

'klonkie ['klonki] n. (-s) small coloured boy.

klont ['klont] n. (-e) lump; clod; v. (ge-) clot, curdle; **-erig** a. (-e) clotty, lumpy; **-jie** dim. small lump.

kloof ['klŏf] n. (klowe) cleft, fissure, gulf, ravine; v. (ge-) cleave, split; chop.

'klooster ['klŏstǝR] n. (-s) cloister, abbey, convent.

klop ['klop] n. (-pe) knock, tap; beat; v. (ge-) knock, tap, rap; beat; palpitate; defeat, lick; **-gees** n. poltergeist; **-jag** n. (-te) police raid; **-hamer** n. mallet; **-lees** n. dolly.

'klopper ['klopǝR] n. (-s) knocker.

klos ['klos] n. (-se) bobbin, reel; spool; coil; v. (ge-) form locks.

klots ['klots] n. lapping (waves); v. (ge-) splash, beat.

klou ['kloa] n. (-e) claw, talon, clutch; v. (ge-) cling, stick; **-erig** a. (-e) sticky; **-tjie** dim.; **-moer** n. dog biscuit.

klou'sule [kloa'sewlə] n. (-s) clause, proviso.

'klouter ['kloatǝR] v. (ge-) clamber, climb.

'kloutjiesolie ['kloakisŏli] n. neat's-foot-oil.

klub ['klʌp] n. (-s) club.

klug ['klʌch] n. (-te) farce; **-tig** a. (-e) farcical.

'kluis ['kloeis] n. (-e) hermitage, cell; strong room.

'kluisenaar ['kloeisǝnāR] n. (-s) recluse.

'kluister ['kloeistǝR] v. (ge-) chain, fetter, shackle.

kluit ['kloeit] n. (-e) lump; **-erig** a. (-e) cloddy, lumpy; **-jie** dim. (-s) dumpling; fib.

kluts ['klʌts] n. die-kwyt wees be at sea, get flurried.

knaag ['knāch] v. (ge-) gnaw; nag.

knaap ['knāp] n. (knape) boy, lad; knapie dim.

knae = knaag; **-nd** a. (-e; -er, -ste) gnawing, ceaselessly; knaging n. (-e, -s) gnawing; pangs (conscience).

knak ['knak] n. (-ke) crack; injury; v. (ge-) crack, snap, break; injure; **-s** av. (-e) at loggerheads.

knal ['knal] n. (-le) explosion, report; v. (ge-) crack, bark, clap; **-demper** n. (-s) silencer, muffler.

knap ['knap] a. (-pe) able, capable, clever; very close fitting, pinching; av. cleverly; -'handig a. (-e) dextrous; -heid n. ability; -sak n. knapsack.

knee ['knē] v. (ge-) knead, mould.

kneg ['knech] n. (-te) servant, slave; v. (ge-) enslave; -s a. (-e) servile.

knel ['knel] v. (ge-) pinch; oppress; jam; -lend a. (-e) oppressive; -ling n. oppression; -verband n. constrictive bandage.

kners ['kneRs] v. (ge-) gnash, grind; grate; -ing n. gnashing.

'knetter ['knetəR] v. (ge-) crackle.

'kneukel ['knœkəl] n. (-s) knuckle.

kneus ['knœs] v. (ge-) bruise; -ing n. bruise, contusion.

'knewel ['knēvəl] n. (-s) whopper.

'knibbel ['knəbəl] v. (ge-) haggle.

knie ['knī] n. (ē-) knee; -skut n. knee-guard; -vering n. knee action (mech.).

kniel ['knīl] v. (ge-) kneel.

knies ['knīs] v. (ge-) fret, mope, sulk; -erig a. (-e) fretful, moping.

knik ['knək] v. (ge-) nod, wink; n. (-ke) nod, knuckle (hinge); -ker n. (-s) marble (in the game).

knip ['knəp] n. (-pe) cut: snip; catch; bolt; v. (ge-) clip; -mes n. clasp knife; -sel n. (-s) cutting, clipping; knip- n. pref. latch-; -lig n. blinker.

'knobbel ['knobəl] n. (-s) knob; nodule.

knoei ['knui] v. (ge-) mess; intrigue; -er n. cheat, intriguer; -ery n. mess, intrigue.

'knoes ['knus] n. (-te) knot, gnarl; -ie dim. nodule.

knoffel ['knofəl] n. garlic.

'knoets ['knuts] n. (-e) burr.

'knokkel ['knokəl] n. (-s) bunion.

knol ['knol] n. (-le) old crock; bulb.

knoop ['knōp] n. (knope) button; knot; stud; oath; bump; v. (ge-) button up; tie; knot; swear.

'knoopsgat ['knōpschat] n. (-gate) button-hole.

knop ['knop] n. (-pe) knob, handle; button; switch; bump; v. (ge-) bud; -pie dim.

'knopkierie ['knopKiRi] n. (-s) knobkerrie, cudgel.

knor ['knoR] v. (ge-) growl, grunt; scold; -rig a. (-e; -er, -ste) peevish.

knot ['knot] v. (ge-) top, prune, truncate, pollard; curtail; -s n. (-e) club, cudgel.

knou ['knoa] n. (-e) gnaw; set back, injury; v. (ge-) gnaw, munch; maul, injure.

'knuppel ['knʌpəl] n. (-s) club, cudgel.

knyp ['knayp] v. (ge-) pinch, squeeze; n. (-e) pinch; in die-wees be in a fix; -er n. (-s) clasper, claw; -tang n. pincers, nippers.

koa'lisie [kōa'lisi] n. coalition.

'koddig ['kodəch] a. (-e; -er, -ste) droll, comical.

'koeël ['kūəl] n. (-s) bullet; -laer n. (-s) ball-bearing; -tjie dim. pellet; -gewrig n. ball and socket joint.

koei ['kui] n. (-e) cow; -tjie dim.

koe'jawel [ku'yāvəl] n. (-s) guava.

koek ['kuk] n. (-e) cake; v. (ge-) clot, knot, cake; -soda n. bicarbonate of soda.

koek'suster [kuk'sʌstəR] n. (-s) sugar-dumpling.

koel ['kul] a. (-e; -er, -ste) cool, fresh; v. (ge-) vent, wreak; cool down; -bloedig a. (-e; -er, -ste) cold-blooded; -erig a. (-e) chilly; -heid n. coolness; -kamer n. (-s) cold-storage; -te n. (-s) coolness; shade; breeze; -room n. cold cream.

'koepel ['kupəl] n. (-s) dome, cupola.

koe'pon [ku'pon] n. (-s) coupon.

'koer ['kuR] v. (ge-) coo.

koe'rant [ku'Rant] n. (-e) newspaper.

koe'rasie [ku'Rāsi] n. courage.

koers ['kuRs] n. (-e) course, route, direction; currency, rate; v. (ge-) head for.

'koester ['kustəR] v. (ge-) cherish, entertain.

koets ['kuts] n. (-e) coach; v. (ge-) crouch, dodge; koets-koets av. continually dodging.

koet'sier [kut'siR] n. (-s) driver, coachman.

koe'vert [ku'fɛRt] n. (-s) envelope.

'koevoet ['kufut] n. (-e) crowbar.

'koffer ['kofəR] n. (-s) box, trunk; coffer; -tjie dim. attaché-case.

'koffie ['kofi] n. coffee.

'koggel ['kochəl] v. (ge-) mimic, imitate, tease; -(a)ry n. mimicry.

kok ['kok] n. (-s) cook, caterer.

koker ['kōkəR] n. (-s) boiler; cooker; sheath; quiver; -ery n. cooking, cookery.

ko'ket [kō'ket] n. coquette, flirt; koke'teer v. (ge-) flirt.

kol ['kol] n. (-le) spot; stain; blaze; kol-kol av. in patches.

'kolffies ['kolfies] n. (-se) retort.

kolk ['kolk] n. (-e) eddy, whirlpool; v. (ge-) eddy, whirl.

kol'lega [kō'lēcha] n. (-s) colleague; kollegi'saal a. (kollegi'ale) as a colleague.

'kollege ['kolitsh] n. (-s) college.

kol'leksie [kō'leksi] n. (-s) collection; kollek'tant n. (-e) collector; kol'lekte n. collection; kollek'teer v. (ge-) collect.

kolo'kwint [kolo'kwənt] n. colocynth.

ko'lonie [kō'lōni] n. (-s) colony; koloni'saal a. (koloni'ale) colonial; kolo'nis n. (-te) colonist.

ko'los [kō'los] n. (-se) colossus; kolo'saal a. (kolo'sale) colossal.

kom ['kom] n. (-me) basin, bowl; coming; v. (ge-) arrive, come; -aan! interj. come along! cheer up! -metjie dim. mug; -s n. arrival, coming.

kom'bers [kom'bɛRs] n. (-e) blanket.

kombi'nasie [kombə'nāsi] n. (-s)

combination; **kombi'neer** v. (ge-) combine.

kom'buis [kom'bœis] n. (-e) kitchen.

ko'medie [kŏ'mēdi] n. (-s) comedy, farce.

ko'miek [kŏ'mik] a. (-e) comic(al), droll; -lik a. (-e; -er, -ste) comic(al), droll.

'komies ['kōmis] a. (-e; -er, -ste) comic(al), funny.

komi'tee [kŏmi'tē] n. (-s) committee.

kom'kommer [kom'kɔməR] n. (-s) cucumber; -tyd n. silly season.

'komma ['koma] n. (-s) comma.

komman'dant [koma'dant] n. (-e) commandant, commander; **komman'deer** v. (ge-) command, commandeer, requisition.

kommen'taar [komən'tāR] n. (kommen'tare) commentary.

'kommer ['komaR] n. care, affliction, grief, anxiety, need; -lik a. (-e) needy; distressed; anxious; -loos a. (-lose) carefree; -nis n. = **kommer**.

'kommetjie ['komaKi] n. (-s) mug, bowl.

kom'missie [ko'misi] n. (-s) commission, committee.

kommuni'kasie [komewni'kāsi] n. communication.

kommu'nis [komew'nəs] n. (-te) communist.

kompan'jie [kompan'yi] n. (-s) company.

kompara'tief [kompaRa'tif] n. comparative (mood).

komparte'ment [kompaRtə'ment] n. (-e) compartment.

kom'pas [kom'pas] n. (-se) compass.

kompen'sasie [kompən'sāsi] n. compensation; **kompen'seer** v. (ge-) compensate.

kompe'tisie [kompə'tisi] n. (-s) competition; **kompe'teer** v. (ge-) compete.

kom'pleet [kom'plēt] a. (kom'plete) complete, utter, positive; av. utterly, completely.

kom'pleks [kom'pleks] n. & a. (-e) complex.

kompli'ment [kompla'ment] n. (-e) compliment; respects.

kom'plot [kom'plot] n. (-te) plot, intrigue.

kompo'nis [kompŏ'nəs] n. (-te) composer.

kom'pres [kom'pRes] n. (-se) compress.

kompro'mis [kompRŏ'məs] n. compromise; **kompromit'teer** v. (ge-) compromise.

konden'sasie [konden'sāsi] n. condensation; **konden'seer** v. (ge-) condense.

kon'disie [kon'disi] n. condition; pl. terms.

konduk'teur [kondʌk'tēR] n. (-s) conductor.

konfede'rasie [konfēdə'Rāsi] n. confederation; **konfede'reer** v. (ge-) confederate.

konfidensi'eel [konfədensi'el] a. (konfidensi'ele) confidential.

konfis'keer [konfəs'kēR] v. (ge-) confiscate.

kon'flik [kon'flək] n. (-te) conflict.

kon'foor [kom'fŏR] n. brazier; chafing-dish.

kon'fyt [kon'fayt] n. jam, preserve; v. (ge-) ge-wees in be accustomed to, be well-versed in.

kon'gres [kauñ'chRes] n. (-se) congress.

'koning ['kŏnəng] n. (-e, -s) king; -'in n. queen; **'koninklik** a. (-e) royal; **'koninkryk** n. kingdom.

'konkel ['konkəl] v. (ge-) plot, wangle, intrigue; -a'ry n. scheming; -werk n. muddle, bad work.

kon'klusie [kong'klewsi] n. (-s) conclusion; **konklu'deer** v. (ge-) conclude.

kon'kreet [kong'kRēt] a. (kon'krete) concrete.

konkur'reer [kongkə'RēR] v. (ge-) compete; **konkur'rensie** n. rivalry.

kon'neksie [ko'neksi] n. (-s) connection.

konse'kwent [konsə'kwent] a. (-e) consistent.

kon'sensie [kauñ'señsi] n. conscience; **konsensi'eus** a. (-e) conscientious.

konsen'treer [konsen'tRēR] v. (ge-) concentrate.

kon'sep [kon'sep] n. (-te) concept, draft.

kon'sepsie [kon'sepsi] n. conception.

kon'sert [kon'seRt] n. (-e) concert.

konserwa'tief [konseRva'tif] n. & a. (konserwatiewe) conservative.

kon'sessie [kon'sesi] n. (-s) concession.

konside'rasie [konsədə'Rāsi] n. consideration; **konside'reer** v. (ge-) consider.

konsili'asie [konsili'āsi] n. conciliation; **konsili'eer** v. (ge-) conciliate.

konsoli'dasie [konsŏlə'dāsi] n. consolidation; **konsoli'deer** v. (ge-) consolidate.

konso'nant [konsŏ'nant] n. (-e) consonant.

kon'stabel [kon'stāvəl] n. (-s) constable.

kon'stant [kon'stant] a. (-e) constant, uniform.

konstel'lasie [konstə'lāsi] n. (-s) constellation.

konster'nasie [kauñstəR'nāsi] n. consternation.

konsti'tusie [kauñstə'tewsi] n. constitution.

kon'struksie [kauñs'tRʌksi] n. construction; **konstrueer** v. (ge-) construct; **konstruk'teur** n. (-s) constructor.

kon'suis [kauñ'sœis] av. quasi.

'konsul ['konsʌl] n. (-s) consul; **konsu'laat** n. consulate; **konsu'lêr** a. (-e) consular.

kon'tak [kon'tak] n. (-te) contact;
-lens n. contact lens.

kon'tant [kon'tant] n. & a. (-e) cash;
impertinent.

konti'nent [konti'nent] n. (-e)
continent.

kontinui'teit [kontənewi'tayt] n.
continuity.

kon'trak [kon'tRak] n. (-te) contract;
-'tant n. (-e) contractor; -'teer v.
(ge-) contract; kontrak'teur n. (-s)
contractor.

kon'tras [kon'tRas] n. (-te) contrast;
kontras'teer v. (ge-) contrast.

kontri'busie [kontRə'bewsi] n. (-s)
contribution.

kon'trole [kon'tRōlə] n. control;
kontro'leer v. (ge-) control; kontro-
'leur n. (-s) controller.

konvensio'neel [kaunfensiō'nēl] a.
(konvensio'nele) conventional.

ko'nyn [ku'nayn] n. (-e) rabbit.

'kooi ['kōi] n. (-e) bed; cage; -goed n.
bedding; bed-clothes.

kook ['kōk] v. (ge-) boil; -s n. coke.

kool ['kōl] n. cabbage; n. (kole) coal,
carbon; -teer n. coal-tar.

koop ['kōp] v. (ge-) buy; -man n.
merchant, chapman; -vereniging n.
co-operative (wholesale) society.

'koopware ['kōpvārə] n. merchandise.

koor ['kōR] n. (kore) choir, chorus.

koord ['kōRt] n. (-e) cord, rope,
string.

ko-ordi'nasie [kō-oRdə'nāsi] n.
co-ordination; ko-ordi'neer v. (ge-)
co-ordinate.

koors ['kōRs] n. fever; -agtig a. (-e)
feverish, hectic; -ig a. (-e) feverish;
-pennetjie n. clinical thermometer.

kop ['kop] n. (-pe) head; hill;
mountain; cob; crest; v. (ge-) form a
cob, form a head (cabbage); -af av.
head off; kop-aan-kop neck and
neck; -klep n. overhead valve; -lamp
n. headlamp; cap lamp; -pie dim.
hillock; cup; -pig a. (-e; -er, -ste)
stubborn; -seer n. headache; -skoot
n. effective reply; -sku a. shy.

'koper ['kōpəR] n. copper; buyer.

'koperkapel ['kōpəRkapel] n. (-le)
cobra.

'kopie ['kōpi] n. bargain.

ko'pie [kō'pi] n. copy; kopi'eer v.
(ge-) copy; -reg n. copyright.

'koppel ['kopəl] v. (ge-) couple, join;
-aar n. (-s) clutch; -naaf n. clutch
hub; -pedaal n. clutch pedal; -veer
n. clutch spring; -rat n. clutch
gear; -ing n. coupling, link; -teken
n. hyphen.

'koppenent ['kopənent] n. head (of
bed).

'kopruimte ['kopRœimtə] n. head-
way.

'kopseer ['kopsēR] n. headache.

kor'daat [koR'dāt] a. & av. bold,
firm.

korf ['koRf] n. (korwe) basket,
hamper, hive; -bal n. basket-ball.

'koring ['kōRəng] n. corn, wheat;
-blom n. cornflower; -kiem n. wheat
germ; -kiemolie n. wheat germ oil.

kor'nuit [kəR'nœit, kəRnōtəR(s)] n.
comrade; henchman; crony.

korpo'rasie [koRpə'Rāsi] n. (-s)
corporation.

korps ['koRps] n. (-e) corps, body.

kor'rek [kō,Rek] a. (-te) correct,
right; kor'reksie n. correction;
korrek'tief n. corrective.

'korrel ['koRəl] n. (-s) grain, pellet;
bead, sight; v. (ge-) aim.

'korrelkop ['koRlkop] n. grouser,
stubborn fellow.

korrespon'dent [koRəspon'dent] n.
(-e) correspondent; korrespon'densie
n. correspondence.

korri'geer [koRə'shēR] v. (ge-)
correct.

kors ['kauRs] n. (-te) crust; v. (ge-)
form a crust; -ie dim. joke; -wel v.
(ge-) banter.

kort ['koRt] a. (-e; -er; -ste) short,
brief; v. (ge-) shorten; -af av.
abrupt; -gebonde a. & av. short-
tempered; -heid n. shortness, brevity; -ing n. rebate; kort-kort av.
frequently; -om av. briefly; -'stondig
a. (-e) short-lived; -weg av. briefly.

'kortgolf'sender ['koRtcholf'send-
əR] n. (-s) short-wave transmitter.

korti'soon [koRtisōn] n. cortisone.

'kortliks ['koRtləks] av. briefly.

'kortsluit ['koRtslœit] v. (-ge-) to
short, fuse; -ing n. short-circuit.

kos ['kos] n. food, fare; v. (ge-) cost;
-baar a. (-bare; -der, -ste) expensive,
costly; -te n. cost, expense; -telik a.
(-e) excellent; -teloos a. (kostelose)
gratis; -vry a. (-e) free of charge.

'koster ['kostəR] n. (-s) church-
warden.

kos'tuum [kos'tewm] n. (-s) costume,
dress.

ko'syn [ku'sayn] n. (-e) frame (door
or window).

kote'let [kotə'let] n. (-te) cutlet, chop.

kou ['koa] n. cage; v. (ge-) chew;
-gom n. chewing-gum; -tjie dim. cud.

koud ['koatl] a. cold; -lei v. (ge-)
walk (a horse) up and down; hoodwink.

'koue ['koaə] n. cold; -ekoors n. ague;
-elik a. (-e) sensitive ot cold; -erig a.
(-e) chilly, coldish; -vuur n. gangrene.

kous ['koas] n. (-e) hose, stocking;
gaiter.

kraag ['kRāch] n. collar, yoke.

kraai ['kRāi] crow; v. (ge-) crow.

kraak ['kRāk] n. (krake) crack; flaw;
fissure; crackle; v. (ge-) crack, creak,
crunch, crackle; -been n. cartilage;
-stem n. grating noise.

kraal ['kRāl] n. (krale) pen, fold,
coral; -tjie dim. (-s) bead.

kraam ['kRām] n. (krame) booth,
stand; childbed; -been n. white leg;
dit pas in sy it suits his purpose.

kraan ['kRǎn] n. (krane) tap, cock; crane; -voël n. (-s) crane.

krabbetjie ['kRavəKi] n. (-s) earring.

kraffie ['kRafi] n. (-s) decanter, carafe.

krag [kRach] n. (-te) strength, force; potency; virtue; -'dadig a. (-e) energetic; -teloos a. (kragtelose) weak; -tens av. by virtue of; -term n. expletive; -tig a. (-e; -er, -ste) strong, powerful; efficacious; cogent; -tig! interj. damn! -vol a. (-e), forcible; -bron n. source of power, power plant; -rem n. power brake; -sentrale n. power station; -stasie n. = kragsentrale; -stuur n. power steering; -verlies n. loss of power; -woord n. expletive.

kragvoer ['kRachfūR] n. concentrates.

kram [kRam] n. (-me) staple; -bout n. U-bolt; - en oorslag n. hasp and staple.

kramer ['kRǎməR] n. (-s) hawker, pedler; cp. **kraam**; -y n. small wares, haberdashery.

krammetjie [kRaməKi] n. (-s) staple.

kramp ['kRamp] n. (-e) cramp, spasm; -agtig a. (-e) convulsive.

kranig ['kRǎnəch] a. (-e; -er, -ste) smart, intelligent, dashing.

krank ['kRank] a. & av. (-e) sick, ill; -e n. (-s) patient, sick person; -heid n. sickness, disease; -'sinnig a. (-e; -er, -ste) crazy, insane, mad; -sinnig maak to dement.

krans ['kRǎns] n. (-e) garland, wreath, chaplet; ledge; whorl; -berge pl. escarpment-mountains; -sie dim. (-s).

krap ['kRap] n. (-pe) crab; scratch; v. (ge-) scratch, claw, paw.

kras ['kRas] a. (-, -se) vigorous, crass, strong; v. (ge-) scratch, scrape; screech; scribe.

krat ['kRat] n. crate.

krater ['kRǎtəR] n. (-s) crater.

krea'tuur [kRěa'tēWR] n. (krea'ture) creature, being.

kre'diet [kRə'dit] n. credit; **kredi-'teer** v. (ge-) credit; **kredi'teur** n. (-s) creditor.

kreef ['kRef] n. (krewe) crawfish, lobster.

kreet ['kRēt] n. (krete) cry, scream, shriek.

krenk ['kRenk] v. (ge-) hurt, offend; -end a. (-e; -er, -ste) offensive; -ing n. (-s) insult.

krenterig ['kRentərəch] a. (-e; -er, -ste) mean, stingy.

kreuk, kreukel ['kRœk, -əl] n. crease, fold; v. (ge-) crease, crumple.

kreun [kRœn] n. (-e) groan; v. (ge-) groan, moan.

kreupel ['kRœpəl] a. cripple, lame; -e n. (-s) a crippled person.

kriek ['kRik] n. (-e) house-cricket; -ie dim.

krieket ['kRikət] n. cricket.

kriesel ['kRisl] n. (-s) bit, morsel.

kriewel ['kRivl] v. (ge-) itch; fidget; -ing n. itching; -rig a. (-e) itchy; fidgety; petulant.

kring ['kRəng] n. (-e) circle, ring, set; v. (ge-) coil, curl, circle; -etjie dim.; -loop n. cycle.

krink ['kRənk] v. (ge-) turn; -arm n. steering arm; -sirkel n. turning circle; -spil n. king pin.

kri'oel [kRi'ul] v. (ge-) swarm, abound, teem.

krisis ['kRisəs] n. (-se) crisis.

Krismis = Kersfees.

kris'tal [kRəs'tal] n. (-le) crystal.

kri'terium [kRi'tēRiʌm] n. criterion.

kri'tiek [kRə'tik] n. criticism, review; a. (-e) critical, crucial; **kri'ties** a. (-e) critical; **kritikus** n. (-se, kritici) critic; **kriti'seer** v. (ge-) criticize.

kroeg [kRuch] n. (kroeë) bar, pub.

kroes ['kRus] a. woolly, frizzy.

krom [kRom] a. (-me; -mer, -ste) bent, crooked; v. (ge-) bend, bow, curve; -hout n. vine; -me n. (-s) curve; -ming n. bend, curve; -trek v. (ge-) buckle, warp.

kromhoutsop ['kRomhoatsop] n. liquor, wine.

kroning ['kRǒnəng] n. (-s) coronation.

kronkel ['kRonkəl] n. (-s) coil, kink; v. (ge-) coil, meander, twist; -pad n. winding road; -end a. (-e) winding; -veer n. coil spring.

kroon ['kRǒn] n. (krone) crown; coronet; head (lettuce); top; castellate; v. (ge-) crown; -rat n. crown wheel; -blaar n. petal; -tjie dim. cowlick; -lugter n. chandelier; -vervolger n. public prosecutor.

kroos ['kRǒs] n. offspring.

krop ['kRop] n. (-pe) crop, gizzard; goitre; head (lettuce); v. (ge-) cram, ek kan dit nie-nie I cannot stand it; -geswel n. goitre.

kropslaai ['kRopslǎi] n. lettuce.

krot ['kRot] n. (-te) hovel, shanty.

kruide'nier [kRœidə'niR] n. (-s) grocer.

kruier [kRœiəR] n. (-s) porter.

kruik ['kRœik] n. (-e) pitcher, jug.

kruin ['kRœin] n. (-e) crown, summit, top; **kruin**- n. pref. crest-, peak-, top-.

kruip ['kRœip] v. (ge-) creep, crawl, cringe; -end a. (-e) creeping; -erig a. (-e) cringing.

kruis ['kRœis] n. cross; v. (ge-) cross; interbreed; crucify; -bande pl. braces; -koppeling n. universal joint; -slang n. cross-bar; **kruis**- n. pref. transposition-, cross-; -ie dim. cross, mark; -verhoor n. cross-examination.

kruisvra ['kRœisfRǎ] v. (ge-) cross-examine.

kruit [kRœit] n. gunpowder.

kruiwa ['kRœivǎ] n. (-ens) wheelbarrow.

kruk ['kRʌk] n. (-ke) crutch; stool; crank; -ker n. crock; -kerig a. (-e) ailing, seedy; -as n. (-te) crankshaft; -aslaer n. crankshaft bearing; -kas n. crankcase.

krul [kRʌl] n. (-le) curl; v. (ge-) curl, frizz; -lerig a. (-e) curly; -letjie dim. (-s) curl, ringlet.

'**krulhare** ['kRʌlhāRə] n. curly hair; 'krulkop n. curly-head.

'**krummel** ['kRʌməl] n. (-s) crumb; v. (ge-) crumble.

'**kruppel** = **kreupel**.

kry ['kRay] v. (ge-) get, receive; catch; acquire, obtain.

kryg ['kRaych] n. war, fight; -s'haftig a. (-e) warlike.

'**krygswet** ['kraychsvet] n. martial law.

krys ['kRays] v. (ge-) scream, shriek, screech.

kryt ['kRayt] n. chalk, crayon; arena.

ku'biek [kew'bik] a. (-e) cube, cubic.

'**kubus** ['kewbʌs] n. (-se) cube.

'**kudde** ['kʌdə] n. (-s) flock.

kug ['kʌch] n. cough; v. (ge-) cough, hem.

'**kuier** ['kœiəR] n. visit, call, outing; v. (ge-) visit, call; stroll; -gas n. (-te) guest.

kuif ['kœif] n. (kuiwe) tuft, forelock, crest.

'**kuiken** ['kœikən] n. (-s) chicken; youngster.

'**kuil** ['kœil] n. (-e) hole, pit, pool; v. (ge-) put in pits, ensile; -tjie dim. (-s) hole; dimple.

'**kuilvoer** ['kœilfūR] n. ensilage.

kuip ['kœip] n. (-e) tub, vat, barrel; cp. Eng. coop; -er n. cooper; schemer; -y n. scheming.

kuis ['kœis] a. (-e) chaste, innocent, pure.

kuit ['kœit] n. (-e) calf (leg); spawn.

kul ['kʌl] v. (ge-) cheat; -lery n. cheating, deceit.

kul'tuur [kʌl'tēwR] n. (kul'ture) culture; cultivation.

'**kunde** ['kʌndə] n. knowledge; 'kundig a. (-e) capable, clever; skilful.

kuns ['kʌns] n. (-te) art; knack; artificial; -greep n. artifice; -leer n. imitation leather; -tenaar n. (-s) artist; -tena'res n. fem. artist; -tig a. (-e) artistic.

kuns'matig [kʌ̃smātəch] a. (-e) artificial.

'**kunsmis** ['kʌ̃sməs] n. fertiliser.

'**kunswerk** ['kʌ̃sveRk] n. (-e) work of art.

'**kurang** = **kierang**.

ku'rator [kew'Rātor] n. (kura'tore) curator, guardian.

kuriosi'teit [kewriosi'tayt] n. curiosity, curio.

kurk ['kʌRk] n. (-e) cork; v. (ge-) cork, close; -droog a. (-droë) bone-dry; -trekker n. (-s) corkscrew.

kur'sief [kʌR'sif] a. (kur'siewe) in italics.

'**kursus** ['kʌRsʌs] n. (-se) course.

'**kurwe** ['kʌRvə] n. (-s) curve, graph.

kus ['kʌs] n. (-se) kiss; n. (-te) coast; te-en te keur of a wide choice; v. (ge-) kiss.

'**kussing** ['kʌsəng] n. (-s) cushion, pillow; -veer n. cushion spring.

'**kussingsloop** ['kʌsəngslôp] n. ('kussingslope) pillow-case.

kuur ['kēwR] n. (kure) cure; caprice.

kwaad ['kwāt] n. evil, wrong, damage; a. & av. angry, annoyed, vexed; -'aardig a. (-e) vicious, malicious; -doener n. (-s) evildoer; -geld n. vir-rondloop loaf about; -heid n. anger; -stook v. (ge-) stir up strife; -stoker n. busybody; -'willig a. (-e) malevolent.

kwaai ['kwāi] a. (-e; -er, -ste) bad-tempered; vicious, strict; -erig a. (-e) tends to be strict; -kop a. irascible person.

kwaak ['kwāk] v. (ge-) quack, croak.

kwaal ['kwāl] n. (kwale) ailment, complaint.

'**kwagga** ['kwacha] n. (-s) quagga.

'**kwajong** ['kwāyong] n. (-ens) imp, urchin, rascal.

'**kwakmiddel** ['kwakmədl] n. (-s) nostrum.

'**kwaksalwer** ['kwaksalvəR] n. (-s) quack; -y n. quackery.

kwalifi'seer [kwalifi-sēR] v. (ge-) qualify.

'**kwalik** ['kwālək] av. hardly, scarcely; amiss.

kwali'teit [kwali'tayt] n. quality.

'**kwansel** ['kwãnsəl] v. (ge-) exchange, barter.

kwanti'teit [kwanti'tayt] n. (-e) quantity.

kwart ['kwaRt] n. (-e) quarter, quart; a. fourth; kwar'taal n. quarter, term; kwar'tet n. quartette; kwar'tier n. (-e) quarter of an hour; quarter, district, quarters.

kwarts ['kwarts] n. quartz.

kwas ['kwas] n. (-te) brush, tuft, tassel; squash; -sie dim.; -terig a. (-e) gnarled; bad-tempered.

kweek ['kwēk] n. quick-grass; v. (ge-) cultivate; -huis n. hothouse; -skool n. seminary; 'kwekeling n. pupil, apprentice; 'kweker n. breeder, grower.

kwel ['kwel] v. (ge-) annoy; worry; -ling n. torment, worry.

kwes ['kwes] v. (ge-) wound, injure; offend.

'**kwessie** ['kwesi] n. (-s) matter, question, issue.

kwik ['kwək] n. mercury; -silwer n. = kwik.

'**kwispel** ['kwəspəl] v. (ge-) wag the tail.

'**kwistig** ['kwəstəch] a. (-e) lavish.

kwi'tansie [kwə'tãsi] n. (-s) receipt.

'**kwota** ['kwōta] n. (-s) quota.

kwyl ['kwayl] n. drivel, slaver; v. (ge-) drivel, slaver; -pomp n. saliva pump.

kwyn ['kwyn] v. (ge-) languish; **-end** a. (-e) languishing.

kwyt ['kwayt] a. & av. be rid of; v. (ge-) acquit oneself of; **-skel** v. (-ge-) forgive; **-skelding** n. waiver.

kyf ['kayf] v. (ge-) dispute, quarrel; **-agtig** a. (-e) quarrelsome.

kyk ['kayk] n. aspect; view; outlook; v. (ge-) see, view, pry; **-er** n. (-s) spectator; pupil (eye); telescope; **-ie** dim. (-s) look, glance; **-gat** n. = loergat; **-spel** n. diorama.

L

laaf ['lāf] v. (ge-) refresh, slake thirst; try to restore consciousness.

laag ['lāch] n. (lae) layer; bed; coating; stratum: ply; a. (lae; laer, -ste) low, base, mean; av. low, lowly, meanly; **-'hartig** a. (-e) base, vile; **-heid** n. lowness; baseness, vileness; **-hout** n. plywood; **-spanning** n. low voltage; **-te** n. (-s) valley, dip; **-water** n. ebb.

laai ['lāi] n. (-e) in ligte -e ablaze; drawer; trick, prank, dodge, habit; v. (ge-) load, charge; **-ruimte** n. tonnage, hold; **-stok** n. ramrod; hy het 'n-ingesluk he is as stiff as a poker; **-tafel** n. chest of drawers; **-tjie** dim.

laaikas ['lāikas] n. (-te) chest of drawers.

laak ['lāk] v. (ge-) blame, find fault with; **-baar** a. & av. (-bare; -der, -ste) blameworthy, reprehensible.

laan ['lān] n. (lane) avenue, lane.

laas ['lās] av. last; **-genoemde** n. latter; **-lede** a. last; **-te** n. last one, a. last, latest; av. last; **-telik** av. finally.

laat ['lāt] a. (-, late) av. late; v. (ge-) allow, let, leave, permit; leave off, refrain from.

laat'dunkend ['lāt'dʌŋkənt] a. (-e) presumptuous, arrogant.

labi'aal [labi'āl] a. (labi'ale) labial.

labora'torium [labōRa'tōRiʌm] n. (-s, labra'toria) laboratory.

'lading ['lādəŋ] n. (-s) load; cargo; charge; cp. laai v.

'lae cp. laag a.

'laer ['lāəR] n. (-s) camp, lager; bearings; **-baan** n. bearing race; **-bus** n. bearing brush; **-dop** n. bearing cap; a. lower, cp. laag a.; **-huis** n. parliament; **-skool** n. primary school; **-wal** av. aan-wees be on the rocks.

'laeveld ['lāfelt] n. low veld.

laf ['laf] a. (lawwe) silly, foolish; insipid; dull; **-aard** n. coward; **-'hartig** a. (-e) cowardly; **-'hartigheid** n. cowardice.

'lafenis ['lāfənəs] n. refreshment; relief; cp. laaf.

lag ['lach] n. laugh, laughter; v. (ge-) laugh, chuckle, titter; **-bui** n. fit of laughter; **-gend** a. (-e) laughing, smiling; av. laughingly; av. (-e)

inclined to laughter, giggling; **-gery** n. laughter; **-gie** dim.; **lag-lag** av. laughingly; with ease; **-lus** n. hilarity; **-siek** a. & av. giggling; **-'wekkend** a. (-e) ludicrous.

lak ['lak] n. sealing-wax; lacquer; seal; v. (ge-) seal; lacquer; v. (ge-) tackle, bring down hard (sport); **-leer** n. patent leather; **-s** a. slack; **-vernis** n. lacquer.

'lakei [lə'kay] n. (-e) lackey.

laken ['lākən] n. (-s) cloth; sheet; **-se** a. -pak cloth suit.

'laklelie ['laklēli] n. (-s) Maltese Cross (lily).

lako'niek [lakō'nik] a. & av. laconic.

laksa'tief [laksa'tif] n. & a. (laksa-'tiewe) laxative; **lak'seer** v. (-ge-) go to stool.

'laksman ['laksman] n. (-ne) hangman; butcher-bird.

lam ['lam] n. (-mers) lamb; a. paralyzed, lame; v. (ge-) give birth (sheep); **-heid** n. paralysis, tiredness; **-'lendig** a. (-e; -er, -ste) miserable, spunkless; **-metjie** dim.; **-sak** n. shirker; **-slaan** v. (-ge-) paralyze.

la'mel [la'mel] n. lamination; **lamel-** a. laminated-.

lamp ['lamp] n. (-e) lamp, valve (wireless); **-ie** dim.; **-i'on** n. Chinese lantern; **-olie** n. paraffin.

land ['lant] n. (-e) land; field; country; v. (ge-) land, disembark; **-bou** n. agriculture; **-dros** n. (-te) magistrate; **-elik** a. (-e) rural; **-erig** a. & av. sulky, blue; **-e'rye** n. cultivated fields; **-genoot** n. (land-genote) fellow countryman; **-goed** n. (-ere) estate; **-ing** n. (-s) landing; **-jie** dim.; **-kaart** n. map; **-loper** n. (-s) tramp; **-meter** n. (-s) surveyor; **-skap** n. landscape; **-sman** n. countryman; **-sreën** n. general rain; **-verhuiser** n. (-s) emigrant; **-verraad** n. high treason; **-weer** n. defence force; **-winning** n. reclamation of land.

'landlyn ['lantlayn] n. land line.

'lanfer ['lʌmfəR] n. crêpe, crape.

lang, lank ['lang, -k] a. & av. long, tall; **-deling** n. long division; **-'dradig** a. (-e) tedious; **-'durig** a. (-e) prolonged, chronic; **-gerek** a. (-te) protracted; **-oog** av. **-wees** be jealous; **-oor** n. donkey; **-s** av. next to, alongside of, along; **-saam** a. & av. (-same; -samer, -ste) slow(ly); **-samerhand** av. gradually; **-slewende** n. survivor; **-vingerig** a. (-e) light-fingered; **-'werpig** a. (-e) oblong.

'laning ['lānəŋ] n. (-s) hedge.

lank = lang; **-al** av. long ago; **-'moedig** a. (-e) patient.

lans ['lāns] n. (-e) lance.

lan'seer [lān'sēR] v. (ge-) launch; pierce.

lap ['lap] n. (-pe) rag, cloth, piece of material; patch; bandage; v. (ge-) patch, mend; **-pie** dim.; **-werk** n. patchwork, patching; tinkering.

'larwe ['laRvə] n. (-s) larva, grub.
las ['las] n. (-te) weld, seam, joint;
burden, load; nuisance; v. (ge-) weld,
join; -dier n. beast of burden; -lap
n. remnant, patch; -plek n. joint;
-pos n. nuisance; -tig a. (-e) difficult,
awkward.
'lasbrief ['lasbRif] n. warrant; cp.
gelas.
'laster ['lastəR] n. slander; -aar n.
slanderer; -ing n. slander; -lik a. (-e)
slanderous.
'lastig ['lastəch] a. (-e; -er, -ste)
troublesome, annoying.
lat ['lat] n. (-te) cane, stick; lath;
batten.
la'tei [la'tay] n. (-e) lintel.
'later ['lâtəR] a. & av. later, later on.
'latwerk ['latveRk] n. lattice, trellis.
La'tyn [la'tayn] n. Latin.
la'ventel [la'fentəl] n. lavender.
lawa ['lâva] n. lava.
la'waai [la'vâi] n. noise, din; v. (ge-)
make a noise; -erig a. (-e) noisy;
-maker n. noisy person; -water n.
liquor.
'lawe = laaf.
lawe'ment [lâve'ment] n. (-e) enema.
'lawwigheid [lavə'chayt] n. silliness,
cp. laf.
lê ['lɛ] n. lying, laying; v. (ge-) put;
lay; lie.
lede ['lêdə] n. pl. = lid; -geld n.
subscription; -lys n. list of members;
-tal n. membership.
'ledemate ['lêdəmâtə] n. limbs;
members of a church; cp. lidmaat.
'ledig ['lêdəch] a. (-e) idle; v. (ge-)
empty; -heid n. idleness.
leed ['lêt] n. harm; sorrow; -vermaak
n. malicious joy; -wese n. regret.
leef ['lêf] v. (-s) live; -tog n. sub-
sistence; -tyd n. lifetime; age;
-tydsgrens n. age-limit; -wyse n.
way of living.
leeg ['lêch] a. (leë) empty; vacant;
av. empty; -heid n. emptiness;
-loper n. (-s) loafer.
'leegte ['lêchtə] n. (-s) void; dale; cp.
laagte.
leek ['lêk] n. (leke) layman.
'leemte ['lêmtə] n. (-s) gap; void;
blank.
leen ['lên] n. feudal tenure; v. (ge-)
borrow, lend; -geld n. borrowed
money; -wese n. feudal system.
leer ['lêR] n. leather; n. (lere)
ladder; n. doctrine; apprenticeship;
v. (ge-) learn; teach; -boek n. text-
book; -gang n. course of study;
-'gierig a. (-e; -er, -ste) studious;
-jonge n. apprentice; -ling n. (-e)
pupil; -looiery n. tannery; -meester
n. tutor; -plan n. curriculum; -saam
a. (-same) informative; -ryk a.
instructive; -'stelling a. (-e) dogmatic; -stoel n. (-e) professorate.
'leër ['lêəR] n. (-s) army; host; v.
(ge-) encamp.
'lêer ['lɛəR] n. (-s) layer; leaguer;
sleeper; file.

lees ['lês] n. (-te) last, boot-tree; v.
(ge-) read; -baar a. (-bare) legible;
-boek n. (-e) reader; -lus n. love of
reading; -stof n. reading-matter;
-teken n. punctuation mark; -woede
n. mania for reading.
leeu ['lêö] n. (-s) lion; -bekkie n.
snapdragon; leeue-aandeel n. lion's
share; -'in n. lioness.
le'geer [lə'chêR] v. (-) to alloy;
le'gering n. alloy.
le'gende [lə'chendə] n. (-s) legend;
legen'daries a. (-e) legendary.
'legio ['lêchiô] n. legion.
legi'oen [lêchi'un] n. (-e) legion.
legiti'meer [ləchiti'mêR] v. (ge-)
legitimize.
'legkaart ['lechkâRt] n. jig-saw
puzzle.
lei ['lay] n. (-e) slate; v. (ge-) lead,
conduct; -band n. leading-strings;
-dak n. slate-roof; -dam n. irriga-
tion-dam; -dend a. (-e) leading,
guiding; passive; -ing n. line,
piping, conduit; lead; -draad n.
clue; -ster n. lodestar; -er n.
leader; guide; -sel n. (-s) reins; -wiel
n. idler; lei- v. pref. lead, guide,
pilot, conduct.
'leidsman ['laytsman] n. (-ne)
leader.
lek ['lek] n. (-ke) leakage, puncture;
v. (ge-) leak; lick; -stroop n. linctus;
-vry a. puncture-proof.
'lekker ['lekəR] n. (-s) sweet,
licker, toady; a. & av. (-der, -ste)
delectable, nice, delicious, fine; -bek
n. epicure; -'bekkig a. (-e) fastidious;
-goed n. sweets; -jeuk n. scabies,
itch; -kry v. (-ge-) be thrilled; -lyf
av. merry, half-tight; -ny n. (-e)
delicacy.
'lektor ['lektoR] n. (lek'tore) lecturer;
lekto'raat n. lectureship; lek'trise n.
fem. lecturer; lek'tuur n. literature,
reading-matter.
'lelie ['lêli] n. (-s) lily; -agtig a. (-e)
lily-like.
'lelik ['lêlək] n. ugly-face; a. (-e; -er,
-ste) ugly, nasty, bad; av. badly,
nastily; -erd n. ugly person; -heid n.
lem ['lem] n. (-me) blade; -metjie
dim. lime; (razor) blade.
le'moen [lə'mun] n. (-e) orange;
-konfyt n. marmalade.
'lende ['lendə] n. (-s; -ne) loin; -jig n.
sciatica; -lam a. ramshackle; -stuk
n. loin-steak.
'lengte ['lengtə] n. (-s) length;
longitude; height; -maat n. linear
measure.
'lenig ['lênəch] a. (-e; -er, -ste) lithe,
supple; v. (ge-) allay, relieve; -heid
n. litheness; -ing n. relief.
'lening ['lênəng] n. (-s) loan.
lens ['lɛns] n. (-e) lens.
'lensie ['lɛnsi] n. (-s) lentil.
'lente ['lentə] n. spring.
'lepel ['lêpəl] n. (-s) spoon, ladle; v.
(ge-) spoon; -lê v. (-ge-) lie close
together, wedged up.

'lêplek ['lɛplek] n. lair, den; room to lie down.
'leraar ['lēRāR] n. (-s) minister; teacher.
'lering ['lēRəng] n. instruction.
les ['les] n. (-se) lesson, lecture; -bes last but not least; v. (ge-) quench, slake.
'leser ['lēsəR] n. (-s) reader; -'es fem. reader.
'lesing ['lēsəng] n. (-s) reading, lecture; version.
'lessenaar ['lesənāR] n. (-s) desk.
let ['let] v. (ge-) -wel please note; mind; attend.
'letsel ['letsəl] n. (-s) injury, damage, scar.
'letter ['letəR] n. (-s) letter; type; v. (ge-) mark, letter; -dief n. plagiarist; -e die- belles lettres; -greep n. (-grepe) syllable; -kunde n. literature; -'kundig a. (-e) literary; -lik a. literally; -setter n. compositor; -tjie n. dim.; -vreter n. bookworm.
'leuen ['lɛn] n. (-s) lie, untruth; -aar n. (-s) liar; -agtig a. (-e) untruthful; -a'res fem. liar.
leun ['lɛn] v. (ge-) lean; -ing n. back, railing, support, banisters; -wa n. semi-trailer.
'leus(e) ['lɛs(ə)] n. (leuse, -s) motto, device; watch-word.
'lewe ['lēvə] n. (-ns) life; v. (ge-) = leef; -nd a. (-e) living; -ndig a. (-e; -er, -ste) living; lively; av. in a lively manner.
'lewens- ['lēvəns-] pref. of life, cp. lewe; -berig n. obituary; -beskouing n. view of life; -duur n. duration of life; -groot a. life-size; -krag n. vitality; -lang a. (-e) lifelong; -loop n. career; -loos a. lifeless; -lot n. fate; -'lustig a. (-e) vivacious; -middele n. provisions; -reg n. life interest; -vatbaar av. viable; -vreugde n. joie de vivre.
'lewensketse ['lēvənskets] n. biography.
'lewer ['lēvəR] n. (-s) liver; v. (ge-) furnish, deliver; -an'sier n. supplier, caterer; -ing n. delivery, supply; -wors n. liver-sausage; lewer- n. pref. hepatic.
'lewertraan ['lēvərtRān] n. cod-liver-oil.
liber'aal [ləbə'Rāl] n. & a. (liber'ale) liberal; libera'listies a. (-e) liberalistic.
lid ['lət] n. (lede) limb: member; -doring n. corn; -maat n. (-mate) member; limb; -maatskap n. membership; -woord n. article.
lied ['lit] n. (-ere) song, hymn, anthem; -jie dim.
'liederlik ['lidəRlək] a. (-e) dirty, filthy.
lief ['lif] a. (liewe) dear, beloved; sweet; nice; kind; av. sweetly, kindly; love; -'dadig a. (-e) charitable; -de n. love; -deloos a. loveless, unkind; -deryk a. & av. loving(ly); -devol a.

(-le) loving; -hê v. (liefgehad) love; -hebber n. (-s) lover, enthusiast, amateur; -hebbery n. hobby; -ie n. dim. sweetheart; -koos v. (ge-) caress, fondle; -kry v. (-ge-) grow fond of, fall in love; -lik a. (-e) lovely; -ling n. darling; -s av. rather; -ste n. dearest; -'tallig a. (-e) sweet, charming.
lieg ['lich] v. (ge-) lie.
lies ['lis] n. (-ie) groin.
'liewers ['livəRs] av. rather = liefs.
lig ['ləch] n. (-te) light; a. (-e; -er, -ste) light, bright, lightweight, slight; av. lightly, easily; v. (ge-) lift, raise; give light; -beeld n. photograph; -dag n. daylight, dawn; -gelowig a. (-e) credulous; -gend a. lying; -geraak a. & av. (-te) touchy; -gevoelig a. (-e) sensitive to light; -'gewend(e) a. & av. incandescent; -gie dim.; -gies av. lightly; -ging n. situation; -krans n. halo; -mis n. libertine; -'sinnig a. (-e) frivolous; -tekooi n. harlot; -ter n. lever.
'liggaam ['ləchām] n. (liggame) body; lig'gaamlik a. (-e) bodily, corporeal.
'ligting ['ləchtəng] n. (-s) collection; draft.
li'keur [li'kœR] n. liquor.
likke'waan [ləkə'vān] n. (likke'wane) iguana.
lik'sens [lək'sɛns] n. licence.
likwi'dasie [likwi'dāsi] n. liquidation; likwe'deer v. (ge-) liquidate.
limf ['ləmf] n. lymph.
limo'nade [ləmõ'nādə] n. lemonade.
lini'aal [lini'āl] n. (line'ale) ruler.
'linie ['lini] n. (-s) line, equator; lini'eer v. (ge-) rule.
'linker ['lənkəR] a. left; -stuur n. left-hand drive.
links ['lənks] a. left-handed; av. on the left; -om! interj. to the left, left turn!; counter clockwise.
'linne ['lənə] n. linen; -goed n. linen; -kas n. linen-press.
lint ['lənt] n. (-e) ribbon; tape; -jie dim.; -wurm n. tape-worm, cestode.
lip ['ləp] n. (-pe) lip; -stif n. lipstick.
li'riek [lə'rik] n. lyric poetry; 'liries a. (-e) lyric; 'lirikus n. lyric poet.
lis ['ləs] n. (-te) stratagem, cunning; noose; -sie dim.; -tig a. (-e; -er, -ste) cunning.
li'sensie = liksens; lisensi'eer v. (ge-) license.
'lispel ['ləspəl] v. (ge-) lisp.
'listig ['ləstəch] a. (-e; -er, -ste) cunning, subtle, sly.
lit ['lət] n. (-te) joint; -teken n. scar.
lite'rator [lətə'Rātor] n. (litera'tore, -a) literary man; liter'tuur n. literature; lite'rêr a. (-e) literary.
li'totes [li'tõtəs] n. litotes.
'lobbes ['lovəs] n. awkward fellow.
'loeder ['ludəR] n. (-s) beast, skunk.
loef ['luf] n. luff, windward side.
loei ['lui] v. (ge-) low roar.
'loën ['lõn] v. (ge-) deny; -ing n, disavowal.

'loënstraf ['lŏnstRaf] v. (ge-) belie.
loer ['lūR] v. (ge-) lie in wait; peep,
spy; -luik n. (-e) inspection eye.
'loesing ['lusəng] n. (-s) hiding,
thrashing.
lof ['lof] n. praise; n. (louwe) foliage;
-lik a. (-e) laudable; -rede n. eulogy;
-'waardig a. (-e) laudable.
log ['loch] a. (logge) clumsy; -heid n.
unwieldiness.
'logies ['lŏchis] a. & av. logical(ly).
lo'jaal [lŏ'yāl] a. (lojale) loyal;
lojali'teit n. loyalty.
lok ['lok] n. (-ke) curl, lock; v. (ge-)
entice, lure; -aas n. bait; -stem n.
lure.
lo'kaal [lŏ'kāl] n. (lo'kale) room; a.
local.
lokomo'tief [lŏkŏmŏ'tif] n. (lokomo-
'tiewe) locomotive.
'lokvoël ['lokfŏl] n. (-s) decoy, trap.
lol ['lol] v. (ge-) be troublesome, nag;
-lerig a. (-e) troublesome; -lery n.
bother, nuisance; -lig a. jolly; -pot
n. nuisance.
'lomerig ['lŏməRəch] a. (-e) drowsy,
sleepy.
'lommer ['loməR] n. foliage, shade;
-ryk a. (-e) shady.
lomp ['lomp] a. (-e; -er, -ste) clumsy;
-e n. rags; -erd n. (-s) bumpkin;
-heid n. clumsiness.
long ['long] n. (-e) lung; -ontsteking
n. pneumonia; -pyp n. windpipe;
-vlies n. pleura.
lont ['lont] n. (-e) fuse; -ruik smell a
rat.
lood ['lŏt] n. lead; plumb-line;
-agtig a. (-e) leaden; -gieter n.
plumber; -lyn n. plumb-line; -reg a.
(-te) perpendicular; -s n. (-e) pilot;
shed, v. (ge-) pilot.
loof ['lŏf] n. foliage; v. (ge-) praise.
loog ['lŏch] n. lye; -agtig a. (-e)
alkaline, like lye; -as n. lye-ash;
-sout n. alkali.
looi ['lŏi] v. (ge-) tan; -bas n.
wattle-bark; -er n. tanner; -ery n.
tannery; -stof n. tannin.
loom ['lŏm] av. drowsy, cp.
lomerig.
loon ['lŏn] n. (lone) wages, reward;
v. (ge-) reward, pay; -staat n. pay-
sheet; -staking n. strike for higher
pay; -tjie dim. boontjie kry sy-
chickens come home to roost;
-trekker n. (-s) wage-earner.
loop ['lŏp] n. walking, walk, gait; v.
(ge-) walk, go; -baan n. career; -jong
n. messenger; -plek n. place for
walking; pasture; -s a. (-e) ruttish;
-ge'selser n. walkie-talkie.
loot ['lŏt] n. (lote) shoot; offspring;
v. (ge-) cast lots; -jie dim. lottery-
ticket.
los ['los] a. (-se; -ser, -ste) loose; av.
loosely; v. (ge-) fire; unload;
redeem; -baar a. (-bare) redeemable;
-bandig a. (-e; -er, -ste) licentious;
-bars v. (ge-) tear; explode;
-barsting n. explosion, outbreak;

-bol n. libertine; -brand v. (-ge-)
discharge; -breek v. (-ge-) break
away; -draai v. (-ge-) loosen,
unscrew; -gaan v. (-ge-) come loose;
-geld n. ransom; -goed n. movable
property; -hande av. with free
hands; -hang v. (-ge-) hang loose;
-heid n. looseness; -knoop v. (-ge-)
unbutton; -kom v. (-ge-) get free;
-koop v. (-ge-) ransom; -kry v. (-ge-)
get loose; -laat v. (-ge-) release;
-loop v. (-ge-) be at large; -maak v.
(-ge-) loosen; -prys n. ransom; -ruk
v. (-ge-) pull loose; -serig a. & av.
loose(ly); -sies av. loosely; -sing n.
discharge; -steek v. (-ge-) lash out;
-weg av. loosely.
'losgespe ['loschespə] n. (losge-)
unbuckle.
lo'seer [lŏ'sēR] v. (ge-) board, lodge;
lo'sies n. board and lodging.
'losie ['lŏsi] n. (-s) lodge; box, loge.
'lostorring ['lostoRəng] v. (losge-)
unpick, rip.
lot ['lot] n. fate, destiny; lot; n.
(lote) lottery-ticket; -e'ry n. lottery;
-genoot n. companion in distress;
-gevalle n. adventures; -ing n.
drawing of lots.
'lotjie ['loiKi] n. van-getik wees, be
crack-brained.
lou ['loa] a. lukewarm; -erig a. (-e)
slightly lukewarm.
lou'rier en 'rum [loa'RiR ən RΛm]
n. bay-rum.
'louter ['loat'əR] a. & av. pure,
sheer; v. (ge-) purify, refine.
'lower ['lŏvəR] n. foliage; -groen a.
bright-green, verdant.
lug ['lΛch] n. (-te) sky; air; atmosphere; scent; smell; v. (ge-) ventilate; -bel n. air-bubble; -droog a.
dry to the touch; -gie dim. breeze;
-'hartig a. (-e) light-hearted; -ledig
a. vacuum; -pos n. air mail; -ruim
n. space; -spoor n. aerial railway;
-streek n. zone; -ster n. chandelier;
-tig a. (-e) airy; nervous; av. airily;
warily; -vaart n. aviation.
'lughawe ['lΛch-hāvə] n. (-s, -ens)
airport.
'lugholte ['lΛch-holtə] n. air pocket.
'lugkasteel ['lΛchkastēl] n. (lug-
kastele) castles in the air.
'luglaat ['lΛchlāt] v. (-ge-) to bleed;
'luglating n. bleeding.
'luggang ['lΛchang] n. flue.
'lugrem ['lΛchRem] n. (-me) pneumatic brake.
'lugspieëling ['lΛchspiləng] n. (-s)
mirage.
'lugsteurings ['lΛchstēwRəngs] n.
atmospherics.
'lugversorging ['lΛchfəRsoRchəng]
n. air-conditioning.
lui ['lœi] n. folk, people; a. lazy; v.
(ge-) ring, peal, toll; -aard, -lak n.
sluggard.
luid ['lœit] a. & av. loud; -ens av.
according to; -'rugtig a. (-e) noisy,
rowdy.

'**luier** ['lœiəR] n. (-s) diaper; v. (ge-) loaf, laze; idle; -**ing** n. idling.

luik ['lœik] n. (-e) shutter, hatch; manhole.

'**luim** ['lœim] n. (-e) mood, humour, whim; -**ig** a. (-e; -er, -ste) humorous, witty.

'**luiperd** ['lœipəRt] n. (-s) leopard, panther.

luis ['lœis] n. (-s) louse.

'**luislang** ['lœislang] n. (-e) python.

'**luister** ['lœistəR] n. lustre, splendour; v. (ge-) listen; listen in; obey; -**aar** n. (-s) listener; -**ryk** a. (-e; -er, -ste) brilliant.

luite'nant [lœitə'nant] n. (-e) lieutenant.

'**luiters** ['lœitəRs] a. innocent.

lu'mier [lə'miR] n. dawn.

'**lummel** ['lʌməl] n. (-s) lout.

lus ['lʌs] n. (-te) desire; loop; v. (ge-) like, desire; -**hof** n. pleasure-garden; paradise; -**oord** n. pleasure-resort; -**teloos** a. listless; -**tig** a. (-e; -er, -ste) gay; **lus**- n. pref. loop-

lu'sern [lew'sɛRəng] n. lucern.

'**luttel** ['lʌtəl] a. (-e) little.

'**luukse** ['lewksə] a. luxury.

ly ['lay] v. (ge-) suffer, endure; -**delik** a. (-e) passive; -**dend** a. (-e) passive; -**dsaam** a. meek; -**er** n. sufferer.

lyf ['layf] n. (lywe) body, figure; -**ie** dim. bodice, figure; -**lik** a. (-e) bodily; -**tog** n. provisions; -**wag** n. bodyguard.

'**lyfrente** ['layfRentə] n. annuity.

lyk ['layk] n. (-e) corpse; v. (ge-) look, seem, appear; -**besorger** n. undertaker; -'**kleurig(e)** a. cadaverous; -**srede** n. funeral service; -**skouing** n. post mortem; -**swa** n. hearse.

lym ['laym] n. glue; v. (ge-) glue; -**erig** a. (-e) sticky.

lyn ['layn] n. line, string, rope; rule, line; -**staan** v. (-ge-) line up, queue; -**reg** a. perpendicular, straight; **lyn**- n. pref. line, circuit.

'**lynolie** ['laynõli] n. linseed-oil; **lynsaad** n. linseed.

lys ['lays] n. (-te) list, register; beading, moulding; cornice; frame; v. (ge-) frame; -**ie** dim.

'**lywig** ['layvəch] a. (-e) corpulent; -**heid** n. body (paint), bulkiness.

M

ma ['mã] n. (-'s) mother.

maag ['mãch] n. (mae, mage) stomach, maw; kinsman; virgin, cp. **maagd**.

maag(d) ['mãch(t)] n. (-e) maiden, virgin; -**delik** a. (-e) maidenly, virginly; -**skap** n. kin, kindred.

maai ['mãi] v. (ge-) mow, cut, reap; -**er** n. (-s) mower; maggot.

maak ['mãk] v. (ge-) make, do, form; -**sel** n. (-s) make, fashion; product, production, creation.

maal ['mãl] n. (male) time; meal; v.

(ge-) grind, mill; paint; multiply; -**gat**, -**stroom** n. whirlpool; -**teken** n. multiplication sign; -**tyd** n. meal.

maan ['mãn] n. (mane) moon; v. (ge-) warn.

maand ['mãnt] n. (-e) month; -**eliks** a. & av. monthly; -**staat** n. monthly return.

'**Maandag** ['mãndach] n. Monday.

'**maanhaar** ['mãnhãR] n. hogsback.

maar ['mãr] prep. but; daar is geen by nie but me no buts; av. but, yet, merely, only, just.

'**maarskalk** ['mãRskalk] n. marshal.

Maart ['mãRt] n. March.

'**maas** ['mãs] n. mesh.

maat ['mãt] n. (mate) measure, size, gauge; time, bar, cadence; n. (-s, maters) mate, comrade; -**band** n. tape-measure; -**glas** n. graduated mea ure; -**recl** n. measure, precaution; -'**skaplik** a. (-e) social; -**skap'py** n. (-e) company, firm; -**staf** n. (-stawwe) measure, standard; -**stok** n. yard-stick.

'**madeliefie** ['mãdəlifi] n. (-s) daisy.

maer ['mãR] a. (-der, -ste) lean, thin, skinny; meagre; attenuate(d); -**merrie** n. shin; -**te** n. leanness.

mag ['mach] n. (-te) power, might, force, strength, authority; v. (mog) may, be allowed; -**dom** n. lots, heaps; -**sgebied** n. sphere of influence; -**teloos** a. (megtelose) powerless, helpless; -**tig** a. (-e; -er, -ste) powerful, potent; -**tig!** interj. Lord! -**tig** v. (ge-) authorize; -**tiging** n. authorization.

maga'syn [macha'sayn] n. (-e) store, warehouse.

'**magies** ['mãchis] a. (-e) magic(al).

magi'straat [machəs'tRãt] n. (magi-'strate) magistrate.

mag'naat [mach'nãt] n. (mag'nate) magnate.

mag'neet [mach'nẽt] n. (mag'nete) magnet; **mag'neties** a. (-e) magnetic.

mag'nesium [mach'nẽsiʌm] n. magnesium.

magni'fiek [manyə'fik] a. magnificent.

ma'hem [ma'hem] n. (-me) crowned crane.

majes'teit ['mãyestayt] n. majesty; majestu'eus a. (-e) majestic.

ma'jeur [ma'yœR] a. major (mus.).

ma'joor [ma'yõR] n. (-s, ma'jore) major.

mak ['mak] a. (-, -ke; -ker, -ste) meek, tame.

ma'keer [mə'kẽR] v. (ge-) ail; lack.

'**makelaar** ['mãkəlãR] n. (-s) broker.

'**maker** ['mãkəR] n. (-s) maker, creator; cp. **maak**.

'**maklik** ['maklək] a. (-e; -er, -ste) easy, comfortable.

ma'kou [mə'koa] n. (-e) Muscovy duck.

'**maksimum** ['maksi'mʌm] n. maximum.

mal ['mal] *a.* (-, *-le*; *-ler*, *-ste*) foolish, silly; mad; **-heid** *n.* folly; **-kop** *n.* silly person, tomboy; **-ligheid** *n.* nonsense; **-praatjies** *n.* nonsense; **-trap** *n.* = **malkop.**

ma'laria [ma'lāRia] *n.* malaria.

Ma'leier [ma'layəR] *n.* (-s) Malay; **Maleis** *a.* (-e) Malay.

'malby ['malbay] *n.* digger bee.

'malmier ['malmiR] *n.* pugnacious ant.

mal'mok [mal'mok] *n.* (-ke) malle-muck, fulmar.

mals ['mals] *a.* (-e) lush, tender.

malva ['malfa] *n.* mallow, geranium.

man ['man] *n.* (-ne, -s) man; husband; **-baar** *a.* (-bare) marriage-able; **-haftig** *a.* (-e; -er, -ste) brave; **-lik** *a.* (-e; -er, -ste) manly, masculine; **-'moedig** *a.* (-e) brave; **-netjie** *n.* (-s) male; **-s** *av.* hy is-s genoeg he is capable of holding his own; **-skap** *n.* (-pe) crew, soldier; **-slag** *n.* homicide.

man'daat [man'dāt] *n.* mandate.

'mandjie ['maing-Ki] *n.* (-s) basket, hamper; **-goed, -werk** *n.* wicker (-work), *cp.* **matjiesgoed.**

ma'nel [mə'nel] *n.* (-le) frockcoat.

ma'neuver [mə'nœ̃vəR] *n.* (-s) manoeuvre.

mane'wales [mānə'vāləs] *n. pl.* antics.

man'gaan [mang'chān] *n.* manganese.

'mangel ['mangəl] *n.* (-s) tonsil; mangle.

'mango ['meng-gō] *n.* (-'s) mango.

'manie ['māni] *n.* mania, craze.

ma'nier [mə'niR] *n.* (-e) manner, fashion, way; **-lik** *a.* (-e) polite; **-tjie** *dim.* mannerism.

mani'fes [manə'fes] *n.* (-te) manifesto.

mani'kuurstel [mani'kē̃wRstel] *n.* (-le) manicure set.

manipu'lasie [manipew'lāsi] *n.* manipulation; **manipu'leer** *v.* (ge-) manipulate.

manji'fiek [manyə'fik] *a.* (-e) magnificent.

mank ['mank] *a.* lame, crippled.

manko'liekerig [mankō'likəRəch] *a.* (-e) ill, seedy.

'mantel ['mantəl] *n.* (-s) mantle; **-draaier** *n.* (-s) turn-coat; **-vlies** *n.* diaphragm.

manu'skrip [manew'skRəp] *n.* (-te) manuscript.

'mare ['māRə] *n.* news, tidings.

ma'rgriet [ma'chRit] *n.* (-e) marguerite, daisy.

mario'net [maRiō'net] *n.* (-te) marionette, puppet.

mark ['maRk] *n.* (-te; -e) market.

'marmer ['maRməR] *n.* marble; **-blad** *n.* marble-top.

mar'motjie [maR'moiKi] *n.* (-s) guinea-pig.

mars ['maRs] *n.* (-e) march; **mar'sjeer** *v.* (ge-) march.

'martel ['martəl] *v.* (ge-) torture, torment; **-aar** *n.* (-s) martyr; **-a'res** *fem.* martyr; **-ing** *n.* torture.

'marter ['maRtəR] *n.* (-s) marten.

Mar'xisme [maRk'səsmə] *n.* Marxism.

mas ['mas] *n.* (-te) mast.

'masels ['māsəls] *n.* measles.

ma'sjien [ma'shin] *n.* (-e) machine, engine; **masji'naal** *a. & av.* mechanical(ly); **masjine'rie** *n.* machinery; **masji'nis** *n.* (-te) machinist, driver; engineer.

'masker ['maskəR] *n.* (-s) mask; **mas'keer** *v.* (ge-) camouflage, mask.

'massa ['masa] *n.* (-s) crowd, mass; lot; **mas'sief** *a.* (mas'siewe) massive, solid.

mas'sage [ma'sāsh] *n.* (-s) massage; **mas'seer** *v.* (ge-) massage; **mas'seur** *n.* (-s) masseur; **mas'seuse** *n.* (-s) masseuse.

mat ['mat] *n.* (-te) mat, door-mat; seat (chair); **deur die-val** come a cropper; *a.* (-te; -ter. -ste) weary, dull; mat; *dim.* ;-**heid** *n.* exhaustion; dullness; **-glas** *n.* opaque glass.

'mate ['mātə] *n.* degree, measure; **-loos** *a.* (-lose) excessive, unlimited; **'matig** *a.* (-e) moderate; **'matigheid** *n.* temperance, continence; **'matiging** *n.* moderation.

mate'maties [matə'mātis] *a.* (-e) mathematical; **matema'tesis** *n.* mathematics.

materi'aal [matēRi'āl] *n.* (materiale) material(s); **materia'lis** *n.* (-te) materialist; **ma'terie** *n.* matter; **materi'eel** *a.* (materiële) material(ly).

'matjiesgoed ['maiKischut] *n.* rushes.

ma'tras [mə'tRas] *n.* (-te) mattress; **-goed** *n.* ticking.

matriar'gaat [matRiaR'chat] *n.* matriarchy; **matriar'gaal** *a.* (matriar'gale) matriarchal.

matriku'lasie [mətrikew'lasi] *n.* matriculation; **matriku'leer** *v.* (ge-) matriculate.

ma'trone [ma'tRōnə] *n.* (-s) matron.

ma'troos [ma'tRōs] *n.* (ma'trose) sailor.

ma'trys [ma'tRays] *n.* (-e) die, matrix.

mayon'naise [mayo'nɛs] *n.* mayonnaise.

mebos ['mēbos] *n.* mebos (salted dried apricots).

me'dalje [mə'dalyə] *n.* (-s) medal.

'mede- ['mēdə] *pref.* co-, fellow-; **-broeder** *n.* colleague; **-burger** *n.* fellow-citizen; **-deling** *n.* (-s) announcement; **-'deelsaam** *a.* (mede-'deelsame) expansive, charitable; **-dinger** *n.* competitor, rival; **-'doë** *n.* compassion; **-gevoel** *n.* sympathy; **-klinker** *n.* (-s) consonant; **-'lye** *n.* compassion; **-'lydend** *a.* (-e) compassionate; **-'pligtig** *a.* (-e) accessory; **-werking** *n.* assistance; **-wete** *n.* knowledge.

'**medemens** ['mɛdəmeñs] n. fellow-man.

'**medewerker** ['mɛdəvɛRkəR] n. (-s) collaborator.

'**medies** ['mēdis] a. (-e) medical; '**medikus** n. doctor; **medisi'naal** a. medicinal; **medi'syne** n. medicine.

medi'tasie [mēdi'tāsi] n. meditation; **medi'teer** v. (ge-) meditate.

'**medium** ['mēdiʌm] n. (-s, '**media**) medium.

mee- = **mede-**; **-bring** v. (-ge-) bring along; entail; **-deel** v. (-ge-) communicate; **-ding** v. (-ge-) compete; **-doen** v. (ge-) join in; **-gaan** v. (-ge-) accompany; agree with; **-gee** v. (-ge-) give; yield; **-help** v. (-ge-) lend a hand; **-kom** v. (-ge-) accompany; **-leef** v. (-ge-) enter into the spirit of; sympathize with; **-maak** v. (-ge-) experience; **-neem** v. (-ge-) take along; carry away; **-praat** v. (-ge-) put in a word; **-reken** v. (-ge-) count, include; **-sleep** v. (-ge-) carry along; sweep before it; **-val** v. (-ge-) surprise agreeably; **-'warig** a. compassionate; **-werk** v. (-ge-) assist, collaborate.

meel ['mēl] n. meal, flour; **-agtig** a. (-e) mealy, floury; **-blom** n. flour; **-bol** n. baked flour (infant food); **-draad** n. stamen.

meen ['mēn] v. (ge-) mean, intend; think.

meent ['mēnt] n. commonage.

meer ['mēR] n. (mere) lake; a. & av. more; **-dere** n. (-s) superior; **-derheid** n. majority; **-der'jarig** a. (-e) of age; **-maal**, **-male** av. frequently; **-'slagtig** a. (-e) polygenous; **-'stemmig** a. (-e) polyphonic; **-voud** n. plural; **-voudig** a. (-e) plural; multiple.

'**meerdoelvoertuig** ['mēRdulfūR-tœich] n. ('**meerdoelvoertuie**) general purpose vehicle.

'**meergraadolie** ['mēRchRātōli] n. multigrade oil.

'**meermin** ['mēRmən] n. (-ne) mermaid.

mees ['mēs] av. cp. **baie** (veel, meer); most(ly); **-(t)al** av. mostly, usually; **-te** a. most, greatest.

'**meester** ['mēstəR] n. (-s) master, teacher; expert; **-lik** a. (-e) masterly; **-skap** n. mastery.

meet ['mēt] n. van-af from the beginning; v. (ge-) measure, gauge; **-baar** a. (-bare) measurable; **-band** n. tape measure; **-ketting** n. surveyor's chain; **-kunde** n. geometry; **-'kundig** a. (-e) geometrical; **-lat** n. dipstick; **-passer** n. callipers; **-stok** n. gauge rod.

meeu ['mēŏ] n. (-e) sea-mew, gull.

me'ganies [mē'chānis] a. (-e) mechanical.

Mei ['may] n. May.

meid ['mayt] n. (-e) maid-servant, servant-girl.

'**meineed** ['maynēt] n. perjury; **mein'edig** a. (-e) forsworn.

'**meisie** ['maysi] n. girl.

me'juffrou [mə'yʌfroa] n. madam, miss, teacher.

me'kaar [mə'kāR] pron. each other, one another.

me'laats [mə'lāts] a. (-e) leprous; **-e** n. (-e) leper.

me'lasse [mə'lasə] n. molasses.

meld ['melt] v. (ge-) announce, mention, state; **-ding** n. mention.

melk ['melk] n. milk; v. (ge-) milk; **-baard** n. milksop; **-bos** n. milkweed; **-ery** n. (-e) dairy; **-koei** n. milch-cow.

melo'die [mēlŏ'di] n. (-ĕ) melody; **me'lodies** a. (-e) melodic; **melodi'eus** a. (-e) melodious.

'**melodrama** ['mēlŏdRāma] n. melodrama; **melodra'maties** a. (-e) melodramatic.

me'morie [mə'mōRi] n. petition, document; **memori'seer** v. (ge-) memorize.

me'neer [mə'nēR] n. (**me'nere**) gentleman, Mr., sir.

meng ['meng] v. (ge-) mix, blend, dilate, adulterate; **-baar** a. (-bare) mixable; **-el** n. mixture; **-elmoes** n. hodge-podge; **-elwerk** n. miscellany; **-er** n. (-s) mixer, blender; **-ing** n. mixing, blending; **-sel** n. blend, mixture.

'**menie** ['mini] n. minium, red-lead.

'**menig** ['mēnəch] pref. many; **-een** pron. many a one; **-e** num. many, several; **-maal** av. frequently; **-te** n. (-s) crowd; **-'vuldig** a. (-e) manifold, abundant.

'**mening** ['mēnəng] n. (-s) idea, opinion; intention; **-sverskil** n. difference of opinion.

mens ['mɛñs] n. (-e) human being, man, person; **-e** pl. men, people; indef. pron. one, they, you; **-dom** n. mankind, humanity; **-heid** n. human race; mankind; **-ie** dim. midget; **-'liewend** a. (-e) humane; **-lik** a. (-e; -er, -ste) human; **-likerwyse** av. humanly; **-vreter** n. (-s) cannibal.

'**menssku** ['mɛñskew] a. shy, unsociable.

mentali'teit [mentali'tayt] n. mentality.

me'nu [mə'new] n. (-'s) menu.

menu'et [mənew'et] n. minuet.

'**merendeels** ['mēRəndēls] av. mostly.

merg = **murg**.

me'riete [mə'Rita] n. merits.

merk ['mɛRk] n. (-e) mark; brand; v. (ge-) mark; notice, perceive; **-baar** a. (-bare) marked, noticeable; **-teken** n. scar; **-'waardig** a. (-e; -er, -ste) curious, remarkable; **merk-** pref. marker-.

'**merrie** ['mɛRi] n. (-s) mare.

mes ['mes] n. (-se) knife; **-hef** n. (-euwwe) haft; **-lem** n. (-me) blade; **-plank** n. knife-board.

'**messel** ['mesəl] v. (ge-) lay bricks; **-aar** n. (-s) bricklayer.

'messing ['mesəng] n. brass.
met ['met] prep. with.
me'taal [mə'tāl] n. metal; -agtig a.
(-e) metallic; -ware n. hardware.
meta'fisika [mēta'fisika] n. metaphysics.
'metafoor ['mētafōR] n. ('metafore)
metaphor.
metallur'gie [mētalʌR'chi] n.
metallurgy.
metamor'fose [mētamoR'fōsə] n.
metamorphosis.
me'tatesis [mə'tātəsəs] n. metathesis.
met'eens [mət'ēns] av. suddenly,
immediately.
mete'oor [mētē'ōR] n. (mete'ore)
meteor; meteorolo'gie n. meteorology; meteoro'loog n. meteorologist.
'meter ['mētəR] n. (-s) meter,
gauge; metre.
'metgesel ['metgəsel] n. (-le)
companion.
me'tode [mə'tōdə] n. (-s) method;
meto'diek n. methodics, methodology; me'todies a. (-e) methodical.
'metries ['mētRis] a. (-e) metric(al).
me'tropolis [mē'tRōpōləs] n.
metropolis.
'metrum ['mētRʌm] n. metre.
'mettertyd ['metəRtayt] av. in due
course.
'metterwoon ['metəRvōn] av. permanently.
'meubel ['mœbəl] n. (-s) article of
furniture, pl. furniture; meubel'leer
v. (ge-) furnish; meubi'lering n.
furniture; -wa n. removal van,
pantechnicon.
'meul(e) ['mœl(ə)] n. (-e(ns)) mill;
-enaar n. miller.
me'vrou [mə'fRoa] n. lady, Mrs.,
madam.
'middag ['mədach] n. noon, midday.
'midde ['mədə] n. middle, midst; in
ons- in our midst.
'middel ['mədəl] n. (-e, -s) means;
remedy; centre; middle; instrument;
waist; -aar n. (-s) mediator; -baar a.
(-bare) average, intermediate; -erwyl
av. meanwhile; 'Middellandse a.
Mediterranean; -lik a. (-e) indirect;
-lyf n. waist; -lyn n. axis, diameter;
-maat n. medium size; average;
-'matig a. (-e) mediocre; -punt n.
centre; -rif n. midriff; -slag n.
middlings; -ste a. middle; -weg n.
the golden mean.
'middel'mannetjie ['mədl'manəKi]
n. dim. = maanhaar.
'middernag ['mədəRnach] n. midnight.
'mied ['mit] n. (-e, -ens) stack, rick.
'mielie ['mili] n. (-s) mealie, maize.
mier ['miR] n. (-e) n. ant; -e hê be
fidgety.
'miershoop ['miRsōp] n. ('miershope)
ant-hill.
miet ['mit] n. mite.
mik ['mək] n. (-ke) forked post

(stick); crotch; v. (ge-) aim; -punt n.
aim, target.
mi'krobe [mi'kRōbe] n. (-s) microbe.
mikro'foon [mikRō'fōn] n. (mikro'
fone) microphone.
mikros'koop [mikRōs'kōp] n. microscope.
mild ['məlt] a. (-e; -er, -ste) generous;
liberal; -elik a. & av. (-e) lavishly.
mil'ieu [məl'yē] n. (-'s) environment, milieu.
mili'têr [mələ'tēR] a. (-e) military.
mil'jard [məl'yaRt] n. (-e) milliard.
mil'joen [məl'yun] n. (-e) million.
milt ['məlt] n. (-e) milt, spleen.
'mimiek [mə'mik] n. mimicry;
'mimies a. (-e) mimic.
mi'mosa [mə'mōsa] n. (-s) mimosa,
wattle.
min ['mən] n. love; a. & av. few,
little; less, minus; -ag v. (ge-)
disdain, disregard; -agtend a. (-e)
contemptuous; -agting n. contempt;
-lik a. (-e; -er, -ste) lovable, friendly;
-naar n. lover; -na'res fem. lover,
paramour; -saam a. (-same; -samer,
-ste) affable.
'minder ['məndəR] a. & av. fewer,
less; inferior; lower; -e n. (-s)
inferior; -heid n. minority; -jarig a.
(-e) minor; -'waardig a. (-e; -er, -ste)
inferior.
mine'raal [mənə'Rāl] n. (mine'rale)
mineral.
mi'neur [mi'nēR] n. minor.
minia'tuur [minia'tēWR] n. (minia'
ture) miniature.
mini'maal [mini'māl] a. (minimale)
minimal.
'minimum ['minimʌm] n. ('minima,
-s) minimum.
mi'nister [mə'nəstəR] n. (-s)
minister, member of cabinet; minis
'terie n. (-s) cabinet, ministry;
ministeri'eel a. (ministeri'ele) ministerial.
'minnewoede ['mənəvude] n.
nymphomania.
'minsiek ['mənsik] a. love-sick.
'minste ['mənstə] av. fewest, least,
slightest.
'minstens ['mənstəns] av. at least.
'minus ['minʌs] av. minus, less.
mi'nuut [mə'nēWt] n. (mi'nute)
minute.
mi'rakel [mə'Rākəl] n. (-s) miracle,
wonder.
mis ['məs] n. (-se) mass; n. (-te) mist,
fog; n. dung, manure, fertilizer; a.
& av. amiss, wrong; -'baar n.
clamour, uproar; -baksel n. monster,
churl; -bredie n. pigweed; -bruik n.
(-e) abuse; -daad n. offence, crime;
-'dadig a. (-e) criminal; -'dadiger n.
(-s) criminal; -dryf n. (-drywe)
offence; -gewas n. deformity,
deformed person; -'gis v. (-) be
mistaken; -'gun v. (-) begrudge;
-'handel v. (-) maltreat; -'ken v. (-)
underrate, misjudge; -'lei v. (-)
mislead, deceive; -'luk v. (-) fail;

-'maak a. (-te) deformed; -'moedig a. (-e) discouraged; -'noeë n. displeasure; -oes n. (-te) bad harvest; failure; -stap n. (-pe) false step, faux pas; -stof n. fertilizer; bad harvest; failure; -tas v. (-ge-) make a blunder; -tig a. (-e) misty, foggy; -'troostig a. (-e) dejected; -verstaan v. (-) misunderstand.

mis'deel [məs'dēl] a. (-de) deprived of; stupid.

mise'rabel [məs'Rābəl] a. (-e) dejected.

mis'gun [məs'chʌn] v. (-) grudge, envy.

mis'haag ['məs-hāch] v. (-) displease.

'mishoop ['məsōp] n. ('mishope) dung-hill.

mis'kien [məs'kin] av. perhaps.

'mislik ['məslək] a. (-e) bilious; rotten, nauseating.

mis'noeë [məs'nuə] n. displeasure; pique.

mis'plaas [məs'plās] a. (-te) misplaced.

'missie ['misi] n. mission.

mis'terie [məs'tēRi] n. (-ë) mystery.

'misverstand ['məsfəRstant] n. misunderstanding; cross-purpose.

'mite ['mitə] n. (-s) myth.

mitolo'gie [mitōlō'chi] n. mythology.

'mits ['məts] conj. provided that.

mo'biel [mō'bil] a. (-e) mobile.

mobili'sasie [mōbələ'sāsi] n. mobilization; mobili'seer v. (ge-) mobilize.

mo'daal [mō.dāl] a. (mo'dale) modal; modali'teit n. modality.

'modder ['modəR] n. mud; -agtig a. (-e) mudlike; -ig a. (-e; -er, -ste) muddy; -vet a. plump as a partridge; -klap n. mud flap.

'mode ['mōdə] n. (-s) fashion, style, mode, vogue; -gek n. dandy;-maakster n. (-s) dressmaker; -pop n. doll, fashionable lady; modi'eus a. (-e) fashionable, stylish; mo'diste n. dressmaker.

mo'del [mō'del] n. (-le) model; -'leer v. (ge-) model, mould.

mode'rator [mōdə'RātoR] n. (-e, -s) moderator.

mo'dern [mō'deRn] a. (-e) modern.

modifi'kasie [mōdifi'kāsi] n. modification; modifi'seer v. (ge-) modify.

moed ['mut] n. courage, nerve, spirit; -e n. te moede at heart; -eloos a. (moedelose) dejected; -ig a. (-e; -er, -ste) brave; -swil n. wilfulness; -s'willig a. (-e) wilfully; -verloor n. & av. -se vlaktes slough of despond.

'moeder ['mudəR] n. (-s) mother; -koek n. placenta; -lik a. (-e) motherly; -loos a. (-lose) motherless; -moord n., -moordenaar n. matricide; -naak a. & av. stark-naked; -sielalleen av. all alone; -skap n. motherhood; -skant n. maternal side; -taal n. native tongue; -vlek n. birth-mark.

'moedermaagd ['mudəRmāch] n. The (Blessed) Virgin.

'moedervlek ['mudəRflek] n. (-ke) birth mark.

moeg ['much] a. & av. (moeë) tired, fatigued, weary.

'moeilik ['muilək] a. & av. (-e; -er, -ste) difficult; -heid n. difficulty.

'moeisaam ['muisām] a. ('moeisame) laborious.

'moeite ['muitə] n. trouble, difficulty; -vol a. (-le) difficult.

'moenie ['muni] v. don't!

moer ['mūR] n. (-e) mother; dam; dregs, grounds; seed (potato).

moe'ras [mu'Ras] n. (-se) marsh.

'moerbei ['mūRbay] n. (-e) mulberry.

'moerdraad ['mūRdRāt] n. female thread.

'moersleutel ['mūRslœtəl] n. spanner.

moes ['mus] n. mash, pulp; v. cp. moet.

'moesie ['musi] n. (-s) mole.

moet ['mut] v. (moes) must, have to.

mof ['mof] n. (mouwe) muff; Hun; wool-sheep; -beeste n. pl. cross-breed cattle; -fie n. mitten; -skaap n. (-skape) wool-sheep.

'moker ['mōkəR] v. (ge-) hammer, hit, strike.

mol ['mol] n. (-le) flat, minor key; mole; -lig a. (-e) plump, soft; -hoop n. mole-cast, mole-hill; -vel n. moleskin; -wa n. trolley.

mole'kule [molə'kewlə] n. (-s) molecule; moleku'lêr a. (-e) molecular.

mo'les [mə'les] n. (-te) trouble, disturbance; moles'teer v. (ge-) molest, annoy; -wa n. riot truck.

molm ['moləm] n. mould.

mom ['mom] n. mask; -bakkies n. mask.

mo'ment [mō'ment] n. (-e) moment; momenteel av. momentary.

'mompel ['mompəl] v. (ge-) mumble, grumble; -ing n.

mo'narg [mō'naRch] n. (-e) monarch; monar'gaal a. (monargale) monarchal; monar'gis n. (-te) monarchist; monar'gisties a. monarchial.

mond ['mont] n. (-e) mouth; estuary; muzzle; -elik, -eling a. & av. (-e) oral(ly), verbal(ly), viva voce; -fluitjie n. mouth-organ; -ig a. (-e) of age; precocious; -ing n. estuary; -klem n. gag.

mon'dering [mon'dēRəng] n. (-s) uniform, equipment.

'monnik ['monək] n. (-ke) monk, friar.

monoco'tyl [mōnōkō'til] n. monocotyledon.

'monoftong ['mōnoftong] n. (-e) monophthong.

monoga'mie [mōnōcha'mi] n. monogamy.

monogra'fie [mōnōchRa'fi] n. monograph.

mono'gram [mōnō'chRam] n. monogram.

mono'loog [mŏnŏ'lŏch] n. (mono'loë) monologue.

monopo'lie [mŏnŏpŏ'li] n. monopoly.

'monster ['maunstəR] n. (-s) monster; freak; sample; v. (ge-) muster; **-agtig** a. (-e) monstrous; **-ing** n. muster; review; **-vergadering** n. mass-meeting.

'monstera ['maunstəRā] n. (plant) delicious monster.

mon'teer [mon'tēR] v. (ge-) mount, assemble; **mon'teur** n. erector, fitter; **mon'tuur** n. frame, setting; **-plaas** n. assembly plant.

monu'ment [monew'ment] n. (-e) monument.

mooi ['mŏi] a. & av. (-er, -ste) beautiful, fine, handsome; mooi-broodjies bak curry favour; **-doenery** n. airs and graces; **-e** n. (-es) beauty; jy is 'n-een you are a fine one; **-heid** n. beauty; **-igheid** n. iets met-regkry get something done by gentle persuasion; **-praat** v. (-ge-) coax; **-s** n. iets- something fine; **-tjies** av. hy moes dit-oordoen he jolly well had to do it again.

'moondheid ['mŏntayt] n. (hede) power.

'moontlik ['mŏntlək] a. & av. (-e; -er, -ste) possible, possibly, perhaps; **-heid** n. possibility.

Moor ['mŏR] n. (more) Moor.

moor ['mŏR] v. (ge-) commit murder; maltreat.

moord ['mŏRt] n. (-e) murder; **-'dadig** a. (-e) murderous; **-enaar** n. (-s) murderer; **moordena'res** n. fem. murderess; **-ery** n. massacre; maltreatment; **-'gierig** a. (-e; -er, -ste) bloodthirsty; **-kuil** n. 'n-van jou hart maak make a coffin of one's heart; **-saak** n. murder-case; **-tuig** n. instrument of murder.

moot ['mŏt] n. (mote) fillet, slice; valley; **-jie** dim.

mop ['mop] n. (-pe) joke.

'mopper ['mopəR] v. (ge-) grumble.

mor = **mopper**.

mo'raal [mŏ'Rāl] n. moral; **morali-'seer** v. (ge-) moralize; **morali'teit** n. morality.

'more, 'môre ['mŏRə, 'mauRə] n. morning, morrow; tomorrow.

mo'reel [mŏ'Rĕl] n. morale; a. (mo'rale) moral.

'morfia ['moRfia] n. morphia.

mor'fien [moR'fin] n. morphine.

'morg ['moRch] n. (-e) morgen (land measure).

mors ['moRs] v. (ge-) spill, mess; waste; **-af** av. clean off; **-dood** av. stone-dead; **-ery** n. messing; wastage; **-ig** a. (-e; -er, -ste) filthy.

mor'tier [moR'tiR] n. (-e, -s) mortar.

mos ['mos] n. (-se) moss; n. must, new wine; av. indeed; **-beskuit** n. rusk; **-doppie** n. billycock; **-konfyt** n. grape-syrup.

Mo'saïes [mŏ'sāis] a. (-e) Mosaic.

'moses ['mŏsəs] n. rival; superior.

'mosie ['mŏsi] n. (-s) motion, vote.

mos'kee [mos'kĕ] n. (-s) mosque.

'mossel ['mosəl] n. (-s) mussel.

'mossie ['mosi] n. (-s) sparrow; -, maar man he may be tiny, but he is a topper.

'moster(d) ['mostəR(t)] n. mustard; **-suur** n. mustard pickles.

mot ['mot] n. (-te) moth; **-jie** ['moiKi] dim. **-by** n. death's-head moth.

mo'tief [mŏ'tif] n. (mo'tiewe) motive, motif; **moti'veer** v. (ge-) motivate.

'motor ['mŏtəR] n. (-s, mo'tore) motor; car; engine; **-anker** n. motor-armature; **-bestuurder** n. driver; **-hawe** n. garage (for repairs); **-ryskool** n. driving school; **mo'tories** a. (-e) motory, motorial; **-'is** n. (-te) motorist; **-loos** a. (-lose) motorless.

'motreën ['motrĕn] n. drizzle.

'motto ['motŏ] n. (-'s) motto, device.

mou ['moa] n. (-e) sleeve.

mout ['moat] n. malt; **-suiker** n. maltose.

mo'veer [mŏ'fĕR] v. (ge-) molest, bait, vex.

mud ['mʌt] n. (-de, -dens) muid, bag; v. (ge-) put in bags; **-sak** n. = mud.

muf ['mʌf] a. (muwwe) musty, mouldy, stale.

'muggie ['mʌchi] n. (-s) gnat; midge.

muil ['mœil] n. (-e) mule; muzzle; **-band** n. gag.

muis ['mœis] n. (-e) mouse; **-hond** n. (-e) polecat, skunk; **-ie** dim.; **-neste** pl. musings, sy kop is vol- he is wool-gathering; **-tand** n. milk-tooth; **-val** n. trap.

muit ['mœit] v. (ge-) rebel, mutiny; **-er** n. (-s) mutineer; **-ery** n. mutiny.

mul ['mʌl] a. (-le) loose, sandy.

'mummie ['mʌmi] n. (-s) mummy.

mu'nisie [mew'nisi] n. munition.

munisipali'teit [mewnisipali'tayt] n. (-e) municipality; **munisi'paal** a. (munisipale) municipal.

munt ['mʌnt] n. (-e) coin; mint; head; v. (ge-) coin, mint; **-goud** n. standard gold; **-kunde** n. numismatics; **-stelsel** n. monetary system; **-stuk** n. coin.

mu'rasie [mew'Rāsi] n. (-s) ruins (of house).

murg ['mʌRch] n. marrow; **-van groente** n. vegetable-marrow.

'murmel ['mʌRməl] v. (ge-) murmur, babble, purl.

murmu'reer [mʌRmə'RĕR] v. (ge-) grumble.

mus ['mʌs] n. (-se) cap, bonnet, cosy.

muse ['mĕWsə] n. muse.

mu'seum [mew'sĕʌm] n. museum.

mu'siek [mew'sik] n. music; piano; harmonium; **-laer** n. theory of music; **musi'kaal** a. (musikale) musical; **musi'kant** n. musician; **'musikus** n. musician; **musi'seer** v. (ge-) play music.

mus'kaat [mʌs'kāt] n. nutmeg; -olie n. nutmeg oil.

muska'del [mʌskə'del] n. muscatel (grapes).

mus'kiet [mʌs'kit] n. (-e) mosquito. -olie n. mosquito oil; -weerder n. mosquito repellent.

'muskus ['mʌskəs] n. musk.

'mussie ['mʌsi] n. (-s) cap, bonnet; cosy.

mu'tasie [mew'tāsi] n. mutation.

muur ['mēwR] n. (mure) wall; -sok n. wall socket.

'muurtapyt ['mēwRtəpayt] n. (-e) tapestry.

my ['may] pron. me; my, mine; v. (ge-) avoid, shun.

myl ['mayl] n. (-e) mile; -geld n. mileage (taxi); -paal n. mile-stone; landmark; -wyser n. speedometer.

'mymer ['mayməR] v. (ge-) muse, ponder, meditate; -aar n. (-s) muser, dreamer; -ing n. reverie.

myn ['mayn] n. (-e) mine; -bou n. mining; -hoop n. dump.

'myne ['mayne] pron. mine, cp. my.

'myntering ['mayntēRəng] n. miners' phthisis pneumoconiosis.

N

''n ['ə] article a, an.

na ['nā] av. near; prep. after; prep. to; conj. -hulle sê it is said.

'na-aap ['nā-āp] v. (-ge-) ape, imitate.

naaf ['nāf] n. (nawe) nave, hub; boss; -dop n. hub cap; -trekker n. hub extractor.

naai ['nāi] v. (ge-) sew, stitch; -goed n. sewing; -masjien n. sewing-machine; -ster n. (-s) seamstress; -werk n. sewing.

naak ['nāk] a. (-te) naked, nude; -theid n.

naald ['nālt] n. (-e) needle; -boom n. conifer; -ekoker n. needle-case; dragon-fly; -werk n. sewing.

naam ['nām] n. (name) name; reputation; -gedig n. acrostic; -genoot n. namesake; -lik av. & conj. namely; -loos a. (-lose) nameless, anonymous; -val n. case; -woord n. noun.

naand ['nānt] interj. good evening!

naar ['nāR] a. (nare) unpleasant; nasty; dismal; faint; bilious; prep. = na; -'geestig a. (-e) dreary; -heid n. unpleasantness; nausea; -stig a. & av. (-e) diligent.

naas ['nās] prep. next, beside; v. (ge-) expropriate; -aan prep. next to; -bestaande n. (-s) next of kin; -eergister av. three days ago; -oormore av. three days hence; -te n. (-s) neighbour; -te a. & av. nearest; -tenby av. roughly, approximately; -ting n. seizure.

'naat ['nāt] n. (nate) seam; -loos a. seamless; -los av. torn in the seams.

'nabetragting ['nābətRachtəng] n. reflection.

naboots ['nābōts] v. (-ge-) imitate; -ing n.

na'burig [nā'bewRəch] a. (-e) neighbouring.

naby ['nābay] a., av. & prep. near; -heid n.

nadat ['nādat] conj. after.

'nadeel ['nādēl] n. ('nadele) disadvantage; harm; loss; na'delig a. (-e; -er, -ste) disadvantageous, detrimental.

'nademaal ['nādəmāl] conj. whereas.

na'denkend [nā'denkənt] a. (-e) meditative.

nader ['nādəR] a. (-, -e) nearer; av. nearer; v. (ge-) approach; -by av. nearer; -end a. (-e) approaching; -hand av. later on, afterwards; -ing n. approach; -ings- approach-.

nadink ['nādənk] v. (-ge-) consider, reflect upon.

nadraai ['nādRāi] n. sequel.

nadruk ['nādRʌk] n. emphasis, stress; reprint; -'druklik a. & av. (-e) emphatic(ally).

'nael ['nāl] n. (-s) nail, claw; navel (on body); v. (ge-) nail; sprint; -band n. umbilical tape; -gordel n. umbilical truss; -loop n. sprint; -skraap av. a close shave; -string n. umbilical cord; -tjies n. cloves.

'nael- ['nāl-] n. pref. nail-; -knipper n. nail clipper; -lak n. nail polish; -potlood n. nail pencil; -room n. nail cream; -skêr n. nail scissors; -vliesskêr n. cuticle scissors; -vyl n. nail file.

nafta ['nafta] n. naphtha.

nag ['nach] n. (-te) night; -dier n. nocturnal animal; -ewening n. equinox; -hemp n. night-dress; -lewe n. night-life; Nagmaal n. Holy Communion; -merrie n. nightmare; -ploeg n. night-shift; -rus n. night's rest; -sê v. (-ge-) say good-night; -skaal n. nightshade; -telik a. (-e) nightly; -vrees n. nyctophobia.

'nagaan ['nāchān] v. (-ge-) trace; check.

'nagalm ['nāchaləm] v. (-ge-) reverberate.

'nageboorte ['nāchəbōRtə] n. after-birth.

'nagedagte ['nāchədachtə] n. after-thought; -nis n. memory.

'nagemaak ['nāchəmāk] a. (-te) imitation, counterfeit.

nagenoeg ['nāchənuch] av. nearly, almost.

nagereg ['nāchəRech] n. (-te) dessert.

nageslag ['nāchəslach] n. posterity.

'naglans ['nāchlāns] n. after-glow.

nagtegaal ['nachtəchāl] n. ('nagte-gale) nightingale.

'nagwag ['nachvach] n. (-te) night watchman.

na'ïef [na'if] a. & av. naive.

'najaag ['nāyāch] v. (-ge-) pursue, chase; 'najaging n. pursuit.

'najaar ['nāyāR] n. autumn.
'nakend ['nākənt] a. (-e) = naak.
'naklank ['nāklank] n. echo.
'nakom ['nākom] v. (-ge-) fulfil.
na'komeling [nā'kōmələng] n. (-e) descendant.
'nakroos ['nākRōs] n. progeny.
'nakyk ['nākayk] v. (-ge-) check; correct.
'nalaat ['nālāt] v. (-ge-) leave behind; neglect; na'latenskap n. estate; na'latig a. (-e) negligent.
'naleef ['nālēf] v. (-ge-) live up to.
'naloop ['nālōp] n. & v. lag.
'namaak ['nāmāk] n. counterfeit; v. (-ge-) imitate; -sel n. (-s) imitation.
na'mate [na'mātə] conj. as, in proportion to.
'namiddag ['nāmədach] n. afternoon.
'nanag ['nānach] n. latter part of night.
'napraat ['nāpRāt] v. (-ge-) repeat (gossip).
nar ['naR] n. (-re) buffoon, jester.
'narigheid ['nāRəchayt] n. misery.
nar'kose [naR'kōsə] n. narcosis; nar'koties a. (-e) narcotic; narkoti'seer v. (ge-) anaesthetize; narkoti'seur n. (-s) anaesthetist.
'narsing ['naRsəng] n. (-s) narcissus.
'nartjie ['naRKi] n. (-s) naartjie, mandarin (fruit).
na'saal [na'sāl] n. & a. ('nasale) nasal; nasa'leer v. (ge-) nasalize.
'nasaat ['nāsāt] n. ('nasate) descendant.
'na-sê ['nāsɛ] v. (-ge-) repeat.
'nasie ['nāsi] n. (-s) nation.
'nasien ['nāsin] v. (-ge-) check, look over, correct.
nasio'naal [nashō'nāl] a. (nasiǒ'nale) national; nasiona'lis n. (-te) nationalist; nasionali'sasie n. nationalization; nasionali'seer v. (ge-) nationalize; nationa'listies a (e) nationalistic; nasionali'teit n. nationality.
'nasit ['nāsət] v. (-ge-) pursue.
'naskrif ['nāskRəf] n. postscript.
'naskryf ['nāskRayf] v. (-ge-) copy; plagiarize.
'naslaan ['nāslān] v. (-ge-) consult, refer to, look up.
'nasleep ['nāslēp] n. sequel.
'nasmaak ['nāsmāk] n. after-taste.
'nasomer ['nāsōmər] n. late summer.
'naspeur ['nāspœR] v. (-ge-) trace, track.
'naspoor = naspeur.
'nastergal = nagskade.
'nastreef ['nāstRēf] v. (-ge-) strive after, pursue.
nat ['nat] n. wet, damp; a. moist, wet, tipsy; -heid n.; -terig a. & av. wettish, slightly wet.
'natlei ['natlay] v. (-ge-) irrigate.
'natreent ['natRēnt] v. (-ge-) become drenched in the rain.
'natrek ['nātRek] v. (-ge-) trace; -ker n. tracer; -papier n. tracing-paper;

-pen n. tracing-pen; -ratjie ['RaiKi] dim. tracing-wheel.
'natrium ['nātriʌm] n. sodium.
natura'lis [natewRa'ləs] n. (-te) naturalist; natura'listies a. (-e) naturalistic.
naturali'sasie [natewRali'sāsi] n. naturalization; naturali'seer v. (ge-) naturalize.
natu'rel [natew'Rel] n. (-le) native.
na'tuur [na'tēwR] nature; -kennis n. natural history, science; -kunde n. physics; -'kundig a. (-e) physical; -'kundige n. physicist; -lik a. (-e; -er, -ste) natural; av. naturally; -likerwyse a. naturally; -skoon n. scenery.
na'tuurgeneser [na'tēwRchənēsəR] n. naturopath.
'navertel ['nāfəRtel] v. (nage-) repeat.
'naverwant ['nāfəRvant] n. (-e) relation; a. (-e) closely related.
'navolg ['nāfolch] v. (-ge-) copy, follow.
'navors ['nāfoRs] v. (-ge-) investigate; do research; -ser n. (-s) investigator; research worker; -ing n. investigation, research.
'navraag ['nāfRāch] n. inquiry.
naweë ['nāvēə] n. afterpains, aftermath.
'naweek ['nāvēk] n. weekend.
'nawerking ['nāveRkəng] n. aftereffects.
'nawinter ['nāvəntəR] n. late winter.
'naywer ['nā-ayvəR] n. jealousy, envy.
'né ['ne] interj. not so!
'nederig ['nēdəRəch] a. (-e; -er, -ste) humble, modest; -heid n.
'nedersetter ['nēdəRsetəR] n. (-s) settler; 'nedersetting n. settlement.
nee ['ne] av. no.
'neef ['nēf] n. (newe) male cousin, nephew.
neem ['nēm] v. (ge-) take; engage, book.
neer ['nēR] av. down; -buig v. (-ge-) bend down; -'buigend a. (-e) condescending; -daal v. (-ge-) descend; -druk v. (-ge-) depress; -kniel v, (-ge-) kneel down; -laag n. defeat; -sit v. (-ge-) put down; -slaan v. (-ge-) fall down; -slag n. sediment; -'slagtig a. (-e) depressed; -stryk v. (-ge-) alight; -trek v. (-ge-) pull down; -vel v. (-ge-) fell.
'neerlê ['nēRlɛ] v. (-ge-) lay down; resign; - by abide by.
neet ['nēt] n. (nete) nit.
ne'gasie [nēchāsi] n. negation; nega-'tief n. & a. (negatiewe) negative.
'nege ['ñegə] num. nine.
ne'geer [nə'chēR] v. (-ge-) ignore, cut.
'negende, neënde ['negəndə, 'nēndə] ordin. ninth.
'negentien, 'neentien ['nēgəntin, 'nēntin] num. nineteen.
'negentig, 'neëntig ['nēgəntəch, 'nēntəch] num. ninety.

'**neger** ['nēchəR] n. (-s) negro; nigger; -'**in** n. negress.

ne'gosie [nə'chōsi] n. wares, goods; -**winkel** n. general store.

negrofi'lis [nēchRōfi'ləs] n. (-te) negrophile.

neig ['naych] v. (ge-) bend, bow, incline; -**ing** n. (-e, -s) inclination, disposition, penchant.

nek ['nek] n. (-ke) neck; -**slag** n. blow in the neck; death-blow.

'**nêrens** ['nɛRǝns] av. nowhere.

nerf [neRf] n. (nerwe) vein, nervure, grain; skin.

'**nering** ['nēRǝng] n. (-e, -s) trade, occupation.

ners ['neRs] n. anus; -**derm** n. rectum.

ner'veus [neRfǣs] a. (-e) nervous.

nes ['nes] n. (-te) nest, haunt, hole; av. = **net soos**; -**sie** dim.; -**skop** v. (-ge-) make a nest; -**tel** v. (ge-) nestle.

net ['net] n. (-te) net; a. neat; av. neatly; exactly; -**heid** n. neatness; -**jies** a. & av. neat(ly); -**nou** av. presently; -**vlies** n. retina.

'**netel** ['nētəl] n. (-s) nettle; -**doek** n. muslin; -**ig** a. (-e; -er, -ste) thorny; critical.

'**netto** ['netō] a. nett.

neuk ['nœk] v. (ge-) hit; flog; plague; pester; -**ery** n. nuisance, mess-up.

neul ['nœl] v. (ge-) be a nuisance; -**erig** a. (-e) troublesome; -**ery** n. nagging.

'**neurie** ['nœRi] v. (ge-) hum.

neurolo'gie [nœRōlōchi] n. neurology; **neuro'logies** a. (-e) neurological; **neuro'loog** n. neurologist; **neu'rose** n. neurosis; **neu'roties** a. (-e) neurotic.

neus ['nœs] n. (-e) nose; prow; nozzle; toe; headland; lobe (cam); **nib;** -**beeld** n. mascot; -**gat** n. (-gate) nostril; -**holte** n. nasal cavity; -**horing** n. rhinoceros; -**wys** a. (-e) conceited.

'**neus-** ['nœs-] a. nasal; -**spoeler** n. nasal douche; -**spuit** n. nasal syringe; -**verstuiwer** n. nose atomizer.

neut ['nœt] n. (-e) nut; nutmeg; -**dop** n. nutshell.

neu'traal [nœ'tRāl] a. (neu'trale) neutral; **neutrali'seer** v. (ge-) neutralize; **neutrali'teit** n. neutrality.

newegeskik ['nēvǝchǝskǝk] a. (-te) co-ordinate.

newel ['nēvǝl] n. (-s) haze, mist, fog; -**agtig** a. (-e) misty, hazy; nebulous; -**ig** a. = **newelagtig**.

newens ['nēvǝns] prep. next to, beside; besides.

newensgaande ['nēvǝnschāndǝ] a. accompanying.

'**neweskikkend** ['nēvǝskǝkǝnt] a. (-e) co-ordinate.

nie ['ni] av. not; un-; non-; -**teenstaande** prep. in spite of; -**temin** conj. & av. nevertheless; **nie-** av.

pref. non-; -**openbaring** n. non-disclosure.

'**niemand** ['nimant] pron. no one.

nier ['niR] n. (-e) kidney.

nies ['nis] v. (ge-) sneeze.

niet ['nit] n. nothing, nothingness; -**ig** a. (-e) insignificant; void; -**igheid** n. insignificance.

nieteen'staande [nitēn'stāndǝ] prep. notwithstanding.

'**nietemin** ['nitǝmǝn] av. none the less.

'**niewers** = **nêrens**.

nig ['nǝch] n. cousin; -**gie** dim. (-s) = **nig**.

nihi'lis [nihi'ləs] n. (-te) nihilist.

'**nikkel** ['nǝkəl] n. nickel.

'**nikker** ['nǝkǝR] n. (-s) nix.

niko'tien [nikō'tin] n. nicotine.

niks ['nǝks] pron. & av. nothing; -**beduidend** a. (-e) insignificant; -**doen** n. idleness; -**nuts** n. (-e) rotter, rascal.

'**nikswerd** ['nǝksvert] a. worthless.

nimf ['nǝmf] n. (-e) nymph.

'**nimmer** ['nǝmǝR] av. never; -**meer** av. never again.

'**nippel** ['nǝpǝl] n. (-s) nipple.

'**nippertjie** ['nǝpǝRKi] n. op die- in the nick of time.

nis ['nǝs] n. (-se) niche, recess.

ni'traat [ni'tRāt] n. nitrate.

nitro'geen [nitRō'chēn] n. nitrogen.

ni'veau [ni'vō] n. level, plane.

'**Noag** ['nōach] n. Noah.

nobel ['nōbǝl] a. (-e) noble.

noc'turne [nok'tʌRnǝ] n. (-s) nocturne.

'**node** ['nōdǝ] av. van-wees be necessary; van-hê require; -**loos** a. (-lose) unnecessary, needless.

'**nodig** ['nōdǝch] a. & av. (-e, -er, -ste) necessary; requisite; v. (ge-) invite; -**e** n. what is necessary; -**heid** n. necessity, need.

noem ['num] v. (ge-) name; mention; -**baar** a. (-bare) mentionable; -**ens-'waardig** a. (-e) worth mentioning; -**er** (-s) denominator.

noen ['nun] n. noon; -**maal** n. lunch.

'**noeste** ['nustǝ] a. diligent; '**noestheid** n.

nog ['noch] conj. neither, nor; a. & av. still, yet, further; -**al** av. rather, quite, fairly; -**maals** av. once again; -**tans** av. yet, still.

nôi ['naui] n. (-ens) sweetheart, girl; missus, lady of the house; -**entjie** dim.

nok ['nok] n. (-ke) ridge, cam; -**as** n. camshaft.

no'made [nō'mādǝ] n. nomads; **no'madies** a. (-e) nomadic.

'**nomen** ['nōmen] n. nomen; **nomi'naal** a. (nomi'nale) nominal.

nomi'nasie [nōmi'nāsi] n. nomination; **nomina'tief** n. nominative; **nomi'neer** v. (ge-) nominate.

'**nommer** ['nomǝR] n. (-s) number; size; v. (ge-) number.

non ['non] n. (-ne) nun.

non- ['non-] *pref.* non-.
noncha'lant [naunѕhəlant] *a.* nonchalant.
'nonna ['nona] *n.* (-s) young mistress; *cp.* **nôi.**
'nonnie = nonna.
'nonsens ['naunѕëns] *n.* nonsense, rubbish.
nood ['nõt] *n.* need, distress; necessity; emergency; nood- *pref.* emergency, temporary, spare; -druf *n.* want, poverty; -lot *n.* destiny; -'lottig *a.* (-e) fatal; -'lydend *a.* (-e) destitute; -saak *n.* necessity; -'saaklik *a* (-e) necessary; -'saaklik *av.* (-e) necessarily; -weer *n.* stormy weather; -'wendig *a.* (-e) necessary; *av.* necessarily.
'nood- [-nõt-] *pref.* stand-by-, emergency-; -deur *n.* emergency door; -luik *n.* emergency escape hatch; -rem *n.* emergency brake; -uitgang *n.* emergency exit; -wiel *n.* spare wheel.
'noodhulp ['nõthʌlp] *n.* first aid.
nooi ['nõi] *n.* = nôi; *v.* (ge-) invite; nooiens *cp.* nôi.
'nooiensvan ['nõyənѕfan] *n.* maiden name.
nooit ['nõit] *av.* never.
noop ['nõp] *v.* (ge-) compel.
Noor ['nõR] *n.* (nore) Norwegian.
noord ['nõRt] *n.*, *a.* & *av.* north; -e *n.* north; -elik *a.* (-e) northern, northerly, northward; -erkeerkring *n.* tropic of Cancer; -pool *n.* north pole.
'noorderbreedte ['nõRdəRbRētə] *n.* northern latitude.
'noorderlig ['nõRdəRlɨəch] *n.* aurora borealis.
'noorkapper ['nõRkapəR] *n.* (-s) grampus.
'Noorman ['nõRman] *n.* Norseman.
noors ['nõRs] *a.* (-e) vicious.
'Noorweë ['nõRvēə] *n.* Norway.
'noot ['nõt] *n.* (note) note.
'noppies ['nopis] *n.* in jou-wees highly delighted.
norm ['noRəm] *n.* (-e) norm, standard; nor'maal *n.* & *a.* normal; normali'sasie *n.* normalization; nor-mali'seer *v.* (ge-) normalize; nor-mali'teit *n.* normality; norma'liter *av.* normally.
'norring ['noRəng] *n.* (-s) big lot, mob, crowd; *cp.* enorm.
nors = noors; -heid *n.* sulky; dour.
'nota ['nõta] *n.* note.
no'taris [nõ'tāRəs] *n.* (-se) notary; notari'eel *a.* (notariële) notarial.
no'tasie [nõ'tāsi] *n.* notation; no'teer *v.* (ge-) note; quote; no'tering *n.* noting, quotation.
'notebalk ['nõtəbalk] *n.* staff, stave.
'notedop ['nõtədop] *n.* cockle-shell.
notifi'kasie [nõtifi'kāsi] *n.* notification; notifi'seer *v.* (ge-) notify.
no'tisie [nõ'tisi] *n.* notice; attention.
notori'teit [nõtõRi'tayt] *n.* notoriety.

no'tule [nõ'tewlə] *n.* minutes; notu-'leer *v.* (ge-) enter, record.
nou ['noa] *n.* straits; *in die-* in a fix; *a.* (-; -er, -ste) narrow; *av.* narrowly; now; *interj.* well! *conj.* now (that); -geset *a.* (-te) scrupulous; meticulous; narrow-minded; -keurig *a.* & *av.* (-e) accurate(ly), careful(ly); -'lettend *a.* & *av.* (-e) precise(ly); -liks *av.* hardly; nou-nou *av.* in a moment, presently; -siende *a.* fastidious; -sluitend *a.* (-e) close-fitting; -strop trek *v.* be hard pressed, struggle; -te *n.* (-s) strait; -en dan *av.* occasionally.
no'velle [nõ'felə] *n.* (-s) novelette; novel'lis *n.* novelist.
No'vember [nõ'feməR] *n.* November.
nu ['new] -en dan = nou en dan; nu-*pref.* new.
nu'anse [new'ansə] *n.* (-s) nuance, nuan'seer *v.* (ge-) shade; nuan'sering *n.* (-s) nuance, shade.
'nugter ['nʌchtəR] *a.* & *av.* (-e; -der, -ste) sober(ly); -heid *n.*
nuk ['nʌk] *n.* (-ke) whim, caprice; -kerig *a.* (-e) sulky, moody.
nu'kleus [new'klēəs] *n.* nucleus.
nul ['nʌl] *n.* (-le) nought, zero; -punt *n.* zero; nul- *pref.* zero-, no-, null.
'Numeri ['newməRi] *n.* Numbers.
nume'riek [newmə'Rik] *a.* & *av.* (-e) numerical(ly); -numero *n.* number.
'nummer = nommer; numme'reer *v.* (ge-) number.
nut ['nʌt] *n.* use; benefit; *v.* (ge-) partake; -teloos *a.* (nutelose; nute-loser, -ste) useless, vain; -tig *a.* & *av.* (-e; -er, -ste) useful(ly).
nuus ['news] *n.* news; -draer *n.* tell-tale; -'kierig *a.* (-e) inquisitive; curious.
nuut ['newt] *a.* (nuwe; nuwer, nuutste) new, fresh.
'nuwe *cp.* nuut; -ling *n.* (-e) new-comer, novice; -rig *a.* (-e) newish; -rwets *a.* (-e) modern; new-fangled; 'nuwigheid *n.* novelty.
'Nuwejaar ['newvəyāR] *n.* New Year.
'nuweling ['newvəling] *n.* (-e) novice; newcomer.
'nuwerig ['newvəRəch] *a.* (-e) newish.
nyd ['nayt] *n.* envy, enmity; -ig *a.* (-e; -er, -ste) angry, jealous; -igheid *n.* anger.
nyg ['naych] *v.* (ge-) bow, curtsy; -ing *n.* bow, curts(e)y.
Nyl ['nayl] *n.* Nile.
'nyweraar ['nayvəRāR] *n.* (-s) industrialist; 'nywerheid *n.* ('nywer-hede) industry.

O

ol ['õ] *interj.* oh! ah! aha!
o'ase [õ'āsə] *n.* (-s) oasis.
ob'jek [ob'yek] *n.* (-te) object, thing;

-sie n. objection; **objek'teer** v. (ge-) object; **objek'tief** a. (objek'tiewe) objective.

obli'gasie [obli'chāsi] n. (-s) bond, debenture.

obser'vasie [opsər'fāsi] n. observation; **obser'veer** v. (ge-) observe.

ob'sessie [op'sesi] n. obsession.

obskuri'teit [opskewRi'tayt] n. obscurity.

obste'trie [opstě'tRi] n. obstetrics; **ob'stetries** a. (-e) obstetrical.

obsti'naat [opstəR'nāt] a. (obstinate) obstinate.

ob'struksie [op'strʌksi] n. obstruction.

oc'tavo [ok'tāvō] n. octavo.

'ode ['ōdə] n. (-s) ode.

Odus'sea [ōdə'sēa] n. Odyssey.

'oë cp. **oog**.

oefen ['ufən] v. (ge-) practise, exercise; **-ing** n. (-e) practice, exercise.

'oënskou ['ōənskoa] n. in-neem inspect, review.

oën'skynlik [ōən'skaynlək] a. & av. (-e) apparent(ly).

'oer- ['uR-] pref. original, first, primeval; **-mens** n. primeval man; **-oud** a. primitive; **-tyd** n. primitive age.

oes ['us] n. (-te) harvest; a. bad, miserable, shabby; indisposed; av. badly; v. (ge-) reap, harvest; **-dors** v. & n. combine (harvester and thresh(er)); **-versekering** n. crop insurance.

'oester ['ustəR] n. (-s) oyster, harvester.

'oewer ['uvəR] n. (-s) bank, shore.

of ['of] conj. or; whether.

offen'sief [ofen'sif] n. & a. (offen'siewe) offensive.

'offer ['ofəR] n. (-s) sacrifice, offering; victim; v. (ge-) sacrifice, offer; **-ande** n. (-s) offering, sacrifice; offertory; **of'ferte** n. (-s) offer; **-'vaardig** a. (-e) willing to make sacrifice.

offisi'eel [ōfisi'ěl] a. & av. official(ly).

offi'sier [ofə'siR] n. (-s, -e) officer.

of'skoon [of'skōn] conj. (al)though.

'ofte ['oftə] conj. nimmer-nooit never.

'oggend ['ochənt] n. (-e) morning.

'ogie ['ōchi] n. dim. (-s) eyelet; **-sdraad** n. wire-netting.

'oker [ōkəR] n. ochre.

ok'kasie [ō'kāsi] n. (-s) occasion.

okker'neut [okəR'nět] n. (-e) walnut.

ok'kult [o'kʌlt] n. & a. (-e) occult.

okku'pasie [okew'pāsi] n. occupation; **okku'peer** v. (ge-) occupy, inhabit.

'oksel ['oksəl] n. (-s) arm-pit.

'okshoof ['okshōf] n. hogshead.

oksi'dasie [oksi'dāsi] n. oxidation; **oksi'deer** v. (ge-) oxidize; **ok'sied** n. (-e) oxide.

ok'taaf [ok'tāf] n. (oktawe) octave.

Ok'tober [ok'tōbəR] n. October.

ok'trooi [ok'tRōi] n. (-e) charter, patent; octroi.

oku'lasie [ōkew'lāsi] n. inoculation, grafting; **oku'leer** v. (ge-) inoculate, graft.

'olie ['ōli] n. oil; v. (ge-) oil, lubricate; **-agtig** a. (-e) oily; **-houdend** a. (-e) oleaginous; **-verf** n. oil colours, oil-paint; **-bad** n. oil-bath; **-bak** n. oil sump; **-damp** n. oil vapour; **-deurweek** a. oil saturated; **-druk** n. oil pressure; **-filter** n. oil filter; **-kan** n. oil can; **-keerder** n. oil retainer; **-koeler** n. oil cooler; **-laag** n. oil film; **-lek** n. oil leak; **-peil** n. oil level; **-peilstok** n. oil dipstick; **-peilwyser** n. oil level indicator; **-pomp** n. oil pump; **-ring** n. oil ring; **-seël** n. oil seal; **-skop** n. dipper; **-skot** n. oil baffle ring; **-smering** n. oil lubrication; **-steen** n. oil stone; **-toeoer** n. oil feed; **-tregter** n. oil funnel; **-vlotter** n. oil float; **-verstuiwer** n. oil atomizer.

'oliejas ['ōliyas] n. oilskin.

olifant ['ōlifant] n. (-e) elephant.

oligar'gie [ōlichaR'chi] n. oligarchy.

'olik ['ōlək] a. (-e) seedy, unwell; **-heid** n.

olm ['oləm] n. elm.

'Olimpies [ō'lɔmpis] a. (-e) Olympic.

o'lyf [ō'layf] n. (olywe) olive.

om ['om] av. round; out; up; over; prep. round, about; at, for; **om te** inf. in order to; **-'arm** v. (ge-) embrace; **-blaai** v. (-ge-) turn over; **-boor** v. (-ge-) hem; **-bou** v. (-ge-) rebuild, convert, remodel; **-beleë** a. immature; **-dop** v. (-ge-) turn inside out; double up; **-dra** v. (-ge-) carry about; nurse; **-draai** v. (-ge-) turn round (back); **-gaan** v. (ge-) go round; associate; **-gang** n. association; **-gee** v. (ge-) care; **-gekeer** a. & av. inverse(ly); **-gekrap** a. (-te) untidy; unruly; **-gewe** v. (-) surround; **-'gewing** n. surroundings; **-gooi** v. (-ge-) upset; **-hein** v. (-ge-) fence; **-'hels** v. embrace; **-'hoog** av. aloft; **-hou** v. (-ge-) keep on; **-'hul** v. (-) envelop; **-mekeer** n. reversal; **-keer** v. (-ge-) invert, reverse; **-keerbaar** a. reversible; **-koop** v. (-ge-) bribe; **-krap** v. (-ge-) disarrange; bungle; upset; **-krul** v. (-ge-) curl up; **-kyk** v. (-ge-) look round; **-'laag** av. below; **-'liggende** a. surrounding; **-loop** n. circulation; ringworm; **-loop** v. (-ge-) make detour; knock down; **-'lyn** v. (-) outline; **-mesientjie** n. in 'n' in a jiffy; **-pad** n. detour; **-praat** v. (-ge-) persuade; **-'ring** v. (-) surround; **-roep** n. broadcast; **-ruil** v. (-ge-) exchange; **-ry** v. (-ge-) knock down; **-sendbrief** n. circular letter; **-set** n. turnover; **-'sigtig** a. (-e) circumspect; **-'singel** v. (-) surround; **-'skep** v. (-) transform; **-'skryf** v. (-) define; **-slaan** v. (-ge-) capsize; **-slag** n. cover; brace; **-'slagtig** a. (-e) tedious; **-'sluier** v. (-) veil, conceal; **-soom** v. (-ge-) **-streeks** av. about; **-streke** n. vicinity; **-trek** n. outline;

-'trent *av.* about; -vang n. extent;
-'vattend *a.* (-e) embracing; -weg n.
(*omweë*) detour; -wend *v.* (-ge-) turn;
-wentel *v.* (*onge-*) rotate; -'wenteling
n. revolution; -werking n. recasting;
-windsel n. wrapper.

'omdat ['omdat] *conj.* because.

o'mega [ő'mēcha] n. omega.

om'gord [om'choRt] *v.* (-) gird on.

'omklink ['omklənk] *v.* (-ge-) rivet.

'omkom [omkom] *v.* (-ge-) perish.

om'lysting [om'laystəng] n. beading,
moulding.

om'muur [om'mēWR] *v.* (-) wall in.

'ompad ['ompat] n. ('*ompaaie*)
detour.

'omploeg ['ompluch] *v.* (-ge-) plough
up.

'omroer ['omRüR] *v.* (-ge-) stir.

'omsetting ['omsetəng] n. conver-
sion.

'omsientjiestyd ['omsingKistayt] n.
in n - in a jiffy; = ommesientjie.

'omsit ['omsət] *v.* (-ge-) put round;
convert; transpose.

'omslaan ['omslän] *v.* (-ge-) capsize.

om'slagtig(e) [om'slachtəch(e)] *a.*
discursive; -heid n. circumlocution.

'omspit ['omspət] *v.* (-ge-) dig up.

om'standig [om'standəch] *a.* (-e)
detailed.

'omstel ['omstel] *v.* (-ge-) reverse.

'omtrek ['omtRek] n. circumference,
perimeter.

'omval ['omfal] *v.* (-ge-) topple over.

om'vangryk [omfang'rək] *a.* (-e)
comprehensive, extensive.

om'vleuel [om'fiőel] *v.* (-) encircle.

on- ['on-] *pref.* un-, in-, im-;
-'aangenaam *a.* unpleasant; -aan-
treklik *a.* (-e) unattractive; -aardig
a. (-e) unpleasant; -afgebroke *a. &
av.* incessant(ly); -'agsaam *a.* careless, inattentive; -be'daarlik *a. &
av.* (-e) violent(ly); -bedag *a.* (-te)
thoughtless; -be'dagsaam *a.* (*onbe-
'dagsame*) thoughtless; -bedug *a.*
(-te) fearless; -beduidend *a.* (-e)
trifling; -be'dwingbaar *a.* indomit-
able; -bedwonge *a.* unsubdued;
-begonne *a.* 'n-taak an impossible
task; -begrepe *a.* not understood;
-beholpe *a.* clumsy; -bekend *a.* (-te)
unknown; -bekook *a.* (-te) rash;
-be'nullig *a.* (-e) trifling, paltry;
-bepaald *a.* (-e) indefinite; -beperk
a. (-te) unlimited; -bereid *a.* (-e)
unprepared, impromptu; -be'rispelik
a. (-e) irreproachable; -be'set *a.*
(-te) unoccupied; -beskof *a.* (-te)
rude, uncouth; -be'sonne *a.* thoughtless; -be'sproke *a.* unreserved;
blameless; -be'suis *a.* (-de) rash;
-be'trede *a.* untrodden; -bevange *a.*
unbias(s)ed; -be'wese *a.* unproved;
-be'wimpeld *a.* candid, frank;
-'billik *a.* (-e) unfair; -bruik n.
disuse; -daad n. misdeed, atrocity;
-danks *av.* notwithstanding; -deug
n. vice; -'deund *a.* (-e) naughty;
-deur'dag *a.* (-te) thoughtless, rash;

-diens n. disservice; -'dig *a.* (-te)
leaky; -ding n. rubbish; absurdity;
-'eens *av.* at variance; -'effe *a.*
uneven; -egtelik *a.* (-e) illegitimate;
-eindig *a. & av.* (-e) endless(ly);
-'enig *av.* at variance; -'ewe *a.* odd;
-ge'ag *a.* (-te) unnoticed, *prep.*
notwithstanding; -ge'daan *a. & av.*
(-*dane*) undone; -ge'deerd *a.* (-e)
unscathed; -ge'durig *a.* (-e) restless;
-ge'ërg *a.* (-de) nonchalant; -ge-
'hinder(d) *av.* (-e) undisturbed,
unhindered; -geluk n. (-ke) accident;
-ge'lukkig *a. & av.* (-e) unfortunate
(.y); -gemak n. discomfort; -ge-
'maklik *a. & av.* (-e) uncomfortable
(-bly); -ge'merk *a. & av.* unper-
ceived, imperceptibly; -ge'poets *a.
& av.* (-e) rude; -ge'regtig *a.* (-e, -de)
unjust; unwarranted; -ge'rep *a.*
(-te) untouched, pure; -ge'seglik *a.*
(-e) refractory; -ge'skonde *a.* undamaged; -ge'sog *a.* (-te) natural,
easy; -ge'stadig *a.* (-e) inconsistent;
fickle; -ge'steld *a. & av.* (-e) indisposed; -ge'trou *a.* (-e) unfaithful;
-geval n. (-le) accident; -geveer *av.*
nearly, approximately; -gewens *a.*
(-te) undesirable; -'nosel *a.* (-e)
stupid, silly; -nut n. rogue, rascal;
-'nutsig *a.* (-e) naughty; -'ooglik *a.*
(-e) unsightly; -ophoudelik *a.* (-e)
incessant; -paar *a.* odd; -raad n.
trouble, danger; -reg n. justice; -sin
n. nonsense; -'sinnig *a.* (-e) foolish;
-'skatbaar *a.* (*on'skatbare*) inesti-
mable; -'stuimig *a.* (-e) stormy,
rough; -'sydig *a.* (-e) neutral; -ver-
'biddelik *a.* (-e) inexorable; -ver-
'drote *a.* untiring; -ver'hoeds *av.*
unexpectedly; -ver'hole *a.* undis-
guised; -ver'mydelik *a.* (-e) inevi-
table; -ver'skillig *a.* (-e) indifferent;
-ver'wags *av.* unexpectedly; -ver-
wyld *av.* immediate; -voor'sien *a.*
(-e) unexpected; -weer n. unsettled
weather; -'willig *a.* (-e) unwilling;
-'wrikbaar *a.* (*on'wrikbare*) un-
yielding.

'onbeksaaf ['ombəskăf] *a.* (-de; -der,
-ste) rude; uncivilized; = onbeskof.

'onbestrede ['ombəstRĕdə] *a.* un-
opposed.

onbe'voeg [ombə'fuch] *a.* (-de) in-
competent, unfit.

onbe'wus [ombə'vʌs] *a.* (-te) un-
aware; unconscious.

'ondank ['ondank] n. ingratitude; -s
prep. notwithstanding.

'onder ['onəR] *av. & prep.* below;
under, underneath, among.

'onderdeel ['ondəRdĕl] n. ('*onder-
dele*) portion; spare part.

'onder- ['onəR-] *pref.* under-, sub-,
vice-, below-; -aan *av.* at the foot of;
-'aards *a.* (-e) subterranean; -arm n.
fore-arm; -baadjie n. waistcoat;
-been n. lower leg; -bly *v.* (-ge-)
remain under; -'breek *v.* (-) inter-
rupt; -daan n. (-*dane*) subject; -dak
n. shelter; -'danig *a.* (-e) submissive;

-druk v. (-ge-) press down; -'druk v. (-) oppress; -'duims a. & av. underhand; -gaan v. (-ge-) set, go down; -'gaan v. (-) undergo, endure; -gang n. setting; destruction; -ge'tekende n. undersigned; -'handel v. (-) negotiate; -'hewig a. (-e) present; -'hewig av. liable (subject) to; -'horig a. & av. dependent, inferior; -houd n. support; interview; -'houdend a. (-e) amusing; -in av. at the bottom; -kant av. below; -ken n. double chin; -kome n. shelter; -koning n. viceroy; -langs prep. along the foot, av. lower down; -'leg av. -wees in well versed in; -'ling a. & av. (-e) mutual(ly); -lyf n. lower part of body; -'maans a. (-e) mundane; -om av. round the bottom; -pak n. underwear; -'rig v. (-) instruct; -'sese [-'sèsə] a. submarine; -'skat v. (-) underrate; -'skei v. (-) distinguish; discern; discriminate; -skeid n. difference; -'skeidelik av. respectively; -'skeiding n. (-e, -s) distinction; -'skep v. (-) intercept; -skikkend a. (-e) subordinate; -soek n. investigation, inquiry; -stam n. root-stock; -staande a. subjoined; -stand n. relief, aid; -standswerke n. relief works; -ste n. lowermost; -'teken v. (-) sign; -toe av. lower down; -'tussen av. meanwhile; -'vind v. (-) experience; -'voed a. (-) underfed; -'vra v. (-) question, interrogate; -'weg av. under way; -wêreld n. lower world; -'werp n. (-e) subject; -'worpe a. & av. submissive; subject to; -'wyl av. meanwhile; conj. while; -wys n. education; teaching; v. (-) teach, instruct; -'wyser n. (-s) teacher; -wyse'res n. fem. teacher.

'onderhandse   'samewerking ['onəRhantsə 'sãməveRkəng] n. collusion.

'ondermaats ['on(d)əRmãts] a. undersized.

'onderpand ['on(d)əRpant] n. collateral; pledge.

'onder'skrywer ['on(d)əR'skRayvəR] n. (-s) underwriter.

'ondervoer ['ondəRfûR] v. (-) starve; -ing n. starvation.

'ondier ['ondiR] n. monster.

'oneg ['onech] a. (-te) spurious.

'ongedierte ['auñchədiRtə] n. vermin, wild beasts.

'ongeneë ['auñchənêə] a. disinclined.

'ongerief ['auñchəRif] n. (ongeriewe), discomfort; -lik a. (-e) inconvenient; uncomfortable.

'ongerus ['auñchəRʌs] a. uneasy.

onge'skik ['auñchəskək] a. unfit; uncouth.

onge'twyfeld ['auñchətwayfəlt] av. undoubtedly.

onge'voelig [āûñchə'fuləch] a. (-e; -er, -ste) apathetic; -heid n. analgesia.

onge'wild ['auñchəvəlt] a. (-e) unpopular.

'onguns ['auñchʌns] n. disfavour; -tig a. unfavourable.

on'handig ['auñ'handəch] a. (-e) clumsy.

'onheil ['onhayl] n. disaster; -spellend a. (-e) ominous.

'onjuis ['auñyœis] a. incorrect.

'onklaar ['aung'klãR] av. out of order.

'onkoste ['aung-kostə] n. expenses.

'onkruid ['aung-kRœit] n. weeds.

'onlangs ['onlangs] a. recently.

'onlus ['aufilʌs] n. (-te) riot.

'onmag ['omach] n. impotence.

'onpadwaardig [ompatvãRdəch] a. (-e) unroadworthy.

on'redelik [auñ'Rèdlək] a. unreasonable.

'onrein ['onRayn] a. unclean.

'onrus ['onRʌs] n. unrest; -'barend a. alarming.

'onskuld ['auñskʌlt] n. innocence; on'skuldig a. (-e) innocent.

'ontug ['ontʌch] n. prostitution; on'tugtig a. unchaste.

'onsame'hangend ['onsãmə'hangənt] a. (-e) desultory.

ont- [ont-] pref. de-, dis-, un-, lack of; commence; -'aard v. (-) degenerate; -beer v. (-) lack, miss; -'bied v. (-) summon; -'bloot v. (-) uncover; a. naked, devoid of; -'boesem v. (-) unburden (oneself); -'brand v. (-) take fire, ignite, break out; -'breek v. (-) lack; -'byt n. breakfast; -'dek v. (-) discover; -'dekking n. discovery; -'dooi v. (-) thaw; -'duik v. (-) dodge; -'eien v. (-) expropriate, dispossess; -'erf v. (-) disinherit; -'ferm v. (-) -oor take pity on; -'gaan v. (-) escape, evade; -'gin v. (-) exploit; -'glip v. (-) slip from; -'gloei v. (-) start to glow, burn; -'gogel v. (-) disillusion; -'groei v. (-) outgrow; -'haal n. (-hale) reception; v. (-) treat; -'hef v. (-) exempt from; -'hou v. (-) refuse; remember; -'hul v. (-) unveil; -'huts a. (-te) upset, disconcerted, dismayed; -'ken v. (-) deny; -'kennend a. (-) negative; -'kom v. (-) escape; -'las v. (-) relieve; -'leed v. (-) analyse; -'leen v. (-) derive, borrow from; -'luik v. (-) bud, develop, open; -'masker v. (-) expose, unmask; -'moedig v. (-) dishearten; -'moedigend a. (-e) disheartening; -'moet v. (-) meet; -'plooi v. (-) reveal, develop, expand; -'rafel v. (-) unravel; -'reddard a. (-e) disabled; -'roer v. (-) move; -'ruim v. (-) vacate; -'sag n. awe; -'set n. relief; -'settend a. (-e) terrible; -'sien v. (-) respect, spare; -'slaan v. (-) dismiss; -'slaap v. (-) pass away; -'slae av. -van rid of; -'slag n. release; -'slape a. deceased; -'snap v. (-) escape; -'spring v. (-)

rise, originate; -'staan n. origin; v. (-) originate; -'stel v. (-) upset; -'stem v. (-) ruffle; -'stentenis n. by-van in default of; -'stig v. (-) offend; -'stoke a. inflamed; -'styg v. (-) rise up from; -'syfer v. (-) decipher; -'vang v. (-) receive; -'vangs n. receipt; reception; -'vanger n. receiver; -'vanklik a. (-e) receptive; -'vlam v. (-) catch fire; -'vlug v. (-) escape, flee; -'voer v. (-) kidnap; -'vou v. (-) unfold; -'waak v. (-) awake; -'war v. (-) unravel; -'werp v. (-) design; n. (-e) design; -'wikkel v. (-) develop, generate; -'wikkeld a. (-e) developed; -'wil n. om my- for my sake; -'wrig v. (-) dislocate; -'wyk v. (-) avoid.

ont'aard [ont'ãRt] v. (-) degenerate, become depraved; a. (-e) depraved; -ing n. depravity.

ont'haarmiddel [ont'hãRmədl] n. (-s) depilatory.

ont'hef [ont'hef] v. (-) discharge.

ont'heilig [ont'hayləch] v. (-) desecrate.

ont'houding [ont'hoadəng] n. continence.

ont'knoping [ont'knõpəng] n. denouement.

ont'lug [ont'lʌch] v. (-) vent, deaerate.

ont'nugter [ont'nʌchtəR] v. (-) disabuse.

ont'steek [ont'stěk] v. (-) fire, ignite; -orde n. firing order.

ont'syfer [ont'sayfəR] v. (-) decipher, decode.

'onverwerk ['onfəRveRk] a. crude, raw.

oog ['õch] n. (oë) eye; -getuie n. eyewitness; -haar n. (-hare) eyelash; -kas n. (-te) eye-socket; -klap n. (-pe) blinker; -knip n. wink; -lid n. (-lede) eye-lid; -'luikend av. iets toelaat connive at; -merk n. (-e) aim; -opslag n. glance; -punt n. point of view; -tand n. (-e) eye-tooth; -verblindend a. (-e) blinding, dazzling; -vlies n. tunicle; -wenk n. moment, twinkling of an eye.

ooi ['ŏi] n. (-e) ewe; -lam n. ewe-lamb; daughter.

'ooievaar ['ŏiəfãR] n. stork.

ooit ['ŏit] av. ever.

ook ['ŏk] conj. & av. also, as well, too, likewise, even.

oom ['õm] n. (-s) uncle; -pie dim.

'oomblik ['õmblək] n. (-ke) moment; 'blikik a. & av. instantaneous(ly).

oond ['õnt] n. (-e) oven, furnace.

oop, 'ope ['õp, 'õpə] a. & av. open; empty; vacant; unbuttoned, unsealed; -bars v. (-ge-) burst open; -draai v. (-ge-) turn on (water); -gaan v. (-ge-) open; -hou v. (-ge-) keep open (unlocked); -spalk v. (-ge-) spread out; -staan v. (-ge-) be open; -stel v. (-ge-) make accessible; -te n. open space.

oor ['ŏR] n. (ore) ear; handle; prep.

over, across, more than, over and above, beyond; av. over, -en weer to and fro; conj. because; -bekend a. & av. (-e) generally known; -bel (-letjie) n. (-s) ear-ring; -belasting n. super-tax; -belig a. (-te) overexposed; -bevolk a. (-te) too densely populated; -blaser n. (-s) scandalmonger; -'bluf v. (-) bluff, frighten; -'bodig a. (-e; -er, -ste) superfluous; -'boord av. overboard; -'brug v. (-) bridge; -daad n. excess; -'dadig a. (-e) excessive; -'dag av. by day; -deel n. judgment, sentence, verdict; v. (ge-) judge, consider, deem; -deel'kundig a. (-e) discerning; -'dink v. (-) consider; -'donder v. (-) bluff, overawe; -'drewe a. & av. exaggerated, excessively; -'dryf v. (-) exaggerate; -'dwars av. athwart; -'eenkom v. (ooreenge-) agree; -een'komstig av. (-e) conformable; -'eenkoms n. agreement; oor-en-oor av. repeatedly; -erf v. (-ge-) inherit; -gang n. crossing; -ganglik a. (-e) transitive; -gawe n. transfer; surrender; -gee v. (-ge-) surrender, deliver, yield; -gehaal a. & av. (-de) cocked, ready; -genoeg av. more than enough; -hand n. upperhand, mastery; -'handig v. (-) hand over, deliver; -'heers v. (-) dominate; -'heersend a. (-e) predominant; -hel v. (-ge-) lean over; -'hoeks a. & av. diagonal(ly); out of sorts; -kant n. the opposite side; -kantel v. (oorge-) topple over; -kleed n. cover; -kom v. (-ge-) come over; recover, befall; -konkel n. box on the ear; -krabbetjie n. (-s) ear-drop; -kruiper n. earwig; -'kruis av. crosswise; -laat v. (-ge-) entrust; -'lams a. (-, -e) clever, handy; -las n. nuisance; -lede a. deceased; -ledene n. (-s) the deceased; -leer n. uppers; -'leg n. deliberation; consultation; judgment; care; -lewer n. (oorge-) give up, yield; -lewering n. tradition; -log n. (-loë) war; -loop v. (-ge-) cross; overflow; -loper n. deserter; -'lyde n. death, decease; -maat n. excess; -mag n. superior numbers; -'meester v. (-) overpower; -merk n. ear-mark; -moed n. rashness; -more, -môre av. the day after tomorrow; -'nag v. (-) pass the night; -name n. taking over; -neem v. (-ge-) take from, take over; -'peins v. (-) ponder over; -plaas v. (-ge-) transfer; -priester n. (-s) high-priest; -'reed v. (-) persuade; -ring n. (-e) ear-ring; -'rompel v. (-) overwhelm; -sien v. (-ge-) excuse, overlook; -sig n. (-te) review; outline; -'skadu v. (-) outshine, eclipse; -'skat v. (-) over-estimate, overrate; -skiet n. left-overs; -skoen n. galosh; -skot n. remains; surplus; -'skry v. (-) exceed; pass beyond; -slaan v. (-ge-) skip, omit; disregard; change to; -sprong n. origin;

-'spronklik a. & av. (-e) original(ly);
-stap v. (-ge-) cross; change; disregard; -'stelp v. (-) overwhelm;
shower upon; -'stroom v. (-) overflow; -tjie n. dim. farthing; -tog n.
passage; -'tollig a. & av. (-e) superfluous(ly); -'treder n. trespasser;
-'treding n. transgression; -'tree v.
(-) transgress, trespass; -'tuiging n.
conviction; -'val v. (-) take by
surprise; -veeg n. box on the ear;
-'vleuel v. (-) outflank; -vloed n.
abundance; -'vloedig a. (-e) abundant; -vol av. full to overflowing;
-waai v. (-) blow over; pass off; -was
n. ear-wax; -kruiper, -wurm n.
earwig; -'weeg v. (-) consider; -weg
n. (-weë) crossing; -'weidig v. (-)
overwhelm; -wig n. preponderance;
-'win v. (-) conquer, defeat; -'winning n. victory; -wins n. excessprofit; -'woë a. considered.

oord ['ŏRt] n. (-e) place, region.
oor'losie [ŏR'lŏsi] n. (-s) watch, cp.
horlosie.
oorsak ['ŏRsäk] n. ('oorsake) cause,
origin; -saaklik a. (-e) causal.
oos ['ŏs] n. & a. east; oos- east-,
eastern; -see n. the Baltic; -sy n.
east-side; -te n. the east; -telik a. &
av. easterly; Oostenryk n. Austria;
-terling n. Oriental; -ters a. (-e)
Oriental.
'ootmed ['ŏtmut] n. humility; ont-
'moedig a. (-) humble.
op ['op] prep. on, upon, in, at; av. up,
on; op- pref. up; -beur v. (-ge-) lift
up, cheer up; -blaas v. (-ge-) blow
up; -bloei v. (-ge-) flourish; -borrel
v. (opge-) bubble up; -bouend a. (-e)
edifying; -brengs n. yield; crop;
-bring v. (-ge-) yield; educate;
arrest; vomit; -daag v. (-ge-) arrive;
-dis v. (-ge-) dish up, serve; -doen v.
(-ge-) acquire, do up; -dok v. (-ge-)
pay up; -draand n. & a. (-e) uphill;
-draans av. uphill; -drag n. (-te)
instruction, order; -'eenvolg v.
(opeenge-) follow each other; -eis v.
(-ge-) claim; -gaaf, -gawe n. (-s)
statement; -gaande a. rising; -gaar
v. (-ge-) accumulate; -gang n.
ascent; success, fame; -geefsel n.
(-s) mirage; -geruimd a. & av. (-e;
-er, -ste) cheerful; -geskort a. (-e)
suspended; -geskote a. grown up,
adolescent; -gesmuk a. (-te) show,
gaudy; -getoë a. elated; -gewek a.
(-te) cheerful; -grawing n. (-s)
excavation; -hef n. fuss; -helder v.
(opge-) clear up; -hemel v. (opge-)
extol; -hits v. (-ge-) incite; -hoop v.
(-ge-) amass; -hou v. (-ge-) hold;
keep on; detain; cease; keep up;
-keil v. (-ge-) wedge up; urge on;
oppose; -klaar v. (-ge-) clear up;
elucidate; -knap v. (-ge-) tidy up;
-koms n. rising; beginning; assembly; -krop v. (-ge-) conceal, restrain,
pent up; -kyk v. (-ge-) look up; -laag
n. edition; -lei v. (-ge-) train;

educate; -let v. (-ge-) attend;
-'lettend a. (-e) attentive; -lewer v.
(-ge-) yield; -loop n. tumult; v. (-ge-)
walk up; slope upwards; mount;
accrue; -los v. (-ge-) dissolve; solve;
-lossing n. solution; -luister v.
(opge-) adorn; -mars n. advance;
-merk v. (-ge-) notice, observe;
-merking n. (-s) remark; -'merklik
a. (-e) remarkable; -'merksaam a.
(op'merksame) observant; attentive;
-meting n. survey; -naaisel n. tuck;
-name n. survey; reception; insertion; taking; -noem v. (-ge-) name,
enumerate; -'nuut av. anew; -offer
v. (-ge-) sacrifice; -pas v. (-ge-) try
on; tend; take care; -'passend a. (-e;
-er, -ste) steady, well-behaved;
-passer n. (-s) nurse, caretaker,
keeper; -raak v. (-ge-) give out;
-raap v. (-ge-) pick up; -raapsel n.
scraps; -rig v. (-ge-) raise, erect;
help up; -rigter n. (-s) founder;
-rigting n. founding, foundation;
-roep n. summons; v. (-ge-) summon,
call; -roer n. rebellion; -'roerig a.
(-e) rebellious, riotous; -rol v. (-ge-)
roll up; -rui v. (-ge-) incite; -ruim
v. (-ge-) clear away; -ruiming n.
clearance; -saal v. (-ge-) saddle; -sê
v. (-ge-) say, recite; call in; renounce;
terminate; -set n. plan, outline,
design; -'setlik a. & av. (-e) deliberate(ly); -sig n. supervision; respect;
-'sigtelik a. (-e) showy; conspicuous;
-sit v. (-ge-) sit up; spoon; raise;
-skep v. (-ge-) serve up; boast; -skiet
v. (-ge-) shoot up, make progress;
-skik v. (-ge-) dress up; -skort v.
(-ge-) postpone, defer; -skrif n.
inscription, heading, title; -skudding
n. commotion; -slaan v. (-ge-) hit,
bounce; cock; pitch; raise; -sluit v.
(-ge-), lock up; -smuk v. (-ge-) dress
up; -soek v. (-ge-) look up, call upon;
look for; -som v. (-ge-) summarise;
-spoor v. (-ge-) trace, track down;
-sprask n. scandal, sensation; -staan
v. (-ge-) stand up; rise; revolt; -stal
n. (-le) premises; -stand n. revolt;
-'standig a. (-e) mutinous; -stel v.
(-ge-) compose; -stel n. (-le) composition; -stook v. (-ge-) incite; -stootjie
n. riot; -stopper n. punch; -styg v.
(-ge-) ascend; rise; mount; -swelg v.
(-ge-) swallow up; -teken v. (-ge-)
note, record; -tel v. (-ge-) add up;
pick up; -telkind n. foundling; -tooi
v. (-ge-) adorn; -trede n. conduct;
appearance; -val v. (-ge-) strike;
-'vallend a. & av. (-e) striking(ly);
-vat v. (-ge-) take up, conceive;
resume; -vatting n. (-s) view, idea;
-veiling n. (-s) auction-sale; -'vlieënd
a. (-e) quick-tempered; -voed v.
(-ge-) educate, train; -voedkunde n.
education, pedagogy; -volg v. (-ge-)
succeed, follow; -vrolik v. (-ge-)
gladden; -vysel v. (-ge-) extol; -weeg
v. (-ge-) -teen counterbalance; -wek
v. (-ge-) rouse, stir up; -wen v. (-ge-)

excite; -'windend a. (-e) exciting.
o'paal [ŏ'pāl] n. (opale) opal.
'opblaas ['oblās] v. (-ge-) bloat.
'opdat ['opdat] conj. in order that, lest.
'opdons ['opdauñs] v. (-ge-) manhandle; spoil; treat carelessly.
op'een [op'ēn] av. one upon another.
op'eens [op'ēñs] av. suddenly.
'opelug ['ŏpəlach] n. open air.
'opelyf ['ŏpəlayf] n. evacuation of the bowels.
'open ['ŏpən] v. (ge-) open; -ing n.; -lik av. openly.
open'baar [ŏpən'bāR] n. public; a. (open'bare) public; v. (ge-) reveal, divulge; open'baring n. revelation, manifestation.
open'hartig [ŏpən'haRtəch] a. (-e) candid.
'opera ['ŏpəRa] n. (-s) opera.
ope'rasie [ŏpə'Rāsi] n. operation.
opera'teur [ŏpəRa'tœR] n. (-s) operator.
opera'tief [ŏpəRa'tif] a. (opera'tiewe) operative.
'opgeskeep ['opchəskēp] a. saddled with.
'opgewonde ['opchəvonə] a. excited.
o'pinie [ŏ'pini] n. opinion.
'opium ['ŏpiʌm] n. opium.
'oplê ['oplɛ] v. (-ge-) superimpose, impose.
'oponthoud ['opontoad] n. delay.
'opper ['opəR] n. (-s) haystack; stook; v. (ge-) suggest, put forward, broach.
'opper- ['opəR-] pref. superlative degree; supreme; head; above; superior; -bes a. av. excellent; -bevel n. supreme command; -heer n. sovereign; -hoof n. chief; -huid n. epidermis; -mag n. supremacy; -'magtig a. (-e) supreme; -mag n. supremacy; -ste a. uppermost, highest; Opperwese n. God.
'oppervlak(te) ['opəRflak(tə)] n. surface; opper'vlakkig a. av. (-e) superficial(ly).
oppo'neer [opə'nēR] v. (ge-) oppose.
oppo'nent [opə'nent] n. (-e) opponent.
opportu'nis [opoRtew'nəs] n. (-te) opportunist.
oppo'sisie [opŏ'sisi] n. opposition.
op'reg [op'Rech] a. (-te) upright, sincere.
'oprit ['opRət] n. (-te) ramp (up); cp. aanrit.
'opsie ['opsi] n. (-s) option.
'opsweep ['opsvēp] v. (-ge-) incite.
'opties ['optis] a. (-e) optical.
opti'mis ['optiməs] n. optimist.
'optog ['optoch] n. (-te) procession; approach.
opu'lent [ŏpew'lent] a. (-e) opulent.
'opvoer ['opfūR] v. (-ge-) perform.
o'rakel [ŏ'Rākəl] n. (-s) oracle.
'orals ['ŏRals] av. everywhere.
o'ranje [ŏ'Ranyə] a. orange.

Oranje-'Vrystaat [ŏRanyə'fRaystāt] n. Orange Free State.
o'rasie [ŏ'Rāsi] n. noise; oration.
o'rator [ŏ'RātoR] n. (-e, -s) orator; ora'tories a. oratorical.
'orde ['oRdə] n. order; -lik a. av. (-e) orderly; -loos a. (-lose) disorderly.
'orden ['oRdən] v. (ge-) ordain; arrange; -ing n. arrangement, ordination.
or'dentlik [oR'dentlik] a. (-e; -er, -ste) decent; av. decently; -heid n.; -'heidshalwe av. for decency's sake.
'order ['oRdəR] n. (-s) command.
ordi'nêr [oRdə'nēR] a. (-e) ordinary.
ordon'nansie [oRdə'nansi] n. (-s) ordinance.
or'ent [ŏR'ent] av. on end, erect.
or'gaan [oR'chān] n. (or'gane) organ; or'ganies a. (-e) organic.
organi'sasie [oRchani'sāsi] n. (-s) organization; organi'seer v. (ge-) organize; organi'seerder n. organizer.
orga'nisme [oRcha'nəsmə] n. (-s) organism.
orgi'dee [oRchi'dē] n. (orgi'deë) orchid.
Ori'ent [ŏRi'ent] n. Orient.
oriën'tasie [ŏRien'tāsi] n. orientation; oriën'teer v. (ge-) orientate oneself; oriën'tering n. orientation.
'orig ['ŏRəch] a. (-e) rest; remaining; meddlesome; lecherous.
'origens ['ŏRəchəñs] av. otherwise.
origi'neel [ŏRichi'nēl] n. a. (origi'nele) original.
or'kaan [oR'kān] n. (or'kane) hurricane.
or'kes [oR'kes] n. (-te) orchestra; orkes'treer v. (ge-) orchestrate.
orna'ment [oRna'ment] n. (-e) ornament; ornamen'teel a. (ornamentele) ornamental; ornamen'teer v. (ge-) ornament.
'orrel ['oRəl] n. (-s) organ; -'is n. (-te) organist.
orto'doks [oRtŏ'doks] a. (-e) orthodox.
ortogra'fie [oRtŏchra'fi] n. orthography.
ortope'die [oRtŏpē'di] n. orthopaedy; orto'pedies a. (-e) orthopaedic.
'os ['os] n. (-se) ox; -stert n. ox-tail; -vel n. hide.
ose'aan [ŏsē'ān] n. (ose'ane) ocean.
os'mose [os'mōsə] n. osmosis.
o'sone [ŏ'sōnə] n. ozone.
'ossewa ['osəvā] n. (-ens) ox-waggon.
'otjie ['oiKi] n. (-s) pig.
'otter ['otəR] n. (-s) otter.
ou ['oa] n. (-ens) old fellow; one, a person; a. (-e, -er, -ste) old, ancient.
'oubaas ['oabās] n. boss, master.
'ouboet ['oabut] n. eldest brother; old chum.
oud ['oat] a. (oue; ouer, -ste) old, aged.
oud- ['oat-] pref. former, ex-, old;

= amptenaar n. ex-official; = soldaat n. ex-soldier; = stryder n. exburger; = student n. old student (boy).

'ouderdom ['oadəRdom] n. age, old age.

'ouderling ['oadəRling] n. (-e) elder.

ouder'wets [oadəR'vets] a. (-e) oldfashioned; precocious.

'oudgediende ['oatchədində] n. veteran.

'oudheid ['oatayt] n. age; antiquity.

oudi'ensie [oadi'ensi] n. (-s) audience.

oudi'teur [oadi'tœR] n. (-s) auditor.

ouds ['oats] av. van- of old; -her av. van- from long ago.

'oudste ['oatstə] n. & a. (-s) oldest, eldest.

'oue ['oaə] n. (-s) old one.

'ouer ['oaəR] n. (-s) parent; a. older, elder; -ig a. (-e) oldish; -lik a. (-e) parental; -loos a. (-lose) parentless, orphan.

'Oujaar ['oayəR] n. the old year; -saand n. New Year's Eve.

'oujongkêrel ['oayong'kɛRəl] n. (-s) bachelor.

'oujongmeisie ['oayongmaysi] n. (-s) spinster.

'oujongnooi ['oayongnõi] n. spinster; cp. oujongmeisie.

'oulaas ['oalâs] av. vir- for the last time.

'oulik ['oalək] a. (-e; -er, -ste) cute, clever; precocious.

'oulap ['oalap] n. penny.

'ouma ['oama] n. grandmother.

'oumense ['oamɛñsə] n. old people.

'oupa ['oapa] n. grandfather.

'outa ['oata] n. old native man.

outen'tiek [oaten'tik] a. (-e) authentic.

ou'teur [oa'tœR] n. (-s) author.

'outjie ['oaKi] n. (-s) old man (girl).

'outo ['oatõ] n. (-'s) automobile.

outobio'graaf [oatõbiõ'chRâf] n. (autobio'grawe) autobiographer.

outo'kraat [oatõ'kRât] n. (outo'krate) autocrat; outo'kraties a. (-e) autocratic.

outo'maties [oatõ'mâtis] a. (-e) automatic.

outo'noom [oatõ'nõm] a. autonomous.

outori'sasie [oatõRi'sâsi] n. authorisation.

outori'teit [oatõRi'tayt] n. authority.

'outyds ['oatayts] a. (-e) oldfashioned; ancient.

'ouvrou ['oafRoa] n. (-e) midwife.

o'vaal [õ'fâl] a. (o'vale) oval.

o'varium [õ'fâRiʌm] n. (o'varia) ovary.

o'vasie [õ'fâsi] n. ovation.

'owerheid ['õvəRayt] n. ('owerhede) authority, government.

'owerigens = origens.

'owerpriester ['õvəRpRistəR] n. (-s) high-priest.

'owerspel ['õvəRspel] n. adultery.

'owerste ['õvəRstə] n. (-s) chief, prior.

P

pa ['pâ] n. (-'s) pa, dad.

'paadjie ['pâiKi] n. dim. cp. pad; path, track, trial; parting of the hair.

paai ['pâi] v. (ge-) coax, stroke, pat.

paai'boelie [pai'buli] n. (-s) bugbear, bogey.

paaie'ment [pâiə'ment] n. (-e) instalment.

paal ['pâl] n. (pale) pole, post, stake; -skerm n. (-s) palisade; -spring n. pole-vault; -tjie dim. (-s) stake; standard; stump (cricket).

paap ['pâp] n. pope, priest; -s a. (-e) papal, popish, papist.

paar ['pâR] n. (pare) pair, couple; v. (ge-) pair, mate, unite; -tjie dim. couple, pair.

'Paasfees ['pâsfês] n. Easter; Passover.

pad ['pat] n. (paaie) road, way, path, walk; -aansluiting n. road junction; -diens n. road service; -flank (-skouer) n. road shoulder; -gevaar n. road menace; -hoflikheid n. road courtesy; -houvermoë n. road holding ability; -kruising (kruispaaie) n. crossroads; -overheid n. road authority; -sin n. road sense; -tekens n. road signs; -toets n. road test; -vark n. road hog; -verlegging n. deviation; -versperring n. road barrier; -vervoer n. road transportation; -viak n. road surface; -wyser n. sign post.

'padda ['paRa] n. (-s) frog; toad; -slyk n. algae; -stoel n. mushroom, toadstool; -vis n. (-se) tadpole.

'padlangs ['patlangs] av. with the road, straight along; -loop v. be straightforward; -praat v. to be outspoken.

'padmaker ['patmâkəR] n. (-s) road-worker.

pag ['pach] v. (ge-) lease; quit-rent; -ter n. lessee; tenant.

'page ['pâshə] n. (-s) page, footboy.

'pagina ['pâchina] n. (-s) page; pagi'neer n. (ge-) paginate.

pa'gode [pa'chõdə] n. pagoda.

pair ['pɛR] n. peer.

pais ['pais] n. peace.

pak ['pak] n. (-ke) pack, package, packet, parcel, bundle, load; flogging; v. (ge-) pack, wrap; seize, grip; -huis n. warehouse; -huisman n. storeman; -kamer n. store-room; -'kaste n. baggage; -kend a. (-e) thrilling; -ker n. packer; -kery n. packing; -kie dim. (-s) packet; -'ket n. (-te) parcel; -king n. packing, boxing; -papier n. wrapping-paper; -stuk n. gasket.

pal ['pal] av. firm, immovable; n. pawl.

pala'taal [pala'tāl] n. & a. palatal;
palati'seer v. (ge-) palatalize; palati-
'sering n. palatalization.

paleontolo'gie [paleõntōlō'chi] n.
paleontology.

pa'leis [pa'lays] n. (-e) palace.

pa'let [pa'let] n. (-te) palette.

'paling ['pāleng] n. (-s) eel.

palis'sade [pali'sādə] n. (-s) palisade.

pal'jas [pal'yas, pol-] n. charm, spell.

palm ['palem] n. (-s) palm; -olie n.
palm-oil.

pal'miet [pal'mit] n. bulrush.

pam'flet [pam'flet] n. (-te) pamphlet.

pampel'moes [pampel'mus] n.
shaddock (grapefruit).

pamper'lang [pampeR'lang] v. (ge-)
cajole, wheedle.

pam'poen [pam'pun] n. (-e) pumpkin; -kop n. dunce; -tjie dim. small
pumpkin; -tjies pl. mumps.

pan ['pan] n. (-ne) pan; tile.

pand ['pant] n. (-e) pledge, security;
v. (ge-) pawn; -jiesbaas n. pawn-
broker; -speel v. (-ge-) play at
forfeits; -gewer n. pledger; -houer n.
pledgee; -reg n. lien.

pa'neel [pa'nēl] n. (-e) panel.

pa'neer [pa'nēR] v. (ge-) coat with
crumbs.

pa'niek [pa'nik] n. panic, scare; -erig
a. (-e) panicky, 'panies a. (-e) panic.

'pannekoek ['panekuk] n. (-e) pancake.

pano'rama [panō'Rāma] n. (-s)
panorama.

pant ['pant] n. (-e) flap, coat-tail.

pante'isme [pantē'esmə] n. pan-
theism.

'panter ['panteR] n. (-s) panther.

pan'toffel [pan'tofəl] n. (-s) slipper;
-blom n. calceolaria.

panto'mime [pantō'mimə] n.
pantomime.

'pantser ['pantseR] n. (-s) armour;
cuirass.

pap ['pap] n. porridge; poultice; a.
& av. (-per, -ste) soft, flabby;
deflated; v. (ge-) poultice, paste;
-nat av. soaking wet; -perig a.
softish.

'pappa ['papa] n. papa, daddy.

pa'paja [pa'pāya] n. (-s) paw-paw.

pa'pawer [pa'pāveR] n. (-s) poppy.

'papbroek ['pabRuk] n. coward,
milksop.

pape'gaai [pape'chāi] n. (-e) parrot.

pape'lellekoors [pape'leləkōRs] n.
sham-fever, trembles.

'papie ['pāpi] n. (-s) cocoon,
chrysalis; -a n. pl. bots.

pa'pier [pa'piR] n. paper; document;
-blom n. (-me) artificial flower;
statice; -mandjie n. waste-paper-
basket.

pa'raaf [pa'Rāf] n. (parawe) initials;
para'feer v. (ge-) initial.

pa'raat [pa'Rāt] a. (pa'rate) ready,
prepared.

para'bel [pa'Ra'bel] n. (-le) parable.

pa'rabool [paRa'bōl] n. (para'bole)
parabola.

pa'rade [pa'Rādə] n. (-s) parade.

para'doks [paRa'doks] n. paradox.

para'dys [paRa'days] n. paradise.

para'graaf [paRa'chRaf] n. (para-
'grawe) paragraph.

paral'lel [para'iel] n. & a. (-le)
parallel.

para'siet [paRa'sit] n. (-e) parasite.

par'don [paR'don] n. pardon.

par'fuum [paR'fēwm] n. perfume,
scent.

'pari ['pāRi] n. par; teen- at par;
-'teit n. parity.

park ['paRk] n. (-e) park; parkeer
v. (ge-) park.

par'ket [paR'ket] n. parquet-floor;
in 'n noeilike-beland be in a quan-
dary.

parle'ment [paRlə'ment] n. parliament; parlementêr a. (-e) parlia-
mentary.

par'mant [paR'mant] a. (-e) cocky,
cheeky, jaunty.

paro'die [paRõ'di] n. (-ë) parody;
parodi'eer v. (ge-) parody.

paro'gie [paRõ'chi] n. parish.

pa'rool [pa'Rōl] n. parole; password.

pars ['paRs] v. (ge-) press.

part ['paRt] n. (-e) part, portion,
share; trick; iemand-e speel play
tricks on a person.

par'tikel [paR'tikəl] n. (-s) particle.

par'ty [pəR'tay] n. (-e) party; a.
some; -dig a.(-e) partial, prejudiced;
-tjie dim. party, social gathering.

par'tykeer [pəR'taykēR] av. sometimes, occasionally.

par'tymaal [peR'taymal] av. —
partykeer.

Par'ys [pa'Rays] n. Paris; -enaar n.
(-s) Parisian.

pas ['pas] n. (-se) pace, step, gait;
pass, defile; pass, passport; te-kom
come in handy; av. just; scarcely;
newly; v. (ge-) fit, fit on; behove;
-gebore a. new-born; -kamer n.
fitting-room; -klaar av. ready-made;
-lik a. (-e; -er, -ste) fitting, becoming;
-munt n. change; -poort n. passport; -'sabel av. passable; -'seer v.
(ge-) pass; -send a. (-e) fitting,
proper.

'Pase ['pāsə] n. Easter.

pasi'ënt [pa'shent] n. (-e) patient.

pasifi'kasie [pasəfi'kāsi] n. pacifica-
tion.

'pasja ['pāsha] n. (-s) pasha.

'pasmaak ['pasmāk] v. (-ge-) fit.

pas'oppens [pə'sopəns] n. in jou-bly
step warily, cp. oppas.

pas'saat [pa'sāt] n. (-e) passage; trade-
wind.

passa'sier [pasə'siR] n. (-s) passenger.

'passer ['pasəR] n. (-s) pair of
compasses.

'passie ['pasi] n. passion; craze.

pas'sief [pa'sif] a. (pas'siewe) passive.

'pasta ['pasta] n. paste.
pas'tei [pə'stay] n. (-e) pie, pasty, pastry; -tjie dim. patty.
pas'tel [pas'tel] n. (-le) pastel.
pas'toor [pas'tōR] n. (pas'tore) pastor; priest.
pasto'rie [pastō'Ri] n. (-e, -s) parsonage, rectory, vicarage.
pa'tat(ta) [pə'tat(a)] n. (-s) sweet potato.
pa'tent [pə'tent] n. (-e) patent; paten'teer v. (ge-) patent.
'pater ['pātəR] n. (-s) father, priest.
pa'teties [pə'tētis] a. (-e) pathetic(al).
pa'tois [pə'tua] n. patois.
patolo'gie [patōlō'chi] n. pathology; pato'loog n. pathologist.
'patos ['pātos] n. pathos.
patri'arg [patRi'arch] n. patriarch.
patri'ot [patRi'ot] n. (-te) patriot; patri'oties a. (-e) patriotic.
pa'trollie [pə'tRoli] n. (-s) patrol; patrol'leer v. (ge-) patrol.
pa'troon [pə'tRōn] n. (pa'trone) patron; pattern; cartridge.
pa'trys [pə'tRays] n. (-e) partridge.
pawil'joen [pavəl'yun] n. (-e) pavilion.
pedago'giek [pēdachō'chik] n. pedagogics, theory of education; peda'gogies a. (-e) pedagogic; peda-'goog n. (peda'goë) pedagogue; educationist.
pe'danties [pē'dantis] a. (-e) pedantic.
peer ['pēR] n. (pere) pear; testis.
pees ['pēs] n. tendon.
peet- ['pēt-] pref. -vader n. godfather; -moeder n. godmother; -ouers n. godparents; -kind n. godchild.
peil ['payl] n. level, gauge; standard; v. (ge-) gauge, sound, plumb; -lood n. plummet; -stok n. dipstick.
peins ['payns] v. (ge-) meditate, ponder; -end a. (-e) pensive; -ing n. meditation.
'pekel ['pēkəl] n. hy is in die- he is in a nice pickle; saltwater, brine; a. salt; v. (ge-) pickle, salt; -water n. brine.
'pelgrim ['pelchRəm] n. (-s) pilgrim.
peli'kaan [pēli'kān] n. (peli'kane) pelican.
pelo'ton [pelə'ton] n. (-ne) platoon.
pels ['pels] = bont.
pen ['pen] n. (ne-) pen; nib; needle; quill; peg, spike, pin; v. (ge-) write; peg; copulate.
pe'narie [pə'nāRi] n. misery, difficulty.
pene'trasie [penə'tRāsi] n. penetration; pene'treer v. (ge-) penetrate.
'penkop ['pen-kop] n. youth, cub.
pens ['pens] n. paunch, belly.
pen'seel [pensēl] n. paint-brush.
pensi'oen [pensi'un] n. (-e) pension; pensioe'naris n. pensioner.
'peper ['pēpəR] n. pepper; -korrel n. pepper-corn; -'ment n. peppermint.
per ['pəR] prep. by, per.

perd ['pɛRt] n. (-e) horse; -fris a healthy; -gerus a. calm.
'perdeby ['pɛRəbay] n. wasp, hornet.
'perdekrag ['pɛRəkRach] n. horsepower.
'pêrel ['pɛRəl] n. (-s) pearl; -oog n. nebula; -saad n. seed-pearl.
per'fek [pəR'fek] a. & av. (-te) perfect; per'feksie n. perfection.
perfo'rasie [pɛRfō'Rāsi] n. perforation; perfo'reer v. (ge-) perforate.
perife'rie [pɛRifə'Ri] n. periphery.
peri'ode [pēRi'ōdə] n. (-s) period; perio'diek a. & av. periodical(ly).
peri'skoop [pēRi'skōp] n. periscope.
perk ['pɛRk] n. (-e) limit; lawn; arena.
perka'ment [pɛRka'ment] n. (-e) parchment, vellum.
per'kussie [pəR'kʌsi] n. percussion.
perle'moen, -moer [pɛRlə'mun, -mūR] n. mother of pearl.
perma'nent [pɛRma'nent] a. (-e) permanent; standing.
per'missie [pəR'misi] n. permission.
per'mit [pəR'mət] n. (-te) permit.
perok'sied [pɛRok'sit] n. peroxide.
per'ron [pə'Ron] n. (-e, -s) platform.
pers ['pɛRs] n. (-) press; v. (ge-) press, squeeze.
pers ['pɛRs] a. purple.
per'seel [pəR'sēl] n. (per'sele) plot, allotment.
per'sent [pəR'sent] n. per cent; persen'tasie n. (-s) percentage.
'persie ['pɛRsi] n. diarrhoea.
'perske [pɛRskə] n. (-s) peach.
'persklaar ['pɛRsklāR] a. ready for the printer.
personali'teit [pɛRsōnali'tayt] n. (-e) personality.
perso'neel [pɛRsō'nēl] n. (perso'nele) personnel.
personifi'kasie [pɛRsōnifi'kāsi] n. personification.
per'soon [pəR'sōn] n. (per'sone) person; head; figure; -lik a. & av. personal(ly).
perspek'tief [pɛRspek'tif] n. perspective.
perti'nent [pɛRti'nent] a. (-e) pertinent, to the point.
per'vers [pɛR'veRs] a. (-e) perverse.
pes ['pes] n. pestilence, plague; pest; v. (ge-) pester.
pessi'mis [pesi'məs] n. (-te) pessimist.
pesti'lensie [pestə'lɛnsi] n. (-s) pestilence, plague.
pet ['pet] n. (-te) cap.
pe'talje [pə'talyə] n. (-s) affair; prank.
pe'tieterig [pə'titəRəch] a. (-e) small, tiny, weak.
pe'tisie [pə'tisi] n. (-s) petition; petisio'neer v. (ge-) petition, request.
'petrol ['petRol] n. petrol.
peul ['pɛl] n. (-e) pod, husk; bolster; v. (ge-) bulge.
'peusel ['pɛsəl] v. (ge-) nibble, peck.
'peuter ['pɛtəR] v. (ge-) potter,

fiddle; -ig a. (-e; -er, -ste) petty, trivial.

pi'ano [pi'ãnõ] n. (-s) piano; pia'nis n. (-te) pianist; pia'niste fem. pianist.

piek ['pik] n. (-e) pike; peak.

'piekel ['pikəl] v. (ge-) lug, drag.

'pieker ['pikəR] v. (ge-) worry, fret.

piekfyn ['pikfayn] av. fine, grand.

'piekniek ['piknik] n. (-s) picnic.

'pieng ['piŋ] n. pink, ignition knock.

piep ['pip] n. pip, roup; v. (ge-) chirp, squeak; -erig a. (-e; -er, -ste) squeaky, weakly.

'piering ['piRəŋ] n. (-s) saucer.

'piesang ['pisaŋ] n. (-s) banana.

pië'teit [piə'tayt] n. piety.

pieter'sielie [pitəR'sili] n. parsley.

piets ['pits] v. (ge-) whip.

pig'ment [pich'ment] n. (-e) pigment, dye.

pi'jama [pə'yãma] n. (-s) pyjamas.

pik ['pək] n. (-ke) pick; peck; pitch; v. (ge-) bite; peck; pick.

pi'kant [pi'kant] a. (-e) piquant.

'pikdonker ['pəkdonkəR] n. & a. pitch dark(ness).

pikke'nien [pikə'nin] n. (-s) piccaninni.

pikke'wyn [pəkə'vayn] n. (-e) penguin.

'pikswart ['pekswaRt] a. pitch black.

pil ['pəl] n. (-le) pill.

pi'laar [pi'lãR] n. (pi'lare) pillar, column.

pi'loot [pi'lõt] n. (pi'lote) pilot.

'pinkie ['pənki] n. (-s) little finger.

'Pinkster ['pənkstəR] n. Pentecost.

pint ['pənt] n. (-e) pint.

pi'on [pi'on] n. (-ne) pawn.

pi'outer [pi'oatəR] n. pewter.

pio'nier [piõ'niR] n. (-s) pioneer.

pi'pet [pi'pet] n. (-te) pipette.

pira'mide [piRa'midə] n. (-s) pyramid.

pi'riet [pi'Rit] n. pyrites.

pis'tool [pə'stõl] n. (pis'tole) pistol.

pit ['pət] n. (-te) stone, pip, kernel, core, pith; -tig a. (-e; -er, -ste) pithy, terse, racy.

'pitboompie ['pətbõmpi] n. seedling (tree).

'pitkos ['pətkos] n. solid food (grain).

'pitsweer ['pətsweR] n. ('pitswere) boil.

pla ['plã] v. (ge-) pester, vex, tease, annoy.

plaag ['plãch] n. (plae) plague; nuisance; -gees n. teaser; -siek a. & av. fond of teasing.

plaas ['plãs] n. (plase) farm; place; v. (ge-) place, put; -gryp v. (ge-) take place, happen; -vervanger n. (-s) deputy, substitute; -vind v. (-ge-) take place, happen.

plaat ['plãt] n. (plate) plate; print; picture; record; patch.

pla'fon [pla'fon] n. (-ne) ceiling.

plagi'aat [plachi'ãt] n. plagiarism.

plak ['plak] n. (-ke) strap, cane; v.

(ge-) paste, glue, gum; -band n. masking tape.

plak'kaat [pla'kãt] n. (plak'kate) placard, poster; edict.

'plakker ['plakəR] n. (-s) paster; paper-hanger; squatter.

'plakkie ['plaki] n. (-s) slice, slab; succulent plant, crassulaceae.

plan ['plan] n. (-ne) plan, project, scheme, design, diagram.

pla'neet [pla'nět] n. (pla'nete) planet.

plank ['plank] n. (-e) plank, board; deal; shelf.

plant ['plant] n. (-e) plant; seedling; herb; v. (ge-) plant; tackle (football); -aardig a. (-e) vegetable-; plan'tasie n. (-s) plantation; -egroei n. vegetation; -er n. (-s) planter; -etend a. (-e) herbivorous; -jie ['plaiŋ'Ki] dim.; -kunde n. botany.

plas ['plas] n. (-se) pool, plash; v. (ge-) splash, pour.

'plasma ['plasma] n. plasma.

plas'tiek [plas'tik] n. plastic art; 'plasties a. (-e) plastic.

plat ['plat] a. horizontal, flat, level, even, smooth; vulgar, coarse; a. flat; -jie ['platKi] dim. flat roof; scamp; -anna n. toad, Xenopus laevis; -dak n. flat roof; -druk v. (-ge-) squeeze, crush; -form n. (-s) platform; -loop v. (-ge-) overrun; finish off; -riem n. strap; -sak av. penniless; -teland n. rural country; backveld, rural parts; -voet n. flat-foot; -weg av. flatly.

'platina ['plãtina] n. platinum.

pla'to [pla'tõ] n. (-'s) plateau.

pla'tonies [pla'tõnis] a. (-e) platonic.

pla'veil [pla'fayl] v. (ge-) pave; -sel n. paving, pavement.

plebs ['pleps] n. pl. rabble.

pleeg ['plěch] v. (ge-) commit.

pleeg- ['plěch-] pref. foster; cp. verpleeg; -kind n. foster-child; -ouers n. foster-parents.

pleg'statig [plech'stãtəch] a. (-e) stately, solemn.

'plegtig ['plechtəch] a. (-e) solemn, stately, ceremonious; -heid n. solemnity; ceremony.

plei'dooi [play'dõi] n. (-e) plea, argument.

plein ['playn] n. (-e) square.

'pleister ['playstəR] n. plaster; v. (ge-) plaster.

pleit ['playt] v. (ge-) plead.

plek ['plek] n. (-ke) place; spot; seat; post.

pleks ['pleks] av. instead of.

ple'sier [plə'siR] n. pleasure, fun; satisfaction; v. (ge-) please; -ig a. (-e; -er, -ste) pleasant, happy.

plet ['plet] v. (ge-) flatten.

plig ['pləch] n. (-te) duty; -pleging n. ceremony; -sgevoel n. sense of duty; -shalwe av. dutifully; -sversuim n. neglect of duty.

'pligsbesef ['pləchsbəsef] n. sense of duty.

'ploeë ['plüə] v. (ge-) plough.

ploeg]'pluch] n. (*ploeë*) plough; batch, team, shift; v. (ge-) = **ploeë**; **-baas** n. foreman, ganger.

ploert ['pluRt] n. (-e) cad; **-ig** a. (-e) caddish.

'**ploeter** ['plutəR] v. (ge-) plod, drudge.

plof ['plof] n. (*plowwe*) thud; v. (ge-) thud, flop, thump.

plomp ['plomp] a. awkward, clumsy, stout.

plooi ['plôi] n. (-e) pleat, fold, crease, wrinkle; v. (ge-) fold, crease, pleat; **-baar** a. (-bare) pliable.

'**plotseling** ['plotsələng] a. & av. (-e) sudden(ly).

pluim ['plœim] n. (-e) plume; **-bal** n. shuttle-cock; **-pie** dim. compliment, feather in the cap; **-vee** n. poultry.

pluis ['plœis] av. in order; v. (ge-) make fluffy, give off fluff; - n. tow; **-ie** dim. plug (*wadding*).

pluk ['plʌk] v. (ge-) pick, pluck, cull; **-sel** n. (-s) picking; crop.

'**plunder** ['plʌndəR] v. (ge-) plunder, loot, rifle, rob; **-ing** n.

plus ['plʌs] av. plus; **-minus** av. approximately.

pneu'maties [pnœ'mātis] a. (-e) pneumatic.

'**poedelnaak** ['pudəlnāk] a. stark naked.

'**poeding** ['pudəng] n. (-s) pudding.

'**poeier** ['puiəR] n. powder; tablet; v. (ge-) powder; **-kwas** n. powder puff; haemanthus, blood flower.

poel ['pul] n. (-e) pool, puddle.

'**poenskop** ['pŭnskop] n. pollard, poll.

poë'sie [pôə'si] n. poetry; **po'ëties** a. (-e) poetic.

poets ['puts] n. (-e) trick; v. (ge-) polish, clean; **-katoen** n. cotton-waste; **-lap** n. polishing cloth.

'**poffertjie** ['pofəRKi] n. (-s) fritter.

'**poging** ['pôchəng] n. (-e, -s) attempt, effort.

'**pokkies** ['pokis] n. pl. small-pox.

pol ['pol] n. (-le) tuft, tussock.

polari'seer [polaRi'sēR] v. (ge-) polarize; **polari'teit** n. polarity.

pole'miek ['pôla'mik] n. controversy, polemic; **po'lemies** a. (-e) controversial, polemic; **polemi'seer** v. (ge-) polemize.

poli'glot [pôli'chlot] n. (-te) polyglot.

'**polis** ['pôləs] n. (-se) policy.

po'lisie [pô'lisi] n. police.

poli'tiek [pôla'tik] n. politics; policy; a. (-e) political; politic; **po'litikus** n. (-se) politician.

poli'toer [poli'tūR] n. polish; v. (ge-) polish.

pols ['pols] n. (-e) pulse; v. (ge-) sound; **-gewrig** n. (-te) wrist; **-band** n. wrist strap.

pol'vy [pol'fay] n. (-e) heel.

po'lys [pô'lays] v. (ge-) polish.

pomp ['pomp] n. (-e) pump; **-band** n. tubeless tyre.

pond f'paunt] n. (-e) pound.

pon'dok [pon'dok] n. (-ke) hovel, hut.

'**ponie** ['pôni] n. (-s) pony.

pons ['paunš] n. punch.

pont ['pont] n. (-e) ferry, pontoon.

'**poog** ['pôch] v. (ge-) try.

pool ['pôl] n. (*pole*) pole.

poort ['pôRt] n. (-e) gate, gateway, entrance; **-wagter** n. gatekeeper.

poot ['pot] n. (*pote*) paw, hoof, foot; v. (ge-) plant; **-jie** n. dim., v. (ge-) trip; **-uit** av. exhausted.

pop ['pop] n. (-pe) doll; **-perig** a. (-e) doll-like, dainty; **-pie** dim.; **-speel** v. (-ge-) play with dolls; trifle.

populari'teit [pôpewlaRi'tayt] n. popularity; **popu'lêr** a. (-e) popular.

popu'lasie [pôpew'lasie] n. population.

popu'lier [popə'liR] n. (-e) poplar.

por ['poR] v. (ge-) prod; spur on; inch.

po'reus [pô'Rês] a. (-e) porous.

po'rie [pô'Ri] n. (-ë) pore.

porno'graaf [poRnô'chRāf] n. (*porno'grawe*) pornographer; **pornogra-'fie** n. pornography; **porno'grafies** a. (-e) pornographic.

porse'lein [poRsə'layn] n. porcelain; purslain.

'**porsie** ['poRsi] n. (-s) portion.

por'taal [por'tāl] n. porch, entrance-hall.

porte'feulje [poRt'fœlye] n. (-s) portfolio.

por'tier [poR'tiR] n. (-e; -s) porter.

'**porto** [poRtô] n. postage.

por'tret [pə'tRet] n. (-te) portrait, photo.

'**Portugal** ['poRtewchal] n. Portugal; **Portu'gees** n. (*Portugese*) Portuguese.

por'tuur [poR'tēWR] n. equal, match.

pos ['pos] n. post; post-office; mail; n. (-te) post, station, sentry; position, job; entry; item; v. (ge-) post; **-bode** n. (-s) postman; **-bus** n. letter-box; **-diens** n. postal service; **-duif** n. carrier pigeon; **-geld** n. postage; **-gids** n. postal directory; **-kantoor** n. post-office; **-kar** n. mail-cart; **-meester** n. postmaster; **-stempel** n. postmark; **-vry** a. post free, frank; **-wissel** n. postal order.

po'seer [pô'sēR] v. (ge-) pose, strike an attitude.

po'sisie [pô'sisi] n. (-s) position.

posi'tief [pôsə'tif] n., a. & av. (*posi'tiewe*) positive; pl. senses, consciousness.

pos'tuur [pos'tēWR] n. figure, shape.

pot ['pot] n. (-te) pot, jar, chamber; game; pool; stakes; v. (ge-) hoard, save up; **-klei** n. potter's clay.

potensi'eel [pôtensi'ēl] a. (-ële) potential.

poten'taat [pôten'tāt] n. (*potentate*) potentate.

'**potlepel** ['potlêpəl] n. (-s) kitchen ladle.

'**potlood** ['potlôt] n. ('*potlode*) lead-pencil.

pot'sierlik [pot'siRlək] a. (-e) ridiculous.

'potyster ['potaystəR] n. cast (pig) iron.

pou ['poa] n. (-e) peacock.

pous ['poas] n. pope.

'pouse ['poasə] n. pause.

'power ['pŏvəR] a. poor.

praal ['pRāl] n. splendour, pomp; v. (ge-) boast; glitter.

praat ['pRāt] v. (ge-) talk; chat, speak; -graag n. tattler; talkative person; -jie dim. ['praiKi] n. talk, rumour, story, gossip; -kous n. tattler; -siek a. garrulous, loquacious.

prag ['pRach] n. beauty, splendour; -liewend a. (-e) ostentatious.

prag'maties [pRach'mātis] a. (-e) pragmatic.

'pragtig ['pRachtəch] a. (-e; -er, -ste) fine, beautiful, lovely.

prak'seer [pRak'sēR] v. (ge-) devise, contrive.

'prakties ['pRaktis] a. (-e) practical; av. practically; prakti'seer v. (ge-) practise; prak'tyk n. practice.

predik ['pRēdək] v. (ge-) preach; predi'kasie n. sermon, homily; -er n. preacher; -ing n. preaching, sermon.

predi'kant [pRēdə'kant] n. (-e) minister, parson, clergyman.

preek ['pRēk] n. (treke) sermon, homily; v. (ge-) preach, cp. predik.

prefer'eer [pRəfə'RēR] v. (ge-) prefer; prefe'rensie n. preference.

'prefiks ['pRēfiks] n. (-e) prefix.

preg'nant [pRech'nant] a. (-e) big with possibilities.

prei ['pRay] n. leek.

prelimi'nêr [pRələmə'nɛR] a. (-e) preliminary.

pre'lude [pRē'lēwdə] n. (-s) prelude.

pre'mie [pRē'mi] n. (-s) premium.

pre'mier [pRə'miR] n. premier.

prent ['pRent] n. (-e) picture, print; -jie dim. ['pRsing-Ki] picture.

prepa'raat [pRəpə'Rāt] n. (prepa-'rate) preparation.

prepo'sisie [pRepə'sisi] n. preposition.

prese'dent [pRəsə'dent] n. precedent.

pre'sent [pRə'sent] n. (-e) present, gift; presen'tasie n. presentation; presen'teer v. (ge-) present, offer; introduce.

presi'dent [pRəsə'dent] n. (-e) president.

pre'sies [pRə'sis] a. & av. (-e) precise(ly).

pre'skripsie [pRə'skRəpsi] n. (-s) prescription.

pres'tasie [pRəs'tāsi] n. (-s) achievement; prakti'seer v. (ge-) achieve, accomplish.

pres'tige [pRes'tish] n. prestige, reputation.

presu'meer [pRəsə'mēR] v. (ge-) presume.

pret ['pRet] n. fun, pleasure; -tig a. (-e; -er, -ste) pleasant, jolly.

pretendeer [pRətən'dēR] v. (ge-) claim, pretend.

pre'tensie [pRə'tēnsi] n. pretence, pretension; pretensi'eus a. (-e) pretentious.

pre'teritum [pRə'tēRitʌm] n. preterite.

preuts ['pRēts] a. (-e) prudish.

'prewel ['pRēvəl] v. (ge-) mutter, mumble.

pri'eel [pRi'ēl] n. (priële) pergola.

priem ['pRim] n. (-e) awl, dagger; v. (ge-) pierce.

priester [pRistəR] n. (-s) priest; -lik a. (-e) priestly.

prik [pRək] v. (ge-) prick; tingle; -kel v. (ge-) excite, irritate; incite; n. (-s) stimulus; spur; prick; goad; -kelbaar a. (prikkelbare) irritable; -kelend a. (-e) exciting; -kellektuur n. sensuous literature; -middel n. excitant.

pril [pRəl] a. (-le) early; -le jeug early youth.

'prima ['pRima] n. prime; pri'mêr a. (-e) primary.

primi'tief [pRəmə'tif] a. (primi-tiewe) primitive.

prins ['pRƏns] n. (-s) prince; -lik a. (-e) princely; prin'ses n. princess.

prinsi'paal [pRənsə'pāl] n. (prinsi-'pale) principal.

prin'sipe [pRən'sipə] n. (-s) principle.

'prisma ['pRəsma] n. prism.

priso'nier [pRəsə'niR] n. (-s) prisoner.

pri'vaat [pRə'fāt] n. privy, w.c.; a. & av. private(ly).

pro ['pRŏ] n. pro; prep. pro.

pro'baat [pRŏ'bāt] a. efficacious.

pro'beer [pRə'bēR] v. (ge-) try, attempt; -sel n. (-s) effort, trial; -slag = probeersel.

pro'bleem [pRŏ'blēm] n. (pro'bleme) problem.

pro'duk [pRŏ'dʌk] n. (-te) product; pro'duksie n. production; produk-'tief a. productive; produ'seer v. (ge-) produce; produ'sent n. producer.

proef ['pRuf] n. (proewe) proof, test, trial; -rit n. trial run; -skrif n. (-te) thesis; -tyd n. probationary period.

'proefplaas ['pRufplās] n. experimental farm.

proe ['pRu] v. (ge-) taste.

proes ['pRus] v. (ge-) sneeze, snort; spitting (carburettor.)

pro'feet [pRŏ'fēt] n. (profete) prophet; profe'sie n. prophecy; profe-'teer v. (ge-) prophesy; pro'feties a. (-e) prophetic.

pro'fessie [pRŏ'fesi] n. profession.

pro'fessor [pRŏ'fesoR] n. (profe'sore) professor.

pro'fiel [pRŏ'fil] n. (-e) profile.

profi'teer [pRŏfi'tēR] v. (ge-) profit.

pro'fyt [pRŏ'fayt] n. (-e) profit, gain; -lik a. profitable.

pro'gram [pRõ'chRam] n. (-me) programme.

progres'sief [pRõchRe'sif] a. (progressiewe) progressive.

projek'teer [pRõyek'tēR] v. (ge-) project; projek'tiel n. (-e) projectile.

prokla'masie [pRõkla'māsi] n. (-s) proclamation; prokla'meer v. (ge-) proclaim, promulgate.

proku'reur [pRõka'RœR] n. (-s) attorney, solicitor.

prole'tariër [pRõlə'tāRiəR] n. (-s) proletarian; proletari'aat n. proletariat(e); prole'taries a. (-e) proletarian.

'proloog ['pRõlõch] n. (proloë) prologue.

prome'nade [pRõmə'nādə] n. promenade.

pro'mosie [pRə'mõsi] n. promotion; pro'motor n. promoter, professor presenting a candidate for a degree; promo'veer v. (ge-) graduate.

pronk ['pRonk] n. pride; v. (ge-) show off; spread, buck; -er n. dandy, coxcomb; -erig a. (-e; -er, -ste) showy = ertjie [=eRKi] n. sweet pea.

pro'nomen [pRõ'nõmen] n. (pronomina) pronoun.

pront ['pRont] a. & av. prompt(ly), punctual(ly); -uit av. flatly.

prooi ['pRõi] n. prey, victim.

prop ['pRop] n. (-pe) cork, stopper, bung, gag, wad, plug; v. (ge-) cram, stuff; -vol av. chock-full, stuffed.

propa'ganda [pRõpa'chanda] n. propaganda; propagan'disties a. (-e) propagandist; propa'geer v. (ge-) propagate.

'proper ['pRõpəR] a. neat, tidy.

propo'nent [pRõpə'nent] n. (-e) candidate for the ministry.

pro'porsie [pRə'poRsi] n. (-s) proportion; proporsio'neel a. (proporsionele) proportional.

'prosa ['pRõsa] n. prose; pro'saïes a. prosaic; prosa'is n. prose-writer.

prose'deer [prosə'dēR] v. (ge-) litigate.

prose'dure [pRõsə'dǝWRə] n. procedure.

pro'ses [pRõ'ses] n. (-se) process; -sie n. procession.

pro'teksie [pRõ'teksi] n. protection.

protekto'raat [pRõtektõ'Rāt] n. (protekto'rate) protectorate.

pro'tes [pRõ'tes] n. (-te) protest; -'teer v. (ge-) protest.

Protes'tant [pRõtəs'tant] n. (-e) Protestant.

'prototipe ['pRõtõtipə] n. (-s) prototype.

pro'vinsie [pRõ'fənsi] n. (-s) province; provinsi'aal a. provincial.

pro'visie [pRõ'fisi] n. provision; provisio'neel a. provisional.

provo'kasie [pRõfõ'kāsi] n. provocation.

pruik ['pRœik] n. (-e) wig, periwig.

pruil ['pRœil] v. (ge-) pout, sulk; -erig a. (-e) sulky.

pruim ['pRœim] n. (-e) plum; v. (ge-) chew.

'pruimpie ['prœimpi] n. (-s) quid.

prul ['pRʌl] n. (-le) trash, rubbish.

'prutsel ['pRʌtsəl] n. (ge-) potter, tinker.

'pruttel ['pRʌtəl] v. (ge-) grumble.

pryk ['pRayk] v. (ge-) shine, be resplendent, show off.

prys ['pRays] n. (-e) price, cost; prize; praise; v. (ge-) assign a price to; -gee v. (-ge-) abandon, give up.

psalm [pə'saləm] n. (-s) psalm.

pseudo'niem [psœdõ'nim] n. (-e) pseudonym.

'psige ['psichə] n. psyche, soul, spirit; 'psigies a. psychic.

psigi'ater [psichi'ātəR] n. (-s) psychiatrist, alienist; psigiatrie n. psychiatry.

psigolo'gie [psichõlõ'chi] n. psychology; psigologies a. (-e) psychological; psigoloog n. (psigoloë) psychologist.

psi'gose [pwi'chõsə] n. psychosis.

puber'teit [pewbəR'tayt] n. puberty.

pu'bliek [pə'blik] n. public; a. & av. (-e) public(ly).

publi'kasie [pəbli'kāsi] n. (-s) publication; publi'seer v. (ge-) publish; publisi'teit n. publicity.

puik [pœik] a. prime, choice, excellent.

'puil ['pœil] v. (ge-) protrude, bulge.

puin ['pœin] n. ruins, debris.

'puisie ['pœisi] n. (-s) pustule, pimple.

punktu'asie [pʌnktew'āsi] n. punctuation; punktu'eer v. (ge-) punctuate.

punt ['pʌnt] n. (-te) point; tip; spot; dot; item; v. (ge-) sharpen; -ig a. (-e) pointed.

punte'nerig [pʌntə'nēRəch] a. (-e) touchy; fastidious.

pu'pil [pew'pəl] n. (-le) pupil.

pur'gasie [pʌR'chāsi] n. purgative; purgation; pur'geer v. (ge-) purge.

pu'ris [pew'Rəs] n. (-te) purist; -ties a. (-e) puristic.

puri'tein [pewRi'tayn] n. (-e) Puritan.

'purper ['pʌRpəR] n. purple.

put ['pʌt] n. (-te) well, pit; v. (ge-) draw; draw on.

'puur ['pēWR] a. (pure; -der, -ste) pure; neat.

'pure ['pewRə] a. sheer.

pyl ['payl] n. (-e) arrow, dart; v. (ge-) dart; -reguit av. dead straight; -snel av. swift as an arrow; -stert n. hawk moth.

pyn ['payn] n. (-e) pain; pine; v. (ge-) ache; -ig v. (ge-) torture; -iging n. torture; -lik a. (-e; -er, -ste) painful, distressing; -loos a. (-lose) painless; -stillend(e) a. analgesic; -stiller n. analgesic.

pyp ['payp] n. (-e) pipe; tube; flue; leg (trouser); -kan n. feeding-bottle; -kan n. (ge-) fool, cheat; -kaneel n. cinnamon; -staal n. tubular steel.

Q

(Refer to KW)

R

R (rand) ['Rant] n. pl. R(and).

R.S.A. ['eResá] n. (*Republiek van Suid-Afrika*) R.S.A. (*Republic of South Africa*).

'raad ['Rãt] n. (*rate, -gewinge, -gewings*) advice, counsel; council, board; -gee v. (ge-) advise; -gewend a. (-e) advisory; -gewer n. (-s) advisor; -pleeg v. (ge-) consult; -saam a. & av. advisable.

'raadsaal ['Rãtsãl] n. ('raadsale) council chamber.

'raadslid ['Rãtslət] n. ('raadslede) councillor.

'raadsman ['Rãtsman] n. (-ne) counsellor.

raai ['Rãi] v. (ge-) advise; guess; -sel n. (-s) riddle, puzzle.

raak ['Rãk] v. (ge-) hit, touch; concern; a. & av. to the point, effective; -skoot n. hit.

raam ['Rãm] n. (rame) frame; window; v. (ge-) frame; estimate.

raap ['Rãp] n. (rape) turnip; v. (ge-) gather, pick up.

raar ['RãR] a. (rare) queer, odd; av. strangely.

raas ['Rãs] v. (ge-) make a noise; rave, storm.

raat ['Rãt] n. (rate) remedy; cp. raad.

ra'barber [Ra'baRbəR] n. rhubarb.

'radeloos ['Rãdəlõs] a. ('radelose) desperate.

radi'kaal [Radi'kãl] a. (radi'kale) radical.

'radio ['Rãdiõ] n. (-'s) radio, wireless; -'gram n. (-me) radiogram; -amateur n. (radio) ham.

'radium ['Rãdiʌm] n. radium.

'radius ['Rãdiʌs] n. (-se) radius.

ra'dys [ra'days] n. (-e) radish.

'rafel ['Rãfl] n. (-s) fray, ravel.

rak ['Rak] n. (-ke) rack, shelf, bracket.

'rakelings ['Rãkələngs] av. -verby graze past.

'rakker ['RakəR] n. (-s) little bounder, rascal.

ram ['Ram] n. (-me) ram.

rame'nas [Ram'nas] n. wild radish.

'rammel ['Ramõl] v. (ge-) rattle, clatter; -aar n. rattle.

'rammelkas ['Raməlkas] n. rattle-trap.

ramp ['Ramp] n. (-e) disaster; -'salig a. (-e) wretched; -spoedig a. (-e) disastrous.

ram'pokker [Ram'pokəR] n. (-s) gangster.

rand ['Rant] n. (-e) ridge; brim; edge; brink; rim; border; boundary; fringe; verge; -eier n. outer egg; wallflower.

'randsteen ['Rantstën] n. ('randstene) kerbstone.

rang ['Rang] n. (-e) rank, position, grade, order; -skik v. (ge-) arrange, range; -telwoord n. ordinal number.

ran'geer [Rãn'shëR] v. (ge-) arrange; shunt; other n. shunter.

rank ['Rank] n. (-e) tendril, shoot; a. (-e) slender, slim; v. (ge-) shoot tendrils, twine.

'rankboon ['Rankbõn] n. ('rankbone) runner bean.

ra'nonkel [Rə'nonkel] n. (-s) ranunculus.

'ransel ['Rãnsəl] v. (ge-) flog, thrash; -eling n. thrashing.

rant = rand; -jie dim.

rant'soen [Rant'sun] n. (-e) ration, allowance; rantsoe'neer v. (ge-) ration; rantsoe'nering n. rationing.

rap'port [Ra'poRt] n. (-e) report; rappor'teer v. (ge-) report; -ryer n. (-s) dispatch-rider.

raps ['Raps] v. (ge-) flick, cut, lash.

rapso'die [Rapsõ'di] n. (-ë) rhapsody.

rari'teit [RaRi'tayt] n. (-e) rarity, oddity.

ras ['Ras] n. (-se) race, strain, stock; a. (-se) swift; av. swiftly, soon; -eg a. (-te) thoroughbred, racy.

'rasend ['Rãsənt] a. (-e) raving, raging, mad, furious, cp. raas; 'raserig a. (-e) noisy; raser'ny n. fury, frenzy; madness.

rasio'neel [Rashõ'nël] a. (rasio'nele) rational; rasiona'listies a. (-e) rationalistic.

'rasper ['RaspəR] n. (-s) rasp, grate; v. (ge-) rasp, grate.

'rassehaat ['Rasəhãt] n. racialism.

'raster ['RastəR] n. (-s) lattice, screen.

rat ['Rat] n. (-te) cog; -jie ['RaiKi] dim.; uit - uit out of gear.

'ratel ['Rãtəl] n. (-s) badge; rattle; v. (ge-) rattle.

'ratelsleutel ['Rãtlslœtl] n. (-s) ratchet wrench.

ratifi'kasie [Ratəfi'kãsi] n. ratification; ratifi'seer v. (ge-) ratify.

'ratkas ['Ratkas] n. (-te) gearbox, transmission.

rats ['Rats] a. (-e; -er, -ste) quick, nimble.

rea'geer [Rëa'chëR] v. (ge-) react; re'aksie n. reaction; reaksionêr a. (-e) reactionary.

rea'lis [Rëa'ləs] n. (-te) realist; reali'sasie n. realization; reali'seer v. (ge-) realize; rea'listies a. (-e) realistic.

re'bel [Rə'bel] n. (-le) rebel; -'leer v. (ge-) rebel, revolt; -lie n. rebellion, insurrection; -s a. & av. rebellious.

red ['Ret] v. (ge-) save, rescue; -deloos av. (reddelose) irretrievably; -ding n. rescue.

re'daksie [Rə'daksi] n. editorial staff; redaksio'neel a. (redaksionele) editorial; redak'teur n. (-s) editor; redak'trise n. fem. editress.

'**rede** ['Rĕdə] n. (-s) reason; understanding; speech; **-deel** n. (-dele) part of speech; **-gewend** a. (-e) casual; **-kawel** v. (ge-) argue, reason; **-lik** a. & av. (-e) reasonable; **-likerwys** av. reasonably; **-loos** a. (-lose) irrational; **-naar** n. (-s) orator; **-'nasie** n. argument; **-'neer** v. (ge-) argue; **-'nering** n. (-s) reasoning; **-twis** v. (ge-) dispute; **-voerder** n. (-s) speaker; **-voering** n. speech.

'**reder** ['RĕdəR] n. (-s) shipowner; **rede'ry** n. shipping-line.

redi'geer [Rədə'chēR] v. (ge-) edit; cp. **redaksie**.

re'duksie [Rĕ'dʌksi] n. reduction.

redupli'kasie [Rĕdewpli'käsi] n. reduplication.

redu'seer [Rĕdew'sēR] v. (ge-) reduce; cp. **reduksie**.

reeds ['Rĕts] av. already.

reeks ['Rĕks] n. (-e) series, row, set.

reël ['Rĕl] n. (-s) line, rule; v. (ge-) arrange, regulate; **-ing** n. arrangement; regulation; **-maat** n. regular order; **-'matigheid** n. regularity; **-'matig** av. (-e) regularly.

reën ['Rĕn] n. (-s) rain; v. (ge-) rain; **-val** n. rainfall.

'**reënboog** ['Rĕmbŏch] n. (reenboē) rainbow.

'**reep** ['Rĕp] n. (repe) strip.

refer'aat [Refə'Rāt] n. (refe'rate) lecture, paper, report; **refe'reer** v. (ge-) refer; **refe'rensie** n. reference.

re'fleks [Rĕfleks] n. (-e) reflex; **-ie** n. reflection; **reflek'teer** v. (ge-) reflect.

refor'masie [RĕfoR'māsi] n. reformation; **refor'meer** v. (ge-) reform.

re'frein [Rə'fRayn] n. refrain, chorus.

reg ['Rech] n. (-te) justice, law; right; a. (-te) right, correct; av. rightly; **-bank** n. court of justice; **-s** av. to the right; right-handed; **-som** av. to the right; **-te** n. rights, laws, duties; **-ter** n. judge.

re'geer [Rə'chēR] v. (ge-) govern, rule; **-der** n. (-s) ruler; **re'gering** n. government.

regene'rasie [Rĕchənə'Rāsi] n. regeneration; **regene'reer** v. (ge-) regenerate.

re'gent [Rə'chent] n. (-e) regent.

reghoek ['Rech'huk] n. (-e) rectangle; **reg'hoekig** a. (-e) rectangular.

'**régie** ['Rĕshi] n. stage-management.

ré'gime [Rə'shim] n. regime.

regi'ment [Rəchə'ment] n. (-e) regiment.

regis'seur [Rəchə'sēR] n. stage manager.

re'gister [Rə'chəstəR] n. (-s) register; **regis'trasie** n. registration; **registra'teur** n. registrar; **regis'treer** v. (ge-) register.

regle'ment [Rəchlə'ment] n. (-e) rules, regulations.

reg'matig [Rech'mātəch] a. (-e) rightful.

regs- ['Rechs-] pref. legal-.

regssinnig [Rech'sənəch] a. (-e) orthodox.

reg'skape [Rech'skäpə] a. upright, honest.

'regsom ['Rechsom] av. clockwise.

regstel ['Rechstel] v. (-ge-) adjust, correct.

'**regstreeks** ['RechstRĕks] av. directly.

regtens ['Rechtəñs] av. de jure.

regter ['RechtəR] n. (-s) judge.

'**regter-** ['RechtəR] pref. a. right; **-arm** n. right arm; **-hand** n. right hand; **-kant** n. right side.

'**regtig** ['Rechtəch] av. really, truly.

re'guit ['Rechœit] a. & av. straight, frank(ly).

regu'lasie [Rəchə'läsi] n. (-s) regulation; **regu'leer** v. (ge-) regulate; **regu'lering** n. adjustment.

reg'verdig [Rech'fƐRdəch] a. (-e) just; v. (ge-) justify; **-e** n. (-s) righteous one; **-ing** n. justification.

rehabili'tasie [Rĕhabili'täsi] n. rehabilitation; **rehabili'teer** v. (ge-) rehabilitate.

'**reier** ['RayəR] n. (-s) heron.

reik ['Rayk] v. (ge-) reach; **-'halsend** av. (-e) yearningly.

rein ['Rayn] a. (-e; -er, -ste) pure, chaste, clean; **-e** n. (-s) pure one; **-heid** n.; **-ig** v. (ge-) purify, cleanse; **-iger** n. (-s) detergent; cleanser.

reinkar'nasie [Rĕəng'kaR'näsi] n. reincarnation.

'**rei(plank)** ['Ray(plank)] n. straight-edge.

reis ['Rays] n. (-e) journey; v. (ge-) travel; **-deken** n. rug; **-iger** n. (-s) traveller; **-siekte** n. travel sickness; **-tas** n. (-se) suit-case; **-'vaardig** av. ready to start.

rek ['Rek] n. (-ke) elastic; catapult; elasticity; v. (ge-) stretch; **-baar** a. (-bare) elastic, ductile; **-verband** n. crepe bandage.

'**reken** ['Rĕkən] v. (ge-) reckon, calculate; count, consider; **-ing** n. (-e, -s) account; calculation; **-meester** n. accountant; **-skap** n. account.

re'klame [Rə'klämə] n. advertisement.

rekomman'deer [Rekomə'dēR] v. (ge-) recommend.

'**rekord** ['RekoRt] n. (-s) record.

re'kruut [Rə'kRewt] n. (re'krute) recruit.

'**rektor** ['RektoR] n. ('rektore) rector, principal.

re'laas [Rə'läs] n. (re'lase) account, narration.

reli'ëf [Rəl'yef] n. relief.

'**reling** ['Rĕləng] n. (-s) railing.

'**relletjie** ['RelǝKi] n. (-s) riot, squabble.

rem ['Rem] n. (-me) brake; v. (ge-) brake, strain; **-hoogte** n. steep hill; **-skoen** n. stick-in-the-mud. obscurant; shoe; **-hefboom** n. brake lever; **-kabel** n. brake cable; **-krag** n.

braking power; **-lig** n. brake light; **-silinder** n. brake cylinder; **-stelsel** n. brake system **-trommel** n. brake drum; **-vloeistof** n. brake fluid.

'**renbaan** ['Renbãn] n. ('renbane) racecourse.

rende'ment [Randə'ment] n. efficiency, interest.

rene'gaat [Rənə'chãt] n. (rene'gate) renegade.

re'noster [Rə'nostəR] n. (-s) rhinoceros.

'**rens** ['Reñs] a. rancid.

'**rente** ['Rentə] n. (-s) interest; **rentmeester** n. steward.

rep ['Rep] n. in-en roer in commotion; v. (ge-) mention; hurry.

repa'rasie [Repə'Rãsi] n. (-s) reparation; **repa'reer** v. (ge-) repair, mend.

repe'teer [Rəpə'tēR] v. (ge-) repeat, rehearse; **repe'tisie** n. repetition, rehearsal.

repro'duksie [RēpRō'dʌksi] n. reproduction; **reprodu'seer** v. (ge-) reproduce.

repu'bliek [Rəpə'blik] n. (-e) republic; **republiekein** n.republican.

repu'tasie [Repə'tãsi] n. reputation.

'**rêrig** [RɛRəch] av. really.

res ['Res] n. (-te) rest.

re'seda [Rə'sēda] n. mignonette.

resen'seer [Rəsen'sēR] v. (ge-) review; **resen'sent** n. reviewer; **re'sensie** n. review.

re'sep [Rə'sep] n. (-te) recipe; prescription.

re'serwe [Rə'seRvə] n. (-s) reserve.

re'ses [Rə'ses] n. recess.

resi'densie [Rəsə'deñsi] n. residence.

resi'tasie [Rəsə'tãsi] n. (-s) recitation; **resi'teer** v. (ge-) recite.

re'spek [Rə'spek] n. respect, regard; **respek'tabel** av. respectable.

restau'rant [Restō'Rant] n. (-e) restaurant.

resul'taat [Rəsʌl'tãt] n. (resultate) result.

reti'reer [Rətə'RēR] v. (ge-) retreat, retire.

re'toer [Rə'tūR] a. return.

re'tories [Rə'tōRis] a. (-e) rhetoric.

reuk [Rœk] n. smell; scent; odour; **-loos** a. (-lose) odourless; scentless; **-orgaan** n. olfactory organ; **-water** n. perfume; **-stafie** n. solid cologne; **-verdrywer** n. deodorant; **-waterspuit** n. scent spray; **-weerder** n. deodorant; **-werend(e)** a. & av. deodorant.

'**reun** ['Rœn] n. (-s) gelding; dog.

reus ['Rœs] n. (-e) giant; **-agtig** a. (-e) gigantic.

re'visie [Rə'visi] n. revision.

re'wolwer [Rə'volvəR] n. (-s) revolver, pistol.

rib ['Rəp] n. (-be, -bes) rib; **-bebeen** n. rib; **-betjie** dim. rib.

'**ridder** ['RədəR] n. (-s) knight; **-lik** a. & av. knightly.

riem ['Rim] n. (-e) thong, strap, oar; ream; **-pie** dim.

'**riemtelegram** ['rimteləchRam] n. (-me) rumour.

riet ['Rit] n. (-e) reed, rush; **-skraal** a. & av. very thin; **-suiker** n. canesugar.

'**rif** ['Rəf] n. (riwwe) reef; ledge, ridge.

'**riffel** ['Rəfəl] n. (-s) wrinkle, ruffle, ripple; v. (ge-) wrinkle, crinkle, ripple; **-rig** a. (-e) crinkled, corrugated.

rig ['Rəch] v. (ge-) aim, direct; align; **-snoer** n. (-e) guide, directing principle; **-ter** n. (-s) guide; **-ting** n. (-e, -s) direction.

ril ['Rəl] v. (ge-) shudder, shiver, **-lerig** a. (-e) creepy; **-ling** n. (-e, -s) shudder.

'**rimpel** ['Rəmpəl] n. (-s) wrinkle, fold, line; v. (ge-) wrinkle, line, pucker; **-room** n. anti-wrinkle cream.

ring ['Rəng] n. (-e) ring; circle; presbytery; **-kop** n. (-pe) stalwart, veteran.

'**ringmuur** ['RəngmēWR] n. encircling wall.

'**rinkel** ['Rənkəl] v. (ge-) jingle.

rin'kink [Rəng'kənk] v. (ge-) rollick, gallivant, caper, frisk.

'**risiko** ['Risikō] n. ('s) risk.

'**rissie** ['Rəsi] n. (-s) chilli.

rit ['Rət] n. (-te) journey; **-jis** ['RəiKi] dim.

'**ritme** ['Rətmə] n. (-s) rhythm, cadence; '**ritmies** a. (-e) rhythmical.

rits ['Rəts] n. series, string; v. (ge-) romp; **-ig** a. (-e) ruttish; **-sel** v. (ge-) rustle.

'**rittel** ['Rətəl] v. (ge-) shiver, shake.

'**ritwyser** ['RətvaysəR] n. trip indicator.

ri'vier [Rə'fiR] n. (-e) river.

rob ['Rop] n. (-be) seal.

'**robot** ['Rōbot] n. (-te) robot.

ro'byn [Rō'bayn] n. (-e) ruby, garnet.

'**roede** ['Rudə] n. (-s) birch; rod; penis.

roei ['Rui] v. (ge-) row, pull.

roei'riem ['RuiRim] n. (-e) oar.

'**roekeloos** ['Rukəlōs] a. ('roekelose) reckless; wicked.

roem ['Rum] n. renown, fame; v. (ge-) boast; praise; **-ryk** a. (-e) famous, splendid.

roep ['Rup] n. call, cry; v. (ge-) call, cry, shout, (hotel) page; **-ende** n. (-s) one who calls; **-ing** n. (-e, -s) calling, vocation.

'**roepstem** ['Rupstem] n. call, voice, summons.

roer ['RuR] n. (-e, -s) rudder; helm; gun, rifle; commotion; v. (ge-) stir; move; touch; **-eier** n. scrambled eggs; **-end** a. (-e) touching, moving; **-ing** n. motion; emotion; **-loos** a. (-lose) motionless; rudderless; **-sel** n. (-e, -s) motion, movement.

roes ['Rus] n. rust; blight; intoxication; v. (ge-) rust; corrode.

'roesvry ['RusfRay] a. stainless.

roet ['Rut] n. soot.

'roete ['Rutə] n. (-s) route.

rog ['Roch] n. rye.

'roggel ['Rochəl] n. gurgle; phlegm; v. (ge-) gurgle, rattle.

rok ['Rok] n. (-ke) skirt, dress, gown.

rol ['Rol] n. (-le) roll; scroll; rôle; cylinder; roller; v. (ge-) roll, tumble; -ler n. roller; -letjie dim. small roll; castor; reel.

'rolbaan ['Rolbān] n. runway, tarmac.

'rollaer ['RolāR] n. (-s) roller bearing.

'rolprent ['Rolprənt] n. (-e) film.

'roltrap ['RoltRap] n. (-pe) escalator.

'rolverband ['rolfəRbant] n. roller bandage.

ro'man [Rô'man] n. (-s) novel.

roman'tiek [Rôman'tik] n. Romantic Movement; -erig a. (-e) tending to be romantic; ro'manties a. (-e) romantic; ro'mantikus n. romanticist.

'Rome ['Rômə] n. Rome; ro'mein n. Roman; ro'meins a. (-e) Roman.

'rommel ['Romel] n. lumber, rubbish; -ry n. rubbish, litter; -waarde n. scrap value.

romp ['Romp] n. trunk, hull; skirt.

rond ['Ront] a. (-e; -er, -ste) round, circular; prep. round; -'borstig a. & av. (-e) open, candid; -ing n. rounding; -loop v. (-ge-) walk around, loaf about; -loper n. (-s) loafer; -te n. round; circle; -uit av. frankly.

ron'dawel [Ron'dāvəl] n. (-s) round hut.

'rondgaande ['Rontchāndə] a. -hof circuit court.

'rondgang ['Rontchang] n. circuit.

rong ['Rong] n. rung.

roof ['Rôf] n. (rowe) scab, crust; robbery; v. (ge-) rob; -dier n. beast of prey.

'roofbou ['Rôfboa] n. overcropping.

rooi ['Rôi] n. red; -word v. (-ge-) blush, turn red; -dag n. dawn; -erig a. (-e) reddish; -kappie n. Red Riding Hood; -nek n. (-ke) Englishman; -water n. Bilharzia.

rook ['Rôk] n. smoke; v. (ge-) smoke; -goed n. smokables, paraphernalia for smoking; -vleis n. smoked beef; -vry a. smokeless.

room ['Rôm] n. cream; -agtig a. (-e) creamy; -ys n. ice-cream.

roos ['Rôs] n. (rose) rose; erysipelas.

roosma'ryn [Rôsma'Rayn] n. rosemary.

'rooster ['RôstəR] n. (-s) grate, grill, grid; timetable, schedule, register; lattice; -brood n. toast; -koek n. girdle cake.

'rosekrans ['RôsəkRāns] n. rosary.

'roskam ['Roskam] n. (-me) currycomb; v. (ge-) curry; rebuke.

ro'syn [Rô'sayn] n. (-e) raisin; -tjie dim. = rosyn.

rot ['Rot] n. (-te) rat; a. rotten; av. -en kaal besteel steal everything a person possesses.

rots ['Rots] n. (-e) rock, cliff; -agtig a. (-e; -er, -ste) rocky; -tuin n. rockery.

'rotsvas ['Rotsfas] a. (-te) firm as a rock.

'rotswand ['Rotsvant] n. cliff.

'rottang ['Rotang] n. (-s) cane.

rou ['Roa] n. mourning; a. raw; hoarse; v. (ge-) mourn; -klag v. (ge-) lament; -koop n. smart-money.

'rousool ['Roasôl] n. untanned leather.

'rower ['RôvəR] n. (-s) robber; -'y n. robbery; cp. roof.

ru ['Rew] a. (ruwe) rough; raw; crude; coarse.

'rubber ['RabəR] n. rubber.

ru'briek [Rə'bRik] n. (-e) category; column; rubric.

rudimen'têr [Rewdimen'tɛR] a. (-e) rudimentary.

rug ['Rach] n. (-ge, -te, rûe) back; n. (-gens. rûens) ridge, hill; -graat n. spine; -graatkromming n. lordosis; -murg n. spinal cord; -murgontsteking n. myelitis; -steun n. support.

'rugbaar ['RachbāR] a. known.

'rugstring ['RachstRəng] n. backbone.

ruig ['Rœich] a. (ruie) shaggy, hairy; bushy; -te n. undergrowth.

ruik ['Rœik] n. = reuk; v. (ge-) smell, scent; -er n. (-s) bouquet.

ruil ['Rœil] n. exchange, barter; v. (ge-) exchange, barter.

ruim ['Rœim] n. (-e) hold; a. (-e; -er, -ste) spacious, roomy; ample; av. amply, abundantly; v. (ge-) empty; remove; -skoots av. amply; -te n. (-s) space; breadth.

ru'ïne [Ru'inə] n. (-s) ruin; rui'neer v. (ge-) ruin.

ruis ['Rœis] v. (ge-) rustle.

ruit ['Rœit] n. (-e) pane; check material; diamond (cards); -er n. (-s) horseman, rider; -erlik av. frankly, openly; -e'ry n. cavalry; -ligter n. window lift; -spuit n. windscreen washer; -veër n. windscreen wiper.

ruk ['Rak] n. (-ke) jerk, tug; period of time; v. (ge-) jerk, pull; -kie dim.

ruma'tiek [Rəmə'tik] n. rheumatism; ru'maties a. (-e) rheumatic.

ru'moer [Rə'mūR] n. noise, din; v. (ge-) make a noise; rumoer'ig a. (-e) noisy.

'runnik ['Ranək] v. (ge-) neigh, whinny.

rus ['Ras] n. rest; peace; pause, caesura; Russian; v. (ge-) rest, repose; -teken n. rest (music); -teloos a. (rustelose) restless; -tend *a.* (-e) resting, retired, dormant; -tig *a.* (-e; -er, -ste) restful, quiet.

'**rusie** ['Rewsi] *n.* (-s) quarrel, brawl; -makerig *a.* (-e) cantankerous.

'**rusoord** ['RʌsõRt] *n.* (-e) place of rest, haven.

'**ruspe(r)** ['Rʌspə(R)] *n.* (-s) caterpillar.

ry ['Ray] *n.* (-e) row, line; series; course; *v.* (ge-) ride, drive; copulate; -tuig *n.* (-tuie) vehicle; -wiel *n.* bicycle; -bewys *n.* (-e) driver's licence.

ryg ['Raych] *v.* (ge-) tack, baste.

ryk ['Rayk] *n.* (-e) kingdom, empire, realm; sphere; *a.* (-e; -er, -ste) rich; *av.* richly; -dom *n.* (-me) wealth; -e *n.* (-s) rich person; -lik *av.* richly.

rym ['Raym] *n.* (-e) rhyme; *v.* (ge-) rhyme; agree, correspond; -pie *dim.*

ryp ['Rayp] *n.* hoar-frost; *a.* (-e; -er, -ste) ripe, mature; *v.* (ge-) frost.

'**ryperd** ['Raypert] *n.* (-e) saddle horse; *interj.* well done!

rys ['Rays] *n.* rice; *v.* (ge-) rise; -ig *a.* (-e) tall; -mier *n.* (-e) termite.

'**ryswater** ['RaysvٰatəR] *n.* rice-water.

S

S.A.U.K. [es-ä-ew-kä] (*Suid-Afrikaanse Uitsaaikorporasie*) *n.* **S.A.B.C.** (*South African Broadcasting Corporation*).

sa ! ['sä] *interj.* catch him!

saad ['sät] *n.* (sade) seed; semen; progeny; germ; -huisie *n.* seed-capsule; -skiet *v.* (-ge-) run to seed.

saag ['sāch] *n.* (sage, sae) saw; *v.* (ge-) saw, cut, rip; -sel *n.* (-s) saw-dust; -tandig *a.* (-e) serrated.

saai ['sāi] *n.* serge; *a. & av.* dull, drab; *v.* (ge-) sow, scatter; -er *n.* sower.

saak ['säk] *n.* (sake) case, matter, concern, affair; -lik *a. & av.* (-e) business-like, to the point; concise; essential; -ryk *a.* (-e) pithy.

saal ['säl] *n.* (sale) hall; *n.* (-s) saddle; *v.* (ge-) saddle.

saam ['säm] *av.* together.

saam-, '**same**= ['säm(ə)-] *pref. cp.* mee= together, co=; -gaan *v.* (-ge-) accompany; go together; -gesteld *a.* (-e) compound, complicated; -hang *n.* context; -smelt *v.* (-ge-) amalgamate; -stel *v.* (-ge-) compose, compile; -stem *v.* (-ge-) agree; -sweer *v.* (-ge-) conspire; -tref *v.* (-ge-) meet; -vat *v.* (-ge-) summarize.

saam'horigheid [säm'hõRəchayt] *n.* solidarity.

saans ['säns] *av.* at night, in the evening.

saat = **saad**.

sabo'tasie [sabo'tāsi] *n.* sabotage; **sabo'teer** *v.* (ge-) sabotage.

sa'dis [sa'dəs] *n.* (-te) sadist; -ties *a.* (-e) sadistic.

saf ['saf] *a. & av.* (-te) soft; mild; light; softly, gently.

sag = **saf**; **saggies** *av.* softly; -'moedig *a.* (-e) mild, gentle; -'sinnig *a.* (-e) gentle, mild.

'**sagtheid** ['sachthayt] *n.* clemency.

'**sago** ['sächõ] *n.* sago.

sak ['sak] *n.* (-ke) bag; pocket; *v.* (ge-) sink, drop, fall, lower, subside; fail.

'**sakboek** [sakbuk] *n.* pocket-book.

'**sakdoek** ['sakduk] *n.* (-e) handkerchief.

'**sakwurm** ['sakvʌrəm] *n.* bagworm.

sal ['sal] *v.* (past tense; sou) shall, will.

sa'laris [sə'lāRəs] *n.* (-se) salary; **salari'eer** *v.* (ge-) pay a salary.

sal'do [sal'dõ] *n.* (-'s) balance, credit.

salf ['salf] *n.* (salwe) ointment, salve; *v.* (ge-) anoint.

'**salig** ['säləch] *a. & av.* (-e) blessed, blissful; -heid *n.* salvation, bliss.

salm ['saləm] *n.* salmon.

'**sandstraal** ['santstRāl] *n.* sand blast.

sa'lon [sa'lon] *n.* (-ne, -s) salon; drawing-room.

salu'tasie [salew'tāsi] *n.* salutation; **salu'eer** *v.* (ge-) salute; **sa'luut** *n.* salute.

sal'vo [sal'võ] *n.* (-'s) salvo, volley.

sam'breel [sam'bRēl] *n.* (sam'brele) umbrella.

'**same** = **saam**; -trekker *n.* contractor; -werking *n.* co-operation.

sampi'oen [sampə'yun] *n.* (-e) mushroom.

sana'torium [sana'tõRiʌm] *n.* (-s) sanatorium.

sand ['sant] *n.* sand, grit, dirt; -erig *a.* (-e) sandy; -lopertjie *n.* hour-glass; -suiker *n.* crystallized sugar.

sang ['sang] *n.* song; singing; verse, poetry; -er *n.* (-s) singer; -e'res *n.* (-se) songstress; -erig *a.* (-e; -er, -ste) melodious, tuneful; -stuk *n.* (-ke) song.

'**sanik** ['sänək] *v.* (ge-) drone, bother, talking shop.

sani'têr [sani'tɛR] *a.* (-e) sanitary.

'**sanksie** ['sanksi] *n.* (-s) sanction.

sap ['sap] *n.* (-pe) juice; sap; -perig *a.* (-e) juicy; -pig *a.* (-e; -er, -ste) choice, juicy, luscious.

sar'dientjie [saR-ding-Ki] *n.* sardine.

sar'kasme [saR'kasmə] *n.* sarcasm; **sar'kasties** *a.* (-e) sarcastic.

'**sarsie** ['saRsi] *n.* (-s) charge, volley.

'**sat** ['sat] *av.* saturated; tired.

'**satan** ['sätang] *n.* Satan; **sa'tanies** *a.* (-e) satanic(al), diabolical; -s *a.* (-e) satanic, hellish.

'**Saterdag** ['sätəRdach] *n.* Saturday.

sa'tire [sa'tiRə] *n.* satire; **sa'tiries** *a.* (-e) satiric(al); **sa'tirikus** *n.* (-se) satirist.

satis'faksie [satəs'faksi] n. satisfaction.

sa'tyn [sə'tayn] n. satin.

se ['sə] pron. of, belonging to, -'s.

sê ['sɛ] n. say; v. (ge-) say, tell.

'sebra ['sebRa] n. (-s) zebra; -oorgang n. zebra crossing.

'sede ['sɛdə] n. (-s) manner, habit; customs; morals; -lik a. (-e) moral, ethical; -loos a. (-lose) immoral; -sedig a. (-e) demure; decorous.

'seder ['sedəR] n. (-s) cedar.

'sedert ['sedəRt] prep. since, for; -'dien av. since then.

'sedig ['sedəch] a. (-e; -er, -ste) modest, coy, demure.

se'disie [sə'disi] n. sedition.

see ['se] n. (see) sea, ocean; flood; multitude.

see- ['se] pref. sea-, marine-; -engte n. strait; -hond n. seal; -hoof n. pier, jetty; -kat n. catfish, squid; -kreef n. lobster; -kwal n. jelly-fish; -meeu n. seagull.

'seekoei ['sekui] n. (-e) hippopotamus.

seel ['sel] n. (-s) certificate.

seël ['sɛl] n. (-s) stamp; seal; v. (ge-) seal, stamp; -merk n. seal; -ring n. signet-ring.

'seemsleer ['semsleR] v. chamois.

'seën ['seən] n. (seëninge, seënings) blessing, benediction; v. (ge-) bless; -ing n. blessing; seine.

seep ['sep] n. soap; -klip n. saponite; -kiskarretjie n. soap-box-cart; -sop n. soap-suds; -water n. soapy water.

'seepsoda ['sepsoda] n. caustic soda.

'seëpraal ['seəpRal] v. (ge-) triumph.

seer ['seR] n. (sere) sore, boil, wound; a. sore, painful; -heid n.; -tjie dim.

'seesiek ['sesik] a. sea-sick.

'seëspieel ['sespil] n. sea-level.

'seevaarder ['sefaRdəR] n. (-s) navigator.

'seëvier ['sefiR] v. (ge-) triumph.

'sege ['sechə] n. victory.

'seggenskap ['sechəngskap] n. say, voice; cp. sê.

segre'gasie [sechRə'chasi] n. segregation; segre'geer v. (ge-) segregate.

'segwyse ['sechswaysə] n. (-s) expression.

seil ['sayl] n. (-e) sail; tarpaulin; canvas; v. (ge-) sail; -sport n. yachting.

sein ['sayn] n. (-e) signal; v. (ge-) signal; telegraph; -wagter n. signal-man.

seis ['says] n. (-e) scythe.

sei'soen [say'sun] n. (-e) season.

'sekel ['sekəl] n. (-s) sickle.

'seker ['sekəR] a. (-, -e) certain; positive; av. surely, certainly, for sure; -e n. the certain; -heid n. certainty, assurance; -heidshalwe av. for safety's sake; -ing n. fuse; -ingdraad n. fuse wire; -ingkas n. fuse box; -lik av. certainly.

se'konde [sə'kondə] n. (-s) second.

sekon'deer [sekon'deR] v. (ge-) second; sekon'dant n. seconder, second.

sekon'dêr [sekon'dɛR] a. (-e) secondary.

sekre'taris [səkRə'taRəs] n. (-se) secretary; sekreta'resse n. (-s) fem. secretary; sekretari'aat n. office of the secretary.

'seks ['seks] n. sex (natural, biological); -loos a. asexual; -manie n. sex mania.

'seksie ['seksi] n. (-s) section; dissection.

seksu'eel [seksew'el] a. (seksu'ele) sexual, sex-.

'sekte ['sektə] n. (-s) sect; sek'taries a. (-e) sectarian.

'sektor ['sektoR] n. (-s. sek'tore) sector.

seku'lêr [sekew'lɛR] a. (-e) secular.

sekuri'teit [səkewRi'tayt] n. security, surety.

se'kuur [sə'kewR] a. (-, se'kure) accurate, precise; av. accurately.

sel ['sel] n. (-le) cell.

'selde ['seldə] av. seldom, rarely.

'seldsaam ['seltsam] a. ('seldsame) rare, scarce.

self ['self] n. self, ego; pron. self; self- pref. self-; -'standig a. (-e) independent; -'sugtig a. (-e) selfish; -werkend a. (-e) automatic. 'selfdig'binneband ['selfdəch'bənəbant] n. self-sealing tube; -digtend a. (-e) self-sealing; -rigtend a. (-e) self-aligning; selfsmeer- pref. self-lubricating (oiling); -voldaan a. complacent.

'selfkant ['selfkant] n. selvedge.

'selfs ['selfs] av. even.

'selspanning ['selspanəng] n. cell voltage.

'semels ['seməls] n. bran.

se'ment [sə'ment] n. cement.

se'mester [sə'mestəR] n. (-s) semester, term.

se'naat [sə'nat] n. senate; se'nator n. (se'natore) senator.

send ['sent] v. (ge-) send, dispatch; -er n. sender; -eling n. missionary; -ing n. mission.

se'niel [sə'nil] a. (-e) senile.

'sening ['senəng] n. (-s) sinew, tendon.

'senior ['senioR] n. (-s) senior.

sen'sasie [sen'sasi] n. (-s) sensation.

sensi'tief [sensə'tif] a. (sensi'tiewe) sensitive.

'sensor ['sensoR] n. (-s) censor.

'sensus ['sensʌs] n. census.

sen'suur [sen'sewR] n. censure.

'sentenaar ['sentənaR] n. (-s) hundredweight.

'senter ['sentəR] n. (-s) centre.

senti'ment [senti'ment] n. (-e) sentiment; sentimen'teel a. (sentimen'tele) sentimental.

sen'trale [sen'tRalə] n. (-s) exchange; power-station; sen'traal a. (sentrale)

central; **sentrali'sasie** n. centralization; **sentrali'seer** v. (ge-) centralize.
'sentrum ['sentrʌm] n. (-s) centre.
'senu = senuwee.
'senuwee ['sɛnəvē] n. nerve.
sepa'rasie [sepə'Rāsi] n. separation.
'sepia ['sēpia] n. sepia.
Sep'tember [səp'teməR] n. September.
'septer ['septəR] n. (-s) sceptre.
'septies ['septis] a. (-e) sceptic.
sere'monie [səRə'mōni] n. (-s) ceremony.
'serie ['sēRi] n. (-s) series.
seri'eus [sɛri'ɵ̄s] a. (-e) serious, earnest.
se'ring [sə'Rəng] n. lilac.
serp ['seRp] n. (-e) scarf.
ser'sant [səR'sant] n. (-e) sergeant.
sertifi'kaat [səRtəfə'kāt] n. (sertifikate) certificate; **sertifi'seer** v. (ge-) certify.
'serum ['sēRʌm] n. serum.
ser'vet [səR'fet] n. (-te) serviette.
ser'vies [səR'fis] n. (-e) set, service.
servi'tuut [seRvi'tēwt] n. (servi'tute) servitude, charge.
ses ['ses] num. six; **-de** ord. sixth.
se'sessie [sə'sesi] n. secession.
sessie ['sesi] n. session; dim. six.
sestien ['sestin] num. sixteen.
sestig ['sestəch] num. sixty.
set ['set] n. (-te) move, trick; set; v. (ge-) set, mount; **-fout** n. misprint; **-sel** n. type.
'setel ['sɛtəl] n. (-s) seat; throne; v. (ge-) reside, be resident; sit.
'setlaar ['setlāR] n. (-s) settler, immigrant.
setmeel ['setmēl] n. starch.
seun ['sɵ̄n] n. (-s) son; boy, chap.
seur ['sɵ̄R] n. (-s) sir, master; v. (ge-) bother, nag.
sewe ['sēvə] num. seven; **-'jaartjie** n. everlasting, immortelle.
'sewentien ['sēvəntin] num. seventeen.
'sewentig ['sēvəntəch] num. seventy.
sfeer ['sfēR] n. (sfere) sphere; **'sferies** a. (-e) spherical.
sfinks ['sfənks] n. sphinx.
siaan [si'ān] n. cyanogen; **sia'nied** n. cyanide.
'sidder ['sədəR] v. (ge-) quake, shiver, tremble; **-ing** n. shudder.
siek ['sik] a. & av. sick, ill, diseased; **-e** n. (-s) patient; **-erig** a. (-e) ailing; **-lik** a. (-e; -er, -ste) ailing; cranky; **-te** n. (-s) sickness; **-estoel** n. invalid chair.
siel ['sil] n. (-e) soul, spirit, mind; **-dodend** a. (-e) dull, monotonous; **-ig** a. (-e) miserable, pitiful; **-siek** av. mentally diseased; **-'togend** av. breathing one's last.
sien ['sin] v (ge-) see, notice, perceive; **-de** a. seeing; **-deroë** av. perceptibly; **-er** n. (-s) visionary; **-lik** a.(-e) visible; **-s** n. tot- goodbye; **-swyse** n. opinion.
sier ['siR] v. (ge-) decorate; **-aad** n.

ornament, trinket; **-kuns** n. decorative art; **-lik** a. (-e; -er, -ste) graceful, elegant.
'sies ['sis] interj. bah, shame!
sif ['səf] n. (siwwe) sieve, strainer, screen.
'sig ['səch] n. sight, visibility; **-afstand** n. length of visibility.
si'gaar [sə'chāR] n. (si'gare) cigar.
siga'ret [səchə'Ret] n. (-te) cigarette.
'sigbaar ['səchbāR] a. (sigbare) visible, clear.
si'geuner [sə'chɵ̄nəR] n. (-s) gipsy.
sigorei [sichōRay] n. chicory.
si'klaam [si'klām] n. cyclamen.
'siklies ['siklis] a. (-e) cyclic.
si'kloon [si'klōn] n. (si'klone) cyclone.
'siks ['səks] interj. by my - strewth!
sili'kose [sili'kōsə] n. silicosis.
si'linder [sə'ləndəR] n. (-s) cylinder; **si'lindries** a. (-e) cylindrical.
sil'labe ['sələbə] n. (-s) syllable.
sil'labus [sə'lābʌs] n. (-se) syllabus.
'silwer ['səlvəR] n. silver; **-agtig** a. (-e) silvery; **-akoon** av. spotlessly clean.
sim'baal [səm'bāl] n. (simbale) cymbal.
sim'bool [səm'bōl] n. (simbole) symbol; **sim'bolies** a. (-e) symbolic; **simboli'seer** v. (ge-) symbolize.
simfo'nie [səmfō'ni] n. symphony; **sim'fonies** a. (-e) symphonic.
simme'trie [səmə'tRi] n. symmetry; **sim'metries** a. (-e) symmetric.
simpa'tie [səmpa'ti] n. sympathy; **simpa'tiek** a. (-e) sympathetic; **simpati'seer** v. (ge-) sympathize.
'simpel ['səmpəl] a. (-e) silly, dotty; simple, plain; mere.
sin ['sən] n. (-ne) sense, mind; wish, fancy, taste; sentence; v. (ge-) muse; **-ledig** a. meaningless; **-lik** a. (-e) sensual; **-nelik** a. (-e) sensuous; **-nigheid** n. liking; **-snede** n. phrase; **-speel** v. (ge-) allude; **-tuig** n. (-tuie) sense-organ; **-'tuiglik** a. (-e) sensory.
'sindelik ['səndələk] a. & av. (-e) clean, tidy.
sinds ['səns] prep. & av. since; for.
sing ['səng] v. (ge-) sing; **-er** n. singer; **sing-sing** n. singing.
'singel ['səngəl] n. (-s) circular (circle) road = **singelpad.**
'sinies ['sinis] a. (-e) cynic(al).
sin'jaal [sən'yāl] n. (sin'jale) signal.
sink ['sənk] n. zinc; v. (ge-) sink; **-dak** n. galvanized roof; **-gat** n. sink-hole; **-lood** n. sinker.
'sinkings ['sənkəngs] n. neuralgia.
'sinnelik ['sənələk] a. (-e) carnal.
si'node [sə'nōdə] n. (-s) synod.
sino'niem [sinō'nim] n. & a. (-e) synonym.
sint ['sənt] n. saint.
'sintel ['səntəl] n. (-s) cinder.
sin'tese [sən'tēsə] n. synthesis; **sin'teties** a. (-e) synthetic.
si'pier [sə'piR] n. (-s) gaoler, warder.

si'pres [sə'pRes] n. cypress.

'sirkel ['səRkel] n. (-s) circle; v. (ge-) circle.

sirku'lasie [səRkew'lãsi] n. circulation; **sirku'leer** v. (ge-) circulate; **sirku'lêre** n. circular letter.

'sirkus ['səRkʌs] n. (-se) circus.

sis ['sɐs] n. chintz; v. (ge-) hiss.

sis'teem [səs'têm] n. (sisteme) system.

si'troen [sə'tRun] n. (-e) citron.

'sitrus ['sitRʌs] n. citrus.

situ'asie [sətew'ãsi] n. (-s) situation.

sjam'panje [sham'panyə] n. champagne.

sjar'mant [shaR'mant] a. (-e) charming.

'sjerrie ['sheRi] n. sherry.

'sjieling ['shiləng] n. (-s) shilling.

'Sjina ['shina] n. China.

sjoko'la [shoka'lã] n. chocolate.

'skaad ['skãt] v. (ge-) damage, harm.

skaaf ['skãf] n. (skawe) plane; v. (ge-) plane; abrade; chafe; **-ring** n. grommet; **-plek** n. abrasion; **-sel** n. (-s) shaving.

skaai ['skãi] v. (ge-) pilfer, pinch.

skaak ['skãk] n. chess; v. (ge-) play chess; abduct; **-mat** v. checkmate.

skaal ['skãl] n. (skale) scale, balance.

skaam ['skãm] a. shy, bashful; v. (ge-) be ashamed; **-been** n. pubis; **-dele** n. private parts; **-te** n. shame, shyness; modesty; **-teloos** a. (skaamtelose) shameless.

skaap ['skãp] n. (skape) sheep; **-agtig** a. (-e) sheepish, sheep-like.

skaar ['skãR] n. (skare) share; notch, chip, nick; crowd; v. (ge-) range, draw up.

skaars ['skãRs] a. & av. scarce(ly); **-heid** n.; **-te** n.

skaats ['skãts] v. (ge-) skate, rink; n. (-e) skate.

'skade ['skãdə] n. damage, harm, injury; shade; **-lik** a. (-e) harmful, deleterious; **-loos** a. (-lose) harmless.

'skadevergoeding ['skãdəfəRchudəng] n. compensation.

'skadu ['skãdew] n. (-'s) shadow.

'skaduwee ['skãdəvê] n. = skadu.

skag ['skach] n. (-te) shaft.

ska'keer [ska'kêR] v. (ge-) variegate, shade; **ska'kering** n. nuance.

skakel ['skãkəl] n. (-s) link; half-back (rugby); switch; v. (ge-) link; switch; connect; **-aar** n. switch.

skalks ['skalks] a. (-e) arch.

'skamel ['skãməl] a. (-, -e) scanty, poor, humble; n. fifth wheel.

'skamper ['skampəR] a. scornful.

skan'daal [skan'dãl] n. (skan'dale) scandal; **skan'dalig** a. (-e) scandalous.

'skande ['skandə] n. disgrace; **-lik** a. (-e; -er, -ste) disgraceful.

skan'dering [skan'dêRəng] a. scansion.

skans ['skãns] n. (-e) rampart, trench.

'skaplik ['skaplək] a. (-e) reasonable, decent.

'skare ['skãRə] n. (-s) crowd, host.

skar'nier [skaR'niR] n. (-e) hinge.

skat ['skat] n. (-te) treasure; v. (ge-) estimate, compute; **-jie** dim. darling; **-lam** n. darling; **-lik** a. (-e) dear; **-tig** a. (-e) sweet.

'skater ['skãtəR] v. (ge-) roar with laughter.

'skaterlag ['skãtəRlach] n. guffaw.

'skede ['skêdə] n. (-s) sheath.

skedel ['skêdəl] n. (-s) skull.

skeef ['skêf] a. (skewe) skew, slanting; av. askew, awry.

skeel ['skêl] a. & av. (skele) squinting; v. (ge-) differ, matter.

'skeeloog ['skêl-ôch] a. squint-eyed.

skeen ['skên] n. (skene) shin.

skeep- pref. ship-cp. skip.

'skeeps- ['skêps-] pref. marine-.

'skeepsruim ['skêpsrœim] n. hold.

skeer ['skêR] v. (ge-) shave; **-kwas** n. shaving brush; **-lemmetjie** n. blade; **-riem** n. strop; **-sel** n. shearings.

'skeermes ['skêRmes] n. (-se) razor.

'skeerseep ['skêRsêp] n. shaving soap.

skei ['skay] n. (-e) yoke-pin; v. (ge-) part, divide; **-baar** a. (-bare) separable; **-ding** n. separation, parting, division; divorce; boundary; **-kunde** n. chemistry.

skel ['skel] a. shrill; glaring; v. (ge-) ring; scold.

'skeldnaam ['skeltnãm] n. nickname, abusive name.

'skeldwoord ['skeltvôRt] n. invective.

ske'let [ska'let] n. (-te) skeleton; **-plant** n. (plant) delicious monster.

skel'lak [ska'lak] n. shellac.

skelm ['skeləm] n. (-s) rogue, rascal; a. (-e) sly, dishonest; **-agtig** a. (-e) dishonest; **-pies** av. slyly; **skelm-skelm** av. furtively.

'skelmstuk ['skeləmstʌk] n. knavery.

'skema ['skêma] n. (-s) scheme, plan, outline; **ske'maties** a. (-e) schematic, sketchy.

'skemer ['skêməR] n. dusk; a. dusky; v. (ge-) grow dusk; **-kelkie** n. sundowner.

skend ['skent] v. (ge-) disfigure; **-ing** n. violation.

skenk ['skenk] v. (ge-) give, grant, present; **-er** n. donor; **-ing** n. grant, gift, donation.

'skennis ['skenəs] n. desecration.

skep ['skep] n. scoop; spoonful; dipper; scoop; v. (ge-) ladle; create; **-per** n. creator; **-pend** a. (-e) creative; **-ping** n. creation; **-sel** n. creature, being.

'**skepties** ['skeptis] *a.* (*-e*) sceptical.

skêr ['skeR] *n.* (*-e*) shears, scissors.

skerf ['skeRf] *n.* (*skerwe*) shard, sherd; chip.

skerm ['skeRəm] *n.* (*-s*) screen, curtain; shield; valance; protector; -bril *n.* goggles; *v.* (ge-) parry.

sker'mutseling [skeR'mʌtsələŋ] *n.* skirmish.

skerp ['skeRp] *a.* (*-e* ; *-er*, *-ste*) sharp; *av.* sharply; -'**sinnig** *a.* (*-e*) sharp, acute; -te *n.* sharpness.

skerpi'oen [skeRpi'un] *n.* (*-e*) scorpion.

'**skerpskutter** ['skeRpskʌtəR] *n.* sniper.

skerts ['skeRts] *n.* joking, jest, fun; *v.* (ge-) make fun, jest; -end *a.* (*-e*) for fun.

skets ['skets] *n.* (*-e*) sketch, draft; *v.* (ge-) sketch, picture; -'**matig** *a.* & *av.* (*-e*) sketchy.

skeur ['skêR] *n.* (*-e*) tear, rent, fissure, cleft; *v.* (ge-) tear, rend, rip; -buik *n.* scurvy; -sel *n.* scrap; -ing *n.* schism.

'**skielik** ['skilək] *a.* & *av.* sudden(ly).

'**skiereiland** ['skiRaylant] *n.* peninsula.

skiet ['skit] *v.* -gee, veer, slack; ease; *v.* (ge-) shoot, fire, blast; lend; -lood *n.* plummet.

skif ['skəf] *v.* (ge-) separate; curdle.

skik ['skək] *n.* pleasure, enjoyment; *v.* (ge-) arrange, order; -king *n.* arrangement; agreement; -lik *a.* (*-e*) obliging.

skil ['skəl] *n.* (*-le*) peel, rind, skin; *v.* (ge-) peel, pare, skin.

skild ['skilt] *n.* (*-e*) shield; escutcheon; badge.

'**skilder** ['skəldəR] *n.* painter; *v.* (ge-) paint; -'**agtig** *a.* (*-e*) picturesque; -ing *n.* depiction; -'y *n.* (*-e*) picture, painting.

'**skildwag** ['skeltvach] *n.* sentry, sentinel.

'**skilfer** ['skəlfəR] *n.* (*-s*) dandruff, scale; *v.* (ge-) scale, flake; -ing *n.* flaking.

'**skilpad** ['skəlpat] *n.* ('*skilpaaie*) tortoise; -jie *dim.* ladybird.

skim ['skəm] *n.* (*-me*) shadow, spectre.

'**skimmel** ['skəməl] *n.* mildew, mould, blight; roan.

skimp ['skəmp] *n.* (*-e*) gibe, jeer; allusion; *v.* (ge-) allude; -naam *n.* nickname.

'**skinder** ['skənəR] *v.* (ge-) slander; -aar *n.* slanderer; -bek *n.* slanderer; -praatjies *n. pl.* gossip, slander.

skink ['skənk] *v.* (ge-) pour, serve; -bord *n.* tray; -er *n.* butler.

skip ['skəp] *n.* (*skepe*) ship, boat; vessel; nave; -breuk *n.* shipwreck; -per *n.* (*-s*) master-boatman; -per *v.* (ge-) wangle.

'**skitter** ['skətəR] *v.* (ge-) sparkle, glitter; -end *a.* (*-e* ; *-er*, *-ste*) sparkling, brilliant; -ing *n.* radiance,

lustre, flashing, glaring; -skerm *n.* anti-dazzle screen; **skitte'ry** *n.* diarrhoea.

'**skobbejak** ['skobəyak] *n.* scoundrel, rogue.

skoei ['skui] *v.* (ge-) shoe; -sel *n.* footwear.

'**skoelapper** ['skulapəR] *n.* (*-s*) butterfly.

skoen ['skun] *n.* (*-e*) shoe, boot; lug; -lepel *n.* shoe-horn.

'**skoenlapper** ['skunlapər] *n.* (*-s*) butterfly = **skoelapper**.

skof ['skof] *n.* (*-te*) shift, stage; *n.* (*skouwe*) hump.

'**skoffel** ['skofəl] *n.* (*-s*) hoe; *v.* (ge-) hoe, weed, 'scuffle'.

skok ['skok] *n.* (*-ke*) shock, jolt, jerk; *v.* (ge-) shake, jolt; -kend *a.* (*-e*) shocking; -brekend *a.* (*-e*) shock absorbing; -breker *n.* shock absorber; -strook *n.* breaker.

sko'lier [skô'liR] *n.* (*-e*) pupil, scholar.

skollie ['skoli] *n.* (*-s*) ragamuffin.

'**skommel** ['skoməl] *v.* (ge-) wobble, roll; fluctuate; -ling *n.*

skone ['skonə] *n.* (*-s*) beauty.

skool ['skôl] *n.* (*skole*) school; shoal; *v.* (ge-) flock together; school; -s *a.* (*-e*) scholastic; school-; -vos *n.* pedant.

skoon ['skôn] *n.* the beautiful; *a.* fine, beautiful; *av.* clear; quite, completely; -dogter *n.* daughter-in-law; -ouers *n.* parents-in-law; -heid *n.* beauty; -skip *av.* -maak make a clean sweep; -veld *av.* clean gone.

'**skoonmoeder** ['skômudəR] *n.* mother-in-law.

'**skoonvader** ['skômfâdəR] *n.* father-in-law.

skoor ['skôR] *n.* (*-soek*) ask for trouble; *v.* (ge-) joke, tease; -voetend *av.* reluctantly.

'**skoorsteen** ['skôRstên] *n.* chimney.

skoot ['skôt] *n.* (*skote*) shot; time, turn; lap, womb, bosom.

skop ['skop] *n.* shovel, scoop; kick; *v.* (ge-) kick, recoil.

'**skopgraaf** ['skopchRâf] *n.* ('*skopgrawe*) shovel.

skor ['skoR] *a.* (*-*, *-e*) hoarse, husky, rough.

'**skorrie'morrie** ['skoRi'moRi] *n.* rabble.

skors ['skoRs] *v.* (ge-) suspend, adjourn; -ing *n.*

skort ['skoRt] *n.* (*-e*) apron; *v.* (ge-) be wrong, wanting (*lacking*); -ing *n.* thing wanting, (what is) the matter.

'**skot** ['skot] *n.* baffle; -plaat *n.* baffle plate; -ruit *n.* baffle window.

'**skotig** ['skôtəch] *a.* gradually sloping.

'**skottel** ['skotəl] *n.* (*-s*) dish, basin; disc.

'**skottelgoed** ['skotlchut] *n.* crockery; -water *n.* swill; -wiel *n.* disc wheel.

skou ['skoa] *v.* (ge-) view; inspect;

survey; -burg n. theatre; -spel n. spectacle, sight.

'skouer ['skoaəR] n. (-s) shoulder.

skraal ['skRāl] a. (-, skrale) thin, lean, poor; bleak, cutting; scanty.

skraap ['skRāp] n. (skrape) scratch; v. (ge-) scrape; pursue, chase; -sel n. scraping; -sug n. stinginess.

'skraus ['skRams] av. grazingly.

'skrander ['skRandəR] a. smart, clever, shrewd.

skrap ['skRap] av. jou -sit make a stand; -s a. & av. scarce(ly) poor(ly).

skrede ['skRēdə] n. (-s) step, stride.

skree ['skRē] n. shout, scream; v. (ge-) shout, scream, cry out.

'skreiend ['skRayənt] a. (-e) glaring.

skreeu ['skRēŏ] = skree; -lelik av. frightfully ugly.

skrif ['skRəf] n. (-te) writing; exercise book; -geleerd a. & av. knowing, cunning; -telik a. (-e) written.

skrik ['skRək] n. fright, terror, alarm; v. (ge-) start, get a fright; -'barend a. (-e) alarming; -beeld n. bugbear, bogy; -kerig a. (-e) jumpy, nervous; -'wekkend a. (-e) alarming.

'skrikkeljaar ['skRəkəlyāR] n. leap-year.

skril ['skRəl] a. (-le) shrill; glaring.

skroef ['skRuf] n. (skroewe) screw; propeller; vice; v. (ge-) screw; -hamer n. wrench, spanner; -draad n. male thread, screw thread; -sleutel n. shifting spanner.

skroei ['skRui] v. (ge-) scorch.

'skrompel ['skRompəl] v. (ge-) shrivel, wither.

skroom ['skRōm] n. diffidence, timidity; v. (ge-) hesitate, dread; -lik av. shamefully; -'vallig a. & av. (-e) diffident, bashful.

'skroot ['skRōt] n. scrap.

skryf ['skRayf] v. (ge-) write, correspond; -behoeftes n. stationery; -masjien n. typewriter; -trant n. style.

'skrynwerk ['skRaynvsRk] n. joinery; -er n. carpenter.

'skrywe = skryf n. letter; -r n. writer; author.

sku ['skew] av. shy, bashful, reserved.

skub ['skʌp] n. (-be) scale.

skud ['skʌt] v. (ge-) shake, tremble, jolt.

'skugter ['skʌchtəR] a. & av. (-, -e) timid, shy, coy.

skuif ['skœif] v. (ge-) push, shove, move; slide, shift; -dak n. sliding roof (hood); -deur n. sliding door; -passer n. calipers; -venster n. sliding window; -meule n. excuse, pretext.

skuil ['skœil] v. (ge-) shelter, hide, take cover; -ing n. cover, shelter; -naam n. pseudonym.

skuim ['skœim] n. foam, scum, skim; v. (ge-) foam, froth, scour; -pie

dim. meringue; -rubber n. foam rubber; -wyn n. sparkling wine.

skuins ['skœifis] a. & av. (-e) slanting(ly), oblique(ly); -te n. slope; -ing n. hypotenuse.

skuit ['skœit] n. (-e) boat; -jie dim.

skuld ['skʌlt] n. (-e) debt; guilt; v. (ge-) owe; -enaar n. (-s) debtor; -ig a. (-e) guilty, culpable; owing; -ige n. (-s) offender, culprit.

skulp ['skʌlp] n. (-e) shell; v. (ge-) scallop; -ie dim.

skulp'tuur [skʌlp'tēWR] n. sculpture.

'skurend ['skēWRənt] a. (-e) abrasive.

skurf ['skʌRf] a. (skurwe) mangy, chapped, scaly; -te n.

skurk ['skʌRk] n. (-e) villain, rogue; -agtig a. & av. vile, blackguardly; -ery n. villainy.

skut ['skʌt] n. (-s) marksman, shot; protection, protector; n. (-e) pound; v. (ge-) protect, guard; impound; -ter n. (-s) marksman, shot; -tery n. militia; -ting n. protection; impounding.

skuur ['skēWR] n. (skure) shed, barn; v. (ge-) rub, scrub, scour, chafe; -doek n. abrasive cloth; cp. skurend; -middel n. abrasive; -plek n. abrasion; -wol n. scouring wool.

skyf ['skayf] n. (skywe) target; slice; disc; -rem n. disc brake; -wiel n. disc wheel; -skiet n. target-shooting.

skyn ['skayn] n. appearance, semblance; glimmer; v. (ge-) shine; appear; -baar a. & av. (-bare) apparent(ly); -beeld n. phantom, -dood n. coma; -geveg n. mock-fight; -'heilig a. (-e) hypocritical; -'heilige n. (-s) hypocrite; -sel n. glow; -vrede n. false peace; -werper n. search-light.

'slae ['släə] n. pl. cuts, blows; cp. slag.

slaaf ['släf] n. (slawe) slave; v. (ge-) slave, toil; -s a. (-e) servile.

slaag ['släch] v. (ge-) succeed; -s av. -raak come to blows.

slaai ['släi] n. salad, lettuce.

slaak ['släk] v. (ge-) breathe, heave, utter.

slaan ['slän] v. (ge-) strike, beat, hit; thrash, slap; -de a. striking; -ding n. cane, whip.

slaap ['släp] n. (slape) temple; sleep; v. (ge-) sleep, be asleep; -been n. temporal bone; -deuntjie n. lullaby; -dronk a. drowsy.

'slaapklere ['släpklēRə] n. pyjamas.

slag ['slach] n. (slae) blow, stroke, beat, lash, clap; trick, turn, twist; kind, ilk; v. (ge-) slaughter, kill; -aar n. artery; -boom n. barrier; -pen n. quill-feather; -tand n. tusk; -ter n. butcher; -tery n. butchery; -ting n. slaughter, carnage; -'vaardig a. (-e) ready for the fray; -yster n. trap.

'slaggat ['slachat] n. (slaggate) pot-hole.

'slaghuis ['slachœis] n. (-e) butchery;
cp. slagter.
'slagoffer ['slachofəR] n. (-s) victim,
dupe.
'slagpale [slachpålə] n. abattoir.
slak ['slak] n. (-ke) snail, slug; slag.
'slak(ke)huis ['slak(ə)hœis] n. cochlea.
'slaklokaas ['slaklok-ås] n. snail bait.
Slams ['slams] a. (-e) Moslem,
Malay.
slang ['slang] n. (-e) snake; hosepipe.
slank ['slank] a. (-, -e) slim, willowy
slender; -heid n.
slap ['slap] a. & av. slack, soft,
weak, lɛx, limp; -heid n.; -pies av.
slackly, weakly; -te n. slackness,
dullness; -hang v. (-ge) sag; -te n.
slack, recession; -tyd n. slack
period; -uur n. slack period.
'slapend ['slåpənt] a. (-e) dormant.
slawer'ny [slåvəR'nay] n. slavery,
bondage; drudgery.
slee ['slē] n. (sleë), sleigh, sledge.
sleep ['slēp] n. drag, tow; train; v.
(ge-) drag, pull, haul, tug, tow; -sel
n. trail; -stang n. towing pole; -tou
n. tow rope; -wa n. trailer; -weer-
stand n. drag; -woonwa n. trailer,
caravan.
sleg ['slech] a. & av. (-te) bad(ly),
evil(ly); -gerig av. poorly; -s av.
only, merely; -te n. the bad; -theid
n. badness, evilness; -ting n.
demolition.
'slenter ['slentəR] v. (ge-) saunter.
'slet ['slet] n. slut.
'sleur ['slœR] n. routine.
sleutel ['slœtəl] n. (-s) key; spanner.
'slik ['slək] n. sludge, cp. slyk.
slim ['sləm] a. (-, -me) smart,
crafty; cunning; -heid n.; -praatjies
n. glib talk.
'slinger ['sləngəR] n. pendulum;
handle; v. (ge-) swing, sway,
wobble; -pad n. winding-path;
-plant n. creeper; -wydte n. amplitude.
slink ['slənk] v. (ge-) shrink,
dwindle; -s a. & av. (-, -e) surrepti-
tious.
slip ['sləp] n. (-pe) tail, flap.
sloer ['slūR] v. (ge-) drag, dawdle.
'sloerie ['sluRi] n. slut.
slof ['slof] v. (ge-) shuffle; -fie n. (-s)
slipper.
slons ['slaufis] n. slut; -erig a. (-e)
slatternly.
sloof ['slōf] v. (ge-) = slaaf v.
sloop ['slōp] n. (slope) slip, pillow-
case; v. (ge-) level, raze.
sloot ['slōt] n. (slote) furrow, trench.
'slopwa ['slopvå] n. sanitary tanker.
'slordig ['sloRdəch] a. & av. (-e; -er,
-ste) untidy, slovenly.
slot ['slot] n. (-te) lock, clasp; castle;
n. end, conclusion; -jie ('sloiKi) dim.
little lock; -veer n. (slotvere) lock
spring.
slu ['slew] a. (-we) crafty, wily.

'sluier ['slœiəR] n. (-s) veil; v. (ge-)
veil, conceal.
sluiks ['slœiks] ter- av. slyly.
'sluimer ['slœiməR] v. (ge-)
slumber, doze; -ing n.
sluip ['slœip] v. (ge-) slink, sneak,
prowl; -moord n. assassination.
sluis ['slœis] n. (-e) sluice, lock;
-deur n. sluice gate.
sluit ['slœit] v. (ge-) close; lock;
conclude; effect; -ing n. closing;
closure; locking; -spier n. sphincter;
- -en-breek n. make and break;
-kas n. locker; -moer n. lock nut,
check nut; -waster n. locking
washer.
sluk ['slʌk] n. (-ke) gulp, mouthful,
draught; pharynx; v. (ge-) swallow,
gulp; -derm n. gullet.
slurp ['slʌRp] n. trunk (elephant);
v. (ge-) guzzle, gulp.
'slyk ['slayk] n. mud, sludge.
slym ['slaym] n. mucus, slime; -erig
a. (-e) slimy.
'slymvlies ['slaymflis] n. (-e)
mucous membrane.
slyp ['slayp] v. (ge-) sharpen, whet,
grind; cut; polish; -ery n. grinding,
cutting-works; -er n. grinder; -mas-
jien n. grinder (machine); -pasta n.
grinding paste; -steen n. grindstone.
slyt ['slayt] v. (ge-) wear out;
sly'tasie n. wear, wastage; -end a.
(-e) wasting; -stuk n. lining; -vlak
n. lined face.
smaad ['småt] n. contumely, abuse,
insult, opprobrium; v. (ge-) malign,
revile; -smadelik a. derisive.
smaak ['såmk] n. taste, flavour,
liking; v. (ge-) taste; enjoy; appear;
seem; -lik a. (-e; -er, -ste) palatable,
delicious; -loos a. (-lose) tasteless;
-vol av. tastefully.
smaal ['småil] v.(ge-) sneer, deride.
smag ['smach] v. (ge-) pine; yearn;
-tend a. (-e) yearning.
smal ['smal] a. & av. (-, -le)
narrow.
sma'rag [sma'Rach] n. (-de)
emerald.
smart ['smaRt] n. (-e) grief,
sorrow; v. (ge-) grieve, pain; -lik a.
(-e; -er, -ste) painful.
smee ['smē] v. (ge-) forge, hammer;
fabricate, hatch; -staal n. forged
steel; -werk n. forging.
smeek ['smēk] v. (ge-) implore,
entreat, beseech.
smeer ['smēR] v. (ge-) smear;
grease; v. (ge-) grease, lubricate;
butter; smear; -boel n. dirty mess;
-goed n. embrocation, liniment; -sel
n. liniment; ointment, dressing;
-der n. lubricator; -gat n. lubricating
hole; -middel n. lubricant; -olie n.
lubricating oil; -winkel n. lubrito-
rium.
'smeerlap ['smēRlap] n. skunk, cad;
-lappery n. filth.
smelt ['smelt] v. (ge-) melt, smelt;
-baar a. (-bare) fusible; -draad n.

fuse; **-ery** n. foundry; **-kroes** n. crucible; **-middel** n. flux; **-room** n. vanishing cream.

'**smerig** ['smĕRəch] a. (-e; -er, -ste) dirty, filthy; *cp.* **smeer**.

'**smering** ['smĕRəng] n. lubrication.

smet ['smet] n. (-te) stain, blot; taint; **-loos** a. (-lose) stainless, immaculate.

smeul ['smĕl] v. (ge-) smoulder.

'**smeulstoof** ['smœlstōf] n. ('smeul-stowe) slow combustion stove.

smid ['smət] n. (smede) = **smit**.

smit ['smət] n. (-te, -s) smith, blacksmith.

smoel ['smul] n. (-e) mug.

'**smokkel** ['smokəl] v. (ge-) smuggle; **-aar** n. smuggler; **-ary** n. smuggling.

smoor ['smōR] av. exceedingly; v. (ge-) smother; **smoor-** *pref.* exceedingly; **-der** a. choke; **-klep** n. choke valve.

'**smorens** ['smŏRŏns] av. in the morning.

smous ['smoas] n. (-e) hawker, pedlar, chapman; v. (ge-) hawk.

smout ['smoat] n. grease, fat, lard; **-werk** n. jobbing.

smul ['smʌl] v. (ge-) feast.

smyt ['smayt] v. (ge-) fling, hurl, cast.

s'n ['sən(ə)] *poss. pron.* -'s; *pa*-father's; *cp.* **syne**.

snaaks ['snăks] a. & av. (-e; -er, -ste) funny, queer, droll; **-erig** a. & av. funny, strange.

'**snaar** ['snăR] n. (snare) string; v. (ge-) string.

snags ['snachs] av. in the night.

snap ['snap] v. (ge-) catch, understand.

'**snaps** ['snaps] n. (-e) tot; **-sie** n. (*dim.*) tot.

'**snater** ['snătəR] n. (-s) mug; v. (ge-) chatter, jabber.

'**snawel** ['snăvəl] n. (-s) bill, beak.

'**snedig** ['snĕdəch] a. (-e) smart, witty.

'**sneespapier** ['snĕspapiR] n. tissue paper.

sneeu ['snĕŏ] n. snow; v. (ge-) snow; **-jag** n. snow-drift.

snel ['snel] a. & av. (-, -le) fast, swift(ly), quick(ly); v. (ge-) hurry, hasten; **-heid** n. speed; **-ler** n. trigger; sprinter; **-skrif** n. shorthand; **-skrywer** n. stenographer; **-gang** n. overdrive; **-gangreëlaar** n. overdrive governor; **-pad(-weg)** n. express way; **-vries** v. (ge-) quick freeze.

'**snerpend** ['sneRpənt] a. (-e) biting, piercing.

snert ['sneRt] n. rubbish, rot, trash.

'**sneuwel** ['snœvəl] v. (ge-) fall, be killed.

snik ['snək] n. (-ke) sob, gasp; v. (ge-) sob; **-heet** av. swelteringly hot.

'**snipper** ['snəpəR] n. (-s) scrap, chip; v. (ge-) snip, shred; **-ig** a. (-e) perky, saucy; **-tjie** n. snippet.

snit ['snət] n. cut; edge; *cp.* **sny**.

snoei ['snui] v. (ge-) prune, trim; **-er** n. pruner.

snoek ['snuk] n. (-e) barracouta, pike, 'snoek'.

snoep ['snup] a. greedy; v. (ge-) eat furtively; **-erig** a. greedy; **-ery** n. sweets, eatables.

snoer ['snūR] n. (-e) line, string; v. (ge-) tie, string; silence a person.

snoet ['snut] n. (-e) snout, muzzle, nose.

snood ['snōt] a. (snoder, -ste) evil, base, vile.

snor ['snauR] n. (-e) moustache; v. (ge-) drone, purr.

snork ['snoRk] n. snoring; snort; v. (ge-) snore; snort.

snot ['snot] n. mucus, snot; **-terig** a. (-e) snotty.

snou ['snoa] v. (ge-) snarl.

'**snuffel** ['snʌfəl] v. (ge-) sniff, nose; pry.

snuif ['snœif] n. snuff; v. (ge-) sniff, take snuff.

'**snuistery** ['snœistəRay] n. (-e) knick-knack.

snuit ['snœit] n. snout, *cp.* **snoet**; v. (ge-) blow one's nose.

'**snuiter** ['snœitəR] n. (-s) youngster; snuffers.

sny ['snay] n. (-e) cut, gash, slice; v. (ge-) cut, castrate; sprint; **-dend** a. (-e) cutting, biting; **-er** n. (-s) tailor, cutter; **-sel** n. (-s) home-made vermicelli; **-tand** n. incisor.

so ['sō] av. so, thus, like this.

'**sober** ['sōbəR] a. frugal.

so'danig [sō'dānəch] *pron.* such, such like.

'**sodat** ['sōdat] *conj.* so that.

'**sodoende** ['sōdundə] av. thus, consequently.

so'dra [sō'dRă] av. as soon as.

'**soebat** ['subat] v. (ge-) coax, cajole, entreat.

soek ['suk] v. (ge-) seek, look for, hunt for.

soen ['sun] n. (-e) kiss; v. (ge-) kiss; **-offer** n. sacrifice of atonement.

'**soepel** ['supəl] a. (-, -e) supple, pliant.

soet ['sut] a. sweet; **-erig** a. (-e) sweetish; **-a'maling** n. tuberose; **-lemoen** n. orange; **-riet** n. sugar-cane; **-sappig** a. (-e) sloppy; **-sopie** n. liqueur.

soewe'rein [suvə'rayn] a. (-e) sovereign.

'**sogenaamd** ['sōchənāmt] a. (-e) so-called; av. ostensibly.

'**soggens** ['sochŏns] av. in the morning.

'**soheentoe** ['sōintu] av. thither.

'**sok** ['sok] n. (-ke) socket; **-sleutel** n. box spanner.

'**sokkie** ['soki] n. (-s) sock.

so'lank ['sōlank] *conj.* for the time being, meanwhile.

sol'daat [sol'dāt] n. (sol'date) soldier.

sol'deer [sol'dēR] v. (ge-) solder; **-sel** n. solder.

'solder ['soləR] n. (-s) loft; ceiling; -ing ['soldəRəng] n. ceiling.

sol'dy [sol'day] n. pay.

solidari'teit [sŏlidaRi'tayt] n. solidarity.

so'lied ['sŏlit] a. (-e) solid, substantial.

solo ['sŏlŏ] n. (-'s) solo.

sol'vent [sol'fent] a. solvent.

som ['som] n. (-me) sum.

somber ['sombəR] a. (-e; -der, -ste) sombre, gloomy; -heid n.

'somer ['sŏməR] n. (-s) summer; -s a. (-e) summer-.

'sommer ['soməR] av. for no reason at all; straight off, without difficulty; -so av. simply; so-so.

'sommige ['soməchə] pron. some.

soms ['soms] av. sometimes, at times.

'somtyds ['somtayts] av. = soms.

son ['son] n. (-ne) sun; -besie n. (-s) cicada; -nig a. (-e) sunny; -onder n. sunset; av. at sunset; -op n. sunrise; av. at sunrise; sonne- = son; sonneblom n. sunflower.

'sonbrand ['sonbRant] n. sunburn; -middel n. sunburn lotion; -olie n. sunburn oil.

'sonbril ['sonbRəl] n. sun glasses.

'sondaar ['sondăR] n. (-s) sinner; sonda'res n. fem. sinner.

'Sondag ['sondach] n. Sunday.

'sonde ['sondə] n. (-s) sin; trouble; -bok n. scapegoat.

'sonder ['sonəR] prep. without; -ling n. eccentric; a. queer.

'sondig ['sondəch] v. (ge-) sin; a. (-e; -er, -ste) sinful, peccable.

'sonkieltjie [săŭñ'kilKi] n. dim. jonquil.

son'net [so'net] n. (-te) sonnet.

soog ['sŏch] v. (ge-) suckle, nurse; -dier n. mammal; -tyd n. period of lactation.

sooi ['sŏi] n. (-e) sod; -brand n. heartburn.

sool ['sŏl] n. (sole) sole.

soölo'gie [sŏ-ŏlŏ'chi] n. zoology.

soom ['sŏm] n. (some) hem; edge, border; seam; v. (ge-) hem, border.

'soontoe = 'soheentoe.

soort ['sŏRt] n. (-e) sort, kind, species; -lik a. (-e) specific; -gelyk a. (-e) similar.

soos ['sŏs] conj. like, such as; just as.

sop ['sop] n. soup; juice; cp. sap; -perig a. (-e) juicy.

sorg ['soRch] n. (-e) care, trouble, worry; one who takes care of; v. (ge-) mind, see, care for, take care of; -'barend a. alarming; -saam a. (-same) painstaking; -'vuldig a. (-e) a. (-e) careful, thorough.

sor'teer [soR'tĕR] v. (ge-) sort, grade; -der n. sorter, grader.

sosi'aal [sŏsi'ăl] a. (sosiale) social; sosialis n. Socialist.

sot ['sot] n. & a. (-te) fool; mad; -ter'ny n. foolishness.

sous ['soas] n. gravy, sauce, relish; v. (ge-) rain, pour.

sout ['soat] n. salt; a. salt, briny; v. (ge-) salt; become immune; -erig a. (-e) saltish, brackish; -igheid n. saltness; savoury; -suur n. hydrochloric acid.

'soveel ['sŏfĕl] av. so much; so many; as much (as).

'sover ['sŏfeR] av. so far, thus far.

so'waar [sŏ'văR] av. actually, to be sure.

'sowat ['sŏvat] av. about, roughly.

so'wel [sŏ'vel] av. & conj. as, as well as.

spaan ['spăn] n. (spane) ladle; oar.

'spaander ['spănəR] n. (-s) chip, splinter; v. (ge-) scoot, run, skedaddle.

spaar ['spăR] v. (ge-) spare; save; -saam a. (-same) thrifty.

'spaarbank ['spăRbank] n. savings bank.

spalk ['spalk] n. (-e) splint; v. (ge-) set, splint.

span ['span] n. (-ne) team; gang; span; v. (ge-) stretch; strain; draw; hobble; -werk n. team-work; -nend a. (-e) exciting; -ning n. tension, strain; -wydte n. spread.

span'deer [span'deR] v. (ge-) spend.

span'spek [spăñ'spek] n. cantaloup.

spar ['spaR] n. (-re) rafter.

'spartel ['spaRtəl] v. (ge-) flounder, struggle; -ing n. struggle.

spasie ['spăsi] n. (-s) space, room, opening.

spat ['spat] n. (-te) splash, spatter, spot; v. (ge-) splash, splutter, spatter; take to one's heels; -sel n. (-s) splash, spot, stain; -bord n. splash board; -skerm n. splash guard; -vlek n. blotch.

'spatlys ['spatlays] n. (-te) skirting.

'speeksel ['spĕksəl] n. spittle, sputum; -pomp n. saliva pump.

speel ['spĕl] v. (ge-) play; act; chime; gamble; -baar a. (-bare) playable; -goed n. toys; -s a. & av. playful; speel-speel av. & a. playing, easily.

spek ['spek] n. bacon, pork; -skiet v. (-ge-) fib; -steen n. French chalk.

spek'takel [spǝk'tăkəl] n. (-s) scene, row, rumpus; sight.

'spektrum ['spektRʌm] n. spectrum.

speku'lant [spǝkǝ'lant] n. (-e) -speculator; speku'lasie n. speculation; speku'leer v. (ge-) speculate.

spel ['spel] n. (spele) game; play; performance; v. (ge-) spell; -etjie dim.; spelling n. spelling, allowance; -ling n. spelling.

speld ['spelt] n. (-e) pin; v. (ge-) pin, fasten.

'speling ['spĕlǝng] n. lash; play; slack.

spe'lonk [spǝ'lonk] n. (-e) cave.

spens ['speñs] n. (-e) pantry.

'sper ['speR] v. (ge-) jam, bar = versper; -rat n. ratchet.

spese'ry [spǝsǝ'Ray] n. (-e) spice.

spesi'aal [spisi'āl] a. & av. (*spesiale*) special(ly); **spesia'lis** n. (-te) specialist; **spesiaali'seer** v. (ge-) specialize.

spesi'fiek [spəsə'fik] a. & av. (-e) specific'ally.

speur ['spœR] v. (ge-) detect; trail; -der n. detective.

'spieël ['spiil] n. (-s) mirror; v. (ge-) mirror, reflect; -beeld n. reflection, image, illusion; -glas n. plate glass.

spier [spiR] n. (-e) muscle; -wit a. snow-white.

spies ['spis] n. (-e) spear, javelin.

spil ['spəl] n. (-le) spigot, axle, arbour, mandrel, pivot, spindle.

'spinnekop ['spənəkop] n. (-pe) spider.

spi'oen [spi'un] n. (-e) spy, scout; v. (ge-) spy, scout; **spioe'nasie** n. espionage; **spioe'neer** v. (ge-) spy, scout.

spi'raal [spi'Rāl] n. spiral.

spiri'tis [spiRi'təs] n. (-te) spiritualist.

spit ['spət] n. (-te) spit, spadeful; lumbago; v. (ge-) dig; -graaf n. spade, cp. **graaf**; -vurk n. garden fork, cp. **vurk**.

spits ['spəts] n. (-e) point; peak; spire; van; a. (-e) pointed; v. (ge-) point; -neus n. pointed nose; -uur n. rush-hour; -'vondig a. (-e) subtle, ingenious.

'spits- ['spəts-] pref. n. crest, peak, top; a. tapered.

spleet ['splēt] n. (*splete*) crack, fissure, gap.

'splint ['splənt] n. (-ers) splinter.

'splinter ['spləntəR] n. (-s) splinter, sliver.

'splinternuut ['spləntəRnewt] a. ('*splinternuwe*) brand-new.

splits ['spləts] v. (ge-) split, cleave; -ing n. fision; -las n. splice; -moer n. split nut; -pen n. cotter pin; -las n. splice.

splyt ['splayt] v. (ge-) split, cleave.

spoed ['sput] n. speed, haste; v. (ge-) hurry, hasten; -eisend a. (-e) urgent; -ig a. & av. (-e; -er, -ste) quick(ly); -waggel n. speed wobble.

spoeg ['spuch] n. s '+tle; v. (ge-) spit, expectorate.

spoel ['spul] n. (-e) spool, shuttle, coil; v. (ge-) flow, wash, rinse; -ing n. n.

spog ['spoch] v. (ge-) boast; brag; -gerig a. (-e; -er, -ste) boastful; showy; -ter n. boaster; -tery n. boasting.

'spokery ['spōkəRay] n. struggle; haunting; cp. **spook**.

spons ['spauñs] n. (-e) sponge: v. (ge-) sponge; -rubber n. sponge rubber.

spon'taan [spon'tān] a. (*spon'tane*) spontaneous.

spook ['spōk] n. (*spoke*) ghost, spook; freak; v. (ge-) haunt; struggle; -agtig a. (-e; -er, -ste) spectral; -sel n. ghost.

spoor ['spōR] n. (*spore*) trail; rail;

trace; track; spur; spore; v. (ge-) trail; travel by rail; spur; align; -slag n. incentive, spur.

'spoorlyn ['spōRlayn] n. railway line; **spoorlynoorgang** n. crossing, level crossing; **'spoorweg** n. (*weë*) railway; **'spoorwegstasie** n. railway station.

spo'radies [spo'Rādis] a. (-e) sporadic(al).

'sporing ['spōRəng] n. *uit -uit* out of alignment.

sport ['spoRt] n. (-e) rung; sport; -baadjie n. blazer; **spor'tief** a. (*sportiewe*) sporting.

spot ['spot] n. scorn, ridicule; mockery; banter; v. (ge-) mock, jeer, jest, joke; -goedkoop av. dirt cheap; -lag n. laugh of derision; -naam n. nickname; byword; -prent n. caricature; -prys n. bargain; -tend a. (-e) jeering; -terny (-te'ry) n. mockery, raillery; -voël n. mocker, teaser.

spraak ['sprāk] n. speech; -saam a. (-same) talkative; **sprake** n. talk, mention.

spreek ['sprēk] v. (ge-) speak; -taal n. spoken language; -woord n. (-e) proverb.

'spreekkamer ['sprēkāməR] n. (-s) consulting room.

'spreekuur ['sprēk-ēwR] n. consulting hour.

spreeu ['sprēö] n. (-s) starling.

sprei ['sprRay] n. (-e) quilt, bedspread; v. (ge-) spread.

spreuk ['sprRēk] n. (-e) motto; proverb.

spring ['sprRəng] v. (ge-) jump, leap, spring; skip; snap; -er n. jumper; -fontein n. fountain; -stof n. explosive.

'sprinkaan ['sprRəng'kān] n. ('*sprinkane*) locust, grasshopper.

sproei ['sprRui] n. spray; v. (ge-) spray, sprinkle; -puit n. spray gun.

sproet ['sprRut] n. (-e) freckle.

'sprokie [sprRōki] n. (-s) fairy tale.

sprong ['sprRong] n. (-e) jump, leap.

spruit ['sprRœit] n. (-e) sprout; offspring; stream; v. (ge-) shoot, sprout; issue, descend.

spuit ['spœit] n. (-e) syringe, squirt; v. (ge-) spout, spray; -water n. aerated water; -verf n. spray paint; v. (ge-) to spray paint.

spul ['spAl] n. lot, caboodle; affair; -letjie dim.

spy ['spay] n. (-e) pin, cotter.

'spyker ['spaykəR] n. (-s) nail.

spyse ['spaysə] n. food; **spysig** v. (ge-) feed; **spyskaart** n. menu.

spyt ['spayt] n. regret, sorrow, compunction; v. (ge-) regret, be sorry.

staaf ['stāf] n. (*stawe*) bar, rod; ingot; v. (ge-) confirm, prove, substantiate.

staak ['stāk] v. (ge-) stop, strike; stall.

staal [stāl] n. steel, sample; v. (ge-) steel; -tjie dim. sample.

staan ['stān] v. (ge-) stand; remain upright; exist; stop; -dak n. pitched roof; -de a. standing, permanent; -koste standing charges; -der n. standard; -spoor n. uit die from the word go; staan-staan av. standing, haltingly.

'staangeld ['stānchelt] n. demurrage.

'staanleer ['stānlēR] n. (staanlere) step ladder.

'staanplek ['stāmplek] n. standing room; parking space.

staar ['stāR] n. pearl-eye; grou-(groen-) glaucoma; v. (ge-) stare, gaze.

staat ['stāt] n. (state) state, condition; position; record; -maker n. stalwart; -sgreep n. coup d'état; -sreg n. constitutional law.

'staatsdiens ['stātsdiñs] n. civil service.

sta'biel [sta'bil] a. (-e) stable; stabili'sasie n. stabilization; stabili-'seer v. (ge-) stabilize; stabili'teit n. stability.

stad ['stat] n. (stede) city, town; -shuis n. city-hall; -sraad n. municipality.

'stadig ['stādəch] n. & a. (-e) slow; -aan av. slowly.

staf ['staf] n. (stawe) staff, mace, support.

'stakker ['stakəR] n. (-s) poor devil. stal ['stal] n. (-le) stable; -letjie dim. booth.

stam ['stam] n. (-me) stem; tribe, race; v. (ge-) form stems; descend from; -boek n. stud-book; -boom n. pedigree; -verwant a. cognate.

'stamel ['stāməl] v. (ge-) stammer.

stamp ['stamp] v. (ge-) knock, pound, crush; -er n. pounder, tamper, jumper, pestle.

stand ['stant] n. position; posture; state; degree, rank; station, class, caste.

stand'aard [stan'dāRt] n. (-e, -s) standard.

'standbeeld ['stantbēlt] n. (-e) statue.

'standerd ['standərt] n. (-s) standard, class.

'standjie ['staingKi] n. (-s) row.

'standpunt [stantpʌnt] n. point of view.

stand'vastig [stant'fastəch] a. (-e) steadfast.

stang ['stang] n. (-e) bit; rod.

stank ['stank] n. stench, stink.

stap ['stap] n. (-pe) step, pace, stride; footstep; v. (ge-) walk; -voets av. at a walking pace.

stapel ['stāpəl] n. (-s) pile; stock; stack; tier; v. (ge-) pile up, stack; -gek av. stark mad.

'stasie ['stāsi] n. (-s) station; stasio-'neer v. (ge-) station.

'statebond ['stātəbont] n. federation of nations.

'staties ['stātis] a. (-e) static.

'statig ['stātəch] a. (-e; -er, -ste) stately, ceremonious.

statis'tiek [statəs'tik] n. statistics; n. pl. (-e) returns.

sta'tuut [sta'tēwt] n. statute; statu-'têr a. (-e) statutory.

'stawel = stapel.

'stawing ['stāvəng] n. cp. staaf v.

steeds ['stēts] a. (-e) urban, town-; av. always, ever.

steek ['stēk] n. (steke) stitch; stab; prod; v. (ge-) prick, stab, jab; burn, smart; -pan n. bed-pan; -proef n. sample; -s a. (-e) jibbing.

steel ['stēl] v. (ge-) steal; n. (stele) handle; stem, stalk; -kant n. blind-side; -s a. & av. stealthy, furtive.

steen ['stēn] n. (stene) brick; rock; -druk n. lithograph; -groef n. quarry; -bouer n. mason; -kool n. coal.

'steggie ['stəchi] n. (-s) cutting, slip.

'steier ['stayəR] n. (-s) scaffolding; v. (ge-) stagger, rear.

steil ['stayl] a. steep, precipitous; -te n. steepness, incline.

stel ['stel] n. (-te) set; lot; chassis; suite; v. (ge-) put, place; adjust; compose; direct, aim; -kunde n. algebra.

stel'lasie [stə'lāsi] n. (-s) scaffolding; frame-work.

'stellig ['steləch] a. & av. positive(ly).

'stelling ['steləng] n. (-s) proposition; premise; thesis.

'stelsel ['stelsəl] n. (-s) system; -'matig a. systematic.

stem ['stem] n. (-me) voice; v. (ge-) vote; tune; -bande n. vocal chords; -buiging n. modulation; -bus n. poll; -hebbend a. (-e) voiced; -loos a. (-lose) voiceless; -mig a. (-e) sedate, demure; -ming n. mood; ballot; -reg n. franchise.

'stempel ['stempəl] n. (-s) stamp, seal, die; v. (ge-) stamp, mark, brand.

'stenig ['stēnəch] v. (ge-) stone.

steno'graaf [stēnō'chRāf] n. (steno-'grawe) stenographer.

ster ['steR] n. (-re) star; -re ['stɛRə] pl. buttocks.

stereo'tiep [stērēō'tip] a. (-e) stereotype.

sterf ['sterf] v. (ge-) die; -bed n. death-bed; -geval n. death; -lik a. (-e; -er, -ste) mortal; -ling n. mortal being; -te n. mortality.

'sterftesyfer ['steRftəsayfəR] n. death rate.

ste'riel [stə'Ril] a. (-e) sterile.

sterk ['steRk] a. (-e; -er, -ste) strong; v. (ge-) strengthen, invigorate; -ing n. strengthening; -te n. strength; -water n. spirits.

stert ['stert] n. (-e) tail, brush; rear; stert- þerf. caudal.

sterwe = sterf.

steun ['stēn] n. support, aid; stay,

prop; v. (ge-) support; groan, moan; -sel n. support.

'steunpunt ['stœmpʌnt] n. fulcrum.

steur ['stœR] v. (ge-) disturb; take notice of; -end a. (-e; -er, -ste) disturbing; -ing n. disturbance; -nis n. disturbance.

'stewel ['stēvəl] n. (-s) boot.

'stewig ['stēvəch] a. (-e; -er, -ste) solid, stout; v. firmly, stiffly.

stief ['stif] a. step; stief- prep. step-.

stier ['stiR] n. bull.

'stiffie ['stəfi] n. (-s) small rod, pin, stick.

stig ['stəch] v. (ge-) found, establish, institute, start; -ter n. founder; -ting n. foundation.

'stigtelik ['stəchtələk] a. (-e) edifying.

stik ['stək] v. (ge-) stitch, suffocate.

'stikstof ['stəkstof] n. nitrogen.

'stil ['stəl] a. (-, -e; -er, -ste) quiet, calm, silent; v. (ge-) allay; hush; -letjies av. quietly; -te n. silence.

sti'lis [sti'ləs] n. (-te) stylist, -'tiek n. style; sti'listies a. (-e) stylistic.

'stilstand ['stəlstant] n. truce; standstill.

stimu'lasie [stimew'lāsi] n. stimulation; stimu'leer v. (ge-) stimulate; stimulus n. (-se) stimulus.

'stingel ['stəngəl] n. (-s) stem, stalk.

stink ['stənk] a. stinking; v. (ge-) stink, smell bad; -end a. (e-) stinking; -besie n. dim. bug; -erd n. stinker; -erig a. (-e) smelly; -hout n. stinkwood.

stip ['stəp] a. & av. (-te) punctual, strict; -telik av. promptly; -theid n. punctuality.

'stippel ['stəpəl] n. (-s) speck, dot; v. (ge-) dot, point; stipple; -lyn n. dotted line.

stipu'lasie [stəpə'lāsi] n. stipulation; stipu'leer v. (ge-) stipulate.

stoei ['stui] v. (ge-) wrestle.

stoel ['stul] n. (-e) chair, seat, stool; v. (ge-) stool; -gang n. stool, motion, defecation.

stoep ['stup] n. (-e) stoep.

stoer ['stūR] a. sturdy, stout, hardy.

stoet ['stut] n. (-e) procession; stud, flock; -ery n. stud; -s a. obtuse, blunt.

stof ['stof] n. (stowwe) dust, powder; stuff, material, matter; v. (ge-) dust; -bril n. goggles; -'fasie n. material, stuff, quality; -'feer v. (ge-) upholster; -fer n. duster; -fig a. (-e; stouwige) dusty; -lik a. (-e) material, corporeal; -nat av. sprinkled, wet on top; -reën n. drizzle; -suier n. vacuum cleaner.

stok ['stok] n. (-ke) stick, staff, pole, club, pointer; v. (ge-) stop, flag; stok- pref. superlative degree; -blind a. & av. stone-blind; -perdjie n. hobby; -kerig a. (-e) stalky, fibrous; stocky.

'stokery ['stōkəRay] n. distillery.

'stokkiesdraai ['stokisdRāi] v. (-gedraai) play truant.

'stokperdjie ['stokpeRKji] n. hobby.

stol ['stol] v. (ge-) freeze, clot, congeal; -ling n.

stom ['stom] a. (-me; -mer, -ste) -dronk a. dead-drunk; -heid n. dumbness; -mi'teit n. blunder.

'stommerik ['stoməRək] n. (-ke) dunce, blunderer.

stomp ['stomp] n. (-e) stub, stump; a. blunt, dull; -ie dim. stub, fag; -'sinnig a. (-e) stupid, dull.

stoof ['stōf] n. (stowe) stove; v. (ge-) stew, cook, broil; swelter.

stook ['stōk] v. (ge-) stoke, fire, burn; distil; stir up.

stoom ['stōm] n. steam; v. (ge-) steam.

stoot ['stōt] n. (stote) push, thrust, stroke; v. (ge-) push, thrust, bump; jostle; butt.

'stootkussing ['stōtkʌsəng] n. buffer.

'stootstoel n. wheelchair.

stop ['stop] n. (-pe) darn; plug; v. (ge-) stop, plug, fill up; darn; stuff; bundle, cram; pull up; halt; -mes n. putty knife; -pel n. stubble; -pelrig a. stubby; -sel n. filling; -verf n. putty.

'storie ['stōRi] n. (-s) story, tale, yarn.

storm ['stoRəm] n. (-s) storm, gale; assault; v. (ge-) storm; -agtig a. (-e; -er, -ste) stormy; -bui n. squall; -loop n. & v. attack; -wind n. gale.

stort ['stoRt] v. (ge-) pour; spill; deposit; plunge; -bad n. shower-bath; -ing n. deposit; -vloed n. flood; -vragmotor n. dump lorry.

'stotter ['stotəR] v. (ge-) stutter, stammer.

stout ['stoat] a. naughty; bad; bold; -erd n. (-s) naughty child; -igheid n. naughtiness; -'moedig a. (-e) bold.

straal ['stRāl] n. (strale) beam, ray, flash; v. (ge-) shine, glow, radiate; -breking n. refraction.

straat ['stRāt] n. (strate) street; strait; v. (ge-) pave.

straf ['stRaf] n. (strawwe) punishment; a. & av. (strawwe; strawwer, -ste) severe, stern; v. (ge-) punish; -baar a. (-bare) punishable, culpable; -heid n. severity; -reg n. criminal law.

strak ['stRak] a. (-, -ke) taut, tight; severe; -kies av. presently; -s av. perhaps; presently.

stram ['stRam] a. (-, -me) stiff, rigid; -merig a. (-e) slightly stiff.

strand ['stRant] n. (-e) beach, seaside; v. (ge-) strand; -'jut n. beach-comber; hyena; -skoen n. sand-shoe.

strate'gie [stRatə'chi] n. strategy; stra'tegies a. (-e) strategic.

'streber ['stRēbəR] n. (-s) = strewer.

streef ['stRêf] v. (ge-) strive, endeavour.

streek ['stRêk] n. (streke) region, area; trick, wile, joke.

streel ['stRêl] v. (ge-) fondle, caress.

streep ['stRêp] n. (strepe) stroke, line; stripe, streak; dash; v. (ge-) mark with a line; lick.

strek ['stRek] v. (ge-) stretch, reach; last; **-king** n. tendency, drift; purport, sense; **-kende voet** n. long foot; **-vermoë** n. coverage.

strem ['stRem] v. (ge-) curdle; strain, hinder; **-ming** n. curdling; hindrance; **-sel** n. curds; rennet.

streng ['stReng] a. (-e; -er, -ste) strict, stringent, vigorous, austere, dour.

'strewe = **streef**.

'strewer ['stRêvəR] n. (-s) (social) climber.

striem ['stRim] n. (-e) weal; v. (ge-) castigate.

strik ['stRək] n. (-ke) knot, bow; snare; a. (-te) strict; v. (ge-) tie a bow; ensnare; **-vraag** n. poser.

string ['stRəng] n. (-e) string; thread; skein; trace.

stroef ['stRuf] a. (stroewe) stiff; gruff, surly.

'strofe ['stRôfə] n. (-s) strophe; **-fies** a. (-e) strophic.

'stroming ['stRomən] n. (-e, -s) stream, current; tendency.

stronk ['stRonk] n. (-e) stalk.

strooi ['stRôi] n. straw; v. (ge-) sow, strew, scatter; **-huis** n. native hut; **-jonker** n. best man; **-meisie** n. bridesmaid; **-suiker** n. castor-sugar.

strook ['stRôk] n. (stroke) strip; frill; counterfoil; v. (ge-) agree, tally.

'strookpad ['stRôkpat] n. (strook-paaie) strip road.

stroom ['stRôm] n. stream, current; torrent; v. (ge-) stream, flow, rush; **-belyn** a. (-de) stream-lined; **-pie** dim.

'stroombaan ['stRômbān] n. circuit (electr.); **'stroomsterkte** n. amperage; **'stroomverbreker** n. cutout.

'stroop ['stRôp] n. syrup, treacle; v. (ge-) strip; pillage, poach; **-soet** a. honey-sweet; **-tog** n. raid.

'stroper ['stRôpəR] n. (-s) poacher; stripper (harvest).

strot ['stRot] n. (-te) throat.

struik ['stRœik] n. (-e) shrub; **-rower** n. highway-robber.

'struikel ['stRœikəl] v. (ge-) stumble, trip.

struk'tuur [stRʌk'têwR] n. (struk-'ture) structure.

'struweling ['stRewvələng] n. (-s) trouble, ruction.

stry ['stRay] v. (ge-) fight, struggle; argue; dispute; contradict; **-ery** n. argument.

stryd ['stRayt] n. fight, battle, struggle, conflict; **-ig** a. (-e) conflicting; **-'vaardig** a. (-e) ready for the fray.

stryk ['stRayk] v. (ge-) walk, stride; smooth, iron; **-goed** n. laundry; **-stok** fiddlestick; **-yster** n. flat iron.

stu ['stew] v. (ge-) push, press; impel; stow; dam up; **-dam** n. weir, barrage; **-wer** n. impeller; **-werblad** n. impeller blade.

stu'deer [stew'dêR] v. (ge-) study; prepare for an examination.

stu'dent [stew'dent] n. (-e) student; **stu'dente** fem. student.

'studie ['stewdi] n. (-s) study.

stug ['stʌch] a. (-, -ge) reserved, stiff, curt.

stuif ['stœif] v. (ge-) be dusty; fly; rush; puff; **-poeier** n. dusting powder; **-sand** n. drift sand.

'stuipe ['stœipə] n. pl. convulsion; **stuipagtig** a. (-e) convulsive; **stuip-trekking** n. convulsion.

stuit ['stœit] v. (ge-) check, arrest, stop; **-end** a. (-e) objectionable; **-ig** a. (-e; -er, -ste) objectionable; **-jie** dim. coccyx.

'stuiwe = **stuif**.

stuk ['stʌk] n. (-ke) piece, fragment; paper, document; play; **-goed** n. piece-goods; **-kend** a. (-e; -er, -ste) in pieces, torn; **-kie** dim. morsel.

stut ['stʌt] n. (-te) prop, support, stay; buttress; strut; v. (ge-) support, prop.

stuur ['stêwR] n. (sture) steering; handles; rudder; v. (ge-) send; drive; steer; **-s** a. (-e) curt, bruff, surly; **-kajuit**, **-kap** n. driver's cab; **-kolom** n. steering column; **-slot** n. steering lock; **-stang** n. steering rod.

styf ['stayf] a. (stywe) stiff, rigid; starched; v. (ge-) starch; **-te** n. stiffness.

styg ['staych] v. (ge-) rise; climb; increase; **-slag** n. upstroke.

styl ['stayl] n. style; post; stanchion.

'stysel ['staysəl] n. starch.

'stywe = **styf**.

subsi'die [sʌp'sidi] n. subsidy.

sub'skripsie [sʌp'skRəpsi] n. subscription.

substan'tief [sʌpstan'tif] n. (substan-'tiewe) substantive noun.

sub'tiel [sʌp'til] a. (-e) subtle.

suf ['sʌf] a. dull, stupid.

'sufferd ['sʌfəRt] n. (-s) dotard.

sug ['sʌch] n. (-te) sigh; desire; pus; v. (ge-) sigh.

sugge'reer [sʌchə'RêR] v. (ge-) suggest.

suid ['sœit] a. south; **suid** pref. south; **-e** n. die- the south; **-elik** a. & av. (-e) southerly; southwards.

'suiderlig ['sœidəRləch] aurora australis.

'suier ['sœiəR] n. (-s) piston, sucker; **-ring** n. piston ring; **-stang** n. piston rod.

suig ['sœich] v. (ge-) suck; **-ing** n. suction; **-eling** n. infant, baby; **-tablet** n. lozenge.

'suiker ['sœikəR] n. sugar.

suil ['sœil] n. (-e) pillar, column, pile.

'**suinig** ['sœinəch] *a.* (-*e*; -*er*, -*ste*) stingy, miserly; -**ies** *av.* sparingly, thriftily.

suip ['sœip] *n.* drinking, booze; *v.* (ge-) guzzle; booze; drink.

suis ['sœis] *v.* (ge-) buzz, sing, sigh; -**ing** *n.* buzzing.

'**suiwel** ['sœivəl] *n.* dairy products.

'**suiwer** ['sœivəR] *a.* (-, -*e*; -*der*, -*ste*) pure, clean; *v.* (ge-) purify, castigate; -**end** *a.* (-*e*) purifying; -**ing** *n.* purification; -**aar** *n.* purifier; -**loop** to run true; -**olie** *n.* straight oil.

'**sukkel** ['sʌkəl] *v.* (ge-) plod, trudge; -**aar** *n.* mug.

suk'ses [sʌk'ses] *n.* (-se) success; -**vol** *a.* (-le) successful.

'**sulke** ['sʌlkə] *a.* & *pron.* such; '**sulks** *pron.* as- as such.

sult ['sʌlt] *n.* brawn.

superi'eur [sewpēRi'œR] *n.* & *a.* superior.

'**suring** ['sēWRəng] *n.* sorel.

'**surplus** ['sʌRplʌs] *n.* (-se) surplus.

sus ['sʌs] *n.* sister - **suster**; *av.* thus; *v.* (ge-) hush, soothe.

sus'pisie [sʌs'pisi] *n.* suspicion.

'**suster** ['sʌstəR] *n.* (-s) sister; -**lik** *av.* sisterly; -**skind** *n.* sister's child (*niece or nephew*).

suur ['sēWR] *n.* (sure) acid; heartburn; acidity; *a.* (-, sure; -*der*, -*ste*) sour, acid, acrid; peevish; -**bestand** *a.* acid-proof; -**deeg** *n.* yeast; -**gehalte** *n.* acidity; -**klontjies** *n.* acid-drops; -**lemoen** *n.* lemon; -**pruim** *n.* kill-joy; -**stof** *n.* oxygen; -**vas** *a.* - **suurbestand**.

'**suutjies** [sewKis] *av.* quietly, stealthily.

'**swaai** ['swāi] *n.* (-*e*) swing; sweep; *v.* (ge-) swing, wield, wave, flourish.

swaan ['swān] *n.* (swane) swan.

swaap ['swāp] *n.* (swape) fool, idiot, dunce, simpleton.

swaar ['swāR] *a.* (-, *sware*) heavy; big, severe; serious; deep; -**moedig** *a.* (-*e*) depressed; -**te** *n.* weight.

swaard ['swāRt] *n.* (-*e*) sword; -**lelie** *n.* gladiolus.

'**swaarte** ['swāRtə] *n.* - **swaarte- krag**.

'**swaartekrag** ['swāRtəkRach] *n.* gravity.

swael ['swāl] *n.* swallow; sulphur; -**stert** *n.* dove-tail; -**stertbaadjie** *n.* tails.

swaer ['swāR] *n.* (-s) brother-in-law.

swak ['swak] *n.* weakness; *a.* (-, -*ke*) weak, feeble; delicate; poor; faint; attenuated; -**keling** *n.* weakling; -**kies** *av.* weakly, poorly; -'**sinnig** *a.* (-*e*) mentally defective; -**te** *n.* weakness.

'**swakheid** ['swakhayt] *n.* debility; weakness.

swam ['swam] *n.* (-*me*) fungus.

'**swanedons** ['swānədauns] *n.* swan's down.

swang ['swang] *n.* in- in vogue.

'**swanger** ['swangəR] *a.* pregnant; -**skap** *n.* gestation.

swart ['swaRt] *n.* black; *a.* (-*e*) black; -**e** *n.* (-s) black one; -'**gallig** *a.* (-*e*) pessimistic; -**sel** *n.* blacking; -**smeer** *v.* (-ge-) blacken.

'**swartmaraai** ['swaRtmə'Rāi] *n.* black Maria.

'**swawel** - **swael**.

'**swawelkruid** ['swāvəlkRœit] *n.* gaillardia.

'**swawelsuur** ['swāvəlsēWR] *n.* sulphuric acid.

sweef ['swēf] *v.* (ge-) float, hover, soar.

'**sweem** ['swēm] *n.* trace, semblance.

sweep ['swēp] *n.* (swepe) whip; -**slag** *n.* lash.

sweer ['swēR] *n.* (swere) ulcer, tumour; *v.* (ge-) fester; swear, take an oath; -**lik** *av.* surely.

sweet ['swēt] *n.* sweat; perspiration; *v.* (ge-) perspire, sweat; cure; -**gat** *n.* pore; -**vos** *n.* sorrel.

sweis ['sways] *v.* (ge-) weld, forge; -**ing** *n.* welding; -**las** *n.* & *v.* weld; -**soldeer** *v.* (ge-) braze; -**staaf** *n.* welding rod; -**werk** *n.* welding.

swel ['swel] *v.* (ge-) swell, dilate; -**ling** *n.* swelling; -**sel** *n.* swelling, tumour.

swelg ['swelch] *v.* (ge-) swill, swallow, guzzle, live voluptuously.

swem ['swem] *v.* (ge-) swim.

'**swendel** ['swendəl] *v.* (ge-) swindle; -**aar** *n.* swindler; -**a'ry** *n.* swindling.

swenk ['swenk] *v.* (ge-) swerve; -**ing** *n.* swerve.

swerf ['swaRf] *v.* (ge-) rove, wander, tramp; -**ling** *n.* wanderer; -**tog** *n.* wandering(s); -**sand** *n.* drift-sand, *cp.* stuifsand.

swerm ['sweRəm] *n.* (-s) swarm, crowd; *v.* (ge-) swarm, cluster, crowd.

'**swernoot** ['sweRnōt] *n.* scoundrel, skunk.

'**swerwe** - **swerf**.

'**swets** ['swets] *v.* (ge-) swear.

'**swier** ['swiR] *n.* elegance, swagger.

'**swewe** - **sweef**.

'**swierig** ['swiRəch] *a.* (-*e*) dashing, jaunty, showy.

swig ['swech] *v.* (ge-) give way, yield.

swik ['swək] *v.* (ge-) stumble.

swoeg ['swuch] *v.* (ge-) toil, drudge, labour (engine).

'**swoel** ['swul] *a.* sultry, close.

'**swye** ['swayə] *n.* silence.

swyg ['swaych] *v.* (ge-) be silent.

sy ['say] *n.* silk; *a.* (-*e*) side, flank; *pron.* she; his, its; *v.* *dit* -so so be it; -**delings** *a.* (-*e*) sidelong, lateral.

'**syfer** ['sayfəR] *n.* (-s) cipher; figure; rate; *v.* (ge-) reckon, calculate, cipher; ooze, filter.

'**syg** ['saych] *v.* (ge-) strain, filter.

'**syne** ['saynə] *pron.* his.

'**sypaadjie** ['saypāiKi] *n.* (-s) sidewalk.

'**sypapier** ['saypəpiR] *n.* tissue paper.

T

taai ['tāi] a. (-e; -er, -ste) tough; sticky; viscous; hardy; **-erig** a. (-e) sticky; **-pit** n. clingstone.

taak ['tāk] n. task.

taal ['tāl] n. (tale) language, speech; **-boek** n. grammar; **-eie** n. idiom; **-geleerde** n. (-s) philologist; **-kunde** n. philology; **-skat** n. vocabulary.

'**taamlik** ['tāmlək] a. & av. (-e) fair(ly), passable(-ly).

ta'bak ['tabak] n. tobacco.

ta'bel [ta'bel] n. (-le) table, list; **-'leer** v. (ge-) = tabuleer.

'**tabbert** ['tavəRt] n. (-s) dress.

tab'let [ta'blet] n. (-te) tablet.

ta'boe [ta'bu] n. taboo.

tabu'leer [tabew'lēR] v. (ge-) tabulate.

taf ['taf] n. taffeta.

'**tafel** ['tāfəl] n. (-s) table, index; **-gebed** n. grace; **-goed** n. table-linen; **-doek** n. tablecloth.

'**tagtig** ['tachtəch] num. eighty.

'**taggentig** = tagtig.

tak ['tak] n. (-ke) branch, bough.

'**takel** ['tākəl] n. (-s) tackle; pulleys; v. (ge-) rig; knock about, maul.

tak'seer [tak'sēR] v. (ge-) tax, value, appraise.

tak'tiek [tak'tik] n. tactics; '**taktikus** n. (-se) tactician.

tal ['tal] n. (-le) number.

ta'lent [ta'lent] n. (-e) talent.

talk ['talk] n. talc.

talm ['taləm] v. (ge-) linger, dawdle.

'**talryk** ['talRək] a. (-e; -er, -ste) numerous.

tam ['tam] a. (-me) weary, fatigued.

ta'maai [ta'māi] a. huge, enormous.

ta'matie [ta'māti] n. (-s) tomato.

tam'boer [tam'būR] n. (-e) drum; drummer.

tamme'letjie [tamə'lɛKi] n. (-s) toffee.

tand ['tant] n. (-e) tooth; prong; tine; **-epasta** n. tooth-paste.

'**tande-** ['tan(d)ə-] pref. tooth-, teething, dental; **-krale** n. plur. teething beads; **-plaat** n. teething ring; **-room** n. dental cream = tandepasta; **-skerm** n. tooth guard; **-vlos** n. dental floss.

tang ['tang] n. (-e) pincers, tongs, pliers.

'**tangens** ['tangchens] n. (tangente) tangent.

'**tannie** ['tani] n. (-s) aunt, lady.

tans ['tans] av. now, nowadays.

'**tante** ['tantə] n. (-s) = tannie.

tap ['tap] n. (-pe) tap; spigot, lug; tenon; v. (ge-) tap, draw off; **-bout** n. stud; **-s** a. tapered.

'**taptoe** ['taptu] n. tattoo.

ta'pyt [ta'payt] n. (-e) carpet.

taren'taal [taRən'tāl] n. (taren'tale) guinea-fowl.

ta'rief [ta'Rif] n. (ta'riewe) tariff.

tart ['tart] v. (ge-) defy, dare, provoke; **-tend** a. (-e) defying, provoking.

tas ['tas] v. (ge-) grope, feel; n. (-te) bag, wallet; **-baar** a. (-bare) tangible; tactile.

'**tawwerd** = tabbert.

te ['tə] prep. at, in, to; av. too.

te'ater [tə'ātəR] n. (-s) theatre.

tee ['tē] n. tea; **-lepel** n. (-s) tea-spoon; **-suiker** n. sugar candy.

teë- ['tē-', tēə-] pref. against = teen.

'**teef** ['tēf] n. (tewe) bitch.

teël ['tēl] n. (-s) tile.

te:l ['tēl] v. (ge-) breed, raise, cultivate; **-t** n. culture; cultivation.

teen ['tēn] n. against, con; prep. against, at, by; **teen-** pref. against; **-deel** n. contrary, opposite; **-kom** n. (-ge-) meet, come up against; **-oor** prep. & av. opposite; over against, in contrast with; **-praat** v. (-ge-) contradict; **-sin** n. dislike; **-sit** v. (-ge-) resist; **-spoed** n. adversity; **-stand** n. resistance; **-stander** n. opponent; **-'strydig** a. (-e) conflicting; **-'swoordig** a. present; av. nowadays; **swerk** v. (-ge-) thwart; **-wig** n. counterbalance; **-'woordig** a. (-e) present.

'**teengestelde** ['tēnchəsteldə] n. (-s) antonym.

'**teengewig** ['tēnchəvəch] n. (-te) counterbalance.

'**teenspoedwa** ['tēnsputvā] n. breakdown van.

'**teenstelling** ['tēnsteləng] n. (-s) contrast.

teer ['tēR] n. tar; a. (tere) tender, frail; v. (ge-) tar, sponge on.

tege'lyk [təchə'layk] av. at the same time; **-ertyd** av. = tegelyk.

teg'niek [tech'nik] n. technics; technique; **-'tegnies** a. (-e) technical.

teiken ['taykən] n. (-s) target.

'**teikenskiet** ['taykənskit] v. (-geskiet) target shooting.

'**teister** ['taystəR] v. (ge-) ravage, afflict.

'**teken** ['tēkən] n. (-s) sign; signal; mark; trace; symptom; v. (ge-) sign, sketch, plot; **-end** a. (-e) characteristic; **-ing** n. signing; drawing.

te'kort [tə'koRt] n. deficit; **-koming** n. (-e) fault, imperfection.

te'kortskiet [tə'koRtskit] v. (-geskiet) fall short of.

teks ['teks] n. (-te) text.

teks'tiel [teks'til] n. textile.

tel ['tel] n. count; v. (ge-) count, number; **-baar** a. (-bare) numerable; **-ling** n. count, numeration; census; score.

tele'drukker [telə'dRʌkəR] n. (-s) teleprinter.

tele'foon ['tēlə'fōn] n. (telefone) telephone; **telefo'neer** v. (ge-) telephone; **tele'fonies** a. (-e) telephonic.

tele'graaf ['tēlə'chRāf] n. telegraph; **telegra'fie** n. telegraphy; **tele-'grafies** a. (-e) telegraphic.

tele'gram [tĕlə'chRam] n. (-me) telegram, wire.

telepa'tie [tĕləpa'ti] n. telepathy.

tele'skoop [tĕlə'skŏp] n. (tele'skope) telescope.

te'leurstel [tə'lĕRstel] v. (teleurge-) disappoint; -ling n. disappointment.

tele'visie [tĕlə'visi] n. television.

'telg ['telch] n. (-e) offspring, scion.

'telkens ['telkŏns] av. time and again.

'teller ['telər] n. (-s) teller, counter.

'telwoord ['telvŏRt] n. numeral.

tem ['tem] n. (ge-) tame, subdue, break in.

'tema ['tĕma] n. (-s) theme, subject.

'temerig ['tĕməRəch] a. (-e) drawling.

'tempel ['tempəl] n. (-s) temple.

'temper ['tempəR] v. (ge-) temper, mitigate, soften.

tempera'ment [tempəRa'ment] n. temperament.

tempera'tuur [tempəRa'tĕwR] n. (tempera'ture) temperature.

'tempo ['tempŏ] n. (-'s) tempo, time.

temp'tasie [tem'tăsi] n. temptation; **temp'teer** v. (ge-) tempt, vex, annoy.

tenk ['tenk] n. (-s) tank.

ten'minste [tə'mŏnstə] av. at least.

ten'sy [ten'say] av. unless.

tent ['tent] n. (-e) tent.

ten'toonstelling [ten'tŏnstelŏng] n. (-s) show.

teolo'gie [tĕŏlŏ'chi] n. theology.

teo'rie [tĕŏ'Ri] n. theory; **teo'reties** a. (-e) theoretical; **teoreti'seer** v. (ge-) theorise.

'tepel ['tĕpəl] n. (-s) nipple, papilla, teat.

te'reg [tə'rech] av. rightly, justly; -**stel** v. (teregge-) put on trial, execute; -**te** av. properly, by rights; -**wys** v. (teregge-) reprove; direct.

terg [teRch] v. (ge-) tease, irritate, provoke; -**end** a. (-e) provoking; -**ery** n. teasing.

'tering ['tĕRəng] n. consumption.

ter'loops [təR'lŏps] a. & av. casual(ly), incidental(ly).

term ['teRəm] n. (-e) term; expression.

'terminus ['teRminʌs] n. (-se) terminus.

'termometer ['teRmŏmĕtəR] n. (-s) thermometer.

ter'myn [təR'mayn] n. (-e) term, period, time; instalment.

ter'nouernood [təR'noaəRnŏt] av. scarcely, hardly.

ter'ras [tə'Ras] n. (-se) terrace.

ter'rein [tə'Rayn] n. (-e) ground, site, plot, terrain, area, sphere.

ter'sluiks [təR'slœiks] av. stealthily.

ter'stond [təR'stont] av. immediately.

ter'sy [təR'say] av. aside.

tert ['teRt] n. (-e) tart.

te'rug ['tRʌch] av. back, backwards; **terug-** pref. back, backwards, re-; -**blik** n. retrospect; -**deins** v.

(terugge-) flinch; -**getrokke** a. reserved; -**houdend** a. (-e) reserved; -**keer** v. (terugge-) return; -**koms** n. return; -**slag** n. repercussion; -**werkend** a. (-e) retrospective; -**wys** v. (terugge-) refer back.

te'rug'kruising [tə'Rʌch'kRœisəng] n. backcross.

te'rugplof [tə'rʌchplof] v. (-ge-) back-fire.

ter'wyl [təR'vayl] conj. while, whilst, whereas.

te'saam [tə'săm] av. together.

te'same = tesaam.

'tesis ['tĕsəs] n. (-se) thesis.

tesou'rie [tesoa'Ri] n. treasury; **tesou'rier** n. treasurer.

testa'ment [təstə'ment] n. (-e) will, testament.

'teuel ['tœəl] n. (-s) bridle, rein.

tever'geefs [təfəR'chĕfs] av. in vain, vainly.

te'vore [tə'fŏRə] av. previously.

te'vrede [tə'fRĕdə] a. satisfied, content; -**nheid** n. satisfaction; complacence.

te'weegbring [tə'vĕchbRəng] v. (-gebring) effect, cause.

'tewens ['tĕvŏns] av. at the same time.

'tiekie ['tiki] n. (-s) tickey, three-pennny-bit.

'tiekiedraai ['tikidrăi] v. (-gedraai) do folk dances.

tien ['tin] num. ten.

tier ['tiR] n. (-s) tiger; S.A. leopard; v. (ge-) thrive; rage; -**melk** n. booze.

tik ['tək] v. (ge-) tick, click, pat, touch; -**ster** n. typist.

'tikmasjien ['təkmashin] n. (-e) typewriter.

'timmer ['təməR] v. (ge-) do carpentry work.

tingerig ['təngəRəch] a. (-e) slender.

'tint ['tənt] v. (ge-) tinge, tint.

'tintel ['təntl] v. (ge-) twinkle, sparkle.

'tipe ['tipə] n. (-s) type; **ti'peer** v. (ge-) typify; **tipies** a. (-e) typical.

'titel ['titl] n. (-s) title.

'tjalie ['tshăli] n. (-s) shawl.

tjank ['tshank] v. (ge-) whine, yelp, howl.

'tjankbalie ['tshankbăli] n. (-s) cry-baby.

tjap ['tshap] n. (-pe) stamp, post-mark; v. (ge-) stamp.

tjek ['tshek] n. (-s) cheque.

'tjoepstil ['tshupstəl] av. absolutely silent.

'tjorrie ['tsyoRi] n. (-s) crock, ramshackle car, jalopy.

toe ['tu] a. closed, shut; av. then, at that time; conj. when; as, while; -**dig** v. (-ge-) impute; -**doen** n. aid; -**gang** n. entrance; -'**ganglik** a. (-e) accessible; -**gee** v. (-ge-) concede; -'**geeflik** a. (-e) indulgent; -**geneë** a. affectionate; -**gif** n. (-te) extra, encore; -**hoorder** n. listener; -**koms** n. future; -**laag** (-lae) n. grant, subsidy; -lig *v.* (-ge-) explain; -nader *v.* (*toege-*) approach; -'reikend *a.* (-e) adequate; -rus *v.* (-ge-) equip; -sig *n.* supervision; -skouer *n.* spectator; -spraak *n.* speech; -staan *v.* (-ge-) accede; -stel *n.* apparatus; -takel *v.* (*toege-*) maul; -tree *v.* (-ge-) join up; -val *n.* chance; -'vallig *a.* & *av.* accidental(ly); -vlug *a.* refuge; -voeg *v.* (-ge-) add; -voegsel *n.* supplement; -voer *n.* supply.

'toejuig [tuy'œich] *v.* (-ge-) cheer, applaud; -ing *n.* applause.

'toelê ['tulɛ] *v.* (-ge-) devote oneself to.

'toeloop ['tulõp] *n.* concourse, throng.

'toename ['tunãmə] *n.* increase.

'toenmaals ['tunmãls] *av.* at that time.

'toepas ['tupas] *v.* (-ge-) apply, put into practice; -lik *a.* suitable.

'toeplak ['tuplak] *v.* (-ge-) cover up; mask (*spray painting*).

toer ['tūR] *n.* tour; toe'ris *n.* (-te) tourist.

toer'nooi [tuR'nõi] *n.* tournament.

'toesê ['tusɛ] *v.* (-ge-) promise.

'toeskroei ['tuskRui] *v.* (-ge-) cauterize.

'toeslag ['tuslach] *n.* surcharge.

'toespeling ['tuspɛləng] *n.* (-s) innuendo.

'toestand ['tustant] *n.* (-e) circumstances.

toet ['tut] *v.* (ge-) hoot; -er *n.* hooter; *v.* (ge-) toot.

toets ['tuts] *n.* test; *v.* (ge-) test, try.

toe'vallig [tu'faləch] *a.* (-e; -er, -ste) accidental, casual; *av.* accidentally; -heid *n.* chance; contingency.

tog ['toch] *n.* (-te) journey, expedition; draught; *av.* nevertheless, still, all the same; -tig *a.* (-e) draughty.

'toiings ['tɔiəngs] *n.* tatters, rags.

toi'let [twa'let] *n.* toilet.

'tokkel ['tokl] *v.* (-ge-) strum.

tok'tokkie [tok'toki] *n.* tapping beetle, toktokkie.

tol ['tol] *n.* (-le) top; toll, customs; bobbin, spool; drum, reel.

'tolbos ['tolbos] *n.* (-se) plume leucadendron.

tolk ['tolk] *n.* (-e) interpreter; mouth-piece.

ton ['ton] *n.* (-ne) ton.

to'neel [tõ'nēl] *n.* (*tonele*) stage; scene; theatre; -agtig *a.* (-e) theatrical; -wese *n.* stage.

tong ['tong] *n.* (-e) tongue; sole; -val *n.* dialect.

'tonnel ['tonəl] *n.* (-s) tunnel; *v.* (ge-) tunnel.

'tontel ['tauntl] *n.* tinder; -doos *n.* tinder-box.

tooi ['tõi] *v.* (ge-) decorate, adorn; -sel *n.* (-s-) trimming.

toom ['tõm] *n.* (-s, *tome*) bridle, check.

toon ['tõn] *n.* (*tone*) toe; tone; *v.* (ge-) show; -bank *n.* counter; -hoogte *n.* pitch; -kuns *n.* music;

-set *v.* (ge-) compose, set to music.

toor ['tõR] *v.* (ge-) conjure; practise witchcraft; -dery *n.* witchcraft; -goed *n.* charms, dope.

'toonbeeld ['tõnbēlt] *n.* paragon.

'toorn [tõRəng] *n.* anger; -ig ['tõRnəch] *av.* angry.

toorts ['tõRts] *n.* (-e) torch.

top ['top] *n.* (-pe) top; peak; tip; *v.* (ge-) top, lop, clip; *interj.* done!

tor ['toR] *n.* (-re) beetle; bumpkin.

'toring ['tõRəng] *n.* (-s) tower.

tor'pedo [toR'pēdõ] *n.* (-'s) torpedo; torpe'deer *v.* (ge-) torpedo.

'torring ['toRəng] *v.* (ge-) unstitch; pester.

tot ['tot] *prep.* till, until, to, as far as; *conj.* till, until.

to'taal [tõ'tãl] *n.* (*to'tale*) total; *a.* (*to'tale*) total; *av.* totally.

'totdat ['todat] *conj.* till, until.

tou ['toa] *n.* (-e) string, rope; queue; *v.* (ge-) follow in a line; -staan *v.* (-ge-) queue; -wys *a.* broken in, tamed.

'toulei ['toalay] *v.* (-ge-) lead a team; -er *n.* leader of team.

'touweefsel ['toavēfsəl] *n.* webbing.

'touwerk ['toavɛRk] *n.* rigging.

'tower = toor; -y *n.* magic.

traag ['tRāch] *a.* (*trae*) sluggish, lazy, inert.

traak ['tRāk] *v.* (ge-) *dit -jou nie* it doesn't concern you.

traan ['tRān] *n.* (*trane*) tear; fish-oil; blubber; *v.* (ge-) water.

tra'disie [tRa'disi] *n.* (-s) tradition.

trag ['tRach] *v.* (ge-) try.

tra'gedie [tRa'chēdi] *n.* (-s) tragedy; 'tragies *a.* (-e) tragic.

trak'teer [tRak'tēR] *v.* (ge-) treat.

'tralie ['tRāli] *n.* (-s) trellis; spike, bar.

tran'saksie [tRãn'saksi] *n.* (-s) transaction.

trans'port [tRãns'poRt] *n.* transport; transfer.

trant ['tRant] *n.* manner, style, way.

trap ['tRap] *n.* (-pe) step; staircase; *v.* (ge-) tread, pedal, thresh; -sgewyse *a.* & *av.* gradual(ly).

tra'want [tRa'vant] *n.* (-e) henchman.

'tred ['tRet] *n.* pace, step, tread.

tree ['tRē] *n.* pace, step; *v.* (ge-) step, walk, tread.

tref ['tRef] *v.* (ge-) strike, hit; find, meet; -fend *a.* (-e) striking; -fer *n.* (-s) hit; -krag *n.* force of impact; -punt *n.* point of impact.

'tregter ['tRechtəR] *n.* (-s) funnel.

trein ['tRayn] *n.* (-e) train.

trek ['tRek] *n.* (-ke) pull, haul, draught; migration; journey; stage; appetite; desire; trait; *v.* (ge-) pull; journey; migrate; move; -ker *n.* trigger; -kings *n.* convulsions; -laken *n.* drawsheet; -pad *n.* trail; -paal *n.* straining post; -pleister *n.* attraction; -sel *n.* enough coffee (tea) for a brew; -skaal *n.* spring balance; **-spanning** n. tension; **-vry** a. draught free; **-watte** n. thermal wool; **-spier** n. extensor.

trem ['tRem] n. (-s; -me) tram.

treur ['tRœR] v. (ge-) grieve, mourn; **-ig** a. (-e; -er, -ste) sad, mournful; **-igheid** n. sadness; sorrow; **-spel** n. tragedy.

'**triestig** ['tRistəch] a. (-e) gloomy, dismal, dreary.

'**trietserig = triestig.**

tril ['tRəl] v. (ge-) tremble, vibrate; **-ling** n. vibration; **-bord** n. flutterboard; **-hare** n. pl. cilia.

trio ['triö] n. (-'s) trio.

tri'omf [tRi'omf] n. triumph; **triom'feer** v. (ge-) triumph; **triom'fantlik** a. & av. (-e) triumphant(ly).

troef ['tRuf] n. (troewe) trump; v. (ge-) trump.

'**troei** ['tRui] interj. back! cp. terug.

'**troepe** ['tRupə] n. pl. troops.

'**troetel** ['tRutəl] v. (ge-) caress, fondle, pamper.

tro'fee [tRo'fē] n. (tro'feë) trophy.

'**troffel** ['tRofəl] n. (-s) trowel.

'**trog** ['tRoch] n. (trôe) chute; trough.

trok ['tRok] n. (-ke) truck; v. (ge-) truck.

'**trollie** ['tRoli] n. (-s) trolley.

trom ['tRom] n. drum; **-mel** n. drum; v. (ge-) drum; **-meldik** a. satiated; **-melvlies** n. ear-drum.

tromp ['tRomp] n. muzzle.

trom'pet [tRom'pet] n. (-te) trumpet.

'**tronie** ['tRöni] n. face, mug.

tronk ['tRonk] n. (-e) goal; **-straf** n. imprisonment.

troon ['tRön] n. (trone) throne.

troos ['tRôs] n. comfort, consolation; v. (ge-) console.

trop ['tRop] n. (-pe) flock, herd.

'**trope** ['tRöpə] n. tropics.

tros ['tRos] n. (-se) bunch, cluster.

trots ['tRots] n. & a. pride, proud.

trot'seer [tRot'sēR] v. (ge-) defy, dare.

trou ['troa] n. fidelity; faith; a. faithful, loyal; v. (ge-) marry, wed; **-breuk** n. breach of faith; **-ens** av. indeed, for that matter; **-breuk** n. perfidy, breach of trust; te goeder - in good faith, bona fide.

tru ['tRew] v. (ge-) reverse, back; **-kaatser** n. (-s) retro-reflector; **-lamp** n. reversing lamp; **-lig** n. reversing light; **-rat** n. reverse gear.

trui ['tRœi] n. (-e) sweater, jersey.

tuberku'lose [tewberkew'lösə] n. tuberculosis.

tug ['tʌch] n. discipline; punishment; v. (ge-) punish, chastise; **-tig** v. (ge-) chastise, punish, castigate.

tuig ['tœich] n. (tuie) harness; rigging; gear.

'**tuimel** ['tœiməl] v. (ge-) tumble.

tuin ['tœin] n. (-e) garden; **-bou** n. horticulture; **tui'nier** n. gardener; **-slang** n. hose.

tuis ['tœis] av. at home; **-hoort** v. (-ge-) belong; **-huis** n. town-house, week-end house; **-koms** n. arrival; **-te** n. home.

tuit ['tœit] n. (-e) spout, nozzle; v. (ge-) tingle.

'**tulband** ['tʌlbant] n. turban.

tulp ['tʌlp] n. (-e) tulip.

turf ['tʌRf] n. peat; turf; clayey soil.

turks'vy [tʌRks'fay] n. (-e) prickly pear.

'**tussen** ['tʌsən] prep. between, among, surrounded by; **-koms** n. intervention; **-werpsel** n. interjection.

'**tussenas** ['tʌsənas] n. countershaft.

'**tussenkap** ['tʌsənkap] n. cowl.

'**tussenrat** ['tʌsənRat] n. idler (gear wheel).

'**tussen'stedelik** ['tʌsən'stēdələk] a. (-e) intercity.

twaalf ['twālf] num. twelve.

twak ['twak] n. = tabak; tobacco; **-praatjies** n. piffle.

twee ['twē] num. two; **-de** ord. second; -'**delig** a. (-e) bipartite; **-drag** n. discord; -'**ledig** a. (-e) binary, binomial; **-ling** n. (-e) twins; **-sprong** n. cross-roads; -'**talig** a. (-e) bilingual.

'**tweebaanpad** ['twēbānpat] n. double-lane road.

'**tweenderangs** ['twēdəRangs] a. second-rate.

'**tweedoel'voertuig** ['twēdul'fuRtœich] n. dual purpose vehicle.

'**tweegangmotor** ['twēchangmötəR] n. two-speed motor.

'**tweeslag** ['twēslach] a. two-stroke.

twee'snydend [twē'snaydənt] a. two-edged.

'**tweewaardigheid** ['twēvāRdəchayt] n. ambivalence.

'**twintig** ['twəntəch] num. twenty.

twis ['twəs] n. (-te) quarrel; v. (ge-) quarrel.

'**twissiek** ['twəsik] a. (-e) quarrelsome.

'**twyfel** ['twayfəl] n. doubt, question, v. (ge-) doubt; -'**agtig** a. (-e) doubtful; **-ing** n. doubt, hesitation.

tyd ['tayt] n. (tye) time; season; tense; **-elik** a. (-e) temporary; **-ens** av. during; **-ig** a. & av. (-e) timely, in good time; **-ing** n. news; tidings; **-perk** n. (-e) period; **-stip** n. moment; **-verdryf** n. pastime.

'**tydfaktor** ['taytfaktoR] n. time factor.

'**tydsloering** ['taytslüRəng] n. time lag.

U

u ['ew] pron. you; your.

u'edele [ew'ēdələ] pron. your honour.

ui ['œi] n. (-e) onion.

'**uier** ['œiəR] n. (-s) udder; **-ontsteking** n. mammitis; **-salf** n. udder paste.

uil ['œil] n. (-e) owl; -skuiken n. blockhead, simpleton; -tjie dim. 'n -knip take forty winks.

'uintjie ['œingKi] n. (-s) nutgrass; edible bulbous plant (lit. small onion).

uit ['œit] prep. out of, in, on, of, through, by, from, among; a. & av. off, out, over, upon; v. (ge-) utter, express, voice; -beeld v. (ge-) depict; -blaker v. (uitge-) blurt out; -boer v. (ge-) become bankrupt; -broei v. (-ge-) hatch; concoct; -buit v. (-ge-) exploit; -'bundig a. (-e) excessive; exuberant; -daag v. (ge-) challenge; -delg v. (ge-) destroy; -doof v. (-ge-) extinguish; -des v. (-ge-) array, attire; -drukking n. (-e, -s) expression; -'druklik a. & av. (-e) definite(ly), explicit(ly); -dy v. (ge-) swell; -eenlopend a. (-e) divergent; -einde n. end; -er v. (ge-) = uit v.; -er'aard av. naturally; -erlik n. exterior; a. & av. apparently, external(ly); -er'mate av. exceedingly; -ers av. utterly, at the utmost; -erste n. (-s) extreme; limit; -gang n. exit; -gawe n. (-s) expense; edition; -gebak a. in disfavour; -gelate a. elated; -geleer a. (-de) cunning; sly; -gelese a. choice; -genome a. excluding; -geslape a. sly, shrewd; -geteer emaciated; -gewer n. publisher; -gewery n. publishing; -haler a. smart; -'heems a. (-e) foreign, exotic; -huisig a. (-e) from home; -ing n. expression; -knikker v. (uitge-) oust; -koms n. outcome; deliverance; -kryt v. (-ge-) decry; -lag v. (-ge-) laugh at, scorn; -lander n. alien; -lating n. remark; -lok v. (-ge-) lure, tempt, elicit; -loop n. outlet, v. (-ge-) walk out, run out; bud; -loopsel n. bud; -munt v. (-ge-) excel; -'muntend a. (-e) excellent; -nodiging n. invitation; -oefen v. (uitge-) exercise; -oorlê v. (uitge-) outwit; -pluis v. (-ge-) sift, investigate, thresh out; -put v. (-ge-) exhaust; -reik v. (-ge-) bestow, present; -rig v. (-ge-) accomplish; -roei v. (-ge-) exterminate; -roep n. interjection; v. (-ge-) shout, declare, proclaim; -saai v. (-ge-) sow, scatter, broadcast; -set n. trousseau; -sig n. prospect; view; -skot n. cullings; -slag n. result, outcome; -'sluitend a. & av. exclusively; -sonder v. (uitge-) exclude; -spansel n. sky; -spraak n. pronunciation; judgment; -stal v. (-ge-) display; -stel n. delay; v. (-ge-) defer, delay; -stof v. (-ge-) beat; -tart v. (-ge-) challenge, provoke; -tog n. (-te) departure; -tree v. (-ge-) retire; -treksel n. (-s) extract; -vaagsel n. dregs; -vaardig v. (-ge-) issue, decree; -vaart n. funeral; -verkore a. chosen, elect; -vlug n. excuse, pretext; -'voerig a. (-e) elaborate, detailed; -weg n. way-

out; loophole; expedient; -werpsel n. excrement; -wis v. (-ge-) erase.

'uitbrand ['œitbRant] v. (-ge-) cauterize.

'uitdraaipad 'œidRāipat] n. (uit-draaipaaie) branch road.

'uitgangs- ['œitchangs-] pref. output-.

'uitgeskakel ['œitchəskākl] a. (-de) out of gear, declutched; eliminated.

'uithol ['œithol] v. (-ge-) to recess.

'uithoutoets ['œithoatuts] n. (-e) endurance test.

'uitlaatgas ['œitlātchas] n. (-se) exhaust gas; uitlaatklep n. exhaust valve.

'uitrafel ['œitRāfəl] v. (-ge-) fray.

'uitrusting ['œitRʌstəng] n. kit; wardrobe, clothing; -sak n. kit bag.

'uitsaksel ['œitsaksəl] n. fallout.

'uitskakel ['œitskākl] v. (-ge-) cut out, disengage, declutch; -aar n. cut-out.

'uitspoel ['œitspul] v. (-ge-) flush.

ulti'matum [ʌltə'mātʌm] n. (-s) ultimatum.

'ultra ['ʌltRa] n. (-s) extremist; ultra-, pref. ultra-.

ultra 'vires [ʌ'tRa 'viRes] ultra vires.

'umlaut ['umlaut] n. umlaut, vowel-mutation.

una'niem [ewna'nim] a. (-e) unanimous.

'unicum ['ewnikʌm] n. unique thing.

'unie [.ewni] n. union.

u'niek [ew'nik] a. (-e) unique.

'uniform ['ewnifoRəm] n. (-s) uniform.

uni'verseel [ewnifeR'sēl] a. (uni-'versele) universal.

universi'teit [ewnifeRsi'tayt] n. (-e) university.

u'raan [ew'Rān] n. uranium.

'urelank ['ewRəlank] av. for hours.

u'reter [ew'Rētə R] n. (-s) ureter.

u'rine [ew'Rinə] n. urine.

urn ['ʌRən] n. (-s) urn.

urolo'gie [ewRōlō'chi] n. urology.

'uterus ['ewtəRʌs] n. uterus.

utili'sasie [ewtili'sāsi] n. utilization.

utili'teit [ewtili'tayt] n. utility.

u'topies [ew'tōpis] a. (-e) utopian.

uur ['ēWR] n. (ure) hour; -werk n. clock; -wyser n. (-s) hour-hand.

'uwe ['ewvə] pron. die- yours truly.

V

vaag ['fāch] a. (vae; vaer, -ste) vague, hazy.

vaak ['fāk] n. sleepiness; a. sleepy.

vaal ['fāl] a. ashen; sallow; faded; drab; -wattel n. silver wattle.

'vaandel ['fāndəl] n. (-s) colours, flag.

vaar ['fāR] n. (-s) sire; v. (ge-) sail; -der n. seafarer; -t n. navigation; speed; -tuig n. vessel.

'**vaardig** ['fãRdəch] *a.* (-e; -er, -ste) clever, deft.

vaar'wel [fãR'vel] *n.* farewell; *interj.* goodbye!

vaas ['fãs] *n.* (*vase*) vase.

'**vaatjie** ['fãiKi] *n.* (-s) keg.

'**vabond** ['fãbont] *n.* (-e) rogue, rascal.

'**vader** ['fãdəR] *n.* (-s) father, sire; -**lands** *a.* (-e) patriotic; -**lik** *a. & av.* (-e) fatherly, paternal(ly); -**moord** *n.* parricide; -**skap** *n.* fatherhood.

'**vadoek** ['fãduk] *n.* (-e) dish-cloth, face-cloth.

vak ['fak] *n.* (-ke) pigeon-hole; profession, trade.

va'kansie [fə'kãnsi] *n.* (-s) holiday(s), vacation.

va'kant [fa'kant] *a.* (-e) vacant.

vaka'ture [faka'tewRə] *n.* (-s) vacancy.

'**vakbond** ['fakbont] *n.* (-e) trade-union.

vak'sine [fak'sinə] *n.* vaccine.

vak'term ['faktɛRəm] *n.* (-s) technical term.

'**vakuum** ['fãkewʌm] *n.* (-s) vacuum.

val ['fal] *n.* (-le) fall; downfall; slope; trap; frill; *v.* (ge-) fall, drop; -**byl** *n.* guillotine; -**deur** *n.* trapdoor; -**skerm** *n.* parachute; -**strik** *n.* trap.

val'lei [fa'lay] *n.* (-e) valley.

'**valluik** ['faləik] *n.* (-e) trapdoor.

valk ['falk] *n.* (-e) hawk, falcon.

'**valletjie** ['faləKi] *n.* (-s) frill.

vals ['fals] *a.* (-e; -er, -ste) false, base, forged, vicious, bogus; *av.* falsely; -**heid** *n.* falseness, treachery.

'**valskerm** ['falskɛRəm] *n.* (-s) parachute.

'**valstrik** ['falstRək] *n.* trap.

'**valtoevoer** ['faltufüR] *n.* gravitation feed; '**valtoevloei** *n.* gravitational flow.

valu'asie [falew'ãsi] *n.* valuation.

va'luta [fa'lewta] *n.* value, rate of exchange.

van ['fan] *n.* (-ne) surname; *prep.* of; from, with, for; by; -'**aand** *av.* this evening, tonight; -'**daan** *av.* where, whence; -'**daar** *av.* hence; -'**dag** *av.* today; -'**een** *av.* asunder; -'**effe** *av.* a moment ago; -**me'kaar** *av.* asunder; -**me'lewe** *av.* formerly; -'**nuuts** *av.* anew; -'**ouds** *av.* of old; -'**self** *av.* by itself; -'**selfsprekend** *a.* (-e) obvious; -'**waar** *av.* whence; -'**weë** *av.* owing to.

vanda'lisme [fanda'ləsmə] *n.* vandalism.

van'dusie [fan'disi] *n.* (-s) auction sale.

vang ['fang] *v.* (ge-) catch; capture.

'**varia** ['fãRia] *n.* miscellanies.

vari'ant [faRi'ant] *n.* (-e) variant.

vari'asie [faRi'ãsi] *n.* (-s) variation; **vari'eer** *v.* (ge-) vary.

'**varing** ['fãRəng] *n.* (-s) fern, bracken.

vark ['faRk] *n.* (-e) pig, swine, hog; -**blom** *n.* arum-lily; -**spek** *n.* bacon; -**vet** *n.* lard.

vars ['faRs] *a.* fresh.

vas ['fas] *a.* (-te; -ter, -ste) fast; firm; fixed; permanent; *av.* firmly; *v.* (ge-) fast; -**berade** *a.* determined; -**beslote** *a.* determined; -**brand** *v.* (-ge-) get stuck; -**heg** *v.* (-ge-) fix, fasten; -**keer** *v.* (-ge-) trap, drive in a corner; -**knoop** *v.* (-ge-) tie; button; -**pen** *v.* (-ge-) peg; -**praat** *v.* (-ge-) talk oneself into a tangle; -**reent** *v.* (-ge-) detained by rain; -**stel** *v.* (-ge-) fix, determine; -**teland** *n.* continent.

'**vasgoed** ['faschut] *n.* fixed property.

'**vashoustrop** ['fashoastRop] *n.* hand strap.

'**vaskeil** ['faskayl] *v.* (-ge-) wedge.

'**vasklem** ['fasklem] *v.* (-ge-) clip, clamp.

'**vaslaan** ['faslãn] *v.* (-ge-) jam, lock.

'**vaste** = *a.* fixed, stationary, solid, permanent, rigid, standing.

'**vaswoel** ['fasvul] *v.* (-ge-) lash.

vat ['fat] *n.* grip, hold; barrel, vat, keg; *v.* (ge-) take, seize, grasp; -**verwyder** *n.* vasodilator.

vee ['fē] *n.* stock, cattle; *v.* (ge-) sweep, wipe; -**teelt** *n.* stock-breeding.

veeg ['fēch] *n.* wipe, swish; *v.* (ge-) wipe; *cp.* vee *v.*

veel ['fēl] *a.* many, much; *av.* much; often, frequently; *v.* (ge-) stand, endure, bear; -**al** *av.* often, mostly; -**eer** *av.* rather, sooner; -**heid** *n.* multitude; -'**ledig** *a.* (-e) multipartite; -**maals** *av.* often; -**meer** *av.* rather; -**soortig** *a.* (-e) multifarious; -'**sydig** *a.* (-e) versatile; -**voud** *n.* multiple; -**vraat** *n.* glutton.

'**veel'belowend** ['fēlbə'lõvənt] *a.* (-e) promising.

'**veelwywery** ['fēlvayvəRay] *n.* polygamy.

veer ['fēr] *n.* (*vere*) feather; spring; ferry; *v.* (ge-) be springy; -**kombers** *n.* quilt; -**krag** *n.* resilience; -**kragtig** *a.* (-e) springy, elastic.

'**veerstoffer** ['fēRstofəR] *n.* (-s) feather duster.

veertien ['fēRtin] *num.* fourteen; -**daags** *a.* fortnightly.

'**veertig** ['fēRtəch] *num.* forty.

veg ['fech] *v.* (ge-) fight; -**ter** *n.* combatant.

vege'tariër [fechə'tãRIəR] *n.* (-s) vegetarian.

'**veilig** ['fayləch] *a.* (-e; -er, -ste) safe, secure; -**heid** *n.* safety; -**heidsgordel** *n.* safety belt; -**heidsklep** *n.* safety valve.

'**veiling** ['fayləng] *n.* public auction.

veins ['fayns] *v.* (ge-) feign, simulate, pretend; -**aard** *n.* hypocrite; -**ery** *n.* hypocrisy.

vel ['fel] *n.* (-le) skin; hide; *v.* (ge-) cut down, fell; flog; **vel-** *pref.* dermal.

veld ['felt] *n.* (-e) veld, field; -**heer** *n.*

general; **-pad** n. track; **-slag** n. battle; **-stoel** n. camp-stool; **-tog** n. (-te) campaign; **-wagter** n. ranger.

'**velerlei** ['fēləRlay] a. various.

'**velling** [feləng] n. (-s) rim.

velt ['felt] n. felt.

'**veltering** ['feltēRəng] n. lupus.

ven'dusie [fan'disi] n. = **vandisie**.

ven'noot [fə'nōt] n. (vennote) partner.

'**venster** ['fenstəR] n. (-s) window.

vent ['fent] n. (-e) fellow; v. (ge-) hawk; **-er** n. hawker, chapman.

venti'lasie [fenti'lāsi] n. ventilation; **venti'leer** v. (ge-) ventilate.

ve'nynig [fə'naynəch] a. (-e; -er, -ste) venomous; vicious.

ver ['feR] a. & av. (-re) far distant; **-af** av. remote.

ver- ['fəR-] pref. to bring about; change into; denotes the bringing about of the condition indicated by the second part of the compound.

ver'ag [fər'ach] v. (-) despise, scorn; **-telik** a. (-e) despicable; **-tend** a. (-e) scornful; **-ting** n. contempt.

ver'al [fəR'al] av. especially.

ver'ander [fəR'anəR] v. (-) change; **-lik** a. (-e) variable.

ver'antwoord [fəR'antvõRt] v. (-) account for; **-elik** a. (-e) responsible.

ver'arm [fəR'aRəm] v. (-) impoverish.

ver'baas [fəR'bās] a. (-de) surprised; v. (-) surprise.

ver'ban [fəR'ban] v. (-) banish.

ver'band [fəR'bant] n. (-e) bond; bandage; **-watte** n. wadding, cotton wool.

ver'beel [fəR'bēl] v. (-) jou imagine, fancy; **-ding** n. imagination, fancy.

ver'been [fəR'bēn] v. (-) ossify.

ver'berg [fəR'beRch] v. (-) hide, conceal.

ver'beter [fəR'bētəR] v. (-) improve; correct; **-baar** a. (-bare) corrigible.

ver'beur [fəR'bœR] v. (-) forfeit, confiscate.

ver'bied [fəR'bit] v. (-) prohibit, forbid.

ver'bind [fəR'bənt] v. (-) join; dress.

ver'bloem [fəR'blum] v. (-s) disguise; gloss over, palliate.

ver'bod [fəR'bot] n. prohibition; **ver'bode** a. prohibited.

ver'bond [fəR'bont] n. (-e) alliance, union, pact, entente.

ver'borge [fəR'bauRgə] a. hidden, latent, esoteric.

ver'brou [fəR'bRoa] v. (-) spoil, bungle.

ver'bruik [fəR'bRœik] n. consumption; v. (-) consume.

ver'brysel [fəR'bRaysəl] v. (-) smash, crush, break.

ver'by [fəR'bay] prep. past, beyond; av. past; over; **-kom** v. (verbyge-) pass; receive a telling off; **-pad** n. by-pass; **-steek** v. (-ge-) by-pass; overtake; **-sein** n. & v. overtake signal.

ver'byster [fəR'baystəR] v. (-) perplex.

ver'daag [fəR'dāch] v. (-) adjourn.

ver'dag [fəR'dach] a. (-te) suspicious.

ver'dedig [fəR'dēdəch] v. (-) defend; **-ing** n. defence.

ver'deel [fəR'dēl] v. (-) divide; **-'deling** n. division; **-deler** n. distributor.

ver'delg [fəR'delch] v. (-) exterminate.

ver'denking [fəR'denkəng] n. suspicion.

'**verder** ['feRdəR] a. & av. (-e) further, farther.

ver'derf [fəR'deRf] n. destruction, ruin; v. (-) ruin, corrupt; **-lik** a. (-e) pernicious, ruinous, deleterious.

ver'dien [fəR'din] v. (-) earn, deserve; **-ste** n. (-s) wages; profit; **-stelik** a. (-e) meritorious.

ver'dig [fəR'dach] a. (-te) fictitious; **-sel** n. figment.

ver'dink [fəR'dənk] v. (-) suspect.

ver'doem [fəR'dum] v. (-) damn.

ver'doesel [fəR'dusəl] v. (-) blurr, gloss over.

ver'doof [fəR'dõf] v. (-) deaden, dull; render insensible.

ver'dowe = **verdoof**.

ver'dra [fəR'dRā] v. (-) endure, bear, tolerate.

ver'drag [fəR'dRach] n. treaty; met- gradually.

ver'driet [fəR'dRit] n. sorrow, grief; **-ig** a. (-e; -er, -ste) sad.

ver'drink [fəR'dRənk] v. (-) drown.

ver'druk [fəR'dRʌk] v. (-) oppress.

ver'dun [fəR'dʌn] v. (-) dilute; **-ner** n. dilutant, thinner.

ver'dwaal ['fəR'dwal] v. (-) get lost, go astray.

ver'eelt [fəR'ēlt] v. (-) to form a callus; a. (-e) callous.

ver'enig [fəR'ēnəch] v. (-) unite; **-ing** n. union; **-baar** a. (-bare) compatible.

ver'erg [fəR'eRch] v. (-) annoy, make angry.

'**verf** ['feRf] n. (verwe) paint; v. (ge-) paint.

ver'foei [fəR'fui] v. (-) detest; **-lik** a. (-e; -er, -ste) odious.

ver'gaan [fəR'chān] v. (-) perish.

ver'gaar [faR'chāR] v. (het-) accumulate, collect.

ver'gader [fəR'chādəR] v. (-) collect, gather; meet; **-ing** n. meeting, conclave.

ver'ganklik [fəR'chanklək] a. (-e) perishable; cp. **vergaan**.

ver'gasser [fəR'chasəR] n. (-s) carburettor, vaporizer; - is versuip carburettor is flooded.

ver'gassing [fəR'chasəng] n. carburation, carburetion.

ver'geef [fəR'chēf] v. (-) forgive; **-lik** a. (-e) pardonable; **-s** a. (-e) fruitless, futile.

ver'geet [fəR'chet] v. (-) forget.

verge'leke [fəRchə'lĕkə] a. -met as compared to (with).

verge'lyk [fəRchə'layk] v. (-) compare; -ing n. comparison.

verge'noeg [fəRchə'nuch] a. content.

verge'sel [fəRchə'sel] v. (-) accompany.

'vergesog ['fɛrchəsoch] a. far-fetched.

ver'gewe [fəR'chĕvə] v. (-) = vergeef.

verge'wis [fəRgə'vəs] v. (-) make sure of.

ver'gif [fəR'chəf] n. (-te) poison; -tig v. (-) poison.

ver'gis [fəR'chəs] v. (-) make a mistake; -sing n. error.

ver'goding [fəR'chŏdəng] n. apotheosis.

ver'godlik [fəR'chodlək] v. (-) deify.

ver'goed [fəR'chut] v. (-) compensate; -ing n. compensation.

ver'groting [fəR'chRŏtəng] n. enlargement.

ver'gryp [fəR'chRayp] v. (-) transgress, infringe.

ver'guis [fəR'chœis] v. (-) abuse, revile.

ver'gul [fəR'chʌl] v. (-) gild.

ver'gun [fəR'chʌn] v. (-) permit; -ning n. permission; permit; concession.

ver'haal [fəR'hāl] n. (ver'hale) story, tale; v. (-) tell.

ver'heel [fəR'hĕl] v. (-) hide, conceal.

ver'hef [fəR'hef] v. (-) lift, raise, elevate, extol; -fend a. (-) ennobling.

ver'hemelte [fəR'hĕməltə] n. (-s) palate.

ver'heug [fəR'hœch] v. (-) gladden, delight.

ver'hewe [fəR'hĕvə] a. exalted, sublime.

ver'hoed [fəR'hut] v. (-) prevent.

ver'hoog [fəR'hŏch] n. platform, dais; v. (-) increase, promote, enhance, raise; -de a. built up, raised, increased.

ver'hoor [fəR'hŏR] n. (ver'hore) hearing; v. (-) answer, fulfil.

ver'houding [fəR'hoadəng] n. (-s) relation.

'vering ['fĕRəng] n. suspension.

ver'kalk [fəR'kalk] v. (-) calcify.

ver'keer [fəR'kĕR] n. intercourse; traffic.

ver'keerd [fəR'kĕRt] a. & av. (-e) wrong, incorrect, unreasonable; -paar to mismate.

ver'keersaanpaksel [fəRkĕRsanpaksəl] n. traffic jam.

ver'ken [fəR'ken] v. (-) reconnoitre; -ner n. scout.

ver'kies [fəR'kis] v. (-) elect; prefer; -ing n. election.

ver'kla [fəR'klā] v. (-) lay a charge against.

ver'klaar [fəR'klāR] v. (-) explain; declare; testify; certify.

ver'kleinwoord [fəR'klaynvŏRt] n. diminutive.

ver'kluim [fəR'klœim] v. (-) grow numb with cold, freeze to death.

ver'knog [fəR'knoch] a. -aan devoted to.

ver'knorsing [fəR'knoRsəng] n. sorry plight, fix.

ver'koelerluik [fəR'kuləRlœik] n. radiator shutter.

ver'koop [fəR'kŏp] v. (-) sell; ver'koping n. sale, auction.

ver'kore [fəR'kŏRə] a. chosen, elect.

ver'kose [fəR'kŏsə] a. chosen, elected.

ver'koue [fəR'koaə] n. cold, chill; a. with a cold.

ver'krag [fəR'kRach] v. (-) violate; ravish, rape.

ver'krampte [fəR'kRamtə] n. (-s) conservative.

ver'krop [fəR'kRop] v. (-) restrain one's feelings.

ver'kwik [fəR'kwək] v. (-) refresh; -kend a. (-e) refreshing.

ver'kwis [fəR'kwəs] v. (-) waste; -tend a. (-e) wasteful.

ver'lang [fəR'lang] v. (-) long; desire, want; -e n. (-ns) longing, desire.

ver'lede [fəR'lĕdə] n. past; a. past, last.

ver'leë [fəR'lĕə] a. bashful, timid; be in need of aid.

ver'leen [fəR'lĕn] v. (-) vest.

ver'lei [fəR'lay] v. (-) seduce; entice; tempt; -delik a. (-e) seductive; -ding n. temptation.

ver'lep [fəR'ləp] v. (-) fade, wilt, wither.

ver'liefderig [fəR'lifdəRəch] a. (-e; -er, -ste) amative.

ver'lies [fəR'lis] n. loss; bereavement.

ver'ligte [fəR'ləchtə] av. & n. (-s) (radically) progressive.

ver'loën [fəR'lŏən] v. (-) deny, repudiate; ver'loëning n. denial.

ver'lof [fəR'lof] n. permission; leave.

ver'loof [fəR'lŏf] v. (-) betroth; -de n. (-s) betrothed.

ver'loop [fəR'lŏp] v. (-) pass, elapse, expire.

ver'loor [fəR'lŏR] v. (-) lose; ver'lore a. lost.

ver'lostang [fəR'lostang] n. obstetric forceps.

ver'lowing [fəR'lŏvəng] n. betrothal; cp. verloof.

ver'maak [fəR'māk] n. pleasure, delight; v. (-) change, alter; amuse; bequeath; make jealous; -lik a. (-e) amusing; -likheid n. entertainment.

ver'maan [fəR'mān] v. (-) admonish, warn.

ver'maard [fəR'māRt] a. (-e) renowned.

ver'maer [fəR'māR] v. (-) macerate.

ver'metel [fəR'mĕtəl] a. (-e) audacious, bold.

ver'mink [fəR'mənk] a. (-te)

maimed, crippled; v. (-) mutilate, maim.

ver'mits [fəR'məts] conj. whereas.

ver'moë [fəR'mŏə] n. (-ns) power, capacity; wealth.

ver'moed [fəR'mut] v. (-) suspect; -e n. (-ns) suspicion, -e van dood presumption of death; -elik a. (-e) probable; av. probably.

ver'moei [fəR'mui] v. (-) tire, fatigue.

ver'mom [fəR'mom] v. (-) disguise.

ver'moor [fəR'mŏR] v. (-) murder.

ver'mors [fəR'moRs] v. (-) waste, squander.

ver'morsel [fəR'moRsəl] v. (-) crush.

ver'my [fəR'may] v. (-) avoid, shun.

ver'naam [fəR'nâm] a. (ver'name) important; av. especially; -lik av. especially.

ver'neder [fəR'nêdəR] v. (-) humble, humiliate.

ver'neem [fəR'nêm] v. (-) hear, understand.

ver'niel [fəR'nil] v. (-) destroy, ruin; ill-treat.

ver'niet [fəR'nit] av. free, gratis; in vain; -ig v. (-) destroy; -igend a. (-e) destructive.

ver'nis [fəR'nəs] n. varnish.

ver'nouing [fəR'noa-əng] n. angina.

ver'nuf [fəR'nʌf] n. ingenuity, genius; wit.

ver'nuwe [fəR'newvə] v. (-) recondition; renew.

ver'oordeel [fəR'ŏRdêl] v. (-) condemn, convict.

ver'orden [fəR'oRdən] v. ordain, decree.

ver'ouder [fəR'oadəR] v. (-) age, grow old.

ver'ower [fəR'ŏvəR] v. (-) conquer.

ver'pleeg [fəR'plêch] v. (-) nurse; -ster n. fem. nurse.

ver'pletter [fəR'pletəR] v. (-) crush, smash.

ver'plig [fəR'pləch] v. (-) force, compel, oblige.

ver'posing [fəR'pŏsəng] n. pause, rest.

ver'pot [fəR'pot] a. (-te) feeble, stunted.

ver'raad [fə'Rât] n. treason; ver-'raai v. (-) betray.

ver'ras [fə'Ras] v. (-) surprise; -sing n. surprise; -send a. (-e) surprising.

ver'rig [fə'Rəch] v. (-) do, perform, execute.

ver'rot ['fRot] v. (ge-) decay, putrefy.

ver'rukkend [fə'rʌkənt] a. (-e) enchanting.

ver'ruklik [fə'Rʌklək] a. (-e; -er, -ste) delectable.

'vers ['feRs] n. (-e) verse, stanza.

'vers ['fɛRs] n. (-e) heifer.

ver'sadig [fəR'sâdəch] v. (-) satisfy (one's appetite).

ver'samel [fəR'sâməl] v. (-) gather.

ver'seg [fəR'sech] v. (-) refuse.

ver'set [fəR'set] n. resistance; v. (-) oppose, resist.

ver'sigtig [fəR'səchtəch] a. (-e) careful, prudent.

ver'sink [fəR'sənk] v. (-) countersink; galvanize; -ing n. countersinking.

ver'skat [fəR'skaf] v. (-) provide.

ver'skerp [fəR'skeRp] v. (-) exacerbate.

ver'skiet [fəR'skit] n. distance.

ver'skil [fəR'skəl] n. (-le) difference; v. (-) differ, vary; -lend a. (-e) different, diversified.

ver'skoning [fəR'skŏnəng] n. (-s) change of clothes; excuse.

ver'skrik [fəR'skRək] a. (-te) frightened; scared; -king n. (-e, -s) terror, horror; -lik a. terrible.

ver'skuldig [fəR'skʌldəch] a. (-de) due.

ver'skyn [fəR'skayn] v. (-) appear; -sel n. phenomenon.

ver'slae [fəR'slâə] a. dismayed.

ver'slag [fəR'slach] n. (verslae) report.

ver'snapering [fəR'snâpəRəng] n. (-e) delicacy, choice morsel.

ver'soek [fəR'suk] n. (-) request; v. (-) request, ask; -ing n. temptation.

ver'soen [fəR'sun] v. (-) reconcile; -lik a. (-e) placable.

ver'sot [fəR'sot] a. -op keen on, doting.

ver'span [fəR'span] v. (-) brace.

ver'sper [fəR'speR] v. (-) block, foul; -ring n.

ver'spil [fəR'spəl] v. (-) waste; -ling n. waste.

ver'spot [fəR'spot] a. (-te) ridiculous, foolish.

ver'spreek [fəR'spRêk] v. make a slip of the tongue.

ver'staan [fəR'stân] v. (-) understand.

ver'stand [fəR'stant] n. intellect, mind; -ig a. (-e; -er, -ste) sensible; wise; av. sensibly, wisely.

ver'star [fəR'staR] a. (-de) rigid, inflexible; v. (-) make rigid, stiffen.

ver'steek [fəR'stêk] v. (-) hide, conceal.

ver'sterf [fəR'steRf] n. death.

ver'stok [fəR'stok] a. (-te) hardened, confirmed.

ver'stoke [fəR'stŏkə] av. -van deprived of.

ver'stoteling [fəR'stŏtələng] n. pariah.

ver'streke [fəR'stRêkə] a. expired, elapsed.

ver'strooid [fəR'stRŏit] a. (-e) absentminded; devious.

ver'stryk [fəR'stRayk] v. (-) elapse, expire.

ver'stuit [fəR'stœit] v. (-) sprain; -ing n.

ver'stuiwer [fəR'stœivəR] n. (-s) atomizer.

ver'suipte [fəR'sœiptə] a. - vergasser flooded carburettor.

ver'swik [fəR'swək] v. (-) sprain;
-king n.

ver'suim [fəR'sœim] n. neglect;
omission, default; v. (-) neglect.

ver'taal [fəR'tāl] v. (-) translate.

'verte ['feRtə] n. (-s) distance.

ver'teer [fəR'tēR] v. (-) consume,
spend, digest.

ver'tel [fəR'tel] v. (-) relate, narrate;
-ling n. story, tale.

verti'kaal [feRti'kāl] a. (verti'kale)
vertical.

ver'toef [fəR'tuf] v. (-) stay.

ver'tolk [fəR'tolk] v. (-) interpret.

ver'toning [fəR'tōnəng] n. (-s)
show, exhibition.

ver'toog [fəR'tōch] n. (vertoē)
representation.

ver'traag [fəR'trāch] v. (-) retard,
decelerate; slug; ver'traging n.
delay; -de a. delayed, belated,
arrested.

ver'troue [fəR'troaə] n. confidence;
ver'troulik a. & av. (-e) confidential
(ly).

ver'twyfel [fəR'twayfəl] v. (-)
despair.

ver'vaardig [fəR'fāRdəch] v. (-)
manufacture.

ver'vangdeel [fəR'fangdēl] n. re-
placement.

ver'veel [fəR'fēl] v. (-) bore;
ver'velend a. (-e) boring.

ver'versing [fəR'feRsəng] n. (-s)
refreshment.

ver'voeging [fəR'fuchəng] n. con-
jugation.

ver'voer [fəR'fūR] n. transport; v.
(-) convey; -ing n. rapture, trance.

ver'vorm [fəR'foRəm] v. (-) distort.

ver'waand [fəR'vānt] a. (-e)
arrogant.

ver'wag [fəR'vach] v. (-) except;
-ting n. expectation.

ver'want [fəR'vant] n. (-e) relative;
a. (-e) related, connate.

ver'weer [fəR'vēR] n. defence; v. (-)
defend; perish; weather; -der n. (-s)
defendant.

ver'welk [fəR'velk] v. (-) fade,
wither.

ver'wen [fəR'ven] v. (-) spoil,
pamper.

ver'werf [fəR'verf] v. (-) gain, win,
achieve.

ver'werp [fəR'veRp] v. (-) reject.

ver'wikkeling [fəR'vəkələng] n.
complication.

ver'wittig [fəR'vətəch] v. (-)
inform, notify.

ver'woed [fəR'vut] a. (-e) fierce,
furious.

ver'woes [fəR'vus] v. (-) destroy;
-tend a. (-e) destructive.

ver'worpe [fəR'voRpə] a. reprobate;
-ling n. castaway.

ver'wronge [fəR'vRongə] a. twisted,
distorted.

ver'wyder [fəR'vaydəR] v. (-)
remove.

ver'wys [fəR'vays] v. (-) refer; -ing
n. reference.

ver'wyt [fəR'vayt] n. (-e) reproach;
blame; v. upbraid, reproach.

ver'ydel [fəR'aydəl] v. (-) frustrate,
confute.

'vesel ['fēsəl] n. (-s) fibre, thread;
-rat n. fibre gear.

'vestig ['festəch] v. (ge-) establish.

vet ['fet] n. fat; a. fat, fatty,
greasy; -koek n. dough-nut.

'veter ['fētəR] n. (-s) (boot-, shoe-)
lace.

'veto ['fētō] n. veto.

vi'breer [fi'bRēR] v. (ge-) vibrate.

vier ['fiR] num. four.

'vierendeel ['fiRəndēl] v. (ge-) quarter.

'vierkant ['fiRkant] n. (-e) square;
vier'kantig a. (-e) square; -swortel
n. square root.

'vierskaar ['fiRskāR] n. tribunal.

vies ['fis] a. & av. annoyed, fed up;
nasty, foul; -erig a. (-e) somewhat
annoyed; -lik a. (-e) filthy, dirty.

vin [fən] n. (-ne) fin.

vind ['fənt] v. (ge-) find; meet; deem;
-ing n. invention.

'vinger ['fəngəR] n. (-s) finger;
-alleen av. all alone; -hoed n. (-e)
thimble; -droog a. touch-dry.

vink ['fənk] n. (-e) finch, weaver-
bird.

'vinkel ['fənkəl] n. fennel.

'vinnig ['fənəch] a. & av. (-e; -er,
-ste) fast, quick(ly); sharp(ly).

vi'ool [fi'yōl] n. (viole) violin; vio'lis
n. (-te) violinist; -tjie dim. violet.

vir ['fəR] prep. for, to, at.

virtu'oos [fəRtew'ōs] n. (virtuose)
virtuoso.

'virus ['fiRʌs] n. virus.

vis ['fəs] n. (-se) fish; -mot n. fish
moth.

visen'teer [fəsən'tēR] v. (ge-)
search, inspect.

'visie ['fisi] n. vision.

vi'sier [fə'siR] n. (-s) visor.

visi'oen [fisi'un] n. vision.

vi'site [fə'sitə] n. visit.

'visum ['fisʌm] n. visa.

vit ['fət] v. (ge-) find fault, cavil;
-terig a. (-e) censorious, cavilling.

vita'mine [fita'minə] n. (-s) vitamin.

vitri'oel [fitrə'yul] n. vitriol.

vla ['flā] n. custard.

vlaag ['flāch] n. (vlae) gust, shower,
paroxysm.

Vlaams ['flāms] a. (-e) Flemish.

vlag ['flach] n. (vlae) flag.

vlak ['flak] n. (-ke) level, plane, face,
flat; a. (-ke) shallow, flat, flush; av.
flatly; -te n. (-s) plain; -klinknael n.
flush rivet.

vlam ['flam] n. (-me) flame, blaze,
flash.

vlas ['flas] n. flax.

vlees ['fles] n. — vleis(-).

'vleeslik ['flēslək] a. (-e) carnal.

vleg ['flech] v. (ge-) plait, wreathe,
weave; -sel n. (-s) plait, tress, braid.

vlei ['flay] n. (-e) marsh, swamp; cp.
v. (ge-) flatter.
vleis ['flays] n. meat, flesh.
vlek ['flek] n. (-ke) stain, spot,
smudge; v. (ge-) stain, soil; flay.
vlerk ['flerk] n. (-e) wing.
'vleuel ['fliǣǝl] n. (-s) wing; vane;
grand piano; -skroef n. thumb-
screw.
vlie = vlieg.
vlieg ['flich] n. (vlieë) fly; v. (ge-)
fly.
vlies ['flis] n. (-e) fleece, membrane.
'vlinder ['flǝndǝR] n. (-s) butterfly.
vloed ['flut] n. flood, river, torrent.
vloei ['flui] v. (ge-) flow, run, stream;
cp. vloed; -stof n. liquid; -politoer
n. liquid polish.
vloek ['fluk] n. (-e) curse, oath; v.
(ge-) swear, curse, damn.
vloer ['fiûR] n. (-e) floor, flooring.
vlok ['flok] n. (-ke) flake, flock.
vlooi ['flôi] n. (-e) flea.
vloot ['flôt] n. (vlote) fleet, navy.
vlot ['flot] n. (-te) float, raft; a.
afloat, adrift; fluent, smooth; av.
fluently; v. (ge-) float, go smoothly;
-tend a. (-e) floating.
vlug ['flʌch] n. flight, escape; a. (-ge)
fast, quick, swift; av. quickly; v.
(ge-) flee, fly; -skrif n. pamphlet;
-sout n. sal volatile; -teling n.
fugitive; -tig a. (-e) cursory.
vlyt ['flayt] n. diligence; -ig a. (-e;
-er, -ste) diligent.
vod ['fot] n. (-de, -dens) rag, tatter.
voed ['fut] v. (ge-) feed, nourish; -ing
n. food, feeding; -saam a. (-same,
-samer, -ste) nutritious; -sel n. food;
-ster n. wet-nurse; -end a. (-e)
nutrient.
voeg ['fuch] n. (voeë) joint, seam; v.
(ge-) add; join, weld.
voel ['ful] v. (ge-) feel, be aware; -ing
n. feeling, touch.
'voël ['fôl] n. (-s) bird; -'ent n. bird-
lime; holly; -tjie dim. little bird;
-vry a. outlawed.
voer ['fûR] n. forage, fodder; v. (ge-)
feed; lead; conduct; line; -ing n.
lining; -tuig n. carriage.
'voert ['fuRt] interj. be gone! scram!
cp. voort.
'voertaal ['fûRtäl] n. medium of
instruction.
'voertsek = voert.
voet ['fut] n. (-e) foot; footing;
bottom, base; rate; -rem n. foot
brake; -skakelaar n. foot-switch;
-ganger n. pedestrian, wingless
locust; -slaan v. (-ge-) walk, slog;
-stuk n. pedestal.
vog ['foch] n. liquid, fluid; -tig a.
(-e; -er, -ste) moist; -brand n. scald.
vo'kaal [fô'käl] n. (vokale) vowel.
vol ['fol] a. (-le) full, filled.
'volbloed ['folblut] a. thoroughbred.
'volbloedigheid ['folbludǝchayt] n.
plethora.
vol'daan [fol'dän] n. receipt; a.
content.

vol'doende [fol'dundǝ] a. sufficient.
vol'donge [fol'dongǝ] a. accom-
plished.
volg ['folch] v. (ge-) follow; pursue;
-eling n. (-e) follower, adherent;
-ende a. following, next; -ens prep.
according to; -orde n. sequence.
vol'hard [fol'haRt] v. (-) persevere,
persist.
volk ['folk] n. (-e) people, nation;
volks- pref. national; -sbuurt n.
people's quarter (of city).
vol'kome [fol'kômǝ] a. & av.
perfect(ly), total(ly).
'volstreep ['folstRêp] n. solid line.
'volksraad ['folksRät] n. House of
Assembly.
vol'ledig [fo'lêdǝch] a. (-e) full,
complete.
'volmag ['folmach] n. power of
attorney; plenary power.
vol'strek [fol'stRek] a. & av. (-te)
absolute(ly).
vol'struis [fol'strœis] n. (-e) ostrich.
vol'tooi [fol'tôi] v. (-) complete,
finish.
vol'trek [fol'tRek] v. (-) execute.
vo'lume [vô'lewmǝ] n. volume.
vol'wasse [fol'vasǝ] a. adult, full-
grown; -ne n. (-s) adult.
vomi'tief [fômǝ'tif] n. emetic.
'vondeling ['fondǝlǝng] n. (-)
foundling.
vonds ['fonts] n. (-e) find, discovery.
vonk ['fonk] n. (-e) spark; v. (ge-)
spark; -el v. (ge-) sparkle; -prop n.
sparking plug; -gaping n. spark gap.
'vonnis ['fonǝs] n. (-se) sentence,
judgment; v. (ge-) pass sentence.
voog ['foch] n. (-de) guardian.
'voor ['fôR] n. (vore) furrow, ditch;
wrinkle; the pros; prep. in front of,
before; a. in front; conj. before;
-aand n. eve; -arm n. fore-arm;
-baat n. by- in anticipation; -beeld
n. (-e) example; -berei v. (-) prepare;
-deel n. advantage, benefit; -geslag
n. (-te) ancestors; -gewend ['fôRchǝ-
vent] a. (-e) pretended, professed;
-grond n. foreground; -hamer n. (-s)
sledge hammer; -'hands a. in stock,
on hand; -heen av. formerly; -hoede
n. vanguard; -hoof n. forehead;
-keur n. preference; -'malig a. (-e)
former; -naam n. Christian name;
-neme n. intention; -oordeel n.
prejudice; -op av. in front; -raad n.
(-rade) supply, stock; -rang n.
precedence; -reg n. privilege; -sê
v. (-ge-) prompt; -sien v. (-) foresee,
supply; -skiet v. (-ge-) advance,
lend; -skot n. loan; -sorg n. precaution; -spoed n. prosperity;
-'spoedig a. (-e) prosperous; -sprong
n. start, advantage; -stad n. (-stede)
suburb; -stel n. proposal; -'uit a. &
av. in front of, before; forward,
beforehand; -'uitgang n. progress;
-uit'strewend a. (-e) progressive;
-vader n. (-s) ancestor; -val n. (-le)
incident; -'waar av. truly; -waarde

n. (-s) condition, stipulation; **wend-sel** n. (-s) pretext; **-werp** n. (-e) object.

'**voorbedag** ['fôRbədach] a. (-te) premeditated.

'**voorbrein** ['fôRbRayn] n. fore-brain.

'**voorgenome** ['fôRchənŏmə] a. intended, proposed.

'**voorgeskrewe** ['fôRchəksRĕvə] a. prescribed.

'**voorgestelde** ['fôRchəstɛldə] a. proposed; bogus.

'**voorhaker** ['fôRhäkəR] n. (-s) mechanical horse.

'**vooringenome** ['fôRəng-chənŏmə] a. bia(s)sed.

'**voorsaal** ['fôRsäl] n. lobby.

voort ['fôRt] av. forward, on, forth, away; **voort-** pref.; -'**durend** a. & av. (-e) continuous(ly); **-plant** v. (-ge-) propagate; **-spruit** v. (-ge-) result from.

'**voorts** ['fôRts] av. moreover, besides.

voos ['fôs] a. (vose) spongy, rotten.

'**vorder** ['fôRdəR] v. (ge-) get on; demand; **-ing** n. progress; claim.

'**vorige** ['fôRəchə] a. former.

vorm ['fôRəm] n. (-s) form, shape, figure; v. (ge-) form.

vors ['fôRs] n. (-te) ridge, capping; monarch; v. (ge-) search, investigate.

'**vort** ['fôRt] av. away, gone; cp. voert, voort.

vou ['foa] n. (-e) fold, pleat; v. (ge-) fold.

vra ['fRä] v. (ge-) ask.

vraag ['fRäch] question; **-teken** n. (-s) question-mark, query.

vrag ['fRach] n. (-te) freight, cargo, load.

'**vratjie** ['fRaiKi] n. (-s) wart.

'**vrede** ['fRĕdə] n. peace; **-saam** a. (-same) peaceful.

vreemd ['fRĕmt] a. (-e) strange; extraneous; queer, funny; av. strangely; **-e** n. (-s) stranger; **-eling** n. (-e) stranger.

vrees ['fRĕs] n. (-se) fear, dread; v. (ge-) fear, be afraid of, dread; -'**agtig** a. (-e) afraid, timid; **-lik** a. & av. (-e; -er, -ste) fearful(ly), dreadful(ly).

vreet ['fRĕt] v. (ge-) feed on (animals).

vrek ['fRek] n. (-ke) miser; v. (ge-) die (animals); **-sel** n. (-s) scoundrel; **-te** n. mortality (animals).

'**vreugde** ['fRœchdə] n. joy.

vriend ['fRint] n. (-e) friend; **-elik** a. & av. (-e) friendly, kindly; **-skap** n. friendship.

vries ['fRis] v. (ge-) freeze.

vrind = **vriend**.

'**vroeër** ['fRûəR] a. & av. earlier, former(ly).

vroeg ['fRuch] a. & av. (vroeë) early; **-te** n. early in the morning; -'**tydig** a. & av. (-e) early.

'**vrolik** ['fRŏlək] a. (-e; -er, -ste) merry, happy, jolly.

vroom ['fRŏm] a. (vrome) pious.

vrot ['fRot] a. rotten, putrid; v. (ge-) rot, decay; cp. verrot.

'**vrotsig** ['fRotsəch] a. (-e; -er, -ste) inefficient.

vrou ['fRoa] n. (-e, -ens) woman, wife, queen; **-lik** a. (-e) womanly, feminine.

vrug ['fRʌch] n. (-te) fruit; foetus; **-baar** a. (-bare) fertile, fecund; **-baarheid** n. fecundity; **-teloos** a. & av. (vrugtelose) fruitless(ly).

vry ['fRay] a. & av. free(ly); v. (ge-) court, woo.

'**Vrydag** ['fRaydach] n. Friday.

vryf ['fRayf] v. (ge-) rub, polish; **-mengsel** n. rubbing compound.

'**vrygesel** ['fRaychəsel] n. bachelor.

'**vryheid** ['fRayhayt] n. freedom.

'**vryloop** ['fRaylŏp] v. (-ge-) coast.

vry'moedig [fRay'mudəch] a. (-e) frank, open.

'**vryry** ['fRayRay] v. (ge-) free-wheel.

'**vrywe** = **vryf**.

'**vrywiel** ['fRayvil] n. free wheel.

vuil ['fœil] n. dirt; a. (-e) dirty; **-goed** n. dirt.

vuis ['fœis] n. (-te) fist.

vul ['fʌl] n. foal; v. (ge-) foal; fill; **-pen** n. fountain-pen.

'**vurig** ['fĕwRəch] a. & av. (-e) ardent(ly), fervent(ly).

vurk ['fʌRk] n. (-e) fork; pitchfork.

vuur ['fĕwR] n. (vure) fire, ardour; v. (ge-) fire; **-pyl** n. (-e) red-hot poker.

vy [fay] n. (vye) fig.

'**vyand** ['fayant] n. (-e) foe, enemy; **vy'andelik** a. hostile; **vy'andig** a. (-e) hostile.

vyf ['fayf] n. five.

vyl ['fayl] n. (-e) file; v. (ge-) file.

'**vywer** ['fayvəR] n. (-s) pond.

W

wa ['vä] n. (-ens) waggon, van, truck, carriage, coach.

waag ['väch] v. (ge-) risk, hazard; **-hals** n. dare-devil; **-skaal** n. balance, scale; **-stuk** n. venture, daring deed.

waai ['väi] n. (-e) hollow of the knee; blow; v. (ge-) blow; float, flutter; **-er** n. fan; **-erband** n. fan belt; **-erblad** n. fan blade.

waak ['väk] v. (ge-) watch, look after, sit up with a patient.

waan ['vän] n. delusion; v. (ge-) imagine; **-sin** n. madness, insanity; -'**sinnig** a. (-e) insane; -'**sinnige** n. (-s) lunatic.

'**waanwys** ['vänvays] a. pedantic, conceited.

waar ['väR] n. (ware) ware, goods; a. (ware) true; av. where; conj. whereas, since; **-aan** pron. what? whom? which? **-agter** pron. behind what (whom, which)? -'**agtig** a. & av. (-e) true, truly, real(ly); **-borg** n.

(-e) guarantee, security; v. (ge-) guarantee, warrant; -lik av. truly, really.

waar- ['vaR] pref. what, where.

'**waarde** ['vaRdə] n. (-s) value; a. dear.

waar'deer [vaR'dēR] v. (ge-) appreciate; appraise; **waar'dering** n. appreciation, valuation.

'**waardeur** ['vaRdœR] av. through (by) which (what).

'**waardig** ['vaRdəch] a. (-e) worthy; dignified.

'**waarheen** ['vaRhēn] pron. where? av. at or to what place.

'**waarheid** ['vaRayt] n. ('waarhede) truth, veracity.

'**waarmee** ['vaRmē] av. with what.

'**waarnatoe** ['vaRnatu] av. where? to which place?

'**waarneem** [vaRnēm] v. (-ge-) perceive; watch; avail; act for someone, hold a temporary appointment; **waar'neembaar** a. (waar-'neembare) perceptible; '**waarne-mend** a. (-e) acting.

'**waarom** ['vaRom] av. why? round what (which)?

'**waarsê** ['vaRsê] v. (-ge-) tell fortune.

'**waarsku** ['vaRskew] v. (ge-) warn, caution; **-wing** n. warning, reminder.

waar'skynlik [vaR'skaynlək] a. & av. probable(-bly).

'**wae** = **waag**.

wag ['vach] n. (-te) watchman, guard; v. (ge-) wait; **-ter** n. watchman, keeper; **-woord** n. password.

'**waggel** ['vachəl] v. (ge-) totter, stagger, reel, wobble; **-wiel** n. wobbly wheel.

'**wakker** ['vakəR] a. awake, vigilant.

waks ['vaks] n. wax, polish.

wal ['val] n. (-le) bank, shore, coast.

walg ['valch] v. (ge-) loathe, nauseate, disgust; **-ing** n. nausea, disgust; **-lik** av. disgustingly.

walm ['valəm] n. (-e, -s) dense smoke; **-kap** n. (-pe) hood (stove).

wals ['vals] n. (-e) waltz; n. & v. roll.

'**walvis** ['valfəs] n. (-se) whale.

wan- ['van-] pref. bad, wrong, false, mal-, mis-; **-begrip** n. false notion; **-daad** n. misdeed; **-gedrog** n. monster; **-hoop** n. despair; **-'kopig** a. (-e) desperate; **-klank** n. discord; **-orde** n. disorder, confusion; **-'skape** a. misshapen; **-trou** v. (ge-) mistrust, distrust.

wand ['vant] n. (-e) wall = **muur**.

'**wandel** ['vandəl] v. (ge-) walk, promenade; **-end** a. (-e) walking; **-ing** n. walk, stroll; **-gang** n. (-e) lobby, cp. **voorsaal**.

wang ['vang] n. (-e) cheek.

'**wankel** ['vankəl] v. (ge-) totter, stagger; waver.

wan'neer ['vanəR, va'nēR] av. & conj. when.

'**wanparing** n. mismating.

want ['vant] conj. because.

'**wapen** ['vapən] n. (-s) weapon, arm(s).

'**wapper** ['vapəR] v. (ge-) flutter, float, fly.

war ['vaR] n. in **die-** in a tangle, in confusion.

'**warboel** ['vaRbul] n. muddle.

warm ['vaRəm] a. & av. warm, hot, fiery; **-as** n. midges, punkies; **-bad** n. hot spring; **-te** n. warmth; **-watte** n. thermal wool.

'**warrel** ['vaRəl] v. (ge-) whirl, swirl.

wars ['vaRs] a. **-van** averse to.

was ['vas] n. wax; growth, rise; laundry; v. (ge-) rise, wax; wash; **-goed** n. laundry; **-vel** n. stencil.

'**wasem** ['vasəm] n. vapour, steam, breath.

wat ['vat] pron. what, who, that, which.

'**water** ['vatəR] n. water; **-ig** a. (-e) watery; **-besem** n. squeegee.

'**watte** ['vatə] n. wadding; **wat'teer** v. (ge-) wad, quilt.

'**watter** ['vatəR] pron. which, what.

web ['vep] n. (-be) web.

wed ['vet] v. (ge-) bet, wager; **-denskap** n. wager.

weder- = **weer** again, re-.

'**wedersyds** ['vēdəRsayts] a. mutual.

'**wedstryd** ['vetstRayt] n. (-e) match, contest.

'**weduwee** ['vēdəvē] n. widow.

'**wedywer** ['vetayvəR] v. (ge-) compete, vie.

wee ['vē] n. woe, grief, pain; **-klag** n. lament; **-moed** n. sadness.

weef ['vēf] v. (ge-) weave; **-sel** n. (-s) tissue, fabric; **-selopbou** n. anabolism.

weeg ['vēch] v. (ge-) weigh; **-skaal** n. balance; **-brug** n. weighbridge.

week ['vēk] n. (weke) week; a. (weke) soft, tender; v. (ge-) soak, steep, soften; **-dier** n. mollusc; **-liks** av. weekly; **-staal** n. mild steel.

'**weelde** ['vēldə] n. luxury, affluence; **-rig** a. (-e) luxurious.

'**weeluis** ['vēlœis] n. (-e) bug.

ween ['vēn] v. (ge-) weep.

weëns ['vēēns] prep. because of, on account of; for.

weer ['vēR] n. weather; av. again; v. (ge-) avert, exclude, defend oneself.

weer'galm [vēR'chaləm] v. (-) echo, resound.

weer'kaats [vēR'kâts] v. (-) reflect.

weer'lê [vēR'lɛ] v. (-) confute.

'**weerlig** ['veRləch] n. lightning.

'**weersin** ['vēRsən] n. aversion.

weer'spieel [vēR'spil] v. (-) reflect.

'**weersyds** = **wedersyds**.

'**weerwraak** ['vēRvRak] n. revenge.

wees ['vēs] n. (wese) orphan; v. (is, was, gewees; inf. om te wees) be; **-huis** n. orphanage; **-kind** n. orphan.

weet ['vēt] v. (wis, ge-) know, know of, be aware of; **-'gierig** a. (-e) eager to learn.

weg ['vech] n. (weĝ) way, road, route; av. away, gone, lost; -kruipertjie n. hide and seek.

'weide ['vaydə] n. (-s) meadow.

wei ['vay] v. (ge-) graze, feed; -veld n. pasturage.

weids ['vayts] a. (-e) grand, stately.

'weier ['vayəR] v. (ge-) refuse, decline, fail; -ing n. refusal; failure.

'weifel ['vayfəl] v. (ge-) waver, hesitate; -ing n. wavering, hesitation; -end a. (-e) hesitating.

'weinig ['vaynəch] a. & av. little, few.

wek ['vek] v. (ge-) wake, awaken, call, rouse, create, cause; -ker n. alarm-clock.

wel ['vel] av. well; v. (ge-) weld; -daad n. benefit, boon; -'dadig a. (-e) benevolent; -dra a. soon; -gemoed a. cheerful; -geskape a. well-formed; -gesteld a. (-e) well-to-do; -gevalle n. pleasure; -iswaar av. indeed; -kom a. (-e) welcome; -'lewend a. (-e) courteous, urbane; -lig av. perhaps; -lus n. lust; delight; prurience; -'riekend a. (-e) fragrant; -sand n. quicksand; -stand n. health; -syn n. welfare; -vaart n. prosperity; -'voeglik a. (-e) decorous, -voeglikheid n. decorum; -'willend a. obliging.

welf ['velf] v. (ge-) vault, arch.

'welig ['vēləch] a. (-e; -er, -ste) luxuriant.

'welke ['velkə] pron. what, which.

welp ['velp] n. (-e) cub; cp. Eng. whelp.

'welwe = welf.

'wemel ['vēməl] v. (ge-) swarm, teem.

wen ['ven] v. (ge-) accustom to; win, gain; gather; harvest; wind; -as n. winch; -tol n. winch drum.

wend ['vent] v. (ge-) turn; -ing n. turn.

wenk ['venk] n. (-e) hint.

wens ['vēns] n. (-e) wish, desire; v. (ge-) wish, desire; -lik a. (-e; -er, -ste) desirable; -denkery n. wishful thinking.

wentel ['ventəl] v. (ge-) revolve, rotate; -ing n. (-e, -s) revolution, rotation.

werd ['vɛRt] a. worth.

'wêreld ['vēRəlt] n. (-e) world; universe; region; -'kundig a. (-e) known to everybody; -lik a. (-e) worldly, carnal; -s a. (-e) worldly; -wys a. (-e) philosophic.

werf ['veRf] n. (werwe) farm, yard, wharf, campus; v. (ge-) recruit, enlist.

werk ['veRk] n. (-e) work, labour, employment; v. (ge-) work; -baas n. foreman; -'dadig a. (-e) effective; -esel n. drudge, slave, glutton for work; -gewer n. employer; -ie dim.; -ing n. action, working, operation; -kaart n. job card; -liede n. pl.

workmen; -lik a. & av. (-e) real(ly), actual(ly); -nemer n. employee; -saam a. diligent; efficacious; -saamheid n. activity; -staking n. strike; -'tuiglik a. (-e) automatic; -woord n. verb.

'werktuig ['veRktœich] n. implement; werk'tuiglik a. automatic.

werp ['veRp] v. (ge-) throw, cast, hurl.

'werskaf ['veRskaf] v. (ge-) be busily engaged on.

werwe = werf.

'werwel ['veRvəl] n. (-s) vertebra; button, latch, swivel.

wes = weste.

'wese ['vēsə] n. (-ns) being, creature; face, looks; substance; existence; -ntlik a. (-e) real, essential; -nloos a. vacant, blank, expressionless.

'weste ['vestə] n. west; buite-unconscious; -lik a. (-e) westerly, wester- pref. western-.

wet ['vet] n. (-te) law, act, statute; v. (ge-) whet; -gewend a. (-e) legislative; -lik a. (-e) legal; -sontwerp n. bill; -tig a. (-e) lawful, legitimate, legal.

wete ['vētə] n. knowledge; cognition; -ns av. knowingly.

'wetenskap ['vētənskap] n. science; knowledge.

'wewenaar ['vēvənaR] n. (-s) widower.

wie ['vi] pron. who, whom.

wieg ['vich] n. (-e) cradle; v. (ge-) rock, lull; dawdle; -elied n. lullaby.

'wiegel ['vichəl] v. (ge-) rock.

wiek ['vik] n. (-e) wing, vane.

wiel ['vil] n. (-e) wheel; -ryer n. cyclist; -balans n. wheel balance; -bandbalans n. tyre balance; -bedding n. wheel seat; -e onruil v. (ge-) change wheels; -ketting n. skid chain; -moer n. wheel nut; -moeromslag n. wheel nut brace; -skyf n. wheel disc; -sleutel n. wheel spanner; -sporing n. wheel alignment; -tapbout n. wheel stud; -trekker n. wheel puller; -waggel n. wheel wobble.

wier ['viR] n. sea-weed; alga(e).

'wierook ['virōk] n. incense.

wig ['vəch] n. (-ge, wie-) wedge.

wik ['vək] v. (ge-) weigh.

'wikkel ['vəkəl] v. (ge-) wrap, envelop; -ing n. winding; -rig a. (-e) wobbly.

wiks ['vəks] v. (ge-) blow, strike, slap, flog.

wil ['vəl] n. will, wish, desire; v. (ge-, wou) want, wish, like.

wild ['vəlt] n. game; a. (-e; -er, -ste) wild, savage, shy; -e n. (-s) savage; wilde- pref. wild; -wingerd n. virginia creeper.

wilg ['vəlch] n. (-e, -ers) willow.

'wilger n. (-s) = wilg.

'willekeur ['vələkœR] n. arbitrariness; wille'keurig a. (-e) arbitrary.

'**willens** ['vələns] av. deliberately.
'**wilskrag** ['vəlskRach] n. will-power.
'**wimpel** ['vəmpəl] n. (-s) pendant.
'**wimper** ['vəmpəR] n. (-s) eyelash.
win = **wen**; **-ner** n. winner; **-ning** n. winning, production, extraction; **-s** n. profit, gain.
wind ['vənt] n. (-e) wind; **-erig** a. (-e) windy; flatulent; **-hond** n. greyhound; **-makerig** a. smart, posh; **-sel** n. bandage; **-streek** n. point of the compass.
'**windbuks** ['vəntbʌks] n. air-gun.
windmaker ['vəntmākəR] n. dandy.
'**windverdrywer** ['vəntfəRdRay-vəR] n. carminative.
'**wingerd** ['vəngəRt] n. (-e) vineyard.
wink ['vənk] v. (ge-) wink, nod, beckon; **-brou** n. (-e) eyebrow.
'**winkel** ['vənkəl] n. (-s) shop, store; **-haak** n. square; **winke'lier** n. (-s) shopkeeper.
'**winter** ['vəntəR] n. (-s) winter; **-s** a. (-e) wintry; **-shande** n. chilblained hands; **-seer** n. (sere) chilblain.
wip ['vəp] v. (ge-) tilt, go up and down, hop; **-neus** n. pug nose; **-perig** a. (-e) wobbly; uppish; **-toestel** n. tipping gear; **-sif** n. jig.
wis ['vəs] a. (-se) certain, sure; v. (ge-) wipe; **-ser** n. eraser; **-kunde** n. mathematics.
wispel'turig ['vəspəl'tēwRəch] a. (-e) fickle, freakish, capricious.
'**wissel** ['vəsəl] n. (-s) bill, draft; points; switch; v. (ge-) exchange; **-geld** n. change; **-ing** n. change; **-tand** n. milk-tooth; -'**vallig** a. (-e) uncertain.
wit ['vət] n. white; a. white; v. (ge-) whitewash; **-mens** n. European; **-sel** n. whiting; **-seerkeel** n. diphtheria; **-voetjie** n. by iemand **-soek** curry favour; **-wortel** n. parsnip.
'**wittebroodsdae** ['vətəbRōtsdā] n. honeymoon.
woed ['vut] v. (ge-) rage; **-e** n. rage, fury, choler; **-end** a. (-e) furious.
'**woeker** ['vukəR] v. (ge-) practise usury; apply diligently.
woel ['vul] v. (ge-) be restless, fidgety; **-ig** a. (-e) restless, fidgety; **-ing** n. agitation.
'**Woensdag** ['vūñsdach] n. Wednesday.
woes ['vus] a. (-te) desolate; savage; **-teling** n. (-e) brute, rough; **-te'ny** n. wilderness; -'**tyn** n. desert.
wol ['vol] n. wool; a. woolly.
wolf ['volf] n. (wolwe) wolf.
wolk ['volk] n. (-e) cloud.
'**wolkruid** ['volkRœit] n. lamb's tail.
wond ['vont] n. (-e) wound.
'**wonder** ['vonəR] n. wonder, miracle; v. (ge-) wonder; **-lik** a. (-e) wonderful, strange.
'**wondnaald** ['vontnālt] n. suture needle.
'**woning** ['vōnəng] n. (-s) dwelling, residence.
woon ['vōn] v. (ge-) dwell, live, stay,

reside; **-plek** n. domicile; habitat; residence; dwelling; **-wa** n. caravan.
woord ['vōRt] n. (-e) word; **-elik** a. (-e) literal, verbal, verbatim.
word ['vōRt] v. (ge-) become, get, turn, grow, be; **-ing** n. birth, origin.
wors ['vauRs] n. (-s) sausage.
'**worstel** ['vōRstəl] v. (ge-) wrestle, struggle; **-ing** n. struggle, wrestling.
'**wortel** ['vōrtəl] n. (-s) root; carrot.
woud ['vɔat] n. wood, forest.
wraak ['vRāk] n. revenge, vengeance; v. (ge-) disapprove; -'**lustig** a. (-e) vindictive.
wrak ['vRak] n. (ke) wreck.
wrang ['vRang] a. (-e) bitter.
wreed ['vRēt] a. (wrede) cruel.
wreek ['vRēk] v. (ge-) revenge, avenge, wreak; cp. **wraak**.
'**wrewel** ['vRēvəl] n. annoyance, spite.
'**wrikbaar** ['vRəkbāR] a. (-'wrikbare) unstable.
wring ['vRəng] v. (ge-) wring, twist; **-ing** n. torsion; **-krag** n. torque.
'**wroeging** ['vruchəng] n. (-e, -s) remorse, compunction.
wrok ['vRok] n. grudge, rancour; cp. **wraak**.
wuif ['vœif] v. (ge-) wave.
'**wulps** ['vʌlps] a. prurient.
wurg ['vʌRch] v. (ge-) strangle, throttle.
wurm ['vʌRəm] n. (-s) worm, grub; **-doder** n. vermicide; **-middel** n. vermifuge.
wy ['vay] v. (ge-) ordain, consecrate.
wyd ['vayt] a. (wye, wyer, -ste) wide, broad, spacious; **-te** n. width, gauge, calibre.
wyf ['vayf] n. (wywe) vixen; **-ie** dim. female (animal).
wyk ['vayk] n. (-e) quarter, ward; v. (ge-) yield, make way.
wyl ['vayl] n. while; conj. since, because; v. (ge-) stop, sojourn; **-e** a. late, deceased.
wyn ['vayn] n. wine; **-gaard** n. vineyard = **wingerd**; **-kelkie** n. wine-glass; **kelkievol** n. wine-glassful; **-ruit** n. rue; **-vomitief** n. ipecacuanha wine.
wys ['vays] v. (ge-) point, show.
'**wyse** ['vaysə] n. (-s) manner, way, fashion; wise one; a. (wise); **-lik** av. wisely.
'**wysgeer** ['vayschēR] n. philosopher.
'**wysheid** ['vaysayt] n. wisdom.
'**wysie** ['vaysi] n. (-s) tune.
wyt ['vayt] v. (ge-) blame (a person for something).

X

'**x-bene** ['eks-bēnə] n. knock-knees.
'**x-strale** ['ekstRālə] n. x-rays.
xilo'foon [ksilŏ'fōn] n. xylophone.

Y

'**YSKOR** ['ayskoR] (Yster- en Staal-

korporasie) abbr. **ISCOR** [Iron & Steel Corporation].

'ydel ['aydəl] *a.* (*-e*) vain; idle, empty; **-heid** *n.* vanity; **-tuit** *n.* vain person.

yk ['ayk] *n.* gauge, verification (*of weights and measures*); *v.* (ge-) gauge, stamp and verify; **-er** *n.* inspector of weights and measures.

yl ['ayl] *a.* thin, rare; *v.* (ge-) be delirious; hasten, hurry; **-'hoofdig** *a.* (*-e*) delirious; **-ings** *av.* hurriedly.

ys ['ays] *n.* ice; *v.* (ge-) shudder, shiver; **-ig** *a.* (*-e*) as cold as ice, icy; **-lik** *a.* (*-e*) horrible; **-tyd** *n.* glacial period.

'yskas ['ayskas] *n.* (*-te*) refrigerator.

'yster ['aystəR] *n.* (*-s*) iron; **-klou** *n.* *-in die grond slaan* take to one's heels, stand firm; **-saag** *n.* hack saw; **-vark** *n.* porcupine; **-ware** *n.* hardware.

'ywer ['ayvəR] *n.* diligence, zeal; **-ig** *a.* (*-e*) diligent.

Z

'zero ['sĕRð] *n.* zero.

'Zeus ['zœs] *n.* Zeus.

'zoeloe ['zulu] *n.* (*-s*) Zulu.

zoem! ['zum] *n.* buzzing; *v.* (ge-) buzz, hum, drone.

ENGELS - AFRIKAANS
ENGLISH - AFRIKAANS

Saamgestel deur
ABEL COETZEE
M.A., D.Litt. (Witwatersrand), D.Lit. et. Phil. (Nijmegen)
Emeritus Professor
Universiteit van die Witwatersrand

AANTEKENINGE OOR DIE ENGELS-AFRIKAANSE GEDEELTE

A. Grammatika

1. *Selfstandige Naamwoorde*

(i) Waar meervoude van *snwe.* gevorm word deur slegs *-s, -es, -en, -ren* by die enkelvoud te voeg, word dit so aangedui ni die Woordeboek:
   horse, (*-s*); **brush,** (*-es*); *d.i.ev.* **horse,** *mv.* **horses;** *ev.* **brush,** *mv.* **brushes.**

(ii) Waar die meervoudsvorm opvallend verskil van die enkelvoud, word die meervousdvorm voluit aangegee, *bv.*:
   mouse, (*mice*), *d.i. ev.* **mouse,** *mv.* **mice.** So ook **tooth,** (teeth); **man,** (*men*), ens.

(iii) Waar dubbele meervoudsvorms voorkom wat albei gangbaar is, word dit so aangedui:
   soprano, (*-s, soprani*), *d.i.* in Engels het **soprano** twee meervoudsvorms: **sopranos** en **soprani.**

(iv) Waar slegs die laaste gedeelte van die *snw.* verandering ondergaan om die meervoud to vorm, word dit as volg aangedui:
   story, (*stories*), *d.i. ev.* **story,** *mv.* **stories.** So ook **wolf,** (*wolves*); **penny,** (*pennies*).

2. *Byvoeglike Naamwoorde en Bywoorde*

(i) Waar die vergrotende en oortreffende trap gevorm word deur bloot *-er, -est,* by die stellende trap te voeg, word dit as volg aangedui in die Woordeboek:
   cold, (*-er, -est*), *d.i.* **cold-colder-coldest.**

(ii) By *bnwe.* wat eindig op *-ly,* vind daar gewoonlik 'n geringe wysiging plaas in die vergrotende en oortreffende trap, wat as volg aangedui word:
   ugly, (*uglier, ugliest*), *d.i.* **ugly-uglier-ugliest.**

(iii) Soms word die vergrotende en oortreffende trap aangedui deur *more* en *most* te gebruik, wat so aangedui word:
   exhilarating, (*more-,most-*), *d.i.* **exhilarating-more exhilarating-most exhilarating.**

(iv) Waar die afwykings groter in omvang is, of heeltemal verskil, word die trappe van vergelyking in hulle geheel aangegee, *bv.*:
   good, (*better, best*).

3. *Werkwoorde*

(i) In Engels word nog twee soorte werkwoorde onderskei: sterk en swak. By sterk werkwoorde word die verlede tyd en die verlede deelwoord gewoonlik aangedui deur middel van klinkerwisselings, gevolglik word diê vorms volledig aangegee in die Woordebork, *bv.*:
   teach, (*taught, taught*); **eat,** (*ate, eaten*).

(ii) By swak werkwoorde word die verlede tyd en die verlede deelwoord gevorm deur die toevoeging van *-ed* aan die teenwoordige tydsvorm wat soms klein wysiginkies veroorsaak, wat as volg aangedu word:
   walk, (*-ed, -ed*), *d.i.* **walk-walked-walked;**
   defy, (*defied, defied*), *d.i.* **defy-defied-defied;**
   refer, (*-red, -red*), *d.i.* **refer-referred-referred.**

(iii) Alle ander afwykinge word ten volle aangegee.

4. *Algemeen*

(i) Wanneer 'n hoofwoord deur middel van 'n voorbeeld verduidelik word, word die hoofwoord nie in die verduideliking herhaal nie, maar om ruimte te bespaar, word dit deur 'n streep vervang, *bv.*:

goose, *sauce for the -, is sauce for the gander.*

(ii) Waar 'n samestelling nie in die Woordeboek opgeneem is nie, moet die aparte bestanddele van die samestelling nageslaan word om die betekenis vas te stel, *bv.*:

railway-station; slaan dan **railway** en **station** apart na.

(iii) Afgeleide woorde en bepaalde samestellinge word gewoonlik nie as aparte hoofwoorde in die Woordeboek aangewys nie, maar meestal as ondergeskikte inskrywing. Dit bring mee dat woorde meestal paragraafsgewyse saamgegropeeer is. Hierop moet die leser bedag wees, anders kan dit gebeur dat iemand te vergeefs na 'n bepaalde woord soek. Om hierdie moeilikheid te beperk, word in besondere gevalle in die woordelys verwys na die plek waar die verklaring wel verstrek word.

(iv) Waar (=) gebruik word, beteken dit dat die twee woorde dieselfde betekenis het; *vgl.* by 'n woord dui aan dat 'n verwysing (vergelyking met) na die betrokke woord meer lig sal bring in verband met die betekenis.

B. Uitspraak

In 'n land waar twee tale daagliks langs mekaar in gebruik is op alle lewensterreine, is dit wenslik dat 'n tweetalige woordeboek van die betrokke tale ook aanduidings sal verstrek van hoe om die woorde juis uit te spreek. Hiervoot het ons 'n stelsel ontwerp waarby 'n kennis van fonetiek nie vereis word nie, maar wat maklik begryp sal word deur enige gewone persoon wat Afrikaanssprekend is. Mens onthou natuurlik daarby dat die klanke van een taal nooit volkome aangedui kan word deur middel van klanke van 'n ander taal nie; derhalwe moet elkeen wat 'n vreemde taal aanleer, sorgvuldig luister hoe die moedertaalsprekers van daardie taal praat, en die klanke suiwer probeer naboots. Sodoende sal die aanduidings wat ons in die Woordeboek verstrek aangaande die uitspraak ook doelmatiger word vir die persoon wat die Woordeboek hanteer.

Hier volg nou 'n uiteensetting van die klankwaarde van die tekens wat aangewend word om die Engelse uitspraak vir die Afrikaanssprekende te benader:

1. *Engelse Medeklinkers*

Engels		Afrikaans
c,	soos **k** in **kan** - - - - - - - - -	k
	soos **s** in **is** - - - - - - - - -	s
ch,	soos **sj** in **masjien** - - - - - - -	sj
	soos **tsj** in **tjank** - - - - - - -	tsj
	soos **k** in **kroon** - - - - - - - -	k
g,	soos **dsj** in **jong** (Maleis) - - - -	dsj
	soos **gh** in **ghoen** - - - - - - -	gh
h,	uitgespreek soos in Afrikaans, maar sonder stem - -	h
j,	soos **dsj** in **jong** (Maleis) - - - - -	dsj
ph,	soos **f** in **pof** - - - - - - - -	f
qu,	soos **kw** in **twak** - - - - - - -	kw
s,	soos **s** in **neus** - - - - - - -	s
	soos **s** in **dis waar** - - - - - -	z
	soos **sj** in **dis jy** - - - - - - -	zj
sh,	soos **sj** in **masjien** - - - - - - -	sj
v,	soos **w** in **wie** - - - - - - - -	v

w,	soos w in **whê**-	-	-	-	-	-	-	-	-	-	-	w
y,	soos j in **Jan**	-	-	-	-	-	-	-	-	-	-	j
z,	soos s in **diswaar**, en z in **Zoeloe**	-	-	-	-	-	-	z
b, f, l, m, n, ng, nk,	soos in Afrikaans	-	-	b, f, l, m, n, ng, nk
k, p, t,	soos in Afrikaans, gevolg deur asemstoot	-	-	k, p, t
r,	uitgespreek met die tongpunt teruggetrek en met lippe			
	getrek soos wanneer mens fluit	-	-	-	-	-	-	r
th,	uitgespreek soos s by iemand wat met tong stoot	-	-	th
dh,	soos th, maar met stem	-	-	-	-	-	-	-	-	dh

Klanke wat „stom" is, word nie by die uitspraak aangetoon nie.

2. *Engelse Klinkers en Tweeklanke*

a,	word byna soos ê uitgespreek	-	-	-	-	-	-	-	æ
	soos a in **vader**	-	-	-	-	-	-	-	-	ā
ai,	soos ê in **bêre** -	-	-	-	-	-	-	-	-	ê
aw,	soos ô in **môre**	-	-	-	-	-	-	-	-	ô
ay,	soos y in **byna**-	-	-	-	-	-	-	-	-	y
e,	soos e in **hen** -	-	-	-	-	-	-	-	-	e
	soos e in **pote** -	-	-	-	-	-	-	-	-	ə
ee,	soos ie in **bier**	-	-	-	-	-	-	-	-	i
ei,	soos ai in **baie**	-	-	-	-	-	-	-	-	ai
	soos y in **byna**	-	-	-	-	-	-	-	-	y
i,	soos ie in **piet**-	-	-	-	-	-	-	-	-	i
	soos ai in **baie**	-	-	-	-	-	-	-	ai, äi
o,	soos o in **rond**	-	-	-	-	-	-	-	-	o
	soos ou in **hout**	-	-	-	-	-	-	-	-	ou
oo,	soos oe in **boet** en **bœr**	-	-	-	-	-	oe, ōē
ou,	soos in **au** en **hout** -	-	-	-	-	-	au, ou
ow,	soos in **au**	-	-	-	-	-	-	-	-	au
oy,	soos oi in **boikot**	-	-	-	-	-	-	-	-	oi
u,	soos joe in **jœrnaal**	-	-	-	-	-	-	-	joe
	byna soos a in **pap** -	-	-	-	-	-	-	-	∆

C. Klem

Die hoofklem van die woorde in hierdie Woordeboek word by die uitspraakaanduidings aangegee deur middel van 'n nadruksteken vóór die lettergreep waarop dit val, bv.:

harmful, [ˈhāmfoel], *d.i.* die klem val op **harm**-.

D. Afkortings wat in hierdie Woordeboek gebruik word

bnw.	-	-	byvoeglike	*tw.*	-	telwoord
			naamwoord	*verl. t.*	-	verlede tyd
bv.	-	-	byvoorbeeld	*verl. dw.*	-	verlede deelwoord
bw.	-	-	bywoord	*vgw.*	-	voegwoord
d.i.	-	-	dit is, dit beteken	*vs.*	-	voorsetsel
d.w.s.	-	-	dit wil sê	*vnw.*	-	voornaamwoord
d.m.v.	-	-	deur middel van	*ww.*	-	werkwoord
ev.	-	-	enkelvoud	*hww.*	-	hulpwerkwoord
mv.	-	-	meervoud	*v.d.*	-	van die
inf.	-	-	infinitief	*verkl.*	-	verkleining,
s.	-	-	selfstandige			verkleinwoord
			naamwoord	*vgl.*	-	vergelyk met
tt.	-	-	teenwoordige tyd	*voors.*	-	voorsetsel
tussenw.	-	tussenwerpsel			

A.1. first-class, *eersteklas.*

A.A. Automobile Association, *A.A.*

A.C. before Christ, *v.C.*

A.D. in the year of our Lord, *n.C.*

ad lib. at pleasure, *ad lib.*

A.D.C. aide-de-camp, *A.D.C.*

a.m. before noon, *vm.*

An. in the year, *in die jaar.*

A.R.A. Associate of the Royal Academy.

A.S. Anglo-Saxon, *Angelsaksies, A.S.*

A.V. Authorised Version, *gemagtigde vertaling.*

avoir. avoirdupois, *avoir.*

b. born, *geb.*

B.B.C. British Broadcasting Corporation.

B.C. before Christ, *v.C.*

B.M.A. British Medical Association, *Britse Mediese Vereniging.*

C. centigrade, *C.*

c. cent.

C.A. chartered accountant.

Cantab. Cantabrigiensis (of Cambridge).

C.E. civil engineer.

cf. confer (compare), *vgl.*

C.I.D. Criminal Investigation Department, *Departement vir Ondersoek van Kriminele Sake.*

C.-in-C. Commander-in-Chief, *opperbevelhebber.*

cir., circ. circa (about), *ongev.*

C.O. commanding officer, *bevelvoerende offisier.*

C.O.D. cash on delivery, *kba.*

Col. Colonel, *kol.*

con. contra (against), *vs.* (*teen*).

cwt. hundredweight, *ct.*

d. died; penny, *oorl.*; *d.*

D.F.C. Distinguished Flying Cross.

D.F.M. Distinguished Flying Medal.

D.P.H. Diploma in Public Health, *Diploma in Volksgesondheid.*

Dr. doctor; debtor, *dr.*; *dt.*

D.S.O. Distinguished Service Order.

e.g. for example, *bv.*

et al. and others, *e.a.*

etc. etcetera, *ens.*

E. & O.E. errors and omissions excepted, *F. & W.U.*

F. Fahrenheit, *F.*

F.D. Defender of the Faith.

F.M. Field-Marshal, *Veldm.*

F.R.C.P. Fellow of the Royal College of Physicians.

F.R.C.S. Fellow of the Royal College of Surgeons.

F.R.G.S. Fellow of the Royal Geographical Society.

F.R.S. Fellow of the Royal Society.

G.B. Great Britain, *G.B.*

G.B.E. Knight (Dame) Grand Cross of the Order of the British Empire.

G.H.Q. general headquarters, *G.H.K.*

G.M.T. Greenwich mean time, *Greenwich-tyd.*

G.P.O. General Post Office, *H.P.K.*

h., hr. hour, *u.*

Hon. Honourable; honorary, *Agb.*; *ere-.*

ib., ibid. in the same place, *ibid.*

id. the same, *dies.*

i.e. that is, *d.i.*

Inc. incorporated, *geinkor.*

incog. incognito (unknown), *onder skuilnaam.*

I.O.U. I owe you, *skuldbrief.*

J.P. Justice of the Peace, *V.R.*

jr., jun. junior, *jr., jun.*

L., lb. pound in weight, *lb.*

£. pound sterling, *£.*

l.c. in the place cited, *t.a.p.*

Lieut., Lt. lieutenant, *luit.*

loc. cit. in place cited, *t.a.p.*

L.R.A.M. Licentiate of Royal Academy of Music.

M. thousand; monsieur, *M., mnr.*

M.B.E. Member of the Order of the British Empire.

M.C. Military Cross.

mem(o). memorandum, *mem(o)*.

Mgr. monseigneur, *Mgr*.

Mlle. mademoiselle, *mej*.

MM. messieurs, *hh*.

M.P. Member of Parliament, *L.V*.

m.p.h. miles per hour, *m.p.u*.

M.P.S. Member of the Pharmaceutical Society, *lid van die aptekersvereniging*.

M.R.C.P. Member of the Royal College of Physicians.

M.R.C.S. Member of the Royal College of Surgeons.

MS(S). manuscript(s), *hs(s)*.

N.C.O. non-commissioned officer *onderoffisier*.

nem. con. no one contradicting, *sonder teenstem*.

ob. died, *oorl*.

O.B.E. Officer of the Order of the British Empire.

O.C. officer commanding, *bevelvoerende offisier*.

O.K. all correct, *alles in orde*.

O.M. Order of Merit.

P.C. Privy Councillor, *lid van die Geheime Raad*.

p.m. afternoon, *nm*.

P.O. Post Office, *Pk*.

pop. population, *bevolking*.

pro tem. for the time being, *pro tem*.

P.S. postscript, *Ns*.

P.T.O. please turn over, *b.o*.

Q.E.D. which was to be demonstrated. *Q.E.D*.

Q.E.F. which was to be done, *Q.E.F*.

R. Rand, *R*.

R.A. Royal Academician.

R.A.C. Royal Automobile Club.

R.A.F. Royal Air Force, *Eng. Kon. Lugmag*.

R.I.P. may he (she) rest in peace, *R.I.P*.

R.N. Royal Navy, *Koninklike Vloot*.

R.N.R. Royal Navy Reserve, *Koninklike Vlootreserwe*.

R.N.V.R. Royal Navy Volunteer Reserve, *Vrywilligerreserwe van die Koninklike Vloot*.

R.S.A. Republic of South Africa, *Republiek van Suid-Afrika*.

R.S.V.P. reply, please, *A. Asb*.

Rt. Hon. Right Honourable, *Ed. Agb*.

R.V. Revised Version.

S.A. State's Advocate (formerly K.C., Q.C.), *S.A. Staatsadvokaat*.

S.O.S. international signal of distress (noodsein), *SOS*.

S.P.C.A. Society for the Prevention of Cruelty to Animals. *Dierebeskermings-Vereniging*.

TB. Tuberculosis, *TB*.

T.N.T. trinitrotoluene (explosive), *springstof*.

Toc H. Talbot House.

T.U.C. Trades Union Congress.

U.K. United Kingdom, *V.K*.

ult. last, *ll*.

U.N.O. United Nations Organization, *V.V., Verenigde Volke*.

UNISA. University of South Africa, *Unisa, Universiteit van Suid-Afrika*.

U.S.A. United States of America, *V.S.A*.

v., vid. vide, see, look, *sien, kyk*.

V.A.D. voluntary aid detachment, *noodhulpdiens*.

V.C. Victoria Cross.

viz. namely; to wit, *nl.; t.w*.

vol. volume, *vol.; dl*.

vs. versus, *vs*.

W. west, *W*.

W.C. water-closet, *toiletkamertjie, gemak*.

W.A.A.F. Women's Auxiliary Air Force.

W.P. Western Province, *W.P*.

W.R.N.S. Women's Royal Navy Service.

Xmas. Christmas, *Kersfees*.

y. year, *jaar, j*.

yd. yard, *jt*.

Y.M.C.A. Young Men's Christian Association, *C.J.V*.

Yr. year, *j*.

yrs. yours, *U dw*.

Y.W.C.A. Young Women's Christian Association, *C.J.V*.

ENGLISH—AFRIKAANS
ENGELS—AFRIKAANS

A

a, an [ə, 'y; 'ən, n] *onbep. lidw.* 'n.

a- ['ə] *voorvoegsel* op, te, na toe, in.

'aardvark ['ǎdvǎk] *s.* (-s) erdvark.

ab- [æb] *voorvoegsel* weg, vanaf, verwyder van.

a'back [ə'bæk] *bw.* agteruit; *taken - verbluf,* verras.

a'bandon [ə'bændən] *ww.* (-ed) opgee, verlaat, in die steek laat; **~s.** oorgawe; losbandigheid; vryheid; **-ed** *bnw.* verlate; losbandig; **-ment** *s.* oorgawe.

a'base [ə'bys] *ww.* (-d) verneder, verlaag; **-ment** *s.* vernedering.

a'bash [ə'bæsj] *ww.* (-ed) verleë maak; verbluf; **-ed** *bnw.* verleë, skaam.

a'bate [ə'byt] *ww.* (-d) verminder, matig, bedaar.

'abattoir ['æbətwǎ] *s.* (-s) slagpaal, slagplek.

'abbey ['æbi] *s.* (-s) abdy, klooster.

ab'breviate [ə'briviyt] *ww.* (-d) verkort, afkort; **abbrevi'ation** *s.*

'abdicate ['æbdikyt] *ww.* (-d) afstand doen van, neerlê.

abdi'cation [æbdi'kysjən] *s.* troonsafstand, abdikasie.

'abdomen ['æbdəmen] *s.* onderbuik, maag.

ab'duct [æb'dʌkt] *ww.* (-ed) ontvoer, skaak.

a'bed [ə'bed] *bw.* in of op die bed.

abe'rration [æbə'rysjən] *s.* afwyking; misstap.

a'bet [ə'bet] *ww.* (-ted) aanspoor, opstook; help, steun; **-tor** *s.* (-s) opstoker; handlanger, medepligtige.

a'beyance [ə'byəns] *s.* stilstand, opskorting.

ab'hor [əb'hô] *ww.* (-red) verafsku, verag; **-rence** *s.*

a'bide [ə'bǎid] *ww.* (-d) vertoef, bly; afwag; verdra; **a'biding** *bnw.* blywende, vaste.

a'bility [ə'biliti] *s.* (*a'bilities*) bekwaamheid, vermoë, talent.

'abject ['æbdsjekt] *bnw.* verworpe, laag, kruipend.

ab'jure [æb'dsjoeə] *ww.* (-d) afsweer, verloën, versaak.

a'blaze [ə'blyz] *bnw. & bw.* aan brand, glansend.

'able ['ybl] *bnw.* (-r, -st) bekwaam, knap, bevoeg; **ably** *bw.* behendig, op bekwame manier.

a'blution [ə'blōěsjən] *s.* afwassing, reiniging, suiwering; **a'bluent** *bnw.* afwassend, reinigend.

'abne'gation [æbni'ghysjən] *s.* ont-

kenning, verloëning; ontsegging; versaking.

ab'normal [æb'nômǝl] *bnw.* abnormaal, afwykend; misvorm; sieklik; **abnor'mality** *s.*

a'board [ə'bôd] *bw. & voors.* aan boord.

a'bode [ə'boud] *s.* (-s) woning, tuiste, verblyf.

a'bolish [ə'bolisj] *ww.* (-ed) afskaf; oplief; herroep; **abo'lition** *s.*

a'bominable [ə'bominəbl] *bnw.* (*more, most*) afskuwelik, walglik; **a'bominate** *ww.* (-d) verafsku, verfoei.

a'bortion [ə'bôsjən] *s.* miskraam; vrugafdrywing; misbaksel.

a'bortive [ə'bôtiv] *bnw.* mislukte, vrugteloos.

a'bound [ə'baund] *ww.* (-ed) volop wees, wemel.

a'bout [ə'baut] *voors.* om, rondom, omstreeks, ongeveer; *bw.* om, rond.

a'bove [ə'bʌv] *voors.* bo, bo-oor, bo-op; bokant; *bw.* omhoog, bo; *bnw.* bostaande.

a'bove-'board [ə'bʌv'bôd] *bnw.* eerlik; rondborstig; billik.

a'brasion [ə'bryzjən] *s.* afskawing, skaafplek, skuurplek; **a'brasive** *bnw.* skurend(e); *s.* skuurmiddel.

a'breast [ə'brest] *bw.* naasmekaar, in gelid.

a'bridge [ə'bridzj] *ww.* (-d) verkort; **-ment** *s.* verkorting.

a'broad [ə'brôd] *bw.* van huis, buitelands.

'abrogate ['æbroghyt] *ww.* (-d) herroep, ophef, afskaf; **abro'gation** *s.* herroeping, opheffing, afskaffing.

a'brupt [ə'brʌpt] *bnw.* (-est) kortaf; skielik; onverwags; steil; **-ly** *bw.* kortaf, plotseling; **-ness** *s.*

'abscess ['æbsis] *s.* geswel, sweer, abses.

ab'scond [əb'skond] *ww.* (-ed) vlug, wegloop.

'absence ['æbsəns] *s.* afwesigheid; verstrooidheid; **'absent** *bnw.* afwesig; afgetrokke, *ww.* (-ed) verwyder, wegbly; **'absentee** *s.* afwesige.

'absinth oil ['æbsinth oil] *s.* alsolie.

'absolute ['æbsəloet] *bnw.* volstrek, totaal, absoluut; **-ly** *bw.* volstrek, heeltemal.

abso'lution [æbsə'lōěsjən] *s.* vergifnis, kwytskelding, absolusie; *vgl.* absolve.

ab'solve [əb'zolv] *ww.* (-d) kwytskeld, vryspreek.

ab'sorb əb'sôb] *ww.* (-*ed*) opsuig,
absorbeer; -ent *bnw.* opsuigend,
absorberend; -ent *gauze s.* absor-
beergaas; **ab'sorption** *s.* absorpsie.

ab'stain [əb'styn] *ww.* (-*ed*) jou
onthou van; wegbly; **'abstinence** *s.*
onthouding, matigheid.

ab'stemious [æb'stimiəs] *bnw.*
onthoudend, matig; **ab'stention** *s.*
onthouding; onttrekking; matigheid.

ab'sterge [əb'stɜdzj] *ww.* (-*d*) afwis,
suiwer, reinig; -nt *bnw.* suiwerend,
reinigend.

'abstract ['æbstɪækt] *bnw.* afgetrokke, abstrak; *ww.* (-*ed*) afskei,
uittrek; *s.* uittreksel, afkooksel,
opsomming.

ab'surd [əb'sɜd] *bnw.* (-*est*) onredelik,
dwaas; -ity *s.*

a'bundance [ə'bʌndəns] *s.* oorvloed,
rykdom; **a'bundant** *bnw.* oorvloedig,
volop.

a'buse [ə'bjôez] *ww.* (-*d*) misbruik;
mishandel; beledig; skend; *s.* (-*s*)
misbruik; **a'busive** *bnw.* beledigend.

a'but [ə'bʌt] *ww.* (-*ted*) grens aan;
-ment *s.* grens.

a'byss [ə'bis] *s.* (-*es*) afgrond.

a'cacia [ə'kysjə] *s.* (-*s*) akasia.

a'cademy [ə'kædəmi] *s.* (*a'cademies*)
akademie, genootskap; **aca'demic**
(al) *bnw.* akademies.

a'canthus [ə'kænthʌs] *s.* akant,
beerklou.

a'carpous [ə'kɑpəs] *bnw.* nie-
vrugdraend.

ac'cede [æk'sid] *ww.* (-*d*) toestem,
aanvaar; toetree.

ac'celerate [æk'seləryt] *ww.* (-*d*)
versnel, verhaas; vervroeg; **ac-
'celerator** *s.* versneller.

'accent ['æksənt] *s.* (-*s*) aksent,
nadruk, klem; uitspraak; stem-
buiging, *ww.* (æk'sent) (-*ed*) betoon,
beklem, nadruk lê op; **ac'centuate**
ww. (-*d*) aksentueer, beklem, betoon.

ac'cept [ak'sept] *ww.* (-*ed*) anneem,
aanvaar, ontvang; -able *bnw.* aanneemlik, welkom; -ance *s.* aanname,
ontvangs; -ed *bnw.* aangenome,
gangbaar.

'access ['ækses] *s.* toegang; toename;
ac'cessible *bnw.* toeganklik.

ac'cessory [æk'sesəri] *s.* medepligtige.

ac'cessory [æk'sesəri] *bnw.* byko-
mend, bykomstig; *s.* (*ac'cessories*)
toebehoorsel, onderdeel, bybehore.

'accident ['æksidənt] *s.* (-*s*) ongeluk,
ongeval; **acci'dental** *bnw.* toevallig;
- insurance *s.* ongeluksversekering;
- rate *s.* ongeluksyfer.

ac'claim [ə'klym] *ww.* (-*ed*) toejuig;
accla'mation *s.* byval.

ac'climatize [ə'klaimətaiz] *ww.* (-*d*)
wen aan die klimaat, aanpas.

ac'clivity [ə'kliviti] *s.* (*ac'clivities*)
opdraande, steilte.

ac'commodate [ə'komədyt] *ww.* (-*d*)
inneem, herberg; aanpas, voeg; guns
bewys; **accommo'dation** *s.* aan-
passing; skikking; herberg

ac'company [ə'kʌmpəni] *ww.*
(*ac'companied*) begelei; vergesel.

ac'complice [ə'kʌmplis] *s.* (-*s*)
medepligtige.

ac'complish [ə'komplisj] *ww.* (-*ed*)
uitvoer, volbring.

ac'cordance [ə'kôdəns] *s.* ooreenstemming; **ac'cordingly** *bw.* gevolglik.

ac'cord [ə'kôd] *ww.* (-*ed*) ooreenstem,
akkordeer; vergun; versoen; *s.* (-*s*)
ooreenstemming, akkoord, ooreenkoms; *with one* - eenparig; *of one's
own* - op eie houtjie.

ac'cost [ə'kost] *ww.* (-*ed*) aanspreek,
aanklamp.

ac'count [ə'kaunt] *s.* (-*s*) rekening;
rekenskap; verslag; *ww.* (-*ed*) beskou,
reken as, hou vir; -ancy *n.* boekhou-
kunde, rekeningkunde; -ant *s.*
rekenmeester, boekhouer.

ac'coutrement [ə'kôtrəmənt] *s.*
opskik, uitrusting.

ac'credit [ə'kredit] *ww.* (-*ed*) in
aansien bring, krediet verskaf;
magtig; erken; -ed *bnw.* amptelik
erken, aanvaar.

ac'crue [ə'krôe] *ww.* (-*d*) toeneem,
oploop, aangroei.

ac'cumulate [ə'kjôemjoelyt] *ww.*
(-*d*) ophoop; vermenigvuldig; opgaar; **accumu'lation** *s.* ophoping,
opgaring, akkumulasie; **ac'cumulative** *bnw.* opstapelend, toenemend.

'accuracy ['ækjoerəsi] *n.* noukeurig-
heid, juistheid, akkuraatheid; **'accurate** *bnw.* noukeurig, presies,
akkuraat.

ac'cursed [ə'kɜsid] *bnw.* vervloek
(te), ellendig(e).

ac'cuse [ə'kjoez] *ww.* (-*d*) beskuldig,
aankla; -d *s.* aangeklaagde; -r *s.*
beskuldiger; **accu'sation** *s.* beskuldiging; **ac'cusative** *s. & bnw.* akkusa-
tief.

ac'custom [ə'kʌstəm] *ww.* (-*ed*) wen
aan, gewoon maak (raak).

'ace ['ys] *s.* (-*s*) aas; bass-.

a'cerbity [ə'sɜbiti] *s.* wrangheid,
bitterheid, bitsigheid.

a'cetic [ə'sitik] *bnw.* suur.

ache ['yk] *s.* (-*s*) pyn, smart; *ww.*
(-*d*) pyn, seer wees.

a'chieve [ə'tsjiv] *ww.* (-*d*) verrig;
bereik; presteer; -ment *s.* (-*s*)
sukses, prestasie.

'acid ['æsid] *bnw.* (-*est*) suur, wrang;
s. (-*s*) suur; **a'cidity** *s.* suurheid,
suurgehalte; -proof *bnw.* suurbestand, suurvas.

a'cidulous [ə'sidjoeləs] *bnw.* suur-
derig.

ack'nowledge [ək'nolidzj] *ww.* (-*d*)
erken; **ac'knowledgement** *s.*

'acme ['ækmi] *s.* toppunt, hoogtepunt.

'acorn ['ykôn] *s.* (-*s*) akker, eikel.

ac'quaint [ə'kwynt] *ww.* (-*ed*)
bekend maak, meedeel; -ance *s.*
kennis; bekende.

acqui'esce [ækwi'es] *ww.* (*-d*) berus; instem; **-nce** *s.* berusting.

ac'quire [ə'kwaiə] *ww.* (*-d*) verwerf, verkry.

acqui'sition [ækwi'zisjən] *s.* (*-s*) verwerwing; aanwins.

ac'quit [ə'kwit] *ww.* (*-ted*) vryspreek, ontslaan.

'acre ['ykə] *s.* (*-s*) akker; **-age** *s.* grootte in akkers.

'acrid ['ækrid] *bnw.* bitter; bitsig; **a'cridity** *s.* bitsigheid.

'acrimony ['ækriməni] *s.* bitterheid; bitsigheid; **acri'monious** *bnw.* bitter; bitsig.

'acrobat ['ækrobæt] *s.* (*-s*) kunstemaker, akrobaat.

acro'batics [ækro'bætiks] *s.* (*mv.*) kunsies, toertjies, toudansery.

a'cross [ə'kros] *voors.* oor, dwarsoor, anderkant; *bw.* dwars, oorkruis.

'act ['ækt] *s.* (*-s*) handeling, daad; bedryf; wet; akte; *ww.* (*-ed*) handel, te werk gaan; optree; **-ing** *bnw.* handelend; waarnemend; **-ion** ['æksjən] *s.* handeling, daad, optrede; **-ionable** *bnw.* afdwingbaar; **-ive** *bnw.* bedrywig, aktief; **ac'tivity** *s.* bedrywigheid.

'actor ['æktə] *s.* (*-s*) toneelspeler; dader; bewerker; **'actress** *s.* aktrise.

'actual ['æktjoeəl] *bnw.* werklik, wesenlik; **-ly** *bw.* werklik, regtig.

'actuary ['æktjoeəri] *s.* ('actuaries) aktuarius, wiskundige adviseur.

'actuate ['æktjoeyt] *ww.* beweeg, moveer, aandryf.

a'cumen [ə'kjöēmən] *s.* skerpsinnigheid.

a'cute [ə'kjoet] *bnw.* (*-st*) skerp, gevat; akuut.

'adage ['ædidzj] *s.* spreekwoord, gesegde.

'adamant ['ædəmənt] *bnw.* adamant, onbuigsaam, onbeweeglik; hard; **ada'mantine** *bnw.* hard, onvermurwbaar.

a'dapt [ə'dæpt] *ww.* (*-ed*) aanpas.

add ['æd] *ww.* (*-ed*) byvoeg, optel; **ad'dition** *s.* toevoeging, optelling; **ad'ditional** *bnw.* addisioneel.

'addict ['ædikt] *ww.* (*-ed*) wy, oorgee.

'additive ['æditiv] *s.* (*-s*) additief, bymiddel.

'addled ['ædld] *bnw.* bedorwe, vrot.

ad'dress [ə'dres] *s.* (*-es*) adres; toespraak; optrede; bekwaamheid; *ww.* (*-ed*) aanspreek; adresseer.

ad'duce [ə'djöēs] *ww.* (*-d*) aanvoer, aanhaal, bybring.

ad'duct [ə'dʌkt] *ww.* (*-ed*) byeentrek, saamtrek.

'adept ['ædept] *s.* (*-s*) ingewyde, meester; *bnw.* ervare.

'adequate ['ædikwit] *bnw.* voldoende, afdoende, geskik.

ad'here [əd'hiə] *ww.* (*-d*) vaskleef; aanhang; staan by.

ad'hesion [əd'hizjən] *s.* vasklewing, adhesie; **ad'hesive** *bnw.* klewerig, taai.

a'dieu [ə'djöē] *tussenw.* (*-s*) vaarwel.

ad'jacent [ə'dzjysənt] *bnw.* aangrensend.

'adjective ['ædzjiktiv] *s.* (*-s*) byvoeglike naamwoord, adjektief.

ad'join [ə'dzjoin] *ww.* (*-ed*) grens aan; aanheg, aanvoeg; **-ing** *bnw.*

ad'journ [ə'dzjən] *ww.* (*-ed*) verdaag, uitstel.

ad'judge [ə'dzjʌdzj] *ww.* (*-d*) beslis, oordeel, toewys, toeken; **ad'judgement** *s.* oordeel, beslissing; toekenning.

ad'judicate [ə'dzjöēdikyt] *ww.* (*-d*) beoordeel, beslis; verklaar, toewys; **adjudi'cation** *s.* beslissing; toewysing; **-tor** *s.* (*-s*) beoordelaar.

'adjunct ['ædzjʌnkt] *bnw.* bygevoeg, toegevoeg, adjunk; hulp-; *s.* byvoegsel, toevoegsel; hoedanigheid, byomstandigheid.

ad'jure [ə'dzjöə] *ww.* (*-d*) besweer; smeek; **adju'ration** *s.* beswering; eed(oplegging).

ad'just [ə'dzjʌst] *ww.* (*-ed*) skik, reël, stel, aansuiwer, regstel, instel.

ad'minister [əd'ministə] *ww.* (*-ed*) bestuur, beheer, administreer; uitoefen; toepas; **ad'minis'tration** *s.* bestuur, beheer; toediening; **ad'ministrative** *bnw.* administratief; **ad'ministrator** *s.* administrateur, bestuurder.

'admiral ['ædmərəl] *s.* (*-s*) admiraal; **-ty** *s.* ('admiralties) admiraliteit, admiraliteitsgebou, admiraalskip.

ad'mire [əd'maiə] *ww.* (*-d*) bewonder, admireer; **'admirable** *bnw.* uitstekend; **admi'ration** *s.* bewondering.

ad'mit [əd'mit] *ww.* (*-ted*) toelaat; toestaan; erken; **ad'mission** *s.* toelating, toegang; erkenning; **-tance** *s.* toegang, toelating.

ad'monish [əd'monisj] *ww.* (*-ed*) vermaan, teregwys.

a'do [ə'döē] *s.* gedoente, ophef, drukte.

ado'lescence [ædo'lesns] *s.* jongelingskap, puberteitsjare.

ado'lescent [ædo'lesnt] *s.* jongeling; *bnw.* opgrociend.

a'dopt [ə'dopt] *ww.* (*-ed*) aanneem, kies.

a'dore [ə'dö] *ww.* (*-d*) aanbid, vereer.

a'dorn [ə'dön] *ww.* (*-ed*) versier, opskik.

a'drift [ə'drift] *bnw.* drywend, los.

a'droit [ə'droit] *bnw.* behendig; takvol.

'adulate ['ædjoelyt] *ww.* (*-d*) vlei, inkruip, lek; **adu'lation** *s.* vleiery; **adu'latory** *bnw.* vleiend, inkruiperig; **'adulator** *s.* (*-s*) vleier, inkruiper.

'adult ['ædʌlt] *s. & bnw.* volwasse(ne).

a'dulterate [ə'dʌltəryt] *ww.* (*-d*) vervals, besmet.

a'dultery [ə'dʌltəri] *s.* owerspel, egbreuk; **a'dulterer** *s.* (*-s*) owerspeler, hoereerder; **a'dulteress** s. owerspeelster, hoer; **a'dulterous** bnw. owerspelig, hoer-.

'adumbrate ['ædʌmbryt] ww. (-d) oorskadu; aandui; voorspel; **adum-'bration** s.

ad'vance [əd'våns] ww. & s. vorder (ing), styg(ing), bevorder(ing); -ment s. vooruitgang; bevordering; voorskot.

ad'vantage [əd'våntidzj] s. voordeel, voorsprong.

'advent ['ædvənt] s. (-s) koms, wederkoms, advent; **'adventist** s. (-s); gelowige in die wederkoms van Christus.

adven'titious [ædvən'tisjəs] bnw. toevallig, bykomstig.

ad'venture [əd'ventsjə] s. (-s) onderneming, waagstuk, awentuur.

'adverb ['ædvəb] s. (-s) bywoord.

'adverse ['ædvəs] bnw. vyandig; teenspoedig; ongunstig; **ad'versary** s. (ad'versaries) teenstander, opponent, vyand; **ad'versity** s. teenspoed.

ad'vert [əd'vət] ww. (-ed) verwys, refereer.

'advertise ['ædvə'taiz] ww. (-d) aankondig, adverteer.

ad'vice [əd'vais] s. raad, advies; berig.

ad'vise [əd'våiz] ww. (-d) aanraai; meedeel; -r s. raadgewer; **ad'visory** bnw. raadgewend.

'advocate ['ædvəkit] s. (-s) advokaat; voorspraak; ww. (-d) verdedig, bepleit, voorstaan.

'aegis ['idsjis] s. skild; beskerming.

'aerate ['əəryt] ww. (-d) met lug (koolsuur) versadig; **aerated water** s. spuitwater; **ae'ration** s. versadiging met lug of koolsuur.

'aeon ['iən] s. (-s) eeu, ewigheid.

'aerial ['əəriəl] s. lugdrade, antenne.

'aerodrome ['əərədroum] s. vliegveld, lughawe.

'aeronaut ['əərənòt] s. (-s) lugskipper, vliegenier; **aero'nautic** bnw. lugvaartkundig, lugvaart-; **aero-'nautics** s. lugvaartkunde, vliegkuns.

'aeroplane ['əərəplyn] s. vliegtuig.

'aesthetic ['isthetik] bnw. esteties.

a'far [ə'få] bw. ver, in die verte.

'affable ['æfəbl] bnw. vriendelik, minsaam.

af'fair [ə'fêə] s. (-s) saak, besigheid, affère, gedoente.

af'fect [ə'fekt] ww. (-ed) voorwend; aantas; **affec'tation** s. aanstellery, gemaaktheid; -ed bnw. aanstellerig; -ion s. aandoening; liefde; siekte; **a'ffectionate** bnw. minsaam, toegeneë.

affi'davit [æfi'dyvit] s. beëdigde verklaring.

af'filiate [ə'filiyt] ww. (-d) aanneem, erken (as kind); aansluit; affilieer; **a'ffili'ation** s. aanneming, erkenning; affiliasie.

af'finity [ə'finiti] s. (af'finities) verwantskap; ooreenkoms; affiniteit.

af'firm [ə'fəm] ww. (-ed) bevestig, bekragtig, verklaar.

af'fix [ə'fiks] ww. (-ed) aanheg; byvoeg; verbind.

af'flatus [æ'flytəs] s. inblasing, ingewing, inspirasie.

af'flict [ə'flikt] ww. (-ed) bedroef, kwel, teister.

'affluence ['æfloeəns] s. oorvloed, weelde; **'affluent** bnw. toevloeiend; oorvloedig, ryk; s. sytak, spruit.

'afflux ['æflʌks] s. toevloei; stroom; vermeerdering.

af'ford [ə'fòd] ww. verskaf; oplewer; bekostig.

affores'tation [æfori'stysjən] s. bebossing.

af'fray [ə'fry] s. (-s) relletjie, vegparty.

af'fright [ə'frait] ww. (-ed) verskrik, skrikmaak.

af'front [ə'frʌnt] s. belediging, a:frontasie.

af'fusion [ə'fjoezn] s. begieting.

a'field [ə'fild] bw. in die veld, op die slagveld; te velde; far - ver van die huis.

a'fire [ə'faiə] bw. aan brand.

a'flame [ə'flym] bw. in ligtelaaie.

a'float [ə'flout] bw. drywend; in die see; aan die gang; in omloop.

a'foot [ə'foet] bnw. & bw. te voet, op die been, op tou.

a'fore [ə'fò] voors. voor; bw. eer; -said bnw. voornoemd; -thought bnw. voorbedag, malice - (bose) opset.

a'fraid [ə'fryd] bnw. bang, bevrees.

Afri'kaans [afri'kåns] s. Afrikaans.

'aft ['åft] bnw., bw. agter.

'after ['åftə] voors. na, agter; bw. agterna, later; -math s. nasleep, nadraai; -'noon s. agtermiddag, namiddag; -thought s. nagedagte; uitvlug; -wards bw. naderhand, later.

a'gain [ə'ghyn] bw. weer, opnuut, verder.

a'gainst [ə'ghynst] voors. teen.

aga'panthus [æghə'pænthʌs] s. agapant, **kandelaar**.

a'gape [ə'ghyp] bw. met oop mond, verstom, dronkgeslaan.

'agate ['æghət] s. (-s) agaat.

a'gave [ə'ghyvi] s. garingboom.

age ['ydzj] s. ouderdom; leeftyd; tyd, eeu; come of - mondig word; ww. (-d) verouder; -d bnw. bejaard.

'agency ['ydzjənsi] s. ('agencies) agentskap; bemiddeling.

a'genda [ə'dzjendə] s. (-s) agenda, program van werksaamhede, sakelys.

'agent ['ydzjeənt] s. (-s) agent; werktuig.

ag'glomerate [ə'ghloməryt] ww. (-d) openhoop; **agglome'ration** s. opeenhoping.

ag'glutinate [ə'ghlöëtinyt] ww. (-d) saamkleef, agglutineer.

'aggravate ['æghrəvyt] ww. (-d) vererger; terg.

'aggregate ['æghrəghit] s. totaal.

ag'gress [ə'ghres] ww. (-ed) aanval, met rusie begin; -ion s. aanranding, aggressie; -ive bnw. parmantig, rusiemakerig; aanvallend; -or s. aanvaller, aanrander.

ag'grieved [ə'ghrivd] bnw. bedroef; gekrenk; veronreg.

a'ghast [ə'ghâst] bnw. versteld.

'agile ['ædzjail] bnw. rats, lenig.

'agitate ['ædzjityt] ww. (-d) beweeg; beroer; agiteer.

a'glow [ə'ghlou] bw. gloeiend, warm; blosend.

a'go [ə'ghou] bw. gelede.

a'gog [ə'ghogh] bw. opgewonde.

'agony ['æghəni] s. pyn. angs, kwelling.

a'gree [ə'ghri] ww. (-d) instem, akkoord gaan; -able bnw. aangenaam; -ment s. ooreenkoms.

agri'culture [æghri'kʌltsjə] landbou(kunde).

a'ground [ə'ghraund] bw. op die grond; gestrand; in verleentheid.

'ague ['yghjoe] s. (-s) koors, kouekoors.

a'head [ə'hed] bw. vooruit, voorop, voor, vooraan.

aid ['yd] ww. (-ed) help, bystaan; s. hulp, bystand.

'aide-de-camp [ydə'kang] s. adjutant.

ail ['yl] ww. (-ed) skeel, skort, siek wees; -ment s. siekte.

aim ['ym] ww. (-ed) mik, korrel; s. doel, oogmerk.

air [ɛə] s. lug, windjie; houding; wysie, lied; ww. (-ed) lug, droogmaak.

'air-base ['ɛəbys] s. (-s) lugbasis, basis van lugmag.

'air-borne ['ɛəbôn] bnw. wat met vliegtuie vervoer word.

'air-brake ['ɛəbryk] s. (-s) lugrem.

'air-con'ditioning ['ɛəkən'disjəning] s. lugversorging.

'air-cooled ['ɛəkôêld] bnw. lugverkoel.

'air-craft ['ɛəkrâft] s. vliegtuig.

'air-cushion ['ɛəkoesjən] s. (-s) luggevulde stootruimte.

'air-filter ['ɛəfiltə] s. (-s) lugsuiweraar.

'air-gun ['ɛəghʌn] s. (-s) windbuks.

'air-line ['ɛəlain] s. (-s) lugdiens; -r s. (-s) vliegtuig van 'n gereëlde lugdiens.

'air-mail ['ɛəmyl] s. lugpos (diens).

'air 'pocket ['ɛə 'pokit] s. (-s) lugholte.

'air-raid ['ɛəryd] s. (-s) lugaanval.

'air-tight ['ɛətait] bnw. lugdig.

'aisle ['ail] s. (-s) vleuel, paadjie.

a'jar [ə'dzjâ] bw. op 'n kier.

a'kimbo [ə'kimbou] bw. with arms - met die hande in die sy.

a'kin [ə'kin] bnw. verwant.

a'larm [ə'lâm] s. alarm; skrik; wekker; ww. (-ed) skrikmaak, waarsku.

a'las [ə'lâs] uitroep. helaas!

al'beit [ôl'biit] voegw. alhoewel.

'alcohol ['ælkəhol] s. alkohol, wyngees.

'alcove ['ælkouv] s. (-s) alkoof; somershuisie.

'ale ['yl] s. (-s) gebroude bier; -house s. biersaal, drinkplek.

a'lert [ə'lôt] bnw. waaksaam, wakker; alarmsein.

'alga ['ælghə] s. (algae) wier.

'algebra ['ældzjibrə] s. algebra, stelkunde.

'alias ['yliəs] s. (-es) aangenome naam.

'alibi ['ælibai] s. (-s) alibi.

a'light [ə'lait] ww. (-ed) afstyg, gaan sit, neerstryk; bnw. aan die brand, verlig.

'alien ['yliən] s. (-s) vreemde.

alie'nist [alêiə'nist] s. (-s) psigiater.

a'lign [ə'lain] ww. (-ed) opstel, rig; in gelid stel; spoor, stel, instel; -ment s. opstelling, rigting; sporing (van wiele).

a'like [ə'laik] bw. gelyk; eenders.

'alimony ['æliməni] s. ('alimonies) onderhoud, onderhoudskoste.

a'live [ə'laiv] bnw. & bw. lewendig.

'alkali ['ælkəlai] s. alkali, loogsout.

all ['ôl] bnw. alger, die hele; vnw. alger, alles; bw. heeltemal, totaal.

al'lay [ə'ly] ww. (-ed) verlig, versag, bedaar.

al'lege [ə'ledzj] ww. (-d) beweer; alle'gation s. bewering.

al'legiance [ə'lidzjəns] s. trou, getrouheid.

'allegory ['ælighəri] s. ('allegories) allegorie, sinnebeeldige voorstelling.

al'lergy [ə'lôdzjiə] s. allergie, prikkelingstoestand van liggaam.

al'leviate [ə'liviyt] ww. (-d) verlig, lenig; al'leviation s.

'alley ['æli] s. (-s) steeg, gang, laan.

al'liance [ə'laiəns] s. (-s) verbond.

'allied ['ælaid] bnw. verbonde, geallieer, verenig.

'allocate ['ælokyt] ww. (-d) aanwys, toeken; allo'cation s. aanwysing, toekenning.

al'lot [ə'lot] ww. (-ted) toewys toeken; -ment s. toewysing: perseel.

al'low [ə'lau] ww. (-ed) toestaan, toelaat; erken; -ance s. permissie; toelae, afslag.

'alloy ['æloi] s. metaalmengsel, legering; allooi, gehalte; kwaliteit; ww. (ə'loi) allieer, legeer.

all-risks policy ['ôl-risks 'polisi] s. alrisikopolis.

al'lude [ə'lôêd] ww. (-d) - to sinspeel op.

al'lure [ə'ljoeə] ww. (-d) aantrek, aanlok.

al'luvial [ə'loeviəl] bnw. aangespoelde, spoel-.

'ally ['æli] s. ('allies) bondgenoot.

'almanac ['ôlmənæk] s. (-s) almanak, kalender.

al'mighty [ôl'maiti] *bnw.* almagtig, yslik.

'almond ['âmənd] *s.* (-s) amandel; mangel.

'almoner ['âmnə] *s.* (-s) aalmoesenier.

'almost ['ôlmoust] *bw.* amper, byna.

alms ['âmz] *s.* aalmoes.

'aloe ['ælou] *s.* (-s) aalwyn.

a'loft [ə'loft] *bw.* bo, omhoog, hoog; in die hoogte.

a'lone [ə'loun] *bnw. & bw.* alleen, eensaam; net.

a'long [ə'long] *voors.* langs, naas; *bw.* aan, vooruit.

a'longside [ə'longsaid] *voors.* naas, naasaan, langsaan.

a'loof [ə'lôef] *bnw. & bw.* apart, ver, opsy.

a'loud [ə'laud] *bw.* hard, hardop, luid.

'alphabet ['ælfəbit] *s.* alfabet.

al'ready [ôl'redi] *bw.* al, alreeds.

'also ['ôlsou] *bw.* ook, eweneens, verder.

'altar ['ôltə] *s.* (-s) altaar; *lead to the* - hu, trou.

'alter ['ôltə] *ww.* (-ed) verander, wysig; **alte'ration** *s.* (-s) verandering, verstelling, wysiging.

alter'cation [ôltə'kysjən] *s.* (-s) woordewisseling, rusie.

'alter 'ego ['altə 'ighou] *s.* 'ander ek', alterego.

al'ternate [ôl'tənit] *bnw.* afwisselend; *ww.* ('ôltənyt) (-d) afwissel; verwissel; **al'ternative** *bnw.* ander; *s.* alternatief, keus.

al'though [ôl'dhou] *vgw.* voeg, al, alhoewel, almiskie.

'altitude ['æltitjôēd] *s.* hoogte.

alto'gether [ôltə'ghedhə] *bw.* altesame, heeltemal.

'always ['ôlwəz] *bw.* altyd, gedurig.

am ['æm] *ww.* (*was, have been*) is.

a'malgam [ə'mælghəm] *s.* mengsel, amalgaam; **-ate** *ww.* (-d) meng, saamsmelt, amalgameer; **a'malga-'mation** *s.* samesmelting, menging.

ama'ranthus [æmə'rænthʌs] *s.* amarant.

a'mass [ə'mæs] *ww.* (-ed) ophoop, byeenvergaar.

'amateur ['æmətə] *s.* amateur, liefhebber.

'amative ['æmətiv] *bnw.* verliefderig.

a'maze [ə'myz] *ww.* (-d) verbaas, verstom; **-ment** *s.* verbasing.

am'bassador [æm'bæsədə] *s.* (-s) gesant.

'amber ['æmbə] *s.* barnsteen.

ambi'dextrous [æmbi'dekstrʌs] *bw.* dubbelhandig.

am'biguous [æm'bighjoeəs] *bnw.* dubbelsinnig, duister.

ambi'lateral [æmbi'lætərəl] *bw.* bilateraal.

am'bition [æm'bisjən] *s.* eersug; doel, strewe; **am'bitious** *bnw.* eersugtig, vooruitstrewend.

am'bivalence [æmbi'vyləns] *s.* tweewaardigheid.

'amble ['æmbl] *ww.* (-d) trippel.

'ambulance ['æmbjoeləns] *s.* ambulans, veldhospitaal.

'ambush ['æmboesj] *s.* hinderlaag, val.

a'meliorate [ə'miliəryt] *ww.* (-d) verbeter, versag; **amelio'ration** *s.* verbetering, versagting.

a'men ['â'men] *s.* uitroep. amen!

a'menable [ə'minəbl] *bnw.* handelbaar, geseglik; - *to* vatbaar vir; **amena'bility** *s.* handelbaarheid, vatbaarheid.

a'mend [ə'mend] *ww.* (-ed) verander, wysig, verbeter; **-s** *s.* vergoeding, herstel.

'amiable ['ymjəbl] *bnw.* vriendelik, beminlik.

'amicable ['æmikəbl] *bnw.* vriendelik, vriendskaplik.

a'midst [ə'midst] *voors.* tussen, onder, te midde van.

a'miss [ə'mis] *bw.* verkeerd, onvanpas; *take* - kwalik neem.

'amity ['æmiti] *s.* vriendskap(likheid).

am'monia [ə'mounjə] *s.* ammoniak.

ammu'nition [æmjoe'nisjən] *n.* ammunisie, skietgoed.

am'nesia [æm'nizjə] *s.* geheueverlies, amnesie.

'amnesty ['æmnesti] *s.* vergifnis, verlies, amnestie.

a'mong, a'mongst [ə'mʌng, ə'mʌnkst] *voors.* onder, tussen.

a'moral [ə'morəl] *bnw.* sonder sedelikheid.

a'morphous [ə'môfəs] *bnw.* vormloos, amorf.

a'mount [ə'maunt] *s.* (-s) bedrag, som, opbrengs, hoeveelheid; *ww.* (-ed) bedra, beloop, beteken.

a'mour [ə'moeə] *s.* liefde, minnary; **'amorous** *bnw.* verlief, liefdes-; **'amorousness** *s.* verliefderigheid.

'amp ['æmp] *s.* (-s) amp (*elektr.*); **-erage** *s.* stroomsterkte.

'ample ['æmpl] *bnw.* (-r, -st) ruim, wyd, breedvoerig, oorvloedig.

'amplify ['æmplifai] *ww.* ('amplified) versterk, vergroot, uitbrei; **'amplifier** *s.* versterker, vergroter; **'amplification** *s.* vergroting, versterking.

'amplitude ['æmplitjôēd] *s.* (-s) wydte, omvang.

'amputate ['æmpjoetyt] *ww.* (-d) afsit, afsny.

a'muck [ə'mʌk] *bw.* *run* - amok maak.

'amulet ['æmjoelit] *s.* (-s) amulet, gelukbringertjie.

a'muse [ə'mjôēz] *ww.* (-d) vermaak, amuseer; **-ment** *s.* vermaaklikheid; **a'musing** *bnw.* (*more, most*) vermaaklik.

'an ['æn, 'ən, 'n] *lidw.* 'n.

ana'bolism [ænæ'boulizm] *s.* weefselopbou.

a'naemic [ə'nimik] *bnw.* bloedarm, anemies.

anaes'thetic [ænis'thetik] *s.* verdowingsmiddel; *bnw.* verdowend.

anal'gesia [ænæl'dzjisia] *s.* ongevoeligheid (vir *pyn*); **anal'gesic** [ænæl'dzjesik] *s.* pynstiller, *bnw.* pynstillend.

a'nalogy [ə'nælədzji] *s.* analogie, ooreenstemming; **a'nalogous** *bnw.* analoog, ooreenkomstig.

'analyse [ˈænəlaiz] *ww.* (-d) ontleed, oplos; **a'nalysis** *s.* ontleding.

'anarchy [ˈænəki] *n.* regeringloosheid, anargie.

a'nathema [ə'næthimə] *s.* vervloeking, ban.

a'natomy [ə'nætəmi] *n.* ontleedkunde, anatomie; liggaam; geraamte.

'ancestor [ˈænsistə] *s.* (-s) voorvader, voorouer; **an'cestral** *bnw.* voorvaderlik, erf-.

'anchor [ˈænkə] *s.* (-s) anker.

'anchovy [ˈæntsjouvi] *s.* ('anchovies) ansjovis.

'ancient [ˈynsjənt] *bnw.* oud, outyds, ouderwets.

an'cillary [ænˈsiləri] *bnw.* hulp-.

and [ˈænd, ənd, ən] *voegw.* en.

'anecdote [ˈænikdout] *s.* (-s) verbaaltjie, anekdote.

a'nemone [ə'neməni] *s.* (-s) anemoon, windroos, seeroos.

a'nent [ə'nent] *voors.* na aanleiding van; met verwysing na.

a'new [ə'njôŭ] *bw.* weer, nogeens.

'angel [ˈyndzjel] *s.* (-s) engel.

'anger [ˈæng-gə] *s.* boosheid, gramskap, woede.

an'gina [ænˈdzjainə] *s.* vernouing; hartkramp, angina.

'angle [ˈæng-ghl] *s.* (-s) hoek, punt; *ww.* (-d) visvang, hengel; **-bracket** *s.* hoeksteun; **- diagonal** *s.* hoeklyn; **-stay** *s.* hoekanker; **- steel** *s.* hoekstaal.

'angry [ˈæng-ghri] *bnw.* boos, kwaad.

'anguish [ˈæng-ghwisj] *s.* angs, pyn, benoudheid.

'animal [ˈæniməl] *s.* (-s) dier; *bnw.* dierlik.

'animate [ˈænimyt] *ww.* (-d) besiel, opwek; **-d** *bnw.* opgewekte, besielde; **ani'mation** *s.* besieling, animo; aansporing.

ani'mosity [æni'mositi] *s.* (ani'mosities) vyandigheid; verbittering.

'ankle [ˈænkl] *s.* (-s) enkel; **-guard** *s.* enkelskut.

'annals [ˈænlz] *s.* kronieke, annale.

an'neal [ə'nil] *ww.* (-ed) temper.

an'nex [ə'neks] *ww.* (-ed) aanheg; inlyf, annekseer; **-ure** *s.* (-s) byvoegsel; **-'ation** *s.* anneksasie.

an'nihilate [ə'naiəlyt] *ww.* (-d) vernietig, uitwis; **annihi'lation** *s.* vernietiging; **annihi'lator** *s.* vernietiger.

anni'versary [æni'vôsəri] *s.* (anni'versaries) gedenkdag, verjaarsdag.

'annotate [ˈænoutyt] *ww.* (-d) van aantekeninge voorsien; **anno'tation** *s.*; **'annotator** *s.* verklaarder.

an'nounce [ə'nauns] *ww.* (-d) aankondig, meld; **-ment** *s.*

an'noy [ə'noi] *ww.* (-ed) lastig val, pla, terg; **-ance** *s.* las, ergernis.

'annual [ˈænjoəl] *bnw.* jaarliks, jaar-; jaarplant.

an'nuity [ə'njoeiti] *s.* (an'nuities) jaargeld, lyfrente, pensioen.

an'nul [ə'nʌl] *ww.* (-led) nietig verklaar; **-ment** *s.*

an'nunciate [ə'nʌnsjiyt] *ww.* (-d) verkondig; **an'nunciation** *s.*

a'noint [ə'noint] *ww.* (-ed) salf, smeer; **-ed** *bnw.* gesalf; **-ing** *s.* salwing; **-ment** *s.* salwing.

a'nomaly [ə'noməli] *s.* (a'nomalies) afwyking.

a'non [ə'non] *bw.* aanstons, netnou; *ever and -* af en toe.

'anonym [ˈænənim] *s.* (-s) naamlose; pseudoniem; **'ano'nimity** *s.* naamloosheid, anonimiteit.

a'nonymous [ə'noniməs] *bnw.* naamloos, anoniem.

a'nother [ə'nʌdhə] *bnw. & vnw.* 'n ander(een), nog een.

'answer [ˈânsə] *s.* (-s) antwoord, verdediging, oplossing; *ww.* (-ed) antwoord, beantwoord.

ant [ˈænt] *s.* (-s) mier.

an'tagonize [ænˈtæghənâiz] *ww.* (-d) teenwerk, bestry, vyandig maak, vervreem.

'antecede [ˈæntisid] *ww.* (-d) voorafgaan; **ante'cedent** *bnw.* voorafgaande, *s.* antesedent; **ante'cedents** *s.* verlede, geskiedenis.

'antedate [ˈæntidyt] *ww.* (-d) vroeër dagteken; vervroeg.

antedi'luvian [ˈæntidi'lôŭviən] *bnw.* voor die sondvloed.

an'tenna [ænˈtenə] *s.* (an'tennae [-ni]) antenne; lugdrade.

an'terior [ænˈtiəriə] *bnw.* verder na vore, voor, vroeër.

an'ticipate [ænˈtisipyt] *ww.* (-d) verwag; voorkom.

anti-'clockwise [ˈænti-ˈklokwäiz] *bw.* linksom, hotom; **= counterclockwise.**

'anti-co'agulant [ˈænti-ko'æghjoelant] *s.* antistolmiddel.

'antics [ˈæntiks] *s.* malstreke.

'anti-dazzle screen [ˈænti-'dæzl] *s.* skitterskerm.

'antidote [ˈæntidout] *s.* (-s) teengif.

an'tipathy [ænˈtipəthi] *s.* antipatie, teensin.

an'tipodes [ænˈtipədiz] *s.* teenvoeters, antipode; **an'tipodal** *bnw.* teengesteld, antipodies.

'antiquate [ˈæntikwyt] *ww.* (-d) verouder, oud maak; **-d** *bnw.* verouder, ouderwets; **anti'quarian** *bnw.* oudheidkundig, antikwaries, *s.* oudheidkundige, antikwaar.

an'tique [æn'tik] *bnw.* oud, antiek; s. (-s) ou kunswerk; **an'tiquity** s. die oudheid.

anti'septic [ænti'septik] *bnw.* antisepties, ontsmettend.

an'tithesis [æn'tithisis] s. teenstelling, antitese; **anti'thetic** *bnw.* teenstellend.

'anti-'wrinkle cream ['ænti-'ringkl] s. rimpelroom.

'antler ['æntlə] s. (-s) horing; -s s. gewei, horings.

antonym ['æntonim] s. (-s) teengestelde.

'anvil ['ænvil] s. (-s) aambeeld.

an'xiety [æng'zaiəti] s. angs, onrus; begeerte.

'anxious ['ænksjəs] *bnw.* besorg, begerig.

'any ['æni] *vnw.* enige, elke; -how *bw.* op 'n manier; in alle geval; *voegw.* hoe dit ook mag wees; in elk geval; -one s. iedereen, enigeen, iemand; -thing s. alles, enigiets; -where *bw.* orals, êrens.

'anybody ['enibodi] s. iedereen, elkeen, iemand.

a'orta [y'ôtə] s. (-s) groot-slagaar, aorta.

a'pace [ə'pys] *bw.* snel, vinnig, sienderoë.

a'part [ə'pât] *bw.* afsonderlik, apart.

a'partment [əpâtmənt] s. (-s) vertrek, kamer.

apa'thetic [æpə'thetik] *bnw.* ongevoelig.

'apathy [æpəthi] s. onverskilligheid, apatie.

'ape ['yp] s. aap; *ww.* (-d) naäap.

a'perient [ə'piəriənt] s. (-s) purgeermiddel, purgasie.

'aperture ['æpətsjoeə] s. opening.

'apex ['ypeks] s. (-es) toppunt.

'aphid ['yfid] s. (-s) (*woolly*-) bloedluis.

'apiary ['ypiəri] s. ('*apiaries*) byehok, korf.

a'piece [ə'pîs] *bw.* per stuk, elk.

a'pology [ə'polədʒi] s. (*a'pologies*) verskoning, ekskuus, apologie; **apo-lo'getic** *bnw.* verontskuldigend; **a-pologize** *ww.* (-d) verontskuldig, verskoning vra, verekskuseer.

'apoplexy ['æpəpleksi] s. beroerte.

a'postate [ə'postit] s. (-s) afvallige; **a'postasy** s. afvalligheid.

a posteriori [y-postiri'ouri] *bnw.* van agter gesien, a posteriori.

a'postle [ə'posl] s. (-s) apostel; -ship s.

a'pothecary [ə'pothikəri] s. (*a'pothecaries*) apteker.

apothe'osis [ypothi'ousis] s. vergoding, hulde, apoteose.

ap'pal [ə'pôl] *ww.* (-led) ontstel, ontset.

appa'ratus [æpə'rytəs] s. toestel, apparaat; orgaan.

ap'parel [ə'pærəl] s. kleding, drag.

ap'parent [ə'pærənt] *bnw.* duidelik, sigbaar.

appa'rition [æpə'risjən] s. (-s) verskyning, gedaante.

ap'peal [ə'pil] s. (-s) beroep, bede, app'el; *ww.* (-ed) appelleer; 'n beroep doen.

ap'pear [ə'piə] *ww.* (-ed) verskyn; blyk; lyk; optree; -ance s. verskyning; verskynsel; optrede.

ap'pease [ə'pîz] *ww.* (-d) bevredig, kalmeer; -hunger (thirst) still, les; **ap'peasable** *bnw.* bevredigbaar; versoenbaar.

ap'pend [ə'pend] *ww.* (-ed) toevoeg, byvoeg, vasknoop, aanhang; -age s. aanhangsel; -ant s. aanhangsel, gevolg; -ix s. bylae; blindederm.

appendi'citis [əpendi'saitis] s. blindedermonsteking.

'appetite ['æpətait] s. eetlus, sin, lus, aptyt; **'appetizing** *bnw.* smaaklik, aantreklik.

ap'plaud [ə'plôd] *ww.* (-ed) toejuig, loof; **ap'plause** s. toejuiging.

'apple ['æpl] s. (-s) appel.

ap'pliance [ə'plaiəns] s. (-s) toestel; aanwending.

'applicant ['æplikənt] s. (-s) applikant; **appli'cation** s. aanwending; aansoek, applikasie; ywer.

ap'ply [ə'plai] *ww.* (*ap'plied*) aanwend, toepas; aansoek doen; toelê op; wend tot.

ap'point [ə'point] *ww.* (-ed) bepaal; benoem; inrig.

ap'portion [ə'pôsjən] *ww.* (-ed) toedeel; -ment s.

'apposite ['æpozit] *bnw.* toepaslik, geskik; -ness s.

appo'sition [æpo'zisjən] s. bystelling, apposisie.

ap'praise [ə'pryz] *ww.* (-d) waardeer, takseer; -r s. waardeerder; **ap'praisal** s. waardeskatting; -ment s. waardeskatting.

ap'preciate [ə'prisjiyt] *ww.* (-d) waardeer, vermeerder; **ap'precia-tion** s.

appre'hend [æpri'hend] *ww.* (-ed) arresteer; begryp; vrees; **appre-'hensible** *bnw.* begryplik; **appre-'hension** s. aanhouding; begrip; vrees; **appre'hensive** *bnw.* bevatlik; bevrees.

ap'prentice [ə'prentis] s. (-s) leerjonge; groentjie; -ship s. leerjongenskap.

ap'prise [ə'praiz] *ww.* (-d) onderrig, berig, meedeel.

ap'proach [ə'proutsj] *ww.* (-ed) nader, nader kom; lyk op; s. nadering, nabyheid, toegang; **approach-** *voorv.* naderings-.

appro'bation [æpro'bysjən] s. byval, goedkeuring; aanbeveling.

ap'prove [ə'prõêv] *ww.* (-d) goedkeur; **ap'proval** s. goedkeuring, byval.

ap'proximate [ə'proksimit] *bnw.* by benadering, geraam; -ly *bw.* ongeveer, naastenby.

ap'purtenance [ə'pâtinəns] s. (-s) toebehore, aanhangsel.

'apricot ['yprikot] s. (-s) appelkoos.
'April ['yprəl] s. April.
'apron ['yprən] s. (-s) voorskoot; skort.
'apt ['æpt] bnw. (-er, -est) geneig tot; geskik; bekwaam; -itude s. aanleg; -ly bw. toepaslik.
'aqueduct ['ækwidʌkt] s. (-s) waterleiding.
'aqueous ['ykwiəs] bnw. waterig, water-.
'arable ['ærəbl] bnw. ploegbaar, beboubaar.
'arbitrary ['ārbitrəri] bnw. willekeurig, arbitrêr; arbi'tration s. arbitrasie.
'arbor ['ābə] s. (-s) spil.
'arbour ['ābə] s. prieel.
arc ['āk] s. (-s) boog.
ar'cade [ā'kyd] s. (-s) oorwelfde gang, deurloop, arkade.
arch ['ātsj] bnw. (-est) aarts-; s. (-es) boog, gewelf; ww. (-ed) buig, welf; -ed bnw. geboë, verwelf; -er s. (-s) boogskutter.
archae'ology [āki'olədzji] s. oudheidkunde, argeologie.
ar'chaic [ā'kyik] bnw. verouderd, argaïes.
archi'pelago [āki'pelighou] s. (-es, -s) argipel, eilandgroep.
'architect ['ākitekt] s. (-s) boumeester, argitek; -ure s. boukunde, argitektuur.
'archive ['ākaiv] s. (-s) argief (gebou).
'arctic ['āktik] bnw. noordelik, noordpool-.
'ardent ['ādənt] bnw. vurig, blakend; 'ardour ['ādə] s. warmte, vuur, ywer.
are ['ā] ww. (were, have been) is; vgl. be.
'area ['eəriə] s. (-s) oppervlakte; gebied, streek, ruimte.
a'rena [ə'rina] s. (-s) strydperk, arena.
'argue ['āghjoe] ww. (-d) redeneer; bewys; stry; 'argument s. redenering, argumentasie; redetwis.
'aria ['āriə] s. (-s) wysie, aria.
'arid ['ærid] bnw. dor, droog, onvrugbaar.
'aristocrat ['æristəkræt] s. (-s) edelman, aristokraat.
a'rithmetic [ə'rithmətik] s. rekenkunde.
ark ['āk] s. ark.
arm ['ām] s. (-s) arm, tak, mou; wapen; ww. (-ed) wapen, bewapen; -ament s. bewapening.
'armature ['āmətsjoeə] s. (-s) bewapening; pantser; anker (van magneet); -winding s. ankerwikkeling.
'armistice ['āmistis] s. wapenstilstand.
'armour ['āmə] s. harnas, pantser; -ed bnw. gepantser.
'arm sling ['ām sling] s. armhangverband.
'army ['āmi] s. ('armies) leër; menigte.

a'roma [ə'roumə] s. geur, aroma; aro'matic bnw. geurig, aromaties.
a'round [ə'raund] bw. rond, in die rondte; voors. rondom, om.
a'rouse [ə'rauz] ww. (-d) wek; in die lewe roep.
ar'raign [ə'ryn] ww. (-ed) daag, aankla; -ment s. beskuldiging, aanklag.
ar'range [ə'ryndzj] ww. (-d) skik, rangskik, reël; af'spreek; -ment s. skikking, ooreenkoms; afspraak.
'arrant ['ærənt] bnw. verstokte; - thief verstokte dief; - nonsense volslae onsin.
ar'ray [ə'ry] ww. (-ed) opstel, uitdos; s. reeks, slagorde, tooisel.
ar'rear [ə'riə] s. (-s) agterstand, agterstallige.
ar'rest [ə'rest] ww. (-ed) stuit, vang, arresteer; s. arrestasie; -ed bnw. vertraagde.
ar'rive [ə'raiv] ww. (-d) aankom, gebeur; ar'rival s. aankoms.
'arrogance ['ærəghəns] s. verwaandheid, aanmatiging; -cy s. = arrogance; 'arrogant bnw. verwaand.
'arrow ['ærou] s. (-s) pyl.
'arson ['āsn] s. brandstigting.
art ['āt] s. (-s) kuns; slag; streek; -ist s. kunstenaar.
'artery ['ātəri] s. ('arteries) slagaar.
ar'thritis [ar'thraitis] s. jig, gewrigsontsteking.
'artichoke ['ātitsjouk] s. (-s) artisjok.
'article ['ātikl] s. (-s) onderdeel, artikel; lidwoord.
ar'ticulate [ā'tikjoelyt] ww. (-ed) artikuleer; uitspreek; articu'lation s. geleding; uitspreek; artikulasie.
'artifice ['ātifis] s. lis, slenter, skelmstreek.
'artificer ['ātifisə] s. (-s) handwerker; uitvinder.
arti'ficial [āti'fisjəl] bnw. kunsmatig; gekunsteld; oneg.
arti'san [āti'zæn] s. (-s) geskoolde ambagsman.
'artist ['ātist] s. (-s) kunstenaar; ar'tiste s. kunstenares; ar'tistic bnw. artistiek, kunsvol.
as ['æz] bw. & voegw. as, net as, soos; terwyl; aangesien; vnw. (as) wat.
'asa'fœtida ['æsə'fetidə] s. duiwelsdrek.
as'cend [ə'send] ww. (-ed) opstyg, klim; as'cent s. bestyging, opgang; -ancy s. oorwig; -ant bnw. opklimmend, oorheersend; as'cension s. bestyging; Hemelvaart.
'ascertain ['æsətyn] ww. (-ed) vasstel, vergewis.
as'cetic [ə'setik] bnw. streng, asketies; s. askeet, kluisenaar.
a'sepsis [y'sepsis] s. ontsmetting; a'septic bnw. ontsmettend.
a'sexual [ə'seksjoeəl] bnw. seksloos.
ash ['æsj] s. (-es) as; es (boom).
a'shamed [ə'sjymd] bnw. beskaamd; skaam, skamerig.

a'shore [ə'sjô] bw. aan wal, gestrand.

'Asia ['ysiə] s. Asië.

a'side [ə'said] s. opmerking weg van die aangesprokene af; bw. opsy, tersy, apart.

ask ['âsk] ww. (-ed) vra, versoek, nooi.

a'skance [ə'skæns] bw. skeef, skuins, van die kant af.

a'slant [ə'slânt] bw. skuins, dwars.

a'sleep [ə'slip] bnw. & bw. aan die slaap, in slaap.

as'paragus [əs'pærəghəs] s. aspersie.

'aspect ['æspekt] s. (-s) aanblik, aansig, voorkoms; gesigspunt, aspek.

as'perity [æs'periti] s. ruheid, strengheid.

as'phyxia [æs'fiksiə] s. verstikking; asfiksie; as'phyxiate ww. (-d) verstik, versmoor.

as'pirant [əs'paiərənt] s. (-s) aspirant, kandidaat.

'aspirate ['æspəryt] ww. (-d) met die h-klank uitspreek; aspireer; s. (-s) aspiraat; aspi'ration s. aspirasie, strewe.

a'spire [ə'spaiə] ww. (-d) strewe; as'piring bnw. eersugtig.

ass ['æs] s. esel; domkop.

as'sailant [ə'sylint] s. (-s) aanrander.

as'sassin [ə'sæsin] s. (-s) sluipmoordenaar; -ate ww. (-d) sluipmoord pleeg.

as'sault [ə'sôlt] s. (-s) aanval, aanranding; ww. (-ed) aanval, aanrand, te lyf gaan.

as'say [ə'sy] s. (-s) toets, proef, keuring; -er s. (-s) toetser, keurder, essaieur; -ing s. keuring, toetsing.

as'semble [ə'sembl] ww. (-d) vergader, versamel, bykeenkom; monteer; as'sembly s. (as'semblies) vergadering, byeenkoms; as'sembly plant s. monteerplaas.

as'sent [ə'sent] s. toestemming; ww. (-ed) toestem.

as'sert [ə'sôt] ww. (-ed) laat geld, handhaaf; verklaar.

as'sess [ə'ses] ww. (-ed) skat; belas; -ment s. raming; belasting; -or s. skatter; belastingheffer; assessor.

'asset ['æset] s. (-s) bate, besit.

as'siduous [ə'sidjoeəs] bnw. volhardend; aandagtig.

as'sign [ə'sain] ww. (-ed) toedeel, toewys; bepaal; -ment s. toedeling; oordrag.

as'similate [ə'similyt] ww. (-d) opneem, assimileer; assimi'lation s. assimilasie, opname.

as'sist [ə'sist] ww. (-ed) bystaan, help; -ance s. hulp; -ant s. helper, handlanger, assistent.

as'size [ə'saiz] ww. (-d) skat, raam; s. vasstelling, gewigsbepaling; -s s. rondgaande hof.

as'sociate [ə'sousjiit] ww. (-ed) verenig; begelei; assosieer; as'soci'ation s. (-s) vereniging, bond, assosiasie.

as'sort [ə'sôt] ww. (-ed) uitsoek, sorteer; -ment s. sortering; verskeidenheid.

as'sume [ə'sjoem] ww. (-d) aanneem, aanvaar, veronderstel.

as'sumption [ə'sʌmpsjən] s. aanname, aanvaarding, veronderstelling, vermoede.

as'sure [ə'sjoeə] ww. (-d) verseker, seker maak, verassureer; as'surance s. versekering; astrantheid; assuransie.

'asterisk ['æstərisk] s. sterretjie.

'asthma ['æsmə] n. asma.

as'tonish [ə'stonisj] ww. (-ed) verbaas, dronkslaan; -ed bnw. verbaas; -ment s. verbasing.

a'stound [ə'staund] ww. (-ed) verbaas, versteld laat staan.

a'stray [əs'try] bw. verdwaal, van die pad af.

a'stride [əs'traid] bw. wydsbeen.

a'stringent [æs'trindzjənt] s. bloedstelpende middel; bnw. sametrekkend; streng.

as'trology [əs'trolədzi] s. sterrewiggelary.

a'stronomy [əs'tronəmi] s. sterrekunde; as'tronomer s. sterrekundige; astro'nomic bnw. sterrekundig, astronomies.

as'tute [əs'tjoet] bnw. slim, geslepe.

a'sunder [ə'sʌndə] bw. uitmekaar, aan stukke.

a'sylum [ə'sailəm] s. (-s) toevlug; asiel; gestig.

at ['æt] voors. op, in, te, by; aan; na; met; teen.

'atheist ['ythiist] s. (-s) godloënaar.

'athlete ['æthlit] s. (-s) atleet, sportsman; ath'letic bnw. atleties, gespierd, lenig; ath'letics s. sport.

a'thwart [ə'thwôt] voors., bw. dwars oor.

'atlas ['ætləs] s. (-es) atlas, landkaartboek.

'atmosphere ['ætməsfiə] s. atmosfeer, dampkring, lug; 'atmospherics s. lugsteurings.

'atom ['ætəm] s. (-s) atoom, greintjie; -ize ww. (-d) atomiseer; verdamp; verstuif; -izer s. verstuiwer.

a'tone [ə'toun] ww. (-d) boete doen, boet; versoen; -ment s. boetedoening; versoening.

a'trocious [ə'trousjəs] bnw. wreedaardig, verskriklik; a'trocity s. wreedaardigheid.

'atrophy ['ætroufi] s. uittering.

at'tach [ə'tætsj] ww. (-ed) vasmaak, bind, aanheg; -ment s. gehegtheid, inhegtenisneming.

at'taché [ə'tæsjy] s. (-s) attaché.

at'tack [ə'tæk] ww. (-ed) aanval, bestorm; s. (-s) aanval.

at'tain [ə'tyn] ww. (-ed) bereik, verkry; -ment s. verkryging; bekwaamheid.

at'tempt [ə'tempt] ww. (-ed) probeer; (-s) poging.

at'tend [ə tɛnd] ww. (-ed) ag gee; bedien; bywoon; -ance s. bediening; geleide; opkoms; -ant s. (-s) bediende, oppasser, gevolg.

at'tention [ə'tɛnʃən] s. aandag; at'tentive bnw. oplettend, aandagtig.

at'tenuate [ə'tɛnjoeyt] ww. (-d) verdun, vermaer; at'tenuation s. verdunning, verswakking.

at'tcst [ə'tɛst] ww. (-ed) getuig, verklaar.

'attic ['ætik] s. (-s) dakkamertjie.

at'tire [ə'taiə] ww. (-d) aanklee, optooi.

'attitude ['ætitjoed] s. (-s) houding, postuur.

at'torney [ə'təni] s. (at'tornies) prokureur.

at'tract [ə'trækt] ww. (-ed) aantrek, boei; -ion s. aantrekking, bekoring; -ive bnw. aanloklik, bekoorlik.

'attribute ['ætribjoet] s. (-s) eienskap, kenmerk.

'auburn ['ôbən] bnw. goudbruin.

'auction ['ôkʃən] s. verkoping, vandisie; auctio'neer s. afslaer.

au'dacity [ô'dæsiti] s. vermetelheid; astrantheid.

'audible ['ôdəbl] bnw. hoorbaar.

'audience ['ôdjəns] s. (-s) gehoor; publiek; oudiënsie.

'audit ['ôdit] s. (-s) verifikasie, ouditering, nasien van boeke; -or s. ouditeur.

audi'torium [ôdi'tôriʌm] s. (audi'toria, -s) gehoorsaal.

'auger ['ôghə] s. (-s) handboor.

'aught ['ôt] s. iets; for - I know sover ek weet.

aug'ment [ôgh'ment] ww. (-ed) vermeerder, vergroot, aanvul; aug'men'tation s., aug'mentative bnw. vermeerderend.

'augur ['ôghə] ww. (-ed) voorspel, waarsê; it -s well dit beloof veel; s. waarsêer; -y s. voorbode.

au'gust [ô'ghʌst] bnw. hoog, verhewe, groots.

'August ['ôghəst] n. Augustus.

aunt(ie) ['ânt(i)] s. (-s) tante, tannie.

'aura ['ôrə] s. (-s) uitstraling; gewaarwording.

'aural ['ôrəl] bnw. oor-, gehoor-.

'auricle ['ôrikl] s. (-s) oor, oorskulp; hartkamer.

au'rora [ô'rôrə] s. (-s) dagbreek; poollig; -australis s. suiderlig; -borealis s. noorderlig.

aus'picious [ôs'piʃəs] bnw. belowend.

aus'tere [ôs'tiə] bnw. (-r, -st) streng; eenvoudig; onkreukbaar; aus'terity s.

'austral ['ôstrəl] bnw. suidelik.

Aus'tralia [ôs'tryljə] s. Australië.

'Austria ['ôstriə] s. Oostenryk.

au'thentic [ô'thɛntik] bnw. eg, outentiek: betroubaar.

'author ['ôthə] s. (-s) dader; oorsaak; skrywer; outeur.

'authorize ['ôthəraiz] ww. (-d) magtig, autoriseer; authori'zation s. magtiging, volmag; authori'tative bnw. gesaghebbend, outoritêr; au'thority s. (au'thorities) gesag, mag; volmag; outoriteit.

'autocrat ['ôtəkræt] s. (-s) outokraat. auto'matic [ôtə'mætik] bnw. werktuiglik, outomaties.

au'tonomy [ô'tɔnəmi] s. selfbestuur; au'tonomous bnw. selfregerend.

'autumn ['ôtəm] s. herfs.

aux'iliary [ôgh'ziljəri] bnw. s. hulp-; helper.

a'vail [ə'vyl] ww. (-ed) baat, help, benut; -able bnw. beskikbaar.

'avalanche ['ævəlânsj] s. (-s) sneeuval, lawine.

'avarice ['ævəris] s. gierigheid, vrekkigheid.

a'venge [ə'vendzj] ww. (-d) wreek, straf.

'avenue ['ævinjoe] s. (-s) toegang, laan.

a'ver [ə'və] ww. (-red) betuig; beweer.

'average ['ævəridzj] s. gemiddelde; awery; bnw. deursnee; ww. (-d) die gemiddelde bereken (bereik).

a'verse [ə'və̃s] bnw. afkerig, onwillig; a'version s.

a'vert [ə'vɛt] ww. (-ed) keer, afwend.

'aviary ['yviəri] s. (aviaries) voëlhok.

'aviate ['yviyt] ww. (-d) vlieg; 'aviator s. (-s) vlieënier; avi'ation s. vliegkuns; lugvaart.

avi'ation [yvi'ysjən] s. vliegkuns.

'avid ['ævid] bnw. begerig, gretig; gierig.

a'void [ə'void] ww. (-ed) vermy, ontwyk.

avoirdu'pois [ævədə'poiz] s. stelsel van mate en gewigte.

a'vow [ə'vau] ww. (-ed) erken, bely; -al s. belydenis; -edly bw. openlik, uitgesproke.

a'wait [ə'wyt] ww. (-ed) wag op, te wagte wees.

a'wake [ə'wyk] ww. (awoke) ontwaak; bnw. wakker.

a'ward [ə'wôd] ww. (-ed) toeken; beslis.

a'ware [ə'weə] bnw. bewus.

a'way [ə'wy] bw. weg, voort.

'awe ['ô] s. vrees, ontsag, eerbied; 'awful bnw. skrikwekkend.

a'while [ə'wail] bw. 'n tydlank, vir 'n rukkie.

'awkward ['ôkwəd] bnw. lomp, onhandig.

awl ['ôl] s. (-s) els.

'awn ['ôn] s. (-s) baard (koring); -ing s. seil, skerm, skutting.

'awning ['ôning] s. (-s) seil, skerm, skutting.

a'wry [ə'rai] bw. skeef, skuins.

'axe ['æks] s. (-s) byl.

'axiom ['æksiəm] s. (-s) aksioom, grondstelling; axio'matic bnw. onbetwisbaar.

'axis ['æksis] s. as, spil.

'axle ['æksl] s. (-s) as; -bearing s. aslaer; -box s. askas; -load s. aslas; back - s. agteras.

'aye ['ai] s. (-s) ja; the -s have it die meerderheid is daarvoor.

'azure ['ysjə] s. asuur, hemelsblou.

B

'babble ['bæbl] ww. (-d) babbel, klets; murmel.

'babe ['byb] s. (-s) babetjie, kind; uilskuiken.

ba'boon [bə'bõen] s. (-s) bobbejaan.

'baby ['bybi] s. (babies) babejtie; wiegsif.

'bachelor ['bætsjələ] s. (-s) vrygesel oujongkêrel.

ba'cillus [bə'siləs] s. basil.

back ['bæk] s. (-s) rug, rugkant; agterspeler; bnw. agterste, agterstallig; bw. terug, agteruit, gelede; ww. (-ed) steun; wed op; tru staan; -bone s. ruggraat; -ing s. steun; -ward(s) bnw. agterwaarts, agterlik, bw. agteruit, agteroor, na agter; -cross s. terugkruising, inteelt; -fire ww. (-d) terugplof; -hand s. handrug; -seat driver s. bekdrywer; -pedal ww. terugtrap; -yard s. agterplaas, werf.

'bacon ['bykən] s. spek.

bac'terium [bæk'tiəriəm] s. bakterie, kiem.

bad ['bæd] bnw. (worse, worst) sleg; stout, nadelig, naar; ongunstig; bederf; vals; -ness s.

badge ['bædzj] s. (-s) kenteken, wapen.

'badger ['bædzjə] s. (-s) dassie, kwas van dassiehaar.

'baffle ['bæfl] ww. (-d) dronkslaan; verydel; s. skot; -plate s. skotplaat; -window s. skotruit.

bag ['bæg] s. (-s) sak, tas.

'baggage ['bæghidzj] n. bagasie; parmant; fierrie.

'bagpipe ['bæghpaip] s.(-s) doedelsak.

'bagworm ['bægwəm] s. (-s) sakwurm.

bail ['byl] s. borg, borgtog; skutting; hoepel; -s s. balkies; ww. (-ed) borgstaan, onder borg vrylaat.

'bailiff ['bylif] s. (-s) balju; geregsbode.

bait ['byt] s. lokaas; ww. aanhits; treiter; lok; afsaal, voergee.

'baize ['byz] s. baai.

'bake ['byk] ww. (-ed) bak; -r s. bakker.

'baked e'namel ['bykd-i'næml] s. brandemalje.

'baking-powder ['byking-'paudə] s. bakpoeier.

'balance ['bæləns] s. (-s) skaal; ewewig; saldo; oorskot; vliegwiel;

balans; ww. (-d) weeg; balanseer; afsluit.

'balcony ['bælkəni] s. ('balconies) balkon.

bald ['bôld] bnw. (-er, -est) kaal, kaalkop.

'balderdash ['bôldədæsj] s. wartaal, onsin.

'bale ['byl] s. (-s) baal; ww. (-d) in bale verpak; uitskep.

'baleful ['bylfoel] bnw. nadelig, verderflik.

'balk, 'baulk ['bôk] s. hindernis; balk; ww. hinder.

ball ['bôl] s. (-s) bal; bol; koeël; kluit; dansparty; ww. (-ed) tot bal vorm; -bearing s. koeëllaer; -syringe s. bolspuit.

'ballast ['bæləst] s. ballas.

bal'loon [bə'lõen] s. (-s) ballon.

'ballot ['bælət] s. (-s) stemming, loting.

balm ['bām] s. balsem, salf; troos.

'balustrade ['bæləstryd] s. (-s) reling, balustrade.

bam'boo [bæm'bõe] s. (-s) bamboes.

bam'boozle [bæm'bõezl] ww. (-d) fop, kul; -ment s. kullery.

ban ['bæn] ww. (-ned) ban, in die ban doen, vloek; s. (-s) banvloek, ban.

ba'nal [bə'nāl] bnw. banaal, alledaags, peuterig.

ba'nana [bə'nānə] s. (-s) piesang.

band ['bænd] s. band, dryfriem; bende; korps; orkes; ww. (-ed) band omsit, verenig.

'bandage ['bændidzj] s. (-s) verband.

'bandy ['bændi] s. hokkiestok; bnw. ('bandier, 'bandiest) krom; ww. ('bandied) - words stry; -legged bnw. hoepelbeen.

'bane ['byn] s. vergif; verderf; -ful bnw. giftig.

'bangle ['bæng-ghl] s. (-s) armband, beenring.

'banish ['bænisj] ww. (-ed) verban, verdryf; -ment s.

'banister ['bænistə] s. (-s) styl van trapleuning; -s s. trapleuning.

bank ['bænk] s. (-s) bank; wal, oewer; ww. (-ed) in die bank sit; staatmaak; -transfer s. bankoordrag.

'bankrupt ['bænk-rʌpt] bnw. bankrot; -cy s. bankrotskap,

'banner ['bænə] s. (-s) banier, vlag, vaandel.

banns ['bænz] s. gebooie.

'banquet ['bænkwit] s. (-s) banket, feesmaal.

'banter ['bæntə] s. gekskeerdery, skerts.

'baobab ['byobæb] s. kremetartboom.

'baptize ['bæptaiz] ww. (-d) doop; 'baptism s. doop.

bar ['bā] s. (-s) staaf; tralie; balie; kroeg; hinderpaal; balk; sluitboom; ww. (-red) afsluit, versper, hinder.

barb ['bāb] s. (-s) weerhaak, prikkel; baard, -er s. kapper.

bar'barian [bā'beəriən] s. (-s) barbaar; *bnw.* barbaars.

'barber ['bābə] s. (-s) kapper, barbier.

'bard ['bād] s. (-s) digter, sanger, bard.

'bare ['beə] *bnw.* (-r, -st) naak, bloot; leeg; *ww.* (-d) ontbloot; **-faced** *bnw.* skaamteloos; **-footed** *bnw.* kaalvoet.

'bargain ['bāghin] s. (-s) ooreenkoms; slag, winskoop.

'barge ['bādzj] s. (-s) vragskuit, trekskuit; **bar'gee** s. skuitvoerder.

bark ['bāk] s. bas, kors, vel; blaf; *ww.* (-ed) bas (kors, vel) afskuur; blaf, hoes.

'barley ['bālj] s. gars; **-sugar** s. bors(bos)suiker.

barn ['bān] s. (-s) skuur.

ba'rometer [bə'romitə] s. (-s) barometer, weerglas.

'baron ['bærən] s. (-s) baron.

'barrage ['bærāzj] s. (-s) damwal; gordynvuur.

'barrel ['bærəl] s. (-s) kuip, vat; geweerloop; buis; trommel, dop.

'barren ['bærən] *bnw.* (-est) kaal; onvrugbaar.

'barricade ['bærikyd] s. (-s) verskansing, barrikade.

'barrier ['bæriə] s. (-s) slagboom, hinderpaal, versperring.

'barrister ['bæristə] s. (-s) advokaat.

'barrow ['bærou] s. (-s) kruiwa; draagbaar, baar.

'barter ['bātə] *ww.* (-ed) verruil, ruil, verkwansel; s. ruil, ruilhandel.

'base ['bys] s. (-s) grondslag, basis; *bnw.* (-r, -st) sleg, laag; onedel; *ww.* (-d) baseer; **-ment** s. fondament; kelder; **-ness** n. laagheid.

'bashful ['bæsjfoel] *bnw.* skaam, verleë.

'basic ['bysik] *bnw.* basies(e), grond-.

'basin ['bysn] s. (-s) skottel, kom; stroomgebied.

'basis ['bysis] s. grondslag, basis.

'bask ['bāsk] *ww.* (-ed) bak, koester.

'basket ['bāskit] s. (-s) mandjie, korf.

'bastard ['bæstəd] s. (-s) baster, halfnaatjie.

'baste ['byst] *ww.* (-d) bedruip; uitlooi; aanmekaar ryg.

bat ['bæt] s. (-s) vlermuis; kolf.

batch ['bætsj] s. (-es) baksel, klomp, stel, trop.

bath ['bāth] s. (-s) bad; badplaas; **-e** ['bydh] *ww.* (-d) baai, swem; bet; **-brush** s. badborsel; **-crystals** s. *mv.* badkristalle; **-oil** s. badolie; **-salts** s. *mv.* badsout; **-soap** s. badseep; **-sponge** s. badspons; **-thermometer** s. badtermometer.

'batman ['bætmən] s. (-men) lyfbediende (militêr) ordonnans.

bat'talion [bə'tæljən] s. (-s) bataljon.

'batten ['bætn] *ww.* (-ed) met latte vasmaak, vaslat; s. lat, klamp.

'batter ['bætə] s. deeg; duik (deuk); hang, skuinste; *ww.* (-ed) oorhel; **-ing-ram** s. stormram.

'battery ['bætərj] s. ('batteries) battery; aanranding, **-acid** s. batterysuur; **-box** s. batterykas; **-box cable** s. batterykaskabel; **-case** s. batterybak; **-cell** s. batterysel; **-charger** s. batterylaaier; **-earth cable** s. batteryaardkabel; **-filler** s. batteryvuller; **-terminal** s. batteryaansluiter; **-tester** s. batterytoetser.

'battle ['bætl] s. (-s) slag, geveg, stryd.

'bauble ['bôbl] s. (-s) speelgoed, tierlantyntjie.

'bawdy ['bôdi] *bnw.* ontugtig, liederlik.

bawl ['bôl] *ww.* (-ed) hard, skreeu.

bay ['by] s. baai; lourier; nis; blaf; *bnw.* vos; *ww.* (-ed) blaf.

'bayonet ['byənit] s. (-s) bajonet.

'bayrum ['byrʌm] s. lourier en rum.

be ['bi] *ww.* (am, is, are; was, were) wees, bestaan.

beach ['bitsj] s. (-es) strand, kus.

'beacon ['bikən] s. (-s) baken, seinvuur, vuurtoring.

bead ['bid] s. (-s) kraletjie; knoppie; balletjie; druppel; korrel.

'beading ['biding] s. omlysting; lys.

'beadle ['bidl] s. (-s) pedel, bode, onderkoster.

beak ['bik] s. (-s) bek, snawel.

'beaker ['bikə] s. (-s) beker.

beam ['bim] s. (-s) balk; straal; bundel; *ww.* (-ed) straal; **-ed** *bnw.* gerig.

bean ['bin] s. (-s) boon (tjie); **-s** s. duite.

bear ['bēə] s. (-s) beer; *ww.* (bore, borne) dra; verdra; toedra; baar; **-able** *bnw.* uithoubaar; **-er** s. draer.

beard ['biəd] s. (-s) baard.

'bearing ['bēaring] s. (-s) houding; rigting; koeëllaer; **-race** s. laerbaan.

beast ['bist] s. (-s) bees; dier; **-ly** *bnw.* dierlik, beesagtig.

beat ['bit] *ww.* (was beaten) slaan; wen; klits; **-ing** s. slae.

be'atify [bi'ætifai] *ww.* (be'atified) heilig verklaar; **beatifi'cation** s. heiligverklaring; **be'atitude** s. geluksaligheid.

'beauty ['bjoēti] s. mooiheid, prag; **'beautiful** *bnw.* pragtig; **-spot** s. moesie.

'beaver ['bivə] s. (-s) bewer; bewerhaarhoed.

be'calm [bi'kām] *ww.* (-ed) kalmeer, stilmaak; **-ed** *bnw.* deur windstilte oorval.

be'cause [bi'koz] *voegw.* omdat, oor.

'beckon ['bekən] *ww.* (-ed) wink, wuif.

be'come [bi'kʌm] *ww.* (became) word; betaam, pas.

bed ['bed] s. (-s) bed, kooi; lêplek; bedding; **-ding** s. beddegoed; **-pan** s. steekpan; **-ridden** *bnw.* bedlêend; **-room** s. slaapkamer; **-stead** s. katel, ledekant.

'bedlam ['bedləm] s. gekkehuis, lawaaispul.

bee ['bi] s. (-s) by.

'beech ['bitsj] s. (-es) beukeboom.

beef ['bif] s. beesvleis; **-steak** s. biefstuk.

beer ['biə] s. bier.

beet ['bit] s. beet.

'beetle ['bitl] s. kewer, tor.

'beetroot ['bitroet] s. beet.

be'fit [bi'fit] ww. (-ted) pas, voeg, betaam.

be'fore [bi'fô] voors. voor; bw. voor, voorop, vooruit; voegw. voor, voordat, eer.

be'forehand [bi'fôhænd] bw. vooraf, van te vore.

be'foul [bi'faul] ww. (-ed) bevuil.

be'friend [bi'frend] ww. (-ed) vriendskap (guns), betoon; steun.

beg ['begh] ww. (-ged) bedel, smeek; **-gar** s. bedelaar; **-garly** bnw. armoedig.

be'get [bi'ghet] ww. (-gat, -gotten) verwek, verkry.

be'gin [bi'ghin] ww. (began, begun) begin, aanvang; aan die gang sit; **-ner** s. beginneling.

be'gone [bi'ghon] uitroep. trap! weg is jy!

be'gotten vgl. beget.

be'grudge [bi'ghrʌdzj] ww. (-d) beny, misgun.

be'guile [bi'ghail] ww. (-d) mislei, bedrieg, flep, bedot.

be'half [bi'hâf] s. ontwil; on your — om jou ontwil.

be'have [bi'hyv] ww. (-d) (jou) gedra; **be'haviour** s. gedrag.

be'head [bi'hed] ww. (-ed) onthoof; **-ing** s. onthoofding.

be'hest [bi'hest] s. bevel, versoek.

be'hind [bi'haind] voors. agter; agterkant; bw. agter, agteraan, agterna, agterom.

be'hold [bi'hould] ww. (beheld) aanskou, beskou.

be'holden [bi'houldən] bw. verplig (teenoor), dank verskuldig aan.

be'hove [bi'houv] ww. pas; it -s you dit betaam jou.

'being ['biing] s. (-s) wese, skepsel; bestaan; deelw. synde.

be'lated [bi'lytid] bnw. vertraag (de).

belch ['beltsj] ww. (-ed) wind opbreek.

'belfry ['belfri] s. kloktoring.

'Belgium ['beldzjəm] s. België.

be'lie [bi'lai] ww. (-d) belieg, loënstraf, weerspreek.

be'lief [bi'lif] s. geloof; be'lieve ww. glo; be'lievable bnw. geloofbaar; be'liever s. gelowige.

be'little [bi'litl] ww. (-d) verklein (eer).

bel'ligerent [bi'lidzjərənt] bnw. oorlogvoerend.

bell ['bel] s. (-s) klok, bel.

'belle ['bel] s. (-s) mooi meisie.

'bellow ['belou] ww. (-ed) brul, bulk; bulder; **-s** s. blaasbalk.

'belly ['belli] s. ('bellies) buik, pens.

be'long [bi'long] ww. (-ed) behoort (aan, by); **-ings** s. eiendom.

be'loved [bi'lʌvd] bnw. geliefde, beminde.

be'low [bi'lou] voors. onder, benede; bw. onder, onderaan, omlaag, benede.

belt ['belt] s. (-s) gort, gordel, lyfband; strook, streep; dryfriem.

bench ['bentsj] s. (-es) bank, draaibank, regbank.

'bend ['bend] ww. (bent, bent) buig; s. buiging, bog, draai.

be'neath [bi'nidh] voors. onder, benede; bw. ondertoe, benede.

bene'diction [beni'diksjən] s. seëning: gebed.

'benefactor ['benifæktə] s. weldoener.

be'neficent [bi'nefisnt] bnw. heilsaam, weldadig.

'benefit ['benifit] ww. (-ed) baat, voordeel trek; begunstig, bevoordeel; s. voordeel, wins, nut.

be'nevolence [bi'nevələns] s. welwillendheid.

be'nevolent [bi'nevələnt] bnw. welwillend; liefdadig.

be'nign [bi'nain] bnw. vriendelik, minsaam; be'nignancy [bi'nighnənsi] s. goedhartigheid; be'nignant bnw. vriendelik, goedhartig; be'nignity s. vriendelikheid.

bent ['bent] s. draai; neiging; trek.

be'queath [bi'kwidh] ww. (-ed) nalaat, bemaak; be'quest s. erfenis.

be'reave [bi'riv] ww. (-d) ontneem; **-ment** s. verlies.

be'reft [bi'reft] verl. deelw. bereave.

'berry ['beri] s. ('berries) bessie.

berth ['bëth] s. (-s) ankerplaas; slaapplek.

be'seech [bi'sitsj] ww. (-ed) smeek.

be'set [bi'set] ww. beleër, insluit; in besit neem; aanval.

be'side [bi'said] voors. naas, langs, behalwe; **-s** bw. behalwe, buitendien.

be'siege [bi'sidzj] ww. (-d) beleër.

be'smirch [bi'smâtsj] ww. (-ed) besoedel, bevuil.

'besom ['bizəm] s. besem.

be'speak [bi'spik] ww. (be'spoke, be'spoken) bespreek; vra: ooreenkom; blyke gee van.

best ['best] bnw. beste; s. bes; bw. liefs; ww. klop; **-man** s. strooijonker.

be'stow [bi'stou] ww. (-ed) bêre; skenk; bestee; **-al** s. skenking.

bet ['bet] s. weddenskap; ww. wed.

be'tray [bi'try] ww. (-ed) verraai, versaak; **-al** s. verraad.

be'troth [bi'troudh] ww. (-ed) verloof; **-al** s. verlowing.

'better ['betə] bnw. beter; bw. beter, liewer; s. meerdere; ww. (-ed) verbeter.

be'tween [bi'twin] voors. tussen, onder.

'bevel ['bevəl] s. skuinste; hoek; ww. (-led) skuins maak, afskuins.

'beverage ['hevəridzj] s. drank.

'bevy ['bevi] s. ('bevies) klompie, paar, vlug.

be'ware [bi'wêə] ww. oppas, in ag neem.

be'wilder [bi'wildə] ww. (-ed) verwar, verbyster.

be'witch [bi'witsj] ww. (-ed) toor, beheks; bekoor.

be'yond [bi'jond] voors. anderkant, oor, verby; bw. verder; s. oorkant.

'bias ['baiəs] s. neiging; vooroordeel, partydigheid.

bib ['bib] s. (-s) borslap.

'Bible ['baibl] s. (-s) Bybel.

'bibulous ['bibjoeləs] bnw. drank-sugtig.

'biceps ['baiseps] s. armspier.

'bicker ['bikə] ww. (-ed) kibbel; -ing s. struweling.

'bicycle ['baisikl] s. (-s) fiets; -lane a. fietslaan; -path s. fietspad.

bid ['bid] s. (-s) bod; ww. (bade) gebied, beveel; bie.

'bier ['biə] s. (-s) baar; vgl. barrow.

big ['bigh] bnw. groot, dik.

'bigamy ['bighəmi] s. tweewywery; 'bigamous bnw. bigamies.

bight ['bait] s. (-s) bog, baai.

'bigot ['bighət] s. (-s) dweper; -ry s. dweepsug.

bile ['bail] s. gal; 'biliary bnw. galagtig; 'bilious bnw. galagtig, mislik.

'bilge ['bildzj] s. buik (van vat); ww. (-d) lek kry, opswel; -water s. ruim-water.

bill ['bil] s. (-s) snawel; briefie; rekening; wissel; wetsontwerp; ww. (-ed) aan (-ed) aanplak, aankondig.

'billet ['bilit] s. (-s) biljet, briefie; betrekking.

'billhook ['bilhoek] s. kapmes.

'billow ['bilou] s. (-s) golf, brander; ww. (-ed) golf, dein; -y bnw. golwend.

bin ['bin] s. (-s) kas, kis, bus, blik.

bind ['baind] ww. (bound) vasmaak, heg, bind; inbind; verplig; bekrag-tig; -er s. band, binddoek; -ing s. band; omboorsel.

'binocle ['binokl] s. verkyker.

bi'noculars [bi'nokjoeləs] s. ver-kyker.

bi'ography [bai'oghrəfi] s. (bio-'graphies) biografie.

bi'ology [bai'olədzji] s. biologie.

'bioscope ['baiəskoup] s. bioskoop.

'biped ['baiped] s. tweevoetige dier.

birch ['bətsj] s. berk.

bird ['bəd] s. (-s) voël; kêrel, vent.

birth ['bəth] s. (-s) geboorte; stand; afkoms; -day s. verjaarsdag; -mark s. moedervlek; -rate s. geboortesy-fer; -right s. geboortereg.

'biscuit ['biskit] s. (-s) beskuit, beskuitjie.

bi'sect ['baisekt] ww. (-ed) halveer.

bit ['bit] s. (-s) hap; bietjie; boor gebit; stang.

bitch ['bitsj] s. (-es) teef.

bite ['bait] ww. (bit, bitten) byt; invreet.

'bitter ['bitə] bnw. (-er, -est) bitter, skerp; griewend.

'bittern ['bitən] s. roerdomp.

'bitumen ['bitjoemin] s. asfalt.

'bivouac ['bivoe'æk] s. kamp.

'blab ['blæb] ww. (-bed) verklap; -ber s. verklikker.

black ['blæk] s. swart; swartsel; roet; rouklere; bnw. (-er, -est) swart, donker, somber; ww. (-ed) swart-maak; -berry s. braambes; -death s. pes; -en ww. (-ed) swartmaak; -guard s. skurk; -head s. puisie, mede-eter; -jack s. wynsak; -lead s. potlood; -mail s. afpersing; black Maria s. tronkwa; -ness s. swart-heid; -pudding s. bloedwors; -smith s. smid.

'bladder ['blædə] s. (-s) blaas.

'blade ['blyd] s. (-s) sprietjie; halm; lem, sabel.

'blame ['blym] ww. (-d) beskuldig; blameer; laak; s. skuld, blaam.

blanch ['blântsj] ww. (-ed) bleik.

blanc-'mange [blə'mondzj] s. bla-maans.

'bland ['blænd] bnw. (-er, -est) innemend; ironies.

blank ['blænk] bnw. (-er, -est) blank, blanko, leeg; wesenloos; s. leegte; ruimte.

'blanket ['blænkit] s. (-s) kombers, deken; -policy s. oordekkende polis.

'blare ['blêə] ww. (-d) sketter, brul.

'blarney ['blâni] s. flikflooiery, vleitaal.

blas'pheme [blæs'fîm] ww. (-d) laster, vloek; 'blasphemy [blæsfəmi] s. godslastering; 'blasphemous bnw. godslasterlik.

blast ['blâst] s. (-s) windstoot; ontploffing; ww. (-ed) ontplof, laat spring; verwoes; vervloek; -ed bnw. vervlakste.

'blatant ['blytənt] bnw. skreeuerig, lawaaierig.

'blaze ['blyz] s. (-s) vlam, gloed; bles; ww. (-d) vlam, skitter; los-brand, skiet.

'blazer ['blyzə] s. (-s) kleurbaadjie.

bleach ['blitzj] ww. (-ed) bleik, verbleik; -ing powder s. bleik-poeier.

'bleak ['blik] bnw. (-er, -est) bleek; guur; onherbergsaam.

'blear ['bliə] bnw. dof, glasig; -eyed bnw. met leepoë.

'bleat ['blit] ww. (-ed) blêr, bulk.

bleed ['blid] ww. (bled) bloei; bloedlaat; afpers; -ing s. luglaat.

'blemish ['blemisj] s. (-es) vlek, klad, smet; ww. (-ed) bevlek, beklad, besmet.

'blend ['blend] ww. (-ed) meng, vermeng; s. (-s) mengsel.

'bless ['bles] ww. (-ed, blest) seën, loof, gelukkig maak; -ed bnw. geseën, geluksalig; vervlakste.

'blight ['blait] s. roes, pes.

'blighter ['blaitə] s. rakker; skobbe-jak.

blind ['blaind] *bnw.* (*-er*, *-est*) blind, verblind; *ww.* (*-ed*) verblind, bedrieg; s. (*-s*) blinding; **-fold** *ww.* (*-ed*) blinddoek; **-approach** s. blinde nadering; **- corner** s. blinde hoek; **- rise** s. blinde bult; **- spot** s. blinde kol.

blink ['blɘŋk] *ww.* (*-ed*) knipoog; **-er** s. (*-s*) kniplig.

bliss ['blis] s. saligheid, geluk, vreugde.

'blister ['blistə] s. (*-s*) blaar.

'blithe ['blaidh] *bnw.* (*-r*, *-st*) bly, opgewek, lustig.

'blizzard ['blizəd] s. (*-s*) sneeustorm.

'bloat ['blout] *ww.* (*-ed*) sout en rook; opblaas; **-ed** *bnw.* opgeblaas; gerook; **-er** s. bokkem, gerookte haring.

'blob ['blob] s. (*-s*) klont; druppel.

block ['blok] s. (*-s*) blok, stomp; vorm; drukplaat; obstruksie; *ww.* (*-ed*) versper, afsluit.

'blockhead ['blokhed] s. (*-s*) domkop, swaap.

blond ['blond] *bnw.* blond, lig; **-e** s. blondine.

blood ['blʌd] s. bloed, sap, familie; **-donor** s. bloedskenker; **-purifier** s. bloedsuiweraar; **-shed** s. bloedvergieting; **-thirsty** *bnw.* bloeddorstig; **-y** *bnw.* bloed(er)ig; vervloekste.

bloom ['blɵ͂m] s. (*-s*) bloeisel; fleur; blos; aanslag (*lens*); *ww.* (*-ed*) bloei; blom; **-ing** *bnw.* bloeiend; vervlakste.

'blossom ['blosəm] s. (*-s*) bloeisel; bloei; *ww.* (*-ed*) bloei, blom.

blot ['blot] s. (*-s*) klad, vlek, smet.

'blotch ['blotsj] s. (*-es*) spatvlek.

'blouse ['blauz] s. (*-s*) bloese.

blow ['blou] s. slag, klap, hou; *ww.* (*blew*, *blown*) waai; blaas; hyg; snuit; **-fly** s. brommer; **-n fuse** s. gesmelte sekering; **-pipe** s. blaaspyp.

'blubber ['blʌbə] s. walvisspek; *ww.* (*-ed*) grens, tjank.

'bludgeon ['blʌdzjən] s. (*-s*) knuppel, knopkierie.

blue ['blɵ͂] *bnw.* blou; bedruk; s. blousel; blou; die lug; *ww.* (*-d*) blou maak, in die blousel steek; **-bottle** s. bloubrommer.

bluff ['blʌf] s. wal; *bnw.* stomp, kortaf; hartlik; *ww.* (*-ed*) oorbluf; uitoorlê; grootpraat.

'blunder ['blʌndə] s. flater, fout; *ww.* (*-ed*) struikel, vergis, flater maak.

blunt ['blʌnt] *bnw.* stomp, bot; kortaf; reguit.

'blur ['blə] s. (*-s*) klad, vlek; *ww.* (*-red*) bevlek, klad; verdof.

'blurt ['blə͂t] *ww.* (*-ed*) uitblaker.

blush ['blʌsj] s. blos, gloed; *ww.* (*-ed*) bloos, rooi word.

'bluster ['blʌstə] *ww.* (*-ed*) raai; swets.

boar ['bôə] s. burg; wildevark.

board ['bôd] s. (*-s*) plank; bord; karton; losies; etes; bestuur; boord; *ww.* (*-ed*) losies verskaf; aan boord gaan; met planke toespyker; voor

'n raad daag; **-er** s. loseerder.

boast ['boust] *ww.* (*-ed*) spog, spog met, grootpraat.

boat ['bout] s. (*-s*) skuit, skip; souspotjie.

'bob ['bob] *ww.* (*-bed*) kort knip; dobber; s. sjieling; **-by** s. konstabel.

'bobbin ['bobin] s. (*-s*) tol, spoeltjie.

'bodice ['bodis] s. (*-s*) lyfie.

'body ['bodi] s. (*'bodies*) liggaam; lyf; persoon; vereniging; massa; *bodily* *bnw.* & *bw.* liggaamlik; heeltemal; **-builder** s. bakbouer; **-work** s. bakwerk.

Boer ['bôə] s. (*-s*) Boer.

bog ['bogh] s. (*-s*) moeras.

'boggle ['boghl] *ww.* (*-d*) skrik; weifel; knoei.

'bogus ['boghəs] *bnw.* vals, voorgewend(e).

bogy ['boughi] s. (*'bogies*) skrikbeeld, duiwel, paaiboelie.

boil ['boil] s. (*-s*) sweer, pitseer, bloedvint; *ww.* (*-ed*) kook; **-er** s. koker, ketel, stoomketel, warmwatertenk; **-er suit** s. ketelpak.

'boisterous ['boistərəs] *bnw.* onstuimig, rumoerig; ru.

bold ['bould] *bnw.* (*-er*, *-est*) dapper, moedig; skerp, duidelik; vrypostig.

'bole ['boul] s. (*-s*) stam.

'bolster ['boulstə] s. (*-s*) peul, kussing, stut; *ww.* (*-ed*) stut.

bolt ['boult] s. (*-s*) grendel; pyl; blitsstraal; *ww.* (*-ed*) grendel; vasskroef; weghardloop; gou wegsluk.

bomb ['bom] s. (*-s*) bom; *ww.* (*-ed*) bombardeer.

'bombard ['bombâd] *ww.* (*-ed*) bombardeer.

'bona'fides ['bounə'faidiz] s. bona fide; *bnw.* in goeie trou.

bond ['bond] s. (*-s*) band; verbond; verband; pakhuis; verpligting; *ww.* (*-ed*) verbind; bind; verband aangaan; in pakhuis opslaan; **-age** s. ['bondidzj] s. knegskap.

'bone ['boun] s. (*-s*) been, graat; **- of** *contention* twisappel; **bony** *bnw.* benerig.

'bonfire ['bonfaiə] s. (*-s*) vreugdevuur, feesvuur.

'bonnet ['bonit] s. (*-s*) mus, kappie, hoedjie; motorkap, enjinkap.

'bonny ['boni] *bnw.* (*-ier*, *-iest*) hups, aanvallig.

'bonus ['bounəs] s. (*-es*) bonus, premie.

'booby ['bôbi] s. (*'boobies*) domoor; **-trap** s. wip, strikval.

book ['boek] s. (*-s*) boek, geskrif; Bybel; renprogram; *ww.* (*-ed*) inskryf; bespreek; **-ie** s. beroepswedder; **-ish** *bnw.* boekagtig, pedanties; **-keeper** s. boekhouer; **-mark** s. bladwyser; **-plate** s. ex libris; **-stall** s. boekwinkeltjie, kraampie.

'boom ['bôĕm] s. (*-s*) slagboom; oplewing; *ww.* dreun.

boon ['bôĕn] s. (*-s*) seën, voordeel, bede, guns; *bnw.* gul, vrolik.

boor ['bōǝ] s. lomperd, onbeskofte vent.

boost ['bōǝst] ww. (-ed) bekend maak deur ywerige reklame; aanja; s. aanjaging; **-er** s. aanjaer.

boot ['bōǝt] s. (-s) skoen, stewel; bagasiekis; voordeel; **-lace** s. skoenveter; **=tree** s. skoenlees.

booth ['bōǝth] s. tent, kraampie, hok.

booty ['bōǝti] s. buit, roof.

booze ['bōǝz] ww. (-d) fuif, suip.

border ['bōdǝ] s. (-s) rant, kant; grens; soom; ww. (-ed) begrens, omrand, omsoom.

bore ['bō] s. (-s) boorwydte; boorgat; vervelige vent; ww. (-d) boor; verveel; **-r** s. (-s) boor; boorder; boorwurm; **-dom** s. verveling.

boreal ['boriǝl] bnw. noordelik, noorder-.

born ['bōn] bnw. gebore.

borne ['bōn] verl. deelw. **bear**.

borough ['bʌrǝ] s. (-s) stad; kiesafdeling.

borrow ['borou] ww. (-ed) leen, ontleen.

bosh ['bosj] s. bog, kaf, onsin.

bosom ['boezǝm] s. (-s) boesem, bors; hart; siel; skoot.

boss ['bos] s. (-es) baas, bobaas; naaf; ww. (-ed) baasspeel.

botany ['botǝni] s. plantkunde, botanie; **bo'tanical** bnw. botanies, plantkundig.

botch ['botsj] ww. (-ed) knoei, konkel; to - your work jou werk afskeep.

bother ['bodhǝ] ww. (-ed) hinder, pla, lol, neul; s. beslommering, las, geneul; **bothe'ration** s. geneul.

bottle ['botl] s. (-s) bottel, fles; pypkan; ww. (-d) bottel, in flesse tap, inmaak, inlê; **'bottling** s. bottelering; **-store** s. drankwinkel.

bottom ['botǝm] s. (-s) boom, bodem; grond; agterent; kiel; bnw. onderste, laaste.

boudoir ['bōdwa] s. private dameskamer.

bough ['bau] s. (-s) tak.

boulder ['bouldǝ] s. (-s) klip, rotsblok.

boulevard ['boelvā] s. breë straat begrens met bome.

bounce ['bauns] ww. (-d) opspring, wip; huppel; opslaan; s. opslag, terugslag; sprong.

bound ['baund] s. grens; perk; sprong; ww. (-ed) begrens; spring.

boundary ['baundǝri] s. ('boundaries) grens, skeiding.

bounder ['baundǝ] s. (-s) rakker, skobbejak.

bounty ['baunti] s. ('bounties) goedertierenheid; gif, gawe; premie; **'bountiful** bnw. mild, oorvloedig.

bouquet ['boeky] s. (-s) ruiker; geur.

bourgeois ['boezjwā] s. middelklas.

bout ['baut] s. (-s) beurt, potjie, rondte; skermutseling.

bovine ['bouwyn] bnw. osagtig; vadsig, bot.

bow ['bau] s. (-s) boog; strykstok; boeg; buiging; knik; ww. (-ed) buig; stryk; **-legged** bnw. hoepelbeen; **-saw** s. spansaag; **-sprit** s. boegspriet; **-window** s. ronde venster.

bowel ['bauǝl] s. endelderm; **-s** mv. ingewande; binneste.

bowl ['boul] s. (-s) kom, bak, beker; kegelbal; ww. (-ed) bal, kegel, boul, rol; **-s** mv. kegelspel; **-er** s. bouler, kegelaar; hardebolkeiltjie.

box ['boks] s. (-es) doos, kis (sie) koffer; losie, afskorting; bus; boksboom; ww. (-ed) afskort; bêre; klap; boks; **-iron** s. hol strykyster; **-office** s. besprekingskantoor; **-spanner** s. dopsleutel, soksleutel.

'Boxing-day ['boksindy] s. Tweede Kersdag.

boy ['boi] s. (-s) jongetjie; seun; jong, bode, bediende; **-hood** s. kinderdae; **-ish** bnw. seunsagtig.

'boycott ['boikǝt] ww. boikot.

brace ['brys] s. klamp; paar, koppe; stut; omslag; ww. (-d) vasmaak, stewig maak, versterk, staal; verspan.

'bracelet ['bryslit] s. (-s) armband; handboei.

'bracken ['brækǝn] s. varing.

'bracket ['brækit] s. (-s) rak; klamp; arm, stut; hakie; ww. (-ed) saamvoeg, tussen hakies plaas.

'brackish ['brækisj] bnw. brak, brakkerig; **-ness** s.

'bradawl ['brædɔl] s. (-s) els.

brag ['brægh] ww. (-ged) spog, grootpraat, bluf, opskep; **-gart** s. grootbek, windmaker.

braid ['bryd] s. (-s) vlegsel; koord, omboorsel, band; ww. (-ed) vleg; omboor.

'braille ['bryl] s. blindeskrif.

brain ['bryn] s. (-s) brein, harsings; verstand; **-fever** s. harsingkoors; **-pan** s. harspan; **-y** bnw. slim.

braise ['bryz] ww. (-d) smoor.

'brake ['bryk] s. bossies, ruigte, kreupelhout; varing, vgl. **bracken**; rem, briek; **-cable** s. remkabel; **-drum** s. remtrommel; **-fluid** s. remvloeistof; **-lining** s. remvoering; **-light** s. remlig; **-shoe** s. remskoen; **-lever** s. remhefboom; **braking power** s. remkrag; **braking system** s. remstelsel.

'bramble ['bræmbl] s. (-s) braambos.

bran ['bræn] s. semels.

branch ['brāntsj] s. (-es) tak, vertakking, vak, afdeling.

brand ['brænd] s. (-s) brandende hout; brandmerk, stempel; swaard; ww. (-ed) brandmerk; inprent; **-iron** s. brandyster; **-new** bnw. splinternuut.

'brandish ['brændisj] ww. (-ed) swaai.

'brandy ['brændi] s. ('brandies) brandewyn.

brass ['brâs] s. geelkoper; geld;
astrantheid; **-band** s. blaasorkes;
-foil s. klatergoud; **-plate** s. naam-
bord; **-y** bnw. koperagtig, koper;
-works s. kopergietery.

brat ['bræt] s. (-s) snuiter, bengel,
skreeubalie.

brattice ['brætis] s. hout afskorting,
skagvoering.

bra'vado [brə'vâdou] s. grootpraat;
uittarting; bluf; bravado.

'brave ['bryv] bnw. (-r, -st) dapper,
moedig, braaf; s. dappere; **-ry** s.
moed, dapperheid.

'bravo ['brâvou] uitroep. mooi!
bravo!

brawl ['brôl] s. (-s) rusie, twis; ww.
(-ed) rusiemaak, twis.

brawn ['brôn] s. spier; spierkrag;
sult, hoofkaas; **-y** bnw. gespierd.

bray ['bry] s. & ww. (-ed) runnik,
balk, skree.

'braze ['bryz] ww. (-d) verbrons,
soldeer met brons, sweissoldeer.

'brazen ['bryzn] bnw. koper-, van
koper, brons-; hard; astrant; brutaal; **-ness** s. astrantheid.

'brazier ['bryziə] s. kopersmid;
konfoor.

Brazil [brə'zil] s. Brasilië.

breach ['britsj] s. bres, breuk;
deurbraak; oortreding; rusie.

bread ['bred] s. (-s) brood.

breadth ['bret-th] s. breedte, wydte;
baan; uitgestrektheid.

'break ['bryk] ww. (broke, broken)
breek, aanbreek, afbreek, verbreek;
s. breuk; onderbreking; **-age** s.
breek, slytasie; breekskade; **-away**
s. wegbraak; **-down** s. instorting,
oponthoud, ongeluk, defek; **-down**
van s. teenspoedwa; **-er** s. temmer;
brander; skokstrook; **-fast** s. ontbyt;
-neck bnw. halsbrekend, gevaarlik;
-through s. deurbraak; **-up** s.
verval; sluiting; **-water** s. hawehoof.

'breaker ['brykə] s. onderbreker;
contact- s. kontakonderbreker;
-points s. onderbrekerpunte; **-gap** s.
onderbrekeropening.

'bream ['brim] ww. skoonbrand; s.
brasem.

breast ['brest] s. (-s) bors; gemoed;
ww. (-ed) trotseer; make a clean -
opblieg; **-work** s. borswering.

breath ['breth] s. asem; luggie; **-e**
['bridh] ww. (-d), asemhaal, asem-
skep; **-less** bnw. uitasem; gespanne;
-ing s. assemhaling.

breech ['britsj] s. (-es) agterste,
agterstuk (kanon); **-es** s. broek;
-loader s. agterlaaier.

breed ['brid] s. (-s) ras, soort; ww.
(bred) verwek, teel; voortbring;
opvoed; **-er** s. verwekker; kweker,
teler.

'breeze ['briz] s. (-s) bries, windjie;
standjie; **'breezy** bnw. winderig;
lewendig.

'breve ['briv] s. (-s) dubbele noot
(mus.).

'breviary ['briviəri] s. ('breviaries)
brevier.

'brevity ['breviti] s. kortheid,
beknoptheid.

brew ['brôë] ww. (-ed) brou, meng;
stook, stig; s. (-s) brousel, mengsel;
-ery s. ('breweries) brouery.

'briar ['braiə] s. wilderoos, doring-
struik; tabakspyp van wilderoos-
hout.

'bribe ['braib] s. (-s) omkoopgeld;
ww. (-d) omkoop; **-ry** s. omkopery.

brick ['brik] s. (-s) baksteen; blok;
gawe kêrel; **-layer** s. messelaar;
-work s. messelwerk.

'bride ['braid] s. (-s) bruid; **-groom**
s. (-s) bruidegom; **-maid** s. strooi-
meisie; **-sman** s. strooijonker;
'bridal bnw. trou-, bruids-; **'bridal**
s. bruilof, trouplegtigheid; **- bouquet**
s. bruidsruiker; **-cake** s. bruids-
koek.

'bridge ['bridzj] s. (-s) brug;
vioolkam; rug van neus; kaartspel;
ww. (-d) oorbrug; **-head** s. brughoof.

'bridle ['braidl] s. (-s) toom, teuel;
dwang, breidel; ww. (-d) optoom;
beteuel; bedwing; **-path** s. voetpad.

brief ['brif] bnw. (-er, -est) kort;
beknop; s. (-s) uittreksel; opdrag;
akte; **-less** bnw. sonder praktyk.

'brier = briar.

brig ['brigh] s. (-s) brik.

brigade [bri'ghyd] s. (-s) brigade,
afdeling; **briga'dier** s. [brighə'diə]
s. (-s) brigade-generaal.

brigand ['brighənd] s. (-s) rower;
-age s. struikrowery.

'brigantine ['brighəntyn] s. (-s)
brigantyn, tweemaster.

bright ['brait] bnw. (-er, -est) helder,
lig; skerp; lewendig; knap; opgeruimd; **-en** ww. (-ed) verlig,
opklaar, opvrolik; **-ness** s. helderheid, glans; **'Bright's disease** s.
nierkwaal, Bright se siekte.

'brilliant ['briljənt] bnw. skitterend,
briljant; s. briljant, geslypte diamant; **'brilliancy** s. skittering,
glans; briljantheid.

brim ['brim] s. (-s) rand, boord,
kant; **-ful** bnw. boordevol; **-stone** s.
swael.

'brindle ['brindl] bnw. gestreep.

'brine ['brain] s. soutwater, pekel;
trane; **'briny** bnw. sout, pekel.

bring ['bring] ww. (brought) bring,
saam (mee) bring.

brink ['brink] s. (-s) rand, kantjie.

brisk ['brisk] bnw. (-er, -est)
lewendig, vlug; verfrissend.

'brisket ['briskit] s. borsvleis,
borsstuk.

'bristle ['brisl] s. (-s) borsel, steek-
haar; ww. (-d) vuurvat, opstuif.

'Britain ['britən] s. Brittanje.

'British ['britisj] bnw. Brits.

'Briton ['britən] s. (-s) Brit.

'brittle ['britl] bnw. (-r, -st) bros.

broach ['broutsj] ww. (-ed) aanbreek, oopslaan; aanroer, opper.

'**broad** ['brôd] *bnw.* (*-er*, *-est*) breed, wyd, ruim; vrysinnig; **-cast** *ww.* (*-ed*) uitsaai; uitbasuin; **-cloth** s. fyn, swart wolstof; **-en** *ww.* (*-ed*) verwyd, rek; **-ly** *bw.* breed, naaste-by, in die algemeen; **-ness** s. breedte, wydte; **-side** s. volle laag.

bro'**cade** [bro'kyd] s. (*-s*) brokaat, goudlaken.

broil ['broil] s. rusie, twis; *ww.* (*-ed*) braai, rooster, bak.

'**broke** ['brouk] *bnw.* platsak, bankrot.

'**broken** ['broukn] *bnw.* gebreek(te); onderbroke.

'**broker** ['broukə] s. (*-s*) makelaar; **-age** s. makelary; makelaarsloon.

'**bromide** ['broumaid] s. (*-s*) bromide.

'**bronchial** ['bronkiəl] *bnw.* bronchiaal, van die lugpyptakke.

bron'chitis [brong-'kaitis] s. brongitis.

'**bronze** ['bronz] s. brons; *bnw.* brons-; **-** ; *ww.* (*-d*) verbrons.

brooch ['broutzj] s. (*-es*) borsspeld.

'**brood** ['brôd] s. (*-s*) broeisel; gespuis; *ww.* (*-ed*) broei; peins; **-y** *bnw.* broeis.

brook ['bruk] s. (*-s*) spruit, beek; *ww.* (*-ed*) verdra, veel.

broom ['brôëm] s. (*-s*) besem; besembos; brem.

broth ['brôth] s. (*-s*) sop, vleiskrag.

'**brother** ['brʌdhə] s. (*-s*) broer, boetie; vriend; **-hood** s. broederskap; **-in-'law** s. swaer; **-ly** *bnw.* broederlik.

brow ['brau] s. (*-s*) winkbrou; **-beat** *ww.* oorbluf, oordonder, bars aanspreek.

brown ['braun] s. bruin (*kleur*); *bnw.* bruin, donker; *ww.* (*-ed*) bruin maak (*word*).

'**browse** ['brauz] *ww.* (*-d*) wei, afvreet.

'**bruise** ['brôëz] *ww.* (*-d*) kneus; s. kneusing, kneusplek.

bru'**nette** [broe'net] s. & *bnw.* (*-s*) brunet.

brunt ['brʌnt] s. skok, spit.

brush ['brʌsj] s. (*-es*) borsel, kwas, besem; skermutseling; *ww.* (*-ed*) afborsel; skrams raak; oorverf.

'**brushwood** ['brʌsjwôëd] s. kreupelhout, struike, ruigte.

brusque ['broesk] *bnw.* kortaf, bruusk.

'**brute** ['brôët] s. (*-s*) bees, ondier, woestaard; *bnw.* dierlik, sinlik; '**brutal** *bnw.* dierlik; onbeskof; woes.

'**bubble** ['bʌbl] s. (*-s*) blaas, bel; skim; *ww.* (*-d*) borrel, kook.

bucca'**neer** [bʌkə'niə] s. (*-s*) seerower, fortuinsoeker.

buck ['bak] s. (*-s*) wildsbokram, mannetjie; *ww.* (*-ed*) bokspring, steeks wees; **-ed** *bnw.* uitgelate, bly.

'**bucket** ['bʌkit] s. (*-s*) emmer, bak.

'**buckle** ['bʌkl] s. (*-s*) gespe; *ww.* (*-d*) vasgespe.

'**buckram** ['bʌkrəm] s. styflinne.

bud ['bʌd] s. (*-s*) bot, knop, kiem; *ww.* (*-ded*) bot, uitloop.

'**Buddha** ['bôëdə] s. Boeddha.

'**budge** ['bʌdzj] *ww.* (*-d*) verroer, beweeg.

'**budget** ['bʌdzjit] s. (*-s*) begroting; *ww.* (*-ed*) begroot.

buff ['bʌf] *bnw.* dofgeel.

'**buffalo** ['bʌfəlou] s. (*-es*) buffel.

'**buffer** ['bʌfə] s. stootkussing; buffer.

'**buffet** ['bʌfit] *ww.* (*-ed*) slaan, stamp; s. slaag; s. ['boefy] verversingslokaal (*toonbank*).

buf'**foon** [bʌ'fôën] s. (*-s*) harlekyn; **-ery** s. geskeerdery.

bug ['bʌgh] s. (*-s*) weeluis; kewer; stinkbesie.

'**bugbear** ['bʌghbèə] s. (*-s*) paaiboelie.

'**bugle** ['bjoeghl] s. (*-s*) beuel, trompet; **-r** s. trompetblaser.

build ['bild] *ww.* (*built*) bou, oprig, maak; s. bou; vorm; **-er** s. bouer; **-ing** s. gebou, bouery.

bulb ['bʌlb] s. (*-s*) bol; gloeilamp, brandpeer.

'**bulge** ['bʌldzj] s. (*-s*) knop; *ww.* (*-d*) uitstaan, swel, uitbult.

'**bulk** ['bʌlk] s. vrag, lading; grootte; massa; meerderheid; **-iness** s. lywigheid.

bull ['boel] s. (*-s*) bul; mannetjie; stier; **-fight** s. stiergeveg; **-frog** s. brulpadda; **-'s-eye** s. kolskoot.

'**bulldozer** ['boeldouzə] s. (*-s*) padskrop, stootskraper.

'**bullet** ['boelit] s. (*-s*) koeël.

'**bulletin** ['boelitin] s. (*-s*) rapport, bulletin.

'**bullheaded** ['boelhedid] *bnw.* onstuimig, woes, driftig.

'**bullion** ['boeljən] s. staafgoud.

'**bullock** ['boelək] s. os.

'**bully** ['boeli] s. & *ww.* bullebak, afknou; **-beef** s. blikkiesvleis.

'**bulrush** ['boelrʌsj] s. (*-es*) palmiet.

'**bulwark** ['boelwək] s. (*-s*) bolwerk, skans.

'**bumble-bee** ['bʌmblbi] s. (*-s*) hommel.

bump ['bʌmp] *ww.* (*-ed*) stoot, stamp; s. (*-s*) slag, knop, bult; **-er** s. stamper; **-er** *bnw.* oorvloedig; **-spring** s. deurslagveer.

'**bumpkin** ['bʌmkin] s. (*-s*) lomperd.

'**bumptious** ['bʌmsjəs] *bnw.* verwaand, aanstellerig.

bun ['bʌn] s. (*-s*) bolletjie; bolla.

bunch ['bʌntsj] s. (*-es*) tros; bondel.

'**bundle** ['bʌndl] s. (*-s*) bondel, hoop, rol; *ww.* (*-d*) saambind.

'**bung** ['bʌng] s. (*-s*) prop, spon.

'**bungalow** ['bʌng-ghəlou] s. (*-s*) enkelverdieping woning (*van weinig pretensie*).

'**bungle** ['bʌng-ghl] *ww.* (*-d*) knoei, verknoei, konkel.

'**bunion** ['bʌnjən] s. (*-s*) eelt (*sweer*), knokkel.

bunk ['bʌnk] s. (-s) kooi; *ww.* (-ed) stokkiesdraai.

bunkum ['bʌnkəm] s. onsin, twak.

bunting ['bʌnting] s. vlagdoek.

buoy ['boi] s. seeboei; *ww.* (-ed) opbeur; **-ancy** s. dryfkrag; veerkragtigheid; lewendigheid; **-ant** *bnw.* drywend; lewendig; veerkragtig.

burden ['bədən] s. (-s) las, vrag; *ww.* (-ed) belas; **-some** *bnw.* lastig, swaar, moeilik.

bu'reau [bjoeə'rou] s. skryftafel; kantoor; buro; **-cracy** s. amptenaarsheerskappy, burokrasie.

burgess ['bədʒiis] (-es) burger.

burgle ['bəghl] *ww.* (-ed) inbreek; **'burglar** s. inbreker; **'burglary** s. inbraak.

bur'lesque [bə'lesk] s. klug, parodie, burlesk.

burly ['bəli] *bnw.* groot, vors, grof.

burn ['bən] *ww.* (burnt) brand, verbrand; bak, warm wees; s. brandplek; **-er** s. brander, pit.

burnish ['bənisj] *ww.* (-ed) poets, polys, vryf, bruineer.

burr ['bə] s. (-s) knoets, klits.

burrow ['bArou] s. hol, lêplek; *ww.* gat grawe; in hol woon.

bursary ['bəsəri] s. ('bursaries) beurs.

burst ['bəst] *ww.* (-ed, burst) bars, oopbreek; s. (-s) bars, skeur; losbarsting.

bury ['beri] *ww.* ('buried) begrawe; **'burial** s. begrafnis.

bus ['bʌs] s. (-es) bus.

bush ['boesj] s. (-es) bos, struik; bosveld; bus.

bushel ['boesjl] s. (-s) boesel.

business ['biznis] s. besigheid; drukte; handel, sake.

bust ['bʌst] s. (-s) borsbeeld; bors.

bustle ['bʌsl] *ww.* (-d) woel, opdruk, aanja; s. drukte.

busy ['bizi] *bnw.* bedrywig; beset; *ww.* ('busied) besighou, bemoei; **-body** s. (busybodies) kwaadstoker, bemoeial.

but ['bʌt, bət] *voegw.* maar, egter, dog; *voors.* behalwe; *bw.* slegs, maar.

butcher ['boetsjə] s. (-s) slagter; **-y** s. slagtery.

butler ['bʌtlə] s. (-s) bottelier, opperhuiskneg.

butt ['bʌt] s. skyf; kolf; stompie; *ww.* (-ed) stamp; afbind.

butter ['bʌtə] s. botter; **-milk** s. karringmelk.

buttercup ['bʌtəkʌp] s. (-s) botterblom, aandblom; **'butterfingers** s. lomperd.

butterfly ['bʌtəflai] s. ('butterflies) skoenlapper.

buttock ['bʌtək] s. (-s) boud.

button ['bʌtn] s. (-s) knoop; **-hole** s. knoopsgat; knoopsgatruiker.

buttress ['bʌtris] s. (-es) steun, stut, beer.

buxom ['bʌksəm] *bnw.* fris, knap, vrolik.

buy ['bai] *ww.* (bought) koop, om-

koop; **-er** s. koper; **-ing society** s. koopvereniging.

buzz ['bʌz] *ww.* (-ed) gons.

buzzard ['bʌzəd] s. (-s) valk; aasvoël.

by ['bai] *voors.* by; met; op; na; volgens; *bw.* verby, opsy.

bye ['bai] s. & *bnw.* (iets) ondergeskik (s); loslopie.

'bygone ['baighon] s. (-s) wat verby is.

'by(e)-law ['bailô] s. (-s) regulasie, verordening.

'by-pass ['baipâs] s. (-es) omweg, ompad, verbypad; *ww.* (-ed) verbysteek.

'by-product ['baiprodəkt] s. (-s) neweproduk.

'by-road ['bairoud] s. (-s) uitdraaipaadjie, nu-paadjie.

'bystander ['baistændə] s. (-s) toeskouer.

'by-word ['baiwəd] s. spreekwoord; skimpnaam.

C

c. ['si] s. cent, *c.* (cent, sent).

C.S.I.R. [Council for Industrial and Scientific Research] s. W.N.N.R. (*Wetenskaplike en Nywerheidsnavorsingsraad*).

cab ['kæb] s. (-s) huurrytuig.

'cabbage ['kæbidzj] s. (-s) kool.

'cabin ['kæbin] s. (-s) kajuit, hut.

'cabinet ['kæbinit] s. (-s) kas; kabinet; ministerie.

'cable ['kybəl] s. (-s) kabel; **-brake** s. kabelrem.

ca'cao [kə'kâou] s. kakao.

'cackle ['kækl] *ww.* (-d) kekkel; babbel.

ca'cophony [kæ'kofəni] s. wangeluit, kakafonie.

cad ['kæd] s. (-s) skobbejak.

ca'daverous [kə'dyverʌs] *bnw.* soos 'n lyk; lykkleurig.

caddy, 'caddie ['kædi] s. (-s) gholfjoggie.

'cadence ['kydəns] s. (-s) kadans, ritme, maat.

'cadge ['kædzj] *ww.* (-d) bedel; smous; **-r** s. klaploper.

caecum ['sikʌm] s. (*anat.*) blindederm.

cae'sura [si'zjoeərə] s. ruspunt.

'café ['kæfy] s. (-s) kafee.

'cage ['kydzj] s. (-s) kooi, hok.

ca'hoot [kə'hôēt] s. (-s) vennootskap, maats; *to go -s* saam maak.

ca'jole [kə'dzjoul] *ww.* (-d) flikflooi, pamperlang.

'cake ['kyk] s. (-s) koek, gebak.

ca'lamity [kə'læməti] s. (*ca'lamities*) ongeluk, ramp.

calceo'laria ['kælsiəlyriə] s. pantoffelblom; pantofeldiertjies.

'calcify ['kælsifai] *ww.* ('calcified) verkalk.

'calcium ['kælsiəm] s. kalsium.

'calculate ['kælkjoelyt] *ww.* (-*d*) bereken; calcu'lation *s.* berekening; 'calculator *s.* rekenaar, rekenmasjien.

'calculus ['kælkjoeləs] *s.* slangsteen; rekenmetode.

'calendar ['kælində] *s.* kalender, almanak.

calf ['kâf] *s.* (*calves*) kalf; kuit; snuiter.

'calibrate ['kælibryt] *ww.* (-*d*) kalibreer, yk.

'calibre ['kælibə] *s.* kaliber; deursnee; gehalte.

call ['kôl] *ww.* (-*ed*) roep; noem; besoek aflê; bel; troef maak; uitlees; *s.* (-*s*) roep, geroep; oproep; kamertjie; lokstem; -ing *s.* geroep; beroep.

'cal(l)ipers ['kælipəs] *s.* meetpasser; skuifpasser.

'callous ['kæləs] *bnw.* gevoelloos, vereelt.

'callow ['kælou] *bnw.* kaal, sonder vere; baar, groen.

'callus ['kæl∧s] *s.* (-*es*, *calli*) eelt.

calm ['kâm] *bnw.* (-*er*, -*est*) kalm, stil; *s.* kalmte; *ww.* (-*ed*) kalmeer, sus.

'calmative ['kâmətiv] *s.* kalmeermiddel.

'calorie ['kæləri] *s.* (-*s*) kalorie.

'calumny ['kæləmni] *s.* lastering.

'calvary ['kælvəri] *s.* ('*calvaries*) Kruisberg, Golgota.

'calyx ['kyliks] *s.* (-*es*) blomkelk.

'cam ['kæm] *s.* nok; -shaft *s.* nokas.

'cambric ['kymbrik] *s.* kamerdoek, batis.

camel ['kæməl] *s.* (-*s*) kameel.

'cameo ['kæmiou] *s.* (-*s*) kamee.

'camera ['kæmərə] *s.* (-*s*) kamera.

'camisole ['kæmisoul] *s.* (-*s*) onderlyfie.

'camouflage ['kæmoefiâzj] *s.* maskering, camouflage.

camp ['kæmp] *s.* (-*s*) kamp, laer; *ww.* (-*ed*) uitkamp, kampeer.

campaign [kæm'pyn] *s.* (-*s*) kampanje, veldtog.

'camphor ['kæmfə] *s.* kanfer.

'campus ['kæmp∧s] *s.* werf, terrein van 'n irrigting.

can ['kæn] *hulpww.* kan, in staat wees, mag; *s.* (-*s*) kan, blik; *ww.* (-*ned*) inlê.

Canada ['kænədə] *s.* Kanada.

ca'nal [kə'næl] *s.* (-*s*) kanaal.

'cancel ['kænsəl] *ww.* (-*led*) kanselleer, afsê, herroep, intrek; cancel'lation *s.* kansellering.

'cancer ['kænsə] *s.* kanker.

'candid ['kændid] *bnw.* openhartig, eerlik, opreg.

'candidate ['kændidit] *s.* (-*s*) kandidaat; applikant; 'candidature *s.* kandidatuur.

'candle ['kændl] *s.* (-*s*) kers; -stick *s.* blaker.

'candour ['kændə] *s.* openhartigheid.

'candy ['kændi] *s.* kandy, suiker-

klontjies, lekkers; *ww.* ('*candied*) versuiker.

'cane ['kyn] *s.* riet, rottang, wandelstok; *ww.* (-*d*) pak slae gee.

'canine ['kænain] *s.* (-*s*) hond; hoektand; *bnw.* honds.

'canister ['kænistə] *s.* (-*s*) blik, kantientjie.

'canker ['kænkə] *s.* (-*s*) kanker; sweer; verpestende invloed.

'canna ['kænə] *s.* (-*s*) kanna, ganna.

'cannibal ['kænibəl] *s.* (-*s*) kannibaal, mensvreter.

'cannon ['kænən] *s.* (-*s*) kanon, geskut; raakskoot.

'canon ['kænən] *s.* (-*s*) kanon, wet; kanunnik.

'canopy ['kænəpi] *s.* ('*canopies*) geweif, dak, hemel.

'cant ['kænt] *ww.* (-*ed*) huigel; -er *s.* (-*s*) huigelaar.

can'tankerous [kən'tæng-kərəs] *bnw.* vitterig, prikkelbaar, dwarskoppig, rusiemakerig.

can'teen [kən'tin] *s.* (-*s*) kantien; veldkombuis; waterkannetjie.

'canter ['kæntə] *ww.* (-*ed*) op 'n handgalop ry.

'canvas ['kænvəs] *s.* seil, doek, skildery; 'canvass *ww.* bespreek, uitpluis, werf; 'canvasser *s.* werwer.

cap ['kæp] *s.* (-*s*) mus, pet; doppie.

'capable ['kypəbl] *bnw.* bekwaam, geskik.

ca'pacity [kə'pæsəti] *s.* (ca'*pacities*) bekwaamheid; hoedanigheid, kapasiteit.

'cape ['kyp] *s.* kaap; mantel.

'capital ['kæpitl] *s.* hoofsom, kapitaal; kapiteel.

ca'pitulate [kə'pitjoelyt] *ww.* (-*d*) kapituleer, oorgee.

'capon ['kypən] *s.* (-*s*) kapoen, gesnyde haan.

ca'price [kə'pris] *s.* bui, nuk, gier; ca'pricious *bnw.* grillig, buierig, wispelturig.

'capsize ['kæpsaiz] *ww.* (-*d*) omval, omslaan; omgooi.

'capstan ['kæpstæn] *s.* kaapstander.

'capsule ['kæps-joel] *s.* kappie, doppie; capsule.

'captain ['kæptin] *s.* (-*s*) kaptein; -cy *s.* kapteinskap.

'captive ['kæptiv] *s.* (-*s*) gevangene; cap'tivity *n.* gevangenskap.

'capture ['kæptsjə] *ww.* (-*d*) vang, roof, inneem.

car ['kâ] *s.* (-*s*) rytuig, wa, motor, trem.

ca'rafe [kə'râf] *s.* (-*s*) kraffie.

cara'van ['kærə'væn] *s.* (-*s*) karavaan, woonwa.

'carbide ['kâbaid] *s.* karbied.

'carbine ['kâbain] *s.* karabyn, buks.

'carbon ['kâbən] *s.* koolstof; -ize *ww.* aankool, -ized *bnw.* aangekool.

'carbonate ['kâbənit] *s.* karbonaat.

'carboy ['kâboi] *s.* (-*s*) karba.

carbu'ration [kabjoe'rysjn] *s.* vergassing.

carburetter, -or ['kâbjoeretə] s. (-s) vergasser.

carcase ['kâkəs] s. (-s) karkas, geraamte.

card ['kâd] s. (-s) kaart; -board s. karton.

cardigan ['kâdighən] s. (-s) gebreide onderbaadjie.

cardinal ['kâdinl] s. (-s) kardinaal; bnw. vernaamste, hoof-.

care ['kêə] s. sorg, hoede; bekommernis; ww. (-d) omgee, bekommer, oppas, versorg; -ful bnw. versigtig; -taker s. oppasser.

ca'reer [kə'riə] s. loopbaan; vaart.

ca'ress [kə'res] s. (-es) liefkosing, streling.

cargo ['kâghou] s. (-es) vrag, lading.

caricature ['kæriki'tsjoeə] s. (-s) karikatuur, drogbeeld.

carmine ['kâmain] s. karmyn;
'**carminative** bnw. windverdrywend;
'**carminative** s. windverdrywer; krampwater.

carnage ['kânidzj] s. slagting, bloedbad.

carnal ['kânl] bnw. vleeslik; wêrelds; sinnelik.

car'nation [kâ'nysjən] s. (-s) angelier.

car'nivorous [kâ'nivərəs] bnw. vleisetend.

carol ['kærəl] s. (-s) Kerslied.

ca'rouse [kə'rauz] ww. (-d) drink, fuif; ca'rousal s. fuifparty.

carp ['kâp] s. karper.

carpenter ['kâpintə] s. (-s) timmerman; 'carpentry s. timmerwerk.

carpet ['kâpit] s. (-s) tapyt.

carriage ['kæridzj] s. (-s) rytuig; onderstel; vervoer; vrag; houding; gedrag.

carrion ['kæriən] s. aas; - beetle, sexton beetle s. aaskewer.

carrot ['kærət] s. (-s) wortel.

carry ['kæri] ww. ('carried) dra; 'carrier s. draer; karweier; posduif.

cart ['kât] s. (-s) kar, voertuig; ww. (-ed) vervoer; -age s. vervoer.

cartilage ['kâtilidzj] s. kraakbeen.

car'toon [kâ'tōēn] s. (-s) spotprent; -ist s. spotprenttekenaar.

cartridge ['kâtridzj] s. (-s) patroon.

cartwright ['kât-rait] s. wa (kar) -maker.

carve ['kâv] ww. (-d) sny, uitsny, beeldsny, kerf; -r s. snyer; mes.

cas'cade [kæs'kyd] w. (-s) watervalletjie; stroom.

case ['kys] s. (-s) geval; saak; naamval; koffer, tas.

casement ['kysmənt] s. raam; venster.

cash ['kæsj] s. kontantgeld; kasgeld; klinkende munt; ww. (-ed) wissel, trek, inkasseer; -ier s. kassier.

cashmere ['kæsjmiə] bnw. kassemier-.

casing ['kysing] s. (-s) buiteband; bekisting, hulsel.

casket ['kâskit] s. (-s) dosie, kissie.

cassock ['kæsək] s. (-s) py, priesterkleed.

cast ['kâst] ww. gooi, werp; vorm; giet; rolle verdeel; s. gooi, worp; rolverdeling; afgietsel; -iron s. gietyster; -steel s. gietstaal.

castaway ['kâstəwy] s. skipbreukeling; uitvaagsel, verworpeling.

caste ['kâst] s. kaste, stand.

castigate ['kæstighyt] ww. (-d) tugtig, kasty; suiwer; casti'gation s. tugtiging.

castle ['kâsl] s. (-s) kasteel, slot.

castor ['kâstə] s. (-s) bewer; strooifiessie; rolwieletjie.

cas'trate ['kæs'tryt] ww. (-d) kastreer, ontman.

casual ['kæs-joeəl] bnw. toevallig; terloops; uitsonderlik; -ty s. ongeval, ongeluk; verlies; dooie.

casu'ist [kæzjoe'ist] s. gewetensregter; drogredenaar.

cat ['kæt] s. (-s) kat; kats; kennetjie.

catalepsy ['kætəlepsi] s. katalepsie, verstywing.

catalogue ['kætəlogh] s. katalogus, lys.

catapult ['kætəpʌlt] s. (-s) rekker, katapult.

ca'tastrophe [kə'tæstrəfi] s. katastrofe, ramp.

catch ['kætsj] ww. (caught) vang, gryp, vasvat; betrap; haal; -word s. slagspreuk, leus; -y bnw. pakkende (e), aanloklik; -ing bnw. besmetlik, aansteeklik.

category ['kætəgəri] s. ('categories) kategorie, klas, soort.

cater ['kytə] ww. (-ed) spyseneer, verversings verskaf; -er s. (-s) leweransier, verskaffer van voedsel, spysenier.

caterpillar ['kætəpilə] s. (-s) ruspe.

caterwaul ['kætəwôl] ww. (-ed) miaau; -ing s. kattegetjank.

catgut ['kæghʌt] s. dermsnaar.

ca'thedral [kə'thidrəl] s. katedraal, domkerk.

catholic ['kæthəlik] bnw. algemeen; katoliek.

cattle ['kætl] s. vee, beeste; stommerik.

caucus ['kôkəs] s. koukus.

caudal ['kôdl] bnw. stert-.

cauldron ['kôldrən] s. (-s) ketel, pot.

caulk ['kôk] s. (-ed) kalfater, stop.

cause ['kôz] s. oorsaak, rede, grond, aanleiding; ww. (-d) veroorsaak; -way s. straatweg.

caustic ['kôstik] bnw. bytend, skerp; sarkasties.

cauterize ['kôtəraiz] ww. (-d) uitbrand, toeskroei.

caution ['kôsjən] s. versigtigheid.

cautious ['kôsjəs] bnw. versigtig.

cava'lier [kævə'liə] s. (-s) ruiter; ridder; begeleide.

cave ['kyv] s. (-s) spelonk, grot.

cavern ['kævən] s. (-s) spelonk, grot; 'cavernous bnw. spelonkagtig.

cavil ['kævil] ww. (-led) vit.

'cavity ['kæviti] s. ('cavities) holte.
'cease ['sis] ww. (-d) ophou, staak, eindig; -less bnw. onophoudelik.
'cede ['sid] ww. (-d) afgee, afstand doen, sedeer, toestem.
'ceiling ['siling] s. (-s) plafon.
'celebrate ['selibryt] ww. (-d) vier; herdink; verheerlik; cele'bration s.; ce'lebrity s. beroemde persoon.
ce'lerity [si'leriti] s. spoed, snelheid.
ce'lestial [si'lestjol] bnw. hemels, hemel-.
'celibacy ['selibosi] s. ongetroude staat.
cell ['sel] s. (-s) sel; hokkie; kluis; graf; -voltage s. selspanning.
'cellar ['selo] s. (-s) kelder.
'cellulose ['seljoelous] s. sellulose, selstof.
ce'ment [si'ment] s. sement.
'cemetery ['semitri] s. ('cemeteries) begraafplaas, kerkhof.
'censor ['senso] s. sensor, keurder, beoordelaar.
'censure ['senso] s. berisping, sensuur; ww. (-d) afkeur, berispe.
'census ['sensos] s. volkstelling, sensus.
cen'tenary [sen'tinori] s. eeufees.
'centigrade ['sentighryd] bnw. honderdgradig.
'centimetre ['sentimito] s. sentimeter.
'centipede ['sentipid] s. duisendpoot.
'centre ['sento] s. middel, middelpunt, sentrum; spil; bnw. middel, middelste.
cen'trifugal [sen'trifjoeghol] bnw. middelpuntvliedend.
cen'tripetal [sen'tripitl] bnw. middelpuntsoekend.
'century ['sentsjoeri] s. ('centuries) eeu; honderdtal.
'cereal ['siariol] s. graansoort; -s s. graan.
'cerebral ['seribrol] bnw. serebraal.
'cerebrum ['seri'brom] s. brein, grootharsings.
'ceremony ['serimoni] s. ('ceremonies) seremonie, plegtigheid; 'ceremonious bnw. plegtig, statig, deftig.
'certain ['sotn] bnw. seker, gewis, stellig; -ly bw. ongetwyfeld; -ty s. sekerheid.
'certify ['sotifai] ww. ('certified) verseker, verklaar, getuig; cer'tificate s. sertifikaat, getuigskrif.
'certitude ['sotitjoêd] s. sekerheid, oortuiging.
ces'sation [se'sysjon] s. staking, einde.
'cession ['sesjon] s. afstand, sessie.
'cesspool ['sespöêl] s. (-s) slykpoel.
'cestoid ['sestoud] s., bnw. lintwurm.
'chafe ['tsjyf] ww. (-d) vryf, skuur, skaaf; erger.
'chaff ['tsjåf] s. kaf; bog.
chagrin ['sjæghrin] s. ergernis, teleurstelling.
chain ['tsjyn] s. (-s) ketting; boeie; gevangeskap.

chair ['tsjêo] s. (-s) stoel; voorsitterstoel: professoraat; -man s. voorsitter.
chalk ['tsjôk] s. kryt, kalk.
'challenge ['tsjælindzj] s. uitdaging; uittarting; protes.
'chamber ['tsjymbo] s. kamer; slot; pot.
'chamberlain ['tsjymbolin] s. (-s) kamerheer (-dienaar).
'chamfer ['sjæmfo] ww. afkant; s. afkanting.
chamois ['sjæmwä] s. gemsbok; -leather s. seemsleer.
'champion ['tsjæmpjon] s. kampioen, baas-.
'chance ['tsjäns] s. (-s) kans, geleentheid; moontlikheid; bnw. toevallig; ww. (-d) waag; toevallig ontmoet.
'chancellor ['tsjänsolo] s. (-s) kanselier.
chande'lier ['sjændo'lio] s. (-s) kroonkandelaar, kroonlugter.
'change ['tsjyndzj] s. (-s) verandering; ruil; kleingeld; omkleding; oorstapping; ww. verander, wissel, ruil, uitruil; -gears oorskakel.
'channel ['tsjænl] s. (-s) kanaal, sloot; -ing s. geutwerk.
chant ['tsjänt] s. (-s) gesang; ww. (-ed) sing.
'chaos ['kyos] s. chaos, warboel; cha'otic bnw. chaoties.
chap ['tsjæp] s. kêrel, vent; bars, skeur; ww. (-ped) bars, spring, skeur.
'chapman ['tsjæpmon] s. koopman, smous, venter.
'chapel ['tsjæpol] s. (-s) kapel, kerk.
'chaperon ['sjæporoun] s. (-es) begeleidster.
'chaplain ['tsjæplin] s. (-s) kapelaan.
'chapter ['tsjæpto] s. (-s) hoofstuk; kapittel.
'char ['tsjä] ww. (-red) brand, verkool.
'character ['kærikto] s. (-s) karakter, kenmerk; hoedanigheid; kenteken; letter; rol; reputasie; -ize ww. (-d) karakteriseer; characte'ristic bnw. kenmerkend.
'charcoal ['tsjäkoul] s. houtskool.
'charge ['tsjädzj] s. (-s) las, skoot, lading; sarsie, aanval; koste; sorg; ww. (-d) laai, belas, beveel; storm; beskuldig; in rekening bring.
'chariot ['tsjæriot] s. (-s) strydwa, triomfwa.
'charitable ['tsjæritobl] bnw. vrygewig; liefdadig.
'charity ['tsjæriti] s. liefdadigheid; aalmoes; vrygewigheid.
charm ['tsjäm] s. (-s) bekoring, sjarme; toormiddel; ww. (-ed) bekoor; betower; -ing bnw. bekoorlik.
chart ['tsjät] s. (-s) tabel, kaart.
'charter ['tsjäto] s. oktrooi; ww. (-ed) huur, bevrag.
'chary ['tsjêori] bnw. ('charier, 'chariest) karig; suinig; spaarsaam.

'chase ['tsjys] s. jag; agtervolging; groef; ww. (-d) jag, jaag, nasit, verdryf.

'chasm ['kæzəm] s. (-s) afgrond, kloof.

'chassis ['sjæsi] s. onderstel, geraamte.

'chaste ['tsjyst] bnw. kuis, rein; 'chastity s. kuisheid.

'chasten ['tsjysn] ww. (-ed) kasty, tugtig.

'chastise ['tsjæstaiz] ww. (-d) kasty, straf, tugtig.

chat ['tsjæt] ww. (-ted) babbel, gesels.

'chattel ['tsjætl] s. (-s) hawe, eiendom.

'chatter ['tsjætə] ww. (-ed) babbel, klets; -box s. babbelkous.

'chauffeur ['sjoufə] s. chauffeur, bestuurder.

cheap ['tsjip] bnw. goedkoop; waardeloos; -en ww. (-ed) goedkoop maak.

cheat ['tsjit] ww. (-ed) bedrieg, fop.

check ['tsjek] s. (-s) stuiting; beletsel; kontrole; bewys; -nut s. sluitmoer.

cheek ['tsjik] s. (-s) wang; astrantheid; -y bnw. astrant.

cheer ['tsjiə] ww. (-ed) toejuig; bemoedig; -ful bnw. opgewek; -y bnw. opgeruimd.

'cheese ['tsjiz] s. (-s) kaas, -paring bnw. suinig.

chef ['sjef] s. (-s) kok, sjef.

'chemical ['kemikəl] s. skeikundige stof; bnw. chemies.

'chemist ['kemist] s. apteker; chemikus; 'chemistry s. skeikunde, chemie.

'cheque ['tsjek] s. tjek, wissel.

'chequer ['tsjekə] ww. (-ed) skakeer; -ed bnw. geruit; geskakeer.

'cherish ['tsjerisj] ww. (-ed) koester, bemin.

'chervil ['tsjɔvil] s. kerwel.

'chess ['tsjes] s. skaak.

chest ['tsjest] s. (-s) kis, kas; borskas.

'chestnut ['tsjestnʌt] s. (-s) kastaiing.

chew ['tsjɔɛ] ww. (-ed) kou, pruim.

chi'canery [sji'kynəri] s. slimstreke, foppery; haarklowery.

'chicken ['tsjikin] s. (-s) kuiken; hoender; snuiter.

'chicory ['tsjikəri] s. sigorei.

'chide ['tsjaid] ww. (-d) berispe, knor.

chief ['tsjif] s. (-s) leier, hoof, voorman; bnw. hoof, eerste, vernaamste.

child ['tsjaild] s. (-ren) kind; -hood s. kinderdae; -ish bnw. kinderagtig; -like bnw. kinderlik.

'children mv. van child.

chill ['tsjil] s. kilheid; koue, verkoue; onvriendelikheid; bnw. koud, kil, fris; koel; ww. (-ed) koud maak (word); afkoel; bevries; -blain s. winterseer.

'chime ['tsjaim] s. klokkespel, klokkelied, deuntjie; ww. (-d) lui, slaan.

chi'mera [kai'miərə] s. hersenskim, inbeelding, droombeeld, paaiboelie.

'chimney ['tsjimni] s. skoorsteen; lampglas.

chin ['tsjin] s. (-s) ken.

'China ['tsjainə] s. Sjina; porselein, breekgoed.

'chink ['tsjink] s. (-s) skrefie, spleet.

'chintz ['tsjints] s. (-es) sis.

'chip ['tsjip] s. (-s) splinter, skerf, brokkie, spaander; -s s. (mv.) ertappelskyfies.

'chirp ['tsjəp] ww. (-ed) tjilp, piep.

'chisel ['tsjizl] s. (-s) bytel.

chi'valrous ['sjivəlrəs] bnw. ruiterlik, ridderlik.

'chloride ['klɔraid] s. chloried.

'chloroform ['klɔrəfɔm] s. chloroform.

chlo'rosis [klə'rousis] s. bleeksug.

'chock-full ['tsjokfoel] bw. propvol.

'chocolate ['tsjokəlit] s. sjokola.

'choice ['tsjois] s. keuse, verkiesing; keur, beste; bnw. uitgelese, keurig.

'choke ['tsjouk] ww. (-d) stik, verwurg, versmoor; demp, verstop; s. smoorder; -valve s. smoorklep.

'choler ['koulə] s. woede; -ic bnw. driftig.

'cholera ['kolərə] s. cholera.

'choose ['tsjɔɛz] ww. (chose, chosen) kies, verkies.

chop ['tsjop] ww. (-ped) kap, kloof; s. (-s) kap, stuk; karmenaadjie, kotelet; golfslag; -per s. byl.

chord ['kɔd] s. (-s) snaar; koord; akkoord.

'chorus ['kɔrəs] s. koor; refrein.

'chose ['tsjouz] verl. t. choose.

Christ ['kraist] s. Christus; -ian s. christen; -mas s. Kersfees.

'christen ['krisn] ww. (-ed) doop.

'chronic ['kronik] bnw. chronies, langdurig, slepend.

chro'nology [krə'nolədzji] s. chronologie, tydrekening.

'chubby ['tsjʌbi] bnw. ('chubbier, 'chubbiest) mollig, rond van wange.

'chuck ['tsjʌk] ww. (-ed) tik; smyt; - it hou op!

'chuckle ['tsjʌkl] ww. (-d) grinnik.

chum ['tsjʌm] s. (-s) maat, vriend.

chunk ['tsjʌnk] s. (-s) stuk, brok.

church ['tsjətsj] s. (-es) kerk; -yard s. kerkhof.

churl ['tsjɔl] s. (-s) vent, lomperd; -ish bnw. onbeskof.

'churn ['tsjɔn] s. (-s) karring.

chute ['sjɔɛt] s. (-s) trog, geut.

ci'cada [si'kɑdə] s. (-s) boomsingertjie.

'cider ['saidə] s. appelwyn.

ci'gar [si'ghɑ] s. (-s) sigaar.

ciga'rette [sighə'ret] s. (-s) sigaret.

'cilia ['silia] s. mv. (enkv. cilium) ooghare, trilhare.

'cinder ['sində] s. sintel.

'cinema ['sinimə] s. (-s) kinema, bioskoop.

'cinnamon ['sinəmən] s. kaneel.

'cipher ['saifə] s. syfer; nul; ww. (-ed) reken, syfer, bereken.

'circle ['sə̄kl] s. (-s) sirkel, ring, kring; galery; ww. (-d) omsluit, omring, omsingel; -road s. singelpad.

'circuit ['sə̄kit] s. (-s) omtrek; rondgang; stroomkring, stroombaan.

'circular ['sə̄kjoelə] s. omsendbrief; bnw. kringvormig, rond, rondgaande.

'circulate ['sə̄kjoelyt] ww. (-d) rondgaan, sirkuleer; circu'lation s. omloop, sirkulasie.

'circumcise ['sə̄kəmsaiz] ww. (-d) besny; circum'cision s. besnydenis.

cir'cumference [sə'kʌmfərəns] s. omtrek.

'circumflex ['sə̄kəmfleks] s. kappie, sirkumfleks.

circumlo'cution [sə̄kʌmlou'kjœsjən] s. omslagtigheid; ontwyking.

'circumscribe ['sə̄kəmskraib] ww. (-d) omskryf, begrens, beperk.

'circumstance ['sə̄kəmstəns] s. (-s) omstandigheid, feit; circum'stantial bnw. bykomstig; omstandig.

circum'vent [sə̄kəm'vent] ww. (-ed) uitoorlê; -ion s. uitoorlegging, bedrog.

'circus ['sə̄kəs] s. (-es) sirkus.

cist [sist] s. (-s) kis.

'cistern ['sistən] s. (-s) tenk, bak, spoelbak.

'citadel ['sitədl] s. (-s) burg, vesting.

'cite ['sait] ww. (-d) dagvaar; aanhaal, siteer.

'citizen ['sitizn] s. (-s) burger, inwoner.

'citron ['sitrən] s. (-s) sitroen; liggeel.

'citrus ['sitrəs] s. sitrus.

'city ['siti] s. ('cities) stad; -hall s. stadshuis; stadsaal.

'civic ['sivik] bnw. burgerlik, burger-; -s. s. burgerleer.

'civil ['sivil] bnw. beleef; burgerlik, burger-; ci'vilian s. burgerman; civili'zation s. beskawing; ci'vility s. beleefdheid.

'clad ['klæd] verl. deelw. clothe.

claim ['klym] ww. (-ed) eis, vorder; beweer; s. (-s) eis, aanspraak, reg; kleim; -ant s. eiser.

clair'voyance [klɛə'voiəns] s. helder-siendheid; clair'voyante s. helder-siende vrou.

'clamber ['klæmbə] ww. (-ed) klouter.

'clammy ['klæmi] bnw. klam, vogtig.

'clamour ['klæmə] s. lawaai, ge-skreeu; 'clamorous bnw. lawaaierig, luidrugtig.

clamp ['klæmp] s. (-s) kram; klem, klamp; ww. (-ed) klem, vasklamp.

'clan ['klæn] s. (-s) stam; kliek.

clandestine ['klændəstin] bnw. skelm, agterbaks, heimlik.

'clang ['klæŋ] ww. (-ed) skal, kletter, lui.

'clank ['klæŋk] ww. (-ed) rammel, klink.

clap ['klæp] ww. (-ped) klap, toejuig; -per s. (-s) klepel; -trap s. mooi-praatjies.

'claret ['klæret] s. klaret, bordeaux-wyn.

'clarify ['klærifai] ww. ('clarified) ophelder, suiwer, opklaar; 'clarity s. helderheid, klaarheid.

'clarinet ['klærənit] s. (-s) klarinet.

'clarion ['klæriən] s. klaroen, trom-pet.

clash ['klæsj] ww. (-ed) bots, bons; indruis teen; s. botsing; gekletter.

clasp ['klæsp] s. klamp, haak, gespe; handdruk; omhelsing; ww. (-ed) vasmaak; omhels.

class ['klâs] s. (-es) klas, rang, stand; orde; kursus; ww. (-es) indeel, klassifiseer; -ify ww. ('classified) klassifiseer.

classic ['klæsik] bnw. klassiek; -s s. klassieke (tale, skrywers).

'clause ['klɔz] s. (-s) klousule, artikel; paragraaf; sinsdeel.

claw ['klɔ] s. (-s) klou, knyper; ww. (-ed) klou, krap.

clay ['kly] s. klei.

clean ['klin] bnw. (-er, -est) skoon, sindelik; rein; netjies; eerlik; bw. skoon, totaal, heeltemal, glad; ww. (-ed) skoonmaak, suiwer, opruim; -ing s.; -ly bnw. & bw. skoon, netjies; -se ww. ['klenz] (-d) reinig.

clear ['kliə] bnw. (-er, -est) helder, duidelik, suiwer, deurdringend; bw. skoon, glad, vry, totaal; ww. (-ed) skoonmaak, opruim; uitklaar, afbe-taal; -ance s. helderheid, opruiming, onbelemmerdheid.

'cleat [klit] s. (-s) klem-, klamp.

'cleave ['kliv] ww. (-d) kloof, splits, klief; getrou bly; -age s. klowing, splitsing.

clef ['klef] s. (-s) sleutel (mus.).

cleft ['kleft] s. (-s) bars, spleet, kloof.

'clement ['klemənt] bnw. genadig, sag; 'clemency s. genadigheid, sagtheid.

clench ['klentsj] ww. (-ed) vasbyt, bal.

'clergy ['klə̄dzji] s. geestelikheid, predikante.

clerk ['klâk] s. (-s) klerk, skriba, koster, griffier.

'clever ['klevə] bnw. (-er, -est) slim, skrander, oulik, handig.

'click ['klik] s. (-s) getik, geklik; click- klik-.

'client ['klaiənt] s. (-s) klant, kliënt; clien'tele ['kliən'tyl] s. klante, klandisie.

cliff ['klif] s. (-s) krans, steilte, rotswand.

'climate ['klaimit] s. (-s) klimaat, weersgesteldheid, lugstreek.

'climax ['klaimæks] s. (-es) klimaks, hoogtepunt.

climb ['klaim] ww. (-ed) klim,

klouter, beklim; -er s. (-s) strewer,
streber; klimmer; rankplant.
'clinch ['klintsj] ww. (-ed) klink;
beklink.
cling ['kling] ww. (clung) kleef, klou,
klem.
'clinic ['klinik] s. (-s) kliniek.
clip ['klip] ww. (-ped) knip, snoei;
kortwiek; vasklou; vasklem; s. (-s)
skeersel; klou, knip, tang; -per s.
knipper, skêr; -ping s. knipsel;
skeersel; clip- klem-.
cloak ['klouk] s. (-s) mantel.
clock ['klok] s. (-s) klok, horlosie;
-wise bnw. bw. regsom, haarom.
'clod ['klod] s. (-s) kluit; knul.
'clog ['klogh] s. (-s) blok, hindernis;
houtskoen.
'cloister ['kloistə] s. (-s) klooster;
suilegang.
'close ['klouz] bnw. gesluit, toe; nou;
bedompig; suinig; naby; s. om-
heining; slot, einde; ww. (-d)
toemaak, sluit; eindig; saamvoeg;
oorenkom; 'closure s. sluiting.
'closet ['klozit] s. (-s) gemakhuisie.
'clot ['klot] s. (-s) klont.
cloth ['kloth] s. laken, tafeldoek,
stuk stof; kleed.
'clothe ['kloudh] ww. (-d) beklee,
inklee, bedek; -s s. klere; clothing s.
kleding, klere.
cloud ['klaud] s. (-s) wolk; ww. (-ed)
bewolk, oorskadu; benewel; under
a - onder verdenking; -ed bnw.
bewolk.
'clout ['klaut] s. (-s) hou, slag.
'clove ['klouv] s. (-s) naeltjie (s);
skyfie.
'cloven ['klouvn] verl. deelw. van
cleave.
'clover ['klouvə] s. klawer.
'clown ['klaun] s. (-s) nar, harlekyn.
club ['klʌb] s. (-s) kierie, knuppel;
gholfstok; klawerkaart; klub; ww.
(-ed) (dood) slaan met knuppel;
bydra; saammaak; -foot s. horrelvoet.
clue ['klōē] s. (-s) wenk, aanduidig,
leidraad.
'clumsy ['klʌmzi] bnw. onhandig,
lomp.
'cluster ['klʌstə] s. (-s) tros, swerm,
trop.
clutch ['klʌtsj] s. (-es) greep, klou;
koppelaar; ww. (-ed) gryp, vat, ruk;
-gear s. koppelrat; -hub s. koppel-
aarnaaf; -pedal s. koppelaarpedaal;
-spring s. koppelaarveer.
'clutter ['klʌtə] s. warboel, verwarring.
coach ['koutsj] s. (-es) koets, rytuig;
breier; oefenmeester; ww. (-ed)
voorberei; brei; oefen.
co'agulate [kou'æghjoelyt] ww. (-d)
stol, klonter.
'coal ['koul] s. steenkool.
coa'lesce [kouə'les] ww. (-d) saam-
groei, verenig.
coa'lition [kouə'lisjən] s. samesmelting, koalisie.

'coal 'tar ['koul 'tā] s. koolteer.
'coarse ['kôs] bnw. (-r, -st) grof,
lomp, onbehoorlik.
coast ['koust] s. (-s) kus; ww. (-ed)
langs kus seil; afdraand gaan,
vrywiel, vryloop.
coat ['kout] s. (-s) baadjie, manel,
mantel, bekleding, pels, vag; laag;
-ed bnw. aangepak; ww. (-ed)
beklee, bedek; verf.
coax ['kouks] ww. (-ed) flikflooi,
pamperlang.
'cob ['kob] s. (-s) mieliekop; poon;
mannetjieswaan; mengsel van strooi
en klei.
'cobble ['kobl] s. (-s) klip, kei; -s
steenkool so groot soos eiers.
'cobra ['koubrə] s. (-s) kobra, kapel.
'cobweb ['kobweb] s. (-s) spinnerak.
'coccyx ['koksiks] s. stuitjie.
'cochlea ['koklia] s. ('cochleae) slakke-
huis.
cock ['kok] s. (-s) haan, mannetjie;
weerhaan; haantjie; kraan; ww.
(-ed) oorhaal.
'cockade [ko'kæd] s. (-s) kokarde.
'cocka'too [koka'tōē] s. (-s) kaketoe.
'cockney ['kokni] s. (-s) Londenaar,
Cockney.
'cockroach ['kokroutsj] s. (-es)
kakkerlak.
'cock'sure ['kok'sjoeə] bw. positief
seker; verwaand.
'cocky ['koki] bnw. ('cockier, 'cockiest)
parmantig.
'cocoa ['koukou] s. kakao; -nut s.
klapper.
co'coon [kə'kōēn] s. (-s) papie, kokon.
cod ['kod] s. kabeljou.
'coddle ['kodl] ww. (-d) troetel,
verwen.
code ['koud] s. (-s) kode.
'codicil ['kodisil] s. (-s) kodisil,
toevoegsel.
co'erce [kou'əs] ww. (-d) dwing,
forseer; co'ercion s. dwang.
'coffee ['kofi] s. koffie; -ground s.
koffiemoer; -strainer s. sif.
'coffer ['kofə] s. (-s) koffer; geldkas.
'coffin ['kofin] s. (-s) doodskis.
'cog ['kogh] s. (-s) kam, tand,
kamrat; -wheel s. kamrat.
'cogency ['koudzənsi] s. bewyskrag;
'cogent bnw. oortuigend, kragtig,
dringend.
'cogitate ['kodzjityt] ww. (-d)
oorweeg, bepeins; cogi'tation s. be-
peinsing.
'cognate ['koghnyt] bnw. verwant;
'cognition s. bewussyn, wete.
'cognizance ['koghnizəns] s. waarneming; jurisdiksie.
co'here [kou'hiə] ww. (-d) saamkleef,
saamhang; co'herence s. verband;
co'herent bnw. samehangend.
co'hesion [kou'hizjn] s. samehang,
verband.
coif'fure [kwa'fjoeə] s. kapsel,
coiffure.
coil ['koil] ww. (-ed) opdraai, oprol,
kronkel; s. (-s) draai, rol, bog,

kronkeling; lok; klos; spoel; **-spring** s. kronkelveer.

coin ['koin] s. (-s) muntstuk; ww. (-ed) geldslaan, munt; versin; **-age** s. muntstelsel.

coin'cide [kouin'said] ww. (-d) saamval, ooreenstem; **co'incidence** s. (-s) sameloop; toeval.

'coke ['kouk] s. (-s) kooks.

cold ['kould] bnw. (-er, -est) koud; s. (-s) koue, verkoue; **-cream** s. koelroom.

col'laborate [kə'læbəryt] ww. (-d) saamwerk, meewerk.

'colander ['kʌləndə] s. (-s) vergiettes.

co'leus [kou'liəs] s. josefskleed.

col'lapse [kə'læps] ww. (-d) instort, in dule val; opvou: misluk.

'collar ['kolə] s. (-s) boordjie, kraag, halsriem.

col'lateral [ko'lætərəl] s. onderpand, dekking.

'colleague ['koligh] s. (-s) kollega, ampsgenoot.

col'lect [kə'lekt] ww. (-ed) versamel, vergader; insamel, kollekteer; **-ion** s. versameling, kolleksie.

'college ['kolidʒi] s. (-s) kollege; raad; **'collegiate** bnw. ingelyfde, geïnkorporeerde.

col'lide [kə'laid] ww. (-d) bots.

'collier ['koliə] s. (-s) steenkoolgrawer.

'colliery ['koljəri] s. ('collieries) steenkoolmyn.

col'lision [kə'lizjən] s. botsing.

col'loquial [kə'loukwiəl] bnw. gemeensaam, behorende tot die omgangstaal.

'colloquy ['koləkwi] s. ('colloquies) onderhoud.

col'lusion [kə'loezjən] s. onderhandse samewerking.

'colocynth ['koləsinth] s. kolokwint, 'bitterappel'.

'colon ['koulən] s. (-s) dubbele punt; dikderm.

'colonel ['kənl] s. (-s) kolonel.

'colony ['kolənl] s. ('colonies) kolonie, nedersetting; **'colonist** s. kolonis, nedersetter; **'colonize** ww. (-d) koloniseer, bevolk; **co'lonial** bnw. koloniaal; s. kolonis.

co'lossal [kə'losl] bnw. kolossaal, reusagtig.

co'lossus [kə'losəs] s. (co'lossi) kolos, reus.

'colour ['kʌlə] s. (-s) kleur, tint; skyn; voorwendsel; ww. (-ed) kleur, verf; oordryf; bloos.

'column ['koləm] s. (-s) kolom; pilaar.

'coma ['koumə] s. (-s) bedwelming, swym, bewusteloosheid, koma.

'comatose ['komətous] bnw. bedwelmd; bewusteloos.

comb ['koum] s. (-s) kam; ww. (-ed) kam; skei.

'combat ['kombət] s. (-s) geveg, stryd, kamp; ww. (-ed) bestry,

beveg; -ant s. stryder; **-ive** bnw. strydlustig.

'combine ['kombain] ww. (-d) verbind, verenig, saamvat; s. oesdors; **combi'nation** s. verbinding, kombinasie; samespanning; hempbroek.

com'bustion [kəm'bʌstjən] s. verbranding, brand.

'come ['kʌm] ww. (came) kom; **-down** s. vernedering.

'comedy ['komidi] s. ('comedies) komedie, blyspel; **co'median** s. komediant.

'comely ['kʌmli] bnw. bevallig, gepas.

'comfort ['kʌmfət] s. (-s) troos; verligting, gerief; welgesteldheid; ww. (-ed) troos, opbeur; **-able** bnw. gerieflik, aangenaam.

'comic ['komik] bnw. komies, komiek, snaaks; s. grappemaker; **-al** bnw. komies, snaaks.

'comity ['komiti] s. beleefheid.

'comma ['komə] s. (-s) komma; inverted **-s** s. aanhalingstekens.

com'mand [kə'mānd] s. (-s) bevel, gebod; aanvoering; beheersing; beskikking; kommando; ww. (-ed) beveel gebied; aanvoer; beskik oor; uitsien op; **-o** s. kommando.

com'memorate [kə'meməryt] ww. (-d) gedenk, herdenk, vier.

com'mence [kə'mens] ww. (-d) begin, aanvang; **-ment** s. aanvang.

com'mend [kə'mend] ww. (-ed) prys, aanbeveel; toevertrou.

com'ment [ko'ment] s. (-s) uitleg, verklaring; opmerking; kommentaar.

com'mensurate [kə'mensjərit] bnw. eweredig, na verhouding.

'commerce ['koməs] s. handel; verkeer; omgang; **com'mercial** bnw. handeldrywend, handels-; verkeers-.

com'mission [kə'misjən] s. (-s) opdrag; volmag; kommissie; **-er** s. kommissielid; opsiener; kommissaris; gemagtigde.

com'mit [kə'mit] ww. (-ted) toevertrou; begaan, pleeg; verbind.

com'mittee [kə'miti] s. (-s) komitee, kommissie.

com'mode [kə'moud] s. (-s) klerekas, laaikas.

com'modity [kə'moditi] s. (com'modities) gerief; handelsartikel.

'common ['komən] bnw. (-er, -est) gewoon, algemeen; publiek; gemeen; gemeenskaplik; laag; **-ly** bw. gewoonlik; **-age** s. dorpsveld, meent.

'commons ['komənz] s. burgery; House of C- Britse Laerhuis.

'commonwealth ['komənwelth] s. gemenebes.

com'motion [kə'mousjən] s. beweging; drukte; opstand.

'communal ['komjoenl] bnw. gemeente-, dorps-.

com'mune [kə'mjőēn] ww. (-d) saam oorlê, oorleg pleeg.

com'municate [kə'mjŏĕnikyt] *ww.*
(-d) meedeel; oorbring; gemeenskap
hou; in verbindig wees, ineenloop;
communi'cation s. meedeling, gesprek; verbinding, verkeermiddels;
kommunikasie.

com'munion [kə'mjŏĕnjən] s. (-s)
gemeenskap; omgang; Nagmaal.

'communism ['komjoenəzəm] s.
kommunisme.

com'munity [kə'mjŏĕniti] s. (com-
'munities) gemeenskap; - of property
gemeenskap van goedere.

com'mute [kə'mjŏĕt] *ww.* (-d)
verander, vervang; -r, s. pendelaar
iemand wat heen en weer reis.

com'pact [kom'pækt] s. ooreenkoms;
bnw. (kəm'pækt) (-er, -est) dig,
beknop.

com'panion [kəm'pænjən] s. (-s)
metgesel.

'company ['kʌmpəni] s. ('companies)
geselskap; deelgenootskap, maatskappy; bemanning.

com'pare [kəm'pɛə] *ww.* (-d)
vergelyk (word); com'parison s.
vergelyking.

com'partment [kəm'pætmənt] s. (-s)
kompartement; afdeling.

'compass ['kʌmpəs] s. (-es) omtrek;
bereik; kompas.

com'passion [kəm'pæsjən] s. medelye, erbarming.

com'patible [kəm'pætibl] *bnw.* vere-
nigbaar.

com'patriot [kəm'pætriət] s. (-s)
landgenoot.

com'pel [kəm'pel] *ww.* (-led) dwing,
verplig; afdwing.

com'pendium [kəm'pendiəm] s. (-s)
samevatting; com'pendious *bnw.*
beknop.

'compensate ['kompensyt] *ww.* (-d)
vergoed; opweeg teen.

com'pete [kəm'pit] *ww.* (-d) wedywer,
meeding; compe'tition s. wedstryd,
mededinging, kompetisie.

'competent ['kompitənt] *bnw.*
bevoeg, bekwaam; 'competence s.
bevoegdheid, bekwaamheid, geskiktheid.

com'pile [kom'pail] *ww.* (-d) versamel, saamstel, insamel.

com'placent [kəm'plysnt] *bnw.*
selfvoldaan, tevrede; com'placence
s. selfgenoegsaamheid, tevredenheid; com'placency s. = complacence.

com'plain [kəm'plyn] *ww.* (-ed) kla;
-t s. klagte, aanklag; kwaal.

comple'mentary [komple'mentəri]
bnw. aanvullend.

com'plete [kəm'plit] *bnw.* (-r, -st)
volledig, voltallig, totaal, volkome;
ww. (-d) voltooi, aanvul.

'complex ['kompleks] *bnw.* ingewik-
keld, samegesteld.

com'plexion [kəm'pleksjən] s. (-s)
gelaatskleur; voorkome, geaardheid.

'complicate ['komplikyt] *ww.* (-d)
ingewikkeld maak, verwikkel; com-

pli'cation s. verwikkeldheid, ver-
wikkeling.

'compliment ['komplimənt] s. (-s)
kompliment, pluimpie; compli'mentary *bnw.* komplimentêr, hoflik, as
huldeblyk.

com'ply [kəm'plai] *ww.* (com'plied)
inwillig, toegee.

com'ponent [kəm'pounənt] s. (-s)
bestanddeel.

com'pose [kəm'pouz] *ww.* (-d)
komponeer; saamstel; compo'sition
s. samestelling; toonsetting; opstel;
settery; com'posure s. kalmte,
gelatenheid.

'compound ['kompaund] *ww.* (-ed)
saamstel; meng; berei; *bnw.* samegesteld; s. (-s) samestelling, mengsel;
kampong.

compre'hend [kompri'hend] *ww.*
(-ed) verstaan; bevat.

com'press [kəm'pres] *ww.* (-ed)
saamdruk; saamvat; s. 'compress
kompres, nat verband.

com'prise [kəm'praiz] *ww.* (-d)
omvat, bevat, insluit.

'compromise ['komprəmaiz] s. (-s)
skikking, ooreenkoms, kompromis.

com'pulsion [kəm'pʌlsjən] s. dwang,
geweld; com'pulsive *bnw.* dwingend,
gedwonge; com'pulsory *bnw.* gedwonge, verpligtend.

com'punction [kəm'pʌnksjən] s.
spyt, berou, wroeging.

com'pute [kəm'pjŏĕt] *ww.* (-d)
bereken, skat; -r s. berekenaar.

'comrade ['komrid] s. (-s) maat,
kameraad.

con ['kon] *voors.* met; -s - pro's and -
voor- en nadele; *ww.* (-ned) aandagtig lees, bestudeer.

'con'cave [kon'kyv] *bnw.* holrond.

con'ceal [kən'sil] *ww.* (-ed) verberg,
wegsteek; verswyg; -ment s.

con'cede [kən'sid] *ww.* (-d) inwillig;
oorgee.

con'ceit [kən'sit] s. verwaandheid.

con'ceive [kən'siv] *ww.* (-d) opvat;
ontvang; uitdink.

'concentrate ['konsentryt] *ww.* (-d)
konsentreer, saamtrek.

con'centric [kon'sentrik] *bnw.* kon-
sentries.

'concept ['konsept] s. (-s) begrip;
konsep.

con'cern [kən'sĕn] *ww.* (-ed) betref,
aangaan, traak; bemoei; aantrek,
bekommer; s. (-s) saak; aangeleentheid; verband; aandeel.

'concert ['konsət] s. konsert;
ooreenstemming, samewerking; *ww.*
(kən'sət) (-ed) ooreenkom, oorlê.

con'cession [kon'sesjən] s. (-s)
bewilliging; vergunning; konsessie;
vgl. concede.

conch ['konk] s. (-es) skulp.

con'ciliate [kən'silliyt] *ww.* (-d)
versoen, paai; oorhaal; concili'ation
s. versoening, konsiliasie; concili-
'atory *bnw.* versoenend.

con'cise [kən'sais] *bnw.* (*-r*, *-st*) beknop, bondig.

'con'clave ['kɔn'klyv] *s.* (*-s*) vergadering.

con'clude [kən'klōēd] *ww.* (*-d*) besluit; eindig; aflei; **con'clusion** *s.* (*-s*) slot, einde; gevolgtrekking; **con'clusive** *bnw.* afdoende.

con'coct [kən'kɔkt] *ww.* (*-ed*) saamflans; brou; beraam; versin; *-tion s.* (*-s*) brousel; versinsel.

con'comitance [kən'kɔmitəns] *s.* samehang; **con'comitant** *bnw.* begeleidend(e).

'con'crete ['kɔn'krit] *bnw.* konkreet, tasbaar; *s.* werklikheid; beton; **con'cretion** *s.* verdikking, stolling; gewas.

con'cur [kən'kə̄] *ww.* (*-red*) instem, saamstem; saamval; meewerk; **con'currence** *s.* instemming, meewerking; *-rent bnw.* saamvallend; instemmend.

con'cussion [kən'kʌsjən] *s.* (*-s*) skudding; skok; botsing.

con'demn [kən'dem] *ww.* (*-ed*) veroordeel, afkeur; **condem'nation** *s.* veroordeling; vonnis; afkeuring.

con'dense [kən'dens] *ww.* (*-d*) kondenseer, verdig, saampers; **conden'sation** *s.* kondensasie, verdigting; *-r s.* kondensator.

conde'scend [kɔndi'send] *ww.* (*-ed*) neerbuig, jou verneder; *-ing bnw.* neerbuigend.

'condiment ['kɔndimənt] *s.* (*-s*) kruiesous.

con'dition [kən'disjən] *s.* (*-s*) toestand; voorwaarde; kondisie; rang; *ww.* (*-ed*) bepaal, oorkom; aanklam; *-al bnw.* voorwaardelik, kondisioneel.

con'dole [kən'doul] *ww.* (*-d*) simpatie betuig.

con'done [kən'doun] *ww.* (*-d*) deur die vingers sien; kondoneer.

con'duce [kən'djōēs] *ww.* (*-d*) bydra, bevorder.

con'ducive [kən'djoesiv] *bnw.* bevorderlik.

'conduct ['kɔnkəkt] *s.* gedrag; bestuur; *ww.* (kən'dʌkt) (*-ed*) gedra, lei, bestuur; **con'ductor** *s.* (*-s*) geleier; kondukteur; dirigent.

'conduit ['kɔndjoeit] *s.* (*-s*) buis, pyp, geleiding.

'cone ['koun] *s.* (*-s*) kegel; dennebol.

con'fabulate [kɔn'fæbjoelyt] *ww.* (*-d*) gesels.

con'fection [kən'feksjən] *s.* vervaardiging; lekkergoed.

con'fectionery [kən'feksjnəri] *s.* lekkergoed.

con'federate [kən'fedərit] *s.* (*-s*) bondgenoot; **confede'ration** *s.* bondgenootskap.

con'fer [kən'fə̄] *ww.* (*-red*) toeken; bydra; bewys; oorlê; *-ence* i'kɔnfərəns] *s.* byeenkoms, bespreking, konferensie.

con'fess [kən'fes] *ww.* (*-ed*) erken,

bely, bieg; *-ion s.* belydenis, erkenning, bieg.

con'fide [kən'faid] *ww.* (*-d*) vertrou, toevertrou; meedeel, opbieg; **'confidence** ['kɔnfidəns] *s.* vertroue, selfvertroue; astrantheid; vertroulike mededeling; **'confidant** *s.* vertrouelîng; **'confident** *bnw.* hoopvol; vrymoedig; astrant; **confi'dential** *bnw.* vertroulik, geheim.

'confine ['kɔnfain] *s.* grens; *ww.* (*-d*) [kən'fain] beperk, begrens; opsluit; **con'finement** *s.* beperking; opsluiting; bevalling.

con'firm [kən'fə̄m] *ww.* (*-ed*) bevestig, goedkeur; aanneem.

'confiscate ['kɔnfiskyt] *ww.* (*-d*) beslag lê op, konfiskeer.

confla'gration [kɔnflə'ghrysjən] *s.* (*-s*) verwoestende brand.

'conflict ['kɔnflikt] *s.* (*-s*) stryd, botsing, konflik; *ww.* (*-ed*) [kən'flikt] stry, bots, in stryd met.

'confluence ['kɔn'floeəns] *s.* samevloeiing.

con'form [kən'fɔ̄m] *ww.* (*-ed*) aanpas by, skik na.

con'found [kən'faund] *ww.* (*-ed*) in die war stuur, dronkslaan; *-ed bnw.* in die war, dronkgeslaan; vervlakste; *-edly bw.* vreeslik, ontsettend.

con'front [kən'frʌnt] *ww.* (*-ed*) teenoorstel, konfronteer.

con'fuse [kən'fjōēz] *ww.* (*-d*) verwar, deurmekaar maak; **con'fusion** *s.* verwarring, wanorde; verleentheid; *-d bnw.* verwar, wanordelik; verleë.

con'fute [kən'fjōēt] *ww.* (*-d*) weerlê, verydel.

con'geal [kən'dzjil] *ww.* (*-ed*) bevries, stol.

con'genial [kən'dzjiniəl] *bnw.* geesverwant; geskik.

con'genital [kən'dzjenitl] *bnw.* aangebore.

con'gest [kən'dzjest] *ww.* (*-ed*) ophoop; strem; oorlaai; *-ion s.* samehoping, kongestie.

con'glomerate ['kɔn'ghloməryt] *s.* sameklonting, konglomeraat.

con'gratulate [kən'ghrætjoelyt] *ww.* (*-d*) gelukwens.

'congregate ['kɔng-ghrighyt] *ww.* (*-d*) versamel, vergader; **congre'gation** *s.* vergadering; gemeente.

'congress ['kɔng-ghres] *s.* (*-es*) kongres, byeenkoms.

'congruence ['kɔng-ghroeəns] *s.* ooreenstemming.

'congruous ['kɔng'ghroeəs] *a.* ooreenstemmend.

con'jecture [kən'dzjektsjə] *s.* (*-s*) gissing.

con'jointly [kɔn'dzjointli] *bw.* gemeenskaplik.

'conjugal ['kɔndzjoeghəl] *bnw.* egtelik.

'conjugate ['kɔndzjoehyt] *ww.* (*-d*) vervoeg.

con'junction [kən'dzjʌnksjən] *s.* (*-s*) verbinding, aansluiting; sameloop;

voegwoord; con'juncture s. tyds-
gewrig, sameloop van omstandig-
hede.

'connate ['konyt] bnw. aangebore,
verwant.

con'nect [kə'nekt] ww. (-ed) verbind;
in verbinding tree, aansluit; -ed
bnw. verbonde; -ion s. (-s) verbinding; aansluiting; gemeenskap;
konneksie.

connois'seur [koni'sӧ] s. (-s)
kenner, fynproewer.

connote [ko'nout] ww (-d) betekenis
hê, beteken.

con'nubial [kə'njoebiəl] bnw. egtelik.

'conquer ['kong'kə] ww. (-ed)
verower, oorwin, verslaan, onderwerp; -or s. oorwinnaar, vero-
weraar.

'conquest ['kong-kwest] s. oorwinning, verowering.

'conscience ['konsjəns] s. gewete,
konsensie; consci'entious [konsji-
'ensjəs] bnw. pliggetrou.

'conscious ['konsjəs] bnw. bewus.

con'scription [kən'skripsjən] s.
verpligte krygsdiens, konskripsie.

'consecrate ['konsikryt] ww. (-d)
heilig, wy, toewy.

con'secutive [kən'sekjoetiv] bnw.
opeenvolgend.

con'sensus [kən'sensəs] s. algemene
opinie.

con'sent [kən'sent] ww. (-ed)
toestem, inwillig; s. toestemming.

'consequence ['konsikwəns] s. (-s)
gevolg, uitwerking; belang, betekenis; 'consequent bnw. gevolglik,
logies; conse'quential bnw. wat
daaruit volg, gevolglik; conse'quent-
ly bw. bygevolg, gevolglik.

con'serve [kən'sӧv] ww. (-d)
bewaar, instandhou; inlê; con-
'servative bnw. konserwatief, behoudend; (verkramp(te)'; conser-
'vation s. bewaring, instandhouding.

con'sider [kən'sidə] ww. (-ed) beskou,
oorweeg, konsidereer; -able bnw.
aansienlik; conside'ration s. be-
skouing; oorweging; -ing voors.
aangesien.

con'sign [kən'sain] ww. (-ed)
toevertrou; oorlewer; afstuur; con-
sig'nee s. ontvanger; -ment s.
oordrag; afsending; besending; con-
'signor s. afsender.

con'sist [kən'sist] ww. (-ed) bestaan
(uit, in).

con'sistence [kən'sistəns] s. (con-
'sistencies) dikte, vastheid, kon-
sistensie; ooreenstemming, konse-
kwensie; con'sistent bnw. konse-
kwent; con'sistency s. = con-
sistence.

con'sole [kən'soul] ww. (-d) troos,
opbeur; conso'lation s. troos, vertroosting.

con'solidate [kən'solidyt] ww. (-d)
set; bevestig; konsolideer; verenig.

'consonant ['konsənənt] s. (-s)
medeklinker.

'consort ['konsӧt] s. (-s) gemaal;
metgesel.

con'spicuous [kon'spikjoeəs] bnw.
opvallend.

con'spire [kən'spaiə] ww. (-d)
saamsweer, saamspan; con'spiracy
s. sameswering, komplot.

'constable ['kʌnstəbl] s. (-s) konstabel, diender.

'constant ['konstənt] bnw. standvastig; bestendig; trou; voortdurend; s. onveranderlike waarde;
'constancy s. standvastigheid, trou;
-ly bw. gedurig, dikwels.

constel'lation [konstə'lysjən] s. (-s)
sterrebeeld, konstellasie.

conster'nation [konstə'nysjən] s.
ontsteltenis, konsternasie.

'constipate ['konstipyt] ww. (-d)
verstop, hardlywig maak; consti-
'pation s. verstopping, hardlywig-
heid.

'constitute ['konstitjӧet] ww. (-d)
saamstel, vorm; stig; konstitueer;
con'stituent s. bestanddeel; kieser;
con'stituency s. kiesafdeling, kiesers;
consti'tution s. samestelling; staatsvorm; grondwet; konstitusie.

con'strain [kən'stryn] ww. (-ed)
bedwing; verplig; noodsaak; opsluit; -t s. dwang; selfbedwang;
opsluiting.

con'strict [ken'strikt] ww. (-ed)
toedruk; beperk; -ion s.; -ive
bandage s. knelverband.

con'struct [kən'strʌkt] ww. (-ed)
saamstel; bou; oprig; konstrueer;
-ion s.

con'strue [kən'strӧё] ww. (-d) uitlê,
verklaar; ontleed; konstrueer.

'consul ['konsəl] s. (-s) konsul; -ar
bnw. konsulêr; -ate s. konsulaatskap.

con'sult [kən'sʌlt] ww. (-ed) raad-
pleeg, beraadslaag; konsulteer; consul'tation s. beraadslaging, konsult;
con'sultative bnw. raadplegend.

con'sume [kən'sjӧёm] ww. (-d)
verteer; verbruik; verkwis; uitteer;
-r s. verbruiker; con'sumption s.
verbruik; tering.

con'summate [kən'sʌmit] bnw.
volslae, volkome; deurtrap.

'contact ['kontækt] s. (-s) aanraking,
kontak; -lens s. kontaklens; ww.
(kən'tækt) (-ed) aanraak, in voeling
kom.

con'tagion [kən'tydzjən] s. besmetting.

con'tagious [kən'tydzjəs] bnw. aansteeklik, besmetlik.

con'tain [kon'tyn] ww. (-ed) inhou,
bevat; bedwing.

con'taminate [kən'tæminyt] ww.
(-d) besoedel, besmet.

con'temn [kən'tem] ww. (-ed) verag,
minag.

'contemplate ['kontemplyt] ww.
(-d) beskou; oorweeg; verwag.

con'temporary [kən'tempərəri] bnw.
gelyktydig; s. (con'temporaries) tyd-
genoot.

con'tempt [kən'tempt] s. veragting, minagting; **-ible** bnw. veragtelik.

con'tend [kən'tend] ww. (-ed) stryd; wedywer; beweer.

'**content** ['kontent] s. tevredenheid, voldaanheid; (-s) s. inhoud, omvang; bnw. (kən'tent) tevrede, voldaan, vergenoeg; **con'tented** bnw. tevrede, voldaan.

con'tention [kən'tensjən] s. twis; bestryding; kontensie.

'**contest** ['kontest] s. (-s) geskil, stryd, kamp; ww. (kən'test) (-ed) bestry, beveg.

'**context** ['kontekst] s. verband, samehang.

conti'guity [konti'ghjoeiti] s. aangrensing; samehang.

con'tiguous [kən'tighjoeəs] bnw. aangrensend, belendend, volgend.

continence ['kontinəns] s. matigheid; kuisheid; onthouding.

continent ['kontinənt] s. (-s) vasteland; **conti'nental** bnw. vastelands.

con'tingency [kən'tindzjənsi] s. toevalligheid.

con'tingent [kən'tindzjənt] bw. gebeurlik; s. afdeling

con'tinue [kən'tinjoe] ww. (-d) aanhou, volhou, volhard, vervolg; bly; **-d** bnw. voortdurend; **con'tinual** bnw. aanhoudend; **con'tinuance** s. voortduring; voortsetting; **con'tinuous** bnw. onafgebroke, aanhoudend.

con'tort [kən'tôt] ww. (-ed) verdraai, verwring.

'**contour** ['kontoeə] s. (-s) omtrek, lyn.

'**contra** ['kontrə] n. oorweging teen; voorvoegsel teen, kontra.

'**contraband** ['kontrəbænd] s. smokkelware.

'**contract** ['kontrækt] s. (-s) ooreenkoms, kontrak; ww. [kən'trækt] (-ed) ooreenkom; saamtrek; sluit; vorm; opdoen; **-or** s. kontraktant, leweransier.

contra'dict [kontrə'dikt] ww. (-ed) weerspreek, teenspreek.

con'traption [kən'træpsjən] s. toestel.

'**contrary** [wkontrəri] bnw. teenoorgesteld; koppig, eiewys.

'**contrast** ['konträst] s. teenstelling, kontras; ww. [kən'träst] (-ed) teenoorstel, vergelyk; verskil, afsteek.

contra'vene [kontrə'vin] ww. (-d) oortree.

con'tribute [kən'tribjoet] ww. (-d) bydra, meewerk.

con'trite [kən'trait] bnw. berouvol, boetvaardig.

con'trive [kən'traiv] ww. (-d) bedink, uitvind; oorlê; **con'trivance** s. uitvindsel; versinsel; lis, plan.

con'trol [kən'troul] s. beheer(sing), bedwang, kontrole; ww. (-led) beheers, bedwing; nagaan; kontroleer.

'**controversy** ['kontrəvəsi] s. ('con-

troversies) strydvraag, twispunt.

'**contumely** ['kontjoemli] s. smaad, hoon; skande.

con'tusion [kən'tjoezjən] s. (-s) kneusing.

co'nundrum [kə'nʌndrəm] s. (-s) raaisel, strikvraag.

conva'lescence [konvə'lesns] s. herstel, beterskap.

con'vene [kən'vin] ww. (-d) byeenroep, belê.

con'venience [kən'vinjəns] s. gerief, gemak, voordeel; **con'venient** bnw. gerieflik.

con'vention [kən'vensjən] s. (-s) byeenkoms; ooreenkoms; konvensie.

con'verge [kən'vədzj] ww. (-d) in een punt saamloop; **-nce** s. sameloping (in een punt); **con'vergent** bnw. samelopend.

con'versant [kon'vəsint] bnw. bekend met, op hoogte van.

conver'sation [konvə'sysjən] s. (-s) gesprek; omgang.

con'verse [kən'vəs] ww. (-d) gesels.

con'version [kən'vəsjn] s. (-s) omsetting (by convert).

con'vert [kən'vət] ww. (-ed) omwissel, bekeer, omset, ombou.

'**con'vex** [kon'veks] bnw. bolrond, konveks.

con'vey [kən'vy] ww. (-ed) vervoer, oortuig; meedeel; beteken; **-ance** s. vervoermiddel; **-ancer** s. transportbesorger.

con'vict [kən'vikt] ww. (-ed) skuldig vind; vonnis; oortuig; s. ['konvikt] (-s) bandiet; **-ion** s. skuldig verklaring; vonnis; oortuiging.

con'vince [kən'vins] ww. (-d) oortuig.

con'vivial [kən'viviəl] bnw. feestelik, vrolik, gesellig.

convo'cation [konvô'kysjən] s. byeenkoms, vergadering; konvokasie.

con'voke [kən'vouk] ww. (-d) byeenroep, belê.

'**convoy** ['konvoi] s. konvooi; geleide.

con'vulse [kən'vʌls] ww. (-d) skud; stuiptrekkings veroorsaak.

cook ['koek] s. (-s) kok; ww. (-ed) kook; vervals, bedissel; **-ery** s. kook kuns.

cool ['kôël] bnw. (-er, -est) koel, fris; kalm; astrant; flou.

'**coop** ['kôëp] s. fuik, hoenderhok; ww. opsluit; **-er** s. kuiper.

co-'operate [kou'operyt] ww. (-d) saamwerk; ko-opereer.

co-'opt [kou'opt] ww. (-ed) koopteer, byhaal.

co-'ordinate [kou'ôdinyt] ww. (-d) gelykskakel; neweskik; ko-ordineer.

cop ['kop] s. (-s) konstabel; ww. (-ped) vang.

'**cope** ['koup] ww. (-d) wedywer, meeding; die hoof bied aan.

'**coping** ['kouping] s. deklaag.

'**copious** ['koupjəs] bnw. oorvloedig, ryk.

'**copper** ['kopə] s. koper; konstabel; *ww.* (-ed) met koper beslaan.

'**coppice** ['kopis] s. (-s) kreupelbos.

'**copy** ['kopi] s. ('copies) kopie; afskrif; namaaksel; reproduksie; eksemplaar; manuskrip; *ww.* ('copied) kopieer; afskrywe; namaak; -**right** s. kopiereg.

co'**quette** [kou'ket] s. behaagsieke vrou.

cord ['kôd] s. tou, lyn, koord; **spinal**- s. ruggraat.

'**cordial** ['kôdiəl] *bnw.* hartlik; s. hartversterking.

'**cordon** ['kôdən] s. (-s) kordon; ring, ketting.

'**corduroy** ['kôdəroi] s. ferweel.

'**core** ['kô] s. (-s) kern, pit, hart, aar; **core**- kern-.

cork ['kôk] s. kurk, prop; dobber; *ww.* (-ed) toekurk; -**screw** s. kurktrekker.

corn ['kôn] s. korrel; graan; mielies; koring; liddoring; *ww.* (-ed) insout.

'**cornea** ['kôniə] s. (-s) horingvlies.

'**corner** ['kônə] s. (-s) hoek; opkoop, spekulasie; *ww.* (-ed) vaskeer, vaslê.

co'**rollary** [kə'roləri] s. (co'rollaries) afleiding, gevolgtrekking.

co'**rona** [kə'rounə] s. (-s) ligkroon; kring; kroonlys; kroon; **coro'nation** s. kroning.

'**coroner** ['korənə] s. (-s) lykskouer.

'**coronet** ['korənit] s. kroontjie.

'**corporal** ['kôpərəl] *bnw.* liggaamlik, stoflik, lyf-, liggaam-; s. korporaal.

'**corporate** ['kôpərit] *bnw.* verbonde, verenig, geïnkorporeerde; **corpo'ration** s. korporasie, vereniging; bestuur; buik.

cor'**poreal** [kô'poriəl] *bnw.* liggaamlik, stoflik, tasbaar.

corps ['kô] s. (-) korps, afdeling; -**e** s. ('kôps) (-s) lyk.

'**corpulent** ['kôpjoelənt] *bnw.* swaarlywig.

cor'**rect** [kə'rekt] *ww.* (-ed) verbeter, nasien, korrigeer; berispe; *bnw.* juis, presies, netjies; -**ion** s. verbetering, korreksie, berisping.

'**correlate** ['korilyt] *ww.* (-d) in korrelasie bring (staan), korreleer.

corre'**spond** [kori'spond] *ww.* (-ed) ooreenkom, klop; briefwisseling voer; korrespondeer; -**ence** s. ooreenkoms; briefwisseling; korrespondensie; -**ent** s. korrespondent.

'**corridor** ['koridô] s. (-s) gang.

'**corrigible** ['koridzjəbl] *bnw.* verbeterbaar.

cor'**roborate** [kə'robəryt] *ww.* (-d) bevestig, versterk; cor'**roborative** *bnw.* bevestigend.

cor'**rode** [kə'roud] *ww.* (-d) verroes, wegvreet; cor'**rosion** s. wegvreting, verroesting; cor'**rosive** *bnw.* wegvretend, s. bytmiddel.

'**corrugate** ['koroeghyt] *ww.* (-d) rimpel, golf; corru'**gation** s. rimpeling, golwing.

cor'**rupt** [kə'rʌpt] *ww.* (-ed) verderf; verknoei; omkoop; *bnw.* bedorwe; omgekoop.

'**corset** ['kôsit] s. (-s) korset, borstrok.

cor'**tège** [kô'tydzj] s. lykstoet, gevolg.

'**cortex** ['kôteks] s. bas, kors.

'**cortisone** ['kôtizoun] s. kortisoon.

'**cosine** ['kousain] s. kosinus.

cos'**metic** [koz'metik] s. kosmetiek.

cosmo'**politan** [kosmô'politən] *bnw.* kosmopolities.

'**cosmos** ['kozmos] s. wêreldstelsel, heelal.

cost ['kost] s. prys, koste; *ww.* (-ed) kos; prys vaastel; -**ly** *bnw.* duur.

'**costume** ['kostjoem] s. (-s) kleding, drag, kostuum.

'**cosy** ['kouzi] *bnw.* behaaglik; s. ('cosies) teemus.

cot ['kot] s. (-s) katel; kinderbed.

co'**tangent** [kou'tændzjənt] s. kotangens.

'**coterie** ['koutəri] s. (-s) kliek.

co'**till(i)on** [kə'tiljən] s. (-s) kotiljons.

'**cottage** ['kotidzj] s. (-s) huisie, hutjie.

'**cotter pin** ['kotə-pin] s. splitpen.

'**cotton** ['kotn] s. katoen; garing; -**wool** s. watte; -**waste** s. poetskatoen.

coty'**ledon** [koti'lidən] s. (-s) saadlob.

couch ['kautsj] s. (-es) rusbank, sofa.

cough ['kof] s. hoes; *ww.* (-ed) hoes.

'**council** ['kaunsl] s. (-s) raad; raadsvergadering; -**lor** s. raadslid.

'**counsel** ['kaunsəl] s. (-s) raad, raadgewing; plan; raadgewer, advokaat; *ww.* (-led) raai, raadgee, adviseer.

count ['kaunt] s. (-s) graaf; tel; telling; rekening; aanklag; *ww.* (-ed) tel, optel; reken, ag, werd wees.

'**countenance** ['kauntinəns] s. gesig, uitdrukking, voorkoms; *ww.* (-d) toelaat, steun.

'**counter** ['kauntə] s. (-s) blokkie; toonbank; teller; boeg; *bnw.* teen-; *bw.* in die teenoorgestelde rigting; *ww.* (-ed) teenwerk, verydel; -**balance** s. teengewig; -**feit** s. namaaksel; -**foil** s. teenblad; -**mand** *ww.* (-ed) herroep, kanselleer; -**pane** s. deken, bedsprei; -**part** s. teenstuk; ewebeeld; -**point** s. kontrapunt.

counterclockwise = **anti-clockwise** linksom, hotom.

'**countershaft** ['kauntəsjäft] s. (-s) tussenas.

'**countersink** ['kauntəsink] *ww.* ('countersank) versink.

'**country** ['kʌntri] s. ('countries) land, landstreek, kontrei; vaderland; platteland.

'**county** ['kaunti] s. ('counties) graafskap, distrik.

coupé ['kôepy] s. koepee.

'**couple** ['kʌpl] s. (-s) paar, span; *ww.* (-d) verbind, koppel; paar.

'**coupon** ['kôepon] s. (-s) koepon, kaartjie.

'**courage** ['kʌridʒ] s. moed, koerasie; cou'**rageous** [kə'rydʒjəs] bnw. moedig, dapper.

'**courier** ['koeriə] s. (-s) koerier, boodskapper.

'**course** ['kôs] s. (-s) loop, gang, vaart; kors; baan; kursus; gereg.

court ['kôt] s. (-s) hof, kantoor; hofhouding; baan; binneplaas; ww. (-ed) vry; uitlok; -**eous** ['kêtiəs] bnw. hoflik; -**esy** ['kêtisi] s. hoflikheid.

'**cousin** ['kʌzn] s. (-s) neef, niggie.

'**cove** ['kouv] s. (-s) inham; gewelf; vent.

'**covenant** ['kʌvinənt] s. (-s) verbond, verdrag.

'**cover** ['kʌvə] ww. (-ed) dek; beskerm; onder die korrel hou; s. (-s) dekking, deksel; band, oortreksel, omslag; skyn; dekkings-fonds; -**ing** s. (-s) hulsel, deksel, bedekking; -**crop** s. (-s) dekgewas; -**age** s. strekvermoë.

'**covert** ['kʌvət] bnw. bedek, geheim, skelm.

'**covet** ['kʌvit] ww. (-ed) begeer; -**ous** bnw. gierig.

'**covey** ['kʌvi] s. (-s) vlug, broeisel, swerm.

cow ['kau] s. (-s) koei; ww. (-ed) oorbluf.

'**coward** ['kauəd] s. (-s) lafaard; -**ice** s. lafhartigheid; -**ly** bnw. lafhartig.

cowl ['kaul] s. (-s) kap, tussenkap.

'**coxcomb** ['kokskoum] s. getande strook rooi doek aan harlekynkap; pronker.

'**coxswain** ['kokswyn, 'koksn] s. stuurman van boot, bootsman.

coy ['koi] bnw. (-er, -est) sedig, bedees.

crab ['kræb] s. (-s) krap, kreef; -**bed** bnw. nors, dwars, stuurs.

'**crab apple** ['kræb 'æpl] s. houtappel.

crack ['kræk] s. (-s) klap; kraak; knak; uithaler-; inbreker; ww. (-ed) kraak, knetter.

'**crackle** ['krækl] ww. (-d) kraak, knetter.

'**cradle** ['krydl] s. (-s) wieg; bakermat.

craft ['krâft] s. (-s) ambag, handwerk; handigheid; vaartuig; -**ty** bnw. slim, slu, listig.

cram ['kræm] ww. (-med) volstop, inpomp, inwors, blok.

cramp ['kræmp] s. (-s) kramp; klamp; -**ed** bnw. nou, gedronge, beklem.

'**crane** ['kryn] s. (-s) kraanvoël; hewel.

'**cranium** ['kryniəm] s. skedel.

crank ['krænk] s. (-s) krukas; kruk; slinger, arm, handvatsel; gril; eksentrieke persoon; ww. (-ed) draai, slinger; -**case** s. kruk'kas; -**shaft** s. krukas; -**shaft bearing** s. krukaslaer.

'**cranky** ['krænki] bnw. (-kier, -kiest) sieklik, eksentriek.

'**crape** ['kryp] s. krip, lanfer.

crash ['kræsj] ww. (-ed) geraas maak;

krakend val; ineenstort; bots; bankrot speel; s. (-es) lawaai; botsing; val; bankrotskap; graslinne.

crass ['kræs] bnw. (-er, -est) kras.

'**crate** ['kryt] s. (-s) krat, mandjie, kis.

'**crater** ['krytə] s. (-s) krater.

crave ['kryv] ww. (-d) bid, smeek, verlang; '**craving** s. verlange, behoefte, begeerte.

'**craven** ['kryvn] bnw. lafhartig.

crawl ['krôl] ww. (-ed) kruip, aansukkel; krioel; s. gekruip, gekriewel.

'**crayon** ['kryən] s. (-s) tekenkryt, pastel.

'**craze** ['kryz] s. (-s) gier, manie; mode; kranksinnigheid.

'**crazy** ['kryzi] bnw. ('crazier, 'craziest) gek, waansinnig; wrak.

creak ['krik] ww. (-ed) kraak, piep, skreeu; s. (-s) gepiep, geskreeu, gekraak.

cream ['krim] s. (-s) room; blom; bnw. roomkleurig; -**ery** s. suiwelfabriek, botterfabriek.

'**crease** ['kris] s. (-s) vou, plooi, rimpel; streep; ww. (-d) vou, plooi, rimpel, kreukel.

cre'**ate** [kri'yt] ww. (-d) skep, in die lewe roep; voortbring; benoem; maak; cre'**ator** s. skepper.

'**creature** ['kritsjə] s. skepsel, mens, kreatuur.

'**credence** ['kridəns] s. geloof, vertroue; cre'**dentials** s. geloofsbriewe, getuigskrif(te); credi'**bility** s. geloofbaarheid; '**credible** bnw. geloofbaar.

'**credit** ['kredit] s. (-s) vertroue, geloof; reputasie; agting; gesag; krediet; -**able** bnw. verdienstelik; gebaar; -**or** s. (-s) skuldeiser.

creed ['krid] s. (-s) geloof.

creek ['krik] s. (-s) inham, bog; spruitjie.

creep ['krip] ww. (crept) kruip, sluip, kriewel; s. (-s) kriewelling; -**er** s. klimplant; -**y** bnw. grillerig.

cre'**mate** [kri'myt] ww. (-d) verbrand, veras; crema'**torium** s. krematorium.

cre'**ole** ['krioul] bnw. kreools; s. (-s) kreool.

'**crêpe** ['krep] s. crêpe, krip, gekrinkelde stof; -**bandage** s. rekverband.

'**crescent** ['kresnt] bnw. groeiend; s. groeiende maan, halfmaan.

cress ['kres] s. (-es) bronkors.

crest ['krest] s. kuif, kam, pluim; kruin; wapen.

'**crevice** ['krevis] s. (-s) skeur, spleet.

crew ['krôē] s. (-s) bemanning.

'**crewel** ['krôēll] s. borduurgaring.

crib ['krib] s. (-s) krip, stal; kinderbed; afkykwerk.

'**cricket** ['krikit] s. (-s) kriek; krieket.

'**crime** ['kraim] s. (-s) misdaad,

wandaad; 'criminal s. (-s) misdadiger.

'crimson ['krimzn] s. karmosyn.

'cringe ['krindzj] ww. (-d) kruip, ineenkrimp; lek.

'crinkle ['krinkl] ww. (-d) krinkel, kreukel.

'cripple ['kripl] bnw. kreupel, mank.

'crisis ['kraisis] s. (crises) keerpunt, krisis.

crisp ['krisp] bnw. (-er, -est) kroes; bros; beslis.

'criss-cross ['kriskros] bw. kruis-endwars.

cri'terion [krai'tiəriən] s. maatstaf, toets, kriterium.

'critic ['kritik] s. kritikus; vitter; -al bnw. haglik, kritiek, krities; -ize ww. (-d) kritiseer.

croak ['krouk] ww. (-ed) kwaak; vrek.

'crochet ['krousjy] ww. (-ed) hekel.

crock ['krok] ww. (-ed) breek, seermaak; s. (-s) tjorrie, uitgediende motor.

'crockery ['krokəri] s. breekgoed.

'crocus ['kroukəs] s. (-es) krokus.

'croft ['kroft] s. stukkie grond; -er s. pagter, klein-boer.

'crony ['krouni] s. ('cronies) boesemvriend.

crook ['kroek] s. (-s) haak, staf; opligter; misdadiger skelm.

croon ['krōĕn] ww. (-ed) neurie.

crop ['krop] s. (-s) krop; steel; rysweep; gewas; oes; knipsel; drag; ww. (-ped) afsny, knip; afeet, pluk; - insurance s. oesversekering.

cross ['kros] s. (-es) kruis; kruising; verneukery; ww. (-ed) kruis, deurkruis; merk; oorsteek; bnw. dwars, oorkruis.

'crossing ['krōsing] s. (-s) kruising; oorweg; level -, railway - s. spooroorgang (gelykgronds).

'cross-purpose ['kros-'pɵpəs] s. misversland.

'crotch ['krotsj] s. (-es) mik, vurk.

'crotchet ['krotsjit] s. kwartnoot; hakie; gier.

crouch ['krautsj] ww. (-ed) hurk, buk, kruip.

crow ['krou] s. (-s) kraai; koevoet; ww. (-ed) kraai, babbel; -bar s. koevoet.

crowd ['kraud] s. (-s) menigte; gedrang.

crown ['kraun] s. (-s) kroon; krans; kruin; - wheel s. kroonrat.

'crucial ['krōĕsjiəl] bnw. kritiek, beslissend.

'crucible ['krōĕsibl] s. (-s) smeltkroes; vuurproef.

'crucifix ['krōĕsifiks] s. (-es) kruis.

cruci'fixion [krōĕsi'fiksjən] s. kruisiging.

'crude ['krōĕd] bnw. onbehoipe; ru, rou; onryp, onsuiwer; onverwerk(te).

'cruel ['kroeil] bnw. (-lest) wreed, wreedaardig.

'cruise ['krōĕz] ww. (-d) kruis, vaar.

crumb ['krʌm] s. (-s) krummel; -le ww. (-d) krummel, brokkel.

'crumple ['krʌmpl] ww. (-d) kreukel, verfrommel.

crunch ['krʌntsj] ww. (-ed) hard kou.

'crusade ['krōĕsyd] s. (-s) kruistog; -r s. kruisvaarder.

crush ['krʌsj] ww. (-ed) plat druk; onderdruk; verpletter.

crust ['krʌst] s. (-s) kors, roof, aanpaksel.

crutch ['krʌtsj] s. (-es) kruk, steun.

cry ['krai] ww. (cried) roep, skreeu, huil, ween; s. (cries) skreeu, kreet, gil; bede; klag; geween.

crypt ['kript] s. (-s) kelder.

'crystal ['kristl] s. (-s) kristal; -lize ww. (-d) kristalliseer.

'cube ['kjōĕb] s. (-s) kubus.

'cubic ['kjōĕbik] bnw. kubiek.

'cubicle ['kjōĕbikl] s. (-s) hok, sel, kraampie, afskorting.

'cuckoo ['koekōĕ] s. (-s) koekoek.

'cucumber ['kjōĕkəmbə] s. (-s) komkommer.

'cud ['kʌd] s. (-s) herkoutjie.

'cuddle ['kʌdl] ww. (-d) liefkoos, omhels.

'cudgel ['kʌdzjəl] s. (-s) kierie, knuppel.

'cue ['kjōĕ] s. (-s) wenk; wagwoord; biljartstok.

'cuff ['kʌf] s. & ww. (-s) omslag, mansjet; klap.

cul'sine [kwi'zin] s. keuken; ete.

'culinary ['kʌlinəri] bnw. kombuis-, kook-, keuken-.

'culminate ['kʌlminyt] ww. (-d) die hoogtepunt bereik.

'culpable ['kʌlpəbl] bnw. skuldig, strafbaar.

'culprit ['kʌlprit] s. (-s) skuldige, boosdoender.

'cultivate ['kʌltivyt] ww. (-d) bewerk; kweek, verbou; ontwikkel; beskaaf; beoefen; ghrop; 'cultivator s. (-s) ghrop.

'culture ['kʌltsjə] s. (-s) verbouing; kultuur.

'culvert ['kʌlvət] s. (-s) riool, duiksloot.

'cumbersome ['kʌmbəsəm] bnw. lastig, lomp.

'cumulate ['kjōĕmjoelit] ww. (-d) ophoop, toeneem; 'cumulative bnw. ophopend, kumulatief; cumu'lation s. ophoping, toename.

'cunning ['kʌning] bnw. slim, geslepe, slu; bedrewe.

cup ['kʌp] s. (-s) koppie, beker, kelkie; - of gold s. gouekelk (blom).

'cupboard ['kʌbəd] s. (-s) kas, muurkas, koskas.

cu'pidity [kjoe'piditi] s. inhaligheid, hebsug.

cur ['kɵ] s. (-s) brak; skurk.

'curate ['kjoeərit] s. (-s) (hulp) predikant.

cu'rator [kjoeə'rytə] s. (-s) opsigter; voog: kurator.

curb ['kɔb] *ww.* (-ed) bedwing, beteuel.

curd ['kɔd] *s.* dikmelk,strems el; -le *ww.* (-d) dik word.

'cure ['kjõẽ] *s.* (-s) geneesmiddel; genesing; kuur; *ww.* (-d) genees; inlê, droogmaak, insout; **'curable** *bnw.* geneeslik (-baar), **'curative** *bnw.* genesend.

'curfew ['kɔfjõẽ] *s.* aandklok.

'curio ['kjoeəriou] *s.* (-s) kunsvoorwerp, rariteit; aandenking.

'curious ['kjoeəriəs] *bnw.* nuuskierig; weetgierig, snaaks, seldsaam.

curl ['kɔl] *s.* (-s) krul, lok; *ww.* (-ed) krul, kronkel.

'currency ['kʌrənsi] *s.* omloop; gangbaarheid; munt, geld.

'current ['kʌrənt] *bnw.* lopend; gangbaar; algemeen; geldig; *s.* (-s) stroom.

cur'riculum [kə'rikjoeləm] *s.* (*curricula*) kursus, leerplan.

'curry ['kʌri] *s.* kerrie.

'curse ['kɔs] *ww.* (-d) vloek, vervloek, laster.

'cursory ['kɔsəri] *bnw.* haastig, oppervlakkig, terloops, vlugtig.

curt ['kɔt] *bnw.* (-er, -est) kortaf, bitsig.

cur'tail [kɔ'tyl] *ww.* (-ed) bekort, besnoei.

'curtain ['kɔtn] *s.* (-s) gordyn, skerm.

'curtsy ['kɔtsi] *s.* kniebuiging.

'curve ['kɔv] *ww.* (-d) buig, draai; *s.* (-s) boog; bog; kromme.

'cushion ['koesjən] *s.* (-s) kussing.

'custard ['kʌstəd] *s.* (-s) vla.

'custody ['kʌstədi] *s.* bewaring; hegtenis; voogdyskap.

'custom ['kʌstəm] *s.* (-s) gewoonte, gebruik; klandisie.

'customer ['kʌstəmə] *s.* (-s) klant.

cut ['kʌt] *ww.* (-) sny, kerf, raps, snoei, knip.

'cute ['kjõẽt] *bnw.* (-r, -st) oulik, slim.

'cuticle ['kjõẽtikl] *s.* (-s) opperhuid; naelvleis; - scissors *s. mv.* naelvleisskêr.

'cutlery ['kʌtləri] *s.* tafelgereedskap.

'cut 'out ['kʌt 'aut] *ww.* (-) afsluit; *s.* (-) afsluiter; uitskakelaar; stroomverbreker.

'cycle ['saikl] *s.* kringloop; fiets; siklus.

'cylinder ['silində] *s.* (-s) silinder.

'cynic ['sinik] *bnw.* sinies; skerp, bytend.

'cynosure ['sinəsjoeə] *s.* (-s) poolster; lei-ster; aantrekking.

D

dB [*decibel*] dB, DB (*desibel*).

dab ['dæb] *ww.* (-bed) tik; bet, sag aandruk teen.

'dabble ['dæbl] *ww.* (-d) 'n stokperdjie beoefen.

'daddy ['dædi] *s.* (*'daddies*) pa, pappie.

'daffodil ['dæfədil] *s.* (-s) affodil.

daft ['dɑft] *bnw.* (-er, -est) dwaas, gek.

'dagger ['dægə] *s.* (-s) dolk.

'daily ['dyli] *bnw.* daagliks; *s.* (*'dailies*) dagblad.

'dainty ['dynti] *bnw.* (*'daintier*, *'daintiest*) fyn, delikaat, lekker, kieskeurig.

'dairy ['dɛəri] *s.* (*'dairies*) melkery, melkkamer.

'dais ['dyis] *s.* (-es) verhoog, troonhemel.

'daisy ['dyzi] *s.* (*'daisies*) madeliefie, margriet.

'dale ['dyl] *s.* (-s) dal, vlei, leegte.

'dally ['dæli] *ww.* (*'dallied*) drentel, talm; dartel.

'dam ['dæm] *s.* (-s) dam, damwal; moeder, moer.

'damage ['dæmidzj] *s.* (-s) skade, nadeel; skadevergoeding; koste; *ww.* (-d) beskadig, bederf.

damn ['dæm] *ww.* (-ed) vervloek; verdoem; afkeur; *s.* vloek; -able *bnw.* verdoemelik; vervloek(s)te; **dam'nation** *s.* verdoemenis, veroordeling; -story *bnw.* verdoemend; -ing *bnw.* verdoemelik; vervloek(s)te.

damp ['dæmp] *bnw.* (-er, -est) vogtig, klam.

'dance ['dɑns] *ww.* (-d) dans; *s.* (-s) dans, bal.

'dandelion ['dændilaiən] *s.* (-s) botterblom.

'dandle ['dændl] *ww.* (-d) wieg, liefkoos.

'dandruff ['dændrəf] *s.* skilfers.

'dandy ['dændi] *s.* (*'dandies*) windmaker, modegek; *bnw.* spoggerig, windmakerig.

'danger ['dyndzjə] *s.* (-s) gevaar; -ous *bnw.* gevaarlik.

'dangle ['dæng-ghl] *ww.* (-d) swaai, slinger; agternaloop; in vooruitsig stel.

'dapper ['dæpə] *bnw.* lewendig.

'dare ['dɛə] *ww.* (-d, durst) durf, waag, trotseer, tart.

dark ['dɑk] *bnw.* (-er, -est) donker, duister; *s.* donkerte, duisternis; -en *ww.* (-ed) donker (maak, word), verduister.

'darling ['dɑling] *s.* (-s) liefling, liefste, skat.

darn ['dɑn] *ww.* (-ed) stop; -ed! *uitroep.* vervlaks!

'darnel ['dɑnl] *s.* drabok (*plant*).

dart ['dɑt] *s.* (-s) spies, pyl; sprong; *ww.* (-ed) gooi, skiet, straal; wegspring.

dash ['dæsj] *ww.* (-ed) smak; slaan; bespat; stuif; vlieg; vernietig; *s.* (-es) smeer; geklots; streep; aanval.

'dastard ['dæstəd] *s.* lafaard; -ly *bw.* lafhartig, laag.

'date ['dyt] *s.* (-s) datum; jaartal; dadel; *ww.* (-d) dagteken, dateer.

'daub ['dôb] *ww.* (*-ed*) besmeer, beplak; *s.* pleistering.

'daughter ['dôtə] *s.* (*-s*) dogter.

'dauntless ['dôntlis] *bnw.* onverskrokke, onversaag.

dawdle ['dôdl] *ww.* (*-d*) draai, seur, drentel.

dawn ['dôn] dagbreek; *ww.* (*-ed*) lig word.

day ['dy] *s.* (*-s*) dag; daglig; dagbreek.

'daze ['dyz] *ww.* (*-d*) verblind; verbyster; bedwelm.

'dazzle ['dæzl] *ww.* (*-d*) verblind; verbyster.

'deacon ['dikən] *s.* (*-s*) diaken; geestelike.

dead ['ded] *bnw.* dood; doods; dom; dooierig; *bw.* in hoë graad; *s.* die oorledene, dooie; *-en ww.* (*-ed*) verdoof, temper; verstomp.

deaf ['def] *bnw.* (*-er*, *-est*) doof.

deal ['dil] *s.* (*-s*) deel, gedeelte; klomp; slag, handelsaak; greinhout; *ww.* (*dealt*) deel, verdeel, gee; sake doen.

'dean ['din] *s.* (*-s*) deken; dekaan.

dear ['diə] *bnw.* (*-er*, *-est*) lief, dierbaar; duur; geagte; *s.* skat, liefste.

dearth ['dôth] *s.* duurte, skaarste.

death ['deth] *s.* (*-s*) dood; sterfte; sterfgeval; - rate *s.* sterftesyfer; -'s-head moth *s.* motby.

de'bacle ['dybâkl] *s.* (*-s*) misluking, fiasko.

de'bar [di'bâ] *ww.* (*-red*) uitsluit, belet.

de'base [di'bys] *ww.* (*-d*) verlaag, verneder; verbals.

de'bate [di'byt] *s.* (*-s*) debat, beraadslaging, redetwis; *ww.* (*-d*) debatteer, beredeneer, bespreek, betwis.

de'bauch [di'bôtsj] *ww.* (*-ed*) bederf; verliederlik; verlaag, verlei; *-ery s.* losbandigheid.

de'benture [di'bentsjə] *s.* (*-s*) skuldbrief.

de'bility [di'biliti] *s.* swakheid, kragteloosheid.

'debit ['debit] *s.* skuld, debet; *ww.* (*-ed*) debiteer, belas.

debo'nair [debə'nêə] *bnw.* joviaal, opgewek, minsaam.

'debris ['dybri] *s.* puin, rommel.

debt ['det] *s.* (*-s*) skuld; *-or s.* skuldenaar.

de'bunk [di'bʌnk] *ww.* (*-ed*) afblaas, uitpak.

'début ['dybôê] *s.* debuut.

'decade ['dekəd] *s.* (*-s*) tiental; dekade.

'decadence ['dekədəns] *s.* verval, dekadensie.

de'camp [di'kæmp] *ww.* (*-ed*) verkas.

de'cant [di'kænt] *ww.* (*-ed*) afgiet; skink.

de'capitate [di'kæpityt] *ww.* (*-d*) onthoof.

de'cay [di'ky] *ww.* (*-ed*) vergaan,

verval, bederf; *s.* agteruitgang, verval, bederf.

de'cease [di'sis] *ww.* (*-d*) sterf; *s.* dood; -d estate *s.* bestorwe boedel.

de'ceit [di'sit] *s.* bedrog.

de'ceive [di'siv] *ww.* (*-ed*) bedrieg, fop, verlei; *-r s.* bedrieër.

de'celerate [di'seləryt] *ww.* (*-d*) vertraag, verminder spoed.

De'cember [di'sembə] *s.* Desember.

'decency ['disnsi] *s.* fatsoenlikheid; 'decent *bnw.* fatsoenlik.

de'centralize [di'sentrəlaiz] *ww.* (*-d*) desentraliseer.

de'ception [di'sepsjən] *s.* bedrog, misleiding.

de'cide [di'said] *ww.* (*-d*) besluit, beslis, oordeel.

de'ciduous [di'sidjoeəs] *bnw.* bladwisselend.

'decimal ['desiməl] *s.* (*-s*) tiendelige breuk.

'decimate ['desimyt] *ww.* (*-d*) uitdun, wegmaai.

de'cipher [di'saifə] *ww.* (*-ed*) ontsyfer.

de'cision [di'sizjən] *s.* (*-s*) beslissing, uitspraak, uitslag.

'deck ['dek] *s.* (*-s*) dek; pak.

de'claim [di'klym] *ww.* (*-ed*) voordra; uitvoer; decla'mation *s.* voordrag.

de'clare [di'klêə] *ww.* (*-d*) verklaar, aankondig; aangee; roep, troefmaak.

de'clension [di'klensjən] *s.* (*-s*) afwyking; verval; verbuiging.

de'cline [di'klain] *ww.* (*-d*) afhel; buig, laat hang; afneem, verval; weier.

de'clivity [di'kliviti] *s.* (*de'clivities*) helling, skuinste.

de'coct [di'kokt] *ww.* (*-ed*) afkook, aftreksel maak deur kook; -ion *s.* (*-s*) afkooksel, aftreksel.

de'code [di'koud] *ww.* (*-d*) ontsyfer, dekodeer.

decom'pose [dikəm'pouz] *ww.* (*-d*) oplos; ontbind; vergaan.

'decorate ['dekəryt] *ww.* (*-d*) versier, dekoreer.

'decorous ['dekərəs] *bnw.* fatsoenlik, deftig.

de'corum [di'kôrəm] *s.* fatsoen, welvoeglikheid.

'decoy ['dikoi] *s.* lokaas; lokvoël.

de'crease [di'kris] *ww.* (*-d*) verminder, afneem.

de'cree [di'kri] *s.* (*-s*) verordening, besluit, dekreet.

de'crepit [di'krepit] *bnw.* vervalle, lendelam, afgeleef.

de'crepitude [di'krepitjoed] *s.* verval, gebreklikheid.

de'cry [di'krai] *ww.* (*de'cried*) uitkryt, verkleiner, beskinder.

'dedicate ['dedikyt] *ww.* (*-d*) toewy, opdra.

de'duce [di'djoes] *ww.* (*-d*) aflei, gevolgtrekking maak.

de'duct [di'dʌkt] *ww.* (*-ed*) aftrek.

deed [′did] s. (-s) daad, handeling; akte; dokument.

deem [′dim] ww. (-ed) oordeel, meen, dink.

deep [′dip] bnw. (-er, -est) diep; diepsinning; grondig; listig; s. (-s) diepte; see; -en ww. (-ed) verdiep.

de'face [di′fys] ww. (-d) skend, vermink; uitwis.

de 'facto [di ′faktou] bnw., bw. daadwerklik, defacto; vgl. **de jure**.

de'famatory [di′fæmətəri] bnw. lasterlik, eerskendend.

de'fault [di′fôlt] s. (-s) gebrek, afwesigheid, ontstentenis; ww. (-ed) versuim, nalaat; -er a. wanbetaler, oortreder, afwesig.

de'feat [di′fit] ww. (-ed) verslaan, oorwin, verydel, vernietig.

'defecate [′defikyt] ww. (-d) reinig, afval uitstoot, ontlas; **'defecation** s. suiwering, ontlasting, stoelgang.

de'fect [di′fekt] s. (-s) gebrek, fout, tekort, defek; **-tive** bnw. gebrekkig, defektief.

de'fence [di′fens] s. (s) verdediging; verweer; bolwerk.

de'fend [di′fend] ww. (-ed) verdedig, verweer; beskerm; **-ant** s. verweerder, beskuldigde; verdediger; **-er** s. verdediger, beskermer.

de'fer [di′fɜ] ww. (-red) uitstel, draal; onderwerp aan, neerlê by.

de'ficient [di′fisjənt] bnw. gebrekkig, ontoereikend; **'deficit** s. tekort; **de'ficiency** s. (de'ficiencies) gebrek, tekort.

de'file [di′fail] ww. (-d) defileer; besmet; onteer.

de'fine [di′fain] ww. (-d) bepaal, omskrywe, omlyn; definieer; **'definite** bnw. bepaald, omskrewe; **defi'nition** s. bepaling, definisie.

de'flate [di′flyt] ww. (-d) afblaas.

de'flect [di′flekt] ww. (-ed) wegbuig, wegskram; deflekteer.

de'flower [di′flauə] ww. (-ed) onteer, ontwy.

de'formity [di′fômiti] s. (de'formities) wanstaltigheid.

de'fraud [di′frôd] ww. (-ed) bedrieg.

de'fray [di′fry] ww. (-ed) bekostig, bestry, betaal.

de'frost [di′frost] ww. (-ed) ontvries.

deft [′deft] bnw. (-er, -est) knap, vaardig.

de'funct [di′fʌnkt] bnw. oorlede.

de'fy [di′fai] ww. (de'fied) trotseer, tart; **de'fiant** bnw. uitdagend, tartend; **de'fiance** s. uittarting, trotsering.

de'generate [di′dzjenərit] bnw. ontaard, versleg.

de'grade [di′ghryd] ww. (-d) verlaag, verneder.

de'gree [di′ghri] s. (-s) graad; klas.

de'hydrate [di′haidryt] ww. (-d) ontwater.

'deify [′di-ifai] ww. (′deified) vergoddelik, verheerlik.

'deign [′dyn] ww. (-ed) jou verwerdig.

'deity [′di-iti] s. (′deities) godheid.

de'jected [di′dzjektəd] bnw. neerslagtig, bek-af.

de' jure [di ′dzjöëri] bnw., bw. regtens; vgl. **de facto**.

de'lay [di′ly] ww. (-ed) vertraag, teenwerk, versuim; - s. vertraging, versuim.

de'lectable [di′lektəbl] bnw. (more -, most -) lekker, verruklik.

'delegate [′delight] s. (-s) afgevaardigde, gemagtigde.

'delegate [′delight] ww. (-d) afvaardig; magtig; opdra; delegeer; **'delegation** s. (-s) afvaardiging, magtiging.

de'lete [di′lit] ww. (-d) uitkrap, skraap, uithaal.

de'leterious [deli′tiəriəs] bnw. skadelik; verwoestend; verderflik.

de'liberate [di′libəryt] bnw. weloorwoë, opsetlik; tydsaam.

'delicate [′delikit] bnw. fyn, teer, tenger; kies; delikaat.

de'licious [di′lisjəs] bnw. heerlik; - monster s. monstera, skeletplant.

de'light [di′lait] s. (-s) genoeë, behae, lus.

de'lineate [di′liniyt] ww. (-d) afbeeld, teken, skets; **deline'ation** s. afbeelding, skets.

de'linquent [di′linkwənt] s. (-s) oortreder, skuldige; **de'linquency** s. vergryp, pligsversuim, oortreding.

de'lirious [di′liriəs] bnw. ylend, waansinning; opgetoë.

de'liver [di′livə] ww. (-ed) bevry, verlos; aflewer; voordra; **-ance** s. bevryding; **-y** s. verlossing; bevalling; aflewering.

de'lude [di′löëd] ww. (-d) mislei, fop.

'deluge [′delöëdzj] s. oorstroming, sondvloed.

de'lusion [di′löëzjn] s. (-s) misleiding; waan, dwaling.

de'mand [di′mänd] ww. (-ed) eis, vra; s. (-s) eis, vereiste; vordering, opvraging.

'demarcate [′dimäkyt] ww. (-d) afbaken, afgrens; **demar'cation** s. afbakening; grens.

de'meanour [di′minə] s. gedrag, houding.

de'ment [di′ment] ww. (-ed) kranksinnig maak, tot raserny dryf.

de'mented [di′mentid] bnw. gek, kranksinnig.

de'mise [di′maiz] s. afsterwe, oorlyde; vererwing.

de'mobilize [dimoubilaiz] ww. (-d) ontbind, demobiliseer.

de'mocracy [di′mokrəsi] s. (de'mocracies) demokrasie; **'democrat** s. demokraat.

de'molish [di′molisj] ww. (-ed) vernietig; sloop.

'demonstrate [′demənstryt] ww. (-d) uitlê; aantoon; vertoon; demonstreer.

de'mur [di′mɜ] ww. (-red) beswaar maak, pruttel.

de'mure [di'mjoeə] bnw. sedig;
preuts; stemmig.

de'murrage [di'mʌridzj] s. staangeld, lêgeld.

'den ['den] s. (-s) hol, lêplek, hok; bof.

'denizen ['denizn] s. (-s) bewoner;
burger; wat inheems is.

de'nominate [di'nominyt] ww. (-d)
aandui, bemoem, betitel; denomi-
'nation s. naam, soort; grootte;
sekte; denomi'national bnw. sektaries.

de'note [di'nout] ww. (-d) aandui;
beteken; te kenne gee.

denouement [dynoe'mãñ] s. ont-
knoping, afloop.

de'nounce [di'nauns] ww. (-d)
aankla; aan die kaak stel.

dense ['dens] bnw. dig; dom.

dent ['dent] s. (-s) deuk, duik.

'dental ['dentl] bnw. tand-; 'denti-
frice s. tandepoetsmiddel; 'dentist
s. tandarts; - cream s. tanderoom;
- floss s. tandevlos; dental- voorv.
tande-.

den'tition [den'tisjən] s. die tandekry; tandestelsel.

'denture ['dentsjə] s. kunsgebit,
kunstande, plaat.

de'nudate [di'njõёdyt] ww. (-d)
blootlê, ont-dek, kaal maak; bnw.
blootgelegde; denu'dation s. bloot-
legging.

de'nude [di'njõёd] ww. (-d) ontbloot,
blootlê.

denunci'ation [dinʌnsi'ysjən] s.
aanklag; aankondiging.

de'ny [di'nai] ww. (de'nied) ontken,
verloën; weier; de'nial s. ontkenning; weiering.

de'odorant [di'oudərənt] s. reukweerder; bnw. reukwerend; de'odor-
ize ww. verdrywing van reuk(e);
de'odorizer s. reukweerder.

de'part [di'pãt] ww. (-ed) vertrek,
heengaan; -ure s. vertrek.

de'partment [di'pãtmənt] s. (-s)
afdeling, departement, tak; depart-
'mental bnw. departementeel.

de'pend [di'pend] ww. (-ed) afhang;
staatmaak op; -able bnw. betroubaar; -ant, -ent s. afhanklike; -ence
s. onderhorigheid.

de'pilate [depilyt] ww. (-d) onthaar,
stroop van hare; de'pilatory bnw.
ontharend; s. onthaarmiddel.

de'plete [di'plit] ww. (-d) ledig,
uitput; uitdun.

de'plore [di'plõ] ww. (-d) betreur,
bekla.

de'port [di'põt] ww. (-ed) gedra,
wegvoer, deporteer; -ment s.
houding; gedrag.

de'pose [di'pouz] ww. (-d) afsit;
getuig.

de'posit [di'pozit] s. (-s) belegging;
deposito; neerslag; ww. (-ed) neersit,
stort, besink.

'depôt ['depou] s. (-s) magasyn;
hoofkwartier; dépôt.

depra'dation [depri'dysjən] s.
plundering, verwoesting.

de'prave [di'pryv] ww. (-d) versleg,
(die sedes) bederf, ontaard, verword;
-d bnw. bedorwe, ontaarde; de-
'pravity s. ontaarding, verslegting.

'deprecate ['deprikyt] ww. (-d)
afkeur.

de'preciate [di'prisjiyt] ww. (-d) in
waarde afneem; minag.

de'press [di'pres] ww. (-ed) neerdruk;
verneder; ontmoedig.

de'pression [di'presjən] s. (-s) daling;
slapte; laagte; neerslagtigheid; de-
pressie.

de'prive [di'praiv] ww. (-d) beroof,
ontneem; ontsê.

depth ['depth] s. (-s) diepte;
diepsinnigheid.

de'pute [di'pjõёt] ww. (-d) afvaardig;
oordra; 'deputy s. ('deputies) plaasvervanger; afgevaardigde; gevolmagtigde; depu'tation s. deputasie.

de'rail [di'ryl] ww. (-ed) ontspoor,
laat ontspoor.

de'range [di'ryndzj] ww. (-d) in die
war stuur.

'derelict ['derilikt] bnw. verlate,
onbeheer.

de'ride [di'raid] ww. (-d) bespot;
de'rision s. bespotting, spot.

de'rive [di'raiv] ww. (-d) aflei; put
uit; vandaan kry; deri'vation s.
afleiding; de'rivative bnw. afgelei.

'dermal- ['dõmi] voorv. huid-, vel-.

'derogate ['deroghyt] ww. (-d) ver-
klein(eer); verlaag; dero'gation s.
afbreuk, verkleinering; de'rogative
bnw. verkleinerend; de'rogatory bnw.
- derogative.

de'rogatory [di'roghetəri] bnw.
benadelend; kleinerend.

derrick ['derik] s. boortoring.

de'scend [di'send] ww. (-ed) af
(neer) daal, afstyg, afkom; afstam;
-ant s. afstammeling; de'scent s.
afstyging; afkoms.

de'scribe [dis'kraib] ww. (-d)
beskrywe, omskrywe; de'scription
s. beskrywing; soort; de'scriptive
bnw. beskrywend.

'desecrate ['desikryt] ww. (-d)
ontheilig, ontwy.

de'sert [di'zət] s. (-s) verdienste,
loon.

'desert ['dezət] s. (-s) woestyn.

de'serve [di'zəv] ww. (-d) verdien;
de'serving bnw. verdienstelik.

'desiccate ['desikyt] ww. (-d) uitdroë, opdroë, droogmaak.

de'sign [di'zain] s. (-s) plan,
ontwerp; doel; ww. (-ed) ontwerp,
skets; bedoel, beoog.

'designate ['dezighnyt] bnw. pas-
benoemde, verkore.

de'sire [di'zaiə] ww. (-d) begeer;
versoek, vra; s. (-s) begeerte;
versoek; de'sirable bnw. begeerlik;
de'sirous bnw. begerig.

de'sist [di'zist] ww. (-ed) ophou,
uitskei met.

desk ['desk] s. (-s) lessenaar; spreekgestoelte.

'**desolate** ['desōlit] bnw. eensaam, verlate, vervalle; bedroef.

de'**spair** [dis'pɛə] s. wanhoop; ww. (-ed) wanhoop, moed opgee.

de'**spatch** [dis'pætsj] ww. (-ed) afstuur, versend.

'**desperate** ['despərit] bnw. wanhopig; roekeloos.

de'**spise** [dis'paiz] ww. (-d) verag; versmaad.

de'**spite** [dis'pait] voors. ondanks.

de'**spondence** [dis'pondəns] s. wanhoop; neerslagtigheid.

de'**spondent** [di'spondənt] bnw. moedeloos, neerslagtig.

'**despot** ['despot] s. (-s) dwingeland, despoot.

des'**sert** [di'zōt] s. (-s) nagereg.

desti'**nation** [desti'nysjən] s. (-s) bestemming; lot.

'**destiny** ['destini] s. ('destinies) bestemming, lot.

'**destitute** ['destitjōēt] bnw. behoeftig, brandarm.

de'**stroy** [dis'troi] ww. (-ed) verniel, verwoes; -er s. torpedojaer.

de'**struction** [dis'trʌksjən] s. verwoesting, vernieling; verderf.

'**desultory** ['desʌltəri] bnw. onsamehangend.

de'**tach** [di'tætsj] ww. (-ed) losmaak; -ment s. losmaking; losheid; afdeling.

'**detail** ['dityl] s. (-s) besonderheid, kleinigheid.

de'**tain** [di'tyn] ww. (-ed) ophou, verhinder; weerhou; gevange hou.

de'**tect** [di'tekt] ww. (-ed) ontdek; betrap; -ion s. ontdekking, opsporing; -ive s. speurder.

de'**tention** [di'tensjən] s. oponthoud; aanhouding; detensie.

de'**ter** [di'tō] ww. (-red) terughou, afskrik.

de'**tergent** [di'tōdzjənt] s. reiniger.

de'**teriorate** [di'tiəriəryt] ww. (-d) versleg, agteruitgaan.

de'**termine** [di'tōmin] ww. (-d) bepaal, besluit; rigting gee; eindig; determi'**nation** s. beslissing; beslistheid.

de'**test** [di'test] ww. (-ed) verfoei, verafsku.

'**detonate** ['detounyt] ww. (-d) ontplof.

de'**tour** [di'tōēə] s. (-s) ompad: padverlegging.

de'**tract** [di'trækt] ww. (-ed) aftrek; onttrek; kleineer; laster.

'**detriment** ['detrimənt] s. nadeel, skade.

'**deuce** ['djōēs] s. duiwel; drommels; twee; gelykop; -d bw, bnw. verduiwelde, verduiwels.

de'**valuate** [di'væljoeyt] ww. verminder in waarde, devalueer; de'**valuation** s. waardevermindering, devaluasie.

'**devastate** ['devəstyt] ww. (-d) verwoes, verniel.

de'**velop** [di'veləp] ww. (-ed) ontwikkel; ontvou; -ment s.

'**deviate** ['diviyt] ww. (-d) afwyk; devi'**ation** s. afwyking; verlegging.

de'**vice** [di'vais] s. (-s) leus; plan; lis; uitvinding, toestel.

'**devil** ['devil] s. (-s) duiwel; -ment s. grap; spokery; -ry s. toordery; boosheid.

'**devious** ['diviəs] bnw. kronkelend, afgeleë, afwykend(e), vgl. deviate.

de'**vise** [di'vaiz] ww. (-d) uitdink, versin, smee.

de'**void** [di'void] bnw. ontbloot, sonder.

de'**volve** [di'volv] ww. (-d) afskuiwe; -on oorgaan op.

de'**vote** [di'vout] ww. (-d) wy, offer; dı'**votion** [di'vousjən] s. toewyding.

de'**vour** [di'vauə] ww. (-ed) verslind, opvreet.

de'**vout** [di'vaut] bnw. vroom, eerbiedig; stigtelik.

dew ['djōē] s. dou.

dex'**terity** [deks'terəti] s. handigheid; regshandigheid.

'**dexterous** ['dekstərəs] bnw. handig, rats.

dia'**betes** [daiə'bitiz] s. suikersiekte.

dia'**bolic** [daiə'bolik] bnw. duiwels, hels, diabolies.

'**diadem** ['daiədem] s. (-s) diadeem.

di'**agnose** ['daiəghnouz] ww. (-d) diagnoseer; diag'**nosis** s. diagnose.

di'**agonal** [dai'æghnl] bnw. diagonaal, oorhoeks.

'**diagram** [daiə'ghræm] s. (-s) diagram, skets.

'**dial** ['daiəl] s. (-s) sonwyser; wyserplaat; ww. (-led) skakel.

'**dialogue** [daiəlogh] s. (-s) dialoog, samespraak.

di'**ameter** [dai'æmitə] s. (-s) middellyn, deursnee.

'**diamond** ['daiəmənd] s. (-s) diamant; ruit.

'**diaphragm** ['daiəfræm] s. (-s) middelrif.

diar'**rhoea** [daiə'riə] s. diaree, buikloop.

'**diary** ['daiəri] s. ('diaries) dagboek.

'**dice** ['dais] s. dobbelsteen.

'**dickey** ['diki] s. (-s) esel; voorskootjie, borsie; bok, agterbak, kattebak.

dic'**tate** [dik'tyt] ww. (-d) dikteer; voorskrywe; ingee; dic'**tation** s. diktee, diktaat; bevel; ingewing; dic'**tator** s. diktator.

'**diction** ['diksjən] s. diksie, segging, styl, trant.

'**dictionary** ['diksjənri] s. ('dictionaries) woordeboek.

di'**dactic** [dai'dæktik] bnw. lerend, didakties.

die ['dai] s. (-s) matrys; (dice) dobbelsteen; ww. (-d) sterf.

'**diet** ['daiət] s. (-s) ryksdag; leefreël, dieet.

'**differ** ['difə] ww. (-ed) verskil; -ence

s. verskil; geskil; **-ent** *bnw.* verskillend; **differenti'ate** *ww.* (-d) onderskeid maak; **diffe'rential** s. ewenaar.

'**difficult** ['difikəlt] *bnw.* moeilik, lastig; **-y** s. ('difficulties) moeilikheid, beswaar.

'**diffident** ['difidənt] *bnw.* bedees, beskeie.

dif'fuse [di'fjöēz] *ww.* (-d) versprei, uitstraal; *bnw.* verstrooi(d), langdradig.

dif'fusion [di'fjöēzjən] s. uitspreiding.

dig ['digh] *ww.* (-ged, dug) grawe, spit; in ribbes stoot.

di'gest [di'dzjest] *ww.* (-ed) verteer, verwerk; verdra; **-ion** s. spysvertering.

'**digit** ['didzjit] s. (-s) vinger, toon; een.

'**dignified** ['dighnifaid] *bnw.* waardig, deftig; verhewe.

'**dignity** ['dighniti] s. waardigheid, adel.

di'gress [dai'ghres] *ww.* (-ed) afdwaal, afwyk.

di'lapidate [di'læpidyt] *ww.* (-d) verval; laat verval.

di'late [dai'lyt] *ww.* (-d) swel, rek; uitwei oor.

di'lemma [di'lemə] s. (-s) dilemma verleentheid.

'**diligent** ['dilidzjənt] *bnw.* vlytig, ywerig.

di'lute [dai'ljöēt] *ww.* (-d) verdun, verswak; **-r** s. verdunner; **-nt** s. verdunner.

dim ['dim] *ww.* (-med) verdof; *bnw.* (-mer, -mest) skemerig, flou, gedemp.

di'mension [di'mensjən] s. (-s) afmeting, grootte, omvang.

di'minish [di'minisj] *ww.* (-ed) verminder, afneem.

di'minutive [di'minjoetiv] s. (-s) verkleinwoord.

'**dimple** ['dimpl] s. (-s) kuiltjie.

din ['din] s. geraas, lawaai.

'**dine** ['dain] *ww.* (-d) eet, dineer.

'**dingy** ['dindzji] *bnw.* donker, vuil.

'**dinner** ['dinə] s. (-s) middagete; dinee; eetmaal.

'**dint** ['dint] s. **by -of** deur middel van.

'**diocese** ['daiəsis] s. (-s) bisdom, biskoplike gebied.

dio'rama [dai-o'rāmə] s. kykspel.

'**dioxide** [dai'oksaid] s. dioksied.

dip ['dip] *ww.* (-ped) insteek, indompel; dip; laat sak; demp (lig); domp(lig); s. indompeling, bad; **-per** s. dompelaar; skoppie.

diph'theria [dif'thiəriə] s. witseerkeel.

di'ploma [di'ploumə] s. (-s) diploma, getuigskrif.

di'plomacy [di'plouməsi] s. diplomasie; oorleg, sluheid.

'**diplomat** ['diplomæt] s. (-s) diplomaat.

'**dipstick** ['dipstik] s. meetlat, peilstok.

'**dire** ['daiə] *bnw.* verskriklik, ontsettend.

di'rect [di'rekt] *bnw.* (-est) regstreeks; *bw.* ronduit, reguit; *ww.* (-ed) rig; aanwys; beveel; **-ion** s. (-s) rigting; bestuur; bevel; **-or** s. direkteur; **- current** s. gelykstroom; **-ional** *bnw.* gerig(te).

'**dirge** ['dödzj] s. (-s) lyksang, klaagsang.

'**dirigible** ['diridzjəbl] *bnw.* bestuurbaar; s. bestuurbare lugballon.

dirt ['döt] s. vuilgoed, vuiligheid; modder; grond; **-y** *bnw.* vuil, smerig.

dis'able [dis'ybl] *ww.* (-d) onbekwaam maak, vermink, wond.

disa'buse [disə'bjöēz] *ww.* (-d) reghelp, uit die droom help, ontnugter, wanindruk verwyder.

disa'gree [disə'ghri] *ww.* (-d) verskil (van mening); twis; **-able** *bnw.* onaangenaam; onplesierig; **-ment** s. verskil, onenigheid.

disap'point [disə'point] *ww.* (-ed) teleurstel.

'**disap'prove** ['disə'pröēv] *ww.* (-d) afkeur.

dis'aster [di'zāstə] s. (-s) ramp, ongeluk; **di'sastrous** *bnw.* noodlottig.

disa'vow [disə'vau] *ww.* (-ed) ontken; afkeur.

dis'burden [dis'bödn] *ww.* (-ed) ontlas, uitstort, verlig, opbieg; **-ment** s. opbiegting, verligting.

dis'burse [dis'bös] *ww.* (-d) uitbetaal, opdok.

disc ['disk] s. (-s) skyf, diskus; **- brake** s. skyfrem; **- wheel** s. skyfwiel, skottelwiel.

dis'card ['diskād] *ww.* (-ed) wegwerp, afdank.

dis'cern [di'sön] *ww.* (-ed) onderskei; uitmaak.

dis'charge [dis'tsjādzj] *ww.* (-d) aflaai; ontplof; losbrand; onthef; nakom; s. ontslag; ontploffing, skoot.

dis'ciple [di'saipl] s. (-s) dissepel.

'**discipline** ['disiplin] s. dissipline, tug, orde; oefening.

dis'claim [dis'klym] *ww.* (-ed) afstand doen van; ontken; **-er** s. ontkenning.

dis'close [dəs'klouz] *ww.* (-d) bloôtlê, openbaar, onthul.

dis'comfort [dis'kʌmfət] s. ongemak, ongerief; kommer.

discom'posure [diskəm'pouzjə] s. verleentheid.

discon'cert [diskən'söt] *ww.* (-ed) verleë maak, uit die veld slaan.

dis'consolate [dis'kɒnsəlit] *bnw.* verslae, troosteloos.

discon'tent ['diskən'tent] s. ontevredenheid, misnoeë.

'**discord** ['diskôd] s. wanklank; twis.

'**discount** ['diskaunt] s. afslag, korting.

dis'courage [dis'kʌridzj] *ww.* (-d) ontmoedig, afraai.

dis'course [dis'kôs] s. (-s) diskoers; gesprek; redevoering.

dis'cover [dis'kʌvə] ww. (-ed) ontdek, ontbloot, onthul.

dis'creet [dis'krit] bnw. verstandig, versigtig; **dis'cretion** s. oordeel, oorleg, verstand, diskressie.

dis'criminate [dis'kriminyt] ww. (-d) onderskei; benadeel, agterstel.

dis'cursive [dis'kəsiv] bnw. omslagtig.

dis'cuss [dis'kʌs] ww. (-ed) bespreek, uitpluis; -ion s. bespreking, diskussie.

dis'ease [di'ziz] s. (-s) siekte, kwaal.

disem'bowel [disim'bauəl] ww. (-led) ontwei, ingewande uithaal.

disen'gage [disen'ghydzj] ww. (-d) uitskakel, ontkoppel.

dis'figure [dis'fighə] ww. (-d) vermink, skend.

dis'gorge [dis'ghôdzj] ww. (-d) uitbraak; teruggee.

dis'grace [dis'ghrys] s. skande.

dis'gruntled [dis'ghrʌntld] bnw. misnoeg, brommerig.

dis'guise [dis'ghaiz] ww. (-d) vermom, verklee; verbloem; s. (-s) vermomming; voorwendsel; masker.

dis'gust [dis'ghʌst] s. teensin, walging.

dish ['disj] s. (-es) skottel; gereg; ww. (-ed) opskep; opdis.

dis'hevel [dis'sjevəl] ww. (-led) hare deurmekaar maak.

'disin'fect ['disin'fekt] ww. (-ed) ontsmet.

'disk, 'disc ['disk] s. (-s) skyf; diskus.

dis'like [dis'laik] s. (-s) afkeer, teensin, hekel.

'dislocate ['dislokyt] ww. (-d) verplaas; ontwrig; verswik.

dis'lodge [dis'lodzj] ww. (-ed) verdryf, uit posisie dwing.

'dis'loyal ['dis'loiəl] bnw. ontrou, dislojaal.

'dismal ['dizməl] bnw. naar, aaklig, somber.

dis'mantle [dis'mæntl] ww. (-d) aftakel.

dis'may [dis'my] s. onsteltenis; ontstel, onthuts.

dis'member [dis'membə] ww. (-ed) verbrokkel, verdeel.

dis'miss [dis'mis] ww. (-ed) wegstuur; ontbind; afdank; uitkry; -al s. ontslag, afdanking; afhandeling.

'diso'bey ['disö'by] ww. (-ed) ongehoorsaam wees.

dis'own [dis'oun] ww. (-ed) weier om te erken; verwerp.

dis'parage [dis'pæridzj] ww. (-d) oneer aandoen, neerhaal; -ment s. kleinering, neerhaling.

dis'parity [dis'pæriti] s. verskil, ongelykheid.

dis'pel [dis'pel] ww. (-led) verdryf; wegruim.

dis'pense [dis'pens] ww. (-d) uitdeel; uitmeet; toeberei; onthef; dis-

'pensable bnw. ontbeerlik; **dis'pensary** s. apteek; **dispen'sation** s. vrystelling.

dis'perse [dis'pəs] ww. (-d) verstrooi; uitmekaar gaan; **dis'persal** s. verstrooiing, verspreiding.

dis'place [dis'plys] ww. (-d) verplaas; vervang; -ment s.

dis'play [dis'ply] s. (-s) vertoning, uitstalling.

dis'pose [dis'pouz] ww. (-d) skik, rangskik; inrig; stem; wegruim; weerlê; **dispo'sition** s. rangskikking; geaardheid; aanleg, neiging.

dis'pute [dis'pjôt] ww. (-d) redetwis; ontken, betwis; twis; **dis'putable** bnw. betwisbaar; **dispu'tation** s. redetwis.

dis're'gard ['disri'ghâd] ww. (-ed) veronagsaam, in die wind slaan.

'disre'spect [disris'pekt] s. oneerbiedigheid.

dis'rupt [dis'rʌpt] ww. (-ed) uiteenskeur.

dis'sect [di'sekt] ww. (-ed) ontleed.

dis'semble [di'sembl] ww. (-d) veins, huigel; ontveins.

dis'sent [di'sent] ww. (-ed) van mening verskil; afskei.

'dissipate ['disipyt] ww. (-d) verstrooi, verkwis.

'dissolute ['disəlöet] bnw. losbandig, liederlik; **disso'lution** s. oplossing, ontbinding; einde; dood.

dis'solve [di'zólv] ww. (-d) oplos, ontbind; **dis'solvent** bnw. oplossend.

dis'suade [di'swyd] ww. (-d) afraai; uit die kop praat.

'distance ['distəns] s. (-s) afstand, verte, distansie; koelheid; **'distant** bnw. ver, verwyder; koel.

'dis'taste ['dis'tyst] s. afkeer, teensin.

dis'temper [dis'tempə] s. muurkalk, witsel.

dis'til [dis'til] ww. (-led) distilleer, stook.

dis'tinct [dis'tinkt] bnw. onderskeie; duidelik; beslis; -ion s. onderskeiding; distinksie.

dis'tinguish [dis'tingwisj] ww. (-ed) onderskei; kenmerk; onderken.

dis'tort [dis'tôt] ww. (-ed) verdraai, verwring, vervorm.

dis'tract [dis'trækt] ww. (-ed) aftrek, aflei; verdeel; verwar.

dis'tress [dis'tres] ww. & s. (-ed) nood, angs, ellende.

dis'tribute [dis'tribjoet] ww. (-d) uitdeel, versprei; **dis'tributor** s. (-s) verdeler; **distributor plate** s. onderbrekerplaat; **distributor valve** s. verdelerklep.

'district ['distrikt] s. distrik; gemeente; wyk; gebied.

dis'trust [dis'trʌst] ww. (-ed) wantrou; s. wantroue, verdenking.

dis'turb [dis'təb] ww. (-ed) steur, pla, hinder; -ance s. (-s) steuring, opskudding.

'dis'use ['dis'jôêz] s. onbruik, ontwenning.

ditch ['ditʃ] s. (-es) sloot, voor.
'ditty ['diti] s. ('ditties) liedjie.
di'van [di'væn] s. (-s) divan, sofa, rusbank.
'dive ['daiv] ww. (-d) duik; insteek; indompel; verdiep in.
di'verge [dai'vədzj] ww. (-d) splits, afwyk; -nce s. (-s) splitsing, afwyking; -nt bnw. afwykend(e).
di'verse [dai'vəs] bnw. verskillend, ongelyk.
di'versify [dai'vəsifai] ww. afwissel, wysig, verander, verskeidenheid aanbring; di'versified bnw. verskillend, verskeie; di'versification s. afwisseling, verskeidenheid.
di'vert [dai'vət] ww. (-ed) aflei; afwend; vermaak.
di'vest [dai'vest] ww. (-ed) ontklee; ontdoen van.
di'vide [di'vaid] ww. (-d) verdeel; skei; sny.
'dividend ['dividənd] s. (-s) divident, aandeel in wins.
di'vine [di'vain] bnw. goddelik.
di'vision [di'viʒn] s. (-s) verdeling; deelsomme; afdeling; skeiding; grens.
di'visor [di'vaizə] s. deler.
di'vorce [di'vɔs] s. (-s) egskeiding.
di'vulge [dai'vʌldzj] ww. (-d) openbaar, verklap.
'dizzy ['dizi] bnw. ('dizzier, 'dizziest) duiselig.
do ['dōē] ww. (doing, did, done) doen, maak, verrig.
'docile ['dousail] bnw. maklik om te leer, geseglik, mak.
'dock ['dok] s. dok; stompstert; stertpit; wilde suring; ww. stert afsny, afkap.
'docket ['dokit] s. (-s) etiket, kaartjie; uittreksel; rol.
'doctor ['doktə] s. (-s) dokter, doktor, arts.
'document ['dokjoemənt] s. (-s) dokument, stuk, akte.
'dodge ['dodzj] ww. (-d) draai; uitoorlê; ontglip; koets.
'doe ['dou] s. (-s) hinde; ree; konynwyfie.
dog ['dogh] s. (-s) hond; reun; kram; -ged bnw. vasberade.
dog 'biscuit [dogh'biskit] s. kloumoer.
'doggerel ['dogherəl] s. gerymel, rymelary.
'doily ['doili] s. ('doilies) doilie, bekerlappie.
'doldrums ['doldrəms] s. streke van die windstilte; neerslagtigheid.
'dole ['doul] s. aalmoes; steun; uitdeling; lot, deel.
doll ['dol] s. (-s) pop.
'dolly ['dōli] s. ('dollies) kloplees.
'dolorous ['dolərəs] bnw. pynlik, klaaglik.
'dolt ['doult] s. swaap, dommerik; -ish bnw. dom, dwaas.
do'main [də'myn] s. (-s) domein, gebied.

'dome ['doum] s. (-s) dom, koepel.
do'mestic [do'mestik] bnw. huis-, huislik; binnelands.
'domicile ['domisail] s. verblyf, woonplek, domisilie.
'dominate ['dominyt] ww. (-d) oorheers, botoon voer.
do'minion [də'minjən] s. (-s) heerskappy; gebied; dominium.
don ['don] ww. (-ned) aantrek.
do'nate [dou'nyt] ww. (-d) skenk, bydra, begiftig.
do'nation [dou'nysjən] s. (-s) skenking, donasie.
'doom ['dōēm] s. vonnis; oordeel; ondergang.
door ['dō] s. (-s) deur; -catch s. deurknip; -latch s. deurklink.
'dope ['doup] ww. (-d) bedwelm maak; s. doepa, bedwelmingsmiddel.
'dormant ['dōmənt] bnw. slapend(e), rustend(e), nie-aktief.
'dormitory ['dōmitri] s. ('dormitories) slaapsaal.
'dormouse ['dōmaus] s. (-mice) slaapmuis, bossertmuis.
'dose ['dous] s. (-s) dosis, dop.
dot ['dot] s. (-s) punt, stippel; kindjie.
'dote ['dout] ww. (-d) kinds wees (word); - on versot wees op; 'dotage s. kindsheid; 'dotard s. sufferd; 'doting bnw. versot; kinds.
'dotty ['doti] bnw. getik, onnosel.
'double ['dʌbl] bnw. & bw. tweevoudig, tweemaal; ww. (-d) dubbel, verdubbel; dubbel vou; s. (-s) die dubbele; dubbelspel; - purpose vehicle s. tweedoelvoertuig; -line road s. tweebaanpad.
doubt ['daut] s. (-s) twyfel, argwaan; ww. (-ed) twyfel, betwyfel.
dough ['dou] s. deeg.
'dour ['doeə] bnw. hard, streng; stuurs, nors.
'dove ['dʌv] s. (-s) duif; -tail s. swaelstert.
'dowdy ['daudi] bnw. ('dowdier, 'dowdiest) slordig.
down ['daun] s. (-s) duin; dons; voors. af, van af; bw. af, neer, onder; bnw. afdraand.
'downstroke ['daunstrouk] s. daalslag.
'doze ['douz] ww. (-d) dut.
'dozen ['dʌzn] s. (-s) dosyn.
'drab ['dræb] bnw. vaal; grou; eentonig, vervelig, saai.
'draft ['drāft] s. (-s) treksel; drankie; ligting; ontwerp, konsep(-).
drag ['dræg] ww. (-ged) sleep, eg, rem; s. sleepweerstand.
'dragon ['dræghən] s. (-s) draak.
'dragonfly ['dræghənflai] s. ('dragonflies) naaldekoker.
dra'goon [drə'ghōēn] s. (-s) dragonder; ww. laat mishandel (dwing).
drain ['dryn] s. (-s) riolering; ww. (-ed) afwater; leegdrink; dreineer, drooglê; aftap; -age s. afwatering, riolering; -plug s. aftapprop.

'**drake** ['dryk] s. (-s) manne-tjieseend.

drape ['dryp] ww. (-ed) omhang, drapeer; -r s. klerasiehandelaar; -ry s. klerasiehandel; kleding-stowwe; drapering.

'**draught** ['dråft] s. (-s) trek, tog; teug, sluk; ontwerp; vgl. **draft**; -free bnw. trekvry.

draw ['drô] ww. (drew, drawn) trek, aantrek, wegtrek; teken, beskryf; -back s. (-s) beswaar, nadeel; -ing s. tekening; tekenkursus; -sheet s. treklaken; -ing **plaster** s. trek-pleister.

'**drawer** ['drôə] s. (-s) trekker; tekenaar; laai; -s s. onderbroek; chest of -s laaikas, laaitafel.

drawl ['drôl] ww. (-ed) temerig praat.

dread ['dred] ww. (-ed) vrees.

dream ['drim] s. (-s) droom.

'**dreary** ['driəri] bnw. ('drearier, 'dreariest) naar; vervelig.

'**dredge** ['dredzj] ww. (-d) bagger.

'**dregs** ['dreghz] s. moer, oorskiet.

drench ['drentsj] ww. (-ed) drenk, deurweek.

dress ['dres] s. (-es) kleed; klere; kleredrag; rok; -ing s. verband; smeersel; garneersel.

drift ['drift] ww. (-ed) afdrywe, wegdrywe; -sand s. swerfsand, stuifsand.

drill ['dril] ww. (-ed) dril, oefen; boor; s. (-s) boor; oefening; duiwel-sterk-stof.

drink ['drink] ww. (drank, drunk) drink.

'**drip** ['drip] ww. (-ped) drup; laat drup; druip.

'**drive** ['draiv] ww. (drove, driven) (aan) drywe, aanja; stuur, bestuur; -r s. bestuurder, drywer; -r's **cab** s. stuurkajuit, stuurkap; **driving** **school** s. motorryskool.

'**drivel** ['drivl] s. kwyl; geklets.

'**drizzle** ['drizl] s. motreent.

'**droll** ['droul] bnw. (-er, -est) snaaks, koddig; -ery s. snaaksheid, koddig-heid, grapmakery.

'**drone** ['droun] s. (-s) waterdraer, hommel; leegloper; gegons.

droop ['drôëp] ww. (-ed) afhang, kwyn; sink.

drop ['drop] s. (-s) druppel; sopie; oorbel; drop; kloutjie; druppel; - **bottle** s. drupbottel; -per s. (-s) drupper.

drought ['draut] s. (-s) droogte.

drown ['draun] ww. (-ed) verdrink, oorstem.

'**drowsy** ['drauzi] bnw. ('drowsier, 'drowsiest) slaperig, lomerig.

'**drudge** ['drʌdzj] s. sloof.

'**drudgery** ['drʌdzjəri] s. sloofwerk.

drug ['drʌgh] s. (-s) geneeskruie, medisyne, artsenymiddel; bedwel-mende middel.

drum ['drʌm] s. (-s) trommel; tamboer; oorvlies; silinder; vat; blik.

drunk ['drʌnk] bnw. dronk; -ard s. dronkaard.

dry ['drai] bnw. (drier, driest) droog, dor; dorstig; ongeërg; -**cleaner** s. droogskoonmaker; **drier** s. droër (droogmaker).

dual ['djoeəl] bnw. tweeledig, dubbel.

'**dubious** ['djoebiəs] bnw. twyfe-lagtig, onseker.

duck ['dʌk] s. (-s) eend; skat, hartlam; nul.

'**ductile** ['dəktil] bnw. rekbaar.

due ['djô] bnw. verplig, skuldig; betaamlik.

du'et [djoe'et] s. (-s) duo.

'**duffer** ['dʌfə] s. (-s) stommerik; bədrieër.

dull ['dʌl] bnw. (-er, -est) dom, bot; dooierig; traag; vervelend; bewolk.

'**dumb** ['dʌm] bnw. stom; spraakloos; stilswyend.

'**dummy** ['dʌmi] s. (dummies) pop; fopspeen.

dump ['dʌmp] ww. (-ed) neergooi, aflaai; damp; rommelstort; -**lorry** s. stortvragmotor.

'**dumpling** ['dʌmpling] s. (-s) kluitjie.

'**dumps** ['dʌmps] s. bedruktheid, naarheid.

'**dun** ['dʌn] bnw. vaalbruin, donker-bruin.

'**dunce** ['dʌns] s. (-s) domkop, stommerik.

'**dunderhead** ['dʌndəhed] s. dom-kop, uilskuiken.

'**dung** ['dʌng] s. mis.

'**dungeon** ['dʌndzjən] s. (-s) tronk, kerker.

dupe ['djôëp] s. (-s) slagoffer, dupe.

'**duplicate** ['djôëplikyt] ww. (-d) dupliseer, in tweevoud vervaardig; s. (-s) duplikaat.

du'ration [djoe'rysjən] s. duur, voortduring.

dusk ['dʌsk] s. skemer.

'**dust** ['dʌst] s. stof; ww. (-ed) bite the - in die stof byt; stuif; -**ing** **powder** s. stuifpoeier.

Dutch ['dʌtsj] s. Hollands, Neder-lands.

'**duty** ['djôëti] s. (duties) plig; diens; belasting; reg(te).

'**dux** ['dʌks] s. (duces) eerste, primus.

dwarf ['dwôf] s. (-s) dwerg.

dwell ['dwel] ww. (dwelt) woon, bly; -ing s. huis.

'**dwindle** ['dwindl] ww. (-d) kleiner word.

dye ['dai] s. (-s) kleurstof.

'**dynasty** ['dinəsti] s. ('dynasties) dinastie, vorstehuis.

dys'pepsia [dis'pepsiə] s. slegte spysvertering.

E

ESCOM ['eskəm] s. (Electricity Supply Commission) EVKOM (Elek-trisiteitvoorsieningskommissie).

each ['itsj] *bnw.* elke, iedere; *vnw.* elk, elkeen, iedereen, stuk.

'eager ['ighə] *bnw.* gretig, begerig; ywerig, vurig.

'eagle ['ighl] *s.* (-s) arend, adelaar.

ear ['iə] *s.* (-s) oor, gehoor; aar, saad, kop.

'earl ['ɔl] *s.* (-s) graaf.

'early ['ɔli] *bw.* ('earlier, 'earliest) vroeg, vroeë.

earn ['ɔn] *ww.* (-ed) verdien; verwerf.

'earnest ['ɔnist] *s.* erns; *bnw.* ernstig; ywerig.

earth ['ɔth] *s.* grond, aarde; gat, hol; grondsluiting; *ww.* (-ed) aard; -en *bnw.* erde-; -cable (strap) *s.* aardkabel.

'earwig ['iəwigh] *s.* (-s) oorkruiper.

'ease ['iz] *s.* gemak, rus, verligting; *ww.* (-d) verlig, stil; skietgee; gerusstel; easy *bnw.* & *bw.* maklik, gerus.

'easel ['izl] *s.* (-s) esel.

east ['ist] *s.* oos(te); *bnw.* & *bw.* oostelik.

'Easter ['istə] *a.* Pase.

eat ['it] *ww.* (ate, eaten) eet; -able *bnw.* eetbaar; -ables *s.* eetgoed.

'eave ['iv] *s.* (-s) dakrand, dakdrup, geut; -sdrop *ww.* (-ped) afluister.

ebb ['eb] *s.* eb.

'ebony ['ebəni] *s.* ebbehout.

ec'centric [ik'sentrik] *bnw.* eksentries, sonderling, snaaks.

'echo ['ekou] *s.* (-es) weerkaatsing, weerklank, eggo.

e'clipse [i'klips] *s.* (-s) verduistering, eklips.

eco'nomic [ikə'nomik] *bnw.* ekonomies; -s *s.* ekonomie; **e'conomize** *ww.* (-d) besuinig, bespaar; **e'conomy** *s.* ekonomie; besuiniging.

'ecstasy ['ekstəsi] *s.* vervoering, ekstase.

'eddy ['edi] *s.* ('eddies) maling, warreling, kolkie.

'edge ['edzj] *s.* (-s) snee; skerpte; kant; 'edging *s.* rand, soom.

'edict ['idikt] *s.* (-s) edik, bevel, verordening.

'edifice ['edifis] *s.* (-s) gebou, gestig.

'edify ['edifai] *ww.* ('edified) stig; edifi'cation *s.* stigting.

'edit ['edit] *ww.* (-ed) redigeer, persklaar maak; **e'dition** *s.* (-s) druk, edisie; -or *s.* (-s) redakteur.

'educable ['edjoekəbl] *bnw.* opvoedbaar.

'educate ['edjoekyt] *ww.* (-d) opvoed, oplei.

edu'cation [edjoe'kysjən] *s.* opvoeding.

'eel ['il] *s.* (-s) paling.

ef'face [i'fys] *ww.* (-d) uitwis; in die skadu stel.

ef'fect [i'fekt] *s.* (-s) uitwerking, gevolg; effek; indruk; *ww.* (-ed) bewerk, bewerkstellig, uitvoer, verwesenlik.

ef'feminate [i'feminyt] *bnw.* verwyf.

effer'vesce [efə'ves] *ww.* (-d) bruis, opbruis.

effer'vescence [efə'vesns] *s.* opbruising.

effi'cacious [efi'kysjəs] *bnw.* werksaam, doeltreffend, kragtig.

ef'ficient [i'fisjənt] *bnw.* doeltreffend; bekwaam; **ef'ficiency** *s.* rendement.

'effigy ['efidzji] *s.* ('effigies) beeld, beeltenis, afbeeldsel.

'effort ['efət] *s.* (-s) poging, kragsinspanning.

ef'fusion [i'fjoëzjən] *s.* uitstorting; ontboeseming.

egg ['egh] *s.* (-s) eier; *ww.* (-ed) - on aanhits.

'ego ['eghou] *s.* (-s) ego, ek.

'egress ['ighres] *s.* (-es) uitgang.

'eiderdown ['aidədaun] *s.* dons, donskombers.

eight ['yt] *s.* agt; -een *s.* agtien; -y *s.* tagtig.

'either ['aidhə] *bnw.* albei, een van beide(twee); *vnw.* albei, enigeen van twee; *bw.* & *voegw.* of.

e'jaculate [i'dzjækjoelyt] *ww.* (-d) uitroep; uitspuit.

e'ject [i'dzjekt] *ww.* (-ed) uitwerp; uitsklet.

'eke ['ik] *ww.* & *bw.* (-d) - out aanvul, vermeerder.

e'laborate [i'læbəryt] *bnw.* uitvoerig; fyn afgewerk.

e'lapse [i'læps] *ww.* (-d) verstryk; verloop.

e'lation [i'lysjən] *s.* opgewektheid, verrukking.

'elbow ['elbou] *s.* (-s) elmboog; bog, kromming.

'elder ['eldə] *bnw.* ouer, *vgl.* old; *s.* ouderling; vlierboom.

'elderly ['eldəli] *bnw.* bejaard.

e'lect [i'lekt] *ww.* (-ed) kies, verkies; -ion *s.* verkiesing.

e'lectric [i'lektrik] *bnw.* elektries; elec'tricity *s.* elektrisiteit.

e'lectrocute [i'lektrəkjoët] *ww.* (-d) dood raak deur elektrisiteit.

'elegance ['elighəns] *s.* elegansie, swier, smaak; **'elegant** *bnw.* sierlik, bevallig, swierig.

'element ['elimənt] *s.* (-s) element, bestanddeel; ele'mentary *bnw.* elementêr, aanvanklik, aanvangs-.

'elements ['elimənts] *s.* beginsels.

'elephant ['elifənt] *s.* (-s) olifant.

'elevate ['elivyt] *ww.* (-d) oplig, ophef; verbef; veredel.

'elevator ['elivytə] *s.* (-s) hyser, hysbak.

e'leven [i'levn] *s.* elf.

elf ['elf] *s.* (elves) elf, kabouter, dwerg.

e'licit [i'lisit] *ww.* (-ed) uittrek, ontlok.

'eligible ['elidzjəbl] *bnw.* verkiesbaar; paslik; verkieslik; geskik, aanneembaar.

e'liminate [i'liminyt] *ww.* (-d) uitskakel; wegwerk; elimineer.

ell ['el] *s.* (-s) el.

'elongate ['ilong'ghyt] *ww.* (-d)
verleng, rek.

e'lope [i'loup] *ww.* (-d) wegloop.

'eloquence ['eloukwəns] *s.* welsprekendheid; 'eloquent *bnw.* welsprekend; veelseggend.

'else ['els] *bw.* anders, nog.

'else'where ['els'wêə] *bw.* elders.

e'lucidate [i'lōēsidyt] *ww.* (-d)
ophelder, toelig.

e'lude [i'lōēd] *ww.* (-d) ontwyk;
ontsnap.

e'maciated [i'mysiytəd] *bnw.* vermaer, uitteer.

'emanate ['emənyt] *ww.* (-d) uitstraal, uitvloei.

e'mancipate [i'mænsipyt] *ww.* (-d)
vrystel, vrylaat, bevry.

em'balm [im'bām] *ww.* (-ed) balsem.

em'bank [im'bænk] *ww.* (-ed) indyk;
afdam; -ment *s.* dyk, wal.

em'bargo [em'bāghou] *s.* (-s) beslag,
embargo.

em'bark [im'bāk] *ww.* (-ed) inskeep;
embar'kation *s.* inskeping.

em'barrass [im'bærəs] *ww.* (-ed)
belas, hinder; verleë maak.

'embassy ['embəsi] *s.* ('embassies)
gesantskap; ambassade.

em'bellish [im'belisj] *ww.* (-ed)
verfraai, opsier.

'ember ['embə] *s.* (-s) as, kole.

em'bezzle [im'bezl] *ww.* (-d) verduister, ontvreem.

'emblem ['embləm] *s.* (-s) sinnebeeld, embleem.

'embolism ['embəlizəm] *s.* (-s)
verstopping (bloedvate), embolie.

em'boss [im'bos] *ww.* (-ed) embosseer.

em'brace [im'brys] *ww.* (-d) omhels,
omvat, insluit.

em'broider [im'broidə] *ww.* (-ed)
borduur; -y *s.* borduursel, borduurwerk.

em'broidery [im'broidəri] *s.* ('broideries) borduurwerk.

em'broil [im'broil] *ww.* (-ed) stryd
veroorsaak.

'embryo ['embriou] *s.* (-s) vrugkiem,
embrio.

e'merge [i'mədzj] *ww.* (-d) vorendag
kom, blyk; e'mergency *s.* nood,
noodgeval.

e'mergency [i'mədzjənsi] *s.* (e'mergencies) nood, noodgeval; - brake *s.*
noodrem; - door *s.* nooddeur;
- escape hatch *s.* noodluik; - exit *s.*
nooduitgang; emergency - *voorv.*
nood-.

'emery ['eməri] *s.* amaril, poleersteen; *ww.* ('emeried) met amaril
poleer.

e'metic [i'metik] *s.* (-s) braakmiddel, vomitief.

'emigrate ['emighryt] *ww.* (-d)
emigreer.

'eminence ['eminəns] *s.* (-s) hoogte;
hoogheid, eminensie.

'eminent ['eminənt] *bnw.* hoog,
verhewe; uitstekend.

'emissary ['emisəri] *s.* ('emissaries)
afgesant; handlanger.

e'mit [i'mit] *ww.* (-ted) uitgee;
uitstraal, afgee.

e'moluments [i'moljoemənts] *s.*
besoldiging.

e'motion [i'mousjən] *s.* (-s) aandoening, emosie.

'emphasis ['emfəsis] *s.* nadruk;
klemtoon; em'phatic *bnw.* nadruklik.

em'ploy [im'ploi] *ww.* (-ed) in diens
hê (neem); aanwend.

'empty ['empti] *bnw.* leeg; hol;
ww. ('emptied) ledig.

'emulate ['emjoelyt] *ww.* (-d)
nastreef; ewenaar.

en'able [i'nybl] *ww.* (-d) in staat stel,
help.

en'act [i'nækt] *ww.* (-ed) verorden;
opvoer.

e'namel [i'næml] *s.* erd, emalje; *ww.*
(-led) vererd, emaljeer.

en'case [in'kys] *ww.* (-d) toemaak,
inwikkel, oortrek.

en'chant [in'tsjānt] *ww.* bekoor;
toor; -ment *s.* bekoring.

en'core [ong'kô] *uitroep.* weer! nog
'n keer!

en'counter [in'kauntə] *ww.* (-ed)
tref, teenkom; slaags raak.

en'courage [in'kʌridzj] *ww.* (-d)
aanmoedig, aanspoor.

en'croach [in'kroutsj] *ww.* (-ed)
inbreuk maak op, indring.

en'cumbrance [in'kʌmbrəns] *s.* (-s)
hindernis, las.

en'cyclical [en'siklikəl] *bnw.* rondgaande, omgaande.

end ['end] *s.* (-s) end, eind, eindpunt;
doel; stompie; *ww.* (-ed) beëindig,
ophou.

en'dear [in'diə] *ww.* (-ed) bemind
maak; -ment *s.* gehegtheid; liefkosing.

en'deavour [in'devə] *ww.* (-ed) streef,
trag, poog.

'endive ['endiv] *s.* andyvie.

en'dorse [in'dôs] *ww.* (-d) endosseer, rugteken; onderskryf;
-ment *s.* endossering; -r *s.* endossant.

en'dow [in'dau] *ww.* (-ed) skenk,
begiftig; -ment *s.* begiftiging, legaat.

en'dure [in'dzjoeə] *ww.* (-d) verdra;
uithou; en'durance *s.* uithouding,
uithouvermoë; verdraagsaamheid,
geduld, gelatenheid; endurance test
s. uithoutoets.

'enema ['enəmə] *s.* (-s) lawement,
spuitmiddel in endelderm, klisma.

'enemy ['enimi] *s.* ('enemies) vyand.

'energy ['enədzji] *s.* energie; krag;
ywer.

en'gage [in'ghydzj] *ww.* (-d) verbind;
verpand; verloof; huur; bespreek;
beset; slaags raak.

'engine ['endzjin] *s.* (-s) masjien,
motor.

engi'neer [endzji'niə] *s.* (-s) ingenieur.

'English ['ing-ghlisj] s. Engels.

en'grave [in'ghryv] s. (-d) graveer; inprent.

en'hance [in'häns] ww. (-d) verhoog, vermeerder.

e'nigma [i'nighmə] s. (-s) raaisel, enigma; enig'matic bnw. duister.

en'joy [in'dzjoi] ww. (-ed) geniet, hou van.

en'list [in'list] ww. (-ed) aanwerf; aansluit.

'enmity ['enmiti] s. vyandigheid.

en'nui [ā'nwi] s. verveling.

e'normous [i'nôməs] bnw. ontsaglik, enorm; ontsettend.

e'nough [i'nʌf] s., bnw. & bw. genoeg, voldoende.

en'quire [in'kwaiə] ww. (-d) vra, navra; vgl. **inquire**.

en'rich [en'ritsj] ww. (-ed) ryker maak (word), verryk; -er s. verryker.

en'rol [in'roul] ww. (-led) inskryf; aansluit.

'ensign ['ensain] s. (-s) teken, vlag, vaandel; vaandrig.

en'sue [in'sjôe] ww. (-d) volg, voortvloei.

en'sure [in'sjoeə] ww. (-d) verseker bewerk; besorg.

en'tail [in'tyl] ww. (-ed) meebring, noodsaak; vassit.

en'tangle [in'tæng-ghl] ww. (-d) verstrik, verwar, verwikkel.

en'tente [an'tänt] s. verbond; - cordiale [kor'diäl] s. minsame (hoflike) verhouding tussen regerings.

'enter ['entə] ww. (-ed) binnegaan; binnedring; inskryf; boek.

ente'ritis [entə'raitis] s. dermontsteking.

'enterprise ['entəpraiz] s. (-s) onderneming; ondernemingsgees.

enter'tain [entə'tyn] ww. (-ed) onderhou; onthaal; oorweeg; koester; -ment s. ontvangs; vermaak.

enthusi'asm [inthôězi'æzəm] s. geesdrif, ywer.

en'tice [in'tais] ww. (-d) verlok, verlei.

en'tire [in'taiə] bnw. heel, totaal, volledig; onbeskadig; -ly bw. heeltemal.

en'title [in'taitl] ww. (-d) betitel; - to reg gee op.

'entity ['entiti] s. ('entities) wese, bestaan, entiteit.

ento'mology [entə'molədzji] s. insektekunde.

'entrails ['entrylz] s. ingewande, harslag.

en'trammel [in'træməl] ww. (-led) hinder, belemmer.

'entrance ['entrəns] s. (-s) ingang; binnekoms; aanvaarding; toegang.

en'treat [in'trit] ww. (-ed) smeek, soebat; bejëen.

en'trench [in'trentsj] ww. (-ed) verskans.

en'trust [in'trʌst] ww. (-ed) toevertrou; opdra.

'entry ['entri] s. ('entries) binnekoms, intog; ingang, toegang, inlaat; aanvaarding; boeking, inskrywing, pos.

e'numerate [i'njôěməryt] ww. (-d) opsom, tel.

e'nunciate [i'nʌnsiyt] ww. (-d) uitspreek; verkondig.

en'velop [ən'veləp] ww. (-ed) inwikkel, omhul.

'envelope ['enviloup] s. (-s) koevert, omslag.

en'vironment [in'vaiənmənt] s. (-s) omgewing, milieu.

en'visage [in'vizidzj] ww. (-d) bəskou; onder die oë sien; voor die gees roep.

'envoy ['envoi] s. (-s) gesant.

'envy ['envi] s. jaloesie, afguns, nyd; ww. ('envied) beny; 'envious bnw. jaloers, afgunstig.

e'phemeral [i'femərəl] bnw. eendaags, verbygaande.

'epicure ['epikjoeə] s. (-s) lekkerbek, genotsoeker.

epi'demic [epi'demik] s. (-s) epidemie.

'epilepsy ['epilepsi] s. vallende siekte, epilepsie.

'episode ['episoud] s. (-s) episode, voorval.

e'pistle [i'pisl] s. (-s) epistel, brief.

'epitaph ['epitäf] s. (-s) grafskrif.

'epithet ['epithet] s. (-s) epitheton; bynaam.

'epoch ['ipok] s. (-s) tydstip, tydvak.

'equal ['ikwəl] bnw. gelyk (waardig); s. (-s) gelyke, weerga; ww. (-led) gelyk wees aan; ewenaar; -ize ww. (-d) ewenaar, gelykstel, effen; -izer s. effenaar; e'quality s. gelykheid, gelykwaardigheid.

e'quate [i'kwyt] ww. (-d) gelykstel; gelykmaking; equation s. (-s) gelykstelling; vergelyking (wisk).

e'quator [i'kwytə] s. ewenaar; middellyn; ekwator.

'equerry [i'kweri] s. ('equerries) stalmeester.

'equi- ['ikwi-] voors. gelyk-, ewe-; -distant bnw. ewe ver; -lateral bnw. gelyksydig; -librium s. ewewig; -valence s. gelykwaardigheid.

'equinox ['ikwinoks] s. (-es) nagewening.

e'quip [i'kwip] ww. (-ped) toerus, uitrus; beman.

'equitable ['ekwitəbl] bnw. billik, onpartydig.

'equity ['ekwiti] s. billikheid.

e'quivalent [i'kwivələnt] bnw. gelykwaardig, ekwiwalent.

'era ['iərə] s. (-s) tydperk; jaartelling.

e'radicate [i'rædikyt] ww. (-d) ontwortel, uitroei, vernietig.

e'rase [i'ryz] ww. (-d) uitwis, uitvee; -r s. wisser.

'ere ['eə] voegw. eer (dat), voor (dat); voors. voor.

e'**rect** [i'rekt] *bnw.* regop, penorent;
ww. (-ed) oprig; stig; opwerp.

'**ermine** [''ɜmin] *s.* hermelyn.

e'**rosion** [i'rouʒən] *s.* wegvreting;
verwering; erosie.

e'**rotic** [i'rotik] *bnw.* eroties, liefde.

err ['ɜ] *ww.* (-ed) sondig, dwaal, jou
vergis.

'**errand** ['erənd] *s.* (-s) boodskap;
opdrag; doel.

'**errant** ['erənt] *bnw.* dwalend.

er'**ratic** [i'rætik] *bnw.* onseker,
wisselend.

er'**roneous** [i'rounjəs] *bnw.* verkeerd, foutief.

'**error** ['erə] *s.* (-s) fout, vergissing;
dwaling; vergryp.

'**erudite** ['eroedait] *bnw.* geleerd,
belese.

e'**rupt** [i'rʌpt] *ww.* (-ed) uitbars,
deurbreek; -ion *s.* (-s) uitbarsting,
deurbraak; e'**ruptive** *bnw.* uitbar-
stend.

'**escalator** ['eskəlytə] *s.* (-s) glytrap.

'**escapade** ['eskəpyd] *s.* (-s) kwa-
jongstreek.

es'**cape** [is'kyp] *ww.* (-d) ontvlug,
ontkom, ontsnap.

es'**carpment** [is'kãpmənt] *s.* skuinste, hang; platorand.

es'**cort** [eskõt] *s.* (-s) geleide; *ww.*
(-ed) [is'kõt] begelei.

eso'**teric** [isou'terik] *bnw.* verborge.

espio'**nage** [espiə'nãʒi] *s.* spionasie,
ver(be)spieding.

espla'**nade** [esplə'nyd] *s.* (-s)
wandelplein, esplanade.

e'**spouse** [is'pauz] *ww.* (-d) trou;
uittrou; omhels, voorstaan; e-
'**spousal** *s.* verlowing; bruilof; omhelsing.

'**essay** ['esy] *s.* (-s) opstel; poging;
ww. (-ed) toets, probeer; -**er** *s.*
keurder, essaieur.

'**essence** ['esns] *s.* (-s) wese, kern;
essens; geur, geursel; es'**sential** *bnw.*
wesenlik; noodsaaklik; essensieel.

es'**tablish** [is'tæblisj] *ww.* (-ed)
vestig; stig; insiel; staaf; -**ment** *s.*
(-s) stigting; nedersetting; inrigting;
stawing.

es'**tate** [is'tyt] *s.* (-s) rang; boedel;
besit; toestand; landgoed.

es'**teem** [is'tim] *ww.* (-ed) skat;
waardeer.

'**estimate** ['estimyt] *ww.* (-d) skat,
raam, waardeer; *s.* (-s) skatting,
waardering; raming; esti'**mation** *s.*
mening; waardering; raming.

e'**strange** [i'stryndʒi] *ww.* (-d)
vervreem; -**ment** *s.* vervreemding.

'**estuary** ['estjoeəri] *s.* ('estuaries)
mond(ing).

'**etch** [etsj] *ww.* (-ed) ets! *s.* -ing ets.

e'**ternal** [i'tɜnl] *bnw.* ewig, ewigdurend; '**eternity** *s.* ewigheid.

'**ether** ['iθə] *s.* eter; lugruim; -**eal**
(ə'thiəriəl] *bnw.* eteries; vlugtig;
hemels.

'**ethics** ['ethiks] *s.* sedeleer, etiek.

'**etiquette** [eti'ket] *s.* etiket, wel-
lewenheidsvorme.

euca'**lyptus** [joekə'liptəs] *s.* (-es)
bloekomboom.

'**eulogy** ['jõĕlədʒji] *s.* lofspraak;
ophemeling.

'**euphemize** ['jõĕfimaiz] *ww.* (-d)
verbloem, versag.

'**euphony** ['jõĕfəni] *s.* welluidendheid.

'**Europe** ['joeərəp] *s.* Europa;
Euro'pean *s.* europeaan.

e'**vacuate** [i'vækjoeyt] *ww.* (-d)
ontruim; leegmaak.

e'**vade** [i'vyd] *ww.* (-d) ontwyk;
ontduik; ontsnap.

e'**valuate** [i'væljoeyt] *ww.* (-d)
bereken, besyfer.

evan'**gelic** [ivæn'dʒjelik] *bnw.* evan-
gelies; Luthers; e'**vangelist** *s.* evan-
gelis.

e'**vaporate** [i'væpəryt] *ww.* (-d)
verdamp, verkook; vervlieg.

e'**vasion** [i'vyʒən] *s.* ontwyking,
uitvlug; e'**vasive** *bnw.* ontwykend.

'**eve** ['iv] *s.* aand; vooraand; -**n** *s.*
aand; -**ning** *s.* aand.

'**even** ['ivən] *bnw.* gelyk; eenvormig;
glad; plag; ewe; *bw.* selfs; *ww.* (-ed)
gelykmaak; effen.

e'**vent** [i'vent] *s.* (-s) gebeurtenis,
voorval; geval; wedstryd; -**ual** *bnw.*
moontlik, gebeurlik.

'**ever** ['evə] *bw.* altyd, immer, ewig,
ooit, weleens; -**green** *bnw.* immer-
groen; -'**lasting** *bnw.* ewigdurend.

'**every** ['evri] *bnw.* elke, iedere; -**body**
vnw. iedereen, elkeen; -**day** *bw.*
aldag, daeliks; -**one** *vnw.* iedereen,
alger; -**thing** *vnw.* alles; -**where** *bw.*
orals.

e'**vict** [i'vikt] *ww.* (-ed) uitsit,
(geregtelik).

'**evidence** ['evidəns] *s.* getuienis,
bewys; blyke; '**evident** *bnw.* duidelik; blykbaar.

'**evil** ['ivl] *bnw.* sleg, kwaad, boos;
bw. sleg; *s.* (-s) kwaad, euwel;
onheil; sonde.

e'**vince** [i'vins] *ww.* (-d) openbaar;
aantoon.

e'**voke** [i'vouk] *ww.* (-d) oproep;
uitlok; voor hoër hof daag.

evo'**lution** [ivə'lõĕsjən] *s.* ontwikkeling; evolusie.

e'**volve** [i'volv] *ww.* (-d) ontvou;
aflei.

'**ewe** ['jõĕ] *s.* ooi.

'**ewer** ['joeə] *s.* (-s) lampetbeker,
waterbeker.

ex- ['eks-] *voorvoegsel.* eks-, gewese.

ex'**acerbate** [eks'ysəbyt] *ww.* (-d)
verskerp.

ex'**act** [igh'zækt] *bnw.* (-er, -est)
noukeurig, presies, juis; akkuraat;
-**ly** *bw.* juis, presies.

ex'**aggerate** [igh'zædzjəryt] *ww.* (-d)
vergroot, oordrywe.

ex'**alt** [igh'zõlt] *ww.* (-ed) verhef;
verheerlik; verdiep; exal'**tation** *s.*
vervoering; verheffing; verdieping.

ex'amine [igh'zæmin] *ww.* (-d)
ondersoek; verhoor; ondervra; ek-
samineer; **ex'aminer** *s.* eksaminator,
ondersoeker; **examin'ation** *s.* (-s)
eksamen; ondersoek.

ex'ample [igh'zāmpl] *s.* (-s) voorbeeld; model; eksemplaar; monster.

ex'asperate [igh'zāspəryt] *ww.* (-d)
vererger, terg.

'excavate ['ekskəvyt] *ww.* (-d)
uitgrawe, opgrawe.

ex'ceed [ik'sid] *ww.* (-ed) oortref;
oorskry; oordryf; **-ingly** *bw.* uiter-
mate.

ex'cel [ik'sel] *ww.* (-led) oortref;
uitblink; **'excellence** *s.* uitmuntend-
heid; **'excellent** *bnw.* uitstekend.

ex'cept [ik'sept] *ww.* (-ed) uitsluit,
uitsonder; *voors* behalwe, uitgenome;
voegw. tensy; **-ion** *s.* uitsondering,
teenwerping.

'excerpt ['eksəpt] *s.* (-s) uittreksel,
ekserp.

ex'cess [ik'ses] *s.* (-es) oormaat;
oorskot; *vgl.* **exceed**; **- payment** *s.*
bybetaling.

ex'change [iks'tsjyndzj] *s.* (-s)
ruiling; wisseling; sentrale; beurs;
ww. (-d) ruil, wissel.

ex'chequer [iks'tsjekə] *s.* (-s) skatkis,
tesourie.

'excise ['eksaiz] *s.* aksyns.

ex'cite [ik'sait] *ww.* (-d) opwind,
prikkel; **-d** *bnw.* opgewonde; **-ment**
s. opwinding, spanning; **ex'citant** *s.*
prikkelmiddel, opwekker.

ex'claim [iks'klym] *ww.* (-ed) uitroep;
excla'mation *s.* (-s) uitroep, kreet.

ex'clude [iks'klōēd] *ww.* (-d) uitsluit.

'excrement ['ekskrimənt] *s.* (-s)
uitwerpsel.

ex'crete [eks'krit] *ww.* (-d) uitwerp,
afskei.

ex'cruciate [iks'krōēsjiyt] *ww.* (-d)
pynig, martel.

ex'cruciating [iks'krōēsjiyting] *bnw.*
pynigend.

ex'cursion [iks'kəsjən] *s.* uitstappie; ekskursie; vakansiekaartjie.

ex'cuse [iks'kjōēz] *ww.* (-d) verontskuldig, verskoon, ekskuseer;
[iks'kjōēs] *s.* (-s) ekskuus, verskoning.

'execute ['eksikjōēt] *ww.* (-d)
uitvoer, voltrek; **exe'cution** *s.* vol-
trekking, uitvoering; teregstelling;
ex'ecutive *bnw.* uitvoerend.

ex'emplary [igh'zempləri] *bnw.*
voorbeeldig.

ex'empt [igh'zempt] *ww.* (-ed)
vrystel, onthef, verskoon; **-ion** *s.*
vrystelling.

'exercise ['eksəsaiz] *s.* (-s) oefening;
opgawe; *ww.* (-d) oefen.

ex'ert [igh'zət] *ww.* (-ed) aanwend, te
pas bring.

ex'hale [eks'hyl] *ww.* (-d) uitasem,
uitdamp.

ex'haust [igh'zōst] *ww.* (-ed) uitput,
leegmaak, gedaan maak; *s.* uitlaat-
pyp (motor); **- valve** *s.* (-s) uitlaat-

klep; **- gas** *s.* uitlaatgas; **-ed** *bnw.*
(more -, most -) uitgeput; **-ion** *s.*
uitputting.

ex'hibit [igh'zibit] *ww.* (-ed) vertoon,
uitstal; **exhi'bition** *s.* (-s) uitstalling;
ingediende bewysstuk.

ex'hilarate [igh'ziləryt] *ww.* (-d)
opvrolik, verfris.

ex'hort [igh'zōt] *ww.* (-ed) vermaan,
waarsku; bepleit; **exhor'tation** *s.*
vermaning; preek.

ex'hume [eks'hjōēm] *ww.* (-d)
opgrawe.

'exigence ['eksidzjəns] *s.* behoefte,
nood, noodgeval; **'exigent** *bnw.*
dringend.

'erile ['eksail] *s.* (-s) verbanning;
banneling; *ww.* (-d) verban.

e'xist [igh'zist] *ww.* (-ed) bestaan;
-ence *s.* bestaan; **-ent** *bnw.* be-
staande.

'exit ['eksit] *s.* (-s) uitgang; dood.

'exodus ['eksədəs] *s.* uittog, eksodus.

ex'onerate [igh'zonəryt] *ww.* (-d)
suiwer; vrypleit; onthef.

ex'orbitant [igh'zōbitənt] *bnw.*
buitensporig.

'exorcise ['eksōsaiz] *ww.* (-d)
besweer, uitdryf, ban.

ex'otic [egh'zotik] *bnw.* uitheems,
vreemd.

ex'pand [iks'pænd] *ww.* (-ed) uitbrei,
uitsit, swel; **ex'panse** *s.* uitgestrektheid; **ex'pansion** *s.* uitbreiding,
toename.

ex'patriate [eks'pætriyt] *ww.* (-d)
verban, uitsit.

ex'pect [iks'pekt] *ww.* (-ed) verwag;
vermoed; **-ance** *s.* verwagting,
vooruitsig; **-ant** *bnw.* verwagtend;
expec'tation *s.* (-s) verwagting,
hoop.

ex'pectorate [eks'pektəryt] *ww.* (-d)
spoeg.

ex'pedience [iks'pidiəns] *s.* dienstig-
heid; gerief; raadsaamheid; **ex-
'pedient** *bnw.* gerieflik, wenslik,
raadsaam.

'expedite ['ekspidait] *ww.* (-d)
bevorder, bespoedig; **expe'dition** *s.*
(-s) bevordering; vesending; ek-
spedisie.

ex'pel [iks'pel] *ww.* (-led) wegja,
verban, vitdryf.

ex'pend [iks'pend] *ww.* (-ed) bestee,
uitgee; verbruik; **-iture** *s.* uitgawe,
koste; **ex'pense** *s.* uitgawe, koste;
ex'pensive *bnw.* duur, kosbaar.

ex'perience [iks'piəriəns] *s.* (-s)
ondervinding, ervaring; bevinding;
ww. (-d) ondervind, ervaar, belewe.

ex'periment [iks'perimənt] *s.* (-s)
eksperiment; *ww.* (-ed) proewe
neem; **-al** *bnw.* proefondervindelik.

'expert [eks'pət] *bnw.* bedrewe; *s.*
(-s) deskundige.

'expiate ['ekspiyt] *ww.* (-d) boet,
vergoeding doen; **expi'ation** *s.* versoening.

ex'pire [iks'paiə] *ww.* (-d) uitasem;
sterf; verstryk; **expi'ration** *s.* uit-

aseming; dood; verval; **expi'ratory** *bnw.* uitasemend.

ex'plain [iks'plyn] *ww.* (-ed) verduidelik, verklaar; **expla'nation** *s.* (-s) verklaring, uitleg; **ex'planatory** *bnw.* verklarend.

ex'pletive [iks'plitiv] *s.* (-s) kragwoord.

ex'plicit [iks'plisit] *bnw.* uitdruklik, duidelik.

ex'plode [iks'ploud] *ww.* (-d) ontplof, spring; laat ontplof; **ex'plosion** *s.* (-s) ontploffing, uitbarsting; **ex'plosive** *s.* springstof.

'exploit ['eksploit] *s.* (-s) prestasie; *ww.* (-ed) ontgin; **exploi'tation** *s.* ontginning.

ex'plore [iks'plô] *ww.* (-d) ondersoek, navors; **-r** *s.* (-s) ontdekker, vorser; **explo'ration** *s.* ondersoeking, navorsing.

'exponent [eks'pounənt] *s.* (-s) vertolker, verklaarder; beliggaming; eksponent.

ex'port [iks'pôt] *ww.* (-ed) uitvoer; *s.* ['ekspôt] uitvoer.

ex'pose [iks'pouz] *ww.* (-d) openbaar, blootlê, ontbloot; **ex'posure** *s.* blootstelling.

ex'postulate [iks'postjoelyt] *ww.* (-d) protesteer; vermaan.

ex'pound [iks'paund] *ww.* (-ed) uiteensit, verklaar, vertolk.

ex'press [iks'pres] *bnw.* uitdruklik; presies; ekspres; *s.* (-es) sneltrein; *ww.* (-ed) uitdruk, vertolk, betuig; **-ion** *s.* uitdrukking; gesegde; **-ive** *bnw.* veelseggend, beeldend; **-ly** *bw.* met opset, nadruklik; **- way** *s.* snelpad, snelweg.

ex'propriate [eks'prouprlyt] *ww.* (-d) onteien.

ex'pulsion [iks'pʌlsjən] *s.* (-s) verbanning, uitdrywing.

ex'punge [eks'pʌndzj] *ww.* (-d) skrap, uitvee, weglaat.

'exquisite ['ekskwizit] *bnw.* uitgesog, uitgelese, keurig.

ex'tant [eks'tænt] *bnw.* voorhande.

ex'tempore [eks'tempəri] *bnw.* onvoorberei.

ex'tend [iks'tend] *ww.* (-ed) uitsteek, uitbrei, verleng, toeroep; **ex'tension** *s.* uitbreiding, verlenging; **ex'tensive** *bnw.* uitgebreid, omvattend; **ex'tent** *s.* omvang.

ex'tenuate [eks'tenjoeyt] *ww.* (-d) versag, vergoelik.

ex'terior [eks'tiəriə] *bnw.* buitenste, van buite; *s.* (-s) buitekant, uiterlike.

ex'terminate [eks'tôminyt] *ww.* (-d) verdelg.

ex'ternal [eks'tônl] *bnw.* buitekantse, buitentste; uiterlik, ekstern.

ex'tinct [iks'tinkt] *bnw.* uitgedoof; uitgesterf.

ex'tinguish [iks'ting'ghwisj] *ww.* (-ed) blus; vernietig; delg.

'extirpate ['ekstôpyt] *ww.* (-d) uitroei, uitdelg.

ex'tol [iks'toul] *ww.* (-led) loof, verheerlik, ophemel.

ex'tort [iks'tôt] *ww.* (-ed) afpers, afdwing; **-ion** *s.* afpersing; **-ionate** *bnw.* dwang-.

'extra ['ekstrə] *bnw.* ekstra; buitengewoon; *s.* (-s) ekstra; toegif; **-dite** *ww.* (-d) uitlewer.

'extract ['ekstrækt] *s.* (-s) ekstrak, aftreksel; uittreksel; *ww.* (-ed) uittrek; aftreksel maak; uithaal; afiei; **-ion** *s.* uittrekking; herkoms.

ex'traneous [eks'trynjəs] *bnw.* buitengewoon, sonderling, snaaks, vreemd(e).

ex'traordinary [iks'trôdnri] *bnw.* buitengewoon; sonderling.

ex'travagance [iks'trævighəns] *s.* oordaad, verkwisting; **ex'travagant** *bnw.* oordadig.

ex'treme [iks'trim] *bnw.* uiterste, verste; *s.* (-s) uiterste; **-ly** *bw.* uiters; **ex'tremity** *s.* uiteinde, uiterste.

ex'tremist [iks'trimist] *s.* (-s) ekstremis, jingo.

'extricate ['ekstrikyt] *ww.* (-d) ontwar; verlos, red.

ex'uberant [igh'zjôëbərənt] *bnw.* weelderig; uitgelate.

ex'ude [igh'zjôëd] *ww.* (-d) uitsweet.

ex'ult [igh'zʌlt] *ww.* (-ed) jubel, juig; **-ant** *bnw.* jubelend; **exul'tation** *s.* jubeling, gejuig.

'eye ['ai] *s.* (-s) oog; *ww.* (-ed) aanskou; dophou; **-bath** *s.* oogbadjie **-dropper** *s.* oogdrupper; **-brow** *s.* (-s) winkbrou; **-let** *s.* ogie; **-lash** *s.* (-es) wimpers; **-sore** *s.* doring-in-die-oog; **-shadow** *s.* oogskadu; **-shield** *s.* oogklap, oogskerm; **-wash** *s.* oogspoelmiddel; bog, voorwendsel, twakpraatjies; **-witness** *s.* ooggetuie.

'eyetooth ['aitôëth] *s.* (-teeth) oogtand.

'eyewash ['aiwôsj] *s.* oogwater; bog.

F

'fable ['fybl] *s.* (-s) fabel, sprokie; versinsel; verhaal; **'fabulous** *bnw.* legendareis, dwaas, ongehoord.

'fabric ['fæbrik] *s.* (-s) weefsel, stof, fabrikaat, struktuur; **-ate** *ww.* (-d) vervaardig, weef; versin; fabriseer; **fabri'cation** *s.* vervaardiging; versinsel.

fa'cade [fə'sâd] *s.* voorgewel, voorkant, gesig.

'face ['fys] *s.* (-s) gesig; voorkom; voorkant; wyserplaat; *ww.* (-d) in die oë sien; trotseer; aandurf; belê, afset.

'facet ['fæsit] *s.* (-s) vlak; faset.

fa'cetious [fə'sisjəs] *bnw.* grappig, geestig.

'facial ['fysjəl] *bnw.* gesigs-, gelaats-.

'facile ['fæsail] *bnw.* gemaklik; vlot; inskiklik; **fa'cilitate** *ww.* (-d) vergemaklik; **fa'cility** s. vaardigheid, gerief.

fac'simile [fæk'simili] s. reproduksie, nabootsing.

fact ['fækt] s. (-s) feit, daadsaak; daad; **-ual** bnw. feitlik, feite-.

'faction ['fæksjən] s. (-s) party; **'factious** bnw. partysugtig.

fac'titious [fæk'tisjəs] bnw. gekunsteld, nagemaak.

'factor ['fæktə] s. (-s) aanleiding; agent; faktor.

'factory ['fæktəri] s. ('factories) kantoor, fabriek, werkplaas.

fac'totum [fæk'toutəm] s. (-s) handlanger, faktotum.

'faculty ['fækəlti] s. ('faculties) aanleg; vermoë; fakulteit.

fad ['fæd] s. (-s) gier, manie.

'fade ['fyd] ww. (-d) verbleek, verlep, kwyn; dein (etergolf); doof.

'faeces ['fisiz] s. uitwerpsels, ontlasting.

fag ['fægh] ww. (-ged) sloof, swoeg; uitpuit; joggie wees; **-end** s. stompie, oorskot.

'faggot ['fæghət] s. (-s) bondel, bos, drag.

fail ['fyl] ww. (-ed) ontbreek, in gebreke bly, kortkom, verswak, in die steek laat; sak; druip; bankrot speel; s. feil, fout, versuim; weier; **-ing** s. gebrek, swak; **-ure** s. mislukking, versuiming, fout, weiering; breuk.

'fain ['fyn] bw. I was - to ek was verplig.

faint ['fynt] bnw. swak, flou, dof, vaag; benoud; ww. (-ed) beswym, flou word, tou opgooi.

fair ['fɛə] bnw. (-er, -est) mooi, fraai, billik; opreg; bw. mooi, eerlik; beleef; **-ly** bw. heeltemal, taamlik, vrywel.

'fairy ['fɛəri] s. ('fairies) fee; bnw. tower-; **-tale** s. sprokie.

faith ['fyth] s. (-s) geloof, vertroue; trou, erewoord; **-ful** bnw. getrou; **-fully** bw. getrou; **-less** bnw. ontrou.

'fake ['fyk] s. (-s) bedrog, lis; namaaksel, vervalsing; ww. (-d) namaak, vervals.

fall ['fôl] ww. (-s) (fell, fallen) val, daal, sink, stort, sak; s. (-s) val, daling, instorting; helling; waterval; reënval.

'fall out ['fôl-aut] s. rusie, herrie; afsaksel, uitsaksel.

'fallacy ['fæləsi] s. ('fallacies) drogrede; bedrog; **fa'llacious** bnw. misleidend, bedrieglik, vals.

'fallible ['fæləbl] bnw. feilbaar.

'fallow ['fælou] bnw. braak, vaalbruin; ww. (-ed) braak.

'false ['fôls] bnw. (-r, -st) vals, onwaar, oneg, onjuis; **-hood** s. (-s) leuen; **falsifi'cation** s. vervalsing; **'falsify** ww. ('falsified) vervals; **'falsity** s. valsheid.

'falter ['fôltə] ww. (-ed) stamel; weifel; strompel, struikel.

'fame ['fym] s. roem; faam, naam; **'famous** bnw. beroemd.

fa'miliar [fə'miljə] bnw. bekend; gemeensaam; vertroud; gewoon; eie; **-ize** ww. (-d) vertroud maak; **famili'arity** s. (famili'arities) vertroudheid; gemeensaamheid.

'family ['fæmili] s. ('families) gesin, familie; geslag; herkoms.

'famine ['fæmin] s. hongersnood, gebrek.

'famish ['fæmisj] ww. (-ed) verhonger, honger ly.

'famous ['fyməs] bnw. beroemd; uitstekend.

fan ['fæn] s. (-s) waaier; bewonderaar; ww. (-ned) waai, koel waai; aanblaas; wan; **-belt** s. waaierband; **-blade** s. waaierblad, waaierlem.

fa'natic [fə'nætik] bnw. dweepsiek; s. (-s) dweper.

'fancy ['fænsi] ww. ('fancied) verbeel; voorstel; glo; opgedaan wees met; kweek; s. ('fancies) verbeelding; fantasie; gier; neiging; **-free** bnw. nie verlief nie; - goods s. snuisterye; **- price** s. afsetersprys.

'fanfare ['fænfɛə] s. trompetgeskal.

fang ['fæng] s. (-s) slagtand, giftand.

'fantasy ['fæntəsi] s. ('fantasies) fantasie; **fan'tastic** bnw. fantasties.

far ['fâ] bnw. ver, afgeleë; bw. ver, verreweg, baie.

'farce ['fâs] s. (-s) klug; **'farcical** bnw. klugtig.

'fare ['fɛə] s. reisgeld; ete, gereg, kos; ww. (-d) gaan, vaar, voed; -'well uitroep vaarwel.

farm ['fâm] s. (-s) plaas, boerdery; ww. (-ed) boer; -er s. (-s) boer, landbouer; **-ing** s. boerdery.

'farrier ['færiə] s. (-s) hoefsmid.

'farther ['fâdhə] bw. verder, buitendien; cp. **far**.

'farthing ['fâdhing] s. (-s) oortjie.

'fascinate ['fæsinyt] ww. (-d) bekoor, boei, vastrek; **fasci'nation** s. bekoring.

'fashion ['fæsjən] s. (-s) mode; manier; fatsoen; **-able** bnw. modieus.

fast ['fâst] bnw. (-er, -est) vas, stewig; blywend; was-eg; vlug; losbandig; bw. ferm, styf; -en ww. (-ed) vasmaak; **-ener** s. hak, knip; **-back** s. vloeidak (motorvoertuig).

fas'tidious [fæs'tidiəs] bnw. kieskeurig.

fat ['fæt] bnw. (-ter, -test) vet, dik, vrugbaar; s. (-s) vet.

'fatal ['fytl] bnw. dodelik, noodlottig; **fa'tality** s. (fa'talities) ongeluk; fataliteit.

'fate ['fyt] s. (-s) noodlot, lot.

'father ['fâdhə] s. (-s) vader.

'fathom ['fædhəm] s. (-s) vaam; ww. (-ed) deurgrond, omvat; peil.

fa'tigue [fə'tigh] s. vermoeienis, afmatting.

'fatuous ['fætjoeəs] bnw. laf, dwaas, onbenullig.

'faucal ['fôkl] bnw. keel-.

'faucet ['fôsit] s. (-s) kraan.
fault ['fôlt] s. (-s) gebrek; fout;
skuld; breuk; lekplek; -y bnw.
gebrekkig, foutief, verkeerd.
'fauna ['fônə] s. fauna, diereryk.
faux 'pas [fô'pa] s. misstap, onbesonnenheid.
'favour ['fyvə] s. (-s) guns; genade;
plesier; ww. (-ed) begunstig, hou van,
voortrek, steun, bevorder; -able
bnw. gunstig, bevorderlik; -ed bnw.
begunstig, bevoorreg; -ite s. (-s)
gunsteling; -itism s. voortrekkery.
fawn ['fôn] bnw. vaalbruin.
fear ['fiə] s. (-s) vrees, angs; ww.
(-ed) vrees, bang wees; -ful bnw.
verskriklik; vreesagtig; -less bnw.
onverskrokke; -some bnw. vreeslik.
'feasible ['fizəbl] bnw. uitvoerbaar,
prakties.
feast ['fist] s. (-s) fees (maal); ww.
(-ed) feesvier, smul, vergas, trakteer.
feat ['fit] s. (-s) kordaatstuk,
prestasie.
'feather ['fedhə] s. (-s) veer, pluim;
ww. (-ed) met vere versier (dek);
-brained bnw. dom, simpel; -weight
s. veergewig; - duster s. veerstoffer.
'feature ['fitsjə] s. (-s) kenmerk; ww.
(-ed) gekenmerk word deur; uitbeeld; vertoon.
febrile ['fibril] bnw. koors-, koorsig;
'febrifuge s. koorsverdrywer, koorsmiddel.
'February ['febroeəri] s. Februarie.
fecund ['fekənd] bnw. vrugbaar;
fe'cundity s. vrugbaarheid.
'federal ['fedərəl] bnw. federaal,
verbonde, bonds-.
'federate ['fedəryt] ww. (-d) federeer;
bnw. ('fedərit) gefedereer; fede'ration s. (-s) bond, federasie.
fee ['fi] s. (-s) honorarium, vergoeding, salaris, inskrywingsgeld.
'feeble ['fibl] bnw. swak; 'feebly bw.
swakkies, flou.
feed ['fid] ww. (fed) voed, voer,
kosgee; s. (-s) voeding, maal, kos;
-er s. (-s) pypkan, suigfles; sytak;
spruit; sylyn.
feel ['fil] ww. (felt) voel, bevoel,
verken; voelhorings uitsteek; s.
gevoel; -er s. voeler, voelhoring;
-ing s. (-s) gevoel, bnw. gevoelig.
feign ['fyn] ww. (-ed) voorwend;
veins, versin.
fe'licitate [fi'lisityt] ww. (-d) gelukwens; felici'tations s. (-s) gelukwensing.
fe'licitous [fi'lisitəs] bnw. gelukkig,
toepaslik.
'feline ['filain] bnw. katte-, katagtig.
fell ['fel] s. (-s) haarvel; berg; kop;
bnw. wreed, woes, fel; ww. (-ed) vel,
platslaan.
'felloe ['felou] s. (-s) velling.
'fellow ['felou] s. (-s) maat; genoot;
lid; weerga; -ship s. kameraadskap;
broederskap; lidmaatskap; studiebeurs.
'felon ['felən] s. (-s) misdadiger.

skurk; fyt; -y s. ('felonies) misdaad.
felt ['felt] s. (-s) velt.
'female ['fimyl] bnw. vroulik, vroue-;
s. (-s) vroumens; vrou; femi'nality
s. vroulikheid; 'feminine bnw.
vroulik; femi'ninity s. vroulikheid;
- thread s. moerdraad.
'femur ['fimə] s. (-s) dybeen.
fen ['fen] s. (-s) veengrond, moeras.
'fence ['fens] s. (-s) draad, heining,
muur; skermkuns; ww. (-d) skerm;
omhein.
fend ['fend] ww. (-ed) weer, verdedig;
sorg.
'fender ['fendə] s. skutyster; aardrand; modderskerm.
fe'nestra [fe'nestrə] s. venster, luik,
opening; -te ww. (-d) opening maak.
'ferment ['fəment] s. (-s) suurdeeg;
gis; gisting; ww. (-ed) gis; laat gis;
aanhits.
fern ['fən] s. (-s) varing.
fe'rocious [fə'rousjəs] bnw. wild,
woes, wreed; fe'rocity s. wildheid,
woestheid.
'ferrule ['feröël] s. (-s) beslag, band.
'ferry ['feri] s. ('ferries) pont.
'fertile ['fətail] bnw. vrugbaar;
fertili'zation s. bevrugting, bemesting; ferti'lizer s. kunsmis; fer'tility
s. vrugbaarheid.
'ferule ['feröël] s. (-s) plak, platriem.
'fervent ['fəvənt] bnw. gloeiend,
vurig; 'fervour s. ywer, gloed.
'fester ['festə] ww. (-ed) etter,
sweer, loop; vreet.
fes'tina 'lente [fəs'tinə 'lenti] bw.
stadig-oor-die-klippe, haas jou langsaam.
'festive ['festiv] bnw. feestelik, fees-;
'festival s. (-s) fees, feesdag;
fes'tivity s. (fes'tivities) feestelikheid, feesvreugde.
fes'toon [fes'tôën] s. (-s) festoen,
loofwerk.
fetch ['fetsj] ww. (-ed) haal, gaan
haal, aanbring, behaal.
'fête ['fyt] s. (-s) fees, feesdag.
fetid ['fitid] bnw. stinkend.
'fetish ['fitisj] s. (-es) fetisj, afgod.
'fetter ['fetə] ww. (-ed) bind, boei,
keten, kluister.
'fettle ['fetl] s. kondisie.
feud ['fjöëd] s. (-s) twis, fete; leen
(goed); -al bnw. leen-, feodaal.
'feuilleton ['föitöng] s. feuilleton,
vlugskrif.
'fever ['fivə] s. (-s) koors.
few ['fjöë] bnw. (-er, -est) min,
weinig.
fi'asco [fi'æskou] s. (-s) mislukking,
fiasko.
'fiat ['faiæt] s. (-s) bevel; toestemming.
fib ['fib] s. (-s) leuen, kluitjie; ww.
(-bed) jok.
'fibre ['faibə] s. (-s) vessel; 'fibrous
bnw. veselagtig; - gear s. veselrat.
'fibula ['fibjoelə] s. (-s) kuitbeen.
'fickle ['fikl] bnw. (-r, -st) wispelturig,
onbestendig.

'fiction ['fiksjən] s. (-s) verdigsel; fiksie; romankuns; fic'titious bnw. denkbeeldig, fiktief; 'fictive bnw. denkbeeldig.

'fiddle ['fidl] s. (-s) viool; ww. (-d) vioolspeel; beusel; -sticks uitroep. onsin, twak.

fi'delity [fi'deliti] s. trou; -guarantee s. getrouheidswaarborg.

'fidget ['fidzjit] ww. (-ed) woel, vroetel.

'fie ['fai] uitroep. foei! sies!

field ['fild] s. (-s) veld, kamp, land, gebied; spelers; ww. (-ed) veldwerk doen, keer; -glass s. verkyker.

fiend [find] s. (-s) bose gees, besetene, derduiwel; -ish bnw. hels, besete, duiwels.

fierce ['fiəs] bnw. (-r, -st) woes; wreed.

'fiery ['faiəri] bnw. vurig; driftig; lewendig.

'fifteen ['fif'tin] s. vyftien.

'fifth 'wheel ['fifth 'wil] s. skamel.

'fifty ['fifti] s. vyftig.

fig ['figh] s. (-s) vy; vyeboom.

'figaro ['figherou] s. koppelaar (minnesake).

fight ['fait] s. (-s) geveg, bakleiery, twis; ww. veg, beveg, bestry; baklei met.

'figment ['fighmənt] s. (-s) versinsel.

'figure ['fighə] s. (-s) gedaante, gestalte, figuur, postuur, vorm; ww. (-d) afbeeld, teken; verteenwoordig; versier; uitreken.

figu'rine [fighə'rin] s. (-s) beeldjie, figuurtjie.

filch ['filtsj] ww. (-d) skaai, gaps.

'file ['fail] s. (-s) vyl; lêer; rol; gelid; ww. (-d) vyl, bywerk.

'filial ['filjəl] bnw. kinderlik.

fili'buster [fili'bʌstə] s. (-s) vrybuiter(y).

'filigree ['filighri] s. werk met silwer en gouddraad.

fill ['fil] ww. (-ed) vul, vol maak, opvul, vervul; versadig; beklee; aanstel; s. bekoms; -er s. tregter; vulsel.

'fillet ['filit] s. (-s) beeshaas; garingvleis; vleis of vis sonder been (opgerol en vasgebind).

'filly ['fili] s. ('fillies) merrievulletjie.

film ['film] s. (-s) laag, vlies; rolprent; newel; mis.

'filter ['filtə] s. (-s) filter, suiweringstoestel; ww. (-ed) filtreer, deursyg, uitlek; fil'trate s. (-s) filtraat; fil'tration s. filtrering.

filth ['filth] s. vuilgoed, smerigheid; -y bnw. smerig, vuil.

fin ['fin] s. (-s) vin.

'final ['fainl] bnw. finaal, laaste, slot-, einde-; s. finale; -e (fi'nāli) s. einde, slot; fi'nality s. afdoendheid; slot, eindpunt.

'finance [fi'næns] s. (-s) finansies, geldwese; ww. (-d) finansier; fi-'nancial bnw. geldelik; fi'nancier s. finansier.

finch ['fintsj] s. (-s) vink.

find ['faind] ww. (found) vind, kry, aantref, verskaf, voorsien; s. (-s) vonds, ontdekking; -er s. vinder; -ing s. (-s) uitspraak, bevinding.

'fine ['fain] bnw. (-r, -st) fyn, dun, skerp; fraai; heerlik; ww. (-d) beboet; suiwer maak; s. (-s) boete; -ry s. tooisel.

fi'nesse [fi'nes] s. geslepenheid, finesse.

'finger ['fing-ghə] s. (-s) vinger; ww. (-ed) beduimel, betas; -print s. vingerafdruk.

'finis ['fainis] s. slot, einde.

'finish ['finisj] ww. (-ed) voltooi, eindig; ophou; afwerk; gedaan maak; s. einde, slot; afwerking; -ing s. afwerking.

'finite ['fainait] bnw. bepaald, definitief, eindig; -verb s. selfstandige werkwoord.

fiord ['fjôd] s. (-s) fjord.

fir ['fə] s. (-s) den.

'fire ['faiə] s. (-s) vuur; brand; hitte; skiet; koors; drif; ww. (-d) aansteek; losbrand; -axe s. brandbyl; -hose s. brandslang; -hydrant s. brandkraan.

firm ['fəm] s. (-s) firma; bnw. vas, hard, massief; stewig; ferm; trou; ww. (-ed) vasstamp; hard word.

first ['fəst] bnw. eerste, vroegste; vernaamste; s. die eerste; bw. eers, eerste; -ly bw. eerstens; -dying s. eerssterwende.

fisc ['fisk] s. skatkis; -al bnw. fiskaal.

'fish ['fisj] s. (-es) vis; ww. (-ed) visvang; hengel; -ery s. ('fisheries) vissery; -monger s. vishandelaar; -y bnw. visryk; verdag; -moth s. vismot.

'fission ['fisjən] s. splitsing, deling.

'fissure ['fisjə] s. (-s) bars, skeur, spleet.

fist ['fist] s. (-s) vuis; poot; handskrif; -ic bnw. boks-, boksers-; -icuffs s. vuisslanery.

fit ['fit] s. (-s) toeval; aanval; bui, nuk; snit; ww. (-ted) pas; passend wees; geskik maak, pasmaak; -ter s. toeruster.

'fitter ['fitər] s. (-s) passer, monteur; - and turner passer en draaier.

'five ['faiv] s. vyf; -r s. vyfpondnoot; -s s. kamertennis.

fix ['fiks] ww. (-ed) bevestig; heg; bepaal, vasstel; beslis; s. (-es) knyp; moeilikheid; fix'ation s. vasstelling; -ative s. kleefmiddel; -ings s. toebehore; -ture s. (-s) spykervaste voorwerp; datum; wedstryd.

fizz ['fiz] ww. (-ed) bruis, borrel; -le ww. (-d) bruis.

'flabbergast ['flæbəghāst] ww. (-ed) dronkslaan.

'flabby ['flæbi] bnw. (flabbier, flabbiest) pap, slap.

flag ['flægh] s. (-s) vlag; plaveisteen; ww. (-ged) sein; plavei.

'flagellate ['flædzjəlyt] ww. (-d) gesel.

flageo'let [flæedzjö'let] s. (-s) oktaaf-
fluitjie.

'**flagon** ['flæghən] s. (-s) flapkan, fles.

'**flagrant** ['flyghrənt] bnw. in die
ooglopend, verregaande, flagrant.

flair ['flêə] s. aanleg.

'**flake** ['flyk] s. (-s) volk; vonk;
brokkie; '**flaky** bnw. vlokkig; **flaking**
s. skilfering.

'**flambeau** ['flæmbou] s. (-s) fakkel,
toorts; **flam'boyant** bnw. vlammend.

'**flame** ['flym] s. (-s) vlam, hitte,
vuur; ww. (-d) vlam, brand, skitter.

fla'mingo [flə'ming-ghou] s. flamink,
volmink.

Flanders ['fländəz] s. Vlaandere.

'**flange** ['fændzj] s. (-s) flens, rand.

flank ['fænk] s. (-s) flank.

'**flannel** ['fænl] s. (-s) flennie;
witbroek; **flanne'lette** s. flennelet.

flap ['flæp] ww. (-ped) flap, klap; s.
(-s) klap, slag; klep.

'**flare** ['flêə] ww. (-s) flikker, gloei;
oopsper; s. (-s) flikkering, vlam;
vertoon; fakkel.

flash ['flæsj] ww. (-ed) skitter,
glinster, flits, skiet; s. (-es) 'flikkering, flits, straal, skig; -y bnw.
pronkerig; -ing s. skittering; beskot.

flask ['flåsk] s. (-s) fles.

flat ['flæt] s. (-s) verdieping; fiat;
gelykte; vlakte; mol (mus.); bnw.
(-ter, -test) plat, gelyk; eentonig;
verslaan; -**iron** s. strykyster; -ly bw.
beslis, botweg; -**race** n. naelwedloop;
-ten ww. (-ed) plet.

'**flatter** ['flætə] ww. (-ed) vlei; fiik-
flooi.

'**flatulence** ['flætjoeləns] s. winderig-
heid; '**flatulent** bnw. opgeblase.

flaunt [flônt] ww. (-ed) swier, spog;
vertoon; wulf.

'**flavour** ['flyvə] s. (-s) geur, smaak;
geursel; ww. (-ed) krui, geur gee;
-ing s. geursel; -**less** bnw. geurloos.

flaw ['flô] s. (-s) bars; fout; gebrek;
defek; vlaag.

'**flax** ['flæks] s. vlas; -**en** bnw. van
vlas, vlas-.

flay ['fly] ww. (-ed) afstroop, afkam.

flea ['fli] s. (-s) vlooi.

fleck ['flek] s. (-s) vlek; sproet.

'**fledged** ['fledzjd] bnw. geveer;
fully - volgroei.

'**fledgling** ['fledzjling] s. (-s) jong
voël; snuiter.

flee ['fli] ww. (fled) vlug, ontvlug.

'**fleece** ['flis] s. (-s) vlies, vag; ww.
(-d) skeer; pluk; plunder; '**fleecy**
bnw. wollerig.

fleet ['flit] s. (-s) vloot; bnw. (-er,
-est) vlug, rats; -**ing** bnw. vlugtig.

'**Fleming** ['fleming] s. (-s) Vlaming.

flesh ['flesj] s. vleis; -y bnw. vlesig,
dik.

flex ['fleks] s. (-es) koord; ww. (-ed)
buig; -**ible** bnw. buigbaar; -**ile** bnw.
buigsaam; -**ion** s. buiging.

'**flick** ['fiik] ww. (-ed) tik; raps; klap.

'**flicker** ['fliikə] ww. (-ed) flikker,
wapper, tril.

flight ['flait] s. (-s) vlug, trek, vaart;
swerm; vliegafstand; -y bnw. lighoof-
dig; wispelturig.

'**flimsy** ['flimzij] bnw. ('flimsier,
'flimsiest) dun, swak, flou.

flinch ['flintsj] ww. (-ed) terugdeins,
aarsel.

fling ['fling] ww. (flung) gooi, werp,
smyt, slinger; s. sprong, dans.

flint ['flint] s. (-s) vuurklip.

'**flip** ['flip] s. (-s) skoot; tik, raps;
drankie.

'**flippant** ['fiipənt] bnw. ligsinnig;
snipperig; '**flippancy** s. ligsinnigheid, snipperigheid.

flirt ['flət] s. (-s) koket; ww. (-ed)
vry, koketteer; flir'tation s. vryery.

flit ['flit] ww. (-ted) sweef; swerf,
trek.

'**float** ['flout] ww. (-ed) drywe, swem,
vlot, dobber; flotteer; s. (-s) vlot;
dobber; blaas; drifsel; vryfplank.

'**flock** ['flok] s. (-s) vlok, pluisie; trop,
kudde; ww. (-ed) saamkom.

floe ['flou] s. (-s) ysskots.

'**flog** ['flogh] ww. (-ged) slaan,
ransel; -**ging** s. loesing.

'**flood** ['flʌd] s. (-s) vloed; stort-
vloed; oorstroming; ww. (-ed) oor-
stroom; vul; -**ed** carburettor s.
versuipte vergasser (ww. versuip);
-**tide** s. hoogwater.

'**floor** ['flôə] s. (-s) vloer, bodem;
verdieping; ww. (-s) vloer; vloerplank.

'**flora** ['flôrə] s. flora, planteryk; -l
bnw. blom(me)-, plante-.

'**floriate** ['flôriyt] ww. (-d) blom;
blompatrone maak op.

'**floriculture** ['flôrikʌltsjə] s. blom-
kwekery.

'**florid** ['florid] bnw. bloemryk.

'**florin** ['florin] s. (-s) floryn.

'**florist** ['florist] s. (-s) bloemis.

'**floss** ['flos] s. vloksy; dons.

'**flotsam** ['flotsəm] s. opdrifsel,
wrakhout.

'**flounce** ['flauns] ww. (-d) strompel,
struikel.

'**flounder** ['flaundə] ww. (-ed)
strompel, ploeter; knoei.

flour ['flauə] s. meelblom; -y bnw.
melerig.

'**flourish** ['flʌrisj] ww. (-ed) bloei,
gedy.

flout ['flaut] ww. (-ed) bespot,
minagtend behandel.

flow ['flou] ww. (-ed) vloei, stroom.

'**flower** ['flauə] s. (-s) blom; fleur;
bloeisel; ww. (-ed) blom, bloei; -y
bnw. bloemryk.

'**fluctuate** ['flʌktjoeyt] ww. (-d)
skommel, wissel; **fluctu'ation** s.
skommeling.

'**flu** ['flôê] s. griep, influensa.

flue ['flôê] s. (-s) windpyp, skoorsteenpyp, luggang.

'**fluent** ['flôêənt] bnw. vloeiend, glad;
'**fluency** s. vlotheid.

fluff ['flʌf] s. (-s) dons, vlokkie; -y
bnw. donserig.

'fluid ['fioeid] s. (-s) vloeistof; bnw. vloeiend.

'fluke ['fiŏĕk] s. (-s) ankerblad; stertpunt; lewerwurm; gelukslag.

fluo'rescence [fioeə'resns] s. fluoresensie.

'flurry ['fiʌrɪ] s. (flurries) windvlaag, drukte; ww. (flurried) jaag, opwind; flurried bnw. opgewonde.

flush ['fiʌsj] ww. (-ed) uitspoel; bloos, gloei; bnw., bw. gelyk; vlak; - rivet s. vlakklinknael.

'fluster ['fiʌstə] ww. (-ed) deurmekaar maak.

'flute ['fiŏĕt] s. (-s) fluit; groefie.

'flutter ['fiʌtə] ww. (-ed) fladder, beef, tril; wapper; opwind; -board s. trilbord.

'flux ['fiʌks] s. (-es) vloed; bloedstorting; fluksie; smeltmiddel, soldeermiddel.

fly ['fiaɪ] ww. (flew, flown) vlieg; vlug; waai; s. (flies) vlieg; vlug; sprong; ligte karretjie; gulp; bnw. oulik; -leaf s. skutblad; -wheel s. vliegwiel.

foal ['foul] s. (-s) vulletjie; ww. (-ed) vul.

foam ['foum] s. skuim; ww. (-ed) skuim; -y bnw. skuimend; -rubber s. skuimrubber.

fob ['fob] s. (-s) kort horlosieketting; horlosiesakkie.

'focus ['foukəs] s. ('foci) brandpunt; ww. (-sed) instel; 'focal bnw. brandpunt.

'fodder ['fodə] s. voer.

foe ['fou] s. (-s) vyand.

'foetus ['fitəs] s. (-es) ongebore vrug; 'foetal bnw. fetaal.

fog ['fogh] s. (-s) mis, newel; -gy bnw. mistig.

foil ['foiil] s. (-s) blad; bladmetaal; foelie; teenstelling; skermsabel; verydeling.

foist ['foist] ww. (-ed) - on one afskuiwe op iemand.

fold ['fould] ww. (-ed) vou; s. (-s) fou, plooi; kraal, kudde; -er s. vouer, lêer.

'foliage ['fouliidzj] s. gebladerte, loof; 'foliate bnw. blaaragtig.

'folio ['fouliou] s. folio; foliant.

folk ['fouk] s. (-s) mense; -lore s. volkskunde.

'follicle ['folikl] s. (-s) saadhuisie.

'follow ['folou] ww. (-ed) volg; agternakom; aanhang; uitoefen; -er s. volgeling; -ing bnw. aanstaande, volgende; s. gevolg.

'folly ['foli] s. ('follies) dwaasheid.

fo'ment [fou'ment] ww. (-ed) fomenteer; aansterk.

fond ['fond] bnw. lief, verlief; -le ww. (-d) troetel, streel; -ly bnw. innig, vurig, liefderyk.

font ['font] s. doopbakkie, bekken.

food ['fŏĕd] s. (-s) voedsel, spyse, kos, stof; -stuffs s. eetware.

fool ['fŏĕl] s. (-s) dwaas, gek, idioot; ww. (-ed) vir die gek hou, om die bos lei; rondbeusel; -ery s. gekkerny; -hardy bnw. onverskillig; -ish bnw. dwaas; -proof bnw. teen verkeerde behandeling bestand, onfeilbaar; -scap s. sotskap; foliopapier.

foot ['foet] s. (feet) voet; voetenent; moer; ww. (-ed) voetslaan; met die voet aanraak; betaal; -hold s. staanplek; -ing s. staanplek; voet; -brake s. voetrem; voetstuk; -note s. voetnoot; -pad s. struikrower; -path s. voetpad; -rule s. duimstok; -sore bnw. met seer voete; -step s. voetstap; -switch s. voetskakelaar; -wear s. skoene.

'footlight ['foetlait] s. (-s) voetlig, verhoolig.

'footprint ['foetprint] s. (-s) spoor.

'footslogger ['foetsloghə] s. (-s) voetslaner.

'fop ['fop] s. (-s) modegek.

'foppish ['fopisj] bnw. windmakerig.

for ['fŏ] voors. vir, om, in plaas van, gedurende; voegw. want, omdat, aangesien, omrede.

'forage ['foridzj] s. voer; ww. (-d) stroop, plunder.

'foray ['fory] ww. (-ed) inval.

for'bear ['fŏbêə] s. (-s) voorsaat; ww. (forbore) afsien van, nalaat, verdra; -ance s. verdraagsaamheid; -ing bnw. verdraagsaam.

for'bid [fə'bid] ww. (forbade, forbidden) belet, verbied; -ding bnw. afstotend.

'force ['fŏs] s. (-s) krag, mag; geweld; strydmag; ww. (-d) dwing; vermeester, oopbreek; kweek; -d bnw. gedwonge; -feed lubrication s. druksmering.

'forceps ['fŏseps] s. tang.

ford ['fŏd] s. (-s) drif; ww. (-ed) deurwaad; -able bnw. deurwaadbaar.

'fore ['fŏə] bnw. voor-; s. voorpunt; boeg; -bode ww. (-d) voorspel; -boding s. voorgevoel; -cast ww. (-ed) voorspel; -close ww. (-d) afwys; -father s. (-s) voorvader; -'going bnw. voorgaande, -'gone bnw. uitgemaakte; -ground s. voorgrond; -head s. voorkop; -lock s. kuif; -man s. voorman; -most bnw. & bw. voorste, allereerste; -noon s. voormiddag; -'see ww. (-saw) vooruitsien; -shore s. strand; -sight s. vooruitsien, oorleg, deursig; -skin s. voorhuid; -'stall ww. (-ed) voorspring; -'taste s. voorsmaak; -tell ww. (-told) voorspel; -thought s. voorsorg, voorbedagtheid; -warn ww. (-ed) vooruit waarsku; -word s. voorwoord.

'forebear ['fŏbêə] s. (-s) voorvader, voorsaat; ww. (-bore) verdra.

'forebrain ['fŏbryn] s. voorbrein.

fore'close [fo'klouz] ww. (-d) oproep, opsê; fore'closure s. opsegging (verband).

'foreign ['forin] bnw. vreemd,

uitheems; **-er** s. vreemde(ling), uitlander.

fo'rensic [fə'rensik] *bnw.* regs-, geregtelik, juridies; **- medicine** s. geregtelike geneeskunde.

fore'runner [fô'rʌnə] s. (-s) voorbode, voorloper.

'foresight ['fôsait] s. vooruitsiendheid.

'forest ['forist] s. (-s) woud, bos; *ww.* (-ed) bos; **-ry** s. bosbou.

fore'stall [fô'stôl] *ww.* (-ed) voorspring.

'forfeit ['fôfit] *ww.* (-ed) verbeur, inboet; **-ure** s. verbeuring.

for'fend [fə'fend] *ww.* (-ed) verhoed.

'forge ['fôdzj] s. (-s) smitswinkel; smeevuur; smeltery, *ww.* (-d) smee; versin; vervals; aandruk; **-ry** s. vervalsing; **-d steel** s. smeestaal; **forging** s. smeewerk.

for'get [fə'ghet] *ww.* (*for'got, for'gotten*) vergeet.

for'give [fə'ghiv] *ww.* (*for'gave, for'given*) vergewe, kwytskeld.

for'go [fə'ghou] *ww.* (*for'went, for'gone*) afsien van, ontbeer, afstand doen van.

fork ['fôk] s. (-s) vurk, gaffel; mik; stemvurk; **-ed** *bnw.* gesplits.

for'lorn [fə'lôn] *bnw.* verlate; hopeloos; ellendig.

form ['fôm] s. (-s) vorm, gedaante, fatsoen; orde; formulier; bank; klas; kondisie; *ww.* (-ed) vorm; maak; kweek; stig; rangskik; **-al** *bnw.* vormlik; formeel; vorm-; for'mality s. (*for'malities*) formaliteit; for'mation s. vorming, formasie; oprigting.

'former ['fômə] *bnw.* vroeër, vorige, gewese; *vnw.* eersgenoemde; **-ly** *bw.* vroeër, vanmelewe.

'formidable ['fômidəbl] *bnw.* gedug.

'formula ['fômjoelə] s. (-s) formule, voorskrif.

'formulate ['fômjoelyt] *ww.* (-d) formuleer.

for'sake [fə'syk] *ww.* (*for'sook, for'saken*) verlaat; versaak.

for'sooth [fə'sôëth] *bw.* wraggies.

for'swear [fə'swèə] *ww.* (*for'swore, for'sworn*) afsweer.

fort ['fôt] s. (-s) fort, vesting; **-ifi'cation** s. verskansing; **-ify** *ww.* ('*fortified*) versterk.

'forte ['fôt] s. krag, sterkte.

forth ['fôth] *bw.* voort, voorwaarts, vooruit; voorts, verder; **-'coming** *bnw.* naderende, aanstaande; **-right** *bnw. & bw.* reguit; meteens; **-with** *bw.* onverwyld.

'fortify ['fôtifai] *ww.* ('*fortified*) versterk.

'fortitude ['fôtitjôëd] s. lewensmoed, gelatenheid.

'fortnight ['fôtnait] s. veertien dae; **-ly** *bnw. & bw.* elke veertien dae, tweeweekliks.

'fortress ['fôtris] s. (-es) fort, vesting.

for'tuitous [fô'tjoeitəs] *bnw.* toevallige.

'fortune ['fôtsjən] s. (-s) geluk, fortuin; vermoë; '**fortunate** *bnw.* gelukkig; gunstig.

'forty ['fôti] s. veertig.

'forum ['fôrəm] s. (-s) forum, regsbank.

'forward ['fôwəd] *bnw.* (-er, -est) voorste; voorwaartse; gevoerd; modern; voorbarig; parmantig; s. voorspeler; *bw.* vooruit, vorentoe; *ww.* (-ed) bevorder; aanstuur; **-ing** s. versending.

'fossil ['fosl] s. (-s) verstening, fossiel.

'foster ['fostə] *ww.* (-ed) oppas, voed, kweek, bevorder; **-parent** s. pleegouer.

foul ['faul] *bnw.* (-er, -est) vuil, smerig; gemeen, vals; skandelik; s. vuilspel; *bw.* vuil; *ww.* (-ed) besmeer; onklaar raak; versper.

found ['faund] *ww.* (-ed) grondves, stig; grond op; giet; smelt; foun-'dation s. fondament, grondslag; stigting; fonds; **-er** s. stigter; metaalgieter; **-ry** s. gietery.

'foundling ['faundling] s. (-s) vondeling.

fount ['faunt] s. (-s) fontein, bronaar, oorsprong.

'fountain ['fauntin] s. (-s) fontein, bron; oorsprong; **-head** s. bron, oorsprong; **-pen** s. vulpen.

four ['fôə] s. vier; **-score** s. tagtig; **-some** s. vierspel.

'fourteen ['fôtin] s. veertien.

fowl ['faul] s. (-s) voël, hoender (*vleis*); **-run** s. hoenderhok.

fox ['foks] s. (-es) vos, jakkals.

'fracas ['frækâ] s. lawaai, rusie, bakleiery.

'fraction ['fræksjən] s. (-s) breking; onderdeel; breuk.

'fracture ['fræktsjə] s. (-s) breuk; 'fractious *bnw.* weerspannig.

'fragile ['frædzjail] *bnw.* teer, tenger, breekbaar.

'fragment ['fræghmənt] s. (-s) stuk, brok, fragment, deel; frag'mentary *bnw.* onvolledig, fragmentaries.

'fragrance ['fryghrəns] s. geur, geurigheid; 'fragrant *bnw.* welriekend, geurig.

frail ['fryl] *bnw.* (-er, -est) teer, tenger; swak.

'frame ['frym] s. (-s) omlysting, lys, raam, kosyn; vorm; ontwerp; geraamte; (gemoed)stemming; *ww.* (-d) omlys, raam; opstel; vorm; maak.

'France ['frâns] s. Frankryk.

'franchise ['fræntsjaiz] s. stemreg.

frank ['frænk] *bnw.* (-er, -est) openhartig, eerlik, reguit; *ww.* (-ed) frankeer; **-ly** *bw.* reguit.

'frankincense ['frænkinsəns] s. wierook.

'frantic ['fræntik] *bnw.* wild, woes; rasend.

fra'ternity [frə'tëniti] s. (*fra'ternities*)

broederskap; **fra'ternal** *bnw.* broederlik; **'fraternize** *ww.* (-d) verbroeder.

'fraud ['frôd] *s.* (-s) bedrog, bedrieëry; bedrieër; mislukking; **-ulence** *s.* bedrog; **-ulent** *bnw.* bedrieglik.

fraught ['frôt] *bnw.* belaai.

fray ['fry] *s.* (-s) rusie, geveg, stryd; *ww.* (-ed) verslyt; rafel, uitrafel.

freak ['frîk] *s.* (-s) gier, gril; **-ish** *bnw.* grillig.

'freckle ['frekl] *s.* (-s) sproet; *ww.* (-d) vol sproete raak; **-d** *bnw.* sproeterig.

free ['fri] *bnw.* (-r, -st) vry; los; astrant; gratis; gul; rojaal; *ww.* (-d) vrymaak, bevry, verlos; **-booter** *s.* vrybuiter; **-born** *bnw.* vrygebore; **-dom** *s.* vryheid; **-handed** *bnw.* vrygewig; **-hold** *s.* erfpag; **-lance** *s.* onafhanklike; **-man** *s.* vryburger; **-mason** *s.* vrymesselaar; **-thinker** *s.* vrydenker; **-wheel** *ww.* vryry; **-wheeling** *s.* vryryery.

'freesia ['frîsiə] *s.* (-s) kammetjie.

'freeze ['frîs] *ww.* (froze, frozen) vries, bevries, verkluim, ryp; **'freezing** *bnw.* vries-, yskoud; **-point** *s.* vriespunt.

freight ['fryt] *s.* (-s) vrag; vraggeld; vervoer; *ww.* (-ed) bevrag; huur; **-er** *s.* skeepshuurder; vragskip.

French ['frenj] *bnw.* Frans; **-man** *s.* Fransman.

'french chalk ['frensj 'tsjôk] *s.* fyntalk, speksteen.

frenzy ['frenzj] *s.* waansin; **'frenzied** *bnw.* waansinnig.

'frequence ['frîkwəns] *s.* frekwensie; **'frequency** *s.* herhaling, frekwensie; **'frequent** *bnw.* veelvuldig; **fre'quentative** *bnw.* herhalend; **fre'quented** *bnw.* besog; **'frequently** *bw.* dikwels.

'fresco ['freskou] *s.* (-s, -es) fresko.

fresh ['fresj] *bnw.* (-er, -est) fris, vars, nuut; astrant; **-en** *ww.* (-ed) verfris, opfris; **-er** *s.* groentjie; nuweling; **-ly** *bw.* onlangs; **-man** *s.* (-men) groentjie, nuweling, *vrl.* **-ette** (-s).

fret ['fret] *ww.* (-ted) prikkel; knies; bekommer; **-ful** *bnw.* prikkelbaar.

'friable ['fraiəbl] *bnw.* bros, brokkelrig.

fricas'see [frikə'sî] *s.* fyn stoofvleis.

'fricative ['frikətiv] *bnw.* skurend, skuur-.

'friction ['friksjən] *s.* wrywing; **-al** *bnw.* wrywings-.

'Friday ['fraidi] *s.* Vrydag.

friend ['frend] *s.* (-s) vriend, kennis; **-ly** *bnw.* ('friendlier, 'friendliest) vriendelik, vriendskaplik; **-ship** *s.* vriendskap.

'frieze ['friz] *s.* (-s) fries.

fright ['frait] *s.* (-s) skrik; **-en** *ww.* (-ed) skrikmaak, verskrik; **-ful** *bnw.* verskriklik.

'frigid ['fridzjid] *bnw.* koud, koel;

styf; lusteloos; **fri'gidity** *n.* koudheid, koelheid.

frill ['fril] *s.* (-s) valletjie; kraag.

'fringe ['frindzj] *s.* (-s) rand; fraiings.

'frippery ['fripəri] *s.* ('fripperies) tierlantyntjies.

frisk ['frisk] *ww.* (-ed) huppel, dartel; **-y** *bnw.* lewendig.

'fritter ['fritə] *s.* (-s) vrugtepannekoek; *ww.* (-ed) verspil, versnipper.

fri'volity [fri'voliti] *s.* (frivolities) ligsinnigheid; **'frivolous** *bnw.* ligsinnig, nietig.

'frizz ['friz] *s.* (-es) krulle; **-le** *ww.* (-d) krul.

fro ['frou] *voors.* to and - heen en weer.

frock ['frok] *s.* (-s) py, toga; trui; manel; rok; kostuum; **-coat** *s.* manel.

frog ['frogh] *s.* (-s) padda; **-hopper** skuimbesie.

'frolic ['frolik] *ww.* (-ked) jakker, pret maak.

from ['from] *voors.* van, vanaf, vandaan; volgens.

front ['frʌnt] *s.* (-s) voorkant, front; gesig; bors; voorop; *ww.* (-ed) teenoor staan, in die oë sien; die hoof bied; **-age** *s.* voorkant, voorbreedte; **-ier** *s.* grens; **-ispiece** *s.* voorgewel; titelblad.

frost ['frost] *s.* vors, ryp; *ww.* (-ed) doodryp, ryp; mat maak; **-bitten** *bnw.* verkluim; **-y** *bnw.* ryperig.

froth ['froth] *s.* skuim; **-y** *bnw.* skuimerig; waardeloos.

frown ['fraun] *ww.* (-ed) frons, nors kyk; *s.* (-s) frons.

'frowsy ['frauzi] *bnw.* bedompig, slordig.

'fructify ['frʌktifai] *ww.* ('fructified) bevrug.

'frugal ['frôghəl] *bnw.* spaarsaam, matig; **fru'gality** *s.*

fruit ['frôët] *s.* (-s) vrugte; **-erer** *s.* vrugtehandelaar; **-ful** *bnw.* vrugbaar; **-ion** *s.* verwesenliking; **-less** *bnw.* vrugteloos, nutteloos; **-y** *bnw.* vrugte-.

frump ['frʌmp] *s.* (-s) flerrie, slons.

'frustrate ['frʌstryt] *ww.* (-d) dwarsboom, verydel; **frus'tration** *s.* verydeling.

fry ['frai] *s.* kleingoed, minderes, langore; *ww.* (fried) braai, bak.

'fuddled ['fʌdld] *bnw.* beskonke, verwar.

'fuel ['fjoeəl] *s.* (-s) brandstof; **-consumption** *s.* brandstofverbruik; **-oil** *s.* brandstofolie; **-pump** *s.* brandstofpomp; **-tank** *s.* brandstoftenk.

'fugitive ['fjôëdzjitiv] *bnw.* voortvlugtig; *s.* (-s) vlugteling.

'fulcrum ['fʌlkrəm] *s.* (-s) steunpunt.

ful'fil [foel'fil] *ww.* (-led) vervul, verwesenlik; **-ment** *s.* vervulling.

full ['foel] *bnw.* vol; volledig; voltallig; gevul; *bw.* vol, ruim;

heeltemal, ten volle; s. volheid;
-**back** s. heelagter; -**blown** bnw.
uitgegroei; -**grown** bnw. volwasse;
-**stop** s. punt; -**y** bw. ten volle.

'**fulminate** ['fʌlminyt] ww. (-d)
bliksem; ontplof; donder; **fulmi-**
'**nation** s.

'**fulsome** ['foelsəm] bnw. walglik,
liederlik.

'**fumble** ['fʌmbl] ww. (-d) knoei,
onhandig wees; -**r** s. sukkelaar,
knoeier.

'**fume** ['fjōĕm] s. (-s) rook, damp;
ww. (-d) rook, damp, kook, briesend
wees; '**fumigate** ww. (-d) uitrook,
ontsmet; **fumi'gation** s. beroking,
ontsmetting, uitswaeling.

fun ['fʌn] s. plesier; grap; -**ny** bnw.
snaaks, grappig.

'**function** ['fʌŋksjən] s. (-s) werk,
werking; amp; plegtigheid; feestelikheid; funksie; -**al** bnw. funk-
sioneel, amps-; -**ary** s. amptenaar.

fund ['fʌnd] s. (-s) voorraad; fonds.

'**fundament** ['fʌndəmənt] s. (-s)
fondament, agterste; funda'**mental**
bnw. fundamenteel, prinsipieel;
fundamental- voorv. grond-.

'**funeral** ['fjōĕnərəl] s. (-s) begrafnis,
lykstasie.

fu'nereal [fjoeeniəriəl] bnw. be-
grafnis-, treur-.

'**fungus** ['fʌngəs] s. swam; '**fungous**
bnw. swamagtig.

fu'nicular [fjoe'nikjoelə] bnw. kabel-,
draad-.

funk ['fʌnk] s. vrees; bangbroek;
ww. (-ed) bang wees; -**y** bnw. bang.

'**funnel** ['fʌnl] s. (-s) tregter;
skoorsteenpyp.

'**funny** ['fʌni] bnw. ('funnier,
'funniest) snaaks, koddig, grappig;
-**bone** s. elmboogbeentjie.

fur ['fə] s. (-s) pels, bont; kim;
beslag; ketelsteen; ww. (-red) voer;
beslaan; aanpak; aanslaan.

'**furbelow** ['fəbilou] s. (-s) valletjie.

'**furbish** ['fəbisj] ww. (-ed) poets,
opvrywe.

'**furcate** ['fəkyt] bnw. gesplits, ge-
vurk.

'**furious** ['fjoeəriəs] bnw. woedend,
rasend.

furl ['fəl] ww. (-ed) opvou, oprol.

'**fur'lough** ['fə'lou] s. (-s) verlof.

'**furnace** ['fənis] s. (-s) oond,
smeltkroes.

'**furnish** ['fənisj] ww. (-ed) meubileer,
uitrus; verskaf; voorsien; -**ings** s.
toebehorens; '**furniture** s. meubels.

'**furniture re'movers** [fənitsjə ri-
mōĕvəs] s. meubelkarweier.

fu'rore [fjoe'rôri] s. (-s) groot
byval(opgang).

'**furrier** ['fʌriə] s. (-s) bontwerker,
bonthandelaar.

'**furrow** ['fʌrou] s. (-s) voor, sloot;
riffel.

'**further** ['fʌdhə] bnw. & bw. verder;
meer, nader; ww. (-ed) bevorder;

-**ance** s. bevordering; -**more** bw.
verder, boonop.

'**furtive** ['fətiv] bnw. skelm, sluipend.

'**fury** ['fjoeəri] s. woed, drif; helle-
veeg.

'**fuse** ['fjōĕz] ww. (-d) smelt;
saamsmelt; s. (-s) lont; sekering;
smeltdraadjie; '**fusion** s. smelting;
- **box** s. sekeringkas; - **wire** s.
sekeringdraad, smeltdraad.

'**fuselage** ['fjōĕzilãzj] s. romp,
geraamte (van vlietuig).

fusil'lade [fjōĕzi'lyd] ww. (-d)
fusilleer, doodskiet.

fuss ['fʌs] s. drukte; -**y** bnw. druk,
rumoerig.

'**fusty** ['fʌsti] bnw. muf.

'**futile** ['fjōĕtail] bnw. vergeefs,
vrugteloos; **fu'tility** s.

'**future** ['fjōĕtsjə] s. (-s) toekoms;
toekomende tyd; bnw. toekomstig,
aanstaande; toekomende; **fu'turity**
s. toekoms.

fuzz ['fʌz] s. dons.

'**fuzzy** ['fʌzi] bnw. ('fuzzier, 'fuzziest)
donserig; vol flemies.

G

'**gab** ['ghæb] s. gebabbel; the gift of
the - wel ter tale; -**ble** ww. (-d)
babbel, klets.

'**gable** ['gybl] s. (-s) gewel.

gad ['ghæd] s. (-s) poryster, stok.

'**gadfly** ['ghædflai] s. ('gadflies)
perdevlieg; brommer; laspos.

gaff ['ghæf] s. (-s) vishaak, viskierie.

gag ['ghægh] ww. (-ged) die mond
stop; muilband; springstang aansit;
s. (-s) prop, springstang.

'**gage** ['ghydzj] s. (-s) pand;
uitdaging, handskoen.

'**gaiety** ['ghyəti] s. vrolikheid, pret,
plesier.

gain ['ghyn] s. wins, profyt, baat;
ww. (-ed) profyt maak, voordeel
trek; -**ings** s. winste; -**say** ww.
(-said) weerspreek, ontken.

gait ['ghyt] s. (-s) gang, stap.

'**gaiter** ['ghytə] s. (-s) slobkous,
kamas, sool, binnesool.

'**gala** ['ghãlə] s. (-s) fees, gala.

'**galaxy** ['ghæləksi] s. ('galaxies)
hemelstraat; skitterende byeenkoms.

'**gale** ['ghyl] s. (-s) stormwind.

Gali'lean [ghæli'liən] s. Galileēr.

'**galipot** ['ghælipot] s. dennegom,
hars.

gall ['ghôl] s. gal; (-s) skaafplek;
kwelling; seerplek; ww. (-ed) skaaf;
kwel, verbitter; -**bladder** s. galblaas;
-**stone** s. galsteen; - **midges** s.
galmuggies; brandassies.

'**gallant** ['ghælənt] bnw. galant;
hoflik; dapper; fler; trots; s. (-s)
galante kêrel; windmaker; verleier;
-**ry** s. galanterie; hoflikheid.

'**galleon** ['ghæliən] s. galjoen.

'**gallery** ['ghælərɪ] s. ('galleries) galery; gang.

'**gallivant** ['ghæli'vænt] ww. (-ed) rondslenter.

'**gallon** ['ghælən] s. (-s) gelling.

'**gallop** ['ghæləp] s. (-s) galop; ww. (-ed) galoppeer.

'**galloway** ['ghælōwy] s. ponie.

'**gallows** ['ghælouz] s. galg.

'**gallstone** ['ghōlstoun] s. (-s) galsteen.

'**gally** ['ghælɪ] s. ('gallies) galei.

ga'**lore** [ghə'lō] bw. volop, soos bossies.

ga'**losh** [ghə'losj] s. (-es) oorskoen.

'**galvanize** ['ghælvənaiz] ww. (-d) galvaniseer, versink; gal'**vanic** bnw. galvanies; galvani'**zation** s. galvanisering.

'**gamble** ['ghæmbl] ww. (-d) dobbel; -r s. dobbelaar; **gambling** s. dobbelry; -r's den s. speelhol.

'**gambol** ['ghæmbəl] ww. (-led) bokspring, huppel; s. bokkesprong.

'**game** ['ghym] s. (-s) spel, speletjie; wedstryd, grap; wild; play the - eerlik speel; bnw. gewillig, bereid; lam, mank; -**keeper** s. boswagter; - **law** s. skietwet; -**ster** s. dobbelaar; '**gaming** s. dobbelary; - **house** s. dobbelhuis; - **table** n. dobbeltafel.

'**gamin** ['ghæmin] s. (-s) straatseun.

'**gamma** ['ghæmə] s. gamma.

'**gammon** ['ghæmən] s. (-s) gerookte ham.

'**gamp** ['ghæmp] s. (-s) tentsambreel.

'**gamut** ['ghæmət] s. (-s) toonladder, gam.

'**gander** ['ghændə] s. (-s) gansmannetjie.

'**gang** ['ghæng] s. (-s) trop, bende; ploeg; -**plank** s. loopplank; -**er** s. ploegbaas, voorman; -**way** s. deurloop, paadjie.

'**ganglion** ['ghæng-ghliən] s. ('ganglia) senuknoop.

'**gangrene** ['ghæng-ghrin] s. kouevuur.

'**gangster** ['ghængstə] s. (-s) rampokker.

'**gantry** ['ghæntrɪ] s. ('gantries) steilasie.

'**gaol** ['dzjyl] s. (-s) tronk; ww. (-ed) in tronk opsluit; -**er** s. bewaarder, sipier.

'**gap** ['ghæp] s. (-s) opening; kloof; gaping; spleet; leemte.

'**gape** ['ghyp] ww. (-d) gaap; oopspalk; s. gaap; -**s** s. gaapsiekte.

'**garage** ['ghærāzj] s. (-s) garage; motorhuis; motorhawe.

'**garb** ['ghāb] s. (-s) kleding, klere; ww. (-ed) klee, uitdos; inklee.

'**garbage** ['ghābidzj] s. afval, vuil.

'**garble** ['ghābl] ww. (-d) sif; verdraai.

'**garden** ['ghādən] s. (-s) tuin; -**er** s. tuinier; -**ing** s. tuinmaak.

gar'**denia** [ghā'dīniə] s. (-s) katjiepiering.

gar'**gantuan** [ghā'ghæntjoeən] bnw. kolossaal.

'**gargle** ['ghāghl] ww. (-d) gorrel; s. (-s) gorrelmiddel.

'**gargoyle** ['ghāghoil] s. (-s) geutspuit.

'**garish** ['ghērisj] bnw. opsigtig, helderkleurig, skreeuend.

'**garland** ['ghālənd] s. (-s) krans; segekrans.

'**garlic** ['ghālik] s. knoffel.

'**garment** ['ghāmənt] s. (-s) kleding(stuk), gewaad.

'**garner** ['ghānə] ww. (-ed) versamel, bêre.

'**garnet** ['ghānit] s. (-s) granaatsteen.

'**garnish** ['ghānisj] ww. (-ed) versier; beslag lê op; -**ing** s. versiering; -**ment** s. wetlike beslaglegging; '**garniture** s. garnituur, versiering.

'**garret** ['ghærət] s. (-s) solderkamer.

'**garrison** ['ghærisn] s. (-s) garnisoen; ww. (-ed) beset.

gar'**rotte** [ghə'rot] ww. (-d) verwurg.

'**garrulity** [ghærðēlitɪ] s. babbelsug; '**garrulous** bnw. babbelsiek.

'**garter** ['ghātə] s. (-s) kousband.

gas ['ghæs] s. (-es) gas; wind; bluf; ww. (-sed) met gas verstik (bedwelm); grootpraat; -**eous** bnw. gasagtig, gas-; **gasco'nade** s. windmakery; kaskenade; - **engine** s. gasmotor.

gash ['ghæsj] s. (-es) sny, keep.

'**gasket** ['ghæskit] s. (-s) vulsel, paksel, patstuk, voering.

gasp ['ghāsp] ww. (-ed) snak, hyg; s. (-s) snik, hyging, asemtog; -**ing** bnw. hygend; verstom.

'**gastric** ['ghæstrik] bnw. gastries, maag-.

'**gate** ['ghyt] s. (-s) hek, poort, ingang, sluis; hekgeld; toeskouers; -**way** s. poort, ingang.

'**gather** ['ghædhə] ww. (-ed) vergader, versamel; opraap, pluk; oes; aflei; plooi; -**ing** s. vergadering; insameling; -**s** s. plooie.

'**gaucherie** ['ghousjərɪ] s. lompheid.

gaud ['ghōd] s. (-s) opskik, siersel; -**y** bnw. ('gaudier, 'gaudiest) opsigtig, spoggerig.

'**gauge** ['ghydzj] s. (-s) maat; kaliber; wydte; meter; ww. (-d) meet, peil; toets; yk; - **rod** s. meetstok.

'**gaunt** ['ghōnt] bnw. maer, vervalle.

'**gauntlet** ['ghōntlit] s. (-s) handskoen; spitsroei.

'**gauze** ['ghōz] s. (-s) gaas; dynserigheid.

gawk ['ghōk] s. (-s) lomperd; skimmelbrood; -**y** bnw. lomp; verskimmel.

gay ['ghy] bnw. (-er, -est) vrolik, uitgelate; kleurig; lugtig.

ga'**zania** [ghə'zyniə] s. (-s) botterblom.

'**gaze** ['ghyz] ww. (-d) staar, tuur; s. (-s) strak blik.

'**gazebo** [ghə'zibou] s. (-s) uitkyktoring.

ga'zelle [ghə'zel] s. (-s) gasel, wildsbok.

ga'zette [ghə'zet] s. (-s) staatskoerant; *ww.* (-d) proklameer.

gear ['ghiə] s. uitrusting; tuig; gereedskap; ratte; versnelling; **out of -** uitgeskakel; **in -** in rat; s. gang; **first -** eerstegang; **top -** s. hoogste gang; **low -** s. laagste gang; **-box** s. ratkas.

'gecko ['ghekou] s. (-s) geitjie.

gela'tine [dzjelə'tin] s. kalfsvoet, gelatien.

geld ['gheld] *ww.* (-ed) sny, ontman; **-ing** s. reun.

gem ['dzjem] s. (-s) edelsteen, juweel.

'gender ['dzjendə] s. (-s) geslag.

gene'alogy [dzjini'ælədzji] s. genealogie, afstamming; stamboom; **genea'logical** *bnw.* genealogies.

'general ['dzjenərəl] s. (-s) generaal, bevelvoerder; *bnw.* algemeen; gewoon; **generali'zation** s. veralgemening; **-ize** *ww.* (-d) saamvat; **-ly** *bw.* gewoonlik.

'generate ['dzjenəryt] *ww.* (-d) voortbring; teel; veroorsaak; ontwikkel; **gene'ration** s. (-s) teling; ontwikkeling; geslag; **'generator** s. voortbrenger; ontwikkelaar; dinamo.

ge'neric [dzji'nerik] *bnw.* generies; algemeen; geslags-.

'generous ['dzjenərəs] *bnw.* edelmoedig, mild; oorvloedig; **gene'rosity** s. edelmoedigheid, mildheid.

'genesis ['dzjenisis] s. genesis, wording, oorsprong.

ge'netic [dzji'netik] *bnw.* geneties.

ge'neva [dzji'nivə] s. jenewer.

'genial ['dzjinjəl] *bnw.* vriendelik, hartlik; aangenaam; **geni'ality** s. vriendelikheid, opgewektheid.

'genie ['dzjini] s. (-s) genius, gees.

'genital ['dzjenitl] s. (-s) geslags-, teel-; **-s** s. geslagsorgane.

'genitive ['dzjenitiv] s. (-s) genitief.

'genius ['dzjinjəs] s. ('genii s. genies; genius; genie.

gent ['dzjent] s. (-s) heer, meneer; *vgl.* **gentleman**.

gen'teel [dzjen'til] *bnw.* fatsoenlik, beskaaf; lieftallig.

'Gentile ['dzjentail] s. (-s) nie-Jood, Christen, heiden.

gen'tility ['dzjentiliti] s. afkoms, stand; deftigheid.

'gentle ['dzjentl] *bnw.* (-r, -st) sag, lief; **gently** *bw.* saggies.

'gentleman ['dzjentlmən] s. (*gentlemen*) heer, meneer; **gentlewoman** s. (*gentlewomen*) dame.

'gentry ['dzjentri] s. burgerstand.

'genuine ['dzjenjoein] *bnw.* waar, opreg, eg.

'genus ['dzjinəs] s. (-es) geslag, soort, klas.

ge'ography [dzji'oghrəfi] s. geografie, aardrykskunde; **geo'graphical** *bnw.* aardrykskundig.

ge'ology [dzji'olədzji] s. geologie, aardkunde; **geo'logical** *bnw.* geologies.

'geomancy ['dzjioumænsi] s. waarsêery; **'geomancer** a. waarsêer.

ge'ometry [dzji'omətri] s. meetkunde; **geo'metrical** *bnw.* geometries.

germ ['dzjəm] s. (-s) kiem; **-inate** *ww.* ontkiem; **-icide** s. kiemdoder; **-ination** s. ontkieming.

'German ['dzjəmən] s. (-s) Duitser; **-y** s. Duitsland.

'germifuge ['dzjəmifjoedzj] s. kiemdrywer.

'germinate ['dzjəminyt] *ww.* (-d) ontkiem, spruit; **germi'nation** s. ontkieming.

'germplasm ['dzjəmplæsm] s. kiemplasma.

gerry'mander ['gherimændə] *ww.* (-ed) knoei met verkiesings.

ges'tation [dzjes'tysjn] s. swangerskap, dragtigheid.

ges'ticulate [dzjes'tikjoelyt] *ww.* (-d) gebare maak; **gesticu'lation** s. gebaar.

'gesture ['dzjestjə] s. (-s) gebaar.

get ['ghet] *ww.* (got) verkry, verwerf, bekom; ontvang; verdien; hê; **'-at-able** *bnw.* bereikbaar; **-'up** s. opmaak; uitvoering.

'geyser ['ghizə] s. (-s) geiser, waterverwarmer.

'ghastly ['ghästli] *bnw.* aaklig; **ghastliness** s. aakligheid.

'gherkin ['ghəkin] s. (-s) agurkie.

'ghetto ['ghetou] s. (-s) ghetto.

ghost ['ghoust] s. (-s) gees, spook; skaduwee; **-like** *bnw.* spookagtig; **-ly** *bnw.* spookagtig.

'ghoulish ['ghŏēlisj] *bnw.* monsteragtig.

'giant ['dzjaiənt] s. (-s) reus.

'gibber ['dzjibə] *ww.* (-ed) brabbel; **-ish** s. brabbeltaal.

'gibbet ['dzjibit] s. (-s) galg; galgdood.

'gibe ['dzjaib] s. (-s) spot, skimp.

'giblets ['dzjiblits] s. gans-afval.

'giddy ['ghidi] *bnw.* ('giddier, 'giddiest) duiselig; opgewonde; ligsinnig; **'giddiness** s.

gift ['ghift] s. (-s) geskenk; gawe; **-ed** *bnw.* begaaf.

'gig ['ghigh] s. (-s) sloep; ligte karretjie.

gi'gantic [dzjai'ghæntik] *bnw.* reusagtig.

'giggle ['ghighl] *ww.* (-d) giggel.

gild ['ghild] *ww.* ('gilt) vergul; **-ing** s. vergulsel.

gill ['ghil] s. (-s) kieu (*mv.* **kiewe**).

gilt ['ghilt] s. vergulsel; skyn.

'gilt-edged ['dzjiilt-'edzjd] *bnw.* doodveilig, eersteklas.

'gimlet ['ghimlit] s. (-s) handboor.

gin ['dzjin] s. jenewer.

'ginger ['dzjindzjə] s. gemmer; vuur, fut; rooikop; **- ale** s. gemmerlimonade; **- beer** s. gemmerbier;

-bread s. peperkoek; -ly bw. behoedsaam.

'gingham ['ghinghəm] s. gestreepte katoen.

'ginned ['dzjind] bnw. gepluisd(e) (saad).

'gipsy ['dzjipsi] s. ('gipsies) sigeuner, heiden; swartoog.

gi'raffe [dzji'rāf] s. (-s) kameelperd.

gird ['ghəd] ww. (-ed) omgord; omsingel; -er s. dwarsbalk; -le s. (-s) gordel; rooster.

girl ['ghəl] s. (-s) meisie; nooi; diensbode, meid; -hood s. meisiesjare; -ish bnw. meisiesagtig.

girth ['ghəth] s. (-s) buikgord, gordel; buik (omvang).

gist ['dzjist] s. hoofsaak, kern.

give ['ghiv] ww. ('gave, 'given) gee, aangee, meegee; versaak; skietgee; -n bnw. gegewe.

'gizzard ['ghizəd] s. (-s) krop.

'glacial ['ghlysiəl] bnw. ys-; 'glaciated bnw. met ys bedek; glaci'ation s. ysvorming; 'glacier s. (-s) gletser.

glad ['ghlæd] bnw. (-der, -dest) bly, verheug; -den ww. (-ed) verbly, opvrolik.

'gladiator ['ghlædiytə] s. (-s) swaardvegter.

gladi'olus [ghlædi'ouləs] s. (-es, gladioli) gladiolus, swaardlelie.

'glamour ['ghlæmə] s. betowering; 'glamorous bnw. betowerend.

'glance ['ghlāns] ww. (-d) flikker; 'n blik werp; vlugtig kyk; s. (-s) oogopslag.

gland ['ghlænd] s. (-s) klier.

glare ['ghlèə] ww. (-d) fel skyn; skerp afsteek, woedend aangluur; 'glaring bnw. verblindend, fel; woes; skittering.

glass ['ghlās] s. (-es) glas; spieël; verkyker; weerglas; ruit; -es s. bril; -paper s. skuurpapier; -ware s. glasgoed, glaswerk; -y bnw. glasig, glasagtig.

glau'coma [ghlô'koumə] s. grou-(groen)staar.

'glaze ['ghlyz] ww. (-d) ruite insit; verglaas; s. (-s) glans, glasuur; -d bnw. verglaas; -r s. ruit-insitter.

gleam ['ghlim] s. straal, skyn, flikkering.

glean ['ghlin] ww. (-ed) versamel, opraap, bymekaarskraap.

glee ['ghli] s. blydskap, vrolikheid.

glen ['ghlen] s. (-s) dal, vlei.

glib ['ghlib] bnw. (-ber, -best) glad, gelyk; beweeglik; -ly bw. glad, vloeiend.

'glide ['ghlaid] ww. (-d) gly, skuiwe, seil; sweef; kruip.

'glimmer ['ghlimə] ww. (-ed) lig, skyn, flikker; -ing s. skynsel, flikkering, skemering.

'glimpse ['ghlimps] s. (-s) glimp; vlugtige blik; kykie.

glint ['ghlint] s. (-s) glinstering, skynsel.

'glitter ['ghlitə] ww. (-ed) skitter, glinster, vonkel.

'glisten ['ghlisn] ww. (-ed) glinster, blink.

'gloaming ['ghlouming] s. skemering.

gloat ['ghlout] ww. (-ed) lekkerkry.

'globe ['ghloub] s. (-s) bol; glaaskap van lamp; aardbol; 'globular bnw. bolvormig.

gloom ['ghlōēm] s. donkerte; somberheid; -y bnw. donker, somber.

'glory ['ghlôri] s. glorie, roem; heerlikheid; 'glorify ww. ('glorified) verheerlik, ophemel; glorifi'cation s. ophemeling; 'glorious bnw. glorieryk.

gloss ['ghlos] s. (-es) verklaring, glos; glans; wanvoorstelling; -ary s. ('glossaries) glossarium; -y bnw. glansend.

'glottis ['ghlotis] s. (-es) stemspleet; 'glottal bnw. stemspleet.

'glove ['ghlʌv] s. (-s) handskoen; -stretcher s. vingerstok.

glow ['ghlou] ww. (-ed) gloei; blaak; brand; s. (-s) gloed, vuur; -er ['ghlauə] ww. (-ed) dreigend kyk; -ing bnw. gloeiend, vurig; -worm s. (-s) glimwurm.

'glucose ['ghlōēkous] s. druiwesuiker.

glue ['ghlōē] s. gom, lym.

glum ['ghlʌm] bnw. (-mer, -mest) bek-af, stuurs.

glut ['ghlʌt] s. (-s) versadiging, oorlading.

'glutton ['ghlʌtn] s. (-s) vraat, gulsigaard; veelvraat.

'glycerine [ghlisə'rin] s. gliserien.

gnarled ['nāld] bnw. kwasterig, knoetserig.

gnash ['næsj] ww. (-ed) kners.

gnat ['næt] s. (-s) muggie.

gnaw ['nô] ww. (-ed) knabbel, knaag.

'gnome ['noum] s. (-s) aardgees, dwerg, kabouter.

gnu ['nōē] s. wildebees.

go ['ghou] ww. (went, gone) gaan, loop, wandel; reis; weggaan; reik; geldig wees; gangbaar wees; s. energie, lewenslus; -between s. tussenganger, bemiddelaar; -ing s. (aan die) gang.

'go ['ghou] s. vaart; dryfkrag; fut; spul.

goad ['ghoud] s. (-s) porstok, prikkel; karwats; ww. (-ed) prikkel; aandrywe.

goal ['ghoul] s. (-s) doel, doelpunt; wenpaal; -keeper s. doelwagter; -line s. doellyn.

goat ['ghout] s. (-s) bok; -ee s. bokbaard.

'gobble ['ghobl] ww. (-d) haastig eet; kloek soos kalkoen; -r s. gulsigaard; kalkoenmannetjie.

'Gobelin ['ghoubelin] s. (-s) behangseltapyt.

'goblet ['ghoblit] s. (-s) roemer, drinkglas.

'goblin ['ghoblin] s. (-s) kabouter.

god ['ghod] s. (-s) afgod; God s. God; -child s. peetkind; -head s. godheid; -ly bnw. godvresend; -send s. onverwagte uitreding.

'godfather ['ghôdfâdhə] s. (-s) peetvader.

'godmother ['ghôdmədhə] s. (-s) peetmoeder.

'goggle ['ghoghl] ww. (-d) uitpeul; oormekaarkyk; -s s. stofbril, skermbril.

'goitre ['ghoitə] s. (-s) kropgeswel, skildklierontsteking.

gold ['ghould] s. goud, geld, rykdom; bnw. goud-, goue; -en bnw. goue, gulde; - foil s. bladgoud; - rush s. (-es) stormloop na 'n nuwe goudveld; -smith s. goudsmid; -fish s. goudvis.

golf ['gholf] gholf; -er s. (-s) gholfspeler; - links s. gholfbaan.

good ['ghood] bnw. ('better, 'best) goed, bekwaam, geskik, gaaf, eg, soet; braaf; s. die goeie; nut, voordeel, welsyn; -s s. goedere; - afternoon uitroep. goeiemiddag; -bye uitroep. vaarwel; -day uitroep. goeiendag; -evening uitroep. goeienaand; -looking bnw. mooi; - will s. welwillendheid; klandisie-, handelswaarde; -y goody-goody bnw. & s. papbroek(erig).

'goose ['ghôes] s. ('geese) gans; -berry s. ('berries) appelderliefde; -flesh s. hoendervleis; -step s. paradepas.

'gore ['ghô] ww. (-d) deurboor.

'gorge ['ghôdzj] ww. (-d) wegsluk, inswelg.

'gorgeous ['ghôdzjəs] bnw. pragtig, skitterend.

go'rilla [ghə'rilə] s. (-s) gorilla.

'gormandize ['ghôməndaiz] ww. (-d) gulsig eet, vreet.

'gory ['ghôri] bnw. ('gorier, 'goriest) bloedig.

'gosling ['ghozling] s. (-s) klein gansie.

'gospel ['ghospəl] s. (-s) evangelie.

'gossamer ['ghosəmə] s. herfsdraad, spinnerak.

'gossip ['ghosip] s. (-s) babbelkous; skinderbek; skinderpraatjies; ww. (-ed) klets, babbel, skinder.

gouge ['ghaudzj] ww. (-d) uitbeitel; uitsteek.

gourd ['ghoeəd] s. (-s) kalbas.

'gourmand ['ghoeəmənd] s. (-s) vraat; fynproewer.

'gourmet ['ghoeəmy] s. (-s) fynproewer.

gout ['ghaut] s. jig; -y bnw. jigtig.

'govern ['ghʌvən] ww. (-ed) regeer, beheer, bestuur, lei; gover'ness s. (-es) goewernante; -ment s. regering; 'governor s. (-s) goewerneur; bestuurder.

gown ['ghaun] s. (-s) rok, tabberd; toga; japon.

grab ['ghræb] ww. (-bed) gryp, skraap, vang.

'grabble ['ghræbl] ww. (-d) gryp, grabbel.

'grace ['ghrys] s. (-s) guns, genade; grasie; swier; bekoorlikheid; fatsoen; tafelgebed; ww. (-d) sier; vereer; begunstig; -ful bnw. bekoorlik; 'gracious bnw. genadig.

gra'date ['ghrə'dyt] ww. (-d) gradeer; gra'dation s. gradering.

'grade ['ghryd] s. (-s) graad; gehalte; helling; ww. (-d) gradeer, klassifiseer; 'gradient s. (-s) helling; 'gradual bnw. geleidelik; 'gradually bw. geleidelik.

'graduate ['ghrædjoeit] s. (-s) gegradueerde; ww. (-d) gradeer; gradueer; -d bnw. gegradeer; gegradueer; gradu'ation s. gradering; graduasie.

graft ['ghrâft] s. (-s) ent; knoeiery; ww. (-ed) ent, oorent.

grail ['ghryl] s. (-s) graal, skottel.

grain ['ghryn] s. (-s) grein; greintjie; verf; draad, nerf; aard; ww. (-ed) korrel; diep verf; haaraf maak; vlam; -'elevator s. (-s) graansuier; -stack s. (-s) graanmied.

gram ['ghræm] s. (-s) gram.

grami'nivorous [ghræmi'nivərəs] bnw. grasetend.

'grammalogue ['ghræməlogh] s. (-s) woordteken.

'grammar ['ghræmə] s. grammatika; gram'marian s. taalkundige; gram'matical bnw. grammatikaal, grammaties.

'gramme = gram.

'gramophone ['ghræməfoun] s. (-s) grammofoon.

'granary ['ghrænəri] s. ('granaries) graanskuur.

grand ['ghrænd] bnw. (-er, -est) groot, hoof-, groots, fraai; -child s. (-ren) kleinkind; -eur s. grootheid; prag; -parents s. grootouers.

'grand-daughter ['ghrænddôtə] s. (-s) kleindogter.

gran'dee [ghræn'di] s. (-s) edelman.

'grandfather ['ghrænfâdhə] s. (-s) oupa, grootvader.

gran'diloquence [ghræn'diləkwəns] s. hoogdrawendheid.

gran'diloquent [ghræn'diləkwənt] bnw. hoogdrawend, spoggerig.

'grandiose ['ghrændious] bnw. groots; spoggerig.

'grandmother ['ghrændmʌdhə] s. (-s) ouma, grootmoeder.

'grandson ['ghrændsən] s. (-s) kleinseun.

'grandstand ['ghrænd'stænd] s. (-s) pawiljoen.

'grange ['ghryndzj] s. (-s) opstal; skuur.

'granite ['ghrænit] s. graniet.

'granny ['ghræni] s. ('grannies) = 'grandmother.

grant ['ghrânt] ww. (-ed) toestaan, vergun; verleen; erken; s. (-s) vergunning; toelae; verlening; skenking.

'**granular** ['ghrænjoelə] *bnw.* korrelagtig; '**granulate** *ww.* (-d) korrel.

'**grape** ['ghryp] *s.* (-s) druif; -**fruit** *s.* (-s) pomelo; - '**hyacinth** *s.* bloudruifie, hiasint.

'**graph** ['ghrāf] *s.* (-s) grafiek.

'**graphic** ['ghræfik] *bnw.* aanskoulik, lewendig.

'**graphite** ['ghræfyt] *s.* grafiet.

gra'**phology** [ghræ'folədʒɪɪ] *s.* handskrifkunde.

'**grapple** ['ghræpl] *s.* (-s) haak, greep; *ww.* (-d) haak, beetpak.

grasp ['ghrāsp] *ww.* (-d) gryp, vat, pak; begryp; *s.* greep; bereik; begrip; -**ing** *bnw.* inhalig.

grass ['ghrās] *s.* (-es) gras, weiveld; -**hopper** *s.* (-s) sprinkaan; -**y** *bnw.* grasryk.

'**grate** ['ghryt] *s.* (-s) herd; rooster; *ww.* (-d) rasper; knars; kraak; skuur; -**ful** *bnw.* dankbaar; -**r** *s.* 'rasper.

'**gratify** ['ghrætifai] *ww.* ('gratified) bevredig, voldoen, verheug; **gratifi-** '**cation** *s.*

'**gratis** ['ghrytis] *bnw.* gratis, kosteloos.

'**gratitude** ['ghrætitjōēd] *s.* dankbaarheid.

gra'**tuitous** [ghre'tjoeitəs] *bnw.* kosteloos; vry; ongevraag.

gra'**tuity** [ghrə'tjoeiti] *s.* ('gra'tuities) toelae, gratifikasie.

'**grave** ['ghryv] *s.* (-s) graf; *bnw.* (-r, -st) ernstig; swaar; -**yard** *s.* kerkhof, begraafplaas.

'**gravel** ['ghrævəl] *s.* gruis; niersteen.

'**gravitate** ['ghrævityt] *ww.* (-d) graviteer, sak, aangetrek word; diamante sif; gravi'**tation** *s.* swaartekrag; aantrekking; **gravity feed** *s.* valtoevoer; '**gravity** *s.* swaarte.

'**gravy** ['ghryvi] *s.* (gravies) sous; -**boat** *s.* sousspotjie.

'**graze** ['ghryz] *ww.* (-d) wei; laat wei; vee oppas; skram, skrams raak, skuur, skaaf.

'**grease** ['ghriz] *s.* (-s) olie, smeer, teer; - **cup** *s.* ghriesdop; - **gun** *s.* ghriesspuit; - **plug** *s.* ghriesprop; **greasy** *bnw.* vetterig, olierig, smerig, lymerig.

great ['ghryt] *bnw.* (-er, -est) groot, tamaal; lank; dik; -**ly** *bw.* grootliks. '**great**'**coat** ['ghryt'kout] *s.* warmjas.

greed ['ghrid] *s.* hebsug, lus, begeerte; -**ily** *bw.* gretig, gulsig; -**y** *bnw.* gulsig, snoep.

green ['ghrin] *bnw.* groen; onervare; fris, jonk; *s.* groen, groenigheid; groente; veld; setperk; jeug; -'**grocer** *s.* groentehandelaar.

'**green**'**gage** ['ghrin'ghydʒj] *s.* (-s) soort groenpruim.

'**greenhorn** ['ghrin'hōn] *s.* (-s) nuweling, groentjie, baar vent.

greet ['ghrit] *ww.* (-d) groet, begroet, verwelkom; -**ing** *s.* groet(e), begroeting.

gre'**garious** [ghrə'ghēðrɪəs] *bnw.* kudde-.

gre'**nade** [ghri'nyd] *s.* (-s) granaat.

grena'**dilla** [ghrenə'dilə] *s.* (-s) grenadella.

grey ['ghry] *bnw.* grys, grou, vaal; *s.* grys kleur; grys klere; skimmelperd; -**hound** *s.* (-s) windhond.

grid ['ghrid] *s.* (-s) rooster, tralie; -**iron** *s.* rooster.

grief ['ghrif] *s.* leed, verdriet.

grieve ['ghriv] *ww.* (-d) bedroef wees; treur; verdriet aandoen; '**grievance** *s.* grief; '**grievous** *bnw.* griewend, bedroewend, ernstig, smartlik.

grill ['ghril] *s.* (-s) rooster; braaivleis; *ww.* (-ed) rooster, braai; -**er** *s.* rooster.

grim ['ghrim] *bnw.* (-mer, -mest) nors, grimmig, streng; -**ace** *s.* grimas, skewebek; *ww.* (-d) grimasse maak.

'**grime** ['ghraim] *s.* vuiligheid, vuilgoed; '**grimy** *bnw.* besmeer, betakel.

grin ['ghrin] *s.* (-s) grynslag; spotlag; glimlag.

grind ['ghraind] *ww.* (ground) maal, kou, fynmaak; knars; slyp; onderdruk; -**er** *s.* meul; maaltand; slyper; -**ing** *s.* slypery; -**ing pasta** *s.* slyppasta; -**stone** *s.* slypsteen.

grip ['ghrip] *s.* (-s) greep, vat; band; beheer; begrip; handvatsel; voortjie; grippie; tas.

'**gripe** ['ghraip] *s.* (-s) greep, mag; koliek, kramp.

'**grisly** ['ghrizli] *bnw.* aaklig, grieselig.

grist ['ghrist] *s.* maalkoring (graan).

grit ['ghrit] *s.* (-s) gruis, grut; grint; energie; -**ty** *bnw.* sanderig.

'**grizzled** ['ghrizld] *bnw.* grys, gespikkelde grys.

'**grizzly** ['ghrizli] *bnw.* grys, grou, valerig.

groan ['ghroun] *ww.* (-ed) kreun, kerm; *s.* (-s) kreun, gekerm.

'**grocer** ['ghrousər] *s.* (-s) kruidenier; -**y** *s.* ('groceries) kruideniersware.

'**groggy** ['ghroghi] *bnw.* ('groggier, 'groggiest) bewerig, slap in die bene.

groin ['ghroin] *s.* lies, sy.

'**grommet** ['ghromit] *s.* (-s) skaafring.

groom ['ghrōēm] *s.* (-s) staljong; bruidegom.

'**groove** ['ghrōēv] *s.* (-s) groef, gleuf; sleur(gang); *ww.* (-d) groef of gleuf maak.

'**grope** ['ghroup] *ww.* (-d) tas, voel in die donker.

gross ['ghrous] *s.* (-es) gros; *bnw.* (-er, -est) geil, vet; grof, lomp; walglik, sinlik.

'**gro**'**tesque** ['ghrou'tesk] *bnw.* grotesk, potsierlik, grillig.

'**grotto** ['ghrotou] *s.* (-s) grot.

ground ['ghraund] *s.* (-s) grond; bodem; beginsel; ondergrond; grondtoon; grondkleur; land; erf;

ww. (*-ed*) grond, grondves, stig; staaf; aflei na die grond; strand; *deelw.* gemaalde; fyn; geslypte; **-less** *bnw.* ongegrond; **- coat** *s.* grondlaag; **-nut** *s.* grondboontjie; **- plan** *s.* plattegrond, grondplan; **-work** *s.* grondslag; geraamte.

group ['ghrŏĕp] *s.* (*-s*) groep, klomp, party; *ww.* (*-ed*) groepeer.

'**grouse** ['ghrauz] *ww.* (*-d*) brom, kla, murmureer; **-r** *s.* brompot.

'**grove** ['ghrouv] *s.* (*-s*) bome, bos.

'**grovel** ['ghrovl] *ww.* (*-led*) kruip.

grow ['ghrou] *ww.* (grew, grown) groei, laat groei, kweek, verbou; **-er** *s.* kweker, verbouer; **-n** *verl. deelw.* volwasse, begroei; **-th** *s.* groei, wasdom.

growl ['ghraul] *s.* (*-s*) knor; gebrom; *ww.* (*-ed*) knor, brom, kla.

grub ['ghrʌb] *s.* (*-s*) maaier; sukkelaar; smerige vent; kosvoorrade; **-by** *bnw.* vol maaiers; smerig.

'**grudge** ['ghrʌdzj] *ww.* (*-d*) misgun, *s.* (*-s*) wrok, hekel; '**grudgingly** *bw.* met teensin.

'**gruel** ['ghroeəl] *s.* dun pap; loesing; **-ling** *bnw.* uitspattend; *s.* loesing.

'**gruesome** ['ghrŏĕsəm] *bnw.* aaklig, afsigtelik.

gruff ['ghrʌf] *bnw.* (*-er*, *-est*) nors, bars, grof.

'**grumble** ['ghrʌmbl] *ww.* (*-d*) brom, pruttel, mor, mopper; dreun.

'**grumpy** ['ghrʌmpi] *bnw.* ('grumpier, 'grumpiest) brommerig, knorrig.

grunt ['ghrʌnt] *ww.* (*-ed*) knor, brom; *s.* (*-s*) geknor, gegrom.

'**guana** ['ghwänə] *s.* likkewaan.

'**guano** ['ghwänou] *s.* ghwano.

guarantee ['ghærənti] *s.* (*-s*) waarborg, garansie; *ww.* (*-d*) garandeer, waarborg, borg staan; '**guarantor** *s.* borg; '**guaranty** *s.* waarborg.

guard ['ghäd] *s.* (*-s*) wag, kondukteur; oppasser; hoede; *ww.* (*-ed*) oppas, bewaak, behoed, skut; **-ian** *s.* (*-s*) bewaker; bewaarder; kurator; beskermer; voog; **-ianship** *s.* bewaking; voogdyskap; **-rail** *s.* leuning, reling.

'**guava** ['ghwävə] *s.* (*-s*) koejawel.

'**gudgeon** ['ghʌdzjən] *s.* uilskuiken.

guer'rilla [ghə'rilə] *s.* sluipsoldaat, sluipvegter.

guess ['ghes] *ww.* (*-ed*) raai, gis, skat; *s.* (*-es*) gissing.

guest ['ghest] *s.* (*-s*) gas, kuiergas.

guf'faw ['ghʌ-fŏ] *ww.* (*-ed*) brullend lag.

'**guide** ['ghaid] *s.* (*-s*) gids; raadgewer; leiding; leidraad; *ww.* (*-d*) lei, rondlei, raadgee, bestuur; '**guidance** *s.* leiding, bestuur; **-book** *s.* reisgids.

guild ['ghild] *s.* (*-s*) gilde, vereniging.

'**guile** ['ghail] *s.* (*-s*) lis, slimheid, bedrog; **-less** *bnw.* argeloos.

guillo'tine [ghilə'tin] *s.* guillotine, valbyl; sluiting.

guilt ['ghilt] *s.* skuld; **-y** *bnw.* (*ier*, *-iest*) skuldig, strafbaar.

'**guinea** ['ghini] *s.* (*-s*) ghienie; **- fowl** *s.* tarentaal; **- pig** *s.* marmotjie.

'**guise** ['ghaiz] *s.* (*-s*) kleding, masker, vermomming.

'**guitar** ['ghitä] *s.* (*-s*) kitaar.

gulch ['ghʌlsj] *s.* (*-s*) kloof.

gulf ['ghʌlf] *s.* (*-s*) golf, baai.

gull ['ghʌl] *s.* (*-s*) seemeeu.

'**gullet** ['ghʌlit] *s.* (*-s*) slukderm.

'**gullible** ['ghʌləbl] *bnw.* liggelowig.

'**gully** ['ghʌli] *s.* ('gullies) kloof; slootjie; geul.

gulp ['ghʌlp] *s.* (*-s*) mondvol, teug; *ww.* (*-ed*) swelg, inslurp.

gum ['ghʌm] *s.* gom; drag; **-s** *s.* tandvleis.

'**gumboil** ['ghʌmboil] *s.* (*-s*) sweertjie aan tandvleis.

'**gumption** ['ghʌmpsjən] *s.* oorleg; fut, pit.

gun ['ghʌn] *s.* (*-s*) geweer; kanon; **-ner** *s.* kanonnier; **-powder** *s.* buskruit.

'**gunny** ['ghʌni] *s.* goiing.

'**gurgle** ['ghŏgl] *ww.* (*-d*) borrel; *s.* borreling.

gush ['ghʌsj] *ww.* (*-ed*) stroom, spuit, oorborrel; dweperig praat of handel.

gust ['ghʌst] *s.* (*-s*) ruk, vlaag, bui; **-y** *bnw.* winderig.

'**gusto** ['ghʌstou] *s.* lus, genot, smaak.

gut ['ghʌt] *s.* (*-s*) derm; snaar; engte; ingewande.

'**gutta-'percha** ['ghʌtə'pŏtsjə] *s.* gomlastiek.

'**gutter** ['ghʌtə] *s.* (*-s*) geut, moddersloot.

guy ['ghai] *s.* (*-s*) stuurtou; tentlyn; gek, dwaas; **-rope** *s.* ankertou.

'**guzzle** ['ghʌzl] *ww.* (*-d*) gulsig eet; **-r** *s.* vraat.

gym'khana [dzjim'känə] *s.* (*-s*) sport.

gym'nasium [dzjim'nyzjəm] *s.* gimnasium; gimnastieksaal.

gym'nastics [dzjim'næstiks] *s.* gimnastiek.

gynae'cology [ghaini'kolədzji] *s.* ginekologie.

'**gypsum** ['dzjipsəm] *s.* gips.

'**gyroscope** ['ghaiərəskoup] *s.* (*-s*) giroskoop.

H

'**haberdasher** ['hæbədæsjə] *s.* (*-s*) kramer, handelaar in garing en band; **-y** *s.* kramery.

'**habit** ['hæbit] *s.* (*-s*) gewoonte; kleed, kostuum; hebbelikheid; *ww.* (*-ed*) klee; **-able** *bnw.* bewoonbaar; **ha'bitual** *bnw.* gewoon, gewoonte-.

habitat ['hæbitæt] *s.* woonplek.

habi'tation [hæbi'tysjn] *s.* (*-s*) woning, woonplek.

'**hack** ['hæk] *s.* (*-s*) knol; broodskrywer; *ww.* holrug ry; kap, kerf; -saw *s.* (-s) ystersaag.

'hackney ['hækni] *s.* (-s) ryperd; sukkelaar; *ww.* (-ed) holrugry.

'haddock ['hædək] *s.* skelvis.

hae'manthus [hi'mænthʌs] *s.* poeierkwas.

'haemorrhage ['heməridzj] *s.* (-s) bloeding.

'haemorrhoids ['heməroids] *s.* aambeie.

haft ['hɑ̈ft] *s.* hef, handvatsel.

'haggard ['hægəd] *bnw.* vervalle; verwilder.

'haggle ['hægl] *ww.* (-d) knibbel, kibbel.

hail ['hyl] *s. & ww.* hael; uitroep. gegroet! *ww.* (-ed) groet, begroet.

hair ['hèə] *s.* (-s) hare, haar; -s' breadth *s.* haarbreedte; -brush *s.* hareborsel; -dresser *s.* haarkapper; -net *s.* haarnetjie; -pin *s.* haarnaald; -splitting *s.* haarklowery; -spring *s.* spriaalveer; - trigger *s.* sneller; -y *bnw.* ('hairier, 'hairiest) harig, behaar.

'hake ['hyk] *s.* (-s) stokvis.

'hale ['hyl] *bnw.* (-r, -st) gesond, fris.

half ['hɑ̈f] *bnw.* half; *s.* ('halves) helfte; halwe; *bw.* half; -blood *s.* halfnaatjie; -breed *s.* baster; -brother *s.* halwe broer; -caste *s.* baster; -crown *s.* halfkroon; -hearted *bnw.* halfhartig; -mast *bw.* halfstok; - time *s.* speeltyd, rustyd; -tone *s.* halfkleurdiepte; -witted *bnw.* halfwys, getik.

'halibut ['hælibət] *s.* heilbot.

hall ['hôl] *s.* (-s) voorportaal, saal; hal; huis; -mark *s.* (-s) stempel, waarmerk.

'hallow ['hælou] *ww.* (-ed) heilig, heilig verklaar.

halluci'nation [həlōēsi'nysjən] *s.* (-s) sinsbedrog, waan.

'halo ['hylou] *s.* (-s) stralekrans, halo, ligkrans.

halt ['hôlt] *ww.* (-ed) stop, halt, tot stilstand kom (bring); *s.* (-s) halte, stopplek; *bnw.* kreupel, mank.

'halter ['hôltə] *s.* (-s) halter.

'halve ['hɑ̈v] *ww.* (-d) halveer, deel.

ham ['hæm] *s.* (-s) ham, dy; (radio) - *s.* radioamateur; -string *ww.* (-strung) haakskeenpese deursny, verlam.

'hamlet ['hæmlit] *s.* (-s) dorpie, gehug.

'hammer ['hæmə] *s.* (-s) hamer; haan (geweer); *ww.* (-ed) hamer, moker, slaan.

'hammock ['hæmək] *s.* (-s) hangmat.

'hamper ['hæmpə] *s.* (-s) mandjie; *ww.* (-ed) hinder, dwarsboom.

hand ['hænd] *s.* (-s) hand; handvol; handskrif; wyser; werksman; *ww.* (-ed) aangee, oorhandig, afgee; -bag *s.* handsak, tas; -barrow *s.* draagbaar; -bill *s.* strooibiljet; -book *s.* handboek, handleiding; - cream *s.* handroom; -cuff *s.* (-s) boei; -feed

ww. (-fed) hans-grootmaak; -icap *s.* voorgee; belemmering; hendikep; -icraft *s.* ambag; -kerchief *s.* sakdoek; -le *s.* handvatsel, steel; -writing *s.* handskrif; -y *bnw.* handig, gerieflik, byderhand; -yman *s.* opknapper, handlanger, faktotum.

'handiwork ['hændiwək] *s.* handewerk.

'handsome ['hændsʌm] *bnw.* mooi, aansienlik;

hang ['hæng] *ww.* ('hung) hang, ophang; behang; *s.* hang.

'hangar ['hængə] *s.* (-s) vliegloods.

hank ['hænk] *s.* (-s) string, wrong.

'hanker ['hænkə] *ww.* (-ed) snak, hunker, verlang; -ing *s.* hunkering, begeerte.

'Hansard ['hænsəd] *s.* volksraadsverslag.

'hansom ['hænsəm] *s.* (-s) (huur)rytuig, keb .

hap'hazard ['hæp'hæzəd] *bnw.* toevallig, wild.

'hapless ['hæplis] *bnw.* ongelukkig.

'happen ['hæpən] *ww.* (-ed) gebeur, plaasvind, voorval.

'happy ['hæpi] (*happier, 'happiest*) gelukkig, bly; raak; -go-lucky *bnw.* onbesorg.

'hara-'kiri ['hɑ̈ra-'kiri] *s.* selfmoord.

ha'rangue [hə'ræng] *ww.* (-d) vurig toespreek, opsweep.

'harass ['hærəs] *ww.* (-ed) teister, pla, kwel.

'harbinger ['hɑ̈bindzjə] *s.* (-s) voorloper, aankondiger.

'harbour ['hɑ̈bə] *s.* (-s) hawe, toevlugsoord; *ww.* (-ed) herberg; -less *bnw.* dakloos.

hard ['hɑ̈d] *bnw.* (-er, -est) hard, styf, moeilik, swaar, streng, skerp; *bw.* hard, swaar; dig; -bitten *bnw.* taai; -en *ww.* (-ed) hard maak(word); verhard; -ihood *s.* astrantheid; -boiled *bnw.* ru, grof, ongevoelig; -fisted *bnw.* suinig; - lines *s.* teenspoed; -ly *bw.* skaars, nouliks; -pressed *bnw.* in nood, agtervolg; -ship *s.* teenspoed; -ware *s.* ysterware; -y *bnw.* sterk, flink, gehard; -up *bnw.* bankrot.

'hare ['hèə] *s.* (-s) haas.

'hare-brained ['hèəbrynd] *bnw.* dwaas, roekeloos, onbeslis.

'harem ['hèərəm] *s.* (-s) harem, vroueverblyf.

'haricot ['hærikou] *s.* bredie.

hark ['hɑ̈k] *ww.* luister.

'harlequin ['hɑ̈likwin] *s.* (-s) harlekyn, hanswors.

harm ['hɑ̈m] *s.* skade, kwaad; *ww.* (-ed) beskadig, benadeel; -ful *bnw.* nadelig, skadelik; -less *bnw.* onskadelik.

'harmony ['hɑ̈məni] *s.* harmonie, eendrag; har'monic *bnw.* harmonies; har'monica *s.* mondfluitjie; har'monics *s.* harmonieleer; harmoniese tone; har'monious *bnw.* harmonieus; 'harmonize *ww.* (-d) harmonieer; har'monium *s.* serafyn.

'harness ['hånis] s. (-es) tuig; harnas; wapenrusting; *ww.* (-ed) optuig, inspan.

harp ['håp] s. (-s) harp; *ww.* (-ed) harpspeel; - *on the same string* op dieselfde aambeeld hamer.

'harpoon ['håpōēn] s. (-s) harpoen.

'harpsichord ['håpsikõd] s. (-s) klawesimbaal.

'harrow ['hærou] *ww.* (-ed) folter, kwel; eg; teister; **-ing** *bnw.* martelend.

'harry ['hæri] *ww.* ('harried) plunder, verniel; beroof; teister.

harsh ['håsj] *bnw.* (-er, -est) ru, grof; fel; wreed.

'harvest ['håvist] s. (-s) oes, oestyd; *ww.* (-ed) oes, insamel; **-er** s. snyer, plukker, oester; snymasjien.

hash ['hæsj] *ww.* (-ed) fynmaak; s. fynvleis; mengelmoes.

'hasp ['håsp] s. (-s) knip, klink, grendel.

'hassock ['hæsək] s. (-s) knielkussing.

'haste ['hyst] s. haas, spoed; *ww.* gou maak; **-n** *ww.* (-ed) gou (haastig) maak; **'hastily** *bw.* haastig; **'hasty** *bnw.* haastig.

hat ['hæt] s. (-s) hoed; **-box** s. hoededoos; **-stand** s. kapstok.

hatch ['hætsj] s. (-es) luik; broeisel; *ww.* (-ed) uitbroei.

'hatchet ['hætsjit] s. (-s) byl.

'hate ['hyt] s. haat; *ww.* (-d) haat; **-d** *bnw.* gehaat; **hatred,** s. haat, wrok.

'hatred ['hytrid] s. haat, wrok, vyandskap.

'haughty ['hôti] *bnw.* ('haughtier, 'haughtiest) hoog, trots, hoogmoedig.

haul ['hôl] *ww.* (-ed) trek, hys, aansleep; s. (-s) trek; vangs; **-age** s. vervoer, sleep.

haunch ['hôntsj] s. (-es) heup, boud, dy.

haunt ['hônt] *ww.* (-ed) êrens boer(lê); rondwaar; lastig val; s. (-s) boerplek.

'have ['hæv] *ww.* ('had) hê, besit; kry, ontvang, neem; gebruik.

'haven ['hyvn] s. (-s) hawe; skuilplek.

'haversack ['hævəsæk] s. (-s) rugsak, knapsak, ransel.

'havoc ['hævək] s. verwoesting.

hawk ['hôk] s. (-s) valk; pylstert (*mot*); *ww.* (-ed) smous, vent; **-er** s. smous, venter, marskramer.

'hawser ['hôzə] s. (-s) tou, kabel.

'hawthorn ['hôthôn] s. (-s) meidoring, haagdoring.

hay ['hy] s. hooi; **-cock** s. mied, opper; **- fever** s. hoolkoors; **-fork** s. hooigaffel; **-rick** s. hooimied; **-stack** s. hooimied.

'hazard ['hæzəd] s. (-s) gevaar, risiko; dobbelspel; kans; *ww.* (-ed) waag; opper; **-ous** *bnw.* gevaarvol, gewaag.

haze ['hyz] s. waas, wasigheid, mis; **'hazy** *bnw.* wasig.

'hazel ['hyzl] s. haselneut; haselaar.

he ['hi] *vnw.* hy; s. mannetjie.

head ['hed] s. (-s) kop; verstand; lewe; bron; leier; koppenent; top; *ww.* (-ed) aanvoer, lei; met die kop stamp; koers vat; **-ache** s. kopseer; **-dress** s. hooftooisel; **-er** s. kopskoot; **-gear** s. hoofdeksel; skagbok; **-light** s. voorste lig, hoof-lig; **-line** s. opskrif; **-long** *bnw.* kopvooruit, *bw.* halsoorkop; **-man** s. hoofman; **-master** s. prinsipaal; **-quarters** s. hoofkwartier; **-stone** s. grafsteen; **-strong** *bnw.* koppig, eiewys; **-waters** s. boloop; **-way** s. vooruitgang; kopruimte; **-wind** s. teenwind; **-y** *bnw.* koppig, driftig.

heal ['hil] *ww.* (-ed) genees; heel; **-th** s. gesondheid, welstand; **-thy** *bnw.* gesond, welvarend.

heap ['hip] s. (-s) hoop, klomp; *ww.* (-ed) stapel.

hear ['hiə] *ww.* (-d) hoor, verneem; luister na; verhoor; **-er** s. toehoorder; **-ing** s. gehoor, verhoor; **-ken** *ww.* (-ed) luister; **-say** s. gerug.

'hearse ['hðs] s. (-s) lykswa, dodebaar.

heart ['håt] s. (-s) hart; boesem; siel; gemoed; moed; kern; **-ache** s. hartseer; **-beat** s. polsslag; **-break** s. hartseer; **-burn** s. sooibrand; **-water** s. hartwater (*beessiekte*); **-en** *ww.* (-ed) bemoedig; **-felt** *bnw.* opreg, innig; **-ily** *bw.* van harte, grondig; **-less** *bnw.* gevoelloos, onverskillig; **-y** *bnw.* hartlik.

hearth ['håth] s. (-s) herd, haard.

heat ['hit] s. hitte, warmte, gloed, vuur, opwinding; bronstigheid; *ww.* (-ed) verhit, verwarm; driftig word; **-ed** *bnw.* verhit; driftig; **-er** s. verwarmer, kaggel.

heath ['hith] s. vlakte; heide; **-er** s. heide.

'heathen ['hithn] s. heiden.

'heave ['hiv] *ww.* ('hove) hef, optel, oplig; dein; swel; gooi; slaak.

'heaven ['hevn] s. (-s) hemel; lug; **-ly** *bnw.* hemels.

'heavy ['hevi] *bnw.* ('heavier, 'heaviest) swaar, moeilik, drukkend.

'heckle ['hekl] *ww.* (-d) hekel, ondervra, strikvrae stel.

'hectic ['hektik] *bnw.* wild, woes; teringagtig.

'hedge ['hedzj] s. (-s) haag, heg, heining, laning; **-hog** s. krimpvarkie; **-row** n. heg, laning.

'hedonism ['hidənism] s. genotsug; genotleer.

heed ['hid] *ww.* (-ed) pas op, let op gee ag; **-less** *bnw.* agteloos.

heel ['hil] s. (-s) hak, hiel; hoef; polvy; *ww.* (-ed) hak aansit, uithak laat oorhel, krink.

'hefty ['hefti] *bnw.* ('heftier, 'heftiest) swaar, gewigtig.

'heifer ['hetə] s. (-s) vers.

height ['halt] s. (-s) hoogte toppunt; **-en** ww. (-ed) verhoog, vermeerder; verhef.

'heinous ['hynəs] bnw. afskuwelik, haatlik.

heir ['êə] s. (-s) arfgenaam; **'heiress** s. erfgename; **-loom** s. erfstuk.

hell ['hel] s. hel; bof; dobbelhol; **-ish** bnw. hels.

'helm ['helm] s. (-s) helmstok; roer.

'helmet ['helmit] s. (-s) helmhoed.

'helot ['helət] s. (-s) heloot, slaaf.

help ['help] ww. (-ed) help, bystaan; bedien; s. hulp, bystand; porsie; **-er** s. helper, hulp.

'helpmate ['helpmyt] s. (-s) wederhelf.

helter'skelter ['heltə'skeltə] bnw. holdersteoldder.

hem ['hem] s. (-s) soom, kant, boord; ww. (-med) soom, omboor; omsingel; **-stitch** s. soomsteek.

heme'ranthic [himə'rænthik] bnw. dagbloeiing.

'hemisphere ['hemisfiə] s. (-s) hemisfeer, halfrond.

'hemlock ['hemlok] s. giftige kerwel.

'hemorrhage = haemorrhage.

'hemorrhoids = haemorrhoids.

hemp ['hemp] s. hennep; tou; dagga.

hen ['hen] s. (-s) hen; **-pecked** bnw. wat onder die pantoffelregering staan.

'hence ['hens] bw. hiervandaan af, hieruit; daarom; **-forth** bw. voortaan.

'henchman ['hentsjmən] s. ('henchmen) agterryer, volgeling.

he'patic- [hi'pætik] voorv. lewer-.

her ['hə] vnw. haar; vgl. **she.**

'herald ['herəld] s. (-s) herout; **-ic** heraldies; **-ry** s. heraldiek, wapenkunde.

herb ['hêb] s. (-s) kruie, bossie; **her'baceous** bnw. kruierig, kruidagtig; **-al** bnw. kruie-; **-alist** s. kruiekundige, drogis; **her'barium** s. herbarium; **her'bivorous** bnw. plantetend.

herd ['hêd] s. (-s) kudde, trop; herder; ww. (-ed) oppas, kyk na; saamhok.

'here ['hiə] bw. hier, hierheen, hiernatoe; **-abouts** bw. hier rond; **-after** bw. hierna, voortaan; **-at** bw. hierby, hierop; **-by** bw. hierby, hierdeur, hiermee; **-under** bw. hierna; **-with** bw. hiermee.

he'redity [hi'rediti] s. erflikheid.

'heresy ['herəsi] s. kettery; **'heretic** s. ketter; **he'retical** bnw. ketters.

'heritage ['heritidzj] s. erfdeel, erfenis.

'hereto'fore ['hiətoe'fô] bw. tevore.

her'maphrodite ['hə'mæfrədait] s. (-s) trassie, dubbelslagtige.

her'metic [hə'metik] bnw. hermeties.

'hermit ['hêmit] s. (-s) kluisenaar; **-age** s. kluis.

'hero [hierou] s. (-es) held; heros; **he'roic** bnw. heldhaftig, dapper; **he'roics** s. hoogdrawendheid, bombas; **-ine** s. heldin.

'herring ['hering] s. (-s) haring.

'hesitate ['hezityt] ww. (-d) aarsel, weifel; **'hesitant** bnw. weifelend; **'hesitancy** s. aarseling; **hesi'tation** s. aarseling.

heu'ristic [hjoeə'ristik] bnw. heuristies, ontdekkend.

hew ['hjöē] ww. (-ed) kap, slaan; **-er** s. kapper.

'heyday ['hydy] s. bloei, fleur.

hi'atus [hai'ytəs] s. (-es) hiaat, gaping, leemte.

'hibernate ['haibənyt] ww. (-d) oorwinter; **hiber'nation** s. winterslaap.

Hi'bernia s. Ierland.

'hiccough ['hikʌp] ww. (-ed) hik.

'hiccup ['hikʌp] (-ped) = hiccough.

'hide ['haid] ww. ('hid, 'hidden) verberg, wegsteek, wegkruip; s. (-s) vel, huid; **-and-'seek** s. wegkruipertjie; **-bound** bnw. vas in die vel; bekrompe; **'hiding** s. loesing; skuilplek.

'hideous ['hidiəs] bnw. afskuwelik.

hie ['hai] ww. (-d) haas, rep.

'hierarch ['haiərâk] s. (-s) hiërarg, kerkhoof; **-y** s. hiërargies.

'hieroglyph ['haiərõghlif] s. hiëroglief; beeldskrif.

high ['hai] bnw. (-er, -est) hoog; verhewe; gunstig; duur; adellik; hewig; edel; bw. hoog; uiters; duur; eg; s. die hoë; **-er** ww. (-ed) verhoog; **-brow** s. intellektueel; **-frequency** s. hoëfrekwensie; **-handed** bnw. eiemagtig; **-land** s. hooglande; **-ly** bw. hoog, hoogs; **-minded** bnw. edelmoedig; **-ness** s. hoogte; hoogheid; **-strung** bnw. hooggespanne; **-water** s. vloed; **-way** s. grootpad.

'hike ['haik] s. voetreis; ww. (-d) te voet reis, stap.

hi'larious [hi'lêəriəs] bnw. vrolik, uitgelate; **hi'larity** s. vrolikheid, uitgelatenheid.

hill ['hil] s. (-s) heuwel, bult, koppie, hoop; **-ock** verkleinw. koppie, bultjie.

hilt ['hilt] s. (-s) handvatsel, greep, geves, hef.

him ['him] vnw. hom; vgl. **he;** **-'self** vnw. homself, hom.

hind ['haind] s. (-s) hinde, ooi; kneg; bnw. agter-, agterste.

'hinder ['hində] ww. (-ed) hinder, belemmer, belet; **'hindrance** s. hindernis, belemmering.

'hindmost ['haindmoust] bnw. agterste, verste.

'Hindu ['hin'dôē] s. (-s) Hindoe, Indiër.

'hinge ['hindzj] s. (-s) skarnier, hingsel, spil; ww. (-d) draai, hang, rus op; skarniere aanbring.

hint ['hint] s. (-s) wenk, toespeling;

ww. (*-ed*) aan die hand doen; sinspeel op.

hip ['hip] *s.* (*-s*) heup; hoekspar.

hippo'potamus [hipə'potəməs] *s.* (*-es*) seekoei.

'hire ['haiə] *s.* huur; loon, huurgeld; *ww.* (*-d*) huur, verhuur; **-ling** *s.* huurling; **-purchase system** *s.* huurkoop.

'hirsute ['həsjōēt] *bnw.* harig, ruig.

his ['hiz] *vnw.* sy syne; *vgl.* **he.**

hiss ['his] *s.* (*-es*) gesis, gefluit, geblaas; *ww.* (*-ed*) sis, fluit, blaas.

'history ['histəri] *s.* (*'histories*) geskiedenis; verhaal, storie; **his'toric** *bnw.* histories, geskiedkundig; **his'torian** *s.* geskiedkundige.

histri'onics [histri'oniks] *s.* toneelkuns.

hit ['hit] *ww.* slaan, moker; tref; *s.* (*-s*) slag, hou; treffer; skimp.

hitch ['hitsj] *ww.* (*-ed*) haak, vashaak; swaai, ruk; *ww.* (*-ed*) ry-stap; **-hike** *ww.* (*-d*) duimry; **-hiker** *s.* (*-s*) duimryer.

'hither ['hidhə] *bw.* hierheen, hiernatoe; **-to** *bw.* tot nog toe; **-ward** *bw.* herwaards.

'hive ['haiv] *s.* (*-s*) bykorf, swerm.

hoar ['hō] *bnw.* grys, grou; **-y** *bnw.* grys, grou.

'hoard ['hōd] *ww.* (*-ed*) ophoop, opstapel, oppot; **-ing** *s.* skutting.

'hoarse ['hōs] *bnw.* hees, skor.

hoax ['houks] *ww.* (*-ed*) fop, om die bos lei.

'hobble ['hobl] *ww.* (*-d*) strompel, hink; span(*perde*).

'hobble-skirt ['hoblskət] *s.* strompelrok.

'hobby ['hobi] *s.* (*'hobbies*) stokperdjie; liefhebbery.

'hobnail ['hobnyl] *s.* (*-s*) dikkopspyker.

'hock ['hok] *s.* (*-s*) hakskeenpees; skenkel; hokwyn.

hockey ['hoki] *s.* hokkie.

hocus-'pocus ['houkəs-'poukəs] *s.* goëlery; harlekynlatyn.

hoe ['hou] *s.* (*-s*) skoffel.

hog ['hogh] *s.* (*-s*) vark, burg; vraat, smeerlap.

'hog'sback ['hoghsbæk] *s.* maanhaar.

'hoist ['hoist] *ww.* (*-ed*) oplig, optel; *s.* hyser.

'hold ['hould] *ww.* (*'held*) hou, inhou, bevat; besit; hê; meen; volhou; vier; *s.* (*-s*) vat; greep; houvas; **-ing** *s.* eiendom.

'hole ['houl] *s.* (*-s*) gat; krot; *ww.* (*-d*) gat grawe; in gat slaan(*gooi*).

'holiday ['holədi] *s.* (*-s*) vakansie.

'hollow ['holou] *bnw.* hol; leeg; oneg; *s.* (*-s*) holte, leegte; *ww.* (*-ed*) uithol.

'holly ['holi] *s.* huls.

'holster ['houlstə] *s.* (*-s*) bolster; pistoolsak.

'holy ['houli] *bnw.* heilig; gewyd.

'homage ['homidzj] *s.* hulde, eerbetoon.

'home ['houm] *s.* (*-s*) tuiste, huis, woonplek; tehuis; bof; vaderland; **-made** *bnw.* tuisgemaak; **- rule** *s.* selfregering; **-sick** *bnw.* be - verlang; **-stead** *s.* opstal; **-work** *s.* huiswerk.

'homicide ['homisaid] *s.* manslag, doodslag; pleger van manslag.

'homily ['homili] *s.* (*'homilies*) kanselrede, preek.

'homonym ['homənim] *s.* (*-s*) gelykluidende woord.

'hone ['houn] *ww.* (*-d*) slyp, aansit.

'honest ['onist] *bnw.* eerlik, opreg; kuis; goed; **-y** *s.* eerlikheid; opregtheid; kuisheid.

'honey ['hʌni] *s.* heuning; **-moon** *s.* wittebroodsdae; **-suckle** *s.* kamferfoelie.

'honorary ['onərəri] *bnw.* ere-, eervol.

'honour ['onə] *s.* eer; eerbewys; eergevoel; *ww.* (*-ed*) eer, vereer; respekteer; honoreer; **-able** *bnw.* eervol, eerbaar.

hood ['hōēd] *s.* (*-s*) kap, dampkap, enjinkap, walmkap; **-wink** *ww.* (*-ed*) blinddoek, flous.

hoof ['hōēf] *s.* (*'hooves*) hoef, klou, poot.

hook ['hoek] *s.* (*-s*) haak, hakie; vishoek.

'hooligan ['hōēlighən] *s.* (*-s*) straatboef.

hoop ['hōēp] *s.* hoepel.

'hooping-cough ['hōēping-kof] *s.* kinkhoes; *vgl.* **whooping cough.**

hoot ['hōēt] *ww.* (*-ed*) jou, uitjou; toet; **-er** *s.* toeter.

'hope ['houp] *ww.* (*-d*) hoop, verwag.

'horde ['hōd] *s.* (*-s*) horde, massa.

ho'rizon [hō'raizn] *s.* (*-s*) horison, gesigseinder.

horn ['hōn] *s.* (*-s*) horing.

'hornet ['hōnit] *s.* (*-s*) wesp, perdeby.

'horrible ['horəbl] *bnw.* verskriklik, aaklig.

'horrid ['horid] *bnw.* aaklig.

'horrify ['horifai] *ww.* (*'horrified*) met afsku vervul.

'horror ['horə] *s.* • (*-s*) afsku, huiwering.

'horse ['hōs] *s.* (*-s*) perd; bok; **-fly** *s.* (*-flies*) blindevlieg, perdevlieg; **-play** *s.* ruwe spel; **-power** *s.* perdekrag; **-shoe** *s.* hoefyster.

'hose ['houz] *s.* (*-s*) kouse; tuinslang; **'hosiery** *s.* kouse en ondergoed.

'hospital ['hospitl] *s.* (*-s*) hospitaal; **hospi'tality** *s.* gasvryheid.

host ['houst] *s.* (*-s*) leër, bende; gasheer; **-age** *s.* gyselaar.

'hostile ['hostail] *bnw.* vyandig, vyandelik.

hot ['hot] *bnw.* (*-ter*, *-test*) warm; vurig; sterk; oulik; **-house** *s.* (*-s*) kweekhuis.

ho'tel [hou'tel] *s.* (*-s*) hotel.

hound ['haund] *s.* (*-s*) jaghond, hond.

hour ['auə] *s.* (*-s*) uur.

'house ['haus] s. (-es) huis; saal; skouburg; volksraad; -breaking s. huisbraak; -hold s. huisgesin; -holder s. (-s) huisbewoner.

'hovel ['hovəl] s. (-s) pondok, afdak.

'hover ['hovə] ww. (-ed) fladder, sweef.

how ['hau] bw. hoe; -'ever bw. egter, maar, nietemin.

howl ['haul] ww. (-ed) tjank, huil; -er s. (-s) flater, stommiteit.

hub ['hʌb] s. (-s) naaf, spil; -bub s. lawaai, rumoer; -cap s. naafdop; -extractor s. naaftrekker.

'huddle ['hʌdl] ww. (-d) opeenhoop, opmekaargooi; oprol; inkrimp.

hue ['hjōē] s. (-s) kleur, tint.

hug ['hʌgh] s. (-s) omhelsing.

'huge ['hjōēdzj] bnw. groot, tamaai.

'Huguenot ['hjōēghənot] s. (-s) Hugenoot.

hulk ['hʌlk] s. (-s) romp.

hull ['hʌl] s. (-s) dop; skil; romp; -ed bnw. gepelde (rys).

hum ['hʌm] ww. (-med) gons, brom.

'human ['hjōēmən] s. (-s) mens; bnw. menslik; hu'mane bnw. mensliewend; hu'manity s. mensheid; menslikheid.

'humble ['hʌmbl] bnw. (-r, -st) nederig, eenvoudig.

'humbug ['hʌmbʌgh] s. bedrog, kullery.

'humdrum ['hʌmdrʌm] bnw. eentonig, saai.

'humerus ['hjōēmərəs] s. humerus, bo-armpyp.

'humid ['hjōēmid] bnw. vogtig; hu'midity s. vogtigheid.

hu'miliate [hjōē'miliyt] ww. (-d) verneder; hu'mility s. nederigheid; humili'ation s. vernedering.

'humour ['hjōēmə] s. bui, luim; humor; geestigheid; -ous bnw. grappig.

'hundred ['hʌndrəd] s. (-s) honderd; -weight s. sentenaar.

'hunger ['hʌng-ghə] s. honger; lus; hunkering; hungry bnw. honger, hongerig.

hunt ['hʌnt] ww. (-ed) jag; jaag; soek na.

'hurdle ['hədl] s. (-s) hekkie; struikelblok.

hurl ['həl] ww. (-ed) smyt, slinger.

'hurricane ['hʌrikən] s. (-s) orkaan.

'hurry ['hʌri] s. haas, haastigheid, gejaagdheid; ww. ('hurried) haastig wees, gou maak, haas, jaag.

hurt ['hət] ww. (-ed) seermaak.

'husband ['hʌzbənd] s. (-s) man, eggenoot; -ry s. landbou.

'hustle ['hʌsl] ww. (-d) dwing, woel, aanjaag.

hut ['hʌt] s. (-s) hut, pondok, strooIS.

'hybrid ['haibrid] s. (-s) baster.

'hydrogen ['haidridzjən] s. waterstof.

'hydro'phobia ['haidrə'foubiə] s. watervrees, hondsdolheid.

'hymn ['him] s. (-s) himne, gesang, lofsang.

hy'perbole [hai'pəbəli] s. (-s) hiperbool, oordrywing.

'hyphen ['haifən] s. (-s) koppelteken.

'hypocrite ['hipōkrit] s. (-s) huigelaar, geveinsde, skynheilige.

hy'potenuse [hai'potnjoes] s. skuinssy.

hy'pothesis [hai'pothisis] s. (hy'potheses) onderstelling, hipotese.

hys'teria [his'tiəriə] s. histerie; hys'teric bnw. histeries.

I

ISCOR (Iron and Steel Corporation) YSKOR Yster- en Staalkorporasie.

I ['ai] vnw. ek.

ice ['ais] s. ys; - age s. ysperiode; -berg s. (-s) ysberg; -bound bnw. vasgevries; -cream s. roomys; 'icicle s. ysnaald; 'icily bw. yskoud, ysig; 'icing s. glasering, versiersuiker; 'icy bnw. yskoud.

'icon ['aikn] s. (-s) beeld, ikon.

'ictus ['iktəs] s. slag, aksent.

i'dea [ai'diə] s. (-s) idee, gedagte; begrip, denkbeeld; plan; -l bnw. ideaal, volmaak; denkbeeldig.

i'dentity [ai'dentiti] s. (i'dentities) identiteit; eenselwigheid; i'dentify ww. (i'dentified) herken; gelykstel; identifiseer.

i'deogram [ai'dioughræm] s. (-s) begripteken.

ide'ology [aidi'olidzji] s. (ide'ologies) ideologie.

'idiom ['idiəm] s. (-s) idioom, wending, segswyse; tongval.

idio'syncrasy [idiō'sinkrəsi] s. (idio'syncrasies) eienaardigheid, eienskap.

'idiot ['idiət] s. (-s) idioot, stommerik; 'idiocy s. idiootheid, sotheid; idi'otic bnw. idioot, dwaas.

'idle ['aidl] bnw. ledig, werkloos; vry, onbeset; tevergeefs; ydel; ww. (-d) leegloop; luier (masjien, enjin); -r gear s. tussenrat, leiwiel; -r s. leegloper; idling s. luiering.

'idol ['aidl] s. (-s) afgod.

'idyll ['aidil] s. (-s) idille.

if ['if] voegw. as, indien, ingeval; of.

ig'nite [igh'nait] ww. (-d) aansteek, ontsteek, ontvlam; ig'nition s. ontbranding, ontsteking.

igno'minious [ighnō'miniəs] bnw. skandelik, smadelik.

igno'ramus [ighnou'rāmʌs] s. domkop.

'ignorance ['ighnərəns] s. onkunde, onwetendheid; 'ignorant bnw. onwetend, onkundig, dom.

ig'nore [igh'nō] ww. (-d) ignoreer, oor die hoof sien.

ilk ['ilk] s. klas, soort.

ill ['il] *bnw.* siek; sleg; moeilik; *bw.* sleg, kwalik; *s.* (-s) kwaad, euwel; -bred *bnw.* onmanierlik.

il'legal [i'lighl] *bnw.* onwettig.

il'legible [i'ledzjəbl] *bnw.* onleesbaar.

ille'gitimate [ili'dzjitimit] *bnw.* onwettig.

il'licit [i'lisit] *bnw.* onwettig.

il'literate [i'litərit] *bnw.* ongeletterd.

'ill-'treat ['il'trit] *ww.* (-ed) mishandel.

il'luminate [i'ljŏĕminyt] *ww.* (-d) verlig; inlig; verduidelik.

il'lusion [i'ljŏĕzjən] *s.* (-s) sinsbedrog, skim, illusie.

'illustrate ['iləstryt] *ww.* (-d) verduidelik; ophelder; illustreer.

il'lustrious [i'lʌstriəs] *bnw.* beroemd, deerlugtig.

'image ['imidzj] *s.* (-s) beeld, beeltenis.

i'magine [i'mædzkin] *ww.* (-d) verbeel, voorstel, bedink, begryp.

'imbecile ['imbisail] *s.* (-s) idioot, imbesiel.

im'bibe [im'baib] *ww.* (-d) drink, opneem.

'imitate ['imityt] *ww.* (-d) navolg, naboots.

im'maculate [i'mækjoelit] *bnw.* onbevlek, rein; onberispelik.

imma'ture [imə'tsjoeə] *bnw.* ombeleë; onvolwasse.

im'mediate [i'midjət] *bnw.* onmiddellik, dadelik.

im'mense [i'mens] *bnw.* ontsaglik; enorm; skitterend.

im'merse [i'məs] *ww.* (-d) indompel, insteek.

'immigrant ['imighrənt] *s.* (-s) immigrant, intrekker.

im'mune [i'mjŏĕn] *bnw.* onvatbaar, vry, gevaad.

imp ['imp] *s.* (-s) rakker, ondeug, kwelgees; -ish *bnw.* duiwels.

'impact ['impækt] *s.* (-s) botsing, skok, slag; force of - trefkrag; point of - trefpunt.

im'pair [im'pèə] *ww.* (-ed) benadeel, verswak.

im'partial [im'pāsjəl] *bnw.* onpartydig.

im'patient [im'pysjənt] *bnw.* ongeduldig, onverdraagsaam.

im'peach [im'pitsj] *ww.* (-ed) beskuldig, aanklal; afkam.

im'pede [im'pid] *ww.* (-d) hinder, belemmer.

im'pel [im'pel] *ww.* (-led) aanspoor, aandryf, stu; -ler *s.* stuwer; -ler blade *s.* stuwerblad.

im'pending [im'pending] *bnw.* dreigend.

im'perative [im'perətiv] *bnw.* bevelend, gebiedend.

im'perial [im'piəriəl] *bnw.* keiserlik, vorstelik.

im'peril [im'peril] *ww.* (-led) in gevaar bring(stel).

im'personate [im'pəsənyt] *ww.* (-d) voorstel, verpersoonlik.

im'pertinent [im'pətinənt] *bnw.* parmantig, astrant; nie tersake.

'im'pervious [im'pəviəs] *bnw.* ondeurdringbaar, ontoeganklik.

im'petuous [im'petjoeəs] *bnw.* voortvarend.

'impetus ['impitəs] *s.* vaart, krag; aandrang.

im'piety [im'paiəti] *s.* goddeloosheid; oneerbiedigheid; **'impious** *bnw.* goddeloos.

im'plant [im'plānt] *ww.* (-ed) implant; inprent.

'implement ['implimənt] *s.* (-s) werktuig, gereedskap; *ww.* (-ed) vervul; aanvul; uitvoer.

'implicate ['implikyt] *ww.* (-d) inwikkel; insluit; meebring.

im'plicit [im'plisit] *bnw.* ingeslote, vanselfsprekend.

im'plore [im'plŏ] *ww.* (-d) smeek.

im'ply [im'plai] *ww.* (im'plied) insluit, behels; bedui; insinueer.

im'port [im'pôt] *ww.* (-ed) invoer; uitdruk.

im'portance [im'pôtəns] *s.* belang (rikheid) betekenis; gewig; **im'portant** *bnw.* belangrik, gewigtig.

im'pose [im'pouz] *ww.* (-d) oplê; inslaan; imponeer; bedrieg.

im'postor [im'postə] *s.* (-s) indringer, bedrieër.

im'possible [im'posbl] *bnw.* onmoontlik; onuitstaanbaar.

'impotence ['impôtəns] *s.* onmag; impotensie; **'impotent** *bnw.* magteloos, impotent.

im'pound [im'paund] *ww.* (-ed) skut, beslag lê op.

im'poverish [im'povərisj] *ww.* (-ed) verarm; uitput.

im'pregnate [im'preghnyt] *ww.* (-d) bevrug; laat deurtrek van; **im'pregnable** *bnw.* onneembaar, onaantasbaar.

im'press [im'pres] *ww.* (-ed) indruk, inprent; tref, indruk maak; -ion *s.* indruk; stempel; oplaag.

im'promptu [im'promptjŏĕ] *bnw. & bw.* uit die vuis.

im'prove [im'prŏĕv] *ww.* (-d) verbeter; bewerk.

'improvise ['imprŏvaiz] *ww.* (-d) uit die vuis lewer.

im'prudent [im'prŏĕdənt] *bnw.* onbedag.

'impudence ['impjoedəns] *s.* brutaliteit.

im'pugn [im'pjŏĕn] *ww.* (-ed) bestry; in twyfel trek.

'impulse ['impʌls] *s.* (-s) drang; prikkel; impuls; **im'pulsive** *bnw.* impulsief.

im'punity [im'pjŏĕniti] *s.* strafloosheid.

im'pute [im'pjŏĕt] *ww.* (-d) toeskryf, wyt.

in ['in] *voors.* in, op, by; *bw.* in, binne; *bnw.* binne; in- *voorsetsel* op, in, na, teen; nie-, on-.

in'adequate [in'ædikwit] *bnw.*, *bw.* ontoereikend.

inad'vertent [inəd'vᵊtənt] *bnw.* onopsetlik; agtelosig.

in'ane [i'nyn] *bnw.* leeg; sinloos; idioot.

in'apt [i'næpt] *bnw.* ongeskik, misplaas.

inas'much [inəz'mʌtsj] *bw.* aangesien, nademaal.

in'augural [i'nôghjoerəl] *bnw.* inwydings-, intree-; **in'augurate** *ww.* (-*d*) inwy, open.

'in'bred ['in'bred] *bnw.* aangebore.

incan'desce [inkæn'dəs] *ww.* (-*d*) gloei, liggee; **-nce** *s.* gloeiing; **-nt** *bnw.* gloeiend, liggewend.

'incan'tation ['inkæn'tysjn] *s.* beswering.

in'carcerate [in'kãsəryt] *ww.* (-*d*) inkerker, opsluit.

in'carnate [in'kãnit] *bnw.* beliggaam, vleeslik.

in'cendiary [in'sendjəri] *bnw.* brandstigtend.

'incense ['insens] *s.* wierook; *ww.* [in'sens] (-*d*) bewierook; vertoorn; **in'centive** *s.* (-*s*) aansporing.

in'ception [in'sepsjən] *s.* begin, aanvang.

in'certitude [in'sᵊtitjôëd] *s.* onsekerheid.

in'cessant [in'sesnt] *bnw.* onophoudelik.

'incest ['insest] *s.* bloedskande.

inch ['intsj] *s.* (-*es*) duim; *ww.* (-*ed*) por.

'inchoative ['inkouytiv] *bnw.* beginnend, inchoatief.

'incident ['insidənt] *s.* (-*s*) voorval; *bnw.* insidenteel; **'incidence** *s.* trefwydte; trefpunt; die voorkoms; **inci'dental** *bnw.* toevallig; **inci'dentally** *bw.* toevallig.

in'cinerate [in'sinəryt] *ww.* (-*d*) verbrand, veras.

in'cipience [in'sipiəns] *s.* aanvang; **in'cipient** *bnw.* aanvangend, beginnend.

in'cision [in'sizjən] *s.* (-*s*) insnyding, kerf, sny; **in'cisor** *s.* (-*s*) snytand.

in'cite [in'sait] *ww.* (-*d*) aanspoor, aanhits; **-ment** *s.* aansporing; aanhitsing.

inci'vility [insi'viliti] *s.* onbeleefdheid.

in'clemency [in'klemənsi] *s.* guurheid; onbarmhartigheid; **in'clement** *bnw.* guur; onbarmhartig.

in'cline [in'klain] *ww.* (-*d*) buig, neig, oorhel; **incli'nation** *s.* helling; neiging.

in'clude [in'klôëd] *ww.* (-*d*) insluit, omvat, meetel; **in'clusion** *s.* insluiting; **in'clusive** *bnw.* insluitend, inklusief.

in'cognito [in'koghnitou] *bnw.* incognito, onder skuilnaam.

inco'herence [inkou'hiərins] *s.* onsamehangendheid; **inco'herent** *bnw.* onsamehangend.

'income ['inkəm] *s.* (-*s*) inkomste; **in'coming** *bnw.* binnelopend.

incom'mode [inkə'moud] *ww.* (-*d*) ontrief, tot oorlas wees.

in'comparable [in'kompərəbl] *bnw.* onvergelyklik, weergaloos.

incom'patible [inkəm'pætbl] *bnw.* teenstrydig, onverenigbaar.

in'competence [in'kompitəns] *s.* onbevoegdheid.

incon'gruity [inkong'ghroeiti] *s.* ongerymdheid; **in'congruous** *bnw.* onverenigbaar.

in'consequence [in'konsikwəns] *s.* inkonsekwensie; **in'consequent** *bnw.* ontoepaslik; misplaas; onlogies.

incon'siderate [inkən'sidərit] *bnw.* onbedagsaam.

incon'sistent [inkən'sistənt] *bnw.* teenstrydig.

incon'solable [inkən'souləbl] *bnw.* ontroosbaar.

in'continence [in'kontinəns] *s.* onmatigheid; **in'continent** *bnw.* onmatig, onbeheers.

incon'venience [inkən'vinjəns] *s.* ongemak, ongerief.

in'corporate [in'kôperit] *bnw.* ingelyf, geïnkorporeer; *ww.* [inkôpə-'ryt] (-*d*) inkorporeer, inlyf.

in'corrigible [in'koridzjəbl] *bnw.* ongeneeslik.

incor'ruptible [inkə'rʌptəbl] *bnw.* onomkoopbaar.

in'crease [in'kris] *ww.* (-*d*) vermeerder; *s.* vermeerdering; toename.

in'credible [in'kredəbl] *bnw.* ongelooflik.

in'credulous [in'kredjôëləs] *bnw.* ongelowig.

'increment ['inkrimənt] *s.* (-*s*) vermeerdering, aanwas.

in'criminate [in'kriminyt] *ww.* (-*d*) beskuldig, intrek.

'incubate ['inkjoebyt] *ww.* (-*d*) uitbroei; broei; **incu'bator** *s.* broeimasjien.

'inculcate ['inkʌlkyt] *ww.* (-*d*) inprent.

in'cumbent [in'kʌmbənt] *bw.* - on rustend op.

in'cur [in'kᵊ] *ww.* (-*red*) blootstel aan, op die hals haal.

in'curable [in'kjoeərəbl] *bnw.* ongeneeslik.

in'cursion [in'kᵊsjən] *s.* (-*s*) inval.

in'debted [in'detid] *bnw.* verskuldig.

in'decency [in'disnsi] *s.* onwelvoeglikheid.

inde'cision [indi'sizjən] *s.* besluiteloosheid.

in'decorous [in'dekərəs] *bnw.* onbehoorlik; ondeftig; **inde'corum** [indi'kôrəm] *s.* ondeftigheid, ongepastheid.

in'deed [in'did] *bw.* werklik, regtig, inderdaad.

in'definite [in'definit] *bnw.* onbepaald.

in'delible [in'delibl] bnw. onuitwisbaar.

in'delicate [in'delikit] bnw. onkies, takloos.

in'demnify [in'demnifai] ww. (in'demnified) skadeloostel; in'demnity s. vergoeding; indemnifi'cation s. vrywaring.

in'dent [in'dent] ww. (-ed) tand, insny, inkerf; bestel; stempel, merk; s. (-s) deuk; stempel; -ure s. formulier, kontrak; bestelling; inkerwing.

inde'terminate [indi'təminit] bnw. onbepaald.

'index ['indeks] s. ('indices) indeks; rigsnoer; wysvinger; register; klapper.

'India ['indjə] s. Indië.

'indicate ['indikyt] ww. (-d) aandui, aanwys, aan die hand gee; indi'cation s. aanwysing aanduiding; in'dicative bnw. aantonend, indikatief; 'indicator s. wyser, aanwyser.

in'dict [in'dait] ww. (-ed) beskuldig, aankla; -ment s. (-s) beskuldiging; verhoor.

in'difference [in'difrəns] s. onverskilligheid, afsydigheid.

'indigence ['indidzjəns] s. behoeftigheid, armoede.

in'digenous [in'didzjinəs] bnw. inheems.

'indigestion ['indidzjestsjən] s. indigestie, slegte spysvertering.

in'dignant [in'dighnənt] bnw. verontwaardig; indig'nation s. verontwaardiging.

in'dignity [in'dighniti] s. (in'dignities) belediging, smaad.

indi'rect [indi'rekt] bnw. indirek, onregstreeks.

indis'creet [indis'krit] bnw., bw. onbesonne, onversigtig; indis'cretion s. onbesonnenheid; glips.

indis'criminate [indis'kriminit] bnw. voor die voet, sonder onderskeid.

indis'posed [indis'pouzd] bnw. ongeneë; ongesteld; afkerig; indispo'sition s. ongeneentheid; ongesteldheid.

'indis'putable ['indis'pjöëtəbl] bnw. onbetwisbaar.

indis'tinct [indis'tinkt] bnw. dof, vaag, onduidelik.

in'dite [in'dait] ww. (-d) opstel, saamstel.

indi'vidual [indi'vidjoeəl] bnw. individueel, afsonderlik; s. (-s) individu, enkeling; individu'ality n. persoonlikheid, eie aard.

'indolence ['indôləns] s. traagheid, luiheid; 'indolent bnw. traag, lui.

in'domitable [in'domətbl] bnw. onbedwingbaar, onversetlik.

'in'doors ['in'dôz] bw. binnenshuis, binne.

in'dorse [in'dôs] ww. (-d) endosseer; vgl. endorse.

in'duce [in'djöës] ww. (-d) oorhaal, beweeg; veroorsaak; -ment s. aanleiding; lokmiddel; oorsaak; aansporing.

in'duct [in'dʌkt] ww. (-ed) inlei, inwy.

in'dulge [in'dʌldzj] ww. (-d) toegee aan; koester; verwen; die vrye loop gee; -nce s. toegewing, verwenning; -nt bnw. toegewend, toegeeflik.

in'dustrial [in'dʌstriəl] bnw. industrieel, nywerheids-; s. nyweraar; in'dustrialist s. fabrikant; in'dustrious bnw. ywerig; naarstig; 'industry s. ('industries) nywerheid; ywer.

in'ebriate [i'nibriyt] bnw. dronk, beskonke; s. dronkaard; inebr'iety s. dronkenskap.

in'effable [in'efəbl] bnw. onsegbaar, onuitspreeklik.

in'equity [in'ekwiti] s. onbillikheid.

in'ert [i'nət] bnw. traag, bewegingloos; i'nertia s. traagheid, inersie.

in'estimable [in'estiməbl] bnw. onskatbaar.

in'exorable [in'eksərəbl] bnw. onverbiddelik.

'infamous ['infəməs] bnw. skandelik, skandalig; eerloos; berug; 'infamy s. skandaligheid; eerloosheid.

'infancy ['infənsi] s. kindsheid, jeug; 'infant s. (-s) kindjie, suigeling; in'fanticide s. kindermoord; 'infantile bnw. kinderlik, kinderagtig, kinder-.

'infantry ['infəntri] s. infanterie, voetvolk.

in'fatuate [in'fætjoeyt] ww. (-d) versot maak verdwaas; -d bnw. versot, gek, verdwaas; verlief; infatu'ation s. versotheid.

in'fect [in'fekt] ww. (-ed) aansteek; besmet; -ion s. besmetting; -ious bnw. aansteeklik, besmetlik; -ive bnw. aansteeklik, besmetlik.

in'fer [in'fə] ww. (-red) aflei; bedoel; 'inference s. gevolgtrekking; infe'rential bnw. afleibaar.

in'ferior [in'fiəriə] bnw. ondergeskik, onder-; minderwaardig; s. (-s) mindere, ondergeskikte.

in'fernal [in'fənl] bnw. hels; in'ferno s. hel, inferno.

in'fest [in'fest] ww. (-ed) vervuil, verpes, teister.

'infidel ['infidəl] s. (-s) ongelowige; bnw. ongelowig; infi'delity s. ongeloof, ontrou.

in'finite ['infinit] bnw. oneindig; s. oneindigheid; -ly bw. oneindig; infini'tesimal bnw. oneindig klein, nietig; in'finitive s. (-s) infinitief, onbepaalde wys; in'finity s. oneindigheid.

in'firm [in'fəm] bnw. swak; -ary s. (in'firmaries) siekehuis; -ity s. (in'firmities) swakheid, sieklikheid.

in'flame [in'flym] ww. (-d) ontsteek; aan die brand steek; aanvuur; inflammasie kry; in'flammable bnw.

brandbaar; **inflam'mation** s. ontsteking.

in'flate [in'flyt] ww. (-d) opblaas; opdryf, opjaag.

in'flect [in'flekt] ww. (-ed) buig, verbuig; **-ed** bnw. verboë; **-ion** s. verbuiging.

in'flict [in'flikt] ww. (-ed) oplê, toebring; **-ion** s. oplegging; leed, straf, kwelling.

influence ['infloeəns] s. (-s) invloed, inwerking; **influ'ential** bnw. invloedryk.

'influx ['inflʌks] s. instroming, toevloed.

in'form [in'fôm] ww. (-ed) meedeel, berig; verklik; **infor'mation** s. inligting; **-ative** bnw. leersaam.

in'formal [in'fôml] bnw. informeel, sonder seremonie; **infor'mality** s. informaliteit.

'infra ['infrə] bnw. & bw. benede, infra-.

in'fraction [in'fræksjən] s. oortreding.

in'fringe [in'frindzj] ww. (-d) oortree, breek, skend.

in'furiate [in'fjoeəriyt] ww. (-d) vertoorn.

in'fuse [in'fjôëz] ww. (-d) inglet, inboesem; laat trek; **in'fusion** s. aftreksel, afkooksel.

in'genious [in'dzjinjəs] bnw. oulik, vindingryk; **ingen'uity** s. vernuftigheid; **in'genuous** bnw. onskuldig.

'ingot ['ing-ghət] s. (-s) staaf, baar.

in'grate [in'ghryt] bnw. ondankbaar; **in'gratiate** ww. (-d) in die guns bring.

in'gredient [in'ghridiənt] s. (-s) bestanddeel.

'ingress ['in-ghres] s. ingang, toegang.

in'habit [in'hæbit] ww. (-ed) bewoon, okkupeer; **-ant** s. inwoner.

in'hale [in'hyl] ww. (-d) inasem, intrek.

in'herent [in'hiərənt] bnw. onafskeidelik verbonde met, inherent.

in'herit [in'herit] ww. (-ed) erf, oorerf; **-ance** s. erfenis.

in'hibit [in'hibit] ww. (-ed) hindei, belet, stuit; **inhi'bition** s. stuiting, inhibisie.

in'imical [i'nimikəl] bnw. vyandelik, vyandig.

in'iquitous [i'nikwitəs] bnw. onregverdig, onbillik; **in'iquity** s. onregverdigheid.

i'nitial [i'nisjəl] bnw. eerste, aanvangs-; s. (-s) voorletter; ww. (-led) parafeer.

i'nitiate [i'nisjiyt] ww. (-d) begin, inwy; **initi'ation** s. inwyding; aanvang; **in'itiative** s. inisiatief.

in'ject [in'dzjekt] ww. (-ed) inspuit; **-ion** s. inspuiting.

in'junction [in'dzjʌnksjən] s. (-s) opdrag, bevel.

'injure ['indzjə] ww. (-d) seerm.ak, beseer; **in'jurious** bnw. nadelig,

skadelik; **'injury** s. ('injuries) besering, wond, letsel; nadeel.

ink ['ink] s. ink.

'inkling ['inkling] s. vermoede, wenk.

'inlet ['inlet] s. opening, inlaat, ingang; inham.

'inmate ['inmyt] s. (-s) bewoner, inwoner.

inn ['in] s. (-s) herberg.

in'nate [i'nyt] bnw. aangebore, ingebore.

'inner ['inə] bnw. binne-, binneste, innerlik; **- tube** s. binnebuis.

'innervate ['inəvyt] ww. (-d) krag gee, staal; besenu.

'innings ['inings] s. beurt.

'innocence ['inəsns] s. onskuld; **'innocent** bnw. onskuldig.

in'nocuous [i'nokjoeəs] bnw. onskadelik.

inno'vation [inə'vysjən] s. (-s) nuwigheid.

innu'endo [injoe'endou] s. (-s) skimp, toespeling.

in'oculate [i'nokjoelyt] ww. (-d) inent; **innocu'lation** s. inenting.

in'ordinate [i'nôdinit] bnw. buitensporig, oordrewe.

inor'ganic [inô'ghænik] bnw. onbewerktuig, anorganies.

'input ['inpoet] s. voorv. ingangs-, aanvangs-.

'inquest ['inkwest] s. (-s) ondersoek, lykskouing.

in'quire [in'kwaiə] ww. (-d) verneem, navra; **in'quiry** s. navraag; ondersoek.

inqui'sition [inkwi'zisjən] s. ondersoek; inkwissie; **in'quisitive** bnw. nuuskierig; **in'quisitor** s. ondersoeker, regter; inkwisiteur.

'inroad ['inroud] s. (-s) inval; inbreuk.

in'sane [in'syn] bnw. kranksinnig, gek; **in'sanity** s. kranksinnigheid.

in'satiate [in'sysjiət] bnw. onversadigbaar; **in'satiable** bnw. onversadiglik.

in'scribe [in'skraib] ww. (-d) inskryf, crskryf; graveer; ingrif: **in'scription** s. inskripsie.

in'scrutable [in'skrôëtəbl] bnw. ondeurgrondelik.

'insect ['insekt] s. (-s) insek, gogga; **-icide** s. insekpoeier.

in'sert [in'sət] ww. (-ed) insteek, invoeg, inlas; opneem; **-ion** s.

'inset ['inset] s. (-s) byvoegsel, bylae; by-portret; inlegsel.

'inside ['insaid] bw. binne(kant, -in) voors. binne.

in'sidious [in'sidiəs] bnw. verraderlik, listig.

in'signia [in'sighniə] s. ordetekens.

in'sinuate [in'sinjoeyt] ww. (-d) insinueer, te verstaan gee; **insinu-'ation** s.

in'sipid [in'sipid] bnw. laf, flou.

in'sist [in'sist] ww. (-ed) nadruk lê, aandring op; aanhou, volhard;

-ence s. aandrang; volharding; **-ently** bw. voortdurend.

'in 'situ ['in 'sitoe] bw. in oorspronklike situasie, op werklike plek van gebeurtenis.

'insolence ['insələns] s. parmantigheid; brutaliteit; **'insolent** bnw. parmantig, brutaal.

in'solvent [in'solvənt] bnw. bankrot.

in'somnia [in'somniə] s. slaaploosheid.

in'spect [in'spekt] ww. (-ed) inspekteer, ondersoek, nasien; **-ion** s. -or s. inspekteur.

in'spire [in'spaiə] ww. (-d) ingee; besiel, aanvuur; inasem; inspireer; **inspi'ration** s. inaseming; ingewing, besieling, inspirasie; **inspi'ratory** bnw. inasemend.

in'stall [in'stôl] ww. (-ed) installeer, bevestig, inrig, aanlê; **instal'lation** s.

in'stalment [in'stôlmənt] s. (-s) gedeelte, termyn; paaiement.

'instance ['instəns] s. (-s) voorbeeld, geval; instansie; aandrang; **'instant** s. oomblik; **instan'taneous** bnw. oombliklik; **'instantly** bw. dadelik.

in'stead [in'sted] bw. - of in plaas van.

'instep ['instep] s. (-s) wreef, brug van voet.

'instigate ['instighyt] ww. (-d) aanspoor, aanhits.

'instinct ['instinkt] s. (-s) aangebore drang, impuls, intuïsie.

'insular ['insjoelə] bnw. insulêr; bekrompe.

'insult ['insʌlt] s. (-s) belediging.

in'superable [in'sjôëpərəbl] bnw. onoorkomelik.

in'surance [in'sjoeərəns] s. assuransie, versekering.

in'surgent [in'sədzjənt] bnw. opstandig, oproerig.

insur'rection [insə'reksjən] s. opstand, oproer.

in'tact [in'tækt] bnw. ongeskonde, ongerep, heel.

in'teger [in'tidzjə] s. heelgetal.

'integral ['intighrəl] bnw. heel, vol, volledig; integraal.

'integrate ['intighryt] ww. (-d) volledig maak, saamstel, intigreer; **in'tegrity** s. eerlikheid.

'intellect ['intilekt] s. (-s) verstand, gees(vermoë), intellek; **intel'lectual** bnw. verstandelik, intellektueel.

in'telligence [in'telidzjəns] s. verstand, oordeel, vernuf, intelligensie; berig, tyding; **in'telligent** bnw. verstandig, intelligent; **intelli'gentsia** s. die geletterde, kultuurlaag van 'n volk.

in'telligible [in'telidzjəbl] bnw. begryplik, bevatlik.

in'temperance [in'tempərəns] s. onmatigheid; dranksug; **in'temperate** bnw. onmatig; dranksugtig.

in'tend [in'tend] ww. (-ed) van voorneme wees; bedoel, bestem vir; **-ed** bnw. bedoelde; **-ing** bnw.

in'tense [in'tens] bnw. (-r, -st) intens, sterk, kragtig; **in'tensity** s. hewigheid, krag, intensiteit.

in'tent [in'tent] bnw. vasbeslote; gespanne.

in'tention [in'tensjən] s. (-s) bedoeling, voornemens.

in'ter [in'tə] ww. (-red) begrawe, ter aarde bestel; **-ment** s.

'inter ['intə] voors. inter, onder, tussen.

inter'cede [intə'sid] ww. (-d) tussenbeide tree, as middelaar optree.

inter'cept [intə'sept] ww. (-ed) onderskep, opvang; stuit.

inter'cession [intə'sesjən] s. bemiddeling; tussenkoms.

'inter'city ['intə'siti] bnw. tussenstedelik.

'intercourse ['intəkôs] s. gemeenskap, omgang.

inter'dict [intə'dikt] s. (-s) verbod; interdik.

'interest ['intrist] s. (-s) belang; belangstelling; deel voordeel; rente; **'interested** bnw. belangstellend; **'interesting** bnw. belangwekkend.

inter'fere [intə'fiə] ww. (-d) jou bemoei met, ingryp.

'interim ['intərim] s. tussentyd.

in'terior [in'tiəriə] s. (-s) binneste; binneland.

inter'ject [intə'dzjekt] ww. (-ed) uitroep; tussenwerp.

inter'linear [intə'liniə] bnw. tussen die reëls (geskryf of gedruk).

inter'locutor [intə'lokjoetə] s. (-s) gesprekgenoot; ondervraer.

'interloper ['intəloupə] s. indringer; onderkruiper.

'interlude ['intəlōëd] s. (-s) tussenspel; pouse.

inter'mediary [intə'midiəri] s. (inter'mediaries) tussenganger, middelaar; **inter'mediate** bnw. intermediêr, tussentyds, tussen-.

inter'mittent [intə'mitənt] bnw. afwisselend, vlaag-vlaag.

in'tern [in'tən] ww. (-ed) interneer, ir.sper.

inter'pose [intə'pouz] ww. (-d) ingryp, tussenbeide tree.

in'terpret [in'təprit] ww. (-ed) tolk; vertolk; verklaar; **interpre'tation** s. (-s) vertolking, uitleg; **-er** s. tolk; vertolker.

inter'punction [intə'pʌnksjən] s. punktuasie.

in'terrogate [in'terōghyt] ww. (-d) ondervra; **inter'rogative** bnw. vraend, ondervraend.

inter'rupt [intə'rʌpt] ww. (-ed) steur, onderbreek; **-ion** s. (-s) onderbreking, steuring, steurnis.

inter'sect [intə'sekt] ww. (-ed) sny, kruis; **inter'section** s. kruispunt.

inter'sperse [intə'spəs] ww. (-d) meng, deurskiet.

in'terstice [in'tɔstis] s. (-s) tussen-ruimte, opening.

'interval ['intəvəl] s. (-s) tussentyd, pouse, rustyd; afstand.

inter'vene [intə'vin] ww. (-d) ingryp; tussenin gebeur; **inter'vention** s. tussenkoms.

'interview ['intəvjōē] ww. (-ed) 'n onderhoud hê met.

in'testate [in'testit] bnw. sonder testament.

in'testine [in'testin] s. (-s) derm, nersderm.

'intimate ['intimit] bnw. vertroulik, gemeensaam, intiem.

inti'mation [inti'mysjən] s. (-s) aanduiding; berig.

in'timidate [in'timidyt] ww.(-d) bang maak, skrik aanja.

'into ['intoe] voors in, tot in.

in'tolerance [in'tolərəns] s. onver-draagsaamheid.

in'tolerant [in'tolərənt] bnw. onver-draagsaam.

in'toxicate [in'toksikyt] ww. (-d) bedwelm, dronk maak; **-d** bnw. dronk, besope; **in'toxicant** s. be-dwelmende drank.

in'trepid [in'trepid] bnw. onversaag, dapper.

'intricate ['intrikit] bnw. ingewik-keld.

in'trigue [in'trigh] s. (-s) knoeiery, kuipery.

in'trinsic [in'trinsik] bnw. innerlik, werklik.

intro'duce [intrə'djōēs] ww. (-d) voorstel, bekendstel, inlei; **intro'duction** s. voorstelling, inleiding, voorbereiding; **intro'ductory** bnw. inleidend.

intro'spection [introu'speksjən] s. selfondersoek, introspeksie.

in'trude [in'trōēd] ww. (-d) indruk; opdring; indring.

in'trusion [in'trōēzjən] s. (-s) indringing.

intu'ition [intjoe'isjən] s. intuïsie, voorgevoel.

'inundate ['inʌndyt] ww. (-d) oor-stroom; oorstelp; **inun'dation** s. oorstroming.

in'ure [i'njoeə] ww. (-d) gewend raak aan; in werking tree.

in'vade [in'vyd] ww. (-d) binnedring; inval in.

'invalid ['invilid] s. (-s) sieke; **-chair** s. (-s) siekestoel.

in'validate [in'vælidyt] ww. (-d) ongeldig maak, ontsenu.

in'valuable [in'væljoeəbl] bnw. on-skatbaar.

in'variable [in'vēəriəbl] bnw. on-veranderlik.

in'vective [in'vektiv] s. (-s) skel-woorde, slegmakery.

in'veigle [in'vighl] ww. (-d) verlei, verlok.

in'vent [in'vent] ww. (-ed) uitvind; bedink.

'inventory ['inventri] s. ('inventories) lys, inventaris.

in'verse ['in'vɔs] bnw. omgekeer.

in'vest [in'vest] ww. (-ed) beklee, belê.

in'vestigate [in'vestighyt] ww. (-d) ondersoek, navors.

investi'gation [investi'ghysjən] s. ondersoek.

in'veterate [in'vetərit] bnw. ver-stokte.

in'vidious [in'vidiəs] bnw. haatlik, aanstootlik; partydig.

in'vigilate [in'vidzjilyt] ww. (-d) toesig hou, oppas; **in'vigilator** s. opsiener, opsigter.

in'vincible [in'vinsəbl] bnw. onoor-winlik.

in'violable [in'vaiələbl] bnw. on-skendbaar.

in'vite [in'vait] ww. (-ed) uitnooi, vra, versoek; **in'viting** bnw. aan-loklik; **invi'tation** s. uitnodiging.

'invoice ['invois] s. (-s) faktuur, geleibrief.

in'voke [in'vouk] ww. (-d) aanroep, inroep, afsmeek.

in'voluntary [in'volentəri] bnw. onwillekeurig.

in'volve [in'volv] ww. (-d) betrek, insleep; insluit; as gevolg hê.

'iodine ['aiədin] s. jodium.

'iota [ai'outə] s. (-s) jota.

'i.o.'u. ['aiou'jōē] s. (-s) skuldbewys.

i'pe'cacuanha [i'pi'kækjoeænə] s. Suid-Amerikaanse rankplant; **-wine** s. wynvomitief.

'ipse 'dixit ['ipsi 'diksit] hy sê dit self.

'ipso 'facto ['ipsou 'fæktou] bw. vanselfsprekend.

i'rascible [i'ræsibl] bnw. driftig.

i'rate [ai'ryt] bnw. kwaad, woedend.

'ire ['aiə] s. woede; **i'rate** bnw. kwaad, woedend.

'iris ['aiəris] s. reenboogvlies; iris; vlap(blom).

'irksome ['ɔksəm] bnw. vermoeiend, vervelend.

'iron ['aiən] s. (-s) yster, brandyster; strykyster; ww. (-ed) stryk; boei; **-monger** s. ysterhandelaar.

'irony ['aiəni] s. ironie.

irradi'ation [irydi'ysjən] s. (-s) uitstraling; stralekrans.

ir'rational [i'ræsjənl] bnw. onredelik, redeloos; irrasioneel.

irre'futable [iri'fjoetəbl] bnw. onomstootlik.

ir'regular [i'reghjoelə] bnw. onreël-matig; wanordelik.

ir'relevant [i'relivənt] bnw. onsaak-lik, nie ter sake.

ir'reparable [i'repərəbl] bnw. on-herstelbaar.

irre'sistible [iri'zistibl] bnw. on-weerstaanbaar.

ir'resolute [i'rezəlōēt] bnw. beslui-teloos.

ir'revocable [i'revəkəbl] bnw. on-herroeplik.

'irrigate ['irighyt] ww. (-d) besproei, natlei; irri'gation s. besproeiing, irrigasie.
'irritate ['irityt] ww. (-d) prikkel, vererg, irriteer.
ir'ruption [i'rʌpsjən] s. (-s) inval, inbraak.
is ['iz] vnw. dit, hy.
'island ['ailənd] s. (-s) eiland.
'isolate ['aisəlyt] ww. (-d) afsonder; iso'lation s.
is'osceles [ai'sǝsiliz] bnw. gelykbenig.
'issue ['isjoe] ww. (-d) voortspruit; uitvaardig; uitgee; versprei; s. (-s) uitvloeisel; kroos; kwessie; uitgawe.
'isthmus ['isməs] s. landengte.
it ['it] vnw. dit, hy.
i'talic [i'tælik] s. (-s) kursiefdruk, kursief.
itch ['itsj] ww. (-ed) jeuk.
'item ['aitəm] s. (-s) item, nommer, artikel.
'iterate ['itəryt] ww. (-d) herhaal; 'iterative s. iteratief.
i'tinerary ['aitinərəri] s. (i'tineraries) reisplan.
its ['its] vnw. sy, van hom, daarvan.
'ivory ['aivəri] s. ivoor.
'ivy ['aivi] s. hedera.
'ixia ['iksiə] s. (-s) kalossie, klossie.

J

jab ['dzjæb] ww. (-bed) steek, stoot.
'jabber ['dzjæbə] ww. (-ed) babbel.
jack ['dzjæk] s. (-s) boer (kaartspel) domkrag; windas.
'jackal ['dzjækôl] s. (-s) jakkals.
'jackass ['dzjækæs] s. (-es) donkiehings; domoor.
'jacket ['dzjækit] s. (-s) baadjie; skil, omslag, vel.
'jade ['dzjyd] s. niersteen; slet; knol, 'n afgeleefde; ww. (-d) uitput, flou wees.
'jagged ['dzjæghid] bnw. ru, skerp, ongelyk.
'jaguar ['dzjæghjoeə] s. (-s) panter, tier (S. Amerikaans).
jail = gaol.
'jalap ['dzjæləp] s. jalap.
jam ['dzjæm] s. (-s) konfyt; gedrang, klomp; ww. (-med) vasdruk, vassit, volprop; bnw. -med geknel, versper, opgehoop; traffic - s. verkeersknoop (ophoping), verkeersversperring.
'January ['dzjænjoeəri] s. Januarie.
jar ['dzjâ] s. (-s) wanklank; skok; twis; fles, kruik; ww. (-red) knars, kraak, kras, skuur.
'jargon ['dzjâghən] s. (-s) brabbeltaal, kombuistaal.
'jaundice ['dzjôndis] s. geelsug.
jaunt ['dzjônt] ww. (-ed) 'n uitstappie maak; -ily bw. swierig.
'javelin ['dzjævlin] s. (-s) werpspies.
jaw ['dzjô] s. (-s) kaak; klou.
jazz ['dzjæz] s. dansmusiek.

'jealous ['dzjeləs] bnw. jaloers; -y s. jaloesie.
jeep ['dzjip] s. (-s) motor vir algemene doeleindes, meerdoel voertuig; kort jas vir vrouens.
jeer ['dzjiə] ww. (-ed) spot, hoon.
'jelly ['dzjeli] s. ('jellies) gelei; -fish s. seekwal.
'jeopardy ['dzjepədi] s. gevaar.
jerk ['dzjək] ww. (-ed) ruk, pluk; -y bnw. rukkerig, hortend.
'jersey ['dzjəzi] s. ('jersies) trui.
jest ['dzjest] s. (-s) grap.
'jetsam ['dzjetsəm] s. opdrifsel.
'jettison ['dzjetisn] ww. (-ed) oorboord gooi.
jet ['dzjet] s. (-s) straal; git.
'jetty ['dzjeti] s. ('jetties) hawehoof, kaai.
Jew ['dzjoē] s. (-s) Jood.
jewel ['dzjoēəl] s. (-s) juweel, kleinood, edelsteen; -ler s. juwelier; -ry s. juwele, juweliersware.
'jiffy ['dzjifi] s. kits.
jig ['dzjigh] s. (-s) horrelpyp; wipsif.
jilt ['dzjilt] ww. (-ed) afsê, fop.
jingle ['dzjing-ghl] s. (-s) gerinkel; rymelary.
'jingo ['dzjing-ghou] s. (-es) jingo, ekstremis.
'jitter ['dzjitə] ww. (-ed) bewe (ook radar).
job ['dzjob] s. (-s) werk, karweitjie, baantjie, spekulasie; - card s. werkkaart.
'jockey ['dzoki] s. ('jockies) jokkie, ruiter.
'jocular ['dzjokjoelə] bnw. grappig, skertsend.
'jocund ['dzjokənd] bnw. vrolik, lustig.
'jog ['dzjogh] ww. (-ged) stamp, ruk; aanstoot.
join ['dzjoin] ww. (-ed) verenig, saamvoeg; aansluit; aangrens; -er s. skrynwerker; oorloper, verraaier; -t s. voeg; bnw. gesamentlik.
'joist ['dzjoist] s. (-s) dwarsbalk.
'joke ['dzjouk] s. (-s) grap; -r s. grapjas; boer(kaartspel).
'jolly ['dzjoli] bnw. jolig, vrolik.
jolt ['dzjoult] s. (-s) stamp, skok.
'jonquil ['dzjong-kwil] s. (-s) narsing, sonkieltjie.
'jostle ['dzjosl] ww. (-d) stamp, stoel, worstel.
'jot ['dzjot] s. (-s) jota, krieseltjie.
'journal ['dzjənl] s. (-s) joernaal, dagboek; tydskrif; journa'lese s. koeranttaal.
'journey ['dzjəni] s. ('journies) reis, tog.
'jovial ['dzjouvjəl] bnw. joviaal, lustig.
jowl ['dzjaul] s. (-s) kaak; keelvel.
joy ['dzjoi] s. (-s) vreugde; -ous bnw. bly, vrolik; -stick s. versneller.
'jubilant ['dzjoēbilənt] bnw. juigend.
'jubilee ['dzjoēbili] s. (-s) jubeljaar, jubileum.
'judge ['dzjʌdzj] s. (-s) regter,

skeidsregter; kenner; -ment s. (-s)
oordeel, vonnis; mening; smaak.
'judicature ['dzjōēdikətsjə] s. (-s)
regspleging; regspraak; geregshof;
regtelik mag.
ju'dicial [dzjōē'disjəl] bnw. regterlik,
geregtelik; oordeelkundig; ju'dicious
bnw. oordeelkundig.
jug ['dzjʌgh] s. (-s) beker, kruik;
tronk.
'juggle ['dzjʌghl] ww. (-d) goël,
knoei.
'jugular ['dzjʌghjoelə] s. (-s)
halsaar, slagaar.
'juice ['dzjōēs] s. (-s) sap; kern;
'juicy bnw. sappig.
Ju'ly [dzjoe'lai] s. Julie.
'jumble ['dzjʌmbl] s. (-s) warboel.
jump ['dzjʌmp] ww. (-ed) spring;
oorspring; steel.
'junction ['dzjʌnksjən] s. (-s)
vereniging, aansluiting, knoop;
'juncture s. (-s) vereniging; tydstip;
voeg.
'June ['dzjōēn] s. Junie.
'jungle ['dzjʌng-ghl] s. (-s) oerwoud;
ruigte; warboel.
'junior ['dzjōēnjə] bnw. junior,
jonger; jongste.
'junk ['dzjʌnk] s. klomp, stuk;
gepluisde tou; soutvleis.
'junket ['dzjʌnkit] s. fuif-, smul-
party; stremsel.
juris'diction [dzjoeəris'diksjən] s.
regsgebied; regspraak, jurisdiksie.
'jury ['dzjōōri] s. ('juries) jurie.
just ['dzjʌst] bnw. regverdig, billik;
presies; bw. net, presies; eenvoudig.
'justice ['dzjʌstis] s. geregtigheid;
reg; regter.
'justify ['dzjʌstifai] ww. ('justified)
verdedig, regverdig; justifi'cation s.
regverdiging.
jut ['dzjʌt] ww. (-ted) vooruitsteek.
'jute ['dzjōēt] s. goiing, juut.
'juvenile ['dzjōēvinail] bnw. jeugdig,
jeug-, jong.

K

'Kaffir ['kæfə] s. (-s) Kaffer.
'Kaiser ['kaizə] s. (-s) keiser.
'kale ['kyl] s. boerkool.
ka'leidoscope [kə'laidəskoup] s. (-s)
kaleidoskoop.
'kanga'roo ['kæng-ghə'rōē] s. (-s)
kangoeroe.
Kar'roo [kə'rōē] s. Karoo.
keel ['kil] s. (-s) kiel.
keen ['kin] bnw. (-er, -est) skerp;
vurig; ywerig; begerig.
keep ['kip] ww. ('kept) hou, behou;
bewaar, oppas; nakom; s. onderhoud, kos; -er s. bewaarder,
oppasser; -ing s. bewaring, sorg;
ooreenstemming; -sake s. aandenking.
keg ['kegh] s. (-s) vaatjie.
'kennel ['kenl] s. (-s) hondehok;
hondefokkery.

kerb ['kəb] s. (-s) rand van sypaadjie; sypaadjie.
'kerchief ['kətsjif] s. (-s) kopdoek,
sakdoek.
'kernel ['kənl] s. (-s) pit; kern.
'kerosene ['kerōsin] s. paraffien.
'ketchup ['ketsjəp] s. blatjang.
'kettle ['ketl] s. (-s) ketel.
key ['ki] s. (-s) sleutel; toonaard;
verklaring; klawer; -board s. toets-
bord, klavier; -hole s. sleutelgat;
-note s. grondtoon; -stone s.
sluitsteen.
'khaki ['kâki] s. (-s) kakie.
'kibosh ['kaibosj] s. kaf, onsin.
kick ['kik] s. (-s) skop; skopper;
krag; pit; ww. (-ed) skop; verset;
-off s. inskop, afskop; -up s.
rumoer, opstand, rusie.
kid ['kid] s. (-s) bokkie; bokvel;
kind, snuiter.
'kidnap ['kidnæp] ww. (-ped) skaak,
steel; ontvoer.
'kidney ['kidni] s. (-s) niertjie.
kill ['kil] ww. (-ed) om die lewe bring.
kiln ['kiln] s. (-s) oond, hoogoond.
'kilo- ['kilou] s. kilo-.
kin ['kin] s. geslag; afkoms;
verwante.
kind ['kaind] s. (-s) soort, klas, ras,
aard, aanleg; natura; bnw. vriendelik, goedhartig.
'kindergarten ['kindəghâtn] s. (-s)
kindertuin, kleuterskool.
'kindle ['kindl] ww. (-d) aansteek.
'kindred ['kindrid] s. bloedver-
wante, bloedverwantskap.
'kinema ['kinəmə] s. bioskoop.
ki'netic [kai'netik] bnw. kineties,
bewegings-.
king ['king] s. (-s) koning, vors;
-dom s. koninkryk; -pin s. krinkspil.
kink ['kink] s. (-s) kinkel, slag.
'kiosk ['kiosk] s. (-s) kiosk;
tuinhuis; winkeltjie.
'kipper ['kipə] s. (-s) rookvis.
kiss ['kis] s. (-es) soen, kus.
kit ['kit] s. ransel; mondering; -bag
s. monderingsak.
'kitchen ['kitsjin] s. (-s) kombuis.
'kite ['kait] s. (-s) valk; vlieër; haai;
proefballon.
'kitten ['kitn] s. (-s) katjie; flerrie.
knack ['næk] s. slag, kuns; gewoonte.
'knapsack ['næpsæk] s. knapsak,
ransel.
knave ['nyv] s. (-s) skurk, skelm;
boer(kaartspel).
knead ['nid] ww. (-ed) knie; hoek,
bog.
'knee ['ni] s. (-s) knie; - action s.
knievering (megan.); -guard s.
knieskut; -cap s. knieskyf; - and
socket joint s. koeëlgewrig.
kneel ['nil] ww. ('knelt) kniel.
knell ['nel] s. (-s) klokslag; doods-
klok.
'knickers ['nikəz] s. kniebroekie.
'knife ['naif] s. ('knives) mes, dolk,
lem.

knight ['nait] s. (-s) ridder; **-ly** bnw. ridderlik.

knit ['nit] ww. (-ted) brei; **-ting** s. breiwerk.

knob ['nob] s. (-s) knop; klont; bult; knobbel; kwas.

knock ['nok] ww. (-ed) klop, slaan, klap; **-er** s. klopper; **-out** s. uitklophou; **knock-for-knock agreement** hou-vir-hou-ooreenkoms (assuran.).

'knock-kneed ['noknid] bnw. met x-bene.

knoll ['noul] s. (-s) bultjie, knoppie.

knot ['not] s. (-s) knoop, strik; knoes; knobbel; bolla; kwas.

'knout ['naut] s. (-s) knoets.

'know ['nou] ww. ('knew, 'known) weet, ken, verstaan, besef; kan; **-ledge** ('nolidzj) s. kennis, wete; begrip.

'knuckle ['nʌkl] s. (-s) kneukel; skinkel; knik(skarnier); **-bone** s. (-s) dolos.

'knurl ['nɔ:l] s., ww. (-ed) kartel.

kraal ['krɑ:l] s. (-s) kraal, stat.

'kudos ['kjoēdos] s. eer, roem.

L

'laager ['lɑ:ghə] s. (-s) kamp, laer.

'label ['lybl] s. (-s) etiket, kaartjie.

'labial ['lybiəl] bnw. van die lippe, labiaal.

la'boratory [lə'borətəri] s. (la'boratories) laboratorium.

'labour ['lybə] ww. (-ed) werk, arbeid; swoeg; sukkel; **la'borious** bnw. met inspanning, moeilik; **-ed** bnw. gekunsteld; **-er** s. arbeider.

'labyrinth ['læbərinth] s. (-s) doolhof.

lac ['læk] s. (-s) lak, lakwerk.

'lace ['lys] s. (-s) veter; rygband; kant; boorsel; ww. (-d) inryg, vasryg; borduur; **'lacing** s. kant; borduursel; loesing.

'lacerate ['læsəryt] ww. (-d) verskeur; seermaak; **lace'ration** s. verskeuring.

lack ['læk] s. gebrek, behoefte, tekort; **-a'daisical** bnw. voorgewende lusteloosheid, geaffekteer(d).

'lackey ['læki] s. (-s) lakei, lyfkneg.

la'conic [lə'konik] bnw. kort en bondig; lakonies; droog.

'lacquer ['lækə] s. lakwerk, vernis, lakvernis.

'lactose ['læktouz] s. laktose, melksuiker.

la'cuna [lə'kjoēnə] s. (-s) hiaat, gaping, leemte.

lad ['læd] s. (-s) seun, knapie.

'ladder ['lædə] s. (-s) leer.

'ladle ['lydl] s. (-s) potlepel, soplepel.

'lady ['lydi] s. ('ladies) dame, vrou; beminde; nôi; **-bird** s. liewenheersbesie, skilpadjie; **-friend** s. vriendin; **-in-waiting** s. hofdame; **-killer** s.

damesveroweraar; **-like** bnw. vroulik, fyn, beskaaf; **-'s-maid** s. kamerjuffrou; **-'s-man** s. meisiegek.

lag ['lægh] ww. (-ged) agterbly, agter raak; beklee; s. naloop.

'laggard ['læghəd] s. (-s) draaikous.

la'goon [lə'ghoēn] s. (-s) strandmeer.

lair ['lēə] s. (-s) lêplek.

'laissez-'faire ['lysy'fēə] s. donsmaar-op.

'lake ['lyk] s. (-s) meer.

lam ['læm] ww. (-med) afransel.

'lama ['lɑ:mə] s. lama.

lamb ['læm] s. (-s) lam, skaapvleis; **-skin** s. lamsvel; **-'s wool** s. lammerwol; **-'s tail** s. wolkruid.

'lame ['lym] bnw. (-r, -st) kruppel, mank, lam, vermink.

lami'nation [læminysjn] s. lamel.

la'ment [lə'ment] s. (-s) weeklag; ww. (-ed) weeklaag, jammer; **'lamentable** bnw. jammerlik.

lamp ['læmp] s. (-s) lamp.

lam'poon [læm'poēn] s. (-s) skimpskrif.

'lance ['lɑ:ns] s. (-s) lans, lansier; ww. (-d) met lans(et) deursteek; oopsny; **-t** s. lanset.

land ['lænd] s. (-s) land, grond, landery, landstreek; nasie; **-ed** bnw. grondbesittend; geland; **-ing** s. landingsplek; trapportaal, trapras; **-lady** s. waardin, hospita; **-line** s. landlyn; **-lord** s. kosbaas, waard; grondeienaar; **-mark** s. (-s) baken; **-owner** s. (-s) grondbesitter.

'landscape ['lændskyp] s. (-s) landskap.

'landslide ['lænd'slaid] s. (-s) grondverskuiwing; stemverskuiwing.

'lane ['lyn] s. (-s) paadjie, deurgang, steeg.

'language ['læng-ghwidzj] s. (-s) taal, spraak.

'languid ['læng-ghwid] bnw. lui, loom; **'languish** ww. (-ed) verswak, verflou, wegkwyn; **'languor** s. matheid, moegheid; **'languorous** bnw. mat, loom.

lank ['lænk] bnw. (-er, -est) dun, rank, skraal, slank.

'lantern ['læntən] s. (-s) lantern.

lap ['læp] s. skoot; oorlel; holte; ww. (-ped) lek, oplek; kabbel; uitsteek; oormekaarslaan; **over**ww. oormekaarslaan; **-dog** s. skoothondjie.

la'pel [lə'pel] s. (-s) lapel, kraagpunt.

'lapidary ['læpidəri] bnw. lapidêr; steen-.

'lapse ['læps] s. (-s) fout, afwyking, verval, verloop; ww. (-d) afdwaal, verval, gly.

'lapsus ['læpsəs] s. fout, vergissing.

'lapwing ['læpwing] s. (-s) kiewiet.

'larceny ['lɑ:sni] s. diefstal.

lard ['lɑ:d] s. varkvet, kookvet; **-er** s. koskas.

'large ['lɑ:dzj] bnw. (-r, -st) groot, ruim, tamaai.

lark ['lɑ:k] s. (-s) grap, pret; ww.

(-ed) pret maak; -spur s. ridderspoor.

'larva ['lāvə] s. ('larvae) larwe.

'larynx ['laerinks] s. (-es) strottehoof.

lash ['læsj] s. (-es) slag, raps, kats; voorslag; speling; ww. (-ed) slaan, gesel, swiep; vasbind.

lass ['laes] s. (-es) meisie.

'lassitude ['læsitjŏĕd] s. afgematheid.

'lasso ['læsou] s. (-es) vangriem.

last ['lāst] s. (-s) lees; las; laaste; uithouvermoë; bnw. laaste, verlede; bw. eindelik, ten slotte; ww. (-ed) aanhou, duur.

latch ['lætsj] s. (-es) knip, klink, knip-.

'late ['lyt] bnw. laat; te laat; vorige, gewese; oorlede; bw. laat, onlangs; -ly bw. onlangs.

'latent ['lytənt] bnw. verborge, sluimerend, latent.

'lateral ['lætərəl] bnw. sydelings, sy-, lateraal.

'latex ['lyteks] s. melksap.

lath ['læth] s. (-s) lat, plankie.

'lathe ['lydh] s. (-s) draaibank.

'lather ['lādhə] s. skuim.

'Latin ['lætin] s. Latyn.

'latitude ['lætitjŏĕd] s. (-s) breedtegraad; speling.

la'trine [lə'trin] s. (-s) latrine, gemak.

'latter ['lætə] bnw. laasgenoemde; -ly bw. onlangs.

'lattice ['lætis] s. traliewerk, rooster.

laud ['lŏd] ww. (-ed) prys, loof; -able bnw. lofwaardig.

'laudatory ['lŏdətəri] bnw. lowend, prysend.

laugh ['lāf] ww. (-ed) lag; s. lag, gelag; -able bnw. bespotlik; -ing bnw. laggend; -ingly bw. lag-lag; -ing-stock s. voorwerp van bespotting; -ter s. gelag.

launch ['lŏntsj] ww. (-ed) van stapel laat loop; uitstuur; begin; s. barkas.

'launder ['lŏndə] ww. (-ed) was; 'laundry s. wassery, wasgoed.

'laureate ['lŏriit] bnw. bekroon; poet – hofdigter.

'laurel ['lŏrəl] s. (-s) lourier.

'lava ['lāvə] s. lawa.

'lavatory ['lævətəri] s. ('lavatories) toiletkamer, gemak.

lave ['lyv] ww. (-d) was: bespoel; 'lavement s. lawement.

'lavender ['lævəndə] s. laventel; laventelbos.

'lavish ['lævisj] bnw. kwistig; -ly bw. kwistig.

law ['lŏ] s. (-s) wet; reg; regspraak; -breaker s. wetsoortreder; -court s. geregshof; -ful bnw. wettig; -less bnw. wetteloos, misdadig; -suit s. hofgeding; -yer s. advokaat, prokureur.

lawn ['lŏn] s. (-s) kamerdoek; grasperk.

lax ['læks] bnw. (-er, -est) laks, los;

-ative bnw. lakserend; -ity s. laksheid.

lay ['ly] ww. ('laid) lê; bedaar; neerlê; bnw. leek; -er s. laag; -man s. leek.

'laze ['lyz] ww. (-d) lui wees; 'lazy bnw. lui, traag.

lead ['led] s. lood, potlood; ww. ['lïd] ('led) lei; met lood omlys; -en bnw. loodswaar; loom; -er s. leier; -ing bnw. voorste, vernaamste; - pencil s. potlood.

leaf ['lïf] s. ('leaves) blaar, blad; velletjie; -age s. blare, lommer; -let verkleinw. blaartjie; traktaatjie; -y bnw. blaarryk.

'league ['lïgh] s. (-s) verbond; liga.

leak ['lïk] ww. (-ed) lek; -age s. lekkasie.

lean ['lïn] bnw. (-er, -est) maer, dun; ww. ('leant, leaned) steun, leun; neig; s. oorhelling; -to s. afdak.

leap ['lïp] ww. ('leapt, leaped) spring, oorspring; s. sprong; -frog s. 'hasie-oor'(spel); - year s. skrikkeljaar.

learn ['lŏn] ww. (-ed, -t) leer, verneem; -ed bnw. geleerd; -er s. leerling, kwekeling; -ing s. geleerdheid.

'lease ['lïs] s. huurkontrak; huur, pag; ww. (-d) huur, verhuur; -hold s. huur, pag.

leash ['lïsj] s. (-es) koppelriem; ww. (-ed) vasbind, vaskoppel.

least ['lïst] s. die minste, vgl. little; bnw. minste; -ways bw. ten minste.

'leather ['ledhə] s. (-s) leer, leerwerk, riem, vel; -ing s. afranseling; -n bnw. leer-, van leer.

'leave ['lïv] s. verlof; ww. ('left) laat, nalaat, verlaat, vertrek, ophou; 'leavings s. oorskot.

'leaven ['levn] s. suurdeeg.

'lecherous ['letsjərəs] bnw. ontugtig, wellustig.

'lecture ['lektsjə] s. (-s) lesing; klas; preek; -r s. lektor; -ship s. lektoraat.

'ledge ['ledzj] s. (-s) muurplaat; lys; -r s. grootboek.

lee ['lï] s. lykant, beskutting.

leech ['lïtsj] s. (-es) bloedsuier.

leek ['lïk] s. prei.

leer ['lïə] ww. (-ed) loer, gluur.

lees ['lïz] s. afsaksel, moer.

'leeway ['liwy] s. agterstand; 'leeward bw. lywaarts.

left ['left] bnw. linker-, links; bw. links; s. (-s) linkerhand; -hand drive s. linkerstuur; -handed bnw. links.

leg ['legh] s. (-s) been; poot; boud; broekspyp; -ging s. kamas.

'legacy ['leghəsi] s. ('legacies) legaat, erfenis.

'legal ['lighl] bnw. wettig, wetlik, regs-; 'legalize ww. (-d) wettig.

'legate ['leghit] s. (-s) legaat; ww. bemaak; lega'tee s. erfgenaam.

le'gation [li'ghysjən] s. gesantskap, legasie.

'legend ['ledzjənd] s. (-s) legende, oorlewering; -ary bnw. legendaries.
'legible ['ledzəbl] bnw. leesbaar.
'legion ['lidzjən] s. (-s) legioen.
'legislate ['ledzjislyt] ww. (-d) wette maak; legis'lation s. wetgewing; 'legislative bnw. wetgewend; 'legislator s. wetgewer; 'legislature s. wetgewende mag.
le'gitimate [li'dzjitimit] bnw. wettig, wetlik; le'gitimize ww. wettig.
le'guminous [le'ghjŏĕminəs] bnw. peuldraend.
'leisure ['lezjə] s. ledige(vrye) tyd.
'lemon ['lemən] s. (-s) suurlemoen; -ade s. limonade; -aquash s. kwas, suurlemoensap.
lend ['lend] ww. ('lent) leen, uitleen; -er s. lener; -ing s. leen, lenery.
length [length] s. (-s) lengte, afstand, duur, grootte; -en ww. (-ed) verleng; -wise bw. in die lengte; -y bnw. lang, vervelend.
'lenience ['liniəns] s. sagtheid; 'lenient bnw. sag, genadig.
lens ['lenz] s. (-es) lens.
lent ['lent] s. vastyd; -en bnw. vas-.
'lentil ['lentil] s. (-s) lensie.
'leopard ['lepəd] s. (-s) luiperd.
'leper ['lepə] s. (-s) melaatse; 'leprosy s. melaatsheid; 'leprous bnw. melaats.
less ['les] bnw. minder, kleiner; voors. min; bw. minder; -en ww. (-ed) verminder.
'lesson ['lesn] s. (-s) les; leesstuk.
lest ['lest] voegw. uit vrees dat, opdat . . . nie.
let ['let] ww. laat, toelaat; verhuur.
'lethal ['lidhl] bnw. dodelik.
le'thargic [le'thădzjik] bnw. suf, slaperig, bot.
'letter ['letə] s. (-s) letter; brief; ww. (-ed) letter; -card s. briefkaart; -ed bnw. geletter; gemerk.
'lettuce ['letis] s. kropslaai.
leucadendron ['ljoekə'dendrən] s. plume - tolbos (proteasoort).
'levee ['levi] s. (-s) oggendresepsie.
'level ['levəl] s. (-s) waterpas pasloogd; peil; hoogte; valk; bnw. horisontaal, waterpas; gelykmatig; ww. (-led) gelykmaak; - crossing s. oorweg.
'lever ['livə] s. (-s) hefboom, ligter; -age s. hefboomkrag.
'levy ['levi] s. ('levies) heffing, aanwerwing.
lewd ['lŏĕd] bnw. (-er, -est) ontugtig.
'lexical ['leksikəl] bnw. van 'n woordeboek.
lexi'cography [leksi'koghrəfi] s. leksikografie.
'lexicon ['leksikən] s. (-s) woordeboek.
'liable ['laiəbl] bnw. verantwoordelik, aanspreeklik; lia'bility s. (lia'bilities) verantwoordelikheid, verpligting, aanspreeklikheid.
li'aison [li'yzông] s. ongeoorloofde liefdesverhouding; liaison; skakel-.

'liar ['laiə] s. (-s) leuenaar.
'lias ['laiəs] s. lias.
'libel ['laibəl] s. (-s) laster; smaadskrif; ww. (-led) belaster; -lous bnw. lasterlik.
'liberal ['libərəl] bnw. mild; vrysinnig; s. liberaal; libe'rality s. gulhartigheid.
'liberate ['libəryt] ww. (-d) bevry, vrylaat; libe'ration s. bevryding, vrylating.
'libertine ['libətain] s. (-s) vrydenker; ligmis.
'liberty ['libəti] s. ('liberties) vryheid.
'libra ['laibrə] s. pond.
'library ['laibrəri] s. ('libraries) biblioteek; li'brarian s. (-s) bibliotekaris.
'licence ['laisəns] s. (-s) liksens, vergunning; verlof; losbandigheid; lisensie; driver's - s. rybewys.
'license ['laisəns] ww. (-d) lisensieer, verlof gee; licen'see s. lisensiehouer; -r s. lisensieverlener; li'centiate s. lisensiaat.
'lichen ['laikən] s. mos; -ous bnw. mosagtig.
'licit ['lisit] bnw. wettig.
lick ['lik] ww. (-ed) lek; klop; s. lekplek, soutplek.
'licorice ['likəris] s. drop; = liquorice.
lid ['lid] s. (-s) deksel; lid.
lie ['lai] s. (-s) leuen; ligging; koers; ww. (-d) lieg; ('lay, 'lain) lê.
lien ['liən] s. pandreg.
lieu ['ljŏĕ] s. in - of in pleks van.
lieu'tenant [lef'tenənt] s. (-s) luitenant.
'life ['laif] s. ('lives) lewe; -belt s. reddingsgordel; -buoy s. reddingsboei; - interest s. lewensreg; -time s. leeftyd; - work s. lewenstaak.
lift ['lift] s. (-s) hysbak, ligter; iemand oplaai; ww. (-ed) oplig, ophef, optel, verhef; steel.
'ligament ['lighəmənt] s. (-s) pees.
'ligature ['lighitsjoeə] s. (-s) verband, band, afbinding.
light ['lait] s. (-s) lig; vuurhoutjie; bnw. (-er, -est) lig; ww. (-ed) opsteek, aansteek, lig maak; bw. lig, los; -en ww. (-ed) verlig, ligter maak; -er s. opsteker, aansteker; -headed bnw. ylhoofdig; -house s. vuurtoring; -ning s. weerlig.
'like ['laik] bnw. soos; gelyk, eners; dieselfde; voors. soos, so; voegw. soos; - enough bw. bes moontlik; s. gelyke, weerga; ww. (-d) hou van; -lihood s. waarskynlikheid; -ly bnw. & bw. waarskynlik; -n ww. (-ed) vergelyk; -ness s. gelykenis, gedaante; -wise bw. netso; 'liking s. sin, lus.
'lilac ['lailək] s. (-s) seringboom.
lili'aceous [lili'ysjəs] bnw. lelieagtig.
lilt ['lilt] s. vrolike liedjie, ritme.
'lily ['lili] s. ('lilies) lelie.
limb ['lim] s. (-s) lit, tak, uitloper.

'**limber** ['limbə] *bnw.* buigsaam, lenig.

'**limbo** ['limbou] *s.* gevangenis; vergetelheid.

'**lime** ['laim] *s.* kalk; lym; lemmetjie; **-light** *s.* kalklig.

'**limit** ['limit] *s.* (*-s*) grens; toppunt; *ww.* (*-ed*) begrens; **limi'tation** *s.* beperking; **-ed** *bnw.* beperk.

limp ['limp] *ww.* (*-ed*) mank wees; *bnw.* slap, pap.

'**limpid** ['limpid] *bnw.* helder.

'**linctus** ['linktəs] *s.* lekstroop.

'**line** ['lain] *s.* (*-s*) tou, lyn; streep; reeks; koers; ewenaar; linie; spoor; besigheid; briefie; soort, gelid; *ww.* (*-d*) strepe trek; in gelid staan; voering insit; dek; **-age** *s.* ['liniidzj] afkoms, geslag; **-al** ['liniəl] *bnw.* lynreg.

'**linear** ['liniə] *bnw.* lineêr, lengte-, lyn-.

'**linen** ['linin] *s.* (*-s*) linne(goed).

'**linger** ['ling-ghə] *ww.* (*-ed*) draal, talm; **-er** *s.* draler.

'**lingerie** ['lènzjəri] *s.* linnegoed, onderklere.

'**linguist** ['ling-ghwist] *s.* (*-s*) taalkenner; linguis; **lin'guistic** *bnw.* taalkundig; **lin'guistics** *s.* taalkunde.

'**liniment** ['linimənt] *s.* (*-s*) smeergoed, smeersel.

'**lining** ['laining] *s.* (*-s*) voering; slytstuk.

link ['link] *s.* (*-s*) skakel; **-s** *s.* mousknope; gholfbaan.

li'noleum [li'nouljəm] *s.* linoleum.

'**linseed** ['linsid] *s.* lynsaad; **- oil** *s.* lynolie.

lint ['lint] *s.* verbandlinne.

'**lintel** ['lintl] *s.* latei.

'**lion** ['laiən] *s.* (*-s*) leeu; **-ize** *ww.* (*-d*) verafgood.

lip ['lip] *s.* (*-s*) lip; astrantheid; rand.

'**lipstick** ['lipstik] *s.* (*-s*) lipstiffie.

'**liquefy** ['likwifai] *ww.* (*'liquefied*) smelt.

li'queur [li'kjoeə] *s.* (*-s*) likeur, soetsopie.

'**liquid** ['likwid] *s.* (*-s*) vloeistof; *bnw.* vloeibaar; '**liquidate** *ww.* (*-d*) likwideer, vereffen; **liqui'dation** *s.* berdedering; **- amber** *s.* amberboom; **- paraffin** *s.* aptekersparaffin; **- polish** *s.* vloeipolitoer.

'**liquor** ['likə] *s.* vog; drank; **-ice** *s.* drop; soethout.

lisp ['lisp] *ww.* (*-ed*) lispel.

list ['list] *s.* (*-s*) lys, rol; strydperk.

'**listen** ['lisn] *ww.* (*-ed*) luister; **-er** *s.* luisteraar.

'**litany** ['litəni] *s.* (*'litanies*) litanie.

'**literal** ['litərəl] *bnw.* letterlik.

'**literary** ['litərəri] *bnw.* letterkundig.

'**literature** ['litəritsjə] *s.* letterkunde.

'**lithe** ['laidhl *bnw.* slap, lenig.

'**litigate** ['litighyt] *ww.* (*-d*) prosedeer; '**litigant** *s.* prosedeerder; **liti'gation** *s.* regsgeding.

'**litmus** ['litməs] *s.* lakmoes.

'**litotes** ['laitōtiz] *s.* litotes.

'**litre** ['litə] *s.* (*-s*) liter.

'**litter** ['litə] *s.* (*-s*) draagbaar; strooi; vuilgoed; worpsel; broeisel.

'**little** ['litl] *bnw.* (*-r, -st; 'less, 'least*) weinig, min; *s.* weinig, min; *bw.* weinig.

'**littoral** ['litərəl] *s.* kusstrook.

'**liturgy** ['litədzji] *s.* liturgie, kerkgebruik.

'**live** ['laiv] *bnw.* lewend; gloeiend; gelaai; *ww.* (*'liv*) (*-d*) lewe, bestaan; woon; **-lihood** *s.* broodwinning.

'**liver** ['livə] *s.* (*-s*) lewer; **-ish** *bnw.* lewersugtig.

'**livery** ['livəri] *s.* (*'liveries*) livrei.

'**livid** ['livid] *bnw.* blou, doodsbleek.

'**living** ['living] *bnw.* lewendig; *s.* broodwinning, bestaan; **- room** *s.* woonkamer.

'**lizard** ['lizəd] *s.* (*-s*) akkedis.

load ['loud] *s.* (*-s*) vrag, lading, las; gewig; pak; *ww.* (*-ed*) laai, bevrag; verswaar.

'**loadstone** ['loudstoun] *s.* (*-s*) magneet, seilsteen.

loaf ['louf] *s.* (*'loaves*) brood; *ww.* (*-ed*) leegloop; **-er** *s.* rondloper; **- sugar** *n.* klontjiesuiker.

loam ['loum] *s.* leem, teelaarde; **-y** *bnw.* kleierig.

loan ['loun] *s.* (*-s*) lening, die geleende; *ww.* (*-ed*) uitleen; **-er** *s.* uitlener; **- office** *s.* voorskotbank.

loath ['louth] *bnw.* ongeneë, onwillig.

'**loathe** ['loudh] *ww.* (*-d*) verafsku; '**loathing** *s.* weersin, walging; **-some** *bnw.* walglik.

lob ['lob] *ww.* (*-bed*) lughou slaan, hoogslaan.

'**lobby** ['lobi] *s.* (*'lobbies*) portaal, voorsaal, wandelgang.

lobe ['loub] *s.* (*-s*) lel, neus.

'**lobster** ['lobstə] *s.* kreef.

'**local** ['loukəl] *bnw.* plaaslik, lokaal; *s.* inwoner; **-ize** *ww.* (*-d*) lokaliseer; **lo'cality** *s.* (*lo'calities*) ligging, plek; **lo'cate** *ww.* (*-d*) plek aanwys, lokaliseer; **lo'cation** *s.* plekbepaling; kampong.

lo'cale [lou'kāl] *s.* plek, oord.

loch ['log] *s.* (*-s*) (*Scottish*) meer.

lock ['lok] *s.* (*-s*) lok, krul; slot; sluis; *ww.* (*-ed*) sluit, opsluit; insluit; vasgryp, vasslaan; 'n sluis aanbring; **-et** *s.* (*-s*) medaljon, hangertjie; **-jaw** *s.* klem in die kake; **-smith** *s.* slotmaker; **-up** *s.* sel; **-nut** *s.* sluitmoer; **-spring** *s.* slotveer.

'**locker** ['lokə] *s.* (*-s*) kassie, kis, laai, sluitkas.

'**lock-jaw** ['lokdzjô] *s.* klem-in-die-kaak.

loco'motion [loukə'mousjən] *s.* beweging; '**locomotive** *s.* (*-s*) lokomotief; *bnw.* bewegend.

'**locum-'tenens** ['loukəm'tenəns] *s.* plaasvervanger.

'**locust** ['loukəst] *s.* (*-s*) sprinkaan.

'**lode** ['loud] *s.* (*s*) watervoor; wateraar.

'lodge ['lodzj] s. (-s) huisie; portierswoning; losie; ww. (-d) huisves, loseer, herberg; indien; deponeer; vassit; -r s. loseerder, kosganger; 'lodging s. huisvesting, losies; indiening.

loft ['loft] s. (-s) solder; -y bnw. hoog, trots.

log ['logh] s. (-s) blok; logboek; puntelys; logaritme; -cabin s. blokhuis.

'loggerhead ['loghǝhed] s. at -s aan die twis.

'logic ['lodzjik] s. logika; -al bnw. logies.

'logos ['loghos] s. Die Woord.

loin ['loin] s. (-s) lende; lendestuk; -cloth s. lendekleed.

'loiter ['loitǝ] ww. (-ed) draal, draai, slenter; -er s. slenteraar; -ing s. rondslentery.

loll ['lol] ww. (-ed) uithang; lustelose houding inneem.

'lollipop ['lolipop] s. draadgetrekte suikerlekkergoed.

'lone ['loun] bnw. eensaam, verlate; -some bnw. eensaam, verlate; -ly bnw. eensaam, verlate; -liness s.

long ['long] bnw. (-er, -est) lang, langdurig, uitgerek; s. 'n lang tyd; bw. lang; ww. (-ed) verlang; -drawn bnw. uitgerek; -eval [lon'dzjivǝl] bnw. langlewend; -evity [lon'dzjeviti] langlewendheid; -hand s. lopende skrif; -headed bnw. uitgeslape; -ing s. verlange; -ish bnw. langerig; -itude s. lengtegraad; -shore s. kus-; -sighted bnw. versiende.

look ['loek] ww. (-ed) kyk, sien; lyk; uitsien; s. (-s) blik, gesig, gelaat; voorkome; -er-on s. toeskouer; -in s. kans; -ing-glass s. spieël; -out s. uitkyk, wagpos, wag, uitsig.

loom ['lōǝm] s. (-s) weeftou; ww. (-ed) opdoem.

'loony ['lōǝni] bnw. getik, mal.

loop ['lōǝp] s. lissie, hingsel; kykgat; -hole s. (-s) loergat, kykgat; skietgat; uitvlug.

'loose ['lōǝs] bnw. (-r, -st) los, slap, ruim; bros; lossinnig; -n ww. (-ed) losmaak, skiet gee; -ly bw. lossies.

loot ['lōǝt] s. roof, buit.

lop ['lop] ww. (-ped) afkap, snoei; -sided bnw. skeef.

'lope ['loup] ww. (-d) met lang springe hardloop.

lo'quacious [lō'kwysjǝs] bnw. spraaksaam, praatsugtig, praatsiek.

lord ['lōd] s. (-s) heer, meester, lord; ww. (-ed) baasspeel; -ling verkleinw. lordjie, meneertjie; -ly bnw. trots, heerssugtig.

lordosis [lō'dousis] s. abnormale kromming van ruggraat, lordose.

'lore ['lō] s. leer, kennis.

'lorgnette ['lōnjet] s. (-s) handbril, lorgnet.

'lorry ['lori] s. ('lorries) vragmotor, lorrie.

'lory ['lōri] s. loerie.

'lose ['lōēz] ww. ('lost) verloor; verbeur; agter raak; ontslae raak; -r s. verloorder; loss, s. verlies.

lot ['lot] s. (-s) lot; perseel, erf; klompie; hoeveelheid.

'lotion ['lousjǝn] s. (-s) wasmiddel.

'lottery ['lotǝri] s. ('lotteries) lotery; -ticket s. loterykaartjie, lootjie.

'lotus ['loutǝs] s. lotosblom.

loud ['laud] bnw. (-er, -est) luid, hard; luidrugtig; opsigtelik; bw. luid, hardop; -en ww. (-ed) luider word; -speaker s. luidspreker.

'lounge ['laundzj] ww. (-ed) slenter, drentel, luier; s. (-s) voorvertrek, sitkamer; -suit s. draagpak.

'louse ['laus] s. ('lice) luis; lousy bnw. luisig, veragtelik.

lout ['laut] s. (-s) tor, japie, takhaar.

'louvre [lēvr] s. (-s) hortjie.

'love ['lʌv] s. liefde, min; liefling; nul; ww. (-d) liefhê, bemin; -affair s. liefdesavontuur; -child s. onegte kind; -letter s. minnebrief; -lorn bnw. smoorverlief; -ly bnw. lieflik; lief; -match s. huwelik uit liefde; -r s. vryer; minnaar; -sick bnw. doodverlief; -song s. minnelied; -story s. liefdesverhaal; 'loving bnw. liefhebbend, liefdevol.

low ['lou] bnw. (-er, -est) laag, plat; sag; gemeen; swak; nederig; min; bw. laag; saggies; ww. (-ed) loei, bulk; -born bnw. van geringe afkoms; -bred bnw. onbeskaaf; -er ww. (-ed) neerhaal, stryk; laer maak; -grade bnw. van lae gehalte; -liness s. nederigheid; -ly bnw. gering, eenvoudig; -spirited bnw. terneergedruk.

'loyal ['loiǝl] bnw. lojaal, getrou; -ty s. getrouheid.

'lozenge ['lozindzj] s. (-s) tabletjie, suigpil, suigtablet.

'lubber ['lʌbǝ] s. (-s) lomperd, tor.

'lubricate ['lōēbrikyt] ww. (-d) smeer, olie gee; 'lubricant s. smeerolie, ghries, bnw. smerend; lubri'cation s. smering; 'lubricator s. smeerder.

'lucent ['ljōēsnt] bnw. (deur) skynend.

lu'cerne ['lōē'sǝn] s. lusern.

'lucid ['lōēsid] bnw. (-est) helder, duidelik; 'lucidity s. helderheid.

luck ['lʌk] s. geluk, toeval; -ily bw. gelukkig; -less bnw. ongelukkig; -y bnw. (-ier, -iest) gelukkig.

'lucre ['lōēkǝ] s. wins, voordeel; 'lucrative bnw. winsgewend, voordelig.

lu'dicrous ['lōēdikrǝs] bnw. belaglik, gek.

lug ['lʌgh] ww. (-ged) sleep, trek; s. tap; klou; skoen.

'luggage ['lʌghidzj] s. bagasie.

lu'gubrious [lōē'ghjōēbriǝs] bnw. treurig, somber.

'lukewarm ['lōēkwôm] bnw. lou.

lull ['lʌl] ww. (-ed) sus, kalmeer; s. rus, verposing.

'lullaby ['lʌləbai] s. (-s) wiegelied.

lum'bago [lʌm'byghou] s. lendepyn, spit.

'lumbar ['lʌmbə] bnw. lumbaal, van die lende.

'lumber ['lʌmbə] ww. (-ed) rammel, dreun; s. rommel; timmerhout; -man s. houtkapper; -room s. rommelkamer.

'luminary ['lōēminəri] s. liggewende voorwerp, voorligter; lumi'niferous bnw. liggewend; lumi'nosity s. skittering; 'luminous bnw. skitterend; 'luminous strip s. glimstrook.

lump ['lʌmp] s. (-s) stuk, klont, klomp; bult, knop; ww. (-ed) opeenhoop, neerplak; ontevrede wees oor; -sugar s. klontjiesuiker; -y bnw. klonterig.

'lunar ['lōēnə] bnw. van die maan, maan-; 'lunacy s. kransinnigheid; 'lunatic s. kransinnige.

lunch ['lʌntsj] s. (-es) middagete; ww. (-ed) middagete nuttig.

lung ['lʌng] s. (-s) long.

'lunge ['lʌndʒ] ww. (-d) stoot, steek, skop, slaan; s. stoot, sprong, uitval.

'lupus ['lōēpəs] s. wolf; veltering.

lurch ['lōtsj] ww. (-d) steier; s. leave in the - in die steek laat.

'lure ['ljoeə] ww. (-d) lok, wegrokkel.

'lurid ['ljoeərid] bnw. bleek, somber, afgryslik.

lurk ['lōk] ww. (-ed) skuil, op die loer lê; -ing-place s. skuilplek.

'luscious ['lʌsjəs] bnw. stroopsoet, lekker.

lush ['lʌsj] bnw. sappig, mals.

lust ['lʌst] s. wellus, sinlike lus, begeerte; -ily bw. kragtig, fiink, fors; bnw. sterk, fris.

'lustrate ['lʌstryt] ww. (-d) reinig, suiwer; 'lustral bnw. reinigings-, lu'stration s. reiniging.

'lustre ['lʌstə] s. glans, luister; roem; ww. blink maak; 'lustrous bnw. luisterryk, glansryk.

'lusty ['lʌsti] bnw. ('lustier, 'lustiest) sterk, fris, fors, fiink.

'lute ['lōēt] s. (-s) luit.

lux'uriance [lʌgh'zjoeəriəns] s. weligheid, geilheid; lux'uriant bnw. geil, welig; lux'urious bnw. weelderig; 'luxury s. ('luxuries) weelde, oorvloed, luukse.

lye ['lai] s. loog.

lymph ['limf] s. vloeistof, limf; lym'phatic bnw. limfaties.

lynch ['lintsj] ww. (-ed) lynch.

lynx ['links] s. (-es) tierkat.

'lyre ['laiə] s. (-s) lier; 'lyric s. (-s) liriese gedig; bnw. liries; 'lyrical bnw. liries.

'lysol ['laisəl] s. lysol.

M

ma ['mā] s. (-s) ma, moeder.

'ma'am ['mæm] s. = madam.

ma'cabre [mə'kābr] bnw. aaklig, grillig, grieselig.

maca'roni [mækə'rouni] s. makaronie.

maca'roon [mækə'rōēn] s. (-s) bitter-, amandelkoekie.

ma'cassar [mə'kæsə] s. makassar (olie).

ma'caw [mə'kō] s. (-s) papegaai.

'mace ['mys] s. (-s) staf, septer, roede; foelie.

'macerate ['mæsəryt] ww. (-d) laat week; afpynig; vermaer.

machi'nation [mæki'nysjən] s. (-s) intrige, sameswering.

ma'chine [mə'sjin] s. (-s) masjien, toestel; -ry s. masjinerie; meganiek; ma'chinist s. masjinis; naaister.

'mackerel ['mækərəl] s. (-s) makriel.

'mackintosh ['mækintosj] s. (-es) reënjas.

'macrocosm ['mækrōkozəm] s. heelal, makrokosmos.

'macula ['mækjoelə] s. ('maculae) vlek; 'maculate bnw. bevlek.

mad ['mæd] bnw. (-der, -dest) gek, dol, mal, rasend; -den ww. (-ed) woedend (mal) word of maak; -ness s. kransinnigheid; dwaasheid; -cap s. dwaas, grapjas; -house s. kransinnige gestig.

'madam ['mædəm] s. (-s) madam, mevrou, juffrou.

mademoi'selle [mædəm'zel] s. (-s) juffrou, mademoiselle.

Ma'donna [mə'donə] s. Maagd Maria.

'madrigal ['mædrighəl] s. (-s) minnelied.

'maelstrom ['mylstroum] s. (-s) draaikolk.

'maestro ['maistrou] s. (-s) meester, komponis, dirigent.

maga'zine [mægh'zin] s. (-s) magasyn, pakhuis; tydskrif; kruithuis.

'maggot ['mæghət] s. (-s) maaier; gril, nuk, luim.

'magic ['mædzjik] s. towerkuns, toorkrag; bnw. magies; toweragtig, ma'gician s. towenaar.

'magistrate ['mædzjistrit] s. (-s) magistraat, landdros; magis'terial bnw. magistraats-; 'magistracy s. magistraatsdistrik; 'magistral bnw. magistraal, meesteragtig.

'Magna 'Charta ['mæghnə'kātə] s. grondwet, Magna Charta.

mag'nanimous [mægh'næniməs] bnw. grootmoedig.

'magnate ['mæghnyt] s. (-s) magnaat, geldman.

mag'nesia [mægh'nisjə] s. magnesia; milk of - magnesiameik.

'magnet ['mæghnit] s. (-s) magneet; mag'netic bnw. magneties; mag-

'netics s. magnetisme; -ize ww. (-d)
magnetiseer; -ism s. magnetisme,
magnetiese verskynsels.

mag'neto ['mægh'nitou] s. (-s)
ontstekingsmagneet; magneet.

mag'nificence [mægh'nifisns] s.
prag, grootsheid; **mag'nificent** bnw.
pragtig, heerlik; groots, magnifiek.

'**magnify** ['mæghnifai] ww. ('mag-
nified) vergroot; ophemel; '**magni-
fier** s. vergrootglas; '**magnitude** s.
grootheid, omvang, grootte.

mag'nolia [mægh'noulje] s. magnolia.

'**magpie** ['mæghpai] s. (-s) ekster;
babbelkous.

'**mahlstick** ['mɔlstik] s. (-s) skilderstok.

ma'hogany [mə'hoghəni] s. mahonie
(hout, boom).

ma'hout [mə'haut] s. (-s) olifant-
drywer.

maid ['myd] s. (-s) meisie, maagd,
jongnôi.

maiden [mydən] s. = **maid**; - over
leë boulberut; - **hair** s. venushaar-
varing; -**hood** s. maagdelikheid; -**ly**
bnw. maagdelik; - **name** s. nooiensvan.

mail ['myl] s. pos, poskar, postrein;
harnas; ww. (-ed) pos; -**bag** s.
possak; -**boat** s. posboot; -**ed** bnw.
gepantser.

maim ['mym] ww. (-ed) vermink,
skend.

main ['myn] s. krag; die oseaan;
hoofleiding; bnw. vernaamste, grootste, eerste; -**land** s. vasteland; -**ly**
bw. hoofsaaklik; -**spring** s. slagveer;
-**stay** s. steunpilaar; **main**- hoof-;
-**light** s. hooflig; -**shaft** s. hoofas;
hoofskag; -**switch** s. hoofskakelaar;
-**bearing** s. hooflaer.

main'tain [men'tyn] ww. (-ed)
volhou; handhaaf; ondersteun; bewaar; **main'tainable** bnw. verdedigbaar; -**er** s. handhawer, verdediger;
'**maintenance** s. handhawing; onderhoud.

'**maize** ['myz] s. mielies.

'**majesty** ['mædzjisti] s. majesteit,
statigheid; **ma'jestic** bnw. majes-
tueus, groots.

'**major** ['mydzjə] s. (-s) majoor;
mondige; majeur; senior; bnw.
groter; hoof-; **ma'jority** s. (ma-
'jorities) meerderheid.

'**make** ['myk] s. (-s) maaksel,
fabrikaat, soort; ww. ('made) maak,
vorm; doen; hou; forseer; begaan;
-**believe** s. skyn; -**r** s. fabrikant,
maker; -**shift** s. hulpmiddel; -**up** s.
grimering; -**ing** s. maaksel; verdienste; -**and-break** s. maak-en-
breek; kontakbreker.

mal ['mæl] voorv. wan-; mis-;
breek; -**formation** s. misvorming;
-**practice** s. wanpraktyk.

mala'droit [mælə'droit] bnw. lomp,
onbeholpe.

'**malady** ['mælədi] s. ('maladies)
siekte, kwaal.

'**mala'fide** ['mylə'faidi] s. mala fide,
kwade trou.

ma'laria [mə'lêəriə] s. malaria,
moeraskoors, muskietkoors.

'**malcontent** ['mælkəntənt] s. (-s)
ontevredene.

'**male** ['myl] s. (-s) mannetjie,
manspersoon; bnw. manlik, mans-.

male'dictory [mæli'diktəri] bnw.
verwensend.

'**malefactor** ['mælifæktə] s. (-s)
boosdoener.

mal'eficent [mə'lefisnt] bnw. skadelik, verderflik; misdadig.

ma'levolent [mə'levələnt] bnw.
kwaadwillig.

'**malice** ['mælis] s. kwaadwilligheid;
ma'licious bnw. boos; kwaadwillig.

ma'lign [mə'lain] ww. (-ed) kwaad-
praat, beskinder; **ma'lignant** bnw.
boosaardig.

ma'lignancy [mə'lighnənsi] s.
kwaadwilligheid; verderflikheid.

ma'linger [mə'ling-ghə] ww. (-ed)
siekte voorwend.

mall ['mɔl] s. (-s) wandellaan;
Pall Mall ['pæl'mæl] s. laan in
London.

'**mallard** ['mæləd] s. (-s) wilde-eend.

'**malleable** ['mæliəbl] bnw. smeebaar;
'**malleate** ww. ('maliyt) (-d) smee,
sweis.

'**mallet** ['mælit] s. (-s) houthamer,
klophamer.

'**mallow** ['mælou] s. malva.

'**malmsey** ['mâmzi] s. malvesywyn.

'**mal'odorous** ['mæl'ouderəs] bnw.
stinkend, slegruikend.

malt ['mɔlt] s. mout; - **liquor** s.
moutdrank.

'**Malta** ['mɔltə] s. Malta; **Maltese
Cross** s. Jerusalemblom, laklelie.

mal'treat [mæl'trit] ww. (-ed) sleg
behandel, mishandel.

mal'treatment [mæl'tritmənt] s.
mishandeling.

mam'ma [mə'mâ] s. (-s) mamma,
moeder; s. ['mæmə] bors, uier,
pram; -l s. soogdier; **mam'malia** s.
soogdiere.

mam'mitis [mæ'maitəs] s. uieront-
steking = **mastitis.**

'**mammon** ['mæmən] s. mammon,
rykdom, skatte.

'**mammoth** ['mæməth] s. (-s)
mammoet.

'**mammy** ['mæmi] s. ('mammies) aia,
nenna.

man ['mæn] s. ('men) man; mens;
eggenoot; onderdaan; arbeider; soldaat; die mensheid; bnw. manlik,
mans-; ww. (-ned) beman, beset;
-**handle** ww. (-d) toetakel; -**hole** s.
valgat, luik; -**kind** s. die mensheid;
-**ly** bnw. (-lier, -liest) manlik;
-**slaughter** s. manslag.

'**manacle** ['mænəkl] ww. (-d) boei.

'**manage** ['mænidzj] ww. (-d)
bestuur; regkry; beheer; behandel;
-**able** bnw. regeerbaar; -**ment** s. (-s)
bestuur; -**r** s. bestuurder; **manage-**

'ress s. bestuurderes; 'managing bnw. besturend; prakties.

'mandarine ['mændərin] s. (-s) nartjie.

'mandate ['mændyt] s. (-s) mandaat; opdrag; volmag; 'mandatory bnw. gebiedend, bevelend.

'mandible ['mændibl] s. (-s) kakebeen; man'dibular bnw. kakebeen.

'mandoline ['mændəlin] s. mandolien.

'mandrel ['mændrəl] s. spil.

'mane ['myn] s. (-s) maanhare.

'manful ['mænfoel] bnw. manhaftig, dapper.

manga'nese [mæng-ghə'niz] s. mangaan.

'mange ['myndzj] s. skurfte.

'mangel ['mæng-ghl] s. (-s) mangelwortel.

'manger ['myndzjə] s. (-s) krip, trog.

'mango ['mæng-ghou] s. (-es) mango.

'mangrove ['mæng-ghrouv] s. (-s) mangoboom; wortelboom.

'mangy ['myndzjl] bnw. ('mangier, 'mangiest) skurftig; onsuiwer.

'mania ['mynlə] s. (-s) manie, gier; kranksinnigheid; -c s. waansinnige, bnw. waansinnig.

'manicure ['mænikjoeə] s. (-s) naelpolitoer; ww. (-d) manikuur; - set s. manikuurstel.

'manifest ['mænifest] s. (-s) manifes; bnw. duidelik; ww. (-ed) duidelik maak, openbaar; manifes'tation s. betoging; mani'festo s. manifes.

'manifold ['mænifould] bnw. menigvuldig, veelsoortig.

'manikin ['mænikin] s. (-s) model, manneken = mannequin.

ma'nipulate [ma'nipjoelyt] ww. (-d) hanteer; knoei; manipu'lation s. bewerking, knoeiery.

man'kind [mæn'kaind] s. die mensdom, die mensheid.

'manna ['mænə] s. manna, geestelike voedsel.

'mannequin ['mænikin] s. (-s) model, modepop, manneken.

'manner ['mænə] s. (-s) manier, wyse; aanwensel; klas; -s s. gedrag, maniere; -ism s. aanwensel; -ly bnw. manierlik, beleefd.

ma'noeuvre [mə'nõëvə] s. maneuwer, plan; ww. (-ed) intrigeer, manipuleer.

'manor ['mænə] s. (-s) landgoed; ma'norial bnw. landheerlik.

'manpower ['mænpauə] s. leërsterkte, strydkrag; werkkragte.

'manse ['mæns] s. (-s) pastorie, predikantswoning.

'mansion ['mænsjən] s. (-s) herewoning.

'manslaughter ['mænslôtə] s. manslag.

man'tilla [mæn'tilə] s. (-s) sluier, mantel.

'mantis ['mæntis] s. (-es) hotnotsgot.

'mantle ['mæntl] s. (-s) mantel; dekmantel; gloeikousie.

'manual ['mænjoeəl] s. (-s) handboek; klaviertoetse; bnw. met die hand; manual- hand-.

manu'facture [mænjoe'fæktsjə] s. (-s) fabrikasie; fabrikaat, maaksel; ww. (-d) vervaardig; bedink; manu'factory s. fabriek; -r s. vervaardiger, fabrikant.

ma'nure [mə'njoeə] s. mis, bemestingstof.

'manuscript ['mænjoeskript] s. (-s) manuskrip; handskrif.

'many ['mæni] s. die menigte; bnw. ('more, 'most) baie, veel; -coloured bnw. bont.

map ['mæp] s. (-s) kaart, landkaart.

'maple ['mypl] s. (-s) esdoring.

mar ['mä] ww. (-red) skend, bederwe.

ma'raud [mə'rôd] ww. (-ed) plunder, stroop; -er s. buiter; -ing s. buitery.

'marble ['mäbl] s. (-s) marmer; albaster.

'marcasite ['mäkəsait] s. piriet, swawelkies.

March ['mätsj] s. Maart.

march ['mätsj] s. (-es) grens, grensland; mars; tog; gang; ww. (-ed) marseer; loop.

'mare ['mêə] s. (-s) merrie.

marga'rine [mädzjə'rin] s. margarine, kunsbotter.

'margin ['mädzjin] s. (-s) rant, kant; wins, speling; grens; -ate ww. (-d) met rant voorsien; -al bnw. aan die rant; margi'nalia s. kanttekeninge.

margue'rite [mäghə'rit] s. (-s) margriet.

'marigold ['merighould] s. (-s) gousblom; 'Afrikaner'.

ma'rine [mə'rin] s. (-s) marine, vloot; seesoldaat; bnw. marine-; 'mariner s. matroos; marine-skeeps-.

mario'nette [mæriə'net] s. (-s) marionet, pop.

'marital ['mæritəl] bnw. huweliks-.

'maritime ['mæritaim] bnw. kus-, see-.

mark ['mäk] s. (-s) merk; teken; stempel; kruisie; ww. (-ed) merk; stempel; teken gee aan; -er s. teller; -ing s. merk; tekening; -sman s. skutter.

'market ['mäkit] s. (-s) mark; afsetgebied; handel; ww. (-ed) bemark, verkoop, handel; -er merk-.

marl ['mäl] s. mergel.

'marmalade ['mäməlyd] s. marmelade.

'marmoset ['mäməzet] s. (-s) klou-apie.

'marmot ['mämət] s. (-s) marmotjie.

ma'roon [mə'rõën] ww. (-ed) agterlaat (op verlate eiland); s. donkerrooi.

mar'quee [mä'ki] s. (-s) veldtent, markee.

'**marrow** ['mærou] s. (-s) murg; murg van groente; -**bone** s. murgbeen.

'**marry** ['mæri] ww. ('married) trou, in die huwelik tree; '**marriage** s. huwelik; '**marriage lines** s. troubewys.

Marseil'laise [māsə'lyz] s. Franse volkslied, Marseillaise.

marsh ['māsj] s. (-es) moeras, vlei; -**gas** s. moerasgas.

'**marshal** ['māsjəl] s. (-s) maarskalk; ww. (-led) rangskik, orden; opstel.

mar'supial [mā'sjōēpiəl] s. (-s) buideldier.

mart ['māt] s. (-s) verkooplokaal, vandusieplek.

'**marten** ['mātin] s. (-s) marter (pels).

'**martial** ['māsjəl] bnw. krygshaftig, oorlogs-, dapper.

marti'net [māti'net] s. (-s) drilmeester.

'**martyr** ['mātə] s. (-s) martelaar; ww. (-ed) martel, pynig.

'**marvel** ['māvəl] s. (-s) wonder; verbasing; ww. (-led) wonder, verbaas wees oor; -**lous** bnw. wonderbaarlik.

marzi'pan [māzi'pæn] s. marsepein.

'**mascot** ['mæskət] s. (-s) gelukbringer, talisman; neusbeeld (motorvoertuig).

'**masculine** ['mæskjoelin] bnw. manlik; managtig; fors.

mash ['mæsj] s. (-es) mengsel; pap; ww. (-ed) meng, fyndruk; -**er** s. hartverowweraar.

mask ['māsk] s. (-s) masker; mombak; voorwendsel; ww. (-ed) vermom; bedek; toeplak (spuitwerf); -**ing tape** s. plakband.

'**mason** ['mysn] s. (-s) messelaar; ww. (-ed) messel; -**ry** s. messelwerk.

'**masquerade** [mæskə'ryd] s. (-s) maskerade; vermomming.

mass ['mæs] s. (-es) mis; massa, hoop, klomp, trop; ww. (-ed) vergader, saamloop; -**ive** bnw. swaar, massief.

'**massacre** ['mæsikə] s. (-s) slagting, bloedbad.

'**massage** ['mæsādzj] s. (-s) massering, massage; ww. (-d) masseer, vrywe; **mas'seur** s. masseerder; **mas'seuse** s. masseerster, masseuse.

mast ['māst] s. (-s) mas; varkenskos.

'**master** ['māstə] s. (-s) meester, baas; besitter; kaptein; weesheer; werkgewer; bobaas; onderwyser; jongeheer; ww. (-ed) oormeester, bemeester; onderwerp; baasraak; baasspeel; heers; -**ful** bnw. baasspelerig; -**ly** bnw. meesterlik; -**key** s. loper, towersleutel; -**piece** s. meesterstuk, kunswerk; -**y** s. beheer, oorhand; **master-** hoof-; - **cylinder** s. hoofsilinder.

'**masticate** ['mæstikyt] ww. (-d) kou, herkou.

'**mastiff** ['mæstif] s. (-s) waghond.

mas'titis [mæs'taitis] s. ontsteking van bors(te) = **mammitis** (bydiere).

'**mastodon** ['mæstədən] s. mastodon.

'**mastoid** ['mæstoid] s. (-s) rotsbeenontsteking.

mat ['mæt] s. (-s) mat; bnw. mat, dof; ww. (-ted) met matte bedek; saamkoek.

Mata'bele [mætə'bili] s. (-s) Matabelie.

'**matador** ['mætədô] s. (-s) matador.

match ['mætsj] s. (-es) vuurhoutjie; gelyke; wedstryd; ww. (-ed) bymekaar pas; opgewasse teen; -**box** s. vuurhoutdosie; -**less** bnw. wergaloos; -**maker** s. koppelaar; -**wood** s. vuurmaakhout, brandhout.

'**mate** ['myt] s. (-s) kameraad, maat; man; hulp; helper; stuurman; mannetjie of wyfie; ww. (-d) paar; verenig; maats maak.

'**mater** ['mytə] s. (-s) moeder; **ma'ternal** bnw. moederlik; **ma'ternity** n. moederskap.

ma'terial [mə'tiəriəl] s. (-s) materiaal, stof; bnw. stoflik; belangrik; **materiali'zation** s. verwesenliking; **ma'terialize** ww. (-d) verwesenlik; materialiseer.

mathe'matics [mithə'mætiks] s. wiskunde; matesis; **mathema'tician** s. wiskundige.

'**matin'ee** ['mætinē] s. (-s) matinee.

'**matriarch** ['mytriāk] s. (-s) stammoeder; -**al** bnw. matriargaal; -**y** s. matriargaat.

ma'tric [mə'trik] s. matriek; -**u'lation** s. matrikulasie; -**ulate** ww. (-d) matrikuleer.

'**matricide** ['mytrisaid] s. moedermoord; moedermoordenaar.

'**matrimony** ['mætriməni] s. huwelik; eg; **matri'monial** bnw. huweliks-.

'**matrix** ['mytriks] s. ('matrices) baarmoeder; moer; matrys.

'**matron** ['mytrən] s. (-s) dame; huisvrou; matrone; huismoeder; -**ly** bnw. huisvroulik; deftig.

'**matter** ['mætə] s. (-s) stof; materie; inhoud; voorwerp; saak; etter; ww. (-ed) van belang wees; -**of-fact** bnw. droog, saaklik.

'**mattock** ['mætək] s. bylpik.

'**mattress** ['mætrəs] s. (-es) matras.

ma'ture [mə'tjoeə] ww. (-d) ryp word, uitgroei; wasdom bereik; bnw. ryp, volwasse, bekwaam; -**d** bnw. ryp; bejeë; **maturate** ww. ryp word; **matu'ration** s. rypwording; rypheid; -**ness** s. rypheid; **ma'turity** s. rypheid.

'**maudlin** ['mōdlin] bnw. sentimenteel.

maul ['mōl] s. (-s) moker; ww. (-ed) moker, kneus, toetakel; - **stick** s. skilderstok.

'**mauser** ['mausə] s. (-s) mausergeweer.

mauso'leum ['mōsə'liəm] s. (-s) praalgraf.

'**mauve** ['mouv] s. & bnw. ligpers.

maw ['mō] s. (-s) maag, pens.

'mawkish ['môkisj] *bnw.* sentimenteel.

max'illa [mæk'silə] *s.* (*max'illae*) bokaak; -ry *bnw.* van die kaak, kaak-.

'maxim ['mæksim] *s.* (-*s*) meksim; grondbeginsel; leus.

'maximum ['mæksiməm] *s.* ('*maxima*) maksimum, grootste hoeveelheid; 'maximize *ww.* (-*d*) vermeerder.

May ['my] *s.* Mei; -flower *s.* meiblom, kerkhofblom; -fly *s.* (-*flies*) eendagsvlieg.

may ['my] *ww.* ('*might*) mag, kan; -be *bw.* miskien; might-have-been *s.* mislukking.

mayon'naise [m야ə'nyz] *s.* mayonnaise (*sous*).

'mayor ['mêə] *s.* (-*s*) burgemeester; -al *bnw.* burgemêesterlik; -'ess *s.* burgemeestersvrou.

'maze ['myz] *s.* (-*s*) doolhof; labirint; *ww.* (-*d*) verbyster.

ma'zurka [mə'zəkə] *s.* (-*s*) masurka.

me ['mi] *vnw.* my; ek; mi (*solfa*).

mead ['mid] *s.* heuningdrank.

'meadow ['medou] *s.* (-*s*) weiland.

'meagre ['migrə] *bnw.* maer, skraal, onvrugbaar, dor.

meal ['mil] *s.* (-*s*) meel; maaltyd, kos; -time *s.* etenstyd; -y *bnw.* melerig; -y-mouthed *bnw.* soetsappig.

'mealie ['mili] *s.* (-*s*) mielie; - borer *s.* mielierusper; - cob *s.* mieliekop; - meal *s.* mieliemeel; - porridge *s.* mieliepap; - stalk *s.* mieliestronk.

mean ['min] *s.* (-*s*) middelweg; gemiddelde; -s *s.* middele; *bnw.* (-*er*, -*est*) gemeen, laag; gemiddelde; *ww.* (*meant*) meen, bedoel, beteken; voornemens wees; -ing *s.* betekenis; -ly *bw.* sleg, min; -ness *s.* gemeenheid; -time *bw.* intussen; -while *bw.* intussen.

me'ander [mi'ændə] *ww.* (-*ed*) kronkel, slinger; -ing *bw.* slingerend.

'measles ['mizlz] *s.* masels; measled *bnw.* vol masels, uitgeslaan; measly *bnw.* siek aan masels; miserabel.

'measure ['mesjə] *s.* (-*s*) maat; maatstaf; maatreël; *ww.* (-*d*) meet; skat; goed bekyk; -d *bnw.* afgemete; -less *bnw.* onmeetlik; -ment *s.* afmeting; 'maat; 'measuring *s.* meting.

meat ['mit] *s.* (-*s*) vleis; kos, maaltyd; -pie *s.* vleispastei; -y *bnw.* vleisig; goed in die vleis; kragtig.

'Mecca ['mekə] *s.* Mekka.

me'chanic [mi'kænik] *s.* (-*s*) ambagsman, werktuigkundige; -al *bnw.* meganies, werktuiglik; -al horse *s.* voorhaker; mecha'nician *s.* werktuigkundige; -s *s.* werktuigkunde; 'mechanize *ww.* (-*d*) meganiseer; 'mechanism *s.* meganisme; tegniek.

'medal ['medl] *s.* (-*s*) penning, medalje; -led *bnw.* vol medaljes;

me'dallion *s.* medaljon; medallist *s.* medaljewenner, bekroonde.

'meddle ['medl] *ww.* (-*d*) bemoei met, inmeng; -r *s.* lolpot, bemoei-al; -some *bnw.* lastig, bemoeisiek.

'medial ['midiəl] *bnw.* middel-, tussen-.

'median ['midiən] *s.* (-*s*) middellyn; -t *s.* mediant.

'mediate ['midiit] *bnw.* middellik; *ww.* (-*d*) bemiddel; medi'ation *s.* bemiddeling; 'mediator *s.* middelaar.

'medical ['medikəl] *s.* (-*s*) medikus, mediese student; *bnw.* medies, geneeskundig; 'medicable *bnw.* geneesbaar; me'dicament *s.* medisyne; 'medicate *ww.* (-*d*) geneeskundig behandel, dokter; 'medico *s.* (-*s*) medikus.

'medicine ['medsin] *s.* (-*s*) medisyne, geneesmiddel; me'dicinal *bnw.* geneeskragtig, medies; - man *s.* toordokter.

medi'eval [medi'ivəl] *bnw.* middelceus.

'mediocre ['midioukə] *bnw.* middelmatig.

'meditate ['meditytt] *ww.* (-*d*) nadink, peins; medi'tation *s.* oorpeinsing; 'meditative *bnw.* peinsend.

Mediter'ranean [meditə'rynjən] *s.* Middel(landse)see.

'medium ['midiəm] *s.* (-*s*) middel; middelweg; voertaal; gemiddelde; medium; *bnw.* middelmatig, matig.

'medley ['medli] *s.* mengelmoes; *bnw.* gemeng, bont.

me'dulla [me'dʌlə] *s.* (-*s*) pit; murg; -ry *bnw.* murg-.

meek ['mik] *bnw.* (-*er*, -*est*) gedwee, sag, beskei.

'meerschaum ['miəsjəm] *s.* (-*s*) meerskuim(pyp).

'meercat ['miəkæt] *s.* (-*s*) meerkat.

meet ['mit] *s.* (-*s*) byeenkoms; *bnw.* paslik; *ww.* ('*met*) ontmoet; bevredig; byeenkom; -ing *s.* (-*s*) ontmoeting; samekoms; vergadering.

megalo'mania [məghælou'myniə] *s.* grootheidswaan.

'megaphone ['meghəfoun] *s.* (-*s*) megafoon.

melan'cholia [melən'kouljə] *s.* melankolie, swaarmoedigheid; melan'cholic *bnw.* melankolies, swaarmoedig; 'melancholy *s.* swartgalligheid; *bnw.* swartgallig.

mé'lange [mê'lãnzj] *s.* mengsel, mélange.

mê'lée [me'ly] *s.* (-*s*) handgemeen, deurmekaar geveg.

'meliorate ['miljərytt] *ww.* (-*d*) versag, verbeter; melio'ration *s.* verbetering.

'mellow ['melou] *bnw.* soet, ryp, sappig; sag; beleë; oud.

'melodrama ['melədrāmə] *s.* melodrama; melodra'matic *bnw.* melodramaties.

'**melody** ['melədi] s. ('*melodies*) wysie, lied, melodie; me'**lodious** bnw. melodieus, sangerig.

'**melon** ['melən] s. (-s) spaanspek; waatlemoen.

melt ['melt] ww. (-ed) smelt, vermurf; ontdooi; oplos.

'**member** ['membə] s. (-s) lid (maat); deel, tak; -**ship** s. lidmaatskap.

'**membrane** ['membryn] s. (-s) vlies, weefsel.

me'**mento** [me'mentou] s. (-es) aandenking.

'**me'moir** ['mem'wa] s. (-s) gedenk-skrif.

'**memory** ['meməri] s. ('*memories*) geheue, herinnering; nagedagtenis; '**memorable** bnw. heuglik; memo'-**randum** s. memorandum; nota; me'**morial** s. gedenkteken; '**memor-ize** ww. (-d) memoriseer, van buite leer.

'**menace** ['menəs] s. (-s) bedreiging; ww. (-d) bedreig; '**menacing** bnw. bedreigend.

me'**nage** [me'nāzj] s. (-s) huis-houding; me'**nagerie** s. dieretuin, diereversameling.

mend ['mend] ww. (-ed) heelmaak, opknap, repareer; herstel.

men'dacity [men'dæsiti] s. leuenag-tigheid; **men'dacious** bnw. leuenag-tig, vals.

'**mendicant** ['mendikənt] s. (-s) bedelaar.

'**menial** ['miniəl] s. (-s) bediende, diensbode; bnw. slaafs; diensbaar.

menin'gitis [menin'dzjaitis] s. har-singvliesontsteking.

'**mental** ['mentl] bnw. geestelik, geestes-, verstands-; **men'tality** s. geeskrag; denkwyse; -**ly** bnw. gees-telik.

'**mention** ['mensjən] ww. (-ed) vermeld, noem; -**able** bnw. noemens-waardig.

'**mentor** ['mentô] s. (-s) raadgewer, leier.

'**menu** ['menjōē] s. (-s) spyskaart.

'**mercantile** ['mākəntail] bnw. handels-; merkantiel.

'**mercenary** ['māsinəri] s. ('*mer-cenaries*) huurling, huursoldaat; bnw. gehuur; omkoopbaar; baatsugtig.

'**mercer** ['māsə] s. (-s) handelaar in weefstowwe; -**ize** ww. (-d) verfklaar maak; -**y** s. weefstowwe.

'**merchandise** ['mātsjəndaiz] s. koopware, negosie.

'**merchant** ['mātsjənt] s. (-s) handelaar, koopman; -**man** s. (-*men*) handelskip; - **service** s. handelsvloot.

'**mercury** ['mākjoeri] s. kwik; **mer'curial** s. kwikmiddel; bnw. lewendig; **mer'curic** bnw. kwikagtig.

'**mercy** ['māsi] s. ('*mercies*) genade; ontferming; '**merciful** bnw. genadig, barmhartig; '**merciless** bnw. on-genadig, hard.

'**mere** [miə] bnw. & bw. net, louter, eenvoudig, bloot; -**ly** bw. net, slegs.

merge ['mādzj] ww. (-d) indompel, oplos, saamsmelt; -**r** s. samesmelt-ing.

me'**ridian** [mə'ridiən] s. (-s) mid-daglyn, meridiaan.

me'**ringue** [mə'ræng] s. (-s) 'skuim-pies', koek of lekkers van suiker met eierwit.

me'**rino** [mə'rinou] s. (-s) merino.

'**merit** ['merit] s. (-s) verdienste; deug; waarde; ww. (-ed) werd wees, verdien; **meri'torious** bnw. verdien-stelik.

'**mermaid** ['māmyd] s. (-s) meermin.

'**merry** ['meri] bnw. ('*merrier*, '*merriest*) vrolik, opgewek, speels; '**merrily** bw. vrolik, opgewek; '**mer-riment** s. vrolikheid, pret; -**go-round** s. mallemeule, rondomtalie; -**making** s. pret; - **thought** s. geluksbeentjie.

'**mesalliance** ['mēsalj ñs] s. mis-huwelik.

me'**seems** [mi'simz] ww. dit lyk vir my.

mesembry'anthemum [mizəmbri-'ænthiməm] s. (-s) vygie.

mesh ['mesj] s. (-es) netwerk, maas; strik.

mess ['mes] s. (-es) gereg, gemeen-skaplike ete; deurmekaarspul, wan-orde; vuilgoed; ww. (-ed) saam-eet; knoei; bemors; -**y** bnw. vuil, morsig.

'**message** ['mesidzj] s. (-s) boodskap, berig.

'**messenger** ['mesindzjə] s. (-s) boodskapper, bode, koerier.

Mes'siah [mi'saiə] s. Messias.

'**metal** ['metl] s. (-s) metaal; me'**tallic** bnw. metaalagtig; -'**liferous** bnw. metaalhoudend; -'**lurgic** bnw. metal-lurgies; -'**lurgy** s. metallurgie, me-taalkunde.

meta'morphose [metə'môfous] ww. verander van gedaante; **meta'mor-phosis** s. gedaanteverwisseling.

'**metaphor** ['metə'fô] s. (-s) beeld-spraak, metafoor; **meta'phoric** bnw. figuurlik, oordragtelik.

meta'physics [metə'fiziks] s. meta-fisika.

'**meteor** ['mitjə] s. (-s) vallende ster; meteoor; -**ic** bnw. meteories; -**ite** s. meteoriet; **meteo'rology** s. meteor-ologie, weekrunde; -o'**logical** bnw. weerkundig.

'**meter** ['mitə] s. (-s) meter.

me'**tier** ['my'tjy] s. beroep, ambag.

me'**thinks** [mi'thinks] ww. dit lyk vir my, my dunk.

'**method** ['methəd] s. (-s) metode, wyse; me'**thodical** bnw. metodies, sistematies; -**ism** s. Metodisme.

'**methylate** ['methilyt] ww. (-d) met methyl meng.

me'**ticulous** [mi'tikjoeləs] bnw. nougeset, angsvallig.

me'**tonymy** [mi'tonimi] s. me-tonimia.

'**metre** ['mitə] s. (-s) digmaat;

metrum; meter; **'metrical** *bnw.* metries.

me'tropolis [mi'tropəlis] s. hoofstad, metropool; **metro'politan** *bnw.* hoofstedelik, metropolitaans.

'mettle ['metl] s. moed, ywer; stoffasie.

mew ['mjōē] s. (-s) meeu; gemiaau; *ww.* (-ed) miaau; -l *ww.* (-ed) miaau, tjank; -s s. stalie.

'Mexico ['meksikou] s. Meksiko.

'mezzanine ['mezənin] s. (-s) tussenverdieping.

mi ['mi] s. mi (*solfa*).

mi'asma [mi'æzmə] s. smetstof, miasma.

miaul = mewl.

'mica ['maikə] s. mika; mi'caceous *bnw.* mika-agtig.

'microbe ['maikroub] s. (-s) mikrobe.

'microcosm ['maikrōkozəm] *a.* mikrokosmos.

'microphone ['maikrəfˌun] s. (-s) mikrofoon.

'microscope ['maikrəskoup] s. (-s) mikroskoop.

mid ['mid] *bnw.* middel, halfpad; *voors.* amid; **-day** s. middag; **-hour** s. middag; **-land** s. binneland; middelland; **-leg** s. middel van been; **-most** *bnw.* middelste; **-night** s. middernag; **-rib** s. middelrib; **-riff** s. middelrif; **-st** *voors.* te midde van; **-summer** s. hartjie van die somer; **-way** s. halfpad; **-winter** s. hartjie van die winter.

'middle ['midl] s. (-s) middel, midde, middelpunt, middelweg; *bnw.* middelste; **-aged** *bnw.* middeljarig; **'midling** *bnw. & bw.* middelmatig, swakkerig; **'midlings** s. middelslag groottes.

'midge ['midzj] s. (-s) muggie, dwerg; **-s** s. *mv.* brandassies, warmas.

'midst ['midst] s. midde, middel.

'midwife ['midwaif] s. ('midwives) vroedvrou; **-ry** s. verloskunde; beoefening van verloskunde; **-ry** forceps s. verlostang.

mien ['min] s. (-s) voorkoms, houding; gesig.

might ['mait] s. mag, krag, vermoë, geweld; *ww. verl.t.* van may; **-y** *bnw.* magtig, kragtig.

'mignonette ['minjonet] s. (-s) reseda.

'migraine ['mighryn] s. skeel hoofpyn.

mi'grate [mai'ghryt] *ww.* (-d) verhuis, trek, swerf; **'migrant** *bnw.* rondswerwende; **mi'gration** s. verhuising; **'migratory** *bnw.* nomadies.

mild ['maild] *bnw.* (-er, -est) sag, sagaardig; vriendelik; lig, swak; - steel s. weekstaal.

'mildew ['mildjōē] s. skimmel.

'mile ['mail] s. (-s) myl; **-age** s. afstand; bedrag per myl; **-stone** s. mylpaal.

'mileage ['mailidzj] s. mylafstand; mylgeld (*taxi*).

'military ['militəri] *bnw.* militêr, oorlogs-; **'militant** *bnw.* vegtend; strydlustig;'**militate** *ww.* (-d) oorlogvoer, stry.

mi'litia [mə'lisjə] s. burgermag.

milk ['milk] s. melk; *ww.* (-ed) melk; **-er** s. melker; melkkoei; **-food** s. melkkos; **-jug** s. melkbeker; **-maid** s. melkmeisie; **-man** s. melkverkoper; **-pail** s. melkemmer, dopemmer; **-sop** s. papbroek; - **tooth** s. melktand, wisseltand; **-y** *bnw.* melkerig, melkagtig; **Milky Way** s. hemelstraat; **-weed** s. (-s) melkbos.

mill ['mil] s. (-s) meule; fabriek; *ww.* (-ed) maal; klop; afransel; ronddraai; **-ed** *bnw.* gemaal; **-er** s. meulenaar.

mil'lennium [mi'leniəm] s. (*millennia*) duisendjarige ryk, Millennium.

'millipede ['milipid] s. (-s) duisendpoot.

'millet ['milit] s. giers.

'milliard ['miljåd] s. (-s) miljard.

'milligramme ['milighræm] s. (-s) milligram; **'millilitre** s. milliliter; **'millimetre** s. millimeter.

'milliner ['milinə] s. (-s) hoedemaakster; modemaakster; **-y** s. hoedemakery; modewinkel.

'million ['miljən] s. (-s) miljoen.

'millstone ['milstoun] s. meulsteen.

milt ['milt] s. milt; hom (*van vis*).

'mime ['maim] s. (-s) klugspel; gebarespel; grapmaker; '**mimic** s. na-aper, mimikus, *bnw.* na-apend, mimies, *ww.* ('mimicked) namaak, na-aap; **'mimicry** s. na-apery, mimiek.

mi'mosa [mi'mouzə] s. (-s) mimosa, doringboom.

'minaret ['minəret] s. (-s) minaret.

'mince ['mins] s. fyngemaalde vleis; *ww.* (-d) maal; bedek; **-meat** s. maalvleis; - **pie** s. vleispasteitjie; **-r** s. vleismeule.

mind ['maind] s. (-s) verstand, opinie; mening; sin, lus; neiging; gees; doel; gedagte; *ww.* herinner, onthou; oppas; omgee; **-ed** *bnw.* gesind, geneig; **-ful** *bnw.* oplettend.

'mine ['main] s. (-s) myn; bron; *vnw.* myne, van my, my; *ww.* (-d) grawe, delf, ontgin; myne lê; **-r** s. delwer.

'mineral ['minərəl] s. (-s) mineraal, delfstof, erts; *bnw.* mineraal-; **-ize** *ww.* (-d) versteen; **mine'rology** s. delfstofkunde.

'mingle ['ming-ghl] *ww.* (-d) meng; deurmekaarloop.

'miniature ['minjə'tsjə] s. (-s) miniatuur.

'minim ['minim] s. (-s) klein bietjie; halwe noot; minim; **-al** *bnw.* minimaal, kleinste; **-ize** *ww.* (-d) verklein; **-um** s. (-a) minste, minimum.

'**minion** ['minjən] s. (-s) gunsteling, aanhanger.

'**minister** ['ministə] s. (-s) minister; dienaar; gesang; predikant; *ww.* (-ed) dien, versorg, help; **minis'terial** *bnw.* ministerieel, amptelik; '**ministry** s. ministerie; bediening.

mink ['mink] s. wesel; weselbont.

'**minor** ['mainə] s. (-s) mindere; minderjarige; mineur; *bnw.* minder; minderjarig; kleiner; ondergeskik; **mi'nority** s. (mi'*norities*) minderheid; onmondigheid.

'**minster** ['minstə] s. (-s) munster, katedraal.

''**minstrel** ['minstrəl] s. (-s) bard, ministreel.

mint ['mint] s. (-s) munt; kruisement; *ww.* (-ed) munt; -**age** s. munt, gemunte geld.

minu'et [minjoe'et] s. (-s) menuet.

'**minus** ['mainəs] s. & *bnw.* minus, min, sonder; negatief.

mi'nute [mai'njoet] *bnw.* (-st) klein, gering; -ly *bw.* haarfyn.

minute ['minit] s. (-s) minuut; oomblik; memorandum; *ww.* (-d) notuleer; -ly *bw.* elke minuut; -s *mv.* notule.

'**minx** ['minks] s. (-es) rissie, uitgelate meisiemens.

'**miracle** ['mirəkl] s. (-s) wonder (werk), mirakel; '**mi'raculous** *bnw.* wonderbaarlik.

mi'rage [mi'r zj] s. (-s) lugspieëling, opgeefsel; bedrog.

'**mire** ['maiə] s. modder, vuiligheid.

'**mirror** ['mirə] s. (-s) spieël.

mirth ['məth] s. vrolikheid; -**ful** *bnw.* vrolik; -**less** *bnw.* treurig.

mis- ['mis-] *voorvoegsel* mis-, wan-, verkeerd, oneg; -**alliance** s. ongelyke huwelik, = **mesalliance** -**anthrope** s. mensehater; -**apprehend** *ww.* (-ed) misverstaan; -**carry** *ww.* ('*miscarried*) misluk, verongeluk; -**cegenation** s. rassevermenging; -**cellanea** s. mengelwerk; -**cel'laneous** *bnw.* deurmekaar, gemeng; -**chief** s. kwaad, onheil, kattekwaad; -**chievous** *bnw.* skadelik, nadelig, ondeuend; -**creant** s. skurk, vabond; -**deed** s. misdaad, oortreding; -**fire** *ww.* (-d) weier, kets; -**fit** s. slegpassend stuk(persoon); -**fortune** s. (-s) ramp; -**give** *ww.* (-gave) twyfel; -**gotten** *bnw.* onregverdig ontvang; -**guide** *ww.* (-d) verkeerd lei; -**hap** s. ongeluk; -**mate** *ww.* verkeerd paar; -**mating** s. wanparing; -**nomer** s. verkeerde benaming; -'**ogamy** s. afkeer van die huwelik; -'**ogyny** s. vrouehaat; -**print** s. drukfout; -**step** s. mistrap; -'**take** s. fout; -'**taken** *bnw.* verkeerd, foutief; -**time** *ww.* (-d) misreken; -**trust** *ww.* (-ed) wantrou.

'**mis'appropriate** ['misə'proupriyt] *ww.* (-d) onwettig toe-eien.

mis'chance [mis'tsjăns] s. ongeluk.

'**mis'construe** ['miskən'strōē] *ww.* (-d) misdui, verkeerd opvat.

'**miser** ['maizə] s. (-s) vrek; ellendeling; -ly *bnw.* gierig.

'**miserable** ['mizərəbl] *bnw.* aaklig, ellendig, miserabel.

'**misery** ['mizəri] s. ('*miseries*) ellende; armoede.

miss ['mis] s. (-es) juffrou; nooientjie; kleinnooi; meisie; misskoot; gemis; *ww.* (-ed) mis; versulm; misskiet; -**ing** *bnw.* verlore.

'**missile** ['misail] s. (-s) werptuig, gooiding.

'**mission** ['misjən] s. (-s) sending, opdrag; roeping; bestemming; -**ary** s. ('*missionaries*) sendeling, *bnw.* sending-.

'**missive** ['misiv] s. (-s) bode; brief.

mist ['mist] s. (-s) mis, newel.

'**mister** ['mistə] s. (-s) meneer.

'**mistletoe** ['misltou] s. mistel(tak), voëlent.

'**mistral** ['mistrəl] s. mistral (*wind*).

'**mistress** ['mistris] s. (-es) mevrou, vrou; meesteres; eienares; geliefde; bysit.

'**mis'use** ['misjōēs] s. misbruik.

'**nite** ['mait] s. (-s) duit, penning; miet; kleintjie.

'**mitigate** ['mitighyt] *ww.* (-d) versag, stil; verswak; verlig; matig; **miti'gation** s. versagting, leniging.

'**mitre** ['maitə] s. myter, biskopshoed.

'**mitten** ['mitn] s. (-s) moffie, duimhandskoen.

mix ['miks] *ww.* (-ed) meng; berei; -**able** *bnw.* mengbaar; -**ed** *bnw.* gemeng; -**er** s. menger; -**ture** s. mengsel, drankie; -**up** s. mengelmoes.

'**mizzle** ['mizl] s. (-s) motreën; mizzly, *bnw.* motreënerig.

moan ['moun] s. (-s) gekreun, gekerm; *ww.* (-ed) kerm, kla; -**ing** s. gekerm.

moat ['mout] s. (-s) grag.

mob ['mob] s. (-s) gepeupel, gespuis, menigte; *ww.* (-bed) omsingel, aanval, molesteer; - **rule** s. beheer deur die gepeupel.

'**mobile** ['moubail] *bnw.* beweeglik, los; **mo'bility** s. beweeglikheid; **mobili'zation** s. mobilisering; '**mobilize** *ww.* (-d) mobiliseer.

'**mocassin** ['mokəsin] s. (-s) mokassin, Rooihuidskoen.

mock ['mok] *ww.* (-ed) bespot; uitkoggel; naboots; -**ery** s. bespotting; - **fight** s. skyngeveg; -**ing** *bnw.* spottend; - **trial** s. skynverhoor; -**turtle** s. nagebootste skilpadsop.

'**modal** ['moudl] *bnw.* modaal, van wyse; **m** '**dality** s. modaliteit.

'**mode** ['moud] s. (-s) manier, wyse; modus; toon; mode; **mo'diste** s. modiste, modemaakster.

'**model** ['modl] s. (-s) model; monster; *bnw.* voorbeeldig; *ww.* (-led) modelleer, boetseer; -**ler** s.

boetseerder; **-ling** s. boetseerkuns; **-ling-clay** s. boetseerklei.

'**moderate** ['moderit] s. (-s) gematigde; *ww.* (-d) matig, temper; *bw.* taamlik, redelik; **-ly** *bw.* gematig, redelik; **mode'ration** s. matigheid; '**moderator** s. moderator, arbiter.

'**modern** ['modən] s. (-s) 'n moderne; *bnw.* modern, nuwerwets; **-ize** *ww.* (-d) moderniseer.

'**modest** ['modist] *bnw.* beskeie, sedig; matig; **-y** s. sedigheid, beskeidenheid.

'**modicum** ['modikəm] s. bietjie, krieseltjie.

'**modify** ['modifai] *ww.* ('modified) wysig; matig; '**modifiable** *bnw.* wysigbaar; '**modification** s. wysiging.

'**modish** ['moudisj] *bnw.* na die mode, mode-.

'**modulate** ['modjoelyt] *ww.* (-d) reguleer, stel; **modu'lation** s. regulering, modulasie; '**module** s. standaard.

'**mohair** ['mouhêə]s. angorahaar.

'**moiety** ['moiəti] s. helfte, deel.

'**moist** ['moist] *bnw.* nat, vogtig; **-en** *ww.* (-ed) bevogtig; **-ure** s. nattigheid, vog.

'**moke** ['mouk] s. (-s) esel.

'**molar** ['moulə] s. (-s) maaltand, kies.

mo'**lasses** [mə'læsəz] s. stroop, melasse.

'**mole** ['moul] s. (-s) moesie; pier, dyk; mol; **-cast** s. molshoop; **-hill** s. molshoop; **-skin** s. molvel; **-snake** s. molslang.

'**molecule** ['molikjôĕl] s. (-s) molekule, stofdeeltjie; mo'**lecular** *bnw.* molekulêr.

mo'**lest** [mô'lest] *ww.* (-ed) molesteer, moveer, hinder, pla; **moles'tation** s. kwellery, lollery.

'**mollify** ['molifai] *ww.* ('mollified) versag, lenig, stil; **mollifi'cation** s. versagting, leniging.

'**mollusc** ['moləsk] s. (-s) weekdier.

'**moment** ['moumənt] s. (-s) oomblik, rukkie, kits; **-ary** *bnw.* kortstondig, vlugtig; **-arily** *bw.* oomblik, momentaal; mo'**mentous** *bnw.* gewigtig, betekenisvol; mo'**mentum** s. dryfkrag, vaart.

'**monarch** ['monək] s. (-s) monarg, koning; mo'**narchical** *bnw.* monargaal; **-ist** s. monargis; **-y** s. monargie.

'**monastery** ['monəstri] s. ('monasteries) klooster; mo'**nastic** *bnw.* klooster-; mo'**nasticism** s. kloosterstelsel.

'**Monday** ['mʌndi] s. Maandag.

'**money** ['mʌni] s. ('monies) geld, munt; vermoë; '**monetary** *bnw.* geldelik, geld-; '**monetize** *ww.* (-d) munt, in omloop bring; '**monied** *bnw.* ryk, bemiddeld; **-grabber** s. geldwolf; **-lender** s. geldskieter; **-order** s. geldwissel.

'**monger** ['mʌng-ghə] s. (-s) handelaar, koopman.

'**mongrel** ['mʌng-ghrəl] s. (-s) baster, brak.

mo'**nition** [mou'nisjən] s. (-s) waarskuwing.

'**monitor** ['monitə] s. (-s) raadgewer.

monk ['mʌnk] s. (-s) monnik.

'**monkey** ['mʌnki] s. ('monkeys) bobbejaan, aap; kruik; **-nut** s. grondboontjie; **-wrench** s. Engelse moersleutel, bobbejaan.

'**monocephalus** ['mounousefələs] *bnw.* eenhoofdig.

monochrome ['mounəkroum] *bnw.* eenkleurig; **monochro'matic** *bnw.* eenkleurig.

'**monocle** ['monokl] s. (-s) oogglas, monokel.

'**monocoty'ledon** ['monoukoti'lidən] s. eensaadlobbige plant.

'**monody** ['monədi] s. ('monodies) alleensang, klaaglied.

mon'**ogamy** [mo'noghəmi] s. monogamie, enkelvoudige huwelik.

'**monoglot** ['monəghlot] s. (-s) eentalige.

'**monogram** ['monəghræm] s. monogram.

'**monologue** ['monəlogh] s. (-s) alleenspraak, monoloog.

'**mono'mania** ['mounou'myniə] s. monomanie.

'**monoph'thong** ['monəf'thong] s. (-s) monoftong, klinker.

'**monoplane** ['monəplyn] s. (-s) eendekker.

mon'**opoly** [mə'nopəli] s. (mon'opolies) monopolie, alleenhandel; mo'**nopolize** *ww.* (-d) monopoliseer.

'**monosyllable** ['monəsilabl] s. (-s) eenlettergrepige woord.

'**monotheism** ['monôthiizəm] s. monoteïsme.

'**monotone** ['monətoun] *bnw.* eentonig; mo'**notonous** *bnw.* eentonig.

mon'**sieur** [mə'sjô] s. (-s) meneer.

mon'**soon** [mon'sôĕn] s. (-s) moesson.

'**monster** ['monstə] s. (-s) monster, gedrog; '**monstrous** *bnw.* monsteragtig; mon'**strosity** s. monster, gedrog.

'**monstrance** ['monstrəns] s. monstrans.

month ['mʌnth] s. (-s) maand; **-ly** *bnw.* maandeliks.

'**monument** ['monjoemənt] s. (-s) monument, standbeeld; monu'**mental** *bnw.* monumentaal.

moo ['môĕ] *ww.* (-ed) loei.

mood ['môĕd] s. (-s) stemming; wyse; modus; **-iness** s. nukkerigheid; **-y** *bnw.* nukkerig.

moon ['môĕn] s. (-s) maan; *ww.* (-ed) droom; **-beam** s. manestraal; **-light** s. maanlig(skyn); **-lit** *bnw.* maanverlig; **-shine** s. maanskyn; smokkeldrank; **-shiner** s. dranksmokkelaar; **-struck** *bnw.* maansiek, mal; **-y** *bnw.* dromerig.

'moon-'blindness['mōen-'blaindnəs] s. nagblindheid.

Moor ['moeə] s. (-s) Moor.

moor ['moeə] s. (-s) heide, vlei; moeras; ww. (-ed) aanlê, anker; -age s. ankerplek; -hen s. bleshoender; -land s. heideveld.

'moose ['mōes] s. (-s) Amerikaanse eland.

moot ['mōet] s. (-s) vergadering; debat; bnw. getwisbaar.

mop ['mop] s. (-s) vryflap, dweil; ww. (-ped) opvrywe, afvee.

'mope ['moup] ww. (-d) knies; suf, moedeloos wees.

mo'raine [mō'ryn] s. (-s) gletserpuin.

'moral ['morəl] s. (-s) moraal, les; sedelike gedrag; bnw. moreel, sedelik; -e [mo'rāl] s. moreel, moed; 'moralize ww. (-d) moraliseer, sedepreek; mo'rality s. sedelikheid.

mo'rass [mə'ræs] s. (-es) moeras.

'morbid ['mōbid] bnw. sieklik, ongesond; -ness s.

'more ['mō] bnw. & rnw. meer, ander, groter, nog; -over bw. verder; origens; daarenbowe.

'morgen ['moghin] s. morg(e).

'morgue ['mōgh] s. (-s) lykhuis, dodehuis; hoogmoed.

'moribund ['moribʌnd] bnw. sterwend.

morn ['mōn] s. more, oggend; -ing s. (-s) oggend, voormiddag.

mo'rose [mə'rous] bnw. stuurs, nors; -ness s.

'morphia ['mōfjə] s. morfia.

mor'phology [mō'folədzjl] s. morfologie; vormleer.

'morrow ['morou] s. (-s) more.

'morse ['mōs] s. morse-stelsel.

'morsel ['mōsəl] s. (-s) brokkie.

'mortal ['mōtl] s. (-s) sterfling; bnw. sterflik; mor'tality s. sterftesyfer; -ly bnw. dodelik.

'mortar ['mōtə] s. vysel; pleister, klei; ww. pleister.

'mortgage ['mōtghidzj] s. (-s) verband; ww. (-d) verpand.

'mortify ['mōtifai] ww. ('mortified) dood, kasty; krenk, beledig; afsterwe; 'mortified bnw. gekrenk, beledig; mortifi'cation s. afsterwing; vernedering.

'mortise ['mōtis] s. (-s) tapgat.

'mortuary ['mōtjoeəri] s. ('mortuaries) dodehuis; kerkhof.

mo'saic [mə'zyik] s. mosaïek.

Mo'selle [mə'zel] s. moeselwyn.

'mosque ['mosk] s. (-s) moskee.

mos'quito [məs'kitou] s. (-es) muskiet; -oil s. muskietolie; - repellent s. muskietweerder.

moss ['mos] s. (-es) mos, moeras, turf; -y bnw. mosagtig.

most ['moust] bnw. & bw. meeste, uiterste; mees, uiters; -ly bw. meestal, grotendeels.

moth ['moth] s. (-s) mot; -eaten, bnw. deur motte gevreet.

mother ['mʌdhə] s. (-s) moeder; abdis; huismoeder; moer; ww. (-ed) vertroetel; kinderlik versorg; -hood s. moederskap; -in-'law s. skoonmoeder; -ly bnw. moederlik; -of-pearl s. perlemoen; -tongue s. moedertaal.

mo'tif [mou'tif] s. (-s) motief, grondidee.

'motion ['mousjən] s. (-s) beweging, gang; voorstel, mosie; ww. (-ed) wink; -less bnw. botstil.

'motivate ['moutivyt] ww. (-d) redes aanvoer, motiveer.

'motive ['moutiv] s. (-s) beweegrede.

'motley ['motli] bnw. bont, deurmekaar.

'motor ['moutə] s. (-s) motor; outo; dryfkrag; - 'bicycle s. motorfiets; -car s. motorkar; -ist s. motoris.

'mottle ['motl] s. (-s) vlek, streep; -d bnw. gevlek, bont.

'motto ['moutou] s. (-es) motto, leus.

'mould ['mould] s. (-s) teelaarde, mulgrond; vorm; matrys, stempel, skimmel, kim; roes; -ing s. fries, beskot, omlysting, lys; -y bnw. beskimmel.

moult ['moult] ww. (-ed) verveer, verhaar, vervel.

mound ['maund] s. (-s) hoop.

mount ['maunt] s. (-s) heuwel; raam; ryperd; ww. (-ed) monteer; bestyg; -able bnw. bestygbaar; -ed bnw. berede; -ing s. montering.

'mountain ['mauntin] s. (-s) berg; - chain s. bergreeks; moun'taineer s. bergklimmer; 'mountainous bnw. bergagtig.

'mountebank ['mauntibænk] s. (-s) kwak.

mourn ['mōn] ww. (-ed) treur, rou, beween; -er s. treurende; -ful bnw. treurig; -ing s. droefheid, rou.

'mouse ['maus] s. ('mice) muis; -r s. muisvanger; -trap s. muisval.

'mousseline ['mʌslin] s. moesselien.

mous'tache [mos'tāsj] s. snor, moestas.

mouth ['mauth] s. (-s) mond, bek, snoet; monding; ww. (-ed) eet, vreet; -organ s. mondfluitjie; -piece s. mondstuk, woordvoerder; -y bnw. grootpraterig.

'move ['mōev] s. (-s) beweging, set; stap; ww. (-d) beweeg, aandrywe; verskuif; trek; voorstel; 'moveable bnw. beweegbaar; -ment s. beweging; ontwikkeling; meganiek; -r s. voorsteller; 'movies s. bioskoop.

mow ['mou] ww. (-ed) maai, sny; -er s. snymasjien, maaier.

Mozam'bique [mouzəm'bik] s. Mosambiek.

much ['mʌtsj] bnw. & bw. ('more, 'most) baie, veel, erg.

'mucilage ['mjōesilidzj] s. gom, slym.

muck ['mʌk] s. vuilgoed, vuilis, gemors.

'mucus ['mjōekəs] s. slym; 'mucous bnw. slymagtig, slymerig; slym-.

mud ['mʌd] s. modder; -dy bnw. modderig, vuil; -guard s. modderskerm; -flap s. modderklap.

'muddle ['mʌdl] s. (-s) verwarring; ww. (-d) verwar; -r s. knoeier.

'muddleheaded ['mʌdlhedid] bnw. deurmekaar, verwar, onnosel.

mu'ezzin [mõe'ezin] s. uitroeper.

muff ['mʌf] s. mof; ww. (-ed) mis, bederwe, verfoes, onhandig doen.

'muffin ['mʌfin] s. (-s) platkoekie.

'muffle ['mʌfl] ww. (-d) toedraai, toemaak; demp; toesnoer; -r s. halsdoek, serp; klankdemper.

'mufti ['mʌfti] s. burgerkleding.

mug ['mʌgh] s. (-s) beker; bakkies; ullskuiken.

'muggy ['mʌghi] bnw. (-ier, -iest) broeiend.

'mulberry ['mʌlbəri] s. ('mulberries) moerbei.

'mulch ['mʌlsj] s. deklaag, kombers (grond); ww. (-ed) deklaag op grond aanbring, bedek.

mulct ['mʌlkt] ww. (-ed) beboet, straf; ontneem van.

'mule ['mjõel] s. (-s) muil; -teer [mjõeli'tiə] s. muildrywer; 'mulish bnw. muilagtig, koppig.

'multi- ['mʌlti] voorvoegsel veel-; -coloured bnw. veelkleurig; -'farious bnw. veelvuldig, veelsoortig; -fold bnw. veelvuldig; -lateral bnw. veelsydig; -partite bnw. veeldelig; -pede s. duisendpoot; -vocal bnw. dubbelsinnig; -grade oil s. meergraadolie.

'multiple ['mʌltipl] s. veelvoud, meervoudig.

'multiply ['mʌltiplai] ww. ('multiplied) vermenigvuldig; multipli'cation s. vermenigvuldiging.

'multitude ['mʌltitjõed] s. (-s) menigte, hoop.

mum ['mʌm] bnw. stil; ww. (-med) vermom.

'mumble ['mʌmbl] ww. (-d) mompel.

'mummy ['mʌmi] s. ('mummies) mummie.

'mump ['mʌmp] ww. pruil; mompel; bedel; fop.

mumps ['mʌmps] s. pampoentjies.

munch ['mʌntsj] ww. (-ed) vreet, kou.

'mundane ['mʌndyn] bnw. aards, wêrelds.

mu'nicipal [mjoe'nisipəl] bnw. munisipaal, gemeente-; munici'pality s. munisipaliteit.

mu'nificent [mjoe'nifisənt] bnw. vrygewig.

mu'nition [mjõe'nisjən] s. ammunisie, krygsvoorraad.

'mural ['mjõerəl] s. (-s) muur-.

'murder ['mədə] s. (-s) moord; ww. (-ed) vermoor, moor, radbraak; -er s. moordenaar; -ous bnw. moorddadig.

'mure ['mjõeə] ww. (-d) ommuur.

'murky ['məki] bnw. ('murkier, 'murkiest) donker.

'murmur ['məmə] s. (-s) geruis, gemor; ww. (-ed) mor, ruis; -er s. murmureerder.

musca'tel [mʌskə'tel] s. muskadel (druiwe wyn).

'muscle ['mʌsl] s. (-s) spier; 'muscular bnw. gespierd.

'Muse ['mjões] s. (-s) sanggodin, Muse.

'muse ['mjões] ww. (-d) peins, mymer.

mu'seum [mjõe'siəm] s. (-s) museum.

'mushroom ['mʌsjroem] s. (-s) paddastoel, sampioen.

'music ['mjõezik] s. musiek; -al bnw. musikaal; mu'sician s. musikus, musikant.

musk ['mʌsk] s. muskus; -iness s. muskusgeur; -ox s. muskusstier; -y bnw. muskusagtig; -melon s. spaanspek.

'musket ['mʌskit] s. (-s) geweer; muske'teer s. musketier; -ry s. infanterie.

'muslin ['mʌzlin] s. neteldoek.

'musquash ['mʌs-kwosj] s. bisamrot; bont van muskusrot.

'mussel ['mʌsl] s. mossel.

must ['mʌst] s. mos, skimmel, kim; bronstigheid; ww. moet, verplig wees.

'mustard ['mʌstəd] s. moster; -poultice s. mosterpleister.

'muster ['mʌstə] ww. (-ed) monster, versamel; - book s. monsterrol.

'musty ['mʌsti] bnw. muf.

'mutable ['mjõetəbl] bnw. veranderlik.

mu'tation [mjõe'tysjən] s. (-s) verandering, wisseling; umlaut.

'mute ['mjõet] s. (-s) stomme; -ly bnw. stom, swygend.

'mutilate ['mjõetilyt] ww. (-d) vermink; muti'lation s.

'mutiny ['mjõetini] s. ('mutinies) opstand, multery; muti'neer s. multer; 'mutinous bnw. oproerig.

'mutter ['mʌtə] ww. (-ed) pruttel, mor.

'mutton ['mʌtn] s. skaapvleis.

'mutual ['mjõetjoeəl] bnw. wederkerig; -ly bw. wederkerig.

'muzzle ['mʌzl] s. (-s) snoet, bek; loop; muilband; -loader s. voorlaaier.

my ['mai] vnw. my; vgl. I.

my'cology [mai'kolədzji] s. swamkunde.

mye'litis [maiə'laitis] s. rugmurgontsteking.

my'opic [mai'opik] bnw. bysiende.

'myriad ['miriəd] s. (-s) menigte, swerm.

'myrmidon ['məmidən] s. (-s) handlanger.

myrrh ['mə] s. mirre.

'myrtle ['mətl] s. mirte.

'mystery ['mistəri] s. ('mysteries) geheim, misterie; mys'terious bnw. geheimsinnig.

'mystic ['mistik] s. mistikus; bnw.

misties; **'mystify** ww. ('mystified)
fop, kul; **mystifi'cation** s. foppery,
kullery.
myth ['mith] s. (-s) mite, storie; **-ic**
bnw. mlties; **my'thology** s. godeleer,
mitologie.

N

NDC (National Development Corporation) s. NOK (Nasionale Ontwikkelingskorporasie).
nab ['næb] ww. (-bed) pak, betrap,
arresteer.
'nadir ['nydia] s. (-s) nadir,
laagtepunt.
nag ['nægh] ww. (-ged) lol, pruttel,
vit; **-ging** bnw. kyfagtig.
nail ['nyl] s. (-s) spyker; nael; ww.
(-ed) vasspyker, vasslaan; betrap;
-brush s. naelborsel; **-clipper** s.
naelknipper; **-cream** s. naelroom;
- file s. naelvyl; **-pencil** s. naelpotlood; **-polish** s. naellak; **- scissors** s.
naelskêr; **- voorv.** nael-.
na'ive [nai'iv] bnw. naïef, eenvoudig,
opreg; **-ty** s. kinderlikheid, naïwiteit.
'naked ['nykid] bnw. naak, kaal,
bloot; **-ness** s.
name ['nym] s. (-s) naam; benaming; ww. (-d) noem, opnoem,
benoem, vernoem, betitel; **-board** s.
naamplaat; **-less** bnw. naamloos,
anoniem; **-ly** bw. naamlik; **-sake** s.
genant.
nap ['næp] s. (-s) dutjie, slapie; ww.
(-ped) dut, slaap.
'nape ['nyp] s. nekholte.
'napery ['nypəri] s. tafellinne.
'naphtha ['næftə] s. nafta; **-lene** s.
naftaline, mottegif.
'napkin ['næpkin] s. (-s) servet; luier.
nar'cissus [nâ'sisəs] s. (-es) narsing.
nar'cosis [nâ'kousis] s. narkose,
verdowing; **nar'cotic** bnw. narkoties,
verdowend, **-s** slaapmiddel; **'narcotize** ww. (-d) verdoof, narkotiseer.
nar'rate [næ'ryt] ww. (-d) verhaal,
vertel; **nar'ration** s. verhaal, relaas;
'narrative s. verhaal, bnw. verhalend; **'nar'rator** s. verhaler.
'narrow ['nærou] bnw. (-er, -est) nou,
smal, knap; **-s** seeëngtes; **-minded**
bnw. bekrompe; **-ness** s. engheid.
'nasal ['nyzəl] s. (-s) neusklank,
nasaal; bnw. nasaal, neus-; **-ize** ww.
(-d) nasaleer; **-ly** bw. deur die neus;
- douche s. neusspoeler; **- syringe** s.
neusspuit.
'nascent ['næsnt] bnw. ontstaan,
begin ontstaan of groei, wordend;
'nascency s. ontstaan, wording,
geboorte.
nas'turtium [nə'stəsjəm] s. (-s)
kappertjie.
'nasty ['nâsti] bnw. ('nastier, 'nastiest)
vuil, vieslik, morsig; gemeen; sleg;
lelik; laag; **'nastiness** s.
'natal ['nytl] bnw. geboorte-.

'nation ['nysjən] s. (-s) nasie, volk;
-al bnw. nasionaal, volks-; **-alize**
ww. (-d) nasionaliseer; **-alist** s.
nasionalis; **natio'nality** s. nasionaliteit.
'native ['nytiv] bnw. aangebore; s.
(-s) inboorling; **-born** bnw. in die
land gebore; **na'tivity** s. geboorte,
herkoms.
'natron ['nytrən] s. natron, loogsout.
'natty ['næti] bnw. netjies, keurig,
fyn.
'nature ['nytsjə] s. (-s) natuur,
geaardheid, aard, karakter; soort;
'natural bnw. natuurlik, ongedwonge, natuur-; **'naturalize** ww.
(-d) naturaliseer; **naturali'zation** s.
naturalisasie; **'naturalism** s. naturalisme; **'naturalist** s. natuurkundige;
'naturally bw. natuurlikerwyse; **-d**
bnw. geaard.
na'turopath [nə'tsjoeropæth] s. (-s)
natuurgeneser.
naught ['nôt] s. (-s) nul; niks.
'naughty ['nôti] bnw. ondeuend,
stout; **'naughtily** bw. ondeuend,
stout; **'naughtiness** n. ondeuendheid, stoutheid.
'nausea ['nôsiə] s. mislikheid;
'nauseate ww. (-d) mislik maak, laat
walg; **'nauseous** bnw. walglik.
'nautical ['nôtikəl] bnw. skeeps-,
see-, seevaart-.
'naval ['nyvəl] bnw. see-, skeeps-,
marine.
'nave ['nyv] s. (-s) naaf; skip (van
kerk).
'navel ['nyvəl] s. (-s) nael; nawellemoen.
'navigate ['nævighyt] ww. (-d)
bevaar; stuur; vaar; **'navigable** bnw.
bevaarbaar; bestuurbaar; **navi'gation** s. skeepvaart; **'navigator** s. (-s)
seevaarder.
'navvy ['nævi] s. ('navvies) dokwerker.
'navy ['nyvi] s. ('navies) oorlogsvloot; **-office** s. admiraliteit; **- yard**
s. arsenaal.
nay ['ny] bw. nee; s. nee, weiering.
'naze ['nyz] s. (-s) kaap, landpunt.
neap-'tide ['nip'taid] s. dooie gety.
'Nazi ['nâtsi] s. lid van die Duitse
Nasionaal-Sosialistiese Party.
near ['niə] bnw. (-er, -est) na, naby;
nouverwant, dierbaar; bw. naby,
digby; voors. by, naby, digby; ww.
(-ed) nader, nader kom; **-ly** bw.
byna, amper; **-ness** s. nabyheid;
-sighted bnw. bysiende, korstigtig.
neat ['nit] bnw. (-er, -est) netjies;
suiwer; keurig; handig; puur; **-ly**
bw. netjies, sindelik; behendig;
-'s-foot oil s. kloutjiesolie.
'nebula ['nebjôëlə] s. ('nebulae,
'nebulas) newelvlek; **'nebular** bnw.
newel-; **'nebulous** bnw. vaag.
'necessary ['nesisəri] bnw. nodig,
noodsaaklik, noodwendig; **'necessarily** bw. noodsaaklikerwyse.
ne'cessity [ni'sesiti] s. (ne'cessities)

nood, noodsaaklikheid, nooddruf; ne'cessitate ww. (-d) noodsaak, verplig; ne'cessitous bnw. behoeftig.

neck ['nek] s. (-s) hals, nek; pas, engte; -band s. hempsboord, halsband; -cloth s. halsdoek; -erchief s. halsdoek; -lace s. halssnoer; -tie s. das.

'nectar ['nektə] s. nektar, godedrank; necta'rine s. kaalperske.

need ['nid] s. (-s) nood, behoefte, gebrek; ww. (-ed) nodig hê; -ful bnw. nodig; -iness s. behoeftigheid; -less bnw. onnodig; -s s. behoeftes, -y bnw. behoeftig.

'needle ['nidl] s. (-s) naald; -case s. naaldekoker; -woman s. naaister; -work s. naaldwerk.

ne'farious [ni'fèəriəs] bnw. goddeloos, gruwelik.

'negate ['nighyt] ww. (-d) ontken, loën; ne'gation s. ontkenning; 'negative bnw. ontkennend; ww. (-d) ontken.

neg'lect [ni'ghlekt] ww. (-ed) verwaarloos, nalaat; s. verwaarlosing; -ful bnw. nalatig; 'negligence s. nalatigheid; 'negligent bnw. nalatig; 'negligible bnw. nietig.

'negligé ['neghlizjy] s. gerieflike loshangende japon.

ne'gotiate [ni'ghousjiyt] ww. (-d) verhandel, handel dryf; onderhandel; ne'gotiable bnw. verhandelbaar; negoti'ation s. verhandeling; onderhandeling.

'negro ['nighrou] s. (-es) neger; ne'gress s. negerin; ne'grophilist s. negrofilis; -'phobia s. negervrees.

neigh ['ny] ww. (-ed) runnik; s. (-s) gerunnik.

'neighbour ['nybə] s. (-s) buurman, buur; naaste; -hood s. buurt; -ing bnw. naburig, aangrensend; -ly bnw. vriendskaplik; -ship s. buurskap.

'neither ['naidhə] vnw. geen van beide; bw. ook nie, ewemin; voegw. neither . . . nor nog . . . nog.

neo'lithic [niou'lithik] bnw. neolities, uit die latere steentyd.

ne'ologism [ni'olədzjizəm] s. (-s) neologisme, nuwe woord.

'neophyte ['nioufait] s. (-s) nuwe bekeerling.

'nephew ['nevjoe] s. (-s) neef.

ne'phritis [ne'fraitis] s. nierontsteking.

'nepotism ['nepōtizəm] s. voortrekkery.

'nerve ['nəv] s. (-s) senuwee, lewe; moed, durf; ww. (-d) staal, verman; -less bnw. kragteloos; 'nervous bnw. senuagtig, skrikkerig; 'nervure s. nervatuur; 'nervy bnw. senuagtig.

'nescience ['nesiəns] s. onwetendheid; 'nescient bnw. onwetend.

ness ['nes] s. (-es) voorgeberge, kaap.

nest ['nest] s. (-s) nes; ww. (-ed) nes maak, nes hê; -egg s. neseier; -le ww. (-d) nestel, nes skop; tuismaak; -ling s. neskuiken.

net ['net] s. (-s) net, strik; ww. (-ted) vang; knoop; binnehaal; -ting s. netwerk; gaas; -work s. gaas.

nett ['net] bnw. netto, suiwer.

'nether ['nedhə] bnw. onderste, laer, benede.

'Netherlands ['nedhələnds] s. Nederland, die Nederlande.

'nettle ['netl] s. (-s) netel, brandnetel; ww. (-d) prikkel; -rash s. uitslag.

'neural ['njoeərəl] bnw. van die senuwees; neu'ralgia s. sinkings; neu'rology s. senuweeleer; neu'rosis s. neurose; neu'rotic s. senulyer, bnw. neuroties.

neu'ritis [njoē'raitis] s. senuontsteking.

neu'rology [njoēə'rolədzji] s. senuleer, neurologie.

'neuter ['njoētə] bnw. onsydig, geslagloos; s. neutrum.

'neutral ['njoētrəl] bnw. neutraal, onsydig, onpartydig; neu'trality s. neutraliteit; -ize ww. (-d) neutraliseer; -i'zation s. neutralisasie.

'never ['nevə] bw. nooit, nimmer; -ceasing bnw. onafgebroke; -dying bnw. ewig; -ending bnw. eindeloos; -failing bnw. onfeilbaar; -more bw. nimmermeer; -theless bw. nietemin, almiskie.

new ['njoē] bnw. (-er, -est) nuut, vars; groen; modern; -born bnw. pasgebore; -comer s. nuweling; -fangled bnw. nuwerwets; -laid bnw. vars; -ly bw. pas, onlangs; -s s. nuus; -spaper s. koerant; - year s. nuwejaar.

'newsmonger ['njoēzmʌng-ghə] s. nuuskramer.

newt ['njoēt] s. (-s) watersalamander.

next ['nekst] bnw. naaste, volgende; langsaam; bw. vervolgens; voors langs, langsaan; s. volgende.

nib ['nib] s. (-s) penpunt.

'nibble ['nibl] ww. (-d) knabbel, peusel.

nice ['nais] bnw. (-r, -st) lekker, aangenaam; mooi, gaaf; fyn; -ness s. -ty s. fynheid.

'niche ['nitsj] s. (-s) nis.

nick ['nik] s. (-s) kerf, keep, skaar; ww. (-ed) kerf, keep; skrams tref.

'nickel ['nikl] s. nikkel; -silver s. argentaan.

'nickname ['niknym] s. (-s) bynaam.

nico'tine ['nikətin] s. nikotine, pypolie.

'niece ['nis] s. (-s) niggie.

'niggardly ['nighədli] bnw. gierig, suinig.

'nigger ['nighə] s. (-s) neger, kaffer, swarte.

nigh ['nai] bw. & voors. naby, byna.

night ['nait] s. (-s) nag, aand; -adder s. nagadder; -cap s. slaapsopie; - club s. nagklub; -dress s. naghemp; -fall s. aand, donker; -gown s. naghemp; -ingale s. nagtegaal; -ly bw. elke nag(aand); -mare s.

nagmerrie; -shade s. nastergal; -watch s. nagwag.

'nihilist ['naililst] s. nihilis.

nil ['nil] s. nul, niks.

'Nile ['nail] s. Nyl.

'nimble ['nimbl] bnw. (-r, -st) rats, vlug.

'nimbus ['nimbəs] s. reënwolk.

'nincompoop ['ninkəmpŏĕp] s. (-s) bog, niksnuts.

'nine ['nain] s. (-s) nege; -teen s. negentien; -ty s. negentig.

'ninny ['nini] s. ('ninnies) uilskuiken, skaap.

nip ['nip] ww. (-ped) byt, knyp; s. byt, knyp; kleintjie; -pers s. knyptang; -py bnw. bytend, fris; rats.

'nipple ['nipl] s. (-s) tepel, speen; nippel.

nit ['nit] s. (-s) neet.

'nitrate ['naitryt] s. (-s) nitraat.

'nitre ['naitə] s. salpeter; 'nitric bnw. salpeter-; 'nitrous bnw. salpeteragtig.

'nitrogen ['naitridzjən] s. stikstof; ni'trogenous bnw. stikstofhoudend.

nix ['niks] s. (-es) niks.

no ['nou] bnw. geen, g'n; bw. nee, niks; -claim bonus s. geeneisbonus (assuran.).

nob ['nob] s. (-s) kop, klapperdop; hoë heer; -by bnw. windmakerig.

'noble ['noubl] s. (-s) edelman; bnw. edel, adellik; no'bility s. adel; -man s. edelman; -minded bnw. edelmoedig.

'nobody ['noubədi] s. niemand.

'noc'turne ['nok'tŏn] s. naglied, nocturne; noc'turnal bnw. nagtelik.

nod ['nod] ww. (-ded) knik, insluimer; s. (-s) knik.

'node ['noud] s. (-s) knoets, kwas; jigknobbel; laagtepunt van golf; 'nodule s. verkleinw. knoesie.

'nohow ['nouhau] bw. glad nie.

'noise ['noiz] s. (-s) geraas, lawaai; -less bnw. stil; 'noisiness s. luidrugtigheid; 'noisy bnw. luidrugtig; -free bnw. geruisloos, geruisvry; -level s. geruispeil.

'noisome ['noisəm] bnw. nadelig, walglik.

'nomad ['noməd] s. (-s) nomade, swerwer; no'madic bnw. nomadies, swerwend.

'nom de 'plume ['nômdə'plŏĕm] s. skuilnaam.

no'menclature [nou'menklətsjə] s. benaming, naam.

'nominal ['nominl] bnw. naamwoordelik, nominaal; -ly bw. in naam; 'nominate ww. (-d) benoem, nomineer; nomi'nation s. benoeming, nominasie; 'nominative bnw. nominatief; nomi'nee s. (-s) benoemde, genomineerde.

non- ['non-] voorvoegsel non-, on-, nie-; -committal bnw. vaag; -descript bnw. sonderling; baster-; -disclosure s. nie-openbaring; -mem-

ber s. nie-lid; -pareil [nonpə'rel] bnw. onvergelyklik; -plus ww. (-sed) verwar; -sense s. onsin; -'sensical bnw. onsinnig, gek.

nonage ['nonidzj] s. onmondigheid, onvolwassenheid.

'nonchalant ['nonsjələnt] bnw. doodbedaard; 'nonchalance s. onverskilligheid, kalmte.

'none ['nʌn] vnw. geneem, niemand, niks; bnw. geen, niks; bw. niks.

no'nentity [no'nentiti] s. (no'nentities) nul.

'noodle ['nŏĕdl] s. (-s) meelsnysels; knul.

nook ['nŏĕk] s. (-s) hoekie, uithoek.

noon ['nŏĕn] s. (-s) middag, twaalfuur.

'noose ['nŏĕz] s. (-s) strik, strop.

nor ['nô] bw. nog, ook nie.

norm ['nôm] s. (-s) norm, standaard; -al bnw. normaal, s. die normale.

north ['nôth] s. die noorde; bnw. noord; bw. noord; -erly bnw. noordelik; -ern bnw. noordelik, noord(er)-; -light s. noorderlig; -wester s. noordwestewind.

'nose ['nouz] s. (-s) neus; reuk; tuit; ww. (-d) ruik, snuffel; - atomizer s. neusverstuiwer; -bag s. voersak; -gay s. ruiker; 'nosy bnw. pure neus; onwelriekend; nuuskierig; 'nostril s. neusgat.

nos'talgia [nos'tældzjiə] s. heimwee.

nostrum ['nostrʌm] s. (-s) geneesmiddel aanbeveel deur sy vervaardiger; kwakmiddel.

'nosy'parker ['nouzi'påkə] s. bemoeial.

not ['not] bw. nie.

'notable ['noutəbl] bnw. merkwaardig; merkbaar; s. belangrike persoon; nota'bility s. merkwaardigheid; 'notably bw. merkbaar.

'notary ['noutəri] s. ('notaries) notaris.

no'tation [nou'tysjən] s. notasie.

notch ['notsj] s. (-es) keep, kerf, skaar; -ing s. keep-.

'note ['nout] s. (-s) nota; toon; aantekening; brief; ww. (-ed) oplet, kennis neem van, opskrywe; -d bnw. beroemd; -paper s. briefpapier; -worthy bnw. opmerkenswaardig.

'nothing ['nΛthing] s. niks, nul.

'notice ['noutis] s. (-s) kennis, aandag, notisie; kennisgewing; berig; ww. (-d) opmerk; -able bnw. merkbaar.

'notify ['noutifai] ww. ('notified) bekendmaak, aankondig, kennis gee; 'notifiable bnw. rapporteerbaar; notifi'cation s. kennisgewing, aankondiging.

'notion ['nousjən] s. (-s) begrip, denkbeeld; -al bnw. denkbeeldig.

noto'riety [noutə'raiəti] s. berugtheid; no'torious bnw. berug, welbekend.

notwith'standing [notwith'stænding] voors. ondanks, ten spyte van.

nought ['nôt] s. niks, nul.

noun ['naun] s. (-s) selfstandige naamwoord.

'nourish ['nʌrisj] ww. (-ed) voed; -ing bnw. voedsaam; -ment s. voeding.

novel ['novəl] bnw. nuut; vreemd; s. (-s) roman; **nove'lette** s. novelle; **'novelist** s. romanskrywer; -ty s. (-ties) nuwigheid.

No'vember [nou'vembə] s. November.

'novice ['novis] s. (-s) groene, nuweling, oningewyde.

now ['nau] bw. nou; s. hede; -a-days bw. teenswoordig.

'no'where ['nou'wêə] bw. nêrens; **'nowise** bw. glad nie.

noxious ['noksjəs] bnw. skadelik.

nozzle ['nozl] s. (-s) neus, snoet; tuit.

nucleus ['njŏěkliəs] s. nukleus, kern.

nude ['njŏěd] bnw. kaal; **'nudity** s. naaktheid.

'nudge ['nʌdzj] ww. (-d) stoot, stamp.

'nugget ['nʌghit] s. (-s) klont, klomp.

'nuisance ['njŏēsns] s. las, plaag, steurnis.

null ['nʌl] bnw. nietig, ongeldig; -ifi'cation s. ongeldigverklaring; -ify ww. (-fied) ongeldig verklaar; -ity s. ongeldigheid.

numb ['nʌm] bnw. gevoelloos, dood; ww. (-ed) verstyf, verdoof; -ness s. styfheid.

'number ['nʌmbə] s. (-s) nommer, getal, aantal, party; ww. (-ed) nommer, nommereer, tel; -less bnw. talloos.

'numeral ['njŏĕmərəl] s. (-s) telwoord; **'numerable** bnw. telbaar; **nume'ration** s. telling, getalstelsel; **nume'rator** s. teller; **nu'merical** bnw. numeries; **'numerous** bnw. talryk.

'numskull ['nʌmskʌl] s. (-s) swaap, domkop.

nun ['nʌn] s. (-s) non; -nery s. nonneklooster.

'nuptial ['nʌpsjəl] bnw. huweliks-, bruilofs-; -s s. bruilof.

'nurse ['nə̄s] s. (-s) verpleegster, suster; kindermeid, kindermeisie; baker; ww. (-d) verpleeg, oppas; versorg; kweek; -maid s. kindermeid; -ry s. (-ries) kinderkamer; kwekery; -ryman s. kweker.

'nurture ['nə̄tsjə] ww. (-d) kweek, opvoed, voed.

nut ['nʌt] s. (-s) neut, moer; klont; modegek; -meg s. neut (muskaat); -meg oil s. muskaatolie; -shell s. neutdop; -ty bnw. neutagtig.

nu'trition [njŏĕ'trisjən] s. voeding, kos, voedsel; **'nutrient** bnw. voedend; **'nutriment** s. kos, voedsel; **nutri'mental** bnw. voedsaam; **nu'tritious** bnw. voedsaam.

'nux 'vomica ['nʌks 'voumikə] s. braakneut, nux vomica.

'nuzzle ['nʌzl] ww. (-d) snuffel, vroetel.

nymph ['nimf] s. (-s) nimf, vroulike natuurgees; bruid.

nympho'mania [nimfou'myniə] s. minnewoede (van vrou), nimfomanie; -c s. lyer aan minnewoede.

O

oak ['ouk] s. (-s) akker, eik; bnw. van eikehout; -en bnw. van eikehout.

'oakum ['oukəm] s. touwerk, pluisgoed.

oar ['ôə] s. (-s) roeispaan, riem; ww. roei; -sman s. roeier; -smanship s. roeikuns.

o'asis [ou'ysis] s. (o'ases) oase.

oath ['outh] s. (-s) eed.

oats ['outs] s. hawer; **'oaten** bnw. hawer-; **'oatmeal** s. hawermeel.

'obdurate ['obdjoerit] bnw. koppig.

o'bedience [ŏ'bidjəns] s. gehoorsaamheid; **o'bedient** bnw. gehoorsaam.

o'beisance [ŏ'bysəns] s. buiging, hulde.

'obelisk ['obilisk] s. (-s) obelisk, gedenknaald.

o'bese [ou'bis] s. bnw. swaarlywig; **o'besity** s. gesetheid.

o'bey [ŏ'by] ww. (-ed) gehoorsaam.

o'bituary [ŏ'bitjoeəri] s. (o'bituaries) sterflys; doodsberig.

'object ['obdzjekt] s. (-s) voorwerp; doel; plan; ww. (-ed) beswaar maak; **ob'jective** ww. (ob'jectified) objektiveer; **ob'jection** s. beswaar; **ob'jectionable** bnw. aanstootlik; **ob'jective** bnw. objektief, s. doel; **-lesson** s. aanskouingsles; **ob'jector** s. beswaarmaker.

o'blige [ə'blaidzj] ww. (-d) verplig; **'obligate** ww. (-d) verplig; **obli'gation** s. verpligting; **o'bligatory** bnw. verpligtend; **o'bliging** bnw. beleef.

o'blique [ŏ'blik] bnw. skuins, skeef.

o'bliterate [ŏ'bliteryt] ww. (-d) uitwis; **o'bliteration** s. uitwissing.

o'blivion [ŏ'bliviən] s. vergetelheid; **o'blivious** bnw. onbewus.

'oblong ['oblong] bnw. langwerpig.

'obloquy ['obləkwi] s. laster, smaad.

ob'noxious [əb'noksjəs] bnw. aanstootlik.

'oboe ['oubou] s. (-s) hobo.

ob'scene [ob'sin] bnw. vuil, liederlik.

ob'scurant [ob'skjoerænt] s. (-s) remskoen; bnw. remskoenagtig; -ism s. bnw. remskoenneiging.

ob'scure [əb'skjoeə] bnw. duister, onduidelik; onbekend; **ob'scurity** s.

ob'sequious ['obsikwiz] bnw. slaafs, onderdanig; kruiperig.

ob'serve [əb'zə̄v] ww. (-d) waarneem; nakom; **ob'servance** s. waarneming, inagneming; **ob'servant** bnw. oplettend; **'observations** (-s) waarneming, opmerking; **ob'serva-**

tory s. (ob'servatories) sterrewag; -r s. waarnemer.

ob'sess [əb'ses] ww. (-ed) lastig val; onophoudelik kwel; beheo met; -ion s. kwelling, obsessie, dwanggedagte.

ob'session [əb'sesjən] s. (-s) kwelling, las, obsessie.

obso'lescent [obsô'lesnt] bnw. verouderend.

'obsolete ['obsôlit] bnw. ouderwets.

'obstacle ['obstekl] s. (-s) hindernis, struikelblok.

ob'stetric 'forceps [əb'stetrik 'fô-səps] s. verlostang.

ob'stetrics [əb'stetriks] s. verloskunde.

'obstinate ['obstinit] bnw. koppig; 'obstinacy s. koppigheid.

ob'streperous [əb'strepərəs] bnw. luidrugtig; astrant.

ob'struct [əb'strʌkt] ww. (-ed) verhinder, dwarstrek; -ion s., -ive bnw. verhinderend.

ob'tain [əb'tyn] ww. (-ed) verkry, verwerf; gebruiklik wees.

ob'trude [əb'trôëd] ww. (-d) opdring.

ob'trusion [əb'trôëzjən] s. opdringing; ob'trusive bnw. indringerig.

ob'tuse [əb'tjôës] bnw. stomp.

'obverse ['obvəs] s. voorkant, omgekeerde.

'obviate ['obviyt] ww. (-d) uit die weg ruim; 'obvious bnw. duidelik.

oc'casion [ə'kyzjən] s. (-s) geleentheid; aanleiding; ww. (-ed) veroorsaak; -al bnw. toevallig; -ally bw. af en toe.

'occident ['oksidənt] s. weste; occi'dental bnw. westers.

'occiput ['oksipʌt] s. (-s) agterkop.

oc'clusion [o'klöëzjən] s. sluiting, verstopping.

oc'cult [o'kʌlt] bnw. verborge, okkult.

occu'pational 'hazard [okjoe'pysjənl 'hæzəd] s. (-s) beroepsgevaar.

'occupy ['okjoepai] ww. ('occupied) beset, besit neem van, beklee, bewoon; 'occupant s. besitter, bewoner; occu'pation s. (-s) besetting, besigheid, ambag; 'occupier s. bewoner, huurder.

oc'cur [ə'kə] ww. (-red) voorkom; gebeur; oc'currence s. voorval, gebeurtenis.

'ocean ['ousjən] s. (-s) oseaan, see; oce'anic bnw. van die oseaan.

'ochre ['oukə] s. oker.

'octave ['oktiv] s. (-s) oktaaf.

Oc'tober [ok'toubə] s. Oktober.

'octopus ['oktəpəs] s. (-s) seekat.

'ocular ['okjoelə] bnw. oog-; 'occulist s. oogdokter.

odd ['od] bnw. ongelyk, onewe; snaaks; -ity s. raarheid, rariteit; -ments s. oorskot; -s s. kanse; oormag; verskil.

ode ['oud] s. (-s) ode.

'odium ['oudiəm] s. haat, blaam; 'odious bnw. haatlik.

'odour ['oudə] s. (-s) geur; 'odorous bnw. geurig.

of ['ov] voors van, aan, deur, op, uit, in.

off ['ôf] bw. af; weg; ver; voors van . . . af; weg; van; bnw. ander, regter, haar; -al s. afval, uitskot.

of'fence [ə'fens] s. (-s) oortreding, belediging, aanstoot; of'fend ww. (-ed) beledig; of'fensive bnw. aanstootlik; walglik.

'offer ['ofə] ww. (-ed) aanbied; offer; s. aanbod; -ing s. offerande.

'off'hand ['ôf'hænd] bnw. uit die vuis; kortaf, onbeleef.

'office ['ofis] s. (-s) kantoor; taak, werk, plig, amp; -bearer s. amptenaar, beampte; -r s. amptenaar; offisier; of'ficial bnw. amptelik; of'ficiate ww. 'n amp waarneem.

of'ficious [ə'fisjəs] bnw. gedienstig; bemoeisiek; offisieus.

'offset ['ôfset] s. spruit, loot; kontras; kompensasie.

'offshoot ['ôfsjôët] s. (-s) loot, spruit, tak.

'offspring ['ôfspring] s. afstammeling, kroos, uitslag.

'often ['ôfn] bw. (-er, -est) dikwels.

'ogle ['oughl] ww. (-d) verliefderig aankyk.

'ogre ['oughə] s. (-s) paaiboelie, monster.

ohm ['oum] s. (-s) ohm, eenheid van weerstand.

oil ['oil] s. (-s) olie; ww. (-ed) olie, smeer; -cake s. lynsaadkoek; -colour s. olieverf; -atomizer s. olieverstuiwer; -bath s. oliebad; -can s. oliekan; -cooler s. oliekoeler; -dipper s. oliekoop; -dipstick s. oliepeilstok; -feed s. olietœvoer; -film s. olielaag; -filter s. oliefilter; -float s. olievlotter; -funnel s. olietregter; -leak s. olielek; -level s. oliepeil; -level indicator s. oliepeilwyser; -lubrication s. oliesmering; -saturated bnw. oliedourweek; -pressure s. oliedruk; -pump s. oliepomp; -retainer s. oliekeerder; -ring s. oliering; -seal s. olieseël; -skin s. oliejas; -sump s. oliebak; -vapour s. oliedamp; -up ww. aanolie, aangeolie raak.

'ointment ['ointmənt] s. (-s) salf, smeergoed.

old ['ould] bnw. (-er, -est) oud, ou; ouderwets; verslete; -en bnw. van ouds.

ole'ander [ouli'ændə] s. (-s) oleander, selonsroos.

ol'factory [ol'fæktəri] s. reukorgaan.

'oligarch ['olighāk] s. (-s) oligarg; -y s. oligargie.

'olive ['oliv] s. (-s) olyf; -oil s. olyfolie.

O'lympus [ou'limpəs] s. Olimpus; o'lympiad s. olimpiade; o'lympian bnw. olimpies.

'omega ['oumighə] s. omega, einde.

'omelet(te) ['omlit] s. (-s) omelet, eierstruif.
'omen ['oumen] s. (-s) voorteken; 'ominous bnw. dreigend.
o'mit [ŏ'mit] ww. (-ted) weglaat; o'mission s. weglating.
omni'farious [omni'fêəriəs] bnw. allerhande, alle soort, veelsoortig.
om'nipotence [om'nipŏtəns] s. almag, alvermoë; om'nipotent bnw. almagtig.
om'nivorous [om'nivərəs] bnw. alles-etend.
on ['on] voors op, by, aan, teen, met, na, oor, te; bw. aan; verder; -and-off switch s. aan-afskakelaar.
once ['wʌns] bw. eenmaal, eenkeer; voegw. sodra; s. eenmaal; bnw. vroeër.
one ['wʌn] s. (-s) een; vnw. mens; een; bnw. een, enigste; -'self vnw. jouself; -sided bnw. eensydig.
'onerous [onərəs] bnw. swaar, drukkend.
'onion ['ʌnjən] s. (-s) ui.
'onlooker ['onloekə] s. (-s) toeskouer.
'only ['ounli] bnw. enigste; bw. maar, slegs, net; voegw. maar, alleen as.
onomato'poeia [onŏmətŏ'piə] s. klanknabootsing.
'onrush ['onrʌsj] s. stormloop.
'onset ['onset] s. aanval.
'onslaught ['onslôt] s. aanval.
'onto [ontŏê] voors op, tot by, na.
'onus ['ounəs] s. las, plig, onus.
'onward ['onwəd] bnw. voorwaarts; bw. voorwaarts, verder.
'onwards = onward.
'ooze ['ŏêz] ww. (-d) syfer, lek; 'oozy bnw. modderig.
'opal ['oupəl] s. (-s) opaal; opa'lescent bnw. opaalagtig.
o'paque [ou'pyk] bnw. ondeurskynend.
'open ['oupən] bnw. oop, openlik; rondborstig; ww. (-ed) oopmaak, oopgaan; begin, inlei; s. ruimte; -ing s. opening; -ly bw. openhartig.
'opera ['opərə] s. (-s) opera; ope'retta s. operetjie, operette.
'operate ['opəryt] ww. (-d) werk; uitwerking hê op; veroorsaak; bestuur; opereer, bedien; ope'ration s. werking; bewerking; werksaamheid; beweging; operasie; bediening; operator s. bediener.
oph'thalmic [of'thælmik] bnw. oog-; - ointment s. oogsalf.
'opiate ['oupiit] s. (-s) slaapdrank.
o'pinion [ə'pinjən] s. (-s) mening, oordeel, opinie.
'opium ['oupjəm] s. opium.
op'ponent [ə'pounənt] s. (-s) teenstander, opponent.
'opportune ['opətjoen] bnw. geleë, gunstig; oppor'tunity s. geleentheid oppor'tunist s. opportunis.
op'pose [ə'pouz] ww. (-d) bestry, opponeer, teenwerk; 'opposite bnw. teenoorgesteld; bw. oorkant; voors.

regoor; oppo'sition s. teenstand, opposisie.
op'press [ə'pres] ww. (-ed) onderdruk, verdruk; -ion s. verdrukking; -ive bnw. onderdrukkend; -or s. verdrukker.
op'probrium [ə'proubriəm] s. oneer, skande, smaad; op'probrious bnw. beledigend, smaadlik.
'optic ['optik] bnw. opties, gesigs-; -al bnw. opties-; op'tician s. brilslyper; -s s. gesigkunde.
'optimism ['optimizəm] s. optimisme.
'option ['opsjən] s. (-s) keuse, voorkeur, opsie; -al bnw. na keuse, opsioneel.
'opulence ['opjoeləns] s. rykdom, weelde; 'opulent bnw. ryk, weelderig.
'opus [oupəs] s. opus, werk, magnum - vernaamste werk.
or ['ô] voegw. & voors. of, anders.
'oracle ['orəkl] s. (-s) orakel.
'oral ['ôrəl] bnw. mondeling, mond-.
'orange ['orindzj] s. (-s) lemoen; oranjekleur; -ade s. lemoensop; - blossom s. lemoenbloeisel.
'orang-'outang ['ôrəng'oetæng] s. (-s) orang-oetang.
o'ration [ŏ'rysjən] s. redevoering, rede; 'orator s. redenaar; ora'torical bnw. oratories; 'oratory s. retoriek.
orb ['ôb] s. (-s) bol, sfeer, hemelliggaam; -it s. baan van hemelliggaam; oogholte.
'orchard ['ôtsjid] s. (-s) boord.
'orchestra ['ôkistrə] s. (-s) orkes; 'orchestrate ww. orkestreer.
'orchid ['ôkid] s. (-s) orgidee.
or'dain [ŏ'dyn] ww. (-ed) orden, bevestig; beveel.
or'deal [ô'dil] s. (-s) beproewing; vuurproef.
'order ['ôdə] s. (-s) orde; rang; stand; klas; volgorde; bevel; bestelling; ww. (-ed) gelas, beveel; bestel; inrig, beskik; - book s. bestelboek; -ly bnw. ordelik, s. ordonnans.
'ordinal ['ôdinl] s. rangtelwoord; bnw. rangskikkend.
'ordinance ['ôdinəns] s. ordonnansie; reglement.
'ordinary ['ôdnri] bnw. gewoon, alledaags.
ore ['ô] s. (-s) erts.
'organ ['ôghən] s. (-s) orrel; orgaan; or'ganic bnw. organies; organi'zation s. organisasie; inrigting; reeling; -ize ww. (-d) organiseer.
'orgasm ['ôghæzəm] s. hewige opwinding.
'orgy ['ôdzji] s. ('orgies) fees, fuif.
'oriel ['ôriəl] s. (-s) spitsvenster.
'orient ['ôriənt] bnw. oosters; ori'ental bnw. oosters; s. oosterling.
orien'tation [ôriən'tysjən] s. oriëntering.
'orifice ['orifis] s. (-s) opening, gaatjie.
'origin ['oridzjin] s. (-s) oorsprong;

o'riginal *bnw.* oorspronklik;
origi'nality *s.* oorspronklikheid;
o'riginally *bw.* eers, oorspronklik;
o'riginate *vww.* (-d) ontstaan, begin.
'ornament ['ɔnəmənt] *s.* (-s)
sieraad, versiersel, ornament;
orna'mental *bnw.* sierlik, dekoratief.
'ornate ['ɔnyt] *bnw.* ryk versier.
orni'thology [ɔni'θolədzji] *s.* voël-
kunde.
'orphan ['ɔfən] *s.* (-s) weeskind;
bnw. wees; -age *s.* weesinrigting.
'orthodox ['ɔθədoks] *bnw.* ortodoks,
regsinnig, behoudend; -y *s.*
or'thography [ɔ'θogrəfi] *s.* orto-
grafie, spelkuns.
'orthopaedy ['ɔθoupidi] *s.* orto-
pedie; ortho'pedic *bnw.* ortopedies.
'oscillate ['osilyt] *vww.* (-d) slinger;
weifel; osileer; oscil'lation *s.* slinge-
ring; weifeling; oscil'latory *bnw.*
swaaiend, weifelend.
'osier ['ouzjə] *s.* (-s) wilger; lat,
mandjiesgoed.
os'mosis [oz'mousis] *s.* osmose;
os'motic *bnw.* osmoties.
'osprey ['ospri] *s.* (-s) see-arend;
aigrettepluim.
'ossicle ['osikl] *s.* beentjie; 'osseous
bnw. beenagtig; ossifi'cation *s.*
beenwording; 'ossify *vww.* verbeen.
os'tensible [os'tensəbl] *bnw.* oënskynlik; os'tensibly *bw.* kastig,
konsuis; osten'tation *s.* vertoon,
pronkery; osten'tatious *bnw.* spoggerig.
oste'ology [osti'olədzji] *s.* osteologie.
'ostler ['oslə] *s.* (-s) staljong.
'ostracize ['ostrəsaiz] *vww.* (-d)
verban, uitdrywe.
'ostrich ['ostritsj] *s.* (-es) volstruis.
'other ['ʌðə] *bnw.* ander(s); *s.*
ander(e); -wise *bw.* anders.
'otter ['otə] *s.* (-s) otter.
ought ['ɔt] *s.* nul; *vww.* moet,
behoort.
'ounce ['auns] *s.* (-s) ons; bergpanter.
our ['auə] *bnw.* ons; -s *vnw. & bnw.*
ons s'n; -'selves *vnw.* onsself.
oust ['aust] *vww.* (-ed) uitdryf;
verdring.
out ['aut] *bw.* uit, buite; dood;
bekend; *voors.* uit, buitekant; *bnw.*
weg van huis; buitegewoon; -bid
vww. oorbie, oortref; -break *s.*
uitbarsting, opstand; -building *s.*
buitegebou; -burst *s.* losbarsting;
-cast *vww.* verban, uitstoot; -class
vww. oortref; -come *s.* uitslag; -crop
s. gevolg; dagsoom; -cry *s.* geskreeu,
lawaai; -'distance *vww.* disnisloop,
oortref; -'do *vww.* oortref; -doors *bw.*
buitenshuis; -er *bnw.* buite, buitenste; -fit *s.* uitrusting, toerusting;
-fitter *s.* uitruster, leweransier;
-flank *vww.* uitoorlê; -going *bnw.*
vertrekkende; -grow *vww.* verby-
groei, vergroei; -house *s.* buitegebou;
-ing *s.* uitstappie; -lander *s.*
uitlander; -'landish *bnw.* uitheems;
-law *s.* balling; voëlvrye; -lay *s.*

uitgawe; -let *s.* mond, afvoerpyp;
-line *s.* omtrek, skets; -look *s.*
vooruitsig; -lying *bnw.* afgeleë;
-most *bnw.* verste, uiterste; -num-
ber *vww.* oortref in getal; -pace *vww.*
disnisloop; -patient *s.* buitepasiënt;
-post *s.* voorpos, buitepos; -put *s.*
produksie; -rage *s.* vergryp; -ra-
geous *bnw.* skandalig; -right *bw.*
geheelenal, volkome; -set *s.* aanvang,
begin; -side *s.* buitekant; -sider
oningewyde, vreemde, indringer;
-size *s.* groot nommer of maat;
-skirts *s.* grense, voorpos; -'spoken
bnw. rondborstig; -standing *bnw.*
belangrik, prominent; -stay *vww.* te
lank vertoef; -'strip *vww.* verbyhard-
loop; verbystreef; -talk *vww.* dood-
praat; -'vote *vww.* oorstem; -ward
bnw. & bw. uiterlik, na die buitekant; -'wit *vww.* uitoorlê.
'outflow ['autflou] *s.* uitstroming,
uitloop.
out'live [aut'liv] *vww.* (-d) oorleef.
'output- ['autpoet] *voorv.* uitgangs-.
out'worn [aut'wôn] *bnw.* afgedra,
verslete.
'oval ['ouvəl] *bnw.* ovaal, eiervormig.
o'vate ['ou'vyt] *bnw.* eierrond; *vgl.*
oval.
'ovary ['ouvəri] *s.* ('ovaries) eierstok,
vrugbeginsel.
o'vation [ou'vyzjən] *s.* toejuiging,
hulde.
'oven ['ʌvn] *s.* (-s) oond.
'over ['ouvə] *bw.* oor; omver; verby;
voors. oor, bo, by, oorkant; *s.* boul-
beurt; -alls *s.* oorpak; -'awe *vww.*
oorbluf; -'bear *vww.* onderdruk;
-bearing *bnw.* baasspelerig; -board
bw. oorboord; -'burden *vww.* oorlaai;
-cast *vww.* bewolk; oorhands naai;
-'charge *vww.* oorbelas; te veel laat
betaal; -'cloud *vww.* bewolk; -coat *s.*
jas; -come *vww.* oormeester, te bowe
kom; -'crowded *bnw.* oorvol, oorbe-
volk; -'do *vww.* oordryf; -done *bnw.*
oordrewe; te gaar; -dose *s.* te groot
dosis; -draft *s.* oortrokke bank-
rekening; -'drive *s.* snelgang; -drive
governor *s.* snelgangreëlaar; -'due
bnw. laat; agterstallig; -'flow *vww.*
oorstroom, oor-loop; -grown *bnw.*
toegegroei, begroei; -'haul *vww.*
deeglik nasien, opknap, *s.* op-
knapping; -'head *bnw.* bo, bo jou
kop, lug-, bogrondse; -head valve
s. kopklep; -'hear *vww.* afluister;
-joyed *bnw.* opgetoë; -'lap *vww.*
mekaar gedeeltelik dek; -'leaf *bw.*
op die volgende bladsy; -live *vww.*
oorleef; -load *vww.* oorlaai, oorbelas;
-look *vww.* uitkyk op; oor die hoof
sien; -master *vww.* oormeester, oorrompel; -'much *bw.* te veel; -night
bw. gedurende die nag; -'power
vww. oorrompel, oorweldig; -print
vww. bo-oor druk; -'rate *vww.*
(-d) oorskat; -'reach *vww.* misreken;
-ride *vww.* tersy stel; -ripe *bnw.*
oorryp; -'rule *vww.* verwerp; -run

ww. oorstroom, platloop; -'seas *bw.*
in die buiteland; -'see *ww.* toesig hou;
-'seer s. opsigter; -shadow *ww.*
oorskadu; -shoe s. oorskoen; -sight
s. vergissing; -size(d) *bnw.* bomaats;
-'sleep *ww.* verslaap; -spill s.
storting; -'state *ww.* oordryf; -step
ww. te buite gaan; -stock *ww.* te
groot voorraad hê; -'strung *bnw.*
oorspanne; -take *ww.* (-took) inhaal;
verbysteek; -take signal s. verby-
steeksein; -throw *ww.* omvergooi;
-time s. oortyd; -tone s. bowetoon;
-trump *ww.* oortroef; -'turn *ww.*
omslaan; -weight s. oorgewig;
-'whelm *ww.* oorrompel; -'work *ww.*
oorwerk; -wrought *bnw.* oorspanne.
'**over'estimate** ['ouvə'estimyt] *ww.*
(-d) oorskat.
'**over'hang** ['ouvə'hæng] *ww.*
(hung) oorhang, uitsteek; dreig.
'**overland** ['ouvəlænd] *bnw.* dwarsdeur die land.
'**over'shoot** ['ouvə'sjōēt] *ww.* (-shot)
verbyskiet, oorheen skiet.
'**overt** ['ouvət] *bnw.* duidelik; openlik.
over'take [ouvə'tyk] *ww.* (-took)
inhaal, oorval.
'**overture** ['ouvətjoeə] s. (-s) voorstel; aanbod; inleiding; begin.
'**oviduct** ['ouvidʌkt] s. (-s) eierleier.
'**oviform** ['ouvifōm] *bnw.* eiervormig.
o'viparous [ou'vipərəs] *bnw.* eier-
lêend.
'**ovoid** ['ouvoid] *bnw.* eiervormig;
vgl. **oval, ovate.**
'**ovum** ['ouvəm] s. ('*ova*) eier.
'**owe** ['ou] *ww.* (-d) skuld; **owing** *bnw.*
verskuldig; **owing** to *voors.* weëns.
owl ['aul] s. (-s) uil; -ish *bnw.*
uilagtig.
own ['oun] *bnw.* eie; *ww.* (-ed) besit;
beken; -er s. eienaar; -ership s.
besitreg.
ox ['oks] s. (-en) os; -eye s. gousblom;
-hide s. beesvel; -tail s. beesstert;
- waggon s. ossewa.
ox'alic [ok'sælik] *bnw.* oksaal.
'**oxide** ['oksaid] s. oksied; '**oxidize**
ww. oksideer; **oxi'dation** s. oksidasie.
'**oxo** ['oksou] s. vleisekstrak.
Ox'onian [ok'sounjən] s. Oxford-
geleerde.
'**oxygen** ['oksidzjen] s. suurstof.
'**oyster** ['oistə] s. (-s) oester; -bed s.
oesterbed.
'**ozone** ['ouzoun] s. oson; **ozo'niferous**
bnw. osonbevattend.

P

pa ['pā] s. (-s) pa, vader.
'**pace** ['pys] s. (-s) tree, pas, tred;
vaart; *ww.* (-d) stap; aftree; pas
aangee; -maker s. gangmaker; -r s.
stapper; trippelaar; gangmaker.
'**pachyderm** ['pækidām] s. (-s)
dikvellige dier.

'**pacify** ['pæsifai] *ww.* ('*pacified*)
paai, kalmeer; vrede herstel; **pa'cific**
bnw. vreedsaam; **pacifi'cation** s.
versoening; **pacifi'catory** *bnw.* versoenend; '**pacifism** s. vredeliewend-
heid; '**pacifist** s. pasifis.
pack ['pæk] s. (-s) pak, bondel;
bende; trop; -age s. pakkie; verpakking; - drill s. saal-dra; -et s.
pakkie; -horse s. pakperd; -ing s.
verpakking; paksel; -ing-needle s.
seilnaald; -saddle s. paksaal;
- thread s. seilgaring.
pact ['pækt] s. (-s) ooreenkoms.
pad ['pæd] s. (-s) kussinkie; stopsel;
beenskut; skryfblok; voetsool; *ww.*
(-ded) stop, vul; -ding s. stopsel.
'**paddle** ['pædl] s. (-s) roeispaan; *ww.*
(-d) roei, in die water plas.
'**paddock** ['pædək] s. kamp, park.
'**padlock** ['pædlok] s. (-s) hangslot.
'**padre** ['pādri] s. (-s) kapelaan.
'**paean** ['piən] s. (-s) danklied,
oorwinningslied.
'**pagan** ['pyghən] s. (-s) heiden; *bnw.*
heidens; -ism s. heidendom.
'**page** ['pydzj] s. (-s) page, livreikneg,
hofknaap, joggie; bladsy; *ww.* (-d)
roep.
'**pageant** ['pædzjənt] s. (-s) vertoning; optog; -ry s. pragtige
vertoning.
pa'goda [pə'ghoudə] s. (-s) afgod-
stempel.
pail ['pyl] s. (-s) emmer.
'**pail(i)asse** [pæl'jæs] s. (-s) matras.
pain ['pyn] s. (-s) pyn, smart; -ful
bnw. pynlik, seer; -killer s. pynstiller; -staking *bnw.* ywerig, fluks.
paint ['pynt] s. verf; *ww.* (-ed) verf,
skilder; beskrywe; -er s. -ing s.
skilderstuk; skilderkuns.
pair ['pèə] s. (-s) paar; *ww.* (-ed)
paar; in pare opstel.
pal ['pæl] s. (-s) maat, vriend.
'**palace** ['pælis] s. (-s) paleis.
'**palate** ['pælit] s. (-s) verhemelte;
smaak; '**palatable** *bnw.* smaaklik;
'**palatal** *bnw.* verhemelte-, palataal;
'**palatalize** *ww.* palataliseer; '**pala-**
tine *bnw.* verhemelte-.
pa'laver [pə'lāvə] s. (-s) bespreking,
konferensie.
'**pale** ['pyl] s. paal; spar; grens;
beyond the - buite perke; *bnw.* (-r,
-st) bleek, dof; *ww.* (-d) bleek word.
'**palette** ['pælit] s. (-s) palet; -knife
s. platmes.
'**palfrey** ['pōlfri] s. damesryperd.
'**paling** ['pyling] s. (-s) paalheining,
skutting.
'**palisade** [pæli'syd] s. (-s) paal-
skans, skutting, borswering.
pall ['pōl] s. doodskleed; *ww.* (-d)
walg; -bearer s. sleepdraer, slip-
draer.
'**palladium** [pə'lydiəm] s. (-s)
bolwerk, waarborg.
'**pallet** ['pælit] s. (-s) strooibed.
'**palliate** ['pæliyt] *ww.* (-d) versag;
verlig; verbloem; **palli'ation** s. ver-

sagting, verbloeming; **'palliative** s. versagtingsmiddel; bnw. versagtend.

'pallid ['pælid] bnw. (-est) bleek, asvaal.

'pallor ['pælə] s. bleekheid.

palm ['pɑ̃m] s. (-s) palm, palmboom; ww. (-ed) betas; wegsteek; omkoop; **-istry** s. handkykery; **-oil** s. palmolie; omkoopgeld; **-y** bnw. palmagtig; **pal'myra** s. waaipalm.

palp ['pælp] s. tasorgaan; **-able** bnw. tasbaar; **pal'pation** s. betasting.

'pal'pate ['pæl'pyt] ww. (-d) tastend ondersoek, betas.

'palpitate ['pælpityt] ww. (-d) klop, pols; **palpi'tation** s. hartklopping, polsslag.

'palsy ['pɔ̃lzi] s. verlamming, beroerte; **'palsied** bnw. verlam.

'paltry ['pɔ̃ltri] bnw. nietig; veragtelik.

'pamper ['pæmpə] ww. (-ed) vertroetel, bederwe.

'pamphlet ['pæmflit] s. (-s) pamflet.

pan ['pæn] s. (-s) pan; bank (ouklip).

pana'cea [pænə'siə] s. (-s) wondermiddel, geneesal, almiddel.

'pancake ['pænkyk] s. (-s) pannekoek.

'pancreas ['pæng-kriəs] s. alvleesklier, soetvleis.

pan'demic [pæn'demik] bnw. algemeen.

pande'monium [pændi'mounjəm] s. hel, groot lawaai.

'pander ['pændə] ww. (-ed) toegee aan; slegte bedoelings bevorder.

'pane ['pyn] s. (-s) ruit.

pane'gyric [pæni'dzjirik] s. (-s) lofrede.

'panel ['pænl] s. (-s) paneel; naamlys; strook; **-ling** s. lambrisering, beskot; **- beater** s. duikklopper; **- beating** s. duikklopping, duikklopwerk.

pang ['pæng] s. (-s) skerp pyn, steek; angs.

'panic ['pænik] s. paniek, plotselinge vrees; bnw. panies; **-y** bnw. paniekerig; **-stricken** bnw. skrikbevange.

'pannier ['pæniə] s. (-s) pakmandjie.

pano'rama [pænə'rɑ̃mə] s. (-s) panorama, vergesig.

'pansy ['pænzi] s. ('pansies) gesiggie.

pant ['pænt] ww. (-ed) hyg, snak.

'panther ['pænthə] s. (-s) panter, luiperd.

pan'technicon [pæn'teknikn] s. (-s) meubelwa.

'pantomime ['pæntəmaim] s. (-s) gebarespel, pantomime.

'pantry ['pæntri] s. ('pantries) spens.

'pants ['pænts] s. broek.

pa'pa [pə'pɑ̃] s. pappa.

'papacy ['pypəsi] s. pousdom; **'papal** bnw. pouslik.

paw'paw [pə'pɔ̃] s. (-s) papajas.

'paper ['pypə] s. (-s) papier; nuusblad; vraestel; verhandeling; plakpapier; wissel; **-s** s. dokumente.

amptelike stukke; ww. (-ed) plak; behang; **- bag** s. kardoes; **- chase** s. snipperjag; **- currency** s. papiergeld; **- cutter** s. papiermes; **- hanger** s. behanger, plakker; **- mill** s. papiermes; **- mill** s. papierfabriek; **-money** s. papiergeld; **papier-maché** s. ['papjy'misjy] papierpap.

pa'pilla [pə'pilə] s. (pa'pillae) tepel.

papula ['pæpjoelə] s. puisie, knobbel.

pa'pyrus [pə'paiərəs] s. (pa'pyri) papirus.

par ['pɑ̃] s. gelykheid, pari; **-ity** s. gelykheid.

pa'rable [pə'ræbl] s. (-s) gelykenis, parabel.

pa'rabola [pə'ræbələ] s. (-s) parabool.

'parachute ['pærəsjŏet] s. (-s) valskerm.

pa'rade [pə'ryd] s. (-s) parade; wapenskou; optog; ww. (-d) optog hou; marsjeer; pronk.

'paradigm ['pærədaim] s. (-s) modelwoord, paradigma.

'paradise ['pærədais] s. paradys, hemel.

paradox ['pærədoks] s. (-es) paradoks, skynbare teenstrydigheid; **para'doxical** bnw. paradoksaal.

'paraffin ['pærəfin] s. lampolie.

'paragon ['pærəghon] s. (-s) model, voorbeeld, toonbeeld.

'paragraph ['pærəghrɑ̃f] s. (-s) paragraaf.

'parakeet ['pærəkit] s. parakiet.

'parallel ['pærələl] bnw. parallel, ewewydig; s. ewewydige lyn; **-ism** s. ewewydigheid, ooreenkoms; **paral'lelogram** s. parallelogram.

'paralyze ['pærəlaiz] ww. (-d) verlam; ontsenu; **pa'ralysis** s. verlamming; **para'lytic** s. verlamde; bnw. verlam.

'paramount ['pærəmaunt] bnw. vernaamste, opper-; **-cy** s. oorwig; hoofskap.

'parapet ['pærəpit] s. (-s) borswering.

pa'raph [pə'rɑ̃f] s. paraaf; ww. parafeer.

parapher'nalia [pærəfə'nyljə] s. uitrusting; mondering; rommel.

'paraphrase ['pærəfryz] s. parafrase; ww. (-d) parafraseer.

'parasite ['pærəsait] s. (-s) parasiet; **para'sitic(al)** bnw. parasietagtig, parasities; **'parasitize** ww. teer op.

para'sol [pærə'sol] s. (-s) sambreel.

'paratrooper ['pærətrŏëpə] s. valskermsoldaat.

'parcel ['pɑ̃sl] s. (-s) pakkie, stuk; klomp; ww. verdeel; inpak; **- post** s. pakkiespos.

parch ['pɑ̃tsj] ww. (-ed) skroei, verdroog, verdor; **-ment** s. perkament.

pard ['pɑ̃d] s. (-s) maat, vennoot.

'pardon ['pɑ̃dn] s. vergifnis, kwytskelding; ww. (-ed) vergewe, kwytskel; **-able** bnw. vergeeflik.

'pare ['pêə] ww. (-d) skil, sny, knip; snoel; **paring** s. skil, skaafsel.

pare'goric [pærə'ghorik] s. pynstillende middel, paragore.

'parent ['pærnt] s. (-s) ouer; **-age** s. afkoms; **pa'rental** bnw. ouerlik.

pa'renthesis [pə'renthisis] s. (pa'renteses) parentese, tussensin.

par'excellence [pår'eksəláns] bw. by uitnemendheid.

'pariah ['pæriə] s. (-s) uitgeworpene, verstoteling.

'parish ['pærisj] s. (-es) gemeente, parogie; **pa'rishioner** s. gemeentelid.

park ['påk] s. (-s) park; ww. (-ed) omhein; parkeer; **-ing** s. staanplek, parkeerplek; parkering.

'parlance ['påləns] s. spreekwyse; **'parley** s. (-s) gesprek, onderhandeling; **'parleyvoo** s. Fransman (skertsend).

'parliament ['påləmənt] s. (-s) volksraad, parlement; **parliamen-'tarian** s. redenaar in parlement; **parlia'mentary** bnw. parlimentêr.

'parlour ['pålə] s. (-s) voorkamer, ontvangkamer; **-maid** s. binnemeisie.

'parlous ['påləs] bnw. gevaarlik.

pa'rochial [pə'roukjəl] bnw. bekrompe.

'parody ['pærədi] s. ('parodies) parodie, spotdig.

pa'role [pə'roul] s. erewoord; wagwoord: parool.

'paroxysm ['pærəksizəm] s. hewige aanval, bui, vlaag.

'parquet ['påky] s. blokkiesvloer.

'parricide ['pærisaid] s. vadermoord.

'parrot ['pærət] s. (-s) papegaai; na-aper.

'parry ['pæri] ww. ('parried) afweer, pareer.

'parse ['påz] ww. (-d) woorde ontleed; **'parsing** s. woordontleding.

'parsimony ['påsiməni] s. spaarsaamheid; gierigheid; **parsi'monious** bnw. spaarsaam, suinig, gierig.

'parsley ['påsli] s. pieterselie.

'parsnip ['påsnip] s. (-s) witwortel.

'parson ['påsn] s. (-s) predikant; **-age** s. pastorie.

part ['påt] s. (-s) deel, gedeelte, stuk, part; rol; aandeel; kant; ww. (-ed) verdeel; uiteengaan; skei; **par'take** ww. (par'took, par'taken) deelneem, deel hê in; geniet, eet; **-ial** bnw. partydig; gedeeltelik; **-i'ality** s. partydigheid; **par'ticipate** ww. (-d) deelneem; **par'ticipant** s. deelnemer; **-i'cipial** bnw. deelwoordelik; **-iciple** s. deelwoord; **-icle** s. deeltjie; partikel; **-ing** s. afskeid, skeiding; **-y** s. party, geselskap; **par'tition** s. verdeling, skeiding; **-itive** bnw. verdelend; **-ly** bw. gedeeltelik; **-ner** s. deelgenoot, venoot.

par'ticular [pə'tikjoelə] bnw. besonder; kieskeurig; s. besonderheid;

-ise ww. spesifiseer; **particu'larity** s. besonderheid, eienaardigheid.

'partimute ['påtimjoet] s. (-s) doofstomme; bnw. doofstom.

parti'san ['påti'zæn] s. (-s) aanhanger; bnw. partydig.

'partner ['påtnə] s. (-s) vennoot, maat, deelgenoot; ww. saamspeel.

'partridge ['påtridzj] s. (-s) patrys.

pass ['pås] ww. (-ed) verbygaan, passeer; deurgaan; toelaat; slaag; vonnis; s. (-es) slaag; handbeweging; pas; bergpas, nek; **-able** bnw. passabel, taamlik, begaanbaar; **-port** s. paspoort.

'passage ['pæsidzj] s. (-s) deurtog; gang; reisgeld.

'pass book ['pås boek] s. (-s) bankboekie.

'passenger ['pæsindzjə] s. (-s) reisiger.

'passion ['pæsjən] s. hartstog, drif; **-ate** bnw. hartstogtelik.

'passive ['pæsiv] bnw. lydend, lydelik, passief, gedwee; s. lydende vorm.

'pass-key ['påski] s. (-s) loper, towersleutel.

'passport ['påspôt] s. (-s) paspoort.

'password ['påswǝd] s. (-s) wagwoord.

past ['påst] bnw. verby, verlede, afgelope; s. verlede; voors. oor, verby; bw. verby.

'paste ['pyst] s. deeg, pap; smeersel; pasta.

'pasteboard ['pystbôd] s. bordpapier; bnw. goedkoop.

'pastel ['pæstəl] s. pastel.

'pasteurize ['pæstəraiz] ww. (-d) pasteuriseer.

'pastille ['pæstil] s. (-s) pil, tablet.

'pastime ['påstaim] s. tydkorting; speletjie.

'pastor ['påstə] s. (-s) pastoor, herder, predikant; **-al** bnw. pastoraal, landelik.

'pastry ['pystri] s. ('pastries) pastei; koek, gebak.

'pasture ['påstjə] s. (-s) weiveld; **'pasturage** s. weiding.

'pasty ['påsti] s. ('pasties) vleispasteitjie.

pat ['pæt] s. (-s) tikkie, kloppie; klontjie; ww. (-ted) tik, klop; platstryk.

patch ['pætsj] s. (-es) lap, pleister; ww. (-ed) lap, heelmaak; **-work** s. laslappies; knoeiwerk; **-y** bnw. gelap; gebrekkig.

'pate ['pyt] s. (-s) harspan.

pa'tella [pə'telə] s. (-s) knieskyf.

'patent ['pytənt] s. (-s) patent, oktrooi; ww. (-ed) patenteer; bnw. gepatenteer; duidelik.

pa'ternity [pə'tǝniti] s. vaderskap; **pa'ternal** bnw. vaderlik.

path ['påth] s. (-s) pad, weg; **-way** s. pad.

pa'thetic [pə'thetik] bnw. aandoenlik, pateties.

pa'thology [pə'tholədʒi] s. patologie; **patho'logical** bnw. patologies; **pa'thologist** s. patoloog.

'pathos ['pythos] s. patos.

'patience ['pysjəns] s. geduld, volharding; soliterspel; **'patient** s. lyer, siekte; bnw. geduldig.

'patois ['pætwa] s. dialek.

'patriarch ['pytriäk] s. (-s) aartsvader, patriarg; **-al** bnw. patriargaal; **-ate** s. patriargaat; **-y** s. patriargale staatsvorm.

pa'trician [pə'trisjən] s. (-s) patrisiër; bnw. patrisies.

'patrimony ['pætriməni] s. vaderlike erfdeel.

'patriot ['pætriət] s. (-s) vaderlander; **patri'otic** bnw. vaderlandsliewend.

pa'trol [pə'troul] s. (-s) patrollie.

'patron ['pytrən] s. (-s) patroon, beskermheer; klant; **-age** s. beskerming; klandisie; **-ize** ww. (-d) beskerm; ondersteun.

patro'nymic [pætrə'nimik] s. (-s) vadersnaam.

'patter ['pætə] s. gebabbel; getrippel.

'pattern ['pætən] s. (-s) patroon; model; voorbeeld.

'patty ['pæti] s. ('patties) pasteitjie, frikkadel.

'paucity ['pòsiti] s. skaarste, skaarsheid.

'paunch ['pòntsj] s. (-es) buik, pens.

'pauper ['pòpə] s. (-s) arme, behoeftige; **-ism** s. armoede.

'pause ['pòz] s. (-s) pouse; ww. (-d) wag, aarsel; rus.

'pave ['pyv] ww. (-d) plavei, uitstraat; **-ment** s. plaveisel, sypaadjie.

pa'vilion [pə'viljən] s. (-s) pawiljoen; tent.

paw ['pò] s. (-s) poot, klou; ww. (-ed) met poot krap; beklou.

'pawl ['pòl] s. (-s) pal.

pawn ['pòn] s. (-s) pand; pion; ww. (-ed) verpand; **-broker** s. pandjiesbaas; **-shop** s. pandjieswinkel.

pay ['py] s. betaling, loon; ww. (paid) betaal; beloon; boet; **-able** bnw. betaalbaar, winsgewend; **-ee** s. ontvanger; **-ment** s. betaling, loon; paaiement.

pea ['pi] s. (-s) ertjie.

'peace ['pis] s. vrede; rus; **-able** bnw. vreedsaam; **-ful** bnw. vreedsaam; **-offering** s. soenoffer.

peach ['pitsj] s. (-es) perske; mooi nooi.

'peacock ['pikok] s. (-s) pou, mannetjiespou.

'peafowl ['pifaul] s. (-s) pou; peacock s. poumannetjie; **peahen** s. pouwyfie.

peak ['pik] s. (-s) punt, spits, piek.

peal ['pil] s. (-s) klokgelui; slag.

'peanut ['pinʌt] s. (-s) grondboontjie.

pear ['pèə] s. (-s) peer.

pearl ['pəl] s. (-s) pêrel; **-y** bnw. pêrelagtig.

'peasant ['pezint] s. (-s) boer,

landbouer; **'peasantry** s. boerestand.

peat ['pit] s. turf; **-y** bnw. turfagtig.

'pebble ['pebl] s. (-s) ronde klippie.

'peccable ['pekəbl] bnw. sondig.

peck ['pek] ww. (-ed) pik na; vit.

'pectoral ['pektərəl] s. borsstuk; bnw. bors-.

pe'culiar [pi'kjöëljə] bnw. besonder, eienaardig; snaaks; **peculi'arity** s. eienaardigheid, eienskap; **-ly** bw. persoonlik, besonder.

pe'cuniary [pi'kjöënəri] bnw. geldelik.

'pedagogy ['pedəghoghi] s. opvoedkunde; **'pedagogue** s. pedagoog, opvoedkundige; **peda'gogic(al)** bnw. voedkundig.

'pedal [pedl] s. (-s) pedaal, trap.

'pedant ['pedənt] s. wysneus; **pe'dantic** bnw. pedanties.

'peddle ['pedl] ww. (-d) smous.

'pedestal ['pedistl] s. (-s) voetstuk.

pe'destrian [pə'destriən] s. (-s) voetganger.

'pedigree ['pedighri] s. (-s) stamboom; afkoms.

'pediment ['pedimənt] s. kroonlys.

'pedlar ['pedlə] s. (-s) smous; vgl. peddle.

peek ['pik] ww. (-ed) loer, kyk.

peel ['pil] s. (-s) skil, dop; ww. (-ed) skil, afdop.

peep ['pip] ww. (-ed) loer; **-hole** s. loergat; **-show** s. kykkas.

peer ['piə] s. (-s) weerga; edelman; ww. (-ed) loer; **-age** s. adelstand; **-less** bnw. weergaloos.

'peevish ['pivisj] bnw. liggeraak.

peg ['pegh] s. (-s) pen; kapstok; ww. (-ged) afpen, vaspen.

'pegamoid ['peghəmoid] s. kunsleer.

pe'jorative [pi'dzjərətiv] bnw. pejoratief, verergerend.

'pelican ['pelikən] s. (-s) pelikaan.

'pellet ['pelət] s. (-s) balletjie; pilletjie; koeëltjie.

'pell-'mell ['pel'mel] bnw. deurmekaar.

pelt ['pelt] s. (-s) vel, huid; ww. (-ed) gooi, neerkletter.

'pelvis ['pelvis] s. bekken; **'pelvic** bnw. bekken-.

pen ['pen] s. (-s) pen; hok; ww. (-ned) inhok; skryf; **-knife** s. sakmes; **-manship** s. skryfkuns; **-name** s. skuilnaam.

'penal [pinl] bnw. strafbaar, straf-; **-ise** ww. (-d) straf, beboet; **-ty** s. straf, boete; **'penance** s. boetedoening.

'pence ['pens] s. = **pennies.**

'penchant ['pensjənt] s. neiging.

'pencil ['pensl] s. (-s) potlood.

'pendant [pendənt] s. (-s) hangertjie.

'pending ['pending] bnw. hangende, onbeslis; voors. gedurende, hangende.

'pendulum ['pendjoeləm] s. (-s) slinger.

'penetrate ['penətryt] ww. (-d) binnedring, deurdring; deurgrond;

pene'tration s. deurdringing, deurgrondig; **'penetrating** *bnw.* deurdringend, skerp; **'penetrative** *bnw.* deurdringend.

'penguin ['peng-ghwin] s. (-s) pikkewyn.

pen'insula [pi'ninsjoelə] s. (-s) skiereiland.

'penitence ['penitəns] s. berou; **'penitent** *bnw.* berouvol; **peni'tentiary** s. (*peni'tentiaries*) verbeteringsgestig.

'pennant ['penənt] s. (-s) wimpel.

'penny ['peni] s. (*'pennies*, *pence*) pennie, oulap; **'penniless** *bnw.* platsaak, brandarm; **-weight** s. 24 grein; **-wise** *bnw.* verkeerd-om suinig; **-worth** s. kleinigheidjie.

'pension ['pensjən] s. (-s) pensioen; [pãngsiông] losieshuis; **-er** s. pensionaris; **-able** *bnw.* geregtig op 'n pensioen.

'pensive ['penziv] *bnw.* piensend.

pent ['pent] *bnw.* opgesluit.

pen'tameter [pen'tæmitə] s. vyfvoetige versreël.

'pentateuch ['pentətjõēk] n. pentateug.

'pentecost ['pentikost] s. pinkster.

'penthouse ['penthaus] s. afdak, skuur; tent; dakwoning.

pen'ultimate [pi'nʌltimit] *bnw.* voorlaaste.

'penury ['pinjoeri] s. armoede, gebrek, behoeftigheid; **pe'nurious** *bnw.* arm.

'people ['pipl] s. (-s) mense; volk; familie; *ww.* (-d) bevolk; **-d** *bnw.* bevolk.

'pep ['pep] s. lewenskrag, lewenslus.

'pepper ['pepə] s. peper; **-and-salt** *bnw.* grys; **-box** s. peperbus; **-corn** s. peperkorrel; **-mint** s. peperment; **-y** *bnw.* gepeper.

'pepsin ['pepsin] s. pepsien.

'peptic ['peptik] *bnw.* spysverterend.

per ['pə] *voors.* deur, per.

per- ['pə] *voorvoegsel* per, deur, heeltemal, hoogste graad van; **-'force** *bw.* noodgedwonge; **-'haps** *bw.* miskien.

per'adventure [pərəd'ventsjə] *bw.* miskien, altemit.

per'ambulate [pə'ræmbjoelyt] *ww.* (-d) rondloop, loop; **per'ambulator** s. kinderwa; **per'ambulation** s. rondwandeling; afloop.

per'ceive [pə'siv] *ww.* (-d) bespeur, sien; begryp.

per'cent [pə'sent] s. persent, per honderd; **-age** s. persentasie.

'percept ['pəsept] s. wat waargeneem is; **per'ceptible** *bnw.* waarneembaar; **per'ception** s. waarneming, begrip; **per'ceptive** *bnw.* waarnemend.

perch ['pətsj] s. (-es) slaapstok; sitplek; baars; *ww.* (-ed) gaan sit.

per'chance [pə'tsjáns] *bw.* dalk, altemit.

per'cipience [pə'sipiəns] s. bewus-

wording; **per'cipient** s. waarnemer.

'percolate ['pəkəlyt] *ww.* (-d) deursyfer; **perco'lation** s. deursyfering; **'percolator** s. filtreerkan, koffiekan.

per'cussion [pə'kʌsjən] s. slag; botsing.

per'dition [pə'disjən] s. verdoemenis.

peregri'nation [perighri'nysjən] s. (-s) rondswerwing.

per'emptory [pə'remptəri] *bnw.* beslis; gebiedend.

per'ennial [pə'renjəl] *bnw.* standhoudend; s. standhoudende plant.

'perfect ['pəfikt] *bnw.* volmaakte; *ww.* (-ed) vooltooi; **per'fection** volmaaktheid.

'perfidy ['pəfidi] s. troubreuk, bedrog; **per'fidious** *bnw.* troueloos.

'perforate ['pəfəryt] *ww.* (-d) deursteek, perforeer; **perfo'ration** s. perforasie.

per'form [pə'fôm] *ww.* (-ed) verrig; uitvoer; opvoer; **-ance** s. opvoering; uitvoering; **-er** s. speler.

'perfume ['pəfjõēm] s. (-s) geur; reukwater; **'perfumer** s. parfumeur; **per'fumery** s. reukwerk.

per'functory [pə'fʌnktəri] *bnw.* slordig.

'pergola ['pəghələ] s. (-s) prieel.

per'haps [pə'hæps, 'præps] *bw.* miskien, dalk.

'peril ['peril] s. (-s) gevaar; **-ous** *bnw.* gevaarlik.

per'imeter [pə'rimitə] s. (-s) omtrek.

'period ['piəriəd] s. (-s) tydperk; voisin; punt; periode; **peri'odical** *bnw.* periodiek; **perio'dicity** s. gereelde terugkeer.

per'iphery [pə'rifəri] s. omtrek; periferie.

'perish ['perisj] *ww.* (-ed) omkom; vergaan, verweer; **-able** *bnw.* verganklik; **-ables** s. bederfbare produkte.

perito'nitis [peritə'naitis] s. peritonitis.

'perjury ['pədzjəri] s. meineed.

'perky ['pēki] *bnw.* (*'perkier*, *'perkiest*) astrant.

'permanence ['pəmənəns] s. duur, vastheid; **'permanent** *bnw.* durend, blywend.

'permeate ['pəmiyt] *ww.* (-d) deurdring; **'permeable** *bnw.* deurdringbaar.

'permit ['pəmit] *ww.* (-ted) toelaat, toestaan; s. verlofbrief, permit; **per'mission** s. verlof, vergunning; **per'missive** *bnw.* vergunnend.

per'mute [pə'mjõēt] *ww.* (-d) omwissel; **permu'tation** s. omwisseling.

per'nicious [pə'nisjəs] *bnw.* dodelik, skadelik.

peror'ation [perõ'rysən] s. redevoering, perorasie.

perpen'dicular [pǝpǝn'dikjoelǝ] *bnw.* loodreg, haaks.

'perpetrate ['pǝpitryt] *ww.* (-*d*) pleeg, begaan; **perpe'tration** *s.* pleging; **'perpetrator** *s.* pleger, dader.

per'petuate [pǝ'petjoeyt] *ww.* (-*d*) verewig; **per'petual** *bnw.* ewigdurend; **perpetu'ation** *s.* bestendiging; **perpe'tuity** *s.* ewigdurendheid.

per'plex [pǝ'pleks] *ww.* (-*ed*) verwar; **-ed** *bnw.* verslae, verleë; **-ity** *s.* verleentheid, verwarring.

'perquisite ['pǝkwisit] *s.* (-*s*) ekstra-inkomste.

'persecute ['pǝsekjōēt] *ww.* (-*d*) vervolg, lastig val; **perse'cution** *s.* vervolging.

perse'vere [pǝsi'viǝ] *ww.* (-*d*) volhou, volhard; **perse'verance** *s.* volharding; **perse'vering** *bnw.* volhardend.

per'sist [pǝ'sist] *ww.* (-*ed*) volhou, volhard; **-ence** *s.* volharding; **-ent** *bnw.* volhardend, koppig.

'person ['pǝsn] *s.* (-*s*) persoon, mens; **-able** *bnw.* aanvallig; **-age** *s.* persoonlikheid; **-al** *bnw.* persoonlik; **-ate** *ww.* (-*d*) deurgaan vir; **-ifi'cation** *s.* verpersoonliking.

person'nel [pǝsǝ'nel] *s.* personeel.

pers'pective [pǝ'spektiv] *s.* perspektief.

perspi'cacious [pǝspi'kysjǝs] *bnw.* skerpsinnig, skrander; **perspi'cacity** *s.* skerpsinnigheid.

perspi'cuity [pǝspi'kjoeiti] *s.* duidelikheid, helderheid; **per'spicuous** *bnw.* duidelik, helder.

per'spire [pǝ'spaiǝ] *ww.* (-*d*) sweet; **perspi'ration** *s.* sweet; **perspi'ratory** *bnw.* sweet-.

per'suade [pǝ'swyd] *ww.* (-*d*) oorreed; beweeg; **per'suasion** *s.* oorreding; **per'suasive** *bnw.* oorredend.

pert ['pǝt] *bnw.* astrant.

'pertinence ['pǝtinǝns] *s.* gepastheid; **'pertinent** *bnw.* gepas.

per'turb [pǝ'tǝb] *ww.* (-*ed*) versteur, verontrus.

per'use [pǝ'rōēz] *ww.* (-*d*) noukeurig deurkyk; **per'usal** *s.* noukeurige deurlees.

per'vade [pǝ'vyd] *ww.* (-*d*) deurtrek; **per'vasion** *s.* deurdringing.

per'verse [pǝ'vǝs] *bnw.* verkeerd, dwars, pervers; **per'versity** *s.* dwarsheid, koppigheid; **'pervert** *ww.* (-*ed*) verdraai; *s.* afgedwaalde.

'pervious ['pēviǝs] *bnw.* vatbaar.

'pessimist ['pesimist] *s.* swaarmoedige; pessimis.

pest ['pest] *s.* pes, plaag; **-er** *ww.* lastig val; **-ilence** *s.* pes, pestilensie.

'pestle ['pestl] *s.* (-*s*) stamper.

pet ['pet] *s.* (-*s*) hansdier; liefling; gunsteling.

'petal ['petl] *s.* (-*s*) blomblaartjie.

'peter ['pitǝ] *ww.* (-*ed*) to - out opraak, doodloop.

pe'tition [pi'tisjǝn] *s.* (-*s*) versoek; petisie.

'petrify ['petrifai] *ww.* ('*petrified*) versteen.

'petrol ['petrol] *s.* petrol; **pe'troleum** *s.* petroleum, lampolie.

'petticoat ['petikout] *s.* (-*s*) onderrok; vrou.

'petty ['peti] *bnw.* niksbeduidend, klein; **'pettiness** *s.* beuselagtigheid; kleingeestigheid.

'petulance ['petjoelǝns] *s.* knorrigheid; **'petulant** *bnw.* knorrig, kriewelrig.

'pew ['pjōē] *s.* (-*s*) kerkbank.

'pewter ['pjōētǝ] *s.* tin; tingoed, piouter.

'phalanx ['fælænks] *s.* (-*es*) falanks.

'phantasy = **fantasy**.

'phantom ['fæntǝm] *s.* (-*s*) spook, skim.

pharma'cology [fāmǝ'kolǝdzji] *s.* artsenyleer, farmakologie; **pharmaco'peia** *s.* [fāmǝkǝ'piǝ] aptekersboek; **'pharmacy** *s.* apteek.

'pharynx ['færinks] *s.* (-*es*) keelholte, fariiks.

'phase ['fyz] *s.* (-*s*) stadium, toestand, fase.

'pheasant ['feznt] *s.* fisant.

'phenol ['finol] *s.* karbolsuur.

phe'nomenon [fi'nominǝn] *s.* (*phe-'nomena*) verskynsel; wonder; **phe-'nomenal** *bnw.* fenomenaal; verbasend.

'phial ['faiǝl] *s.* flessie.

phi'lander [fi'lændǝ] *ww.* (-*ed*) vry, flirt.

phi'lanthropy [fi'lænthrǝpi] *s.* liefdadigheid, filantropie.

phi'lately [fi'lætǝli] *s.* versameling van posseëls.

phi'lology [fi'lolǝdzji] *s.* taalkunde, filologie.

phi'losophy [fi'losǝfi] *s.* wysbegeerte; **phi'losopher** *s.* wysgeer; **philo'sophical** *bnw.* wysgerig; gelate.

'philtre ['filtǝ] *s.* (-*s*) minnedrank.

phlegm ['flem] *s.* slym; fluim; **phleg'matic** *bnw.* flegmaties.

'phone ['foun] *s.* telefoon; *ww.* (-*d*) telefoneer, oplui.

pho'netics [fō'netiks] *s.* fonetiek, klankleer.

'phoney ['founi] *bnw.* koddig; oneg; vals.

'phonogram ['founǝghræm] *s.* (-*s*) fonogram.

'phosphate ['fosfyt] *s.* (-*s*) fostaat.

'phosphorous ['fosfǝrǝs] *s.* fosfor; **phospho'rescent** *bnw.* glimmend.

'photo ['foutǝ] *s.* (-*s*) foto; ugl. **photograph**; **- flash bulb** *s.* fotoflitslamp.

'photograph ['foutǝghrāf] *s.* (-*s*) portret, foto; **pho'tographer** *s.* fotograaf; **pho'tography** *s.* fotografie; **photo'graphic** *bnw.* fotografies; **photogra'vure** *s.* fotogravure.

'phrase ['fryz] *s.* (-*s*) segswyse,

uitdrukking, frase; **phrase'ology** s. bewoording, woordkeus.

phre'nology [fri'nolədʒi] s. skedelleer.

'phthisis ['thaisis] s. myntering.

phyl'loxera [fi'loksiərə] s. druifluis.

'physic ['fizik] s. medisyne; **-s** s. natuurkunde; **-al** bnw. fisies; **phy'sician** s. geneesheer; **-ist** s. natuurkundige.

physi'ognomy [fizi'onəmi] s. gelaat, gesig, voorkome.

physi'ology [fizi'olədʒi] s. fisiologie.

'physique ['fizik] s. liggaamsbou.

'piano ['pjænou] s. (-s) klavier, piano.

'piccalilli ['pikəlili] s. atjar.

'piccaninny ['pikənini] s. (*'piccaninnies*) klonkie.

pick ['pik] s. (-s) pik, kielhouer; keuse; ww. (-ed) pik, kap; kies; **-pocket** s. goudief; **-up** (*radar*) s. beeldopnemer.

'pick-a-back ['pikəbæk] bw. op die rug; abba.

'pickaxe ['pikæks] s. (-s) kielhouer.

'picket ['pikit] s. (-s) brandwag; paal.

'pickle ['pikl] s. pekel; **-s** s. atjar, suur.

'picnic ['piknik] s. (-s) piekniek.

'picture ['pikstjə] s. (-s) prent, skildery; **pic'torial** bnw. skilderagtig; **pictu'resque** bnw. skilderagtig.

pie ['pai] s. (-s) pastei; **-bald** bnw. bont.

'piece ['pis] s. (-s) stuk, deel, lap; geskut; ww. (-d) saamvoeg; **-meal** bnw. & bw. stuksgewyse.

pier [piə] s. (-s) hawehoof.

'pierce ['piəs] ww. (-d) deursteek, deurboor.

'piety ['paiəti] s. piëteit, verering.

'piffle ['pifl] s. twak, kaf, bog.

'pig ['pigh] s. (-s) vark; varkvleis; smeerlap; **-'headed** bnw. koppig, dwars; **-skin** s. varkleer; **-sty** s. varkhok; **-tail** s. pruikstert, haarvlegsel.

'pigeon ['pidʒin] s. (-s) duif; **-hole** s. skuiwergat; briewebus; hokkie.

'pigment ['pighmənt] s. kleurstof, pigment.

'pigweed ['pighwid] n. misbredie.

'pike ['paik] s. (-s) spies; snoek.

'pilchard ['piltsjəd] s. (-s) sardientjie.

'pile ['pail] s. (-s) paal; stapel; pluis; **-s** s. aambeie; ww. hel; **piling** helwerk; **piling stake** s. heipaal.

pilfer ['pilfə] ww. (-ed) ontfutsel, steel; **-er** s. dief.

'pilgrim ['pilghrim] s. (-s) pelgrim; **-age** s. pelgrimstog.

pill ['pil] s. (-s) pil.

'pillage ['pilidʒj] ww. (-d) plunder; s. plundering.

'pillar ['pilə] s. (-s) pilaar, suil; **-box** s. briewebus.

'pillion ['piljən] s. (-s) vrouesaal; agtersaaltjie.

'pillory ['piləri] s. (*'pillories*) skandpaal.

'pillow ['pilou] s. (-s) kussing; **-case** s. kussingsloop.

'pilot ['pailət] s. (-s) stuurman, gids, loods, vlieënier; **-** s. klik-.

'pimple ['pimpl] s. (-s) puisie; **-d** bnw. puisterig.

pin ['pin] s. (-s) speld; nael; stif; spyker; ww. (-ned) vassteek, vasspyker; **-cushion** s. speldekussing.

'pinafore ['pinəfô] s. (-s) voorskoot.

'pincers ['pinsəs] s. knyptang, tang.

pinch ['pintzj] s. (-es) knyp, knypie; snuifie; nood; verleentheid; ww. (-ed) knyp, knel; besuinig.

'pine ['pain] s. (-s) denneboom; ww. (-d) kwyn; **-apple** s. pynappel; **- tar** s. denneteer.

'pinion ['pinjən] s. (-s) vleuel, vlerk; slagveer; wiek.

pink ['pink] s. ligrooskleur; grasangelier; pieng; ontstekingsklop.

'pinnacle ['pinəkl] s. (-s) torinkie; toppunt.

'pinprick ['pinprik] s. (-s)speldeprik.

pint ['paint] s. (-s) pint.

pio'neer [paiə'niə] s. (-s) baanbreker; pionier.

'pious ['paiəs] bnw. vroom.

pip ['pip] s. piep; pit.

'pipe ['paip] s. (-s) pyp; buis; fluit; ww. (-d) piep; omboor; fluitspeel; **-r** s. fluitspeler; **'piping** s. fluitspel; boorsel; pype.

pi'pette [pi'pet] s. (-s) pipet.

'pique ['pik] s. wrok, hekel, misnoeë; **'piquancy** s. skerpheid, pikanterie; **'piquant** bnw. skerp, pikant.

'pirate ['paiərit] s. (-s) seerower; rowerskip; **'piracy** s. seeroof.

'pistol ['pistl] s. (-s) pistool, rewolwer.

'piston ['pistn] s. (-s) suier, klep; **-ring** s. suierveer, suierring; **-rod** s. suierstang.

pit ['pit] s. (-s) put, kuil; **-fall** s. vanggat, val.

pitch ['pitsj] s. (-s) pik; baan; toonhoogte; helling. ww. (-ed) teer; opslaan; toon aangee; kampeer; steek; **-dark** bnw. pikdonker; **-er** s. kruik; **-fork** s. gaffel, goolgaffel.

pith ['pith] s. pit, kern; murg; wese; krag; **-less** bnw. futloos.

'pittance ['pitəns] s. toelagie.

'pitted ['pitd] bnw. ingevreet, pokdalig; **'pitting** s. invreting.

'pity ['piti] s. medelye, jammerte; **'piteous** bnw. jammerlik, ellendig; **'pitiable** bnw. bejammerenswaardig; **'pitiful** bnw. ellendig, treurig; **'pitiless** bnw. wreed.

'pivot ['pivət] s. (-s) spil.

'placable ['plykəbl] bnw. versoenbaar, inskiklik.

'placard ['plækəd] s. (-s) plakkaat.

pla'cate [plə'kyt] ww. (-d) paai, versoen.

'place ['plys] s. (-s) plek, plaas, dorp; huis; stand; ww. (-d) neersit, regsit; belê; aan betrekking help; **-kick** s. stelskop; **-r** s. mineraalgrond.

pla'centa [plə'sentə] s. nageboorte.

'placid ['plæsid] bnw. vreedsaam, stil, kalm.

'plagiarism ['plydzjərizəm] s. plagiaat.

'plague ['plygh] s. (-s) plaag, pes; ww. (-d) verpes.

plain ['plyn] s. (-s) vlakte; bnw. (-er, -est) duidelik, helder; bw. duidelik; -ly bw. duidelik; **-spoken** bnw. rondborstig.

plaint ['plynt] s. (-s) aanklag, klag; -iff s. klaer.

plait ['plæt] s. (-s) vlegsel, plooi.

plan ['plæn] s. (-s) plan; voorneme; metode; skets.

'plane ['plyn] s. (-s) plataanboom; skaaf; vlak, peil; vliegtuig; ww. (-d) vlieg; skawe.

'planet ['plænit] s. (-s) planeet.

plank ['plænk] s. (-s) plank.

plant ['plânt] s. (-s) plant, gewas; masjinerie, gereedskap; aanleg; ww. (-ed) beplant, vestig; **plan'tation** s. plantasie.

plaque ['plâk] s. (-s) medalje.

'plaster ['plâstə] s. pleister; ww. (-ed) bepleister.

'plaster of paris ['plâstəv'pæris] s. gebrande gips; **- bandage** s. gipsverband; **- shears** s. gipsskêr; **- splint** s. gipsspalk.

'plastic ['plæstik] bnw. plasties; **plas'ticity** bnw. plastisiteit; **'plasticine** s. boetseerklei.

'plate ['plyt] s. (-s) plaat; bord; tafelsilwer, goudwerk; bekerwedren; ww. (-d) versilwer, verguld.

'plateau ['plætou] s. (-s) plato, tafelland, hoogvlakte.

plate 'glass ['plyt 'ghlâs] s. spieëlglas.

platform ['plætfôm] s. (-s) verhoog; perron; beleid.

'platinum ['plætinəm] s. platina.

'platitude ['plætitjôēd] s. gemeenplaas.

'plausible ['plôzəbl] bnw. aanneemlik.

play ['ply] s. (-s) spel; vermaak; toneelstuk; ww. (-ed) speel, baljaar; bespeel; **-er** s. speler; **-ful** bnw. uitgelate, spelerig; **-ground** s. speelgrond; **-house** s. skouburg; **-wright** s. toneelskrywer.

'playtime ['plytaim] s. (-s) speeltyd, pouse.

'plaything ['plything] s. (-s) speelding, tydverdryf.

plea ['pli] s. (-s) pleidooi; **-d** ww. (-ed) pleit, bepleit; **-ding** s. pleit, pleidooi.

'please ['pliz] ww. (-d) behaag, genoeë verskaf; **-d** bnw. tevrede, voldaan; **'pleasance** s. plesier, genot; **'pleasant** bnw. aangenaam; **'pleasantry** s. geestigheid; **'pleasing** bnw. aangenaam; **'pleasure** s. genot.

pleat ['plit] s. (-s) plooi.

'plebiscite ['plebisit] s. (-s) volkstemming.

'plectrum ['plektrəm] s. (-s) plektron, krappertjie.

'pledge ['pledzj] s. (-s) pand; dekking; belofte; ww. (-d) verpand, beloof; **-r** s. pandgewer; **-e** [pled'zji] s. pandhouer, pandjiesbaas.

'plenary ['plinəri] bnw. volkome, onbeperk.

'plenty ['plenti] s. oorvloed; bw. oorvloedig; **'plentiful** bnw. oorvloedig.

'pleonasm ['pliənæzəm] s. pleonasme.

ple'thora ['ple'thourə] s. volbloedigheid.

'pleura ['ploeərə] s. borsvlie; **'pleural** bnw. borsvlies-.

'pleurisy ['ploerisi] s. borsvliesontsteking.

'pliant ['plaiənt] bnw. buigsaam, slap.

'pliers ['plaiəz] s. knyptang.

plight ['plait] ww. (-ed) verpand, beloof; s. belofte, verlowing; toestand.

plod ['plod] ww. (-ded) swoeg, beur, sloof; **-der** s. ploeteraar.

plot ['plot] s. (-s) erf, bouperseel, hoewe; intrige; komplot; ww. (-ted) skets; saamsweer.

plough ['plau] s. (-s) ploeg; ww. (-ed) ploeë, ploeg; **-share** s. ploegskaar.

'plover ['plʌvə] s. (-s) waterkiewietjie; strandloper.

pluck ['plʌk] s. ruk, pluk; slag; moed; ww. (-ed) kaalpluk; bedrieg; **-y** bnw. moedig.

plug ['plʌgh] s. (-s) prop, pluisie; pruimpie; ww. (-ged) toestop; beskiet.

plum ['plʌm] s. (-s) pruim; die beste.

'plumage ['plôēmidzj] s. vere.

'plumb ['plʌm] s. skietlood; out of - nie loodreg.

'plumber ['plʌmə] s. (-s) loodgieter.

'plume ['plôēm] s. (-s) pluim, veer(bos); **'plumage** s. vere; **'plumose** bnw. gepluim; **'plumy** bnw. pluimagtig.

'plummet ['plʌmit] s. (-s) dieplood, skietlood, peillood.

plump ['plʌmp] bnw. (-er, -est) dik, rond, vet; mollig.

'plunder ['plʌndə] s. roof; ww. (-ed) beroof; **-age** s. buit.

'plunge ['plʌndzj] s. sprong; indompeling; waagstuk; **-r** s. suier.

'plural ['ploeərəl] s. (-s) meervoud.

plus ['plʌs] s. (-ses) plusteken.

plush ['plʌsj] s. (-es) pluis, pluche, verweel.

'plutocrat ['plôētōkræt] s. kapitalis, plutokraat.

ply ['plai] s. ('plies) laag, vou; dikte; draad; ww. ('plied) hanteer; gebruik; oefen.

'plywood ['plaiwood] s. laaghout.

pneu'matic [njôē'mætik] bnw. lug-, wind-, lugdruk-; **- brake** s. lugrem; **- drill** s. lugboor.

pneu'monia [njōē'mounjə] s. long-ontsteking.

poach ['poutsj] ww. (-ed) eier kaal kook; steel; stroop; -er s. stroper, wilddief.

pock ['pok] s. (-s) pokkie.

'pocket ['pokit] s. (-s) sak; holte; ww. (-ed) in die sak steek; -book s. sakboekie; - expenses s. geringe uitgawe; - money s. sakgeld.

pod ['pod] s. (-s) peul; ww. (-ded) uitdop.

'podge ['podzj] s. dikkerd; 'podgy bnw. dik, vet.

'poem ['pouim] s. (-s) gedig.

'poet ['pouit] s. (-s) digter; po'etic bnw. digterlik; -ry s. poësie, digkuns.

'poignancy ['poinənsi] s. skerpheid; 'poignant bnw. skerp, pynlik.

point ['point] s. (-s) puntjie, punt; stippeltjie; eienskap; wissel; ww. (-ed) skerp maak, toelig; -blank bw. botweg; -duty s. verkeersdiens; -ed bnw. skerp; gevat; -er s. stok, wyser; jaghond; -less bnw. stomp; laf; -sman s. wisselwagter.

'poise ['poiz] s. ewewig; houding; ww. (-d) balanseer.

'poison ['poizn] s. (-s) gif; ww. (-ed) vergiftig; -ing s. vergifting; -ous bnw. giftig.

'poke ['pouk] s. (-s) stamp, stoot; tuit; -r s. pookyster; poker(spel); -bonnet s. tuitkappie; 'poky bnw. nou, beknop; vuil.

'pole ['poul] s. (-s) pool; paal; 'polar bnw. pool-; 'polarize ww. (-d) polariseer; po'larity s. polariteit; -cat s. muishond; -star s. poolster.

po'lemic [pō'lemik] s. polemiek, pennestryd; -s s. polemiek; 'polemize ww polemiseer.

po'lice [pə'lis] s. polisie; -court s. magistraatshof; -man s. diener, konstabel; -station s. polisiepos, klagkantoor.

'policy ['polisi] s. ('policies) beleid; polis.

'polish ['polisj] ww. (-ed) skoonmaak, poleer, poets; s. (-es) poetsmiddel, waks; glans.

po'lite [pə'lait] bnw. beleefd, vriendelik.

po'litic [pə'litik] bnw. verstandig, slim; -al bnw. staatkundig; poli-'tician s. politikus; -s s. politiek; staatsleer.

'polka ['polkə] s. polka.

poll ['poul] s. (-s) kop; stemming; uw. snoei; bnw. poenskop(bees); -ing s. stemming; -tax s. hoofbelasting.

'pollen ['polin] s. stuifmeel; -ate ww. bestuif.

'pollinate ['polinyt] ww. (-d) bestuif; vgl. pollen.

po'lute [pə'lōēt] ww. (-d) besoedel, besmet; pol'lution s. besmetting, bevlekking.

'polo ['poulou] s. polo.

polo'naise]polə'nyz] s. polonaise.

po'lony [pə'louni] s. (po'lonies) polonie, wors.

pol'troon [pol'trōēn] s. (-s) lafaard; lamsak.

'polyandry ['poliændri] s. veelmannery.

po'lygamy [po'lighəmi] s. veelwywery.

'polyglot ['polighlot] s. (-s) veeltalige persoon.

'polyp ['polip] s. (-s) poliep.

'polysyllable ['polisiləbl] s. meer-lettergrepige woord.

'polytheism ['polithiizəm] s. politeïsme, veelgodery.

po'made [pə'mād] s. (-s) pomade, haarolie.

pomp ['pomp] s. prag, praal; pom'posity s. vertoon; -ous bnw. luisterryk.

'pompom ['pompom] s. pom-pom, bommeksim.

'pompon ['pômpông] s. pompon, kwassie.

pond ['pond] s. (-s) dam, poel.

'ponder ['pondə] ww. (-ed) bepeins, oorweeg; -able bnw. weegbaar; -ous bnw. swaar.

'poniard ['ponjəd] s. (-s) dolk.

pon'tifical [pon'tifikəl] bnw. pouslik, hoëpriesterlik.

pon'toon [pon'tōēn] s. (-s) pont.

'pony ['pouni] s. ('ponies) ponie.

'poodle ['pōēdl] s. (-s) poedelhond.

pool ['pōēl] s. (-s) dam, poel, plas, kuil; vereniging; pot; ww. grawe; winste deel; verenig.

'poop ['pōēp] s. agterstewe, agterdek.

poor ['poeə] bnw. arm; swak; skraal; -ly bw. min, ellendig; bnw. sleg.

pop ['pop] s. knal, plof; -corn s. springmielies; -gun s. propgeweer.

'pope ['poup] s. pous; -ry s. papistery; 'popish bnw. paaps.

'poplar ['poplə] s. (-s) poppelier.

'poplin ['poplin] s. popelin.

'poppy ['popi] s. ('poppies) papawer.

'populace ['popjoeləs] s. gepeupel; menigte; 'popular bnw. populêr, gewild; 'popularize ww. gewild maak; popu'larity s. gewildheid; 'populate ww. (-d) bevolk; popu'lation s. bevolking; 'populous bnw. volkryk.

'porcelain ['pōslin] s. porselein, breekgoed.

porch ['pōtsj] s. (-es) portaal.

'porcupine ['pōkjoepain] s. (-s) ystervark.

'pore ['pō] s. (-s) sweetgaatjie, porie; ww. (-d) kyk, staar; 'porous bnw. poreus.

pork ['pōk] s. varkvleis; -er s. slagvark.

por'nography [pô'noghrəfi] s. pornografie.

'porpoise ['pôpəs] s. (-s) bruinvis, seevark.

'porridge ['poridz] s. pap.

'porringer ['poringdzjə] s. (-s) kommetjie, bakkie, diepbord.

port ['pôt] s. (-s) hawe; poort;

houding; bakboord; portwyn; -able
bnw. draagbaar; -age *s.* vervoerloon;
-al *s.* poort; -al-vein *s.* poortaar;
port'cullis *s.* valdeur; -er *s.* portier;
draer.

por'tend ['pô'tend] *ww.* (-ed) voorspel, beteken.

'porter ['pôtə] *s.* (-s) deurbewaarder;
kruier; -age *s.* kruiersloon.

port'folio [pôt'fouljou] *s.* (-s)
portfeulje.

'porthole ['pôthoul] *s.* (-s) patrys-
poort.

'portico ['pôtikou] *s.* portiek.

'portion ['pôsjən] *s.* (-s) deel, porsie,
aandeel.

'portly ['pôtli] *bnw.* ('portlier, 'port-
liest) geset; deftig.

'portrait ['pôtrit] *s.* (-s) portret; -ure
s. portret, afbeelding; por'tray *ww.*
(-ed) skilder, beskrywe.

'pose ['pouz] *s.* (-s) houding; *ww.*
(-d) poseer, houding aanneem; -r *s.*
raaisel, strikvraag.

po'sition [pə'zisjən] *s.* (-s) posisie,
stelling.

'positive ['pozətiv] *bnw.* positief,
bepaald; *s.* stellende trap.

'posse ['posi] *s.* polisiemag.

pos'sess [pə'zes] *ww.* (-ed) besit, eien;
-ion *s.* besitting, eiendom; -ive
bnw. besittend; -or *s.* eienaar.

'possible ['posəbl] *bnw.* moontlik; *s.*
uiterste; 'possibly *bw.* dalk; possi-
'bility *s.* moontlikheid.

'post ['poust] *s.* (-s) paal, pos,
poskantoor; posisie; fort; *ww.* (-ed)
pos; jaag; wagte opstel; -age *s.*
posgeld; postal *bnw.* pos-; -card *s.*
poskaart; -date *ww.* vooruit dateer;
-er *s.* aanplakbiljet; -free *bnw.*
franko, posvry; -humous *bnw.*
nagelate, posthuum; -man *s.* briewe-
besteller; -mark *s.* posstempel;
-master *s.* posmeester; -meridian *s.*
namiddag; -'mortem *s.* lykskouing;
-office *s.* poskantoor; -'pone *ww.*
(-d) uitstel; -'ponement *s.* uitstel;
-script *s.* naskrif.

pos'terior [pos'tiəriə] *s.* agterste;
bnw. later, agter-.

pos'terity [pos'teriti] *s.* nageslag.

'postern ['poustən] *s.* agterdeur
sydeur.

pos'til(l)ion [pəs'tiljən] *s.* voorryer.

'postulate ['postjoelyt] *s.* stelling;
ww. (-d) veronderstel, postuleer;
postu'lation *s.*

'posture ['postsjə] *s.* (-s) houding,
postuur.

'posy ['pouzi] *s.* ('posies) ruiker,
blomtuil.

pot ['pot] *s.* (-s) kan; pot; blompot;
ww. (-ted) inmaak; neerskiet; in-
palm; -luck *s.* wat die pot verskaf;
-sherd *s.* potskerf; -shot *s.* potskoot;
-tage *s.* sop; -ter *s.* pottebakker;
-tery *s.* pottebakkery.

'potash ['potæsj] *s.* = potassium.

pot'assium [pə'tæsjəm] *s.* kalium.

po'tato [pə'tytou] *s.* (-es) ertappel.

'potency ['poutənsl] *s.* mag, vermoë;
'potent *bnw.* sterk; 'potentate *s.* (-s)
heerser, potentaat; po'tential *bnw.*
moontlik; po'tentiality *s.* moontlikheid.

'pothole ['pothoul] *s.* (-s) slaggat;
kolkgat, maalgat.

'potion ['pousjən] *s.* (-s) drank.

pouch ['pautsj] *s.* (-es) sak, beurs,
buidel.

'poultice ['poultis] *s.* (-s) pap.

'poultry ['poultri] *s.* pluimvee;
'poulterer *s.* pluimveehandelaar.

'pounce ['pauns] *ww.* (-d) neerskiet
op, bevlie.

pound ['paund] *s.* (-s) pond; *ww.*
(-ed) skut; fynstamp; -age *s.* skut-
geld; -er *s.* stamper; -keeper *s.*
skutmeester.

pour ['pô] *ww.* (-ed) giet, gooi,
skink, stort, stroom.

pout ['paut] *ww.* (-ed) pruil, dikmond
wees.

'poverty ['povəti] *s.* armoede,
gebrek; -'stricken *bnw.* arm.

'powder ['paudə] *s.* (-s) poeier; stof;
kruit; *ww.* (-ed) poeier; verpoeier;
- horn *s.* kruithoring; - magazine *s.*
kruithuis; -y *bnw.* poeieragtig.

'powder-puff ['paudəpʌf] *s.* (-s)
poeierkwas.

'power ['pauə] *s.* (-s) mag, krag;
vermoë; gesag; -ful *bnw.* sterk;
invloedryk; -less *bnw.* magteloos;
-station *s.* sentrale; - brake *s.* (-s)
kragrem; - steering *s.* kragstuur.

'practice ['præktis] *s.* (-s) praktyk,
gewoonte; uitvoering; 'practicable
bnw. moontlik, uitvoerbaar, doenlik;
'practical *bnw.* prakties, doelmatig;
'practically *bw.* feitlik; prac'tition-
er *s.* arts.

'practise ['præktis] *ww.* (-d) beoefen;
praktiseer; oefen.

'prairie ['prêri] *s.* ('prairies) prairie,
grasvlakte.

'praise ['pryz] *s.* lof, roem; *ww.* (-d)
loof, eer; -worthy *bnw.* loflik.

pram ['præm] *s.* (-s) kinder-
waentjie.

'prance ['prâns] *ww.* (-d) bokspring,
pronk.

prank ['prænk] *s.* (-s) poets, kaskenade.

'prate ['pryt] *ww.* (-d) babbel, klets.

'prattle ['prætl] *ww.* (-d) babbel,
klets.

prawn ['prôn] *s.* (-s) seegarnaal.

pray ['pry] *ww.* (-ed) bid; smeek;
versoek; -er *s.* (-s) gebed; prayer
meeting *s.* biduur.

preach ['pritsj] *ww.* (-ed) preek; *s.*
preek; -er *s.* prediker.

pre- ['pri-] *voorvoegsel* voor vooraf,
voor-.

'pre'amble [priæmbl] *s.* (-s)
inleiding, voorrede.

pre'carious [pri'kêəriəs] *bnw.* onseker, wisselvallig.

pre'caution [pri'kôsjən] *s.* voorsorg
(maatreël); -ary *bnw.* voorsorgs-.

pre'cede [pri'sïd] *ww.* (-d) voorgaan, voorrang kry; -nce *s.* voorrang; -nt ['prisident] *s.* voorbeeld, presedent; **pre'ceding** *bnw.* vorige.

'precept [prisept] *s.* (-s) bevel, voorskrif.

'precinct ['prïsinkt] *s.* gebied; -s grenslyn.

'precious ['presjəs] *bnw.* kosbaar; *bw.* drommels.

'precipice ['presipis] *s.* (-s) afgrond.

pre'cipitate [pri'sipityt] *s.* besinksel, neerslag; *ww.* (-d) neerstort; versnel, bespoedig; neerslaan, besink; *bnw.* halsoorkop, gejaag; **pre'cipitance** *s.* oorhaasting; **precipi'tation** *s.* neerslag; oorhaasting.

'précis ['prysï] *s.* (-) opsomming, oorsig.

pre'cise [pri'saïs] *bnw.* presies, sekuur; juis; -ly *bw.* juistement; **pre'cision** *s.* juistheid.

pre'clude [pri'klöëd] *ww.* (-d) uitsluit.

pre'cocity [pri'kositi] *s.* vroegrypheid; **pre'cocious** *bnw.* [pri'kousjəs] vroegryp, oulik.

'pre-cooked ['prï-koekd] *bnw.* klaargaar-.

pre'cursor [pri'kə̀sə] *s.* (-s) voorloper; **pre'cursory** *bnw.* inleidend.

'predatory ['predətəri] *bnw.* roofsugtig, plundersiek.

'predecessor ['prïdisesə] *s.* (-s) voorganger.

predesti'nation [prïdesti'nysjən] *s.* uitverkiesing.

pre'dicament [pri'dikəmənt] *s.* moeilike posisie.

'predicate ['predikyt] *s.* (-s) gesegde; eienskap.

pre'dict [pri'dikt] *ww.* (-ed) voorspel.

pre'dominate [pri'dominyt] *ww.* (-d) oorheers; **pre'dominant** *bnw.* oorheersend.

preen ['prïn] *ww.* (-ed) die vere gladstryk.

'preface ['prefis] *s.* voorrede, voorwoord.

'prefect ['prïfekt] *s.* hoof, prefek.

pre'fer [pri'fə̀] *ww.* (-red) verkies; indien; **'preferable** *bnw.* verkieslik; **'preference** *s.* voorkeur.

'prefix ['prïfiks] *s.* voorvoegsel.

'pregnable ['preghnəbl] *bnw.* kwesbaar, verowerbaar.

'prejudice ['predzjoedis] *s.* vooroordeel; -d *bnw.* bevooroordeeld.

'prelate ['prelit] *s.* (-s) prelaat, biskop, kerkvader.

pre'liminary [pri'liminəri] *s.* (**pre'liminaries**) voorafgaande, preliminêr.

'prelude ['preljöëd] *s.* (-s) voorspel, prelude.

'premier ['premjə] *s.* (-s) eerste minister; *bnw.* eerste.

'premise ['premis] *s.* (-s) stelling, premis.

'premium ['prïmjəm] *s.* (-s) premie.

premo'nition [prïmö'nisjən] *s.* voorteken.

pre'pare [pri'pêə] *ww.* (-d) voorberei; **prepa'ration** *s.* voorbereiding; **pre'paratory** *bnw.* voorbereidend.

pre'ponderate [pri'pondəryt] *ww.* (-d) oorweeg, oortref; **pre'ponderance** *s.* oorwig; **pre'ponderant** *bnw.* oorweënd.

prepo'sition [prepə'zisjən] *s.* voorsetsel.

pre'posterous [pri'postərəs] *bnw.* ongerymd, gek.

'prepuce ['prïpjöës] *s.* voorhuid.

'prerequisite ['prï'rïkwizit] *s.* (-s) voorvereiste.

pre'rogative [pri'roghətiv] *s.* (-s) prerogatief, reg.

'presage ['presidzj] *s.* (-s) voorteken.

pre'scribe [pris'kraïb] *ww.* (-d) voorskryf; **pre'scription** *s.* voorskrif, resep, preskripsie.

'presence ['prezns] *s.* aanwesigheid; **'present** *bnw.* aanwesig; huidig; *s.* (-s) geskenk.

pre'sent [pri'zent] *ww.* (-ed) aanbied; **presen'tation** *s.* aanbieding.

pre'sentiment [pri'zentimənt] *s.* voorgevoel.

'presently ['prezntli] *bw.* aanstons.

pre'serve [pri'zə̀v] *ww.* (-d) inlê; bewaar; *s.* konfyt; ingelegde vrugte.

pre'side [pri'zaïd] *ww.* (-d) voorsit, lei, bestuur.

'president ['prezidənt] *s.* (-s) voorsitter; president; **presi'dential** *bnw.* voorsitters-.

press ['pres] *s.* druk, drukte, menigte; pers, drukkery; *ww.* (-ed) druk, platdruk; druk uitoefen; -ing *bnw.* dringend; -man *s.* joernalis, -sure *s.* druk, drukking, spanning; **pressure indicator** *s.* drukwyser.

pres'tige [pres'tïzj] *s.* reputasie; gesag, prestige.

pre'sume [pri'zjöëm] *ww.* (-d) veronderstel, vermoed; **pre'sumably** *bw.* vermoedelik; **pre'suming** *bnw.* verwaand; **pre'sumption** *s.* vermoede, veronderstelling; **pre'sumptive** *bnw.* waarskynlik; **pre'sumptuous** *bnw.* verwaand; **presumption of death** vermoede van dood.

pre'tend [pri'tend] *ww.* (-ed) voorgee, beweer; **pre'tence** *s.* skyn, voorwendsel; -er *s.* pretendent; -ing *bnw.* aanmatigend; **pre'tension** *s.* aanspraak; **pre'tentious** *bnw.* aanmatigend.

'preterite ['pretərit] *s.* verledetyd.

'pretext ['prïtekst] *s.* voorwendsel.

'pretty ['priti] *bnw.* (**'prettier**, **'prettiest**) mooi, lief; *bw.* taamlik.

pre'vail [pri'vyl] *ww.* (-ed) die oorhand kry; heers; oorreed; -ing *bnw.* heersend, algemeen; **'prevalence** *s.* oorwig; algemeenheid; **'prevalent** *bnw.* oorwegend, algemeen.

prevari'cation [prïværi'kysjən] *s.* bontpratery.

pre'vent [pri'vent] *ww.* (-ed) verhinder; voorkom; **-ion** s. verhindering; afwering; **-(a)tive** bnw. afwerend.

'**previous** ['privjəs] bnw. vorige; voorbarig; bw. voordat; **-ly** bw. vooraf.

prey ['pry] s. (-s) prooi; buit; ww. (-ed) roof, plunder.

price ['prais] s. (-s) prys, waarde; ww. (-d) prysmaak; **- list** s. pryslys; **-less** bnw. onskatbaar.

prick ['prik] s. (-s) steek, prik(kel); kwelling; ww. (-ed) prik, steek; aanspoor; kwel; **-er** s. priem, els; **-le** s. prikkel, doring, pen; **-ly** bnw. doringrig, prikkelend.

'**pride** ['praid] s. hoogmoed.

priest ['prist] s. priester, geestelike; **-hood** s. priesterskap; **-ly** bnw. priesterlike; **-ridden** bnw. onder priesterlike dwang.

prig ['prigh] s. pedant, wysneus; **-gish** bnw. eiewys.

prim ['prim] bnw. netjies; styf, aanstellerig.

'**prima-'donna** ['primə'donə] s. (-s) hoofsangeres in opera.

'**primal** ['praiməl] bnw. primitief, grond-.

'**primary** ['praiməri] bnw. vroegste, oorspronklike; primère; elementêre; vernaamste.

'**primate** ['praimit] s. aartsbiskop, primaat.

'**prime** ['praim] s. begin; bnw. vernaamste, prima; primêr; ww. (-d) laai; inpomp; grondlaag verf; **-r** s. leesboekie; **pri'meval** bnw. primitief, oer-; '**priming** s. pankruit; grondverf; '**primitive** bnw. eerste, primitief.

prince ['prins] s. (-s) prins, vors, heerser; **-ly** bnw. vorstelik; '**princess** s. prinses.

'**principal** ['prinsəpl] s. (-s) hoof; bnw. belangrikste; **-ly** bw. vernaamlik.

'**principle**]'prinsəpl] s. (-s) beginsel; prinsiepe; **-d** bnw. beginselvas.

print ['print] s. druk; teken; prent; ww. (-ed) afdruk, merk, stempel; druk; **-er** s. drukker; **-ing** s. drukwerk; **-ing-ink** s. drukink.

'**prior** ['praiə] bnw. & bw. vroeër, voor(afgaande); **pri'ority** s. voorkeur.

priory ['praiəri] s. kloosterhoof.

'**prise** vgl. **prize**.

prism ['prizəm] s. (-s) prisma.

'**prison** ['prizn] s. (-s) gevangenis, tronk; **-er** s. gevangene, bandiet.

'**private** ['praivit] bnw. privaat, persoonlik, s. gewone soldaat, manskap; '**privacy** s. afsondering, stilte, geheimhouding; **-ly** bw. privaat, onder vier oë; **pri'vation** s. ontbering, gebrek.

'**privilege** ['privilidzj] s. (-s) voorreg; **-d** bnw. bevoorreg.

'**privy** ['privi] s. gemakhuisie; bnw. geheim.

'**prize** ['praiz] s. (-s) prys; buit; ww. (-d) waardeer, op prys stel; prysmaak; **-fight** s. vuisgeveg.

pro ['prou] = **professional**.

pro ['prou] voors. voor; **- and con** voor en teen.

'**probable** ['probəbl] bnw. waarskynlik; '**probably** bw. vermoedelik.

pro'bation [prə'bysjən] s. proeftyd; **-ary** bnw. proef-; **-er** s. proefleerling.

'**probe** ['proub] ww. (-d) peil, ondersoek, nagaan.

'**problem** ['problem] s. (-s) probleem, vraagstuk; raaisel; **proble'matic** bnw. onseker, problematies.

pro'ceed [prə'sid] ww. (-d) voortgaan; **pro'cedure** s. handelwyse; prosedure; **-ing** s. verrigtinge; '**proceeds** s. opbrings, wins.

'**process** ['prouses] n. voortgang, ontwikkeling; metode; hofsaak; **pro'cession** s. optog.

pro'claim [prə'klym] ww. (-ed) aankondig, proklameer; **procla'mation** s. aankondiging, proklamasie.

pro'clivity [prə'kliviti] s. (pro'clivities) neiging.

pro'cure [prə'kjoeə] ww. (-d) kry, verkry; veroorsaak; **pro'curable** bnw. verkrybaar; **procu'ration** s. verkryging; volmag.

prod ['prod] s. (-s) porstok, priem, prikkel.

'**prodigal** ['prodighəl] s. verkwister.

'**prodigy** ['prodidzji] s. wondermens; **pro'digious** bnw. wonderbaarlik.

'**produce** ['prodjões] s. produkte, oes; **pro'duce** ww. (-d) opbring, oplewer; **pro'ducer** s. produsent; opvoerder; '**product** s. produk; **pro'duction** s. produksie, voortbrengsel, produk; **pro'ductive** bnw. produktief, vrugbaar.

pro'fane [prə'fyn] bnw. heidens; goddeloos; **pro'fanity** s. goddeloosheid; godslastering.

pro'fess [prə'fes] ww. (-ed) verklaar, erken; bely; aanspraak maak op; onderwys gee; **-ed** bnw. erkende; **-ion** s. verklaring, beroep; **-ional** bnw. professioneel; s. beroepspeler; **-or** s. belyer; professor, hoogleraar; **pro-fes'sorial** bnw. professoraal.

'**proffer** ['profə] ww. (-ed) aanbied.

pro'ficient [prə'fisjənt] bnw. bekwaam.

'**profile** ['proufail] s. (-s) profiel, loodregte deursnee.

'**profit** ['profit] s. wins, voordeel, nut; ww. (-ed) profiteer, wins maak; voordeel trek uit; baat; **-able** bnw. voordelig; **profi'teer** ww. woekerwins maak; **profi'teering** s. woekerwins.

'**profligate** ['proflighit] bnw. losbandig.

pro'found [prə'faund] bnw. diepgaande, deeglik, grondig; **pro'fundity** s. diepte, diepsinnigheid.

pro'fuse [prə'fjõez] bnw. mild,

kwistig; volop; **pro'fusion** s. oorvloed, oordaad.

'progeny ['prodzjini] s. nageslag.

prog'nosis [progh'nousis] s. voorspelling, prognose.

prog'nosticate [progh'nostikyt] *ww.* (-d) voorspel, aandui.

'pro'gramme ['prou'ghræm] s. (-s) program.

'progress ['proughres] s. vordering; **pro'gressive** *bnw.* progressief, s. (*radical*) verlig(te).

pro'hibit [prə'hibit] *ww.* (-ed) belet, verbied, **prohi'bition** s. verbod, drankverbod; **prohibitio'nist** s. afskaffer; -ive *bnw.* verbiedend.

project ['prodzjekt] s. (-s) plan, skema; -ile s. projektiel, bom.

pro'lific [prə'lifik] *bnw.* vrugbaar.

'pro'logue [prou'logh] s. (-s) voorspel, proloog.

pro'long [prə'long] *ww.* (-ed) verleng, uitrek.

prome'nade [promi'nād] s. (-s) wandelpad, promenade.

'prominent ['prominənt] *bnw.* voortreflik, hoog, promenent; **'prominence** s. vernaamheid; hoogte; punt.

promis'cuity [promis'kjõëiti] s. gemengdheid, verwarring.

'promise ['promis] s. (-s) belofte; *ww.* (-d) belowe; **'promising** *bnw.* belowend; **pro'missory** *bnw.* belowend; **pro'missory note** s. skuldbewys, promesse.

'promontory ['proməntri] s. ('*promontories*) kaap, voorgebergte.

pro'mote [prə'mout] *ww.* (-d) bevorder, bespoedig; promoveer; oprig; **pro'moter** s. voorstander; promotor; **pro'motion** s. bevordering, promosie.

prompt [promt] *bnw.* (-er, -est) vlug, snel, spoedig; pront; kontant; *ww.* (-ed) aanhits; besiel; voorsê; influister; -er s. voorsêer, fluisteraar; -itude s. stiptheid, prontheid.

promul'gation [proməl'ghysjən] s. bekendmaking, proklamasie.

'prone ['proun] *bnw.* vooroor, plat op die gesig, uitgestrek; - to geneig tot, onderhewig aan.

prong ['prong] s. (-s) gaffel; tand (*van vurk*).

'pronoun ['prounaun] s. (-s) voornaamwoord.

pro'nounce [prə'nauns] *ww.* (-d) uitspreek; verklaar; -ment s. verklaring; **pronunci'ation** s. uitspraak.

proof ['prõëf] s. (-s) bewys; blyk; toets; proef; *bnw.* bestand; ondeurdringbaar; *ww.* (-ed) ondeurdringbaar maak, *vgl. ook* prove; -reader s. proefleser.

prop ['prop] s. (-s) stut, steunpilaar; staatmaker.

propa'ganda [propə'ghændə] s. propaganda.

propa'gate [propə'ghyt] *ww.* (-d)

voortplant; propageer; **propa'gation** s.

pro'pel [prə'pel] *ww.* (-led) voortdryf, beweeg; -lor s. skroef.

pro'pensity [prə'pensiti] s. (*pro'pensities*) neiging; hebbelikheid.

'proper ['propə] *bnw.* eie; geskik; juis; eg; behoorlik; -ly *bw.* behoorlik, fatsoenlik; -ty s. eiendom; eienskap.

'prophet ['profit] s. (-s) profeet; **'prophecy** s. profesie, voorspelling; **'prophesy** *ww.* profeteer; **pro'phetic** *bnw.* profeties.

pro'pinquity [prə'ping-kwiti] s. (*pro'pinquities*) buurt; ooreenkoms; verwantskap.

pro'pitiate [prə'pisjiyt] *ww.* (-d) versoen; paai; **pro'pitious** *bnw.* gunstig, genadig.

pro'portion [prə'pôsjən] s. verhouding, eweredigheid; -al *bnw.* eweredig; -ally *bw.* na eweredigheid; -ate *bnw.* eweredig.

pro'pose [prə'pouz] *ww.* (-d) voorstel; **pro'posal** s. voorstel; **propo'sition** s. (-s) voorstel; stelling.

pro'pound [prə'paund] *ww.* (-ed) voorstel, voorlê.

pro'prietor [prə'praiətə] s. besitter, eienaar; **pro'prietary** s. eiendomsreg; eienaars; **proprietary item** s. eiendomsartikel; **pro'priety** s. juistheid; korrektheid.

props ['props] s. toneelbenodighede.

pro'rogue [prə'rough] *ww.* (-d) verdaag; **pro'rogation** s. verdaging.

pro'scribe [pros'kraib] *ww.* (-d) verban; voëlvryverklaar.

'prose ['prouz] s. prosa; alledaagsheid; **pro'saic** *bnw.* prosaïes, alledaags.

'prosecute ['prosikjõët] *ww.* (-d) vervolg; voortsit; **prose'cution** s. vervolging; **'prosecutor** s. vervolger; aanklaer.

'prosody ['prosədi] s. prosodie.

'prospect ['prospekt] s. (-s) uitsig; vooruitsig, hoop; **pros'pective** *bnw.* aanstaande, te wagte.

'prosper ['prospə] *ww.* (-ed) bloei, floreer; **pros'perity** s. voorspoed, welvaart; -ous *bnw.* voorspoedig, welvarend.

'prostrate ['prostryt] *bnw.* uitgestrek, plat.

pro'tect [prə'tekt] *ww.* (-ed) beskerm, vrywaar; -ion s. beskerming; -ive *bnw.* beskermend; -or s. beskermer; skerm; -orate s. protektoraat.

'protégé ['proutazjy] s. beskermeling.

'protest ['proutest] s. (-s) protes; **protes'tation** s. protes, betuiging.

'Protestant ['protistənt] s. (-s) Protestant.

protocol ['proutəkol] s. protokol, oorkonde.

'prototype ['proutətaip] s. (-s) model, prototiepe.

pro'trude [prə'tröĕd] *ww.* (-d) vooruitsteek.

'proud ['praud] *bnw.* hoogmoedig; trots; fier.

'provender ['prouvĭndə] *s.* voer, kos; proviand.

'proverb ['provŏb] *s.* (-s) spreekwoord, spreuk; -ial *bnw.* spreekwoordelik.

pro'vide [prə'vaid] *ww.* (-d) voorsien, verskaf, sorg; -d *voegw.* mits; **'providence** *s.* voorsiening, voorsorg.

'province ['provins] *s.* (-s) provinsie, gewes; **pro'vincial** *bnw.* provinsiaal.

pro'vision [prə'vizjən] *s.* (-s) voorsiening, voorsorg.

pro'viso [prə'vaizou] *s.* (-s) voorwaarde.

pro'voke [prə'vouk] *ww.* (-d) aanhits, prikkel; **provoking** *bnw.* uitdagend; **pro'vocative** *bnw.* tergend.

'provost ['provəst] *s.* hoof, opsiener, provoos.

'prow ['prau] *s.* boeg, voorstewe.

'prowess ['prauis] *s.* dapperheid, moed.

prowl ['praul] *ww.* (-ed) rondsluip.

'proximate ['proksimit] *bnw.* naaste, onmiddellik.

prox'imity [prok'simiti] *s.* nabyheid.

'proxy ['proksi] *s.* volmag; gevolmagtigde.

'prude ['prŏĕd] *s.* preutse persoon; **'prudish** *bnw.* preuts; **-ry** *s.* preutsheid.

'prudence ['prŏĕdns] *s.* versigtigheid; wysheid; **'prudent** *bnw.* versigtig; **pru'dential** *bnw.* versigtig.

'prune ['prŏĕn] *s.* (-s) gedroogde pruimedant; *ww.* (-d) snoei.

'prurience ['prŏĕriəns] *s.* wellus; **'prurient** *bnw.* wulps.

'prussic 'acid ['prʌsik'æsid] *s.* blousuur.

pry ['prai] *ww.* ('pried) loer; **-ing** *bnw.* snuffend, nuuskierig.

psalm ['sām] *s.* (-s) psalm.

'pseudo ['psjŏĕdou] *bnw.* oneg, vals, pseudo.

'psyche ['psaiki] *s.* gees, siel; **'psychic** *bnw.* psigies, geestes-.

psy'chiatry [sai'kaiətri] *s.* psigiatrie; **psy'chiater** *s.* psigiater; **psychi'atric** *bnw.* psigiatries.

psy'chology [sai'kolədzji] *s.* sielkunde; **psycho'logical** *bnw.* sielkundig; **psy'chologist** *s.* psigoloog, sielkundige.

pto'maine [tou'myn] *s.* voedsel (vergifting).

pub ['pʌb] *s.* (-s) kantien.

'puberty ['pjŏĕbəti] *s.* puberteit, geslagsrypheid.

pu'bescent [pjœ'besnt] *bnw.* donsharig.

'public ['pʌblik] *s.* publiek; **pu'blicity** *s.* publisiteit.

publi'cation [pʌbli'kysjən] *s.* (-s) publikasie; openbaarmaking.

'publish ['pʌblisj] *ww.* (-ed) publi-

seer; bekendstel; **-er** *s.* uitgewer.

'pucker ['pʌkə] *s.* (-s) plooi, vou.

'pudding ['poeding] *s.* (-s) poeding, nagereg.

'puddle ['pʌdl] *s.* modder, modderplas, klei; porrel.

'pudency ['pjoednsi] *s.* skaamte.

'puerile ['pjoeəraiļ] *bnw.* kinderagtig.

puff ['pʌf] *s.* (-ed) blaas, hyg; opswel; ophemel.

'pugilist ['pjŏĕdzjilist] *s.* bokser, vuisvegter.

pug'nacity [pʌg'næsiti] *s.* strydlustigheid; **pug'nacious** *bnw.* veglustig.

pull ['poel] *s.* ruk, pluk; trekker; eerste drukproef; teug; *ww.* (-ed) ruk, trek, roei; **-man** *s.* passasierswa; **-over** *s.* trui; **-through** *s.* deurtrekker(*geweer*).

'pullet ['poelit] *s.* (-s) hoender, kuiken.

'pulley ['poeli] *s.* (-s) katrol.

'pulmonary ['pʌlmənəri] *bnw.* long-.

pulp ['pʌlp] *s.* pap, pulp, kos (*van vrugte*).

'pulpit ['poelpit] *s.* (-s) preekstoel.

'pulse ['pʌls] *s.* (-s) pols, polsslag; peulvrug; *ww.* (-d) klop, tril; **pul'sate** *ww.* klop, tril; **pul'sation** *s.* klopping, hartslag; **pul'satory** *bnw.* kloppend.

'pulverize ['pʌlveraiz] *ww.* (-d) verpoeier.

'pumice ['pʌmis] *s.* puimsteen.

pump ['pʌmp] *s.* (-s) dansskoen; *s. & ww.* pomp.

'pumpkin ['pʌmpkin] *s.* (-s) pampoen.

pun ['pʌn] *s.* (-s) woordspeling.

punch ['pʌntsj] *s.* (-es) deurslag; dryfyster; vuisslag; pons; hanswors.

punc'tilious [pʌnk'tiliəs] *bnw.* punteneurig, vol flemies.

'punctual ['pʌnktjoeəl] *bnw.* presies, stip, noukeurig.

'punctuate ['pʌnktjoeyt] *ww.* (-ed) punktueer; **punctu'ation** *s.* leestekens, punktuasie.

'puncture ['pʌnktsjə] *s.* (-s) gaatjie, lekplek; **-proof** *bnw.* lekvry.

'pungent ['pʌndzjənt] *bnw.* skerp, bytend, deurdringend(*geur*).

'punish ['pʌnisj] *ww.* (-ed) straf, kasty; **-ment** *s.* straf, boete; **'punitive** *bnw.* straffend.

'punkies ['pʌnkis] *s. mv.* warmas, brandassies.

punt ['pʌnt] *s.* (-s) pont, platboomskuit; *ww.* skuit vooruitboom; hoog skop(*voetbal*).

'puny ['pjŏĕni] *bnw.* klein, tingerig; niksbeduidend.

pup ['pʌp] *s.* (-s) klein hondjie; snuiter.

'pupa ['pjŏĕpə] *s.* (-s) papie.

'pupil ['pjŏĕpl] *s.* (-s) leerling; oogappel; pupil; **-teacher** *s.* kwekeling.

'**purchase** ['pətʃjəs] *ww.* (-d) koop, aankoop; -er *s.* koper.

'**pure** ['pjoeə] *bnw.* (-r, -st) rein, suiwer, skoon; kuis; puur, louter.

'**purge** ['pədʒj] *ww.* (-d) suiwer, reinig; **pur'gation** *s.* purgasie; '**purgative** *s.* purgeermiddel.

'**purify** ['pjoeərifai] *ww.* ('purified) reinig, suiwer, louter; skoonmaak; purifi'cation *s.* reiniging; puri'fier *s.* reiniger, suiweraar; '**purist** *s.* puris, taalsuiweraar; '**purity** *s.* reinheid.

purl ['pəl] *bnw.* aweregse breisteek; *ww.* (-ed) aweregs brei.

'**purlieu** ['pəljoē] *s.* (-s) grens, perk.

pur'loin [pə'loin] *ww.* (-ed) steel, ontfutsel.

'**purple** ['pəpl] *s. & bnw.* purper, pers.

'**purport** ['pəpət] *s.* betekenis, strekking, inhoud.

'**purpose** ['pəpəs] *s.* (-s) oogmerk, plan, opset, doel; -ful *bnw.* doelbewus; -ly *bw.* opsetlik.

purr ['pə] *ww.* (-ed) spin, snor, snork.

'**purse** ['pəs] *s.* (-s) beursie; -r *s.* betaalmeester; -strings *s.* snoerkoord van die beursie.

'**purslane** ['pəslin] *s.* postelein, fynbeslein, porselein.

pur'sue [pə'sjoe] *ww.* (-d) vervolg; nastreef; agtervolg; **pur'suit** *s.* vervolging; najaging; agtervolging; -s *s.* belange, arbeid, werk, studie.

pur'veyor [pə'vyə] *s.* (-s) leweransier.

'**purview** ['pəvjoē] *s.* strekking, omvang; gesigskring.

pus ['pʌs] *s.* etter.

push ['poesj] *s.* stoot, stamp; volharding; nood, knyp; *ww.* (-ed) stoot, druk; deurdryf; aanhelp; bevorder; -bike *s.* trapfiets; -ing *bnw.* ondernemend.

puss ['poes] *s.* kat; -y *s.* katjie; pussy willow *s.* katwilg.

'**pustule** ['pʌstjoēl] *s.* (-s) puisie.

put ['poet] *s.* (-s) stoot, gooi; *ww.* (-) sit, steek, stoot; uitdruk, sê.

'**putrid** ['pjoētrid] *bnw.* vrot, bedorwe, stink; '**putrify** *ww.* ('putrified) sleg word, vrot; sweer.

'**puttee** ['pʌti] *s.* (-s) beenwindsel.

'**putty** ['pʌti] *s.* stopverf.

'**puzzle** ['pʌzl] *s.* (-s) raaisel, probleem, moeilikheid; *ww.* (-d) verwar, hoofbrekens besorg.

'**pygmy** ['pighmi] *s.* ('pygmies) dwerg; onbeduidende persoon.

py'jamas [pə'dʒāməs] *s.* slaapklere, pijamas.

'**pyramid** ['pirəmid] *s.* (-s) piramide.

'**pyre** ['paiə] *s.* (-s) brandstapel.

'**python** ['paithən] *s.* (-s) reuseslang, luislang.

Q

quack ['kwæk] *s.* gekwaak; kwaksalwer; *ww.* (-ed) kwaak; -ery *s.* kwaksalwery.

quad'rangle [kwo'dræng-ghl] *s.* (-s) binneplein; vierkant.

'**quadrate** ['kwodrit] *s.* (-s) vierkant.

qua'drille [kwə'dril] *s.* (-s) kadriel.

'**quadruped** ['kwodroeped] *s.* (-s) viervoetige dier.

'**quadruple** ['kwodroepl] *s.* viervoud; *bnw.* viervoudig; -t *s.* viertal; -ts *s.* vierling; '**quadruplex** *bnw.* viervoudig.

quaff ['kwof] *ww.* (-ed) drink, sluk.

quag ['kwægh] *s.* (-s) moeras; -gy *bnw.* moerasagtig; -mire *s.* moeras, vlei.

'**quagga** ['kwæghə, 'kwacha] *s.* (-s) kwagga.

quail ['kwyl] *s.* (-s) kwartel; *ww.* (-ed) bang word.

quaint ['kwynt] *bnw.* (-er, -est) einaardig, sonderling.

'**quake** ['kwyk] *s.* (-s) trilling, skudding; *ww.* (-d) skud, bewe.

'**Quaker** ['kwykə] *s.* Kwaker.

'**qualify** ['kwolifai] *ww.* ('qualified) bekwaam maak, bevoeg wees (maak); kwalifiseer; qualifi'cation *s.* kwalifikasie; bekwaamheid; '**qualified** *bnw.* gekwalifiseer, bevoeg.

'**quality** ['kwoliti] *s.* ('qualities) gehalte; eienskap; rang; kwaliteit; '**qualitative** *bnw.* kwalitatief.

qualm ['kwŏm] *s.* (-s) wroeging; twyfel; naarheid.

quan'dary [kwon'dèəri] *s.* moeilikheid, vorknorsing.

'**quantity** ['kwŏntiti] *s.* ('quantities) kwantiteit, hoeveelheid; - surveyor *s.* bestekopmaker; '**quantum** *s.* hoeveelheid, kwantum.

'**quarantine** ['kworəntin] *s.* kwarantyn, afsondering.

'**quarrel** ['kworəl] *s.* (-s) twis, geskik, onenigheid; *ww.* (-led) twis, kyf, skoor; -some *bnw.* twissiek, kyfagtig.

'**quarry** ['kwori] *s.* ('quarries) prooi, slagoffer; steengroef, gruisgat; *ww.* ('quarried) uitgrawe; -man *s.* steengroefwerker.

quart ['kwŏt] *s.* (-s) kwart; 2 pinte; -er *s.* kwart; kwartier; kwartaal; wyk; genade; *ww.* (-ed) vierendeel; inkwartier; -erly *s.* kwartaalblad, *bnw.* kwartaalliks, *bw.* kwartaalsgewyse; '**quartet** *s.* viertal; '**quarto** *s.* kwarto(*formaat*).

quartz ['kwŏts] *s.* kwarts.

quash ['kwosj] *ww.* (-ed) nietig verklaar; verpletter.

quasi ['kwysai] *voegw.* kastig, konsuis, kwasie.

'**quassia** ['kwosjə] '**quassie 'chips** *s.* bitterwortel, bitterhoutjies.

qua'ternary [kwə'tənəri] *bnw.* vierdelig.

'**quatrain** ['kwotryn] *s.* kwatryn.

quaver ['kwyvə] *s.* (-s) agtstenoot, trilling; *ww.* (-ed) tril, bewe.

quay ['ki] *s.* kaai, hawehoof.

queen ['kwin] *s.* (-s) koningin; vrou;

ww. (*-ed*) koningin speel; **-bee** *s.* bykoningin; **-ly** *bnw.* vorstelik.

queer ['kwiə] *bnw.* (*-er*, *-est*) sonderling, snaaks; *ww.* (*-ed*) bederwe, verbrou.

quell ['kwel] *ww.* (*-ed*) onderdruk, bedwing.

quench ['kwentʃ] *ww.* (*-ed*) blus; les; smoor.

quern ['kwən] *s.* (*-s*) handmeul.

'query ['kwiəri] *s.* (*'queries*) vraag (teken); *ww.* (*'queried*) vra, betwyfel; **'querulous** *bnw.* ontevrede, klaerig, brommerig.

quest ['kwest] *s.* (*-s*) ondersoek; soektog.

'question ['kwestʃən] *s.* (*-s*) vraag, vraagstuk; twyfel; *ww.* (*-ed*) vra, ondervra; betwyfel; **-able** *bnw.* twyfelagtig; **-mark** *s.* vraagteken.

queue ['kjōē] *s.* (*-s*) stert, vlegsel; tou, streep.

'quibble ['kwibl] *ww.* (*-d*) uitvlugte soek.

quick ['kwik] *s.* lewe; *bnw.* lewendig, snel, vlug, gou; *bw.* vinnig; gou; **-en** *ww.* opwek, aanvuur; **-ening** *s.* verlewendiging; **-freeze** *ww.* snelvries; **- grass** *s.* kweekgras; **-lime** *s.* ongebluste kalk; **-ly** *bw.* vinnig; **- march** *s.* versnelde pas; **-sand** *s.* wilsand; **-set** *s.* heining, haag; **-tempered** *bnw.* opvlieend; **-witted** *bnw.* gevat.

'quicksilver ['kwiksilvə] *s.* kwik- (silwer).

quid ['kwid] *s.* pond; pruimpie.

'quiet ['kwaiət] *s.* stilte, rus; *bnw.* (*-er*, *-est*) stil, rustig, kalm; *ww.* tot bedaring bring; bedaar; **-ude** *s.* rus, kalmte.

quill ['kwil] *s.* (*-s*) slagveer; skag; pen.

quilt ['kwilt] *s.* (*-s*) gestikte deken, donskombers.

quince ['kwins] *s.* (*-s*) kweper.

qui'nine [kwi'nin] *s.* kina.

'quinsy ['kwinzi] *s.* keelontsteking, keelsweer.

quint ['kwint] *s.* kwint; **-essence** [kwin'tesns] *s.* kern; **-et** *s.* vyftal.

quip ['kwip] *s.* (*-s*) kwinkslag, skimp.

'quire ['kwaiə] *s.* boek (24 vel papier).

quit ['kwit] *ww.* (*-ted*) verlaat, laat vaar, bes gee; vergeld; **-rent** *s.* erfpag; **-s** *bnw.* kiets; **-tance** *s.* kwytskelding, kwitansie.

'quite ['kwait] *bw.* heeltemal.

'quiver ['kwivə] *s.* pylkoker; trilling; *ww.* (*-ed*) bewe, tril.

quix'otic [kwik'sotik] *bnw.* buitensporig, dwaas.

quiz ['kwiz] *s.* vasvrawedstryd.

'quizzical ['kwizikl] *bnw.* grappig, snaaks, tergerig.

quod ['kwod] *s.* tronk.

quoit ['koit] *s.* (*-s*) werpskyf.

'quorum ['kwôrəm] *s.* (*-s*) kworum.

'quota ['kwoutə] *s.* (*-s*) kwota, toegewese deel.

'quote ['kwout] *ww.* (*-d*) kwoteer, aanhaal; **quo'tation** *s.* aanhaling; **quo'tation-marks** *s.* aanhalings-tekens.

'quotient ['kwousjənt] *s.* kwosiënt, uitslag.

R

R. (Rand) *s.* R. (*Rand*).

R.S.A. (Republic of South Africa) *s.* R.S.A. (*Republiek van Suid-Afrika*).

'rabbi ['ræbai] *s.* (*-s*) rabbyn, **rab'binical** *bnw.* rabbyns.

'rabbit ['ræbit] *s.* (*-s*) konyn; **-hutch** *s.* konynhok.

'rabble ['ræbl] *s.* gespuis, gepeupel.

'rabid ['ræbid] *bnw.* (*-est*) woes, dol, rasend.

'rabies ['ræbiiz] *s.* hondsdolheid.

'race ['rys] *s.* (*-s*) wedren, wedloop; ras, geslag, soort; *ww.* (*-d*) hardloop, jaag; **-course** *s.* renbaan; **-horse** *s.* renperd; **-meeting** *s.* reisies; **'racialism** *s.* rassehaat.

ra'chitis [ræ'kaitis] *s.* rachitis, Engelse siekte.

'raciness ['rysinis] *s.* geurigheid, rasegtheid.

rack ['ræk] *s.* (*-s*) rak, kapstok; pynbank; *ww.* (*-ed*) folter, pynig; **-rent** *s.* woekerwins; **- wheel** *s.* kamrat.

'racket ['rækit] *s.* raket, tennisspaan; swendelary, bedrogspul.

'racy ['rysi] *bnw.* (*'racier*, *'raciest*) geurig, sterk, geestig; ras-eg.

'radiate ['rydiyt] *ww.* (*-d*) skitter; uitstraal; versprei; **'radial** *bnw.* straalvorming; **'radiance** *s.* glinstering, glans, straling; **'radiant** *bnw.* stralend, skitterend; **radi'ation** *s.* uitstraling; **'radiator** *s.* verkoeler (*motorkar*); **radiator shutter** *s.* verkoelerluik.

'radical ['rædikəl] *s.* radikaal; *bnw.* radikaal, fundamenteel.

'radio ['rydiou] *s.* radio, draadloos.

'radish ['rædiʃ] *s.* (*-es*) radys.

'radium ['rydiəm] *s.* radium.

'radius ['rydiəs] *s.* radius, straal; speekbeen.

'raffia ['ræfiə] *s.* raffia, palmvesel.

'raffle ['ræfl] *s.* (*-s*) lotery.

raft ['râft] *s.* (*-s*) vlot; **-er** *s.* dakspar, balk.

rag ['ræg] *s.* (*-s*) vlenter, vod, lap, vadoek, toiing; jool.

'ragamuffin ['rægəmʌfin] *s.* skobbejak, smeerlap.

'rage ['rydzj] *s.* woede; gier, mode; *ww.* (*-d*) woed, raas, tier.

'rag-fair ['ræghfêə] *s.* rommelverkoping.

'ragged ['ræghid] *bnw.* ru, ongelyk, geskeur, toiingrig.

'ragout ['ræghôē] *s.* stoofvleis, bredie.

raid ['ryd] s. (-s) inval, strooptog; ww. (-ed) inval doen, roof.

rail ['ryl] s. dwarspaal; leuning; spoorstaaf; ww. (-ed) traliewerk aanbring; per spoor stuur; spot, smaal; -ing s. traliewerk, leuning, reling; -lery s. korswel, skerts, tergery; -road s. spoorweg; -way s. spoorweg.

'**raiment** ['rymənt] s. kleding, gewaad.

rain ['ryn] s. (-s) reën; -bow s. reënboog; -fall s. reënval; -gauge s. reënmeter; -y bnw. reënerig; - locust s. langasemsprinkaan.

'**raincoat** ['rynkout] s. (-s) reënjas.

'**raise** ['ryz] ww. (-d) optel, ophelp, oplig; oprig; versamel; teel; veroorsaak; verhef.

'**raisin** ['ryzn] s. (-s) rosyntjie.

'**rake** ['ryk] s. (-s) hark; **rakish** bnw. losbandig; - comb s. growwekam.

'**rally** ['ræli] ww. ('rallied) herenig; herstel, moed skep; 'n sarsie maak.

'**ram** ['ræm] s. (-s) ram; stormram; stamper.

'**ramble** ['ræmbl] ww. (-d) ronddwaal; afdwaal; -r s. omswerwer; klimplant; '**rambling** s. omswerwing, bnw. deurmekaar.

'**ramify** ['ræmifai] ww. vertak; ramifi'cation s.

ramp ['ræmp] s. helling, skuinste, oprit, afrit, aanrit; -age s. uitgelatenheid; -ant bnw. heersend; geil; -art s. skans, borswering.

'**ramrod** ['ræmrod] s. laaistok.

'**ramshackle** ['ræmsjækl] bnw. bouvallig, lendelam.

ranch ['rāntsj] s. veeplaas.

'**rancid** ['rænsid] bnw. galsterig.

'**rancour** ['rænkə] s. wrok, haat; 'rancorous bnw. haatdraend, wrokkend.

'**random** ['rændəm] s. toeval, geluk; at - blindweg, op geluk af; bnw ewekansig.

range ['ryndzj] s. (-s) reeks; rigting; perke, bereik; draagwydte; kaggel, stoof; ww. (-d) opstel, plek inneem; uitstrek; -r s. veldwagter.

'**rank** ['rænk] s. (-s) gelid; stand; staanplek; ww. (-ed) in orde stel, klassifiseer; bnw. welig, geil; walglik; flagrant.

'**rankle** ['rænkl] ww. (-d) sweer; leed veroorsaak; knaag.

'**ransack** ['rænsæk] ww. (-ed) deursnuffel; plunder.

'**ransom** ['rænsəm] s. losprys.

rant ['rænt] s. bombastiese taal.

rap ['ræp] s. (-s) slag, hou, tik; duit, sier.

ra'pacious [rə'pysjəs] bnw. roofgierig.

'**rape** ['ryp] ww. (-d) onteer, verkrag.

'**rapid** ['ræpid] bnw. (-est) vlug, snel, vinnig; -s s. stroomversnelling; ra'pidity s. snelheid.

rap'port [ræ'pòl] s. mededeling.

'**rapt** ['ræpt] bnw. meegevoer; verruk; versonke.

'**rapture** ['ræptsjə] s. verrukking, ekstase; '**rapturous** bnw. verruk, opgetoë.

'**rare** ['rèə] bnw. seldsaam; skaars; ongewoon; -ly bw. selde; -fy ww. verdun, yl maak; verfyn; '**rarity** s. seldsaamheid; ylheid.

'**rascal** ['ràskəl] s. (-s) skurk, rakker, skelm, vabond.

rash ['ræsj] s. uitslag; bnw. (-er, -est) onbesonne.

'**rasher** ['ræsjə] s. snytjie ham (spek).

rasp ['ràsp] s. (-s) rasper; -berry s. framboos.

rat ['ræt] s. (-s) rot; onderkruiper.

'**ratchet** ['rætsjit] s. sperrat; - wrench s. ratelsleutel.

'**rate** ['ryt] s. (-s) tarief; prys; belasting; snelheid; klas; syfer; voet; ww. (-d) skat, waardeer, takseer; uitskel; '**rateable** bnw. belasbaar; -s s. munisipale belasting; -payer s. belastingbetaler (stedelik); '**rating** s. klas; aanslag.

'**rather** ['ràdhə] bw. liewers, eerder; enigsins.

'**ratify** ['rætifai] ww. ('ratified) bekragtig; ratifi'cation s.

'**ratio** ['rysjiou] s. verhouding.

'**ration** ['ræsjən] s. (-s) rantsoen.

'**rational** ['ræsjnl] bnw. redelik, billik.

'**rattle** ['rætl] s. (-s) gerammel; ww. (-d) rammel, raas; -snake s. ratelslang; -r s. rammelaar.

'**raucous** ['ròkəs] bnw. hees, skor.

'**ravage** ['rævidzj] ww. (-d) verniel, plunder.

'**rave** ['ryv] ww. (-d) raas, uitvaar; dweep met.

'**ravel** ['rævəl] ww. (-led) verwar; ontwar.

'**raven** ['ryvn] s. (-s) raaf, kraai; -ous bnw. roofsugtig; vraatsugtig, uitgehonger.

ra'vine [rə'vin] s. (-s) bergkloof, skeur.

'**ravish** ['rævisj] ww. (-ed) wegvoer; verkrag; bekoor; -ment s.

raw ['rò] bnw. rou; ru; dom, baar; seer; -boned bnw. brandmaer; -ish bnw. rouerig.

ray ['ry] s. (-s) straal; rogvis.

'**raze** ['ryz] ww. (-d) uitwis; vernietig, verwoes, afbreek.

'**razor** ['ryzə] s. (-s) skeermes; -back s. spitsrug; - edge s. snykant van skeermes; - strop s. skeermesriem.

reach ['ritsj] s. (-es) bereik; omvang; uitgestrektheid; ww. (-ed) bereik, bykom; aangee.

re- ['rl-] voorvoegsel re-, weer, terug, nogeens, teen.

re'act [ri'ækt] ww. (-ed) reageer; -ion s. reaksie; -ionary bnw. teenwerkend, reaksionêr; s. opstandeling.

read ['rid] ww. lees; uitlê; raai; studeer; -able bnw. sigbaar; leesbaar; -er s. leesboek; leser; lektor; reviseur; -ership s. lektorskap; -ing

s. lesing, verklaring, uitleg; leesstof; -ing-desk s. lessenaar; -ing-room s. leeskamer.

ready ['redi] bnw. gereed, bereid; 'readily bw. geredelik; 'readiness s. gereedheid, bereidwilligheid; -made bnw. klaargemaak; -reckoner s. rekenboekie.

re'agent [ri'ydzjənt] s. reagens.

real [riəl] bnw. werklik, waar; -ly bw. waarlik.

realize ['riəlaiz] ww. (-d) besef; verwesenlik; tot geld maak; reali-'zation s.; 'realist s. realis; rea'listic bnw. realisties; re'ality s. werklikheid; realty, s. vaste eiendom.

realm ['relm] s. (-s) koninkryk, ryk.

ream ['rim] s. riem(papier); ww. (-ed) ruimer maak; -er s. ruimerboor.

reap ['rip] ww. (-ed) oes, insamel, maai; -er s. maaier.

rear [riə] s. agterhoede; agtergrond; agterstand; ww. (-ed) grootmaak; teel; steier; -guard s. agterhoede; -ward bnw. agterste; -wards bw. agterwaards; - brake s. agterrem; - lamp s. agterlamp; - light s. agterlig.

reason ['rizn] s. (-s) rede; verstand; dryfveer; ww. (-ed) redeneer; -able bnw. billik; -ed bnw. beredeneerde; -ing s. redenering, redenasie.

reave ['riv] ww. (-d) ontroof, ontneem.

re'bate [ri'byt] s. korting, rabat.

rebel ['rebl] s. (-s) rebel, opstandeling; bnw. rebels; ww. (-led) rebelleer; re'bellion s. rebellie; re'bellious bnw. rebels.

re'buff [ri'bʌf] s. afjak; afwysing.

re'buke [ri'bjõёk] s. (-s) teregwysing; ww. (-d) teregwys.

re'but [ri'bʌt] s. afweer, terugslag.

re'calcitrant [ri'kælsitrənt] bnw. weerspannig.

re'cant [ri'kænt] ww. (-ed) herroep, terugtrek.

reca'pitulate [rikə'pitjoelyt] ww. (-d) saamvat; reca'pitulatory bnw. saamvattend.

re'cede [ri'sid] ww. (-d) terugwyk, daal, sak, verdwyn.

re'ceipt [ri'sit] s. (-s) kwitansie, bewys; ww. (-ed) voldaan maak.

re'ceive [ri'siv] ww. (-d) ontvang; onthaal; re'ceivable bnw. aanneemlik, ontvangbaar; -r s. ontvanger; gehoorstal.

'recency ['risnsi] s. resente dagtekening; 'recent bnw. pasgebeur; 'recently bw. onlangs.

re'ceptacle [ri'septəkl] s. (-s) bak, bewaarplek; re'ception s. ontvangs, resepsie; re'ception room s. ontvangskamer; re'ceptive bnw. ontvanklik.

re'cess [ri'ses] s. vakansie, onderbreking, reses; hoek, alkoof, nis; inlaat; ww. uithol; -ion s. terugwyking; afstand.

re'cidivism [ri'cidivizm] s. terug-

valling (in vorige toestand, opvattings).

'recipe ['resipi] s. resep, voorskrif.

re'cipient [ri'sipiənt] s. ontvanger; vgl. receiver.

re'ciprocate [ri'siprəkyt] ww. (-d) vergeld, vergoed, op gelyke wyse behandel; re'ciprocal bnw. wederkerig; reci'procity s. wederkerigheid.

re'cite [ri'sait] ww. (-d) opsê, resiteer; opsom; re'cital s. opsomming; voordrag; reci'tation s. resitasie; voordrag; opsomming; re-cita'tive s. [resita'tiv] resitatief; -r s. resiteerder, voordraer.

'reckless ['reklis] bnw. roekeloos, onverskillig.

'reckon ['rekn] ww. (-ed) reken, tel; dink, meen; -ing s. afrekening, berekening.

re'claim [ri'klym] ww. (-d) terugwin, verbeter; ontgin; mak maak.

recla'mation [reklə'mysjən] s. herwinning, verbetering; ontginning.

re'cline [ri'klain] ww. (-d) lê, leun, rus.

re'cluse [ri'klõёz] s. kluisenaar.

'recognize ['rekəghnaiz] ww. (-d) herken; besef; recog'nizable bnw. herkenbaar; re'cognizance s. verbintenis, erkenning; borgtog; recog-'nition s. erkenning, herkenning.

re'coil [ri'koil] ww. (-ed) terugslaan; terugdeins.

recol'lect [rekə'lekt] ww. (-ed) onthou, herinner; -ion s.

recom'mend [rekə'mend] ww. (-ed) aanbeveel, aanraai; recommen'dation s. aanbeveling; recom'mendatory bnw. aanbevelings-.

'recompense ['rekəmpens] s. beloning, vergoeding.

'reconcile ['rekənsail] ww. (-d) versoen; recon'cilable bnw. versoenbaar; reconcili'ation s. versoening; recon'ciliatory bnw. versoenend.

recon'dition [rikən'disjn] ww. (-ed) vernuwe, herstel.

re'connaissance [ri'konisəns] s. verkenning.

recon'noitre [rekə'noitə] ww. (-d) verken.

'record ['rekôd] s. (-s) rekord; register; geskiedrol; verslag; plaat; ww. (-ed) (ri'kôd) opteken, aanteken, vermeld; -er s. argivaris.

re'count [ri'kaunt] ww. (-ed) verhaal, oortel.

re'coup [ri'kõёp] ww. (-ed) terughou; skadeloosstel.

re'course [ri'kôs] s. toevlug.

re'cover [ri'kʌvə] ww. (-ed) terugkry, herwin; herstel; goed maak; herbeklee; -y s. herstel, herwinning.

'recreant ['rekriənt] s. (-s) afvallige.

recre'ation [rekri'ysjən] s. ontspanning, vermaak; recre'ative bnw. ontspannend, vermaaklik.

re'criminate [ri'kriminyt] ww. (-d) wedersyds beskuldig.

re'cruit [ri'krŏĕt] s. rekruut, nuweling.

'rectangle ['rektæng-ghl] s. (-s) reghoek; **rect'angular** bnw. reghoekig.

'rectify ['rektifai] ww. ('rectified) herstel, verbeter; **'rectifiable** bnw. herstelbaar; **rectifi'cation** s. verbetering.

recti'linear [rekti'linjə] bnw. reglynig.

'rectitude ['rektitjŏĕd] s. opregtheid; korrektheid.

'rector ['rektə] s. (-s) rektor; predikant; -y s. pastorie.

'rectum ['rektəm] s. endelderm.

re'cumbent [ri'kʌmbənt] bnw. rustend, leunend.

re'cuperate [ri'kjŏĕpəryt] ww. (-d) herstel, opknap; **recupe'ration** s. herstel; **re'cuperative** bnw. versterkend.

re'cur [ri'kə] ww. (-red) herhaal, weer gebeur; **-rence** s. terugkeer, herhaling; **-rent** bnw. herhalend.

'recusant ['rekjoezənt] bnw. opstandig; weierend.

red ['red] bnw. rooi; **-breast** s. rooiborsie; **-den** ww. (-ed) rooi word; **-dish** bnw. rooierig; **-handed** bnw. op heter daad; **-hot** bnw. roolwarm, gloeiend warm; **-hot poker** s. vuurpyl; **-letter** bnw. gedenkwaardig; **-skin** s. Rooihuid; **- tape** s. burokrasie.

re'deem [ri'dim] ww. (-ed) terugkoop, vrykoop, verlos; inlos; **Redeemer** s. Verlosser; **re'demption** s. verlossing, bevryding; **re'demptive** bnw. verlossend; **re'demptory** bnw. verlossings-.

'redolence ['redŏlǝns] s. geur; **'redolent** bnw. geurig.

re'doubt [ri'daut] s. vesting, skans; **-able** bnw. gedug.

re'dound [ri'daund] ww. (-ed) bydra; terugval; voortvloei.

re'dress [ri'dres] s. herstel, vergoeding; ww. (-ed) verhelp, vergoed.

re'duce [ri'djŏĕs] ww. (-d) herlei; minder maak; **re'ducible** bnw. herleibaar; **re'duction** s. vermindering; afslag; herleiding.

re'dundance [ri'dʌndəns] s. oortolligheid; **re'dundancy** s. oortolligheid; **re'dundant** bnw. oortollig.

reed ['rid] s. (-s) riet; mondstuk; fluit.

reef ['rif] s. (-s) rif, rotsbank.

reek ['rik] s. rook, walm; stank; **-y** bnw. vuil.

reel ['ril] s. (-s) rolletjie, klos; riel; ww. (-ed) oprol; wankel.

re'fection [ri'feksjən] s. verversing; **re'fectory** s. eetkamer.

re'fer [ri'fə] ww. (-red) verwys; vermeld; refereer; **refe'ree** s. skeidsregter; **'reference** s. verwysing; getuigskrif; bewysplaas; **refe'rendum** s. referendum.

re'fill [ri'fil] s. (-s) hervulling; ww. (-ed) hervul.

re'fine [ri'fain] ww. (-d) suiwer louter; verfyn; -d bnw. gesuiwer beskaaf; **-ment** s. suiwering, ver edeling; **-ry** s. suiweringsfabriek.

re'flect [ri'flekt] ww. (-ed) weerkaats peins; **-ion** s. weerkaatsing; oor weging; blaam; **-ive** bnw. peinsend wederkerend; **-or** s. reflektor.

'reflex ['rifleks] s. weerkaatsing refleksbeweging.

re'formatory [ri'fômətəri] s. verbeteringshuis.

re'fract [ri'frækt] ww. (-ed) breek (van strale); **-ion** s. straalbreking; **-ive** bnw. straalbrekend; **-or** s. refraktor; **-ory** bnw. koppig.

re'frain [ri'fryn] s. refrein; ww. (-ed) bedwing, beteuel.

re'fresh [ri'fresj] ww. (-ed) verkwik, verfris; **-ment** s. verversing; **-ing** a. verkwikkend.

re'frigerate [ri'fridzjəryt] ww. (-d) verkoel; **refrige'ration** s. verkoeling; **re'frigerator** s. koelkamer, yskas.

'refuge ['refjŏĕdzj] s. (-s) toevlug, skuiling; **refu'gee** s. vlugteling.

'refund ['rifʌnd] ww. (-ed) terugbetaal.

'refuse ['refjŏĕs] s. oorskot, oorskiet, afval; ww. [ri'fjŏĕz] (-d) weier, van die hand wys; **re'fusal** s. weiering; opsie.

re'fute [ri'fjŏĕt] ww. (-d) weerlè, teenspreek; **refu'tation** s. weerlegging.

'regal ['righəl] bnw. koninklik; **re'galia** s. koninklike ordetekens.

re'gale [ri'ghyl] ww. (-d) onthaal, vergas; **-ment** s. onthaal.

re'gard [ri'ghâd] s. agting; opsig; aandag; **-s** s. groete; ww. (-ed) bekyk, beskou, ag slaan op; **-ful** bnw. opmerksaam; **-ing** bnw. betreffende; **-less** bnw. onverskillig.

re'generate [ri'dzjenəryt] ww. (-d) laat herlewe; opwek; hervorm.

regent ['ridzjant] s. regent; **'regency** s. regentskap.

re'gime [ry'zjim] s. stelsel, beheer.

re'gimen [rə'dzjimən] s. streng gereëlde behandeling.

'regiment ['redzjimənt] s. regiment; **regi'mental** bnw. regiments-.

'region ['ridzjən] s. (-s) streek; gebied; gewes.

'register ['redzjistə] s. (-s) register; lys; rol; ww. (-ed) registreer; **'registrar** s. registrateur; **regis'tration** s. registrasie; **'registry** s. registrasiekantoor.

re'gress [ri'ghres] s. teruggang; **-ive** bnw. regressief, terugwerkend.

re'gret [ri'ghret] s. (-s) verdriet, smart, spyt; ww. (-ted) treur, betreur, berou, spyt hê(wees); **-ful** bnw. berouvol; **-able** bnw. te betreur.

'regulate ['reghjoelyt] ww. (-d)

kontroleer, reguleer; **regu'lation** s. kontrole; regulasie; **'regular** bnw.
gereëld, reëlmatig; **regu'larity** s. reëlmatigheid.

reha'bilitate [riə'bilityt] ww. (-d) herstel, rehabiliteer.

re'hearse [ri'hǝs] ww. (-d) opsê, herhaal, repeteer; **re'hearsal** s. repitisie.

'reign ['ryn] s. (-s) leisel, teuel; bewind.

'rein ['ryn] ww. (-ed) stuur; beteuel, in toom hou.

'reindeer ['ryndiǝ] s. (-s) rendier.

rein'force [riin'fôs] ww. (-d) versterk; bewapen.

rein'state [ri'in'styt] ww. (-d) herstel.

re'iterate [ri'itǝryt] ww. (-d) herhaal.

re'ject [ri'dzjekt] ww. (-ed) verwerp, afwys; **re'jection** s. verwerping, afwysing; **-able** bnw. verwerplik.

re'joice [ri'dzjois] ww. (-d) verbly, verheug wees; **re'joicing** s. vreugde.

re'joinder [ri'dzjoindǝ] s. (-s) antwoord, wederwoord.

re'lapse [ri'læps] ww. (-d) terugval, weer instort.

re'late [ri'lyt] ww. (-d) verhaal, vertel; in verband bring met; **-d** bnw. verwant; **re'lation** s. verwantskap; familiebetrekking; verslag; **'relative** s. bloedverwant, bnw. betreklik, relatief.

re'lax [ri'læks] ww. (-ed) verslap; versag; ontspan; **relax'ation** s. verslapping; ontspanning.

're'lay ['ri'ly] ww. ('re'laid) aflos, wissel; uitsaai, deursend, heruitsend; **- race** s. afloswedren.

re'lease [ri'lis] ww. (-d) loslaat, vrystel.

'relegate ['relighyt] ww. (-d) verban, verplaas.

re'lent [ri'lent] ww. (-ed) toegee; **-less** bnw. onverbiddelik.

'relevance ['relivǝns] s. verband; **'relevant** bnw. ter sake.

re'liable [ri'laiǝbl] bnw. vertroubaar, betroubaar; **re'liance** s. vertroue; vgl. **rely.**

'relic ['relik] s. (-s) oorblyfsel.

re'lief [ri'lif] s. verligting; reliëf.

re'lieve [ri'liv] ww. (-d) verlig; bevry; aflos; ontset.

re'ligion [ri'lidzjǝn] s. (-s) godsdiens, geloof; **re'ligious** bnw. godsdienstig.

re'linquish [ri'linkwisj] ww. (-ed) laat vaar; loslaat; **-ment** s. loslating; afstanddoening.

'relish ['relisj] ww. (-ed) hou van, behae skep in.

re'luctance [ri'lʌktǝns] s. teensin, huiwering; **re'luctant** bnw. teensinnig.

re'ly [ri'lai] ww. (re'lied) vertrou op, staatmaak op.

re'main [ri'myn] ww. (-ed) oorbly, oorskiet; bly; **-s** s. oorskot; **-der** s. res.

re'mand [ri'mǎnd] ww. (-ed) 'n saak uitstel; terugroep.

re'mark [ri'mǎk] s. (-s) opmerking; **-able** bnw. opmerklik.

'remedy ['remidi] s. ('remedies) geneesmiddel, remedie; **re'mediable** bnw. herstelbaar; **re'medial** bnw. heilsaam, genesend.

re'member [ri'membǝ] ww. (-ed) onthou, herinner, byval; **re'membrance** s. herinnering, geheue; **re'membrancer** s. persoon wat in herinnering roep.

re'mind [ri'maind] ww. (-ed) herinner; **-er** s. herinnering; **remi'niscence** s. herinnering; **remi'niscent** bnw. laat dink aan.

re'miss [ri'mis] bw. agtelosig, nalatig.

re'mit [ri'mit] ww. (-ted) vergewe; terugstuur; oormaak; **re'mission** s. vergifnis; afslag; **-tal** s. vergifnis; **-tance** s. betaling, oormaking.

'remnant ['remnǝnt] s. (-s) oorblyfsel; lappie; brokkie; oorskotjie.

re'monstrate [ri'monstryt] ww. (-d) protesteer, beswaar maak; **re'monstrance** s. portes; **re'monstrant** bnw. protesterend.

re'morse [ri'môs] s. berou; **-ful** bnw. berouvol; **-less** bnw. meedoënloos.

re'mote [ri'mout] bnw. (-r, -st) afgeleë; gering; **-ness** s. groot afstand, afgeleënheid.

re'mould [ri'mould] ww. (-ed) herbou, ombou.

re'munerate [ri'mjǒěnǝryt] ww. (-d) beloon; vergoed; **re'muneration** s. beloning, vergoeding; **re'munerative** bnw. lonend.

re'naissance [rǝ'nysǝns] s. herlewing; Renaissance.

rend ['rend] ww. (-ed) skeur; verdeel.

'render ['rendǝ] ww. (-ed) vergeld; gee; vertolk.

'rendezvous ['rondivǒě] s. vergaderplek.

'renegade ['renighyd] s. (-s) renegaat, verraaier.

re'new [ri'njǒě] ww. (-ed) vernuwe, hernuwe; **-al** s. hernuwing.

'rennet ['renit] s. stremsel.

re'nounce [ri'nauns] ww. (-d) afstand doen van; opgee, versaak; **-ment** s. versaking, verloëning.

'renovate ['renǒvyt] ww. (-d) vernuwe, herstel; **reno'vation** s.

re'nown [ri'naun] s. faam, roem; **-ed** bnw. beroemd, befaamd.

rent ['rent] s. (-s) skeur; huur; nag; **-able** bnw. huurbaar; **-al** s. huurgeld; **-free** bnw. huurvry.

re'pair [ri'pèǝ] ww. (-ed) regmaak, verstel, herstel; **-s** s. herstelwerk; **'reparable** bnw. herstelbaar.

re'partee [re'pǎti] s. (-s) gevatte antwoord.

re'past [ri'pǎst] s. maal.

re'patriate [ri'pætriyt] ww. (-d) repatrieer; **repatri'ation** s.

re'peal [ri'pil] ww. (-ed) herroep, afskaf.

re'peat [ri'pit] ww. (-ed) herhaal; **-edly** bw. herhaaldelik; **-ing** bnw.

repeterend; **repe'tition** s. herhaling;
- prescription s. herhaalvoorskrif.

re'pel [ri'pel] ww. (-led) afweer,
verslaan; **-lent** bnw. afwerend;
insect -lent s. insekweerder.

re'pent [ri'pent] ww. (-ed) berou hê;
-ance s. berou; **-ant** bnw. berouvol.

'repertoire ['repətwā] s. (-s) repertoire.

'repertory ['repətəri] s. lys, register,
gids; repertorium.

re'place [ri'plys] ww. (-d) vervang;
-ment s. vervanging; vervangdeel.

re'plenish [ri'plenisj] ww. (-ed)
aanvul.

re'plete [ri'plit] bnw. vol, gevul, sat.

'replica ['replikə] s. (-s) kopie.

re'ply [ri'plai] ww. (re'plied) antwoord; s. antwoord.

re'port [ri'pôt] s. (-s) gerug, verslag,
berig; knal; **-er** s. verslaggewer.

re'pose [ri'pouz] ww. (-d) rus; lê.

re'pository [ri'pozitəri] s. bewaarplek.

repre'hensible [repri'hensəbl] bnw.
laakbaar.

repre'sent [repri'zənt] ww. (-ed)
voorstel; beweer; verteenwoordig;
represen'tation s. voorstelling; ver-
teenwoordiging; **repre'sentative** s.
verteenwoordiger; bnw. verteen-
woordigend.

re'press [ri'pres] ww. (-ed) onderdruk; **re'pression** s.; **-ive** bnw. onderdrukkend.

re'prieve [ri'priv] ww. (-d) uitstel,
opskort.

'reprimand ['reprimānd] s. (-s)
teregwysing, verwyt.

re'prisal [ri'praizəl] s. (-s) weerwraak.

re'proach [ri'proutsj] s. (-es)
verwyt; **-ful** bnw. verwytend.

reprobate ['reprōbyt] bnw. goddeloos, sleg.

repro'duce [riprə'djōēs] ww. (-d)
voortbring; **repro'duction** s. kopie;
weergawe; voortplanting.

re'proof [ri'prōēf] s. (-s) berisping.

re'prove [ri'prōēv] ww. (-d) berispe;
re'proval s. teregwysing.

'reptile ['reptail] s. (-s) reptiel,
kruipende dier.

re'public [ri'pΛblik] s. (-s) republiek;
-an bnw. republikeins.

re'pudiate [ri'pjōēdiyt] ww. (-d)
verwerp; **re'pudiation** s.

re'pugnance [ri'pΛghnəns] s. afkeur,
weersin; **re'pugnant** bnw. walglik,
afstotend.

re'pulse [ri'pΛls] ww. (-d) afslaan;
afskrik; **re'pulsive** bnw. haatlik;
re'pulsion s. weersin, afsku; af-
stoting.

re'pute [ri'pjōēt] s. naam, reputasie;
'reputable bnw. fatsoenlik; **repu'tation** s. goeie naam, reputasie.

re'quest [ri'kwest] s. (-s) versoek;
ww. versoek.

re'quire [ri'kwaiə] ww. (-d) vereis;
begeer; nodig hê; **-ment** s. vereiste.

'requisite ['rekwizit] bnw. nodig,
vereis; **requi'sition** s. aansoek, eis.

re'quite [ri'kwait] ww. vergeld;
beloon.

re'scind [ri'sind] ww. (-ed) herroep,
ophef.

'rescue ['reskjōē] ww. (-d) red, bevry.

re'search [ri'sətsj] s. navorsing.

re'semble [ri'zembl] ww. (-d) lyk na,
aard na, trek na; **re'semblance** s.
gelykenis, ooreenkoms.

re'sent [ri'zent] ww. (-ed) kwalik
neem; **-ful** bnw. boos, beledig;
haatdraend; **-ment** s. wrok.

re'serve [ri'zəv] ww. (-d) terughou,
agterhou; bespreek; bestem; voor-
behou; s. reserwe; d bnw. besproke;
reser'vation s. bespreking; **'reservoir** ('rezəvwā] s. (-s) dam.

re'side [ri'said] ww. (-d) woon, bly;
'residence s. woning, woonplek;
inwoning; s. residensie; **'resident** s.
inwoner; **resi'dential** bnw. inwon-
end, wonings-, woon-.

'residue ['rezidjoe] s. oorblyfsel, res;
re'sidual bnw. oorblywend; **re'sidu-
ary** bnw. orig.

re'sign [ri'zain] ww. (-ed) bedank;
onderwerp aan; **resig'nation** s. be-
danking; gelatenheid.

re'silience [ri'ziliəns] s. veerkrag;
re'silient bnw. veerkragtig.

'resin ['rezin] s. hars, harpuis; **-ous**
bnw. harsagtig.

re'sist [ri'zist] ww. (-ed) weerstaan;
-ance s. weerstand; **-ible** bnw.
weerstaanbaar; **-less** bnw. sonder
weerstand.

'resolute ['rezəlōēt] bnw. vasberade; **reso'lution** s. besluit.

re'solve [ri'zolv] ww. (-d) besluit;
-d bnw. vasberade.

'resonance ['reznəns] s. weerklank,
resonansie; **'resonant** bnw. weer-
galmend; **'resonator** s. klankbord.

re'sort [ri'zôt] ww. (-ed) toevlug
neem tot; s. toevlug; oord.

re'sound [ri'zaund] ww. (-ed)
weergalm.

re'source [ri'sôs] s. (-s) toevlug;
vindingrykheid; **-s** s. middele; **-ful**
bnw. vindingryk; **-less** bnw. hopeloos, radeloos.

re'spect [ri'spekt] s. eerbied; opsig;
betrekking; ww. (-ed) ag, respekteer;
-able bnw. fatsoenlik; **-a'bility** s.
fatsoenlikheid; **-ful** bnw. eerbiedig;
-fully bw. beleef; **-ive** bnw. respek-
tief; besonder; **-ively** bw. respektie-
welik.

re'spire [ris'paiə] ww. (-d) asemhaal;
respi'ration s. asemhaling; **respi-
'ratory** bnw. asemhalings-.

'respite ['respait] s. uitstel, respyt.

re'splendent [ri'splendənt] bnw.
glinsterend, skitterend.

re'spond [ris'pond] ww. (-ed)
reageer; **re'sponse** s. antwoord; **-ent**
s. verweerder.

re'sponsible [ris'ponsəbl] bnw. verantwoordelik.

est ['rest] *ww.* (*-ed*) rus; oorbly; rus gee; *s.* rus, slaap; oorskot, res; -**ful** *bnw.* rustig; -**ive** *bnw.* steeks.

restaurant ['restərăng] *s.* (*-s*) restaurant.

esti'tution [resti'tŏēsjən] *s.* teruggawe; herstel.

e'store [ri'stŏ] *ww.* (*-d*) herstel; terugbesorg; vernuwe; genees; re-'**storable** *bnw.* herstelbaar; **re'stora-tive** *s.* geneesmiddel; **resto'ration** *s.* herstel.

e'straint [ri'strynt] *s.* dwang, bedwang.

re'strict [ri'strikt] *ww.* (*-ed*) beperk; -**ion** *s.*; -**ive** *bnw.* beperkend.

re'sult [ri'zʌlt] *s.* (*-s*) uitslag, resultaat; -**ant** *s.* resultant.

re'sume [ri'zjŏēm] *ww.* hervat; **re'sumption** *s.* hervatting.

'résumé ['rezjoemy] *s.* oorsig.

resur'rection [rezə'reksjən] *s.* opstanding.

re'suscitate [ri'sʌsityt] *ww.* (*-d*) opwek, laat herlewe; bykom, bewussyn herwin.

'retail ['rityl] *s.* kleinhandel; - **dealer** *s.* kleinhandelaar.

re'tain [ri'tyn] *ww.* (*-ed*) behou; -**er** *s.* volgeling, onderhorige; -**ing fee** *s.* honorarium; **re'tention** *s.* behoud.

re'taliate [ri'tæliyt] *ww.* (*-d*) vergeld; **retali'ation** *s.*; **retali'atory** *bnw.* vergeldend.

re'tard [ri'tăd] *ww.* (*-ed*) vertraag.

'retch ['ritsj] *ww.* (*-ed*) opgooi, jongosse-inspan; vomeer.

'reticence ['retisəns] *s.* swygsaamheid; **reticent** *bnw.* swygsaam.

'retina ['retinə] *s.* netvlies.

'retinue ['retinjŏē] *s.* (*-s*) gevolg, stoet.

re'tire [ri'talə] *ww.* (*-d*) vlug; jou afsonder; aftree; -**d** *bnw.* stil; afgetrede; -**ment** *s.* afsondering; aftreding; **re'tiring** *bnw.* stil, afgetrokke.

re'tort [ri'tŏt] *s.* (*-s*) gevatte antwoord; kolffles, retort.

re'tract [ri'trækt] *ww.* (*-ed*) terugtrek; intrek; herroep.

re'treat [ri'trit] *s.* (*-s*) terugtog; rusplek; *ww.* (*-ed*) terugwyk.

re'trench [ri'trentsj] *ww.* (*-ed*) verminder, besuinig; -**ment** *s.* besuiniging.

retri'bution [retri'bjŏēsjən] *s.* (*-s*) vergelding.

re'trieve [ri'triv] *ww.* (*-d*) terugvind; herstel; red; -**r** *s.* jaghond.

'retrograde ['retroughryd] *bnw.* verslegtend.

'retrogress ['retroughres] *ww.* (*-ed*) versleg; -**ion** *s.* verslegting.

'retro-re'flector ['ritrou-ri'flektŏ] *s.* trukaatser.

'retrospect ['retrouspekt] *s.* terugblik; **retro'spective** *bnw.* terugwerkend.

re'turn [ri'tŏn] *ww.* (*-ed*) terugkom;

terugbesorg; *s.* terugkoms; wins; teruggawe.

re'veal [ri'vil] *ww.* (*-ed*) openbaar; **reve'lation** *s.* openbaring.

'revel ['revl] *ww.* (*-led*) pret maak, vrolik wees; -**ler** *s.* pretmaker; -**ry** *s.* pretmakery.

re'venge [ri'vendzj] *s.* wraak; -**ful** *bnw.* wraaksugtig.

'revenue ['revinjŏē] *s.* inkomste.

re'verberate [ri'vəbəryt] *ww.* (*-d*) weergalm.

re'vere [ri'viə] *ww.* (*-d*) vereer, eer; '**reverence** *s.* eerbied; '**reverend** *s.* eerwaarde; '**reverent** *bnw.* eerbiedig.

'reverie ['revəri] *s.* (*-s*) mymering.

re'verse [ri'vŏs] *bnw.* omgekeer; *ww.* omdraai, omstel; **re'version** *s.* terugval; **re'vert** *ww.* terugval; reversing tru; **reversing lamp** *s.* trulamp; **reversing gear** *s.* trurat; **reversible** *bnw.* omkeerbaar.

re'vile [ri'vail] *ww.* (*-d*) beskimp, slegmaak.

re'vise [ri'vaiz] *ww.* (*-d*) hersien; **re'vision** *s.*

re'vive [ri'vaiv] *ww.* (*-d*) herlewe, weer oplewe; weer opwek, besiel; hernuwe, herstel.

re'voke [ri'vouk] *ww.* (*-d*) herroep; **revo'cation** *s.*

re'volt [ri'voult] *ww.* (*-ed*) opstaan, rebelleer; *s.* opstand; -**ing** *bnw.* oproerig; walglik; **revo'lution** *s.* opstand, omwenteling.

re'volve [ri'volv] *ww.* (*-d*) draai; -**r** *s.* pistool, rewolwer.

'rev 'up ['rev 'ʌp] *ww.* (*revved -*) opjaag.

re'ward [ri'wŏd] *s.* (*-s*) beloning.

'rhapsody ['ræpsədi] *s.* rapsodie.

'rhetoric ['retərik] *s.* retorika; -**al** *bnw.* retories.

'rheumatism ['rŏēmətizəm] *s.* rumatiek; **rheu'matic** *bnw.* rumaties.

rhi'noceros [rai'nosərəs] *s.* renoster.

rhomb ['rom] *s.* ruit; -**oid** *s.* langwerpige ruit; -**us** = **rhomb**.

'rhubarb ['rŏēbăb] *s.* rabarber.

'rhyme ['raim] *s.* rym(pie); -**less** *bnw.* rymloos.

rhythm ['ridhəm] *s.* ritme, maat; -**ical** *bnw.* ritmies.

'rib ['rib] *s.* (*-s*) ribbetjie; ribstuk; ribbebeen; ribbe.

'ribald ['ribəld] *bnw.* liederlik; -**ry** *s.* smerige taal.

'ribbon ['ribən] *s.* (*-s*) lint, band; - **grass** *s.* lintgras.

rice ['rais] *s.* rys.

rich ['ritsj] *bnw.* ryk; kostelik; kleurryk; -**es** rykdom, skatte.

rick ['rik] *s.* (*-s*) mied.

'rickets *s.* = **rachitis**; '**rickety** *bnw.* swak, lamlendig.

'rickshaw ['riksjŏ] *s.* (*-s*) riksja.

'ricochet ['rikəsjet] *ww.* (*-ted*) opslaan.

rid ['rid] *ww.* (*-ded*) bevry, ontslaan; -**dance** *s.* bevryding, verlossing.

'riddle ['ridl] s. (-s) raaisel; ww. (-d) vol gate skiet.

ride ['raid] ww. ('rode, 'ridden) ry; s. rit; -r s. ruiter.

ridge ['ridzj] s. (-s) rug, rant, rif; vors, nok; maanhaar; 'ridgy bnw. heuwelagtig.

'ridicule [ridi'kjõēl] s. belaglikheid, spot; ri'diculous bnw. belaglik.

rife ['raif] bnw. heersend, algemeen.

'rifle ['raifl] s. (-s) geweer; ww. (-d) roof, plunder; -man s. skutter; - range s. skietbaan.

rift ['rift] s. (-s) bars, skeur.

'rig ['righ] ww. (-ged) van tuig of touwerk voorsien.

'rigging ['righing] s. (-s) touwerk, tuigasie, uitrusting.

right ['rait] bnw. reg; regverdig; billik; regter, haar; ww. (-ed) in orde bring, herstel; s. reg; aanspraak; regterhand; bw. presies; regs; -about bnw. regsom; -eous bnw. regverdig, regskape; -ful bnw. wettig; -handed bnw. regs; -minded bnw. reggeaard.

rigid ['ridzjid] bnw. styf; streng; ri'gidity s. styfheid; strengheid.

'rigmarole ['righməroul] s. geklets, onsamehangende praatjies.

'rigour ['righə] s. strengheid, hardheid; 'rigorous bnw. streng, hard.

'rile ['rail] ww. (-d) boos maak, siel uittrek.

rim ['rim] s. rant, kant; velling.

'rime ['raim] s. ryp.

rind ['rind] s. skil, bas, kors.

ring ['ring] s. (-s) ring; kring; sirkel, kartel; ww. ('rang, 'rung) 'n ring aansit; lui; weerklink; bel; -leader s. belhamel; -worm s. omloop.

rink ['rink] s. (-s) skaatsbaan.

'rinse ['rins] ww. (-d) afspoel, uitspoel.

riot ['raiət] s. (-s) drinkgelag; oproer; muitery; -er s. oproermaker; -ous bnw. oproerig; -ry s. oproerigheid; - truck s. moleswa.

ripe ['raip] bnw. (-r, -st) ryp; -n ww. (-ed) ryp word, ryp maak.

rise ['raiz] ww. ('rose, 'risen) opstaan; opkom; rys, styg; s. opgang; verhoging; opdraand, bult; 'rising bnw. opgaande, s. opstand.

risk ['risk] s. (-s) gevaar; waagstuk; -y bnw. gevaarlik.

'rite ['rait] s. (-s) ritus, kerkgebruik; 'ritual bnw. ritueel.

'rival ['raivəl] s. (-s) teenstander, mededinger; -ry s. mededinging.

'river ['rivə] s. (-s) rivier; -bed s. rivierbedding; -side s. rivieroewer.

'rivet ['rivit] s. (-s) klinknael, bout.

road ['road] s. (-s) pad, weg; ankerplek; - book s. roeteboek; - hog s. padluis, jaagduiwel; -side s. kant van die pad; -ster s. ryperd, fiets; -worthy bnw. padvaardig; - authority s. padowerheid; - barrier s. padblok(kade), padversperring; - courtesy s. padhoflikheid; cross-s s.

padkruising, kruispaaie; - deviation s. padverlegging; -holding ability s. padhouvermoë; - junction s. padaansluiting; - menace s. pad gevaar; -sense s. padsin; - service s. paddiens; - shoulder s. padflank - signs s. padtekens; - signpost s. padwyser; - test s. padtoets; transportation s. padvervoer.

roam ['roum] ww. (-ed) swerf ronddool.

roar ['rõ] ww. (-ed) brul, bulder raas, dreun; -ing bnw. brullend.

roast ['roust] ww. (-ed) braai, brand; s. braaivleis; -er s. braaier; brander oond.

rob ['rob] ww. (-bed) steel, roof; -ber s. rower; -bery s. roof.

robe ['roub] s. (-s) tabberd, kleed.

'robin ['robin] s. (-s) rooiborsie.

ro'bust [rõ'bʌst] bnw. sterk, kragtig.

'rock ['rok] s. (-s) rots; ww. (-ed) wieg; wankel; - crystal s. berg-kristal; -ery s. rotstuin; -ing-chair s. rystoel; - oil s. steenolie; - pigeon s. bosduif; -y bnw. rotsagtig.

'rocket ['rokit] s. (-s) pyl.

rod ['rod] s. (-s) roede, stok, staf, staaf; stang.

'rodent ['roudənt] s. (-s) knaagdier.

'rogue ['rough] s. (-s) skurk, skelm; -ry s. skelmery; 'roguish bnw. skelmagtig.

'rôle ['roul] s. (-s) (toneel) rol.

roll ['roul] s. (-s) rol, register, naamlys; broodjie; ww. (-ed) rol, oprol; - call s. monstering, appél; -er s. roller, rolstok; - bandage s. rolverband; -er bearing s. rollaer; -er blind s. blinding; -er-skate s. rolskaats; -ing bnw. rollend, golwend; -ing-pin s. rolstok; -ing-press s. rolpers; -ed bnw. gewals(te).

ro'mance [rə'mæns] s. romanse; -r s. romanskrywer; ro'mantic bnw. romanties.

romp ['romp] ww. (-ed) baljaar, jakker.

rood ['rõēd] s. (-s) roede; kruis.

roof ['roef] s. dak; -ing s. materiaal vir dakwerk; -less bnw. dakloos, sonder dak; - tree s. nokbalk; - garden s. daktuin; - carrier s. (-s) dakrak, dakrooster.

rook ['roek] s. (-s) kraai; bedrieër; -ery s. kraaines.

room ['roem] s. (-s) kamer; ruimte; geleentheid; -y bnw. ruim; -iness s. ruimheid.

roost ['rõēst] s. stellasie; slaapplek; ww. gaan slaap; -er s. haan.

root ['rõēt] s. wortel; ww. (-ed) wortelskiet; -let s. worteltjie; -stock s. onderstam.

'rope ['roup] s. (-s) tou, lyn; ww. (-d) vasmaak, vang met tou; -dancer s. koorddanser; -ladder s. touleer; -yarn s. kaalgaar; 'ropey bnw. draderig.

'rose ['rouz] s. (-s) roos; 'rosary s. ('rosaries) roostuin, rosekrans; -ate

['rouziit] *bnw.* rooskleurig; **-bud** *s.*
roosknop; **-coloured** *bnw.* rooskleurig; **- diamond** *s.* rosetsteen;
-mary *s.* roosmaryn; **-ola** *s.* uitslag;
- rash *s.* roothond; ro'**sette** *s.* roset,
kokarde; **-wood** *s.* palissanderhout;
'**rosy** *bnw.* blosend.

'**rosemary** ['rouzməri] *s.* rosemaryn.

'**rosin** ['rozin] *s.* harpuis, hars; **-y**
bnw. harpuisagtig.

'**roster** ['rousta] *s.* rooster, lys.

'**rostrum** ['rostrəm] *s.* spreekgestoelte.

rot ['rot] *s.* vrotheid, verrotting;
kaf, onsin; *ww.* (-ted) vrot, sleg
word, vergaan; **-ten** *bnw.* vrot,
ellendig.

'**rota** ['routə] *s.* (-s) rooster, lys.

ro'**tate** [rou'tyt] *ww.* (-d) roteer,
draai; afwissel; '**rotary** *bnw.* draaiend; ro'**tation** *s.* draaiing, wenteling; ro'**tator** *s.* draaispier.

'**rotavator** ['routəvytər] *s.* (-s) kapploeg.

'**rote** ['rout] *s.* gewoonte; *learning
by* - van buite leer.

ro'**tund** [rou'tʌnd] *bnw.* rond,
bolvormig; **-ity** *s.* rondheid.

'**rouge** ['rōēzj] *bnw.* rooi; *s.* rooiverf;
blanketsel; rouge.

'**rough** ['rʌf] *bnw.* (-er, -est) grof, ru,
hard; ongemanierd; onstuimig; *s.*
oneffenheid; skurk; **-and-ready** *bnw.*
grof, onafgewerk; **-and-tumble** *bnw.*
slordig, deurmekaar; **-cast** *bnw.*
gerofkas; **-ly** *bw.* naasteby; **-shod**
bnw. meedoënloos; **-age** *s.* growwe
bestanddeel van voedsel; **-rider** *s.*
perdetemmer.

round ['raund] *bnw.* (-er, -est) rond;
s. kring; bol; rondte; *voors.* rondom;
bw. om; *ww.* (-ed) afrond; omseil;
-about *bnw.* wydlopig; **-ly** *bw.*
kortaf.

'**rouse** ['rauz] *ww.* (-d) opwek,
aanspoor; '**rousing** *bnw.* opwekkend,
besielend.

rout ['raut] *ww.* (-ed) verslaan, op
vlug jaag.

'**route** ['rōēt] *s.* (-s) roete, koers, pad,
weg.

rou'**tine** ['rōē'tin] *s.* roetine, sleur,
gewoonte.

'**rove** ['rouv] *ww.* (-d) swerf; **-r** *s.*
swerwer; losspeler.

row ['rou] *s.* (-s) ry, reeks; *ww.* (-ed)
roei.

row ['rau] *s.* (-s) rusie, twis; lawaai;
ww. (-ed) rusie maak; **-dy** *bnw.*
luidrugtig; **-dyism** *s.* lawaai, oproerigheid.

'**rowlock** ['rolək] *s.* (-s) roeimik, dol.

'**royal** ['roiəl] *bnw.* koninklik, vorstelik; rojaal; **-ist** *s.* koningsgesinde;
-ty *s.* die koninklike familie.

rub ['rʌb] *ww.* (-bed) vrywe; polys;
s. vrywing; moeilikheid; **- down** *s.*
bewerk met roskam, flinke afvrywing van liggaam; **-bing compound**
s. vryfmengsel.

'**rubber** ['rʌbə] *s.* gomlastiek;
wisser; pot, spelreeks.

'**rubbish** ['rʌbisj] *s.* vuilgoed,
rommel.

'**rubble** ['rʌbl] *s.* afval, rommel.

'**ruby** ['rōēbi] *s.* ('*rubies*) robyn.

'**ruction** ['rʌksjən] *s.* (-s) onenigheid,
twis.

'**rudder** ['rʌdə] *s.* (-s) roer, stuur.

'**ruddy** ['rʌdi] *bnw.* ('*ruddier*, '*ruddiest*) blosend.

'**rude** ['rōēd] *bnw.* (-r, -st) ru, grof;
onbeskof; onbeskaaf.

'**rudiment** ['rōēdimənt] *s.* (-s)
grondslag; halfontwikkelde orgaan;
rudi'**mentary** *bnw.* rudimentêr.

rue ['rōē] *ww.* (-d) betreur, berou; *s.*
wynruit; **-ful** *bnw.* verdrietig.

ruff ['rʌf] *s.* geplooide kraag.

'**ruffian** ['rʌfjən] *s.* (-s) skurk.

'**ruffle** ['rʌfl] *ww.* (-d) frommel,
deurmekaar maak.

rug ['rʌgh] *s.* (-s) reisdeken;
vloerkleed.

'**rugby** ['rʌghbi] *s.* rugbie-voetbal.

'**rugged** ['rʌghid] *bnw.* ruig, ru;
streng; lomp.

'**ruin** ['rōēin] *s.* (-s) verderf; bouval;
murasie; *ww.* (-ed) ruïneer; **rui'nation** *s.* ondergang, renewasie; **-ous**
bnw. verderflik; nadelig; vervalle.

'**rule** ['rōēl] *s.* (-s) reël, bepaling;
voorskrif; bestuur, gesag; liniaal,
duimstok; *ww.* (-d) regeer, beheer
voer, beheers; linieer; **-r** *s.* heerser;
liniaal; '**ruling** *bnw.* heersend; *s.*
beslissing.

'**rum** ['rʌm] *bnw.* (-mer, -mest)
sonderling, snaaks; *s.* rum (drank).

'**rumble** ['rʌmbl] *ww.* (-d) dreun,
ratel, rommel.

'**ruminate** ['rōēminyt] *ww.* (-d)
herkou.

'**rummage** ['rʌmidzj] *ww.* (-d)
deursnuffel, visenteer.

'**rumour** ['rōēmə] *s.* (-s) gerug.

rump ['rʌmp] *s.* stuitjie, agterste
deel, romp.

run ['rʌn] *ww.* ('*ran*) hardloop, hol;
stroom, vloei; smokkel; lui; *s.* lopie;
toeloop; aanvraag; wedren; uitstappie; **-about** *bnw.* rondswerwend;
-away *s.* droster, wegloper; **-ner** *s.*
hardloper, renbode, bode; **-ning**
bnw. lopend; **-ning foot** *s.* strekkende
voet; **-ning in** *ww.* inry, inslyt;
-ning in period *s.* inrytyd, inslyttyd.

'**rune** ['rōēn] *s.* (-s) runeskrif (teken).

'**rupture** ['rʌptsjə] *s.* (-s) breuk;
tweespalk; *ww.* (-d) 'n breuk kry.

'**rural** ['roeərəl] *bnw.* plattelands,
landelik.

'**ruse** ['rōēz] *s.* (-s) streek, lis.

rush ['rʌsj] *s.* (-es) biesie, palmiet,
vaart, stormloop, drukte; *ww.* (-ed)
hardloop, storm, voortsnel.

rusk ['rʌsk] *s.* (-s) beskuit.

russet ['rʌsit] *bnw.* rooibruin.

rust ['rʌst] *s.* roes; *ww.* (-ed) verroes
-y *bnw.* geroes.

'**rustic** ['rʌstik] *bnw.* landelik; *s.*

boer, plaasjapie; **-ate** *ww.* (-*d*)
verboers; **rus'ticity** *s.* landelikheid.
'**rustle** ['rʌsl] *ww.* (-*d*) ritsel, ruis.
rut ['rʌt] *s.* (-*s*) groef.
'**ruthless** ['rōěthlis] *bnw.* meedoënloos.
'**rye** ['rai] *s.* rog; **- bread** *s.* rogbrood.

S

S.A.B.C. (South African Broadcasting Corporation) S.A.U.K.
(*Suid-Afrikaanse Uitsaaikorporasie*).
sabba'tarian [sæbə'těəriən] *s.*
sabbatariër.
'**sabbath** ['sæbəth] *s.* sabbat, rusdag.
'**sable** ['sybl] *s.* sabeldier; sabelbont;
swart.
'**sabotage** ['sæbotāzj] *s.* sabotasie.
'**sabre** ['sybə] *s.* (-*s.*) sabel; **-tache**
[-tæsj] *s.* sabeltas.
sac ['sæk] *s.* sak; **-cule** *s.* sakkie.
'**saccharine** ['sækərin] *s.* saccharine.
sacer'dotal [sæsə'doutl] *bnw.* priest-
erlik.
sack ['sæk] *s.* (-*s*) sak; plundering;
ww. (-*ed*) ontslaan, afsê; plunder;
-cloth *s.* saklinne; **-race** *s.* sak-
wedren.
'**sacrament** ['sækrəmənt] *s.* (-*s*)
sakrament; **sacra'mental** *bnw.* sa-
kramenteel.
'**sacred** ['sykrid] *bnw.* heilig, gewyd.
'**sacrifice** ['sækrifais] *s.* (-*s*) offerande; offer; opoffering; *ww.* (-*d*)
opoffer, offer; afstaan; **sacri'ficial**
bnw. offer-.
'**sacrilege** ['sækrilidzj] *s.* heilig-
skennis, kerkroof; **sacri'legious** *bnw.*
ontheiligend.
sacro'sanct [sækrou'sænkt] *bnw.*
heilig, onskendbaar.
'**sacrum** ['sykrəm] *s.* heiligbeen.
sad ['sæd] *bnw.* (-*der*, -*dest*) treurig,
droewig; **-den** *ww.* (-*ed*) bedroef,
treurig stem.
'**saddle** ['sædl] *s.* saal; bergrug; *ww.*
(-*d*) opsaal; belas; **-bag** *s.* saalsak;
-bow *s.* saalknop; **-cloth** *s.* saal-
kleedjie; **-horse** *s.* ryperd; **-r** *s.*
saalmaker; **-ry** *s.* saalmakery; **-tree**
s. saalboom.
'**sadism** ['sædizəm] *s.* sadisme.
'**safe** ['syf] *s.* brandkas; koskas; *bnw.*
(-*r*, -*st*) veilig, seker; ongedeerd;
-conduct *s.* vrygeleide; **-deposit**
bnw. brandkas; **-guard** *s.* beskerming, *ww.* beskerm; **-keeping** *s.*
bewaring; **-ly** *bw.* veilig; **-ty** *s.*
veiligheid; **-ty-belt** *s.* veiligheids-
gordel; **-ty-catch** *s.* rus(*geweerslot*);
-ty-curtain *s.* brandskerm; **-ty-lamp**
s. veiligheidslamp **-ty-match** *s.*
vuurhoutjie; **-ty-pin** *s.* haakspeld;
-ty-razor *s.* veiligheidskeermes; **-ty-
valve** *s.* veiligheidsklep.
'**saffron** ['sæfrən] *s.* saffraan.
sag ['sægh] *ww.* (-*ged*) uitsak, afsak,
skiet, slap hang, deurhang.
'**saga** ['sāghə] *s.* (-*s*) saga.

sa'gacity [sə'ghæsiti] *s.* skerpsinnigheid; **sa'gacious** *bnw.* skerpsinnig.
'**sage** ['sydzj] *s.* (-*s*) wyse; salie; *bnw.*
wys.
'**sago** ['syghou] *s.* sago.
'**Sahara** [sə'hārə] *s.* Sahara.
sail ['syl] *s.* (-*s*) seil; *ww.* (-*ed*) vaar;
-cloth *s.* seildoek; **-er** *s.* seilskip; **-ing**
s. vertrek(*van skip*); **-or** *s.* matroos.
saint ['synt, 'sint] *s.* (-*s*) heilige,
vrome; **-ed** *bnw.* heilig, vroom; **-like**
bnw. heilig; **-liness** heiligheid; **-ly**
bnw. vroom; **-vitus-dance** *s.* trek-
kings.
'**sake** ['syk] *s.* *for my* **-** terwille van
my.
'**salad** ['sæləd] *s.* slaai; **- dressing** *s.*
slaaisous; **-oil** *s.* slaai-olie, soetolie.
'**salary** ['sæləri] *s.* (*'salaries*) salaris,
besoldiging.
'**sale** ['syl] *s.* (-*s*) verkoping; veiling;
-sman *s.* verkoper.
'**salient** ['syljənt] *bnw.* in die oog
lopend, opvallend.
sa'line [sə'lain] *s.* (-*s*) sout; **sa'linity**
s. southeid.
sa'liva [sə'laivə] *s.* speeksel, spoeg,
kwyl; '**salivary** *bnw.* speeksel-;
- pump *s.* kwylpomp, speekselpomp.
'**sallow** ['sælou] *bnw.* bleek, sieklik.
'**sally** ['sæli] *s.* (*'sallies*) uitval,
kwinkslag; *ww.* (*'sallied*) uitstorm,
uittrek; **-port** *s.* uitvalpoort.
'**salmon** ['sæmən] *s.* salm.
sa'loon [sə'lōēn] *s.* (-*s*) salon, saal,
eetsaal; drinkplek; **-carriage** *s.*
salonwa; **-rifle** *s.* salongeweertjie.
salt ['sōlt] *s.* sout; pikbroek; *bnw.*
(-*ier*, -*iest*) sout, pekel, skerp; *ww.*
(-*ed*) sout, insout; **-cellar** *s.* sout-
potjie, soutbussie; **-ed** *bnw.* gesout,
pekel-; **-ish** *bnw.* souterig; **-lick** *s.*
soutlekplek; **- pan** *s.* soutpan; **-petre**
s. salpeter; **-works** *s.* soutmakery; **-y**
bnw. sout, souterig.
sa'lubrity [sə'lōēbriti] *s.* heilsaam-
heid, gesondheid; **sa'lubrious** *bnw.*
heilsaam, gesond.
'**salutary** ['sæljoetəri] *bnw.* heilsaam.
salu'tation [sæljoe'tysjən] *s.* begroeting.
sa'lute [sə'lōēt] *s.* (-*s*) groet, saluut;
ww. (-*d*) groet, salueer.
'**salvage** ['sælvidzj] *s.* berging,
redding; *ww.* (-*d*) berg, red.
'**salve** ['sælv] *ww.* (-*d*) red; **sal'vation**
s. redding; **-r** *s.* skinkbord, pre-
senteerblad.
'**Salvia** ['sælvia] *s.* salie.
'**salvo** ['sælvou] *s.* (-*s*) salvo, sarsie.
sal vo'latile [sælvə'lætəli] *s.* vlugsout.
'**same** ['sym] *bnw.* dieselfde, einste;
-ness *s.* gelykheid, eentonigheid.
'**sample** ['sāmpl] *s.* (-*s*) monster,
voorbeeld, staaltjie; **-r** *s.* monster-
aar, toetser; iemand wat monsters
insamel.
sana'torium [sænə'tôriəm] *s.* (-*s*)
gesondheidsoord, verpleeginrigting.

sanctify ['sæŋktifai] ww. ('sanctified) heilig, heilig maak, wy; sanctifi'cation s. heiliging, wyding; 'sanctitude s. heiligheid; 'sanctity s. heiligheid.

sancti'monious [sæŋkti'mounjəs] bnw. skynheilig.

sanction ['sæŋksjən] s. (-s) goedkeuring; sanksie; strafmaatreëls.

sanctuary ['sæŋktjoeəri] s. ('sanctuaries) heiligdom; toevlugsoord.

sand ['sænd] s. (-s) sand; -bag s. sandsak; -blast s. sandstraal; -glass s. sandloper; -paper s. skuurpapier; -shoe s. strandskoen, seilskoen; -stone s. sandklip, sandsteen; -y bnw. sanderig.

'sandal ['sændl] s. (-s) sandaal; -wood s. sandelhout.

'sandwich ['sændwidzj] s. (-es) toebroodjie.

sane ['syn] bnw. (-r, -st) verstandig.

'sangfroid ['sæŋg-frɔ̃ã] s. bedaardheid.

'sanguine ['sæŋ-ghwin] bnw. bloedrooi; astrant; optimisties; 'sanguinary bnw. bloedig; bloeddorstig.

sanitary ['sænitəri] bnw. gesondheids-, sanitêr; sani'tation s. riolering; - tanker s. slopwa.

sanity ['sæniti] s. gesondheid van verstand; vgl. sane.

sans ['sænz, 'sɔ̃ŋ] voors. sonder.

Sanskrit ['sænskrit] s. Sanskrit.

'Santa 'Claus ['sæntə'klɔ̃z] s. Sinterklaas.

sap ['sæp] s. sap, vog; loopgraaf; moeite, swaar werk; ww. (-ped) tap; ondermyn; ingrawe; -less bnw. saploos; droog; uitgeput; -ling s. boompie; -per s. myngrawer.

'sapience ['sypiəns] s. wysheid; 'sapient bnw. eiewys, waanwys.

sa'ponify [sæ'pɔnifai] ww. (sa'ponified) verseep; saponifi'cation s. verseping; sapo'naceous bnw. seepagtig.

'sapor ['sæpə] s. geur; 'sapid bnw. geurig; sa'pidity s. geurigheid.

'sapphire ['sæfaiə] s. (-s) saffier.

'saraband ['særəbænd] s. sarabande.

'Saracen ['særəsn] s. Saraseen.

'sarcasm ['sãkæzəm] s. sarkasme; sar'castic bnw. sarkasties.

sar'cophagus [sã'kofəghəs] s. sarkofaag.

sar'dine [sã'din] s. (-s) sardientjie.

sar'donic [sã'donik] bnw. bitter, sinies, sardonies.

'sardonyx ['sãdəniks] s. sardoniks.

'sarong ['sãrong] s. sarong, Maleise romp.

sarsapa'rilla [sãsəpə'rilə] s. sarsaparilla.

sar'torial [sã'tôriəl] bnw. kleremakers-.

sash ['sæsj] s. (-es) serp, gord, lyfband; skuifraam.

'Satan ['sytən] s. Satan; sa'tanic bnw. duiwels.

'satchel ['sætsjəl] s. (-s) sakkie.

'sate ['syt] ww. (-d) versadig;

'satiable bnw. versadigbaar; 'satiate ww. (-d) versadig; sati'ation s. versadiging; sa'tiety s. satheid, volheid.

sa'teen [sæ'tin] s. wolsatyn.

'satellite ['sætəlait] s. (-s) satelliet.

'satin ['sætin] s. satyn; - finish s. satynglans; -wood s. satynhout; -y bnw. satynagtig.

'satire ['sætaiə] s. spotskrif, hekelskrif, satire; sa'tiric bnw. satiries; sa'tirical bnw. satiries; 'satirize ww. hekel; 'satirist s. satirikus.

'satisfy ['sætisfai] ww. ('satisfied) bevredig, voldoen; oortuig; satis'faction s. bevrediging; satis'factory bnw. bevredigend.

saturate ['sætjəryt] ww. (-d) deurweek, versadig; 'saturable bnw. deurweekbaar; satu'ration s. deurweking.

'Saturday ['sætədi] s. Saterdag.

'Saturn ['sætən] s. Saturnus; -ic bnw. lydende aan loodvergifting; -ine bnw. swaarmoedig.

satur'nalia [sætə'nyljə] s. uitspattinge.

'satyr ['sætə] s. sater, bosgod; wellusteling.

'sauce ['sôs] s. sous; astrantheid; -boat s. souspotjie; -pan s. kastrol; -r s. piering; 'saucy bnw. astrant; - tureen s. souspotjie.

'saunter ['sôntə] ww. (-ed) slenter; s. slentergang.

'sausage ['sosidzj] s. (-s) wors.

'savage ['sævidzj] bnw. (-st) wild, woes, barbaars; woedend; s. barbaar; ww. (-d) toetakel; -ry s. barbaarsheid.

sa'vanna(h) [sə'vænə] s. grasvlakte.

'savant ['sævənt] s. geleerde.

'save ['syv] ww. (-d) red; bewaar; spaar; voors. behalwe; voegw. tensy; 'saving bnw. reddend, s. redding; voors. behalwe; 'savings s. spaargeld; 'savings-bank s. spaarbank.

'Saviour ['syvjə] s. Heiland.

'savour ['syvə] s. geur; 'savouriness s. geurigheid; -y bnw. geurig.

sa'voy [sə'vɔi] s. (-s) savojekool.

'savvy ['sævi] ww. (savvied) begryp, snap.

saw ['sô] s. (-s) spreuk; saag; ww. (-ed) saag; -bones s. sjirurg; -dust s. saagsel; -fish s. saagvis; -horse s. saagbok; -mill s. saagmeul; - pit s. saagkuil; - set s. tandsetter; -yer s. saer.

'saxifrage ['sæksifridzj] s. steenbreek.

'Saxon ['sæksən] s. Sakser; Saksies.

'saxophone ['sæksəfoun] s. (-s) saksofoon.

say ['sy] ww. ('said) sê, beweer; opsê; s. mening; bewering; seggingskap; -ing s. gesegde.

scab ['skæb] s. (-s) skurfte; brandsiekte; kors; roof; onderkruiper; -by bnw. skurftig; 'scabies s.

skurfte; '**scabious** *bnw.* skurf; -**rous**
bnw. skurfagtig.

'**scabbard** ['skæbəd] s. (-s) skede.

'**scabies** ['skybiiz] s. skurfte.

'**scaffold** ['skæfəld] s. (-s) skavot;
steier; -**ing** s. steierhout.

scald ['skôld] *ww.* (-ed) brand met
kookwater; skroei; uitkook; s.
brandwond, vogbrand; digter,
skalde; -**ing** *bnw.* gloeiend.

'**scale** ['skyl] s. (-s) skub, dop; skaal;
touleer; *ww.* (-d) uitdop, afdop;
weeg; beklim; '**scalable** *bnw.* be-
klimbaar; '**scaly** *bnw.* skubbig; -
insects s. dopluise.

'**scallop** ['skôləp] s. skulp, skulpwerk;
-**ed** *bnw.* uitgeskulp.

scalp ['skælp] s. (-s) skedel; kopvel.

'**scalpel** ['skælpəl] s. (-s) ontleedmes.

scamp ['skæmp] s. (-s) skurk,
skelm, vabond; -**er** *ww.* (-ed)
hardloop, weghol; s. galop.

scan ['skæn] *ww.* (-ned) skandeer;
noukeurig ondersoek; aftas (*radar*).

'**scandal** ['skændl] s. skandaal;
skande; skindery; -**ise** *ww.* beskinder, beledig; -**monger** s. skinderbek; -**ous** *bnw.* lasterlik.

'**scansion** ['skænsjən] s. skandering.

'**scant** ['skænt] *bnw.* karig, skraal;
-**ily** *bw.* karig; -**ling** s. balkie; -**y**
bnw. skaars.

'**scapegoat** ['skypghout] s. sondebok.

'**scapegrace** ['skypghrys] s. deugniet,
niksnuts.

'**scapula** ['skæpjoelə] s. skouerbeen.

scar ['skâ] s. (-s) litteken, merk.

'**scarab** ['skærəb] s. (-s) heilige
kewer (*Egipte*).

'**scarce** ['skɛəs] *bnw.* (-r, -st) skaars,
seldsaam; -**ly** *bw.* nouliks.

'**scare** ['skɛə] *ww.* (-d) laat skrik,
skrik; s. vrees; -**crow** s. voëlver-
skrikker; -**monger** s. onrussaaier.

scarf ['skâf] s. (*scarves*) serp, halsdoek; -**pin** s. dasspeld.

'**scarify** ['skɛərifai] *ww.* (*scarified*)
insnydinge in vel maak, kop;
scarifi'cation s. insnyding, kopping.

scarla'tina [skâlə'tinə] s. skar-
lakenkoors.

'**scarlet** ['skâlit] s. (-s) skarlaken; *bnw.*
skarlakenrooi; -**fever** s. skarlaken-
koors.

scarp ['skâp] s. (-s) steilte, helling.

'**scathe** ['skydh] *ww.* (-d) beskadig,
beseer; s. letsel; -**less** *bnw.* ongedeerd; '**scathing** *bnw.* vlymend.

'**scatter** ['skætə] *ww.* (-ed) strool,
verstrooi; uitmekaar jaag; -**brain** s.
warkop; -**brained** *bnw.* warhoofdig.

'**scavenge** ['skævindzj] *ww.* (-d)
straat vee; -**r** s. straatveër; aasdier;
-**r beetle** s. miskruier.

scene ['sin] s. (-s) toneel, tafereel;
voorval; standjie; -**painter** s. to-
neeldekorateur; -**ry** s. natuurtoneel;
-**shifter** s. toneelhandlanger; '**scenic**
bnw. skilderagtig.

scent ['sent] s. (-s) geur; reukwater;
lawentel; lug; *ww.* (-ed) ruik, insnuif,

vermoed; -**bottle** s. reukflessie;
- **spray** s. reukwaterspuit.

'**sceptic** ['skeptik] s. twyfelaar; -**al**
bnw. skepties; **scepsis** s. twyfel(sug).

'**sceptre** ['septə] s. (-s) septer, staf.

'**schedule** ['sjedjôël] s. (-s) lys,
staat, tabel, rooster.

'**scheme** ['skîm] s. (-s) skema; *ww.*
(-d) knoei; **sche'matic** *bnw.* ske-
maties; -**r** s. konkelaar.

schism ['sizəm] s. skeuring; **schis-**
'**matic** s. verdeler, *bnw.* verdeler.

schist ['sjist] s. leisteen; -**ose** *bnw.*
leisteenagtig.

'**scholar** ['skolə] s. (-s) skolier;
geleerde; -**ly** *bnw.* geleerd; -**ship** s.
geleeredheid; beurs.

scho'lastic [ska'læstik] s. skolastikus,
bnw. skolasties.

school ['skôël] s. (-s) skool; leer-
skool; *ww.* (-ed) leer; skole vorm;
- **board** s. skoolraad; -**boy** s. skool-
seun; -**fellow** s. skoolmaat; -**house**
s. skoolgebou; -**ing** s. opvoeding,
afrigting; -**master** s. onderwyser;
-**mistress** s. onderwyseres; -**room** s.
klaskamer; -**teacher** s. onderwyser
(es).

'**schooner** ['skôënə] s. (-s) skoener.

sci'atica [sai'ætikə] s. heupjig;
sci'atic *bnw.* heup-.

'**science** ['saiəns] s. wetenskap;
natuurwetenskap; **scien'tific** *bnw.*
(natuur)wetenskaplik; '**scientist** s.
(natuur)wetenskaplike.

'**scintilla** [sin'tilə] s. (-s) vonkie;
'**scintillate** *ww.* (-d) vonkel; **scintil-**
'**lation** s. vonkeling.

'**scion** ['saiən] s. (-s) spruit;
afstammeling.

'**scirrhus** ['sirəs] s. kankergewas.

'**scission** ['sizjən] s. (-s) snyding,
splitsing.

'**scissors** ['sizəz] s. skêr.

scle'rosis [sklia'rousis] s. sklerose;
scle'rotic *bnw.* hard.

scoff ['skof] *ww.* (-ed) spot, skimp;
-**er** s. spotter.

scold ['skould] *ww.* (-ed) uitskel;
berispe.

'**scone** ['skon] s. (-s) botterkoekie.

scoop ['skôëp] s. (-s) skop; skep;
wins; slag; *ww.* (-ed) skep; uithol; 'n
slag slaan.

scoot ['skôët] *ww.* (-ed) laat spat,
weghol.

'**scope** ['skoup] s. beweegruimte.

scorch ['skôtsj] *ww.* (-ed) brand,
skroei, verseng; -**er** s. iets wat skroei;
woesteling.

'**score** ['skô] s. (-s) telling; keep;
rekening; partituur; *ww.* (-d) inkeep;
tel; op musiek stel; -**r** s. teller.

scorn ['skôn] s. veragting, hoon;
ww. (-ed) hoon verag; -**ful** *bnw.*
veragtelik; minagtend.

'**scorpion** ['skôpjən] s. (-s) skerpioen.

Scot ['skot] s. Skot; -**ch** *bnw.* Skots;
-**chman** s. Skot; -**land** s. Skotland;
-**tish** *bnw.* Skots.

scot'free ['skot'fri] *bnw.* belasting-vry, vry; ongestraf.

scoundrel ['skaundrəl] *s.* skurk, skobbejak.

cour ['skauə] *ww.* (-ed) skuur; *ww.* skuur; rondswerwe; deursoek; **-ing wool** *s.* skuurwol.

scourge ['skədzj] *s.* gesel; plaag; kastyding; *ww.* (-d) gesel, kasty, teister.

scout ['skaut] *s.* (-s) verkenner, padvinder; **-master** *s.* leier van groep verkenners.

scowl ['skaul] *ww.* (-ed) frons; **-ing** *bnw.* fronsend.

scraggy ['skræghi] *bnw.* ('scraggier, 'scraggiest) maer, skraal.

scramble ['skræmbl] *ww.* (-d) klouter; worstel; **-d egg** *s.* roereier.

scrap ['skræp] *s.* (-s) snipper, vodjie, brokkie, afval, rommel, skroot; bakleiery; *ww.* (-ped) weggooi; baklei; **-book** *s.* knipselboek, plakboek; **-heap** *s.* afvalhoop; **-iron** *s.* roesyster; **- value** *s.* rommelwaarde.

'scrape ['skryp] *ww.* (-d) skraap; krap; skuur; **-r** *s.* skraper; **'scrapings** *s.* skraapsels, snippers.

scratch ['skrætsj] *ww.* (-ed) krap, skraap, skrap; *s.* krap, skrapie, streep; **- race** *s.* gelykstaan-wedstryd; **-y** *bnw.* deurmekaar, onduidelik.

scrawl ['skrɔl] *s.* slegte skrif, hanepote, krabbel.

scream ['skrim] *ww.* (-ed) skreeu, gil.

screech ['skritzj] *ww.* (-ed) gil, skreeu; **-owl** *s.* kerkuil.

screen ['skrin] *s.* (-s) skerm, beskutting; doek; sif; *ww.* beskerm, beskut; sif; **-wiper** *s.* skermveër.

screw ['skrōē] *s.* (-s) skroef; salaris; *ww.* vasskroewe; opdruk; afpers; **-driver** *s.* skroewedraaier; **-jack** *s.* domkrag; **- propeller** *s.* skroef(skip); **-wrench** *s.* skroefhamer; **-worm** (*cattle*) *s.* beesbrommer.

'scribble ['skribl] *ww.* (-d) krabbel.

'scribe ['skraib] *s.* (-s) skrywer; klerk; skrifgeleerde; *ww.* (-d) kras.

'scrimmage ['skrimidzj] *s.* stoeiery, bakleiery; skrum.

scrip ['skrip] *s.* briefie, bewys, aandelesertifikaat.

script ['skript] *s.* (-s) manuskrip; skrif; skryfletter.

'scripture ['skriptsjə] *s.* (-s) die Heilige Skrif; **'scriptural** *bnw.* skriftuurlik.

scroll ['skroul] *s.* (-s) rol, lys; krul.

'scrotum ['skroutəm] *s.* balsak.

'scrounge ['skraundzj] *ww.* (-d) kaap, skaai; klaploop.

scrub ['skrʌb] *s.* ruigte; armoedige dier; *ww.* (-bed) skrop; **-bing-board** *s.* wasplank; **-bing-brush** *s.* skropborsel; **-by** *bnw.* niksbeduidend; ruig; **-oak** *s.* dwergeik.

scruff ['skrʌf] *s.* (-s) nek.

scrum ['skrʌm] *s.* (-s) skrum; **-mage** *s.* = **scrimmage.**

'scrumptious ['skrʌmpsjəs] *bnw.* uitstekend, heerlik.

'scruple ['skrōēpl] *s.* (-s) beswaar; *ww.* (-d) aarsel, swarigheid sien; **'scrupulous** *bnw.* nougeset.

'scrutiny ['skrōētini] *s.* noukeurige ondersoek; **'scrutinize** *ww.* (-d) goed deurkyk; **scruti'neer** *s.* stemopnemer.

'scuffle ['skʌfl] *ww.* (-d) worstel, baklei, stoei.

scull ['skʌl] *ww.* (-ed) skifroei.

'scullery ['skʌləri] *s.* ('sculleries) opwasplek; **'scullion** *s.* skottelwasser.

'sculptor ['skʌlptə] *s.* beeldhouer; **'sculptural** *bnw.* beeldhou-; **'sculpture** *s.* beeldhoukuns.

scum ['skʌm] *s.* skuim, uitvaagsel; *ww.* (-med) afskuim.

'scupper ['skʌpə] *s.* (-s) spuigat.

'scurf ['skəf] *s.* rofie; skilfer; korsie; skurfte.

'scurrilous ['skʌriləs] *bnw.* laag, gemeen.

'scurry ['skʌri] *ww.* ('scurried) weghardloop, yl.

'scurvy ['skəvi] *s.* skeurbuik; *bnw.* ('scurvier, 'scurviest) gemeen, laag.

'scuttle ['skʌtl] *s.* (-s) koolemmer; luik.

'scythe ['saidh] *s.* (-s) sens.

sea ['si] *s.* (-s) see, oseaan; golf; deining; **- air** *s.* seelug; **- anemone** *s.* see- anemoon; **-board** *s.* seekus; **-borne** *bnw.* uit verre lande; **-breeze** *s.* seewind; **- coast** *s.* kus; **-dog** *s.* rob; **-faring** *bnw.* seevarend; **- front** *s.* seekant; **-going** *bnw.* seevarend; **-gull** *s.* seemeeu; **-hog** *s.* seevark, bruinvis; **-horse** *s.* walrus; **-legs** *s.* seebene; **- level** *s.* seespieël; **- line** *s.* kim; **-port** *s.* hawe; **-rover** *s.* kaper; **-scape** *s.* seegesig, seetoneel; **-shore** *s.* seekus, strand; **-sick** *bnw.* seesiek; **-side** *s.* seekus, strand; **- urchin** *s.* see-egel; **-ward** *bnw.* seewaarts; **-weed** *s.* seewier; **-worthy** *bnw.* seevaardig.

seal ['sil] *s.* (-s) rob; seël; **-er** *s.* robbevanger; **-skin** *s.* robbevel; *ww.* seël, verseël; afdig; **-ing ring** *s.* afdigting; **-ing ring** *s.* digtingsring.

'sealing-wax ['silingwæks] *s.* lak.

seam ['sim] *s.* (-s) naat, soom; litteken; laag; **-less** *bnw.* sonder naat of las; **-stress** ['semtstris] *s.* naaister; **-y** *bnw.* met nate; verkeerde, ongunstige; **-y side** *s.* selfkant, keerkant van iets; ongunstige kant.

sear ['siə] *bnw.* dor; *ww.* (-ed) brand, skroei, verseng.

search ['sətsj] *ww.* (-ed) soek; ondersoek, visenteer; peil; *s.* soektog; ondersoek; visentasie; **-ing** *bnw.* deudringend, skerp; **-light** *s.* soeklig; **- party** *s.* soekgeselskap; **- warrant** *s.* lasbrief tot huissoeking.

'**season** ['sizn] s. (-s) seisoen, jaargety;
gepaste tyd; ww. (-ed) geskik, ryp
gemaak; smaaklik maak; matig;
-able bnw. geleë, tydig; **-ing** s.
toebereiding; kruie; sous; **- ticket**
s. seisoenkaartjie.

seat ['sit] s. (-s) sitplek; bank, stoel ,
setel; landgoed; ww. (-ed) laat sit;
-ing s. sitplek, sitgeriewe, sitplek-
voorsiening; bed(ding); **-ing comfort**
s. sitgemak, sitgerief; **- adjuster** s.
banksteller; **- cover** s. bankoortrek-
sel.

'**secant** ['sikənt] s. snylyn.

se'cede [si'sīd] s. (-d) afskei; **se'cession** s. afskeiding.

se'clude [si'klōēd] ww. (-d) uitsluit;
afsonder; **-d** bnw. afgesonder, stil;
se'clusion s. afsondering.

'**second** ['sekənd] s. (-s) sekonde;
getuie, sekondant; tweede, ander;
bnw. tweede; ww. (-ed) bystaan;
sekondeer; **-ary** bnw. sekondêr;
ondergeskik; **-class** bnw. tweede
klas, tweederangs; **-er** s. sekondant;
-hand bnw. halfslyt, tweedehands;
-ly bw. tweedens; **-rate** bnw.
tweederangs, minderwaardig, **-sight**
s. sienersgawe.

'**secret** ['sikrit] s. (-s) geheim;
bnw. geheim; '**secrecy** s. geheimhouding; **se'crete** ww. (-d) wegsteek;
afskei; **secretive** bnw. geheimsinnig; **se'cretion** s. verberging; afskeiding; **-ly** bw. stilletjies.

'**secretary** ['sekrətri] s. ('secretaries)
sekretaris;   minister;   **secre'tarial**
bnw. van die sekretaris; **secre'tariat**
s. sekretariaat; **-bird** s. sekretaris.

sect ['sekt] s. (-s) sekte; **sec'tarian**
bnw. sektaries.

'**section** ['seksjən] s. (-s) verdeling,
deel; deursnee; ww. (-ed) in seksies
verdeel; **-al** bnw. afdelings-.

'**sector** ['sektə] s. (-s) sektor.

'**secular** ['sekjoelə] bnw. wêreldlik;
sekulêr; **-ize** ww. sekulariseer; **-iza-
tion** s. sekularisasie; **secu'larity** s.
wêreldlikheid.

'**se'cure** [si'kjoeə] bnw. veilig, seker,
gerus; ww. (-d) beveilig; sluit;
vrywaar; **se'curity** s. sekuriteit;
waarborg, borg; veiligheid; **security
bond** s. borgakte.

se'dan [si'dæn] s. (-s) sedan; **- chair**
s. draagstoel.

se'date [si'dēt] bnw. bedaard, besadig, kalm; '**sedative** bnw. kalmerend;
s. kalmeermiddel.

'**sedentary** ['sedntəri] bnw. sittend.

'**sedge** ['sedʒ] s. watergras.

'**sediment** ['sedimənt] s. (-s) afsaksel,
moer.

se'dition [si'disjən] s. opruiïng;
oproer; muitery; sedisie; **se'ditious**
bnw. oproerig; ophitsend.

se'duce [si'djōēs] ww. (-d) verlei; **-r**
s. verleier; **se'ducible** bnw. verlei-
baar; **se'duction** s. verleiding; **se-
'ductive** bnw. verleidelik.

see ['si] ww. ('saw, 'seen) sien; kyk;

begryp; sorgdra; besoek; s. bisdom,
-ing voors. aangesien.

seed ['sid] s. (-s) saad; nakomelings-
kap; ww. saadskiet; **-bed** s. saadak-
kertjie; **- bud** s. saadknop; **-corn** s.
saadkoring; **-ling** s. plantjie; **- potato**
s. moer; **-sman** s. saadhandelaar; **-y**
bnw. vol saad; siekerig, oes; toiingrig.

seek ['sik] ww. ('sought) soek; poog
begeer.

seem ['sim] ww. (-ed) lyk, skyn; **-ing**
bnw. oënskynlik; **-ingly** bw. na dit
skyn; **-ly** bnw. betaamlik.

seer ['siə] s. (-s) siener.

'**see'saw** ['si'sô] s. wipplank; bnw. &
bw. heen en weer.

'**seethe** [sidh] ww. (-d) sied, kook;
'**seething** bnw. wiedend, kokend.

'**segment** ['seghmənt] s. (-s) segment,
gedeelte; **segmen'tation** s. verdeling
in segmente.

'**segregate** ['seghrighyt] ww. (-d)
afsonder, afskei, segregeer; **segre-
'gation** s. afskeiding, segregasie.

seine ['syn] s. seën, treknet.

'**seismograph** ['saizmōghrāf] s.
seismograaf; **seis'mography** s. seis-
mografie.

seis'mology [saiz'molədzji] s. seis-
mologie.

'**seize** ['siz] ww. (-d) vat, gryp, neem;
beslag lê op; '**seizable** bnw. gryp-
baar; '**seizure** s. beslaglegging.

'**seldom** ['seldəm] bw. selde, min.

se'lect [si'lekt] ww. (-ed) uitsoek,
kies; bnw. uitgesoek, uitgelese; **-ion**
s. keuse, seleksie.

self ['self] s. self, eie persoonlikheid;
-abuse s. selfbevlekking; **-acting**
bnw. outomaties; **-aligning** bnw.
selfrigtend; **-assertion** s. aanmatiging; **-binder** s. selfbinder; **-colour** s.
natuurlike, effe kleur; **-command**
s. selfbeheer; **-conceit** s. eiedunk;
-conscious bnw. verleë, bedeesd;
-evident bnw. klaarblyklik; **-forget-
ful** bnw. onbaatsugtig; **-lubricating**
bnw. selfsmeer-; **-opinion** s. eiewaan;
-righteous bnw. eiegeregtig; **-same**
bnw. einste; **-sealing** bnw. selfdig-
tend; **-seeking** bnw. selfsugtig;
-starter s. aansitter; **-styled** bnw.
selfbetitelde; **-suggestion** s. outo-
suggestie; **-will** s. koppigheid.

'**selfhelp** ['selfhelp] s. bnw. selfhulp,
selfbediening.

'**selfish** ['selfisj] bnw. selfsugtig,
baatsugtig.

sell ['sel] ww. ('sold) verkoop; verrai;
fop.

'**selvage** ['selvidzj] s. (-s) selfkant.

'**selvedge** = selvage.

se'mantic [si'mæntik] bnw. seman-
ties; betekenis-; **-s** s. semantiek,
betekenisleer.

semasi'ology [simysi'olədzji] s.
betekenisleer, semantiek, semasio-
logie.

'**semblance** ['sembl₍ ns] s. skyn,
voorkome.

'semen ['simən] s. saad; 'seminal bnw. saad-, kiem; semi'nation s. saadoordrag.

se'mester [si'mestə] s. semester, halfjaar.

'semi- ['semi-] voorvoegsel half-; -breve s. hele noot; -colon s. kommapunt; -final s. halfeindwedstryd; -fluid s. taai vloeistof; -tone s. halwe toon; -trailer s. leunwa; -vowel s. halfvokaal; -quaver s. sestiende noot.

'seminary ['seminəri] s. ('seminaries) semenarie, kweekskool.

'Semite ['simait] s. (-s) Semiet; se'mitic bnw. Semities.

'sempstress ['sempstris] s. = seamstress.

'senate ['senit] s. senaat, hoërhuis; 'senator s. senator; sena'torial bnw. senaats-.

send ['send] ww. ('sent) stuur, uitstuur, wegstuur; -er s. afsender; -off s. afskeid.

'senile ['sinail] bnw. seniel, ouderdoms-; se'nility s. ouderdomsverval.

'senior ['sinjə] bnw. senior, ouer, hoër in rang; s. (-s) superieur, hoof; seni'ority s. voorrang, senioriteit.

'senna ['senə] s. seneblare.

sen'sation [sen'sysjən] s. (-s) gewaarwording, sensasie; opskudding; -al bnw. opsienbarend; -alism s. sensasiebejag.

'sense ['sens] s. (-s) sin, sintuig, gevoel; besef; betekenis'; ww. (-d) gewaarword, aanvoel; besef; -less bnw. gevoelloos; bewusteloos; onsinnig; sensi'bility s. gevoeligheid; 'sensible bnw. waarneembaar; verstandig; 'sensitize ww. (-d) gevoelig maak; 'sensitive bnw. gevoelig; sensi'tivity s. gevoeligheid; 'sensory bnw. sintuiglik; 'sensual bnw. sinlik, wellustig; 'sensuous bnw. sinlik.

'sensor ['sensə] s. (-s) aanvoeler.

'sentence ['sentəns] s. (-s) sin; vonnis; ww. (-d) veroordeel, vonnis.

sen'tentious [sen'tensjəs] bnw. bondig, pittig.

'sentiment ['sentimənt] s. (-s) sentiment, gevoel; mening; gedagte; -al bnw. sentimenteel; sentimen'tality s. oorgevoeligheid.

'sentinel ['sentinl] s. (-s) wag, brandwag.

'sentry ['sentri] s. ('sentries) wag, brandwag; -box s. waghuisie.

'separate ['sepəryt] ww. (-d) skei, afskei; uiteengaan; s. afdruk; bnw. afsonderlik; 'separable bnw. skeibaar; sepa'ration s. skeiding; sepa-'rator s. roomafskeier.

'sepia ['sipjə] s. sepia.

'sepsis ['sepsis] s. ontsteking, verrotting; septic, bnw. septies, ontstoke.

Sep'tember [səp'tembə] s. September.

'sepulchre ['sepəlkə] s. (-s) graf.

'sequel ['sikwəl] s. (-s) nasleep;

vervolg; 'sequence s. reeks, volgorde.

se'quester [si'kwestə] ww. (-ed) afsonder; in bewaring neem.

'sequestrate ['sikwestryt] ww. (-d) sekwestreer, beslag lê op; seques'tration s. beslaglegging.

'seraph ['serəf] s. (-s) engel; se'raphic bnw. hemels, engelagtig.

'serenade [serinyd] s. (-s) serenade.

se'rene [si'rin] bnw. helder, kalm, stil; se'renity s. helderheid, kalmte, rus.

serf ['səf] s. (-s) slaaf; -dom s. lyfeienskap.

'serge ['sədzj] s. serge.

'sergeant ['sadzjənt] s. (-s) sersant.

'serial ['siəriəl] s. vervolgstorie; tydskrif; bnw. in opeenvolgende aflewerings; -ly bw. in aflewerings; seri'atim bw. een na die ander.

'series ['siəriz] s. serie, reeks.

'serious ['siəriəs] bnw. ernstig; stemmig; -ly bw. ernstig; -ness s. erns.

'sermon ['səmən] s. (-s) preek; vermaning.

'serpent ['səpənt] s. (-s) slang; 'serpentine bnw. slangagtig.

'serrate ['serit] bnw. getand; -d bnw. saagtandig.

'serum ['siərəm] s. serum, spuitstof, entstof.

'servant ['səvənt] s. (-s) bediende; bode; dienaar; amptenaar.

'serve ['səv] ww. (-d) dien; diens bewys, help; baat; dek; afslaan (tennis).

'service ['səvis] s. (-s) diens; servies; die inslaan; -able bnw. diensbaar, dienlik; servi'ette s. servet; 'servile bnw. slaafs, kruipend; ser'vility s. slaafsheid; 'servitude s. slawerny.

'session ['sesjən] s. (-s) sitting, sessie.

set ['set] ww. sit; plaas; stel; aansit; spalk; bepaal; stol; ondergaan(son); s. stel, servies; kliek; steggie; bnw. vas, bepaal; -back s. teenslag; -down s. teregwysing; -off s. kontras; -tee s. (-s) rusbank; -ter s. jaghond; -ting s. raam; montering; milieu; setting lotion s. kartelmiddel; -tle ww. (-d) jou vestig; tot bedaring kom; bepaal; -tled bnw. vasgestel; bestendig; opgedaan; -tler s. setlaar.

'seven ['sevn] s. sewe; -teen s. sewentien; -ty s. sewentig.

'sever ['sevə] ww. (-red) skei afskaf; -al bnw. verskeie; -ance s. afskeiding.

se'vere [si'viə] bnw. streng; wreed; swaar; se'verity s. strengheid, erns.

sew ['sou] ww. (-ed) naai; -ing s. naaldwerk; -ing-machine s. naaimasjien.

'sewage ['sjoeidzj] s. rioolslyk.

'sewer ['sjoeə] s. riool; -age s. riolering.

sex ['seks] s. (-es) geslag; -less bnw. geslagloos; -ual bnw. seksueel, geslags; -u'ality s. seksualiteit.

'sextant ['sekstənt] s. hoogtemeter, sekstant.

'sextet [seks'tet] s. (-s) sekstet.

'sexton ['sekstən] s. (-s) koster.

'shabby ['sjæbi] bnw. ('shabbier, 'shabbiest) laag, gemeen; slordig, armsalig.

'shackle ['sjækl] s. (-s) boei; shakel; kram; koppeling.

'shaddock ['sjædak] s. pompelmoes.

'shade ['sjyd] s. skaduwee, koelte; tint; skerm; skim; 'n aks; ww. (-d) beskadu, oorskadu; 'shadiness s. skadurykheid; 'shady bnw. lommerryk; verdag.

'shadow ['sjædou] s. = shade.

shaft ['sjāft] s. (-s) spies; disselboom; skag; as; ligstraal.

shag ['sjægh] s. (-s) ruie haarbos; kerftabak; -gy bnw. harig, ruig.

'shake ['sjyk] ww. ('shook, 'shaken) skud, bewe; laat wankel; 'shaking s. skudding; 'shaky bnw. onvas.

'shale ['sjyl] s. leiklip.

shall ['sjæl] ww. ('should) sal, moet.

shal'lot [sjə'lot] s. (-s) salot.

'shallow ['sjælou] bnw. (-er, -est) valk, ondiep; oppervlakkig.

sham ['sjæm] ww. (-med) voorgee, veins; s. bedrog; bnw. vals; = fight s. skyngeveg; -mer s. fopper; -my s. seemsleer.

'shamble ['sjæmbl] ww. (-d) slof, sleepvoet loop.

'shame ['sjym] s. skaamte; skande; ww. (-d) beskaam; oneer aandoen; -faced bnw. bedees, beskeie; -ful bnw. skandelik; -less bnw. onbeskaamd.

sham'poo [sjæm'pōё] s. haarwasmiddel, haarwaspoeier.

'shamrock ['sjæmrok] s. klawer.

'shandy ['sjændi] s. half-om-half (bier en limonade).

shank ['sjænk] s. (-s) been, skeen, skinkel.

'shanty ['sjænti] s. ('shanties) pondok.

'shape ['sjyp] s. (-s) fatsoen, vorm; gestalte; -less bnw. vormloos; -ly bnw. mooi gevorm.

'share ['sjèə] s. (-s) deel; aandeel; skaar; ww. (-d) deel, verdeel; -holder s. aandeelhouer; -r s. deelhebber.

shark ['sjåk] s. (-s) haai; woekeraar.

sharp ['sjåp] bnw. (-er, -est) skerp; spits; bitsig; slim; geslepe; haastig; ww. (-ed) bedrieg; bw. gou, presies; s. kruis(mus); -en ww. (-ed) skerp maak; -er s. swendelaar; -shooter s. skerpskutter; -witted bnw. skrander.

'shatter ['sjætə] ww. (-ed) verpletter.

'shave ['sjyv] ww. (-d) skeer; skawe; 'shaving s. skaafsel, krul; skeer.

shawl [sjōl] s. (-s) tjalie.

she ['sji] vnw. sy.

sheaf ['siif] s. ('sheaves) gerf, bundel.

shear ['sjiə] ww. ('shorn) skeer, knip; -s s. skaapskèr.

sheath ['sjith] s. (-s) skede; dop, huls(el); -e ww. (-ed) in skede steek.

she'been [sji'bin] s. (-s) kantien, smokkelkroeg.

shed ['sjed] s. (-s) skuur, loods; ww. stort, verloor.

sheen ['sjin] s. glans.

sheep ['sjip] s. (-) skaap, skape; -dip s. skaapdip; -dog s. skaaphond; -farmer s. skaapboer; -fold s. skaapkraal; -ish bnw. skaapagtig; -skin s. skaapvel.

sheer ['sjiə] bnw. louter, puur; regaf; bw. loodreg, regaf; ww. (-ed) wegswaai.

sheet ['sjit] s. (-s) laken; plaat; vel; -ing s. lakenlinne; - iron s. plaatyster; - lightning s. weerlig.

'shekel ['sjikəl] s. (-s) sikkel.

shelf ['sjelf] s. ('shelves) rak; bank; sandbank.

shell ['sjel] s. (-s) dop, skulp; bom; ww. (-ed) uitdop; bombaardeer; -proof bnw. bomvry; -y bnw. vol skulpe.

shel'lac [sjə'læk] s. skellak.

'shellfish ['sjelfisj] s. skulpvis.

'shelter ['sjeltə] s. (-s) beskutting, skerm; ww. (-ed) beskut, beskerm; -less bnw. dakloos.

'shelve ['sjelv] ww. (-d) op rak plaas; vgl. shelf; 'shelving s. rakke, rakplanke.

'shepherd ['sjepəd] s. (-s) herder, skaapwagter.

sherd ['sjəd] s. (-s) potskerf.

'sheriff ['sjerif] s. (-s) balju.

'sherry ['sjeri] s. sjerriewyn.

shield ['sjild] s. (-s) skild, skut, skerm; ww. (-ed) beskut, beskerm.

shift ['sjift] ww. (-ed) verskuiwe; verhuis; omruil; s. (-s) verandering; ploeg; skof; redmiddel; -less bnw. radeloos; -y bnw. skelm; -ing spanner s. skroefsleutel.

'shilling ['sjiling] s. (-s) sjieling.

'shimmer ['sjimə] ww. (-ed) glinster, skemer.

shin ['sjin] s. (-s) skeen, maermerrie; -guard s. beenskut.

'shinbone ['sjinboun] s. (-s) skeen, maermerrie.

'shine ['sjain] ww. ('shone) skyn, blink, glinster; uitblink; 'shining bnw. glansend; 'shiny bnw. blink.

'shingle ['sjing-ghl] s. (-s) dakspaan, ronde klippies; gordelroos.

ship ['sjip] s. (-s) skip, vaartuig; -board s. skeepsboord; -builder s. skeepsbouer; -chandler s. skeepsleweransier; -load s. skeepsvrag; -master s. kaptein van handelskip; -mate s. skeepskameraad; -ment s. lading; -per s. verskeper; -ping s. skepe, skeepsmag; verskeping; -shape bnw. netjies in orde; -wreck s. skipbreuk; -yard s. skeepswerf.

'shipwright ['sjiprait] s. (-s) skeepsboumeester (-timmerman).

shirk ['sjə̄k] *ww.* (-ed) ontduik, ontvlug; -er *s.* pligversaker.

shirt ['sjə̄t] *s.* (-s) hemp; -sleeve *s.* hempsmou; -ing *s.* hemdegoed.

'shirtfront ['sjə̄tfrʌnt] *s.* (hemps) borsie.

'shiver ['sjivə] *ww.* (-ed) bewe, rittel, sidder, ril.

'shoal ['sjoul] *s.* (-s) skool (visse); klomp, hoop.

shock ['sjok] *s.* (-s) skok, botsing; *ww.* (-ed) skok, aanstoot gee; -absorber *s.* skokdemper; -ing *bnw.* ergerlik, gruwelik; -absorbing *bnw.* skokbrekend.

'shoddy ['sjodi] *bnw.* nagemaak, prullerig.

shoe ['sjōē] *s.* (-s) skoen; hoefyster; remskoen; *ww.* ('shod) beslaan; van skoen voorsien; -black *s.* skoenpoetser; -horn *s.* skoenlepel; -lace *s.* skoenveter; -maker *s.* skoenmaker; -string *s.* skoenveter, skoenband.

shoot ['sjōēt] *ww.* ('shot) skiet; bot; *s.* loot; stroomversnelling; jagtog; skietwedstryd; -er *s.* skutter; -ing *s.* skiet; jag.

shop ['sjop] *s.* (-s) winkel; werkplek; *ww.* (-ped) inkopies doen; -keeper *s.* winkelier; -lifter *s.* winkeldief; -man *s.* winkelier; -ping *s.* inkopies; -soiled *bnw.* verbleik; -walker *s.* wegwyser vir klandisie in winkel; -worn *bnw.* verbleik.

'shore ['sjō] *s.* (-s) kus, strand, oewer.

short ['sjōt] *ww.* (-ed) kortsluit; *bnw.* kort, klein; kortaf; beknop; *bw.* plotseling, skielik; -age *s.* tekort; -bread *s.* broskoek; -circuit *s.* kortsluiting; -coming *s.* gebrek, tekortkoming; -en *ww.* (-ed) verkort, korter maak (word); -hand *s.* snelskrif; -lived *bnw.* kortstondig; -ly *bw.* binnekort; -s *s.* kort broek; -sighted *bnw.* bysiende; kortsigtig; -winded *bnw.* kortasem.

shot ['sjot] *s.* (-s) skoot; hael; skutter; -gun *s.* haelgeweer.

'shoulder ['sjouldə] *s.* (-s) skouer; skouerstuk; blad; *ww.* (-ed) stamp met skouer; las opneem.

shout ['sjaut] *ww.* (-ed) skreeu; hard roep; juig.

'shove ['sjʌv] *ww.* (-ed) stoot, skuif, stamp.

'shovel ['sjʌvl] *s.* (-s) graaf, skopgraaf; *ww.* (-led) skep.

show ['sjou] *ww.* (-ed) wys, toon, laat sien; vertoon; aantoon; *s.* (-s) tentoonstelling; vertoning; vertoon, praal; skyn; -case *s.* uitstalkas.

'shower ['sjauə] *s.* (-s) reënbui; stroom.

'showroom ['sjouroem] *s.* (-s) uitstalkamer.

shred ['sjred] *s.* (-s) repie, stukkie, lappie.

shrew ['sjrōē] *s.* (-s) wyf, heks, feeks.

shrewd ['sjrōēd] *bnw.* skerpsinnig.

shriek ['sjrik] *ww.* (-ed) gil; skaterlag; *s.* (-s) gil.

shrill ['sjril] *bnw.* (-er, -est) skril, skerp.

shrimp ['sjrimp] *s.* (-s) garnaal; dwerg.

'shrine ['sjrain] *s.* (-s) heiligdom, altaar, tempel.

shrink ['sjrink] *ww.* ('shrank, 'shrunk) krimp; -age *s.* inkrimping.

'shrivel ['sjrivl] *ww.* (-led) krimp, verskrompel.

shroud ['sjraud] *s.* (-s) doodskleed.

shrub ['sjrʌb] *s.* (-s) struik; -bery *s.* struikgewas; -by *bnw.* ruig, struikagtig.

shrug ['sjrʌgh] *ww.* (-ged) die skouers ophaal.

'shudder ['sjʌdə] *ww.* (-ed) huiwer, sidder, gril.

'shuffle ['sjʌfl] *ww.* (-d) skuif; skud; skuifel.

shun ['sjʌn] *ww.* (-ned) vermy, ontwyk.

shunt ['sjʌnt] *ww.* (-ed) rangeer, regstoot.

shut ['sjʌt] *ww.* sluit, toemaak, toegaan; -ter *s.* hortjie, luik; sluiting; sluiter.

'shuttle ['sjʌtl] *s.* (-s) spoel; -cock *s.* pluimbal.

shy ['sjai] *bnw.* ('shier, 'shiest) sku, skaam; *ww.* ('shied) skrik, wegspring; **shyly** *bw.* skaam, skaamskaam.

sick ['sik] *bnw.* (-er, -est) siek; mislik; -bed *s.* siekbed; -en *ww.* (-ed) siek word; - leave *s.* siekteverlof; - list *s.* siekelys; -ly *bnw.* (-lier, -liest) sieklik, swak; -ening *bnw.* walglik; -ness *s.* siekte; -room *s.* siekekamer.

'sickle ['sikl] *s.* (-s) sekel.

'side ['said] *s.* (-s) klant; helling; aanstellings; -board *s.* buffet; -car *s.* syspanwa; -dish *s.* bygereg; - face *s.* profiel; -issue *s.* bysaak; -light *s.* sydelingse inligting; -line *s.* byverdienste; -long *bnw.* sydelings; -saddle *s.* meisiesaal; -show *s.* kraampie; -step *ww.* pypkan; - valve *s.* syklep; -view *s.* profiel; -walk *s.* sypaadjie; -wards *bw.* sydelings; -ways *bw.* sydelings, skuins; -whiskers *s.* bakbaard; **'sidle** *ww.* (-d) skuins loop.

'siding ['saiding] *s.* (-s) halte; syspoor, wisselspoor.

'siege ['sidzj] *s.* (-s) beleg.

si'esta [si'esta] *s.* middagslapie.

'sieve ['siv] *s.* (-s) sif.

sift ['sift] *ww.* (-ed) sif; uitpluis.

sigh ['sai] *ww.* (-ed) sug.

sight ['sait] *s.* (-s) gesig; sig; vertoning; skouspel; korrel, visier; -less *bnw.* blind; -ly *bnw.* mooi; -seeing *s.* besigtiging van besienswaardighede; -seer *s.* kykgierige; - distance *s.* sigafstand.

sign ['sain] *s.* (-s) teken, voorteken; wagwoord; sinnebeeld; *ww.* (-ed) teken, onderteken; teken gee; -board *s.* uithangbord; -post *s.* wegwyser.

'signal ['sighnl] s. (-s) teken, sein, sinjaal; -box s. sinjaalhuisie; -gun s. seinskoot; -man s. seinwagter.

'signature ['sighnitsjə] s. (-s) handtekening, ondertekening; 'signatory s. ondertekenaar.

'signet ['sighnit] s. seëlring.

'signify ['sighnifai] ww. ('signified) aandui; beteken; sig'nificance s. betekenis; sig'nificant bnw. betekenisvol; signifi'cation s. betekenis; sig'nicative bnw. aanduidend.

'signor ['sinjo] s. (-s) meneer; -a s. mevrou; -ina s. mejuffrou.

'silage ['sailidzj] s. kuilvoer; vgl. silo.

'silence ['sailəns] s. stilte; stilswye; -r s. knaldemper, klankdemper; 'silent bnw. stil, swyend.

silhou'ette [silöě'et] s. (-s) silhoeët.

silk ['silk] s. sy; -en bnw. syagtig, van sy; -stockings s. sykouse; -worm s. sywurm; -y bnw. syagtig, glad; stroperig.

sill ['sil] s. (-s) vensterbank, drumpel.

'silly ['sili] bnw. ('sillier, 'silliest) verspot, laf.

'silo ['sailou] s. (-s) voerkuil.

silt ['silt] s. modder, slyk.

'silver ['silvə] s. silwer; silwergeld; silwergoed; -fish s. silwervis; -fox s. silwerjakkals; -grey bnw. silwergrys; -plated bnw. versilwer; -smith s. silwersmid; -ware s. tafelsilwer; -y bnw. silweragtig.

'simian ['simiən] s. aap.

'similar ['similə] bnw. eenders; simi'larity s. eendersheid; -ly bw. net so.

'simile ['simili] s. (-s) vergelyking.

'simmer ['simə] ww. (-ed) borrel; sing(ketel).

'simple ['simpl] bnw. (-r, -st) eenvoudig; enkel; louter; onskuldig; onnosel; -ton s. swaap; sim'plicity s. eenvoud, onskuld; simplifi'cation s. vereenvoudiging; 'simplify ww. vereenvoudig; 'simply bw. eenvoudig.

'simulate ['simjoelyt] ww. (-d) veins, voorgee.

simul'taneous [siməl'tynjəs] bnw. gelyktydig.

sin ['sin] s. (-s) sonde; oortreding; -ful bnw. sondig; -ner s. sondaar; -offering s. soenoffer.

since ['sins] bw. daarna, gelede; voegw. nadat, sedert.

'sincere ['sinsiə] bnw. openhartig, opreg; -ly bw. opreg, openhartig; sin'cerity s. opregtheid.

'sinecure ['sainəkjoeə] s. luibaantjie.

'sinew ['sinjöě] s. (-s) sening, spier; -y bnw. seningrig; gespierd.

sing ['sing] ww. ('sang, 'sung) sing; besing; gons; -er s. sanger; -ing s. sang, sangkuns; gesuis.

'singe ['sindzj] ww. (-d) skroei, verseng.

'single ['sing-ghl] bnw. enkel; s. enkelspel; ww. (-d) - out uitkies;

-handed bw. alleen, sonder hulp; -t s. onderhempie; 'singly bw. afsonderlik.

'singular ['sing-ghjoelə] bnw. enkelvoudig; buitengewoon; s. enkel voud; singu'larity s. merkwaardigheid.

'sinister ['sinistə] bnw. onheilspellend.

sink ['sink] ww. ('sank, 'sunk) sink, sak, daal; s. afwasbak; riool; -er s. dieplood; -ing bnw. sinkend.

'sinkhole ['sinkhoul] s. (-s) sinkgat.

'sinuous ['sinjoeəs] bnw. kronkelend, bogtig.

'sinus ['sainəs] s. (-es) holte; bog; opening.

sip ['sip] ww. (-ped) slurp, met klein teugies drink.

'siphon ['saifən] s. (-s) spuitwaterfies; hewel.

sir ['sə] s. (-s) meneer, seur, sir.

'sire ['saiə] ww. (-d) teel, die vader wees van (by perde).

'siren ['sairin] s. (-s) mishoring; sirene.

'sirloin ['səloin] s. lendestuk (beesvleis).

'sister ['sistə] s. (-s) suster; non; verpleegster; -in-law s. skoonsuster; -ly bw. susterlik.

sit ['sit] ww. ('sat) sit, sitting hê; broei; poseer; -ter s. sitter; model; broeihen; -ting s. sitting; broeisel eiers; sitplek; bnw. sittend; -tingroom s. sitkamer.

'site ['sait] s. (-s) ligging, terrein.

'situated ['sitjoeytid] bnw. geleë; situ'ation s. ligging, situasie.

six ['siks] s. ses; -pence s. sikspens; -teen s. sestien; -ty s. sestig.

'size ['saiz] s. (-s) groote, omvang; nommer; formaat; gomwater; sizable bnw. groot.

'sizzle ['sizl] ww. (-d) braai.

'skate ['skyt] s. (-s) skaats; ww. (-d) skaatsry; skating rink s. skaatsbaan.

skein ['skyn] s. string; knoedel.

'skeleton ['skelitn] s. (-s) geraamte; 'skeletal bnw. van 'n geraamte; -key s. towersleutel, loper.

sketch ['sketsj] s. (-es) skets; -book s. sketsboek; -y bnw. onafgewerk, onsamehangend.

skew ['skjöě] bnw. skeef, skuins; -eyed bnw. skeel.

'skewer ['skjoeə] s. (-s) vleispen, sosatiepen.

ski ['sji] s. (-s) ski, sneeuskaats.

skid ['skid] ww. (-ded) gly; skuiwe, dwarsgly.

skiff ['skif] s. (-s) bootjie; skif.

skill ['skil] s. bekwaamheid; handigheid; 'skilful bnw. bekwaam, knap; -ed bnw. bekwaam, opgelei.

'skillet ['skilit] s. kookpotjie.

skim ['skim] ww. (-med) afskuim, afroom; rakelings gly oor; -mer s. skuimspaan.

skimp ['skimp] ww. (-ed) suinig of

vrekkig wees; **-y** *bnw.* skrap, skraal.
skin ['skin] *s.* (*-s*) vel, huid; skil; *ww.*
(*-ned*) afskil; **-flint** *s.* vrek, gierigaard; **-ner** *s.* afslagter; **-ny** *bnw.*
maer.
skip ['skip] *ww.* (*-ped*) spring;
riemspring; oorslaan; *s.* hysbak;
-per *s.* skipper; kaptein; **'skipping
rope** *s.* springtou.
'skirmish ['skŏmisj] *s.* (*-es*) skermutseling.
skirt ['skŏt] *s.* (*-s*) romp, rok; soom,
-ing *s.* beskot, spatlys, vloerlys; **-ing
board** *s.* spatlys.
skit ['skit] *s.* parodie.
'skittle ['skitl] *s.* (*-s*) kegel.
'skulk ['skʌlk] *ww.* (*-ed*) loer.
skull ['skʌl] *s.* (*-s*) skedel; **-cap** *s.*
kalotjie.
skunk ['skʌnk] *s.* (*-s*) muishond;
smeerlap.
sky ['skai] *s.* ('*skies*) lug, hemel; **-lark**
s. leeuerik; **-light** *s.* vallig; **-rocket**
s. vuurpyl; **-scraper** *s.* wolkkrapper.
slab ['slæb] *s.* (*-s*) piat klip; plaat;
plak.
slack ['slæk] *bnw.* slap, los; traag;
-en *ww.* (*-ed*) slap word, verslap; *s.*
speling; slapte.
slag ['slægh] *s.* metaalskuim, slak.
'slake ['slyk] *ww.* (*-d*) les; blus.
slam ['slæm] *ww.* (*-med*) toeklap.
'slander ['slåndə] *ww.* (*-ed*) belaster,
beskinder; **-er** *s.* lasteraar; skinderbek; **-ous** *bnw.* lasterlik.
slang ['slæng] *s.* plattaal.
slant ['slånt] *s.* skuinste; **-ing** *bnw.*
skuins.
slap ['slæp] *ww.* (*-ped*) klap.
slash ['slæsj] *ww.* (*-ed*) sny; slaan;
raps.
'slate ['slyt] *s.* (*-s*) lei; leiklip;
- pencil *s.* griffel.
'slattern ['slætən] *s.* sloerie, slet.
'slaughter ['slôtə] *s.* slagting; *ww.*
(*-ed*) slag; vermoor; **-er** *s.* slagter;
moordenaar; **-house** *s.* slagplek;
-ous *bnw.* moorddadig.
'slave ['slyv] *s.* (*-s*) slaaf; *ww.* (*-d*)
sloof; **-ry** *s.* slawerny.
slay ['sly] *ww.* ('*slew*, '*slain*) doodmaak, vermoor.
sled ['sled] *s.* (*-s*) slee.
'sledge ['sledzj] *s.* (*-s*) slee; **-hammer**
s. voorhamer.
sleek ['slik] *bnw.* (*-er*, *-est*) glad,
blink.
sleep ['slip] *ww.* ('*slept*) slaap; *s.*
slaap; vaak; rus; **-er** *s.* slaper;
dwarslêer; **-walker** *s.* slaapwandelaar; **-y** *bnw.* vaak.
'sleet ['slit] *s.* nat sneeu.
'sleeve ['sliv] *s.* (*-s*) mou; huls; **-less**
bnw. sonder moue; **-link** *s.* mansjetknoop.
sleigh ['sly] *s.* = **sled.**
'sleight ['slait] *s.* handigheid,
behendigheid, streek.
'slender ['slendə] *bnw.* (*-er*, *-est*) dun,
slank.

'sleuthhound ['slŏethhaund] *s.*
bloedhond.
'slice ['slais] *s.* (*-s*) sny; skyf.
'slide ['slaid] *ww.* ('*slid*) gly, glip,
skuif; **sliding door** *s.* skuifdeur;
sliding roof(hood) *s.* skuifdak;
sliding window *s.* skuifvenster.
slight ['slait] *bnw.* (*-er*, *-est*) tinger;
gering; **-ly** *bw.* effentjies.
slim ['slim] *bnw.* (*-mer*, *-mest*) skraal;
tinger.
'slime ['slaim] *s.* slym, slyk,
modder; **'slimy** *bnw.* slymerig;
inkruiperig.
'sling ['sling] *ww.* (*-slung*) swaai; *s.*
slingervel; draagband.
'slink ['slink] *ww.* ('*slank*, '*slunk*)
wegsluip.
slip ['slip] *ww.* (*-ped*) gly, glip; ontglip; *s.* fout; vergissing; sloop;
lyfie.
'slipper ['slipə] *s.* (*-s*) pantoffel; **-y**
bnw. glyerig; slu.
'slipshod ['slipsjod] *bnw.* slordig.
slit ['slit] *s.* (*-s*) sny, skeur, spleet.
slog ['slogh] *ww.* (*-ged*) slaan, moker.
'slogan ['sloughən] *s.* strydkreet.
'slope ['sloup] *s.* helling, skuinste,
hang; '**sloping** *bnw.* skuins.
'slop pail ['sloppyl] *s.* toiletemmer,
slopemmer.
'sloppy ['slopi] *bnw.* morsig, slordig;
week.
slops ['slops] *s.* vuil water.
slot ['slot] *s.* gleuf.
sloth ['sloth] *s.* luiheid, traagheid;
-ful *bnw.* lui, traag.
slouch ['slautsj] *ww.* (*-ed*) paphang.
slough ['slau] *s.* modderpoel, moeras.
'sloven ['slʌvn] *s.* slordige persoon;
-ly *bnw.* slordig.
slow ['slou] *bnw.* (*-er*, *-est*) stadig;
lomerig; **-ly** *bw.* stadig, langsaam;
-coach *s.* draaikous.
'sludge ['slədzj] *s.* slik, slyk; *ww.* (*-d*)
verslik, aanslik.
slug ['slʌgh] *s.* (*-s*) slak.
'slug ['sləgh] *ww. bnw.* vertraag.
'sluggard ['slʌghəd] *s.* (*-s*) luiaard;
'**sluggish** *bnw.* traag.
'sluice ['sloēs] *s.* (*-s*) sluis.
slum ['slʌm] *s.* (*-s*) agterbuurte.
'slumber ['slʌmbə] *ww.* (*-ed*)
sluimer.
slump ['slʌmp] *s.* slapte.
slur ['slə] *s.* klad, smet.
slush ['slʌsj] *s.* modder, slyk.
sly ['slai] *bnw.* skelm, slu.
smack ['smæk] *s.* klap; klapsoen;
smakie.
small ['smôl] *bnw.* (*-er*, *-est*) klein,
weinig, min; kleingeestig; **-ish** *bnw.*
kleinerig; **-pox** *s.* waterpokkies.
smart ['småt] *ww.* (*-ed*) pyn, brand;
ly; *bnw.* (*-er*, *-est*) skerp; gevat;
piekfyn, swierig; **-ing** *bnw.* smerterig.
'smattering ['smætəring] *s.* mondjievol; oppervlakkige kennis.
smash ['smæsj] *ww.* (*-ed*) stukkend
breek(slaan); bankrot gaan.

smell ['smel] s. (-s) reuk, geur; ww. (-ed) ruik; snuffel; **smelling-salts** s. vlugsout; **-y** bnw. stinkend.

'smile ['smail] s. & ww. glimlag.

smirch ['smə̄tsj] ww. (-ed) besmeer.

smirk ['smə̄k] s. grimlag, gemaakte laggie.

'smite ['smait] ww. ('smote, 'smitten) slaan, tref, kasty.

smith ['smith] s. smid; **-y** s. smidswinkel.

'smithe'reens ['smidhə'rins] s. stukkies, gruiselemente.

'smoke ['smouk] s. rook, damp; **-d** bnw. gerook; **-less** bnw. rookloos; **-r** s. roker; **rookkoepee; -stack** s. skoorsteenpyp; **'smoky** bnw. rokerig.

smooth ['smōēdh] bnw. (-er, -est) glad; vlejerig; **-e** ww. (-d) gelykmaak; **-tongued** bnw. vleiend.

'smother ['smʌdhə] ww. (-ed) smoor, stik; geheim hou; **-y** bnw. verstikkend, benoud.

'smoulder ['smouldə] ww. (-ed) smeul.

'smudge ['smʌdzjl] ww. (-d) bemors, besmeer; **'smudgy** bnw. smerig, morsig.

smug ['smʌgh] bnw. selfvoldaan.

'smuggle ['smʌghl] ww. (-d) smokkel; **-r** s. smokkelaar; **-ry** s. smokkelary.

smut ['smʌt] s. roetvlek, roet; brand; **-ty** bnw. (-tier, -tiest) vuil, morsig.

snack ['snæk] s. happie, ligte maaltyd.

snail ['snyl] s. (-s) slak; **-bite** s. slaklokaas.

'snake ['snyk] s. slang; **'snaky** bnw. slangagtig.

snap ['snæp] ww. (-ped) hap, gryp; knal; kiek; toesnou; s. klap, knal; byt, hap; kiekie; veerkrag; **-dragon** s. leeubekkie; **-pish** bnw. vinnig, bitsig; **-py** bnw. lewendig; **-shot** s. kiekie.

'snare ['snēə] s. (-s) strik, val.

snarl ['snāl] ww. (-ed) knor, snou.

snatch ['snætsj] ww. (-ed) gryp, wegruk.

sneak ['snik] s. sluiper, valsaard.

sneer ['sniə] ww. (-ed) bespot, hoon; **-ing** bnw. honend.

'sneeze ['sniz] s. (-s) nies; **-wood** s. nieshout.

sniff ['snif] ww. (-ed) snuif, snuffel.

'snipe ['snaip] s. (-s) snip.

'snivel ['snivəl] ww. (-led) snotter, grens.

snob ['snob] s. (-s) ploert, snob; **-bery** s. snobbisme; **-bish** bnw. snobagtig.

'snooze ['snōēz] ww. (-d) dut, indommel.

'snore ['snōə] ww. (-d) snork.

snort ['snōt] ww. (-ed) proes, snork.

snout ['snaut] s. (-s) snoet.

snow ['snou] s. sneeu; **-ball** s. sneeuubal; **-bound** bnw. vasgesneeu; **-drift** s. sneeuval; **-drop** s. sneeuklokkie; **-flake** s. sneeuvlokkie.

-storm s. sneeustorm; **'snowy** bnw. sneeuagtig.

snub ['snʌb] ww. (-bed) afjak.

snuff ['snʌf] s. snuif, snuf.

'snuffle ['snʌfl] ww. (-d) snuiwe, deur die neus praat.

snug ['snʌgh] bnw. (-ger, -gest) knus, gesellig; **-gle** ww. (-d) inkruip.

so ['sou] bw. so, sodanig, dus.

soak ['souk] ww. (-ed) week, deurweek; **-ing** bnw. deurdringend.

soap ['soup] s. seep; **-suds** s. seepsop; **-y** bnw. seep-; **-box cart** s. seepkiswæntjie.

soar ['sōə] ww. (-ed) swewe, opstyg.

sob ['sob] ww. (-bed) snik.

'sober ['soubə] bnw. nugter, sober; matig; **so'briety** s. matigheid; bedaardheid.

so(u)briquet ['soubriky] s. bynaam.

'sobstuff ['sobstʌf] s. melodrama.

'social ['sousjəl] bnw. gesellig; sosiaal; maatskaplik; s. geselligheid; **'sociable** bnw. gesellig; gemaklik in die omgang; **-ism** s. sosialisme; **-security** s. bestaansbeveiliging.

so'ciety [sou'saiəti] s. (so'cieties) gemeenskap, samelewing; maatskappy; genootskap.

soci'ology [sousi'olədzjl] s. sosiologie; **socio'logical** bnw. sosiologies.

sock]'sok] s. (-s) sokkie.

'socket ['sokit] s. (-s) holte; kas; potjie, sok; **- joint** s. koeëlgewrig.

sod ['sod] s. (-s) sooi; smeerlap.

'soda ['soudə] s. soda; **-fountain** s. spuitfontein; **-water** s. spuitwater, sodawater.

'sodden ['sodn] bnw. deurweek, papnat.

'sodium ['soudjəm] s. natrium.

'sofa ['soufə] s. (-s) sofa, rusbank.

soft ['soft] bnw. sag, pap; teer; onnosel; **-en** ww. (-ed) versag; temper; **-ening** bnw. versagtend; **-hearted** bnw. teerhartig; **- soap** s. groenseep; vleiery; **-y** s. sukkelaar, papperd.

'soggy ['soghi] bnw. ('soggier, 'soggiest) papnat.

soil ['soil] s. grond; bodem; vlek; ww. (-ed) vuil maak, besmet; besoedel.

'soiree ['swāry] s. aandparty.

'sojourn ['sodzjə̄n] s. verblyf.

'solace ['soləs] s. troos, vertroosting.

'solar ['soulə] bnw. sons-; **- plexus** s. senunet op krop van maag.

'solder ['soldə] s. soldeersel.

'soldier ['souldzjə] s. (-s) soldaat, krygsman; **-ly** bnw. krygshaftig, soldaat; **-y** s. krygshaftig, soldaat-; **-y** s. krygsvolk.

'sole ['soul] s. (-s) sool; voetsool; tongvis.

'solemn ['soləm] bnw. plegtig; deftig; **-ize** ww. vier; voltrek; **so'lemnity** s. plegtigheid.

so'licit [sə'lisit] ww. (-ed) versoek, vra; aansoek doen om; **-or** s.

prokureur; -ous bnw. begerig; so-'licitude s. besorgdheid.
solid ['solid] bnw. (-est) vas, solied; eenparig; eg; **soli'darity** s. solidariteit, eenheid; **so'lidify** ww. verdig; **so'lidity** s. vastheid, stewigheid; - **cologne** s. reukstafie; - **line** s. volstreep.
so'liloquy [sə'liləkwi] s. (so'liloquies) alleenspraak.
soli'taire [soli'tɛə] s. solitêrspel; solitêrsteen; **'solitary** bnw. eensaam, verlaat.
'solitude ['solitjōēd] s. stilte, verlatenheid, eensaamheid.
'solo ['soulou] s. solo.
'solstice ['solstis] s. sonstilstand.
soluble ['soljoebl] bnw. oplosbaar; **solu'bility** s. oplosbaarheid; **so'lution** s. oplossing.
solve ['solv] ww. (-d) oplos; **'solvable** bnw. oplosbaar; **solva'bility** s. oplosbaarheid; -ncy s. solventskap; -nt bnw. solvent.
'sombre ['somə] bnw. (-st) somber, swartgallig.
'some ['sʌm] bnw. sommige, party; sowat; vnw. sommige, party; bw. net, danig; -body s. iemand; -how bw. op een of ander manier; -one vnw. iemand; -thing s. iets; -time bw. voormalig; -times bw. soms; -what bw. enigsins; -where bw. êrens.
'somersault ['sʌməsōlt] s. bolmakiesiesprong.
som'nambulism [som'næmbjoelizəm] s. slaapwandeling.
son ['sʌn] s. (-s) seun; -in-law s. skoonseun.
so'nata [sə'nātə] s. (-s) sonate.
song ['song] s. lied, sang; sangstuk.
sonnet ['sonit] s. (-s) sonnet.
so'nority [sə'noriti] s. welluidendheid; **'sonorous** bnw. welluidend.
soon ['sōēn] bw. gou, spoedig, weldra.
soot ['sōēt] s. roet; -y bnw. roetagtig.
'soothe ['sōēdh] ww. (-d) kalmeer; **soothing syrup** s. kalmeerstroop.
sop ['sop] s. sop; troosmiddel.
so'phism [so'fism] s. opsetlike vals argument.
so'phisticated [so'fistikytid] bnw. oulik, ouderwets.
'sophistry ['sofistri] s. drogredenering.
sopo'rific [soupə'rifik] s. slaapmiddel.
so'prano [sə'prānou] s. sopraan.
'sorcery ['sōsəri] s. towery; **'sorcerer** s. (-s) towenaar.
'sordid ['sodid] bnw. laag, vuil.
'sore ['sō] bnw. seer.
'sorrel ['sorəl] s. suring.
'sorrow ['sorou] s. smart, leed; -ful bnw. treurig; **'sorry** bnw. jammer, spyt.
sort ['sōt] s. soort, klas.
sough ['sau] s. gesuis, sug.

soul ['soul] s. siel; wese; -ful bnw. hartroerend.
sound ['saund] s. klank, geluid; see-engte; bnw. (-er, -est) gesond, sterk; bw. vas; ww. (-ed) klink, lui; -ly bw. terdeê.
soup ['sōēp] s. (-s) sop.
sour ['sauə] bnw. suur, nors.
'source ['sōs] s. (-s) oorsprong, bron.
south ['sauth] s. suide; -erly bnw. suidelik; -wester ['sau'westə] s. suidwestewind.
souve'nir [sōēvəniə] s. (-s) aandenking; soewenier.
'sovereign ['sovrin] s. vors, heerser; pond.
sow ['sou] ww. (-ed) saai; versprei; -er s. saaier.
'space ['spys] s. (-s) ruimte, plek; tydsduur; **'spacious** bnw. ruim.
spade ['spyd] s. (-s) graaf, spitgraaf; skoppens; -work s. aanvoorwerk.
'spangle ['spæng-ghl] s. goud- of silwerversierseltjie.
'spaniel ['spænjəl] s. (-s) patryshond; kruiper.
spank ['spænk] ww. (-ed) pak gee, looi; -ing s. pak slae, loesing.
'spanner ['spænə] s. (-s) skroefhamer.
spar ['spā] s. (-s) spar; spriet; mas; vuisgeveg.
spa'raxis [spə'ræksis] s. ferweeltjie.
'spare ['spɛə] bnw. skraal, maer; vry; - **wheel** s. noodwiel.
spark ['spāk] s. (-s) vonk; sprankie; -ing s. ontsteking; - **gap** s. vonkgaping.
'sparkle ['spākl] ww. (-d) vonkel, skitter.
'sparrow ['spærou] s. (-s) mossie.
'sparse ['spās] bnw. dun, skaars.
spasm ['spæzəm] s. (-s) kramp; trekking; **spas'modic** bnw. krampagtig.
'spate ['spyt] s. vloed, oorstroming.
'spatter ['spætə] ww. (-ed) spat, bemors; beklad.
spawn ['spôn] s. eiertjies, kuit, saad, broeisel.
speak ['spik] ww. ('spoke, 'spoken) praat, spreek, sê; -er s. spreker; -ing bnw. pratend; sprekend.
spear ['spiə] s. (-s) spies, lans, speer.
'special ['spesjl] bnw. spesiaal; ekstra; -ize ww. spesialiseer; -ist s. spesialis; -ty s. spesialiteit.
'specie ['spisji] s. (-s) spesie, klinkende munt; -s s. soort.
spe'cific [spi'sifik] bnw. spesifiek, bepaald, soortlik; **specifi'cation** s. spesifikasie; **'specify** ww. ('specified) spesifiseer.
'specimen ['spesimin] s. (-s) monster, proef, voorbeeld.
'specious ['spisjəs] bnw. bevallig, skoonklinkend.
speck ['spek] s. (-s) stippel.
'speckled ['spekld] bnw. gespikkel.
'spectacle ['spektəkl] s. (-s) gesig,

skouspel; **-s** s. bril; **spec'tacular** bnw. skouspelagtig, aanskoulik.

spec'tator [spek'tytə] s. (-s) toeskouer.

'spectre ['spektə] s. (-s) spook, skim; **-tral** bnw. spookagtig.

'spectrum ['spektrəm] s. spektrum.

'speculate ['spekjoelyt] ww. (-d) bepeins; spekuleer; **specu'lation** s. oorpeinsing; spekulasie; **'speculative** bnw. spekulatief; **'speculator** s. spekulant.

speech ['spits̩] s. (-es) spraak, taal; redevoering; **-less** bnw. spraakloos.

speed ['spid] s. (-s) snelheid, spoed; **-y** bnw. spoedig; **-ster** s. (-s) jaagduiwel; **-cop** s. verkeerskonstabel; **-trap** s. jaagstrik; **-wobble** s. spoedwaggel.

spee'dometer [spi'domitə] s. (-s) mylmeter.

spell ['spel] s. (-s) towerspreuk; betowering; beurt; **-bound** bnw. betower; **-ing** s. spelling.

spend ['spend] ww. ('spent) uitgee, bestee; verteer; deurbring; **-thrift** s. verkwister.

spew ['spjoε] ww. opbring, uitspoeg.

sphere ['sfiə] s. (-s) bol, bal, sfeer; kring.

'sphincter ['svinktə] s. sluitspier.

sphinx ['sfinks] s. (-es) sfinks.

'spice ['spais] s. (-s) spesery; kruie; **'spicy** bnw. kruidagtig, pikant; onbetaainlik.

'spick and 'span ['spikn'spæn] bnw. agtermekaar.

'spider ['spaidə] s. (-s) spinnekop.

'spigot ['spighət] s. (-s) tap.

'spike ['spaik] s. (-s) punt, pen, lang spyker, doring.

spill ['spil] ww. (-ed, spilt) stort, mors.

spin ['spin] ww. ('span, 'spun) spin; laat draai.

'spinach ['spinidzj] s. spinasie.

'spindle ['spindl] s. (-s) spoel, spil, as.

'spine ['spain] s. (-s) ruggraat; doring; **'spinal** bnw. van die ruggraat; **-less** bnw. sonder ruggraat, pap; doringloos; **'spiny** bnw. vol dorings; moeilik.

'spinster ['spinstə] s. (-s) oujongnooi.

'spiral ['spaiərəl] s. (-s) spiraal.

'spire ['spaiə] s. (-s) toringspits.

'spirit ['spirit] s. (-s) gees, moed; geesdrif; sterk drank, stemming; **-s** s. brandstof; geesryke drank; **-ed** bnw. vurig; **-less** bnw. sonder gees, doods; **-level** s. waterpas; **'spiritual** bnw. geestelik; **'spiritualist** s. spiritis; **'spirituous** bnw. geesryk, alkoholies.

'spit ['spit] s. braaispit; ww. deurboor; spoeg; **-ting** (carbur.) s. proes.

'spite ['spait] s. wrok; nyd; **-ful** bnw. haatlik, nydig.

'spitfire ['spitfaiə] s. rissie; soort vliegtuig.

'spittle ['spitl] s. spoeg.

spit'toon [spi'tὄεn] s. spoegbakkie, kwispedoor.

'splash ['splæsj] ww. (-ed) spat; **-board** s. spatbord; **-guard** s. spatskerm.

'splay ['sply] ww. (-ed) skuins maak, verstuit.

'spleen ['splin] s. milt; swaarmoedigheid.

'splendid ['splendid] bnw. pragtig, kostelik.

'splendour ['splendə] s. prag, luister, praal.

'splice ['splais] s. ww. splitslas.

splint ['splint] s. spalk; splinter; kuitbeen; **-er** s. splinter.

split ['split] ww. (-) splits, splyt, bars, kloof; **-nut** s. splitmoer; **-pin** s. spy.

spoil ['spoil] ww. (-ed, -t) bederwe, verniel; **-er** s. plunderaar; **-sport** s. sportbederwer.

'spoke ['spouk] s. (-s) speek.

'spokesman ['spouksmən] s. mondstuk.

spoli'ation [spouli'ysjən] s. plundering; afpersing.

'sponge ['spandzj] s. (-s) spons; parasiet; ww. (-d) afspons; uitwis; teer op; **-r** s. klaploper, parasiet; **'spongy** bnw. sponsagtig; **-rubber** s. sponsrubber.

'sponsor ['sponsə] s. (-s) peetvader, peet.

sponta'neity ['pontə'niiti] s. spontaneiteit, ongedwongenheid.

spon'taneous [spon'tynjəs] bnw. spontaan, ongedwonge.

spool ['spὄεl] s. (-s) spoel, rolletjie, tolletjie.

spoon ['spὄεn] s. (-s) lepel; **-y** bnw. gek; verlief.

spo'radic [spὄ'rædik] bnw. sporadies.

sport ['spɔt] s. (-s) pret, korswel; tydverdryf; speletjie; sport; gawe ou, ou doring; **-ing** bnw. spelend; sportief.

spot ['spot] s. (-s) plek, vlek, kol, klad; **-less** bnw. vlekloos; **-light** s. soeklig; **-ted** bnw. gespikkel, bont; **-ty** bnw. gespikkel.

'spot fine ['spotfain] s. (-s) afkoopboete.

'spouse ['spauz] s. (-s) eggenoot; **'spousal** s. bruilof.

spout ['spaut] s. (-s) spuit; geut; tuit.

sprain ['spryn] ww. (-ed) verstuit, verswik, verrek; s. verswikking, verstuiting.

sprawl ['sprὄl] ww. (-ed) uitrek, uitgerek lê.

spray ['spry] s. takkie; skuim; motreën; **-gun** s. sproeispuit; **-paint** s. ww. spuitverf.

spread ['spred] ww. (-) sprei, versprei; uitstrooi; smeer; s. spanwydte.

spree ['spri] s. fuif.

sprig ['sprigh] s. takkie.

'sprightly ['spraitli] bnw. ('spright-

lier, '*sprightliest*) vrolik, lewendig.
spring ['spring] *ww.* ('*sprang,
'sprung*) spring, opspring; ontspruit;
kraak; - **tide** s. hoogwater, spring-
vloed; lente; - **balance** s. trekskaal.
'**springboard** ['springbôd] *s.* duik-
plank.
'**sprinkle** ['sprinkl] *ww.* (-*d*) sprinkel,
strooi.
'**sprite** ['sprait] *s.* (-*s*) kabouter, fee;
spook, gedaante.
'**sprout** ['spraut] *s.* (-*s*) spruit, loot.
'**spruce** ['sprôes] *bnw.* (-*r*, -*st*) netjies,
viets.
spruit ['sprôët] '*spruit s.* (-*s*) spruit,
sloot.
spry ['sprai] *bnw.* lewendig, rats.
spur ['spê] *s.* (-*s*) spoor; spoorslag;
uitloper.
'**spurious** ['spjoeəriəs] *bnw.* oneg,
vals.
spurn ['spên] *ww.* (-*ed*) versmaad,
verag.
spurt ['spêt] *s.* (-*s*) uitbarsting,
kragsinspanning.
'**sputter** ['spʌtə] *ww.* (-*ed*) spat,
spoeg; babbel.
spy ['spai] *s.* ('*spies*) spioen; *ww.*
('*spied*) spioen; -**glass** s. verkyker.
'**squabble** ['skwobl] *ww.* (-*d*)
kibbel, twis, stry.
squad ['skwod] *s.* (-*s*) seksie,
klompie; -**ron** s. eskader; **flying** - s.
blitspatrollie; **flying - car** s. blits-
motor.
'**squalid** ['skwolid] *bnw.* (-*est*) vuil,
morsig.
'**squall** ['skwol] *s.* (-*s*) windvlaag;
gil.
'**squander** ['skwondə] *ww.* (-*ed*)
verkwis, verspil; -**er** s. verkwister.
'**square** ['skwêə] *bnw.* (-*est*) vier-
kantig; eerlik; in orde; haaks.
squash ['skwosj] *ww.* (-*ed*) plat druk,
pap druk; s. vroeë pampoen skorsie;
moes; kwas.
squat ['skwot] *ww.* (-*ted*) hurk;
bnw. gehurk; -**ter** s. plakker.
squeak ['skwik] *ww.* (-*ed*) piep;
kraak; s. gepiep.
squeal ['skwil] *ww.* (-*ed*) gil;
verklik; -**er** s. verklikker.
'**squeamish** ['skwimisj] *bnw.* kieskeurig; puntenerig; nougeset.
'**squeegee** ['skwidzji] *s.* (-*s*) water-
besem.
'**squeeze** ['skwiz] *ww.* (-*d*) druk;
afpers; afdruk; -**r** s. drukker, pers.
squint ['skwint] *s.* (-*s*) skeel oë; *ww.*
(-*ed*) skeel kyk; -**eyed** *bnw.* skeeloog.
squirm ['skwêm] *ww.* (-*ed*) kriewel,
krimp.
'**squirt** ['skwêt] *ww.* (-*ed*) spuit.
stab ['stæb] *ww.* (-*bed*) steek, wond;
grief.
'**stable** ['stybl] *bnw.* stabiel, vas;
vasberade; s. (-*s*) stal; **sta'bility** s.
standvastigheid; vastheid; *ww.* (-*d*)
op stal sit(hou).
stack ['stæk] *s.* (-*s*) stapel, hoop;
mied.

staff ['stäf] *s.* (-*s*) staf, stok;
personeel; - **notation** s. balkskrif.
stag ['stægh] *s.* (-*s*) takbok, hert.
'**stage** ['stydzj] *s.* (-*s*) toneel;
stadium; *ww.* (-*d*) opvoer; -**coach** s.
poskoets; -**manager** s. regisseur;
-**struck** *bnw.* versot op die toneel;
-**whisper** s. hoorbare fluistering.
'**stagger** ['stæghə] *ww.* (-*ed*) wankel;
waggel; verstom; -**ing** *bnw.* wagge-
lend.
'**stagnate** ['stæghnyt] *ww.* (-*d*)
stilstaan; lui word; **stag'nation** s.
stilstand; '**stagnant** *bnw.* stilstaande;
lui, traag.
staid ['styd] *bnw.* bedaard, stemmig.
stain ['styn] *s.* (-*s*) vlek, kol;
skande; *ww.* (-*ed*) vlek, beklad;
kleur; -**er** s. verwer; -**less** *bnw.*
onbevlek, rein; vlekvry.
stair ['stêə] *s.* (-*s*) trappie, treetjie;
-**case** s. trap, trapkoker.
stake ['styk] *s.* (-*s*) paal; brandstapel; wedgeld.
'**stalactite** ['stæləktait] *s.* druipsteen aan dak van grot.
'**stalagmite** ['stæləghmait] *s.*
druipsteen op vloer van grot.
'**stale** ['styl] *bnw.* (-*r*, -*st*) oud, muf;
-**mate** s. skaakmat.
stalk ['stôk] *ww.* (-*ed*) deftig stap;
bekruip; s. stingel.
'**stall** ['stôl] *ww.* (-*ed*) gaan staan,
staak; vassit in die modder; op stal
hou; s. kraampie; -**s** (*teater*) s. stalles.
'**stallion** ['stæljən] *s.* (-*s*) hings.
'**stalwart** ['stôlwət] *s.* (-*s*) staatmaker.
'**stamen** ['stymən] *s.* (-*s*) meel-
draad.
'**stamina** ['stæminə] *s.* uithouvermoë.
'**stammer** ['stæmə] *ww.* (-*ed*) stotter,
hakkel, stamel; -**er** s. hakkelaar.
stamp ['stæmp] *s.* (-*s*) seël,
stempel; tjap; stamper; -**duty** s.
seëlreg.
'**stampede** ['stæmpid] *ww.* (-*d*) op
loop sit of jaag.
'**stance** ['stæns] s. houding.
'**stanch** ['stântsj] *ww.* stelp =
staunch.
'**stanchion** ['stânsjən] s. pilaar, stut,
styl.
stand ['stænd] *ww.* ('*stood*) staan;
gaan; uithou; s. stilstand;. stelling;
standertjie; pawiljoen; -**ing** s. stand,
rang; -**point** s. standpunt; -**still** s.
stilstand.
'**standard** ['stændəd] *s.* (-*s*) vlag;
standaard; maatstaf; stander; -**ize**
ww. (-*d*) standaardiseer.
'**stand-by** ['stænd-'bai] *s. bnw.* nood-.
'**stand'offish** ['stænd'ofisj] *bnw.*
terughoudend.
'**standpoint** ['stændpoint] *s.* (-*s*)
standpunt.
'**stanza** ['stænzə] *s.* (-*s*) vers,
koeplet, stansa.
'**staple** ['stypl] *s.* (-*s*) kram;
vernaamste produk; draad; -**r** s.

wolsorteerder; **hasp and - s.** kram en oorslag.

star ['stā] s. (-s) ster; hooffiguur; **-board** s. stuurboord; **-spangled** bnw. met sterre besaai.

starch ['stātsj] s. stysel; ww. (-ed) stywe; bnw. gestyf; **-y** bnw. styselagtig.

'**stare** ['stēə] ww. (-d) staar, tuur, aangaap.

stark ['stāk] bnw. styf; louter; bw. gans, stapel-.

start ['stāt] ww. (-ed) skrik, opspring; begin; aan die gang sit of kom; s. sprong; aanvang; voorsprong; **-er** s. aansitter; afsitter.

'**startle** ['stātl] ww. (-d) skrik maak; '**startling** bnw. ontstellend.

'**starve** ['stāv] ww. (-d) honger ly, van honger omkom; ondervoed, ondervoer; **star'vation** s. verhongering.

'**state** ['styt] s. staat; toestand; rang; ww. (-d) verklaar; vasstel; **-craft** s. diplomasie; **-ly** bnw. statig, deftig; **-ment** s. verklaring, bewering; **-sman** s. staatsman.

'**statice** ['stætis] s. papierblom.

'**station** ['stysjən] s. (-s) stasie; status; staanplek; **-ary** bnw. stilstaande.

'**stationer** ['stysjən] s.(-s), handelaar in skryfbehoeftes; **-y** s. skryfbehoeftes.

sta'tistics [stə'tistiks] s. statistieke.

'**statue** ['stætjoe] s. (-s) standbeeld; '**statuary** s. beeldhoukuns; **statu-'esque** bnw. soos 'n standbeeld; **statu'ette** s. beeldjie.

'**stature** ['stætsjə] s. lengte, gestalte.

'**status** ['stytəs] s. status, rang, posisie.

'**statute** ['stætjŏēt] s. (-s) statuut, wet, instelling; '**statutory** bnw. wetlik.

staunch ['stônsj] bnw. trou, betroubaar; ww. stelp.

'**stave** ['styv] ww. (-d; stove) in duie slaan; duie insit; **-off** afweer, afwend.

stay ['sty] ww. (-ed) weerhou; stuit; opskort; bly; vertoef; loseer; s. verblyf; uitstel; opskorting; stut; anker; **-s** s. korset.

stead ['sted] s. stede, plek; diens, nut; **-fast** bnw. standvastig; **-y** bnw. (steadier, steadiest) vas; gestadig; besadig.

steak ['styk] s. (-s) biefstuk.

steal ['stīl] ww. (stole, stolen) steel; sluip; **-th** s. geheimsinnige optrede; onderduimsheid; **-thy** bnw. skelm, heimlik.

steam ['stīm] s. stoom, wasem, damp; **-boat** s. stoomboot; **-engine** s. stoommasjien; **-er** s. stoomskip; **-power** s. stoomkrag; **-ship** s. stoomskip.

steed ['stīd] s. strydros.

steel ['stīl] s. staal; ww. (-ed) verhard; **-clad** bnw. gepantser;

-plated bnw. gepantser; **-y** bnw. soos staal; hard.

steep ['stīp] bnw. (-er, -est) steil; kras; ww. (-ed) week, indompel; **-en** ww. steiler word.

'**steeple** ['stīpl] s. (-s) toring; **-jack** s. toringwerker; '**steeply** bnw. steilerig.

'**steeplechase** ['stīpltsjys] s. hinderniswedren.

steer ['stīə] ww. (-ed) stuur; koers vat; s. (-s) stier, bulletjie; **-age** s. stuur; tussendek; **-ing** s. stuurtoestel, stuur; **-ing column** s. stuurkolom; **-ing lock** s. stuurslot; **-ing rod** s. stuurstang.

stem ['stem] s. (-s) stam, stingel, steel; ww. (-med) stuit.

stench ['stentsj] s. stank.

'**stencil** ['stensil] s. (-s) tekenpatroon, sjablon, wasvel.

sten'ography [ste'noghrəfi] s. stenografie; snelskrif; **sten'ographer** s. stenograaf; snelskrywer.

step ['step] s. (-s) tree, stap, pas; trappie; leer; ww. (-ped) loop, stap; **-child** s. stiefkind; **-parents** s. stiefouers; **-ladder** s. (-s) staanleer, trapleer.

'**stepbrother** ['stepbrʌdhə] s. stiefbroer.

'**stepping-stone** ['steping-stoun] s. (-s) vastrappiek; oorspring'klip.

'**sterile** ['sterail] bnw. onvrugbaar; kiemvry; **sterili'zation** s. sterilisasie; **ste'rility** s. onvrugbaarheid; '**sterilize** ww. (-d) onvrugbaar maak.

'**sterling** ['stöling] s. sterling; eg.

stern ['stön] bnw. streng; ernstig, stug.

'**sternum** ['stönəm] s. borsbeen.

'**stevedore** ['stividô] s. (-s) stuwadoor.

stew ['stjŏē] ww. (-ed) stowe; s. gestoofde vleis, bredie.

'**steward** ['stjoeəd] s. (-s) rentmeester; kelner.

stick ['stik] ww. (-ed) steek; vassteek; vasklewe; aanhou; s. (-s) stok; jandooi; lummel; **-ing-plaster** s. hegpleister; **-y** bnw. klewerig, taai.

stiff ['stif] bnw. styf, stram; swaar; sterk; **-en** ww. (-ed) styf maak, verstywe; **-necked** bnw. hardkoppig.

'**stifle** ['staifl] ww. (-d) versmoor; onderdruk.

'**stigma** ['stighmə] s. brandmerk; skandvlek.

stile ['stail] s. (-s) trappie, oorklimtrap.

still ['stil] bnw. (-er, -est) stil, kalm; ww. stil maak, kalmeer; bw. nog, steeds; s. distileerketel; **-born** bnw. doodgebore.

'**stilt** ['stilt] s. (-s) stelt; **-ed** bnw. onnatuurlik.

'**stimulate** ['stimjoelyt] ww. (-d) prikkel, opwek; '**stimulant** bnw. prikkelend, s. prikkelmiddel; **stimu'lation** s. prikkeling; '**stimulus** s. prikkel.

sting ['sting] *ww.* (*stung*) steek, prik; s. angel; prikkel.

'stingy ['stindzji] *bnw.* (*stingier, stingiest*) vrekkig, inhalig.

stink ['stink] s. stank; *vgl.* **stench;** -wood s. stinkhout.

stint ['stint] *ww.* (*-ed*) beperk; suinig wees.

'stipend ['staipend] s. (*-s*) besoldiging, loon.

'stipulate ['stipjoelyt] *ww.* (*-d*) stipuleer, bepaal; **stipu'lation** s. bepaling, voorwaarde.

stir ['stö] *ww.* (*-red*) roer, verroer; beweeg; s. beweging; oproer.

'stirrup ['stirəp] s. stiebeuel.

stitch ['stitsj] s. (*-es*) steek; *ww.* (*-ed*) stik, naal.

stock ['stok] s. (*-s*) stam; steel; geslag; voorraad; effekte; *ww.* (*-ed*) in voorraad hou, voorsien; **-ade** s. verskansing; **-breeder** s. beesboer; **-broker** s. aandelemakelaar; **- exchange** s. beurs; **-fish** s. stokvis; **-in-trade** s. voorraad; **- phrase** s. staande uitdrukking, gesegde; **-taking** s. voorraadopname; **-yard** s. veekraal.

'stocking ['stoking] s. (*-s*) kous.

'stodgy ['stodzji] *bnw.* (*stodgier, stodgiest*) swaar.

stoke ['stouk] *ww.* (*-d*) stook; **-r** s. stoker.

'stolid ['stolid] *bnw.* (*-est*) bot; koppig.

'stomach ['stʌmək] s. (*-s*) maag, pens; eetlus.

'stone ['stoun] s. (*-s*) klip, steen; pit; 14 pond; *ww.* (*-d*) stenig; pitte verwyder; **'stony** *bnw.* klipperig.

'stook ['stöëk] s. (*-s*) opper, hooihopie.

stool ['stöël] s. (*-s*) stoeltjie; stoelgang.

stoop ['stöëp] *ww.* (*-ed*) buk, buig, krom loop.

stop ['stop] s. (*-s*) stilstand; halte; leessteken; register(*orrel*); *ww.* (*-ped*) stop; toestop; beëindig; stilhou; ophou; **-cock** s. kraan; **-gap** s. noodhulp, plaasvervanger; **-page** s. stilstand, onderbreking; **-per** s. prop.

'store ['stö] *ww.* (*-d*) bêre, bewaar, opgaar; s. voorraad; winkel; skuur; **'storage** s. opbergloon; **-house** s. skuur; **-keeper** s. winkelier; **-man** s. (*-men*) pakhuisman.

'storey ['störi] s. (*-s*) verdieping.

stork ['störk] s. (*-s*) ooievaar.

storm ['störm] s. (*-s*) storm; aanval; *ww.* (*-ed*) aanval, woed; **-y** *bnw.* stormagtig.

'story ['störi] s. (*stories*) storie, geskiedenis, verhaal; **-book** s. storieboek; **-teller** s. verteller, verhaler.

stout ['staut] *bnw.* sterk, kragtig, geset.

'stove ['stouv] s. (*-s*) stoof.

stow ['stou] *ww.* (*-ed*) bêre; **-age** s. bêreplek; **-away** s. verstekelingpassasier.

'straddle ['strædl] *ww.* (*-d*) wydsbeen (staan, ry); **- truck** s. buidelwa.

'straggle ['stræghl] *ww.* (*-d*) afdwaal, verdwaal; **-r** s. verdwaalde, agterblyer.

straight ['stryt] *bnw.* (*-er, -est*) reguit; openhartig; *bw.* reguit, onmiddelik; s. reguit stuk; **-en** *ww.* (*-ed*) reguit maak; **-forward** *bnw.* eerlik, padlangs; **- edge** s. reiplank; **-jacket** s. dwangbaadjie, dwangbuis; **-oil** s. suiwer olie.

strain ['stryn] *ww.* (*-ed*) trek; oorspan; verrek; deursif; s. inspanning; spanning; **-ed** *bnw.* gespanne; **-er** s. sif, sygdoek.

straining 'post ['stryning'poust] s. (*-s*) trekpaal.

strait ['stryt] s. (*-s*) seestraat; **-en** *ww.* (*-ed*) beperk; **- jacket** s. dwangbuis; **-laced** *bnw.* eng, preuts.

strand ['strænd] s. strand, kus; *ww.* (*-ed*) strand; s. (*-s*) string, draad.

'strange ['stryndzj] *bnw.* (*-r, -st*) vreemd, onbekend; sonderling; **-r** s. vreemdeling.

'strangle ['stræng-ghl] *ww.* (*-d*) verwurg; **'strangulate** *ww.* verwurg.

strap ['stræp] s. (*-s*) riem, platriem, plak; **-ping** *bnw.* frisgebou.

'stratagem ['strætidzjəm] s. krygslis, streek.

'strategy ['strætədzji] s. strategie; **stra'tegic** *bnw.* strategies; **'strategist** s. strateeg.

'stratum ['strytəm] s. (*'strata*) stratum.

'stratus ['strytəs] s. stratuswolk.

straw ['strö] s. strooi; **-berry** s. (*-berries*) aarbei.

stray ['stry] *ww.* (*-ed*) dwaal, afdwaal, verdwaal.

streak ['strik] s. (*-s*) streep, strook; **-ed** *bnw.* gestreep; **-y** *bnw.* vol strepe.

stream ['strim] s. stroom, stroming; rivier, spruit; **-er** s. wimpel; **-ing** *bnw.* stromend; **-let** s. stroompie.

street ['strit] s. (*-s*) straat.

strength ['strength] s. sterkte, krag; **-en** *ww.* (*-ed*) versterk, sterk maak.

'strenuous ['strenjoeəs] *bnw.* ywerig; wat groot inspanning verg.

stress ['stres] s. (*-es*) drang; spanning; klem; aksent.

stretch ['stretsj] s. (*-es*) rek, spanning; uitgestrektheid; *ww.* (*-ed*) rek; uitrek; oordrywe; **-er** s. draagbaar; kateltjie.

striate, 'striated ['striət, 'striytəd] *bnw.* gestreep.

strict ['strikt] *bnw.* (*-er, -est*) streng; stip; presies; eng; **-ure** s. afkeuring; ongunstige kritiek; vernouing.

'stride ['straid] s. (*-s*) stap, lang tree.

'strife ['straif] s. stryd, twis, tweedrag.

'strike ['straik] *ww.* (*struck, stricken*) slaan, stoot, bots; lyk, skyn; staak; **-r** s. staker; **'striking** *bnw.* treffend.

string ['string] s. (*-s*) lyn, tou; snaar; snoer; reeks; *ww.* (*strung*)

inryg; besnaar; afhaar; **-band** s.
strykorkes; **-y** bnw. (-ier, -iest)
draderig.

'**stringency** ['strindzjənsi] s. strengheid; skaarste.

strip ['strip] ww. (-ped) uittrek;
plunder; melk; afdraai, doldraai;
stroop; **-per** s. stroper; **-ling** s.
opgeskote seun; **- road** s. strookpad.

'**stripe** ['straip] s. (-s) streep; striem;
'**stripy** bnw. gestreep.

'**strive** ['straiv] ww. (strove, striven)
strewe; wedywer.

'**stroke** ['strouk] s. (-s) hou, slag;
aanval; trek; ww. (-d) streel,
liefkoos.

stroll ['stroul] ww. (-ed) loop, luier,
slenter.

'**strong** ['strong] bnw. (-er, -est) sterk,
kragtig; geweldig; kras; **-box** s.
brandkas; **-hold** s. vesting; **-minded**
bnw. beslis; **-room** s. kluis.

strop ['strop] s. (-s) skeerriem.

'**strophe** ['stroufi] s. (-s) strofe.

'**structure** ['strΛktsjə] s. (-s) bou;
struktuur; gebou; '**structural** bnw.
wat die bou betref.

'**struggle** ['strΛgl] ww. (-d) worstel,
stoei, sukkel.

strut ['strΛt] ww. (-ted) deftig stap,
pronk; s. stut.

'**strychnine** ['striknin] s. wolwegif.

stub ['stΛb] s. stompie.

'**stubble** ['stΛbl] s. stoppels.

'**stubborn** ['stΛbən] bnw. (-est) koppig, halsstarrig.

'**stuck-'up** ['stΛk'Λp] bnw. verwaand,
trots.

stud ['stΛd] s. (-s) knop; nael;
halsknopie; stut; tapbout.

'**student** ['stjoēdənt] s. (-s) student,
leerling; navorser.

'**study** ['stΛdi] s. (studies) studie;
studeerkamer; ww. (studied) studeer,
bestudeer; beoefen; '**studied** bnw.
opsetlik; '**studio** s. ateljee; '**studious**
bnw. ywerig, vlytig.

stuff ['stΛf] s. stof, goed; ww. (-ed)
stop, volstop, opstop; **-ing** s. vulsel;
-y bnw. (-ier, -iest) bedompig.

'**stultify** ['stΛltifai] ww. (stultified)
belaglik maak.

'**stumble** ['stΛmbl] ww. (-d) struikel,
strompel; '**stumbling-block** s.
struikelblok.

stump ['stΛmp] s. (-s) stomp,
stompie; paaltjie; **-y** bnw. (-ier, -iest)
kort, geset.

stun ['stΛn] ww. (-ned) verdoof,
dronkslaan; **-ner** s. doodhou; **-ning**
bnw. bedwelmend; verrukkend.

stunt ['stΛnt] ww. (-ed) knot, die
groei belemmer; s. (-s) streek,
kunsie.

'**stupefy** ['stjoēpifai] ww. (stupefied)
bedwelm, verdoof; **stupe'faction** s.
bedwelming; stu'**pendous** bnw. verbasend; '**stupor** s. bedwelming.

'**stupid** ['stjoēpid] bnw. (-est) dom,
onnosel; stu'**pidity** s. domheid,
onnoselheid.

'**sturdy** ['stədi] bnw. (sturdier,
sturdiest) stoer, sterk.

'**sturgeon** ['stədzjən] s. steur.

'**stutter** ['stΛtə] ww. (-ed) hakkel,
stotter, stamel; **-er** s. hakkelaar,
stotteraar.

sty]'stai] s. (sties) varkhok; karkatjie.

'**style** ['stail] s. stilus; stif; styl;
skryfwyse; naam; '**stylish** bnw.
deftig.

'**styptic 'pencil** ['stiptik 'pensl] s.
(-s) bloedstelpstiffie.

'**suave** ['swyv] bnw. (-r, -st) vriendelik, sag, goed.

'**subaltern** ['sΛbltn] s. (-s) ondergeskikte.

sub- [sΛb-] voorvoegsel onder-, sub-;
-cutaneous bnw. onderhuids; **-jacent**
bnw. laer geleë; **-ject** s. onderdaan,
ww. onderwerp; **-jection** s. onderwerping; **-join** ww. byvoeg; **-jugate**
ww. onderwerp; **-'junctive** s. aanvoegende wyse; **-let** ww. onderverhuur; **-'ordinate** bnw. ondergeskik; **-sequence** s. opvolging;
-tenant s. onderhuurder; **-ter'ranean** bnw. onderaards; **-'vert** ww.
onderwerp.

sub'due [səb'djoē] ww. (-d) onderwerp, beteuel; **-d** bnw. stil, gelate.

sub'lime [sə'blaim] bnw. (-r, -st)
subliem, verhewe, heerlik; '**sublimate** ww. veredel, verfyn; **sublimation** s. veredeling; su'**blimity** s.
verhewen, held.

'**submarine** ['sΛbmərin] s. (-s) duikboot.

sub'merge [səb'mədz] ww. (-d)
onderdompel; sub'**mersion** s. oorstroming.

sub'mit [səb'mit] ww. (-ted) onderwerp; voorlê; beweer; sub'**mission**
s. onderwerping; voorlegging.

sub'ordinate [sə'bôdinyt] ww. (-d)
ondergeskik maak; bnw. ondergeskik; subordi'**nation** s. ondergeskiktheid.

sub'poena [sə'pinə] ww. (-ed) dagvaar; s. dagvaarding.

sub'scribe [səb'skraib] ww. (-d)
onderteken; inteken; **-r** s. intekenaar; sub'**scription** s. intekening, intekengeld; bydrae.

'**subsequent** ['sΛbsikwənt] bnw.
daaropvolgende; **-ly** bw. daarna.

sub'servience [səb'səvians] s. onderdanigheid; sub'**servient** bnw. dienstig, onderdanig, kruiperig.

sub'side [səb'said] ww. (-d) sak,
wegsak; sub'**sidence** s. sakking.

sub'sidiary [səb'sidiəri] bnw. hulp-;
s. (subsidiaries) vertakking, sytak.

'**subsidy** ['sΛbsidi] s. toelaag, steun,
subsidie.

sub'sist [səb'sist] ww. (-ed) bestaan,
lewe; **-ence** s. leeftog.

'**subsoil** ['sΛbsoil] s. onder-grondlaag,
laag grond onder teelaarde; **-er** s.
(-s) bladbreker.

'**substance** ['sΛbstəns] s. stof; fut;
kern; wese; substansie; sub'**stantial**

bnw. werklik, wesenlik; belangrik.

sub'stantiate [sʌb'stænsjiyt] *ww.* (-*d*) staaf.

'**substitute** ['sʌbstitjōēt] *ww.* (-*d*) vervang; **substi'tution** *s.* vervanging.

'**subterfuge** ['sʌbtəfjōēdzj] *s.* uitvlug, voorwendsel.

'**subtile** =subtle.

'**subtle** ['sʌtl] *bnw.* (-*r*, -*st*) subtiel, teer, fyn; spitsvondig.

sub'tract [səb'trækt] *ww.* (-*ed*) aftrek; **sub'traction** *s.* aftrekking.

'**suburb** ['sʌbəb] *s.* (-*s*) voorstad; -**an** *bnw.* voorstedelik.

sub'vention [səb'vensjən] *s.* onderstand, geldelike steun.

'**subway** ['sʌbwy] *s.* (-*s*) duikweg, tonnel.

suc'ceed [sək'sid] *ww.* (-*ed*) opvolg; slaag.

suc'cess [sək'ses] *s.* sukses, welslae; voorspoed; -**ful** *bnw.* suksesvol; -**ion** *s.* opvolging, erfopvolging; -**ive** *bnw.* agtereenvolgend; -**ively** *bw.* agtereenvolgens; -**or** *s.* opvolger.

suc'cinct [sək'sinkt] *bnw.* beknop, bondig.

'**succour** ['sʌkə] *s.* hulp, steun, bystand.

'**succulence** ['sykjoeləns] *s.* sappig, heid; '**succulent** *bnw.* sappig.

suc'cumb [sə'kəm] *ww.* (-*ed*) beswyk, swyg.

such ['sʌtsj] *bnw.* (-*ed*) suig, insuig, uitsuig; suip; drink; -**er** *s.* suier; loot; -**ing** *bnw.* suigend, piepjonk; -**ing-pig** *s.* speenvark; -**le** *ww.* (-*d*) soog; -**ling** *s.* suigeling.

such ['sʌtsj] *bnw.* (-*ed*) suig, insuig, uitsuig; suip; drink; -**er** *s.* suier; loot; -**ing** *bnw.* suigend, piepjonk; -**ing-pig** *s.* speenvark; -**le** *ww.* (-*d*) soog; -**ling** *s.* suigeling.

'**suction** ['sʌksjən] *s.* suiging.

'**sudden** ['sʌdn] *bnw.* (-*est*) skielik, plotseling.

suds ['sʌdz] *s.* seepsop, seepwater, seepskuim.

sue ['sjōē] *ww.* (-*d*) geregtelik vervolg; dagvaar; aanskrywe; -**r** *s.* eiser.

'**suède** ['swyd] *s.* sweedse leer, suède.

'**suet** ['sjoeit] *s.* niervet.

'**suffer** ['sʌfə] *ww.* (-*ed*) ly; uithou; boet; gedoog; -**able** *bnw.* toelaatbaar, duldbaar; -**ance** *s.* toelating, toestemming; -**er** *s.* lyer; -**ing** *bnw.* lydend; -**ings** *s.* lyding.

'**suffice** [sə'fais] *ww.* (-*d*) voldoende wees; toereik; **suf'ficiency** *s.* genoegsaamheid; **suf'ficient** *bnw.* genoegsaam, genoeg.

'**suffix** ['sʌfiks] *s.* (-*es*) agtervoegsel, suffiks.

'**suffocate** ['sʌfəkyt] *ww.* (-*d*) stuk, versmoor; **suffo'cation** *s.* versmoring.

'**suffrage** ['sʌfridzj] *s.* stemreg; **suffragette** *s.* suffrajet, vrou wat stemreg eis.

suf'fuse [sə'fjōēz] *ww.* (-*d*) oordek; kleur, stroom oor.

'**sugar** ['sjoeghə] *s.* suiker; *ww.* (-*ed*) versuiker; -**basin** *s.* suikerpot; -**candy** *s.* suikerklontjies; -**cane** *s.* suikerriet; -**loaf** *s.* suikerbrood; -**y** *bnw.* suikerig; soet; vleierig.

sug'gest [sə'dzjest] *ww.* (-*ed*) aan die hand doen, voorstel, opper, suggereer; -**ible** *bnw.* ontvanklik; -**ion** *s.* suggestie; ingewing, wenk; -**ive** *bnw.* suggestief.

'**suicide** ['s-joeisaid] *s.* (-*s*) selfmoord; selfmoordenaar; **sui'cidal** *bnw.* selfvernietigend.

suit ['s-jōēt] *s.* (-*s*) pak klere; regsgeding; *ww.* (-*ed*) pas; -**able** *bnw.* geskik; -**a'bility** *s.* geskiktheid; -**case** *s.* handkoffer, tas; -**or** *s.* vryer.

'**suite** ['swit] *s.* (-*s*) gevolg; stel.

'**suitor** ['s-jōētə] *s.* (-*s*) vryer; party in hofsaak.

sulk ['sʌlk] *ww.* (-*ed*) pruil, nukkerig wees; -**s** *s.* nukkerigheid; -**y** *bnw.* (-*ier*, -*iest*) nors, nukkerig.

'**sullen** ['sʌlən] *bnw.* (-*est*) knorrig, stuurs, bot.

'**sully** ['sʌli] *ww.* (*sullied*) besmet, besmeer.

'**sulphate** ['sʌlfyt] *s.* sulfaat.

'**sulphide** ['sʌlfaid] *s.* (-*s*) sulfied.

'**sulphur** ['sʌlfə] *s.* swawel.

'**sultan** ['sʌltən] *s.* (-*s*) sultan.

sul'tana [səl'tānə] *s.* (-*s*) sultanarosyntjie(-druiwe).

'**sultry** ['sʌltri] *bnw.* (*sultrier*, *sultriest*) bedompig, swoel.

sum ['sʌm] *s.* (-*s*) som; bedrag; totaal.

'**summary** ['sʌməri] *s.* ('*summaries*) opsomming.

'**summer** ['sʌmə] *s.* (-*s*) somer; -*y* *bnw.* someragtig, somers.

'**summit** ['sʌmit] *s.* (-*s*) toppunt.

'**summon** ['sʌmən] *ww.* (-*ed*) dagvaar; oproep; ontbied; -**s** *s.* dagvaarding, oproep.

'**sumptuous** ['sʌmptjoeəs] *bnw.* weelderig.

sun ['sʌn] *s.* son, sonlig, sonskyn; -**beam** *s.* sonstraal; -**bonnet** *s.* kappie; -**down** *s.* sononder; -**flower** *s.* sonneblom; -**glasses** *s.* sonbril; -**ny** *bnw.* sonnig; -**rise** *s.* sonop; -**shade** *s.* sambreel; -**stroke** *s.* sonsteek, sonstraal.

'**sunburn** ['sʌnbən] *s.* sonbrand; -**lotion** *s.* sonbrandmiddel; -**oil** *s.* sonbrandolie.

'**Sunday** ['sʌndi] *s.* Sondag.

'**sunder** ['sʌndə] *ww.* (-*ed*) skei; afkap; afsny.

'**sundial** ['sʌndaiəl] *s.* (-*s*) sonwyser.

'**sundry** ['sʌndri] *bnw.* verskillende, diverse.

'**sunset** ['sʌnset] *s.* (-*s*) sonsondergang.

'**sunshine** ['sʌnsjain] *s.* sonskyn.

sup ['sʌp] *ww.* (-*ped*) aandete gebruik; *s.* mondjievol, slukkie.

'**super-** ['s-jōēpə-] voorvoegsel bo, bo-op, meer as, die hoogste graad, super-.

su'perb [s-jŏĕ'pŏb] *bnw.* voortreflik, pragtig.

super'cilious [s-joepə'siliəz] *bnw.* trots, verwaand.

super'ficial [s-jŏĕpə'fisjəl] *bnw.* oppervlakkig, vlak.

su'perfluous [s-joe'pəfloeəs] *bnw.* oortollig.

'superimpose ['sjŏĕpəimpouz] *ww.* (-d) oplê.

superin'tendent [s-joepə-in'tendənt] *s.* direkteur, superintendent.

su'perior [s-joe'piəriə] *bnw.* hoër, beter, superieur; **superi'ority** *s.* hoër rang, voorrang, superioriteit.

su'perlative [s-joe'pŏlətiv] *bnw.* oortreffend; voortreflik.

'superman ['s-jŏĕpəmæn] *s.* (-men) oppermens.

super'sede [s-joepə'sid] *ww.* (-d) vervang, afdank.

super'stition [s-joepə'stisjən] *s.* bygeloof.

'supertax ['s-jŏĕpətæks] *s.* super-belasting, oorbelasting.

'supervise ['s-joepəvaiz] *ww.* (-d) toesig hou.

'supine ['sjŏĕpain] *bnw.* agteroor; traag, vadsig.

'supper ['sʌpə] *s.* aandete.

sup'plant [sə'plänt] *ww.* (-ed) verdring.

'supple ['sʌpl] *bnw.* slap, buigsaam; **-ment** *s.* aanhangsel, aanvulling; **-'mentary** *bnw.* supplementêr, aanvullings-.

'suppliant ['sʌpliənt] *s.* (-s) smekeling.

'supplicate ['sʌplikyt] *ww.* (-d) smeek; **suppli'cation** *s.* versoekskrif.

sup'ply [sə'plai] *ww.* (supplied) voorsien, verskaf; **sup'plies** *s.* voorrade.

sup'port [sə'pŏt] *ww.* (-ed) steun, ondersteun, help; *s.* steun, hulp, bystand; **-er** *s.* ondersteuner.

sup'pose [sə'pouz] *ww.* (-d) veronderstel.

sup'press [sə'pres] *ww.* (-ed) onderdruk; verswyg.

'suppurate ['sʌpjoeryt] *ww.* (-d) sweer, etter; **suppu'ration** *s.* ettering.

su'preme [s-joe'prim] *bnw.* hoogste, opperste; **su'premacy** *s.* [su'preməsi] *s.* opperheerskappy, oppermag.

'sur- ['sə-] voorvoegsel bo-, oor-, super.

'surcharge ['sətsjädzj] *s.* oorlading, ekstrabedrag, toeslag.

'surcoat ['sŏkout] *s.* oorkleed.

sure ['sjoeə] *bnw.* (-r, -st) seker, gewis; onfeilbaar; veilig; *bw.* seker, waarlik; **-ly** *bw.* seker, tog.

'surety ['sjoeəti] *s.* (sureties) borg, pand.

'surf ['sŏf] *s.* branding, branders.

'surface ['sŏfis] *s.* oppervlakte; vlak.

'surfeit ['sŏfit] *s.* oorversadiging, satheid.

'surge ['sŏdzj] (-d) dein, golf.

'surgeon ['sŏdzjən] *s.* snydokter, sjirurg; **'surgery** *s.* heelkunde.

'surly ['sŏli] *bnw.* (surlier, surliest) nors, stuurs.

'surmise ['sŏmaiz] *s.* vermoede, gissing.

sur'mount [sŏ'maunt] *ww.* (-ed) oorwin, te bowe kom.

'surname ['sŏnym] *s.* van, familie-naam.

'surplice ['sŏplis] *s.* (-s) koorkleed (-hemp).

'surplus ['sŏpləs] *s.* (-es) oorskot, surplus.

sur'prise [sə'praiz] *s.* verrassing; verbasing; **sur'prising** *bnw.* verbasend.

sur'render [sə'rendə] *ww.* (-ed) oorgee; uitlewer, afkoop.

surrep'titious [sʌrəp'tisjəs] *bnw.* onderduims, slinks.

sur'round [sə'raund] *ww.* (-ed) omring, omsingel; **-ing** *s.* omsingeling; **-ings** *s.* omgewing.

'survey [sŏ'vy] *ww.* (-ed) bekyk; opneem; opmeet; *s.* opmeting.

sur'vive [sə'vaiv] *ww.* (-d) oorlewe; behoue bly; **sur'vivor** *s.* oorlewende, langslewende.

sus'ceptible [sə'septəbl] *bnw.* vatbaar, gevoelig; **suscepti'bility** *s.* gevoeligheid.

sus'pect [sʌs'pekt] *ww.* (-ed) vermoed, verdink.

sus'pend [sʌs'pend] *ww.* (-ed) opskort; ophang; **sus'pense** *s.* spanning; twyfel.

sus'pension [sʌs'pensjn] *s.* vering.

sus'picion [səs'pisjən] *s.* argwaan, suspisie; **sus'picious** *bnw.* agterdogtig.

sus'tain [səs'tyn] *ww.* (-ed) dra, steun; uithou; volhou; handhaaf.

'sustenance ['sʌstinəns] *s.* voedsel, onderhoud.

'suture needle ['sjŏĕtsjŏ-nidl] *s.* hegnaald, wondnaald.

'swab ['swob] *s.* (-s) skropbesem; lap; pluisie; depper; **- forceps** *s.* deppertang.

'swaddle ['swodl] *ww.* (-ed) toedraai.

'swagger ['swægə] *ww.* (-ed) groot-praat.

'swain ['swyn] *s.* (-s) kêrel, vryer.

'swallow ['swolou] *ww.* (-ed) sluk, insluk; *s.* (-s) swaeltjie.

'swamp ['swomp] *s.* (-s) moeras, vlei.

swan ['swon] *s.* (-s) swaan.

'swank ['swænk] *ww.* (-ed) spog.

'sward ['swŏd] *s.* (-s) grasveld.

swarm ['swŏm] *s.* (-s) swerm; menigte.

'swarthy ['swŏdhi] *s.* swart, donker, blas.

'swash ['swosj] *ww.* (-ed) klots, plas.

'swathe ['swydh] *ww.* (-d) verbind; indraai.

'sway ['swy] *ww.* (-ed) swaai, slinger; beheers.

swear ['swēə] *ww.* (swore, sworn) sweer, 'n eed aflê; vloek.

sweat ['swet] *ww.* (-ed) sweet; *s.* sweet; -er *s.* trui.

sweep ['swip] *ww.* (swept) vee, wegvee, uitveeg; aftas (radar); *s.* (-s) swaai, veeg; skoorsteenveër; -ing *bnw.* omvattend.

sweet ['swit] *bnw.* (-er, -est) soet, lekker; -s *s.* lekkergoed; -en *ww.* soet maak; -bread *s.* soetvleis; -heart *s.* liefling; -ish *bnw.* soeterig; -meat *s.* lekkergoed; -oil *s.* soetolie; -potato *s.* patatta.

'sweetgum ['switghʌm] *s.* (-s) amberboom.

'sweet-pea ['swit'pi] *s.* pronkertjie.

sweet-William [swit 'wiljəm] *s.* (-s) baardangelier.

'swelling ['sweling] *s.* swelsel, geswel.

swelter ['sweltə] *ww.* (-ed) versmag, verskroei; benoud wees.

'swerve ['swɜv] *ww.* (-d) afwyk; swenk.

swift ['swift] *bnw.* (-er, -est) vlug, gou, rats; *bw.* gou, vinnig.

'swill ['swil] *ww.* (-ed) spoel; suip.

swim ['swim] *ww.* (swam, swum) swem.

'swindle ['swindl] *s.* (-s) bedrog, swendelary.

'swine ['swain] *s.* (-s) vark, swyn.

swing ['swing] *ww.* (swang, swung) swaai, skommel.

swirl ['swɜl] *ww.* (-ed) draai, warrel.

'swish ['swisj] *ww.* (-ed) siets; suis, ruis.

switch ['switsj] *s.* lat; vals haarvlegsel; wisselspoor; skakelaar; stroomwisselaar.

'swivel ['swivl] *ww.* (-led) op 'n spil draai; *s.* werwel.

swoon ['swôẽn] *ww.* (-ed) vlou val, beswym.

swoop ['swôẽp] *ww.* (-ed) neerskiet.

sword ['sôd] *s.* (-s) swaard, sabel.

swot ['swot] *ww.* (-ted) blok.

'syllable ['siləbl] *s.* (-s) lettergreep.

'syllabus ['siləbəs] *s.* (-es, i) sillabus, leerplan.

symbol ['simbəl] *s.* (-s) simbool, sinnebeeld, teken.

'symmetry ['simitri] *s.* simmetrie, eweredigheid.

'sympathy ['simpəthi] *s.* simpatie, medelye.

'symphony ['simfəni] *s.* (symphonies) simfonie.

symptom ['simptəm] *s.* simptoom, teken, verskynsel.

syndicate ['sindikit] *s.* (-s) sindikaat, kartel.

'synod ['sinəd] *s.* (-s) sinode, kerkvergadering.

'synonym ['sinənim] *s.* (-s) sinoniem.

sy'nopsis [si'nopsis] *s.* (syn'opses) oorsig, sinopsis.

'syntax ['sintæks] *s.* sintaksis.

sy'ringe [si'rindzj] *s.* (-s) spuit.

'syrup ['sirəp] *s.* stroop.

'system ['sistim] *s.* sisteem, stelsel.

T

tab ['tæb] *s.* (-s) strokie; kenkaartjie.

'tabernacle ['tæbənækl] *s.* tabernakel, tent, hut; liggaam.

'table ['tybl] *s.* (-s) tafel; plato; tabel; lys; - centre *s.* tafellap; -cloth *s.* tafeldoek; -knife *s.* tafelmes; -land *s.* plato; - linen *s.* tafelline; -spoon *s.* eetlepel.

'tableau ['tæblou] *s.* (-s) tablo.

'tablet ['tæblit] *s.* (-s) tablet, pil.

'tabloid ['tæbloid] *s.* (-s) tablet, pil.

ta'boo [tə'bô] *s.* verbod, taboe.

'tabouret ['tæbərit] *s.* tamboeryntjie.

'tabulate ['tæbjoelyt] *ww.* (-d) tabuleer; 'tabular *bnw.* tafel-.

'tacit ['tæsit] *bnw.* stilswyend.

'taciturn ['tæsitɜn] *bnw.* stil, swygsaam.

'tack ['tæk] *ww.* (-ed) vasslaan; vasryg.

'tackle ['tækl] *ww.* (-d) aanpak; neertrek.

'tacky ['tæki] *bnw.* klewerig.

tact ['tækt] *s.* tak, slag; -ful *bnw.* takvol.

'tactics ['tæktiks] *s.* taktiek.

'tactile ['tæktil] *bnw.* tasbaar, voelbaar.

'tactual ['tæktsjoeəl] *bnw.* tas-, van die tassin.

'tadpole ['tædpoul] *s.* (-s) paddavissie.

'taffeta ['tæfitə] *s.* taf.

tag ['tægh] *s.* (-s) etiket, adreskaart.

tail ['tyl] *s.* (-s) stert; pant, slip.

'tail'light ['tyl'lait] *s.* agterlamp.

'tailor ['tylə] *s.* kleremaker, snyer; *ww.* kleremaak; -ing *s.* kleremakery.

taint ['tynt] *ww.* (-ed) besmet; aansteek; *s.* bysmaak; -ed *bnw.* met bysmaak bederf.

'take ['tyk] *ww.* (took, taken) neem, vat, gryp; takings *s.* ontvangste.

'take-in ['tykin] *s.* bedrieëry.

'tale ['tyl] *s.* (-s) verhaal, storie; getal; -bearer *s.* nuusbek.

'talent ['tælənt] *s.* talent, gawe; -ed *bnw.* begaaf.

'talisman ['tælizmən] *s.* talisman; gelukbringertjie.

talk ['tôk] *ww.* (-ed) praat, gesels; *s.* gesprek; praatjie; 'talkative *bnw.* spraaksaam; -ie *s.* klankfilm; -ing *bnw.* sprekend; -ing-to *s.* skrobbering.

tall ['tôl] *bnw.* (-er, -est) groot, kras; -boy *s.* laaikas.

'tallow ['tælou] *s.* kersvet, harde vet; talk.

'tally ['tæli] *s.* (tallies) getal; kerfstok.

'talon ['tælən] *s.* (-s) klou; -ed *bnw.* met kloue.

'tambour ['tæmboeə] *s.* (-s) tamboer, trom; -ine *s.* tamboeryn.

'tame ['tym] *ww.* (-d) tem; -d *bnw.* mak; -r *s.* temmer; 'tamable *bnw.* tembaar.

'**tamper** ['tæmpə] *ww.* (*-ed*) - with omkoop, knoei met; *s.* stamper.

tandem ['tændəm] *s.* (*-s*) tandem; tweepersoonsfiets.

tan ['tæn] *ww.* (*-ned*) looi; verbrand; *bnw.* bruin; *-nery s.* looiery.

tang ['tæng] *s.* geur, smaak.

tangent ['tændzjənt] *s.* raaklyn.

tangerine ['tændzjə'rin] *s.* nartjie.

tangible ['tændzjəbl] *bnw.* tasbaar.

tangle ['tæng-ghl] *s.* (*-s*) verwarring, knoop.

tank ['tænk] *s.* (*-s*) tenk; *-ard s.* drinkkan.

tantalize ['tæntəlaiz] *ww.* (*-d*) tempteer.

'**tantamount** ['tæntəmaunt] *bw.* diselfde as.

'**tantrum** ['tæntrəm] *s.* (*-s*) slegte bui, luim.

tap ['tæp] *s.* (*-s*) kraan; drinkplek; *ww.* (*-ped*) uittap; uitvra; tik; klop.

'**tape** ['typ] *s.* (*-s*) band; lint; strook; maatband; - recorder *s.* bandopnemer; -worm *s.* lintwurm.

taper ['typə] *ww.* (*-ed*) spits uitloop; *-ing bnw.* spits; *-ed bnw.* spits-, taps.

'**tapestry** ['tæpəstri] *s.* (*tapestries*) behangsel; '**tapestried** *bnw.* behang.

'**tapioca** ['tæpioukə] *s.* tapioka.

'**tappet** ['tæpit] *s.* klepveer; klepstoter.

'**tapping 'beetle** ['tæping 'bitl] *s.* (*-s*) toktokkie.

tar ['tå] *s.* teer; *-brush s.* teerkwas.

'**tare** ['tèə] *s.* (*-s*) onkruid; elegewig; tarra.

'**tardy** ['tådi] *bnw.* (*tardier, tardiest*) traag, stadig, onwillig.

'**target** ['tåghit] *s.* (*-s*) skyf; mikpunt.

'**tariff** ['tærif] *s.* (*-s*) tarief.

'**tarmac** ['tåmæk] *s.* (*-s*) teerblad, aanloopbaan (lughawe).

'**tarnish** ['tånisj] *ww.* (*-ed*) dof maak, aanslaan; bevlek; besoedel.

tar'paulin ['tå'pôlin] *s.* (*-s*) bokseil.

'**tarry** ['tæri] *ww.* (*tarried*) wag, draal.

'**tarsus** ['tåsəs] *s.* voetwortel.

tart ['tåt] *s.* (*-s*) tert; flerrie; *bnw.* bitsig.

tar'taric ['tå'tærik] *bnw.* wynsteen-.

task ['tåsk] *s.* (*-s*) taak, werk; *-master s.* baas.

'**tassel** ['tæsəl] *s.* (*-s*) kwassie, klossie, fraiing.

'**taste** ['tyst] *ww.* (*-d*) proe, smaak; *s.* smaak; voorliefde; happie; *-ful bnw.* smaakvol; *-less bnw.* smaakloos; '**tasty** *bnw.* (*tastier, tastiest*) smaaklik.

'**tatter** ['tætə] *s.* (*-s*) flenter, toiing; *-ed bnw.* verflenter.

'**tattle** ['tætl] *ww.* (*-d*) babbel, klets, skinder; *-r s.* babbelaar.

tat'too [tə'tôê] *s.* taptoe; *ww.* tatoe-eer.

taunt ['tônt] *s.* (*-s*) smaad, hoon, beledging; *-ing bnw.* beledigend, honend.

taut ['tôt] *bnw.* strak, styf gespanne; *-en ww.* stywer span.

'**tavern** ['tævən] *s.* (*-s*) kroeg, drinkplek.

'**tawdry** ['tôdri] *bnw.* (*tawdrier, tawdriest*) opgeskik, uitspattig.

'**tawny** ['tôni] *bnw.* taankleurig.

tax ['tæks] *s.* (*-es*) belasting; las; *-able bnw.* belasbaar; '**-ation** *s.* belasting; *-collector s.* belastinggaarder; *-free bnw.* belastingvry; *-payer s.* belastingbetaler.

'**taxi** ['tæksi] *s.* (*-s*) huurmotor.

tea ['ti] *s.* tee; *-caddy s.* teebus; *-cloth s.* teekleedjie; *-cosy s.* teemus; *-cup s.* teekoppie; *-party s.* teeparty; *-pot s.* teepot; *-room s.* kafee; *-set s.* teeservies; *-spoon s.* teelepel.

teach ['titsj] *ww.* (*taught*) leer, onderwys gee, onderrig; *-er s.* onderwyser(es); *-ing s.* onderwys.

teak ['tik] *s.* kiaat.

'**team** ['tim] *s.* (*-s*) span; *-ster s.* drywer.

tear ['tiə] *s.* (*-s*) skeur, traan; *ww.* (*tore, torn*) skeur, trek, pluk; vlieg.

'**tease** ['tiz] *ww.* (*-d*) terg.

teat ['tit] *s.* tiet, tepel, speen.

tech'nique [tek'nik] *s.* tegniek; '**technical** *bnw.* tegnies; **tech'nology** *s.* tegnologie.

'**tedium** ['tidiəm] *s.* verveling; '**tedious** *bnw.* vervelend.

tee ['ti] *s.* bof.

teem ['tim] *ww.* (*-ed*) wemel, krioel.

teens ['tins] *s.* die jare tussen 13-19, tiendertyd.

'**teethe** ['tidh] *ww.* (*-d*) tandekry; **teething** *voorv.* tande-; **teething beads** *s. mv.* tandekrale; **teething ring** *s.* tandering.

tee'totaller [ti'toutlə] *s.* afskaffer.

'**tegument** ['teghjoemənt] *s.* vel, huid, hulsel.

'**telegram** ['telighræm] *s.* telegram.

'**telegraph** ['telighråf] *s.* telegraaf; **te'legraphy** *s.* telegrafie.

te'lepathy [ti'lepəthi] *s.* telepatie.

'**telephone** ['telifoun] *s.* (*-s*) telefoon.

'**teleprinter** ['teləprintə] *s.* teledrukker.

'**telescope** ['teliskoup] *s.* teleskoop, verkyker.

'**television** ['telivizjn] *s.* televisie, beeldradio.

tell ['tel] *ww.* (*told*) vertel, meld; onderskei; tel; *-er s.* verteller; teller; *-tale s.* nuusdraer.

te'merity [ti'meriti] *s.* vermetelheid.

'**temper** ['tempə] *s.* humeur; stemming; temper; *-ament s.* geaardheid; *-ate bnw.* matig, gematig.

'**temperature** ['tempritsjə] *s.* temperatuur, warmtegraad.

'**tempest** ['tempist] *s.* (*-s*) storm, orkaan; **tem'pestuous** *bnw.* stormagtig.

'**temple** ['templ] *s.* (*-s*) tempel; slaap; *bnw.* slaap-.

'**tempo** ['tempou] *s.* (*-s*) tempo.

'**temporary** ['tempərəri] *bnw.* tydelik; 'temporal *bnw.* tydelik; 'temporise *ww.* draal, sloer.

tempt ['tempt] *ww.* (-ed) versoek, verlok, verlei; temp'tation *s.* versoeking; -er *s.* verleier; -ing *bnw.* verleidelik; 'temptress *s.* verleidster.

ten ['ten] *s.* tien.

'tenable ['tenəbl] *bnw.* verdedigbaar.

te'nacity [ti'næsiti] *s.* taaiheid, hardnekkigheid; te'nacious *bnw.* taai, hardnekkig.

'tenant ['tenənt] *s.* (-s) huurder.

tend ['tend] *ww.* (-ed) gaan; geneig wees; oppas; ten'dentious *bnw.* tendensieus.

'tender ['tendə] *ww.* (-ed) aanbied; *s.* aanbod; *bnw.* sag; tingerig; liefhebbend; -izer *s.* beukelaar, vleissagmaker; -foot *s.* groene.

'tendon ['tendən] *s.* (-s) sening.

'tendril ['tendril] *s.* (-s) rank.

'tenement ['tenimənt] *s.* (-s) verblyf; huurkamers.

'tenet ['tinət] *s.* leer, beginsel.

'tenon ['tenən] *s.* (-s) tap, pen.

'tenor ['tenə] *s.* koers, gang; strekking; tenoor.

'tense ['tens] *s.* tyd; *bnw.* styf, gespanne; 'tension *s.* spanning; trekspanning; 'tensile *bnw.* rekbaar.

tent ['tent] *s.* (-s) tent.

'tentacle ['tentəkl] *s.* (-s) voelhoring.

'tentative ['tentətiv] *bnw.* tentatief.

'tenuous ['tenjoeəs] *bnw.* tingerig, dun, klein.

'tenure ['tenjoeə] *s.* eiendomsreg, besit.

'tepid ['tepid] *bnw.* (-est) lou.

tercen'tenary [təsen'tinəri] *s.* derde eeufees.

term ['təm] *s.* (-s) perk; termyn; kwartaal; semester; term, uitdrukking; bewoording.

'terminate ['təminyt] *ww.* (-d) eindig, beëindig.

termi'nology [təmi'nolədzji] *s.* terminologie.

'terminus ['təminəs] *s.* (termini, terminuses) terminus, eindpunt.

'termite ['təmait] *s.* (-s) rysmier.

'terra ['terə] *s.* aarde; -firma vaste grond; -cotta *s.* terra-cotta.

'terrace ['terəs] *s.* (-s) terras.

ter'restrial [ti'restrial] *bnw.* aards.

'terrible ['terəbl] *bnw.* vreeslik, verskriklik.

'terrier ['teriə] *s.* (-s) terriër.

'terrify ['terifai] *ww.* (terrified) verskrik; ter'rific *bnw.* verskriklik.

'territory ['teritəri] *s.* (territories) gebied, landstreek; terri'torial *bnw.* territoriaal.

'terror ['terə] *s.* (-s) vrees, skrik; -ize *ww.* skrik aanja; -ist *s.* terroris; -stricken *bnw.* skrikbevange.

'terse ['təs] *bnw.* (-r, -st) pittig, bondig.

test ['test] *s.* (-s) toets; proef; wedstryd.

'testament ['testəmənt] *s.* (-s)

testament; testa'mentary *bnw.* testamentêr.

tes'tator [tes'tytə] *s.* (-s) erflater.

'testify ['testifai] *ww.* (testified) getuig.

'testimony ['testiməni] *s.* (testimonies) getuienis; testi'monial *s.* getuigskrif.

'testy ['testi] *bnw.* (testier, testiest) prikkelbaar; 'testily *bw.* knorrig; 'testiness *s.* prikkelbaarheid.

'tether ['tedhə] *s.* (-s) tou, riem; *ww.* op lyn slaan.

text ['tekst] *s.* (-s) teks; onderwerp; inhoud; -book *s.* handboek.

'textile ['tekstail] *s.* (-s) weefstof.

'texture ['tekstsjə] *s.* weefsel, tekstuur, bou.

than ['dhæn] *bw. & voors.* as, dan.

thank ['thænk] *ww.* (-ed) dankie sê, bedank; -ful *bnw.* dankbaar; -less *bnw.* ondankbaar; -s *s.* dank.

that ['dhæt] *vnw.* daardie, die; wat; *bw.* so; *voegw.* dat, sodat; *bnw.* sodanig.

thatch ['thætsj] *s.* (-es) grasdak, strooidak.

thaw ['thô] *ww.* (-ed) dooi, smelt, ontdooi.

the ['dhə, 'dhi] *lidw.* die.

'theatre ['thiətə] *s.* (-s) teater, skouburg; the'atrical *bnw.* teatraal.

thee ['dhi] *vnw.* u.

theft ['theft] *s.* (-s) diefstal.

their ['dhɛə] *vnw.* hulle; -s *vnw.* hulle s'n.

them ['dhem] *vnw.* hulle; *vgl.* they.

'theme ['thim] *s.* (-s) temaonderwerp.

then ['dhen] *bw.* toe; dan; vervolgens; *bnw.* toenmalig; *voegw.* dus.

'thence ['dhens] *bw.* daarvandaan af, vandaar, derhalwe.

'thenceforth ['dhensfôth] *bw.* sedertdien.

the'ology [thi'olədzji] *s.* teologie.

'theorem ['thiərəm] *s.* teorema, stelling.

'theory ['thiəri] *s.* (theories) teorie; theo'retical *bnw.* teoreties.

thera'peutic [therə'pjŏětik] *bnw.* terapeuties, geneeskundig; -s *s.* terapie.

'there ['dhɛə] *bw.* daar; daarheen; soontoe; -after *bw.* daarna; daarvolgens; -by *bw.* daardeur; -fore *bw.* daarom, dus; -in *bw.* daarin; -to *bw.* daartoe; behalwe; -upon *bw.* daarna; -withal *bw.* buitendien.

therm ['thəm] *s.* (-s) warmte-eenheid; -al wool *s.* warmwatte, trekwatte.

ther'mometer [thə'momitə] *s.* (-s) termometer, koorspennetjie.

'these ['dhiz] *vnw.* meerv. *van* this.

'thesis ['thisis] *s.* stelling; tesis, dissertasie, proefskrif.

they ['dhai] *vnw.* hulle.

thick ['thik] *bnw.* dik; troebel; bot; *s.* dikte; *bw.* dig, dik; -en *ww.* (-ed) aandik, verdik; -et *s.* ruigte; -head *s.* dikkop; -headed *bnw.* bot, dom;

-ish *bnw.* dikkerig; -set *bnw.* dig begroei.

thief ['thif] *s.* (*thieves*) dief.

'**thieve** ['thiv] *ww.* (-d) steel; -ry *s.* diewery, diefstal; '**thievish** *bnw.* diefagtig.

thigh ['thai] *s.* (-s) dy; - stockings *s.* dykouse.

'**thimble** ['thimbl] *s.* (-s) vingerhoed.

thin ['thin] *bnw.* dun; *ww.* vermaer; verdun.

'**thine** ['dhain] *vnw.* u, van u.

thing ['thing] *s.* (-s) ding, iets, saak; -s *s.* goed, goeters.

'**thingummy** ['thingəmi] *s.* dinges.

think ['think] *ww.* (*thought*) dink; meen; van plan wees; -ing *bnw.* dinkend, redelik.

third ['thəd] *bnw.* derde; -ly *bw.* derdens; *vgl.* **three.**

thirst ['thəst] *s.* dors; *ww.* (-ed) dors hê, vurig verlang na; -y *bnw.* dors, dorstig.

'**thirteen** ['thə'tin] *s.* dertien.

'**thirty** ['thəti] *s.* dertig.

this ['dhis] *vnw. & bnw.* dit, hierdie, die.

'**thistle** ['thisl] *s.* (-s) dissel.

'**thither** ['dhidhə] *bw.* daarheen.

'**thole** ['thoul] *s.* (-s) dolpen, roeipen.

'**thong** ['thŏng] *s.* (-s) riem.

'**thorax** ['thŏræks] *s.* (-es) bors, borsstuk, borskas.

thorn ['thŏn] *s.* (-s) doring; doringbos; -y *bnw.* vol dorings, netelig.

'**thorough** ['thʌrə] *bnw.* deeglik, grondig; volledig; -bred *bnw.* volbloed-, opreggeteel; -fare *s.* deurgang; -going *bnw.* deurtastend; -ly *bw.* deeglik, terdeë.

thorp(e) ['hŏp] *s.* dorpie.

'**those** ['dhouz] *vnw.* daardie, diegenes, *vgl.* **that.**

though ['dhŏ] *voegw.* ofskoon, alhoewel, al.

thought ['thŏt] *s.* (-s) gedagte, oorpeinsing, idee; -ful *bnw.* bedagsaam; peinsend; -less *bnw.* onbesonne.

'**thousand** ['thauzind] *s.* (-s) duisend.

thrall ['thrŏl] *s.* (-s) slaaf.

thrash ['thræsj] *ww.* (-ed) slaan; dors; -er *s.* dorsmasjien; -ing *s.* dorsery; loesing.

thread ['thred] *s.* (-s) draad; garing; *ww.* garing insteek; -bare *bnw.* verslyt.

threat ['thret] *s.* (-s) dreigement; -en *ww.* (-ed) bedreig; -ening *bnw.* dreigend.

three ['thri] *s.* drie; -pence *s.* trippens; -ply *bnw.* driedraads.

thresh =**thrash.**

'**threshold** ['thresjhould] *s.* drumpel, ingang.

'**thrice** ['thrais] *bw.* driemaal, *vgl.* **three.**

thrift ['thrift] *s.* spaarsaamheid; -less *bnw.* verkwistend; -y *bnw.* (-ier, -iest) spaarsaam, welvarend.

thrill ['thril] *s.* (-s) trilling, rilling;

tinteling; *ww.* (-ed) tril, ril, sidder; -ing *bnw.* trillend; spannend.

'**thrips** ['thrips] *s. mv.* blaaspootjies.

thrive ['thraiv] *ww.* (*throve, thriven*) vooruitkom; '**thriving** *bnw.* voorspoedig.

throat ['throut] *s.* (-s) keel; - atomizer *s.* keelverstuiwer; - brush *s.* keelkwassie; - paint *s.* keelverf.

throb ['throb] *ww.* (-bed) klop, pols.

throes ['throuz] *s.* wee, pyn, angs.

'**throne** ['throun] *s.* (-s) troon.

'**throng** ['throng] *s.* (-s) gedrang, menigte; *ww.* (-ed) verdring, (toe)stroom.

'**throttle** ['throtl] *s.* (-s) strot, lugpyp, gorrel; klep.

through ['thrŏĕ] *voors.* deur, uit; *bw.* deur, deur-en-deur; *bnw.* deurgaande; -'out *bw.* dwarsdeur, deurgaans, *voors.* dwarsdeur.

throw ['throu] *ww.* (*threw, thrown*) gooi, werp; ondergooi; *s.* gooi, worp.

thrust ['thrʌst] *ww.* (-ed) stoot, steek.

thud ['thʌd] *s.* (-s) dowwe slag, plof.

'**thug** ['thʌgh] *s.* (-s) sluipmoordenaar, wurger.

thumb ['thʌm] *s.* (-s) duim; -screw *s.* (-s) duimskroef; vleuelskroef.

'**thump** ['thʌmp] *ww.* (-ed) stamp, slaan, moker, bons.

'**thunder** ['thʌndə] *s.* donder, donderweer; -bolt *s.* donderslag, blits, straal.

Thursday ['thəzdi] *s.* Donderdag.

thus ['dhʌs] *bw.* dus, aldus, so.

thwart ['thwŏt] *ww.* (-d) dwarsboom, belemmer.

'**thyme** ['taim] *s.* tiemie.

ti'ara [ti'ãrə] *s.* (-s) tiara.

tick ['tik] *s.* tik; merkie; bosluis; krediet.

'**ticket** ['tikit] *s.* kaartjie; - collector *s.* kaartjiesknipper; - examiner *s.* kaartjiesknipper.

'**tickle** ['tikl] *ww.* (-d) kielie, streel; '**ticklish** *bnw.* kielierig.

'**tide** ['taid] *s.* (-s) gety; tyd, stroom.

'**tidings** ['taidings] *s.* tyding, nuus, berig.

'**tidy** ['taidi] *bnw.* netjies; tidily *bw.* netjies; *ww.* (*tidied*) aan die kant maak.

tie ['tai] *ww.* (-d) bind, vasbind; *s.* band, knoop; das; - rod *s.* koppelstang; -up *s.* staking.

'**tier** ['tiə] *s.* (-s) ry, reeks.

tiff ['tif] *s.* (-s) rusie.

'**tiger** ['taighə] *s.* (-s) tier; -cat *s.* tierkat; -lily *s.* tierlelie; '**tig(e)rish** *bnw.* tieragtig; venynig.

tight ['tait] *bnw.* styf, stewig, dig; beskonke; *bw.* styf; -en *ww.* (-ed) stywer maak; -fisted *bnw.* suinig; -laced *bnw.* bekrompe; -s *s.* spanbroek.

'**tile** ['tail] *s.* (-s) teël, dakpan.

till ['til] *ww.* (-ed) bewerk; *s.* geldlaai; *voors.* tot; *voegw.* tot, totdat; -able *bnw.* beboubaar; -age *s.*

akkerbou; **-er** s. landbouer; roerpen.
tilt ['tilt] s. (-s) kap, tent, seil; *ww.* (-ed) skuins staan, wip, kantel.
'**timber** ['timbə] s. hout, timmerhout; bos, woud; **-headed** *bnw.* dom, bot; **-yard** s. timmerhoutwerf.
'**timbre** ['tɛmbə] s. toonkleur.
'**timbrel** ['timbrəl] s. tamboeryn.
'**time** ['taim] s. (-s) tyd, keer; tempo; *ww.* (-d) reël, reguleer; bereken; maat hou; **-honoured** *bnw.* eerbiedwaardig; '**timing** s. regulering; **-keeper** s. tydopnemer; **-lag** s. tydsloering; **-ly** *bnw.* tydig, bytyds; **-piece** s. horlosie; **-table** s. rooster; **-worn** *bnw.* verslyt.
'**timid** ['timid] *bnw.* (-est) skamerig, bangerig, bedees, beskroom; ti'**midity** s. beskroomdheid, skugterheid; '**timorous** *bnw.* skroomvallig, beskroom.
tin ['tin] s. tin, blik; geld; **-foil** s. bladtin, blinkpapier; **-sel** s. klatergoud.
'**tincture** ['tinktsjə] s. (-s) tinktuur.
'**tinder** ['tində] s. tontel, tonteldoek.
'**tine** ['tain] s. (-s) tand(e).
'**tinge** ['tindzj] s. (-s) tint, kleur; sweempie.
'**tingle** ['ting-ghl] *ww.* (-d) tuit, jeuk, prikkel; '**tingling** s. prikkeling, getuit.
'**tinker** ['tinkə] *ww.* (-ed) heelmaak; lap; knoei.
'**tin'opener** ['tin'oupənə] s. (-s) bliksnyer.
tint ['tint] s. (-s) kleur, tint.
'**tiny** ['taini] *bnw.* (tinier, tiniest) klein.
tip ['tip] s. (-s) punt, top; fooitjie; wenk; **-toe** *ww.* op punte van tone loop, kantel; **-top** *bnw.* prima, eersteklas; side- truck s. kantelwa.
'**tippet** ['tipit] s. (-s) pelskraag.
'**tipsy** ['tipsi] *bnw.* (tipsier, tipsiest) dronk; **-cake** s. wynkoek.
ti'**rade** [ti'ryd] s. (-s) tirade, woordvloed.
'**tire** ['taiə] *ww.* (-d) moeg word; **-d** *bnw.* moeg, tam; **-less** *bnw.* onvermoeid; **-some** *bnw.* vermoeiend, vervelig.
'**tissue** ['tis-jōē] s. (-s) weefsel; **-paper** s. sypapier, sneespapier.
tit ['tit] s. (-s) tepel, tiet; *vgl.* teat; **-bit** d. lekkerhappie.
ti'**tanic** [tai'tænik] *bnw.* titanies, reusagtig.
'**tithe** ['taidh] s. tiende.
'**titillate** ['titilyt] *ww.* (-d) kielie, streel.
'**title** ['taitl] s. (-s) titel; opskrif; naam; aanspraak; *ww.* betitel; **-d** *bnw.* met titel; **-deed** s. eiendomsbewys; **-role** s. hoofrol, titelrol.
'**titter** ['titə] *ww.* (-ed) giggel.
'**tittle-tattle** ['titltætli] s. geklets, gebabbel.
'**titular** ['titjoelə] *bnw.* titulêr, slegs in naam.
to ['tōē] *voors.* na, tot, vir, voor, aan, te (*om inf. in te lui*); *bw.* toe.
toad ['toud] s. (-s) padda; haatlike

mens; **-stool** s. paddastoel; **-y** *bnw.* witvoetsoekerig; **-yism** s. witvoetsoekery.
toast ['toust] s. braaibrood; heildronk; *ww.* (-ed) rooster, braai; **-er** s. broodbraaier; insteller van heildronk.
to'**bacco** [tə'bækou] s. tabak; **-nist** s. tabakverkoper.
to'**day** [tə'dy] *bw.* vandag, teenswoordig.
'**toddle** ['todl] *ww.* (-d) waggel; **-r** s. kleintjie, kleuter.
toe ['tou] s. (-s) toon; **-s** s. neus (*skoen*); **-nail** s. toonnael.
'**toffee** ['tofi] s. tammeletjie, toffie.
tog ['togh] s. **-s** klere, mondering; *ww.* (-ged) aantrek.
'**toga** ['toughə] s. (-s) toga.
to'**gether** [tə'ghedhə] *bw.* saam, bymekaar, gelyk.
toil ['toil] *ww.* (-ed) swoeg, sloof, arbei; **-s** s. net, strik; **-er** s. werkesel; **-some** *bnw.* swaar, vermoeiend.
'**toilet** ['toilit] s. toilet, toilettafel; **-paper** s. toiletpapier; **-set** s. wastafelstel.
'**token** ['toukən] s. (-s) aandenking; teken.
'**tolerate** ['toleryt] *ww.* (-d) verdra, duld; '**tolerable** *bnw.* draaglik; redelik; '**tolerably** *bw.* taamlik; '**tolerance** s. verdraagsaamheid; '**tolerant** *bnw.* verdraagsaam; **tole'ration** s. verdraagsaamheid.
toll ['toul] s. tol.
to'**mato** [tə'mātou] s. (-es) tamatie; **-sauce** s. tamatiesous.
tomb ['tōēm] s. (-s) grafkelder, graf; **-stone** s. grafsteen.
'**tomboy** ['tomboi] s. (-s) rabbedoe.
'**tom'cat** ['tom'kæt] s. (-s) mannetjieskat.
'**tome** ['toum] s. (-s) lywige boekdeel.
tom'foolery ['tom'fōēləri] s. gekkestreke.
'**Tommy** ['tomi] s. (Tommies) tommie, Britse soldaat.
to'**morrow** [tə'morou] *bw.* more.
ton ['tʌn] s. (-s) ton; **-nage** s. tonnemaat.
'**tone** ['toun] s. (-s) toon, klank; kleur, tint; gees; *ww.* (-d) toon-; '**tonal** *bnw.* toon-; to'**nality** s. toonaard; kleurafwisseling.
tongs ['tongz] s. tangetjie.
'**tongue** ['tʌng] s. (-s) tong; taal; klepel; landpunt; **-tied** *bnw.* stom, met mond vol tande.
'**tonic** ['tonik] s. (-s) versterkmiddel.
to'**night** [tə'nait] s. vanaand; *bw.* vanaand, vannag.
'**tonsil** ['tonsil] s. (-s) mangel; tonsi'**litis** s. mangelontsteking.
'**tonsure** ['tonsjə] s. tonsuur; ton'**sorial** *bnw.* barbiers-.
too ['tōē] *bw.* te, alte.
tool ['tōēl] s. (-s) gereedskap, werktuig.
toot ['tōēt] *ww.* (-ed) blaas, toeter.
tooth ['tōēth] s. (teeth) tand; **-ache** s.

tandpyn; -**brush** s. tandeborsel; -**ful**
s. mondjievol; -**less** bnw. tandeloos;
- **guard** s. tandeskerm; -**paste** s.
tendepasta; -**pick** s. tandeskraper;
-**powder** s. tandepoeier; -**some** s.
lekker; **tooth**- voorv. tande-.

top ['top] s. (-s) top, kruin; hoof;
kap; tol; -**boots** s. kapstewels; -**coat**
s. oorjas; - **dog** s. bobaas; - **dress** ww.
grondkombers aanbring, bo-bemes-
ting toedien; - **dressing** s. bobe-
mesting; - **gear** s. hoogste versnelling; -**most** bnw.; - **up** ww. byvul;
-**ping up** s. byvulling.

'topaz ['toupæz] s. (-es) topaas.

'toper ['toupǝ] s. suiplap.

'topic ['topik] s. (-s) onderwerp; -**al**
bnw. aktueeel.

to'pography [tǝ'poghrǝfi] s. topo-
grafie.

'topper ['topǝ] s. (-s) pluiskeil; gawe
kêrel.

'topping ['toping] bnw. uitstekend,
gaaf.

'topple ['topl] ww. (-d) omkantel,
omtuimel.

'topsy'turvy ['topsi'tǝvi] bw. onderstebo.

'toque ['touk] s. (-s) klein, nouslui-
tende dameshoed sonder rand.

torch ['tôtsj] s. (-es) toorts, fakkel.

tor'ment [tô'ment] s. .kwelling;
pyniging; ww. (-ed) kwel, folter; -**or**
s. kwelgees.

tor'nado [tô'nydou] s. (-s) tornado,
orkaan.

tor'pedo [tô'pidou] s. (-es) torpedo.

'torpid ['tôpid] bnw. slapend; traag;
tor'pidity s. slaap; doodsheid;
'torpor s. =torpidity.

'torque ['tôk] s. (-s) halsband; s.
wringkrag.

'torrefy ['torifai] ww. (torrefied)
uitdroë, brand.

'torrent ['torǝnt] s. (-s) stroom;
tor'rential bnw. geweldig.

'torrid ['torid] bnw. versengend,
brandend; tor'ridity s. skroeihitte,
dorheid.

'torsion ['tôsjǝn] s. kronkeling,
torsie; wringing.

'torso ['tôsou] s. romp van 'n standbeeld.

'tortoise ['tôtǝs] s. (-s) skilpad;
-**shell** s. skilpaddop.

'tortuous ['tôtjoeǝs] bnw. gekronkel,
slinks, skelm.

'torture ['tôtsjǝ] s. foltering: mar-
teling; ww. (-ed) martel, pynig; -**r** s.
folteraar.

toss ['tos] ww. (-ed) gooi, opgooi,
rondgooi, skud; -**up** s. onsekerheid.

tot ['tot] s. (-s) sopie, dop; kleuter-
tjie.

'total ['toutl] s. (-s) totaal, volle
bedrag; to'tality s. totaliteit; -**isator**
s. totalisator.

'totem ['toutǝm] s. totem.

'totter ['totǝ] ww. (-ed) wankel,
slinger; -**ing** bnw. onseker, onvas.

touch ['tʌtsj] ww. (-ed) raak, voel

aan; aanslaan; tref; aandoen; s.
aanraking; aanslag; tassin; -**able**
bnw. tasbaar; -**and-go** bnw. onseker;
-**ing** bnw. roerend; -**line** s. buitelyn;
-**dry** bnw. vingerdroog; -**me-not** s.
kruidjieroer-my-nie; -**stone** s. toets-
steen; -**wood** s. swam; -**y** bnw.
liggeraak.

tough ['tʌf] bnw. (-er, -est) taai, hard,
styf; kopig; -**en** ww. (-ed) taai maak;
-**ish** bnw. taaierig.

tour ['toeǝ] s. (-s) reis, toer; ww.
(-ed) rondreis; -**er** s. toermodel; -**ist**
s. toeris.

'tournament ['toeǝnǝmǝnt] s. (-s)
wedstryd, toernooi.

'tourney ['toeǝni] s. (-s) toernooi.

'tourniquet ['toeǝniky] s. (-s)
aarpers.

'tow ['tou] ww. (-ed) trek, op sleeptou
neem, sleep; pluis; -**rope** s. sleeptou;
-**ing pole** s. sleepstang.

'toward ['touwǝd] bnw. volgsaam;
voors. [tǝ'wôd] na, na toe; teen;
tenoor; tot; naby; bw. op hande.

'towel ['tauǝl] s. (-s) handdoek;
-**horse** s. handdoekrak; -**ling** s.
handdoekstof.

'tower ['tauǝ] s. (-s) toring; -**ed** ww.
met torings; -**ing** bnw. baie hoog,
geweldig.

town ['taun] s. (-s) dorp; -**clerk** s.
stadsklerk; - **council** s. stadsraad;
- **hall** s. stadshuis; - **planning** s.
stadsaanleg; -**sfolk** s. stedelinge;
-**ship** dorpsgebied, dorpie; -**speople**
s. stedelinge.

'toxin ['toksin] s. toksine, gif; 'toxic
bnw. giftig; 'toxicant s. gif, bnw.
giftig; toxi'cology s. toksikologie.

toy ['toi] s. (-s) speelding, speelbal,
speelgoed; - **soldier** s. popsoldaatjie.

'trace ['trys] s. (-s) spoor, teken;
string; ww. (-d) natrek; opspoor;
traseer; -**r** s. natrekker; tracing
paper s. natrekpapier; tracing pen
s. natrekpen; tracing wheel s.
natrekwiel.

'trachea ['trykiǝ] s. (tracheae) lugpyp.

track ['træk] s. (-s) spoor, pad, weg,
baan; -**er** s. speurder.

tract ['trækt] s. (-s) streek; traktaatjie; -**able** bnw. hanteerbaar, gedwee.

'traction ['træksjǝn] s. trekking;
'tractor s. treklokomotief; trekker.

'trade ['tryd] s. (-s) handel, bedryf,
beroep; die persone in die handel;
-**mark** s. handelsmerk; -**er** s. handelaar; -**sman** s. handelaar; - **union** s.
vakbond; - **wind** s. passaatwind;
'trading bnw. handeldrywend; -**in**
ww. inruil; s. inruilartikel.

tra'dition [trǝ'disjǝn] s. tradisie,
oorlewering; -**al** bnw. tradisioneel.

tra'duce [trǝ'djôǝs] ww. (-d)
belaster; -**r** s. lasteraar.

'traffic ['træfik] s. handel, verkeer;
- **jam** s. verkeersaanpaksel.

'tragedy ['trædzjidi] s. (tragedies)
tragedie, treurspel; 'tragic bnw.
tragies.

trail ['tryl] s. (-s) sleep; streep; spoor; pad, trekpad; **-er** s. rankplant; sleepwaentjie; **-er caravan** s. sleepwoonwa.

train ['tryn] ww. (-ed) oefen, brei; dril; snoei; s. trein; **-er** s. afrigter; sleep; **-ing** s. oefening.

trait ['tryt] s. (-s) trek, eienskap.

'**traitor** ['trytə] s. (-s) verraaier.

tra'jectory [tra'dzjektəri] s. (trajectories) baan.

tram ['træm] s. (-s) trem; koolwa; **-way** s. tremspoor.

'**trammel** ['træməl] s. (-s) treknet, sleepnet.

tramp ['træmp] s. (-s) boemelaar.

'**trample** ['træmpl] ww. (-d) trap, vertrap.

'**trance** ['trāns] s. (-s) ekstase; beswyming, vervoering.

'**tranquil** ['træng-'kwil] bnw. kalm, stil, rustig; **-lity** s. rus, kalmte.

trans- ['træns-] voorvoegsel. trans-, oor, oorkant.

'**tran'sact** ['træn'zækt] ww. (-ed) verrig, afhandel; **tran'saction** s. transaksie; handeling; ooreenkoms; **-or** s. verrigter, onderhandelaar.

'**transat'lantic** ['trænzæt'læntik] bnw. transatlanties.

tran'scend [træn'send] ww. (-ed) oortref, te bowe gaan; **-ence** s. voortreflikheid; **-ent** bnw. voortreflik; **transcen'dental** bnw. transendentaal, bowe-sinlik.

'**transconti'nental** ['trænzkonti-'nentl] bnw. transkontinentaal.

tran'scribe [trans'kraib] ww. (-d) afskryf, oorskryf; **-r** s. kopiis; **tran'scription** s. transkripsie; kopie.

'**transfer** ['trænsfə] s. (-s) oordrag, transport, verplasing.

'**transfigure** ['trænsfighə] ww. (-d) van gedaante verwissel.

trans'fix [træns'fiks] ww. (-ed) deursteek, deurboor.

trans'form [træns'fôm] ww. (-ed) verander, vervorm; **transfor'mation** s. vervorming; **-able** bnw. veranderbaar; **-er** s. transformator (elektr.).

trans'fusion [træns'fjōězjən] s. oortapping, transfusie.

trans'gression [træns'ghresjən] s. oortreding, sonde; **trans'gressor** s. oortreder.

'**transient** ['trænziənt] bnw. kortstondig, verganklik.

'**transit** ['trænsit] s. vervoer, deurvoer; oorgang; **tran'sition** s. oorgang; **tran'sitional** bnw. oorgangs-; **-ive** bnw. oorganklik; **-ory** bnw. kortstondig, vlugtig.

trans'late [trāns'lyt] ww. (-d) vertaal; **trans'lation** s. vertaling; **trans'lator** s. vertaler.

'**trans'lucent** ['trænz'lōěsnt] bnw. deurskynend.

transmi'gration [trænzmai'ghrysjən] s. landverhuising.

trans'mit [trænz'mit] ww. (-ted) aanstuur, deurstuur; **trans'mission**

s. aanstuur; oorhandiging; oorerwing; transmissie; ratkas; **-ter** s. aanstuurder, versender.

transmu'tation [trænzmjōě'tysjən] s. vormverwisseling.

trans'parent [træns'pêərənt] bnw. deursigtig.

trans'pire [træns'paiə] ww. (-d) sweet; **transpi'ration** s. sweet, transpirasie.

trans'plant ['træns'plänt] ww. (-ed) oorplant, verplant.

trans'port [træns'pôt] ww. (-ed) vervoer; **-able** bnw. vervoerbaar; **transpor'tation** s. vervoer, transport; '**transporter** s. vervoerder, transportryer.

trans'pose ['trænz'pouz] ww. (-d) omwissel; **transpo'sition** s. omwissel ing, kruis-.

transub'stantiate [trænsəb'stænsjiyt] ww. van vorm verander.

'**transverse** ['trænzvəs] bnw. dwars-.

trap ['træp] s. (-s) wip, strik, val, slagyster; **-door** s. valdeur, valluik **-per** s. pelsjagter.

tra'peze [trə'piz] s. sweefstok, trapesium.

tra'pezium = **trapeze**.

'**trappings** ['træpings] s. tuig, tooisel, opskik.

trash ['træsj] s. prul, bog, kaf; **-y** bnw. prullerig.

'**travail** ['trævyl] s. (-s) barenswee; trawal.

'**travel** ['trævl] ww. (-led) reis; s. reis; beweging; **-ler** s. (-s) reisiger; **-ling** s. reis; **-stained** bnw. vuil van die reis; **- sickness** s. reissiekte.

'**traverse** ['trævəs] ww. (-d) afreis, deurkruis.

'**travesty** ['trævəsti] s. parodie, belaglike voorstelling.

trawl ['trôl] s. (-s) treil, sleepnet; **-er** s. treiler.

tray ['try] s. (-s) skinkbord; platkissie.

'**treachery** ['tretsjəri] s. verraad, valsheid; '**treacherous** bnw. verraderlik, vals.

'**treacle** ['trikl] s. swart stroop.

tread ['tred] ww. (trod, trodden) trap; stap; betree; **-le** s. trap, pedaal; **-mill** s. trapmeule.

'**treason** ['trizn] s. verraad; **-able** bnw. verraderlik.

'**treasure** ['trezjə] s. (-s) skat, rykdom; **-house** s. skatkamer; **-er** s. penningmeester, tesourier; **treasury** s. skatkis, departement van finansies.

treat ['trit] ww. (-ed) behandel; onthaal; s. onthaal, traktasie; **-ise** s. verhandeling; **-ment** s. behandeling; **-y** s. verdrag.

'**treble** ['trebl] s. driekeer soveel; sopraan.

tree ['tri] s. (-s) boom; as; lees; saalboom.

'**trefoil** ['trefoil] s. klawer.

'**trellis** ['trelis] s. traliewerk, prieel.

'**tremble** ['treml] *ww.* (-*d*) bewe, sidder, gril; '**trembly** *bnw.* bewerig.

tre'**mendous** [tri'mendəs] *bnw.* verskriklik, geweldig, yslik.

'**tremor** ['tremə] *s.* (-s) bewing, trilling.

'**tremulous** ['tremjoeləs] *bnw.* bewend, trillend.

trench ['trentsj] *s.* (-es) sloot; loopgraaf; *ww.* (-*ed*) dolwe.

'**trenchant** ['trensjənt] *bnw.* skerp; vlymend; beslis.

trend ['trend] *s.* (-s) loop, neiging, rigting.

tre'**pan** [tri'pæn] *ww.* (-*ned*) die skedel deurboor.

trepi'**dation** [trepi'dysjən] *s.* angs; bewerasie.

'**trespass** ['trespəs] *ww.* (-*ed*) oortree; misbruik maak van; -**er** *s.* oortreder.

tress ['tres] *s.* (-es) haarlok, vlegsel.

'**trestle** ['tresl] *s.* (-s) bok, stut.

'**trial** ['traiəl] *s.* (-s) toets, proefneming; verhoor; beproewing, besoeking; - **and error** *s. bnw.* gissing en vergissing; - **run** *s.* proefrit.

'**triangle** ['trai-æng-ghl] *s.* (-s) driehoek; tri'**angular** *bnw.* driehoekig.

'**tribe** ['traib] *s.* (-s) stam; geslag; '**tribal** *bnw.* stam-; -**sman** *s.* lid van 'n stam.

tri'**bulation** [tribjoe'lysjən] *s.* beproewing.

'**tribune** [tribjŏěn] *s.* spreekgestoelte; verhoor; verteenwoordiger; tri'**bunal** *s.* regbank.

'**tribute** ['tribjŏět] *s.* (-s) skatting; skatpligtigheid; hulde; '**tributary** *bnw.* skatpligtig; tak-; *s.* skatpligtige; takrivier, spruit.

'**trice** ['trais] *s.* oomblik, kits.

trick ['trik] *s.* (-s) lis, skelmstreek, kunsie, slag; *ww.* (-*ed*) fop, streke uithaal; -**er** *s.* fopper; -**ery** *s.* kullery; -**ish** *bnw.* bedrieglik; -**y** *bnw.* vol streke.

'**trickle** ['trikl] *ww.* (-*d*) drup, tap; biggel.

'**tricolour** ['trikələ] *s.* driekleur.

'**tricot** ['trikou] *s.* tricot, masjiengebreide goed.

'**tricycle** ['traisikl] *s.* driewiel.

'**trident** ['traidənt] *s.* drietand.

'**trifle** ['traifl] *s.* (-s) nietigheid, kleinigheid; koekpoeding; -**r** *s.* beuselaar; '**trifling** *bnw.* niksbeduidend.

'**trigger** ['trighə] *s.* (-s) sneller.

trigo'**nometry** [trighə'nomitri] *s.* driehoeksmeting.

'**trilogy** ['trilədzji] *s.* trilogie.

trim ['trim] *ww.* (-*med*) in orde bring; knip; snoei; versier; *bnw.* netjies, fyn; -**ming** *s.* garnering, belegsel, fralings, bekleding.

'**trinity** ['triniti] *s.* (*trinities*) drietal; drie-eenheid.

'**trinket** ['trinkit] *s.* (-s) sieraad; -**box** *s.* juweelkissie.

'**trio** ['triou] *s.* (-s) drietal, trio.

trip ['trip] *ww.* (-*ped*) struikel

pootjie; fout begaan; *s.* (-s) toggie.

'**tripe** ['traip] *s.* ingewande, binnegoed, pens; bog, kaf.

'**triple** ['tripl] *bnw.* drievoudig; -**t** *s.* drietal; drieling.

'**triplicate** ['triplikit] *bnw.* drievoudig.

'**tripod** ['traipod] *s.* drievoet.

'**trite** ['trait] *bnw.* (-*r*, -*st*) afgesaag, uitgedien.

'**triumph** ['traiəmf] *s.* (-s) triomf, oorwinning; segetog; -**al** *bnw.* triomf-, sege-; -**ant** *bnw.* seëvierend, triomfantelik.

'**trivial** ['trivəl] *bnw.* niksbeduidend; trivi'**ality** *s.* beuselagtigheid.

'**tro'chee** ['trou'ki] *s.* (-s) trogee.

'**trolley** ['troli] *s.* (-s) trollie, molwa.

trom'bone [trom'boun] *s.* ᵤ(-s) skuiftrompet.

troop ['trŏěp] *s.* (-s) klomp, trop, troep; -**s** *s.* troepe; -**er** *s.* ruiter.

'**trope** ['troup] *s.* (-s) beeldspraak, troop.

'**trophy** ['troufi] *s.* (*trophies*) trofee; prys; beker.

'**tropic** ['tropik] *s.* (-s) keerkring; *bnw.* tropies; -**al** *bnw.* tropies.

trot ['trot] *ww.* (-*ted*) draf; -**ter** *s.* pootjie; -**ters** *s.* tripe *and* -**ters** afval.

'**trouble** ['trʌbl] *s.* (-s) moeilikheid, las; kwaal; verdriet, kwelling-; -**some** *bnw.* lastig; '**troublous** *bnw.* moeilik.

trough ['trof] *s.* (-s) trog, bak.

'**trounce** ['trauns] *ww.* (-*d*) afransel, klop, slaan; '**trouncing** *s.* loesing.

'**troupe** ['trŏěp] *s.* (-s) geselskap, troep.

'**trousers** ['trauziz] *s.* broek; '**trousering** *s.* broekstof.

'**trousseau** ['trŏěsou] *s.* uitset, bruidsuitrusting.

trout ['traut] *s.* forel.

'**trowel** ['trauəl] *s.* (-s) troffel.

troy ['troi] *s.* troy-gewig; fyngewig.

'**truant** ['trŏěənt] *s.* (-s) stokkiesdraaier; '**truancy** *s.* stokkiesdraaiery.

'**truce** ['trŏěs] *s.* wapenstilstand; verposing.

truck ['trʌk] *s.* ruilhandel; smousware; kaf, bog; goederewa, vragwa.

'**truculence** ['trʌkjoeləns] *s.* wildheid; '**truculent** *bnw.* wild, woes.

'**trudge** ['trʌdzji] *ww.* (-*d*) aansukkel.

true ['trŏě] *bnw.* (-*r*, -*st*) waar, suiwer, eg; opreg; getrou; juis; -**born** *bnw.* eg; '**truly** *bw.* waarlik, regtig, opreg; **run** - *ww.* suiwer loop.

trump ['trʌmp] *s.* (-s) trompet; troefkaart; staatmaker; -**ery** *s.* klatergoud; -**et** *s.* trompet; -**eter** *s.* trompetblaser.

'**truncate** ['trʌnkyt] *ww.* (-*d*) top, afknot.

'**truncheon** ['trʌntsjən] *s.* mokerstok; staf.

'**trundle** ['trʌndl] *ww.* (-*d*) rol; *s.* wielietjie; rolwa.

trunk ['trʌnk] *s.* stam, stomp; romp; trommel; slurp; -**call** *s.* hooflynop-

roep; -s s. kortbroek; -road s. hoof-
weg; -line s. hooflyn.

truss ['trʌs] s. stut; tros; breukband.

trust ['trʌst] s. vertroue, geloof;
krediet; trust, kartel; bewaring;
stigting; trus'tee trustee, kurator.
-ful bnw. vol vertroue; -worthy bnw.
betroubaar; -y bnw. vertroubaar.

truth ['trōēth] s. waarheid; -ful bnw.
waarheidliewend; -less bnw. vals;
vgl. true.

try ['trai] ww. (tried) probeer, poog;
toets; ondersoek; -ing bnw. lastig;
vermoeiend.

tryst ['trist] s. afgesproke vergaderplek.

tub ['tʌb] s. (-s) vat, balie, kuip.

'tube ['tjōēb] s. (-s) buis, pyp; binneband; -r s. knol; 'tubing s. pyp;
'tubular bnw. buisvormig; -less tyre
s. pompband.

'tubercle ['tjōēbəkl] s. knoppie,
puisie; tu'bercular bnw. tuberkuleus,
vol knoppies; tubercu'losis s. tering,
tuberkulose; tu'berculous bnw. tuberkuleus.

'tuberose ['tjōēbərouz] s. soeta-
maling.

tuck ['tʌk] s. (-s) opnaaisel, plooi.

'Tuesday ['tjōēzdi] s. Dinsdag.

tuft ['tʌft] s. bossie, klossie, kwassie,
polietjie.

tug ['tʌgh] ww. (-ged) trek, pluk,
sleep; -boat s. sleepboot; -of-war s.
toutrek.

tu'ition ['tjōē'isjən] s. onderrig,
onderwys; klasgeld.

'tulip ['tjōēlip] s. tulp.

'tulle ['tjōēl] s. netsy, tule.

'tumble ['tʌmbl] ww. (-d) tuimel, val;
bolmakiesie slaan; -down bnw.
bouvallig; -r s. drinkglas.

'tummy ['tʌmi] s. (tummies) magie.

'tumour ['tjōēmə] s. (-s) geswel.

'tumult ['tjōēmʌlt] s. opskudding,
tumult; tu'multuous bnw. oproerig,
lawaaierig.

'tune ['tjōēn] s. (-s) toon, melodie,
wysie; ww. (-d) stem, instel; -ful bnw.
melodieus, welluidend; -less bnw.
klankloos; 'tuning-fork s. stemvurk.

'tunic ['tjōēnik] s. soldaatbaadjie.

'tunnel ['tʌnl] s. (-s) tonnel, skag.

'tunny ['tʌni] s. tonyn.

'turban ['tʌbən] s. tulband.

'turbine ['tʌbin] s. (-s) turbine.

'turbulence ['tʌbjoeləns] s. on-
stuimigheid; 'turbulent bnw. onstuimig, oproerig.

tu'reen [tə'rin] s. (-s) sopkom.

turf ['tʌf] s. turf, kweek; turfgrond.

'turkey ['tʌki] s. (-s) kalkoen.

'turmeric ['tʌmərik] s. borrie.

'turmoil ['tʌmoil] s. gewoel, onrus.

turn ['tʌn] ww. (-ed) draai, afdraai;
krink; omkeer; omblaai; s. draai,
bog, wending; aard; -bench s. draaibank; -coat s. manteldraaier; -er s.
draaibankwerker; -ery s. draaiwerk;
-over s. omset; -table s. draaiskyf.

'turn-out ['tʌnaut] s. opkoms;
produksie.

'turnip ['tēnip] s. raap.

'turnkey ['tʌn-ki] s. tronkbewaar-
der, sipier.

'turpentine ['tʌpəntain] s. terpentyn.

'turnpike ['tʌnpaik] s. (-s) draaihek,
slagboom.

'turnstile ['tʌnstail] s. (-s) draaihek.

'turquoise ['tʌkwāz] s. turkoois.

'turret ['tʌrit] s. (-s) torinkie.

'turtle ['tʌtl] s. (-s) tortelduif;
seeskilpad.

tusk ['tʌsk] s. (-s) slagtand; -er s.
olifant met slagtande.

'tussle ['tʌsl] s. (-s) gestoel, bakleiery.

'tussock ['tʌsək] s. (-s) graspol.

'tutelage ['tjoetilidzj] s. voogdyskap, voogdy.

tutor ['tjōētə] s. dosent, leermeester,
breier; voog; tu'torial s. breiklas.

'twaddle ['twodl] s. geklets, gesanik.

twain ['twyn] bnw. s. twee; cut in -
aan twee sny.

twang ['twæng] s. snaarklank;
neusklank.

tweak ['twik] ww. (-ed) knyp, draai.

tweed ['twid] s. (-s) tweed.

'tweezers ['twizəz] s. haartangetjie.

twelve ['twelv] s. twaalf.

'twenty ['twenti] s. twintig.

'twice ['twais] bw. tweekeer.

twig ['twigh] s. (-s) tak, twyg.

'twilight ['twailait] s. skemering.

twill ['twil] s. keperstof.

twin ['twin] s. (-s) tweeling;
dubbelganger.

'twine ['twain] s. tou, seilgaring.

'twinge ['twindzj] s. (-s) steek, pyn.

'twinkle ['twinkl] ww. (-d) flikker;
'twinkling s. flikkering.

twirl ['twəl] ww. (-ed) in rondte draai,
swaai.

twist ['twist] ww. (-ed) draai, vleg;
kronkel.

twit ['twit] ww. (-ted) terg, pla,
verwyt.

twitch ['twitsj] s. (-es) trek, ruk.

'twitter ['twitə] ww. (-ed) tjilp,
kwetter; giggel.

two ['tōē] s. twee; -fold bnw. dubbel;
-pence s. twee pennies; -ply bnw.
tweedraads; -some s. spel of dans vir
twee; -speed motor s. tweegangmotor (tweespoed-); -stroke s. tweeslag, tweetak.

'two-edged ['tōē-edzjəd] bnw. twee-
snydend.

'tympan ['timpən] s. (-s) ysterraam,
vlies.

'type ['taip] s. tipe, soort, voorbeeld; ww. tik; tipeer; -setter s.
lettersetter; -write ww. tik; -writer
s. tikmasjien; 'typist s. tikster.

'typhoid ['taifoid] s. maagkoors,
tifus.

ty'phoon [tai'fōēn] s. (-s) tifoon.

'typhus ['taifəs] s. tifus.

'typical ['tipikl] bnw. tipies.

'tyranny ['tirəni] s. dwingelandy;
tyr'rannical bnw. tiranniek; 'tyran-

pize *ww.* tlrannlseer; **'tyrant** *s.* tiran, dwingeland.

'tyre ['taiə] *s.* (-s) buiteband; - **failure** *s.* bandbreuk; - **lever** *s.* bandligter; - **paint** *s.* buitebandverf; - **pressure** *s.* banddruk; - **size** *s.* bandgrootte; - **tread** *s.* bandloopvlak; - **retreading** *s.* bandversoling; - **wall** *s.* bandwand.

U

U'NISA [joe'nisə] (University of South Africa) UNISA (*Universiteit van Suid-Afrika*).

u'biquity [jōē'bikwiti] *s.* alomteenwoordigheid; **u'biquitous** *bnw.* alomteenwoordig.

'u-'bolt ['jōē-'boult] *s.* krambout, u-bout.

'udder ['ʌdə] *s.* (-s) uier; - **paste** *s.* uiersalf.

'ugly ['ʌghli] *bnw.* (*uglier, ugliest*) lelik.

'Uitlander ['ytlændə] *s.* Uitlander.

'ulcer ['ʌlsə] *s.* (-s) sweer; -**ate** *ww.* versweer; **ulce'ration** *s.* verswering.

'ulna ['ʌlnə] *s.* ellepyp.

'ulster ['ʌlstə] *s.* reёnjas.

ul'terior [ʌl'tiəriə] *bnw.* verder, later; verborge.

'ultimate ['ʌltimit] *bnw.* uiteindelik.

ulti'matum [ʌlti'mytəm] *s.* ultimatum.

'ultimo ['ʌltimou] *bw.* laaslede.

'ultra ['ʌltrə] *bnw.* ekstremisties, ultra.

ultra'montane [ʌltrə'montyn] *bnw.* geleё besuide die Alpe.

ululate ['jōēljoelyt] *ww.* (-d) huil, skreeu; **ulu'lation** *s.* gehuil, getjank.

um'bilicus [ʌm'bilikəs] *s.* nawel; **um'bilical** *bnw.* nawel-; **um'bilical cord** *s.* nawelstring; **umbilical tape** *s.* naelband.

'umbrage ['ʌmbridʒ] *s.* koelte; belediging.

'umbrella ['ʌmbrelə] *s.* (-s) sambreel.

'umlaut ['oemlaut] *s.* umlaut.

'umpire ['ʌmpaiə] *s.* (-s) skeidsregter, eindbeslisser.

un- ['ʌn-] *voorvoegsel.* on-, nie-, ont-.

un'animous [joe'næniməs] *bnw.* eenstemmig.

una'wares ['ʌnə'wēəs] *bw.* onverwags, skielik; onwetend.

'unbe'known ['ʌnbi'noun] *bw.* onbekend, sonder medewete.

'unbe'lief ['ʌnbi'lif] *s.* ongeloof.

'un'bias(s)ed ['ʌnbaiəst] *bnw.* onbevooroordeel.

'unbred ['ʌnbred] *bnw.* onopgevoed, ongepoets.

un'burden [ʌn'bədn] *ww.* (-ed) ontboesem, lug.

un'called for [ʌn'kōld fô] *bw.* onvanpas, onnodig.

un'canny [ʌn'kæni] *bnw.* (*uncannier, uncanniest*) geheimsinnig, angswekkend.

'uncial ['ʌnsiəl] *s.* hoofletter.

'uncle ['ʌnkl] *s.* (-s) oom.

'unco ['ʌnkou] *bnw.* vreemd.

un'coil [ʌn'koil] *ww.* (-ed) afdraai, losdraai.

un'couth [ʌn'kōēth] *bnw.* lomp, baar, ongepoets.

'unction ['ʌnksjən] *s.* salwing; vleiery; **'unctuous** *bnw.* salwend; vleiend.

un'daunted [ʌn'dôntid] *bnw.* onverskrokke.

'under ['ʌndə] *voors* onder, benede; *bw.* onder; *bnw.* onder-, onderste-; **under-** *voorvoegsel* onder-; -**cut** *ww.* insny.

'underdone ['ʌndə'dʌn] *bnw.* halfgaar.

'under'fed ['ʌndə'fed] *bnw.* ondervoed.

under'go [ʌndə'ghou] *ww.* (*underwent, -ne*) ondergaan.

'underlying ['ʌndelai-ing] *s.* (-s) handlanger, ondergeskikte.

'under'neath ['ʌndə'nith] *voors* onder, benede; *bw.* onder.

'undersize ['ʌndəsaiz] *bnw.* ondermaats.

'under'stand ['ʌndə'stænd] *ww.* (*understood*) begryp, verstaan; -**ing** *bnw.* intelligent.

'understudy ['ʌndəstʌdi] *s.* plaasvervanger.

'under'take ['ʌndə'tyk] *ww.* (*undertook*) onderneem; aanvaar; -**r** *s.* lykbesorger; **'undertaking** *s.* onderneming.

'under'tone ['ʌndə'toun] *s.* fluisterstem.

'underwear ['ʌndəwēə] *s.* onderklere.

'underwood ['ʌndəwood] *s.* struikgewas.

'underworld ['ʌndəwōld] *s.* doderyk; agterbuurte.

'underwrite ['ʌndərait] *ww.* (*underwrote, underwritten*) onderteken, verseker; -**r** *s.* versekeraar; onderskrywer.

'un'do ['ʌn'dōē] *ww.* (*undid, undone*) losmaak; -**ing** *s.* ongeluk; vernietiging, ondergang.

'un'due ['ʌndjōē] *bnw.* oordrewe; **un'duly** *bw.* oormatig.

'undulate ['ʌndjoelyt] *bnw.* golwend; **'undulating** *bnw.* golwend; **undu'lation** *s.* golwing.

un'earth'y [ʌn'əthli] *bnw.* bowenatuurlik; spookagtig.

un'failing [ʌn'fyling] *bnw.* onfeilbaar; standhoudend, getrou.

'unguent ['ʌng-ghwent] *s.* salf, olie.

un'heard of [ʌn'hədov] *bnw.* ongehoorde.

'uni- ['jōēni-] *voorvoegsel.* een-.

'unicorn ['jōēnikôn] *s.* eenhoring.

'uniform ['jōēnifôm] *s.* uniform; *bnw.* eenvormig; -**ity** *s.* eenvormigheid.

'unify ['jōēnifai] *ww.* (*unified*) verenig; **unifi'cation** *s.* vereniging.

'**unilateral** ['jōĕni'lætəril] *bnw.* een-sydig.

'**union** ['jōĕnjən] *s.* vereniging, unie; **-ist** *s.* vakbondlid.

u'**nique** [jōĕ'nĭk] *bnw.* uniek, sonder weerga.

u'**nison** ['jōĕnizn] *s.* harmonie, eensgesingheid.

'**unit** ['jōĕnit] *s.* (-s) eenheid.

u'**nite** [jōĕ'nait] *ww.* (-d) verenig; **-d** *bnw.* verenig; '**unity** *s.* eenheid.

'**universe** ['jōĕnivəs] *s.* heelal; uni'**versal** *bnw.* algemeen; **universal joint** *s.* kruiskoppeling; uni'**versalize** *ww.* algemeen maak; univer'**sality** *s.* algemeenheid.

uni'**versity** [joeni'vəsiti] *s.* (*universities*) universiteit.

'**un'kempt** ['ʌn'kempt] *bnw.* ongekam, slordig.

un'**laden** [ʌn'lydn] *bnw.* onbelas.

un'**learning** [ʌn'ləning] *ww.* afleer, afwen, ontwen.

un'**leash** [ʌn'lisj] *ww.* (-ed) bevry van leiband.

un'**less** [ən'les] *voegw.* tensy, behalwe.

un'**mitigated** [ʌn'mitighytid] *bnw.* onversag, onverminder; deurtrap.

un'**principled** [ʌn'prinsəpld] *bnw.* gewetenloos, beginselloos.

un'**ravel** [ʌn'rævl] *ww.* (-led) uitrafel, ontwar; ontsyfer.

un'**ruly** [ʌn'rōĕli] *bnw.* (*unrulier*, *unruliest*) bandeloos.

un'**scrupulous** [ʌn'skrōĕpjoeləs] *bnw.* gewetenloos.

un'**seemly** [ʌn'simli] *bnw., bw.* onbetaamlik, onwelvoeglik.

un'**speakable** [ʌn'spikəbl] *bnw.* onuitspreeklik.

'**unto** ['ʌntoe] *voors.* aan, tot, vir.

'**un'told** ['ʌn'tould] *bnw.* onvermeld, talloos.

un'**toward** [ʌn'touəd] *bnw.* eiesinnig, eiewys.

un'**wieldy** [ʌn'wildi] *bnw.* (*unwieldier*, *unwieldiest*) onhandig, lomp.

up ['ʌp] *bw.* op, boontoe, na bo; *voors.* op; *s.* -s and downs wisselvallighede.

up'**braid** ['ʌp'bryd] *ww.* (-ed) berispe.

up'**braiding** [ʌp'bryding] *s.* berisping.

'**upbringing** ['ʌpbringing] *s.* opvoeding.

up'**country** ['ʌp'kʌntri] *bnw. & bw.* binneland, onderveld.

up'**heaval** [ʌp'hivl] *s.* omwenteling; opheffing.

up'**hill** ['ʌp'hil] *bnw.* opdraand; *bw.* moeilik.

up'**holster** [ʌp'houlstə] *ww.* (-ed) beklee; **-er** *s.* bekleër, stoffeerder; **-y** *s.* bekleding, bekleedsel.

'**upkeep** ['ʌpkip] *s.* onderhoud.

up'**on** [ə'pon] *voors.* op, bo-op, by.

'**upper** ['ʌpə] *bnw.* bo-, hoër; boonste; **-s** *s.* bo-leer; **-most** *bnw.* hoogste, boonste-.

'**uppish** ['ʌpisj] *bnw.* vrypostig, astrant.

'**upright** ['ʌprait] *bnw.* opreg; loodreg.

'**up'roar** ['ʌp'rō] *s.* lawaai, oproer, geraas; **-ious** *bnw.* lawaaierig.

up'**set** [ʌp'set] *ww.* omgooi; ontstel.

'**upshot** ['ʌpsjot] *s.* gevolg, uiteinde, uitslag.

upside-'**down** ['ʌpsaid'daun] *bnw.* onderstebo, deurmekaar.

'**upstart** [ʌp'stāt] *s.* parvenu, vrypostige persoon.

'**upstroke** ['ʌpstrouk] *s.* (-s) stygslag.

up-to-'**date** ['ʌptoedyt] *bnw.* op datum.

'**upward** ['ʌpwəd] *bnw. & bw.* opwaarts, boontoe, na bo.

'**urban** ['əbən] *bnw.* stedelik, stads-; ur'**bane** *bnw.* hoflik; ur'**banity** *s.* hoflikheid.

'**urchin** ['ətsjin] *s.* deugniet, rakker, vabond.

'**urge** ['ədzj] *ww.* (-d) aanspoor; aandring; **-nt** *bnw.* dringend; **-ncy** *s.* dringendheid.

'**urine** ['joeərin] *s.* water, urine; '**urinate** *ww.* water laat; uri'**nation** *s.* waterlosing.

urn ['ən] *s.* (-s) urn, vaas, kruik.

us ['ʌs] *vnw.* ons.

use ['jōĕs] *s.* gebruik, gewoonte; *ww.* (-d) gebruik, verbruik; '**usage** *s.* behandeling; gewoonte; '**usance** *s.* handelsgebruik; **-d** *bnw.* gewoond, gewend; **-ful** *bnw.* nuttig; **-less** *bnw.* nutteloos; **-r** *s.* gebruiker, verbruiker; '**usual** *bnw.* gewoon, gebruiklik; '**usually** *bw.* gewoonlik.

'**usher** ['ʌsjə] *s.* (-s) deurwagter, deurwaarder; *ww.* (-ed) binnelei; ushe'**rette** *s.* plekaanwyser(vroulik); **-ing** *s.* plekaanwysing.

'**usufruct** ['jōĕsjoefrʌkt] *s.* vruggebruik.

'**usurp** [jōĕzəp] *ww.* (-ed) wederregtelik in besit neem; **-er** *s.* oorweldiger, indringer.

'**usury** ['jōĕzjoeri] *s.* woekering, woekerwins; '**usurer** *s.* woekeraar; u'**surious** *bnw.* woekerend.

u'**tensil** [joe'tensl] *s.* (-s) gereedskap, werktuig; **-s** *s.* kombuisgoed.

'**utilize** ['jōĕtilaiz] *ww.* (-d) gebruik, aanwend; utili'**zation** *s.* gebruikmaking, aanwending.

u'**tility** [joe'tiliti] *s.* nut, nuttigheid; utiliteit; utili'**tarian** *bnw.* utilitaristies; **-man** *s.* handlanger.

'**utmost** ['ʌtmoust] *bnw.* uiterste, verste, meeste.

U'**topia** [jōĕ'toupjə] *s.* Utopië; **-n** *bnw.* utopies.

'**utter** ['ʌtə] *ww.* (-ed) opper; *bnw.* totaal, volkome; **-able** *bnw.* wat geuit kan word; **-ance** *s.* uitlating; **-ly** *bw.* volkome; **-most** *bnw.* uiterste, verste.

'**uvula** ['jōĕvjoelə] *s.* kleintongetjie; **-r** *bnw.* van die kleintongetjie, uvulêr.

V

V.H.F. (very high frequency) **B.H.F.** (bale hoë frekwensie).

'vacant ['vykənt] *bnw.* vakant, leeg; onbeset; vry; dom; **'vacancy** s. vakature; **va'cate** *ww.* (-d) ontruim; **va'cation** s. ontruiming; vakansie.

'vaccinate ['væksinyt] *ww.* (-d) inent; **vacci'nation** s. inenting; **'vaccine** s. entstof; **vac'cinia** s. koelpokke.

'vacillate ['væsilyt] *ww.* (-s) slinger, swaai; aarsel; **vacil'lation** s. aarseling.

'vacuum ['vækjoeəm] s. lugleë ruimte; - **brake** s. lugrem; **-cleaner** s. stofsuier; **-flask** s. koffiefles; **vac'uity** s. leegheid; **'vacuole** s. holtetjie; **'vacuous** *bnw.* leeg, dom.

'vade-'mecum ['vydi'mikəm] s. vademecum, handleiding.

'vagabond ['væghəbənd] s. rondloper, swerwer; **-age** s. landlopery.

va'gary [və'ghêəri] s. gril, gier, luim.

'vagrant ['vyghrənt] *bnw.* rondtrekkend; s. leegloper; **'vagrancy** s. rondlopery, leeglopery.

'vague ['vygh] *bnw.* (-r, -st) vaag; onseker.

'vain ['vyn] *bnw.* (-er, -est) nutteloos, vergeefs; ydel, verwaand; **-'glorious** *bnw.* verwaand; **-'glory** s. verwaandheid, ydelheid.

'valance ['væləns] s. skerm.

'vale ['vyl] s. vallei, dal, sloot.

vale'diction [væli'diksjən] s. vaarwel, afskeid.

'valence ['vyləns] s. valensie.

va'lerian [və'liəriən] s. balderjan.

'valet ['vælit] s. (-s) lyfbediende.

'valiant ['væljənt] *bnw.* dapper, moedig.

'valid ['vælid] *bnw.* gegrond, geldig; **-ate** *ww.* (-d) bekragtig; **vali'dation** s. bekragtiging; **va'lidity** s. geldigheid.

va'lise [və'liz] s. handsakkie, valies.

'valkyr ['vælkiə] s. walkure.

'valley ['væli] s. (-s) vallei, dal; - **period** s. slap tyd.

'valour ['vælə] s. moed; **'valorous** *bnw.* moedig.

value ['væljõë] s. waarde, prys, betekenis; **'valuable** *bnw.* kosbaar; **'valuables** s. kosbaarhede; **valu'ation** s. waardering; skatting; **-less** *bnw.* waardeloos; **-r** s. skatter, waardeerder.

'valve ['vælv] s. (-s) klep; skulp, skaal; - **grinder** s. klepslyper; - **head** s. klepkop; - **lifter** s. klepligter; - **spring** s. klepveer; - **timing** s. klepreëling.

vamp ['væmp] s. oorleer; geïmproviseerde begeleiding.

'vampire ['væmpaiə] s. vampier; bloedsuier; woekeraar.

van ['væn] s. (-s) voorhoede; bagasiewa; vervoerwa; **-guard** s. voorhoede.

'vane ['vyn] s. (-s) weerhaan; wiek; lem.

va'nilla [və'nilə] s. vanieltje.

'vanish ['vænisj] *ww.* (-ed) verdwyn, wegraak; **-ing cream** s. smeltroom.

'vanity ['væniti] s. (vanities) ydelheid; - **bag** s. poeierkwassakkie.

'vanquish ['væng-kwisj] *ww.* (-ed) verslaan, oorwin.

'vantage ['vântidzj] s. voordeel.

'vapour ['vypə] s. (-s) damp, stoom, mis; **vapo'rific** *bnw.* verdampend; **'vaporize** *ww.* laat verdamp; **vapori'zation** s. verdamping; **'vaporizer** s. verdamper, verstuiwer; **'vaporous** *bnw.* dampagtig; **-ish** *bnw.* winderig; **-y** *bnw.* damperig.

'variable ['vêəriəbl] *bnw.* veranderlik, onbestendig; **varia'bility** s. veranderlikheid.

'variance ['vêəriəns] s. verskil, stryd, teenstrydigheid, geskil; **'variant** *bnw.* verskillend, veranderlik, s. variant.

vari'ation [vêəri'ysjən] s. verandering, afwyking, variasie.

vari'cella [væri'selə] s. waterpokkies.

'varicose ['værikous] *bnw.* spataar-; - **veins** s. spatare.

'varied ['vêərid] *bnw.* verskillend.

'variegate ['vêərighyt] *ww.* bont maak, afwissel; **-d** *bnw.* bont, gevlek; **varie'gation** s. bontheid, veelkleurigheid.

va'riety [və'raiəti] s. (varieties) verskeidenheid; afwisseling.

'variform ['vêərifôm] *bnw.* veelvormig.

'various ['vêəriəs] *bnw.* verskillend; verskeie.

'varlet ['vâlit] s. (-s) skelm.

'varmint ['vâmint] s. swernoot; skelm.

'varnish ['vânisj] s. vernis; verbloeming.

'varsity ['vâsiti] s. universiteit.

vary ['vêəri] *ww.* (varied) verander, afwissel, afwyk.

'vase ['vâs] s. (-s) blompot.

'vasodilator ['væsə'dailytə] s. vatverwyder.

vas'sal [væ'sæl] s. (-s) leenman, vasal.

vast ['vâst] *bnw.* (-er, -est) omvangryk, groot, uitgebrei.

vat ['væt] s. (-s) vat, kuip.

vault ['vôlt] s. (-s) gewelf, verwulf; *ww.* oorwelf; spring.

vaunt ['vônt] *ww.* (-ed) spog, grootpraat.

veal ['vil] s. kalfsvleis.

'Veda ['vydə] s. Veda; **'Vedic** *bnw.* Vedies.

veer ['viə] *ww.* (-ed) draai, omspring.

'vega ['vyghə] s. moeras, vlei.

'vegetable ['vedzjitəbl] s. (-s) plant; **-s** s. groente; **'vegetal** *bnw.* plantaardig; **vege'tarian** s. vegetariër; **'vegetate** *ww.* (-d) groei, vegeteer;

vege'tation s. plantegroei; 'vegeta-
tive bnw. groeiend soos plante.

ve'hemence ['vilməns] s. geweld;
vuur, hartstog; 'vehement bnw.
geweldig, vurig.

'vehicle ['viikl] s. (-s) rytuig, voertuig.

veil ['vyl] s. (-s) sluier; gordyn;
masker.

vein ['vyn] s. (-s) aar; stemming;
trant; aard.

'velar ['vilə] s. (-s) velaar; klank by
die sagte verhemelte gevorm; bnw.
velêr.

'vellum ['veləm] s. fyn perkament,
velyn.

ve'locity [vi'lositi] s. snelheid.

'velum ['viləm] s. sagte verhemelte,
velum.

'velvet ['velvit] s. ferweel, fluweel;
velve'teen s. katoenverweel; -ing s.
pluis; -y bnw. ferweelagtig.

vend ['vend] ww. (-ed) verkoop;
vent; -er, -or s. verkoper, venter;
-ible bnw. verkoopbaar; -ibility s.
verkoopbaarheid.

ven'detta [ven'detə] s. bloedwraak.

ve'neer [və'niə] ww. (-ed) inlê; vernis;
verbloem.

'venerate ['venəryt] ww. (-d)
eerbiedig; eer; 'venerable bnw.
eerbiedwaardig; vene'ration s. eerbied, ontsag, eerbetoon.

ve'nereal [vi'niəriəl] bnw. geslags-,
veneries.

ve'netian blind [vi'nisjən blaind] s.
skuifblinder.

'vengeance ['vendzjəns] s. wraak;
vengeful bnw. wraaksugtig.

'vengefulness ['vendzjfoel] s. wraak-
sugtigheid.

'venison ['venzn] s. wildsvleis.

'venom ['venəm] s. gif; -ous bnw.
giftig.

vent ['vent] s. gat, luggat, opening;
ww. ontlug.

'ventail ['ventil] s. klep, ventiel.

'ventilate ww. (-d) ventileer, lug;
venti'lation s. lugverversing, venti-
lasie, lugtoevoer; -ator s. luggat,
ventilator.

'ventral ['ventrəl] bnw. van die buik,
buik.

'ventricle ['ventrikl] s. holte.

ven'triloquist [ven'triləkwist] s.
buikspreker.

'venture ['ventsjə] s. (-s) waagstuk;
onderneming; ww. (-d) waag; -some
bnw. waaghalsig.

'venue ['venjōē] s. (-s) plek, (van
misdaad, waar iets moet gebeur).

ver'acious [və'rysjəs] bnw. waarheidliewend.

verb ['vəb] s. werkwoord; -al bnw.
woordelik, mondeling; verbaal; -alize
ww. tot werkwoord maak; -alism s.
woordevittery; ver'batim bnw. woordelik; -iage s. omhaal van woorde;
-ose s. langdradigheid.

'verdancy ['vədənsi] s. groenheid;

'verdant bnw. groen; 'verdure s.
groenheid.

'verdict ['vədikt] s. (-s) uitspraak.

'verdigris ['vədighris] s. kopergroen.

'verge ['vədzj] s. kant; grens; roede;
-r s. koster, stafdraer.

'verify ['verifai] ww. (verified) bewys;
ondersoek; nagaan; 'verifier s.
kontroleerder; verifi'cation s. bewys,
bevestiging.

'verily ['verili] bw. voorwaar, waarlik.

'verity ['veriti] s. waarheid; 'veritable
bnw. waar, eg.

'vermian ['vəmiən] bnw. wurmagtig;
'vermicide s. wurmgif; ver'micular
bnw. wurmvormig; ver'miculate
bnw. wurmvormig; vermicu'lation
s. wurmvormige beweging; ver'micu-
lose bnw. vol wurms; 'vermiform s.
wurmvormig; 'vermifuge s. wurm-
drywende middel; 'vermigrade bnw.
voortkronkelend.

vermi'celli ['vəmi'seli] s. vermicelli.

'vermicide ['vəmisaid] s. wurmdo-
der.

ver'million [və'miljən] s. vermiljoen.

'vermin ['vəmin] s. ongedierte.

ver'nacular [və'nækjoelə] s. lands-
taal, dialek.

'versatile ['vəsətail] bnw. veelsydig;
versa'tility s. veelsydigheid.

'verse ['vəs] s. (-s) vers, versreël; -d
bnw. bedrewe, ervare; versifi'cation
s. beryming; versbou; verskuns.

'version ['vəsjən] s. (-s) vertaling.

'versus ['vəsəs] voors. teen, versus.

vert ['vət] s. groen.

'vertebra ['vətibrə] s. werwelbeen,
vertebra; -l bnw. gewerwel verte-
braal, werwel-; 'vertebrate bnw.
gewerwel, s. gewerwelde dier.

'vertex ['vəteks] s. top, toppunt;
kruin.

'vertical ['vətikəl] bnw. vertikaal,
loodreg; -ly bw. regaf, regop.

'vertigo ['vətighou] s. duiseling,
duiseligheid.

'verve ['vēəv] s. geesdrif, vuur,
gloed.

'very ['veri] bnw. eg, waar, opreg;
bw. baie, erg, uiters.

'vesicle ['vesikl] s. (-s) blasie;
selletjie.

'vessel ['vesl] s. (-s) vat; fles; bloed-
vat; vaartuig.

vest ['vest] s. (-s) onderhemp; frok;
onderbaadjie; ww. (-ed) beklee met,
oordra; berus by, verleen; -ment s.
gewaad.

'vestibule ['vestibjōēl] s. (-s) portaal.

'vestige ['vestidzj] s. (-s) spoor,
teken, bewys.

'veteran ['vetərən] s. (-s) veteraan.

'veterinary ['vetnri] s. (veterinaries)
veearts.

'veto ['vitou] s. vetoreg; verbod.

vex ['veks] ww. (-ed) vererg; lastig
val; -'ation s. ergernis; plaery; las;
-'atious bnw. ergerlik, lastig.

'via ['vaiə] bw. oor, langs, via.

'viable ['vaiəbl] *bnw.* (*more -, most -*) lewens vatbaar.

'via'duct ['vaiə'dʌkt] *s.* (*-s*) viaduk, boogbrug.

'vial [vaiəl] *s.* (*-s*) flessie, nool.

'viands ['vaiəndz] *s.* kos, lewensmiddele.

vi'brate [vai'bryt] *ww.* (*-d*) tril, vibreer; vi'bration *s.* trilling, vibrering; vi'bratory *bnw.* trillend.

'vicar ['vikə] *s.* (*-s*) vikaris, predikant; -age *s.* vikariaat, pastorie.

'vice ['vais] *s.* (*-s*) ondeug, gebrek, fout; skroef, klem; voors. in die plek van; voorvoegsel. visie-, onder-; -roy *s.* onderkoning; 'vicious *bnw.* sleg, bedorwe.

i'cinity [vi'siniti] *s.* nabyheid, buurt, omgewing.

'vicious ['visjəs] *bnw.* bedorwe; boosaardig; wys.

vi'cissitude [vi'sisitjōēd] *s.* wisselvalligheid, afwisseling.

'victim ['viktim] *s.* (*-s*) slagoffer, prooi; -ize *ww.* (*-d*) verongelyk, veronreg; -i'zation *s.* verongelyking, veronregting.

'victor ['viktə] *s.* (*-s*) oorwinnaar; vic'torious *bnw.* oorwinnend; -y *s.* oorwinning.

'victual ['vitl] *s.* (*-s*) kos, voedsel; -ler *s.* proviandmeester.

vie ['vai] *ww.* (*-d*) wedywer, ding.

view ['vjōē] *s.* (*-s*) uitsig, gesig; mening; doel; besigtiging.

'vigil ['vidzjil] *s.* (nag) waak; -ance *s.* waaksaamheid; -ant *bnw.* waaksaam.

'vigour ['vighə] *s.* krag; 'vigorous *bnw.* krag.

'vile ['vail] *bnw.* (*-r, -st*) laag, gemeen, vuil; ellendig; vrot.

'vilify ['vilifai] *ww.* (vilified) belaster; 'vilifier lasteraar.

'villa ['vilə] *s.* (*-s*) villa, alleenstaande voorstedelike woning.

'village ['vilidzj] *s.* (*-s*) dorp; -r *s.* dorpenaar.

'villain ['vilən] *s.* (*-s*) skurk; -ous *bnw.* skurkagtig; -y *s.* skurkagtigheid.

vim ['vim] *s.* pit, krag, energie.

'vincible ['vinsibl] *bnw.* oorwinlik.

'vindicate ['vindikyt] *ww.* (*-d*) verdedig, regverdig; vin'dicable *bnw.* regverdigbaar; vindi'cation *s.* regverdiging, verdediging; 'vindicator *s.* verdediger, voorspraak; vin'dicatory *bnw.* verdedigend; vin'dicative *bnw.* verdedigend.

vin'dictive [vin'diktiv] *bnw.* wraakgierig, wraaksugtig.

'vine ['vain] *s.* (*-s*) wingerdstok; rankplant; vi'naceous *bnw.* van wyn of druiwe; wyn-, druiwe-; - grower *s.* wynboer; -ry *s.* broeikas vir wingerdstokke; -yard *s.* wingerd; viniculture, *s.* wynbou; vi'niferous *bnw.* wynproduserend; vinous *bnw.* wyn-, wynagtig; vint *ww.* wyn-; maak;

'vintage *s.* wynoes; wyn; 'vintner *s.* wynkoper.

'vinegar ['vinighə] *s.* asyn; - flies *s.* asynvliegies.

vi'ola [vi'oulə] *s.* altviool, altspeler.

'violate ['vaiəlyt] *ww.* (*-d*) skend, verkrag; vio'lation *s.* skending; verkragting; inbraak; 'violator *s.* skender.

'violence ['vaiələns] *s.* geweld; 'violent *bnw.* geweldig, hewig.

'violet ['vaiəlit] *s.* (*-s*) viooltjie; perskleur.

vio'lin [vaiə'lin] *s.* (*-s*) viool; 'violinist *s.* vioolspeler; -cello *s.* [-'tsjelou] *s.* tjello; -'cellist *s.* tjellospeler.

'viper ['vaipə] *s.* (*-s*) adder; -ish *bnw.* adderagtig.

vi'rago [vi'ryghou] *s.* kyfagtige vrou, feeks, rissiepit.

'virgin ['vədzjin] *s.* (*-s*) maagd; -al *bnw.* maagdelik, rein; vir'ginity *s.* maagdelikheid.

Vir'ginia 'creeper [və'dzjiniə 'kripə] *s.* wildewingerd.

'virile ['virail] *bnw.* manlik, gespierd; vi'rility *s.* manlikheid.

'virtue ['vətjōē] *s.* (*-s*) deug, reinheid; 'virtual *bnw.* eintlik; 'virtually *bw.* feitlik; virtu'osity *s.* virtuositeit; virtu'oso *s.* virtuoos, kunstenaar; 'virtuous *bnw.* deugsaam.

'virus ['vaiərəs] *s.* venyn, smetstof; virus; 'virulence *s.* venynigheid; 'virulent *bnw.* giftig, venynig.

'visa ['vizə] *s.* visum.

'visage ['visidzj] *s.* (*-s*) gelaat.

vis-a-vis ['vizāvi] *bw.* teenoor mekaar.

'viscera ['visərə] *s.* ingewande.

'viscid ['visid] *bnw.* taai, klewerig; vis'cidity *s.* klewerigheid; vis'cosity *s.* klewerigheid, taaiheid; 'viscous *bnw.* klewerig.

vis'cosity [vis'kositi] *s.* klewerigheid; 'viscous *bnw.* klewerig, taai.

'viscount ['vaikaunt] *s.* burggraaf.

'visible ['vizəbl] *bnw.* sigbaar, duidelik; visi'bility *s.* sigbaarheid, lig.

'vision ['vizjən] *s.* (*-s*) gesig, visioen; droomgesig; -ary *bnw.* denkbeeldig, ingebeeld.

'visit ['vizit] *s.* (*-s*) besoek; *ww.* (*-ed*) besoek, kuier(by); visenteer; -ant *bnw.* besoekende; visi'tation *s.* besoeking; ondersoek; inspeksie; visiting-card *s.* visitekaartjie; visiting-day *s.* ontvangdag; -or *s.* besoeker.

'vista ['vistə] *s.* (*-s*) uitsig, vergesig, verskiet.

'visual ['viz-joeəl] *bnw.* gesigs-; -ize *ww.* voor die gees roep; visualiseer; -i'zation *s.* voorstelling.

'vital ['vaitl] *bnw.* lewens-; allergrootste; -s *s.* lewensorgane; -ize *ww.* lewe gee, verlewendig; vi'tality *s.* lewenskrag.

'vitamin ['vitəmin] *s.* (*-s*) vitamine.

'vitric ['vitrik] *bnw.* glasagtig; -s *s.* glasgoed; 'vitreous *bnw.* glasagtig; vitre'osity *s.* glasagtigheid; vi'tres-

cence s. verglasing; **vi'trescent** bnw.
verglasend; **vitrifi'cation** s. verglasing; **vitrify** ww. verglaas; **'vitrifiable** bnw. verglaasbaar.

'vitriol ['vitriəl] s. blouvitriool.

vitupe'ration [vitjoepə'rysjən] s. siegmakery.

vi'vacity [vi'væsiti] s. lewenslustigheid; **vi'vacious** bnw. lewendig, lewenslustig.

'viva'voce ['vaivə'vousi] bnw. mondeling.

'vivid ['vivid] bnw. helder, glansend.

'vivify ['vivifai] ww. (vivified) verlewendig, opwek.

vi'viparous [vi'vipərəs] bnw. lewendbarend.

vivi'section [vivi'seksjən] s. viviseksie.

'vixen ['viksn] s. jakkalsteef; feeks; rissie.

'vocable ['voukəbl] s. (-s) woordvorm; **vo'cabulary** s. woordeskat, woordelys.

'vocal ['voukəl] s. (-s) vokaal, klinker ; bnw. stem-; mondeling; **vo'calic** bnw. soos 'n klinker, stemhebbend; **-ize** ww. uitspreek; stemhebbend maak; **-ism** s. vokaalstelsel; **-ist** s. vokaalsanger.

vo'cation [vou'kysjən] s. roeping, beroep, ambag; **vo'cational** bnw. beroeps-.

vo'ciferate [vou'sifəryt] ww. (-d) raas; **vocife'ration** s. geraas.

vo'ciferous [vou'sifərəs] bnw. luidrugtig.

'vogue ['vough] s. (-s) mode.

'voice ['vois] s. (-s) stem, spraak, klank; ww. (-d) uiting gee aan; **-d** bnw stemhebbend; **-less** bnw. spraakloos ; stemloos.

void ['void] bnw. nietig; vakant; leeg; ongeldig; s. leegte; leemte.

'volatile ['volətail] bnw. vlugtig; lewendig; vlug-.

vol'cano [vol'kynou] s. (-es) vulkaan; **vol'canic** bnw. vulkanies.

vo'lition [vou'lisjən] s. wil, wilskrag.

'volley ['voli] s. (-s) sarsie, salvo; stroom, vloed.

volt ['voult] s. (-s) volt; **-age** s. spanning.

'voluble ['voljoebl] bnw. glad, vlot; **volu'bility** s. vlotheid, woorderykheid.

'volume ['voljoem] s. (-s) boekdeel; grootte; massa; **vo'luminous** bnw. omvangryk.

'voluntary ['voləntəri] bnw. vrywillig, ongedwonge; **volun'teer** s. (-s) vrywilliger.

vol'uptuous [və'lʌptjoeəs] bnw. wellustig.

'vomit ['vomit] ww. (-ted) vermeer, opgooi; **-ive** s. vomitief.

'voodoo ['vōēdōē] s. toordery.

vor'acious [və'rysjəs] bnw. gulsig; **vor'acity** s. gulsigheid.

'vortex ['vôteks] s. draaikolk.

'votary ['voutəri] s. (votaries) aanbidder; bewonderaar.

'vote ['vout] s. (-s) stem; stemming stemreg; **-r** s. kieser; **'voting** s. stemmery; **'voting paper** s. stembriefie.

'vouch ['vautsj] ww. (-ed) bevestig, waarborg, instaan; **-er** s. kwitansie, teenblad; **-'safe** ww. vergun, inwillig.

vow ['vau] s. (-s) eed, gelofte; ww. (-ed) 'n gelofte doen, sweer, plegtig belowe.

'vowel ['vauəl] s. (-s) klinker, vokaal; **- gradation** s. ablaut; **- mutation** s. umlaut.

'voyage ['voiidzj] s. (-s) seereis; **-r** s. seereisiger.

'vulcanize ['vʌlkənaiz] ww. (-d) vulkaniseer.

'vulgar ['vʌlghə] bnw. (-est) plat, grof, ongepoets; **-ism** s. plat uitdrukking; **vul'garity** s. onbeskoftheid, laagheid, platheid.

'vulnerable ['vʌlnərəbl] bnw. kwesbaar.

'vulture ['vʌltsjə] s. (-s) aasvoël.

W

wad ['wôd] s. (-s) prop, pluisie; **-ding** s. watte, verbandwatte.

'waddle ['wodl] ww. (-d) waggel.

'wade ['wyd] ww. (-d) deurwaad; **-r** s. wader, strandloper.

'wadi ['wodi] s. droë rivierloop.

'wafer ['wyfə] s. (-s) wafel, oblietjie.

'waffle ['wofi] s. (-s) wafel.

waft ['wâft] ww. (-ed) liggies meevoer deur lug.

wag ['waegh] ww. (-ged) waai, skud, kwispel; s. swaai, skud; spotvoël; **-gery** s. tergery; **-tail** s. kwikstertjie.

'wage ['wydzj] s. (-s) loon, verdienste; **-r** s. weddenskap.

'waggish ['waeghisj] bnw. ondeund.

'waggon ['waeghən] s. (-s) wa; trok.

waif ['wyf] s. (-s) swerwer, daklose, opdrifsel.

'wail ['wyl] ww. (-ed) weeklaag, huil, kerm.

'wainscot ['wynskət] s. beskot; **-(t)ing** s. beskot.

waist ['wyst] s. (-s) middel; lyfie; **-coat** s. onderbaadjie.

'waistband ['wystbænd] s. broeksband; gordel.

wait ['wyt] ww. (-ed) wag; versuim; **-er** s. tafelbediende, kelner; **-ing** s. wagtery; bediening; **waiting-room** s. wagkamer; **-ress** s. kelnerin.

'waive ['wyv] ww. (-d) afsien van, laat vaar; **-r** s. afstand; kwytskelding.

'wake ['wyk] ww. (woke, waked; waked, woken) wakker word of maak; **-ful** bnw. slaaploos; waaksaam.

'waken ['wykn] ww. (-ed) wakker maak of word.

walk ['wôk] ww. (-ed) loop, stap, wandel; s. pas, gang; **-er** s. wandelaar; **-ing** s. lopery, geloop, bnw. lopend; **-over** s. maklike oorwinnig.

'**walkie-talkie** ['wôki-'tôki] s. loopgeselser.

wall ['wôl] s. (-s) muur; wal; **-flower** s. muurblom; **-paper** s. plakpapier.

'**wallet** ['wolit] s. (-s) sakkie, portfeulje.

'**wallop** ['wôləp] ww. (-ed) uitlooi, slaan; **-ing** s. drag slae.

'**wallow** ['wolou] ww. (-ed) rol, wentel.

'**walnut** ['wôlnət] s. okkerneut.

'**walrus** ['wôlrəs] s. walrus.

'**waltz** ['wôls] s. (-es) wals.

wan ['wôn] bnw. (-ner, -nest) bleek, naar.

wand ['wond] s. staf, stok.

'**wander** ['wôndə] ww. (-ed) dwaal, swerwe, dool; **-er** s. swerwer, swerweling; **-ings** s. omswerwinge.

'**wane** ['wyn] ww. (-d) taan, verbleek, verflou.

want ['wont] s. (-s) gebrek, behoefte; ww. (-ed) nodig hê, begeer; **-ing** bnw. sonder.

'**wanton** ['wontən] bnw. dartel, weelderig, wellustig; onverantwoordelik.

war ['wô] s. (-s) oorlog, stryd, kryg; **-cry** s. oorlogskreet; **- cloud** s. oorlogswolk; **-dance** s. krygsdans; **-horse** s. strydros; **-like** bnw. krygshaftig; **-path** s. oorlogspad; **-fare** s. oorlog, kryg.

'**warble** ['wôbl] ww. (-d) sing, kweel.

ward ['wôd] s. (-s) pleegkind; beskermeling; voogdyskap; afdeling; ww. bewaar, beskerm; **-en** s. voog, bewaarder; **-er** s. bewaarder, sipier.

'**wardrobe** ['wôdroub] s. (-s) hangkas, klerekas.

'**wardroom** ['wôdroem] s. offisierskajuit.

'**ware** ['wêə] s. (-s) goed, ware; **-s** s. koopware; **-house** pakhuis; winkel.

'**warfare** ['wôfêə] s. oorlog, kryg.

warm ['wôm] bnw. (-er, -est) warm, heet; vurig; hartlik; ww. (-ed) verwarm; verhit; **-ing** s. loesing; **-th** s. warmte; hartlikheid.

warn ['wôn] ww. (-ed) waarsku; kennisgee; vermaan; **-ing** s. waarskuwing.

warp ['wôp] s. skering; skeefheid, kromtrekking; ww. (-ed) kromtrek, bederf; **-ed** bnw. kromgetrek, verwronge.

'**warrant** ['worənt] s. (-s) volmag; versskering; lasbrief; **-y** s. volmag.

'**warrior** ['woriə] s. (-s) kryger, krygsman.

wart ['wôt] s. (-s) vratjie; **-hog** s. vlakvark; **-y** bnw. vratterig.

'**wary** ['wêəri] bnw. (warier, wariest) behoedsaam; '**wariness** s. behoedsaamheid.

wash ['wosj] ww. (-ed) was, uitwas, afwas, spoel; s. wasgoed; was; spoeling; **-able** bnw. wasbaar; **-away** s. verspoeling; **-basin** s. waskom; **-board** s. wasplank; **-day** s. wasdag; **-er** s. waster; **-house** s. wasinrigting;

-ing s. wasgoed; **-out** s. misoes; **-tub** s. wasbalie; **-y** bnw. waterig.

'**washed-out** ['wôsjtaut] bnw. bleek, vaal, neerslagtig.

'**wash-stand** ['wôsjstænd] s. wastafel.

wasp ['wosp] s. (-s) perdeby, wesp.

'**waste** ['wyst] ww. (-d) verspil, verkwis; '**wastage** s. verspilling, verkwisting; woesteny; **-basket** s. snippermandjie; **-ful** bnw. verkwistend; **-r** s. verkwister; '**wastrel** s. misbaksel, verkwister.

watch ['wotsj] s. (-es) wag, waak; horlosie; **-dog** s. waghond; **-ful** bnw. waaksaam, lugtig; **-man** s. wag; **-word** s. wagwoord.

'**watchmaker** ['wôtsjmykə] s. horlosiemaker, juwelier.

'**water** ['wôtə] s. water; ww. natmaak, natgooi; **-borne** bnw. oor die water vervoer, deur water aangevoer; **-closet** s. waterkloset, gemak; **-colour** s. waterverf; **-course** s. watervoor; **-cress** s. bronkors; **-fall** s. waterval; **-fowl** s. waterhoender; **-logged** bnw. deurweek; **-mark** s. watermerk; **-melon** s. waatlemoen; **-power** s. waterkrag; **-proof** bnw. waterdig; **-shed** s. waterskeiding; **-tight** bnw. waterdig; **-works** s. waterwerke; **-y** bnw. waterig, flou.

'**watering-can** ['wôtering-kæn] s. gieter.

'**water-line** ['wôtəlain] s. waterlyn.

'**waterspout** ['wôtəspaut] s. waterhoos.

watt ['wot] s. (-s) watt.

'**wattle** ['wotl] s. latwerk; akasia; basboom, vaalbas.

'**wave** ['wyv] s. (-s) golf; golwing; kartel; ww. (-d) kartel; **-length** s. golflengte.

'**waver** ['wyvə] ww. (-ed) weifel; bewe; **-er** s. weifelaar; **-ingly** bw. weifelend.

wax ['wæks] s. was, lak; **-en** bnw. wasagtig, van was; **-y** bnw. wasagtig.

'**waxwork** ['wæks'wôk] s. wasbeeld.

way ['wy] s. (-s) weg, pad; wyse, manier; **-bill** s. vragbrief; **-farer** s. reisiger; **-'lay** ww. (-laid) voorlê, inwag; **-side** bnw. langs die pad; **-ward** bnw. eiesinnig.

'**way out** ['wy-aut] s. uitgang.

we ['wi] vnw. ons.

weak ['wik] bnw. (-er, -est) swak, tingerig, flou, sieklik; **-en** ww. (-ed) verswak; **-kneed** bnw. papbroekig; **-ly** bnw. sieklik; **-ness** s. swakheid.

weal ['wil] s. weivaart, welsyn.

wealth ['welth] s. rykdom; **-y** bnw. welgesteld.

wean ['win] ww. (-ed) speen, afwen.

'**weapon** ['wepən] s. (-s) wapen.

wear ['wêə] ww. (wore, worn) dra, uitslyt, afmat; s. slytasie; **-able** bnw. draagbaar; **-er** s. draer.

'**weary** ['wiəri] bnw. (wearier, weariest) vermoeid, moeg; ww. (wearied) vermoei, afmat, verveel.

'**weasel** ['wizl] s. wesel (muishond).

'weather ['weðǝ] s. weer; ww. oorleef; -beaten bnw. verweer.
'weathercock ['weðǝkok] s. (-s)
weerhaan.
'weave ['wiv] ww. (wove, woven) weef,
vleg.
web ['web] s. (-s) web, spinnerak;
-bing s. touweefsel.
wed ['wed] ww. (-ded) trou; -ding s.
bruilof.
'wedge ['wedzj] s. (-s) wig, keil; ww.
vaskeil.
'wedlock ['wedlok] s. huwelik, eg.
'Wednesday ['wenzdi] s. Woensdag.
wee ['wi] bnw. (-er, -est) baie klein.
weed ['wid] s. (-s) onkruid; -s s.
onkruid; -y bnw. vervuil.
week ['wik] s. (-s) week; -end s.
naweek; -ly bnw. & bw. weekliks, s.
weekblad.
weep ['wip] ww. (wept) huil, wen.
'weevil ['wivil] s. (-s) kalander.
weigh ['wy] ww. (-ed) weeg; oorweeg;
-t s. gewig; -ty bnw. swaar, gewigtig.
'weigh'bridge ['wy'bridzj] s. (-s)
weegbrug.
weird ['wiǝd] bnw. (-er, -est) bowenatuurlik, grillig.
'welcome ['welkǝm] ww. (-d)
verwelkom.
weld ['weld] s. las, smeeplek; ww.
sweis; -ing s. sweising, sweiswerk;
-ing rod s. sweisstaaf.
'welfare ['welfɛǝ] s. welsyn.
well ['wel] s. (-s) bron, put; ww.
opwel, bw. goed, wel; bnw. goed,
wel, gesond; -nigh bw. byna; -to-do
bnw. welgesteld.
'welter ['weltǝ] bnw. swaargewig-.
wench ['wentsj] s. (-es) meisie.
wend ['wend] ww. (-ed) gaan.
west ['west] s. die weste.
wet ['wet] bnw. (-ter, -test) nat, vogtig.
'wether ['weðǝ] s. hamel.
'whale ['wyl] s. (-s) walvis; -bone s.
balein; -oil s. visolie, walvistraan;
-r s. walvisvaarder.
'wharf ['wôf] s. (-s, wharves) kaai;
-age s. kaaigeld.
what ['wot] bnw. watter, wat; vnw.
wat; hoe; -'ever bnw. wat ook al.
wheat ['wit] s. koring; -en bnw. van
koring; -germ s. koringkiem; -germ
oil s. koringkiemolie.
'wheedle ['widl] ww. (-d) flikflooi.
wheel ['wil] s. (-s) wiel; rat; swen-
king; -barrow s. kruiwa; -chair s.
siekestoel; -wright s. wamaker;
- alignment s. wielsporing; - balance
s. wielbalans; - chain s. wielketting;
-disc s. wielskyf; - nut s. wielmoer;
-nut brace s. wielmoeromslag;
- puller s. wieltrekker; - seat s.
wielbedding; - wobble s. wielwaggel;
change -s ww. wiele omruil; -chair
s. stootstoel.
'wheezy ['wizi] bnw. kortasem.
'whelp ['welp] s. (-s) welp, klein
hondjie.
when ['wen] bw. wanneer, toe, as;
vnw. from - van wanneer af.

'whence ['wens] bw. waarvandaan.
'where ['wɛǝ] bw. waar, waarheen;
vnw. waarvandaan; -abouts s. ver-
blyfplek.
where'as [wɛǝr'æz] voegw. aangesien,
nademaal.
'wherefore ['wɛǝfô] bw. waarom,
hoekom.
whet ['wet] ww. (-ted) slyp, wet;
-stone s. slypsteen.
'whether ['weðǝ] bnw. & bw.
watter(een); voegw. of, ditsy.
'whey ['wy] s. wei, dikmelkwater.
which ['witsj] bnw. watter; vnw.
watter, wie, wat.
'while ['wail] s. tydjie, oomblik;
voegw. terwyl.
whilst ['wailst] = while voegw.
whim ['wim] s. (-s) gril, nuk; -sical
bnw. vol nukke.
'whimper ['wimpǝ] ww. (-ed) huil,
grens.
'whine ['wain] ww. (-d) huil, tjank.
'whinny ['wini] ww. (whinnied)
runnik.
whip ['wip] s. (-s) sweep, peits,
karwats; -hand s. oorhand.
'whipcord ['wipkôd] s. ferweel.
whirl ['wôl] ww. (-ed) dwarrel, draai;
-pool s. draaikolk; -wind s. dwarrel-
wind.
'whiskers ['wiskǝs] s. snorbaard.
'whisper ['wispǝ] ww. (-ed) fluister;
-ing s. gefluister.
'whistle ['wisl] s. (-s) fluitjie, fluit;
ww. (-ed) fluit.
whit ['wit] s. 'n ietsie.
'white ['wait] bnw. (-r, -st) wit, blank;
bleek; -en ww. (-ed) wit word (maak);
-wash ww. (-ed) wit; s. witsel.
whither ['wiðǝ] bw. waarheen.
'whitlow ['witlou] s. fyt.
'whittle ['witl] ww. (-d) sny, afsny,
afsnipper.
who ['hŏê] vnw. wie, wat; -m vnw.
van wie, wie s'n.
'whole ['houl] bnw. heel, onbeskadig;
-sale s. groothandel; -some bnw.
gesond, heilsaam; -ly bw. geheelenal.
'whooping-cough ['hŏêping-kof] s.
kinkhoes.
'whorl ['hwôl] s. krans.
why ['wai] bw. waarom, hoekom.
'wicked ['wikid] bnw. (-er, -est)
goddeloos, sondig.
'wicker ['wikǝ] s. biesies, matjiesgoed.
'wicket ['wikit] s. (-s) hekkie, poort-
jie; paaltjies; -keeper s. paaltjies-
wagter.
'wide ['waid] bnw. (-r, -st) wyd, breed,
ruim; -awake bnw. nugter; -n ww.
(-ed) wyer maak of word; -spread
bnw. oral; width s. wydte.
'widow ['widou] s. (-s) weduwee; -er
s. wewenaar.
'wield ['wild] ww. (-ed) uitoefen,
beheer, swaai, hanteer.
'wife ['waif] s. (wives) vrou, eggenote;
-ly bnw. huisvroulik.
'wig ['wigh] s. (-s) pruik.

wild ['waild] *bnw.* (*-er, -est*) wild, woes, dol, rasend; roekeloos; *bw.* halsoorkop; **-s** s. wildernis; **-erness** s. wildernis; woesteny.

'**wile** ['wail] s. (*-s*) streek, lis; **wily** *bnw.* listig; **wiliness** s. listigheid.

will ['wil] *ww.* (*-ed; would*) wil, begeer; *hulp. ww.* (*would*) sal; s. testament; wilskrag; **-ing** *bnw.* gewillig; **-ingly** *bw.* gewilliglik; **-power** s. wilskrag.

'**willow** ['wilou] s. (*-s*) wilgerboom; **-y** *bnw.* met wilgers begroei.

'**willy-'nilly** ['wili'nili] *bw.* of hy wil of nie.

wilt ['wilt] *ww.* (*-ed*) kwyn, verwelk, verlep.

'**wimple** ['wimpl] s. (*-s*) sluier, kap.

win ['win] *ww.* (*won*) wen; behaal; verdien.

'**wince** ['wins] *ww.* (*-d*) krimp, terugdeins, huiwer.

'**winch** ['wintsj] s. (*-es*) wenas; **-drum** s. wentol.

wind ['waind] *ww.* (*wound*) opwen; **-ing** *bnw.* kronkelend; **-up** *ww.* afsluit.

wind ['wind] s. (*-s*) wind, lug; reuk; *ww.* (*-ed*) uitasem raak; laat blaas; **-bag** s. windsak; **-fall** s. afgewaaide vrugte; meevaller; **-lass** s. windas; **-mill** s. windpomp; **-pipe** s. lugpyp; **-y** *bnw.* winderig;‖

'**winding'up** ['wainding'ʌp] s. afsluiting, slot.

'**window** ['windou] s. (*-s*) venster, raam; **-lift** s. ruitligter.

'**windscreen** ['windskrin] s. windskerm; **-washer** s. ruitspuit.

'**wine** ['wain] s. (*-s*) wyn; **-glass** s. wynkelkie.

wing ['wing] s. (*-s*) vlerk, vleuel; **-ed** *bnw.* gevleuel.

wink ['wink] *ww.* (*-ed*) knipoog, knik.

'**winsome** ['winsəm] *bnw.* innemend, bevallig.

'**winter** ['wintə] s. (*-s*) winter; '**wintry** *bnw.* winteragtig, koud.

'**wipe** ['waip] *ww.* (*-d*) afvee, skoonvee, afdroë.

'**wire** ['waiə] s. (*-s*) draad; telegram; **-edge** s. braam; **-less** s. radio; '**wiring** s. drade; elektriese geleiding ; '**wiry** *bnw.* draderig; gehard.

'**wisdom** ['wizdəm] s. wysheid, verstand; **-tooth** s. verstandtand.

'**wise** ['waiz] *bnw.* (*-r, -st*) verstandig, wys; **-acre** s. alweter.

wish ['wisj] *ww.* (*-ed*) wens, begeer, verlang; s. wens, begeerte; **-bone** s. geluksbeentjie; **-ful** *bnw.* verlangend; **-ful thinking** s. wensdenkery.

wisp ['wisp] s. (*-s*) bossie, toutjie.

wis'taria [wis'teriə] s. bloureën, wisteria.

'**wistful** ['wistfoel] *bnw.* hunkerend.

wit ['wit] s. vernuf, vernuftigheid; geestigheid; **-s** s. teenwoordigheid van gees, verstand.

witch ['witsj] s. (*-es*) heks, towerares; **-craft** s. toordery; **-ery** s. toorkuns.

with ['widh] *bw.* met, saam met, by, van; **-'draw** *ww.* (*-drew*) terugtrek, herroep; **-'drawal** s. terugtrekking.

with'al [wi'dhol] *bw.* boonop, buitendien.

'**wither** ['widhə] *ww.* (*-ed*) verwelk, verlep.

with'hold [widh'hould] *ww.* (*-held*) weerhou, onthou.

with'stand [widh'stænd] *ww.* (*-stood*) weerstaan.

'**witness** ['witnis] s. (*-es*) getuie; getuienis.

'**witticism** ['witisizm] s. kwinkslag.

'**wittingly** ['witingli] *bnw.* wetend, bewus, opsetlik.

'**witty** ['witi] *bnw.* geestig.

'**wizard** ['wizəd] s. towenaar, waarsêer; **-ry** s. towery.

'**wizened** ['wiznd] *bnw.* verrimpelde.

'**wobble** ['wobl] *ww.* (*-d*) waggel, slinger.

woe ['wou] s. (*-s*) wee, nood, ellende; **-begone** *bnw.* armsalig; **-ful** *bnw.* treurig.

'**wold** ['would] s. (*-s*) bosveld, vlakte.

wolf ['woelf] s. (*wolves*) wolf; vraat; **-ish** *bnw.* wolfagtig, wreed, vraterig.

'**woman** ['woemən] s. (*women*) vrou; **-ly** *bnw.* vroulik; **-like** *bnw.* soos 'n vrou.

'**wonder** ['wʌndə] *ww.* (*-ed*) wonder, wonderwerk; **-ful** *bnw.* wonderlik; '**wondrous** *bnw.* wonderbaarlik.

'**wont** ['wount] *bnw.* gewoond, gewend.

woo ['woȇ] *ww.* (*-ed*) vry na; **-ing** s. vryery.

wood ['woed] s. (*-s*) woud, bos, hout; **-y** *bnw.* bosagtig; **-tar** s. houtteer; **-wool** s. houtwol.

'**woodcut** ['woedkʌt] s. (*-s*) houtsnee.

wool ['woel] s. (*-s*) wol; **-len** *bnw.* van wol, wol-.

word ['wȇd] s. (*-s*) woord; berig; bevel; **-ing** s. bewoording.

work ['wȇk] s. (*-s*) werk, arbeid; *ww.* (*-ed*) werk, bewerk, arbei; **-able** *bnw.* bewerkbaar; uitvoerbaar.

world ['wȇld] s. (*-s*) wêreld; **-ly** *bnw.* wêrelds.

worm ['wȇm] s. (*-s*) wurm; **-y** *bnw.* vol wurms.

'**worn-'out** ['wȏn-'aut] *bnw.* verslete, moeg.

'**worry** ['wʌri] *ww.* (*worried*) bekommer; '**worries** s. moeite, kommer.

'**worse** ['wȏs] *bnw.* erger, slegter; *vgl.* **bad.**

'**worship** ['wȏsjip] *ww.* (*-ped*) vereer, aanbid.

'**worsted** ['woestid] s. kamstof.

worth ['wȏth] s. waarde; **-y** *bnw.* waardig.

'**would-be** ['woedbi] *bnw.* kastig, sogenoemd; aspirant-.

wound ['woȇnd] s. (*-s*) wond, besering; *ww.* (*-ed*) wond, beseer.

'**wraith** ['ryth] s. (*-s*) gees, skim.

'**wrangle** ['ræng-ghl] *ww.* (*-d*) kyf, twis.

wrap ['ræp] *ww.* (*-ped*) toedraai, toemaak, inpak; **-per** *s.* omslag; **-ping** *s.* omslag, huls; **-ping paper** *s.* pakpapier.

wrath ['rôth] *s.* toorn, woede.

'wreak ['rik] *ww.* (*-ed*) wreek.

wreath ['rith] *s.* (*-s*) krans.

'wreathe ['ridh] *ww.* (*-d*) bekrans; kronkel; omstrengel.

wreck ['rek] *s.* wrak; **-age** *s.* wrak, wrakhout.

wrench ['rentsj] *s.* (*-es*) skroefhamer.

'wrench ['rentsj] *ww.* (*-ed*) ruk, draai; verwring.

'wrest ['rest] *ww.* (*-ed*) draai; afpers; **-ler** *s.* stoeier.

'wrestle ['resl] *ww.* (*-d*) stoei, worstel.

wretch ['retsj] *s.* (*-es*) ellendeling; skelm.

'wriggle ['rigl] *ww.* (*-d*) kriewel, wikkel.

wring ['ring] *ww.* (*wrung*) wring, draai.

'wrinkle ['rinkl] *s.* plooi, rimpel.

wrist ['rist] *s.* (*-s*) pols, handgewrig; **-strap** *s.* polsband.

'writ ['rit] *s.* (*-s*) skrif; bevel; dagvaarding.

'write ['rait] *ww.* (*wrote, written*) skryf.

'writhe ['raidh] *ww.* (*-d*) krimp; draai; verwring.

wrong ['rông] *bnw.* verkeerd, nie in die haak nie.

'wry ['rai] *bnw.* (*wrier, wriest*) skeef.

X

'x-ray ['eks'ry] *s.* (*-s*) x-straal, rontgenstraal.

'xylophone ['zailəfoun] *s.* (*-s*) xilofoon.

Y

yacht ['jot] *s.* (*-s*) jag.

'Yankee ['jæng-ki] *s.* Amerikaner.

yap ['jæp] *ww.* (*-ped*) kef, blaf.

yard ['jâd] *s.* (*-s*) jaart, tree; werf.

yarn ['jân] *s.* garing; verhaal.

yaw ['jô] *s.* (*-s*) afwyking.

'yawl ['jôl] *ww.* (*-ed*) skreeu, brul.

yawn ['jôn] *s.* (*-s*) gaap; *ww.* (*-ed*) gaap.

'yea ['jy] *bw.* ja.

year ['jə] *s.* (*-s*) jaar; **-ly** *bnw.* jaarliks.

'yearling ['jəling] *s.* (*-s*) eenjarige dier.

yearn ['jən] *ww.* (*-ed*) verlang, hunker; **-ing** *s.* verlange, hunkering.

yeast ['jist] *s.* suurdeeg, gis.

yell ['jel] *ww.* (*-ed*) gil, skreeu.

'yellow ['jelou] *s.* geel.

'yelp ['jelp] *ww.* (*-ed*) tjank, kef.

yes ['jəs] *bw.* ja.

'yes-man ['jəs-mæn] *s.* (*-men*) jabroer; handlanger.

'yesterday ['jəstədi] *s.* gister.

yet ['jet] *bw.* nog, nogtans, totnogtoe.

yield ['jild] *ww.* (*-ed*) oplewer, opbring.

yoke ['jouk] *s.* (*-s*) juk.

yolk ['jouk] *s.* dooier.

'yonder ['jondə] *bw.* daar, gunter.

'yore ['jô] *s.* (*of -*) vanmelewe.

you ['jôê] *vnw.* jy, jou, julle, u.

young ['jʌng] *bnw.* (*-er, -est*) jong, jonk, klein; onervare; **-ster** *s.* jongeling.

your ['jô] *vnw.* joue, van u.

youth ['jôêth] *s.* jeug, jonkheid.

'Yule ['jôêl] *s.* Kersfees.

Z

zeal ['zil] *s.* ywer, erns.

'zealous ['seləs] *bnw.* vurig, ywerig.

'zebra ['zibrə] *s.* (*-s*) sebra; **- crossing** *s.* sebraoorgang.

'zenith ['zenith] *s.* toppunt.

'zephyr ['zefə] *s.* windjie, luggie.

'zero ['ziərou] *s.* nul, nulpunt.

zest ['zest] *s.* gretigheid, lus.

'zigzag ['zighzægh] *bnw.* kronkelend.

zinc ['zink] *s.* sink.

'zip ['zip] *s.* (*-s*) ritssluiting.

'zone ['zoun] *s.* sone, streek.

zoo ['zôê] *s.* (*-s*) dieretuin.

zo'ology [zou'olədzji] *s.* dierkunde.

'Zulu ['zôêloe] *s.* (*-s*) Zoeloe.